First Published in 2021 by Echo Books
Echo Books is an imprint of Superscript Publishing Pty Ltd, ABN 76 644 812 395
Registered Office: Suite 401, 140 Bourke St, Melbourne, VIC, 3000
www.echobooks.com.au
Copyright © Jeffrey E Hatwell 2017
Creator: Hatwell, Jeff: Author.
Title: Brave Days: The Fourth Australian Division in the Great War
ISBN: 978-0-6485540-8-0 (hardcover)

A catalogue record for this book is available from the National Library of Australia

Book layout and design by Peter Gamble, Canberra.
Set in Garamond Premier Pro Display, 12/15, Trajan Pro and MinervaModern
www.echobooks.com.au
Front cover image: *The 4th Division moving up through the 3rd, 8th August 1918*
H. Septimus Power, 1930. Australian War Memorial (ART12208).
Other books by the Author: *No Ordinary Determination*, Fremantle Press, 2005 and 2014.
With Elspeth Langford: *The Swans of Ypres*, Echo Books, 2020

BRAVE DAYS

The Fourth Australian Division
in the Great War

Jeff Hatwell

Contents

Introduction and Acknowledgements	vii
Maps	x
Abbreviations	xii
1: The Veteran Battalions	1
2: Gunners, Sappers, Pioneers and others	13
3: The 'Heads': the Division Takes Shape	27
4: The Nursery	47
5: Inferno on the Somme	65
6: Mouquet Farm	99
7: Holding the Line	123
8: Action at Gueudecourt	151
9: Pursuit to the Hindenburg Line	179
10: Bullecourt	199
11: The Gun-Line—Lagnicourt and Second Bullecourt	253
12: Black and Green Lines at Messines	271
13: In And Out Of The Line	307
14: Bite and Hold	331
15: Depot Division	369
16: *Vous Les Tiendrez*–Hébuterne	401
17: Dernancourt	423
18: Three Weeks in April	473
19: The Right of the Line	513
20: Astonishment of a Continent	535
21: The Monash Touch	569
22: Etinehem and Madame Wood	613
23: Outpost Line	637
24: Armistice	677
Appendix	713
13th Battalion's attack at Mouquet Farm	713
14/15 August 1916	713
Bibliography	723
Index	729

Introduction and Acknowledgements

This book arose mainly from my previous publication, No Ordinary Determination, on the subject of two First AIF soldiers, Harry Murray and Percy Black. Both were members of infantry units within the 4th Division, and it seemed that there would be a place for a more broadly-focussed history of that overall body. A division being the smallest Army formation that includes elements of the main arms and services under a single command, such a work gives the opportunity to examine the functions of those elements and how they fitted together to achieve the tactical aims of the higher command. There was something of a gap in the record as far as the 4th Division was concerned (as is also the case with the 2nd Division) which I believed could be filled by a detailed narrative history.

Unique among the five Australian divisions in sourcing the majority of its personnel from the less-populated states of the Commonwealth, the 4th Division had its own collective personality, as well as the individual personalities who left their impression on history. The 4th Division had its share of victory and defeat, developing its skills and methods leading up to the triumphs of late 1918. In this book I have tried to show something of the rhythm and routines of life for the soldier on the Western Front, as the Division rotated between the front line – experiencing the occasional major battle, the frequent smaller engagements and the slog of holding the line – and the areas behind the lines, either in close support, reserve or resting.

In general, I have taken as a model the 5th Division history by Captain Alexander Ellis, *The Story of the Fifth Australian Division*, first published in 1920. Captain Ellis did not have the benefit of instant communication and ready access to a variety of sources that the Internet affords today, but he did have the great advantage of having been personally involved in many of the events of which he wrote (as both a regimental and staff officer), and of knowing personally many of the people concerned – something, of course, that no present-day author can match. In this book I have tried to follow his example of giving some attention to all of the different elements of a division, while giving prominence to the infantry as the most numerous component and the most exposed to danger. I have also followed Ellis's practice of periodically giving an Order of Battle, to outline the divisional structure by units and identify the senior officers at particular times.

C E W Bean's six volumes of the *Official History of Australia in the War of 1914–18* are of course indispensible in a work such as this. On going through original sources, I have found a few instances where Bean appears to have been in error or to have misinterpreted some minor details, and the same applies to some other authors (including myself, in my earlier work) and to a few commonly accepted impressions. In most of those cases I have relegated the reasons for my views to the chapter notes, so as not to distract from the overall narrative. With respect to each combat action I have mentioned some of the resulting decorations awarded to individual soldiers, but those instances are not intended to be comprehensive lists; all awards of the Victoria Cross to 4th Division members are, however, described in some detail. Most if not all infantry battalion unit histories include lists of all award recipients in the unit, in some cases including the text of the recommendations, and each 4th Division battalion has had at least one published history – the set was completed with the publication of Craig Deayton's history of the 47th Battalion, *Battle Scarred* (2012).

The Australian forces in France and Belgium formed a small part of the British Expeditionary Force (BEF) and officially their unit and formation titles included the adjective 'Australian', as in 4th Australian Division, 24th Australian Machine Gun Company, 12th Australian Field Ambulance and so on, to distinguish them from British units with the same number; Canadian units were identified in a similar manner. At the time, the expression '4th Division' without the qualifier would have been taken to mean the British Army's 4th Division. For an Australian readership, I have reversed this terminology, specifically identifying British units as such, at least when first mentioned; readers outside Australia are asked to forgive this somewhat parochial approach. Measurements are shown in metric terms except where a direct quotation mentions an Imperial measure; in those cases an approximate metric conversion is added. Where an Imperial term is part of the name of a weapon or other item (e.g. 18-pounder field gun) it is used without conversion.

My thanks are due to the Army History Unit for contributing to my expenses via a research grant in 2008. My greatest personal support has been from Elspeth Langford, who took on the marathon task of reading all of the draft chapters, noting corrections and asking pertinent questions, and maintained the enthusiasm that was of such value in my previous work. The late Mr George Franki, co-author of *Mad Harry: Australia's Most Decorated Soldier*, who was my friend and mentor for many years, also read many of the early chapters and gave much valuable input. The group of Western Australian military historians and writers, Neville Browning, Wes Olsen, Ian Gill, Murray Ewen and Andrew Pittaway, set the example for endeavour and for the overriding importance of 'getting it right;' thanks to Murray also for the loan of numerous books, many of which I had not heard of before and were not easy to obtain otherwise. Thanks also to Greg O'Reilly, whose advice ensured that I did not overlook the machine gun units.

Dr Andrew Richardson, presently working with the Australian War Memorial and previously with the Army History Unit, gave generously of his time in providing valuable detailed advice. The encouragement and advice received from Dr Roger Lee, also with both of those organisations, was greatly appreciated also. Everyone with an interest in Australian military history owes thanks to the management and staff of the War Memorial and the National Archives of Australia, who over a long period organised the digitisation of most of the documents and personnel records relevant to the First World War. That work has enabled ready access, without charge, to researchers like myself located on the other side of the continent from Canberra.

For granting permission to quote from copyright material, I thank: the Australian War Memorial; the family of the late Dr C E W Bean, for material from the 'Bean Papers' in the AWM collection (arranged through Stuart Bennington at the AWM); Dr P A Pedersen; Andrew Barnes, for extracts from *Jacka's Mob* by E J Rule; the Royal Artillery Institution; Peter Davies, for material from the T S Louch Memoirs. I have also quoted several extracts from *Backs to the Wall* by the late G D Mitchell; it appears from other works that have quoted Mitchell that attempts to trace the copyright holders for his work have not been successful. The publishers of several other works quoted herein have also been approached for the appropriate permissions, and the sources of all quoted passages have been identified and referenced.

Special thanks to Graham James for his efforts in preparing the maps, often with the vaguest of guidelines from the author (any errors in the maps are of course my responsibility). Guidance from the principals at Echo Books, Ian Gordon at the beginning through to Marcus Fielding most recently, ensured that this project would come to fruition.

Jeff Hatwell
Perth, Western Australia
December 2020

Maps

1.	Egypt: II Anzac area of operations, 1916	34
2.	Western Front, May 1916	49
3.	Armentières area	52
4.	Somme sector rear area, north of Amiens	66
5.	Somme sector, area around Pozières	69
6.	Pozières/Mouquet Farm battlefield, August – September 1916	76
7.	Mouquet Farm: attack by 13th Brigade, 3 to 5 September 1916	115
8.	Ypres sector, 1916	125
9.	Gueudecourt area	136
10.	Operations at Stormy Trench, February 1917	166
11.	Advance to the Hindenburg Line, March/April 1917	184
12.	13th Brigade's action at Noreuil, 2 April 1917	189
13.	First Battle of Bullecourt, 11 April 1917	227
14.	Battle of Messines, 7 June 1917, 4th Division's attack on the Oosttaverne Line; positions reached before retreat in the evening	285
15.	Battle of Messines 8 to 12 June 1917: second phase of 4th Division's operations	297
16.	Battle of Polygon Wood, 26 September 1917	338
17.	First Battle of Passchendaele, situation at end of 12th Brigade's advance	354
18.	Area of 4th Division's movement from Flanders, March 1918	403
19.	4th Brigade's defence of Hébuterne, March/April 1918	410
20.	Dernancourt area	427
21.	Second Battle of Dernancourt, 5 April 1918	451
22.	Environs of the Somme, Ancre and Hallue Rivers between Amiens and Albert	479
23.	Second Battle of Villers-Bretonneux: counter-attack by the 13th and 15th Brigades, 24/25 April 1918	495

24.	48th Battalion's action at Monument Wood, 3 May 1918	521
25.	Battle of Hamel, 4 July 1918	557
26.	Battle of Amiens, 8 August 1918, 4th Division sector	593
27.	Etinehem Peninsula, Somme River: 13th Brigade's operations, 10 to 13 August 1918	620
28.	Lieutenant Lawrence McCarthy's exploit near Madame Wood, 23 August 1918	627
29.	Péronne to the Hindenburg Line, September 1918	639
30.	Battle of the Hindenburg Outpost Line, 18 September 1918, 4th Division sector	654
31.	Area of Fourth Army's advance east of the Hindenburg Line, October/November 1918	689
32.	Area of advance into Belgium after the Armistice	696

Abbreviations

2IC	Second in Command
2nd Lt	Second Lieutenant
AA&QMG	Assistant Adjutant and Quartermaster General
AAMC	Australian Army Medical Corps
AASC	Australian Army Service Corps
AAVC	Australian Army Veterinary Corps
ADC	Aide-de-camp
ADMS	Assistant Director of Medical Services
ADS	Advanced Dressing Station
ADVS	Assistant Director of Veterinary Services
AFA	Australian Field Artillery
AFC	Australian Flying Corps
AIF	Australian Imperial Force
AWL	Absent Without Leave
AWM	Australian War Memorial
Bde	Brigade
Bdr	Bombardier
BEF	British Expeditionary Force
Bn	Battalion
Brig Gen	Brigadier General
Capt	Captain
CB	Companion of the Order of the Bath
CCS	Casualty Clearing Station
CGS	Chief of the General Staff

CMG	Companion of the Order of St Michael and St George
CO	Commanding Officer
Col	Colonel
Coy	Company
Cpl	Corporal
CQMS	Company Quartermaster Sergeant
CRA	Commander Royal Artillery
CRE	Commander Royal Engineers
CSI	Companion of the Order of the Star of India
CSM	Company Sergeant Major
CWGC	Commonwealth War Graves Commission
DAA&QMG	Deputy Assistant Adjutant and Quartermaster General
DAAG	Deputy Assistant Adjutant General
DAC	Divisional Ammunition Column
DADMS	Deputy Assistant Director of Medical Services
DADOS	Deputy Assistant Director of Ordnance Services
DADVS	Deputy Assistant Director of Veterinary Services
DAQMG	Deputy Assistant Quartermaster General
DCM	Distinguished Conduct Medal
DDMS	Deputy Director of Medical Services
DHQ	Divisional Headquarters
Divn	Division
DSO	Distinguished Service Order
DTMO	Divisional Trench Mortar Officer
FOO	Forward Observation Officer
GCB	Knight Grand Cross of the Order of the Bath
Gen	General
GHQ	General Headquarters (of the BEF)
Gnr	Gunner
GOC	General Officer Commanding
GS	General Staff
GSO1	General Staff Officer Grade 1
GSO2	General Staff Officer Grade 2
GSO3	General Staff Officer Grade 3
HE	High Explosive
HQ	Headquarters

HTM	Heavy Trench Mortar
IO	Intelligence Officer
KBE	Knight Commander of the Order of the British Empire
KCB	Knight Commander of the Order of the Bath
KCMG	Knight Commander of the Order of St Michael and St George
Lcpl	Lance Corporal
Lt	Lieutenant
Lt Col	Lieutenant Colonel
Lt Gen	Lieutenant General
LTM	Light Trench Mortar
MAC	Motor Ambulance Convoy
Maj	Major
Maj Gen	Major General
MC	Military Cross
MDS	Main Dressing Station
MG	Machine Gun
MM	Military Medal
MTM	Medium Trench Mortar
NCO	Non-commissioned Officer
NSW	New South Wales
NZ	New Zealand
NZ & A	New Zealand and Australian (Division)
OC	Officer Commanding
OIC	Officer in Charge
OR	Other Rank(s)
psc	passed staff college
Pte	Private
QF	Quick Firing
Qld	Queensland
RAF	Royal Air Force
RAP	Regimental Aid Post
RE	Royal Engineers
RFA	Royal Field Artillery
RFC	Royal Flying Corps
RHA	Royal Horse Artillery
RMO	Regimental Medical Officer

RNAS	Royal Naval Air Service
RSM	Regimental Sergeant Major
SA	South Australia
SAA	Small Arms Ammunition
Sgt	Sergeant
Spr	Sapper
Tas	Tasmania
VC	Victoria Cross
Vic	Victoria
WA	Western Australia

1: The Veteran Battalions

The evacuation had been going on for more than a week by the night of 19 December 1915 when the final 10,000 soldiers of the Australian and New Zealand Army Corps began quietly filing down from the heights above Anzac Cove towards the beaches and the boats that would take them away from the Gallipoli peninsula. In the abandoned firing line up on the ridges, the occasional shot still cracked out from rifles set up to fire automatically at the Turkish lines. The last few hundred men, the 'Diehards,' were on the boats before sunrise, and the bloody eight-month Gallipoli campaign was over for the Anzacs.

Regarded at different times as an unmitigated disaster, or a brilliant strategic concept undone by inadequate resources and inept leadership, or anything in between, the campaign was clearly a major defeat for the allied cause in the war. As far as the Australian Imperial Force was concerned, its part in the Gallipoli operations had cost over 26,000 casualties, including 8,141 deaths. The war had still to be won and the abandonment of the expedition meant in the long run that the Force would be deployed elsewhere. The Turks were still a threat in Egypt and Palestine, but most of the AIF could now expect to be sent to Europe to fight the Germans on the Western Front.

Against the human and material losses of the campaign, it was possible to find some intangible positives as far as the Australians were concerned. The young nation had begun to establish itself, in its own eyes and those of the world, as an entity separate from its Imperial origins and with its own special characteristics. Reflecting the national pride aroused at home at the performance of Australia's soldiers was the establishment of an extraordinarily strong *esprit de corps* within the AIF itself. The units and formations of Gallipoli, in existence for less than a year at the time of the Landing, had created their own traditions in the heat of battle. Identification of those units by a simple numbering scheme, without the romantic unit names found in the British and Indian armies, did not diminish their members' pride at all.

The 1st Division of the AIF, formed in August 1914 in the first flush of Australian enthusiasm when the British Empire had first declared war on Germany and Austria-Hungary, had as its major component twelve infantry battalions, formed into three brigades. The 1st Brigade (1st to 4th Battalions) was recruited from New South Wales, the 2nd Brigade (5th to 8th Battalions) from Victoria, and the 3rd Brigade (9th to 12th Battalions) from what were then often referred to as the 'Outer States'—Queensland, South Australia, Western Australia and Tasmania. The Division's other arms, the artillery, engineers, medical units and others, had similar origins. Such had been the fervour to enlist that there were easily enough recruits to make up a further infantry brigade and accordingly the 4th Australian Infantry Brigade came into being in September 1914. By contrast with the brigades of the 1st Division, the 4th Brigade was made up of a battalion each from New South Wales (the 13th), Victoria (14th), Queensland and Tasmania (15th) and Western and South Australia (16th).

By the time of the Gallipoli Landing, the 4th Brigade had been grouped with New Zealand units and an Australian Light Horse Brigade to form a composite formation known as the New Zealand and Australian ('NZ & A') Division. The circumstances of the NZ & A's creation meant that it was underprovided with supporting arms. Most of its small artillery and engineer component was supplied by New Zealand. The new 2nd Australian Division, fit and fully equipped but short of training and experience, arrived at Gallipoli late in the campaign. Increasing numbers of volunteers were continuing to throng the recruiting offices in Australia (reaching a peak of over 36,000 enlistments in July 1915 alone), as the news from the war fronts made it plain that the war would go on for much longer and the maximum contribution would be needed.

After staging through Lemnos Island off the Gallipoli coast, the troops were shipped back to Egypt, whence they had departed the previous April for the ill-fated venture. The NZ & A Division initially settled at Moascar Camp near the Suez Canal, with the others being based at a new camp at Tel-el-Kebir, 112 kilometres from Cairo. The AIF was well under strength in numbers, about 14,000 men short of establishment overall, owing to battle casualties and disease. Many of those still on strength were weakened by illness and poor nutrition. On the other hand, there were over 45,000 reinforcements in Egypt, mostly partly-trained recruits from Australia (and New Zealand), but including numerous experienced men recently discharged from Egyptian hospitals after recovering from wounds or illness. Held back from Gallipoli because of the planned evacuation, the reinforcements had been dividing their time between desultory training and causing trouble in the disorderly entertainment venues of Cairo.

Together with the tens of thousands of new recruits still in Australia, there were now sufficient troops available to offer several new formations to the allied war effort. Consultations between the Australian government and the British War Office suggested that the best approach would be to add three new infantry divisions to the AIF. The idea was taken up by Major General Sir Alexander Godley, commanding the New Zealand troops and the NZ & A Division and acting in command of the combined ANZAC forces in Egypt (in the temporary absence of Lieutenant General Sir William Birdwood). Godley, a mediocre field commander but an effective administrator, saw the opportunity of converting the NZ & A to a full New Zealand division and at the same time creating two new Australian divisions from the troops then available in Egypt (a further Australian division—the 3rd - would be formed in Australia). The new divisions in Egypt would need a total of six infantry brigades (24 battalions). Two of these brigades were already available: the 4th, Gallipoli veterans, and the 8th, which like the 4th had been formed independently of the Australian divisions, but which had not seen action.

Four new brigades (16 battalions) would therefore need to be formed. That was the number of existing infantry formations, the 1st to 4th Brigades (1st to 16th Battalions), that had first landed on Gallipoli. General Birdwood, resuming command of the Corps on 19 January 1916, decided that the new units would be formed by splitting those originals in half and building each half into a full unit. The 2nd Division, considerably less experienced than the 1st Division and the 4th Brigade, would be left intact to complete its training and development. Birdwood's chief of staff, Brigadier General C B B White, ordered the process to begin on 12 February 1916 with the first of his notable series of memoranda, which formed the framework for the AIF's reorganisation:

> Out of the sixteen veteran battalions in the A. and N.Z. Army Corps (1st to 16th) it is intended to form 16 new battalions. This will be done by dividing the veteran battalions into two wings ... Both wings will then be filled up by reinforcements ... Companies will be fairly divided into two parts ...[1]

The two new divisions would be numbered the 4th and 5th, and it was the 4th Brigade which was to form the nucleus of the 4th Division's infantry.

The 4th Australian Infantry Brigade's inaugural commander was Colonel John Monash, a Melbourne civil engineer and part-time citizen soldier. Little known at the time outside of Victoria's business and social circles, he would in time be recognised as one of the greatest of all Australians, perhaps the greatest.[2] The units in his new brigade came from all around the young nation, and were said to include a higher proportion of country recruits than did the 1st Division units, such men having taken longer to make their way to the recruiting centres in the state capitals.

The 13th Battalion of New South Wales assembled at Rosehill Racecourse near Sydney in September 1914, and according to the battalion history, its men were all of unusually large stature.[3] Victoria's 14th Battalion was formed at Broadmeadows to the north of Melbourne. The 15th Battalion was made up of three-quarters Queensland recruits and one quarter Tasmanian, many members from both states being tough miners and rural workers. The unit did not come together until the whole brigade assembled at Broadmeadows in November 1914. Similarly, the 16th Battalion was recruited mostly from Western Australia with a smaller South Australian element and joined together at Broadmeadows. Again many of the men were hard-bitten bushmen, timber workers and goldfields veterans, 'big loose-limbed fellows ... from the backblocks.'[4]

After a period of brigade training at Broadmeadows, the 4th Brigade followed the 1st Division to Egypt, and thence to Gallipoli. Elements of the Brigade landed at Anzac Cove late on the first Anzac Day. Parts of the 16th and 15th Battalions clambered up Monash Valley that evening and took up positions on Pope's Hill. The rest of the Brigade followed, and for the vital first weeks on the beachhead they held the precarious posts at the head of Monash Valley—Quinn's Post ('the spearhead of Anzac'[5]), Courtney's Post and Pope's Hill. After repulsing their share of the major Turkish attack of 19 May 1915, the Brigade's area was visited by the great C E W Bean, the official war correspondent:

> the men were fine breezy chaps, but they were far more amateurish and casual than in any of the lines we had so far gone through. And one of the officers spoken to by Colonel White was almost disobedient—had to be told twice to stand below the parapet and acted then in a way intended to show that he resented the order ... However when we got along a bit to Quinn's there was more reason for the attitude of the men ...[6]

That incident was in some ways perhaps characteristic of the 4th Brigade and later the 4th Division, but by 1917 Bean would have completely revised his opinions of them; by the time he came to write the *Official History*, Bean stated that the Brigade's holding of the head of Monash Valley was one of the greatest feats of the 1st AIF.[7] It was during the battle of 19 May that a young 4th Brigade soldier, Private (acting Lance Corporal) Albert Jacka of the 14th Battalion, won Australia's first Victoria Cross of the war, single-handedly recapturing a section of the Courtney's Post trenches from a Turkish force.

The Brigade was relieved in the Monash Valley positions in June 1915, and its next major campaign on Gallipoli was the August offensive. Much ground to the north of Anzac Cove was occupied, but, debilitated by sickness, the brigade was unable to take its final and crucial objective, Hill 971, in the impossible terrain. Suffering heavy casualties in this operation, the brigade took further losses in two attacks at Hill 60, and spent the rest of the campaign defending its line in the northern sector. Its 13th and 16th Battalions stayed to the last, pulling out late on the final night of the evacuation.

The 4th Brigade, like the rest of the AIF, was in the process of recovering its strength in February 1916 when the process of forming the new divisions commenced. Monash (now Brigadier General as were all brigade commanders[8]) was still leading the brigade. The 13th Battalion was commanded by Lieutenant Colonel Leslie Tilney, transferred from the 16th Battalion during the Gallipoli campaign. The unit's officers included another originally from the 16th who would achieve unmatched distinction—Lieutenant Henry 'Harry' Murray, an energetic 35 year old who had enlisted as a private in the machine gun section of the 16th in Western Australia and had been commissioned as the 13th's Machine Gun Officer during the August operations at Anzac. The 14th Battalion's CO was Lieutenant Colonel Charles Dare, who had led the attack at Hill 60 and was currently the AIF's youngest battalion commander. The most notable of the 14th's members was the hero of Courtney's Post, the extraordinary Albert Jacka VC, now a Company Sergeant Major (CSM) and soon to be commissioned.

Queenslander Lieutenant Colonel James Cannan had been the 15th Battalion's CO almost since the beginning of the war, leading the unit ashore at the Landing and later garrison commander of Quinn's Post. His adjutant at Quinn's and now second-in-command of the Battalion itself was Major Terence McSharry ('Jockey Mac' to the troops), originally a member of the Light Horse The 15th had suffered the highest total casualties of all the Gallipoli battalions. Completing the 4th Brigade's component units was the 16th Battalion, under its Gallipoli commander Lieutenant Colonel Harold Pope, after whom Pope's Hill had been named. Outstanding among his officers was Captain Percy Black, a moustachioed 38 year old gold miner ('the old prospector' as Bean called him[9]) who had enlisted as a private and been 'number one' on a machine gun during the first weeks at Gallipoli (with Harry Murray, now in the 13th Battalion, as his 'number two'). Commissioned in May 1915, Black had proved to be a natural leader and would shortly be promoted to major after only 20 months in the army.

With the break-up of the NZ & A Division, the 4th Brigade moved by train from Moascar to the big AIF camp at Tel-el-Kebir on 26 February 1916. The AIF expansion plan called for the 4th Brigade's battalions to form the new 12th Brigade units from their ranks. Both old and new brigades would be part of the 4th Division. The situation of the Division's remaining infantry brigade was slightly different: the new 13th Brigade was formed from the original 3rd Brigade battalions of the 1st Division, with the 'parent' units remaining with their original division. Recruited from the 'outer' states, the 3rd Brigade comprised the 9th (Queensland), 10th (South Australia), 11th (Western Australia) and 12th (SA, WA, Tasmania) Battalions. The units took pride in their status as their respective state's first infantry units to be formed. Brigadier General Ewen Sinclair-MacLagan had led the 3rd Brigade since the beginning of the war, and his command had had the honour of being first ashore at the Landing, as the covering force for the whole operation

Sinclair-MacLagan remained with the 1st Division when the great AIF re-organisation took place, but he would become part of the 4th Division's history later in the war. Among the 3rd Brigade members who were chosen for the new units, several names stood out. Major Raymond Leane of the 11th Battalion had established his reputation on Gallipoli with his leadership of a raid on Turkish positions at Gaba Tepe; although finally forced to withdraw, he had shown his ability to handle men in critical situations. Later in the campaign he led a successful assault on the position that became known as Leane's Trench. A tall, imposing man, he was obviously a potential unit commander at least. A fellow officer in the 11th Battalion, Major Edmund Drake-Brockman, was similarly highly regarded; he was due to return to his unit after recovering from a Gallipoli wound, and although not initially going to the 4th Division, he would join the new formation soon.

Majors Miles Beevor, Francis Lorenzo and Frederick Hurcombe, all 10th Battalion officers, would play key roles with the new division. Among noted current and former 3rd Brigade officers who initially stayed with the 1st Division but later crossed to the 4th were

Major Alfred Salisbury of the 9th Battalion, brigade staff officer Major John Peck, and Major John Whitham, who had distinguished himself with the 12th Battalion on Gallipoli and was currently on the 2nd Brigade staff. The eight distinguished battalions of the 4th and 3rd Brigades, which had forged their first traditions in the heat of battle, would now go through the administratively and emotionally taxing process of splitting themselves in two.

Brigadier General[10] Duncan Glasfurd took command of the new 12th Brigade as of 1 March 1916. He was a 42 year old British regular officer of the Argyll and Sutherland Highlanders, seconded to the Australian regular army at the time that the war broke out. Chosen for General Bridges' 1st Division staff, Glasfurd had gone ashore on the first morning on Gallipoli and, under fire, had been instrumental in establishing some sort of order out of the initial disorganisation on the beach and inland. The official historian C E W Bean described him as being at this time 'one of the bravest and most conscientious officers upon the Staff'[11] and later that his great value as a commander was 'accurate judgment of men and ... strength in enforcing [his] judgments.'[12] Before the war he had been Director of Military Training in Australia, and had supervised the 1st Division's training in Egypt prior to the Gallipoli expedition.

The veteran 4th Brigade now faced the trauma of splitting up to produce General Glasfurd's new command. The initial split for each battalion envisaged two 'wings', the first (headquarters) wing to include the original battalion headquarters (less a few specialists - signallers and pioneers), the machine-gun section, the battalion transport, and half of the rifle company members. The second wing would comprise basically the other half of the rifle companies, and would need to create its own ancillary sub-units. Both wings would take in reinforcements to build up to full battalion establishment. In oddly feminine style, the new units were often called the 'daughters' of the original parent battalions.

The 13th and 14th Battalions paraded on 2 March[13] to be given their orders. The 13th was to form the new 45th Battalion, and had adopted the simple method of allocating two full rifle companies to its 'daughter;' it was a 'particularly sad moment'[14] for the troops, as the battalion history recorded. The 13th's second in command, Major Sydney Herring, went to the new battalion as its first CO, with promotion to lieutenant colonel. The reaction of the 14th Battalion to its formation of the new 46th was, perhaps characteristically, rather more militant. CSM Albert Jacka VC, who had made his own feelings about the split quite clear, paraded his company and began to read out the names of the NCOs posted to the 46th. He was interrupted by a chorus of protest. 'To think that a man has never left the battalion and been in every stunt, and now he's to be chucked out like this' complained a hard-bitten sergeant.[15] Jacka himself remained with the 14th. The 46th's inaugural commander was British regular Lieutenant Colonel Geoffrey Lee, formerly of the King's Royal Rifle Corps.

The 15th Battalion gave birth, no doubt as reluctantly as the others, to the 47th on the next day, also providing the latter unit's CO, Lieutenant Colonel Robert Eccles Snowden, among other officers. Also on 3 March, a group of four officers and 350 'ORs' from the 16th Battalion paraded at Tel-el-Kebir to hear a farewell address from their CO, Lieutenant Colonel Pope. 'Even as the colonel spoke they eyed with some resentment a tall officer standing near to him … to them he was an alien, of another Battalion, indeed of another Brigade, and the soldier is ever a regimental bigot.'[16] The tall officer was Major (shortly confirmed as Lieutenant Colonel) Raymond Leane, formerly of the 11th Battalion, nominated commanding officer of the new 48th Battalion, and as Leane gave the orders for the group to march off, 'their inclusion in the 48th was an accomplished fact before their gloomy anticipation of it had ceased.'[17]

The 13th Infantry Brigade had begun to form a few days earlier. Appointed to command was a Light Horse officer, William Glasgow, veteran of both the Boer War and Gallipoli. This 39 year old Queensland citizen soldier was a grazier in civilian life. C E W Bean characterised him as

> the most forcible of the three strong brigadiers of the 4th Division … with puckered humorous brows as shaggy as a deerhounds; with the bushman's difficulty of verbal expression but sure sense of character and situations.[18]

Glasgow had commanded the garrison of Pope's Hill at Gallipoli, when the Light Horse took over that position from the 4th Infantry Brigade. On his appointment to the 13th Brigade, Glasgow brought with him from the Light Horse Major John Cecil Ridley and Captain Alan Steele as staff officers, as well as a number of NCOs whom he had selected as potential infantry officers. Among the latter were two towering Tasmanian brothers, Arthur and Duncan Maxwell, both granted commissions in the new 52nd Battalion, and Quartermaster Lieutenant Robert Christie, commissioned into the 51st. This type of headhunting quickly became rife throughout the AIF as its expansion proceeded.

The 3rd Brigade gave reluctant birth to its 'daughters'. Major Harry Seager (10th and 50th Battalions) wrote that 'poor General MacLagan was broken hearted at losing half his old brigade. There was not an officer, NCO or man on parade who had not a lump in his throat when he had finished his farewell speech.'[19] Seager did acknowledge, however, that 'everybody realised it was essential to stiffen up the new troops to keep up the splendid name of Australia.'[20] The Queenslanders of the 9th Battalion produced the 49th, the new commanding officer of which was Lieutenant Colonel Francis Lorenzo, a 36 year old regular officer who was serving in the 10th Battalion at the time. The 10th itself, a South Australian unit, provided the troops for the new 50th Battalion, as well as its CO, Lieutenant Colonel Frederick Hurcombe, previous second in command of the 10th. Aged 49, he was an exception to the emerging AIF policy of appointing younger men to unit command. It was a measure of the esteem in which the 50th's new CO was held that the unit's nickname quickly became 'Hurcombe's Hungry Half Hundred.'[21]

The 11th Battalion, Western Australia, gave birth to the 51st Battalion, achieving the split by retaining its odd-numbered infantry sections and transferring the even-numbered sections to the new unit. 'In this way an impartial division was made and the new battalion started its new career with exactly the same quality of personnel as the older battalion'[22] (this of course was the basic object of the scheme). The new Lieutenant Colonel to command the 51st was British regular officer Arthur Ross, 37, promoted from his current posting as brigade major on the 3rd Brigade staff. The 12th Battalion's new 'daughter' was the 52nd, both units being mainly Tasmanian with elements from South and Western Australia. Major P K Baker was initially appointed to command the 52nd, but he had fallen seriously ill and was soon succeeded by Lieutenant Colonel Miles Beevor, a 33 year old former accountant from South Australia. Beevor was another 10th Battalion original, that unit having now supplied three of the four 13th Brigade COs.

To sum up, the Fourth Division's infantry element was made up as follows (senior officers' ranks are shown as they were when promotions were confirmed; short-term acting COs are not included):

4th Infantry Brigade:	Brigadier General J Monash
13th Battalion (NSW)	Lieutenant Colonel L E Tilney
14th Battalion (Vic)	Lieutenant Colonel C M M Dare
15th Battalion (Qld and Tas)	Lieutenant Colonel J H Cannan
16th Battalion (WA and SA)	Lieutenant Colonel H Pope
12th Infantry Brigade:	Brigadier General D J Glasfurd
45th Battalion (NSW)	Lieutenant Colonel S C E Herring
46th Battalion (Vic)	Lieutenant Colonel G T Lee
47th Battalion (Qld and Tas)	Lieutenant Colonel R E Snowden
48th Battalion (WA and SA)	Lieutenant Colonel R L Leane
13th Infantry Brigade:	Brigadier General T W Glasgow
49th Battalion (Qld)	Lieutenant Colonel F M deF Lorenzo
50th Battalion (SA)	Lieutenant Colonel F W Hurcombe
51st Battalion (WA)	Lieutenant Colonel A M Ross
52nd Battalion (Tas, SA, WA)	Lieutenant Colonel M F Beevor

Apparent from the above is an important contributing factor to the 4th Division's unique character among the five infantry divisions of the First AIF. Two-thirds of its most numerous arm was recruited from the less-populated or 'outer' states, and only one-third from the heavily-populated states of New South Wales and Victoria—the reverse of the situation in the other four AIF infantry divisions. The proportion of recruitment by state for the division's other arms was similar, if not as pronounced as in the infantry.

The infantry of the new division was concentrated at Tel-el-Kebir, the tented camp being expanded to accommodate the new units. All units set to work absorbing their reinforcements and implementing training programmes. Some training had to be fairly basic, most of the new recruits having arrived from Australia only partially trained. Apart from elementary drill work, many were without rifles and needed initial musketry training. Reinforcements continued to be added over the next few weeks, some being organised contingents originally designated for the 'old' battalions but now sent straight to the new ones. In the 45th Battalion for example, on 16 March 1916 the unit received five officers and 459 other ranks as reinforcements, consisting of the 14th Reinforcements of the 1st Battalion, the 2nd Reinforcements of the 30th Battalion and the 10th, 11th and 12th Reinforcements of the 13th Battalion, these all being recruited from New South Wales. Others were from less reliable sources; the 13th Battalion history noted that in late March the unit 'had to take on our strength 200 rejects from the 1st Brigade—very hard after losing our splendid men to the 45th and other units.' In time, however, many of this group put their previous misconduct behind them and proved to be useful soldiers, at least in the field: they 'perhaps troubled their officers, but they troubled the enemy more.'[23]

A major difficulty for all units was the provision of officers and NCOs. The battalions had started with, at most, half of their normal establishment and vacancies had to be filled as a matter of urgency. By this time, very few AIF officers (only the limited number of Duntroon graduates) were directly commissioned, the great majority being selected from the ranks. Some were commissioned during training and became officers in the various reinforcement contingents, but most were selected in the field from NCOs and men who had proven their leadership qualities in action. Battalion commanders now began to search the ranks for suitable candidates, not only in their own units but in other units and different branches of the service. The Light Horse in particular was heavily raided, but there were plenty of instances of poaching between different infantry units. Even the new formations were on the receiving end of such activities. Brigadier General Glasfurd was sufficiently irritated as to record his feelings in the 12th Brigade's official War Diary. He wrote of

> ... a scramble between new units for good officers and a good deal of 'officer snatching' took place. Some commanding officers and even brigade commanders exceeded the limits of courtesy and common sense by sending emissaries to my lines to offer my officers better positions in other units. The great flow of promotions also unsettled several officers, NCOs and men who lacked ballast. Very ordinary subalterns expected to be offered positions as senior majors and several privates were promoted sergeants straight away.[24]

Despite the difficulties encountered and the genuine anguish of the 'original' personnel, there can be little doubt that General Birdwood's method of forming the new units was the best way. It ensured that each new unit had an experienced core around which to develop its military capacity. While the original battalions had of course lost a large proportion of their veterans, they had retained enough to ensure a rapid return to efficiency, backed up emotionally by their established traditions. Conscious of this factor, AIF Headquarters ruled that the identifying colour patches worn on the shoulders of the new battalions should use the same colours as the parent units, but shaped differently. These scraps of fabric were regarded with considerable pride, and it was some consolation to those transferred to new units that they could continue to wear their original battalion's colours. The 'daughter' units at first wore their patches as vertical rectangles instead of the horizontal rectangles of the originals, but the 12th and 13th Brigades changed to the standard circular shape of the 4th Division in 1917;

the 4th Brigade retained its horizontal rectangles throughout the war, in recognition of its part at the Landing. A strong sense of brotherhood was to prevail between the old and new units (in the case of the 13th Brigade, such links were with the 1st Division's 3rd Brigade) throughout the war. The new units would build their own traditions on the Western Front, as General Birdwood had anticipated; the general was well aware that 'every individual was fully satisfied that his particular battalion was the best, not only in the AIF but in the British Empire or even in the world.'[25] This confident attitude played its part in the 1st AIF's effectiveness in the war.

In any case such considerations were overshadowed by the amount of work required by all units to meet the challenges of administration and training presented by the reorganisation. Similar difficulties, in some cases more serious than those of the infantry, were being faced by the other elements of the new division, these in turn impinging on the infantry. The 13th Battalion's experience was typical, being required to release 37 machine gunners to the 4th Brigade Machine Gun Company, 53 other members to the 4th Division artillery, 26 to the 4th Pioneer Battalion, and five to the Divisional Signal Company. It is to those units that this account will now turn.

1 Notes

1. C E W Bean, *The Official History of Australia in the War of 1914-18* (hereinafter *Official History*), Vol III, p.41.
2. See, for example, P A Pedersen, *The Anzacs*, p.408.
3. T A White, *The Fighting Thirteenth*, p. 15.
4. W Devine, *The Story of a Battalion* (48th Battalion history), p. 3.
5. *Official History*, Vol IV, p. 294.
6. Bean Diary AWM38 3DRL606/8/1, 24 May 1915 (Page 91 in PDF).
7. *Official History*, Vol IV, p. 488n.
8. Strictly speaking, the rank was 'Colonel and Temporary Brigadier General.'
9. *Official History*, Vol IV, p. 293.
10. The new brigadiers (Glasfurd and Glasgow) initially held the rank of colonel, and were confirmed as brigadier generals shortly afterwards. For convenience, they will herinafter be referred to as brigadier generals from the beginning of their commands.
11. *Official History*, Vol I, p. 486.
12. *Ibid*, Vol III, p. 52.
13. Dates for 4th Brigade split-ups are taken from battalion histories. The *Official History* gives 4 March 1916 for the formation of the 45th and 46th Battalions, 7 march for the 47th and 48th.

14   White, *Op Cit*, p. 58.
15   E J Rule, *Jacka's Mob*, p. 14.
16   Devine, *Op Cit*, p. 2.
17   Ibid.
18   *Official History*, Vol III, p. 848 - 9.
19   R R Freeman, *Hurcombes's Hungry Half Hundred*, p. 4..
20   Ibid.
21   Ibid, p.1.
22   W C Belford, *Legs Eleven*, p. 198.
23   White, *Op Cit*, p. 61.
24   12th Brigade War Diary for February to March 1916.
25   J E Lee, *The Chronicle of the 45th Battalion AIF*, p. 6.

2: Gunners, Sappers, Pioneers and others

In 1916, a division was essentially the smallest army formation to include all branches of the service—a self-contained formation capable of coordinating all arms in battle. The core of an infantry division, and its most numerous element, was of course its twelve infantry battalions. Second in numbers and controlling the division's heaviest firepower was the divisional **artillery**. The big guns, in conjunction with the chattering machine guns, dominated the battlefields of the Western Front. It was the artillery that caused the most casualties over the course of the war and blasted the war zone to a wasteland.

The heaviest-calibre artillery weapons were controlled at Corps and Army level, but each British and Empire infantry division was provided with its own lighter weapons as field artillery. The structure and organisation of the divisional artillery elements underwent considerable change during the war, but in early 1916 a division on the Western Front included three units (brigades) of field guns, each brigade divided into four batteries of four guns each, and one brigade of howitzers divided into three batteries, each also having four weapons. Artillery brigades were each commanded by a Lieutenant Colonel. Each brigade had its ammunition column, the horse-drawn transport echelon, shortly to be consolidated into a divisional ammunition column. Divisional artillery was under the command of an officer of the rank of Brigadier General, designated as the Commander Royal Artillery (CRA). Briefly, the standard field gun was the 18-pounder (8 kilograms, the weight of its standard shell) Quick Firing (QF) gun, which fired shrapnel and high explosive (HE) shells, and later gas and smoke shell also, at reasonably high velocity and low trajectory over a range of 6,400 metres; improved marks could reach over 9,000 metres later in the war. At the divisional level, the standard howitzer (technically a howitzer and not a 'gun') was the 4.5 inch (114 mm) QF firing 16-kilogram HE shells up to 6,000 metres. Howitzers shot at a lower velocity and higher trajectory than field guns, lobbing their shells over obstacles and into the enemy's trenches.

Although the divisional artillery organisation described above was now standard in France, the 1st and 2nd Divisions of the AIF had only been equipped on a lower scale of three field gun

An 18-pounder field gun of the 38th Battery, 10th AFA Brigade, in action near Zonnebeke, Belgium, October 1917, photographed by Frank Hurley. (AWM E01209)

A 4.5-inch field howitzer of the 111th Battery, 11th AFA Brigade, near Ravine Wood, Ypres sector, Belgium. (AWM C04390)

brigades each with three batteries, and no howitzers. Thus while the new 4th and 5th Divisions had to create their artillery from scratch, even the existing divisions were each short of one battery per field gun brigade and their entire howitzer brigade of three batteries. It was decided at first to stay with the original lower scale and begin forming the new divisions' artillery by transferring a field brigade from each of the existing divisions, together with further personnel from which to build up the necessary new brigades. The 1st Division's 3rd Australian Field

Artillery (AFA) Brigade was transferred to the 4th Division and renumbered as the 12th AFA Brigade. The new division would form also the 10th and 11th Brigades beginning in late February, then next month the 24th (Howitzer) Brigade, the decision having been made to establish howitzer units in all divisions. The Gallipoli veteran Lieutenant Colonel Charles Rosenthal, promoted from field brigade commander in the 1st Division to brigadier general, was appointed CRA of the 4th Division.

Rosenthal was 41 years old and had served in the citizen forces artillery since he was 17. It was largely through his forceful leadership that field guns had been emplaced in the steep tangled terrain at Anzac. He was an architect in civilian life and apart from soldiering General Rosenthal's other main outside interest was music; he had a fine reputation as a singer and was also an accomplished pianist, 'a man with a breezy, thrusting personality and keen, simple enthusiasms.'[1] He was now faced with a military task that would need all of his considerable energy, building up the full artillery component of an imperial division with severely limited time and resources.

Brigadier General (Sir) Charles Rosenthal KCB CMG DSO (1875-1954), CRA 4th Division to August 1917; later commander 9th Infantry Brigade (3rd Division) then, as major general, GOC 2nd Division.
(AWM H19207)

Transfer of the first personnel and equipment to the 4th Division took place on 21 February 1916, and the Division now had a small core of trained artillerymen on which to build. Some of these were perhaps not of the highest standard. Some crafty officers took the opportunity to send away certain of their less desirable personnel; at least one such officer was soon horrified to be informed that he also had been transferred to the 4th Division, to take command of the same troublemakers that he had just rid himself of.[2] Training of the extra personnel needed to bring the artillery up to full strength (at this time, about 3,000 officers and other ranks) presented a major challenge. The technical expertise required to operate the complex destructive weapons could not be acquired easily and qualified instructors were at a premium. The task had scarcely begun when a sudden change of plans made it even more difficult. The 1st and 2nd Divisions were warned for imminent transfer to France and almost at the last minute it was ordered that those divisions must be equipped up to the full artillery establishment for service in that theatre. On 2 March Brigadier General Rosenthal was required to give back virtually all of the field brigade personnel that had been transferred to him only 11 days earlier. The 4th Division artillery was left with about 150 officers and men, and the work had to start again. The remaining source of men was mainly the infantry and light horse, and the necessary numbers began to come in over the next two weeks. Equipment was also in short supply, with the 1st and 2nd Divisions having priority, and the same applied to horses—divisional artillery needed about 2,000 horses, with 280 vehicles, to move the guns and for the ammunition columns.[3]

Training recommenced, the few trained artillery officers employing ingenuity and hard work to achieve results. The *Official History* cites the example of the 12th AFA Brigade commanded by Lieutenant Colonel Reginald Rabett. The Colonel gave his new junior officers two hours of instruction starting at 4:30 am after which they joined their men to begin the day's gun drill under the four battery commanders, the only officers with any previous experience. The new officers were able to begin providing training to their men within a fortnight, in effect the teachers staying a page ahead of the students. For the first few weeks the 4th Division artillery had the advantage of a good training area at Tel-el-Kebir, with a hutted camp, reliable water supply and 'an excellent manoeuvre area with gravel surface.'[4] This changed much for the worse at the end of the month with the division's move to Serapeum in the Suez Canal area (of which more later). The gunners now found themselves 'in the midst of a sandy waste where empty vehicles could only with difficulty be drawn by the teams, and manoeuvre was quite impossible.'[5] All ranks persevered, coping at the same time also with operational tasks—defence of the camp, and provision of two batteries and an ammunition column supporting a mobile force operating east of the Canal.

Training in the desert proceeded through all difficulties, concluding with elementary shooting practice for the last three weeks of May 1916, at which time the division began preparing for its move to Europe. The artillery units at that time were composed and commanded as follows (batteries were individually numbered, howitzer batteries being allocated three-digit numbers):

CRA: Brigadier General C Rosenthal
10th AFA Brigade (nominally recruited from NSW[6]) Lieutenant Colonel G H M King
(37th, 38th, 39th and 40th Batteries)
11th AFA Brigade (Queensland) Lieutenant Colonel F A Hughes
(41st, 42nd, 43rd and 44th Batteries)
12th AFA Brigade (Victoria) Lieutenant Colonel R L R Rabett
(45th, 46th, 47th and 48th Batteries)
24th AFA Brigade (all states) Lieutenant-Colonel W C N Waite
(110th, 111th and 112th Howitzer Batteries)

The Brigade COs were all pre-war militia officers and Gallipoli veterans (Colonel Waite had also served in South Africa). Colonels King and Rabett were from New South Wales, Waite from South Australia and Hughes from Queensland. General Rosenthal reported some interesting statistics. As of the end of May, the origins of the divisional artillery's personnel were:

Artillery	457
Light Horse	1,198
Infantry	1,171
Other arms	151
(Total	**2,977)**

Of the 85 officers, 24 were militia artillery officers and 12 were artillerymen commissioned from the ranks. In both categories some had only a few months experience. The remaining 49 were mostly from the Light Horse with no previous artillery experience. There were no regular artillery officers at all. Even the 5th Division, which faced similar difficulties forming its artillery, had 12 regular officers. General Rosenthal ventured 'to say that no Divisional artillery in the British Army today [May 1917] can point to such an extraordinary constructional record.'[7] The official historian commented 'It had fallen upon a handful of Australian militia officers to create in two months this specialised force. It is unlikely that such a task was ever attempted among any other troops destined for the Western Front.'[8]

Machine guns formed another vital element of a division's firepower. The 1st AIF had gone to Gallipoli with the standard British Army allocation of machine guns, two Maxim guns and their crews per infantry battalion, under command of battalion headquarters. Early in the campaign it was found necessary to group the guns by brigades, under a brigade machine gun officer, to provide integrated firepower in defence of the precarious foothold at Anzac. This system was particularly employed in the positions at the head of Monash Valley, held for the first crucial weeks by the 4th Brigade. Late in the campaign, the establishment was doubled to four guns and crews, the 2nd Division being so equipped when it arrived at the front. A few of the early model Vickers guns, an improved and lighter version of the Maxim, arrived at Gallipoli towards the end of the campaign. That weapon, belt-fed, water-cooled and tripod-mounted, was such a sound design that it was still being used effectively by Commonwealth forces in the Korean War. There were still a number of the older Maxims with the AIF in Egypt, but these were steadily being replaced by Vickers guns.

The British Army's first year of combat on the Western Front had also shown the desirability of grouping machine guns into larger units, and late in 1915 the Machine Gun Corps was created. The Army's machine guns and gunners were progressively formed into machine gun companies, separate from the infantry battalions and directly controlled at brigade level. The new policy was applied in the AIF as part of its reorganisation in Egypt, and the 4th Division was required to form three new machine gun companies, to be numbered according to their respective brigades. Each company when fully equipped would have 16 Vickers guns, the equivalent of four infantry battalions' previous allocation of four guns each. The companies were first established about two weeks after the split-up of the original infantry battalions; those had initially retained their machine gun sections, with the new battalions having to create their own. This process was now overtaken by the new arrangements, and the 4th Brigade battalions released their machine gunners and weapons to make up the 4th Machine Gun (MG) Company. The two new brigades would have to look further afield to fill their establishments, although the 4th Company provided some assistance; the 12th MG Company's first four guns (Maxims) were transferred from the 4th. Full establishment of a machine gun company was six officers and 200 other ranks, the 16 guns and crews divided into four sections of four guns each under a subaltern officer; companies had their own allocation

Vickers machine guns, 12th MG Company. The weapon on the left has an auxiliary tripod attached under the water jacket. The officers in this 1917 photograph are: back row, left to right: : Second Lieutenant Bernard O'Reilly; 2nd Lt Claude King; 2nd Lt Edward Cullimore; 2nd Lt William Gregson.
Front row: Lieutenant Peter Grieveson; Captain Harry Crouch; Capt David Martin; Lt Allan Taylor; Lt Errol Upton. (AWM H00177)

of vehicles and horses for transport of equipment and ammunition. It would take some time for the MG companies to build up to full strength; the 12th Company reported on 14 March that training had commenced with 32 NCOs and men, rising to 80 a few days later.

The 4th MG Company's first commander was Major Eric Wilton, a regular officer who transferred in from the 16th Battalion infantry. Captain Edgar Sawer was placed in command of the 12th Company; he had served with the 10th Battalion machine guns at Gallipoli, and had recently been reassigned to the new 48th Battalion before the MG companies were established. The 13th Company was first led by Captain Roy Morell, a former Light Horse machine gun officer, one of a number of Light Horse members brought into the 13th Brigade by Brigadier General Glasgow (Morell later served on General Glasgow's staff at both brigade and division level, and was Australian Corps Machine Gun Officer in 1918). In common with the rest of the reconstituted AIF, the new MG companies now took on the challenge of intensive training and building up to full strength in men and material.

The weaponry of a division on the Western Front included a number of trench **mortar** batteries. Each infantry brigade was allotted a light trench mortar (LTM) battery, equipped with eight of the new Stokes 3-inch (76mm) mortars, and designated by the brigade number; the Stokes fired a 4.5 kilogram bomb. The divisional artillery controlled the heavier mortars: three batteries each with four 'medium' mortars and one battery of four 'heavies'. The medium trench mortar (MTM) was of 2-inch (50mm) calibre but fired a 19-kilogram spherical bomb, the small calibre being because the bomb was attached to a steel rod or tail which fitted into the mortar barrel. These were later replaced by the 6-inch (152mm) Newton mortars. The standard 9.45-inch (240mm) heavy trench mortar (HTM) fired a monster 69-kilogram bomb—the 'Flying Pig'. The artillery's mortar batteries were identified by code numbers: in the 4th Division, the heavy battery was numbered V4A, the medium batteries X4A, Y4A and Z4A. Personnel were allotted to the infantry and artillery mortar batteries while the Division was still in Egypt; however, the weapons and proper training facilities would not become available until the division reached France, so in practice the batteries were not formed until then.

Another specialised element of a Great War Imperial infantry division, the military **engineers** ('sappers'), had responsibility for the myriad construction and demolition tasks necessary in operations. The divisional engineers consisted of three field companies, each of which was commanded by a major and comprised six officers and about 200 other ranks, plus transport including 70 horses and mules and 50 vehicles. Each field company was informally linked to one of the division's infantry brigades but officially controlled by Division HQ through the divisional Commander Royal Engineers (CRE), an officer of the rank of lieutenant-colonel. The 4th Division's inaugural CRE was Lieutenant Colonel Gilbert Elliott, an experienced 43 year old British regular officer of the Royal Engineers. Colonel Elliott was another of the senior British Army officers who had been serving with the Australian permanent forces at the outbreak of the war. He had gone to Gallipoli as CRE of the 1st Division—that is, he was the first leader in battle of Australian engineers.

The nucleus of the 4th Division engineers was the 4th Field Company. This was a 2nd Division unit,[9] originally formed in Egypt in August 1915. It had gone to Gallipoli after training and played its part in the constant tunnelling, mining and general field works undertaken during that campaign. In late February 1916 the unit moved from the Canal zone to Tel-el-Kebir and began the process of evolving into three companies. Numbering of engineer units during the AIF expansion was a source of some confusion—there were two separate '5th' companies at one stage, for instance. As far as the 4th Division was concerned, its new engineer field companies were numbered the 4th, 12th and 13th, and so conformed to the division's infantry brigade numbers. The 12th and 13th Field Companies took their initial personnel from the 4th company, and filled up to establishment with reinforcements. These mostly came from the pool of specialist engineer personnel held at the Base Detail Camp at Zeitoun (location of the Imperial School of Instruction), but also included a number of infantrymen. Volunteers had been sought from the battalions, and this source provided a number of men with trade or technical qualifications who had enlisted when there was a lack of vacancies in the specialist arms, and now took up the opportunities in both of the new divisions.[10]

The CRE also controlled the divisional **signal** company—Signals was not established as a separate corps until 1925. The company was responsible for all communications between divisional units, by telephone, telegraph, visual signalling and the developing technology of wireless telegraphy. A section of motorcycle couriers (the DRLS, Despatch Rider Letter Service) handled distribution of the division's written correspondence. The signal company, commanded by a major, originally had a personnel establishment similar to that of an engineer field company but by 1918 had expanded to 16 officers and 350 other ranks, with 40 vehicles (including two motor lorries) and 120 horses and mules. The personnel numbers included several detachments of an officer and 20 ORs normally attached to the artillery headquarters, each artillery brigade and each infantry brigade (at battalion level, the infantry provided its own signalling officer and signallers. Major John Fraser was appointed officer commanding the 4th Division Signal Company. Incidentally, one of the NCOs in the Division's despatch rider group was 19 year old Corporal Charles Kingsford Smith, transferred from the 2nd Division signals.[11] 'Smithy' went to France with the 4th Division, later to be commissioned as a pilot in the Royal Flying Corps (RFC) and go on to post-war immortality as one of the great pioneers of civil aviation.

As of April 1916, the 4th Division engineer units and their commanding officers were:[12]

CRE:	Lieutenant Colonel G C E Elliott
4th Field Company:	Major R V Cutler
12th Field Company:	Major E A E Andrewartha
13th Field Company:	Major M J G Colyer
4th Division Signal Company:	Major J E Fraser

A new type of unit, closely associated with the engineers, had come into being in the British Army late in 1914. These were the **pioneer** battalions, formed to meet increasing demands for skilled labour on the construction and maintenance of trenches, general earthworks, roadways and the like, as the Western Front rapidly settled into the stalemate of trench warfare. Allocated on the basis of one per division, the pioneer battalions formed something of a hybrid between infantry and engineers, with infantry training and weaponry but composed as far as possible of skilled 'pick and shovel men' and tradesmen, particularly from the building trades. Ideally up to half of the battalion would possess a recognised trade. Pioneer battalions were structured like infantry battalions, commanded by a lieutenant colonel and divided into four companies. Their role has been summed up as 'fighting infantry, capable of providing "organised and intelligent labour" for engineering operations,'[13] or more simply as 'the handy man of the division ... just as useful to it as is a handy man about a house or farm.'[14] The battalion CO reported to the divisional commander, but was expected to work closely with, and often under the direction of, the CRE (the infantry battalions each had a small pioneer section also, to carry out minor works).

AIF pioneer battalions were numbered according to their division number. The 4th Pioneer Battalion was formed in early March 1916 at Tel-el-Kebir. Lieutenant Colonel James Corlette,[15] an Australian militia officer of engineers who had commanded the 1st Field Company at Gallipoli, was detailed to organise and command the unit. Corlette soon encountered a common problem confronting commanders of new units during this period. Personnel were allocated from the infantry battalions, and each company and battalion commander seized upon the opportunity to get rid of undesirable or troublesome characters, and as a result the drafts contained an undue proportion of such men, though, of course, also containing many men of good character.[16]

That was only the beginning of Colonel Corlette's difficulties. Allocated a bare area of desert on the outskirts of Tel-el-Kebir, the Battalion had no tents or transport at first, and had only six officers on strength. The next ten days were spent setting up the campsite and some training was started. Scarcely had the camp been put into shape, however, when the Pioneers had to move with the rest of the Division to Serapeum on the Canal. Training in infantry and engineering work got under way again, hampered by frequent cases of absence without leave and other minor offences among the less reliable of the troops. The Battalion was also called on to undertake works around the divisional area almost straight away.

The CO worked assiduously to bring his unit up to scratch, arranging commissions for a number of men with engineering backgrounds (although with little military experience) and attempting, with limited success, to extract more tradesmen from other units. The Battalion was still well short of optimum efficiency, and well below full strength in numbers, when it was ordered to take over part of the outer defence line ten miles east of the Canal, both to garrison the line and to continue construction of defensive works. Corlette made his objections to this move clear to divisional headquarters, and it was not long afterwards (9 May 1916) that he found himself being transferred to the Engineering Training Depot at Tel-el-Kebir, reverting to his substantive rank of major. Command of the 4th Pioneer Battalion was taken on by Major Ernest Williams, transferred from the divisional headquarters staff. It was an unfortunate start for the new unit but it would perform well in France and Belgium.[17]

Within a division, the duties of attending to the illnesses and wounds suffered by the personnel were undertaken by members of the Australian Army **Medical** Corps (AAMC), under the control of the division's Assistant Director of Medical Services (ADMS), assisted by a deputy (DADMS). Appointed on 18 February 1916, the 4th Division's first ADMS was the forthright Colonel George Barber, a militia medical officer from Kalgoorlie in the Western Australian goldfields. Colonel Barber was 47 years old in February 1916; English born and raised, he had qualified in medicine in England before migrating to Australia at the age of about 27. Joining the AIF from the citizen forces in 1914, he had served throughout the Gallipoli campaign, as second in command and later commanding officer of the 2nd Australian Stationary Hospital, based at Lemnos Island. Major Alexander Marks was appointed as DADMS.

AAMC personnel under the command of the ADMS included each Regimental Medical Officer (RMO) and his orderlies at unit level (such as an infantry battalion), but the main medical corps units in the division were the three Field Ambulances. These each consisted of 10 officers, with a lieutenant colonel in command, (all qualified medical practitioners) and 250 'ORs', about 150 of whom were stretcher-bearers and the remainder belonged to the 'tent' subdivision, responsible for tending the wounded at the field ambulance's treatment centre. A field ambulance unit was normally made up of three sections, each with its complement of stretcher-bearer and tent personnel, commanded by a major or captain and capable (in theory) of looking after up to 50 patients each. Initially, however, the new units in Egypt had only two sections, as did the reconstituted existing units. This change simplified creation

Colonel George Barber CB DSO (1868–1951), ADMS 4th Division; later DDMS Australian Corps. (AWM H19364)

of the new units, but shortly before leaving for France the Australian field ambulances were ordered to re-expand to three sections. Each field ambulance also had a small dental unit attached to it. The divisional medical services were also responsible for hygiene issues, and the ADMS controlled the decidedly unglamorous but essential divisional Sanitary Section, of one officer and 27 other ranks.

The new field ambulances were formed in a similar manner to the other new units, existing units being split to provide the basis for the new ones, and were numbered similarly to the infantry brigades. The 1st and 2nd Divisions were ordered to release the 'C' Sections of their existing field ambulances to the new divisions. In the 4th Division, the 4th Field Ambulance was already in existence, having been part of the old NZ & A Division with the 4th Infantry Brigade. The 4th Field Ambulance retained its 'A' (mainly recruited from Victoria with a few New South Welshmen) and 'B' (South Australia) Sections, and released 'C' Section (Western Australia) to become 'A' Section of the new 12th Field Ambulance. 'C' Section (Victoria) of the existing 6th Field Ambulance (2nd Division) then became 'B' Section of the new 12th. The 13th Field Ambulance was created similarly from the transferred sections of the 3rd (1st Division) and 7th (2nd Division) Field Ambulances; both were from the 'outer' states—Queensland, Tasmania, South Australia and Western Australia. The commencing organisation of the 4th Division medical services was:

ADMS:	Colonel G W Barber
DADMS:	Major A H Marks
4th Field Ambulance:	Lieutenant Colonel A J Meikle
12th Field Ambulance:	Lieutenant Colonel T G Ross
13th Field Ambulance:	Lieutenant Colonel J B StV Welch

The medical units were immediately occupied in their day to day functions of dealing with sickness and injuries among the troops in camp, while building up to strength with reinforcements and training the new men. During the period at the new base at Serapeum, these latter included further numbers to restore the units' third sections. Many of those reinforcements came in straight from Australia; in the case of the 4th Field Ambulance, from New South Wales, adding another State to that unit's recruitment background.[18]

The Australian Army Service Corps (AASC) provided the personnel for the Divisional Train, the division's main **transport and supply** organisation. The Divisional Train carried rations and various other supplies (but not ammunition, which was transported by the artillery's ammunition column for both artillery and infantry) from the division's main supply depot to collection points at brigade level, where individual units' transport took over. The Train also carried the division's heavy baggage when it was on the march. At full strength, a divisional train comprised about 20 officers and 400 other ranks; they were equipped with 180 horse-drawn vehicles with 400 horses, the drivers 'usually a fine type of up-country Australian accustomed to horses.'[19] Motor transport was provided to cover situations where distances were too great for horses, comprising about 80 three-ton lorries. This group, given several different titles over the course of the war, was manned by nine officers and 350 other ranks by 1918, and included workshop facilities for maintenance of all of the division's motor vehicles; MT Companies were not permanently part of each division, however, and were allocated by Corps HQ as necessary.

The Divisional Train was commanded by a lieutenant-colonel, and was divided into four companies: one for each infantry brigade and its attached troops, and the fourth (Headquarters) company looking after the divisional troops including artillery and pioneers. To create the transport units needed for the new divisions, the now familiar method of splitting up existing units and expanding the resulting components was continued. In the case of the AASC, there happened to be three companies available which were surplus to the requirements of the existing AIF divisions and these were used for the new divisions. Half of the original 20th AASC Company became the 14th (Headquarters) Company of the 4th Division; the original 7th AASC Company became the 7th, 26th and 27th Companies, and all set about expanding to full strength, taking on reinforcements from various sources. There was no attempt to align the unit numbers with their associated infantry brigades. Boer War veteran Major Albert Holdsworth was promoted to lieutenant colonel and took command of the 4th Divisional Train, with the following subordinate commanders:

14th Company (Headquarters):	Major J R Charlton
7th Company (grouped with the 4th Infantry Brigade):	Captain M H Cleeve
26th Company (12th Brigade):	Captain V J P Hennessy
27th Company (13th Brigade):	Captain S A Robertson

With many units being closely linked with particular infantry brigades, it was now becoming the practice to refer to 'brigade groups', consisting of the infantry brigade and its associated arms and services: machine gun company, engineer field company, field ambulance, AASC company and light trench mortar battery.

Aside from ammunition and rations, supply of equipment such as clothing, boots, weapons, vehicles and the rest of the myriad goods needed by an army, was administered by an officer and 50 ORs of the Army Ordnance Corps reporting to divisional headquarters. There were also several 'Lines of Communication' supply units of the AASC which were linked with the Division but not directly controlled by it. These included the 4th Field Bakery and 4th Field Butchery, and five (the 16th to 20th) Depot Units of Supply, overseeing the dispatch of supplies from the base depots along the lines of communication to the division.

To look after the health of its thousands of horses and mules, each infantry division was provided with five officers and 40 other ranks of the Australian Army **Veterinary** Corps (AAVC). In a manner analogous to the Medical Corps' arrangements, certain of the personnel were attached to various units, notably the artillery and the train, to attend to the animals' day-to-day needs, and others formed a Mobile Veterinary Section which operated like a Field Ambulance, providing immediate treatment for battle casualties and arranging evacuation to a base veterinary hospital where necessary. The veterinary members were under the command of an Assistant Director of Veterinary Services (ADVS) at division headquarters; Major William Kendall was initially appointed to that post in the 4th Division, the title of which was later changed to Deputy Assistant Director (DADVS) when a position of ADVS was established at Corps level. Captain Edward James commanded the Mobile Veterinary Section.

A division included a detachment of **military police**, consisting of an officer and 26 other ranks of the Australian Provost Corps. The officer in charge was entitled the Assistant Provost Marshal (APM), Captain F K Prideaux-Brune being the 4th Division's first APM. In France, a Traffic Control Detachment (an officer and 50 men) was added, to oversight movements of the myriad vehicles in each divisional area. Another element added in France was the Divisional **Salvage** Company, an officer and 70 ORs responsible for collecting any recyclable material from the huge quantities of discarded equipment and stores that littered the battlefields of the Western Front.

Divisional headquarters included a number of personnel looking after the various **administrative** functions of the division, including the divisional paymaster and his staff of the Army Pay Corps. A Claims Officer, processing claims by the civilian population for property damage and the like, was added in France, as was the French Mission, a French liaison officer and several interpreters. In 1917 each division appointed a Burials Officer responsible for recording the locations of graves and processing the personal effects of the dead. Chaplains of various religious denominations were attached to the division, usually about 12 working in the various units. Civilian welfare organisations, the Australian Comforts Fund and the YMCA, had representatives attached to the division, which had its divisional canteen as well. The divisions also formed concert parties from such members who had some talent as entertainers, putting on performances whenever possible. The 4th Division troupe, known as 'The Smart Set,' was formed in late 1917, and earlier the brigades had set up concert parties (or 'Pierrots'); performances by the latter troupes were considered somewhat more risqué than those of the Smart Set.[20]

While in Egypt, the divisions were allocated troops from the Australian Light Horse to form a mounted unit, B Squadron of the 13th Light Horse Regiment in the 4th Division's case; the 4th Cyclist Company was also included at this time, but both units were detached on arrival in France and transferred to Corps control.

The complex collection of front line and administrative troops that constituted an imperial infantry division in 1916 comprised, at full strength, approximately 850 officers and

19,000 other ranks, with their weapons and equipment, as well as about 4,000 draught animals and 1,000 vehicles—full strength was, of course, rarely if ever attained once the division had gone into action and began to suffer casualties. A division was commanded by an officer of the rank of major general, the General Officer Commanding (GOC), assisted by his headquarters staff. The 4th Australian Division's first GOC was Major General Sir Herbert Vaughan Cox, a British officer of the Indian Army. General Cox faced the task of bringing together his new formation from its disparate sources, and developing its military capacity to the level needed to play its part in the savage fighting on the Western Front.

2 Notes

1. *Official History*, Vol V, p. 300.
2. D Horner, *The Gunners: A History of Australian Artillery*, p. 113.
3. A D Ellis, *The Story of the Fifth Australian Division*, p. 4.
4. Brig-General C Rosenthal, 'Fourth Australian Divisional Artillery, A Brief Outline of Its History', 20 May 1917, AWM 224, item MSS 5.
5. Ibid.
6. State affiliations of the artillery brigades are mentioned in 4th Division Artillery Order No 57, in the appendices to the Artillery HQ War Diary for January 1917.
7. Rosenthal, 'Brief Outline', as for Note 3 above. The *Official History* (Vol III, p. 295n) erroneously says the personnel figures were for the 5th Division artillery, as pointed out by Horner, *Op Cit*.
8. *Official History*, Vol III, p. 297.
9. Not NZ & A Division as is sometimes stated, although the unit was attached to the New Zealand Division for two weeks in February 1916 before joining the 4th Division (see AWM4, 14/23/9).
10. Ellis, *Op Cit*, p. 20.
11. Kingsford Smith had originally left Australia with the 4th Light Horse Brigade Signal Troop, but the 4th LH had been temporarily broken up shortly after reaching the Mediterranean and the signal personnel, among others, were attached to the 2nd Division.
12. Names of OCs are taken from the 4th Division HQ (General Staff) War Diary for April 1916, Appendix VIII. The names given in R McNicoll, *The Royal Australian Engineers*, Vol 2 p.60 as 'after the great reorganisation' are not all correct, at least as far as the 4th Divison is concerned (confirmed by a check of the officers' service records). That list also shows J M C Corlette as OC of a 5th Division field company, whereas he was only in that unit for a few days before being appointed commanding officer of the 4th Pioneer Battalion.
13. K W Mitchinson, *Pioneer Battalions in the Great War*, p. xi.
14. Ellis, *Op Cit*, p. 6.
15. In the National Archives of Australia system, his Army Service Record is indexed as 'Corlett'.
16. AWM 224, MSS 90, notes by Colonel Corlette on formation of 4th Pioneer Battalion. Most of the summary that follows is from that document.

17 'Monty' Corlette later became CRE of the 2nd Division on the Western Front, winning the CMG and DSO, and reached the rank of brigadier in the citizen forces between the wars. See the article on J M C Corlette by P J Greville in the *Australian Dictionary of Biography*.
18 AWM 224, MSS 289, 4th Field Ambulance Historical Material.
19 *Official History*, Vol III, p. 14.
20 Rule, *Op Cit*, p. 116.

3: The 'Heads': the Division Takes Shape

Sir Herbert Cox was 56 years old in March 1916, a professional soldier of the British Indian Army. He had commanded the 29th Indian Infantry Brigade for most of the Gallipoli campaign, firstly at Cape Helles and then north of Anzac in the offensives of August 1915. The latter operations had brought him into close contact with Australian troops, when he had been in overall command of the column assaulting the heights around Hill 971. Cox's brigade was grouped with Monash's 4th Australian Brigade in this force, Cox as a major general being in overall command of the column.[1] After the failure of the Hill 971 efforts, Cox and Monash were also associated in the fighting at Hill 60.

Major General Sir Herbert Cox GCB KCMG CSI (1860–1923), GOC 4th Division to the end of 1916. (AWM A01509A)

At the beginning of the AIF's expansion in Egypt, Major General Cox was appointed 'GOC Australian Provisional Formations,' responsible for the initial setting up and training of the new 4th and 5th Divisions. Shortly afterwards he was nominated by Sir William Birdwood, GOC AIF, for the command of the 4th Division, subject to approval by the Australian government. At first, there was some difficulty with the government over General Cox's appointment. Senator George Pearce, Minister for Defence, pressed Birdwood to reconsider selecting Australians from among the present brigadiers for the new divisional commands—Birdwood had also nominated another British officer, H A Lawrence, as GOC 5th Division. General Birdwood wrote to the minister to explain his thinking on the selections, commenting on General Cox:

[he] has been in command of the whole of our new formations since they were started, and has organised the big camp for the two divisions at

Tel-el-Kebir. This work he has done quite admirably, and has I am sure already gained the full confidence of all our officers and men—indeed, I do not think the work could have been better done, while I have every confidence of his proving a thoroughly good divisional general in the field. He has great experience, and has determination, force of character and a thorough grip of his work.[2]

General Cox's appointment to the 4th Division command was confirmed, although General Birdwood did finally appoint an Australian, J W McCay, to the 5th Division. Reactions to the new GOC 4th Division were varied. Brigadier General Monash, a man who never underestimated his own abilities, had felt that he himself had strong claims to the position, and was considerably displeased at being overlooked.[3] Monash had been less than impressed with Cox when under the latter's command in the August campaign on Gallipoli, although it would be difficult to find any commander, Monash included, who had distinguished himself at that time. By the end of the 4th Division's time in Egypt, however, the two officers had developed a great mutual respect and worked well together as GOC and senior infantry brigadier. Monash left a much-quoted description of Cox in a letter to his (Monash's) daughter in May 1916: 'he is one of those crotchety, peppery, livery old Indian officers, whom the climate has dried and shrivelled up into a bag of nerves. But he is very able and knows his job thoroughly.'[4] The 48th Battalion historian (Padre William Devine, the 48th's Roman Catholic chaplain) noted that the General had a more affable side to his personality, which he showed when chatting to the troops at Christmas 1916.[5]

With a divisional GOC came his headquarters staff officers, about whom opinions tended to be strong, both in a general and particular sense. Captain Harry Seager (50th Battalion, 13th Brigade), commented:

> General Cox of the Ghurkas is our Divisional Commander (Butcher Cox), a real fighting man but we have not a high opinion of his staff. Mostly cold-footed birds of SS Aragon (chuckouts from the British Army), who every Anzac despises.[6]

The *Aragon* was a ship moored at Lemnos island during the Gallipoli campaign, on which the British lines-of-communication staff were accommodated in considerable comfort; they had built an unenviable reputation for inefficiency and obstructiveness.[7]

The Staff, those officers who assist a general to administer his command and manage it in battle, have been the object of unfavourable reactions from the frontline soldier virtually since the beginning of organised military forces. A classic illustration of this attitude can be found in Shakespeare's *Henry IV Part I*, where the fighting man Harry Hotspur proclaims:

> ... I remember, when the fight was done
> When I was dry with rage and extreme toil,
> Breathless and faint, leaning upon my sword,
> Came there a certain lord, neat, and trimly dress'd,
> Fresh as a bridegroom; and his chin new reap'd,
> ...
> He question'd me ...

> *I then, all smarting with my wounds being cold,*
> *To be so pestered with a popinjay,*
> *Out of my grief and my impatience,*
> *Answered neglectingly I know not what ...*[8]

The war of 1914-18 produced the unforgettable popular conception of an incompetent collection of staff officers, living in luxury in some French chateau while sending the fighting men to their deaths. Underlying this image was the principle that the work of the staff was fundamental to the success or otherwise of an armed force in war. If incompetence of the staff produced failure of the force as a whole, then conversely an efficient staff would make a major contribution to success. A war is being fought and good men will be killed in the process—but if the army is properly equipped, fed, trained, paid and cared for in case of sickness or wounds, and is given objectives that are actually achievable and clear orders as to how the battle is to be conducted, then the chances of success are greatly improved. The staff is mostly noticed when it fails, not so much when things are well organised. At the same time, while the man in the front rank is more likely to be aware when matters at headquarters are being handled badly, the more perceptive are very conscious of when they are being backed up efficiently. Morale and fighting spirit are lifted and a factor is removed from the strain of battle.

British and Imperial Army staffs were broadly structured in three branches, known as 'G', 'A' and 'Q'. The 'G' (General) Branch was responsible for the planning of operations, converting the general's decisions for conduct of the battle into detailed orders, and ensuring that the troops were properly trained to play their parts; Intelligence also came under the 'G' Branch. 'A' means the Adjutant-General's Branch, which looked after all matters of personnel—discipline, promotions, pay, leave, movements, and medical administration. The Quartermaster-General's, 'Q', Branch had the responsibility for all supply, transport and accommodation matters.

These staff branches existed at every level of command down to infantry brigades and their equivalents. For an imperial infantry division during this period the senior staff officer, the divisional GOC's chief of staff, was the General Staff Officer Grade 1 (GSO1). That officer worked closely with the GOC and controlled the preparation of most divisional orders, which went out over his signature. The position of GSO1 was a lieutenant colonel's appointment. The GSO1's deputy, with the rank of major, was the GSO2, who assisted with much of the actual drafting of orders and operational correspondence. Completing the division's 'G' Branch officers was the GSO3, usually a captain but sometimes also a major, who assisted his two seniors and had particular responsibility for the collation and issue of Intelligence information. Another staff officer was added to divisions later in the war, so that one officer could specialise in Intelligence.

The 'A' and 'Q' Branches were represented at divisional level by three staff officers, all with traditional unwieldy titles. In overall control of both branches was the Assistant Adjutant and Quartermaster-General (AA&QMG), with the rank of lieutenant colonel. Under the AA&QMG the 'A' Branch functions were carried out by the Deputy Assistant Adjutant and Quartermaster-General (DAA&QMG), usually a major (in April 1917, this position was given a somewhat less confusing title of Deputy Assistant Adjutant General or DAAG[9]). Another major or captain was responsible for 'Q' matters, the Deputy Assistant Quartermaster-General (DAQMG). The latter officer worked closely with the chief Ordnance Corps officer attached to the staff, (the DADOS, Deputy Assistant Director of Ordnance Services) to ensure timely supply of equipment from base depots. Ideally, in a well-organised staff the three branches would work closely together.

The three 'G' and three 'A' and 'Q' specialist staff officers formed the divisional staff in the narrow sense, but the various senior officers directly commanding the divisional arms and services—such as the CRA, CRE, ADMS and others mentioned in the previous chapter - were also considered broadly as part of the GOC's staff. The General also had two aides de camp (ADCs), his personal assistants. These were usually captains or subalterns, the senior of whom had the duties of HQ camp commandant, looking after accommodation and offices as well as administering the clerks, drivers, signallers, runners and others, numbering about 70 altogether, who supported the HQ officers.[10]

At one command level down, infantry brigade and divisional artillery, two staff officers were provided: the brigade major and the staff captain (the same titles were used for the artillery HQ staff officers). The brigade major was the brigadier's (or the CRA's) 'G' officer and hence chief of staff, while the staff captain looked after both 'A' and 'Q' matters. The ranks of the officers in the two positions were usually as implied by their titles, although it was not unknown for a brigade major to have the rank of captain or a staff captain to be a lieutenant. Most brigades also had one or more officers attached for practical training in staff work, and postings of assistant brigade major and assistant staff captain were later added. An infantry brigadier also had the brigade's specialist officers attached to his headquarters, such as the brigade machine gun officer (also Officer Commanding [OC] the brigade machine gun company), trench mortar officer (similarly commanding the LTM battery), signal officer, intelligence officer and others. At unit level, such as an infantry battalion, there were no staff officers in the strict sense, but the CO had his second-in-command, adjutant, quartermaster and again his various specialist officers—transport, musketry, 'bombing' (grenades), Lewis guns, intelligence, signals—to assist him in managing the battalion.

Finding officers to fill positions on the staff was no simple task. Ideally, the staff officer would have graduated from a course at one of the Imperial staff colleges, at Camberley in England or Quetta in India; such officers were designated by the initials 'psc' for 'passed staff college'. This qualification was certainly not a prerequisite for a staff appointment, however, particularly with the enormous expansion of the British and Empire forces since the outbreak of the war and consequent greatly increased requirements for staff officers. Officers who lacked the formal qualification but who showed a flair for staff work were in demand, in particular regular officers with their background of lengthy and detailed training, or long-serving militia officers with pre-war experience. Officers commissioned during the war were not necessarily excluded from the 'true' staff (and many were on battalion and brigade headquarters as weapons specialists), but would probably need a longer training period - on a steep learning curve we would now say. Short courses for potential staff officers were soon introduced.

In 1914 there were only eleven officers available to the AIF who could claim the 'psc' qualification, four of whom were British officers on secondment to the Australian forces.[11] Consequently, early in the war Australian staffs at all command levels often included several British officers with some experience in staff work, even if not all possessed formal qualifications. In the long term the AIF and the Australian Government aimed for fully Australian staffs, which had been largely but not completely achieved during 1918. In the 4th Division on its formation in February 1916, however, four of the six headquarters staff officers were members of the British Army rather than the AIF. The two ADCs were also British—not unreasonably, since it was the GOC's prerogative to personally pick his ADCs, and General Cox would naturally choose officers with a similar career background to his (one was his son, Lieutenant Cecil Cox).

The 4th Division's original staff officers were:[12]

GSO1	Lieutenant Colonel J Duncan, Royal Scots Fusiliers
GSO2	Major E M Williams, AIF
GSO3	Captain P A F Spence, Royal Highlanders
AA&QMG	Lieutenant Colonel E Armstrong, Highland Light Infantry
DAA&QMG	Major J G Ramsay, Cameron Highlanders
DAQMG	Captain W Fowler-Brownsworth, AIF
ADCs	Lieutenant D Gillies-Reyburn, Indian Army
	Lieutenant C H V Cox, Leicestershire Regiment

To what extent any of these were Captain Seager's 'chuckouts from the British Army' is difficult to determine. Lieutenant Colonel John Duncan was succeeded as GSO1 by Lieutenant Colonel Denis (D J C K) Bernard, another British officer, in April 1916 while the division was still in the early stages of its training in Egypt, but this does not necessarily indicate a lack of competence. Duncan eventually became a major general with a knighthood, as did Bernard. The latter officer served as chief of staff to three successive 4th Division GOCs, and only left the Division at the end of 1917 when a concerted effort was being made to 'Australianise' AIF staffs. Lieutenant Colonel Edward Armstrong similarly stayed as the Division's AA&QMG until August 1917. In the broader sense of the staff, the chiefs of the arms and services attached to divisional headquarters were all AIF officers, including the CRE, Lieutenant Colonel Elliott, who although a British regular was also a member of the AIF. The 4th Division's initial infantry brigade staff officers, all members of the AIF, were (brigade major/staff captain):

4th Brigade: Major J M A Durrant; Captain W J M Locke

12th **Brigade:**	Major J H Peck; Lieutenant W Inglis
13th **Brigade:**	Major J C T E C Ridley; Captain W A B Steele

At divisional artillery headquarters, the CRA, Brigadier General Rosenthal, was assisted by Captain E W Richards (AIF) as brigade major and Captain F E Forrest (AIF) as staff captain (Major William Waite had initially been appointed as brigade major, but General Rosenthal wanted him as a field brigade CO and he was quickly promoted to command the 24th AFA Brigade).

Staffs at all levels were faced with very heavy workloads as the new units developed, their tasks complicated by the need for the 4th Division to relocate to a new base late in March. The Australian and New Zealand forces in Egypt had been organised into two army corps—I Anzac Corps, comprising the 1st and 2nd Australian Divisions and the New Zealand Division, and II Anzac Corps comprising the 4th and 5th Australian Divisions (army headquarters was aware of the tautology in these titles, in that the 'c' in Anzac stood for 'Corps', but the word had already become a general term rather than an acronym). Since late January 1916 I Anzac had been responsible, together with several British and Indian divisions, for garrisoning the defence line of the Suez Canal, guarding against a possible invasion of Egypt by the Turks. The Anzac forces in the centre of the line used two base camps near the canal banks, Serapeum and Ferry Post, from which light railways had been laid to link with the main defensive line of trenches in the desert about 13 kilometres east of the canal. As well as occupying the trenches, the defence scheme required the garrison to periodically send mobile columns further into the desert seeking enemy activity. Duty at the canal defences was uncomfortable, thirsty work but not particularly dangerous. In spite of the higher command's initial fears there proved to be no real danger of a major Turkish attack. The need for additional troops on the Western Front was, however, becoming urgent.

General Sir Archibald Murray, commanding the British and Empire forces in the canal area, was already under orders to send several of his divisions, including the Australians, to France once their re-equipment and training had reached a satisfactory level. It was expected that the transfers could begin at the end of March, but events on the Western Front produced an acceleration in the programme. The massive German attack on the French at Verdun, beginning in February, placed the British Army in the position of having to provide maximum support to its ally and all available manpower was needed urgently. General Murray was ordered to commence transferring troops to the Western Front at once. The general had a low opinion of the Australians, based mainly on their casual attitude to the ceremonial aspects of army discipline. For this reason he had been inclined to hold back the Australian divisions as being unsuitable for service in France without considerable further training, but in view of the new strategic situation he now felt that the 1st and 2nd Divisions had made enough progress to be sent to Europe. Being completely new formations, the 4th and 5th Divisions were seen as being less advanced in preparation and would be required to stay longer in Egypt.

On 29 February 1916 General Murray ordered that the 1st and 2nd Divisions were to embark for France within the next two weeks (the New Zealanders followed a few weeks later). They would be replaced in the Suez Canal defensive zone by the 4th and 5th Divisions. At the same time, as described in the previous chapter, the 4th and 5th were required to give up nearly all of their newly-forming artillery elements to the 1st and 2nd Divisions, so that the latter would have something close to their full establishment of artillery on embarkation. On 5 March the older divisions, forming I Anzac Corps under General Birdwood as Corps Commander, began entraining for their move in from the desert. Elements of the Anzac Mounted Division relieved them in the line, pending the arrival of the 4th and 5th Divisions, now comprising II Anzac Corps with General Godley appointed as Corps Commander. The movement of those divisions from their present base at Tel-el-Kebir to the canal area would prove to be a harrowing experience. Transport of I Anzac to Alexandria for embarkation was carried out by train and its units were given priority in the use of the available railway rolling-stock. Headquarters accordingly decided that the 4th and 5th Divisions would move to the canal area on foot by route march. The march was conceived as an organised exercise and a test of the new units' fitness and discipline in the field. Although the ostensible reason for the march was the lack of trains, it is not clear why some trains could not have been back-loaded to the canal with the relieving troops. Certainly some were available and were used to transport some elements of the divisions. The infantry advance parties were transported by train—the 16th Battalion from the 4th Division and the 8th Brigade, 5th Division. The divisional artillery also travelled by train, although several days later than the other troops.

On 25 March Lieutenant-Colonel Duncan (GSO1) issued the 4th Division's first formal Operation Order, outlining the march procedure. The Division was split into three 'flights' each corresponding roughly to a brigade group, with some other troops attached, and each commanded by the appropriate infantry brigadier; detailed planning for the march was delegated to the brigades. The distance to be covered was about 64 kilometres, to be completed over three days in what were thought to be easy stages: 24 kilometres from Tel-el-Kebir to Mahsama on the first day, a similar distance to Moascar on the second day, and finishing with a shorter stage to the Division's new base at Serapeum on the third. This did not appear unreasonable, but marching over desert sand in high temperatures with full equipment would not be easy. Many of the Gallipoli veteran troops were still not fully recovered from illness and poor nutrition, and the new reinforcements were still short of full fitness. As well, most of the men were suffering from the side effects of recent inoculations.

The first flight consisted of the 4th Brigade Group plus the Pioneers and the divisional Sanitary Section, and was scheduled to leave Tel-el-Kebir on 26 March. The second flight would begin on the next day; this was formed from the 12th Brigade Group with the divisional signals and military police. Finally the 13th Brigade Group with the divisional mounted troops, the third flight, would start its journey on 31 March. The 4th Field Ambulance, starting out with the 4th Brigade Group, would drop one of its sections at Mahsama at the end of the first stage, and another section at Moascar (second stage) to provide medical services for the troops

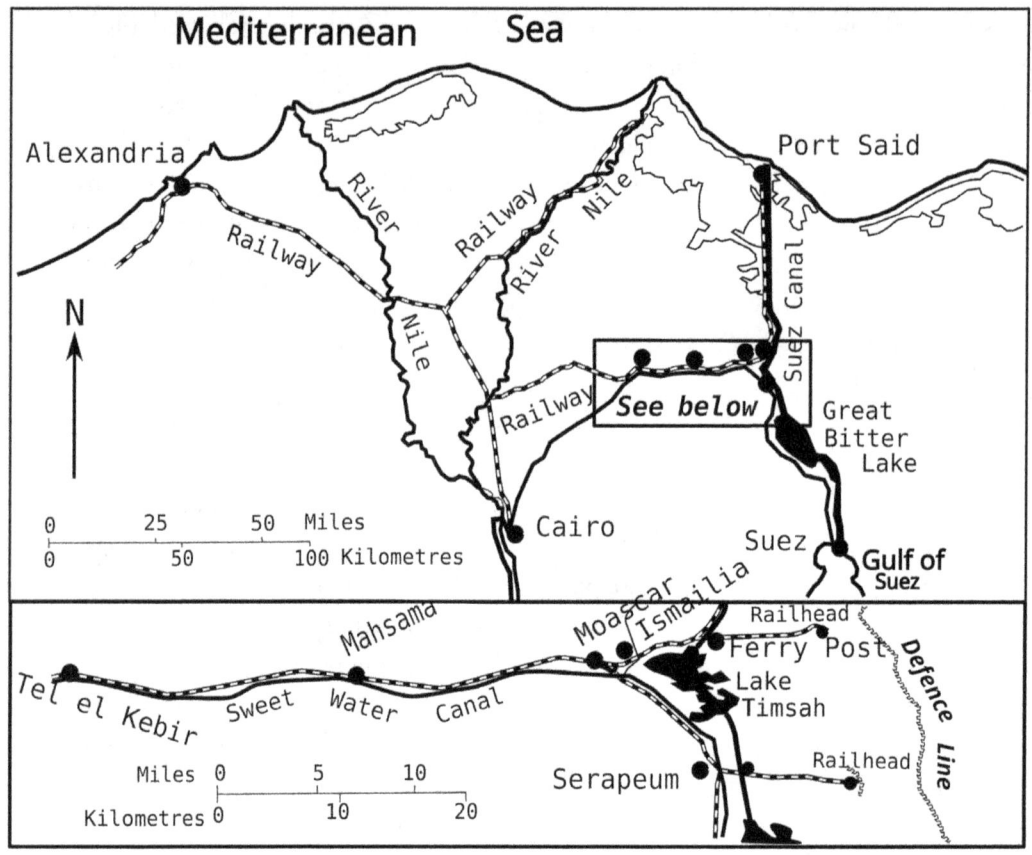

Egypt: II Anzac area of operations, 1916

following behind. Each section would then join up with the third flight when it came through and march with them on the final stage to Serapeum.

Each flight was allocated 250 camels to carry some of the infantry's supplies—officers' baggage, a day's rations and the men's blankets. The infantrymen all had to carry full packs, their rifles and 120 rounds of ammunition, as well as their single full water bottle each. All ranks were issued with British-style sun helmets—the weather was getting increasingly hot. The march route, through sand of varying firmness, was near the railway and the line of the so-called 'Sweet-water Canal'; this had been dug originally to provide drinking water for the workers constructing the Suez Canal itself, but the quality of its water had deteriorated over the years and it was now unfit for human consumption. The field ambulance units (at least the 12th and 13th) hired Arab dhows to carry their stores and equipment via that watercourse.[13] Engineer field companies similarly used rafts to transport their stores and heavy equipment to the new base—presumably barrel rafts constructed by themselves.[14]

The 4th Brigade, setting out first on 26 March, had originally planned to start at dawn but was delayed by the need for daylight to begin loading the accompanying camel train. The column took regular ten minute halts every hour, and rested for three hours between midday and 3 pm in the worst of the heat. Marching over reasonably firm ground for most of the distance the troops reached the first night's bivouac area at Mahsama in the late afternoon. Fourteen men had dropped out en route, six of whom were medically evacuated by the 4th Field Ambulance.[15] That unit's aid post also treated over 100 men for sore feet, mainly due to new boots;[16] foot problems would become a major issue for the rest of the march. Generally, the 4th Brigade group (the 'First Flight') had come through the first stage reasonably well.

Things began to deteriorate towards the end of the second day's march, which began at 6 am in a thick fog. By 9 am the fog had burnt off and the temperature was climbing rapidly. After the prescribed midday rest, the column set out again through a three-kilometre stretch of very heavy sand, in continuing heat. Increasing numbers of men began to fall out along the route following that stage, a total of 132 by the time the main body reached the bivouac area at Moascar. Most of these managed to rejoin during the evening, but again several had to be evacuated.

The third stage of the march, although considerably shorter than the others, proved to be the most trying, the men suffering increasingly from the cumulative effects of the first days' heat and exertion, as well as many having their feet already painfully blistered. The going was heavier than before, the temperature hotter, and many of the troops were unable to resist emptying their water bottles early in the day. The midday halt was cut short when clouds of tormenting insects descended on the column—it was felt that continuing the march was better than staying. Those without water began to disobey orders and head for the 'Sweet-water' canal, risking contracting disease from its tainted water. The troops' mood was not improved by the sight of several empty railway trains going past in the same direction.[17] In the 14th Battalion,

> by three o'clock men's tongues were swollen, and the tropical sunshine, streaming down white-hot from overhead, turned the place into a furnace. Men began to drop, and lay beside the road ... The man who was marching in front of me wobbled suddenly to the side of the road, and collapsed on the sand. A newly joined soldier, Harry Danman [a pseudonym for Victor Hall] , went to his assistance and ... placed his own water bottle to the man's lips ... Danman himself sank to the sand shortly after.[18]

The worst straggling occurred when the goal of Serapeum camp was in sight a mile or two away, the column becoming ragged and disorganised. Brigadier General Monash antagonised some of the men by berating them for lack of discipline, telling some of the 14th Battalion that their sisters could do as well (the fact that the brigadier was riding a horse would not have improved the troops attitude).[19] The 4th Brigade reported a total of 460 stragglers, of whom 413 rejoined their units later in the day.[20] The weary, footsore men settled into their new camp, spending March 29 resting before taking up their duties in the defence lines and resuming the training programme.

The second flight, the 12th Brigade group and attached troops under Brigadier General

Glasfurd, started out on the afternoon of 27 March. The troops arrived at their first night's bivouac location (Kassassin) around 8 pm. Glasfurd and his staff had planned a slightly different approach to that of the first flight, starting their next stage as early as possible, marching for a few hours in the morning then taking a long rest until late afternoon, and continuing the march later into the evening, the intention being to avoid the heat of the day as much as possible. The 12th Brigade also appears to have taken a more flexible approach to water supply than did the 4th, treating the refilling of the troop's water bottles as a priority.[21] Although the second flight consequently experienced fewer problems with heat and thirst, there were still many cases of painful feet, despite the brigade staff's careful orders about precautions for boots and feet.[22] The head of the second flight's column began arriving at Serapeum camp on the morning of 30 March. The numbers who fell out during the march had been considerably less than in the first flight, although the 12th Brigade had a larger number sent to hospital.[23] The brigadier noted the 'trying circumstances' of the march in his report and commented that there was 'considerable room for improvement in march discipline and a great deal has yet to be learnt, especially by Company Officers and NCO[s].'[24]

The 4th Division's third flight, Brigadier General Glasgow's 13th Brigade group plus the divisional mounted troops, left Tel-el-Kebir early in the morning on 31 March. The column was fortunate to encounter cooler conditions than the first two groups, and appears to have taken extra precautions over water supply and the troops' condition—possibly benefiting from the experiences of the earlier columns. The first stage of the march, for instance, finished at 11:45 am and the column did not set out again until the next morning.[25] The 13th Brigade group arrived at Serapeum around midday on 2 April, recording a considerably lower total of men falling out or hospitalised than had the previous two columns. General Cox sent his written congratulations to the brigadier on the performance. Notwithstanding the 13th Brigade's experience, most of those who took part in the desert march remembered it as a nightmare. The 5th Division, in particular its 14th Brigade, suffered even more on the march. At the end of the second stage, the 14th Brigade was 'practically out of hand ... like the remnant of a broken army.'[26] The 5th Division GOC, Major General J W McCay, considered the 14th Brigade's arrangements for the march and the performance of its commander to be inadequate. The brigadier was removed from his command. His replacement was one of the 4th Division's original Gallipoli unit COs, Lieutenant Colonel Harold Pope of the 16th Battalion, who was made up to temporary colonel and transferred to command the 14th Brigade—to his cost eventually: he was also to run afoul of General McCay in France later that year.

To replace Pope, Major Edmund Drake-Brockman[27] from the 11th Battalion (3rd Brigade, 1st Division) was promoted into the 16th Battalion a few weeks later as its new CO. He was also a Gallipoli veteran, having distinguished himself from the start of that campaign, reorganising the 11th under fire during the confusion of the first day. He had been seriously wounded later in the campaign, and had only recently returned from convalescence in Australia. A militia officer before the war, Drake-Brockman was a member of one of Western Australia's most noted pioneer families, on both sides—his mother was the former Grace Bussell, who had become a national heroine as a teenager through her part in the rescue of survivors from a shipwreck on the WA coast. Lieutenant Colonel Drake-Brockman remained as CO of the 16th Battalion for most of the war.

The 4th Division completed its concentration in the Serapeum area over the first few days of April 1916, the main body of the divisional artillery arriving by train over 4 and 5 April. The new location had its drawbacks: 'quite the most horrible place of any we have yet been in,' wrote Brigadier General Monash to his wife.

> Between eleven and four it is almost unbearably hot in the sun, although the nights are cool; but with the slightest breeze, the fine dust of the desert lifts and travels in clouds so dense that one cannot see for fifty yards, and the dust covers everything, food and all, with a fine layer. Intense heat, dust and myriads of savage flies and sandflies ...[28]

The conditions meant that training could only be carried out effectively in the early mornings and evenings. Within those periods training activities were intensive, for there was plenty to do.

The infantry, in addition to basic training, tactical exercises and musketry, had new weapons to learn. Having lost their heavy Vickers machine guns to the brigade MG companies, the battalions were now to be issued with the Lewis gun which restored some of their firepower. This was a light machine gun (or automatic rifle) that was light enough, although still weighing nearly 14 kilograms loaded, to be carried at the spearhead of an infantry attack. The Lewis used a 47-round horizontal drum magazine and was air cooled with a cylindrical barrel shroud fitted with cooling fins inside. The Lewis was normally fired resting on its bipod mounting, but a strong man could fire one effectively from the hip, and a special sling was later provided for that purpose. The Lewis had its disadvantages: it tended to jam easily and had to be cleaned very frequently, often under fire, to keep it operating; a drum of ammunition would usually be fired off very quickly, so a team of ammunition carriers was necessary. The weapon's portability, however, made it so useful in combat that the initial allocation of one per British and Empire infantry company was quickly increased to four, and eight by mid 1918.[29] For the 4th Division infantry in Egypt only one Lewis per battalion was available for training at first, but supplies gradually came through and specialist instructional schools were established to train the selected gun teams. This type of weapon was something that the German army on the Western Front was unable to match, despite its expertise with machine guns in general.

The hand grenade (commonly called a 'bomb' during the war) was another weapon of major tactical significance. During the Gallipoli fighting, the Imperial forces had famously used their improvised 'jam tin bombs' against the Turks' purpose-made, though still crude,

Lewis guns. The photograph, taken by Lt Harry Downes, shows members of the 48th Battalion training in the snow near Péronne, France, December 1917. (AWM P10688.035.007)

bombs. Almost at the time of the Gallipoli evacuation, and so too late to be used effectively, the AIF had received a consignment of a new grenade, the British Mills bomb. This was now in common use on the Western Front. It was a highly efficient weapon, with a powerful explosive charge and a segmented casing that broke into deadly flying pieces on bursting. Its pin-and-lever fuse was a major improvement over all previous methods of exploders. The Division's infantry battalions began to send men to training schools to learn the new weapon. Specialist 'bombing' platoons were formed under a battalion bombing officer, and all ranks in the rifle companies received training on the Mills bomb over the period in Egypt. The infantryman's basic weapon remained the reliable Lee-Enfield .303 rifle, with its murderous 420mm sword bayonet. The rifle could also be fitted with an adapter for projecting a grenade from the barrel using a blank cartridge.

While these infantry specialist courses were being run (battalion signallers and stretcher-bearers also had their schools) the bulk of the infantry personnel proceeded with routine training at the new camp. The battalions arranged detailed timetables to cover a variety of subjects and skills at platoon and company level, moving up to exercises involving the whole battalion. Brigade and finally division exercises would follow in time. Basics like close order drill, extended order drill, shooting and bayonet fighting were undertaken on most days, and the programme included tactical exercises by both day and night, practicing attack and defence, setting up outposts, forming rear guards and the like. Some of the troops needed more attention than others. It was mentioned in Chapter 1 that the 13th Battalion had found itself taking on a number of 'rejects' as reinforcements at this time. That situation was experienced throughout the 4th Division's infantry units at Serapeum. The *Official History* notes that the 1st and 2nd Divisions had left behind at Serapeum over 2,000 men who were considered to be unsatisfactory soldiers for one reason or another.[30] These had been blandly described by their divisions as simply needing further training. The GOC AIF, General Birdwood (who was also now GOC I Anzac Corps), had not been fully informed on the situation and regarded the 'rejects' as surplus reinforcements who should readily be absorbed by the 4th and 5th Divisions. It was so ordered, and the new divisions had to bear the consequences of what appears to have been a piece of sharp practice. The battalions did manage to get a proportion of the most troublesome individuals removed from the units' primary establishment, but most of these were still retained in the general reinforcement pool attached to the divisions.

All arms and services in the Division became heavily engaged in training, particularly of their new members with no experience in the work of their units. The difficulties faced by the divisional artillery in particular were mentioned in Chapter 2, and much hard work was required from all ranks. A limited amount of guns and ammunition was available for practice, and sufficient weapons had to be emplaced and manned for the defence of the front line against the Turks. By April 1916 the threat of a major enemy offensive against Egypt and the Canal had receded considerably, but the British position still had to be defended. The tactical plan for this had changed by the time the two new divisions arrived at the front line. The main trench line defending the Canal was set about 13 kilometres to its east, to keep a potential invasion force out of artillery range of the vital waterway. Originally these trenches were fully manned by infantry, but by April it had been decided to occupy the front line thinly and leave the bulk of the defending troops further to the rear in support, to move up rapidly in the (unlikely) case of a serious attack. The defence line was divided up into sections and sub-sections, and the 4th Division now assumed responsibility for the southern sub-section of the AIF's section of the line.

A narrow-gauge light railway had been constructed from Serapeum to a point in the desert about eight kilometres east of the Canal, accompanied by a rough road that continued for the rest of the distance to the front line. The railway carried equipment and supplies to its terminus and those were then taken by camel to the front line outposts, as was water which was piped as far as the railhead. A camp was established at the railhead as the forward base for the outpost defenders' support elements. The defence scheme employed an infantry brigade with its machine gun company and a section of the attached field ambulance; one battalion, and later a section of four machine guns, was to be distributed along the outpost line. The rest of the troops remained at the railhead camp, from which units were periodically sent to relieve those at the outposts. An artillery brigade and two engineer field companies were also in support at the railhead base.

The 12th Infantry Brigade was the first to occupy the Division's area of responsibility. On

4 April, a few days after marching to Serapeum, the 45th Battalion moved to the railhead and thence to the outpost line.[31] The remainder of the brigade followed two days later by route march, stores and baggage being carried by the light railway. Camp was established near the railhead, and training programmes were resumed immediatesly. Training also continued with some intensity at the main Serapeum camp. All ranks were aware that the Division's move to France was imminent, as soon as its equipping was completed and training had reached a sufficient standard. General Cox anticipated that this point would be reached by the end of May and his message to that effect was read out to the troops on parade.[32]

There were, however, some breaks from the training programme. One of these was an act of nature, when a Khamsin, the destructive North African desert wind, struck the whole area on 13 April. The storm caused havoc in both camps and the defence line, also hitting the 5th Division further north. General Monash wrote that the wind

> reached hurricane force, and seemed to lift the desert up bodily into the air ... the sun and sky were blotted completely out, and the air for a height of hundreds of feet was thick with dust and grit and sand and even pebbles of gravel ... down went one building after another. [Many tents were blasted away, and in those that stood], the fine dust was even forced *through* the fabric of the canvas.[33]

There was at least one fatality, when a man blinded by the dust was hit by the light railway train. By the time the storm died down after about 24 hours, the light rail line itself and the main line back to the west were buried under sand and had to be found and dug out before traffic could resume. The same had to be done with the front line trenches and barbed wire entanglements, and repair works took priority for the next few days.

On a far more pleasant note the whole Division (except for the front line battalion, the 46th by this time) was given a holiday on 25th April to celebrate the first anniversary of the Landing—already being referred to, within the army at least, as Anzac Day. There were morning church parades followed by sports and an aquatic carnival on the Canal in the afternoon. The Corps Commander, General Godley, visited the Division during the day as did the Prince of Wales, later King Edward VIII and later still the Duke of Windsor, who was serving with the British Army in the area. His Royal Highness was later entertained by the senior officers of the Division, a function that was hampered when it was discovered that several cases of whisky were missing. Those had been purloined by certain enterprising cooks of the 51st Battalion.[34] Training resumed after the welcome break, and an exercise for the full Division was carried out on 28 April, with the 12th Brigade, acting as the 'enemy' at its railhead location, being attacked by the other two brigades. Throughout this period, General Cox had kept a close eye on his Division's progress, frequently visiting the units, observing their training schools and conferring with his subordinate commanders.[35]

For the units in the front line outposts, there was more to do than just occupying their positions and continuing with training. Improvements to the defensive earthworks were required, with some new trenches to be dug and the layout of others modified, as well as laying out additional barbed wire. The works were organised by the engineers of the 4th Field Company; as was the standard practice, the actual labouring work was to be done by the infantry, after the engineers had arranged supply of materials. Divisional orders specifically included the comment that the infantry officer in charge of a section of the line 'is responsible for completing the defence works, and that the Engineer Officers and personnel are only present for the purpose of supervising...and giving technical advice and assistance.'[36] It was also specified that each man was to do at least six hours work per day. That type of duty was often a source of friction between infantry and engineers.

The 46th Battalion, which relieved the 45th in the outpost line on 21 April, reported that most of its first two weeks in the line was spent working on the defences. The importance of the work was given some urgency when intelligence reports suggested that the Turks were planning an attack, supposedly to occur on 12 May. To meet the threat, the front line garrison was doubled. The 4th Pioneer Battalion moved into the line (over the objections of its acting CO, as noted in the previous chapter) as did the 12th Brigade's 45th and 48th Battalions, the 47th being kept in reserve. At the same time, the 13th Brigade group was moved forward to the railhead area in support. Generals Murray (Commander in Chief) and Godley (Corps Commander) inspected the front line on 11 May to satisfy themselves that all was in readiness to receive the predicted enemy attack. It soon became apparent that this was not going to eventuate, but the strengthened front line garrison was retained for the time being. Normal reliefs were resumed, as was the training programme.

On 16 May, the 13th Brigade infantry battalions and MG company began to relieve the 12th Brigade units and the Pioneers in the front line positions, with the 12th moving back to support. At about this time, some changes occurred in the 4th Division's headquarters. Lieutenant Colonel Denis Bernard, British Army, had already taken over as GSO1 during April, and both the GSO2 and GSO3 changed during May. The original GSO2, Major Williams AIF, was transferred to command the 4th Pioneer Battalion and his replacement was Major Henry McRae, a British officer from the Indian Army. GSO3 Captain Spence, another British officer, had also transferred out and was replaced by an AIF officer, Major George Dickinson from the 15th Battalion, 4th Brigade. A change also occurred in the 12th Brigade's HQ when Major John Peck, the brigade major, was transferred to command the 12th Training Battalion (the unit that provided advanced training for 12th Brigade reinforcements). An Australian-born British Army regular, Captain Edward Salier, took over as brigade major.

The time for the 4th Division's move to France was fast approaching and all units continued with their training. The operational conditions in Egypt were not really comparable to what would be found on the Western Front, and many of the formation tactical exercises were to be of little value in that theatre. Nevertheless the Division had made great advances on where it had been when it first formed. In the 46th Battalion for instance, Lieutenant Colonel Lee commented in the unit's War Diary that the period occupying the front line:

> ... gave many opportunities of exercising all ranks in trench warfare, outposts,

patrols, and musketry. Many valuable lessons were learned, more especially in siting trenches, tactical use of wire entanglements, and fire control from trenches. It also gave many opportunities for OC Companies and OC Posts for exercising independent command.[37]

The end of May 1916 became the firm target for the move of the 4th and 5th Divisions to France. The area Commander-in-Chief, Sir Archibald Murray, still had some doubts about the divisions' level of training, but he had been favourably impressed by what he had seen during his inspections. As well, the excellent efforts of the Australian and New Zealand mounted troops in several difficult assignments in the desert had caused him to revise his opinion of the value of the troops from the Antipodes. Although the divisional artillery was still somewhat short of full efficiency, General Murray acknowledged the difficulties it had faced, as a technical arm formed very recently and with the great majority of its personnel having no artillery background. Considerable progress had been made, and the gunners completed their basic firing practice with live ammunition—150 rounds for each 18-pounder battery and 120 for each howitzer battery—shortly before the units began to prepare for embarkation.

The 4th Division staff now tackled the highly complex task of moving more than 19,000 men with their equipment and weapons, as well as thousands of horses and mules, from camps in the Egyptian desert across the Mediterranean to France. A preliminary order for the move was issued by Lieutenant-Colonel Armstrong (AA & QMG) on 23 May, followed by detailed schedules and timetables giving itineraries for each unit of the division. As had been done with the Serapeum route march, a system of grouping the divisional units into three 'flights' was adopted, each flight being built around one of the infantry brigade groups. The flights were preceded by an advance party under the GSO2, Major McRae, to make arrangements for the Division's eventual disembarkation at Marseille, the point of arrival in France. The first flight consisted of the 4th Brigade Group with the 11th AFA Brigade, the Sanitary Section, Divisional Train headquarters and the AASC's Divisional Units of Supply. On 31 May, the troops and equipment departed by railway trains from Serapeum, travelling overnight to the Alexandria docks to board their ships on 1 June.

The other two infantry brigades and attached troops were at the Railhead camp and the front line defensive positions. Those troops were relieved by British units in the first days of June, marching back to Serapeum to board their trains for Alexandria. The second flight comprised the 12th Brigade Group and several other units including the divisional headquarters, the 4th Pioneer Battalion and both the 12th and 24th AFA Brigades. Larger than the first flight, these troops arrived at Alexandria over three days, all embarking by the early morning of 4 June. The third flight (13th Brigade Group, 10th AFA Brigade, Divisional Ammunition Column and other units) similarly took several days to complete the journey to the docks, the 13th Brigade troops being hit by another Khamsin while on the march to the Serapeum railway siding. The third flight's final elements arrived at the docks for embarkation early on 6 June, and later that day the whole of the 4th Division was at sea, at different stages of the voyage, on a total of 13 transport vessels.[38]

In the main, the Division departed Egypt fully equipped, although there were several deficiencies. The number of draught animals was well under full establishment, as were transport vehicles, but the shortages would be made up once the Division reached the front. Weapons such as Lewis guns and trench mortars would also be supplied in France. The divisional artillery had embarked with 44 field guns and howitzers,[39] full establishment being 60, and was well short of horses and vehicles also. The artillery was also faced with two separate reorganisations, ordered virtually on the eve of their departure from Egypt. Firstly, the Brigade Ammunition Columns were ordered to be disbanded and their personnel and equipment consolidated into the Divisional Ammunition Column (DAC). The officer commanding the DAC, Lieutenant Colonel Hugh Vernon, made hasty arrangements for taking over the stores and equipment of the brigade columns and getting all ready for collection at the railway siding. As with the other divisional artillery units, few of the personnel in Colonel Vernon's expanded unit were originally artillerymen (50 out of about 800).

As well, orders were received by Brigadier General Rosenthal and his staff to carry out a basic change in the way that the field artillery brigades were constituted, fitting in with a reorganisation that was occurring in all British forces on the Western Front. Currently divisional artillery included three brigades of 18-pounder field guns (each brigade having four batteries) and one brigade of 4.5-inch howitzers (three batteries). The new structure required all four brigades to comprise three field gun batteries and one howitzer battery, that is, without a separate howitzer brigade. Since the existing howitzer brigade only had three batteries, this meant that one of the four restructured brigades would have its three field batteries but no howitzers to begin with. The intention was to form a further howitzer battery later, but a further reorganisation supervened before that could be done. There was no time for the CRA and his staff to do anything before the Division sailed, but the arrangements were worked out on board ship and the necessary orders issued for implementation on arrival in France.[40] The 4th Division's new artillery brigade structure was:

10th AFA Brigade—37th, 38th, 39th field batteries, 110th howitzer battery
11th AFA Brigade—41st, 42nd, 43rd field batteries, 111th howitzer battery
12th AFA Brigade—45th, 46th, 47th field batteries (no howitzer battery)
24th AFA Brigade—40th, 44th, 48th field batteries, 112th howitzer battery[41]

The voyage from Alexandria to Marseille took about six days, each group of ships arriving in port progressively over the period 7 to 11 June 1916. While some further training activities had been carried out on board ship, most of the Division's units seem to have given their men an easy time after their exertions of the previous months. By all accounts, the voyage was pleasant and uneventful, and everyone was happy to be leaving the oppressive climate and primitive conditions of Egypt behind them. There was a general feeling of eager anticipation at the prospect of going to a country of western culture and temperate weather, and of being involved in mighty events, joining the other Australian divisions in the allied armies fighting the main enemy. It was probably beyond the imagination of anyone to anticipate the ordeals that would have to be endured in the time to come.

3 Notes

1. According to G Corrigan ('The Gurkhas at Gallipoli' in R Johnson, *The British Indian Army*, pp. 82–3) 'because brigade commanders in India were usually district commanders too, they often held, as did Cox, a rank higher than would be justified by command of a brigade.' His promotion to major general appeared in the *London Gazette* of 16 August 1915 but was backdated to 17 February 1915.
2. General Birdwood to Senator Pearce, 24 March 1916, National Archives of Australia Item 694581.
3. Pedersen, *Monash as Military Commander*, p. 209.
4. *Ibid*, p.157. Often only the first sentence of this extract is quoted.
5. Devine, *Op Cit*, p. 31.
6. Freeman, *Op Cit*, p. 4.
7. See, for example, the *Official History*, Vol II, p. 386n and p. 782.
8. *Henry IV Part I*, Act I Scene III.
9. It seems that a separate posting of DAAG existed early in the war, with the DAA&QMG being the second in charge to the AA&QMG. The 1st Australian division had four A/Q staff officers in 1914-15.
10. The 4th Division Administrative Staff War Diary over the period November 1916 to February 1917 shows a 'war establishment' varying around 70 ORs. Sir John Monash, when GOC 3rd Division, gave a figure of 80 in a letter of 18 July 1916 (*War Letters of General Monash*, ed. F M Cutlack).
11. Ross Mallett, article 'Division Headquarters', on Australian Defence Force Academy internet site www.unsw.adfa.edu.au.
12. *Official History*, Vol III, p. 289n.
13. AWM 224, MSS 313, 13th Field Ambulance historical notes by Lt Col D. Cade.
14. War Diaries of 12th Field Company and HQ 4th Division Engineers for March 1916. The 13th Brigade War Diary (Colonel Glasgow's report on the march, Appendix D March 1916) indicates that 13th Field Company personnel also travelled part of the distance by raft.
15. 4th Brigade War Diary for March 1916. The figure probably refers to the infantry only. The 4th Field Ambulance recorded 30 men evacuated (AWM 224, MSS 290/1, historical notes on 4th Field Ambulance).
16. AWM 224, MSS 290/1, *Op Cit.*.
17. Rule, *Op Cit*, p. 15, and White, *Op Cit*, p. 60.
18. Rule, *Loc cit*.

19 Rule, *Loc cit*. See also T P Chataway, *History of the Fifteenth Battalion*, p.105.
20 4th Brigade War Diary for March 1916. White, *Op Cit*, p. 60, says 480 stragglers.
21 Lee, *Op Cit*, pp. 14-15.
22 12th Brigade War Diary for March 1916.
23 4th Division General Staff War Diary for March 1916.
24 12th Brigade War Diary for March 1916.
25 13th Brigade War Diary for March 1916, Appendix D.
26 *Official History*, Vol III p. 291.
27 His name is often rendered as Drake Brockman without the hyphen (or just as Brockman) in contemporary sources, but the more recent hyphenated style will be used in this book.
28 Cutlack, *War Letters, Op Cit*, p. 108, letter of 29 March 1916.
29 R Holmes, *Tommy*, p. 393.
30 *Official History* Vol III, pp. 57–8 and 292–3.
31 Presumably relieving the 16th Battalion, which had been sent to Serapeum in advance of the main body of the division.
32 12th Brigade War Diary for April 1916, Appendix II.
33 Cutlack, *War Letters, Op Cit*, p. 110, letter of 15 April.
34 R Christie, '51st Bn's First CO', *Reveille*, August 1933, p. 61.
35 See extracts from Sir H V Cox's diary for April and May 1916, AWM 1DRL 0221.
36 4th Division General Staff War Diary for April 1916, Appendix VII.
37 46th Battalion War Diary, 18 May 1916.
38 The brigade groups were each accommodated on three ships, but the 4th Division Admin Staff War Diary for May 1916 indicates that each of the second and third 'flights' used two additional ships for excess troops from various units. This does not include two further ships carrying the first reinforcement elements for both the 4th and 5th Divisions (see the *Official History*, Vol III p. 73n).
39 4th Division Admin Staff War Diary for May 1916, Appendix I.
40 'Fourth Australian Division Artillery—A Brief Outline of its History', *op cit*.
41 *Official History*, Vol V, p. 681.

4: The Nursery

On 7 June 1916 the first troopships of the 4th Australian Division entered the French Mediterranean port of Marseille. As each ship berthed over the succeeding days, the troops disembarked and marched to the railway station to board trains for northern France and the battle zone. The authorities had expected misbehaviour from the Australians while passing through Marseille through their supposed indiscipline, but the earlier passage of the 1st and 2nd Divisions had produced no trouble. The only reported problems with the 4th Division occurred when the two ships carrying the reinforcements arrived, a few days after the main body. These troops included a high proportion of the 'undesirables' that the Division had been compelled to accept in Egypt, and these appear to have been the ringleaders of an attempt to break into the town. A group from one ship succeeded and had to be rounded up the next day, but those from the other ship were stopped by one of the 4th Brigade's disembarkation officers, Lieutenant Harold F Murray of the 13th Battalion.[1] Lieutenant Murray drew his revolver and faced down the would-be rioters, forcing them to return to the ship.

The train journey from Marseille to the battle zone took the troops through the beautiful, peaceful countryside of southern France, a memorable experience. The final destination for the main body was the area around the town of Merris in French Flanders, although some elements of the Division were initially diverted to other places. The artillery's trains travelled to Le Havre, to the big British ordnance depot near that city. Here they were issued with field guns, howitzers, vehicles and draught animals to bring the brigades up to full strength in their equipment. Those guns that had been brought from Egypt were given a full overhaul at the ordnance workshops. Each artillery brigade spent several days at the Le Havre depot completing their equipment, then entrained again for their concentration area around the village of Caestre, near the divisional HQ at Merris. In the same way the transport elements of the other units, as well as the Divisional Train, were sent to another depot at Abbeville to draw wagons and horses, which they then drove to their various billeting areas.

These covered an area of about 60 square kilometres just on the French side of the France-Belgium border, about seven kilometres behind the allied front line at its closest point. The Division's area ran in a narrow strip about 20 kilometres long into the back area, between the towns of Bailleul and Cassel. The troop trains arrived progressively over a period of eight days, the units detraining at various stations in the region and marching to their allocated billeting areas. By now the troops had discovered that northern France was somewhat different from the sunny south. Steady rain began to fall shortly after the first units arrived, and the mutter of the guns at the front could now be heard. Divisional headquarters was set up at Merris village on 10 June, and the first infantry units, the battalions of the 4th Brigade, established themselves near Bailleul and La Crèche within the next two days. The last of the Division's principal units had arrived by 18 June. The various unit transport elements and the Divisional Train came in progressively over the next week, having driven their own horse-drawn vehicles from the Abbeville depot. Before then, the 4th Brigade Group had already moved on preparatory to going into the front line.

The situation in which the 4th Division found itself had been developing since the outbreak of the war in August 1914. The massive German offensive which had overrun most of Belgium and large areas of northern France had been stopped at the Battle of the Marne, just north of Paris, in early September 1914. From that point, each side had tried to outflank the other to the north, the so-called 'race to the sea'. Neither succeeded, and the battle-front settled into a 760-kilometre long line of defensive earthworks stretching from the France/Switzerland border to Nieuport on the North Sea coast of Belgium, in the small corner of that country not under German occupation. Both sides made several attempts to break through their enemy's lines in 1914 and 1915 but all ended in bloody failure. The trench lines were improved and strengthened, and the fighting front settled into a narrow ribbon of desolate earth and ruined villages running through the green countryside of northern France, while the high commands of the Allies and the Central Powers sought to find a method of breaking the stalemate.

By the time the divisions of the AIF began to arrive at the front in March 1916 the British Expeditionary Force (BEF) had 49 divisions holding most of the northern section of the Allied front line. By early July the number of divisions had increased to 60, including the 1st, 2nd, 4th and 5th Australian Divisions. Belgian and French troops held a small sector on the North Sea coast. The British part of the line then ran south for about 130 kilometres, with a distinct bulge—the infamous Ypres Salient—around the Belgian city of Ypres (Ieper), to the River Somme which formed the boundary between the British and French sectors. From that point, the French Army of over 100 divisions held the remaining three-quarters of the front. Facing the Allied line were 120 German divisions. Each side's engineers had constructed increasingly elaborate fortifications, particularly on the German side. A front-line trench system usually comprised at least three parallel lines of excavations: the actual front or firing line, the support trench and the reserve trench, although there could be

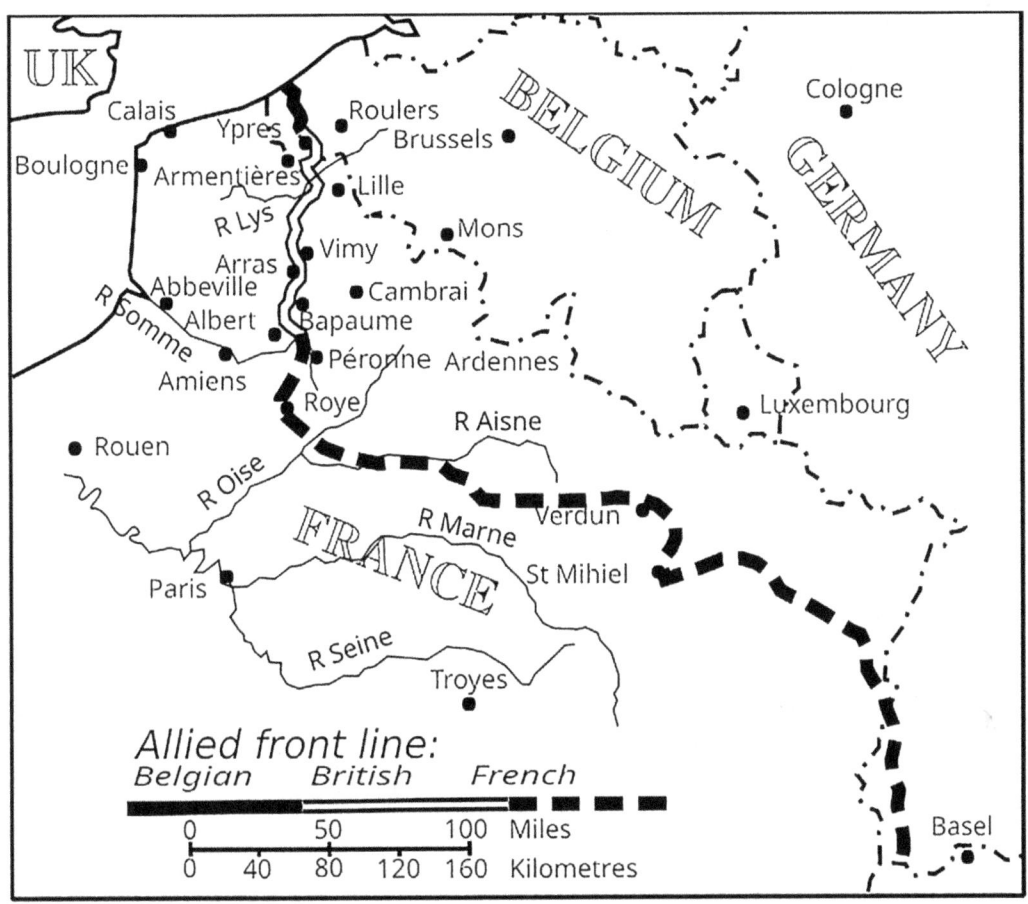

Western Front, May 1916

several more lines in some areas. At least 1600 metres further back were more positions for troops in reserve. Each line was linked to the others by communication trenches, allowing protected movement between the lines.

Each trench was constructed with firing bays interspersed with traverses, short sections that ran at right angles to the front. If an enemy party managed to enter the trench, the traverses prevented them firing up its whole length and also limited the range of shell splinters if an artillery shell happened to burst directly in the trench. Communication trenches were not usually traversed, but were laid out in zigzags or curves. The edges of the trenches were raised by sandbag walls, the parapet at the front and the parados at the rear. Deep dugouts were excavated below the trench walls to provide some protection against artillery fire. The lines were protected in front by barbed-wire entanglements, usually positioned just out of grenade-throwing range. Trenches would usually be nearly two metres deep, sometimes up to three metres including the sandbagged parapet. A 'firestep' was provided for the troops of the garrison to stand on, so as to shoot from the trench. Between the opposing front lines ran No Man's Land, often overgrown with long grass and weeds, and of varying width depending on the sector concerned. In the area first occupied by the AIF, around the large town of Armentières in French Flanders, it was over 360 metres wide in some places, although the gap was usually considerably narrower.

The 2nd Australian Division led the way for the AIF on the Western Front, two of its infantry brigades taking over front line positions from British units south-east of Armentières on 7 April 1916, followed a week later by the 1st Division going into the line on the right of the 2nd. At this stage of the war the sector here was comparatively quiet, and it was therefore a suitable area for introducing new troops to conditions on the Western Front. It was known as 'the Nursery.' Arriving in the rear of the sector early in June, the 4th Division went through an intensive period of induction into Western Front conditions before taking its turn in the front line. New equipment was issued, in particular steel helmets and gas masks, the latter initially cloth hoods but later replaced by the more effective Box Respirator—the use of poison gas by both sides was something that the AIF had not experienced in the Gallipoli campaign. Infantry and pioneers completed their allocation of Lewis guns. Specialised training commenced immediately: the 46th Battalion, for example, reported sending groups of officers and NCOs to grenade, musketry and sniping schools as well as a Stokes mortar school for personnel allotted to the brigade LTM battery.[2] These infantry-based mortar units were now set up and equipped, and as soon as the divisional artillery arrived in the sector, it commenced forming and training its HTM battery and its three MTM batteries.[3]

Each infantry battalion also set up a 'scout' platoon of 30 NCOs and men under the battalion intelligence officer. The divisional GSO1's memorandum ordering creation of this group noted that it was to be made up of 'expert observers, snipers and scouts, all of whom will be men specially selected for this work.'[4] The duties of the scouts included gathering

> all information concerning the enemy up to and including his parapet, including precise topographical details of the ground between our own and the enemy's lines, frequent reports on the enemy's wire, location of the enemy's observation posts, M[achine] G[un] emplacements, listening posts etc.[5]

Hazardous duty, somewhat compensated by the scouts being exempted from the usual 'fatigue' duties. Routine infantry training continued, somewhat hampered at sub-unit level by the absences of NCOs and junior officers on various specialist courses. Leave was now available for all ranks, and as many officers and men as could be spared were released. Major General Cox himself took the opportunity for a week in London after his years of overseas service; the CRA, Brigadier General Rosenthal, acted as GOC for the period. A longer-term change also took place at divisional headquarters when the DAA & QMG, Major Ramsay, was taken seriously ill and went on extended sick leave. He was replaced by Major Hubert Ford, AIF, transferred from the 13th Battalion.

In the flat Flanders landscape, where a slight rise counted as important high ground, the very high water table meant that conventional trenches could not be dug without becoming flooded almost immediately. Instead the fighting lines consisted of sandbag breastworks built above ground level (technically 'parapet trenches' or 'box trenches'). The walls of sandbags were up to six metres thick at the base, and would usually stop a bullet or shell splinter, although a direct hit by a high explosive shell would do considerable damage to the wall. Communication 'trenches' were constructed in a similar manner, gradually sloping down to ground level as they approached the rear areas.

Strategically, the situation was dominated by the huge battle in progress on the French front at Verdun. The battle had commenced in February 1916, the German supreme command having decided to launch a massive assault there in an effort to knock France out of the war, while remaining on the defensive elsewhere. The Germans sought to force the French to commit more and more troops to defending the sector, seeking to make the French army gradually 'bleed to death'. The efforts of the defenders, however, ensured that the attacking Germans also suffered huge casualties, and the grim struggle was still going on with no end in sight in June of 1916. Nevertheless, by taking the initiative and attacking at Verdun, the Germans had forestalled the Allies strategic plans for 1916.

At the end of the previous year, the French and British high commands had developed a general scheme for a major coordinated offensive on the Western Front, to be mounted along the axis of the River Somme. Their Russian and Italian allies were also to launch powerful drives on their respective fronts. Verdun, drawing in division after division of the French army, changed the nature of the proposed Somme offensive. The British contribution had originally been intended as support for the French, but now the main strength on the Somme would be provided by the BEF. The need to relieve some of the pressure on the French at Verdun became an overriding reason for undertaking the operation. The BEF needed the maximum possible resources to conduct the Somme offensive and hold the line on the rest of the Front, and it was for that reason that the transfer of the ANZAC troops to France had been expedited. Although the AIF would not be directly involved in the Somme battle until some weeks after it began, the preliminary preparations for the battle heavily influenced operations in the Armentières sector.

The 1st and 2nd Divisions had already undertaken several raids on the German trenches in their area, part of an increase in activity intended to distract the Germans from the British build-up further south. Arriving in the rear of the sector in mid-June 1916, the 4th Division (nominally part of II Anzac Corps) was attached to I Anzac Corps under General Birdwood. I Anzac formed part of Second Army, under General Sir Herbert Plumer, who in turn reported to Field Marshal Sir Douglas Haig, Commander in Chief of the BEF, at General Headquarters (GHQ). General Birdwood soon informed General Cox that his Division would be required to progressively take over a sector of the front line as soon as possible. The 1st and 2nd Divisions had been ordered to prepare for a move further north, to the Messines sector, to take part in projected operations intended to divert German attention from the Somme offensive 100 kilometres to the south, which was planned to begin on 1 July. In the event, the Messines plans were soon shelved, to be revived on a much larger scale in 1917, and I Anzac had not completed its move before it was diverted to the Somme.

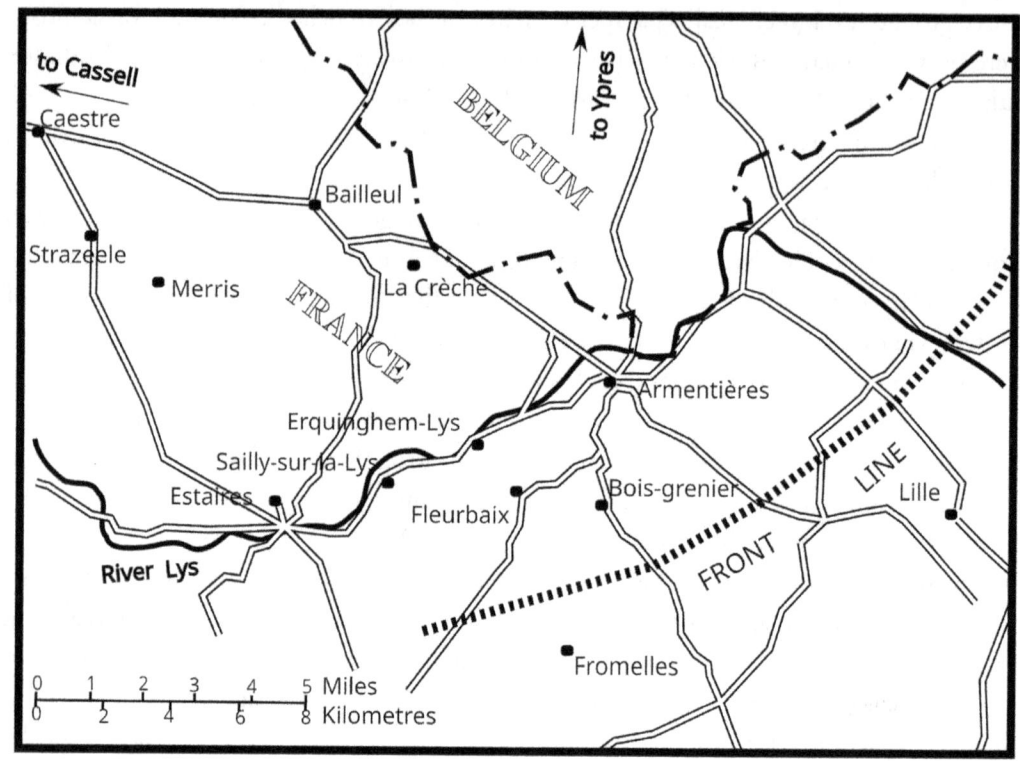

Armentières area

In the meantime, however, the 4th Division began to relieve the 1st and 2nd in the line. Brigadier General Monash's 4th Infantry Brigade and the units grouped with it moved forward between 17 and 19 June, establishing headquarters at Erquinghem-Lys, and relieved the 2nd Division's 7th Brigade in reserve. Here the 4th Brigade temporarily came under command of 2nd Division HQ and began to send parties from its infantry units into the front line around the village of Bois-Grenier for familiarisation with the situation in the trenches. A week later the formal relief began with the 13th and 14th Battalions going forward, and by 30 June the 4th Brigade infantry was fully on duty in the front line, with Brigadier General Monash in command of the sector. Other elements of the brigade group moved up also, with the 4th MG Company, 4th Field Company and 4th Field Ambulance relieving their 2nd Division counterparts.

On 22 June the 4th Pioneer Battalion relieved the 2nd Pioneers and within a few days was engaged in works on communication trenches within reach of enemy long range artillery. The Pioneers had a change of CO early in the next month, Major Williams being promoted to command I Anzac's mounted troops. He was replaced by Lieutenant Colonel Albert Fewtrell, former commander of the Australian Mining Battalion, who had a background in both military and civil engineering. At about the same time the 4th Division's artillery began relieving that of the 1st and 2nd Divisions, completing the handover by 4 July.

> Thus guns' crews consisting almost entirely of men who on March 14th had been privates in the infantry and light horse—with section commanders of whom a large proportion had in March been infantry or light horse sergeants—became on July 4th responsible for the artillery defence of a sector of the Western Front.[6]

There was a change of personnel in the artillery headquarters on 8 July. The acting brigade major, Captain Richards, was promoted to major and returned to his former unit, the 12th AFA Brigade, as a battery commander. A British officer, Major Cecil Bates of the Royal Artillery, joined the Division as the new brigade major.

The 13th Brigade Group was ordered forward on 19 June, with brigade headquarters at Sailly-sur-la-Lys, the brigade temporarily coming under 1st Division orders as the divisional reserve. Again selected officers and NCOs were first sent up to the line for familiarisation, and full relief of the equivalent 1st Division units was completed by 29 June, except for the brigade LTM battery which was still in the process of formation. Brigadier General Glasgow was now in command of this sector of the front line, around Petillon village. The brigade that the 13th relieved happened to be its 'parent', the 3rd, and the Official Historian commented that 'the meeting between the two was an incident long remembered by those who were present.'[7] The 12th Brigade Group was the last element of the division to move up. In the first few days of July, the 12th Brigade infantry and its attached units relieved the 1st Brigade (1st Division) in the portion of the line in front of Fleurbaix village, Brigadier General Glasfurd formally taking over command of this section on 4 July. The 4th Division was now responsible for defending the sector of the front line previously held by the 1st Division and one brigade of the 2nd Division (the New Zealand Division, next north in the line, extended its right to take over from the remainder of the 2nd). Divisional HQ moved forward from Merris to Sailly-sur-la-Lys, and Major General Cox was now in overall command of the sector. At the same time, the Division came again under the control of II Anzac Corps (General Godley), while the 5th Australian Division was now arriving in the rear of the sector.

In what was to be a short period of duty in this area, the 4th Division now began to gain experience with the operational methods that had been developing since the establishment of the trench-lines. In a corps zone (a corps usually consisting of three divisions), it had become normal practice for two divisions to be 'in the line' with one in reserve, up to 24 kilometres from the front, resting and training. In turn, a division in the line would usually have two of its infantry brigade groups at the front and the third brigade 1,600 metres or more behind in reserve, although in some circumstances a division would have all three brigades in the line, as the 4th Division and the New Zealanders to their north were now required to do at Armentières. Within the front line brigades, there would usually be two infantry battalions in the actual forward trench, each having another battalion behind in the support trenches. The 12th Brigade, for example, took over its section of the front on the night of 3/4 July with the 45th and 46th Battalions in the fire-trench, supported respectively by the 47th and 48th Battalions. At sub-unit level, each battalion rotated which of its four companies, and the four platoons within each company, would actually be manning the parapet at any one time. Rotation took place at all levels, with the hope of relieving some of the physical and mental strain on the troops. The periodic changeovers have been likened to 'an eightsome reel, with muddy and heavily laden dancers treading out their prescribed steps.'[8]

The relief of one unit or formation by another was an exercise in itself with its own procedures, as well as its difficulties and dangers. The infantry taking over the front line system would move up in single file, trudging with full packs, weapons and equipment through the narrow communication trenches, almost always at night and often through thick mud. Usually there would be the regular harassing artillery fire from the enemy to endure, and the chance of making a wrong turn in the maze of trenches. Having found its final position with the help of guides from the current occupants, the relieving troops would post sentries and begin to settle in while their predecessors filed back along the communication trench to the rear. Company officers would take over charge of the 'trench stores'—reserves of ammunition and grenades, signal rockets, empty sandbags, spare coils of barbed wire, metal pickets for the wire and so forth. The formality of signing for the items was gone through with even though the relieving officer was rarely able to actually check the stores in the dark.

Just before dawn all of the garrison would 'stand to', rifles in hand and bayonets fixed, at the ready in case of a surprise attack by the enemy in the half-light. 'Stand down' came when full daylight arrived, and the men would clean their rifles (half of the garrison at a time) followed by breakfast, then the routine work of the day would begin. This might include improvements to the trench and dugouts, filling sandbags and other manual tasks, while keeping below the parapet to avoid sniping: carelessness in that precaution was often fatal. Sentries by this time were normally using periscopes during the day rather than taking the risk of snatching quick glances over the parapet. Dusk would bring another stand-to. After dark the garrison stood down and sentries (the number doubled at night) continued on duty, desperately trying to stay awake through their shifts. The level of activity in the line increased markedly at night despite the protective darkness periodically being dispelled by flares or star shells. Carrying parties set out from the rear, bringing supplies, ammunition and rations up to the front lines. Patrols crept into No Man's Land to gather information—on the British side, this was when the battalion intelligence officer would set out with a party of his scouts to reconnoitre the enemy's position. The rifle companies might also send out patrols, as well as working parties to carry out repairs on the barbed wire protecting the trench. Occasional clashes with enemy groups on similar errands would produce casualties and prisoners to each side. The 14th Battalion, relieving the 19th Battalion (2nd Division) in the front line on 27 June, sent out their first patrol on the same night. Encountering a German patrol, they had one man wounded, and a 19th Battalion officer acting as guide was fatally hit. Three wounded prisoners from the German 50th Prussian Reserve Division (231st Regiment) were brought in, two of whom subsequently died.[9]

Both sides took steps to interfere with enemy activity. Every night, artillery batteries fired planned 'shoots' at targets in the enemy lines, including communication routes in the back areas. Machine guns carried out similar tasks, firing at predetermined points or sweeping along the enemy parapet with long bursts. During this first period in the line, the 46th Battalion reported the disconcerting experience of an enemy gun being able to shoot into the rear of the Australian parapet, through some peculiarity in the positioning of the opposing trench lines.[10] Trench mortars also delivered harassing fire at times. The LTM batteries made themselves unpopular with the infantrymen, arriving in the front line trench to set up their weapons, firing a few bombs at the enemy, then packing up and withdrawing before the usual retaliatory fire arrived on the heads of the garrison. The mortar-men were of course only following orders, and in different circumstances the close support value of the mortars came to be appreciated by the infantry. Just occupying the front line, without any outright combat, produced casualties. For example, the 13th Brigade lost seven killed and 34 wounded in its first five days in the line.[11]

Life in the front line trench even in routine line-holding was always uncomfortable as well as dangerous. Cramped conditions, rain, mud and cold were exacerbated by ever-present vermin. Gallipoli veterans had experienced lice infestation, and they found that the Western Front trenches were also rife with the irritating little creatures, usually referred to as 'chats,' which everyone picked up rapidly. Also present were countless rats, grown large on an unlimited supply of food provided by discarded rations and the corpses of humans and draught animals. The discomfort of the troops was capped off by the all-pervading odours of the front—unwashed men, human waste, explosives residue and decomposing corpses—which the almost-universal smoking did little to conceal. The unhealthy conditions contributed to the contraction of various diseases, including those known as trench fever, a flu-like complaint spread by lice, and trench foot, an inflammation caused by immersion of the feet in water seeping inside the soldiers' boots.

The constant strain on the troops meant that efforts were made to limit the period of a tour in the front line, and units were usually relieved after one or two weeks, even in relatively quiet sectors. Rotation back to the reserve or support lines rarely meant a 'rest' for the men. Various labouring tasks were required of the resting units, such things as road making and repairs, burying of telephone cables, carrying supplies and the like. Often these tasks were performed within enemy artillery range. Further back, the troops resumed routine training, but had the opportunity for some relaxation and entertainment during their off-duty hours in the numerous village taverns (*estaminets*).

While full-scale battle was comparatively rare, the type of operation known as trench-raiding was carried out with some regularity by both sides. As well as inflicting casualties on the enemy, these enterprises were mainly intended to gather intelligence, by capturing prisoners and bringing them back for interrogation, or at least coming away with some kind of enemy unit identification. A further justification for raiding, as far as the higher command was concerned, was a desire to maintain an aggressive attitude among the troops. After some experience of heavy casualties with few definite benefits in return, those at the front line were less convinced of the value of raiding. A raid would usually begin with a short sharp artillery and mortar bombardment on the selected segment of the enemy trench and the barbed wire in front of it, followed by the guns shifting target to place a curtain of shell-bursts behind and on each side of the objective (a 'box barrage') to isolate it from potential reinforcements. The infantry raiding party, which could number 80 or more in a big operation, would follow up the barrage as soon as possible, hoping to find the wire cut by the shells and mortars and the enemy garrison cowering in their dugouts. Only a few minutes was allowed in the enemy trench, during which the raiders would try to kill as many of the enemy as they could, except for snatching a few prisoners. Grenades, pistols, bayonets and various homemade clubs were used in the brief, savage mêlée. The raiders then headed back to their own lines, usually through a gauntlet of machine gun and artillery fire from the alerted enemy.

Shortly before the 4th Division arrived in the Armentières sector, the number of raids on the German lines had increased under orders from GHQ. The intention was to draw the Germans' attention away from the build-up further south in preparation for the Somme offensive, and the 'Nursery' sector was no longer as quiet as before. The 1st and 2nd Divisions and the New Zealanders had already carried out a series of raids, some more successful than others, by the time the 4th Division began to take over the line. The Germans had retaliated by staging their own raids. General Cox was informed that his division would be required to begin mounting raids as soon as possible. Conscious of the troops' inexperience, his approach was that

> 'for a first attempt the raid should not be on too ambitious a scale,' that it should be undertaken on the latest practicable date, and that the team should be sent into the trenches in advance of its brigade.[12]

That brigade was Brigadier-General Monash's 4th, the first of the 4th Division troops to go into the line and seen as the most experienced, although the splitting of the original units had supposedly levelled out old and new units in that respect.

The brigadier in turn selected the 14th Battalion to mount the first raid. An all-volunteer team of six officers and 83 others was selected. The majority of these would directly attack the objective, but some were detailed to various other tasks such as flank guards, scouts, stretcher bearers and signallers. Captain Arthur Cox was in overall command and the actual storming party would be led by Lieutenant Harold Wanliss, a young officer with no combat experience but one whom 'everyone liked and admired'[13] for his obvious fine qualities. Other officers in the party were equally new to fighting, but they were backed up by several battle-hardened NCOs, veterans of Gallipoli. The raiders spent several days training for the operation, which was planned to take place on the night of 2/3 July. General Cox observed the team's final 'full dress rehearsal' of the attack, for which they used a replica of the objective constructed in a back area. Artillery support, including medium trench mortars to cut the enemy wire, would be provided by the 2nd Division, as the 4th's artillery had not yet completed relief.

The opposing trenches were about 300 metres apart at the point chosen for the raid. After dark on 2 July the raiding party crept out into No Man's Land so as to be closer to the objective when the barrage ceased. The guns and mortars opened fire at 11:30 pm, lengthening the range from the enemy front line trench to the support positions after a few minutes. The raiders charged, only to find that the German barbed wire was mostly intact. The MTM bombs had landed in open space between wire belts, and although an unlucky enemy patrol had been caught by the mortars, the 14th Battalion raiders now had to struggle through the obstacle any way they could. German machine guns and artillery reacted immediately. Many of the raiders were hit in the wire, and enemy fire was also directed at No Man's Land and the Australian lines, shell bursts cutting the telephone lines that the Australian signallers had laid out behind them. Communication with headquarters now relied on runners. Lieutenant Wanliss and three other officers were wounded, but Wanliss continued on to the enemy parapet, from where he directed the fighting. With only a few minutes before their own artillery was due to fire on the German front line again, those Australians who had succeeded in reaching the enemy trench threw grenades into dugouts trying to do as much damage as possible, then Wanliss gave the order to retire. He was wounded again returning through the wire, tried to continue but collapsed, and was then hit a third time while being carried out by several of his men. The Australians had been forced to leave several casualties in the German position and now ran the gauntlet of machine guns and shrapnel on the return journey. The raiders took cover in a stream-bed in No Man's Land until the German fire died down, then cautiously made their way back to their own lines.

The raid had achieved little despite good preparation and the gallantry of all ranks. The 14th had lost 10 killed and 28 wounded in a few minutes of fighting; it was optimistically claimed that 50 Germans had been killed by the bombardment and the fighting in the trench, but it appears that the enemy losses were actually six killed and 46 wounded.[14] Brigadier General Monash's report praised the behaviour of officers and men, but had to acknowledge that 'the enterprise cannot be considered to have been successful.'[15] Whatever the outcome, Lieutenant Wanliss had proven himself in action. His courage and leadership resulted in the award of the Distinguished Service Order (DSO), the first time that decoration had been awarded to an AIF subaltern.

The Germans reacted immediately, launching a raid on the Australian line during the following night. By chance or design, the blow fell on the 14th Battalion's sector in its turn. It also happened to be the night that the 4th Division artillery was completing the takeover of responsibilities from the 2nd Division gunners. Control and communication were still settling in, resulting in artillery support for the infantry being not as prompt as it might have been.[16] The German raid began with an hour-long bombardment, using high explosive shells and *minenwerfer* (mortar) bombs on the targeted section of the Australian breastwork, blowing it in and burying a number of men under the tumbled sandbags. The German raiding party followed up and some of them succeeded in entering the wrecked trench. After a short, fierce fight with grenades and bayonets, the raiders withdrew, taking an Australia private with them as a prisoner. Casualties in 'D' Company of the 14th Battalion amounted to 43, 10 of them killed or missing. In these pointless operations on the two nights, some of the Division's infantry had quickly gained experience of Western Front trench warfare in both attack and defence, but at a high price.

The divisional artillery went into action shortly afterwards, beginning a series of routine shooting tasks in the sector. The CRA reported

> 8th July 10.30 pm: Left group consisting of 40th, 44th, 47th and 112th (How[itzer]) Bty 4th Aust Div Art[iller]y bombarded BRIDOUX SALIENT ... in cooperation with light trench mortars. Ammunition expended 816 R[oun]ds Shrapnel and High Explosive.
>
> 9th July 4 pm: All Batteries cooperated in destroying front line parapet at [map reference]. Expended 1000 HE 18 p[ounde]r and 200 HE 4.5 How.
>
> 9/10 July 9.30 pm to 4 am: All batteries shelled back roads and lines of approach at intervals. Expended 576 Shrapnel.[17]

The reference to the 'Left Group' above refers to the method of artillery command and control used on the Western Front. Artillery in a defensive sector or supporting a division in attack was divided into groups, usually two (Left and Right) or three (Left, Centre and Right). The division's field artillery brigades would be distributed across the groups, each of which was under command of a senior brigade CO; in many cases the artillery of two or more divisions, and sometimes elements of the Corps artillery, was combined into such groups. When the main body of a division went into reserve it was not uncommon for its artillery to continue defending the line or to be detached for the purpose of supporting other troops in a particular operation. The 4th Division artillery would soon be required to undertake that type of duty.

The 4th Division's stint in the Armentières sector was destined to be of short duration. Events on the Somme front had begun to dominate the deployment of the BEF, the great offensive having been launched on 1 July 1916. The attack had been preceded by a week of artillery bombardment which had been confidently expected to obliterate the German front line and open the way for a walkover advance by the infantry. Although the Germans had suffered heavy casualties and been badly shaken, their deep, strong dugouts had provided good protection for their highly-efficient machine gunners, who emerged when the bombardment ceased and proceeded to mow down the advancing lines of the British infantry. The casualty list for the first day of the battle was unprecedented, with 19,240 killed out of a total of 57,470 including wounded, missing and prisoners.[18] Scarcely any progress was made along most of the front, but some territory was captured at the southern end of the 35-kilometre attack line. In succeeding days, the British and supporting French elements concentrated on forcing their way forward in that area. The next two weeks saw more ground gained but at a terrible cost of 40,000 more casualties. The need for fresh divisions was urgent, both to replace those shattered in the fighting and to increase the pressure where some success had been achieved. At the same time it was important to discourage the Germans from transferring troops to the crucial sector.

Accordingly, the 1st and 2nd Australian Divisions (I Anzac Corps), relieved in the Armentières sector by the 4th Division, had moved south to the Somme. BEF GHQ then decided to also send the 4th Division with them—a decision that 'had not been arrived at without some hesitation' as the official historian wrote[19] owing to lingering doubts as to whether their training was sufficiently advanced for large-scale operations. In any case, General Cox was informed late on 7 July that the 4th Division would be required to rejoin I Anzac and move to the Somme area as part of the GHQ Reserve. The Division would be relieved in the Armentières line by the newly-arrived 5th Division. At this point the units of the 4th Division had been in full occupation of the front line for a maximum of 10 days in the case of the 4th Brigade Group, with the 12th Brigade and the artillery only since 4 July. Of the infantry, only a portion of the 14th Battalion had taken part in any significant combat. Now the Division found itself handing over to even less experienced troops and initiating them to the conditions of the front line.

The relief was done in some haste, the infantry brigade groups changing over during the two nights of 10 and 11 July. The divisional artillery completed their handover two nights later, the two divisions taking over each other's guns and ammunition supplies. It had been intended that the 4th Division artillery would divert to the St Omer area, well to the rear, to undergo extra training, but the next day a counter-order was issued: the 4th Division artillery was now required to go back into the line to support that of the 5th Division in certain 'special operations' that had suddenly emerged (except for the artillery-based mortar batteries, which continued on to their training programme). By this time the incoming division's gunners had occupied the existing properly-constructed protective pits in the gun-line, and the returning 4th Division gunners had to improvise new positions, hurriedly digging in and setting up communications. The batteries were re-established during the night of 15/16 July, distributed over three groups of the 5th Division artillery and under command of the 5th Division CRA.

The 'special operations' in which the 4th Division's artillery became involved developed into the Battle of Fromelles. A project intended to deter the Germans from transferring troops from the sector to reinforce their Somme front, after numerous changes of plan the operation now took the form of a full assault on the German lines. This was to be carried out by two divisions, the 5th Australian and the 61st British—the former having just arrived in the war zone, the latter under strength after having been used to provide reinforcements for other divisions. The 5th Division, with the 4th Division artillery attached, was temporarily transferred to the control of XI Corps (General Sir Richard Haking), under First Army. The 5th Australian Division infantry was required to attack the German first line trench system on a front of 1,800 metres across a No Man's Land that was up to 365 metres wide at one point. Their supporting artillery would include a group of British heavy guns and howitzers from Corps and Army level, as well as the batteries of the two Australian divisions. Some of the 'heavies' personnel were also of limited experience, and the supply of artillery ammunition was less than desirable—the Somme front had priority. With his infantry and artillery both being comparatively raw in Western Front conditions, General Haking optimistically pushed ahead with his plans, overcoming the doubts of GHQ—and the fact that he had recently arranged a similar attack on his front that had failed with heavy losses.

As far as the 4th Division artillery was concerned, their tasks were straightforward supporting fire for the infantry attack. The enemy front and support lines were to be bombarded with HE shell, both to wreck the parapets and cut the defensive barbed wire. The guns would then 'lift', lengthening the range by about 100 metres to a designated 'barrage line' and lay down a curtain of fire to interfere with enemy reinforcements. The plan called for several such lifts, each of a few minutes duration, after which the guns would suddenly revert to the enemy front line and switch to shrapnel shell, hoping to catch the defenders emerging from cover. The final lift would then stay on the barrage line while the infantry advanced. The attached corps heavy artillery was also tasked with shelling enemy batteries (counter-battery fire). The final plan called for the full bombardment by all guns to last for five hours before the last lift. Each group of guns was allotted to covering one of the infantry brigades that would be sent in.

After several postponements the operation was set for 19 July. For several days leading up to then the artillery had attempted to register on their designated targets, with observers noting the fall of shot and advising aiming corrections. Observation was mainly by aircraft of the Royal Flying Corps (RFC), and adverse weather had restricted their effectiveness. Some preliminary wire-cutting shoots were also carried out prior to 19 July, all of this activity making it plain to the Germans (the 6th Bavarian Reserve Division in this sector) that a significant operation was imminent; they also had direct observation of the opposing line from the high ground of Aubers Ridge. The artillery opened proceedings at 11 am on the day with intensive registration shooting in the now clear weather, building up steadily to the full bombardment of the enemy lines. All guns and mortars were in action by 3 pm. The planned 'false lifts' took place but apparently without catching the defenders out—an artillery Forward Observation Officer (FOO) in the infantry front line reported that the Germans did not seem to be manning their parapet during the brief respite. Nevertheless the waiting infantry was encouraged by the sight of the destruction wrought on the German front line breastworks, but they were soon suffering themselves as the enemy batteries began retaliating. The German shells caused numerous casualties to the infantry waiting in the assembly trenches and they were able to keep up this shooting without serious interference, the counter-battery fire of the British 'heavies' being ineffective.

At 6 pm the artillery made its final lift and the infantry went forward. The sacrifice of the 5th Division infantry at Fromelles on that tragic night has only recently begun to receive its rightful recognition in Australian public knowledge, although C E W Bean did his best to present the full story in the *Official History*,[20] adding to the account in the 5th Division's history.[21] The brief artillery preparation had not been enough to completely suppress the German defenders and the wide, flat No Man's Land was swept by the fire of their machine guns and rifles. Most of the Australian infantry had never been in combat before and they had only been at the front for a few days, but courage and determination took them into the enemy front line in spite of enormous casualties. After hanging on there through most of the night they were forced to retreat, still under heavy fire, back to their original line. From the artillery's point of view, their tasks were carried out according to plan, and the divisional guns responded through the night as best they could to messages from the infantry, shifting target or increasing the rate of fire to defend against counter-attacks. At a few times it appeared that some guns were shelling their own troops. The official historian commented that

> some of the guns were undoubtedly firing erratically, and, with artillery so new to its work, the error could not be easily traced or prevented. The defect was the direct outcome of the rapidity with which this artillery had been raised in Egypt.[22]

Similar instances occurred throughout the war, however, regardless of the level of artillery experience. Finally, the guns were confined to covering the retreat of the shattered infantry brigades and laying down a barrage against any possible counter-attack. Essentially, the artillery had failed in the battle; the number of guns, the ammunition supply and the period of bombardment were all inadequate to properly support the infantry, and those drawbacks were compounded by the overall inexperience of all elements.[23]

The 5th Division's casualties in this ill-advised operation totalled over 5,500 including 1,917 killed; the 5th was effectively broken as a fighting force for many months to come. General Haking commented in his report that the attack had done the 5th Division (and the 61st British Division, which also lost heavily) 'a great deal of good.' No doubt he meant the survivors. Casualties in the artillery were very light, neither side having done any effective counter-battery shooting. The 4th Division gunners had one officer (Captain Gordon Thompson, commander of the 48th Battery, 24th AFA Brigade) and one OR killed plus a total of 18 wounded.[24] In a different sense, another casualty of the battle was the former 16th Battalion CO Colonel Harold Pope, now acting in command of the 5th Division's 14th Brigade. After many hours awake conducting his brigade in the battle, he had fallen into an exhausted sleep during the following afternoon. The GOC, General McCay, tried to wake him and jumped to the conclusion that he was drunk. Pope was relieved of his command and sent back to Australia; determined to clear his name, he would eventually return to the 4th Division.

In the aftermath of the battle the 4th Division artillery was split up for a short time. The 10th AFA Brigade remained attached to the 5th Division while the 11th was attached to the New Zealand Division artillery, each being supported by detachments of the DAC. The other two brigades and the rest of the DAC pulled back to their former billets in the reserve area around Croix du Bac. The detached troops subsequently rejoined and the full 4th Division artillery moved to Second Army's training area at Lumbres, west of St Omer, on 7 August to undergo two weeks of intensive training exercises. At Fromelles they had become the first element of the 4th Division to be involved in a full-scale action on the Western Front—and in time they would also be the last. In the meantime the rest of the 4th Division had moved south to take part in the drama and tragedy of the Somme.

4 Notes

1. Not, it seems, Captain Henry William 'Harry' Murray, also of the 13th Battalion—later Lieutenant Colonel Murray VC CMG DSO DCM, Australia's most highly decorated soldier. The official historian, C E W Bean, identified H W Murray as the officer involved in this incident (*Official History*, Vol III, p. 73n) and other writers have subsequently followed that - including the present author, in *No Ordinary Determination* (2005). In that book, however, I mentioned in a chapter note that there was a possibility that Harold Murray had actually been the protagonist, based on the officer's rank being stated as lieutenant, whereas Henry 'Harry' Murray had been a captain for some time when the incident occurred. I have since found in the 4th Division Admin Staff War Diary (May 1916, Appendix 9) a list of the 4th Division's disembarkation officers appointed for duty at Marseille. Each brigade was ordered to nominate one captain and two subalterns, and the 4th Brigade officers were Captain W R Wadsworth of the 14th Battalion, Lieutenant A W Potts, 16th Battalion (in World War II, Brigadier Arnold Potts of Kokoda Track fame) and Lieutenant H F Murray, 13th Battalion. It would not be the only time that the presence of two officers named H Murray in the same battalion caused confusion—each officer's service record contains at least one entry that actually relates to the other one. H W 'Harry' Murray never claimed to have taken part in such an incident, and probably was not aware that it had been claimed for him. A man of considerable modesty, he was disinclined to read anything about himself. Lieutenant Harold F Murray was wounded at Mouquet Farm in August 1916, so severely that he was returned to Australia and discharged as permanently unfit for duty.
2. 46th Battalion War Diary, 12 June 1916.
3. 4th Division Artillery HQ War Diary, 26 June 1916.
4. 4th Division General Staff War Diary for June 1916, Appendix M.
5. *Ibid*.
6. *Official History*, Vol III, p. 300. The *Official History* implies that the 4th Division artillery only relieved that of the 2nd Division, but the War Diaries of the three divisions' artillery headquarters indicate clearly that the 1st Division artillery was also replaced by 4th Division units. Overall, the 4th Division took over the entire front of the 1st Division and part of the 2nd Division's front.
7. *Ibid*, p. 305n.
8. Holmes, *Op Cit*, p.275–6.
9. Rule, *Op Cit*, p. 19–20
10. 46th Battalion War Diary, 11 July 1916.

11	13th Brigade War Diary, 30 June 1916.
12	*Official History*, Vol III, p.300.
13	Rule, *Op Cit*, p. 21.
14	*Official History*, Vol III, p. 302n.
15	4th Division General Staff War Diary for July 1916, Appendix D.
16	*Official History*, Vol III, p. 303.
17	4th Division Artillery HQ War Diary, 8/9 July 1916.
18	M. Middlebrook, *The First Day on the Somme*, p. 263 (noting that the figures are taken from the British Official History).
19	*Official History*, Vol III, p. 334.
20	*Ibid*, Vol III, pp. 328–447.
21	Ellis, *Op Cit*, pp. 81–116. W. H Downing's memoir *To The Last Ridge* (1920, 1998) is another contemporary work to include an account of the battle.
22	*Official History*, Vol III, p. 357.
23	At the time of writing, military historian Peter Barton was engaged in researching German records of the battle, on behalf of the Australian Army History Unit. Among other things, the records confirmed the overall ineffectiveness of the Australian and British artillery work from the German point of view.
24	It is possible that some or all of these losses were not the result of enemy action. The *Official History* comments that some casualties in the artillery were caused by faulty shells bursting prematurely (Vol III, p. 357n). The relevant war diaries do not detail the causes of the casualties, nor does Captain Thompson's service record.

5: Inferno on the Somme

The 4th Division infantry and other elements had handed over their Armentières front-line positions to the 5th Division by the night of 11 July. The troops retraced their steps to the reserve area that they had occupied less than a month earlier, concentrating around Merris village. From here the elaborate process of entraining the division took place, the various units marching to Bailleul to board 24 railway trains at two stations, departing for the south on 13 and 14 July (motor vehicles of the field ambulances and the supply column went by road under their own power). The 4th Division was now back under I Anzac Corps, which in turn was intended to be part of Fourth Army in the Somme area. Having left its artillery behind at Armentières to support the 5th Division, the 4th Division would now be covered by the former artillery element of the Indian Army's Lahore Division. The Indian Army itself had minimal artillery of its own, the Royal Artillery usually providing that arm at divisional level. The Lahore Division infantry had recently been transferred to the Mesopotamia front, but its (British) artillery had stayed in France. In July 1916 the guns (5th, 11th and 18th Brigades Royal Field Artillery and the Ammunition Column) were in the Ypres Salient attached to the 3rd Canadian Division, with which they had recently been in heavy action at the battle of Mount Sorrel. The Lahore artillery was now transferred to the 4th Australian Division, and also entrained on 13 and 14 July to accompany their new division to the Somme. At that point they were joined by the Medium and Heavy Trench Mortar batteries of the 4th. The Lahore artillery commander, Brigadier General Edward Hoare-Nairne, would be *de facto* CRA 4th Australian Division.

The infantry brigade groups detrained at the town of Doullens on 13 July then marched to billets around various villages at distances of about 20 kilometres. Most units found the march an exhausting one, the men's feet suffering in particular from the unaccustomed marching on hard cobbled roads. The 4th Brigade Group billeted at Domart-en-Ponthieu and St-Ouen, the 12th at Bertaucourt-les-Dames and the 13th at Halloy-les-Pernois with the Pioneer Battalion nearby at Canaples. Divisional HQ was also established in Domart. The territory from here east to the front line constituted the back area of I Anzac. Twenty kilometres to the south lay the city of Amiens,

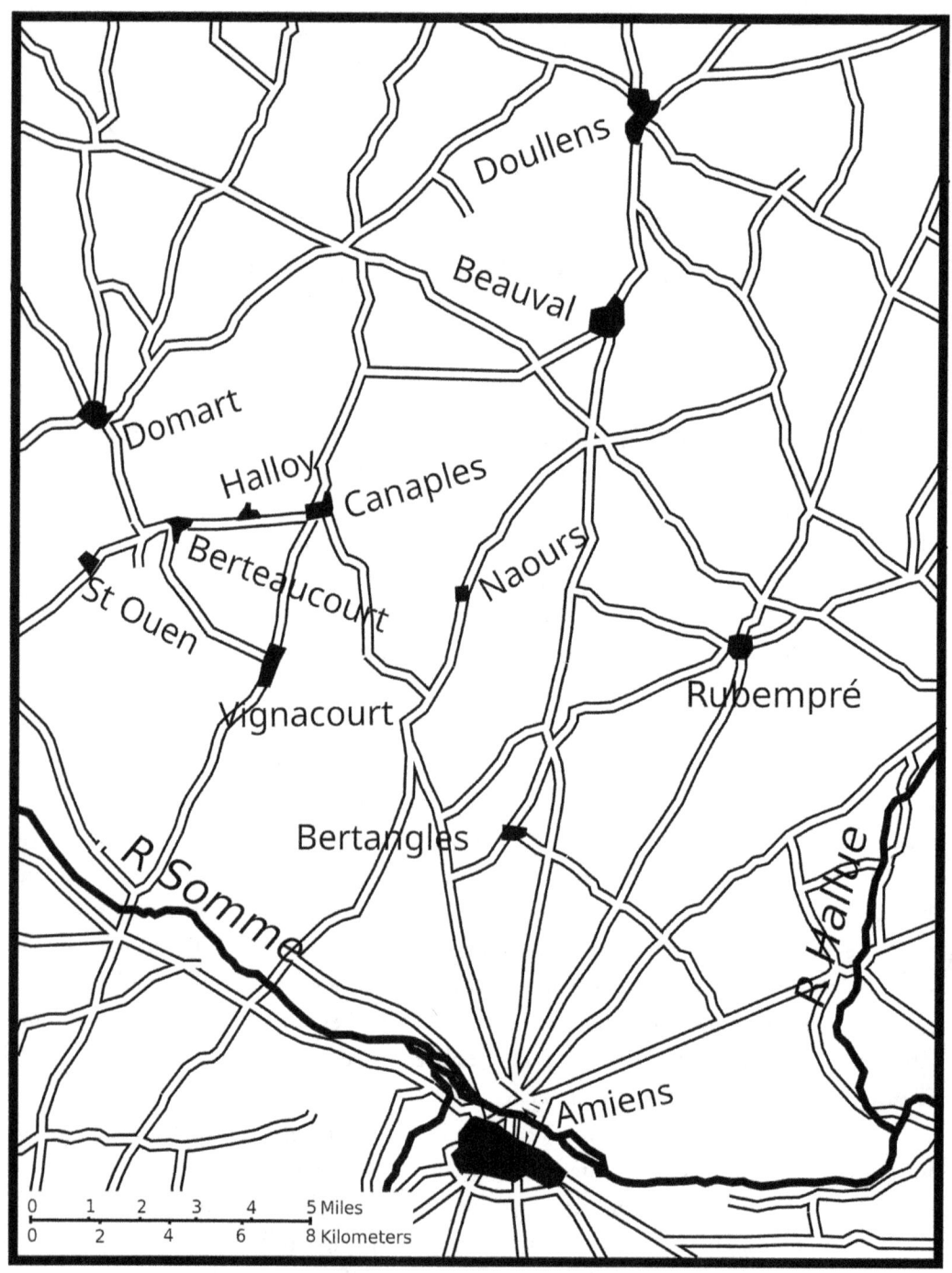

Somme sector rear area, north of Amiens

> a miniature Paris, far beyond shell range, practically undamaged, the important streets and boulevards thronged with a bright population not visibly affected by the war; hotels, shops, cafes, cabarets and newspaper kiosks carried on a brisk trade.[1]

It was at Domart on 14 July that Brigadier General John Monash, who had led the 4th Brigade since it was raised in 1914, left the brigade and the 4th Division. He had been promoted to major general as GOC of the new 3rd Australian Division, a formation that had been recruited in Australia and sent directly to England for training. Monash's skills as an administrator, trainer and planner were well suited to divisional command, and he had now reached the next rung on the ladder leading to the highest operational command in the 1st AIF.

There was some ambivalence towards Monash in the 4th Brigade, the 15th Battalion history noting his 'aloofness'[2] in comparison to his successor, Colonel (shortly Brigadier General) Charles Brand. A 42-year-old Queenslander, Brand was a pre-war regular who had been an original officer of the 1st Division. As brigade major of the 3rd Brigade, he had been among the first ashore at the Landing, winning the DSO, the first Australian to be awarded that decoration on Gallipoli. The new brigadier made an unfortunate first impression on the troops. At a parade shortly after taking over he had several defaulters exhibited, then delivered a speech, of which Sergeant E J Rule (14th Battalion) recalled:

> he started to tell us of his own exploits and to let us know that he was no dud ... 'I won my DSO before any of you were on Gallipoli' ... no end of murmuring went round, for the old 4th Brigade had landed on Gallipoli only about six hours later than the 1st Division. When the parade was over the old Brig was just about the most unpopular man in France.[3]

Fortunately that impression was soon overturned. Brigadier-General Brand's 'care for the men's wants soon brought him their confidence and he became generally popular.'[4] That comment was of particular note as coming from a 14th Battalion source, as the brigadier's relationship with that unit was often less than harmonious. Brand became known by several nicknames among the brigade troops —'The Old Brig', 'Charlie', and 'Steve'.

The brigadier's unfortunate speech had occurred on 21 July. By that time the 4th Brigade infantry and machine guns had moved from Domart/St Ouen to billets around Naours, about 10 kilometres closer to the front line. The 1st and 2nd Divisions had preceded the 4th Division, and on the previous night units of the 1st had taken over a sector of the Somme front. It was here at the southern end of the battlefield that some partial progress had been made since the battle started on 1 July, albeit at a terrible price in British blood. The unattained objectives set for the first day of the battle included the fortified village of Thiepval and the high ground running south-east from there for about 10 kilometres to Guillemont; between those points was the village of Pozières, also heavily fortified and close to the highest point of the ridge. The British attacks had been repulsed there on 1 July, and new assaults were made in the following two weeks.

Although the Thiepval – Pozières ridge remained in German hands, some success was gained further to the south. The advancing British captured enough territory to swing their front line across the German second line trenches; the British front in that sector now ran roughly east-west, facing the flank of the ridge to its north. The next step would be a major assault to drive the Germans from the high ground. Two successive attacks on Pozières by units of the British III Corps on 15 and 17 July were repulsed by the machine guns and artillery of the German garrison, despite a huge bombardment by the British artillery that almost demolished the village itself. Responsibility for the sector was now transferred from Fourth Army to Reserve Army, under General Sir Hubert Gough. It was at this point that I Anzac became involved, its divisions being attached to the largely cavalry Reserve Army as part of a major increase to its infantry resources. This was the first time that the Australians had encountered General Gough, but it would not be the last.

The 1st Australian Division was 'put in' on 23 July, after another furious artillery bombardment that obliterated what remained of the village. By dawn they had captured the position and were digging in. The Germans in their turn now pounded the area with artillery and launched counter-attacks. All were beaten off, and further attacks by the 1st Division expanded the captured area. The cost was terrible: after suffering over 5,000 casualties, the exhausted 1st Division was relieved by the 2nd, which continued to press forward despite initial setbacks. Their eventual capture of the highest point of Pozières Ridge cost the 2nd the huge total of 6,846 casualties by 5 August. Now it was the 4th Division's turn.

Since arriving in the reserve area, the Division had been undertaking intensive training. Infantry units in particular undertook several route marches to toughen up the men, and considerable attention was also placed on grenade fighting or 'bombing' (at least in the 4th Brigade[5]) and bayonet work. The troops also took part in a series of tactical exercises that reflected the lessons learned during the first weeks of the Somme battle. Co-operation between infantry and artillery was now being emphasised; it had been recognised that the infantry had to be given a chance to keep up with the 'lifts' in the artillery barrage, in time and distance. The infantry battalions worked with batteries of the Lahore artillery, practising the technique of closely following the barrage to their first objective. While the barrage was lifting to the next objective, another wave of infantry would pass through the first wave and move on to that point. The exercises were valuable training, but would not necessarily guarantee success against an objective that shot back, and when the effectiveness of the supporting artillery was less than perfect.

On 25 July the Division began to march forward by stages towards the front line. By 27 July the 4th Brigade Group was billeted around Warloy-Baillon, about 19 kilometres from the battlefield, where they encountered troops of the 1st Division returning from the heavy fighting for Pozières. The obvious exhaustion, both physical and mental, of these survivors gave the 4th Brigade troops some inkling of what was in store for them; 'in all my experience I've never seen men so shaken up as these' recalled Sergeant Rule[6] (14th Battalion). The 12th Brigade came up close to the 4th on 29 July, billeting around several villages near Warloy. On the same day the 13th Brigade, following a stage behind the other two in reserve, marched from billets around Halloy to the area of Rubempré and Hérissart. This march proved to be rather farcical. The previous night, the survivors of the 1st Division's 3rd Brigade, on their way back to rest from the Pozières fighting, had bivouacked near the 13th's area. The 3rd was the 13th's 'parent' brigade and the opportunity was taken to renew old acquaintances in nearby village *estaminets* once the troops were off duty. Next morning the 13th Brigade troops were unpleasantly surprised to find themselves faced with a long route march with all of their equipment (orders for the march had not been issued until 11:30 pm the previous night), and the mostly hung-over men were something of a rabble. To make matters worse, the GOC, Major General Cox, had decided to observe the march with his staff and Brigadier General Glasgow. Rather surprisingly, General Cox took the brigade's poor performance in his stride, saying to the mortified brigadier, 'Don't worry, Glasgow, if your men don't march too well. The Germans are all flat-footed.'[7] It appears that the brigade's battalion COs were not quite as understanding.[8]

The next stage of the approach march took the 12th and 4th Brigade Groups to the large open billeting area known as the 'Brickfields,' just outside the town of Albert; both brigades were in place there by 4 August. The troops were now within long artillery range of the enemy, and Albert itself had been bombarded several times. A famous landmark was the tower of the Albert cathedral, where a shell had knocked the statue of the Virgin and Child into a precarious horizontal position, hanging over the street; this became a familiar sight to everyone who passed through on the way to and from the front line. Elements of the 4th and 12th Brigades were under orders to move to the front line on the night of 5/6 August.

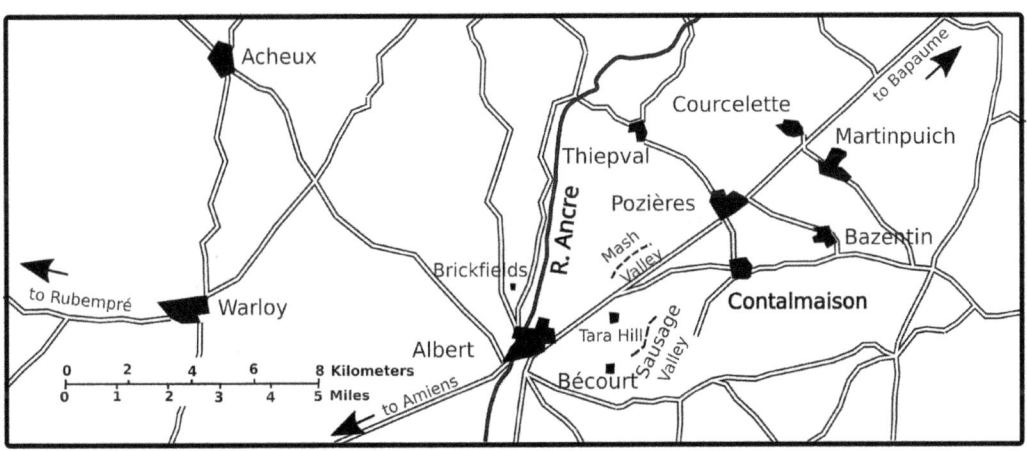

Somme sector, area around Pozières

The 4th Division was going into a battlefield situation where intense fighting was taking place constantly, from infantry clashes to the impersonal, devastating artillery bombardments. The geography of the battlefield, although barely recognisable under the constant shelling, was a pattern of roads, trenches and other fieldworks, ridges and valleys, that soon became almost as well known by their nicknames as had the various landmarks at Gallipoli. The axis was the straight Roman road (now the D929) between Albert and Bapaume, the latter town being about 12 kilometres behind the German lines. The road passed through the place where Pozières village had once been. Just outside Albert was the rise known as Tara Hill, the final staging point before the front line, where 4th Division HQ was established on 6 August. Beyond Tara Hill the ground sloped down to the long, shallow Sausage Valley (or Gully) south of the Roman road, a re-entrant leading off Pozières ridge. North of the road, in the British sector, was a similar depression known as Mash Valley. Sausage Valley formed the main line of approach to the front for men and material, and also accommodated numerous artillery batteries. The German second-line fieldworks ran behind Pozières village along the ridge in this sector; this double trench system was referred to as the 'OG' (for Old German) Lines—OG 1 was the front trench, and OG 2 the support trench behind it. Part of 'K' Trench, an intermediate segment of the German defensive system, was now in British hands and was being used as a communication trench to the front line on the ridge. A kilometre south of the main road was a small quarry known as the Chalk Pit, used as an ammunition dump, as a temporary refuge for resting infantry and sometimes for emplacement of mortars.

With the capture of Pozières and the adjacent part of the OG lines by the 1st and 2nd Australian Divisions, operations would soon focus on Thiepval to the north-west. Blocking the way to Thiepval was a further network of recently-constructed German trenches, and in particular the strongpoint of Mouquet Farm. The farm buildings had been destroyed by shelling like everything else in the area, but the farmhouse had extensive cellars which had been extended by the Germans to provide an underground system of protective bunkers. Manned by a determined garrison well provided with weapons, that hornets' nest was an immensely strong position—just how strong was not at first realised by the British and Australian commanders. Constant shelling by both sides had made the battlefield in general a scene of almost total devastation. The official historian, C E W Bean, was there:

> ... the flayed land, shell-hole bordering shell-hole, corpses of young men lying against the trench walls or in shell holes; some—except for the dust settling on them—seeming to sleep; others torn in half; others rotting, swollen, and discoloured ... the air fetid with their stench or at times pungent with the chemical reek of high explosive; the troops of both sides—always in desperate need of sleep—working or fighting by night and living by day in niches scooped in the trench side—dangerous places perilously shaken with the crashing thump of each heavy shell whose burst might all too easily shovel them on top of their occupants.[9]

The difficulties of the battlefield extended back to affect the issues of supply to the front line fighters and evacuation of casualties. Supply responsibilities at divisional level came under the Divisional Train for rations and water, and the artillery's Divisional Ammunition Column (DAC) for both infantry and artillery ammunition. A massive organisation existed behind the lines for bringing vast quantities of supplies from British factories through the base system on the coast to the vicinity of the fighting front. From the base depots, transport was usually by railway train to a railhead perhaps 16 kilometres or more behind the lines. From here the supplies would be taken to divisional distribution points, usually by means of motor lorries allocated to the division. Here the mainly horse-drawn vehicles of the Divisional Train units would take over to carry their allocated loads to brigade group 'refilling points;' the divisional train vehicles could also collect directly from the railhead depending on its distance from the front. At the brigade points, unit transport sections would collect their rations for delivery to the men in the firing line. This never-ending process, added to other military traffic on the muddy roads, produced a scene of constant activity behind the lines.

It was the task of the divisional 'Q' staff to familiarise themselves with the supply situation in the division's sector and ensure that all units were informed of what had to be done. Several days before the 4th Division was due to take over the Pozières sector, the AA & QMG, Lieutenant Colonel Armstrong, issued a circular to all units describing the arrangements that would apply. The divisional railhead was at Acheux, about 11 kilometres north-west of Albert, close enough to the front for the Divisional Train to collect supplies directly from the railhead and transport them to refilling points in the Brickfields area. Parties under the various unit quartermasters then drew their unit's rations from the Brickfields points for carrying to the trenches. This process was helped by a light railway or 'trench tramway' that had been built forward to a location called Gordon Dump at the head of Sausage Valley; from there fatigue parties from the reserve infantry brigade would carry rations to the unit cookers, which were to be established as far forward as possible, and thence to the troops in the front line. Water was pumped from the back areas to storage tanks near Gordon Dump, from which containers (usually used petrol tins) were filled for carrying forward. Ammunition—that is, Small Arms Ammunition (SAA) for rifles and machine guns, as well as grenades, flares, and light mortar rounds—was similarly conveyed by the DAC from rear dumps to the tramway and thence to Gordon Dump and by working parties to brigade ammunition dumps. From those dumps it was up to the brigade staffs to arrange drawing and delivery of ammunition to the trenches, again employing carrying parties from the units. Artillery ammunition was delivered by the DAC to separate dumps serving the gun-line.

The system seemed well organised on paper and usually worked with reasonable efficiency in the back areas. The closer the supplies came to the fighting front, however, the more the enemy began to interfere. Harassing artillery fire could disrupt road traffic within its range, killing men and animals and cratering the roads. At the end of the supply line the unit carriers, lugging containers ('dixies') of stew from the cookers, water tins or boxes of grenades, found themselves struggling through muddy, partly wrecked communication trenches, often under bombardment, to reach the men in the front line. The trip was nearly always done at night and the carriers tried to pick the rare quiet times, but a ration party could still get caught by shelling in their determination to get through to their mates if at all possible. As well as rations and ammunition, further dumps were maintained by the divisional engineers to hold great quantities of 'engineer stores'—timber, corrugated iron, barbed wire, pickets, tools, sandbags and the like—needed for construction work in the division's area. The main engineer dumps in the rear of the Pozières were at Acheux and Méricourt-l'Abbé, from where motor lorries brought consignments forward to intermediate locations at Bécourt Wood and La Boiselle. Items for the artillery and other units behind the front line were drawn from these dumps. Stores for the forward area were brought up to Gordon Dump, Copse Avenue and The Chalk Pit from where the field companies, pioneers and infantry working parties obtained supplies for works in the battle area.

The casualty clearance system was also one of stages or relays, but working in the opposite direction, away from the front and towards the back area. At the point of combat, each unit's regimental stretcher-bearers picked up wounded stretcher cases (as opposed to 'walking wounded' who could make their own way to the rear). The casualty would be carried back to his unit's Regimental Aid Post (RAP), where he was taken over by Medical Corps personnel—the Regimental Medical Officer (RMO) and his orderlies. The RAP could be as close as 300 metres to the front line, housed where possible in a well-protected dugout. The wounded man would receive basic first aid here and wait to be sent on for the next stage of treatment. AAMC stretcher-bearers from the Field Ambulance units collected casualties at the RAPs and carried them on the next stage, to an Advanced Dressing Station (ADS) controlled by a nominated Field Ambulance. Each ADS could receive wounded from at least four RAPs. An ADS was normally established near a road to allow for wheeled transport on the next stage, and was also dug-in for protection from shellfire (intermediate divisional collection points could also be set up between RAP and ADS). The ADS medical staff provided further treatment to urgent cases and sent their patients on as quickly as possible, by vehicle from there—either horse-drawn or motor ambulance. The last point of the process that was still under divisional control was the Main Dressing Station (MDS), which also formed the headquarters of the division's Field Ambulances. The MDS was usually far enough back to be out of effective artillery range. Here the casualties were further cared for and the less serious cases could complete their treatment at the MDS. Those that needed surgery and other longer-term treatment were sent on again to a Casualty Clearing Station (CCS), a corps-level establishment that included full hospital facilities, with operating theatres and a staff including surgeons and nurses. Following treatment at the CCS the patient would often be transported to a hospital in England for follow-up treatment and convalescence. Sadly, treatment was not always successful, and military cemeteries tended to form near CCS locations.

The casualty handling system looked an orderly and effective one on paper, but the practical problems of the front line meant that its functioning was often less than ideal. Normal trench 'wastage,' that is the steady stream of wounded and sick men that resulted from static trench warfare, could usually be handled without major difficulties, but heavy action put a great strain on the system. Each infantry battalion had an allocation of 16 regimental stretcher bearers. Even at two to a stretcher this was inadequate to handle a large number of casualties, and in anything approaching heavy conditions four bearers were usually needed per stretcher. Bearers from the Field Ambulance units would often have to be brought in to assist in the front line, and units from divisions in reserve could be required to assist the division in action. The system could be swamped by the wounded resulting from a pitched battle—such as that going on in the Pozières sector, which the 4th Division was about to enter. Here the 2nd Division's recent advance had left the established RAPs in the battle area up to 1,600 metres behind the new front line, an excessive 'carry' for the regimental bearers and their patients, especially in the torn-up ground. The 4th Division's medical services took over the sector from 6 August, with the 12th Field Ambulance assuming control of the ADS at Bécourt Chateau near the lower end of Sausage Valley. Over the next few days Colonel Barber, the ADMS, arranged for RAPs to be established much closer to the front line, in dugouts north of the Pozières townsite, at the village cemetery and in 'Tramway Trench,' presumably using former German dugouts.[10] The 4th Field Ambulance had already begun treating battle casualties as early as 27 July, when its 'tent' subdivision was brought in to assist the 1st Field Ambulance (1st Division) in the MDS at Warloy. The 4th then took over control of the MDS from 30 July. Hundreds of wounded from the heavy fighting at Pozières were treated over the next few days. Most of these patients would have been from the 2nd Division, which had relieved the 1st on 27 July. The Warloy MDS

> consisted of a long low dressing hut about 50 feet by 10 [15 metres by 3] which was a very inconvenient size when we were busy as it was rather dark and we had to try and accommodate 4 working trestles. We had in addition ten marquees ... four for those waiting attention, four for those waiting evacuation and two were fitted out as an operating theatre.[11]

The 4th Field Ambulance tent personnel continued to maintain the MDS until relieved in their turn by the 1st Division, while its stretcher-bearers were sent forward to help the other medical units in evacuating casualties.

Although the 4th Division infantry did not begin to take over the front line until the night of 5/6 August, the 4th Pioneer Battalion and some of the divisional engineers were sent in earlier to assist the 2nd Division with urgent work on communications routes. German artillery was continuing to pound the battlefield area; as well as killing and wounding troops, the shelling was collapsing the few communication trenches and destroying roadways. The vital links with the front line had to be kept open at all costs. On the night of 1/2 August the 13th Field Company of engineers was attached to the 2nd Division's 6th Brigade and set to work clearing K (or 'Kay') Trench—'this is ranged on and shelled severely, and is much filled with dead men. It is one of the only two communication trenches leading to the 6th Brigade front line, however.'[12] The next day work continued on K Trench in daylight. This time the engineers were allocated working parties from the 6th Brigade to do the digging. The activity drew another storm of enemy shellfire, and the men, understandably shaken by the experiences of the last few days, abandoned the work to seek cover. The work had to be persevered with, however. The 13th Field Company was now under the command of Major James Mirams, who had replaced the original OC, Captain Colyer.

The 4th Pioneer Battalion became involved in the battle from 1 August also, working on communication trenches in support of the 2nd Division infantry. The pioneers concentrated particularly on the trench called Copse Avenue to the east of Pozières, which was to be used as an approach trench for the troops attacking the ridge, as well as digging and clearing other trenches in the maze of earthworks that was developing on the battlefield. When the 2nd Division launched its attack on the OG Lines on the night of 4/5 August, the 4th Pioneers, together with the 13th Field Company, were among the troops that followed up the infantry to construct communications trenches and strong-points. Some of the pioneers became involved in the fighting; Captain Spencer Adams (formerly of the 16th Battalion, a 'Diehard' at the Gallipoli evacuation) led a party of his own 4th Pioneer men and some infantry to 'mop up' survivors of a failed German counter-attack.[13] After its unpromising beginnings in Egypt, the 4th Pioneer Battalion, in a major action for the first time, stuck to its thankless task for the next 10 days under constant bombardment. Digging out blown-in trenches and keeping communications open to the front line cost the unit 230 members killed and wounded in that time.[14] From 3 August, the 46th Infantry Battalion (12th Brigade) was also put in to support the 2nd Division, providing carrying parties for the attacking infantry.[15]

After their first attempt had failed with heavy casualties, the 2nd Division infantry had captured their objectives in the OG Lines (that is, the segment of those lines that ran along the crest of the ridge behind Pozières) on the night of 4/5 August. Their losses had again been heavy and the newly-taken positions were mainly occupied by the dead, both Australian and German. The 2nd Division infantry had just enough strength left to repel some weak counter-attacks on 5 August, but the survivors now had nothing more to give. The Reserve Army commander, the impulsive General Sir Hubert Gough, was characteristically eager to continue the advance towards Mouquet Farm and Thiepval immediately, but even he soon realised that fresh troops were needed. The 4th Division infantry began to move in that night. Such had been the 2nd Division's losses that its battalions had been reduced to the size of companies or less, and one or two 4th Division battalions had easily enough troops to relieve a 2nd Division brigade. The 15th Battalion (4th Brigade) was sent in on the left of the line, the 48th and 45th (12th Brigade) on the right. In between the 15th and 48th, some 2nd Division troops would have to remain in position until the following night when they were relieved by the 14th Battalion (4th Brigade). 'Dead and wounded lay everywhere, some killed on their stretchers, with the stretcher-bearers lying dead beside them.'[16] The 4th Division troops took over the captured ground just in time to receive the full force of the enemy's counter-stroke. As soon as it was clear that they had lost the ridge position, the German forces (the IX Reserve Corps under General von Boehn) had commenced a furious artillery bombardment of what was now the new Australian line. The advance had driven a salient into the enemy line, which meant that the Germans could bring in batteries to fire from the left and right of the position as well as in front. Although lacking good aerial observation for their guns—the RFC held air superiority over the battlefield—the Germans were shooting at targets that were precisely mapped and they were able to find the range quickly. Using mostly high-explosive shells from weapons of all calibres from heavy howitzers to the light 77 mm 'whizz-bangs', the German gunners

> ... first registered carefully upon their allotted trenches and, during the hours which followed, methodically placed their shells along them, from one flank to the other; then to the rear along a communication trench; then down the support line to the other flank, and thence back to the front line. In some sectors two howitzers seemed to work in opposite directions, their lines of fire crossing, parting, and then returning to cross again.[17]

In anticipation of such a response, orders from Army and Corps level had already recommended that the garrison of the new position should be minimal, particularly in OG 2, the German support line which was now the Australian front line. OG 1, now the Australian support line, had a number of deep dugouts that could shelter the troops, unlike OG 2 which was in any case in the process of being almost obliterated by shellfire. In the 12th Brigade, now coming into the front line, there was an immediate clash between commanders over the tactics to hold the trenches. Conscious that the bombardment was likely to be followed by a counter-attack, Brigadier General Glasfurd ordered the 48th Battalion to occupy the OG lines with two of its companies, with the other two in support, in Tramway Trench about 400 metres to the rear. The 48th's forceful CO, Lieutenant Colonel Raymond Leane, believed that this would result in unnecessary casualties and intended to place only one company in the OG lines, a second in Tramway Trench and keep the other two in reserve, further back to the south of the Pozières village site (as it happened, his views coincided with those of Corps HQ). Colonel Leane had personally experienced the intensity of the German shelling, having earlier been caught in a barrage when going forward with his company commanders to reconnoitre. The brigadier repeated his orders in writing. Leane deferred to the extent of placing two companies in the front line as ordered, but only one in Tramway Trench; the fourth he still kept in reserve behind Pozières. Although Glasfurd apparently did nothing official about this instance of insubordination—in the event, Leane's approach turned out to be justified—there was considerable tension between the two officers thereafter.[18]

For the moment, there were few German ground troops in front of the 48th Battalion as the men struggled forward to the front line, but the enemy artillery continued to rain shells on the OG lines and the approach routes to them. The battalion suffered heavy casualties on the way in, and those reaching the front unhurt had difficulty even finding their new positions. Most of the 2nd Division troops, at the end of their tethers, had already fallen back without waiting for the formal relief. The line of OG 1 was eventually found and occupied by about 10:30 pm, the men starting to dig out its collapsed walls, but OG 2 had almost disappeared under the shelling. A platoon under Lieutenant Derwas Cumming probed forward well beyond OG 2's actual location. Identifying it on their return, Cumming's men

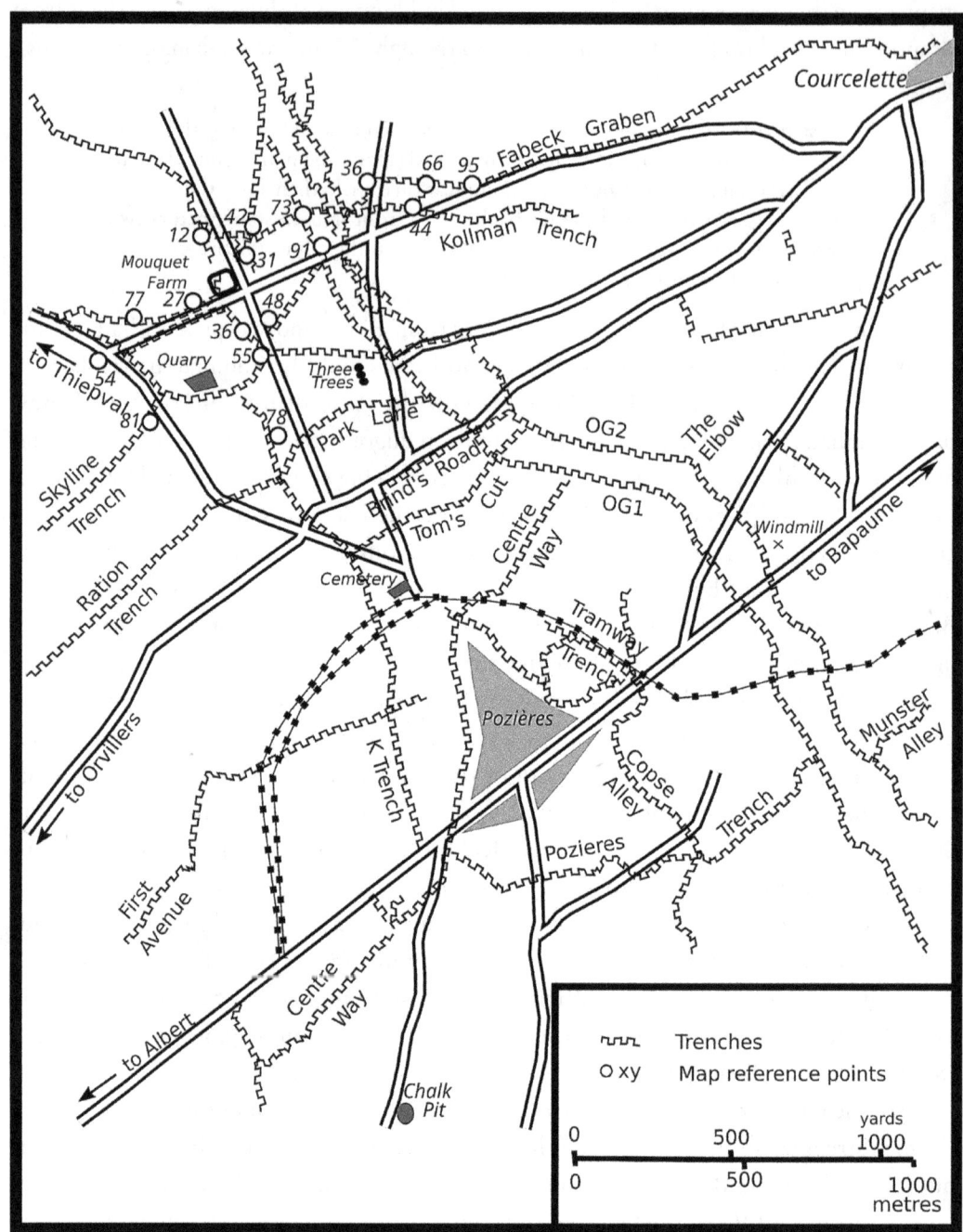

Pozières/Mouquet Farm battlefield, August – September 1916

occupied what had become a series of shell-holes and set to work with their shovels to restore some semblance of a trench. Another patrol, 10 of the battalion scouts under Sergeant David Twining, set up an outpost a little in advance of OG 2, near the ruins of 'The Windmill' on the top of the ridge.

On the left, the 15th Battalion (4th Brigade) also encountered devastating shellfire as it went forward through K Trench. Only the battalion's Lewis gun section and two platoons of its 'B' company managed to reach the front line that night. The rest of the battalion was pinned down by the bombardment and could not complete their relief until the next morning. The 15th had lost about 200 dead and wounded during the night.[19]

> It was the unit's first real experience of concentrated shellfire, and the first taste of warfare for many of its ranks. It was impossible to penetrate this devastating curtain of fire in platoon or any other form of close formation without suffering heavy casualties, so throughout the early morning the battalion filtered through in small parties.[20]

By 5 am on 6 August the 15th had two companies in the front line, but it was 2 pm before the unit had fully occupied its allotted positions. The right of the 4th Division's line was taken up by the 45th Battalion (12th Brigade). This unit also found itself struggling through an inferno of shell bursts to its position south of the main road near the German-occupied trench called Munster Alley. The 45th suffered 32 killed and 70 wounded in its first 24 hours in action.[21] One of the dead was the battalion's senior company commander, Major Duncan Chapman— thought to have been the first Australian ashore at the Landing.[22] During the evening of 6 August the 45th sent its 'B' Company and the battalion 'bombing' platoon to assist the 8th Yorkshire Regiment on the right in an attack on the German position in Munster Alley. The Yorkshiremen and New South Welshmen combined to capture the objective, the 45th reporting the taking of 30 prisoners in the battalion's first important action.[23]

The enemy bombardment continued almost unabated throughout the day of 6 August and into the night. The two companies of the 48th Battalion that were holding that unit's front line took particularly heavy casualties. During the afternoon Colonel Leane pulled out the survivors and sent in the company that he had carefully held back in reserve behind Pozières. By the early morning of 7 August the 4th Division had completed taking over the front line of I Anzac Corps. Artillery cover was initially provided by the 2nd Division; the 4th's attached Lahore Division guns were still coming up, progressively relieving units of the 1st and 2nd Divisions' artillery before assuming over control of the divisional sector on 9 August. The 4th Brigade had its 15th Battalion on the left, with two companies in a cross trench at 'Brind's Road' facing north-west and a third in OG 2 facing north-east, the line thus taking a roughly right-angled bend at this point. Next on the right was the 14th Battalion position. Lieutenant Colonel Dare, the 14th's CO, had been even more reluctant than Leane of the 48th to crowd his front line, and only one company was 'up', with a platoon in each of OG 1 and OG 2 and a third in Centre Way a little to the rear behind OG 1. One company was in support and the other two further back in reserve. The troops in the 14th's front line had suffered heavy losses in the bombardment, but there does not seem to have been any attempt to relieve them with a fresh company (as the 48th had done) so the 14th's line had become dangerously weak. The platoon in OG 1 (under Lieutenant Albert Jacka VC, the hero of Courtney's Post at Gallipoli) was meant to be in support to that garrisoning OG 2, but the latter had slipped somewhat to the left of Jacka's platoon which thus had no-one between it and the enemy; both groups were badly depleted by casualties.

Between the 4th Brigade and the 12th Brigade on the right of the line, a 150-metre gap had been left, unnoticed in the darkness and constant shelling. This was at the point known as 'The Elbow' where the OG lines made a pronounced change in direction. The 48th Battalion formed the garrison next on the right, with the comparatively fresh company brought up by the CO in OG 1, the support line. OG 2 was occupied by several small posts with Lewis guns, as well as the few remaining men of Sergeant Twining's small band near the Windmill. The 45th Battalion then occupied the remainder of the sector towards Munster Alley. Some Vickers gun sections of the 4th and 12th MG Companies were posted wherever any semblance of cover could be found, as well as a few 2nd Division guns that had not yet been withdrawn; the shelling had 'blown out' several guns and caused casualties in the crews. At some time between 4 am and 5 am (accounts differ) on 7 August, the enemy bombardment lifted away from the OG lines and began to fall in the rear areas—one of these shells burst near the 48th Battalion cookers, killing 26 men of the companies that had been relieved in the front line earlier. In the half-light, a force of German infantry advanced on the 4th Division's lines in a major counter-attack.

The Germans, two full battalions of the 63rd Infantry Regiment, had by accident or design chosen the gap in the Australian line as the focus of their attack. They had managed to achieve almost complete surprise, most of the Australians being still in the OG 1 dugouts for sheer survival under the bombardment. The order for 'Stand To' was just being called along the line when the German troops appeared, advancing over the few isolated posts in OG 2, passing through OG 1 and down the slope towards Pozières. On the way their right flank quickly came under fire from the 15th Battalion and the platoon of the 14th that was in OG 2, with the 48th, including Sergeant Twining's small advanced post, opening fire on the German left flank. The fire did not prevent them from penetrating deep into the Australian position, in the process cutting off and capturing 40 men of a 48th Battalion post in OG 1—the post commander had been mortally wounded and another officer (also wounded[24]) had ordered surrender, perhaps prematurely. The Australian prisoners were being escorted back to the enemy lines when the tide suddenly turned. SOS flares called in the supporting British and Australian artillery, which brought down a barrage that cut off the Germans from their supports. At the same time the Germans within the Australian line were counter-attacked from a totally unexpected source.

Lieutenant Jacka's depleted platoon of the 14th had been sheltering in their dugout in

Captain Albert Jacka VC MC and Bar (1893–1932), 14th Battalion. (AWM A02868)

OG 1, under the impression that they were only in support of the front line, when a German grenade rolled down the dugout steps and exploded, wounding two men. Jacka reacted instantly, firing his revolver up the steps and leading the seven or eight unwounded men of the platoon out into the open. He immediately grasped what had happened and set out to fight his way back to the reserve position. Seeing the party of prisoners from the 48th Battalion being taken back to the enemy lines, Jacka quickly changed his plans and led his small group in a charge against the German guards, some of whom surrendered immediately. Others fired back at the attackers while some began to shoot the 48th prisoners, who had broken away from their guards, grabbed German rifles and joined in the fight. The struggle quickly spread over the battlefield as other groups of Australians saw what was going on and moved with fixed bayonets towards the enemy force that had penetrated the lines. Reinforcements from the 15th, 14th and 48th Battalions came up and joined in the wild mêlée that developed on the slope of the ridge. Of Jacka's small group that had initiated the counterstroke, all had been wounded, including their leader, but Jacka continued to fight with the controlled ferocity that characterised him in action. Presumably he had discarded his revolver for a rifle and bayonet, and he now took on a group of four Germans in a shell hole, who fired at him as he charged. Jacka was hit three times; each time he was knocked down but, almost incredibly, bounced to his feet and kept coming. The Germans, who must have been terrified at being attacked by what was apparently some supernatural creature, tried to surrender. Jacka could not afford to take prisoners, however. At least one of his wounds was serious, the bullet having gone through his body, and he knew that he could not keep going much longer. He shot three of his opponents and bayoneted the fourth. Another German then attacked him from behind but Jacka managed to kill him also. That was almost the end of his strength, but he managed to drag himself closer to the Australian lines where he was picked up by stretcher bearers.

'The bravest man in the Aussie army,' commented a bearer to Sergeant Rule as the stretcher party passed through the 14th Battalion's lines. 'I wouldn't give a Gyppo piastre for him; he is knocked about dreadfully.'[25] That he certainly was, having been wounded seven times altogether, and close to death. In the meantime the German incursion had been thoroughly repulsed, many surrendering and the others falling back to their own lines. Jacka's extraordinary effort of leadership and personal combat had been the catalyst that led to this outcome. Jacka was evacuated all the way back to England and it would be many months before he was fit to return to duty. This fight is famous not only for Jacka's deeds but also because he was not awarded a second VC in recognition, as he had unquestionably earned; he was decorated, but with the lesser award of the Military Cross (MC). It does appear that the full details of his action only emerged some time later, but it would not have been impossible to upgrade the recommendation to the higher award afterwards. Such a procedure was rare but not unheard of in the British Empire forces.[26]

Following the morning's dramatic events, the 4th and 12th Brigades reoccupied their positions and settled back in to holding the line for the time being. The infantrymen, as well as pioneers and engineers, and the weary stretcher-bearers, resumed the never-ending task of repairing damaged trenches and clearing the dead and wounded. After a pause during the infantry combat, the German artillery resumed its bombardment of the Australian positions, before easing off again later in the day. The 4th MG Company's commander, Major Wilton, was wounded by shrapnel during this shelling; Lieutenant (later Captain) Albert Mitchell took over command of the unit. The 12th MG Company had lost three Vickers guns in the German attack and the crew of one was reported to be missing.[27]

On the right of the 4th Division's line, the 12th Brigade decided to relieve its front-line battalions immediately, and during the night the 46th and 47th Battalions came up to take over from the 45th and 48th, those units moving back to the support line. The 48th Battalion had been hit particularly hard, losing 180 officers and ORs killed or missing and 418 wounded, mostly caused by artillery fire. 'Wounded' could mean anything from comparatively minor injuries where the soldier could sooner or later be back on duty, to loss of limbs, or the dreadful mutilations caused by the hurtling, razor-sharp pieces of HE shell casings. Sometimes 'wounded' can seem like a euphemism. As well as physical injury, the stress of battle, particularly exposure to constant artillery bombardment, could cause the mental and emotional collapse, not fully understood at the time, known as 'shell shock.' The impersonal shellfire sought out both the novice and the veteran equally. Among the 48th officers killed was Lieutenant Jack Cosson, 'a cheery, shrewd old bookmaker of the West'[28] who had enlisted in the 16th Battalion as a private at the age of 44 and had won the Distinguished Conduct Medal (DCM) at Gallipoli.[29]

There were no further attempts by the Germans to mount a counter attack on their lost positions in this sector, and Reserve Army planning now turned towards resuming the thrust towards Thiepval. The tactics employed over the next few weeks of battle have been justifiably condemned, both at the time and in retrospect. The ground taken by I Anzac since 23 July had created a deep salient in the German lines, and it was General Gough's intention to force this still deeper behind the enemy position until Thiepval could be taken from the rear. This approach ensured that the advance would have to be made on a narrow front, in turn restricting the size of the attacking force that could be used. Although the new phase would begin with several successful small advances, the more ground that was taken the more the enemy artillery could concentrate its fire from three sides. Maintenance of communications to the front line became increasingly difficult, as did the provision of supports and reinforcements to back up a successful local attack. The overall intention of Reserve Army's operations soon became apparent to the enemy, who could usually anticipate the objectives of a particular attack and prepare an appropriate reception. The troops found themselves fighting on ground that became so churned up by shellfire as to make it almost impossible to accurately identify their own position on the map, a factor affecting cooperation between infantry and artillery. The lack of landmarks led to an informal system of numbered 'points' to identify locations, using two-digit numbers based on abbreviations of grid references on the standard maps.[30] With Reserve Army's determination to pursue its tactics of hammering a wedge into the enemy's front (as C E W Bean put it), commanders at corps and divisional level were obliged to stay within that framework when planning their own units' tactics.

I Anzac Corps issued orders on 7 August, the same day as the defeat of the German counter-attack, for the 4th Division to begin the new series of attacks on the following night. The advance would begin from the trench at Brind's Road, facing north-west towards Mouquet Farm and presently held by two companies of the 15th Battalion. Two roughly parallel lines of partly-wrecked German trenches, Park Lane and Skyline Trench, lay between the Australian line and the Farm, and Major General Cox decided that those would be tackled first in successive attacks. Success would open the way to then attack the Farm position itself and the trench called the Fabeck Graben that ran north-east from it. The 15th Battalion (4th Brigade) being already in position, that unit was selected to carry out the first step, the capture of Park Lane.

On the morning of 8 August, Cox and his staff held a conference at 4th Division HQ, Tara Hill with Brigadier General Brand and Lieutenant Colonel Cannan, the 15th Battalion CO, as well as senior artillery officers and the GOC and brigade and battalion commanders from the 12th British Division which would be cooperating on the left of the advance.[31] The results were summarised in an operation order issued by the 4th Division GSO1, Lieutenant Colonel Bernard, that afternoon. An intense artillery barrage was ordered, including 'heavies' on the enemy support lines; the German front line would be hit by the field artillery of the 2nd Division and the two brigades of the Lahore Division that had just come into the line. 'Zero' was planned for 9:20 pm that night. The barrage, mostly of shrapnel from the field guns, would stay on the enemy front line for three minutes before lifting into the rear areas, the infantry following closely behind to get into the German trench before the garrison could recover—an early attempt at the 'creeping barrage' that was perfected later in the war. Further fire support was provided by the 4th Brigade's MG company and LTM battery.

The 15th Battalion 'hopped the bags' at Zero as planned, attacking with all four companies in line, in three waves. The first wave comprised two platoons from each company plus several Lewis guns, the other two waves each having one platoon of each company; senior officer in the attack force was Major Charles Johnston, who led the second wave. The 16th Battalion sent one of its companies forward from reserve to take over the 15th's position in the Australian front line. On the left of the 15th Battalion, British troops (the 7th Battalion, Suffolk Regiment) were to attack a key enemy machine gun nest at 'Point 78'—those guns had already shattered two previous attacks on them. The 15th's advance worked to plan at first, the troops in the first wave closely following their barrage and getting into the enemy trench before the German infantry could recover from the shelling—those not killed surrendered or ran. Captain Hubert Brettingham-Moore, commanding the left company ('D') of the 15th, was wounded during the fight but was able to continue leading as well as fighting in person. His men occupied their part of the objective in Park Lane and began the work of consolidating—the process of setting up the captured position to defend against counter-attack. The right and centre of the attack reached the objective, overrunning it in the dark and occupying positions about 100 metres beyond it. The second and third waves were disorganised by the enemy counter-barrage, but scattered elements of those waves pushed on through the shelling and reached the objective. The 15th's companies had lost touch with each other, but had succeeded in occupying parts of the enemy position.[32] The unit's casualties included two company commanders, Captains John Corrigan and Cyril Corser, both seriously wounded.

On the 15th's left, the attack by the 7th Suffolks had again foundered in front of the German machine guns at Point 78, and a further attempt also failed. Reports coming in to Battalion HQ showed Colonel Cannan that his left flank was 'in the air,' and at 4 am he ordered Captain Brettingham-Moore to withdraw his company to its original line (the latter was awarded the DSO for his efforts that night[33]). The remainder of the Battalion continued to hold its gains on the right, but the line was disconnected and still uncertain of its actual position. Reserve Army ordered the attack repeated on the following night, and the 4th Division's sector was now extended to the left to include responsibility for taking the Point 78 position and the trenches near it. This task was given to the 16th Battalion, and three companies of that unit were brought up during the evening (9 August) to join its advanced company in the front line.

The 16th's CO, Lieutenant Colonel Drake-Brockman, had received his orders earlier in the day. After studying the ground from the front line, he decided against repeating the frontal attacks on Point 78 and instead ordered the position attacked from the flank. The troops were then to wheel to their right and go on to take the western segment (called 'Circular Trench') of Park Lane. Zero was set for midnight, supported by a short, intense artillery barrage on the enemy front line, similar to that of the previous night and again including the brigade's LTM battery. The 16th's intelligence officer, Lieutenant Bill Lynas, carried out a daring reconnaissance of No Man's land with some of his scouts after dark. They went over the whole area that would be covered by the advance, and went close to the enemy front line to place markers for guiding the advancing companies—these were electric torches with shaded lenses, dug in to the earth so that their faint light was only visible to the attackers. For his work on this and the next few nights, during which he was buried by shell-bursts four times, Lynas was awarded the first of his eventual three MCs.

The supporting artillery barrage came down on the German front line at 11:55pm, the 4th LTM battery joining in with its Stokes guns concentrating on Circular Trench. The 16th Battalion infantry moved forward as the fire lifted at midnight, led by the unit's senior company commander, Major Percy Black. The attack swept over the Point 78 machine guns then swung right and took its next objective in Circular Trench as well. The troops set about consolidating the captured position, and by 4 am the commanders knew that the operation had succeeded. On the right of the 16th, the 15th Battalion moved up to reoccupy the positions that they had captured in their earlier advance. With some determined shovel-work the new line was consolidated by daybreak and communication trenches had been dug. On the right of the 4th Brigade's sector, the 14th Battalion gained some ground on their front also.

The morning of 10 August found the 4th Brigade in possession of a new front line about 200 metres in advance of its original position. Although it was not a continuous line, all of the posts in it were at least in touch with each other and it was strongly held. Casualties had been comparatively light. Many of those who had been wounded during the advance had been brought in by a 16th Battalion soldier, Private Martin O'Meara, one of Lieutenant Lynas's scouts, who had taken it upon himself to search for wounded men when he was not needed for scouting duties. He had done the same thing during the previous night, assisting wounded from the 15th Battalion and the Suffolks. The German artillery was unusually slow to react to the loss of their trenches and the troops had several hours respite before the terrible bombardment descended again. During this comparatively quiet period, the 15th Battalion, which had suffered heavy losses in the past few days, was relieved by the 13th Battalion coming up from reserve. During its past few days in Sausage Valley, the 13th Battalion had put in plenty of hard manual work at the usual duties of a brigade reserve unit. Parties toiled at digging and carrying tasks, and the unit suffered 36 casualties from enemy shellfire. Most of these were in ration parties taking food and water up to the front line twice a day: 'they had never, so far, been more than five minutes late, and had spilt only two dixies. Men from the front line showed themselves exceedingly well pleased with this service.'[34] To supplement the uninteresting rations, Brigadier-General Brand had arranged for canteen goods to be brought right up to the front line for sale. The 4th Brigade troops in the trenches were able to buy extra food items, such as cakes and tinned fruit, small luxuries that can often produce a disproportionate lift in the morale of men under severe strain. 'Does not sound very wonderful,' Brand later wrote, 'but when the conditions at that period were considered it was a good effort.'[35]

By late afternoon on 10 August, the German shelling had again built up to its usual intensity. Much of it was directed at the new Australian front line, but the back areas were shelled as well; the Lahore Artillery's 5th Brigade RFA in Sausage Valley was hit, losing four senior officers killed.[36] General Cox now ordered a further small advance to be made that night by the 4th Brigade. The 13th Battalion, newly in the line, was ordered to capture a trench about 100 metres to its front, while the 16th would also advance to gain ground towards the feature called 'The Quarry.' The 16th also extended its left to take over a section of front line in Ration Trench from a British unit. Both battalions were ordered to

The Pozières/Mouquet Farm battlefield, looking from Centre Way trench towards Mouquet Farm
(AWM EZ0100)

push out fighting patrols ('bombing parties') beyond their objectives. The usual support from 'heavies,' field artillery, mortars and machine guns was arranged. There was some concern that the troops would be in danger of shelling from their own guns—the uncertain geography of the battlefield was making it increasingly difficult to identify exact positions of the units themselves and their objectives. The heavy artillery was due to deliver an hour-long bombardment of the 13th's objective trench early in the night, and as a precaution the Battalion was ordered to pull back 200 metres from its position during the shelling, then reoccupy the line when it ceased. After the heavy bombardment, the field artillery kept up a slow fire of shrapnel on the German trench until Zero (1 am) when an intense 3-minute barrage came down and two companies of the 13th advanced, getting as close to the shell bursts as they could before the barrage lifted.'The night was not only very dark, but a heavy fog had descended, rendering observation even a yard in front a matter of difficulty. There was nothing to do but stumble forward behind the bursting shells ...'[37] There was minimal opposition from enemy infantry and the troops, led by Captains Hugh Pulling and Francis 'Toby' Barton, went well beyond their objective. Unable to locate exactly the positions that they were supposed to occupy, the troops stopped and dug in when the creeping barrage became stationary. Two men and an officer advanced even further and were taken prisoner when they ran into German-held positions. Captain Barton disappeared without trace while reconnoitring. The troops now became involved in some stiff fighting against local German counter-attacks, all of which failed.[38] Overall, the 13th's losses had been comparatively light.

On the left, also at 1 am, the 16th Battalion went forward through enemy shelling to establish a new line of posts, finding that the trench that they were supposed to capture had been mostly obliterated. The troops settled into shell holes and the remnants of the trenches, and began digging to make some sort of continuous line. This now formed a small salient about 200 metres from the original line at its furthest point, and partly on a forward slope under enemy observation. The inevitable retaliatory shelling landed behind the captured position at first, but the Germans found the range when daybreak came and launched a tremendous bombardment on the new line, hitting the 16th Battalion particularly hard. The pounding went on for hours, inflicting heavy losses and forcing the troops to withdraw a short distance from the captured posts and seek cover in shell holes and old dugouts. The 16th stayed alert for a possible counter-attack, however. This came at 2:45 pm; preceded by an even heavier burst of shellfire, German troops appeared from the direction of Mouquet Farm. Moving in small groups at first, they soon coalesced into a strong line and advanced on the Australian positions. The 16th's troops quickly reoccupied their original posts, setting up their Lewis guns and calling in artillery support. As the German line advanced, its flank became exposed to outposts of the 13th Battalion on the right of the Australian line. Heavy fire from the 13th's Lewis gunners and riflemen caught the enemy line in enfilade, while the 16th poured in frontal fire. With the support of an 18-pounder barrage, the German attack was quickly shattered. The 4th Brigade troops rejoiced in the chance to hit back at real enemies in daylight after suffering under the dreadful shelling of the past few days. The action was over in twenty minutes, the surviving Germans scattering back to look for cover around The Quarry. Here their demoralisation was completed by a barrage from the heavy artillery called in by Colonel Drake-Brockman (the message was sent by carrier-pigeon).

Defeat of the enemy infantry attack only brought a renewal of the shelling, which pounded the Australian lines for the rest of the afternoon, through the night and into the morning of 12 August. The 16th Battalion reported its casualties from the artillery fire as 'severe' and noted that the shelling seemed to be coming from an easterly direction[39]—a consequence of the advance thrusting a narrow front into the German line. The 16th nevertheless managed to send patrols ahead to probe the wilderness of shell holes and wrecked trenches beyond their position, as did the 13th on the right, but nothing positive could be achieved under the shelling.

Throughout the fighting of these nights, Private O'Meara had continued his self-imposed task of finding and bringing in the 16th Battalion's wounded, working in the open and ignoring the enemy artillery and machine gun fire. He also volunteered to bring up ammunition to the front line, twice making the return trip through the barrage to the battalion dump, again in the open since the communication trenches had been blown in. O'Meara seemed to be everywhere during this chaotic time. On the morning of 12 August, the trench occupied by Major Black's 'B' Company was subjected to a particularly heavy pounding; Black withdrew his men from the trench away from the line of shell bursts, but one soldier was buried under

Private (later Sergeant) Martin O'Meara VC (1885–1935), 16th Battalion. (AWM H12763)

collapsed earth. O'Meara appeared and dug the man out in spite of the barrage roaring all around him. During the past four days and nights of intense fighting he was thought to have personally rescued at least 25 wounded as well as carrying ammunition and water to the front line and carrying out his normal scouting duties, always under heavy fire. It was only his own wounding late on 12 August that stopped him. O'Meara's efforts brought him the Victoria Cross. The recommendation for the award was a remarkable document, including full statements by no less than seven officers, headed by the CO and Major Black, who had observed him in action at different times. 'Private O'Meara is the most fearless and gallant soldier that I have ever seen' wrote Lieutenant Lynas. O'Meara was a 30 year old Irish immigrant who had been working as a sleeper-cutter in the Western Australian timber industry before enlisting in August 1915. His VC was the second for the 4th Brigade (after Albert Jacka at Gallipoli) but the first for the 4th Division as such.

The situation on 12 August was that the front line had been carried forward about 300 metres towards Mouquet Farm, the wedge becoming steadily deeper and narrower. The brunt of the attacking tasks so far had fallen to units of the 4th Brigade, first the 15th Battalion then the 16th and 13th. The 14th Battalion had remained holding the line on the right of the 4th Brigade's sector, dangerous enough duty at Pozières, but it was noticeable that the Battalion had not been used in any major attacks.

> During this week the brigade 'hopped the bags' three times in all, [wrote Sergeant Rule] but for some reason or other our battalion only had to go out one night, to straighten out a kink ... The reason for our immunity I don't know ... I always feel that we were not given our proper share of work.⁴⁰

This may have been simply due to the Battalion's position being unsuitable from which to launch an attack, but it could also be concluded that Brigadier General Brand did not have full confidence in the unit's leadership.

The 12th Brigade remained posted further to the right, away from the main axis of the thrust into the German position, holding the line and patrolling No Man's Land, with the brigade machine guns and mortars regularly harassing the German lines opposite. The 13th Brigade group was still in reserve at the Brickfields for the moment, apart from its linked medical and engineer units working with the other brigades. The battered 4th Brigade was due for relief, and the 13th Brigade was warned to prepare for taking over the front line. The relief was planned for 13 August, following a further night attack to be sent in by the 4th Brigade, but it was realised that the heavily-strained 16th Battalion needed to be withdrawn immediately. As the exposed tip of the wedge, that unit had endured an especially severe pounding from the enemy's ferocious bombardments. The 50th Battalion was detached from the 13th Brigade and ordered to relieve the 16th during the morning of 12 August, coming temporarily under the 4th Brigade's control. The 50th Battalion had already begun moving up with the intention of initially relieving the 15th in the reserve position at Wire Trench three kilometres from the front, but it was now ordered to continue into the front line and take over the 16th's positions. The relief proved to be an ordeal in itself. The Germans had apparently observed the movements, and launched a 'terrific shelling of all our positions, paying particular attention to Kay Trench, 1st Avenue and Centre Way, leading down to Chalk Pits'[41]—that is, the main communication routes. The troops from both units were crowded into the trenches together, and it was nearly three hours before the last of the 16th men struggled clear and made their way to the rear, heading for the Brickfields billeting area. The unit had achieved all of the objectives set for it during its period in the line, but at a cost of 406 casualties, of which 58 were killed or missing. Most of these had been the result of artillery fire; as with the rest of the 4th Brigade, the unit had proven its superiority whenever the enemy infantry had been encountered. For his front-line leadership in this period of intense combat, Major Black was later awarded the DSO.

The shelling continued unabated as the 50th Battalion settled into the front line and prepared to take part in Reserve Army's next advance that night. The objective was the position identified as Skyline Trench, the capture of which would bring the line very close to the Mouquet Farm strongpoint. Units of the 12th British Division would attack the western part of Skyline Trench to the left of the 4th Brigade, which would advance across the shallow depression between its present positions and a line just short of The Quarry, about 250 metres away. The 50th Battalion would form the left wing of this attack, with the 13th Battalion advancing on its right. Zero was set for 10:30 pm. Artillery cover for the attack was provided mainly by the Lahore guns playing on the objective, with the heavy guns and howitzers of I Anzac Corps and II (British) Corps joining in, concentrating on particular strong points and the enemy support positions. As had become normal practice, the targets were to be pounded for several hours before the infantry attack went in, when the barrage would increase to a crescendo, 'creeping' in three lifts to the objective ahead of the infantry.

The 50th Battalion's lead-up to the attack had been less than ideal, rushed into the line at short notice and having to prepare and disseminate orders under fire, working with another brigade's staff. The Battalion had already taken losses from the enemy bombardment, which fell heavily around the headquarters dugout as well as well as on the troops in the line. There was only time for companies to pass on brief verbal orders to platoon commanders.

Nevertheless, the South Australians went forward on time, with the 13th Battalion on their right, that unit starting from a line somewhat closer to the objective. The troops of the 50th had been shaken by the difficulties of the relief, but their morale was boosted by the sight of the barrage flaying the enemy lines.

> The Lahore Divisional Artillery put up a splendid barrage,' [recalled a 50th member]. 'The whole battalion could be seen by the flames of it—a continuous flash of shrapnel... when the 50th saw the barrage their spirits changed completely.[42]

Keeping close to the barrage and overcoming scattered resistance from the enemy infantry, the advancing troops occupied their objective, as far as the leaders could tell in the mass of craters and partly destroyed trenches. Messages eventually got through to the rear reporting success. The line had indeed been advanced but the 50th's new position was actually 100 metres short of Point 55, where its right was intended to be. As well, the companies in the centre of the attack had inadvertently crowded to their right during the advance, resulting in a wide gap in the line near the Quarry feature. Beyond this gap, the extreme left of the 50th's line was held by a platoon under Lieutenant William Hoggarth, who had advanced as far as the outskirts of Mouquet Farm itself before returning to occupy his correct objective at 'Point 81'—'more by luck than good management,'[43] On the whole, the 50th had achieved success in its first major action, despite its line being disconnected and its correct location uncertain, 'possibly due to certain weak spots in the regimental and company leadership not unusual in new battalions' in C E W Bean's view.[44]

On the right of the 4th Brigade's attack, the 13th Battalion's advance had also gone successfully and the troops were established in a rough line on the slope leading up to the Farm, seizing two large enemy dugouts on the way. Their advance having outstripped that of the 50th Battalion, the 13th's left flank was open and strenuous efforts were made to dig a trench angling back to the point called 'Three Trees' to link up with the 50th's right. The 13th Battalion's line thus formed a small salient about 100 metres in advance of the 50th. This situation proved to be an advantage when the Germans sent in an infantry counter-attack in the early morning gloom (13 August). Directed at the right of the 50th's position, the enemy force collided with the 13th's left. After a brief close-range duel with grenades and small arms the attack was beaten off, mainly by the 13th's Lewis guns firing in enfilade. The German artillery took over again. The Australian communications and support line had been heavily shelled during the night, and now the new front line was the target. There was nothing the troops could do except try to endure the strain until their unit was relieved, and it appears that their own artillery was unable to deliver any effective counter-battery fire—not unusual at this stage of the war. To make matters worse, lack of communication trenches made it even more difficult to get basic supplies through to the front line.

The 4th Brigade advance was not the only action on the battlefield during the night of 12/13 August. On both flanks, operations took place to enable the remainder of the line to keep pace with the main axis of the advance (or the 'wedge'). The 12th British Division successfully attacked Skyline Trench on the left of the line, and the 4th Division's 12th Brigade, still holding the line on the right of the divisional sector, was involved in an operation by the 15th (Scottish) Division to force the Germans out of the Munster Alley trench. Part of this position had been taken earlier, and the 46th Battalion again contributed 'bombers' and working parties to assist the Scots in taking the remainder of the trench, up to where it joined the main German position in 'Switch Trench'. Plans were now made for the next stage of the northward advance towards Mouquet Farm. This would be undertaken by the 13th Brigade, which completed its relief of the 4th Brigade in the front line during the day of 13 August. Of the 4th Brigade units, the 15th and 16th Battalions had already been withdrawn, and it was decided that the 13th Battalion should stay in the line, coming under 13th Brigade command. The 14th Battalion was therefore the only 4th Brigade infantry unit to be withdrawn, replaced by the 49th Battalion on the right of the wedge, facing north-east. The 13th MG Company and LTM Battery relieved their 4th Brigade counterparts during the afternoon, and Brigadier General Glasgow took over command of the sector at 4 pm. The front line was reorganised shortly afterwards. The 13th Battalion edged to its left to make room for two companies of the 51st Battalion to move up, with a third company squeezing in later; the remaining company of the 51st had to find space in communication trenches leading to the firing line. The 13th Brigade's line now consisted of the 49th Battalion holding the right, the 51st next, then the 13th (detached from the 4th Brigade), with the 50th on the left flank. The latter unit's irregular position, occupied the previous night, had been partly consolidated and its isolated post at Point 81 was still held. The 52nd Battalion remained in Wire Trench as the brigade support unit.

Brigadier General Brudenell White, Chief of Staff at I Anzac, had given considerable thought to the next stage of the advance. On 12 August he had written to Major General Cox outlining his views and suggesting how to approach future operations. The aim was to occupy a line beyond Mouquet Farm, at which point I Anzac could be required to stand on the defensive while the capture of Thiepval proceeded. 'The deciding factor is our hold on the high ground,' wrote White.[45] That meant advancing beyond the Farm, which was 'slightly in the "dip"' below the highest level of the shallow depression in which it was located. To the east of the Farm the suggested objective included a strong enemy trench usually called by its German name, the Fabeck Graben. This was some 400 metres from the Australian front line and ran across the old OG 1 and OG 2 trenches which extended to the north-west in this sector. White believed that an advance on this flank would need to be done in two stages, the first establishing an intermediate line before assaulting the final objective. The attack would probably have to extend to Point 77, about 250 metres west of Mouquet Farm. That part of the advance, including capture of the Farm itself, would be included in the suggested second stage, after establishing patrol posts closer to the objective as a preliminary. Both Corps and Division staff had no real idea of how strong the bastion of Mouquet Farm actually was, and General Cox's overly optimistic judgement was that the whole objective could be taken in a single operation.[46] This was accepted by I Anzac, which issued an operation order at 7 am on 14 August for an attack that night, giving the 4th Division an objective line which included the Fabeck Graben and extended across to the west of Mouquet Farm and at a distance of about 100 metres beyond it. From here the line would bend back in a dog-leg to join up with the British 48th Division in the recently-captured Skyline Trench.

Almost immediately, the situation was found to have changed overnight. A German counter-attack had retaken most of Skyline Trench from the British, exposing the 4th Division's left flank, still represented by the small post of the 50th Battalion at Point 81. A series of contradictory reports came in during the early morning. At first it was thought that the 50th had also been forced to retire, but it was later established that the troops at Point 81 (now under Captain James Churchill Smith[47]) had held on and established a barricade in their trench. The situation on the left flank remained precarious, however, and plans for the attack that night were hurriedly modified. The eastern or right sector of the original objective was retained, that is the Fabeck Graben, but only to Point 73, 250 metres east of Mouquet Farm. From here the objective line for the left sector of the attack was changed, initially by I Anzac and then further modified by the Division. The left objective now angled back roughly south down OG 1 from Point 73, then ran south-west, skirting the south-east corner of the Farm about 100 metres short of it. The new objective continued past The Quarry to join the present front line at the disputed Point 81 ('with left flank refused' in the words of the amended Corps order). The area just in front of the Farm and to its west would therefore not be attacked at this stage, the new objective in this sector being similar to that first suggested by General White at Corps HQ. It might have been better, given the disruption caused by the enemy attack, to have postponed the operation altogether until the situation had stabilised, even if only for 24 hours. It seems likely that I Anzac, and therefore the 4th Division, were under pressure from Reserve Army to keep the advance going at all costs. Also, as the 4th Division was scheduled to be relieved by the 1st after this night's operations, a further postponement would probably have been necessary while the 1st Division was settling in. Even if it was accepted that the advance needed to keep going, both Corps and Division HQs could have reconsidered General White's earlier suggestion and brought back the objective on the right also, to an intermediate line short of the Fabeck Graben. No such change was made, however, and Brigadier General Glasgow and his staff set about organising the 13th Brigade for the operation.

Major Ridley, the brigade major, got the Brigade operation order out at 5 pm, little more than an hour after receiving the divisional order giving the final objective for the night. On the left, the 50th Battalion, pivoting on its post at Point 81, would advance over a distance averaging about 150 metres to a line north of The Quarry, running north-east for about 350 metres to Point 36, south of Mouquet Farm. The 50th was also tasked with extending its left from Point 81 for about 100 metres south-west towards the British, who would be making another attempt to re-take Skyline Trench. The centre battalion, the 13th, which had been in the front line longest and so was the most reduced in numbers, was given a shorter objective. This line continued that of the 50th's objective for a further 300 metres north-east, from Point 36 to Point 91, the latter being on the line of the road running in front of Mouquet Farm to Courcelette village. There was thought to be an enemy trench close to the road. The plans called for the 13th Battalion to advance over a distance varying from 200 metres for its right flank to 100 metres on its left. This assumed that the left was at Point 55, but it was actually 100 metres further back,[48] so that the 13th's whole line would need to cover about 200 metres to the objective.

The heaviest task was allotted to the 51st Battalion, 'a fine, comparatively fresh Western Australian unit … Although as a battalion it was new, it contained a fair proportion of veteran officers and men.'[49] The extreme right of the 51st's objective was Point 95 in the Fabeck Graben; from there it extended left along that trench across the junction with OG 2 to Point 73 in OG 1. From there the objective ran 150 metres south down OG 1 to join the right of the 13th Battalion at Point 91. Altogether the 51st would advance for a distance of over 350 metres to capture a front of about 600 metres—a challenging task to say the least. The 49th Battalion, holding the right face of the wedge facing north-east, would extend to its left to form a defensive flank, linking up with the 51st's right at the objective; one company of the 49th was allocated to the 51st as a reinforcement if required. The 52nd Battalion remained in support and would provide carrying parties for the attacking units. The 13th MG Company was detailed to lay harassing fire on two road junctions in the German rear area, impeding enemy approaches to the 51st Battalion's objective. Four Vickers guns emplaced south of Pozières would be firing at ranges of 2,500 metres and more, over the heads of the advancing infantry. Communication trenches at several points behind the attacking front would be worked on by the 13th Field Company, assisted by elements of the 4th Field Company and the 4th Pioneer Battalion made available to the 13th Brigade for the operation. There seems to have been no particular task allotted to the Brigade LTM battery.

The field artillery's supporting shrapnel barrage was arranged to fall in four successive, roughly parallel, lines lifting ahead of the infantry before stopping 150 metres beyond the main objective to interfere with enemy reinforcements. The first two barrage lines were along the line of the Courcelette road (about 100 metres in front of the main objective, the Fabeck Graben) and on the objective itself. The intense barrage would begin at 'Zero' and last for three minutes on both of these lines, then all guns would concentrate on the objective line for another two minutes before lifting ahead to allow the infantry in. The planned barrage lines do not seem to have been changed greatly to allow for the change of objective, with the result that the 13th Battalion's new objective would not be bombarded. The Lahore howitzers, however, now had the task of dropping HE shells along OG 1 between Points 73 and 91 (part of the 51st's modified objective) for three minutes, as well as hitting OG 2 south of the Fabeck Graben. The right flank of the advance would be protected by barrages from three brigades of the 1st Division artillery, now back in the line and grouped with the Lahore guns. During the day and night leading up to the advance, both the field artillery and the Corps heavy artillery kept up a regular pounding of the enemy positions. Zero was set for 10 pm.

While the planning and briefing was taking place in various headquarters dugouts, the troops in the front line were waiting in their trenches under the incessant German shelling. 'Terrific bombardment all day,' reported the 50th Battalion. 'Enemy guns blowing trenches and saps to pieces.'[50] The Germans' examination of captured British orders had put them particularly on the alert for an attack, and any signs of movement were greeted with a storm of shellfire. Communication trenches, support lines and back areas were bombarded as well as the front line, and it became almost impossible to get supplies up to the troops in the front trenches. The support trench called Tom's Cut (a short length of a former German communication trench north of Pozières) became particularly notorious as a shell-trap. Casualties mounted up and food and water ran short. The shelling kept on all day and into the night, while the British artillery kept up its own fire into the German lines in preparation for the night's attack. There were reports of some of the 'friendly' shells falling on the Australian front line—few things are more damaging to infantry morale than being shelled by their own artillery.

The situation in the front line was highly unfavourable for mounting an attack but there was no thought of postponement. Towards evening, battalion commanders received their written orders and began verbally briefing their attack leaders. Almost immediately, 50th Battalion HQ was shaken when the CO, Colonel Hurcombe, was suddenly incapacitated with what was described as shell shock. The Battalion second-in-command, Major Ross Jacob, took over.[51] Each of the attacking battalions planned an advance using the recommended tactics, three companies in two waves, including Lewis gunners and 'bombers', with the fourth company to follow up in support. Deployment for the attack began after dark (about 8:30 pm), an awkward movement in itself, as many of the waiting troops had been crammed into a tangle of short trenches often running at a sharp angle to the line of the advance. Enemy shelling continued as the battalions waited for Zero, numbers steadily decreasing as more and more men were hit. The remorseless German bombardment on the Australian support lines also pinned down the engineers attempting to improve communication trenches. The 13th Field Company's casualties included its commander of only three weeks, Major Mirams, who was badly wounded and died a few days later. He was succeeded by an attached officer of the Royal Engineers, Captain H.A. Reid. Messages began to come in from the infantry in the front line to battalion and brigade HQs reporting the havoc caused by the shelling. The 51st Battalion CO, Colonel Ross, was prompted to notify Brigade HQ that 'Both 13th CO thinks, and it is my genuine (not depressed) opinion that it would be a mistake to press the offensive locally in this salient'[52] (the 51st and 13th Battalion HQs were sharing a dugout about 400 metres behind the front line).

The 50th Battalion was hit particularly hard. There was apparently some panic in the ranks as well as an attempt to have the advance cancelled, but the orders were unchanged. The three battalions' attacking waves were deployed by 10 pm when the covering bombardment came down on the objectives, and the lines of infantry went forward. On the left, the 50th managed to get through the continuing enemy shelling to reach its objective beyond The Quarry. Here the troops tried to dig in, but the line was now swept by German machine guns firing from positions on the left flank; with further heavy losses, the battalion was driven back to its original position. The 50th's RMO, Major Lewis Jeffries, was later awarded the DSO for his work with the wounded on this and the two previous nights. He had personally led the stretcher bearers into the front line under fire, treating wounded men on the battlefield before helping to carry them to the rear.

The 51st Battalion, attacking the Fabeck Graben on the right, started well but with over 300 metres to cover, its right flank had only gone about half-way before the covering barrage lifted off the objective. Beyond the 51st's right, the barrage covering the flank proved to be ineffective, and four German machine guns on the slope towards Courcelette fired through it, pinning down the battalion's 'A' Company on that side. Further to the left, some small groups from the other companies managed to penetrate the enemy trench but were driven out again in heavy fighting. Like the right flank, the troops on the left had not had time to reach the trench before the barrage moved on, allowing the full enemy garrison to emerge from the dugouts in time to meet the assault. Although forced to withdraw, the troops in that sector dug in about 60 metres short of the objective and hung on there. It appears, however, that the 51st was unable to make any attempt on the extreme left of their objective, the 150-metre length of OG 1 running back to the south-east, where it was meant to join with the 13th Battalion's objective.

That unit, the centre battalion of the advance, had been tasked with taking a line roughly along the Courcelette road, 200 metres out from their own position. The covering barrage was falling beyond this line, in accordance with the artillery orders but of no help to the attackers; the 13th did have the advantage, however, of being less exposed to flanking machine guns than the other battalions. Reduced by the enemy shelling to about 180 men, the three companies of the 13th's attacking waves went forward at Zero, led by the dynamic Captain Harry Murray, commander of 'A' Company. About 75 metres from their start line the 13th ran into an unexpected enemy position, an outpost line of connected shell holes. The 13th made short work of those Germans and then continued the advance to their main objective, cheering and shouting as they went. The objective proved to be a trench 'full of Germans,'[53] who opened a heavy but ineffective fire, and the position was quickly taken after a sharp fight. Many of the Germans fled into the night, and the 13th captured 11 prisoners and a machine gun. Captain Murray set about consolidating the captured position, a trench extending from Point 91 in OG 1 for 300 metres south-west to Point 36, about 100 metres south of Mouquet Farm (not the western segment of the Fabeck Graben, contrary to what has been written elsewhere[54]). The riflemen were posted along the trench, interspersed with three Lewis guns, and an advanced party with another Lewis gun was sent

40 metres further forward along OG 1 towards Point 73.

At 11:15 pm Captain Murray sent back a message by runner to advise Battalion HQ that the objective had been secured. He attempted to link up with the 50th Battalion on his left but could not make contact—in fact the 50th had already been forced back before the 13th had reached its objective. There was also no sign of the 51st on the other flank. According to the plan, some troops from that unit should be working back down OG 1 from the north by now. By midnight it was apparent that the 13th Battalion was isolated, and parties of Germans were beginning to probe at the open flanks. In the moonlight, a body of troops was seen approaching from ahead along the line of OG 1. These might have been a linking-up party from the 51st Battalion, but they proved to be Germans and opened fire when challenged. Lewis gun fire drove this group off but many others were seen closing in from three sides, and it was now obvious that the 13th Battalion would have to withdraw to avoid being cut off and surrounded. Murray sent his wounded back to the Australian lines and quickly organised a staged retreat, setting up several successive strong-points as the troops fell back. The Germans pressed hard, but the 13th fought them off with Lewis guns and grenades at each post along the line of retreat. Nearing the Australian lines, grenades were running short but the battalion 'bombers' now arrived and covered the final stage of the retreat, driving the pursuing Germans back to their own lines. Although the 13th had suffered some losses during the withdrawal, including several taken prisoner, Captain Murray had managed to extricate most of his men from a very dangerous situation.

This did not alter the fact, however, that the operation had failed. Some groups of the 51st Battalion were still dug in near the Fabeck Graben but these were unsupported and pulled back during the early morning (15 August). The whole attacking force had been forced back to its original front line, except where part of a shallow jumping-off trench started by the 51st Battalion had been deepened and incorporated into the front line. As far as possible under continuing shellfire, the surviving troops turned to strengthening the line in case of a follow-up enemy attack, which did not eventuate. The rebuff of 14/15 August was the first check to the 4th Division's steady advance—the 'wedge' was now meeting its strongest resistance so far, as it inched deeper into the enemy position. This was the last operation of the Division's first period on the Pozières/Mouquet Farm front. The 1st Division was now coming up to relieve the 4th in the line and continue the thrust forward.

> Brought in on the night of August 5th, the 4th Division had in nine days not only borne the brunt of the German counter-measures against Pozières heights, but in six successive night attacks ... had brought the line within striking distance of Mouquet Farm.[55]

5 Notes

1. *Official History*, Vol III, p.448.
2. Chataway, *Op Cit*, p. 112.
3. Rule, *Op Cit*, p. 24.
4. *Ibid*.
5. *Ibid*, p. 25.
6. *Ibid*.
7. P Edgar, *To Villers-Bretonneux*, p. 67.
8. N Browning, *For King and Cobbers*, p. 35.
9. *Official History*, Vol III, p. 728.
10. *Official History*, Vol III, p. 704n and p. 542.
11. *4th Australian Field Ambulance: Historical Material*, AWM224, MSS 289/290. This document, probably written by Lt Col Meikle (CO 4th Field Ambulance), gives figures for casualties handled during this period that are slightly different from those in the unit's War Diary for August 1916. The discrepancy seems to be caused by different dates being considered in the two documents.
12. 13th Field Company War Diary, 1/2 August 1916.
13. *Official History*, Vol III, p. 695n.
14. *Ibid*, p. 669.
15. According to the Battalion's War Diary for August 1916, all four companies were employed on these tasks, under the command of the battalion second-in-command, Major Howard Denham.
16. *Official History*, Vol III, p. 709.
17. *Ibid*, p. 702.
18. *Ibid*, p. 708.
19. The *Official History* gives a total of 430 casualties for the 15th's first 'tour' at Pozières; the battalion history says that about half of the total occurred on that night (Chataway, *Op Cit*, p. 118.)
20. Chataway, *Op Cit*, p. 120.
21. 45th Battalion War Diary for August 1916, also Lee, *Op Cit*, p. 26.
22. *Official History*, Vol 1, p. xlvi in UQP edition.

23 The Battalion's War Diary notes that a 'weak' enemy counter attack was made on the morning of 6 August 'which was easily repulsed'; the *Official History* treats this report cautiously, mentioning it only in a footnote (Vol III, p. 711n). The phrasing in the Diary is very similar to that used in describing the counter attack that unquestionably took place on the following day, and it is possible that the compiler gained a false impression that two attacks took place rather than one.

24 See the Bean Papers, AWM38 3DRL606/244/1, folios 49 to 53.

25 Rule, *Op Cit*, p.29.

26 Three of the Lancashire Fusiliers' famous 'Six VCs before breakfast' at Gallipoli were awarded after being initially turned down by higher authority; lesser decorations granted to two of the soldiers were cancelled and replaced by the VC. The circumstances were admittedly a little different to Jacka's case, but the episode does show that it was possible for a decoration to be upgraded (see S Snelling, *VCs of the First World War: Gallipoli*, pp 16–17).

27 12th MG Company War Diary, 7 Aug 1916.

28 Devine, *Op Cit*, p. 44.

29 According to Cosson's service record he was born in 1871, although information provided by his widow in 1927 for the Australian War Memorial Roll of Honour states that he was 50 at the time of his death.

30 The main map sheets were divided into 6000 yard squares, each designated by a capital letter. These were in turn divided into 36 numbered 1000 yard squares, which themselves were divided into four 500 yard squares, identified as a, b, c, d. These had ten 50-yard divisions on the vertical (south-north) and horizontal (west-east) sides, which were used to identify the coordinates of a particular point. The 4th Division's operations on this front were mostly confined to the square subdivisions 33, 34, 27 and 28 in Square 'R' of the main map of the area. Thus the full reference for a point right at the centre of the 500-yard square 'b' in subdivision 33 would be R.33.b.5.5. This became 'Point 55', about 200 metres south-east of Mouquet Farm. Presumably someone on the staff tried to ensure that point numbers were not doubled up, as the final two coordinates would be the same for a similar point in another square. If this was unavoidable, the longer reference would be used. Formal written orders normally used the full reference.

31 4th Division General Staff War Diary, 8 August 1916.

32 Chataway, *Op Cit*, pp. 123–9

33 Brettingham-Moore had been wounded in the legs and buttocks by grenade fragments and a bullet. After hospitalisation he returned to duty, but soon suffered a serious deterioration in his eyesight and was eventually discharged from the army. His given name is incorrectly shown as 'Herbert' in some documents.

34 *Official History*, Vol III, p. 735n.

35 Chataway, *Op Cit*, p. 120.

36 Lahore Artillery War Diary, 10 August 1916.

37 White, *Op Cit*, p. 65.

38 *Ibid*, p. 65.

39 16th Battalion War Diary, 11 August 1916.

40 Rule, *Op Cit*, p. 34.

41 16th Battalion War Diary, 12 August 1916.

42 Bean Papers, AWM38 3DRL 606/227/1, p. 228a (p.33 in PDF).

43 Edgar, *Op Cit*, p. 70.

44   *Official History*, Vol III, p. 757.
45   4th Division General Staff War Diary, August 1916, Appendix XV.
46   *Official History*, Vol III, p. 759.
47   See Edgar, *Op. Cit.*, p. 72 for Churchill Smith's experiences at Point 81.
48   I Anzac's Intelligence Summary for 15/16 August identified the line as 'running along South edge of QUARRY to point 100 yards South of R.33.b.5.5 [Point 55]' (I Anzac Intelligence War Diary for August 1916 Part 2).
49   *Official History*, Vol III, p. 764.
50   50th Battalion War Diary, 14 August 1916.
51   The unfortunate Colonel Hurcombe's service record shows that, during the Gallipoli campaign, he had also been hospitalised suffering from a nervous breakdown—a circumstance that apparently sounded no warning bells when selecting him for the highly stressful task of commanding an infantry battalion on the Western Front. On that occasion he had also been relieved by Major Jacob, both officers being members of the 10th Battalion at the time.
52   *Official History*, Vol III, p.763. Ross's comment suggests that he had heard about Colonel Hurcombe's difficulties.
53   13th Battalion War Diary, 14 August 1916.
54   Including by the present author and in the *Official History*, among many others. The reasons for this statement, which contradicts the *Official History*, are given in the Appendix.
55   *Official History*, Vol III, p. 770

6: Mouquet Farm

Over the next two days, relief of the 4th Division by the 1st Division was completed. The 4th Brigade, less the 13th Battalion, had already moved back to the Brickfields bivouac area near Albert during 13 August. The 13th Battalion was withdrawn from the front line early on 15 August, straight after its night attack, with the 51st taking over the position temporarily. Coming out, the 13th lost twelve casualties, eight of them to a single shell while passing through the notorious gauntlet of Tom's Cut. By now the remainder of the 4th Brigade had moved about 19 kilometres further back to Warloy-Baillon, where the 13th Battalion rejoined late on the night of 15 August, greeted with a 'tremendous ovation'[1] from the other units of the Brigade.

The 12th Brigade handed over its front line positions to incoming 1st Division units during 15 August also, and the troops made their way to the Brickfields that evening, then on to Warloy the next day, the marching column being joined by the 4th Pioneers and the 13th Field Company, also relieved by 1st Division units. The 4th Division medical units were relieved by their 1st Division equivalents on 15 August also. The 13th Brigade continued to hold the front line facing Mouquet Farm until the next morning when its relief was completed; the Brigade units followed in the footsteps of the others to Warloy. 4th Division HQ moved back from Tara Hill to Rubempré, 22 kilometres from the front line. All units spent a few days at Warloy, where the troops had the rare pleasure of a hot bath and a change of clothing, free of lice for an all too brief period. From Warloy the Division's units made their way to the rest and training area further to the rear, billeting in various villages around the divisional HQ's new location at Canaples, 40 kilometres behind the front line.

The human cost of the 4th Division's first 'tour' in the Pozières/Mouquet Farm sector, if not quite as high as that suffered earlier by the 1st and 2nd Divisions, had been severe. The divisional administrative staff calculated a total of 4,761 casualties between 29 July and 16 August,[2] including the Lahore artillery's losses. This total included 1,073 killed or missing. While the 'missing' (of which there were 369 recorded) included a few prisoners, the majority would have been killed, their deaths unobserved and their bodies lost in the wasteland of the battlefield. All but 190 of the total casualties had been suffered by the infantry and pioneers. Of the infantry brigades, the 12th had the most casualties and its 48th Battalion the highest total among the infantry battalions. The 12th Brigade had not been used in the series of northward attacks towards the Farm position, and its units' involvement in infantry combat had been limited to fighting the German attack of 7 August and later a few minor operations supporting British units. Most of the brigade's losses had come while holding the trenches of the right (eastern or 'windmill') sector of the 4th Division's line, under constant bombardment, emphasising the devastating effect of the German artillery.

With the Division now out of the line for a short period, several units received new commanding officers. The 50th Battalion (13th Brigade) had lost Lieutenant Colonel Hurcombe to 'shell shock', and his replacement was Major (shortly Lieutenant Colonel) Alfred Salisbury, transferred from the 9th Battalion (3rd Brigade, 1st Division). Salisbury was a Queenslander, 31 years old and an experienced soldier. He had been a pre-war militia officer and had served with the 9th Battalion at Gallipoli, being among the first ashore at the Landing. At the time of the AIF's expansion in Egypt, there had been some expectation that Salisbury would be given a command in the 4th Division, but this had not eventuated.[3] He had gone to France with the 9th Battalion and fought in the 1st Division's recent stint at Pozières. Now as his unit was moving up to the front line again, Salisbury was notified of his new command, and joined the 50th Battalion on 18 August.

Lieutenant Colonel Tilney, CO of the 13th Battalion (4th Brigade) had been ill with heart trouble for some time, and his condition had now become so serious that Brigadier General Brand decided to rest him on extended sick leave. Major James Durrant, the present brigade major of the 4th Brigade, was promoted to lieutenant colonel and took command of the 13th Battalion on 20 August. Colonel Durrant was returning to familiar territory, having served with the 13th at Gallipoli, firstly as its adjutant and later as second-in-command. He was a pre-war regular, aged 31, born in South Australia, a confident and effective officer. His replacement as brigade major at 4th Brigade HQ was Major John Peck (of whom more later), transferred from commanding the 12th Training Battalion in England.

The 12th Field Company of the divisional engineers was another unit needing a new commander. Major Andrewartha, who had commanded the unit since its formation, had found himself unable to bear the strain of combat during the Pozières fighting, and as soon as his unit came out of the line he had asked to be relieved of his command and reduced to captain. This was granted, and he was transferred to an engineer training depot in England (such options were more readily available to officers than to other ranks). Command of the 12th Field Company was given to Major Consett Carre Riddell, an outstanding officer (and a relative of General Sir William Birdwood), promoted into the 12th from the 4th Field Company.

Most of the infantry battalions were seriously under strength and needed to take on numerous reinforcements. Several drafts had arrived in the area during the fighting and had been waiting in bivouacs, and these were now allocated to their units together with further reinforcements who marched in over the next week. Some of these were lightly wounded returning to duty, but most were new recruits who would need further training with the units before going into action—not that anything could really prepare them for the experiences of the Mouquet Farm battlefield, to which the Division would soon be returning. The troops were given a few days of rest and light duties and the units re-organised and re-equipped. Some formal parades were held, with inspections by the GOC, Sir Herbert Cox. At these parades, General Cox presented what were described as 'congratulatory cards' to everyone who had been recommended for a decoration during the recent fighting. Intended to raise morale, this practice may have missed the mark in some cases—the 13th Battalion history noted that the cards were referred to as 'soup tickets' and were often used as score sheets during card games.[4]

Training soon resumed, both individual skills work and unit tactical exercises, although the troops now had some off-duty time and the opportunity for a bit of relaxation in the village *estaminets*. The infantry brigades all carried out practice attacks, working on the technique of attacking in waves behind a creeping barrage, the leading waves taking a simulated front line trench and following waves leapfrogging through to capture a support line. Particular attention was paid to co-operation with reconnaissance aircraft, an area which had been unsatisfactory during the earlier operations and which had raised concern as high as Army level. It was the task of 'contact patrol' aircraft to determine the position of the front line after an attack, and the infantry were supposed to light flares to enable the airmen to spot them. The troops were understandably reluctant to do this, fearing that the Germans would also detect them and know exactly where to shoot. For the gallant pilots and observers of 7 Squadron RFC, the unit allocated to support I Anzac, flying low over the battlefield in their lumbering two-seater BE2Cs, it was a frustrating as well as dangerous experience for little result. Brigade and unit commanders ordered that training exercises should emphasise the importance of accurately identifying the position of the front line, the advantages outweighing the immediate risks. Each infantry brigade's exercises included signalling an aircraft as the final stage of the attack, although the process miscarried several times when the aircraft failed to appear on time for one reason or another. In the case of the 4th Brigade's practice attack on 22 August, the exercise was called off before reaching this stage when urgent orders arrived for the brigade to move forward forthwith. Rotation of the three Australian divisions was continuing and it was the 4th Division's turn to go into the front line again.

Some thought had been given to the difficulties experienced during the Division's first tour. The 51st Battalion CO, Lieutenant Colonel Arthur Ross, had made a number of recommendations, in both a message written straight after the fighting of 14/15 August and in a more formal report prepared a few days later.[5] Ross took particular note of the issue of communications, in the broader sense of routes for troop movements and supplies as well as transmission of messages. 'It is a great mistake to keep on a series of small offensives without properly consolidating and fixing communication trenches *first*,' he wrote.

> Many lives are thrown away in approaching the firing line and to suffer casualties *before* going into action is very demoralising ... I did not see one single good communication trench within one mile of the firing line.
>
> Unless such trenches *in* the firing line are built, it is very difficult to deploy squarely ... loss of direction in attack is only to be expected when troops have no time to cut saps and improve communications solidly ...[6]
>
> (emphasis in the original)

Colonel Ross was also critical of the artillery support provided to his battalion, commenting that a five-minute barrage was too short considering that the unit had to conduct an advance of 300 yards. He recommended an intense barrage lasting 20 minutes. As it was, the barrage had not been heavy enough to suppress flanking enemy machine guns which had been able to pin down the 51st. The situation had not been helped by the lack of an artillery Forward Observation Officer (FOO) working with the battalion—'though I hate blaming artillery' the colonel added.[7] Ross made several other suggestions before reiterating that 'high casualties must be expected if troops are ordered to hold or fight on in a salient, *without perfect communication trenches*.[8] It is not clear how much notice was taken of Colonel Ross's views at higher levels, but there does seem to have been some effort to improve communications.[9] The divisional staff also prepared a memorandum, circulated on 25 August, pointing out the lessons resulting from the recent fighting. In tactical matters, units were urged to avoid crowding the front line and to hold captured positions with as few troops as possible, to minimise casualties:

> Lewis guns must be got up at once, also reserve ammunition, water and bombs. Continuous trenches are not necessary ... provided posts are mutually supporting. Counter attacks can be dealt with by the Artillery and Vickers Guns place in rear covering the gaps ... The line should be thinly held, never more than a few men in any shell hole or Lewis Gun position. Immediately the objective has been gained, Communication trenches must be commenced.[10]

Among other items, the staff also noted the difficulty of finding one's way in the maze of the trench lines. The importance of firm organisation of traffic in communication trenches was urged, and the basic but vital matter of notice boards and signposts (an engineer responsibility) was pointed out. In the conditions of the Pozières/Mouquet Farm battlefield, though, such things were perhaps easier said than done. Colonel Ross's report had implied some criticism of pioneers and engineers, and the staff of the 12th Brigade had also noted difficulties with cooperation between infantry and engineers. A memo from the brigade major, Captain Salier, (presumably with Brigadier General Glasfurd's approval) pointed out that the 'responsibilities of the completion of the work and the question of whether the shell fire permits of work or not is one for the [officer in charge of the] Infantry working party to decide—not for the Engineer officer.'[11]

The 4th Brigade Group, leading off the Division's return to the front during the afternoon and evening of 22 August, marched via Talmas and Vadencourt to reach the Brickfields area near Albert four days later. That was the final staging point before the battlefield and the remainder of the Division was now coming up also. After a two-day interval the 12th Brigade Group left its rest area and marched over the same route to the Brickfields, followed by the 13th Brigade Group at a further two days' interval. The 13th reached the Brickfields on 29 August, and on that day was visited by the corps commander, General Sir William Birdwood. The general presented medal ribbons to thirteen members of the brigade who had been awarded the Military Medal (MM) during the fighting earlier in the month. This was a frequent practice of General Birdwood, presenting a ribbon soon after an award was confirmed, before the medal itself became available. On this occasion there was some ill-feeling in the brigade, directed at the 49th Battalion. Captain Max Gore of the 50th Battalion commented:

> Imagine the chagrin of the rest of the brigade when the only battalion that had not been in the action, because it had been in reserve, received seventy-five percent of all the decorations, through the imaginative recommendations of a flamboyant commanding officer of Italian extraction [i.e. Lieutenant Colonel Lorenzo]. Somehow he managed to snare a DSO for himself as well.
>
> ... There may have been several reasons for this fiasco:
> 1. The brigadier was a Queenslander.
> 2. The battalion was of Queensland men.
> 3. The commanding officer of the battalion was a Queenslander.[12]

The incident inspired a bard in the 50th to compose some verses which included the lines

> Good old Birdy came to Albert, making speeches mighty fine,
> Shaking hands and giving medals, gave the lot to forty-nine.[13]

Captain Gore was perhaps being a little unfair here. Firstly, Colonel Lorenzo's DSO had been awarded in November 1915, for services at Gallipoli. As well, the 49th had not actually been the 13th Brigade's reserve battalion during the fighting. The 52nd Battalion had been in reserve, while the 49th had held the eastern or 'windmill' sector of the line, although it had not been directly involved in the attack of 14/15 August. Nevertheless, perception counts and it appears that interstate rivalries continued to flourish. In any case, both the 49th and 52nd Battalions would soon be thrown into very heavy fighting and such carping would be forgotten.

Units of the 4th Brigade began to take over the front line during the night of 26 August, only a few hours after reaching the Brickfields and less than two weeks after being relieved in its first 'tour' at Mouquet Farm. The 4th Division infantry units were virtually all under strength to some extent, and now included a number of reinforcements who could not have known what to expect when they reached the front; the veterans of the first fighting knew only too well. The situation was little different to that which had confronted the 4th Division when it had been relieved earlier in the month. The 1st Division had managed to edge forward in front of Mouquet Farm, establishing a position running for 200 metres along the Courcelette road east of the Farm and occupying the short segment of OG 1 south of the road previously held by the enemy. The 2nd Division then relieved the 1st, and launched an attack with the objective of straightening the line along the road to the west of the farm. The attack made some progress but the troops were eventually forced back with heavy losses. One small party from the 21st Battalion did, however, establish themselves at Point 77, in enemy-held territory about 200 metres ahead of the Quarry position. The operation had been carried out on 26 August, and the 4th Brigade moved up that night to relieve. The Brigade temporarily came under command of the 2nd Division and was immediately tasked with resuming the attack to the west of the Farm.

Brigadier General Brand sent the 14th and 15th Battalions into the line first, on the left and right respectively, with the 16th and 13th in the support lines. The 15th was initially required to occupy a position stretching 1,500 metres around to the 'Windmill' section of the firing line. It was quickly realised that this was excessive, and a battalion was sent up from the 2nd Division reserve to take over part of the line on the right. The 14th Battalion took over the left of the line from the 21st, sending out a patrol which found the isolated post at Point 77 and relieved (in more ways than one) its garrison. A start was made on digging a communication trench back to the Quarry. In a repeat of the attempt by the 21st Battalion to establish a line west of the Farm, the 14th Battalion was now instructed by Brigade to make an attack to its front. The Battalion was given the task of capturing Points 54 and 27, the left and right extremities of a 400-metre front (Point 77 was between the two), which would provide an intermediate position for attacking the Farm itself. The force allocated to the operation was inexplicably light: the Battalion 'bombing' platoon, half to each strongpoint, with each half supported by two rifle platoons. Another two platoons would advance to Point 77, then extend to both sides to complete the new line. Less than half of the Battalion was to be used to attack strong positions that had defied a force of more than twice that size two days earlier.

The attack was set for midnight on the night of 27/28 August. It was already apparent to the troops that the operation was ill-conceived, the platoon sergeant of the bombers, Edgar Rule, commenting in his memoirs,

> the arrangements were rotten—the battalion staff work could not have been worse, and it was more by good luck than good management that any of us came out of the show.[14]

The attacking infantry went forward on time and found their fire support to be less than adequate. What artillery fire there was proved to be inaccurate, and a medium trench mortar quickly went out of action. The group attacking Point 54 had only a light Stokes mortar to provide a covering bombardment. The LTM crew did well, firing quickly and accurately while themselves under German shelling, but they could not take the place of a full barrage. The OC of the Brigade LTM Battery, Lieutenant Arnold Potts, had been in that posting for only a week; he personally directed the mortar fire and was later awarded the MC for his work on that and subsequent nights. In the Second World War, Brigadier Potts would find controversial fame on the Kokoda Track.[15] The bombing sections got into the German strong-points behind their bursting grenades, but they had been steadily depleted by casualties and were not strong enough to hold off the inevitable heavy counter-attacks. The supporting rifle platoons were unable, or perhaps unwilling, to come up in time to hold the Germans off. Before dawn the attackers were back in their original front line, having suffered 75 casualties;[16] of these, the deaths fortunately were only four. The bombing platoon commander, Lieutenant Archibald Dean, had been badly wounded in the head and died three months later. The operation had produced no positive results, despite claims that it had been a 'successful raid,' and had done no good to the morale of the 14th Battalion.[17] Point 77 was, however, still held.

During the day of 28 August 4th Division HQ moved up to Tara Hill, and from noon the Division took over command of the sector from the 2nd. The rest of the Division was now coming up: the 12th Brigade Group reached the Brickfields during the day, sending its 48th and 47th Battalions further forward to Tara Hill and La Boisselle where they became the divisional reserve. While here, the 48th was required to supply a working party of 300 men—almost the full strength of the unit—to the divisional Signal Company to bury a telephone cable up to the Pozières position. On 29 August, the 45th and 46th Battalions went into the line on the Windmill sector of the front, relieving units of the 2nd Division. On the same day the 13th Brigade Group moved up to the Brickfields. Other divisional units progressively took over from their 2nd Division counterparts. The engineers and pioneers continued the constant work on communication trenches and roads, while the Divisional Train took over control of the transport routes and depots serving the front line. The medical services assumed responsibility for the network of intermediate dressing stations behind the front. The 13th Field Ambulance became the controlling medical unit, converting an Advanced Dressing Station (ADS) in the school house at Albert into a Main Dressing Station (MDS). Field artillery support was again provided by the Lahore Division guns, still in the line, and by the four brigades of the 2nd Division artillery.

During their previous period at the front, the troops had at least been spared the hardship of mud, the weather having stayed mostly fine. Now, however, persistent heavy rain began to descend on the battlefield, quickly turning the pulverised earth into a soupy quagmire. The combination of shellfire and rain caused trench walls to crumble, and the men in the damaged trenches would often be waist-deep in mud and water. Rifles and Lewis guns could not be kept clean and workable and it became almost impossible to get any hot food or drinks up to the troops in the front line. The devastating German shelling continued as before on the front and support lines, although it does seem to have become somewhat lighter on the rear areas and in the Windmill sector. A policy of relieving front-line infantry battalions every 48 hours had recently been adopted, none too soon in the circumstances. Hence the 14th and 15th Battalions facing Mouquet Farm were relieved on 29 August by the 16th and 13th Battalions. The latter units would now conduct the next major attack, planned for the same night; a company each from the 14th and 15th would remain in support. The objectives as determined by the Division were now extended to include the Farm itself and a line just beyond it (forgoing capture of the intermediate position along the road first), and the Fabeck Graben trench running to the east. Orders from I Anzac to the Division had only specified capturing the line of the Fabeck to Point 42 north-east of the Farm, leaving it up to the division to decide how to go about taking the Farm and linking back to the original front line.[18] The Corps order included a comment that Mouquet Farm 'despite our bombardment is, according to latest information, still a point of some strength. Special and determined measures will be taken for the capture and consolidation of this position.'[19] It appears that I Anzac had suggested using a full brigade in the attack, but General Cox and his staff were optimistic enough to believe that two battalions could do the job.[20]

Divisional HQ issued the operation order for the attack to the 4th Brigade during the night of 28 August, and the brigade issued its order at noon the next day, specifying 'Zero' as 11 pm that night. The 16th Battalion was given Mouquet Farm and the trenches on either side as its objectives, and the 13th would attack the greater portion of the Fabeck Graben, with its left at Point 73 where the Fabeck crossed OG 1. To reach the objective, the 13th Battalion would also have to overrun a newly-dug outpost line (Kollmann Trench) 100 metres in front of the Fabeck. Four of the 4th MG Company's Vickers guns would go forward with the 16th Battalion and one with the 13th, while other guns put indirect fire onto German trenches leading to the objectives. Field artillery support would be provided by the Lahore Division guns, firing a barrage on four successive lines at 100 metre intervals, two minutes on each line. Corps and Army heavy artillery would bombard the objectives during the day—an arrangement that would have unintended consequences. Several mortars from the Brigade LTM battery were allocated to the battalions for additional fire support. The 16th Battalion arranged to use three companies and the bombing platoon to attack the Farm and its immediate vicinity, with the fourth company securing the left flank and providing close support to the others. The 13th Battalion would use all four companies in line, each with a segment of the Fabeck Graben as its objective; the Battalion bombers would advance up OG 1 from Point 91 to Point 73 on the left of the 13th's attack. That line formed the boundary between the two units. Both battalions established 'fighting' HQs close to the front line.

The wet weather continued.

> Never has anyone seen a more miserable dawn than that of the 29th August, 1916, [the 13th Battalion history noted.] Those who have been at sea on a black day will remember the depressiveness of the dreary, black water wastes. From our trenches the outlook was even more foreboding; nothing but twisted, heaped and churned mud, with jagged stumps and ragged wire.[21]

As the day wore on the troops manning the front line trenches were pounded by the German artillery and at times by their own guns, while the rain increased. The 'heavies', tasked with bombarding particular points in the German lines, frequently dropped short onto the Australian front line. The 13th Battalion was hit particularly hard by friendly fire, some of the artillery targets being only 50 metres from the infantry's positions. Although the troops were dispersed away from the trench line and into shell holes, the 13th suffered 90 casualties during the day to shells from both sides. The 16th Battalion also took punishment from the heavy artillery. The unit intelligence officer, Lieutenant Bill Lynas, reported afterwards that

> the heavies will persist in shelling our lines. Some of our own shells lob as much as 200 yards in rear of our own lines ... this is disconcerting to say the least. Heavy artillery should not ... be used at close distances unless the most perfect communication is arranged ... before we can redirect the heavies their tour of bombardment is over ... many of our people have been killed and at least 200 yards of our trenches levelled today by our own guns.[22]

After dark, the battalions deployed into their jumping-off positions. The intelligence officers of the two battalions, Lynas of the 16th and Lieutenant Gordon Mills of the 13th, led parties of scouts into the mud between the lines to reconnoitre and to mark out lines for guiding the attacking troops, the 16th using fabric tapes and the 13th coloured lamps. Both officers remained in no man's land to assist in the attack, and both were awarded the MC for their efforts (in Bill Lynas' case, a Bar to the MC that he had won two weeks earlier for similar exploits). The companies were in position by 10:45 pm ready for the covering barrage, although wet and muddy and with numbers depleted by the day's losses. At Zero, 11 pm, the Lahore field guns opened up, bursting their shrapnel with good accuracy on the barrage lines, two minutes on each line before lifting 100 metres on to the next. The infantry orders were to keep as close to the barrage as possible but the troops were slowed down by the muddy ground. At several points along the objectives the German infantry had time to make ready before the attackers arrived, and their defensive artillery fire descended on the battlefield. In the 13th Battalion's sector, the right-flank companies ran into enfilading machine gun fire coming from the direction of Courcelette, as the 51st Battalion had done two weeks earlier. Despite heavy losses, small groups managed to occupy Kollmann Trench briefly, and a few men got into parts of the Fabeck Graben, but the survivors were unable to hang on against counter-attacks.

There was some success on the left of the 13th's line. Captain Harry Murray's 'A' Company, which had been reduced to 64 men by casualties during the day, followed the barrage closely and managed to capture its objective in the Fabeck Graben. At the same time the Battalion bombers, under Lieutenant Bob Henderson, advanced on Murray's left along OG 1 to Point 73. The bombers were assisted strongly by Stokes mortars of the Brigade LTM battery, lobbing mortar rounds ahead of the grenade men and increasing their range by 15 metres after every three rounds.[23] Corporal Thomas Baxter's good work in charge of one of the mortars was rewarded with the DCM, and the officer in command, Second Lieutenant James Robin, won the MC. Fighting mainly with grenades and bayonets since most of their rifles were clogged with mud, Captain Murray's men captured 150 metres of the Fabeck Graben and now faced the task of holding on to their gains. Murray had started the attack with low numbers, and his company's strength had steadily melted away as men were hit; he now had only 28 to defend the captured position. He divided the available men into seven posts of three each with the remainder as a mobile reserve to reinforce threatened points. Murray was now in an almost identical situation to that which he had faced in the 13th Battalion's operation two weeks earlier, in possession of his objective but dependent on the situation on both flanks.

On the left of the attack front the 16th Battalion advanced on Mouquet Farm and the trenches on either side of it. The company tasked with securing Point 54 on the extreme left ('D', under Captain Charles Ahearn) was caught by the German defensive shelling and eventually forced back. Captain Albert McLeod's 'C' Company, next on the right, advanced into the wilderness to the west of the Farm but was unable to locate its actual objective and eventually had to withdraw. 'B' Company, led by Major Percy Black, attacked Mouquet Farm itself and quickly occupied the position. Black personally shot an enemy machine gunner who was preparing to open fire, but was then badly wounded in the neck by grenade splinters. His men were in possession of the Farm position, however, and on the right of the 16th's line, 'A' Company (Captain Ross Harwood) kept up with the covering barrage and gained their objectives around Points 31 and 42. The fighting in this area now intensified as the Germans launched heavy counter attacks from nearby positions. At the Farm, the 'B' Company troops and the battalion bombing platoon under Lieutenant Vernon Wilton attempted to 'mop up' the warren of dugouts and cellars but they were unable to locate all of the entrances in the dark. German infantry (good troops of the 4th Guard Division) swarmed up from below ground and gradually gained the upper hand in fierce fighting. Outnumbered and counter-attacked from all directions, the Australians were forced out of the Farm again. Sergeant George Dow, platoon sergeant of the bombers, distinguished himself both in the initial advance and in covering the withdrawal, and was later awarded the DCM. Captain Harwood's force beyond the Farm was also heavily counter attacked by superior numbers; the line was split into small groups and almost surrounded. The survivors eventually made their way back to the original front line after intense fighting, which had prevented any attempt to link up with the 13th Battalion to their right.

Of that unit, only Captain Murray's small force in the Fabeck Graben was still in the objective, and was also under pressure from counter attacks. Two launched from the right were repulsed, mainly by the use of grenades, but it was apparent that the right flank was open. Murray now tried to gain touch with the 16th on his left. Taking two men with him, he probed westwards from Point 73 for about 80 metres. Here the patrol encountered a group of five Germans who announced their presence by throwing grenades which wounded all three Australians. One of the men lost a foot and the other was blinded in one eye. Murray himself was hit in the leg and back by splinters (one penetrated a lung), but shot two of the Germans with his revolver. The others fled, but there was no sign of any support on this flank either. The battered patrol struggled back to the captured position to find another counter-attack in progress. This was repulsed as was a further attempt, but it was apparent that there was no future in remaining in the objective any longer. The company now had only 16 unwounded men, according to the battalion history,[24] and it was isolated in the enemy's lines with no support on either flank and under increasing artillery fire. Carrying their wounded, 'A' Company withdrew back to the original front line. Numerous wounded men from both sides still lay in the mud of No Man's Land. With daylight an unofficial truce emerged on the battlefield, parties of German and Australian stretcher-bearers going out under red-cross flags to bring in their wounded.

Mouquet Farm remained in German hands despite the best efforts of the two battalions. Each had suffered heavy casualties and fought with great determination but the task had been too heavy for their limited numbers. Decorations had been awarded despite the lack of success. Some have been mentioned previously, and among others were a DSO for Captain Harwood and a DCM for Sergeant Henry Bradley of the 16th Battalion, and a DSO for Captain Murray of the 13th. The 16th Battalion's losses in the operation totalled 231, including 81 killed and missing, while the 13th had 217 casualties of whom 73 were killed or missing.[25] Both units had lost three of their four company commanders wounded—Captains Theodore Wells and Robert Browning as well as Harry Murray in the 13th Battalion, and Major Black and Captains Harwood and McLeod in the 16th. Clearly the capture of Mouquet Farm and the trenches east of it was too difficult a task for two under-strength battalions to tackle, particularly in the prevailing weather conditions and with artillery support that had proven to be less than ideal. In his report written after the action,[26] Lieutenant Lynas of the 16th Battalion expressed the opinion that a full battalion would be needed to capture and consolidate the Farm itself—one company could take the position, as 'B' Company had done, but a large force would be needed for mopping-up. The report made several other suggestions for future attacks, including attacking Point 54 south-west of the Farm by mortar fire rather than infantry. Lynas, the battalion intelligence officer, had gone out with the stretcher parties on the morning of 30 August, and it is apparent that he had taken the opportunity to reconnoitre the German positions at close range ('We had a good look at Mouquet Farm from right, left and front, at about 40 to 15 yards distance'[27]). Each side often accused the other of taking advantage of the Red Cross in this manner, while denying that they themselves ever did so.

I Anzac was due to be rested away from the Somme front, and the 1st and 2nd Divisions were already on their way north. Advance units of the Canadian Corps were moving up to relieve the 4th Division, but one more attack was ordered before the Division was withdrawn. The operation was scheduled for 3 September, giving several days for preparation. As a first step, the 4th Brigade's two front line battalions (13th and 16th) were relieved by the 48th and 47th Battalions of the 12th Brigade, coming up from reserve. The 45th and 46th Battalions were already holding the Windmill sector of the line, and those units were now joined on their right by troops of the 1st Canadian Brigade, temporarily under the 4th Division's control. The actual attack would be delivered by the 13th Brigade, at the moment waiting in reserve at La Boiselle, Tara Valley and the Brickfields. Units further forward were given preparation tasks to be completed before the attack went in. Up to now the higher commands had insisted on attacks virtually every 24 hours with consequent hasty preparation. Although still scarcely adequate, the few days available for planning the new operation were at least an improvement. There was an attempt to address several of the issues raised after the earlier operations, and there are signs that notice was being taken of suggestions from the front line. The first priority was to improve communication trenches and provide adequate 'jumping-off' positions for the attacking troops—digging, in a word. As early as 30 August, straight after the failed attack of the previous night, the divisional staff had ordered construction of new earthworks and improvements of existing ones. Working parties were allocated from the front-line infantry battalions (now the 47th and 48th), the Pioneers and two British cavalry units, and from the 14th and 15th Battalions of the 4th Brigade which were still in reserve at Wire Trench. The divisional CRE, Lieutenant Colonel Gilbert Elliott, was responsible for coordinating the work.

Progress on these tasks was slow to begin with, the 15th Battalion noting that it was very difficult for the working parties to even reach their areas, the few routes being congested by units moving to and from the front line. The divisional staff, while acknowledging that the muddy ground and the exhaustion of the troops were factors, found it necessary to apply some pressure: 'certain officers were directed to appear at DHQ and were exhorted to do better in future.'[28] Officers in charge of working parties were also called in for a personal briefing by the CRE. A big effort was put in and most of the works were ready for the attacking force by the evening of 2 September. Assembly trenches roughly parallel to the enemy position, although barely deep enough, had been dug to accommodate the attacking troops on the right and centre, who would not occupy these lines until just before the assault. The 47th Battalion's working parties had made particularly slow progress. General Cox, intervening personally, attributed their poor performance to a want of energy by the Battalion CO, Lieutenant Colonel Snowden, in driving the work through. Cox immediately relieved Snowden of his command.[29] The unit's second-in-command, Major Thomas Flintoff, took over. Most of the digging had been done at night, German shelling preventing work during daylight. Shells frequently cut telephone communications to the front also and unit and divisional signallers were constantly going out under fire to repair damaged cables. Corporals Joseph Climpson and Edwin Fennell of the 4th Division Signal Company were among signallers decorated for such work, each being awarded the MM for keeping the lines in operation between 12th Brigade HQ and its front-line units during both periods in the Mouquet Farm sector.

Where the previous series of attacks had been launched at night, Zero for this operation was set for 5:10 am on 3 September, just before dawn. A dawn attack had been suggested by Lieutenant Lynas of the 16th Battalion,[30] although he had envisaged a 'silent' attack without a preliminary bombardment. An elaborate supporting barrage was planned for the operation of 3 September (the 2nd Division had carried out a dawn attack, unsuccessfully, a week earlier). The divisional operation order was issued to the 13th Brigade on the night of 1 September, again with the objectives of the Fabeck Graben and the Farm, extending to the Point 77 outpost on the left (west) of the latter. The strength of the Farm position was recognised, the order stating that the main attack against Mouquet Farm will be in great strength and depth ... A very strong 'mopping up party' will be detailed to clear the cellars and dug-outs in and near the farm ... Very rapid consolidation of this locality is essential.[31]

Division HQ sent Major George Dickinson, the GSO3, to assist brigade officers in reconnoitring routes to the assembly positions—the presence of a staff officer near the front line was usually a good indication to the troops that an attack was imminent, if there had been any doubt. Brigadier General Glasgow's orders for his 13th Brigade were produced early the following morning. Three battalions, the 49th, 51st and 52nd, would make the attack, with the 50th remaining in reserve in the Park Lane trench but also with a small party attached to the 51st and occupying the outpost at Point 77. On the right, the 49th Battalion had two objectives: firstly Kollmann Trench, the outpost position 100 metres in front of the Fabeck Graben, then advancing to the section of the Fabeck between Points 95 and 36. The 52nd Battalion was allocated the rest of the Fabeck Graben to Point 42 north-east of the Farm, with half a company (i.e. two platoons) to face west and attack the outskirts of the Farm position. Here they would link with the 51st Battalion, which had the task of taking the Farm itself, including mopping-up the dangerous dugouts, cellars and strong points that had frustrated previous attempts. The 13th MG Company was tasked with firing on enemy communication trenches leading to the objectives, over the heads of the attacking infantry, and with laying down covering fire on the left flank. The 1st Canadian Brigade's MG Company was also brought in to cover the right flank. As well as this long-range indirect fire, the 13th Company also positioned two guns on each flank of the front line to give direct close support to the infantry if opportunity arose. The 13th LTM battery's main task was to bombard the strong German post at Point 54, beyond the left of the attack front. At the same time, several British divisions of Reserve Army would be attacking towards Thiepval to the west, while Fourth Army to the east would attack Ginchy and Guillemont. In the event, the latter operation did not get under way until several hours after the 13th Brigade's attack was launched. Both British operations involved two or more divisions on a comparatively broad front, instead of three battalions pushing into a narrow salient as the 13th Brigade was required to do.

The 13th Brigade infantry began moving up to the front line on the night of 1/2 September, relieving the units of the 12th Brigade. Initially each battalion sent only one company into the front trenches, to avoid overcrowding prior to the attack. The remaining companies did not begin moving up until the next night, 2/3 September, deploying for the dawn attack. The efforts made to improve communication trenches and provide 'jumping-off' positions paid dividends:

> Routes to be followed were laid down and Staff Officers detailed to regulate traffic. The whole of the attacking troops ... arrived in position without any delay or confusion, with very few casualties and without being discovered by the enemy.[32]

noted the Brigade report. The CO of the 49th Battalion, Lieutenant Colonel Lorenzo, might not have agreed with the brigade staff on this point; when the time came for his unit to occupy its assembly trench, he found some of the 52nd Battalion already in it. The latter insisted that they were in the right position and refused Lorenzo's orders to move out.

Apart from this hitch, the attacking force was successfully deployed into its starting positions with most of the men reasonably fresh and rested, having being held back from the front line until close to Zero. The 52nd Battalion had received a setback during the afternoon of 2 September when the CO, Lieutenant Colonel Miles Beevor, was wounded and evacuated.[33] Major Denis Lane, the second-in-command, took over the Battalion. A distressing, but fortunately rare, incident in the 49th Battalion had caused a change in a key post also. When that unit's advance company began to occupy the front line on the night of 1 September, the company commander was found to be drunk. He was removed from command and arrested.[34] Lieutenant Leonard Keid took charge of the company and was killed leading it in action two days later.

The Corps artillery staff had arranged a comprehensive barrage for the operation. The objective line and the Farm were pounded for several days beforehand, and the available field artillery was tasked with laying down a moving barrage to protect the infantry in the actual attack. The guns of the Lahore artillery, continuing its attachment to the 4th Division, and those of the 2nd Division artillery which were still in the line, would form the 13th Brigade's fire support. On the right flank, where enemy machine gun fire had disrupted two previous attacks on the Fabeck Graben, three brigades of the 2nd Division's guns would deliver an intense barrage for eight minutes. Heavy artillery batteries were assigned to bombard the general area beyond, towards Courcelette. The left flank of the attack, west of Mouquet Farm and in the Point 54 area, was similarly protected, aided by a smoke-screen to be laid down by a Royal Engineer unit. In the centre, the main line of the barrage would lie on the first objective trenches for five minutes before lifting to the second objective for a further three minutes. The barrage would then move on to the German support line. The three infantry battalions had each worked out their own tactical plans for the operation, all involving variations on the use of several attacking waves which had been practised during the Division's recent period out of the line.

The artillery opened promptly at 5:10 am as first light was appearing in the sky. At the same time mortars of the 13th LTM battery, mounted in the Quarry, bombarded the German post at Point 54; 60 rounds were fired before the infantry attack went in. This completed the LTM's task, but a number of the mortar men then formed carrying parties to bring ammunition forward for the infantry on the right flank. The machine-gunners continued the harassing fire that had commenced earlier in the night, firing 64,000 rounds into the German rear areas during the operation. By all accounts the field artillery's shrapnel barrage was accurate and heavy, and the infantrymen were able to follow the shell-bursts closely to the first objectives.

On the right the 49th Battalion went forward in four waves, each company forming a wave. The first wave was to capture the first objective (Kollmann Trench) and occupy it, with the second wave passing through to form a screen in front of the captured position, using shell holes for cover. The third wave's task was to capture the Battalion's second objective (Fabeck Graben) with the fourth wave going further to form a screen beyond that trench. Several parties were detailed to dig communication trenches, and the second and fourth waves carried picks and shovels which would be dropped at the captured positions to use in consolidation. The first stage of the 49th's attack went according to plan, the first wave keeping up with the barrage and meeting little resistance at Kollmann Trench, which was easily captured. The attack of the third wave on the second objective did not go so smoothly, however. The barrage was timed to last for only three minutes on the Fabeck Graben, barely sufficient in any case, and the advancing infantrymen were slowed down by the muddy ground. By the time they reached the enemy trench the barrage had lifted and the Germans were ready to fight. After heavy fighting with rifles and grenades, 'C' Company of the 49th was in possession of the right-hand (eastern) part of its objective between Points 66 and 95, but had been forced out into shell holes west of Point 66. The Queenslanders set up barricades in the captured section of trench and prepared to defend it. The eastern part of the Fabeck Graben was now reasonably firmly in Australian hands. There were no reports of the flanking machine gun fire that had stopped the two earlier attacks in this area, indicating that the covering barrage on the right had managed to suppress that danger. It is also possible that the guns may have been distracted by the bombardment preceding Fourth Army's attack on Guillemont to the east.

In the centre of the 13th Brigade's advance, the 52nd Battalion, going into its first major action, employed three of its companies and two platoons of the fourth in line abreast, to attack the western sector of the Fabeck Graben from Point 36 to Point 42 north-east of the Farm. The remaining two platoons (of 'B' Company) were allocated to support the 51st Battalion's right flank in that unit's attack on the Farm itself. The 52nd's operation order was somewhat vague as to the tactics to be employed—in particular, it appears to have been left up to each company to decide how many waves to use.[35] The unit's after-action report noted that 'all companies were in position with their 1st wave in front trench and other waves (in some cases two and others three) in assembly trenches.'[36] The Official Historian, C E W Bean, commented that the 52nd was 'most unevenly commanded.'[37] It had fallen to the Battalion intelligence officer, Lieutenant Arthur Maxwell, to go around all companies to ensure that they were in position and aware of their lines of advance—he found that 'D' Company on the right flank was facing at right angles to their correct line and hastily repositioned it just before Zero. Maxwell was one of two lofty brothers in the 52nd; the other, Lieutenant Duncan Maxwell, commanded a platoon in 'A' Company.

The 52nd's 'D', 'A' and 'C' companies all appear to have reached their objectives but encountered heavy machine gun fire from the German positions. 'D' on the right flank took heavy casualties, including its commander killed and several other officers killed or wounded, and the survivors were driven back (this was the point near where the left of the 49th Battalion had been stopped short of the enemy trench). The next company to the left, 'A', was also hit hard, losing among others the veteran Captain Charles Littler, one of the AIF's great 'characters,'[38] mortally wounded. Lieutenant Duncan Maxwell immediately took over the leadership of the company and managed to occupy a segment of the objective with a small party, including a few men from 'D' Company. 'C' Company, centre-left in the attack, appears to have reached its objective, but went too far beyond it and ran into its own supporting barrage and heavy machine gun fire from the German support positions. The company commander and several other officers were killed, and the company fell apart, the survivors struggling back to their original line. On the 52nd's extreme left, the remnants of two platoons (about 20 men under an NCO, Sergeant Harry Cutts) had reached the western end of the Fabeck Graben near Point 42 and the remaining two platoons were in position to support the 51st Battalion's attack on Mouquet Farm itself.

The 51st had advanced successfully on the Farm, with three of its companies attacking and also using wave tactics.[39] The remaining company ('A') occupied the existing front line, with parties set to dig communication trenches forward to the captured position and others 'carrying' for the attacking troops. The unit intelligence officer, Lieutenant Thomas Louch, had been out with his scouts during the hours of darkness, laying down white fabric guide-tapes to indicate the direction of advance; Louch continued in No Man's Land during the attack to guide the attacking waves, winning the MC for his efforts. The Western Australians followed the barrage (described as 'perfect') so closely that the troops were able to occupy the Farm before the garrison could emerge to mount an effective defence. The first two companies moved further forward to establish defence lines 100 metres beyond the Farm, while the following waves, 'C' Company and the bombers, set about mopping up, clearing the warren of dugouts that made the German stronghold such a difficult proposition. Those troops tossed grenades into all the dugout entrances that could be seen, at one point firing a Lewis gun down the stairs of a passageway. The two detached platoons from the 52nd Battalion joined in to clear the north-east corner of the position. Eventually resistance in the underground chambers was overcome and 60 German prisoners were sent back. The troops at the Farm set about digging a support line across the position, at the same time sapping forward to link up with the lines of the two advanced companies and to the rear to meet 'A' Company parties sapping forward from the original front line. It seemed that Mouquet Farm was firmly in Australian hands at last.

The main assault had ended with the situation along the line uneven. On the extreme right, the 49th Battalion was in possession of part of its objective in the Fabeck Graben, working strenuously with pick and shovel to consolidate and link up with the original front line. The left of the 49th had been unable to hold its segment of the German trench but was hanging on in shell holes just short of it. Lieutenant Maxwell's small group of the 52nd Battalion was isolated to the 49th's left, and trying to gain touch on both flanks. Further to the left, where part of the

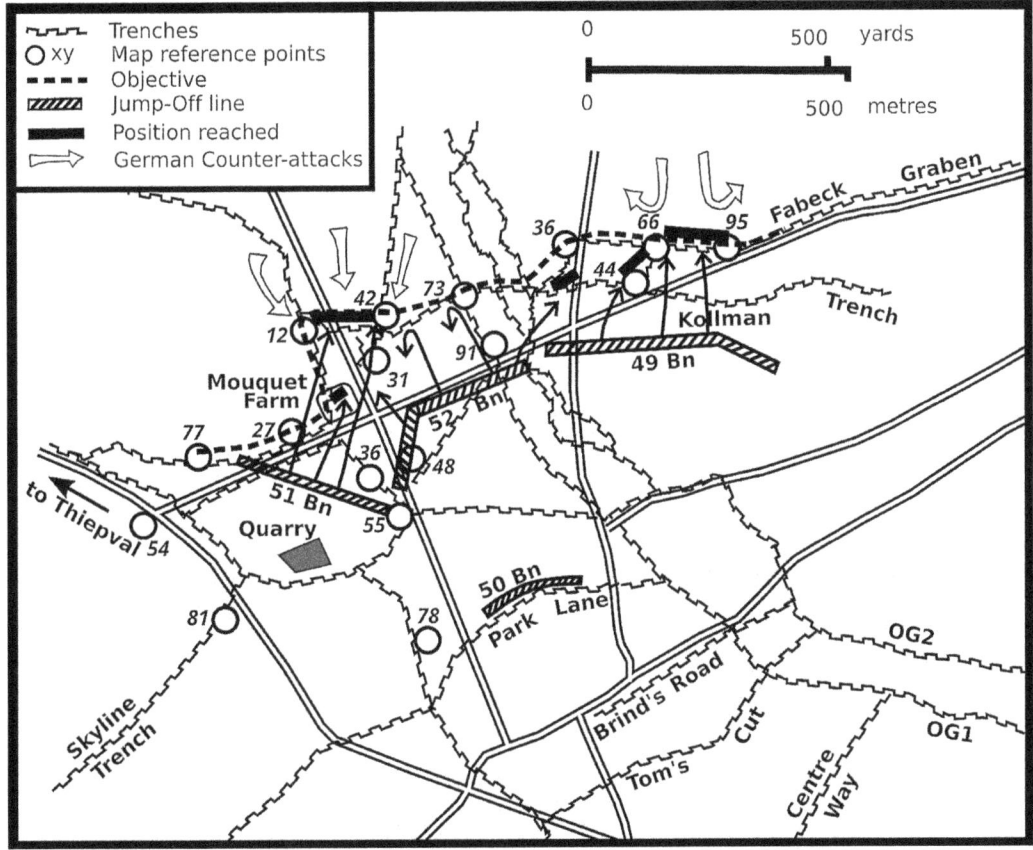

Mouquet Farm: attack by 13th Brigade, 3 to 5 September 1916.

52nd had been repulsed, a wide gap existed to its depleted platoons supporting the 51st at the Farm. The latter unit was in possession of its objectives and preparing to defend them against the inevitable German counterstroke, which was already under way and gathering strength. Increasingly heavy machine gun fire was directed at the Farm position from the enemy rear, and at about 8 am the German heavy artillery began to bombard their lost position. German infantry appeared probing towards Point 42 between the 51st's position and that of the two 52nd platoons at the western end of the Fabeck Graben. The latter group, badly outnumbered, was forced to pull back to the vicinity of the Farm and join the 51st troops.

The right flank of the Mouquet Farm position was now in the air, and the two companies in the advanced line beyond the Farm were becoming isolated. Fifty men were sent forward from the support line to reinforce them, but the German shelling intensified and the support line itself was suffering heavy losses. The Farm quickly became untenable. The two officers and 20 men of 'C' company remaining on their feet, out of 200 who had started with the mopping-up wave,[40] finally evacuated the Farm and made their way back to the old front line. The advanced companies were soon surrounded by German infantry who closed in with grenades. The troops stood and fought but were overwhelmed and virtually wiped out. Some were taken prisoner by the Germans, but many more died in the trenches. A patrol of the 50th Battalion, scouting the area some hours later, found a trench in which 'the dead bodies of Australian soldiers lay in profusion, in all sorts of attitudes just as they had died ... most of them were of the 51st Battalion.'[41] The *Official History* noted that eight years later 'officials of the Graves Commission found beyond Mouquet Farm a trench filled with the bodies of Australians. There is little doubt that they were a remnant of the lost companies.'[42] In hindsight, the advanced companies should have pulled back earlier, but the commanders' original orders had been to hold on at all costs and they had done so until it was too late for a successful withdrawal. While the plan for the actual capture of the Farm had worked well, it appears that rather less thought had gone into the subsequent defence of the position against counter-attack. In particular, there does not seem to have been any firm arrangement for a defensive artillery barrage that could have been called in to suppress the enemy infantry, despite the presence of a liaison officer from the Lahore artillery at 51st Battalion HQ.[43] The German artillery had also suffered little if any interference from counter-battery fire by the Allied heavy artillery and was able to accurately drop its shells on the captured position. It would not have helped matters that the I Anzac artillery was in the process of handing over to the Canadian Corps when the attack took place, a poorly-timed relief in the midst of heavy fighting.[44]

The assault had ultimately failed on the left and centre of the line and the Germans were once more in possession of Mouquet Farm and the adjacent trenches to its east. Further east, however, the 49th Battalion still held the ground that it had won, with Lieutenant Maxwell's group of the 52nd hanging on also. Maxwell had collected about 90 men, including a few reinforcements who came up during the morning. Probing to his right, he succeeded in making contact with the left of the 49th after one of his men shot the crew of a German machine gun that was barring the way. Forty German grenadiers caught between the two forces were taken prisoner. There was no sign of any friendly troops on the left, however, and the 52nd troops barricaded the trenches on that flank and prepared to defend their position and cover the 49th Battalion's left. A German counter-attack was driven off at about 11 am and during the afternoon the 52nd troops received a welcome reinforcement when a company of the 13th Canadian Battalion joined them in the trench. These troops had been placed under command of the 52nd and Major Lane had immediately sent them up to support Duncan Maxwell, whose brother Arthur, the 52nd's Intelligence Officer, personally guided the newcomers through the wilderness to the front line. The Canadians were at full strength (250 men) and their commander, Captain J. H. Lovett, outranked Lieutenant Maxwell, but the latter was the man on the spot and thus familiar with the situation. With sound common sense, Captain Lovett placed himself under the orders of the beanpole young Australian subaltern. This segment of the line was now adequately garrisoned, for the time being at least. Late in the day an attempt by the Canadians to extend the line to the left was unsuccessful, and the combined force settled down to defend its position, as the 49th Battalion was doing on the extreme right.

After the 49th had seized its objectives in the Fabeck Graben in the dawn rush, they had about two hours' grace before the Germans began to react in strength. The Queenslanders made the most of this respite, with their picks and shovels deepening the battered trench and digging back to open communications with the original front line. Leading the defence of the captured position was the officer commanding 'C' Company, Captain Charles Fortescue, a veteran of the 9th Battalion at Gallipoli. The captured trench ran along the crest of the ridge and the 49th had a view over Courcelette and beyond. The unit had lost heavily during the fighting for the trench and Colonel Lorenzo called for reinforcements to help in consolidating and manning the new line. The 50th Battalion, in reserve, sent up its 'A' Company which itself only had a strength of three officers and 37 men. They were first put to work repairing and deepening the former German outpost line (Kollmann Trench), which was now the 49th's support line, then moved up to reinforce the garrison of the new front line in the Fabeck Graben. The CO also sent forward his adjutant, Captain Harry Swain, and Regimental Sergeant Major (RSM) Robert Hannah to assist with coordinating the defence and maintaining the flow of supplies to the new front line. The first German counter-attacks when they came were tentative and were repelled without great difficulty, and energetic digging through the day got the main trench down to a depth of two metres, with the right-hand communication trench nearly as deep. Night brought increased German shelling but few casualties, the troops being well protected by the deepened trenches. The pressure increased when morning came on 4 September, at which time Captain Fortescue first realised that the whole objective had not been taken and that his left was bent back from Point 66 to 44. Westward beyond there, the line was held by Lieutenant Maxwell's group of the 52nd Battalion and the 13th Canadian Battalion.

The Germans launched three infantry counter-attacks against the 49th during the day. The first two, at 9 am and 11 am, were attempted without artillery cover and were driven off by rifle and Lewis gun fire. The 49th called for a defensive ('SOS') barrage from the own guns but with no response, again probably due to the artillery relief in progress at the time. The third attack, directed at the left flank, came at 4:15pm and was preceded by a heavy half-hour bombardment on the front and support lines. This time the 49th's SOS signal brought a barrage down on the German infantry and helped to stop the attack. The Battalion's Lewis gun crews were particularly prominent in the day's fighting, keeping the attackers under fire and taking heavy casualties themselves as the Germans tried to knock out the guns with grenades. Relief was on the way, with more Canadian troops now coming into the line. During the day a Canadian company took over the 49th's right flank back to the original front line, and at 8 pm another two companies joined the troops in the captured position. Meanwhile Lieutenant Maxwell's force had been holding out on the 49th's left. At dawn a German infantry advance on the trench held by the 52nd and Canadians was stopped and then dispersed with help from the 49th, but at about 3:30 pm a heavy and accurate artillery barrage fell on the left 140 metres of the position. The troops in that section of the trench were almost annihilated by the fire, and Maxwell was forced to abandon it, pulling back to his right and setting up a new barricade. Among the casualties were the Canadian OC, Captain Lovett, and the 52nd's Sergeant Allan Black, both seriously wounded. Black had ably assisted Maxwell throughout the action, and now refused to be evacuated as long as he was capable of at least advising the troops. Maxwell himself, with five Australian and Canadian troops, manned the post at the new barricade. The expected infantry attack did not come, but 'the enemy artillery ... quickly located the new barrier, and a howitzer battery began to feel for it, the four shells falling every three minutes close about the barrier ...'[45] Eventually one shell burst on target; somehow Maxwell was unhurt, but the rest of his small group were killed or wounded. By this time the combined Australian-Canadian force had been reduced to only 40 fit men. Fortunately there were no further infantry attacks in that part of the field, and artillery was called in to lay down a protective barrage in front of the line. German shelling continued through the night, however. So weary were the men that some of them slept under the bombardment,[46] but Lieutenant Maxwell grimly stayed awake all night—as he had been for over 48 hours since the attack had jumped off—guarding the flank. At 1:30 am on 5 September a company of the 16th Canadian Battalion came up to relieve the remaining troops of the 52nd, and the exhausted men with their fine young officer made their way back to the old front line. The 52nd Battalion may have failed elsewhere on the battlefield but Maxwell's group had maintained their unit's honour.

Meantime the 49th Battalion and its Canadian reinforcements were holding on to the right of the captured position. Three counter attacks had been repulsed during the day and the German infantry next tried a night attack with grenades at about 10 pm. This was detected, and broken up with heavy fire from rifles and Lewis guns, the Australians firing Very-light flares to illuminate the scene. A further attempt at about midnight was driven off as well. Relief was at last on the way for the weary Queenslanders and by 7 am on 5 September the captured position had been handed over to the remaining companies of the 16th Canadians. Three hours later the 49th Battalion troops began arriving at the Brickfields billets near Albert, the last element of the 4th Division to come out of the front line. The unit had been the object of some head-shaking in the 13th Brigade over what had been seen as a large share of decorations for minimal fighting in its first 'tour' at Mouquet Farm. This time there were again plenty of medals recommended by Lieutenant Colonel Lorenzo, but the achievements of the unit could not be questioned. The 49th had captured an objective, or at least a major portion of it, that had defied several previous attempts by units of its own Division and the 1st Division, and then held it for two days and nights against heavy counter attacks and shelling. The soldiers had used both shovels and weapons effectively, following plans that perhaps been over-complicated but had in the main succeeded. Among the decorations awarded to the unit were the DSO for Captain Fortescue, the DCM for RSM Hannah and the MC for the adjutant, Captain Swain. Colonel Lorenzo gave particular credit to the Lewis gunners for holding off the counter attacks, and a number of NCOs and men received MMs, while the

Lewis gun officer, Lieutenant Thomas Steele, was awarded the MC. The 49th's success owed much to the outstanding effort in support of its left flank by Lieutenant Duncan Maxwell's party of the 52nd Battalion, and that officer received the MC, perhaps the least reward that could have been given for his tireless gallantry and leadership. The same decoration was awarded to his brother Arthur, the unit intelligence officer, and others in the 52nd included the DCM for Sergeant Black. The Brigade intelligence officer, Lieutenant Tennyson Clark,[47] had also spent the night in No Man's Land leading up reinforcements under fire, and he was another officer to be awarded the MC.

By the time the 49th Battalion came out of the front line, Major General Cox had already (at noon on 4 September) handed over command of the sector to the GOC of the 1st Canadian Division, Major General Arthur Currie, future GOC Canadian Corps. HQ 4th Division moved back from Tara Hill to Rubempré, where part of the 4th Brigade was already billeted. The remaining units of the 4th Division moved to the rear areas over the next few days, finishing with the 13th Brigade Group's move from the Brickfields to Warloy on 6 September. The Division's second tour of the Mouquet Farm sector had been about the same length of time as the first but its casualty total had been somewhat lower, at 2,487 (as reported by the divisional Admin staff; there were another 375 casualties in attached units, including 283 in the 1st Canadian Brigade[48]) compared to 4,761. Most units being below strength to begin with, the proportion of casualties to effective strength would be closer to that incurred in the first tour, however. Of the total casualties, 788 were recorded as killed or missing, compared to 1,073 in the first tour. The 'missing' figure reported at the time was extraordinarily high at 539, and the majority of these were from the 13th Brigade, indicative of the ferocity of the fighting in the final attack. The 51st Battalion in particular could not be more exact about the fate of its two cut-off companies which had disappeared in the wilderness beyond the Farm. That unit had now been badly cut up in both periods of fighting in the sector, and the morale of the survivors was seriously affected—including that of the CO, Lieutenant Colonel Ross, as would become apparent later. The 49th and 52nd Battalions had suffered heavily also, the latter unit's losses being the highest in the Division. Altogether the 13th Brigade had incurred 1,358 casualties.

Casualties in the 4th Brigade totalled 754, while the 12th Brigade, which had suffered the most in the first tour, lost 266. Since the 12th Brigade had been restricted to line-holding, the latter figure suggests that the German artillery bombardments were not as heavy as in the first tour, and that the new practice of holding the front line with a thin garrison had kept casualties down. Again the vast majority of the losses were with the infantry. The next heaviest were suffered by the divisional engineers, with a total of 52. The Pioneer Battalion had not been as much under fire as in the first tour, and its losses, at 28, were consequently much lighter than before. Of the other units, the 13th Field Ambulance had lost fourteen stretcher bearers 'missing' who, together with five regimental bearers from the 48th Battalion, had strayed into the German lines and been captured.[49] The price had again been high, particularly when the only positive result was the capture of 300 metres or so of battered trench. Nevertheless, the Germans did consider the Fabeck Graben to be a position of considerable importance and soon made a strenuous effort to recover it. A formal counter attack on 8 September, preceded by a two-day bombardment, recaptured the position from its Canadian garrison.[50] Several more unsuccessful narrow-front attacks on Mouquet Farm were made by the Canadians before this method was finally abandoned by Reserve Army. On 26 September a well-prepared advance by four divisions on a broad front, as should have been done in the first place, finally captured Thiepval, overrunning the Farm in the process.[51] Altogether, the divisions of I Anzac Corps had suffered about 23,000 casualties in the operations at Pozières and Mouquet Farm. For those who had survived the experience, it had been a painful step in the slow and bloody learning process for all ranks in the British and Empire armies. That process would eventually bring victory, but such a conclusion seemed a long way off in September 1916.

6 Notes

1. 13th Battalion War Diary, 15 August 1916.
2. 4th Division Admin Staff War Diary for August 1916, Appendix 4. The *Official History* (Vol III, p.770) gives a total of 4649, perhaps using slightly different dates.
3. Edgar, *Op Cit*, p. 58.
4. White, *Op Cit*, p. 70.
5. It is probably the latter report that Bean had in mind when mentioning Colonel Ross's views (*Official History*, Vol III, p. 773 and 773n) rather than the brief signal that he had sent during the battle.
6. 51st Battalion War Diary for August 1916, Appendix 2.
7. *Ibid*, Appendix 3.
8. *Ibid*, Appendix 2.
9. *Official History*, Vol III, p.773.
10. 4th Division General Staff War Diary for August 1916, Appendix 43.
11. 12th Brigade War Diary for August 1916, Appendix 21A. The distribution list for this memo did not include the 12th Field Company or the CRE.
12. Quoted in Freeman, *Op Cit*, p.73.
13. *Ibid*. Captain Gore had the presentation occurring on the way back from the first period of fighting, within a day or two of the brigade's relief. It is highly unlikely, however, that any decorations would have been confirmed in such a short time. The 13th Brigade War Diary says that General Birdwood made the presentations at Albert on 29 August, and the 50th Battalion War Diary also gives that date.
14. Rule, *Op Cit*, p. 41.
15. For Potts' biography, see Bill Edgar, *Warrior of Kokoda* (1999).
16. *Official History*, Vol III, p. 827. Unit records give slightly different figures.

17 E J Rule's account of this fighting is the most informative (*Op Cit,* pp. 39–44), and was quoted extensively in the *Official History*. The relevant entries in Bean's notebooks (AWM38, 3DRL606/135/1) and diaries (AWM38, 3DRL606/56/1) are of interest; the latter reference contains a severe preliminary judgement on the operation. The 14th Battalion War Diary entry was obviously written to put the best possible face on events. The Battalion's written orders have not come to light; a copy was apparently appended to the brigade diary, but the August appendices are missing from that document.

18 I Anzac General Staff War Diary for August 1916 Part 2, Appendix 3 (Order No. 39).

19 *Ibid.*

20 *Official History*, Vol III p. 828.

21 White, *Op Cit*, p. 72.

22 16th Battalion War Diary for August 1916, Appendix 5.

23 White, *Op Cit*, p.74.

24 *Ibid.*

25 These figures are from the battalion War Diaries and are slightly different from those given in the *Official History*.

26 16th Battalion War Diary for August 1916, Appendix 5.

27 *Ibid.*

28 4th Division General Staff War Diary for 1 September 1916.

29 Correspondence in Colonel Snowden's service record (National Archives) has the details of this incident.

30 16th Battalion War Diary for August 1916, Appendix 5.

31 4th Division General Staff War Diary for September 1916, Appendix 3.

32 13th Brigade War Diary for September 1916, Appendix 5(a), 'Summary of Operations near Mouquet Farm—period 1st–5th Sept 1916'.

33 Lt Colonel Beevor's service record shows that he received a 'GSW' (gunshot wound) in the thigh. This suggests a sniper, but the colonel was in a trench at the time and it is more likely that he was hit by a shrapnel ball, as mentioned by C E W Bean in his diary (AWM 3DRL606/58/1).

34 49th Battalion War Diary, 1 September 1916, and the officer's service record.

35 52nd Battalion War Diary for September 1916, appendix to 'Report on Attack on Mouquet Farm'.

36 *Ibid*, main report.

37 *Official History*, Vol III, p. 846. In his diary, Bean made some scathing comments on Lt Col Beevor and other officers, and alleges that Brigadier General Glasgow was of the same opinion.

38 Littler was 48 years old and had led an adventurous life before joining the AIF. At Gallipoli, he had been in charge of the beach details, gaining the nickname 'Duke of Anzac'. Littler was something of an eccentric, and went into battle carrying only his swagger-stick. He was a first cousin of the 13th Battalion's Captain Harry Murray.

39 Colonel Ross's report on the operation (51st Battalion War Diary for September 1916, Appendix I) says that the battalion deployed in seven waves in its jumping-off positions. It then says that for the attack formation was six waves, 'each Coy [of the three attacking] of two waves 50 yards apart.' In the attack itself, after the two leading companies came the '3rd Line, C Coy and Battalion Grenadiers who formed the Battalion mopping up party.' Unfortunately there is no clear diagram (there is a sketch in C E W Bean's diary, AWM 3DRL 606/58/1, which is not fully consistent with the written descriptions). It seems most likely that 'B' and 'D' companies

advanced one behind the other, each in two waves, followed by 'C' and the bombers also in two waves, but it is also possible that the two leading companies, although each in two waves, were alongside each other thus forming two extended lines. The third 'line' would then be 'C' and the bombers as mentioned in the battalion report.

40 51st Battalion War Diary for September 1916, Appendix I. The *Official History* (Vol III, p. 851) says there were 30 men. The figure is not easy to make out in the Diary document.
41 Freeman, *Op Cit*, p. 68.
42 *Official History*, Vol III, p. 852.
43 51st Battalion War Diary for September 1916, Appendix I.
44 *Official History*, Vol III, p. 856n, also War Diaries for I Anzac Artillery and 2nd Division Artillery.
45 *Official History*, Vol III, p. 857.
46 *Ibid*.
47 This appears to be the correct spelling, rather than Clarke.
48 4th Division Admin Staff War Diary for September 1916, Appendix C. Casualty figures for individual units were not as comprehensively reported as those for the first Mouquet Farm tour, and the *Official History* is less precise also.
49 N. Browning, *Leane's Battalion*, p. 54.
50 *Official History*, Vol III, p. 860–61.
51 *Ibid*, p. 861n.

7: Holding the Line

The 4th Division made ready for its move to the area of the Ypres Salient – usually the last place to go for a rest from heavy fighting, but it was comparatively quiet at this time when both sides were focussing on the Somme front. The Division's units marched away from the front in stages, by the familiar routes through the Brickfields to Warloy and Vadencourt, then to Rubempré and other villages nearby. Most units were able to pause for a day or two to rest and refit, before the marchers turned north, covering 20 kilometres to concentrate at the Doullens railhead. Here the division boarded 24 trains at three stations, the departures starting in the early morning of 8 September and continuing into the next day. Their destination was the area between Hazebrouck and Poperinghe (Poperinge) in Flanders, straddling the France/Belgium border, about 15 kilometres west of the front line at Ypres.

The 15th Battalion travelled with a new commanding officer, the unit's original CO, Lieutenant Colonel James Cannan, having been promoted to brigadier general and transferred to the 3rd Division in England, under General Monash. The 15th Battalion's second-in-command, Major Terence McSharry, moved straight into the vacancy as of 30 August as acting lieutenant colonel. A small man with a high voice and an energetic manner, McSharry made quite a contrast to his tall, reserved predecessor. The 15th's new CO was a Queenslander born and raised, and had originally been a member of the Light Horse. He had transferred to the 15th Battalion when appointed as permanent adjutant of Quinn's Post on Gallipoli. McSharry proved to be a highly effective CO, popular with the men despite a sharp tongue on occasion; he 'breathed confidence wherever he went ... [and gained] a respect and an obedience of the men to his commands that was amazing.'[1]

The first of the Division's trains began arriving at their detraining stations in Flanders during the morning of 8 September, after a six-hour journey of about 80 kilometres (as the crow flies) from Doullens. The final trains pulled in early the next morning, units marching off to their designated billeting areas as they detrained. Divisional HQ was established at the village of Reninghelst (Reningelst), just on the Belgian side of the border, on 12 September.

A number of hutted camps had been established in the area, many with Canadian names from their previous occupants, and most units were accommodated in these. The 4th Brigade Group occupied huts in seven camps to the south of Reninghelst, and the other brigades spread out over an area 10 kilometres to the west as far as the village of Steenvoorde in France. Here the Division was in a reserve position, rejoining the 1st and 2nd Divisions as part of I Anzac Corps again. The Corps was now under the control of Second Army, which was commanded by the avuncular, cautious General Sir Herbert Plumer.

Wherever possible, infantry units gave their men an opportunity for a few days rest before regular training increased in intensity. The Division GSO1, Lieutenant Colonel Bernard, circularised the brigades on 11 September outlining the facilities and areas available for training and urging units to take advantage of the comparatively quiet period.[2] Battle exercises up to brigade strength were planned, as well as individual specialist training. Particular attention was given to training in Lewis gunnery and hand grenades, getting as many men as possible skilled in the use of those vital weapons. Another priority was 'gas drill'—the use of poison gas was prevalent in the sector, and it was at about this time that all ranks were issued with the new Box Respirator gas mask, a considerable improvement over earlier devices. Heavy casualties among the officers at Mouquet Farm meant that there were many subalterns newly commissioned from the ranks, and schools were organised at brigade level to provide practical training in handling troops in tactical situations. There was a great need for training of reinforcements as well—all units were under strength, and reinforcements came in steadily, both new troops and those returning from hospital. The Division reported a total of 38 officers and 1,732 other ranks arriving during September.[3] Although this was well under the number needed to replace losses, more gradually came in and units began to build up their numerical strength.

The 4th Division was due to take over a sector of the front line on the night 16/17 September and the 4th Brigade, out of the line for the longest, would go in first. At the same time the divisional artillery was finally reunited with the main body. It will be recalled that when the Division had moved to the Somme front in July, the artillery had been detached to remain in the north, where it had taken part in the Battle of Fromelles. Following that grim night the artillery brigades spent a short period attached to other formations then on 7 August moved to the training range near St Omer for a fortnight of intensive training. This involved not only shooting practice, but also numerous exercises in the movement and positioning of batteries, the ammunition supply system and laying telephone cable networks. On the Western Front, divisional or field artillery batteries' gun lines were usually positioned from 2,400 to 3,200 metres behind the front line trenches, depending on the width of No Man's Land and hence the range to the enemy front line (the 'Heavies' were further to the rear). Each battery had its observation post (OP) established closer to the front line in a suitable concealed location. The batteries had their immediate ammunition supply of 24 rounds per gun (12 per howitzer) carried in the gun limbers on the move, with an additional 76 rounds (48 for howitzers)

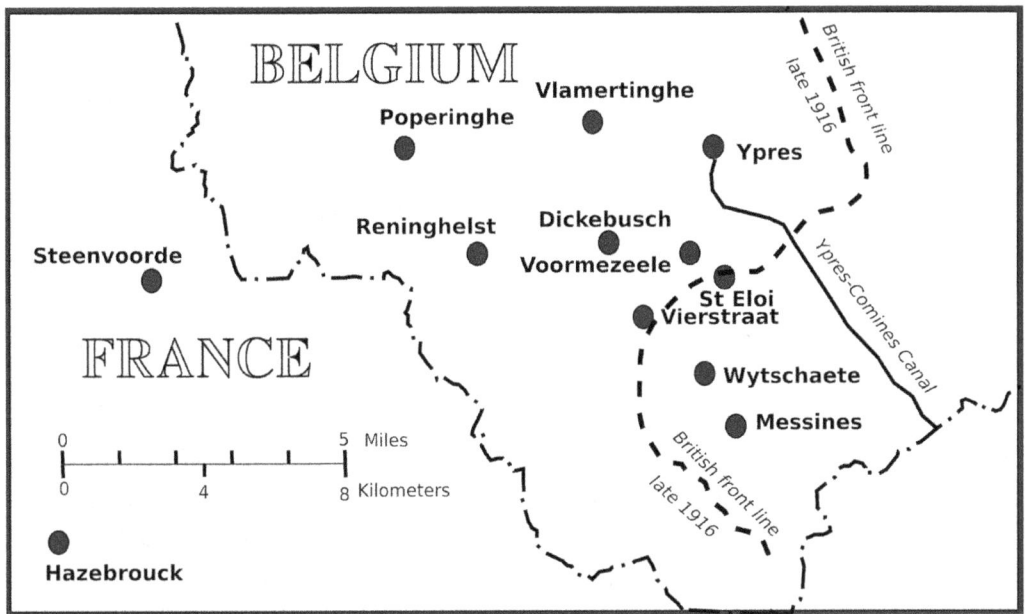

Ypres sector, 1916.

in a wagon and limber accompanying each section of two guns. Further supplies were held about four kilometres back in the wagon lines, and from there ammunition would be brought forward to the guns, once emplaced, in the batteries' horse-drawn vehicles as required. Large stocks were built up at each gun position for planned bombardments in major operations.[4] The wagon lines were re-stocked from the Divisional Ammunition Column's dumps, further still to the rear. Telephone lines linked the various sub-units in the gun and wagon lines, as well as running to brigade and divisional HQs and the DAC, and forward to the OPs, with signallers keeping the vital wires in operation.

On completion of the training programme the 4th Division artillery came under the orders of the Canadian Corps and prepared to return to the front line. The guns were in position in the area forward of Reninghelst on the night of 26/27 August, responsible for covering, coincidentally, the 4th Canadian Division in the St Eloi sector of the front line. The divisional artillery HQ was located at Reninghelst and the DAC HQ at Vlamertinghe (Vlamertinge), just west of Ypres itself. Lieutenant Colonel Hugh Vernon, commanding the DAC, noted that the main ammunition dump was 'about 7,800 yards [7,100 metres] from either side of the Ypres salient'[5]—that is within reach of long-range enemy guns. In the flat countryside, the dump could be observed from German positions on the ridge at Wytschaete (Wijtschate) to the south-east, and a hessian screen had been erected to block the view—this was sometimes blown down in rainstorms and had to be hurriedly repaired. The 10th, 11th and 24th AFA Brigades were allocated to the St Eloi sector, while the 12th Brigade was temporarily attached to the 4th (British) Division, in another coincidence of numbering, north of the Ypres-Comines canal. Routine artillery work was commenced straight away, the guns bombarding selected targets in the German lines and harassing the enemy's working parties.

These tasks continued through September, excepting the night of 16/17 when the artillery provided support for three raids carried out by the 4th Canadian Division infantry, firing over 3,000 18-pounder and 600 howitzer rounds. Two of the raids were assessed as successful. In the meantime, the MTM and HTM personnel arrived from the Somme where they had been attached to the Lahore artillery. The 12th AFA Brigade also rejoined from the neighbouring sector. On 17/18 September the 4th Australian Infantry Brigade came into the front line and that morning the 'GOC 4th Australian Division assumed command and the 4th Australian Divisional Artillery rejoined their own division from which they have been absent since July 12th.'[6]

The 4th Brigade, relieving the 11th Canadian Brigade, sent the 13th, 15th, and 16th Battalions into the front line trenches with the 14th Battalion in reserve. The Brigade MG company and LTM battery similarly took over the positions of their Canadian equivalents. So quiet was the sector at this time that although the various reliefs took place partly during daylight no casualties were suffered in the process. The units of the 12th Brigade moved up to the area vacated by the 4th to form the divisional reserve for the time being, with the 13th Brigade staying around Steenvoorde as the Corps reserve. The 4th Division's left or northern boundary was on the Ypres-Comines canal, on the right of the 1st Division which was deployed north of the canal. On 20 September the 12th Brigade moved up to take over the front line to the south-west of the Diependaal Beek (stream), on the 4th Brigade's right. The 12th Brigade put its 46th and 47th Battalions into the front line first, with the 45th in support and the 48th in reserve. This deployment extended the 4th Division's front a further 2,000 metres south-west, to the line of the Vierstraat-Wytschaete road; the Division now held a total frontage of 4,400 metres.[7] The new part of the sector was covered by an artillery group from the 3rd Canadian Division until the end of the month, when the 4th Division artillery was redeployed to cover the whole of the Division's sector. The guns were organised into two groups: Right, with five 18-pounder batteries, one howitzer battery and one MTM battery, covering the 12th Infantry Brigade, and Left, covering the 4th Brigade, with seven batteries of 18-pounders, two of howitzers and two MTM batteries. Three Belgian field gun batteries were also attached to the Left group.[8] All divisions of I Anzac were now in the line, with the 1st and 2nd Divisions to the left of the 4th. Further south near Armentières, the 5th Division, barely recovered from Fromelles, was back in the line as part of II Anzac.

The 4th Division now began a period of routine line-holding typical of the periods between major battles on the Western Front. The infantry battalions held their firing line trenches with light forces, mainly Lewis gunners, with the majority of the troops in the support and reserve trenches. Movement was limited during the day but at night patrols went out into No Man's Land to reconnoitre, and 'listening posts' were manned. Apart from the capture of two Germans by the 15th Battalion on the night of 20 September, the 4th Brigade units' patrols found that they had No Man's Land to themselves. The Germans relied mainly on flares and machine gun fire to interfere with the Australian patrols, while intermittently bombarding the front trenches with mortars. The German *minenwerfer* fired a large slow-moving shell (called a 'rum-jar' by BEF troops; the weapon was known as a 'Minnie') that could be seen in flight as it fell, a nerve-wracking experience for those in the target area. A direct hit on a trench by a rum-jar could be devastating, but the German artillery fire was light and comparatively ineffective. The 4th Division's artillery, mortars and machine guns carried out regular harassment of the enemy lines, firing on a variety of targets. The artillery mainly concentrated on trenches and suspected machine gun posts and strong points. As well as shooting at similar targets, the medium mortars also attempted to cut sections of the German barbed wire,[9] while the machine guns fired thousands of rounds each night into enemy communication trenches and transport routes. Mortar batteries were also instructed to retaliate for any rum-jars fired by the Germans, and the infantry LTM batteries at times engaged in duels with their opposite numbers on the other side of No Man's Land. The snipers of both sides presented a constant danger to an enemy raising his head above the parapet.

A program of field engineering works was instituted to improve the trenches, communications and transport routes in the sector. Parts of the front line were assessed as in poor condition and badly drained, a situation exacerbated by periods of heavy rain. The infantry units manning the front line worked on maintaining and improving the trenches that they occupied, with the reserve battalions supplying large working parties to the engineer field companies for works in the reserve lines. The Pioneer Battalion divided its resources between maintaining and extending the 'Decauville'—the light railway or tramway forming part of the supply route to the front—and working on drainage systems for the trenches. All efforts at improving drainage could not prevent the trenches from often being up to knee-deep in water, increasing the risk of the men developing 'trench foot'. An issue of rubber thigh-boots helped somewhat, but the troops were urged to make every effort to prevent the condition. In the 4th Brigade, Major John Peck, brigade major, included in the Brigade Standing Orders the comment that 'It should be a point of honour and pride for a Platoon Commander to be able to say no member of his Platoon developed "Trench feet" during the Brigade's tour of duty in the front line.'[10] Officers were required to ensure that their men changed their socks frequently, dried their feet and rubbed them with whale oil, and kept up circulation with exercise. When the troops were occupying a flooded front-line trench this was, of course, easier said than done. It is questionable how effective the whale-oil treatment actually was—George Mitchell (48th Battalion) maintained that a massive application of the waterproofing compound Dubbin to the boots was far better at keeping one's feet dry.[11]

Towards the end of September and into October the infantry units undertook several aggressive operations to probe the German lines, in the hope also of providing some diversion from renewed offensives on the Somme front. Some of these operations were similar to the big trench raids mounted earlier in the year, with large parties and heavy artillery preparation, but in other instances a different method was also tried. The raids of July had involved parties numbering eighty or more but the new approach was to use small groups of one officer and 10 to 15 NCOs and men. Instead of the preliminary bombardment the raiders would now make a stealthy approach to their objective without the artillery firing, hoping to catch the enemy by surprise. Once they were within grenade range the infantry leader would call in the guns to lay down a curtain of fire to isolate the section of trench being attacked. Ideally, communication with the guns would be by field telephone, signallers unreeling wires behind them as the raiding party crept forward. As the shells crashed down the raiders would fling their grenades and rush the enemy trench with the aim of inflicting casualties and taking prisoners in a few minutes of sharp fighting. The raiders would then head back across No Man's Land, dragging the prisoners with them, after signalling the artillery to shift target to cover the withdrawal. Particular objectives would be selected from sections of the enemy line where the wire was believed to have already been cut by routine artillery and mortar fire. Brigade and battalion orders tended to avoid the term 'raid' and referred to 'strong patrols' and 'minor enterprises'. Although the theory appeared reasonable, the troops soon found that things were not so straightforward in practice.

The first of these 'minor enterprises' was undertaken by the 16th Battalion on the night of 25/26 September. The party (one officer, two NCOs and 10 men) reached the enemy line undetected and called in the artillery. The telephone wires had failed so a runner was sent back to pass the message and the party waited until the first gun fired before beginning their attack. They found that the supposed gap in the wire had been partly repaired and still presented too much of an obstacle to penetrate the German line. The raiders contented themselves with tossing grenades at the trench before withdrawing under cover of artillery fire. The troops got to back to their lines, the only casualty being one man slightly wounded. The battalion reported that the enemy 'trenches seem to be more strongly garrisoned at night than was previously thought,' and noted that the 'Artillery co-operation was good, and the shooting excellent.'[12] This, incidentally, was the first time that a 4th Division infantry operation had been given fire support by the artillery of its own Division.

On the following night, 26/27 September, the 15th Battalion sent a 'strong patrol,' again an officer and 12 others, against another section of the enemy line. This group was also foiled by enemy barbed wire, in this case a previously undetected entanglement behind the damaged first line of wire. The patrol returned to its own lines without loss after an hour in No Man's Land. It is notable that the officers in charge of both of these operations were not prepared to risk unnecessary casualties in their small squads by trying to force a way through obstacles under close-range fire from an alerted enemy. The next night saw the 13th Battalion launching another of these enterprises, with a group of one officer and 13 others. The battalion scouts had reconnoitred the German lines in their sector over several previous nights, and a section of trench near the landmark called Piccadilly Farm was selected for the raid. The raiding party leader was a highly respected officer, Lieutenant Frank Fitzpatrick, who had gone with the scouts on each night and was thoroughly familiar with the terrain. It was planned that the raiders would creep almost to the enemy parapet before calling in the artillery by field telephone, when the guns would lay down a box barrage around the section of trench while the infantry made their rush. Despite the careful preparations the raid went disastrously wrong on the night. Lieutenant Fitzpatrick somehow lost his way in No Man's Land and led the party too far to the left, into the target line for the barrage on that flank. When he gave the signal for the guns to open, the shells fell all too accurately onto the raiders. Fitzpatrick himself paid the ultimate price for his error, and a wounded corporal was taken prisoner by the Germans. The rest of the troops regained the own lines with three wounded and nothing to show for their endeavours.

The Division's next operation against the enemy lines was mounted by the 12th Brigade. The Brigade reverted to earlier tactics, organising an old-style large raiding party preceded by an artillery barrage. The 46th Battalion was selected to mount the operation, using a team of four officers and 66 men divided into several sub-groups to carry out various tasks. The plan allowed for a maximum of 15 minutes in the enemy trench. Artillery support consisted of seven 18-pounder batteries, two howitzer batteries and four MTMs, as well as six Stokes mortars of the brigade LTM battery. The 12th MG Company was also tasked with laying down fire into the German rear areas. At the same time as the large operation, a small party from the 47th Battalion would attempt a 'silent' raid on another part of the line, following the methods tried by the 4th Brigade over recent nights. The raids took place on the night of 30 September/1 October, the 46th Battalion's party passing through the 48th, holding the front line, to take up its assembly position. The artillery barrage started at 10 pm, falling on the enemy trenches for five minutes before lifting and forming a box around the objective. The infantry assault force rushed the trench as the barrage lifted and succeeded in entering it against sporadic resistance. After a brief occupation of the enemy position the raiders returned across No Man's Land with a wounded prisoner. The troops were back in their own lines about 40 minutes after the lifting of the barrage, having lost one of their number killed, with three others wounded.

Retaliation by the German artillery was not particularly heavy, but one shell burst in the Australian front line trench amid some of the returned raiders of the 46th and the garrison of the 48th, killing seven and wounding three. Added to the casualties in the raid itself, these losses would seem to be a heavy price to pay for capturing one prisoner and some documents, but the raid was officially regarded as a success and reported as such. The 47th Battalion's small group of 'silent' raiders had reached their objective undetected, but finding the enemy wire mostly intact had prudently abandoned the enterprise. These operations had achieved little, and neither had those carried out by the other divisions of I and II Anzac Corps during the same period.[13] The routine patrolling that went on most nights had maintained superiority in No Man's Land and brought in occasional prisoners at less cost than the formal raids. The enthusiasm of the higher command for raiding was unaffected, however. The Germans tried a raid of their own on the 4th Brigade's lines on the night of 4 October. At 5 pm German artillery and mortars began a heavy bombardment of a sector of the 16th Battalion's front line. Most of the garrison was quickly withdrawn to the flanks and rear, minimising casualties, but the trench was badly damaged. After 90 minutes of shelling, two parties of German infantry, each estimated at 50 in number, advanced across No Man's Land. One group only reached about half-way before it was stopped and driven back by the 16th's Lewis gunners. The second reached the Australian parapet, but was finally repulsed in its turn. This fight and the preliminary bombardment cost the battalion seven killed[14] and eight wounded. The enemy casualties could not be ascertained and it was theorised that the Germans had carried all of their dead and wounded back to their own lines. This action was the most serious involving the 4th Division units during that period in the front line. The damage caused to the trenches meant several days' hard labour for the troops in making repairs before the 4th Brigade was relieved by the 13th Brigade on 7 October.

The 13th Brigade's 52nd and 49th Battalions took over from the 13th and 16th Battalions in the front line during that evening, with the 51st Battalion replacing the 15th the next day to complete the front line deployment—a movement in daylight which again saw no casualties. The brigade relief was completed by the 50th Battalion taking over from the 14th as the reserve unit, the 50th having just rejoined its brigade after detachment to the training area near St Omer during the previous few weeks. The mortar and machine gun units also changed over as usual, and the 4th Brigade Group marched back to the divisional reserve billets in the Reninghelst area. At the same time, there was a change in the 13th Brigade's HQ personnel, Captain Roy Morell transferring in from the 13th MG Company to replace Captain Alan Steele as staff captain; the latter officer was posted to the 52nd Battalion. Lieutenant (soon Captain) Charles Duchatel took over command of the MG Company. The 13th Brigade now began to prepare for a 'minor enterprise' of its own, to be launched on the night of 12 October. The 49th Battalion was selected to carry out the raid, which would employ a substantial party of three officers and 34 others with strong artillery support.

Despite careful planning and preliminary training the raid miscarried on the night. Originally it had been intended that the infantry commander would call in the barrage by field telephone once his party was fully deployed in position and ready to advance. Higher authority had then ordered, however, that the operation had to commence at a fixed time, 6:30 pm, as it was one of sixteen raids being mounted in Second Army's sector and it was intended that all should begin simultaneously. The 49th Battalion group had to wait until dark to leave the trenches and make its way to the selected assembly position in No Man's Land, and was further delayed by an inconvenient burst of flare-shooting by the Germans. As a result only nine of the raiding party had been able to get into position by 6:30 when the artillery opened fire. By the time the group would have been ready to advance, the advantage of surprise would have been lost, and the raid commander called off the operation. The barrage itself had been 'excellent' and the battalion reported its disappointment at not being able to take advantage of it because of the loss of flexibility in the plan. German artillery retaliation killed two men and wounded three others in the 49th Battalion's lines. The 4th Division's final raid of this period was mounted by the 12th Brigade on the night of 15/16 October. The 45th Battalion sent a forty-man party with strong artillery support against a German trench at Bois Quarante, a small salient where the enemy line was within 100 metres of the Battalion's front. The raiders entered the trench successfully behind accurate shooting by the divisional artillery but the 50-metre stretch that they occupied was found to be empty of enemies. Although the raiding during this period had produced minimal results, the 12th Brigade commander, Brigadier General Glasfurd, saw a positive in the development of infantry/artillery cooperation. Despite restrictions on ammunition supplies, the divisional artillery's supporting barrages had generally been accurate and timely; 'even if no other result had been obtained, the confidence of all [infantry] ranks in our artillery support would have ... repaid us for making the raid.'[15] The brigadier also noted how closely the raid commanders and artillery FOOs had worked together. It was another small step in the slow learning process.

It had originally been expected that the divisions of I Anzac would remain at Ypres for several months, but as early as 9 October GHQ had issued orders to prepare for moving back to the Somme. The 1st Division was pulled out of the line on 12/13 October and moved back to the St Omer area. The sector of the line where the 1st had been was temporarily filled by the 2nd Division extending to its right and the 4th extending to its left. The 4th Brigade Group returned to the front line after a week in reserve and relieved the 1st Brigade in what was known as the Bluff sector. The 4th Division now had all three of its brigades in the line for a brief period. On 19 October the 4th Brigade was again relieved, this time by British units, and marched back to reserve positions as the 4th Division prepared to follow the 1st and 2nd back to the Somme. The 12th Brigade was relieved, also by British units, on 22 October, as was the 13th Brigade the next day. Before that, however, 13th Brigade units had been involved in a burst of heavy fighting. The Germans, although relatively quiescent in day-to-day operations, had been working underground, steadily mining towards the British lines. One tunnel had reached the front line trench just to the left of the 52nd Battalion's position, and the charge in it was blown early on the morning of 22 October. The explosion wiped out the British garrison at that point (where the 14th Battalion had been relieved only the previous night) and a German infantry force rushed to occupy the crater. The 52nd turned several of its Lewis guns onto the area, firing across the canal to support British counter-attacks. The 13th MG Company also got involved. Lieutenant Duchatel set four of his Vickers guns to interfere with the enemy's communications and supports, the machine gunners getting off 20,000 rounds at those targets. British infantry eventually drove off the German force and the line was restored.

At this time the AIF was voting on the first Australian conscription referendum, and having ceased fire the personnel of the 13th MG Company then registered their votes,[16] as all units had been doing over the last few days. The overall AIF vote was narrowly in favour of conscription, the referendum being lost through civilian votes, but the underlying attitude of the AIF was the subject of some comment and theorising. In the vehement opinion of the 14th

Battalion historian, Newton Wanliss,

> the fighting members of the AIF (except the officers) voted overwhelmingly 'No'... the Australian troops had many grievances ... somewhat vaguely attributed by them to the 'Heads' ... and as they knew the 'Heads' wanted an affirmative vote they voted in the negative. There was a large 'Yes' vote in the AIF but it came from the non-fighting sections of that organisation ... These men had safe, remunerative and comfortable billets ... They feared that the dwindling of reinforcements would result in them being sent to the front, and voted 'Yes' accordingly, to obviate the danger of such an unpleasant contingency.[17]

C E W Bean felt that the main motive for negative votes by front-line men was a reluctance to force others to face the horrors of war.[18]

By 26 October most of the 4th Division units had moved from their billeting areas to designated railway stations to entrain for the south. The exceptions were the divisional artillery, which was to stay in the line at Ypres for the time being (covering the British 41st Division), and part of the divisional transport. The artillery carried out mostly routine tasks for the next three weeks, particularly night shelling of enemy transport routes. There were also two special operations. On the afternoon of 4 November, the 4th Division artillery combined with that of two British divisions to deliver a hurricane one-hour bombardment on the German front line. The Division's MTMs joined in with the guns, firing 712 rounds in the hour. On 10 November the MTMs improved on that performance when they bombarded the enemy front line on their own, twelve mortars putting 798 bombs into the target in an hour; one mortar crew got off 125 rounds.[19] On the night of 12/13 November elements of the 41st British Division artillery arrived to take over the gun lines. The relief was completed by the following night and the 4th Division artillery prepared to follow the rest of its Division to the Somme.

Over the period 16 September to 23 October, the 4th Division had suffered a total of 288 casualties,[20] of whom 86 had been killed (plus two missing)—an average of less than eight casualties per day, low enough to fall into the euphemistic category of 'wastage.' This meant a comparatively easy time for the medical units; 'the line ... was very quiet and consequently all hands had a fair amount of spare time' wrote a member of the 4th Field Ambulance.[21] That unit had recently lost its original commanding officer, Lieutenant Colonel Alexander Meikle, who had fallen seriously ill with emphysema and been hospitalised in England. Major Roy McGregor took over the command temporarily, before Lieutenant Colonel Harold Follit arrived as the permanent CO in November, by which time the Division was back on the Somme. The 12th Field Ambulance also had a change of CO in November, when Lieutenant Colonel Thomas Ross was posted to the 2nd Australian General Hospital. His replacement was Lieutenant Colonel John Newell who was transferred from the 8th Field Ambulance (5th Division); Colonel Newell himself was reassigned the following February, when Major Basil Kennedy took over the command.

The trains carrying the main body of the Division began arriving at stations in the Fourth

Army back area in the Somme sector during the early morning of 27 October. Divisional HQ was established in the village of Ailly-le-Haut-Clocher, about 30 kilometres north-west of Amiens, with the divisional units spread out in billets around nearby villages, from Pont-Remy on the Somme itself north to Oneux. A new member of the HQ Staff at this time was Major Henry Wynter, a permanent Australian officer who joined from the 3rd Division as DAA&QMG, replacing Major Hubert Ford who had been acting in that posting for the past four months. Major Wynter, a Queenslander, would go on to a distinguished military career in various mainly staff appointments, reaching the rank of Lieutenant General in World War II. Another change took place at Division HQ during the following month, when the GSO3, Major Dickinson, was posted to the 5th Division. Captain Arthur Keighley came in from the 13th MG Company as GSO3.

The 4th Division in its new area continued as part of I Anzac Corps with the 1st and 2nd Divisions, as well as the 5th Division, now also under I Anzac, which therefore now controlled four divisions. I Anzac in turn was now part of Fourth Army, commanded by General Sir Henry Rawlinson. The Somme battle was in its final stages at this time. Since early September when I Anzac had left the area, the British line had advanced painfully to capture the third line of German defences, including the villages of Thiepval, Gueudecourt and Flers. Fourth Army occupied a sector running roughly north-west to south-east facing the enemy-occupied town of Bapaume. The advance over previous weeks had taken the British line into a shallow valley between two low ridges so it was in the undesirable position of occupying low ground with winter coming on, and with the enemy having the advantage of observation. During the weeks preceding I Anzac's arrival, efforts to improve the army's position for the winter had seen several attacks mounted on the new German line on the ridge in front of Bapaume, all of which had failed with heavy losses.

The Fourth Army's advance had taken it on to ground that had been devastated by artillery bombardments and was being turned into a quagmire by the heavy rains that arrived during October.

> The continuous pressing of the attack had made it impossible to devote adequate labour or even thought to precautions against rainy conditions, and consequently, when the weather broke, the Fourth Army had found itself with seven miles of unorganised crater-field behind its front-line troops. This area had been churned by the advancing battle into wild moorland, bare of dwellings, trees, or hedges, flayed in most parts even of grass, and its drainage almost everywhere blocked by innumerable craters ... [even] a light rain converted the trenches to mere muddy ditches, and rendered the cross-country tracks distressingly heavy for men and horses and impassable by wheeled traffic.[22]

On the map the forward zone included numerous small villages, but these were mostly reduced to piles of rubble. Carriage of food and ammunition supplies forward to the front line and of wounded to the rear was an extreme challenge in these conditions. It was virtually impossible for the front line troops to receive hot food and they had to make do with cold emergency rations - bully beef and biscuits. Getting artillery ammunition forward was a slow and difficult process by pack-horse or mule to guns occupying unstable positions in the mud. There was no spare transport capacity to bring up the engineering stores that might have improved the situation. Relieving troops would arrive in the front line utterly exhausted after dragging themselves for hours through the glutinous mud. Any attack across No Man's Land would be slowed down and disorganised by the mud, making the troops easy targets for the defenders' fire.

Such were the conditions in which I Anzac took over a sector of Fourth Army's line from XV Corps on 30 October. The normal deployment of a four-division corps on this front consisted of two divisions in the front line or fighting zone, another in what was called the 'R' (reserve and approach) area and the remaining division in the 'T' (training and rest) area, with frequent rotations between the divisions. The 4th Division, having been last to leave Ypres, was fortunate that its first position in the rotation was in the 'T' area. The 1st and 2nd Divisions were sent into several costly and unsuccessful attacks on German positions through the rain and mud before those operations were finally abandoned. The Somme battle itself ended on 15 November with the capture of Beaumont Hamel by Fifth Army in the northern part of the battle zone. The 4th Division began to move towards the front line over 1 to 3 November, moving into the 'T' area with HQ at Vignacourt. There all units carried on with routine training and tactical exercises, often carried out in soaking rain. Among the most urgent issues for the Division staff was to organise the transport of supplies to the front line. Following the recent experience of the other divisions, a Pack Transport Troop was formed by pooling the pack-mules and their drivers from the infantry units. The Troop came under the Divisional Train and was commanded by Captain Clement Walsh of the 7th Company AASC. Once the Division took over the front line the Pack Transport Troop was responsible for carriage between the railheads and the headquarters of the forward area battalions. The mule convoys carried their loads up nightly in the open through the muddy, torn-up ground under constant enemy shelling. A month later the GOC, Major General Cox, issued a Special Order of the Day congratulating the Division on its endurance in the terrible conditions. So vital was the work of the Pack Transport Troop that the General singled out that unit, and Captain Walsh personally, for special praise.[23] For his leadership under fire, Walsh was recommended for the MC, which was eventually awarded to him in 1917 after further good work, a rare 'fighting' decoration for an AASC member. Sixteen NCOs and drivers, seconded from the infantry battalions and the AASC companies, won MMs for their service with the Troop.

The numerical strength of the Division continued to build up. By now several 4th Brigade infantry battalions were reporting themselves up to full strength again, or nearly so, and units from the other brigades were approaching that point. As well as the arrival of inexperienced new recruits, the return of men recovered from wounds or illness boosted numbers also. During this period units of the 4th Brigade welcomed back several outstanding battlefield leaders wounded during the Pozières/Mouquet Farm fighting: Captain Harry Murray (13th Battalion) in October, Major Percy Black (16th) and Captain John Corrigan (15th) in November and Lieutenant Albert Jacka (14th) in December.

The 12th Brigade was first to go into the front line in the new sector. On 6 November units of the Brigade left their billets around Flesselles village to travel to Dernancourt, near Albert in the 'R' area, being transported for that stage of the journey by the novel means of French motor-busses. Dernancourt was a name that would acquire great significance for the Brigade and the Division in 1918, but for the moment it was just an unimportant village with particularly squalid billeting for the troops. Division HQ moved to Ribemont on 8 November, before moving further up to Pommiers Redoubt, between Mametz and Montauban, a week later. The 12th Brigade units paused at Dernancourt for several days, mostly occupied with continuing training, before marching during 11 November to Fricourt, about 12 kilometres behind the front line at Gueudecourt. Early the next day the units marched by increasingly difficult roads to Bernafay Wood from where the final long slog through the mud to the front line began. The Brigade commander, Brigadier General Duncan Glasfurd, went up ahead of his troops to examine the ground that they would occupy. In the support trench (or muddy ditch) called Cheese Road, a splinter from a bursting enemy HE shell struck him in the abdomen. So difficult were the conditions that it took 10 agonising hours to get the badly-wounded brigadier from the trenches through the ADS at Bernafay Wood to where he could be given adequate treatment, but nothing could be done for him and General Glasfurd died that night in the CCS at Heilly, a further 13 kilometres away.[24] Perhaps he could have been saved had it been possible to attend to him more quickly, as would also have been the case with many other casualties during this period. The 12th Brigade War Diary recorded that 'His loss was a great one to the Brigade. His fine example of courage, unselfishness and steadfast devotion to duty was one that could well be followed by everyone.'[25] General Cox wrote that Glasfurd was 'the best of my brigadiers ... I shall miss him very much indeed.'[26] As a tactician, Glasfurd had displayed a certain lack of flexibility when his Brigade was faced with the shelling at Pozières/Mouquet Farm. Circumstances meant that he had not had an opportunity to handle his units in a major offensive operation, but he never ceased his efforts to instil military professionalism into his officers and men. Lieutenant Colonel Sydney Herring, CO of the 45th Battalion, was placed in temporary command of the Brigade.

The 46th and 47th Battalions relieved 1st Division units in the front line during the night of 12 November.

> Companies were led across the open in the dark to their positions, the going was very bad owing to many disused trenches, shell holes and wire ... only two C[ommunication] T[renches] for last 2000 yards [1830 metres] and these were impassable ...[27]

The 12th Brigade occupied the right-hand section of the divisional front with two of its battalions in the firing line trenches in accordance with the standard disposition of units in this part of the line. On the Brigade right, the 46th Battalion took over positions in Grease Trench which ended in the small, awkward salient called Goodwin's Post. The 47th occupied the left segment of the Brigade line, in Biscuit Trench and Petrol Lane (the usual arbitrary

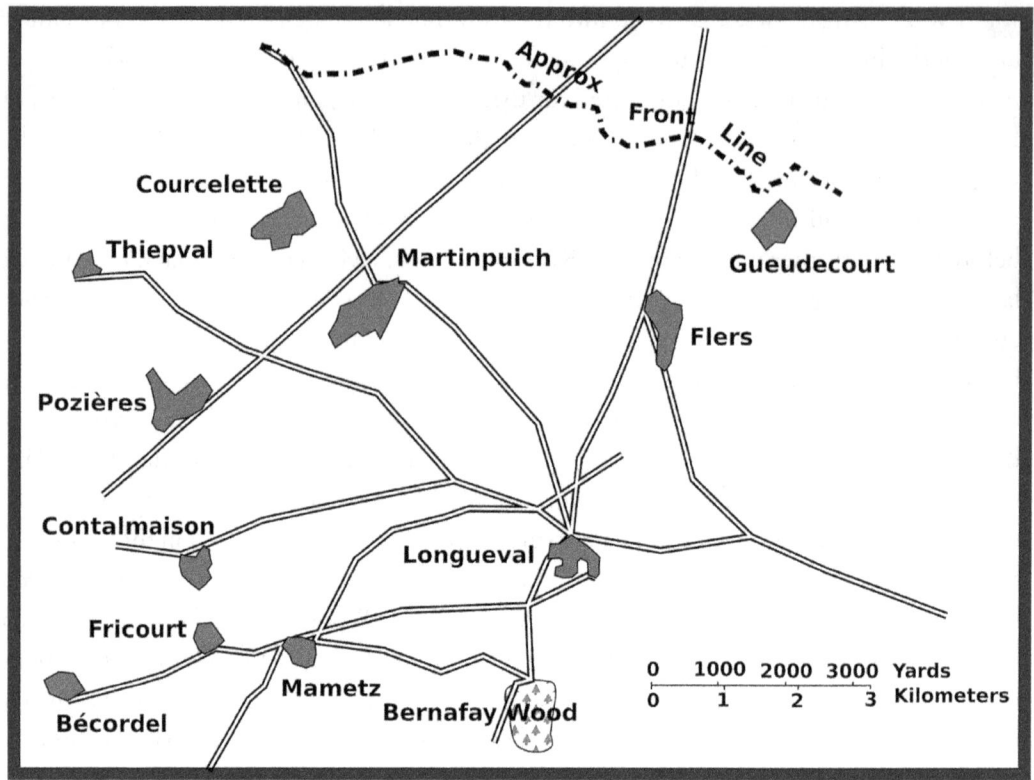

Gueudecourt area.

names were applied to the trenches, often those of ration items in this area). For now the 48th Battalion held the support line in Switch Trench with the 45th held in reserve further back in the Bernafay Wood area; those units rotated into the front line a week later. The 4th Division initially held the right-flank sector of the I Anzac line with the 2nd Division on its left, but the Corps boundaries were changed several days later. The 2nd Division was relieved by British units and the 4th Division thus became the left of I Anzac, with the 5th Division coming back into the line to take up the right flank position. The front line battalions began to incur casualties from regular German shelling. Having lost its brigadier killed in action on 12 November, the 12th Brigade had another senior officer casualty on 14 November, when the 47th Battalion CO, Lieutenant Colonel Thomas Flintoff, was seriously wounded and evacuated.[28] The unit's second in command, Major Eric Lewis, took over the command.

The remainder of the 4th Division's sector of the front was allotted to the 13th Brigade. On 13 November the Brigade took over the left of the divisional front, a narrower sector where one battalion occupied the front line (the 50th initially) with another in support and the remaining two further back in reserve. The 4th Brigade formed the divisional reserve for the time being, billeted around Ribemont village. The rotation scheme would see the 12th Brigade relieved by the 4th after two weeks in the front line, while the 13th Brigade, with only one battalion 'up', carried out its own relief by rotating its battalions between reserve, support

The 'Cheese Road' trench, near Flers, where Brigadier General Duncan Glasfurd was mortally wounded on 12 November 1916. (AWM E00576)

and firing line; the 13th MG Company relieved its front-line Vickers gun sections every few days. Most of the troops from the infantry units in reserve were employed on working parties (as labourers, in other words) assisting the engineers and pioneers as the Corps worked on improving road and rail communications across the wasteland of the former battlefield. The Division CRE, Lieutenant Colonel Gilbert Elliott, divided his resources between front line works and the reserve areas. The 12th and 13th Field Companies were assigned to support the infantry brigades in the front line, working on support trenches, dugouts, drainage and communication trenches. These companies also built duckboard tracks across the mud in the immediate rear of the front line. The 4th Field Company, which had moved up a few days in advance of the main body, was allocated to road-works linking the front and rear areas, concentrating particularly on the Flers-Longueval road, constructing new surfacing and repairing frequent damage caused by the inevitable enemy shelling. The 4th Company also carried out some track-laying on the Decauville light railway or tramway lines linking the broad-gauge railheads in the rear to points closer to the front. The Decauville, however, was mainly the responsibility of the 4th Pioneer Battalion. The Battalion was at first divided between the tramway and working on roads and communication trenches, but by the end of the month the whole unit, with infantry working parties, was concentrating on the maintenance and extension of the Decauville. The Pioneers had some recent experience with tramway work at Ypres, but the task on the Flers/Gueudecourt front was considerably heavier. Lieutenant Colonel Albert Fewtrell, CO of the 4th Pioneers, had wide expertise with railways from civilian life and so was particularly suited to managing that vital task.

Continuing the routines of relief, the 4th Division medical units took over from their 1st Division equivalents. The 4th Field Ambulance relieved the 2nd, based at the ADS near Bernafay Wood on the Longueval road and became responsible for the evacuation of casualties brought in from the front line. The bearer sub-divisions of the 12th and 13th Field

Ambulances were also sent to the ADS to assist those of the 4th. The evacuation route from the front line RAPs to the ADS involved a carry for stretcher bearers of up to five kilometres through the mud to a wagon rendezvous point on the Flers-Longueval road. It was exhausting work which could take six hours or more and usually employed thirty-six bearers per casualty, working in several relays of six or eight to a stretcher.[29] Several relay posts where the bearers could change over were established between the ADS and the front line. Where possible, wooden sledges drawn by two horses were used which reduced the carry time to two hours, but these were in short supply. It was often necessary for infantry units to detail large numbers of men to reinforce the Field Ambulance stretcher-bearers, the reverse of the usual situation. There was a stretch of light railway which could be used for part of this section if the train was available, but hand-carrying was often necessary. Horse-drawn ambulance wagons took the patients from the rendezvous point the next 2,400 metres to the ADS. From the ADS, serious casualties were sent on to the MDS at Bécordel, eight kilometres away. On this front the MDS was controlled by Corps and administered by the 15th Field Ambulance (5th Division) with attached elements from several divisions. At first, patients for the MDS were carried in motor-ambulances, but so bad was the road that the vehicles could take up to seven hours to cover the distance. By the end of the month, however, the broad gauge railway had been extended to Quarry Siding and trains were allocated for transport of casualties to Bécordel.[30] Two sections of the 13th Field Ambulance tent personnel were allocated to the Quarry Siding ambulance post,[31] the remainder joining with the tent sub-divisions of the 12th for duty at the MDS.

For the infantry in the front line, the misery of life in the mud was added to the dangers of enemy action. 'The conditions on the fighting front imposed on the troops the extreme limit of sordid discomfort and suffering in the process of dying for their country.'[32] The trenches were regularly shelled by the Germans and snipers were active. The battalions sent out nightly patrols to slog through the morass of No Man's Land, and despite the conditions these were often successful in bringing in prisoners. The MG companies and LTM batteries continued their routine tasks of harassing the enemy positions, with the infantry's Lewis gunners joining in—on the night of 26/27 November, gunners of the 48th Battalion were credited with helping the artillery to destroy a German working party detected in the open.[33] The troops' main enemies, however, were the weather and the terrain. Even before reaching the front line, conditions were miserable enough. Coming up through the reserve area in late November, the 14th Battalion stopped at the bivouac area grandiosely named Carlton Camp:

> we pulled up on the top of a ridge as bare as a bald head—mud everywhere, nothing else ... this was Carlton Camp, and was to be our home ... we lined up and each was given a sheet of six-foot galvanised iron ... everyone set to dig holes in the ground, to be covered by four sheets of iron ... a driving sleet now commenced ...[34]

It was not so much a case of continuous rain at this time—4th Division war diaries in November report rain on no more than nine days during the month, some of these when the Division did not have units in the front line. There were several bitterly cold days, including one with snow. The heavy rains of October on the churned-up earth had done the damage, however, and there were never enough consecutive fine days for the ground to even begin to dry out, particularly with non-existent drainage. December saw a great increase in wet days, with more snow and the temperature continuing to go down; this winter would be regarded as France's worst in forty years.

Private Edward Lynch, whose remarkable (if partly fictionalised[35]) memoir of an infantry private's life in the trenches was not published until 2006, was a recent reinforcement in the 45th Battalion. He found that on reaching the front line trench after an exhausting struggle through the quagmire,

> [we] put in a miserable night standing in the mud. Nowhere to lie or even sit. The best we can do is to lean back against the wet wall of the trench, but that's not comfortable as we slide down as soon as we doze. We stand in the mud. A quarter of an hour's standing and we find we have sunk to our knees so pull our legs out of the freezing bog and stand in a fresh place ... again we sink into the mud, only quicker ... [the day is] no different from the night except that we can see the mud a little better ...[36]

The numbers of men evacuated due to sickness exceeded those from battle wounds; the 4th Field Ambulance reported that a daily average of 80 sick and 26 wounded men passed through the Bernafay ADS between 14 and 30 November.[37] 'Trench Foot' had been a problem at Ypres in September/October, and not surprisingly it was rife in the conditions on the Somme front; many men developed bronchial complaints also. The 4th Division's measures to control Trench Foot did have some success, however—the 4th's figures for losses due to sickness were noticeably better than those of the other divisions in I Anzac,[38] to the credit of the unit medical officers and the divisional ADMS, Colonel George Barber. The establishment of a Corps Rest Station near the Bécordel MDS provided a facility where the less seriously ill could recuperate for several weeks before being returned to their units. Some aspects of the Rest Station were less than satisfactory, and similar facilities set up at the battalion level seem to have involved an element of statistical manipulation, to the detriment of sufferers retained on strength when they perhaps should have been evacuated.[39]

The front line trenches were in a constant state of disrepair, deep in watery mud and with sides frequently falling in from the rain and enemy shelling. The units in occupation laboured to drain their trench, dig out collapsed sections and shore up the sides, but any improvement was very temporary. Relieving units found the trench in deplorable condition, put in much hard work to improve it, then handed over in turn to their relief who also found the trench deplorable. Gradually, however, some progress was made. Some timber was obtained for a start to be made on providing duckboards along the trench floors and revetments for the sides. Considerable efforts were put in to get cooked food to the men in the firing line. The 48th Battalion, coming up to the front line on 19 November, organised for two hot meals to be brought up each day by fatigue parties (a particularly apt term in the circumstances) over a distance of 1,500 metres through the mud from the cookers located at Flers. Other units followed the example. The food was carried in crudely-insulated containers and while it may not have been actually hot by the time it reached the troops, any small comfort was welcome. The issue of 'tommy cookers', small stoves using a block of solid fuel, enabled the men in the front line to heat a tin of bully beef or water for tea—often the water was drawn from a convenient flooded shell-hole, and on more than one occasion a hole was later found to also contain a corpse. Sheepskin waistcoats and rubber wading-boots were issued to provide some protection from the weather. There were improvements to billeting in the reserve areas with construction of huts in bivouac areas at Mametz, Fricourt and Montauban as well as similar camps closer to the front at Bernafay and Bazentin[40]—'Comfortless wooden huts like toy boats at anchor in a sea of mud'[41] but far better than holes in the ground. The Division's horses and mules suffered as much as the men. Over the two months of November and December, the 4th Mobile Veterinary Section under Major Edward James treated and evacuated about 2,000 animals for sickness and wounds, well over ten times the usual numbers for similar periods, and another 700 were treated in January 1917.[42]

A new commander for the 12th Brigade arrived on 19 November. This was Lieutenant Colonel (soon temporary Brigadier General) James Robertson, who was posted from the 1st Division, where he had been CO of the 9th Battalion. The new brigadier was a Queenslander, 38 years old, a pre-war militia officer. All of his service so far had been with the 9th Battalion, of which unit he was second-in-command at the Gallipoli Landing where he had been wounded but returned to take command of the battalion in the later stages of the campaign. Robertson had taken the 9th to France and led it through the 1st Division's fighting at Pozières and Mouquet Farm.

The 4th Division's artillery began arriving from the north on 23 November, setting up its HQ with Division HQ at Pommiers Redoubt; the DAC was based at nearby Montauban. Over the next few days the field brigades relieved their counterparts of the 2nd Division artillery in the gun lines. Because of the difficulty of moving artillery pieces in the quagmire, the gunners took over the weapons that were already in place from the outgoing units, parking their own in the rear area, where they were to be taken over by other units in reserve. Not surprisingly, there were complaints from 4th Division gunners about the condition of the pieces that they had inherited:

> Guns taken over from outgoing people in a very unsatisfactory condition ... nearly all the trouble is through wear, caused by neglect ... 2 guns were taken over out of action owing to spring troubles.[43]

The 4th Division CRA, Brigadier General Charles Rosenthal, took over tactical control of the sector artillery, now covering the left division front of I Anzac's area following the change in the Corps boundaries; his command included elements of the 1st Division artillery. Each division had three of its four field brigades in the line, with the fourth in reserve and training.

On 27 November the 4th Brigade infantry and supporting arms relieved those of the 12th Brigade, which moved back to camps in the Bazentin and Mametz areas. The 13th and 14th Battalions went into the front line first, with the 16th in support and 15th in reserve, both of the latter units providing large working parties for road and trench works, as well as assisting with transport of artillery ammunition. The 13th Battalion on the right of the line had its left occupying the difficult position at Goodwin's Post, while the 14th's line, as the left battalion, extended to several old gun pits which were incorporated in the defences. Both of these outposts were in close proximity to German positions in Lard Trench and Hilt Trench, and in the sunken road known as Fritz's Folly. Edgar Rule, 14th Battalion, recalled that the Germans were only twenty yards away from the Gun Pits, 'around the corner' in the sunken road where they could be heard coughing, and that the bodies of Australians killed in earlier failed attacks were close by, still caught in the mud.[44] There was an advantage to both sides in occupying this area, however—with the front lines being so close, neither side was prepared to risk hitting its own troops with artillery bombardments. The front line battalions continued the constant work of improving their trenches while maintaining pressure on the enemy. The 13th Battalion became involved in some sharp night-fighting around Goodwin's Post, patrolling aggressively and dispersing enemy working parties with fire from Lewis guns, of which the unit had six positioned in the front line. Meanwhile the 14th Battalion was due to undertake an operation against the German positions in Fritz's Folly which ultimately miscarried in extraordinary circumstances.

On 1 December, the 14th received a draft order for the attack, classified 'Secret' as usual, from 4th Brigade HQ. The unit CO, Lieutenant Colonel Charles Dare, decided to send the document by runner into the forward area for comment by the commander of the front line company. The company commander in turn had the runner take the order to one of his platoon commanders in the front line trench. In attempting to return from there to company HQ the runner took a wrong turn and wandered into the German lines, where he and the plans were captured. With the proposed operation now compromised the Division took swift action against the officers whose carelessness with secret documents had caused the situation. Colonel Dare and the company and platoon commanders were immediately placed under arrest and a Court of Enquiry was held the next day. Although no courts-martial resulted, the company commander was soon discharged from the army and sent home, while Colonel Dare was removed from his command and posted to AIF headquarters in the UK; from there he was later sent back to Australia for staff duties and eventually discharged also. No blame was attached to the platoon commander, Lieutenant Frederick Appleton, who continued to serve with the unit and was killed at Amiens in 1918. Colonel Dare was unquestionably a brave fighter, having won the DSO at Gallipoli leading the 4th Brigade's attack on Hill 60 through a storm of fire. It had become apparent in France, however, that he did not have the right qualities for a successful unit commander, and it appears that the battalion itself and Brigadier General Brand had already lost confidence in him by this time.[45]

Next day, by a remarkable coincidence, a German runner became lost and walked into the Australian lines in the same area. He was found to be carrying plans for withdrawal from the Fritz's Folly salient, which the Germans duly carried out a few days later. In a sense the loss of the Australian plans had saved lives by causing the abandonment of an attack which would have been unnecessary. This episode marked the end of the 4th Division's current tour in the front line with the regular rotation now bringing the 1st Division in to relieve the 4th. The 13th Brigade was relieved on the night of 5/6 December by the 3rd Brigade, with the 4th Brigade being relieved by the 2nd Brigade on the following night. The 12th Brigade had already begun moving back from the reserve area on 4 December. The 4th Brigade's reserve battalion, the 15th, stayed in position near Bazentin and continued with its numerous fatigue tasks. The Battalion historian saw a positive in this: 'They at least had freedom of movement and enough exercise to keep the blood circulating, whereas their unfortunate sister battalions were living in mud one moment and ice the next.'[46]

As was now routine, the divisional artillery stayed in the line as part of the group covering the 1st Division, now coming under tactical control of the 1st Division CRA. The greater part of the engineer, pioneer and medical units also remained in position for the time being, continuing their roles in support of the incoming division. By this time, the broad-gauge railway in the back areas had been extended to Quarry Siding, near Bernafay Wood, and units leaving the forward area marched to the siding from where they were carried by train for the next stage of the journey to rear billets. The train trip was not a particularly pleasant experience—the men usually had to stand for hours in open cattle trucks in the freezing weather.[47] The 4th Division's troops spent about ten days in the 'R' area around Dernancourt, Buire and Ribemont with Division HQ at the latter village, where the men were able to get a welcome bath. After a few days of rest and refitting units began some light training with short route marches and shooting practice. The Division then moved further back to Vignacourt (HQ from 19 December), Flesselles, Cardonette and other nearby villages in the area north of Amiens, taking its turn again in the Fourth Army's rest and training area. As well as training programmes for the units, battalion sports were organised, both activities being carried out with some difficulty due to the continuing wet weather. There was also the opportunity for the fortunate few to take local leave (official or unofficial) in Amiens. The period in the Flers/Gueudecourt front line had cost the Division 579 casualties, 147 of whom were killed or missing,[48] nearly all as a result of enemy artillery fire. Among the infantry units those of the 12th Brigade had been the hardest hit, with a total casualty list of 239 during November. Many more had been evacuated with various illnesses, but most of these would be expected to return sooner or later.

The Division could expect a period of two to three weeks in the rear before moving up to the line again, and considerable attention was given to training. General Cox ordered that units should concentrate on realistic tactical exercises in the training area, practicing advances, attacks and deployments. The exercises were to include machine guns, Lewis guns, 'bombers' and rifle grenadiers supporting the riflemen. The tactical work was to be interspersed with shooting on the range and physical fitness programs, including running and route marches. The GOC was also concerned about the training of expected 'partly trained reinforcements ... Their training must be pushed on as rapidly as possible ... They will be absorbed into the establishment of their Battalions as they become efficient.'[49]

At this time, BEF divisions were establishing divisional training schools where newly-promoted officers and NCOs could receive instruction in their new duties. The 4th Division's infantry school had been set up on 29 November at La Chaussée, its first commandant being Major (temporary Lieutenant Colonel) Hubert Ford, ex-13th Battalion and until recently Division DAA&QMG. The school was set up to conduct three-week courses for platoon commanders and section leader NCOs, initially twenty students in each category, but this was soon increased to 26 officers and 104 NCOs per course. A signals school was also established during December to train signallers from all elements of the Division. At the end of November the Division had also set up an artillery school at Naours, under the command of Lieutenant Colonel Reginald Rabett, CO of the 12th AFA Brigade. Colonel Rabett had made a major contribution to the initial training of the 4th Division's gunners in Egypt, but he seems to have encountered difficulties with the new school. There was some tension between the divisional general staff and the artillery chiefs over the school. The GSO2, Major McRae, wrote in the staff war diary that

> the GSO1 visited our Artillery School at the request of [I] ANZAC—apparently all is not well and it is not a success being badly founded. This is not surprising as it was all done at a moment's notice without plans or forethought, without sufficient staff or suitable accommodation. Apparently the GOC RA [at Corps] ordered the CRA to have the school opened at very short notice ... All help from the Divisional General Staff was refused and now having failed they ask the General Staff to help them out of their difficulties.[50]

Presumably by 'they' Major McRae was referring to the Corps artillery staff rather than that of the Division. In any event, the school had a short life, being wound up in late January 1917 and replaced by a school at Corps level, as part of the major reorganisation of the artillery arm which occurred at that time.

During this period there were several more changes of commanding officer in the infantry units. The circumstances were dramatic in the case of the 51st Battalion. It had been apparent for some time to the unit's senior officers that the behaviour of the CO, Lieutenant Colonel Arthur Ross, was becoming increasingly erratic. Having seen the battalion that he had commanded from its inception being twice shattered at Mouquet Farm, Ross had steadily sunk into what would probably today be diagnosed as severe depression. By December he had ceased to communicate with his officers, banning several from the mess altogether, and had lost his effectiveness as a commander. The Battalion adjutant, Captain Thomas Louch, was prevailed upon to report the situation to 13th Brigade HQ. After an initially frosty reception, Louch was able to convince Brigadier General Glasgow that something needed to be done.

Colonel Ross was interviewed by the ADMS, Colonel Barber, who immediately sent him on extended sick leave.[51] Major Robert Christie, the Battalion second-in-command, took over as temporary CO. Colonel Ross's valuable career with the AIF was by no means over, however. By the new year he had recovered and was appointed commandant of the I Anzac Corps School, where his ability as a trainer of officers and NCOs came to the fore. In May 1917, Edgar Rule, by then a lieutenant, attended a course at the Corps school and remembered Ross as

> the most able instructor I'd ever seen, and I've heard others say the same. Many officers in the AIF felt his influence to the end of the war and moulded themselves on him... Like many other English officers who have had much to do with our forces, he became very much attached to them, and I remember him telling us that we had records every bit as good as the Guards.[52]

Colonel Ross finished the war on Major General William Glasgow's staff in the 1st Division.

Another British officer commanding a 4th Division battalion was Lieutenant Colonel Geoffrey Lee, who had led the 46th Battalion efficiently since its formation in Egypt. On 2 December, Colonel Lee was posted to command a battalion of his original British Army regiment, the Kings Royal Rifles. He was succeeded as CO of the 46th by the battalion second-in-command, Major (shortly Lieutenant Colonel) Howard Denham, a 33-year old from Sydney, a former militia officer who had transferred into the 46th, a Victorian unit, from the 30th (NSW, 8th Brigade) in Egypt. In the 4th Brigade, another Victorian battalion came under the command of a Sydneysider when the 14th Battalion received a new CO on 14 December. This was the current brigade major of the 4th Brigade, Major John Peck, promoted to lieutenant colonel and posted to the 14th to replace the unfortunate Colonel Dare. Peck was a pre-war regular officer, 30 years old, a Gallipoli veteran who had served in several regimental and staff appointments since 1914. Colonel Peck combined an infectious sense of humour with a thorough knowledge of his business, and he had an immediate positive impact on his unit's morale and efficiency. The 14th appears to have been a dispirited lot at this time, through unsatisfactory leadership as much as conditions in the line, but 'this merry, efficient manager of men'[53] brought about a rapid transformation. The return from hospital of the inspiring Albert Jacka at about the same time was another positive factor for the 14th Battalion. At 4th Brigade HQ, Peck was succeeded as brigade major by Major Charles Johnston, formerly of the 15th Battalion. There had also been a recent change of staff captain, Captain William Locke having returned to his original unit, the 13th Battalion, early in November. His replacement was Captain Alexander Fraser, posted in from the 52nd Battalion.

It was apparent that the greater part of the Division, particularly the infantry brigade groups, would be out of the line at Christmas, so battalion committees put in some time planning special events and meals for Christmas Day. Funds were raised to buy appetising food items in Amiens and nearby villages, supplemented by gifts from the Australian Comforts Fund. The new GSO3 at Division HQ, Captain Keighley, was a theatrical producer in civilian life and he put together a troupe to provide entertainment over the festive period. Christmas Day gave the troops a rare and very welcome day off from the war and the constant round of training, apart from the unlucky few who were detailed for essential duties. Church services in the morning were followed by Christmas lunch with poultry, hams, vegetables, puddings and beer, served to the men by their officers in the old Army tradition. Sports were held in the afternoon and the officers' messes held their own dinners in the evening. General Cox visited the billets to observe the festivities: 'the men are having a great blow-out and I have been motoring around to see them all day.'[54] It was back to work for all ranks on Boxing Day when training resumed. For those elements of the Division still near the front line, particularly the divisional artillery, Christmas made little difference to the war. The 24th AFA Brigade's battery positions and HQ location had been subjected to intermittent counter-battery shelling by German medium guns through December, including gas shells on one occasion. Several gunners were killed and others wounded, and a few guns put out of action temporarily, but the Brigade's regular tasks of harassing the enemy's 'back country' were not interrupted. On 20 December the CRA, Brigadier General Charles Rosenthal, had been slightly wounded in the leg but was back on duty after a day resting at the CCS[55]—the CRA was not one to spend all of his time in his office, and this was neither the first nor the last time that he was hit by enemy fire. The 11th AFA Brigade came up from reserve the next day to relieve the 24th Brigade in the gun-line and like its predecessor encountered accurate enemy shelling of the battery locations. The 11th Brigade lost three killed and 15 wounded over three days, with a particularly violent exchange of fire occurring on the night of Christmas Eve.

The Germans put down a heavy bombardment on the Australian front line trench, and in case this presaged an attack the infantry called for the 'SOS' barrage on the enemy lines. The 11th Brigade fired over 600 rounds in that barrage and in reply its positions were heavily bombarded by the enemy guns. Two gun-pits took direct hits, causing several casualties and damaging the guns. There would be no repetition of the unofficial Christmas truces of previous years and the guns of both sides kept up the shelling on Christmas Day. So concerned was the Brigade commander, Lieutenant Colonel Francis Hughes, that his battery positions had been pinpointed by the enemy that he ordered his guns not to fire for the next few days. Colonel Hughes believed that the gun-flashes were being spotted, although the battery positions may well have been picked up by enemy aerial reconnaissance and photography—the Germans held a degree of air superiority over the front at this time, and their machines were often seen overhead. The shelling of the 11th's gun-line continued and on 30 December the Brigade HQ was badly hit. A dugout was blown in during the afternoon, killing two gunners, and at 9 pm a direct hit

> blew in passage from office to dugout, blocking the latter and burying [the adjutant and the orderly officer] ... after one and a half hours digging they were got out uninjured. As the shelling continued, headquarters were withdrawn to battery dug-outs ...[56]

The enemy guns kept up their accurate shelling for the next two weeks, causing further casualties and damage, before a rearrangement of artillery groupings between the 4th and 1st Divisions in mid-January saw the 11th's batteries relocated.

Except for the 12th Field Company, the Division's engineers and pioneers remained camped fairly close to the front line, within range of enemy artillery, continuing with their work on communication routes. The 4th Pioneers were billeted variously at Mametz, Quarry Siding and Trones wood while working on the light railways. The Pioneer CO, Lieutenant Colonel Fewtrell, had demonstrated his expertise in managing the railway works, and on 24 December he was detached from the 4th Division to become CO of the I Anzac Light Railway Company. The 4th Pioneers' second-in-command, Major Norman Macrae, took over as acting CO of the Battalion. The 4th Field Company was at Montauban and Longueval and continued with roadworks, as well as some construction of camp huts. The 13th Field Company, also based at Longueval, worked under fire on extensions and repairs of the front line trenches until relieved of those tasks by the incoming 1st Field Company on 9 December. The 12th Field Company, which had spent most of its tour working in the front line and support trenches, was relieved on 12 December and moved back to join the main body of the Division in the rest area, billeting at Vignacourt. Here the Company was allocated to work on the troops' accommodation, including facilities for the recently-established divisional schools at La Chaussée and Naours. Of the medical units, the tent sub-divisions of the 12th and 13th Field Ambulances continued their work at the Bécordel MDS, the Corps Rest Station at Buire and the Quarry Siding reception post. The bearer sections of those units were relieved from their front line duties and moved to the Bécordel and Buire facilities, while the whole of the 4th Field Ambulance was relieved at the ADS and went back with the main body, splitting its personnel to provide services to each of the three brigade groups. Colonel Barber took the opportunity to rotate a number of his medical officers between the field ambulances and unit RMO postings, a fairly regular process. One of these was the current 50th Battalion RMO, Major Lewis Jeffries, but at about this time, the DADMS, Major Alexander Marks, was promoted to command a 1st Division field ambulance, and Major Jeffries replaced him as DADMS.

November and December had seen a number of changes in senior officer postings, and the final change of the year occurred at the top when Major General Sir Herbert Cox left the Division to take up an appointment as Military Secretary to the India Office, with promotion to lieutenant general. His chosen replacement was Brigadier General William Holmes, currently commanding the 5th Infantry Brigade (2nd Division). As the 4th Division's first GOC, General Cox had overseen the original forming of the Division from diverse material and its gradual evolution into an effective fighting force. The General's lifetime of military experience had been put into the organisation and training of the division, and by his frequent inspections and visits to units he kept a close awareness of how his officers and men were developing. On the battlefield General Cox had led the division in its initiation to the Western Front at Armentières and then the savage fighting at Pozières/Mouquet Farm. In the latter campaign his tactics after the successful early fighting could be questioned. His approach appeared to be reactive: orthodox plans were made in what was a highly unusual situation, then changes were made for the next attempt when the first approach failed, only for the general to find that the conditions had changed and that he was in effect fighting yesterday's battle today. General Cox, and perhaps his 'G' staff at HQ, seemed to take insufficient notice of the generally sound suggestions of General White at Corps HQ until after their own methods had failed. On the other hand, there are signs that comments coming up the line from unit officers were taken into account in developing modified plans. Of course, division commanders were constrained by orders from Corps and more particularly from General Gough and Army HQ, and there was limited scope for initiative at division level. It is doubtful if many other commanders could have done noticeably better than General Cox, considering what he was faced with—the situation at Mouquet Farm would have tested a Marlborough or a Lee—and his experience and professionalism were unquestionably what was needed to lead the 4th Division in its first year of existence. General Holmes arrived at Vignacourt on 28 December for a brief familiarisation before taking over command, accompanying General Cox on a round of visits to the brigades, during which the latter said his farewells to senior officers. The change of command took place on the last day of 1916, and the 4th Division went into the new year under an Australian-born general.

7 Notes

1. These comments are taken from an anonymous document by a 15th Battalion soldier which appears in a collection of notes compiled by the late Mr Ian Black, which the present author obtained when researching a previous work. The document, which is obviously authentic, is in the form of a printer's proof for what would be part of the soldier's memoirs. The author has been unable to identify the soldier. He may have been Lieutenant Peter Ohlson, but this is little more than a guess.
2. 4th Division General Staff War Diary for September 1916, Appendix 19.
3. 4th Division Admin Staff War Diary for September 1916, Appendix B.
4. M Farndale, *History of the Royal Regiment of Artillery: Western Front 1914–18*, p. 4 and p. 142.
5. 4th Division DAC War Diary, 31 August 1916.
6. 4th Division Artillery HQ War Diary, 17/18 September 1916.
7. 4th Division General Staff War Diary, 19 September 1916
8. 4th Division Artillery HQ War Diary for September 1916 Appendices (Order No. 30).
9. 4th Brigade War Diary for September 1916, Appendix 11.
10. 4th Brigade War Diary for September 1916, Appendix 10.
11. G D Mitchell, *Backs to the Wall*, p. 28.
12. 16th Battalion War Diary for September 1916, Appendix 6.
13. *Official History*, Vol III, pp. 881–886.
14. Ian Gill, *Bloody Angle, Bullecourt and Beyond* (16th Battalion), p. 26; the AWM Roll of Honour confirms seven fatalities (the unit War Diary says six).

15   12th Infantry Brigade War Diary for October 1916, Appendix 25.
16   13th MG Company War Diary, 22 October 1916.
17   N Wanliss, *The History of the Fourteenth Battalion AIF*, pp. 164–5.
18   *Official History*, Vol III, p. 892.
19   4th Division Artillery HQ War Diary, 10 November 1916
20   4th Division Admin Staff War Diary for September (Appendix C) and October (Appendix D) 1916.
21   AWM 224, MSS 291/1: 4th Australian Field Ambulance: History 1916–18.
22   *Official History*, Vol III, p. 897.
23   4th Division General Staff War Diary for December 1916, Appendix 4.
24   Accounts of General Glasfurd's ordeal have some inconsistencies. It is described in the *Official History* (Vol III, p. 955) as a ten-hour stretcher journey between the front line and the ADS. The Bernafay Wood ADS was under the 2nd Field Ambulance at the time, and that unit's War Diary (November 1916, App I) details the usual evacuation route from the front line RAPs to the ADS, covering about 7000 yards in total, part of which was by horse-drawn ambulance. The 4th Division GS War Diary for November says that it took ten hours to get the General to the *Casualty Clearing Station (CCS)*, not the ADS; this seems unlikely given the distance and road conditions, but is not impossible. The time that Glasfurd was hit is not recorded, but the 12th Brigade HQ was scheduled to leave Fricourt for Bernafay Wood and the front line at 8 am on 12 November. Lt Col Ray Leane recorded in the 48th Battalion War diary that he saw the wounded Brigadier at the 2nd Field Ambulance 'in the morning,' suggesting that it took less than ten hours to get him to the ADS; it is recorded that General Glasfurd died in the evening. Accounts do not mention if he received any treatment at the next staging point, the MDS, before being moved to the CCS, but the Australian Dictionary of Biography mentions that Glasfurd's brother spoke to him at Bécordel (i.e. the MDS).
25   12th Brigade War Diary, 12 November 1916
26   Letter of General Cox in AWM 1DRL/0221.
27   46th Battalion War Diary, 12 to 19 November 1916.
28   Colonel Flintoff's service record states that he was hospitalised with multiple gunshot wounds (GSW) but he may well have been hit by shrapnel. No details of the circumstances are given.
29   A G Butler, *Official History of the Australian Army Medical Services* (hereinafter *Medical History*), Vol II, p. 85.
30   2nd Field Ambulance War Diary for November 1916, Appendix I. See also AWM224, MSS 289/290.
31   The *Medical History* noted the success of this group 'under a particularly energetic officer [Lt Col J B StV Welch, CO of the 13th Field Ambulance]' (Vol II, p. 88).
32   *Ibid*, p. 89.
33   48th Battalion War Diary for November 1916. See also N. Browning, *Leane's Battalion*, pp. 74–5.
34   Rule, *Op Cit*, pp. 56–7.
35   See W. Davies, *In the Footsteps of Private Lynch*, passim.
36   E.P.F. Lynch, *Somme Mud* (ed. Will Davies), pp. 31–2.
37   4th Field Ambulance War Diary for 30 November 1916.
38   *Medical History*, Vol II, p. 98.

39 *Medical History,* Vol II, p. 97 and Mitchell, *Op Cit*, p. 47. Mitchell's criticism was made of the 48th Battalion, a good unit with a CO (Lt Col R A Leane) noted for his care for the men.
40 *Official History*, Vol III, p. 925.
41 Devine, *Op Cit*, p. 67.
42 4th Mobile Veterinary Section War Diary for December 1917, Appendix I (statistics for April 1916 to December 1917).
43 24th AFA Brigade War Diary, 25 November 1916.
44 Rule, *Op Cit*, p. 58.
45 See for example Rule, *Op Cit*, pp. 24, 37 and 41. The unit history (Wanliss, *Op Cit*, pp. 168–71) makes no comment on Dare's qualities as a CO but emphasises the improvements in the management of the unit brought about by his successor, Lt Col John Peck.
46 Chataway, *Op Cit*, p. 142.
47 Browning, *For King and Cobbers, Op Cit*, pp. 90, 93.
48 This includes a few casualties in the units that remained near the front line throughout December after the main body of the Division had been withdrawn to the rest area. The numbers were extracted from the 4th Division and I Anzac Admin Staff War Diaries for November and December 1916.
49 4th Division General Staff War Diary for December 1916, Appendix 18.
50 4th Division General Staff War Diary, 9 December 1916.
51 Browning, *For King and Cobbers, Op Cit*, pp. 88–9; P. Edgar, *To Villers-Bretonneux*, pp. 101–3.
52 Rule, *Op Cit*, p. 84.
53 *Ibid*, p. 62.
54 Letter of General Cox in AWM 1DRL/0221.
55 C Rosenthal, *Diary 1 January 1916 to 31 December 1918*, entries 20 to 22 December 1916.
56 11th AFA Brigade War Diary for 30 December 1916.

8: Action at Gueudecourt

William Holmes was promoted to temporary major general from 1 January 1917 on taking command of the 4th Division. He was 54 years old, born and resident in Sydney, and he had been a member of the citizen forces since the age of 10, when he joined the 1st Infantry Regiment of the NSW Militia as a boy bugler. By 1886 he was a second lieutenant in the regiment and was making his living as a civil servant in the NSW public service. In 1895 he was made secretary of the Metropolitan Board of Water Supply and Sewerage, a very responsible position for a comparatively young man. In 1899 Holmes volunteered for the NSW contingent being sent to South Africa to fight the Boers, where he was wounded and won the DSO in action with the 1st NSW Mounted Rifles. He resumed Militia service on returning to Australia and was a colonel commanding an infantry brigade when war broke out in 1914. Shortly afterwards, Colonel Holmes was appointed to command the Australian Naval and Military Expeditionary Force, which was formed to occupy German colonies in New Guinea and nearby territories. The task was accomplished swiftly and Holmes was made Administrator of the region.

He returned to Australia in January 1915 and next month transferred to the AIF as brigadier of the 5th Infantry Brigade in the new 2nd Division. Holmes took his brigade to Gallipoli for the final stages of the fighting,

Major General William Holmes CMG DSO (1862–1917), GOC 4th Division January to July 1917. (AWM I33440)

where he showed no hesitation in visiting the most dangerous parts of the front line. C E W Bean noted that Holmes was noticeably more physically active that other senior officers of similar age, and 'possessed also fine moral qualities, transparent sincerity, energy and courage.'[1] He had been under consideration for command of a division when the AIF expansion took place early in 1916, but General Birdwood felt that he was not ready at the time. Holmes led the 5th Brigade to France where it took part in the capture of the OG lines at Pozières. In November Holmes had commanded the 2nd Division's unsuccessful attack through the mud at Flers, an action that reflected no particular credit on him. His tactics on that occasion 'in simply ordering the 26th Battalion to repeat an attack which had failed, appear to have incurred some criticism from higher authority.'[2] That uncharacteristic lapse did not, however, prevent his selection for divisional command.

The 4th Division enjoyed a holiday with sports on New Year's Day, the day before it was due to move out for its next turn in the front line. The new year brought a number of awards for senior officers in recognition of leadership over recent months, particularly during the Mouquet Farm operations. Brigadier General Charles Brand (4th Brigade) was made a Companion of the Order of St Michael and St George (CMG), and there were DSOs for infantry COs Lieutenant Colonels James Durrant (13th Battalion) and Sydney Herring (45th), and the former CO of the 4th Pioneer Battalion, Lieutenant Colonel Albert Fewtrell. The ADMS, Colonel George Barber, and his former deputy, Major Alexander Marks, both received the DSO, as did the CO of the 13th Field Ambulance, Lieutenant Colonel John St Vincent Welch and the former CO of the 12th Field Ambulance, Lieutenant Colonel Thomas Ross. Lieutenant Colonel Francis Hughes, CO of the 11th AFA Brigade, was also awarded the DSO, for his work during the artillery's detachment in the Armentières sector. The Division CRE, Lieutenant Colonel Gilbert Elliott, had already been awarded the DSO in November. Colonel Elliott had been hospitalised at the end of December suffering from bronchitis and general fatigue, and the 1st Division CRE, Lieutenant Colonel A M Martyn, was managing the 4th Division engineers for the time being while his own division was out of the line.

The 4th Division began its move forward on 2 January with the 4th and 12th Brigade Groups leading off and marching in stages along the now-familiar routes towards the front. The 13th Brigade Group marched the next day. By 7 January the 12th Brigade infantry was moving into the front line to relieve units of the 1st Division on the right of the divisional sector, occupying a two-battalion front as in the previous tour. The 13th Brigade came in during 8 January and took over the one-battalion front on the left to complete the 4th Division's sector. The 4th Brigade formed the divisional reserve at Mametz, supplying the usual working parties for a variety of tasks behind the lines. The Division's other elements again went through the routine relief of their 1st Division counterparts, and 4th Division HQ was re-established at Pommiers Redoubt on 9 January. The weather continued to deteriorate, several wet days early in the month making the mud worse than ever. Some snow was reported on 10 January, followed by more rain, and then came a change with a heavy snowfall on 17 January. Falls were interspersed by clear, bright frosty days, and the snow remained frozen on the ground as the temperature fell rapidly to well below freezing point. The underlying mud soon froze as well, to a depth of several feet.

For the men on working parties, 'with every blow of the pick splinters of ice penetrated hands and faces, causing cuts and scratches that were most difficult to heal.'[3] Towards the end of the month, Private George Mitchell (48th Battalion) noted that in the reserve camps at night, the men wore all the clothing that they could find, and

> Where our breath touched the wool, there icicles formed ... it was useless to try to drink from the water-bottle that had been a pillow. The water inside was always frozen.

A mate tried to write a letter home:

> He heated the bottle of ink. Before he could write a single word the ink on the nib would be frozen ... All this was inside the hut. Outside it was really cold. Tea was taken by us in our dixies, boiling from the cookers. In the twenty paces that we hurried back to the hut, thin ice had formed around the edges. If the slightest wind was blowing men had to walk with the head averted from the direction of the current. The pain caused by the moving air on the eyes made it impossible to look for more than a second or so to windward. Bare hands were numbed beyond use after five seconds exposure.[4]

The temperature did not seem to bother the lice and rats, unfortunately. For all the adverse effects of the cold, it did have the great benefit of freezing the mud hard. The men could at least stay dry and movement through the trenches and across open ground became far less fatiguing. Digging to improve a trench was more difficult, but the frozen trench walls were much less prone to collapsing. The white covering on the ground did, however, make it easier for each side to detect the other's traffic patterns by aircraft reconnaissance and observation balloons, and harassment by the opposing artilleries became uncomfortably accurate.

The routine of holding the line continued for the infantry units, brigades rotating their battalions through the firing-line trenches about every ten days. As usual, the troops worked on maintaining and improving their trenches. The regular night patrols went out into No Man's Land until the combination of snow and moonlight later in the month made the troops too visible to the enemy. There was a steady drain of losses through German shelling of the lines, but no formal raids were attempted by the Division during this period. The enemy did, however, mount a raid in the 12th Brigade's sector on 16 January when a party of about 50 German infantry was seen advancing on a post of the 45th Battalion. The attackers were driven off by the 45th's fire, leaving four dead on the field.

The strategic situation on the Western Front at the beginning of 1917 was in a state of radical change. At the Chantilly conference in late 1916, the Allies' representatives had agreed to mount further offensives on all fronts in the early spring. On the Western Front the British and French would again attack along the axis of the Somme but with greater force than in 1916. It was loosely arranged that offensives on the Russian and Italian fronts would be launched at around the same time. Preliminary movements began in December 1916 with a view to beginning the Anglo-French operation in February 1917, but a sudden change of plans put a stop to preparations. The French commander-in-chief, General Joseph Joffre, lost his position and was replaced by the rising officer General Robert Nivelle, who had different ideas for the coming year. Nivelle had risen to prominence almost overnight through his conduct of a series of brilliant attacks late in 1916 that had regained most of the ground lost to the Germans at Verdun and put the seal on the German failure in that battle. Now in operational control of the French armies on the Western Front, General Nivelle conceived an ambitious scheme for an offensive that would end the war virtually at a stroke, using the tactics that had recently succeeded for him at Verdun. Broadly, his methods involved a short but intense artillery bombardment of the objective, followed by a creeping barrage behind which the infantry advanced, using a flexible system of small-unit tactics that the French had been developing. Although the Nivelle offensive ultimately failed when it was launched later in the year, his methods were not unsound in themselves—the creeping barrage, when perfected, could protect advancing infantry, and the BEF would soon introduce a new system of platoon structure and tactics that owed much to those developed by the French at Verdun.[5] In that fighting, however, General Nivelle had been in command of a single army with comparatively limited objectives, and his new plan involved three armies attacking on a broad front against the main German defensive line. As Winston Churchill commented,

> it does not follow in war or in some other spheres that methods which work well on a small scale will work well on a great scale. As military operations become larger, they become more ponderous, and the time factor begins to set up complex reactions. Where days of preparation had sufficed, months may be required. Secrets that can be kept for days are apt to wear out in months. Surprise, the key to victory, becomes harder to secure with every additional man and gun.[6]

Instead of the British and French armies attacking eastwards on both sides of the Somme against the western face of the huge salient formed by the German line, the new plan called for the main effort to be a decisive French attack on its southern face, on the river Aisne. Subsidiary offensives further north would be launched to keep the German reserves occupied while the main blow was delivered, with the BEF attacking in the region of Arras. To allow General Nivelle to assemble the divisions required for his great offensive, the French requested that the British take over a sector of the line presently held by two French armies. The whole scheme, including issues of overall command, was the subject of stressful negotiations at the highest level, which eventually resulted in broad agreement to follow the Nivelle strategy. It was at this point that the new plans began to affect the divisions of I Anzac, holding the line in the Flers/Gueudecourt sector. A British corps was pulled out of the line on the left of I Anzac and sent to relieve French forces to the south. I Anzac was required to extend its front to its left to cover the gap, putting all four of its divisions into the line. The 1st and 2nd Divisions took over their new sectors on the left of the 4th and 5th Divisions between 28 January and 3 February. The divisions continued to rotate their brigades between firing line and reserve, but they no longer had the opportunity for a period of complete rest away from the front line and for comprehensive training programs.

In late January a major reorganisation of the BEF infantry divisions' artillery resources took place. With the aim of improved flexibility in the distribution of field artillery, BEF HQ directed that all divisional artillery was to be reduced from four field brigades to two with the surplus being formed into unattached 'Army' brigades. These would then be available for use by GHQ wherever required on the front, usually coming under an Army command and from that level allotted to a corps. At the same time the number of guns or howitzers per battery was increased from four to six. The number of 18-pounders controlled by divisions was now 36 (six batteries, three per brigade), reduced from 48, although the number of 4.5-inch howitzers remained at 12 (two batteries, one per brigade) because of the increase in the number of weapons per battery. The DACs also had portion of their personnel, vehicles and draught animals allocated to the new Army brigades. Personnel establishment of the divisions' artillery was reduced from 111 officers and 2,988 other ranks to 70 officers and 2,289 other ranks.[7] As far as the 4th Division was concerned the reorganisation meant the disbandment of the 24th AFA Brigade and the re-assignment of the 12th AFA, under Lieutenant Colonel Reginald Rabett, as an Army brigade, leaving only the 10th and 11th AFAs (plus the medium and heavy mortars) comprising the divisional artillery. The weapons and personnel of the 24th AFA were absorbed by the 10th and 11th to provide for their increased establishment and there were some changes made to the artillery groupings and battery positions in the line. Lieutenant Colonel Giffard King remained in command of the 10th AFA, while Lieutenant Colonel William Waite was transferred from the disbanded 24th to command the 11th AFA. The nominal commander of the 11th, Lieutenant Colonel Francis Hughes, had recently gone on sick leave with influenza and found himself unattached when he recovered; Colonel Hughes was posted to the 5th Division in February as CO of its DAC.

The artillery reorganisation took place at a time of intensified fighting on the I Anzac front. In order to increase the pressure on the Germans prior to the major spring offensives, Fourth Army ordered the adoption of a more aggressive approach, and several small local operations against the enemy lines were conceived. The intention was to take and hold ground, rather than just raiding. The freeze had made attacks more practicable by temporarily removing the paralysing mud as a factor, and I Anzac urged that these operations be undertaken as soon as possible to take advantage of the conditions before the inevitable thaw set in. The 4th Division was given the task of capturing the Stormy Trench/Cloudy Trench system, a position running along rising ground about 100 metres away from the Australian front line in Grease and Shine Trenches, north-east of Gueudecourt. The attack was planned for 1 February and would be undertaken by the 4th Brigade, which had relieved the 12th as the right-hand brigade in the front line on 24 January. The objective was about opposite the point where the 4th and 5th Divisions' fronts met, so elements of the latter division would be expected to co-operate. It was to be a one-battalion operation and Brigadier General Brand selected the 15th Battalion to make the attack. On 28 January, the brigadier conferred with the Battalion CO, Lieutenant Colonel McSharry, and his senior company commander, Major William Mundell, to develop a scheme for the operation. The enemy position was protected by a five-metre wide barbed wire entanglement, and the first priority was to cut the wire and open the way for the infantry. It was felt that this task would best be done by medium trench mortars. It was arranged that the division's X4A MTM battery, which was already in a suitable position (the freeze had enabled firm emplacements to be made), would bombard the wire on 30 January and again the next day if necessary. The X5A battery of the neighbouring 5th Division would join in as well, targeting the wire on the right of the objective. Night patrols by the infantry would check the success or otherwise of the wire-cutting before the main attack went in. This was planned for the night of 1/2 February and would involve the four platoons of Major Mundell's company plus two from Captain David Dunworth's company—a total of about 220 men, a barely adequate force to capture and hold an important enemy position, but it seemed sufficient to the planners given that Stormy Trench had been assessed as weakly held by the enemy. The Division's newly re-organised 11th and 10th AFA Brigades (by now designated on this front as Numbers 1 and 2 Groups, 'B' Division Artillery) would provide the covering barrage, supported by the 5th and 1st Division guns firing on the enemy support lines.

The preliminaries of the operation began on the afternoon of 30 January as planned with 4th and 5th Division MTMs firing their 19-kilogram 'Plum Pudding' bombs at the German wire in front of the objective. The task soon proved to be a difficult one: Lieutenant Werner McPherson, in charge of X4A's two mortars, noted that many of the bombs seemed to bounce on the frozen ground before detonating, limiting their effect on the wire.[8] The ammunition (that is, the cordite charges propelling the bombs) proved to be unreliable: one of the guns, with no change in its elevation, had some of its shots sail well over the target and others land well short, with two rounds falling on the edge of the gun pit. The shoot ended with less than satisfactory results, although the 5th Division mortars did not report any particular problems. That night, infantry patrols found the wire to be partly cut on the left of the objective but still almost intact on the right. The heavy artillery was scheduled to bombard the enemy front and support lines for two hours the next afternoon, 31 January, so the wire was included in the targets. The 4th and 5th Division MTMs opened up again after the artillery ceased fire. X4A battery did some effective shooting but again had trouble with faulty ammunition. A round from one gun fell on the parapet of the emplacement, where it exploded, killing one man and wounding two others, one of whom later died from his wounds. A reconnaissance that night found that the wire was still an obstacle on the right, so another shoot by the 'heavies' and the 5th Division mortars was arranged for the next day, 1 February[9] (X4A was not needed). The infantry attack was to go in that same night, and to reduce the risk of the Germans observing the assembly of the troops during the day, it was decided that the right flank group, Captain Dunworth's half-company, should move up to their jumping-off trench in the dark of early morning. As a result, those troops had to lie out in a forward position, a new trench dug by the 15th Brigade, when the final bombardment came down on the German position only 80 metres away. The front line troops had been withdrawn for safety during the previous day's shelling, but now a 15th Battalion officer wrote that

> Our 60lb [sic] trench mortar bombs and our heavy artillery had a go at the enemy wire on the front we were tackling ... we should really have been withdrawn to escape the back-lash of our heavies, but movement out of the trench in daylight was impossible ... We were peppered with showers of frozen earth and fragments of shell which came hissing into the snow about us, but had great luck in getting no one hit, though shells were falling close to the trench both in front and behind.[10]

In spite of this bombardment the wire at this point was still not sufficiently cut, although the X5A mortars believed that they had blasted a lane through the entanglement.[11] Captain Dunworth reported at 4 pm that the wire in front of him was still intact, but there seems to have no thought of delaying the operation. The left group, Major Mundell's company, began filing into their assembly positions in Grease Trench as darkness was falling, and the troops were ready to advance when the covering barrage came down. 'Zero' was set for 7 pm, and two minutes before Zero the 11th AFA Brigade 18-pounders fired a few rounds beyond the objective to warm the guns before shortening their range on to Stormy Trench promptly at 7, bursting their shrapnel accurately along the objective. The guns of the 10th AFA Brigade also opened up, targeting the part of the trench to the left of the infantry's objective, while the 5th Division guns did the same on the right as the infantry rose from the assembly trenches and went forward. The covering barrage was planned to last for only two minutes before shifting to a line beyond the objective, but with the hard ground and a fairly short distance to cover, the 15th Battalion troops on the left flank moved fast and entered the enemy trench almost simultaneously with the lift of the barrage, which had been very accurate. The right-flank group, frustrated by the uncut wire in front of them, could only advance as far as the wire, from where they grenaded the enemy trench in the hopes of distracting the defenders. A platoon of this group had been detached to reinforce Major Mundell's company on the left, which quickly surprised and overwhelmed the German garrison on that flank, most of whom surrendered without resistance. The attackers bombed down the trench to the right and succeeded in occupying most of the planned objective. The left group's only casualties at this point were two men slightly wounded, although the right group had at least two killed as well as several wounded in front of the uncut wire.[12] The troops set about consolidating the captured trench, quickly setting up barricades ('bomb stops' or blocks) at each end of the occupied segment. Three Lewis guns were posted forward, as was a Vickers gun of the 4th MG Company which had been sent up with the third wave of infantry. Parties of the troops still holding the original front line began digging a communication sap through to the new position. At this point it appeared that the planners' assessment of weak opposition had been correct, but the picture changed rapidly as the enemy launched a series of counter-attacks.

At 7:15 the German counter-bombardment came down on the captured position and across No Man's Land, causing heavy casualties among the carrying parties bringing up ammunition to the troops in the captured position. The shelling on the trench then ceased while German infantry launched a counter-attack with grenades on the left flank; that was beaten off and the German bombardment resumed. The Lewis gun outposts, in the open in front of the captured trench, were vulnerable to the shelling and one was destroyed by a direct hit. Another Lewis was out of action through continual stoppages, thought to be caused by the oil freezing, and Major Mundell decided to withdraw the guns, including the Vickers, to the comparative safety of the trench—a move which subsequently drew some criticism from the higher commanders. Between 1 am and 2 am several probing attacks came in from parties of German infantry, the most serious at about 1:30. This was repulsed with the help of a protective barrage by the 11th AFA Brigade, called in by its liaison officer with the infantry,[13] but the 15th troops had now used up almost all of their grenades. A supply of German stick grenades and 'egg bombs' found in the dugouts temporarily relieved the situation, but the heavy enemy shelling of No Man's Land was blocking further grenade supplies coming forward from the Australian lines. Early in the action a carrying party, at some cost in casualties, had managed to get through with a few boxes of grenades but these proved to be useless—through some blunder behind the lines their detonators had not been fitted.[14]

The captured position appeared to be firmly held, however, and success had been confidently reported to higher command when the situation suddenly deteriorated. The German counter-attack units, although so far repulsed, had already shown much more determination than the original garrison of the trench. At about 4 am another heavy counter-attack developed, launched by specially-trained storm troops of the German 4th Guards Division on the right flank, after another heavy bombardment. The moon had just set and the battlefield was in complete darkness—according to the 15th Battalion history, to the advantage of the Germans who knew the ground.[15] The 15th attempted to fire an SOS signal flare to call in covering artillery but it failed to burn. The guns had kept up a slow bombardment of the German approach routes for most of the night, but this was not heavy enough to deter the storm troops. Apparently the supply of shells was limited—the artillery group commander, Lieutenant Colonel Waite, had already expressed concern about ammunition expenditure and 'was desirous all evening of curtailing the fire.'[16] The artillery was unaware of the SOS situation until about 4:30 am, when a signal sent up by Battalion HQ was seen and the guns fired off most of their remaining ammunition in response. By then it was too late—assailed by showers of grenades from attackers invisible in the darkness, the 15th soon used up their few remaining grenades and could make no effective resistance. The right flank was driven in, and with further assaults being mounted against the centre and no artillery support, Major Mundell gave the order to retire. Some men could not get out of the trench in time and were taken prisoner; by the time the artillery opened fire, the survivors of the infantry were back in the original front line. The 15th Battalion had suffered 146 casualties in the battle, including

55 killed and missing; the German losses were about the same.[17] Two mortars of the 4th LTM Battery, emplaced in No Man's Land to assist the infantry, had been knocked out by enemy shelling. The mortar officer, Lieutenant James Robin, and three of his men were killed and two others wounded.[18]

There was some dismay at the command level, after the sudden collapse of the operation when success had seemed assured and had been reported as such. Within a few hours of the 15th's retreat, General Holmes conducted a searching interview with Colonel McSharry at the latter's headquarters.[19] The GOC was accompanied by the CRA, General Rosenthal, the 4th Brigade commander, General Brand, and Major Johnston, brigade major. The 15th Battalion was due to be relieved in the front line by the 13th, and the latter unit's CO, Colonel Durrant, was also present. General Holmes' conclusions ascribed the failure partly to misuse of the Lewis guns, which he believed should have been kept forward to interfere with enemy counter-attacks. The General, and Colonel McSharry, may not have been aware that two of the three guns were out of action at the crucial time. Communication between infantry and artillery was another important issue, one particularly noted by General Rosenthal. In hindsight the numerical strength of the attacking party was now seen to be inadequate. The arrangements for dealing with counter-attacks appeared to be faulty, and the GOC gained the impression that the troops had not shown enough determination—surely unfair in the light of the casualty list, their initial capture of the objective and repulse of several earlier counter-attacks, and the breakdown in the supply of grenades. General Holmes did acknowledge that Colonel McSharry had not had time to review all the reports and messages relating to the action, and that he was suffering from lack of sleep. The colonel's main source of information was Major Mundell, who had also not slept, and had been personally engaged in desperate combat all night. The Battalion history, unusually for such publications, was also critical:

> The Battalion staff work at Gueudecourt was not up to its usual standard ... there could have been no excuse for assuming that the assault would meet with only little opposition. Apparently Battalion Headquarters considered that the latter would actually be the case, as companies were sent into the fight with a totally inadequate supply of bombs, and with no provision made for their support once the position was occupied.[20]

By 'Battalion Headquarters' the writer presumably meant the CO, showing that even a fine commander like Colonel McSharry was capable of the occasional lapse under pressure. It should be noted, however, that the initial plans were made in conjunction with the brigadier and his staff, who no doubt had some influence on the approach that was taken.

At the meeting on the morning of the repulse (2 February), General Holmes decided that the 4th Brigade would repeat the attack on the night of 4/5 February. The 13th Battalion, due to relieve the 15th in the front line, was given the task. The 13th's CO, Colonel Durrant, having been present at the meeting, had some advance notice to begin his preparations before the official brigade order came through at 8pm on 3 February.[21] The 15th Battalion's experience had highlighted several important factors that Durrant paid particular attention to in his plans. In the first place, the 13th would use the whole battalion, less the nucleus 'left out of battle', to attack what was essentially the same objective, although extended by about 180 metres on the left flank.[22] This was about half as long again as the objective that the 15th had attempted with one and a half companies. Colonel Durrant later reported that a total of 671 officers and men took part in the attack.[23] Supply of grenades had been another major failing, and Durrant arranged for a stock of 20,000 grenades to be fed forward to the objective once it was taken. 12,000 of these were brought up to the front line trench and the remainder to the Battalion's forward HQ at the feature called Chalk Pit (or Chalk Cliff), with the intention of reducing the distance to be covered by carriers, who would probably be under fire from enemy artillery. For immediate use each rifleman would carry six grenades in his pockets (in the attack the men wore their greatcoats against the cold) and each company's 36 'bombers' were to carry 20 per man. Each company also detailed a group of 20 carriers to go forward with the second wave of the attack, each with a further 24 grenades (two boxes). The hand grenades were supplemented by 1,000 rifle grenades, fitted with adaptors and launched with a blank cartridge from rifles, these having a significant range advantage over hand-thrown grenades. The use of these weapons was suggested to the CO by Lieutenant George McDowell, the Battalion bombing officer.[24]

Much attention was given to improving the level of artillery support. The main covering barrage for the 15th Battalion's initial assault had been very effective, but the protective shelling afterwards had been too light to seriously interfere with German counter-attacks and the supply of artillery ammunition had proved to be inadequate. The 4th and 5th Division guns had fired about 8,600 shells during the operation, 'little more than would be used in a trench-raid.'[25], Extra artillery was provided for the renewed attack. The 10th AFA Brigade was due to be relieved by the 6th (Army) AFA Brigade but it was decided to delay the relief and leave the 10th in the line until after the operation, while bringing forward the 18-pounder batteries of the 6th Brigade into temporary emplacements. Those guns would join with Lieutenant Colonel Waite's No 1 Group (essentially the 11th AFA Brigade) in laying down the covering barrage on the objective then switching to protective fire. To improve the level of co-operation between infantry and artillery, Colonel Waite would command his guns from the infantry battalion's forward HQ. Telephone links were provided from there back to the battery positions and the ammunition supply for the guns was increased.

The 13th Battalion relieved the 15th in the front line (Grease and Shine Trenches) after dark on 2 February, placing a light garrison in the firing line—two platoons each from 'A' and 'B' companies—with the remainder of the battalion deployed in support positions. The 'A' Company commander, Captain Harry Murray, lost no time in making a personal reconnaissance of the ground that night, crawling across No Man's Land with his scouts up to the enemy wire. Captain Donald Wells, 'B' Company OC, did the same. Definite orders for the operation came through on the following night and Colonel Durrant called in all company commanders to go through the details. Afterwards the commanders of the two companies in support—Captain Norman MacDonald of 'C' and Lieutenant William Bone of 'D'—went up to the front line and also explored the ground where the attack would take place, as did Major Charles Johnston, the brigade major. The operation would be on the next night (4 February) and during that day the company commanders briefed their officers, who in turn explained the plans to their men—Colonel Durrant intended that everyone would be fully informed of what was expected well before the attack was launched. Those officers and NCOs who had not yet seen the ground came up to the front line during the day, risking snipers by observing over the parapet. Such was the morale in the 13th that eight men due to go on leave postponed it so as to take part in the operation. Captain Murray had come down with a bad case of influenza, but refused to be evacuated. Shivering with fever, he took his place at the head of his company, and one of Murray's officers, Lieutenant Ralph Kell, joined the attack despite suffering from dysentery.

The Germans would probably have made some efforts to repair their wire since the earlier attack and the objective had now been extended. Lieutenant McPherson's X4A MTM battery was again given the wire-cutting task. Following a bombardment of the objective by the I Anzac heavy artillery during the afternoon, the mortars began lobbing their big shells into the wire towards the left end of the objective. The mortars fired 25 rounds, most of which were observed to hit the target, although there was still considerable risk to the mortarmen from faulty cartridges. Five shells fell short, one of those landing only 30 metres from the gun, and there were a few overshoots which were believed to have burst in the German trench. The accurate shots were seen to have cut the entanglement in several places.[26] There still appeared to be insufficient damage to the wire on the extreme right of the objective, but this was allowed for in the 13th's tactics on the night. No stone was left unturned by the Battalion. On the theory that the Lewis gun stoppages experienced by the 15th Battalion had been caused by the oil freezing up, the 13th's gunners stripped their weapons down, removed all the oil and grease from the working parts and applied kerosene instead. Whether for this reason or not, the 13th had much less trouble with Lewis stoppages during the fighting.

After sunset on 4 February the assault force began moving from the support lines into their jumping-off positions in and near the front-line trench. The men had wrapped sand-bags around their boots to muffle the sound of tramping feet. Zero was set for 10 pm. A full moon meant that the approach route of 'D' Company on the left was open to enemy observation, so the men had to move up in small groups. Some were still coming up when Zero arrived but most of the battalion was in position forty minutes earlier. There was not enough space in the front line for the whole force so a platoon of 'A' Company on the right flank had to start 100 metres behind the rest of the company. The troops, waiting in the bitter cold, were warmed by a rum issue—normal practice before an attack in most of the BEF but unusual in the AIF, where rum was normally distributed after battle.

At 10 pm the barrage crashed out, and the infantry rose from their positions and set out across the frozen No Man's Land, those groups forced to start from rearward positions hurrying to catch up with the main line. As they left the trench, Captain Stewart Hansen's company of the 14th Battalion filed into it to hold the line and provide extra support for the attack force. The 13th advanced in one main wave of riflemen and bombers with the Lewis gunners and carrying parties following closely behind. A German machine gun set up in No Man's Land was overrun and captured, its crew all killed or wounded. The barrage fell with precise accuracy, the flashes of the 18-pounder shrapnel shells forming almost a straight line in the air along the enemy trench. 'The shooting of the artillery was wonderfully good,' wrote Colonel Durrant in his after-action report. 'The assaulting wave was actually able to get to 5 or 6 yards from the barrage, which previously I have often said was impossible.' [27] The artillery was using thirty 18-pounders in five batteries on the line of the objective itself and a short distance to either side, each gun firing five rounds per minute. The barrage was timed for two minutes, the same as in the earlier operation but with more guns, 300 shells falling in the allotted time. The troops crawled the last few yards to the objective, so close to the barrage that the shells were bursting behind them, blasting the shrapnel pellets over their heads into the enemy trench. As the barrage lifted away to fall on the enemy support lines, the 13th rushed the trench.

The companies on the left and centre had no trouble getting through the gaps in the wire and were on top of the German garrison troops before they could emerge from their dugouts. Lieutenant Bone's company on the left was able to work further up the trench beyond their original objective. Lieutenant McDowell brought his bombers up and constructed a barricade to defend that flank. On the right, Captain Murray's 'A' Company was held up by a 75 metre stretch of uncut wire, but this was no surprise and the troops quickly swung around the left end of the entanglement and advanced down the trench to the right. The short delay had given time for the defenders to come up from their dugouts, however, and a stiff fight quickly developed, both sides mainly using grenades. 'A' Company, pressing forward both on the floor of the trench and in the open along the parapet, killed or captured many of their opponents and drove the survivors back along the trench. The company was still about 100 metres short of their objective point on the right when this first fighting died down, but Murray decided to hold where he was rather than attempting to advance further. Writing after the war, Murray pointed out that going further would have put his men at the bottom of a slope, throwing grenades uphill against an enemy throwing downhill when the inevitable counter-attacks came in.[28] As well, the German counter-bombardment had started and was falling heavily in and around the area. A barricade was put up and the capture of Stormy Trench was complete—the problem now would be to hold it. The green flares signalling success were fired along the line, but during this process the 'C' Company commander, Captain MacDonald, was killed by a sniper. A Gallipoli veteran, he had only been back with the Battalion for a week after being attached to the Camel Corps in Egypt.

The troops now set to work on the vital work of consolidation to put the captured trench in a state of defence. It was over two metres deep in sections so fire steps had to be cut in what had been the back wall. Picks and shovels had been brought with the assault force but the frozen earth made for slow work. The Battalion's Lewis guns had come up and were posted to screen the front of the position and at the flanking barricades. About 40 Germans had been killed and more than 60 taken prisoner—the latter were quickly hustled across No Man's Land to the Australian lines, where their unit was identified as the 10th Company, 362nd Regiment. That information reached BEF HQ within an hour of the attack—the 4th Division staff believed the time to be a record. Not all of the prisoners reached the rear, however. Some were caught by their own counter-barrage which now fell on the lost position, and on No Man's Land and the original Australian front line. The Germans poured in a fierce bombardment, using both HE and shrapnel shells and casualties began to mount up. After half an hour's pounding the shelling died down on the right flank. There was a pause of about ten minutes, then at 10:50 pm an infantry counter-attack was heralded by a shower of German grenades which burst at 'A' Company's barricade, almost wiping out the group of bombers posted there. The troops nearby fell back but they were rallied by Captain Murray, who led them back to the barricade. Private Malcolm Robertson brought up more bombers, and a fierce grenade duel began. Murray ordered the SOS signal rocket to be fired. It was spotted almost immediately by observers at the forward HQ and within thirty seconds the artillery was laying an accurate curtain of fire along the prearranged SOS line—'a beautiful barrage' as Colonel Durrant described it.[29] The barrage prevented any reinforcements from reaching the German force, but the grenade fight at the trench went on.

The Germans, throwing from shell-holes and old trenches and outranging the Australians, were beginning to gain the advantage when Captain Murray changed his tactics and called for a bayonet charge over the top against the enemy bombers, who broke and fled. Murray personally shot three with his revolver and captured another three. The company Lewis gunners had kept up a covering fire from their exposed positions as the bayonet-men charged. At the same time, the Germans occupying the main trench beyond the barricade were tackled by a group led by Corporal Roy Withers ('a big strong lad, who could hurl our bombs 60 yards [55 metres]'[30]) who ignored a leg wound and ran along the trench-line in the open, flinging grenades down into it. He was supported by Private Robertson, skilfully lobbing rifle-grenades further along the trench. Robertson had also been wounded, hit in the face by grenade splinters. The first German counter-attack on the right had failed and shortly afterwards their artillery resumed its bombardment of the captured position. Captain Murray stayed in the open for some time looking for wounded, carrying three back to the trench one by one. The Germans had also launched a counter-attack at about 11 pm on the left flank, held by Lieutenant Bone's 'D' Company. Here again the SOS signal had brought a swift and accurate response from the artillery, and in another grenade battle 'D' Company drove off the attackers, with Lieutenant McDowell's bombers being particularly prominent. Fighting now died down on that flank but heavy pressure continued against 'A' Company on the right.

Around midnight, that Company was again counter-attacked by a German infantry force. The previous pattern was repeated, with the Australian artillery reacting promptly to the SOS signal to lay down the protective barrage and the two sides' grenadiers battling for the advantage. Over a period of 20 minutes the Germans made five attempts to dislodge 'A' Company before admitting defeat and pulling back. Private Robertson again distinguished himself, continuing his self-appointed role as leader of a bombing section—which he twice had to reorganise as casualties mounted up—and tormenting the Germans with accurate rifle grenades. Corporal Withers also repeated his efforts of the earlier fighting. He had gone back through the barrage to the old front line to get his knee-wound dressed, helping another wounded man on the way, then had insisted on going back to the fighting. He returned to Stormy Trench carrying a load of flares and ammunition then made the hazardous return trip several more times, carrying wounded men back and ammunition forward. In between trips he joined in the grenade-fight with his powerful throwing. After the final attack in this phase had been repulsed there was a period of comparative calm in the vicinity of the trench. Captain Murray and Private Robertson took the opportunity to reconnoitre the surrounding area, identifying likely spots where the German grenadiers could shelter in the event of another counter-attack.

This came at about 3 am, preceded by another ferocious bombardment, which included heavy 'rum jar' mortar bombs.[31] The survivors of 'A' company braced themselves for another battle and the alert artillery gunners once again brought down their barrage on the SOS line. Once more the grenade fighting was brought to an end when Murray, 'with his revolver in one hand and a bomb in the other,'[32] led bayonet charges that drove off the German grenadiers in disorder. This proved to be the enemy's final attempt to retake the lost position but they continued to pound the area with artillery and mortars. By the time dawn broke on 5 February the trench had been almost demolished on the right, HE shells breaking the frozen earth into rubble and vaporising the snow all around.[33] 'A' Company was now down to about 60 unwounded members out of 149 who had jumped off at Zero but the position was firmly held all along the line and the 13th Battalion had won its battle.

The result could not have been achieved without the great effort of the carrying parties to get ammunition, and particularly supplies of grenades, to the fighting line. The fierce shelling on No Man's Land had continued throughout the infantry battle, and carriers struggling up to Stormy Trench with their loads suffered heavy casualties. The German guns also pounded the original Australian front line continuously, and the two platoons of the 14th Battalion's 'C' Company occupying Shine Trench were particularly heavily hit. By the end of the battle, the 14th had suffered 72 casualties[34] from artillery fire. Of these, 27 were killed or died from their wounds, including Captain Hansen who was hit in the head by a shell splinter and died three days later. The 13th Battalion's carriers had kept on through the storm of shell fire, and Lance Corporal John Rankin and Private Frederick McQueen particularly distinguished themselves in this heavy, highly dangerous work. The carriers were losing men all the time, however, and

Captain Alfred 'Lofty' Williamson, now in charge of 'C' Company of the 14th, organised parties of his men to assist the 13th in the task. At one stage in the fighting, the 14th sent up a Lewis gun under Corporal Percy Muir to replace one that had been knocked out on the right flank; Muir and his crew fought all night alongside 'A' Company of the 13th.

The occupied section of Stormy Trench was now regarded as part of the Australian front line and efforts began to consolidate it for defence and link it to the original front by communication trenches. For the time being the 13th Battalion would form the garrison, but Captain Murray sent back a message requesting relief for his battered 'A' Company, which had taken the main weight of the German counter-attacks and suffered by far the highest casualties of the companies. That night, the 16th Battalion, holding the left of the 4th Brigade sector, sent up one of its reserve companies under Captain Charles Ahearn to take over the right of the firing line. The 'A' Company survivors returned to the acclaim of peers and commanders for their epic fight, and many decorations were recommended by Colonel Durrant shortly afterwards. The outstanding efforts of Captain Murray, Corporal Withers and Private Robertson were recognised by recommendations for the VC. In the event, Withers and Robertson were awarded the DCM instead, but during March it was announced that Murray's VC had been approved.

Captain (later Lieutenant Colonel) Henry 'Harry' Murray VC CMG DSO and Bar DCM (1880–1966), 13th Battalion.
(State Library NSW 179524))

Henry William 'Harry' Murray was a Tasmanian by birth and upbringing, and a Western Australian by residence and enlistment when he joined the AIF in 1914, as a private in the 16th Battalion. He had started as a machine gunner, in the same Maxim gun team as his great friend Percy Black, and had served throughout the Gallipoli campaign from the Landing to the evacuation, apart from short periods in hospital with illness and a wound. During the campaign Murray had been commissioned into the 13th Battalion (NSW) as its MG officer, and had remained with that unit as an infantry officer when the machine guns were detached into independent companies. The fighting at Mouquet Farm had demonstrated his outstanding abilities as a front-line leader and now he had excelled himself at Stormy Trench. He had the knack of keeping an overview of the battle situation while fighting for his life in hand-to-hand combat. His VC, added to the DSO and DCM that he had been awarded previously, put him ahead of Albert Jacka and the late Alfred Shout, both with the VC and MC, as the most highly decorated Australian serviceman. Murray retains that distinction to this day, and he was to be decorated several more times during the war. His VC was the third to be awarded to a 4th Brigade soldier. Harry Murray was 36 years and two months of age at the time of the battle, among the oldest of VC winners.[35] Other decorations awarded to the 13th Battalion for Stormy Trench included MCs to Lieutenants McDowell and Bone for their firm defence on the left flank, and for the unit's RMO, Captain Norman Shierlaw, who patched up the wounded for 48 hours under fire. Sergeant Andrew Gove was awarded the DCM for his work with the carrying parties and for an incident several days after the battle when he smothered a burning box of grenades that had been set alight by a German shell. Fourteen MMs were awarded to 13th Battalion soldiers, including ammunition carriers Lance Corporal Rankin and Private McQueen and stretcher bearer Private Victor Corby, all of whom had run the gauntlet of No Man's Land throughout the night. The 14th Battalion Lewis gunner, Private Muir, was also awarded the MM, as was Private Percy Hume of that unit, a stretcher bearer who had single-handedly attended to the 14th's many casualties in Shine Trench all night under savage shellfire.

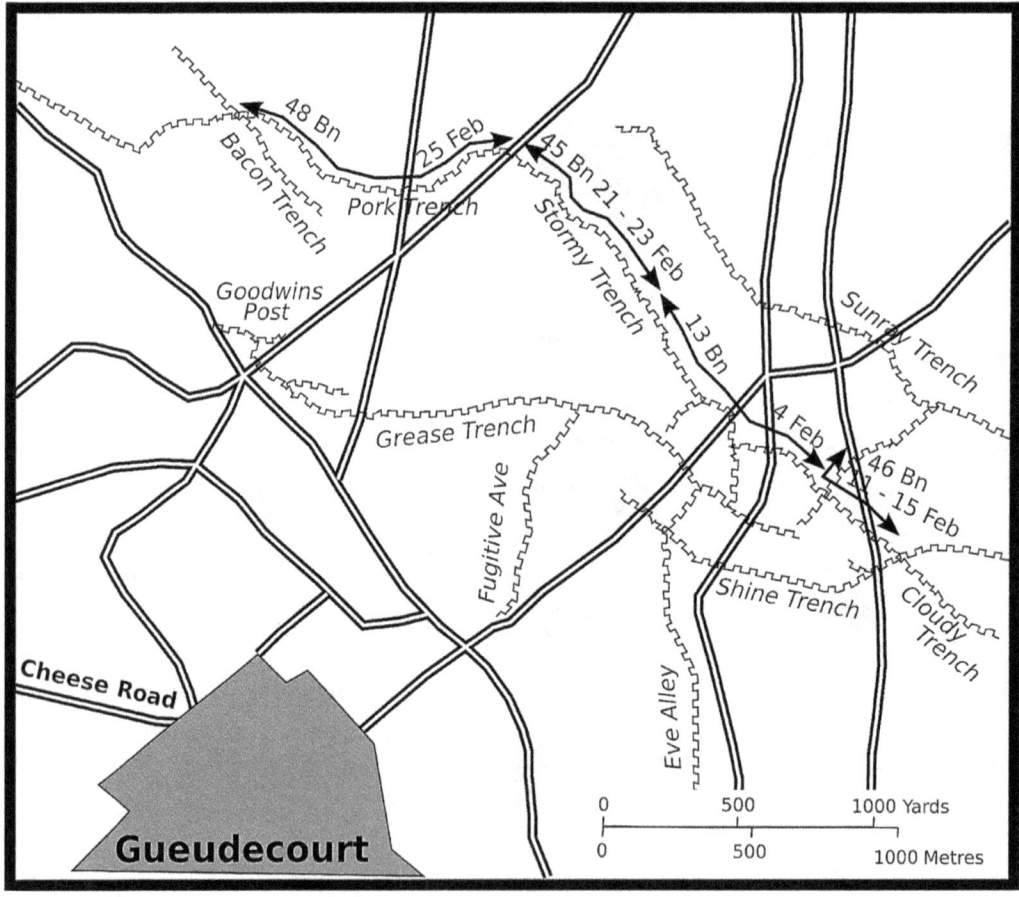

Operations at Stormy Trench, February 1917.

The pressing issue now was to hold and if possible extend the new front line position in Stormy Trench. The 4th MG Company had sent up a Vickers gun as soon as the trench had been captured and another was mounted on 6 February to give defensive firepower, added to the battalion Lewis guns posted along the line. Work continued on communication trenches and one was put through from Grease Trench on the night of 6/7 February—dug in ten hours by a party from the 14th Battalion and named Fourteenth Alley in recognition of that unit's part in the operation. It had been intended that the neighbouring 15th Brigade (5th Division) would dig a trench from their front to link with the right of the original objective position. The heavy fighting on that flank, however, had prevented the 13th Battalion from pushing far enough along to make the connecting trench a practical proposition yet. For the next few days nothing further was attempted, apart from night work to improve the new position. Proper firesteps were cut, the original parapet and parados were reversed and a start was made on barbed wire entanglements on what was now the enemy's side. The three companies of the 13th and one of the 16th Battalion continued to garrison the trench under regular enemy shelling, with the Germans occupying the same trench beyond the barricades on each flank. The captured position was about 600 metres long and more than two metres deep, with sufficient dugouts to accommodate at least 150 men. Running along elevated ground, it offered observation of the enemy rear area, and its occupation by friendly troops made traffic in Grease Trench and the communication trench Fugitive Alley secure from enemy observation. The operation had in many ways been a model of planning, with the 13th Battalion leadership making advance arrangements to meet most eventualities that might be encountered by the troops. The details of the first attack by the 15th Battalion had been studied closely, and the defects in that rather unlucky unit's arrangements had been largely rectified. Co-operation between infantry and artillery had been exemplary, and the sharing of headquarters by Colonels Waite and Durrant had worked well. The allocation of more guns and more ammunition than had been allowed in the previous attack was a major factor in success—the artillery reported firing more than 20,000 rounds (mostly 18-pounders) on 4/5 February,[36] well over twice the amount expended in the first attack. For all of this, however, at the crisis of the battle it all came down to the determination, skill and discipline of the men fighting with grenade, Lewis gun and bayonet in the front line, and the leadership of their officers and NCOs.

The 4th Brigade was relieved by the 12th on the night of 9 February, with the 47th and 46th Battalions initially manning the firing line. The 47th took over from the 16th in Grease Trench on the left of the brigade sector, and the 46th replaced the 13th on the right—that is, the forward position in Stormy Trench. The 4th Brigade units moved back to Mametz and Bécourt, while the 12th Brigade prepared to follow up the initial success by widening the foothold in Stormy Trench. The 46th Battalion was given the task of pushing the right flank further along the trench, which was designated as Cloudy Trench in that area, and an operation was organised for the night of 11/12 February. This took the form of a grenade attack to be launched from the temporary barricade or block established by the 13th Battalion. A very small force was allocated, comprising two groups of seven 'bombers,' each group under an NCO, supported by six rifle-grenadiers and a working party of two NCOs and ten men who would be responsible for constructing a new barricade. Lieutenant William Syme was in command of the attack force. The rifle-grenadiers provided the main direct fire support; the nature of the operation made the use of artillery impractical, and there were no LTMs in suitable emplacements to shoot at the enemy section of the trench. The two front-line Vickers guns (now manned by the 12th MG Company), together with the Battalion Lewis guns, would sweep the area in front of the objective to deter enemy supports.

The attack was launched at 11:40 pm. The rifle-grenadiers, firing from the existing block, put down a shower of projectiles onto the first 45 metres of the enemy's trench section. After three minutes the aim was lifted 30 metres further along the trench to interfere with enemy supports, and the bombing squads took over with hand grenades. Gaining the upper hand over the German garrison, the bombers advanced steadily up the trench, tossing grenades into dugouts as they went. The rifle-grenadiers kept their barrage moving ahead of the advance and the Germans were unable to rally. After 25 minutes fighting the 46th troops had advanced more than 100 metres along the trench. There the bombers halted to cover the following working party, who quickly constructed two barricades, 25 metres apart. These were completed within 20 minutes, and the bombers then withdrew behind the advanced block and prepared to meet German counter-attacks. The first of these came at 1:00 am but was quickly driven off, mainly by rifle grenades. All was quiet until 4:40 am when a determined attack got inside the rifle grenade barrage and drove the 46th bombers back from the first barricade. The Victorians rallied and quickly recaptured it, led by Corporal Harold Ritter and Lance Corporal Samuel Browse, who stood their ground and drove back their opponents with accurate throwing. The forward block was not intended to be permanently occupied, however, and the attack force finally withdrew behind the stronger second block and completed the consolidation of the captured segment. A length of between 80 and 100 metres of trench had been added to the new front line[37] and access was gained to an old sap running towards the 5th Division's front line on the right. The intention was to deepen and extend the sap to link up the two divisional fronts. The cost had been light—the 46th had lost two killed and four wounded from a total force of 35. Five German dead were found in the trench, and one prisoner was captured; presumably the Germans would have suffered some wounded also.

Three nights later, on 14/15 February, the 46th Battalion mounted another thrust along the trench, again using a small party of bombers and rifle-grenadiers under Lieutenant Syme. This was timed to coincide with a large-scale raid by 5th Division troops on the German position in Sunray Trench to the north-east. Using the same tactics as before, the 46th captured another 45 metres of trench and set up a new block. The 46th bombing squad led by Lance Sergeant Stanley Goldsmith lost five of its seven men to German grenades at the start, but Goldsmith and the others hung on and drove back their opponents. The most serious losses to the 46th occurred with the troops holding the main position, who were caught by the German barrage fired in retaliation for the Sunray Trench raid and suffered 27 casualties.[38] The two attacks brought a number of decorations to 46th members, including the MC to Lieutenant Syme and MMs to Corporals Ritter and Browse and Sergeant Goldsmith. A further small operation by the 57th Battalion (5th Division) on the right saw the Australian line linked up on that flank.

Shortly after this burst of fighting, the 12th Brigade changed over its front-line battalions, the 45th relieving the 46th on the right in Stormy Trench, and the 48th relieving the 47th on the left in Grease Trench, during the night of 17 February. The 12th Brigade now concentrated on extending the Stormy Trench position to the left (west), for a considerably greater distance than that gained on the right. The 45th Battalion was given this task and its CO, Lieutenant Colonel Sydney Herring, initially planned an elaborate and ambitious operation to capture over 400 metres of trench. The attack force was to comprise 10 officers and 250 ORs, with a further two officers and 100 ORs in immediate support, covered by an artillery barrage and LTMs. The attack was to be launched early on 20 February but the weather intervened. The great frost had effectively ended on 16 February, when temperatures began to increase; the snow was replaced by rain the next day, and within a short time the mud was back. At first it formed a shallow layer above the still-frozen ground, but within a day of the rain starting, Private George Mitchell (48th Battalion) recorded that his party, coming up through Fritz's Folly, were 'bogged to the thighs. Last night our boots were on frozen ground at ankle-depth.'[39] By the night of 19 February conditions in the front line and its approaches were so bad that the 45th Battalion operation was called off. The constant traffic of carrying parties bringing up supplies for the attack had churned the trench floors into a morass. The attack commander, Captain Harold Howden, sent an unequivocal message to Colonel Herring beginning

> I want you to exercise your full right and cry the stunt off. Conditions are exceptionally fierce as regards mud ... [the trenches] are thigh deep and Fourteenth Alley is impassable ... what men who have arrived here are absolutely done in.[40]

Captain Howden, who had been a private at Gallipoli with the 13th Battalion before being commissioned into the 'daughter' 45th, went on to point out that both the attack force and the parties following with supplies of grenades would be fatally bogged down by the mud and the operation was likely to fail with heavy losses. Colonel Herring was convinced, and immediately recommended to Brigade HQ that the attack be postponed. Brigadier General Robertson, after obtaining confirmation through a staff officer, ordered the operation called off, just in time to stop the covering artillery barrage from opening up. Robertson, incidentally, had shown a degree of flexibility in this incident which goes against a later assessment of him by C E W Bean as being rigidly insistent on orders being carried out.[41]

The brigadier wanted the operation attempted again as soon as possible, but he took the opportunity to order that the numbers involved be scaled down considerably. Perhaps by now aware of the success achieved by small parties of the 46th and 57th Battalions at the other end of the Stormy Trench position, the planners quickly drew up a simplified scheme using only two 17-man teams of 'bombers' with carriers, two rifle-grenadier teams, two Lewis gun teams, and a dozen men for escorting prisoners. Artillery support was dispensed with except for a protective 'SOS' barrage to be called in if necessary. Direct fire support would be confined to the two Stokes mortars of the 12th LTM battery, with covering fire from Vickers guns of the 12th MG Company. Rather than attempting to overwhelm the whole objective of the original scheme in one assault, the orders called for 240 metres of trench to be captured if possible, but allowed for the attack to be stopped if progress became too difficult. The modified operation was ordered for only 24 hours after the original scheme had been called off. While there was no expectation that conditions in the trenches would be any better by then, the men would have had some rest and the smaller and more flexible groups might be better able to cope with the mud. Shortly before 3 am (the 'Zero' time) on 21 February, the bombing parties, under Lieutenants Robert Murray and Edmund Cornish, left their trench and took up position in the open, where the going was slightly better than that in the trench. At Zero the mortars opened up on the enemy's block, bombarding it for three minutes before lifting 150 metres along the trench. The infantrymen pushed their way through the mud into the German position. Taken by surprise, the Germans put up little resistance on the flank and the attackers began to work their way up the trench. Led by Sergeant William Gocher, the rifle-grenadiers came up and added their missiles to the mortar-bombs falling along the enemy position while the bombers pushed on through the slush of the trench floor, driving their opponents before them. A particularly muddy patch trapped three men, who were not dug out until the next day,[42] and the carrying parties struggled to get through with supplies of grenades. Hampered by their heavy loads, one group was unable to get out of the jumping-off trench until Lieutenant Herbert Maiden got down on his knees in the mud to use his back as a step-ladder.[43] Extra carriers were brought up from the support line, among them Private Ted Lynch:

> We reach a great squashy patch of churned up mud. There ahead of us we see [our officer] beckoning us on whilst we hear our attackers shouting desperately for bombs. Our two leading carriers go down to their waists in the mud and are bogged ... [the officer] pulls them out and on they go. Another fellow gets bogged whilst 'Bombs! Pass the word for bombs!' is being roared out from on ahead where the fighting is hottest.[44]

The 45th attackers chased the enemy down the trench for 260 metres, beyond the range of the LTM covering fire, before resistance stiffened. In accordance with the orders, a block was quickly thrown up to defend the captured position while the mortars were moved up and re-emplaced to meet any counter-attack. This came just before daylight and was easily beaten off, mainly by the mortars and rifle-grenades. The new segment of trench was in poor condition, comparatively shallow and muddy, which made the task of consolidation an exhausting one. The 45th's losses in the attack itself had been slight, with only seven ORs and an officer wounded,[45] although retaliatory shelling later in the morning caused another 30 casualties in the front line. The 45th took 29 prisoners in this fight and estimated that the

Germans had lost another 80 men killed or wounded, in all a satisfying small victory for the Battalion, albeit against unimpressive opposition. Plans were immediately made to follow up this success with another attack along the trench on the next night, 22/23 February. The new objective for the 45th Battalion was set as a sunken road intersecting the trench about 150 metres from the block established in the previous attack. The recent operations had extended the line held by the 45th, nominally the right-hand unit of the brigade, well to its left (west), so that it was now in advance of the left battalion, the 48th, occupying positions in the Grease Trench vicinity. The 48th was given a task in the new operation, to capture the next segment of enemy trench, known as Pork Trench, running further west from the sunken road. Once the 45th had secured its objective, the 48th would continue the attack with a 60-strong force advancing from Goodwin's Post for about 200 metres across No Man's Land. The attackers would enter the trench and advance along it by 'bombing,' with the objective of capturing a further 150 metres, up to another road crossing. Fire support for both battalions would again be provided by Stokes mortars of the 12th LTM Battery and their own rifle grenadiers, with the 12th MG Company delivering indirect fire into the enemy rear area.

The 45th Battalion force was again under the overall command of Captain Howden, this time with Lieutenants Leon Ferguson and Alexander Muir in charge of the bombers. The 45th's attack was launched at midnight behind a barrage of mortar rounds and was almost a repetition of the previous attack, with the German garrison putting up little resistance. Although slowed down by the mud the attacking infantry pushed through to secure its objective at the sunken road, taking 32 prisoners while losing only three wounded themselves; Sergeant Reynold Scott was among those prominent in the fighting, leading a section of bombers and organising the rifle grenadiers in keeping the enemy under pressure. The 48th Battalion's operation, however, struck problems. Hampered by fog as well as deep mud in No Man's Land, the 48th's party had difficulty keeping direction and then encountered three successive belts of barbed wire. The men managed to cross the first two but the third proved to be impassable. It was close to the enemy trench, which was strongly manned at this point, and the troops came under heavy fire. Although the 48th's rifle grenades probably did some damage to the Germans the infantrymen were unable to advance. After the attack group had been pinned down for two hours in the mud, the officers reluctantly made the decision to withdraw and the troops made their way back to the original line, crawling for much of the way. Three men had been wounded, one of whom later died in hospital. A disappointed Colonel Leane ordered that another attempt be made to capture Pork Trench on the night of 24 February, just before the battalion was due to be relieved in the front line. Careful preparations were made[46] and after dark the attacking party advanced cautiously towards the objective. Entering the trench at 8:15 pm the troops were surprised to find that it was now deserted, and the position was soon occupied by the 48th party. This bloodless capture represented the 12th Brigade's final operation on the Gueudecourt front, both the 45th and 48th Battalions being relieved that night by the 58th Battalion (5th Division) in what was now the front line.

The 12th Brigade had extended the territory initially captured by the 4th Brigade at the start of the month, advancing the I Anzac front to the line Cloudy Trench-Stormy Trench-Pork Trench along the rising ground north-east of the original Flers-Gueudecourt position. These operations were the first in which the 12th Brigade had been tasked with taking and holding ground, and although there had been little serious opposition offered by the enemy—for reasons that would soon become apparent—the Brigade units had performed with efficiency and dash. Up to now the Brigade's combat experience had mainly been with holding the front line, usually under heavy bombardment as at Pozières, together with the raiding and patrolling inherent in that duty. The two successful attacks made by the 45th Battalion in particular were rewarded with numerous decorations. These included MCs to Captain Howden (a Bar to the MC that he had won at Pozières), Lieutenants Murray, Cornish and Ferguson, and CSM Thomas Crooks, who had organised the carrying parties, under fire, in both attacks—the MC could be awarded to warrant officers as well as commissioned officers. Sergeant Scott was awarded the DCM for his work in the second attack, and 17 MMs included awards to Sergeant Gocher (a Bar), stretcher bearer Private Hans Nielsen, signaller Private Gilbert Turner, rifle grenadier Private Walter Worner, and Lewis gunner Private Thomas Blunden.

The operations of the 4th and 12th Brigades during February had included much work with picks, shovels and sandbags as well as with rifles and grenades. Captured enemy fieldworks had to be consolidated with firesteps, transposition of parapet and parados, construction of blocks or 'bomb stops', stringing of barbed wire, establishment of machine gun posts, and construction of communication trenches back to the original line. Unusually, it appears that the infantry carried out this work with little or no assistance from the divisional engineers and pioneers. Those units were still heavily engaged in upgrading the infrastructure immediately behind the front line but it should have been possible to release a few officers or NCOs to provide advice and direction to the infantry—of course, the latter may not have requested any assistance, or some may have been provided but simply not recorded.[47] During February, the 4th Field Company was mainly engaged in work on the camps and headquarters accommodation, while the 12th and 13th Field Companies worked on improvements to the reserve and communications trenches in their brigade sectors; both of those companies incurred some casualties from shell fire and snipers. The 4th Pioneer Battalion continued with the constant work of extending and maintaining the Decauville light railway tracks in the forward area.

The Pioneers received a new CO in February, Lieutenant Colonel Vernon Sturdee, who was arguably the most distinguished regular officer to serve with the 4th Division (Monash being a militiaman). Sturdee was a Victorian, 26 years old, a member of a family with some distinction in the armed services of the Empire. His father, Alfred Sturdee, was a medical practitioner who had emigrated from England to Australia and was currently a colonel in the AAMC, until recently ADMS of the 1st Division. An uncle was Admiral Sir Doveton Sturdee RN, victor of the Battle of the Falklands in 1914. Vernon Sturdee had been an officer of the Australian Engineers in the permanent forces since 1911. Transferring to the AIF, he had served at Gallipoli (as had his father), and was a major commanding the 8th Field Company (5th Division) when he was promoted to command the 4th Pioneers. The future would see General Sir Vernon Sturdee as Chief of the Australian General Staff in World War Two and afterwards. A change of command also took place in the 4th Field Company during February, when Major Cutler was posted to command the Engineer Training Depot in England; Captain Clarence Mills took over as acting OC for the time being.

The circumstance whereby two infantry battalions of the 4th Division had been relieved in the front line by one of the 5th Division reflected the development of the allies' plans for the year. As C E W Bean wryly noted:

> To staff officers' batmen and car drivers, French *estaminet* proprietors, and other observant and well-informed persons behind the Somme front, it was at this time obvious that the launching of a great British offensive farther north was approaching.[48]

That was the planned attack against the German front near Arras, in conjunction with the main blow to be struck by the French to the south under General Nivelle's grand scheme. A change in the higher command arrangements had taken place on 15 February, with I Anzac transferring from Fourth Army to Fifth Army—the former Reserve Army, commanded by the ominous figure of General Sir Hubert Gough, the same who had presided over the carnage at Mouquet Farm. Fifth Army, in particular I Anzac Corps, would play a part on its front with a thrust towards Bapaume in support of the main British effort at Arras. All four of I Anzac's divisions had been in the front line for some time, and the Corps commander, Sir William Birdwood, was anxious to give the troops even a brief rest before they faced the demands of major offensive operations. There was also a requirement, officially announced as recently as 14 February, for comprehensive re-training of the infantry battalions in a new system of platoon-based tactics, a task best done out of the line. General Birdwood decided to withdraw one division at a time and hold the line more thinly with the other three. The 4th Division after a month of heavy fighting was selected to be relieved first; the gap was covered by the 5th Division extending its left and the 1st Division its right.

The 4th Division units again went through the process of handing over to their reliefs and moving back to the rear areas. The 4th Infantry Brigade, already in reserve around Mametz, began its move to Ribemont-sur-Ancre on 22 February. Units from the 5th Division relieved those of the 12th Brigade on 24 February, and the latter moved back to Hénencourt. The 13th Brigade, which had been holding its one-battalion front on the left of the Division sector throughout the period, was relieved by 1st Division units on 24 February, moving to Bresle. During its tour the 13th Brigade had not been required to undertake any offensive operations like those carried out by the other two brigades, although preparations had begun for an attack on the enemy position in Scabbard Trench late in the month. The operation was called off when it became apparent that the Division was about to be relieved. The Division General Staff War Diary noted that this was something of a disappointment: 'the 13th Brigade are most anxious to show what they can do'[49]—a staff officer's view that may not have been shared by the average rifleman in the ranks. The 13th Brigade had some changes to its senior officers during February, Brigadier General Glasgow promoting his trusted brigade major, Cecil Ridley,[50] to Lieutenant Colonel commanding the 51st Battalion, replacing the temporary CO, Major Robert Christie. Christie, who reverted to second in command of the unit, was highly thought of but presumably the brigadier felt that he was not yet ready for the permanent command. Captain Roy Morell, the staff captain, moved up to the brigade major posting with the commensurate promotion and Captain Arthur Nicholson came in from the 52nd Battalion as staff captain.

Most of the Division's units made their way back to the Corps Training Area over the next few days, including the medical, engineer and artillery units, which had generally been on duty in the forward area behind the front line since November. Division HQ was set up at Baizieux on 25 February and HQ of the divisional artillery was established five kilometres away at Bavelincourt Chateau on the next day. The 11th AFA Brigade remained in the line for a short period, attached to the 5th Division, not rejoining its own division until 6 March. The 10th AFA Brigade arrived in the area on 28 February. The 10th had been attached to the 2nd British Division near Courcelette since 9 February, following the initial Stormy Trench operations, to assist in a projected British attack towards Miraumont. That advance, launched on 24 February, made the astounding discovery that the Germans had abandoned their positions. Patrols and minor operations on I Anzac's front on previous nights, including the 48th Battalion's occupation of Pork Trench, had revealed that some of the enemy advanced positions were empty. It was only now realised, however, that an extensive German retirement was actually taking place and that contact with the enemy had been lost over a large segment of the front. This momentous development did not immediately affect the 4th Division, coinciding as it did with the Division's relief from the front line, but in six weeks' time the full implications would appear. About this time, the units and senior officers of the 4th Division were as follows:

4th Australian Division Order of Battle, late February 1917

	GOC	Major General W Holmes
	GSO1	Lieutenant Colonel D J C K Bernard
	GSO2	Major H S M McRae
	GSO3	Captain A S Keighley
	AA&QMG	Lieutenant Colonel E Armstrong
	DAA&QMG	Major H D Wynter
	DAQMG	Captain W Fowler-Brownsworth
	ADCs	Lieutenant D Gillies-Reyburn, Lieutenant K A Ferguson
Infantry		
	4th Brigade:	Brigadier General C H Brand
	Brigade Major:	Major C M Johnston
	Staff Captain:	Captain A H Fraser

13th Battalion:	Lieutenant Colonel J M A Durrant
14th Battalion:	Lieutenant Colonel J H Peck
15th Battalion:	Lieutenant Colonel T P McSharry
16th Battalion:	Lieutenant Colonel E A Drake-Brockman
4th MG Company:	Captain A Mitchell
4th LTM Battery:	Captain A W Potts

12th Brigade: Brigadier General J C Robertson
Brigade Major: Captain E L Salier
Staff Captain: Major W Inglis
45th Battalion: Lieutenant Colonel S C E Herring
46th Battalion: Lieutenant Colonel H K Denham
47th Battalion: Lieutenant Colonel E StL Lewis
48th Battalion: Lieutenant Colonel R L Leane
12th MG Company: Captain E G Sawer
12th LTM Battery: Captain J Johnstone

13th Brigade: Brigadier General T W Glasgow
Brigade Major: Major R Morell
Staff Captain: Captain A Nicholson
49th Battalion: Major W L Arrell
50th Battalion: Lieutenant Colonel A G Salisbury
51st Battalion: Lieutenant Colonel J C T E C Ridley
52nd Battalion: Lieutenant Colonel D A Lane
13th MG Company: Captain C F Duchatel
13th LTM Battery: Captain S C Morris

Artillery

CRA:	Brigadier General C Rosenthal
Brigade Major:	Major C M Bates
Staff Captain:	Captain F E Forrest
10th Field Artillery Brigade:	Lieutenant Colonel G H M King
(37th, 38th, 39th, 110th Batteries)	
11th Field Artillery Brigade:	Lieutenant Colonel W C N Waite
(41st, 42nd, 43rd, 111th Batteries)	
Divisional Ammunition Column:	Lieutenant Colonel H V Vernon
Divisional Trench Mortar Officer:	Captain S J Fox
(X4A, Y4A, Z4A MTM Batteries; V4A HTM Battery)	

Engineers

CRE:	Lieutenant Colonel G C E Elliott
4th Field Company:	Captain C F Mills
12th Field Company:	Major C C Riddell
13th Field Company:	Captain H A Reid
4th Division Signal Company:	Major J E Fraser

Pioneers

4th Pioneer Battalion:	Lieutenant Colonel V A H Sturdee

Medical

ADMS:	Colonel G W Barber
DADMS:	Major L W Jeffries
4th Field Ambulance:	Lieutenant Colonel H H B Follit
12th Field Ambulance:	Major B C Kennedy
13th Field Ambulance:	Lieutenant Colonel J B StV Welch

Veterinary

ADVS:	Major R H F Macindoe (acting *vice* Major W A Kendall, on sick leave)
4th Mobile Veterinary Section:	Major E S James

Transport (Divisional Train)

CO:	Lieutenant Colonel A A Holdsworth (Lt Col F Henley temporarily)
7th Company AASC:	Captain J W Blanch
14th Company AASC:	Major J R Charlton
26th Company AASC:	Captain V J P Hennessy
27th Company AASC:	Captain S A Robertson

8 Notes

1. *Official History*, Vol II, p. 810.
2. *Ibid*, Vol III, p. 940.
3. Chataway, *Op. Cit.*, p. 148.
4. Mitchell, *Op. Cit.*, p. 49.
5. *Official History*, Vol IV, p. 18.
6. W S Churchill, *The World Crisis* (abridged edition), p.704.
7. Ellis, *Op Cit*, p. 168.
8. 4th Australian Divisional Trench Mortar Officer(DTMO) War Diary, 1 February 1917.

Lieutenant McPherson's records and MC recommendation indicate that he was nominally with Z4A battery, not X4A, but the shoot was certainly carried out by X4A. Probably McPherson was temporarily relieving another officer.

9   The *Official History* (Vol III p. 28) and General Holmes' after-action report (4th Division GS War Diary for February 1917, Appendix 20, dated 8 February 1917) both state that the heavy artillery was used during the day on 1 February, but the I Anzac Heavy Artillery war diary does not mention such a task, which would have been arranged at short notice, perhaps without written orders.

10 Lieutenant Tom Heffer, quoted in Chataway, *Op Cit*, pp. 150–51.

11 5th Australian DTMO War Diary, 1 February 1917.

12 Chataway, *Op Cit*, p. 152; 4th Division GS War Diary for February 1917, Appendix 20.

13 The times mentioned here are taken from the 4th Division Artillery's Daily Operations Report for 1 to 2 February, appendix to the artillery HQ War Diary for February 1917. The *Official History* (Vol IV, p. 29) gives 1:55 am for this counter-attack. There are several discrepancies in times given in the various war diaries and official reports.

14 Chataway, *Op Cit*, p. 154. Mills grenades were packed 12 to a box with the detonators in a separate container in the box, for safety reasons during transport. Before action, for each grenade the base plug had to be unscrewed, using a special tool also in the box, the detonator inserted and the plug screwed on again. There does not seem to have been any fixed responsibility for this task, and it did occasionally happen that a box of grenades reached the firing line without detonators fitted. It would not have been easy to fit the detonators in the middle of a hot fight in the dark, assuming the grenade boxes were intact.

15 *Ibid*, p. 149.

16 General Holmes' notes, 4th Division GS War Diary for February 1917, Appendix 6.

17 *Official History*, Vol IV, p. 31 for German losses. The figure of 146 for the Australian casualties comes from General Holmes' after-action report of 8 February; the *Official History* says 144.

18 *Official History*, Vol III, p. 30; 4th Division GS War Diary for February 1917, Appendix 20; 4th LTM Battery War Diary, 2 February 1917.

19 'Attack of 15th Battalion on Enemy Salient on 1st February 1917. Notes of an interview with Lt Col McSharry,' 4th Division GS War Diary for February 1917, Appendix 6.

20 Chataway, *Op Cit*, pp. 148–9.

21 The *Official History* (Vol IV, p. 31n) says that Colonel Durrant 'did not hear' of the operation until 8 pm on 3 Feb, which was when the unit War Diary states that the orders were received. However, General Holmes' notes on the debriefing with Colonel McSharry (4th Division GS War Diary for February 1917, Appendix 6) state that the meeting was held at 10.30am on 2 February and that Colonel Durrant was present. The General's more detailed report on the Stormy Trench operations (Appendix 20 of the February diary) states that the decision to re-attack with the 13th Battalion on 4/5 February was taken at that meeting. Durrant would have had time to at least give some thought to the operation before formal orders came through.

22 This is apparent from the map references given in the various orders and reports, and is also mentioned in the Artillery HQ War Diary. Colonel Durrant's report in the 13th Battalion War Diary states only that the objective was the same as that of the previous attack.

23 13th Battalion War Diary for February 1917, Appendix B23.

24 Noted in Lt McDowell's MC recommendation (AWM Honours and Awards records).

25 *Official History*, Vol IV, p. 30. In the 4th Division Artillery HQ War Diary for February 1917, the Daily Operations Report for 1–2 February gives a total expenditure of 6,872 18-pounder shells

for the two divisions plus 641 howitzer shells for the 5th Division only, no figure being available for the 4th Division howitzers—presumably those made up the difference.

26 4th Australian DTMO War Diary, 4 February 1917.
27 As for Note 23.
28 H W Murray, 'Capture of Stormy Trench', *Reveille*, December 1937, pp. 10–11, 62–5.
29 As for Note 23.
30 White, *Op Cit*, p. 86.
31 *Ibid*, p. 88.
32 Murray's VC recommendation (AWM Honours and Awards records).
33 H W Murray, 'Stormy Trench', *Op Cit*.
34 As recorded in the 14th Battalion War Diary for February 1917. Wanliss (*Op Cit*, p. 179) uses this figure also. The *Official History* (Vol IV, p. 37n) says 95 casualties, perhaps following Rule (*Op Cit*, p. 66).
35 As far as the Army was concerned, Murray was 33; he had understated his age on enlistment in 1914.
36 General Rosenthal's report, appendix to 4th Division Artillery HQ War Diary for February 1917.
37 The relevant war diaries and reports are inconsistent as to the length of trench occupied. The *Official History* says 150 yards [137 metres], while Colonel Denham's report in the 46th Battalion War Diary states that the party advanced about 200 yards [183 metres] up the trench. A report in the 12th Brigade diary has the distance as 125 yards [114 metres]. Both of the latter, however, are clear that the distance was that reached by the covering party, who then withdrew to the barricades, built somewhat to the rear of that point. The map references (admittedly not fully consistent and unlikely to be completely accurate) given for the old and new blocks indicate a distance of between 80 and 100 yards [73 and 91 metres] between them. The 12th MG Company War Diary says 100 yards, although this was probably not meant to be any more than a rough estimate.
38 *Official History*, Vol IV p. 38. The 46th Battalion War Diary does not specify its losses for particular dates, except for the six casualties on 11/12 February, but says that the total for February was 14 killed and 77 wounded.
39 Mitchell, *Op Cit*, p. 64.
40 12th Brigade War Diary for February 1917, Appendix 16.
41 Bean Diary, AWM 38 3DRL606/107/1, 16 April 1918.
42 Lt Col Herring's report in the 45th Battalion War Diary for February 1917, Appendix 3.
43 *Ibid*.
44 Lynch ed Davies, *Op Cit*, p. 116. Lynch used pseudonyms in his account.
45 In Lynch's account, he mentions four men killed, and two officers and two ORs wounded
46 N. Browning, *Leane's Battalion, Op Cit*, p. 89.
47 On the other hand, the 14th Battalion War Diary for 7 February 1917 records that after that unit had dug the 'Fourteenth Alley' trench, a fatigue party was 'handed over to A[ustralian] E[ngineers] Sapper [and] in usual manner was put on the wrong work by that Sapper'.
48 *Official History*, Vol IV, p. 41.
49 4th Division General Staff War Diary, 21 February 1917.
50 Colonel Ridley had five given names—John Cecil Thomas Edmund Charles. He signed his name as 'C C Ridley' and was referred to in that way in the brigade and battalion War Diaries.

9: Pursuit to the Hindenburg Line

The beginning of March 1917 saw the units of the 4th Division billeted in several locations in the Corps Training Area, a few kilometres to the west of Albert. Division HQ was at Baizieux with the artillery HQ at Bavelincourt and the artillery units nearby. Of the infantry brigades the 4th was at Ribemont, the 12th at Bresle and the 13th at Buire. The men had had the welcome opportunity for a bath and a change of clothes before training programmes resumed. During its February tour in the line the Division had suffered a total of 855 casualties. Of those 193 were recorded as killed or missing. A further 1,055 had been evacuated with illness during the same period.[1] The 4th Brigade's casualties had been much the highest among the infantry elements in February, at 148 killed or missing and 408 wounded. Those losses had mostly occurred in the 15th and 13th Battalions' attacks on Stormy Trench early in the month, when tough opposition had been offered by the enemy. The later operations by the 12th Brigade units had met only weak resistance, at least partly because of the imminence of the planned German withdrawal.[2] As well, it is likely that by then the Germans had already been picking out their stoutest troops from the line to form rearguards, which would put up heavy resistance to the pursuing forces in the coming weeks.

The German retirement reflected their new overall strategy for the conduct of the war. Their command team, nominal commander-in-chief Field Marshal Paul von Hindenburg and his forceful, ruthless chief of staff, General Erich Ludendorff, had developed a plan to stand on the defensive on the Western Front and win the war at sea, with an unrestricted U-boat campaign starving Britain out. For months the Germans had been constructing a formidable defensive line, running roughly from Arras to Soissons, forming a chord across the large salient between those points. This soon became known to the allies as the Hindenburg Line, although the Germans called it the Siegfried Line. In some places the new system was up to 48 kilometres to the rear (east) of the present front. Falling back to the position would have the effect, in a time-honoured military stratagem, of shortening the line to be defended and thus saving troops—in this case, as many as 13 divisions.[3] Withdrawing to the Hindenburg Line would also delay the impact of an allied offensive in the area—which the Germans anticipated would be launched soon—and generally disrupt the allied plans. The strength of the new line would be such that the German army could expect to hold it indefinitely while the U-boats went about their work.

As far as the BEF was concerned, the situation required that the retreating Germans be followed up strongly. At first, though, the Commander-in-Chief, Field Marshal Sir Douglas Haig, and his Army commanders ordered cautious tactics. If a planned retreat to a shorter line was a traditional stratagem, so was a feigned retreat to draw on and disorganise a pursuing enemy before turning on him in counter-attack, and such a possibility was rightly feared by GHQ. The abandoned trenches in front of I Anzac's line represented the Germans' preliminary move before their general retreat began in mid-March and for the moment the enemy positions on either flank continued to be strongly defended. The empty trenches could be dangerous also—troops of the 1st Division encountered explosive booby-traps set up in the dugouts. As the full retreat got under way the Germans implemented a savage scorched-earth policy on the territory in front of the Hindenburg Line, mostly untouched by the war until now. Everything that could conceivably be of use to the pursuing allies was destroyed, down to fruit trees and household furniture. Wells were poisoned and delayed-action mines concealed in wrecked buildings and cellars. The German rearguards would prove to be dangerous opponents, not content with temporarily holding up the pursuers but usually defending their positions grimly and often launching strong counter-attacks.

It would be several weeks before the 4th Division returned to combat and encountered those conditions. For the time being, the Division made use of its break from the front line to re-equip and train. The battalions implemented individual, platoon and company training, and all infantry brigades took part in several combined field exercises. Practice attacks on defended positions were carried out and the brigades began working on open warfare techniques—the Division expected to come up against an enemy on the move in its next period of combat and there was a need to break away from the tactics and general mind-set of static trench warfare. As well, during February GHQ had issued new instructions for the tactics and structure of infantry platoons, which were now recognised as the basic element of infantry operations. The infantry companies currently used specialist groups of Lewis gunners, bombers and rifle grenadiers in support of their four platoons of riflemen. The new scheme required that all weapons be incorporated within each platoon, which would be organised into four integrated sections—one section each of riflemen, Lewis gunners, bombers and rifle grenadiers. The number of Lewis guns per battalion was increased from twelve to sixteen, one per platoon. At the same time some changes were made to the battalions' administrative organisation.

There appears to have been some unevenness in the extent to which the new platoon structure was implemented by individual battalions in the early stages, but the principles were established at least. New tactics for attacks at platoon and company level needed considerable practice before full efficiency could be achieved, and the two or three weeks that the

4th Division had out of the line would not have been enough for this. The other divisions, on the move following up the retreating Germans, had even less opportunity to master the new system and it would be well into the year before the AIF, and the BEF overall, was able to fully exploit it.[4] The 4th Division's training proceeded through the first three weeks of March in continuing bad weather, including several falls of snow. The infantry brigades exercised in their allocated areas of farmland, each practicing battalion and full brigade attacks on dummy trench lines. The technique of advancing behind artillery cover was practised, with the creeping and standing barrages represented by lines of horsemen.[5] The brigades each conducted an 'open warfare' exercise to give the troops some training for advancing in columns across open country and dealing with enemy ambushes and rearguard parties, a novelty after the weary months of trench warfare. Communications received attention as well, with a divisional signals exercise conducted on 19 March. An attack by the full division was simulated, with the various command levels, of both infantry and artillery, practising the transmission of orders and information on the progress of the battle by field telephone, runner and power buzzer (a device to transmit and receive Morse through an earth connection). This was the last major exercise in the training area before the Division began to move forward again.

The divisional artillery units had been continuously in the line since the previous November, apart from brief rotations among the brigades. They had had little opportunity for rest during the first part of the Division's period in the rear, however. The 10th AFA Brigade had arrived in the rear area on 28 February with the 11th Brigade following a week later, but by 12 March both brigades were again on the march up to the front line. The guns had been ordered to support the 2nd Division, in the front line around Le Sars, in an attack on positions believed to be still held by the Germans in front of Loupart Wood. Before the attack could be launched, however, patrols found that the enemy had withdrawn to their next line of resistance along the heights near the town of Bapaume. The proposed operation was called off and the 4th Division artillery brigades retraced their steps to rejoin their Division in the rest area around Bavelincourt. For the next two weeks the gunners worked on overhauling their equipment and practicing gun drills, with the transport drivers attending to the condition of their horses and selected personnel taking part in the divisional signals exercise on 19 March.

The 4th Division's return to the combat zone began on 21 March with the 13th Brigade Group moving out of the Buire area up to Mametz, east of Albert. Two days earlier the CO of the 52nd Battalion, Lieutenant Colonel Lane, had been posted to command the Brigade training establishment, the 13th Training Battalion, in England. His replacement was Lieutenant Colonel Harold Pope, founding CO of the 16th Battalion in the original 4th Brigade, the experienced veteran after whom Pope's Hill on Gallipoli had been named. It will be recalled that Pope had been acting brigadier of the 14th Brigade at Fromelles and had been unjustly dismissed from his command and sent home after the battle. The punishment culminated in his AIF appointment being terminated, but Pope was determined to clear his name and his unceasing agitation resulted in an appointment as OIC Troops on a troopship to England. Once there he was able to convince General Birdwood to reinstate him in his old rank, and he was offered the posting to the 52nd.[6] Although at 43 Colonel Pope was now a little older than the current run of infantry COs, he had the experience and 'that happy knack of getting things done well and without friction.'[7]

The 4th Brigade Group departed its billets on 22 March, with the 12th moving out on the next day, less its 47th Battalion and 12th Field Company. Those units had been detached a few days earlier and sent 60 kilometres by train in the opposite direction, to the area around Abbeville, where they were attached to XIII Corps for duties salvaging unused stores and building materials in that Corps' back area; the reasoning behind the choice of those particular units for such duties is not immediately apparent. The 12th MG Company marched without its OC, Captain Edgar Sawer, who had suddenly been taken seriously ill with what was diagnosed as a gastric ulcer but was probably cancer of the stomach or bowel;[8] the condition was to kill him a little over a year later. Lieutenant (later Captain) Harry Crouch took command of the Company. Divisional HQ moved from Baizieux to Fricourt, just east of Albert, on 23 March. At about the same time, a change in HQ personnel saw the able staff officer Major Henry Wynter, the DAA & QMG, posted to I Anzac HQ. His replacement was Lieutenant Colonel Richard Dowse, previously CO of the 3rd Division Train. Colonel Dowse was 50 years old, a pre-war regular officer and a veteran of the Boer War, in which he had served with the Queensland Mounted Rifles (during April, the position was re-named Deputy Assistant Adjutant General—DAAG). Earlier in the month the GSO2, Major McRae, writer of the chatty and informative entries in the divisional General Staff war diary, had also gone to a Corps HQ posting, in II Anzac. Major Charles Miles came in from the 1st Division artillery as the new GSO2.

Fricourt, Mametz and their vicinity were in the present reserve area, and the 4th Division troops took over the billets of the 1st Division, recently relieved from the line and now going into the rest area. The fighting front continued to move eastward as it followed up the retreating enemy. The advance had now gone beyond the large town of Bapaume, thoroughly wrecked by the retreating Germans, which had been occupied by 5th Division units on 17 March. Columns from the 5th and 2nd Divisions continued the pursuit, with the latter division's 6th Brigade (Brigadier General John Gellibrand) taking the village of Vaulx-Vraucourt on 18 March, within sight of the Hindenburg Line itself. On 20 March the 6th Brigade advanced further to attack the village of Noreuil but met strong resistance and was repulsed with serious losses. Falling back to its original line at Vaulx-Vraucourt, the 6th Brigade was temporarily relieved by the 7th Brigade of its own Division, before the 4th Division came up to relieve the 2nd in the left sector of I Anzac's front.

The 13th Brigade Group led the way for the Division, taking up positions at the forward edge of the fighting zone in front of Vaulx-Vraucourt. Brigadier General Glasgow became commander of the left sector Advanced Guard from 28 March. The Brigade deployed with the 51st, 50th and 52nd Battalions in the front line with the 49th in support. The battalions pushed companies and platoons into outpost positions and sentry posts, while the 13th MG Company disposed its Vickers guns along the front. There was little entrenchment done. The region was crossed by numerous sunken roads which provided reasonable cover and the troops dug niches in the road-banks for shelter—miserable enough accommodation in the cold and rainy weather. Behind the Advanced Guard, the 4th Brigade occupied positions designated as the Main Defensive System, but with one battalion (the 16th then the 15th) sent forward and attached to the 13th Brigade as an extra reserve. The 12th Brigade, less the 47th Battalion still detached at Abbeville, was deployed further back near Bapaume in what was called the Intermediate System. The 4th Division artillery had not yet come up, having been given an extra week in the rest area, so for the time being artillery cover was provided by the two field brigades of the 2nd Division's artillery and the 12th (Army) AFA Brigade, the former 4th Division unit. Of the medical units, the 13th Field Ambulance had some of its bearers at relay posts in the 13th Brigade Advanced Guard area and others assisting the 4th Field Ambulance upgrading the ADS in Bapaume to an MDS as the fighting front continued to advance. The main body of the 12th Field Ambulance, now commanded by Lieutenant Colonel Charles Wassell, accompanied its infantry brigade to the Intermediate System area. The engineers of the 4th and 13th Field Companies were operating in the areas of their associated infantry brigades, working mostly on water supply tasks and road repair. The 12th Field Company returned to the Division area from detachment on 7 April and began work on the roads between Favreuil and Noreuil. At that time the unit's Captain Howard Tolley was promoted to major and posted to the 4th Field Company as its new OC. Major Tolley had built up an excellent reputation as Major Consett Riddell's second-in-command in the 12th Company (a big fellow, 183 cm tall and weighing 77 kg, Tolley made quite a contrast physically to the slight, bespectacled Riddell). The 4th Pioneers continued their ceaseless construction work on the Decauville tramway as it followed the advancing front eastwards.

Most of the Divisional Train moved to Bapaume on 28 March, less one company 'feeding' the artillery from Albert. At Bapaume, the Train supply units provided services for 'Army and Corps units congregated here, also attached units of II Aust Div including II Div Artillery,'[9] as well as its own Division. The 4th Division's HQ moved up from Fricourt to Bapaume also on 28 March. Three days later, the GOC, General Holmes, carried out a personal inspection of an infantry outpost in daylight. The General was always prepared to risk the dangers of the front line, which were intensified by his insistence on wearing his red-banded cap and thus increasing the chances of attracting enemy fire ('drawing the crabs'). On this occasion his aide-de-camp, Lieutenant Keith Ferguson,[10] was hit by a sniper and the outpost was then shelled, wounding Ferguson again, so seriously that he was later invalided home and discharged. There were casualties among the infantrymen in the post also—front line visits by generals do not always have a positive effect on morale. Lieutenant Duncan Maxwell, one of the 52nd Battalion's best officers, was posted as the new ADC.

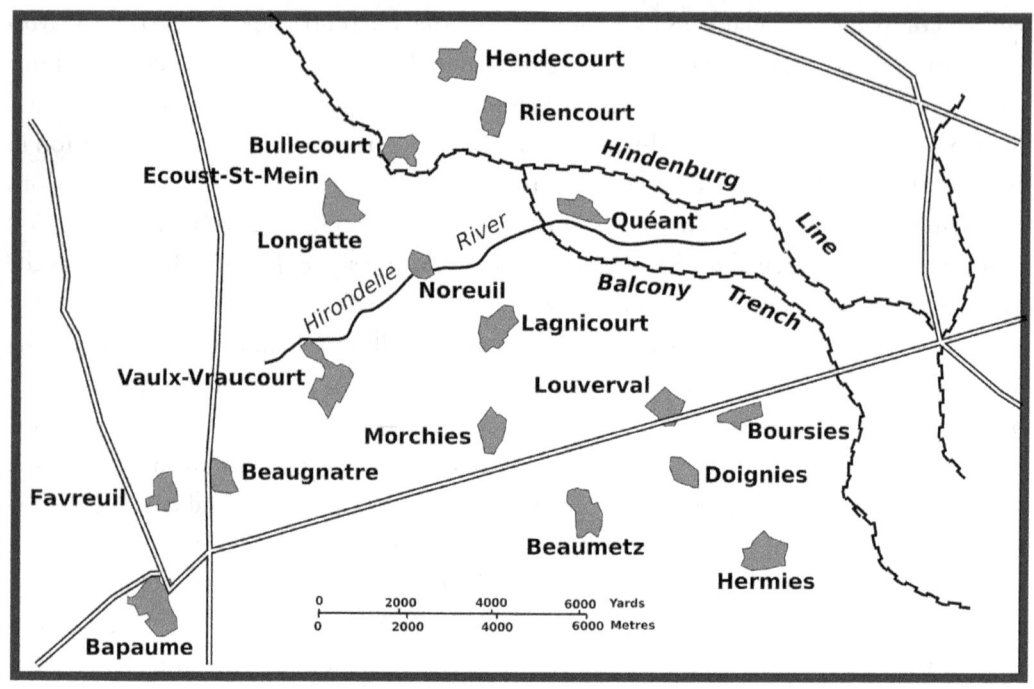

Advance to the Hindenburg Line, March/April 1917.

As the Advanced Guard of the Division, the 13th Brigade was within five kilometres of the Hindenburg Line trenches; the Line itself was screened by a chain of fortified villages running roughly parallel to it—the 'outpost villages.' Preparations were almost complete for Third Army's attack at Arras to the north, planned to open on 9 April, and the great offensive by the French under General Nivelle was due to be launched in the south shortly afterwards—the latter operation being no secret to the Germans, owing to extraordinarily lax security. Fifth Army to the south of Third Army's sector would support the Arras offensive by assaulting part of the Hindenburg Line, but before that could be done the outpost villages had to be captured. The Army commander, General Gough, now ordered simultaneous operations to seize those strong-points. The date for the attacks was set as 2 April. On the right of the 4th Division's sector of the front, one of the villages, Lagnicourt, was already in Australian hands, having been taken by the 7th Brigade a few days earlier and now occupied by the 52nd Battalion. It would now be the 13th Brigade's task to capture Noreuil, the next village to the north-west, which had already defied an attack by the 6th Brigade on 20 March.

Noreuil was about three kilometres from Lagnicourt with the linked villages of Ecoust-St-Mein and Longatte (held by the enemy) a similar distance further north-west, in the V Corps sector; Ecoust/Longatte was to be taken by the 7th British Division of that Corps. The next two villages to the south-east of Lagnicourt, Louverval and Doignies, would be attacked by the 5th Division, holding the right of the I Anzac sector. Cursory orders for the Noreuil operation came down from Corps and Division to the 13th Brigade on 30 March and the

Brigade staff got their orders out to the battalions at 11 pm that night. Brigadier General Glasgow's plan set the Brigade's final objective as a line 800 metres beyond Noreuil village in the road running from Lagnicourt to the ominous village of Bullecourt in the Hindenburg Line. The brigadier decided on a two-pronged attack. The 51st Battalion, posted in front of Vaulx-Vraucourt on the left, was given the task of advancing south-west to north-east directly towards the objective road, with its right flank company clearing the northern outskirts of Noreuil. Before reaching the final objective the 51st would have to cross the parallel Noreuil-Longatte sunken road, almost certainly defended by the enemy. The 50th Battalion in the centre, occupying positions in front of Lagnicourt, would attack from the south and secure the major portion of Noreuil village before wheeling to its right and continuing on to the final objective in the road. On the right flank of the operation, the 52nd Battalion was holding Lagnicourt, the southern end of the objective road, and had the task of extending its left up the road to cover the right of the 50th.

The 13th MG Company provided two Vickers guns to each of the 50th and 51st to give close fire support in the advance and others were positioned to provide covering fire across the front, including an additional four guns attached from the 4th MG Company. Patrols had located a number of German strong-points outposted in the roads near Noreuil and to deal with those each battalion would be accompanied by a section of two Stokes mortars from the brigade LTM Battery. A supporting artillery barrage for the attack would be provided by the field brigades covering the 4th Division sector (the 4th and 5th AFA Brigades of the 2nd Division, reinforced by two 18-pounder batteries from the 12th 'Army' AFA Brigade)—barely adequate considering the extent of the objectives and the distance that the infantry was required to cover. The 50th Battalion would have to advance roughly a kilometre before reaching Noreuil, then another kilometre to the final objective in the road, and the 51st had almost as much ground to cover. Such distances would have been out of the question in the close trench warfare of previous months but were not unreasonable in the more open conditions of the present fighting, provided that effective fire support was given to the infantry.

Detailed planning was left to the battalions. For the 51st, Colonel Ridley's orders called for three companies in the attack with the fourth in reserve. The left and centre companies, advancing over open ground north of Noreuil on a total frontage of 730 metres, would each deploy in a single wave of two lines. The right-flank company, which would penetrate the northern part of the village, was more concentrated, deployed on a front of 230 metres in two waves, each of two lines with 70 metres between waves. The jumping-off line, 640 metres from the village and parallel to the Longatte road, would be marked with tapes by the Battalion scouts during the night, with the main body advancing 275 metres up to the tapes an hour before Zero. The 50th Battalion, attacking from the south, was assigned to capture the greater portion of the village as its first objective, and Colonel Salisbury allocated the greatest weight to his left and centre companies which had that task. They were formed in two waves of two lines per wave, on a frontage of 165 metres each. A mopping-up party of 60 men was to clear any isolated points of resistance while the main body swept through the village. The right flank company, which would skirt the southern edge of the village and operate mostly in open ground, was in a single wave covering a front of 330 metres. The Battalion's fourth company would follow in reserve. The ground was a series of low ridges or spurs divided by gently sloping valleys, features which ran roughly parallel to the final direction of advance and at right angles to the objective road. Noreuil was located on the southern slope of one of these spurs, slightly below the crest, with the ground descending into a shallow valley before rising again to the next spur to the south, on which Lagnicourt was situated. On the northern side of the Noreuil spur, the ground sloped down into another valley before rising again to form the ridge on which Ecoust/Longatte stood. A network of roads and tracks, mostly sunken, covered the area and ran into and out of the villages, and the cutting of a light railway ran along the southern side of Noreuil. The 51st Battalion's line would face north-east with its right and centre on the higher ground of the Noreuil spur and its left down the slope of the valley between Noreuil and Longatte. The 50th would form up facing north along the Lagnicourt spur, overlooking Noreuil, and advance down into the valley to attack the village before wheeling to line up with the 51st for the final advance to the objective road.

Although the heavy and field artillery had been carrying out routine shelling of the village and its approaches in previous days, a formal preliminary bombardment before the attack was dispensed with, to improve the chances of achieving surprise. At Zero, set for first light at 5:15 am on 2 April, the field artillery would open the covering barrage on two lines forming a rough 'L' shape immediately south and west of Noreuil, including the Noreuil-Longatte road, generally in parallel with the 50th and 51st Battalions' fronts; the two available howitzer batteries concentrated on the edges of the village itself. After 10 minutes some batteries would lengthen on to the area to the north and east of the village with the remainder joining in after a further 10 minutes. This would allow the infantry battalions 20 minutes to advance from their jumping-off lines to the outskirts of the village, distances of 640 metres for the 51st and 915 metres for the 50th. The barrage would then take 10 minutes to advance to its next target line, about half-way between the village and the final objective, the guns spreading their fire over the intervening area by varying direction and elevation ('sweep' and 'search', rather than a true creeping barrage). For several of the batteries, their target for the intermediate barrage line was identified as a length of trench running north-west to south-east, roughly parallel with the final objective.[11] This trench is not mentioned in the infantry's orders, either at brigade or battalion level; it was not marked on maps at the time, and was probably detected from an aerial photograph. It appears that the infantry staff failed to notice the reference in the artillery orders. The barrage would stay on the intermediate line for 10 minutes before lifting on to the line of the final objective, where it would stay for a further 20 minutes then advance again to a protective line 300 metres beyond. The 50th Battalion's right wheel at the village made for a complicated fireplan, with the batteries covering that unit having to swing their barrage line through ninety degrees to conform to the infantry movement.

Wet weather during the day of 1 April gave way to a cold but clear night and early morning, and the troops assembled then moved up to the tapes marking their jumping-off positions in good time for the zero hour. As they lined up, the 51st Battalion found a number of other troops were attempting to form up in the same position. These turned out to be Scots of the Gordon Highlanders, one of the 7th British Division battalions meant to be attacking Ecoust/Longatte. Through some blunder of navigation the Gordons' tapes had been laid in the wrong position, facing Noreuil instead of Longatte. There was no time to reorganise before Zero and many of the Scots advanced with the 51st. Promptly at 5:15 am the barrage crashed out and the infantry moved forward. It was soon apparent that the barrage was too thin to completely suppress the German defenders—for the 51st Battalion's attack each six-gun battery was required to cover 275 metres of front, while one of the batteries supporting the 50th had to cover twice that distance at the eastern end of the railway cutting. The guns were firing a mixture of HE and shrapnel at two rounds per minute—half the highest normal rate in barrage fire.

The 51st, advancing north-eastward towards the Noreuil-Longatte sunken road, met machine gun fire from both flanks and the road itself as the German gunners fired through the barrage. The Western Australians lost eighty killed and wounded in a few minutes and were forced to ground short of the road, which was found to be protected by barbed wire. The deadlock on the right flank was broken by a platoon commander, Lieutenant Roy Earl, who crawled under the wire with a few of his men and managed to get into the road. Outflanking one of the German machine guns, Earl shot the crew with his revolver then led his men up the road to attack the rest of the enemy guns with grenades and Lewis gun fire. Two more posts were wiped out and three others surrendered,[12] while on the left flank another was eliminated by Lance Corporal John Magee, firing his Lewis gun from the hip as he advanced, despite a wounded hand. The Battalion rushed the road with the bayonet and quickly overcame the remaining resistance there as well as clearing the northern edge of the village. Enemy machine gun fire was still coming from the direction of Longatte on the 51st's left, where the 7th British Division attack was well behind schedule due to the Gordons' loss of direction. The 51st established a post in the road to secure the left flank, consisting of a bombing team, a Lewis gun and a captured German machine gun, later strengthened by one of the 13th MG Company's Vickers guns. The barrage had moved on to the final objective by now, and the Battalion pushed on over the open ground north of the village, on the way overrunning a German post in a sunken road junction. The advance had gone beyond the village and was within 250 metres of the objective when the troops encountered an empty shallow trench running at an angle across their front. This was almost certainly the one identified in the artillery orders—it ran in the same direction, although the infantry's estimated position was about 200 metres east of that used by the artillery. The infantry had not been informed that the feature existed, but it offered a convenient place to pause while the barrage continued on the final objective. So far the 51st's attack had made reasonable progress but it was soon realised that the line was coming under fire from the right rear, in the direction of Noreuil. Although the 51st had by now gained touch with elements of the 50th on their right, it was apparent that the latter unit had struck trouble taking the village.

The 50th, attacking Noreuil from the south, had moved off down the valley slope on time as the barrage came down. Heavy machine gun fire from ahead showed that the barrage was too light to suppress the defenders, but the line pushed on in spite of casualties, many of the troops firing from the hip as they advanced. The Germans had strong-points in the two sunken roads that ran into the village at right angles to the 50th's line. These were taken on by the Stokes mortars of the Brigade LTM battery, which had moved up with the infantry, and the bombing platoon. Both posts were quickly silenced, that on the left (west) by grenades and the other by the mortar bombs.[13] One of the mortarmen, Private Stan Coombs, went forward alone and captured the survivors of one machine gun crew, who were so shaken that they failed to realise that Coombs was unarmed. The greater part of the right flank company, 'A' under Captain David Todd, was advancing across open ground south of the village, but its left was on the Noreuil-Lagnicourt road and brushed through the south-east corner of the village. There was some confused fighting among the ruined houses, both sides losing casualties and prisoners before the company continued its advance. Although temporarily disconcerted by an unexpected line of barbed wire, the company pushed through to the line of the Quéant road running west to east through the village, and made its wheel to face the final objective. Forming the inside of the wheel, 'A' Company now waited for the other companies to come up and complete the line.

On the left of the advance, 'D' Company, under Captain James Churchill Smith, who had held the Point 81 outpost at Mouquet Farm, passed the knocked-out enemy post in the western road only to encounter another strong point that the Germans had established in the cemetery near the south-west corner of the village. The machine gun in that post caught 'D' Company in enfilade, causing many casualties including three platoon commanders killed. Among these were Lieutenant William Hoggarth, first officer to enter Mouquet Farm, and the bombing officer, Lieutenant Wilfred Bidstrup, whose entire platoon was killed or wounded. Captain Harold Armitage's 'C' Company in the centre now encountered a second enemy machine gun post behind a barricade in the eastern sunken road (the Noreuil/Lagnicourt road), which checked the advance. The mortars attempted to knock out that post also but this time they were unable to get a direct hit.

With vital time being lost there, the company bypassed the area and pushed on into the village while Sergeant James Wilson, in charge of the company's second wave, detached a squad of six bombers to deal with the enemy machine gun. One of the men, Private William O'Connor, opened fire on the post with his rifle and managed to pick off the German 'Number One' on the gun. At this, Danish-born Private Joergen Jensen dashed forward alone up to the barricade and threw a grenade into the post. Jumping on to the barricade holding another grenade, Jensen found himself confronting at least 29 Germans.[14]

PURSUIT TO THE HINDENBURG LINE

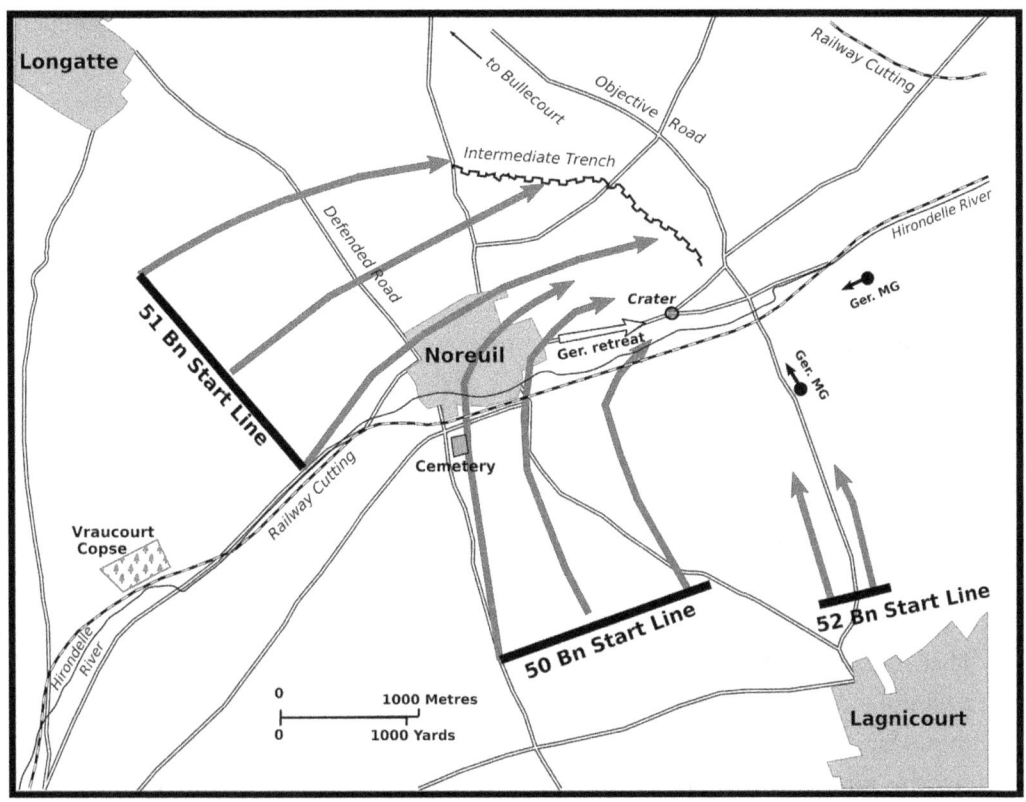

13th Brigade's action at Noreuil, 2 April 1917

He took a further grenade from his pocket and drew out the pin with his teeth. Threatening the Germans with the grenades, Jensen, who spoke German, told them that they were surrounded and demanded their surrender. This they did, and Jensen then sent one of his prisoners to another enemy squad nearby who were engaging one of the Stokes mortars and that group was also persuaded to surrender. For good measure Jensen also freed several members of 'A' Company who had been taken prisoner by the Germans in the initial fighting at the edge of the village (including another Scandinavian, Swedish-born Sergeant Andrew Johanson). As the German prisoners, now numbering over 40, came out of their position towards the Australian lines they were fired on by some Australians who did not realise that they had surrendered. Jensen, having risked his life against enemy fire moments before, now risked it again to friendly fire. He jumped on to the parapet and waved his steel helmet, at which signal the firing ceased and the prisoners trooped into captivity.

The left and centre companies meanwhile had fought their way into the village past the enemy post in the cemetery, and a burst of close-range fighting among the ruined buildings followed. In accordance with the plan, the main bodies of the companies pushed on through the village and wheeled into line for the advance to the final objective, leaving behind their teams of bombers to mop up any remaining resistance in buildings and dugouts. The right of 'C' Company gained touch with the left of the waiting 'A' Company and the united line began its final advance, straddling the Noreuil/Quéant sunken road and with the 51st Battalion in touch on the far left. Before long, however, the line began to lose cohesion. Although it was daylight by now, the configuration of the ground and the road banks made visual contact difficult and the line soon came under heavy machine gun fire. This was particularly directed at 'A' Company on the right flank and that company was forced to take cover behind the banks, losing touch with the rest of the battalion and itself splitting into two segments where the road forked about 500 metres east of the village. Captain Todd with most of his company was pinned down in and near the left-hand fork of the road but on the extreme right of the line, following the right-hand fork, Lieutenant Max Gore's platoon of 'A' tried to keep the advance going forward—after an instance of near-mutiny[15]—by moving in single file along the road behind its low southern bank. The head of the column reached the point where the road crossed the final objective, but here the platoon was stopped by the enemy machine guns. The fire was coming from higher ground part-way up the slope along the objective road to the right (south), the flank that was meant to have been secured by the 52nd Battalion advancing from Lagnicourt.

That unit, with what appeared to be the most straightforward task of the day, had sent a reinforced company to occupy the line of the Lagnicourt-Bullecourt road up to the right boundary of the 50th Battalion's objective. Presumably through some failure in map-reading, this force had actually stopped and was digging in about 100 metres short of its objective, behind the crest of the Lagnicourt spur. The map reference for the objective in the Battalion orders was clearly, by the contour lines, a location in the road some way down the slope. The orders did not identify any particular enemy posts to be attacked, but in fact the Germans had established a barricaded strongpoint on the slope between the correct objective and the position that was actually occupied by the 52nd. It was machine gun fire from that post that was enfilading the right of the 50th. The German position was out of sight from that held by the 52nd, but is difficult to understand how those troops could not have been aware that heavy machine gun fire, directed at the flank of the next unit, was coming from a nearby location. Nevertheless, the company of the 52nd reported that they were holding their assigned objective and the report was accepted without question at Battalion HQ. This was an error for which the CO, Lieutenant Colonel Pope, must bear some responsibility, allowing that he had only been with the Battalion for a fortnight and may not have been fully familiar with his officers' capabilities. The situation lasted all day and it was not until evening that the Battalion intelligence officer established that the troops were not in the correct position. The gap was finally closed after dark, the end of an inglorious episode in the history of the 52nd Battalion.

Meanwhile in the village itself the 50th Battalion mopping-up teams found themselves facing unexpectedly heavy odds. There were still several hundred Germans remaining in the precincts of the village, considerably outnumbering the Australians. In a series of small fights in the ruins both sides lost heavily but the Germans (mostly members of the 119th Reserve Infantry Regiment) gained the upper hand and the survivors of the bombers were forced to surrender. The Germans, however, were in an untenable position themselves, in grave danger of being completely cut off, with enemies in their rear and on both sides and two company commanders dead. At about 6:30 am they evacuated the village and streamed east down the Quéant road, hustling the Australian prisoners along in front. As the German column approached the road fork it came on to the rear of the 50th's 'A' Company, pinned down in the roads by the flanking machine gun fire. Taken by surprise and outnumbered, the company could put up little resistance, especially as the Australian prisoners were at the front of the column and in the line of fire. The company was soon split into small groups and most were forced to surrender. The prisoners were sent under escort to the German lines—the closest point being the sunken road that was the final Australian objective. A number of the Germans stayed in the area of the forked road and turned their attention to the rest of the Australian force to their north. The column of prisoners with their German escorts was continuing from the sunken road towards the German rear area when a tragic error brought more loss of life. The 13th MG Company had emplaced two Vickers guns on the high ground north of Lagnicourt, from where they had been laying down supporting fire onto the northern flank of the objective during the early stages of the attack. Having completed this task about 6 am, the gunners looked for more targets and spotted the column at a range of about 1,500 metres. The distant figures, understandably, were mistaken for an exclusively enemy party and the guns opened fire, killing up to twenty of the Australian prisoners.[16]

The 50th's other two companies had reached the trench discovered by the 51st, short of the final objective, and had linked up with that unit. The line came under heavy frontal fire from Germans occupying the objective road and the officers on the spot decided to consolidate in the trench for the time being, particularly as the final objective would be exposed to fire from the Hindenburg Line itself. Because of the destruction of 'A' Company, however, the 50th's right flank in the trench was wide open, and soon came under attack from the Germans in the forked road. The machine gun on the slope to the south joined in, enfilading the trench, and there was some danger that the Australian line would be rolled up. Captains Smith and Armitage sent messages back to Battalion HQ reporting the situation, but shortly after sending a second message at 8:45 am Armitage bravely risked raising his head to observe and was killed by a sniper. The loss of their popular OC left 'C' Company, holding the extreme flank, with no officers on the spot. The highly capable NCO Sergeant Wilson now took charge of the company, however, and proved more than equal to the task. The Germans were pressing up the trench with grenades and after three attacks had been beaten off by Wilson's men he organised the construction of a barricade. Wilson then withdrew his men 25 metres from the barricade and allowed the Germans to crowd up to it. The attackers were then broken by a shower of grenades and fire from Lewis guns.

This repulse put an end to the direct German attacks on the trench, and the survivors of the enemy force settled back behind the bank of the flanking sunken road and contented themselves with firing into the Australian position. The situation was still precarious but reinforcements were now on the way for the South Australians. Lieutenant Colonel Salisbury had earlier sent two platoons of his reserve 'B' Company under Captain Seager into Noreuil village to complete the mopping up. On receiving the first message from 'C' Company reporting the gap on its right, he then sent a further platoon under Lieutenant Esson Rule to assist 'A' Company. The platoon moved up through the railway cutting south of the village, but by this time 'A' Company had already been eliminated and the platoon came under heavy enemy fire which mortally wounded its commander. In the meantime Salisbury, anxious to clarify the situation on the ground, had sent forward the battalion second-in-command, Major Noel Loutit, to take charge. Loutit, a very experienced soldier who as a subaltern at the Gallipoli Landing had gone the furthest inland of any ANZAC officer, came up to the platoon shortly after 9 am. He soon observed the fighting to his front where the German party in the forked sunken road was still firing into the trench occupied by the main body of the 50th. Loutit resolved to attack these Germans immediately and led the platoon into the southern fork of the road, behind the Germans in the northern fork. A carefully-aimed volley killed or wounded a number of the enemy and the survivors broke for the main German line in the objective road.

The pressure on the Australian right flank in the trench was now relieved but Loutit's force in the road now came under accurate fire from the German machine gun on the slope of the Lagnicourt spur. There was a large mine-crater where the road forked, and Loutit withdrew the platoon to the crater and set up a strong-point, positioning two Lewis guns to command the roads. He was soon reinforced by Captain Seager with the other two reserve platoons, which had passed through the village and completed the mopping-up. The final objective in the Lagnicourt-Bullecourt road remained in enemy hands, however, and the decision was taken—it is not clear whether by Loutit or Seager—to make an immediate attack on the road. Without covering fire (the barrage had moved on by now) or co-ordination with the troops in the trench on their left, two attempts to advance up the valley failed with heavy losses in the face of enemy machine gun fire. The officers admitted defeat and the survivors pulled back to the mine-crater. Perhaps one attempt on the road was worth a try when there was a chance of catching the enemy unprepared, but the judgement could be questioned that sent the troops forward a second time. Loutit reported the situation to the CO from an advanced telephone post, and was recalled to HQ to report in person, leaving Seager in charge. 'B' Company settled in to consolidate the post in the crater and maintained fire on the enemy positions from there. Their fire-power was soon augmented by a Vickers gun of the 13th MG Company. This was one of a two-gun section that had advanced with the 50th's line in the initial attack on the village, but the section was caught by enemy fire and lost its officer, Second Lieutenant Bernard Holloway, badly wounded. Most of the crewmen were hit also and one gun was put out of action but Corporal Frank Bennetts continued forward with the other and the few unhurt men and reached the vicinity of the crater, where he reported to Captain Seager. The gun was emplaced where it could sweep the valley and for the rest of the day Bennetts, supported by the riflemen and Lewis gunners, covered the gap in the line with his fire and suppressed the German machine gun on the slope.

The right flank was no longer in danger and the situation had now stabilised. Although the Germans still held the final objective in the Lagnicourt-Bullecourt road, Noreuil village itself was now firmly in Australian hands and the trench occupied by the 50th and 51st formed a strong intermediate position with good observation of the ground to its front. The battalion COs decided to suspend any further attempts on the road for the time being. During the late afternoon and evening, amid several flurries of snow, German forces were twice observed forming up as if to launch counter-attacks but these were quickly broken up by artillery fire.[17] At 2:30 am the next morning (3 April), on the assumption that the objective road would be attacked again at dawn, Captain Seager led a patrol of 'B' Company 50th Battalion forward to reconnoitre, only to find that the Germans had abandoned the entire position during the night. The company quickly set up posts in the road, finding several badly wounded 50th men who had been taken prisoner then left behind when the Germans withdrew. At around the same time, the right of the 50th was finally linked with the left of the 52nd. Later in the day the 51st Battalion occupied the section of the road to their front, and the final objective now formed the 13th Brigade's front line. That night the battered 50th and 51st were relieved in the new line by the 49th coming up from reserve. The 49th sent its scouts out under Sergeant Walter King, to locate the enemy's forward posts. The Germans were found to be occupying the cuttings and embankments of a light railway that ran parallel to the Hindenburg Line, about 800 metres from the Australian line, with an advanced post in a crater 200 metres closer.

The railway cutting was now the next objective and 'C' Company of the 49th was ordered to capture a 550 metre segment of it in a pre-dawn attack on 5 April. Led by Major Charles Fortescue, who had led in the capture of the Fabeck Graben the previous September, 120 men of the company advanced under a hastily-arranged barrage and took the objective without great difficulty. There was some resistance from Germans posted further to the left (west) in the cutting, however, and the troops built a barricade to protect that flank. Daylight brought an escalation in the fighting. A German machine gun began to fire in enfilade along the cutting and parties of the enemy tried to rush the barricade. Despite losing nearly half of its strength killed or wounded,[18] 'C' Company held on in heavy fighting. Sergeant Vic Cross particularly distinguished himself in the fight, as did Sergeant King of the Battalion scouts, who had guided the attacking party and joined in the fight at the barricade. The next morning, two more of the 49th's companies came up and occupied the section of the cutting on 'C' Company's left, the Germans having withdrawn to the Hindenburg line during the night.

On the morning of 5 April Brigadier General Glasgow had moved his headquarters forward to Noreuil. In five days of hard fighting, the 13th Brigade had advanced the divisional front to the line of the railway cutting, pushing the enemy back in that sector from their last position before the Hindenburg Line itself. The cost had been high. The exact number of casualties suffered by the Brigade in the battle varies depending on which source is used, but the total was close to 650, including the 49th Battalion's losses in the fight for the railway cutting. Of these, over 250 had been killed or were missing, the latter estimated to include 60 taken prisoner. The prisoners were all from the 50th Battalion which had suffered particularly heavily with one of its companies, having been almost wiped out, apart from the nucleus left out of battle. Outside of actual battle the units had taken the usual 'wastage' in holding the old and new lines, mostly to enemy shelling, and the Brigade reported a total of 704 casualties for the week ending on the morning of 6 April. It is questionable whether the elaborate battle plan employed at Noreuil was really necessary—possibly the Brigade staff succumbed to the temptation to produce a brilliant tactical coup when a simpler approach might well have produced the same result with fewer losses. Captain Max Gore (he had been promoted while a prisoner) later wrote, still bitter from the experience of captivity, that the plan was 'one of the most grandiose and stupid ever drawn up.'[19] That harsh description could be applied to numerous battle plans in this war, including the one that the 4th Division would try to carry out within a week of Noreuil. The main complication was the requirement for the 50th Battalion to attack from the south and then for its whole line to wheel to the right, finishing at right angles to its original direction, with the left flank of the line having to fight its way through the village. It is to the credit of the troops' level of training that they carried out the manoeuvre successfully, under fire and in poor light. It was perhaps inevitable, however, that concentration on accomplishing the wheel distracted from the basic need to crush the enemy resistance in the village. This was compounded by underestimation of the German numbers in the village and consequent inadequate strength allocated to the mopping-up parties. The lessons of the Mouquet Farm fighting seem to have been forgotten, although the 50th Battalion had not been directly involved in the attacks on the Farm strongpoint itself, unlike the 51st Battalion. If the latter unit had been tasked with the main responsibility for Noreuil village, it is conceivable that officers who had survived the Farm would have influenced the amount of weight given to mopping-up. As it was, the 50th Battalion, having gone beyond the village, was left with an active enemy in its rear, a situation which was made worse by the 52nd's failure to eliminate the enemy post on the right flank.

Attacking from two directions had the further drawback of stretching the available artillery resources, which were barely adequate to begin with. Both infantry battalions found that the barrage, though accurate, was too thin to keep the defenders heads down completely, the German machine gunners firing through the barrage. An alternative plan might have been for the two battalions to attack directly from the south-west, with the 50th filing out to assemble in one line with the 51st. The 52nd, much under-utilised in the battle plan, could then have masked the village from the south against a breakout as well as occupying the Lagnicourt end of the objective road. A more important task might have resulted in that unit's junior leaders taking the operation more seriously. The right flank still had to be covered and the existing line held, but the Brigade had the 49th Battalion and the borrowed 15th available for that task. The artillery, given a simpler fire plan, could then have concentrated on a shorter barrage line, with more field guns available to hit the enemy positions in the sunken Noreuil-Longatte road. Another alternative to a direct assault would have been to envelop the village on both sides then move a strong force in to mop up. That method had achieved success in preceding weeks during the pursuit and was also used effectively on the same day as the Noreuil battle by the 5th Division at Louverval and Doignies, and by British units at Croisilles as well as a few days later by the 1st Division at Boursies, Demicourt and Hermies. Those successes had cost casualties—the German rearguards fought hard—but in proportion considerably less than those suffered by the 13th Brigade. As it was, the Brigade's plan was neither one thing nor the other—a partial envelopment by the 51st Battalion north of the village and a direct assault by the 50th from the south. A year later, Brigadier General Glasgow and his staff would use a considerably simpler plan at Villers-Bretonneux.

Regardless of the merits or otherwise of the plan, the soldiers on the battlefield had fought well and won their objectives in the end. A number of outstanding individual efforts were acknowledged by decorations, headed by the award of the Victoria Cross to Private Joergen Jensen of the 50th Battalion for his single-handed elimination of an enemy strongpoint. He also received his first promotion, to Lance Corporal, a few days after the battle. The 26 year old Dane had migrated to Australia in 1909 and been naturalised in September 1914, a month after the outbreak of the war. Before Noreuil his army record had been notable mostly for several instances of absence without leave and the consequent punishments, although he must have shown something positive to have been selected for the demanding job of scout. Jensen was one of the countless instances of soldiers whose finest qualities come out in the heat of battle rather than on the parade ground. His VC was the first in the Division to be awarded outside the 4th Infantry Brigade.

Other 50th Battalion decorations included a Bar to the DSO to Major Loutit[20] and the MC to Captain Seager. Sergeant Wilson received the DCM for his stout defence of the right flank gap, as did his colleague Corporal Arthur Verrier. In the 51st Battalion, decorations included MCs won by Captain Norman Owen for his skilful leadership of 'A' Company on the crucial right flank of the Battalion's attack and by his platoon commander Lieutenant Earl, who had first penetrated the Longatte road position. The Lewis gunner Lance Corporal Magee was awarded the DCM for his successful duel with an enemy machine gun post. Another DCM was won by Corporal Joseph Blenkinsop, who had taken command of his platoon after its officer and senior NCOs had all become casualties and had led it successfully through the heavy fighting. Outside of the infantry battalions, the machine gunner Corporal Bennetts, 13th MG Company, was another who won the DCM. Troops awarded MMs included Sergeants King and Cross of the 49th Battalion, and Private Coombs of the 13th LTM Battery.

On 5 April elements of the 4th Division artillery began arriving in the battle area to rejoin their division, Brigadier General Rosenthal establishing his headquarters near Bapaume. It

Private (later Corporal) Joergen Jensen VC (1891–1922), 50th Battalion.
(AWM H06203A)

had been expected that the 2nd Division guns would be relieved by those of the 4th, but new orders were issued for the former to stay in the line and come under the orders of the 4th Division. I Anzac's preliminary operations in front of the Hindenburg Line were still in progress, with the 1st Division about to attack the outpost villages on the right of the sector, but the Corps was beginning to deploy its available forces for the projected assault on the Line itself. Circumstances would put the 4th Division in the forefront of the battle.

9 Notes

1. Figures from 4th Division Admin Staff War Diary for February 1917, Appendices 4 and 5.
2. See the *Official History*, Vol IV, pp. 80–81.
3. Pedersen, *The Anzacs*, p. 189.
4. C E W Bean stated that it was not until Messines (June 1917) that the Australian divisions were able to employ the new method effectively (*Official History*, Vol IV p. 18). The 2nd Division did not have an opportunity to introduce the new structure until the end of March, when it was relieved by the 4th (2nd Division GS War Diary). Monash's 3rd Division, training in England, adopted the system from the outset (see Pedersen, *Monash as Military Commander*, p. 169).
5. The brigade and unit orders for the exercises use realistic phrasing in describing the artillery arrangements, but the use of horsemen to indicate the barrage lines is made clear in the 12th Brigade orders and those of the 50th Battalion (13th Brigade), in their respective War Diaries for March 1917. The 12th Brigade diary mentions that each battalion was required to supply ten horsemen for the brigade exercises.
6. See the *Australian Dictionary of Biography*, article on 'Pope, Harold' by Suzann Welborn (this article incorrectly identifies the 13th Brigade commander as General Talbot Hobbs instead of General Glasgow).
7. Letter of Lieutenant R. Morris (16th and 48th Battalions), 1 Feb 1916. Copy made available to the author by David Hagan and Mark Palmer.
8. By the time of Edgar Sawer's death, the condition was being described as 'malignant disease of the pylorus' in his service record (p. 176 of that document, in the National Archives). After returning to Australia in July 1917, he had somehow been passed fit and was sent back to England to resume duty. The disease soon recurred and he was again sent home, dying within a few days of arrival.
9. 4th Divisional Train War Diary, 1 April 1917.
10. Lieutenant Ferguson had been appointed as ADC to General Holmes in January when the latter became GOC of the Division.
11. Specified in the 2nd Division artillery's orders for the operation (2nd Division Artillery HQ War Diary for March 1917 Appendices, Order No. 24 of 31 March).
12. Browning, *For King and Cobbers, Op Cit*, p. 109.
13. According to Bean's notes (Bean Papers, 1917 Notebook, AWM38 3DRL606/148/1, p. 29), and Major Churchill-Smith's account quoted in Freeman, *Op Cit*, p. 99. The 50th Battalion orders (Operation Order 18, War Diary for April 1917, Appendix 6) called for the mortars to engage both enemy posts.

14 According to Bean's notes (Bean Papers, 1917 Notebook, AWM38 3DRL606/148/1-1917, p.35).
15 Freeman, *Op Cit*, p. 101.
16 *Official History*, Vol IV, p. 219n, and 13th MG Company War Diary, 2 April 1917.
17 The 51st Battalion War Diary records that the barrage was called in at 5 pm and at 8 pm, but the 2nd Division Artillery War Diary records firing an 'SOS' barrage at 8 pm only.
18 The *Official History* (Vol IV, p.221) says that 'C' Company lost one officer (Lieutenant Darcy Maunder) killed and 53 men 'shot down', as Bean had recorded in a notebook (AWM38 3DRL606/126/1, p.46). The casualty figures reported to I Anzac for ORs were 20 killed and 33 wounded (I Anzac Admin Staff War Diary for April 1917, casualty report for 24 hours ended 12 noon 6/4/1917).
19 Quoted in Freeman, *Op Cit*, p.100.
20 The initial recommendation was simply for the DSO, but there was another DSO recommendation in the system for his work in the Mouquet Farm campaign. This was approved in the interim, so his Noreuil decoration was awarded as a Bar to the DSO.

10: Bullecourt

Following a lengthy period of planning and the deployment of an overwhelming force of artillery, the First and Third Armies were about to launch their great offensive against the German positions east of Arras. The battle area was 13 kilometers north of the position now held by Fifth Army, which was expected to assist Third Army by assaulting the Hindenburg Line position, thereby threatening the enemy's left flank and rear. Except for a sector on the Third Army's right, the main Arras attack would be made from a stable position against the original enemy line as it had been at the beginning of the year. Fifth Army, however, was deploying at the end of a long pursuit and facing a new and unfamiliar German position. General Gough was nevertheless keen to do his part, and some preliminary planning work had been done over the past few weeks. Artillery support was the key to the projected operation, and as each heavy and field battery came up to within range of the Hindenburg Line it opened fire on the enemy defences.

The main Hindenburg position consisted of a double trench system, with the front line trench protected by a formidable barbed wire entanglement comprising several separate belts. There were at least two such wire belts everywhere along the position, with three belts in some parts and four in a section of the front that would shortly be attacked by the 12th Brigade. Each belt was up to eight metres in depth and the lines were angled to channel an attacking force into killing grounds for the defending machine guns. The support trench, 150 to 200 metres behind the front line, was protected by another single belt of wire in the open space between, and the two lines were linked by several communication trenches. The trenches themselves were well constructed, two metres deep with numerous traverses and dugouts. On maps and aerial photographs the system showed a strong resemblance to the 'OG' lines encountered at Mouquet Farm in 1916, so the Australian staffs referred to them as OG 1 (front line) and OG 2 (support line). Formidable as it was, the Hindenburg Line could have been even stronger. Fifth Army's pursuit had been faster than the Germans had anticipated and some features of the Line were still incomplete in early April. A series of concrete bunkers had been planned but the work had barely begun and the network of communication trenches was well short of complete.[1]

Part of the reason for Fifth Army's rapid advance was the work of the engineers and pioneers in restoring the transport infrastructure close behind the infantry. Speed had been achieved at some expense in durability, however. Attempts to rush the Corps and Army heavy artillery forward on the new roads in wet weather proved to be counter-productive, with the big guns and their tractor tows bogging and breaking down. A conflict of priorities arose between the transport of road-making materials and that of artillery ammunition.[2] These factors combined to delay the heavy artillery in bringing its full available strength to bear on bombardment of the Hindenburg Line. That strength had already been reduced to a minimum by the need to transfer numerous heavy batteries to First and Third Armies to support the Arras operation. It had been decided at GHQ that Fifth Army's attack on the Hindenburg Line would be launched 24 hours after the main offensive, notwithstanding that artillery preparation would potentially be inadequate.

The attack at Arras went in on 9 April and quickly gained unprecedented success—the Canadian Corps brilliantly captured the strong position of Vimy Ridge, and Third Army was able to advance up to five kilometres on parts of its front. On that day in Fifth Army's sector, the 1st Australian Division completed the capture of the final three outpost villages on I Anzac's front. Fifth Army had now stabilised a line facing the Hindenburg Line and roughly parallel to it but time was running out to make an effective contribution to the Arras operation. I Anzac held the right of the line at a distance averaging about a kilometre from the newly-occupied railway cutting to the enemy front line trench, which in this sector ran roughly north-west to south-east. The 1st Division now held the right sector of I Anzac's line, thinly spread to cover 12 kilometres of front.[3] The 4th Division, holding the Corps left sector, was much more concentrated—it was from that part of the front that the main assault on the Hindenburg Line would be launched.

On I Anzac's left, and so on the left of the 4th Division, was the British V Corps' sector, with its 62nd Division in the line. On the German side of No Man's Land opposite the junction of the 62nd British and the 4th Australian was the fortified village of Bullecourt, forming a projecting bastion in the Hindenburg Line. Either side of Bullecourt, just on the reverse slope of a low, curved ridge, ran the German trench-lines, set back from the line of the village and so forming re-entrants.[4] To the east of the village (German left, British right) the re-entrant ran for about 2,500 metres to the trench system in advance of the village of Quéant, where the line curved out again towards the British front. Quéant had not been incorporated in the original Hindenburg Line, but had recently been enclosed by a hastily-dug trench known as Balcony Trench. Near Quéant another trench system (the Wotan Line or Drocourt-Quéant Switch) ran north behind the main German line near Arras, forming a fall-back position in case of a major British break-through in that area. Beyond the Hindenburg Line lay the villages of Riencourt-les-Cagnicourt and Hendecourt-les-Cagnicourt.

The 4th Division's infantry attack would be carried out by the 4th and 12th Brigades, which moved into the front line (that is, the railway cutting) on the night of 7/8 April, relieving the 13th Brigade units after their heavy losses in the hard fighting at Noreuil. The 4th Brigade took over the right sector of the Division front with its 14th and 16th Battalions in the front line. On the left the 12th Brigade put in the 46th and 48th Battalions. The battalions each had one company in the front line, with the remainder and the support battalions posted in the vicinity of Noreuil and further to the rear at Favreuil. A series of orders came down through Army, Corps, Division and Brigade command levels for the preparation and execution of the Hindenburg attack and the front line infantry units sent out reconnaissance patrols and began to improve their positions as soon as the troops came up. The 12th Brigade units started excavating jumping-off trenches outside the line of the railway cutting, while on the 4th Brigade's front a patrol from the 14th Battalion—led by Albert Jacka, now a captain and the unit Intelligence Officer—discovered an unoccupied sunken lane 250 metres beyond the cutting and roughly parallel to it. This made a convenient assembly position and the front-line companies of the 14th and 16th battalions quickly occupied the lane,[5] while on the left the 46th Battalion's jumping-off trench intersected it.

Behind the infantry, the field artillery was organising to cover the imminent operation. The 2nd Division artillery was already in the line, and with the arrival of the 4th Division's own artillery on 5 April and that of the 1st Division over the next few days, the guns and howitzers of three divisions were available. The combined force was designated as the Left Sector artillery, under the overall command of the 4th's CRA, Brigadier General Rosenthal. The Left Sector was divided into three groups:

'P' Group—the 4th Division artillery (the 10th and 11th AFA Brigades) under Lieutenant Colonel King, CO of the 10th Brigade. This group was responsible for the left of the divisional sector, covering the 12th Infantry Brigade, and including the enemy lines on the east side of Bullecourt village;

'Q' Group—the 2nd Division artillery (the 4th and 5th AFA Brigades), reinforced by the 12th (Army) AFA Brigade, the former 4th Division unit. The CO of the 12th, Lieutenant Colonel Rabett, commanded this group, which covered the right-centre of the front where the 4th Infantry Brigade would be operating;

'M' Group—the 1st Division artillery (the 1st and 2nd AFA Brigades), commanded by Lieutenant Colonel G I Stevenson, CO of the 2nd Brigade. This group covered the right of the sector, the part of the enemy line in front of Quéant.

The guns were positioned near the outpost villages of Ecoust-Longatte, Noreuil and Lagnicourt. The 4th Division batteries, 'P' Group, were emplaced behind Ecoust, 'Q' and 'M' Groups in the shallow parallel valleys between the villages, valleys that ran roughly at right angles to the Hindenburg Line. Bombardment of targets in the Hindenburg Line began as soon as each battery got into position, but the Australian guns were quickly subjected to enemy counter-battery fire. Their positions were predictable by the enemy, if not yet directly pinpointed, and searching fire up and down the valleys began to cause regular casualties among the gunners and other personnel.[6] As well as their field and medium artillery, the Germans also employed some very heavy guns to deliver harassing fire on the Australian back area. On 7 April a long-range shell hit the bivouac of the 4th Divisional Train's 7th Company AASC at Bapaume, killing or fatally wounding five men; another lost a leg. Fifteen horses were also killed and eight more were injured. Intelligence later assessed that the German gun was a 240mm weapon firing from the vicinity of Bourlon Wood, a range of about 20 kilometres.[7] Three days later another single high velocity shell, possibly from the same gun, made a direct hit on the headquarters dugout of the 4th AFA Brigade (2nd Division, supporting the 4th Infantry Brigade). The Brigade CO, Lieutenant Colonel Bertram Watts, was killed instantly together with the three officers of his staff.

The preliminary artillery programme called for the field brigades' 4.5-inch howitzers to bombard the enemy's Bullecourt village positions and to begin wire-cutting across the projected front of the attack to the east of the village. The 18-pounders were tasked with firing along the wire through the night to interfere with the work of repair parties. The Corps and Army heavy artillery continued pounding Bullecourt and Quéant as well as adding their weight to the wire cutting task. Without serious damage to the wire an infantry attack would almost certainly fail, and the staffs waited anxiously for reports on the results of the shelling. Artillery observation officers were teamed with infantry officers to observe from ground level, a task made more difficult by the location of the German line on the reverse slope. Aerial observation by the RFC gave a wider picture but flying was often restricted by the weather, which continued abysmal, with sleet or snow, or both, on most days. The RFC fliers had other problems too: this was the period when the Germans held the greatest technological advantage of the aerial war, and the antiquated British reconnaissance machines were easy victims for the vastly superior Albatros fighters of Baron von Richthofen and his colleagues, who were operating over the Arras/Bullecourt front at this time. The month became known as 'Bloody April', summing up the consequences of the RFC's brave but costly policy of continuing to operate offensively regardless of losses.

As of 8 April reports reaching I Anzac headquarters made it clear that 'the state of the wire in front of [V Corps and I Anzac] precludes the possibility of either Corps effecting on the 9th or 10th [of April] the co-operation outlined'[8]—that is, the operations in support of the Arras offensive. The wire-cutting fire was to continue 'vigorously' however, and in the meantime other avenues would be explored. An idea had taken root in Army HQ that the Germans would not hold the Hindenburg Line and were in the process of a further withdrawal. The front line units were ordered to send out nocturnal patrols to determine if that piece of wishful thinking was in fact correct. As a secondary objective, the patrols would also make a close-up check of the extent of damage done to the enemy wire by the shelling. On the night of 8/9 April the 48th Battalion sent out a patrol under the scout sergeant, Frederick Hammond, to examine the enemy lines in the vicinity of Bullecourt itself.

The scouts, working their way through three belts of wire up to a fourth belt in front of the German parapet, found no sign of any evacuation. One of the scouts, Private Tom Arnold, a 19 year old South Australian sheep farmer (later commissioned and three times decorated), recalled observing 'men on duty in each bay, machine guns mounted, flares were fired often so we could see splendidly. [The trench seemed] strongly held by the talking that was going on and [the] number of men on duty.'[9] There was some damage to the wire, but the scouts had got through it mostly by crawling through craters made by heavy artillery shells that had burst without actually breaking the strands. Patrols sent out by the 62nd Division (V Corps) on their front had similar results, finding minimal damage to the wire and the enemy still holding his trenches in strength.[10] A patrol from the 14th Battalion, on the other hand, reported that the wire on that unit's front was 'very badly knocked about and cut in many places,' and did not detect much in the way of enemy activity. Captain Jacka's report for the night noted that 'the shooting of our artillery was very accurate ... the heavies and field guns playing well onto wire all along the front,' although one 18-pounder battery was firing consistently short.[11]

Events now moved swiftly. The preliminary orders that foreshadowed the attack on the Hindenburg Line had assumed that the enemy wire obstacle would have been largely neutralised, but by the time I Anzac's Order Number 123 was issued on 8 April the opposite assumption had been made and it was apparent that the operation would probably have to be postponed. The 4th Division was nevertheless ordered to hold itself ready for immediate action should an opportunity arise, with its operations conforming to the scheme already outlined at Army and Corps level. Broadly, the intention was for the 12th Brigade on the left to use two battalions, with a third in reserve, to attack the Hindenburg Line immediately to the east of Bullecourt village, while the 62nd British Division attacked west of the village. Bullecourt itself was to be bypassed for the time being, to be taken later. The 4th Brigade would use all four of its battalions against the centre and right of the Line to its front, west of Quéant. The landmark forming the right-hand limit of the objective was the *Moulin* (mill) *Sans Souci*—a name, translating as 'carefree,' that would soon prove to have a certain bitter irony. Having taken the German front and support lines, designated units of the brigade would then go on to capture the village of Riencourt, nearly a kilometre beyond the trenches. To complete the enemy's discomfiture the British 4th Cavalry Division would then pass through the lines into the German rear area. C E W Bean recorded in the *Official History* that General Gough had originally proposed a further grandiose objective, intending that the I Anzac troops, having captured the Hindenburg Line and Riencourt, would then wheel to their right and advance a further 1,600 metres to confront the Drocourt-Quéant switch line—'victory might have been sought almost as reasonably by a plan to capture the moon.'[12] Fortunately, the general was persuaded to abandon that idea.

The 4th Division was allocated extra resources to support its infantry. Most importantly, a company of British tanks—officially No. 11 Company, D Battalion, Heavy Branch,

Machine Gun Corps—had just arrived in the area. Commanded by Major William Watson, the company nominally consisted of 12 tanks, but one had broken down on the way in, although the staff do not seem to have been aware of that at the time—the plans that came out over the next few days assumed 12 tanks rather than 11 were available. The Corps order specified that a section of those tanks (i.e., four machines) was 'placed at the disposal of the GOC 4th Australian Division and will be employed as that divisional commander may decide upon orders which will be issued by him direct to the section commander.'[13]

Also at the Division's disposal were the sinister facilities of No.1 Special Company, Royal Engineers. That unit was equipped with a number of mortar-like devices called Livens Projectors, the purpose of which was to fire cylinders of poison gas into the enemy lines. Extra machine guns were also allocated in the form of the 2nd Division's 6th and 7th MG Companies as well as part of the 13th Company. The 5th Division, in Corps reserve, was ordered to make an infantry brigade available to move up if needed. At this stage of the planning, it was assumed that a routine artillery barrage would provide the main support to carry the infantry into the enemy's line,[14] and the Division's preliminary instructions to the Brigades were on that basis. The Brigade staffs in turn instructed their battalions accordingly. Most of the communication at this stage appears to have been verbal, either by field telephone or in person, with a few memoranda or messages delivered by courier. The 4th and 12th Brigade staffs had, however, been able to produce some written orders which, although swiftly superseded, show what the original thinking was for the conduct of the imminent battle.

Brigadier General Brand's initial operation order for the 4th Brigade, issued at 10 am on 9 April, could only say that the Brigade would attack the Hindenburg Line 'on a date to be notified hereafter.'[15] A fairly standard artillery fire plan was described in the order, with the barrage falling on the enemy front line at zero hour, which of course could not be specified yet, and staying there for 16 minutes before lifting to fall between the front and support lines. After a further eight minutes, the barrage would begin to creep ahead to settle on the enemy support line, and a further series of lifts would take it to a covering line beyond the trenches. After an hour, the barrage would move on again to the Brigade's third objective, Riencourt village. This arrangement was presumably agreed between the infantry and artillery staffs in accordance with the artillery's instructions from Corps level,[16] but did not reach the stage of detailed orders before other events supervened.

Brand had evidently decided to accept the offer of assistance from the section of tanks that had been made available to the Division. The 4th Brigade's order states that '[One] section of tanks, two on either flank of the brigade, will co-operate. COs are responsible [that] all ranks are familiar with the signals to be used when working with tanks.'[17] It appears from the order that the 4th Brigade expected to also have the 52nd Battalion attached for operations:[18] the first and second objectives were allocated to the 14th, 15th and 16th Battalions, with the 13th and 52nd to attack the third objective. In the 12th Brigade, Brigadier General Robertson's preliminary order outlined the proposed operation very briefly, noting that the 46th and 48th Battalions would capture the Brigade's first and second objectives respectively, after which the 47th would pass through to attack a third objective—'which will be defined later.'[19] Again a routine covering barrage by the artillery was envisaged with lifts following the same pattern as that specified for the 4th Brigade. No assistance from tanks is mentioned. The brigadier may have seen no role for them or it may simply be that the 4th Brigade had got in first, bearing in mind that at this stage it was still intended that only one section of four tanks would be available to the 4th Division.

Both brigades arranged for elements of their own supporting arms, Stokes mortars and Vickers machine guns, to accompany the infantry in the attack. The role of the additional machine guns attached from the 6th, 7th and 13th MG Companies, defined in an order dated 8 April from divisional level,[20] was to provide fire support on the flanks of the attack and defend against possible counter-attacks. A considerable weight of fire was directed at covering the right flank of the 4th Brigade's advance, with 12 guns to barrage the enemy positions towards Quéant and eight guns of the 6th Company dug in along the railway cutting, positioned to interfere with any counter-attack mounted from the enemy lines near Quéant, considered the most likely direction. On the left, four guns of the 7th MG Company would reinforce six of the 12th MG Company in laying down fire on the trenches in front of Bullecourt village; another three guns would fire on the roads to Riencourt. Although I Anzac's warning order had mentioned that 'if tanks are used measures will be taken by means of artillery and machine gun fire to drown the noise caused by the tanks approaching,'[21] this factor does not seem to have been considered in the Division and Brigade planning for the machine guns and neither was it prominent in the artillery arrangements.

Before the end of the day on 9 April, the situation had changed dramatically. The story is well known and the key factor in the events of the First Battle of Bullecourt. Major Watson, commander of the tank company, had been working on a scheme using his tanks to break through the wire as the spearhead of the attack instead of in a supporting role:

> ... my tanks, concentrated on a narrow front of a thousand yards and supported as strongly as possible by all the infantry and guns available, should steal up to the Hindenburg Line without a barrage. As they entered the German trenches down would come the barrage, and under cover of the barrage and the tanks the infantry would sweep through ...[22]

The scheme was short on detail, in particular as to how the noisy machines could 'steal up without a barrage' across nearly a kilometre to an enemy position where there could be assumed to be at least a few sentries awake, but the major presented his idea to his battalion commander, Lieutenant Colonel Hardress Lloyd, on the morning of 9 April. The colonel was so impressed that he decided to take the proposal to General Gough, and the two tank officers saw the general at Fifth Army HQ that afternoon. It was an opportune moment. Reports of the First and Third Armies' initial success at Arras had come through, and the General was mortified that his command could do nothing to assist the offensive while the

German wire remained intact. Now he was presented with a means of breaking through the obstacle at one stroke and he jumped at the chance. Somewhat to their own surprise, the tank officers were ordered to make the necessary preparations and launch their attack at dawn the next day. The I Anzac leadership was called in and ordered to arrange for the 4th Division infantry to make its attack in conjunction with the tanks. General Birdwood and his chief of staff, General White, had their doubts about the wisdom of the scheme—Birdwood apparently more so than the normally cautious White[23]—but Gough was undeterred. There was still believed to be some chance, however, that the Germans may have been withdrawing and that a formal attack might not be necessary. A final reconnaissance was ordered to be undertaken that night. If the Germans had actually gone, a designated advance party would occupy the abandoned positions, otherwise the attack would go ahead.

At 4th Division HQ, according to General Holmes' after-action report,

> On April 9th, about 4 pm, verbal instructions were received that—as it was possible that the enemy would shortly evacuate the Hindenburg Line—strong patrols were to be sent out to reconnoitre it ... in the event of it being still held and the Army Commander ordering it to be attacked, the attack was to be carried out at dawn in co-operation with 12 tanks.[24]

Instead of a few tanks being available as extra support for the infantry if required, the full tank company had suddenly become the centrepiece of the operation. The tank commander, Major Watson, issued hastily-prepared orders to his crews and arranged for the clumsy machines to begin moving towards the front. He then made his way to 4th Division HQ during the evening to confer with the staff over the final arrangements. The Division issued two memoranda that evening following up the earlier verbal orders. The initial memo included the first written mention that the full company of twelve tanks would take part in the operation and precede the infantry to the enemy line, but still specified that 'the attack will be carried out under a barrage.' The second memo, issued at 9:30 pm, advised that the artillery support was changed to flank barrages only, to begin at 4:30 am, the same time as Zero for the attack, but at some point the barrage time was changed to 4:45.[25] In extreme haste, the infantry brigades and the artillery groups were informed of the new plans, and in turn rushed to get their units and leaders organised to implement them. Although produced with the best of intentions (like those with which the road to hell is paved), the tankers' plan would prove in the end to be a catalyst for disaster. As a new weapon, the tanks were well short of being fully developed, both mechanically and in terms of tactics. The machines used by the 11th Company were an early version, the Mark II (apart from two even older Mark Is), which had been superseded by improved versions and were in the process of being relegated to training duties. Very slow—a man walking briskly could outpace them—they were mechanically unreliable, and choking fumes from the engine usually got into the crew compartment. The crew's discomfort, combined with the severely restricted vision to the outside, made it very difficult for them to operate efficiently. Apart from being vulnerable to artillery fire, the Mark II's boiler-plate hull could be penetrated by armour-piercing bullets from enemy machine guns—it was only the new, not yet available, models that had true armour plating. On the other hand, the very presence of a tank could unnerve enemy riflemen in a front-line trench, unprotected against a metal monster armed with light artillery weapons and machine guns, and a tank was certainly capable of crushing a wire entanglement—provided, that is, that the tank could actually reach the enemy line.

Any doubts about the tanks' effectiveness were given little weight in the hasty preparations that now followed. The infantry and artillery staff and troops had no experience with tank operations, and the tank personnel had little themselves. Major Watson was comparatively new to his branch of the service and only a few of his officers had actually served with tanks in action. The plans for the imminent battle assumed that artillery and tanks could not be used together, although the tank commanders' original scheme does not seem to have explicitly stated this. The artillery fire-plan was hastily revised to take account of the presence of the tanks, which were now to be the principle—the only—means of penetrating the German wire. As Division HQ's memorandum stated, instead of a normal barrage the guns would now fire only on to the flanks of the attack, on the German positions at Bullecourt village on the left and at Balcony Trench in front of Quéant on the right. There would be no artillery fire on the actual frontage of the attack except for some shelling of the area behind the Hindenburg Line trenches in the vicinity of Riencourt, intended to interfere with German reserves coming forward.

The proposal to bypass Bullecourt village had been dropped and the British 62nd Division would no longer be attacking in direct conjunction with the 4th Australian. Instead two battalions of the 12th Brigade, protected by the four tanks allocated to them, were to capture the trench lines east of Bullecourt. The tanks would then turn left and enter Bullecourt, followed by one of the 12th Brigade battalions. Only when firm foothold had been gained would units of the 62nd Division be signalled to move forward and complete the capture of the village; the reasons for the relegation of that division to such a passive role remain unclear. On the right, the 4th Brigade's task remained as before except that the 52nd Battalion was no longer attached. Two of the brigade's battalions were to occupy the enemy trench lines and two to pass through and capture Riencourt. This would be accomplished with the assistance of four of the tanks and no artillery. Between the fronts of the two infantry brigades was a wide shallow depression leading towards the enemy line, with a road (the 'Central Road') running along it. The feature 'might ... form a deadly channel for the enemy's machine-gun fire'[26] against the infantry, so it was decided that this part of the attack would be undertaken by tanks alone. The remaining four tanks (actually only three were available) were given that task.

Orders, necessarily sketchy with the limited time available, were got out by various means to the units involved and hasty briefings were done. The infantry brigades arranged to bring forward their reserves into position for the battle. Firstly though, the front line battalions were ordered to make their last-minute reconnaissance of the Hindenburg Line. The 4th Brigade sent out a combined patrol from the 14th and 16th Battalions under the 14th's Intelligence Officer, Captain Jacka, and including his counterpart in the 16th, Lieutenant Frank Wadge, and another 16th officer, Lieutenant Henry Bradley. The patrol went out after dark, at 9:50pm, following the line of a minor road dividing the two battalions' sectors. It was about 700 metres to the outer edge of the German wire, and Jacka managed to penetrate some distance into the entanglement, where he could observe the damage and listen for signs of enemy activity in the trenches. After almost being detected by a German patrol, he made his way back to his patrol and they returned to the Australian lines. In his handwritten report,[27] Jacka stated that he had examined a 200 metre stretch of wire[28] and found that it was 'very badly broken and cut to pieces' in that sector. Enemy parties could be heard repairing damaged wire close to the front trench and a machine gun was firing. Although a number of sources assert that Jacka added that other parts of the wire were intact, his report (which, to repeat, was in handwriting rather than being typed up at some later time) does not say so.[29] The condition of the wire, however, was not the main object of the reconnaissance—it was to determine whether or not the Germans were still holding the Hindenburg Line in strength, and Jacka's patrol confirmed that they certainly were. Patrols sent out by the 12th Brigade's 46th and 48th Battalions on the left and left-centre of the divisional front also reported signs that the Line was strongly held. The 48th patrol found no significant damage to the wire south-east of Bullecourt, although that from the 46th, checking the frontage further to the east, reported it 'well cut for stretches of 20 yards [18 metres]'[30] (it appears that the 12th Brigade had initially misunderstood the orders from Division for the patrols, and Brigadier General Robertson had given a verbal order to the 48th Battalion to send a single company to attack Bullecourt village itself. Faced with an apparent suicide mission, Colonel Leane had insisted on getting the order in writing, but the mistake was corrected by a divisional staff officer before anything was done[31]). The consensus was that the Germans were not withdrawing and hence the attack was 'on' for the early morning of 10 April. Zero time would be 4:30 am. At I Anzac HQ Generals Birdwood and White were having increasing doubts about the wisdom of the operation, and they made a last-minute appeal to General Gough to call it off. By now news was coming through that the Arras offensive to the north had stalled in the face of heavy enemy resistance and there was no longer any point in trying to assist with a major breakthrough. To General Gough, however, this only increased the need for Fifth Army to make an effort on its front, and he reiterated that the attack must go ahead.

The infantry units began their assembly. The 12th Brigade's two attacking battalions, already in the front line, brought up their support companies and moved into the shallow assembly trenches prepared during the previous night. Two companies of the 47th Battalion, attached to the 46th as a reserve, came up into close support positions. The 4th Brigade's reserve units, the 13th and 15th Battalions, had set out between 9:30 and 10 pm on the 11-kilometre march from their billets near Favreuil to the front line. By 4 am those troops were settling in to their forming-up positions along the line of the railway cutting, backing up the 14th and 16th in the forward positions in and around the sunken track. 'The night was wild and bitterly cold, with a fierce wind and occasional sleet and snow.'[32] Arriving at 4th Brigade HQ in Noreuil for a last-minute briefing, the battalion COs 'found Brigadier General Brand apparently despondent. Then and only then we learned that the orders had been altered.'[33] The COs were informed, to their consternation, that the plan now called for the barrage to be dispensed with, and the infantry's support would be provided by tanks only. In the meantime the first actions of the battle had taken place at 1 am, when the Special Company RE fired a number of cylinders filled with Phosgene gas into the German positions in Bullecourt village. The Germans were taken by surprise and lost 200 casualties to the deadly fumes before the bombardment ceased. At about 2 am Captain Jacka took some of his 4th Brigade scouting patrol out into No Man's Land again, this time to lay out tapes to guide the advance. A famous incident took place as the patrol was finishing this work, when 'two of the enemy were seen boldly advancing onto [the] tape on the jumping off mark.'[34] The Germans would almost certainly detect the tapes. They could not be allowed to give the alarm, so Jacka hurried back to the line and brought out a Lewis gunner to cut off their escape route. He then stalked the two, who he had now identified as an officer and a private, and would have the shot the officer if his pistol had not misfired. The Germans nevertheless surrendered and Jacka hustled them back to the Australian line and captivity, encouraging the officer to keep moving by giving him a crack on the head with the pistol.

Despite the haste and changes in orders the troops were in position in the snow ready to advance by 4 am, by many accounts in good spirits even if their senior officers were not. The 4th and 12th Brigade battalions had experienced victory in their most recent fighting at Stormy Trench and since then had been rested away from the front. Regular training during that period had enabled most units to reach high levels of efficiency, and for the most part they had developed a set of fine officers and NCOs. 'The boys were in great nick,' wrote Lance Corporal George Mitchell of his 48th Battalion.

> The battalion was up to its full strength and pride, trained to the minute. The hardships of the winter were history, and the big, fit men were laughing and joking as they marched.[35]

Word soon reached the troops that they would now be attacking in conjunction with tanks, news that initially received a favourable reaction: 'The Australian infantry had never seen tanks in action, and were full of characteristic curiosity to see them.'[36] The arrangement had been that the tanks would be formed up in front of the infantry before 4:30, at which time they would set out for the Hindenburg Line. Having reached the enemy trench and crushed the wire, the tanks were to announce their success by displaying a green disc, the signal to the infantry to 'come on' according to the Division and Brigade orders. How the signal was to be detected in half-dark from a distance of 700 metres or more was not specified, and it seems to have been assumed that the Germans would obligingly refrain from taking any countermeasures while the infantry walked across that distance to join the tanks in the objective. As zero hour approached, however, there was no sign or sound of the tanks, the key to the whole operation. The tanks, which had been based nearly 10 kilometres behind the front, had begun their journey to the start line after dark at 8 pm but had soon struck difficulties finding their way in the pitch dark over unfamiliar territory. A heavy snowstorm compounded the problems and it was after 3 am when a tank officer reported to Major Watson, waiting at 4th Division HQ, that they were still three kilometres short of Noreuil and had no chance of reaching the jumping-off position on time. A half-hour postponement of the infantry advance requested by Brigadier General Brand at 4th Brigade[37] was apparently authorised, but by 5 am the tanks had still not arrived and the first signs of dawn were showing in the sky. If caught in the open by the enemy artillery—the jumping-off trenches were little more than ditches, not intended to provide full cover—the infantry would be cut to pieces, and General Holmes gave the order to abandon the operation: 'I think there is just time to get the boys back.'[38]

There was no time for an orderly withdrawal. As soon as the word reached the battalions lying out in the snow, the troops simply got to their feet and walked back to the main and reserve lines, looking like, as a number of witnesses recalled, a crowd leaving a football match. A fortuitous snow storm swept across the area, hiding the movement from enemy observation, and for the most part the troops got away unscathed. In the later stages of the withdrawal, however, a German artillery bombardment descended on the 48th Battalion's rearguard company in the railway cutting. Among the five killed was the battalion second-in-command Major Ben Leane, brother of the CO, Lieutenant Colonel Ray Leane, and another seventeen men were wounded before the firing died down. Major Leane caught a direct hit from a German 77mm shell. Early the next morning, Colonel Leane personally gathered up his brother's mutilated remains and buried them, at unimaginable emotional cost, then got on with the business of commanding his battalion in battle.[39]

It later emerged that the German barrage had been called down in response to a British probe against the Bullecourt village position. The 62nd Division's orders were to advance on the village only when it had been entered by tanks and the 12th Brigade infantry, following a signal to that effect. The 62nd had, however, also been ordered to push strong patrols up to the village when the Australian attack started at 4:30 am, the original Zero time. Unaware of the half-hour postponement of the 4th Division's operation, six patrols went forward on schedule and were caught in the Bullecourt wire by German machine guns, and by a bombardment from their own artillery as well. Before the patrols could extricate themselves, the British battalions lost 162 casualties. Once General Holmes decided to call the operation off altogether the 62nd Division was informed promptly —the message was recorded as being received at 4:55 am, presumably by telephone, and most accounts have General Holmes reaching his decision at about 5 am[40]—but by then it was too late to recall the patrols. Naturally, this incident was the cause of much bad feeling between the British and Australians. In later accounts, the 4th Division staff came in for some criticism for not informing the 62nd that the attack had been cancelled, but they actually had done so and the issue was rather with the initial half-hour postponement. There is some doubt that the staff was even aware of the British patrols and of the postponement,[41] which in any case was not so much that the infantry were ordered to delay their advance, but that they could not move until the tanks had reached the Hindenburg Line as the orders specified. The circumstances of excessive haste, imprecise orders and imperfect communications were the real problem.

The confusion and muddle of the morning had, not surprisingly, undermined the morale of the troops. For the 4th Brigade's reserve battalions, retracing their steps 11 kilometres to the billeting area at Favreuil, feeling was strong against the 'heads.'

> So, dog-tired, disappointed and more pessimistic than at any other period in their history concerning the higher authorities, they [the 13th Battalion] struggled on over the snow ... the last were only limping into Favreuil late that afternoon, falling asleep immediately on arrival.[42]

Because the plan had fallen down essentially due to the non-arrival of the tanks, that overriding issue tended to draw attention away from other flaws. There was a general understanding in the infantry brigades that the noise of the approaching tanks would be drowned out by that of the artillery barrage on the flanks of the advance, assisted by the covering fire of some of the allocated machine guns in position along the front line. The tanks were supposed to be in position in front of the infantry jumping-off line before 4:30 am, but it does not seem to have been considered at the command level that their 'hideous barking ... squeals, screeches and sparks'[43] might well be detected by the enemy some time earlier, during their approach to the start line. The machine guns were ordered to open fire only at Zero, 4:30am, while the field artillery orders[44] actually said that the guns of 'P' and 'M' Groups, shooting on the flanks, were to cease their normal night firing at 4:30 am and pause for 15 minutes to prepare for the flank barrage, which was to open at 4:45. 'Q' Group covering the actual attack frontage would simply continue its regular nocturnal shelling of the area beyond the Hindenburg Line around Riencourt. The Corps heavy artillery would similarly continue to shell Bullecourt, Riencourt and Quéant before lifting away at 5:15 am to allow the tanks to enter those locations. From 4:30 to 4:45 it was only the machine guns that had any role in covering the tanks' noise. The staff planners do not seem to have questioned whether the sound of six Vickers guns firing from over a kilometre away from the Hindenburg Line would be loud enough to drown out the sounds of a dozen tanks, particularly when the tanks, unlike the guns, would be steadily getting closer to the listeners.

This may not have been important if the failure of 10 April had led to a complete change of plans, but a conference at Fifth Army HQ at noon on that day resulted in orders to repeat the operation the next morning, at the same time of 4:30 am, and using essentially the same tactics. North at Arras, Third Army was about to attack again in an attempt to revive the stalled offensive, and again Fifth Army was required to put in a supporting attack. The I Anzac commanders again objected strongly, citing in particular the comprehensive failure of the tanks in the first attempt. In the end, however, General Gough was not to be dissuaded.

After (so he said) conferring by telephone with the Commander in Chief, Sir Douglas Haig, the Army commander gave the definite order to proceed with the operation. General Birdwood in turn conferred with General Holmes and the 4th Division staff during the afternoon to make the final arrangements. These were mostly as for the previous morning, with the exception that the impractical idea of the tanks signalling to the infantry when to advance was discarded, and the infantry would now simply start fifteen minutes after the tanks. The orders specified that six tanks would form up in front of each brigade (the staff were still under the impression that twelve were available). Of those supporting the 4th Brigade, the two on the extreme right once they had reached the Hindenburg trench would turn to their right and cover the Brigade's flank by engaging the enemy positions in Balcony Trench and Quéant. On the left in the 12th Brigade's sector, the four tanks on the left of the line would assist the infantry to capture the trenches then turn to their left to lead the advance into Bullecourt itself, at which point the 62nd British Division would begin its advance. In the centre of the attack front, the 12th Brigade's right and the 4th Brigade's left, four tanks (actually three) would advance up the depression between the two brigades. Except for those breaking off on the left and right, the remaining tanks would then continue forward to support the final advance on Riencourt and Hendecourt.

Verbal or telegraphed orders were sent to the 4th and 12th Brigades in mid-afternoon, followed up with a brief written operation order at 6 pm.[45] The orders for the field artillery were issued also, from Brigadier General Rosenthal's Left Sector HQ; those confirmed the arrangements for the previous morning. Two 'SOS' protective barrage lines were specified: one beyond the final objective (Riencourt) and another about 460 metres north of the Hindenburg Line, in case the infantry and tanks were unable to advance beyond the trenches. The two infantry brigades in turn got word out to the battalions and prepared their own written orders. Both brigades called in their battalion COs to confer late in the night, the 12th Brigade at 10:15 pm and the 4th at midnight. There was no time for the battalions (except for the 46th) to issue written orders, and the COs quickly got their company commanders together for verbal briefing. It was at the 16th Battalion briefing, which finished at 2 am, that Major Percy Black, the unit's senior company commander and unofficial elder statesman, was recorded as saying to Colonel Drake-Brockman, 'I mayn't come back, but we'll get the Hindenburg Line.'[46] It is apparent that both brigades' staffs were at first still under the impression that the flanking artillery barrages, which were expected to help drown the noise of the tanks, would open at 4:30 am, and this was stated in the first set of written orders. Each brigade issued a supplementary order later in the night correcting this to show that the barrage would actually start at 4:45, the same time that the infantry jumped off. It is possible that this point was not picked up by the battalions—certainly when the battalion histories came to be written, some of them complained that the artillery was silent at zero hour. Brigadier General Brand 'rang up Divisional Headquarters to know if this provision [for artillery-fire] had been made and was told "yes".'[47] It is difficult to believe that no-one mentioned times during this conversation, yet that seems to be the case. The opportunity was lost to argue for an earlier start to the barrage. The details of the machine gun barrage, in particular its timing, do not seem to have been discussed.

In the meantime word had been sent back to the reserve battalions and the weary troops were again slogging up to the front. The battalions already in the front line had their intelligence officers and scouts out in No Man's Land making a final reconnaissance and re-laying guide tapes; the 4th Brigade gave Captain Jacka the duty of directing the tanks into position when they arrived. By 3:30 am the infantry units had assembled in their jumping-off positions along the attack front. It had been snowing again and the ground was covered with a white mantle. On the right, the 4th Brigade had its 14th and 16th Battalions leading off from positions in advance of the sunken track, each unit with all of its four companies in line and each company in four waves formed by its four platoons. The 14th on the Brigade left had its left flank resting on the central road that bisected the battlefield from north to south, on the edge of the shallow depression dividing the two brigades. In the second line, positioned along the railway cutting, the 15th Battalion on the left and 13th on the right assembled in the looser 'artillery formation', ready to back up the 14th and 16th respectively. The 4th MG Company's Vickers guns were attached to the infantry, four to each battalion, and the 14th and 16th Battalions each had three Stokes mortars of the 4th LTM Battery allotted to them.[48] The battalions all established forward headquarters in the railway cutting, with the 14th and 16th HQs located together. Westwards, the 12th Brigade on the left of the attack front had the 46th Battalion leading off, lined up in the shallow assembly trenches running across the sunken track. Behind them the 48th Battalion was in the open ground in front of the railway cutting,[49] lying in the snow. The 47th, in support under the orders of the 46th but not involved in the initial advance, assembled in the Noreuil-Longatte sunken road. Brigadier General Robertson had decided not to send machine guns and mortars forward at first, and elements of those arms waited in the railway position to be called forward when the enemy trench line was gained. Several of the 12th MG Company's guns, together with the attached guns from the 7th Company, were positioned to barrage the trenches on the east side of the Bullecourt position up until 5 am.[50] As with the 4th Brigade, battalion HQs were set up along the railway. Both brigades had their headquarters in dugouts and cellars in Noreuil. The existing front line would be held by the 13th Brigade when the attacking force went forward, the 51st and 52nd Battalions coming in to take up their positions.

Command and control would obviously be an issue, even more so than was usual on the Western Front, with the battalion objectives being located at least 700 metres from the forward units' jumping-off positions. There was some attempt made to set up adequate communications and the 4th Division staff had outlined the arrangements in a Signalling Instructions memo issued on 9 April.[51] Behind the front line a network of telephone wires interconnected divisional HQ, the infantry brigades and the artillery groups, most of the wires being simply laid across the open ground, there being no time to bury them.

Marching infantry and the movements of the tanks frequently broke the wires, which were, of course, extremely vulnerable to enemy shelling as well. Signallers were constantly out repairing broken wires. Each infantry brigade was to carry two of the Power Buzzer morse signalling devices forward in the advance, with the brigade HQs having receiving stations. One battalion in each brigade was detailed to carry with it a field telephone connected to Brigade HQ behind its last wave in the advance, the signallers reeling out the wires as they went. Wireless telegraphy was being experimented with at this time and a trench wireless set was made available to the 4th Brigade, to be carried by three men to the final objective (Riencourt)—if this apparatus could have been successfully set up and used it might have made a great difference to the conduct of the forthcoming battle, but it was destroyed by a German shell while still packed up and waiting in the assembly area.[52] The usual flares, rockets and runners were available to the officers in the fighting area, as was the odd but sometimes useful method of carrier pigeons. In the event, none of the communication methods worked effectively in the crisis of the battle. Even if they had, it is doubtful if the battle could have been successfully controlled from headquarters at such a distance from the fighting, under Western Front conditions as they were in April 1917. In practice the battalions would be on their own tactically. Each brigade had a senior company commander in the attack force— Major Percy Black, 16th Battalion, in the 4th Brigade, and Major Victor Waine, 46th Battalion, in the 12th Brigade—who would be able to exert some control over their brigade's actions by virtue of rank, but who did not have formal authority outside their own units.

To the infantry waiting in the snow the immediate concern was the arrival of the tanks, which were now dispersed in the Noreuil valley, considerably closer to the front line than the previous morning. According to the Division order, the tanks were to be in position and formed up ready to advance by 3:30 am, an hour before zero. On the 4th Brigade front, where six tanks were expected, one had arrived in the sector at about 3 am and by 3:20 had been guided up by Captain Jacka to its starting position in front of the infantry. Jacka encountered the tank section commander—probably Captain Wilfred Wyatt; the tank section commanders were not travelling with their machines, but were observing from the jumping-off positions—and asked him if the tanks could actually reach the Hindenburg Line in the 15 minutes allowed for in the plan.[53] On being told that this was impossible, Jacka took the tank officer to the joint HQ of the 14th and 16th Battalions, where the two COs were informed. This meant that the infantry would be likely to reach the wire before the tanks. Colonel Drake-Brockman immediately phoned Brigade HQ and asked for the infantry advance to be delayed by 15 minutes. The request was referred up the line to Division HQ but General Holmes was not prepared to change the programme.[54] In the meantime the tanks were still straggling up. Only another two had managed to reach the start line by 4:30. One more had arrived in the vicinity but the crew had ignored Jacka's instructions and got their machine ditched in the sunken track. The tank could not be extricated in time for Zero, but it seems to have got going later, after the infantry had advanced.[55] Another was held up by mechanical trouble some distance from the start line. At 4:30 the three tanks that were in position, 150 metres ahead of the infantry, moved off towards the enemy line. At that time the machine guns covering the right flank opened fire—the 6th MG Company later reported that its guns each fired 3,000 rounds over the next two hours into target areas in the Quéant/Balcony Trench sector, and continued to fire at a reduced rate for another six hours.[56] Also at 4:30 the field artillery's routine bombardment on the flanks ceased in accordance with its orders, although the heavy artillery continued its regular shelling on Bullecourt, Quéant and Riencourt.

Within a few minutes flares were seen rising from the Hindenburg Line as the defenders, good troops of the 27th Württemberg Division, spotted the activity. A few machine guns opened fire and the German artillery's defensive barrage began to come down on No Man's Land and on the Australian front line along the railway, scattered at first but steadily increasing in intensity. Some of the first shots were all too accurate. A '5.9' shell wiped out the right-hand LTM section, three mortar crews and their weapons, waiting in the sunken track.[57] A late-arriving tank then unaccountably fired a machine gun burst from behind the track, killing three members of the mortar section's carrying party. Another shell-burst knocked Captain Jacka off his feet and mortally wounded his assistant, Lieutenant Harry McKinley. At 4:45 the field artillery opened fire again, laying the flank barrages on Bullecourt and Quéant. At the same time, 'punctual to the second,'[58] the 4th Brigade infantry moved off, the 16th and 14th Battalions forming the leading waves, four long lines in perfect order. Behind them followed the 13th and 15th Battalions in the second line. For the first few minutes the leading infantry, moving briskly over firm and almost flat ground, advanced with little interference from the enemy, who were concentrating their fire on the three tanks. As had been feared, however, the infantry caught up with the tanks about half-way through the approach—two of them had actually stopped and were firing in the general direction of the enemy line. There was some hesitation and at the same time the German machine gun fire shifted onto the infantry, from in front and both flanks. Gaps opened up in the long lines and red patches began to appear on the snow. It was at this point or shortly afterwards that both of the lead battalions lost a company commander, Captain Bob Orr of the 14th, seriously wounded and later killed by a shell in No Man's Land, and Captain Virgil Tucker of the 16th, killed instantly by a machine gun bullet.

The troops could not stay where they were and they would be under heavy fire and without cover whether they advanced or retreated. Without the tanks in front there was no support if the advance continued, but to turn back now would have been almost as dangerous and in any case was morally out of the question. On the extreme right of the line the 16th Battalion's 'B' Company was rallied and led forward by its commander, Major Percy Black, with his famous call of 'Come on boys, bugger the tanks!' The momentum was picked up along the rest of the 16th's line and it surged towards the wire, with the other company commanders—Captains Robert Somerville and Horace Hummerston, and Lieutenant Dan Aarons, who had taken over from Captain Tucker—taking the lead. The 14th Battalion on the left pressed forward also under the hail of fire, its left-hand company taking particularly heavy losses from machine guns, including some firing at long range from the direction of Bullecourt[59] (in that part of the battlefield, the Germans' attention should have been occupied by the 12th Brigade's attack, but in fact that attack had not even been launched yet). Like the 16th, the 14th Battalion was led in the field by a highly effective group of officers. 'Before or since, we've never had such a combination of company commanders,' wrote Edgar Rule.[60] One of these, Captain Orr, had already been badly hit, but Captains William Wadsworth, Frederick Stanton and the Carlton footballer Alfred 'Lofty' Williamson led their men into the wire.

In some places, the troops found that the entanglement had been badly damaged by heavy artillery shells and was comparatively easy to cross, particularly on the 14th Battalion's right, confirming Captain Jacka's observations on the previous night. In other places the wire was scarcely damaged but there were some avenues to be found, either the few gaps made by shells or the narrow access lanes used by German patrols. The men tended to bunch up at these points and made easy targets for the defenders. The fire of rifles and machine guns rose to a crescendo, the Germans firing along their wire and cutting down the troops struggling through it. Showers of sparks flew as bullets ricocheted from the strands. There is no definite number for the killed and wounded in this part of the battle but it may have been as high as 450 between the two battalions,[61] many of the bodies caught up in the barbs. Undaunted, the survivors forced their way through and made for the enemy front line trench, 'OG 1'. This was quickly taken with grenade and bayonet, many of the garrison, apparently disconcerted by the tanks as well as by the aggression of the attacking infantry, retreating into dugouts or running back to 'OG 2,' their support line.

The battle plan called for the leading battalions to press on immediately to OG 2, and as soon as OG 1 was secured the depleted units resumed the advance. OG 2 was protected by only a single belt of wire, which was undamaged. If anything, that obstacle proved to be at least as dangerous as the multiple entanglements protecting OG 1, particularly on the left where the 14th Battalion again came under intense enfilade fire from well-placed machine guns. Here their heavy losses included two more company commanders, Captains Stanton and Williamson, both killed leading attempted rushes. Finally a party from the 14th under Lieutenant Stan Thompson got into OG 2 through a communication trench, clearing out the German garrison on that flank; Lieutenant Thompson, whose twin brother was also a 14th officer, was himself killed in the attack. On the right Major Black led the 16th Battalion across the gap against OG 2 under heavy fire. Reaching the wire belt, he searched along it, found a patrol lane and sent his men through the opening. Here he gave his runner, Private Charles Ellis, a verbal message for Battalion headquarters: 'The first objective is gained and I am pushing on to the second.' In the same moment, Black was killed, shot through the head by a German bullet. The 16th Battalion's great battlefield leader was gone, but his men rushed OG 2 and engaged the enemy garrison at close quarters. This must have been at about 5 am or a little later; Private Ellis reached the HQ in the railway cutting at 5:16 am with his message,[62] half an hour after the line of infantry had first moved off into the attack.

Major Percy Black DSO DCM (1877–1917), (C A Longmore, The Old Sixteenth)

On his way Ellis would have passed through the waves of the 13th and 15th Battalions, coming up quickly in support of the first waves. Those units, starting at the same time as the lead battalions but 500 metres to the rear, ran into the enemy defensive barrage falling along the Australian front line and began to lose casualties from the start. One of the 13th's company commanders, Captain Theodore Wells, was seriously wounded at this stage. Halfway across No Man's Land the battalions came under increasingly heavy flanking fire from the now fully alerted enemy. Captain Harry Murray's 'A' Company, leading the 13th Battalion's advance, was caught in enfilade by traversing machine gun fire from their right and lost 30 casualties in a few seconds, including three platoon commanders. The 15th Battalion on the left had heavy losses also, company commander Captain Robert McIntosh being among the seriously wounded, but both units now opened out their formations and continued forward at the double up to the wire. One of the tanks had reached the wire by now but after breaking a path into the first belt it had become entangled in the strands, with its crew working hard to free it. Parts of the 13th Battalion made for this point, taking heavy casualties from an enemy machine gun firing from a forward sap near the tank. The German crew kept firing 'with death certain and imminent'[63] until they were killed. Fire from the flanking machine guns continued as the 13th and 15th troops forced their way through the wire by any means, losses mounting up all the time; the 15th Battalion estimated that it had 100 casualties during this stage of the fighting;[64] those killed included a second company commander, Captain John Watson.[65] The survivors kept on to the OG 1 trench. The first line battalions, having captured the trench, had now moved on and some of the 13th and 15th troops mopped up in OG 1, rolling grenades into the dugouts and taking prisoner 60 of the surviving Germans in the trench. These were sent back under escort, but many of them were cut down in No Man's Land by their own machine guns. The 13th and 15th went forward again to join the lead battalions still fighting in OG 2, taking further casualties as they crossed the open space between the lines and struggled through the wire belt; another 15th Battalion company commander, Captain Francis Leslie, was killed there.[66] It was about this time that Harry Murray realised that his old friend Percy Black had been killed: 'I saw his body within fifteen minutes of his being hit ... as I was assisting the 16th attack on the support line I had not time to even take his personal effects.'[67] The arrival of those reinforcements finished the fight in OG 2 for the time being, the surviving Germans retreating along the trench to the flanks or running to the rear towards Riencourt.

It was then probably about 5:30 am. The plan now called for the 13th and 15th Battalions to continue forward to the final objective, Riencourt, but the crippling losses suffered in the half-hour of fighting made success in that venture highly doubtful. Led by Captain David Dunworth, a group from the 15th with a few 14th men nevertheless made an attempt, attacking on the left towards the communication trench known as Ostrich Avenue, which ran alongside the Central Road to Riencourt. The attempt failed, the party being practically wiped out by machine gun fire. Captain Dunworth himself was wounded in the shoulder but managed to crawl back to OG 2. He was the only 15th Battalion company commander still in action and he continued to lead until weakened by loss of blood. The 16th Battalion succeeded in establishing a post in another communication trench, Emu Alley, 150 metres beyond OG 2, but from here they faced open ground covered by enemy fire and could get no further. The troops in this post were later joined by a party from the 13th under Lieutenant Bernard Rose, and for the rest of the battle that group was involved in heavy fighting against enemy troops trying to advance down the trench. Two 13th Battalion rifle grenadiers, Corporal Wilfred Patten and Private Charles Knight, particularly distinguished themselves in that fighting.

Ammunition was running short, particularly grenades—apart from the supplies carried by the specialist bombing sections, the men had been ordered to carry only the standard two each, in the optimistic expectation that most of the fighting would be in the open rather than in the trenches. The barrage had already lifted away from Bullecourt on the left and Riencourt in the centre, supposedly to allow the entry of tanks and infantry, and also temporarily from Balcony Trench on the right, to allow the tanks to pass along it. The right flank barrage recommenced after half an hour, but at a considerably reduced rate of fire. The tank caught in the OG 1 wire managed to get free at about 5:30 and tried to continue its advance, by one account mistakenly shooting at the Australian troops now occupying OG 2,[68] but it was soon knocked out by artillery fire. Another tank on the far right crossed the wire of Balcony Trench and drove alone down the German line, shooting at the defenders, but it soon came within range of a machine gun firing armour-piercing ammunition. Shot through by the steel-cored bullets, the tank caught fire; the survivors of its gallant crew baled out and were captured. Enemy fire from the flanks and Riencourt was unimpeded and machine guns were already sweeping the tops of the captured Hindenburg trenches. On the left and right of the section occupied by the 4th Brigade, the trench lines were still strongly held by the enemy, particularly on the left, in the 400-metre gap between the 4th and 12th Brigade objectives which was meant to have been covered by the tanks. It was apparent to the surviving senior officers of the 4th Brigade in the captured position that any further advance was out of the question, and the most that could be done now was to hang on to the ground gained. That was certainly how Captain Murray of the 13th Battalion assessed the situation, and his views had much weight in the Brigade:

> After the death of Major Black, many officers from all parts of the brigade sector ... tended naturally to seek out and consult Captain Murray for direction that would unite their effort. Murray was not the sole or senior company commander in OG 2 ... but he was the leader best known to all the brigade.[69]

Murray took on the responsibility without hesitation and set out along the whole length of the captured trenches to see the overall situation for himself.

One point that would have been obvious was that the 12th Brigade had not made the expected progress on the left of the battlefront. The timing of the 12th Brigade attack was meant to be the same as that for the 4th Brigade on the right, with the infantry jumping off at 4:45 am. The intention was said to be that the infantry would begin its advance at that time regardless of what progress the tanks might have made, and the timing of the fire support, limited as that might have been, was based on that premise. In fact the 12th Brigade infantry advance began half an hour late, a crucial delay. The 46th Battalion was to lead off the attack, but by what may or may not have been a misunderstanding that unit's command group had gained the impression that the infantry was to wait for fifteen minutes after the tanks had passed the jumping-off line before starting. When the first tank did not even arrive at the line until 4:45 the infantry continued to wait. The confusion in the orders has never been fully explained, although obviously the result of the extreme haste in which the arrangements had been made. The 46th Battalion seems to have been the only unit in the operation, in either brigade, that produced a written order to supplement its verbal briefing, and this order included the instruction 'The infantry will not advance until fifteen minutes after the tanks pass the Jumping Off Trench.'[70] The 46th Battalion CO, Lieutenant Colonel Howard Denham, reported after the battle that the plan was 'carefully explained by me, personally, to the company commanders concerned and a copy of these orders handed by me to them.'[71] The 46th's senior company commander, Major Victor Waine, mentioned in a post-war talk with C E W Bean that he had asked the CO at the conference what to do if the tanks did not arrive, a reasonable question in view of the recent fiasco. Colonel Denham's answer was 'If no tanks turn up, of course you will have to go forward alone. But they will turn up.'[72] There was apparently no discussion of what the timing should be in that eventuality.

The battalion orders were the outcome of the conference at Brigade HQ held at 10:15 pm.[73] The final written Brigade order, No 137, does not have a time of issue endorsed but Brigadier General Robertson's after-action report notes that the order was issued at 10:30, and probably it was typed and duplicated in time to give a copy to the battalion COs before the conference broke up (although the 47th Battalion War Diary says that unit did not receive the order until 3 am). That order does show the correct timing for the infantry advance, but the first Brigade order, No 136 endorsed as issued at 7 pm, still shows the original arrangement for the tanks to advance first, occupy the line, and then signal the infantry to advance; the relevant typed paragraph was crossed out and marked 'cancelled' by hand, but it is not clear if that was done before or after distribution. That order also states that the flank barrage would commence at 4:30 am, which was corrected to 4:45 in the final order (the 4th Brigade's first order also included the 'green disk' arrangement and had the wrong timing for the flank barrage; those points were corrected by a memo issued at 10:45pm[74]). Although the *Official History* says that the error in the 46th Battalion's order was not detected by the Brigade staff,[75] the Battalion did not necessarily send a copy of the order to Brigade. In the haste and confusion of order and counter-order, there was considerable potential for misunderstanding, for which the Brigade staff must take some of the responsibility.

Whatever the reasons were for the mistake, it was the 12th Brigade troops lined out in the snow who were about to suffer the consequences. By 4:30, with the German defensive barrage now beginning to fall on the infantry position, none of the tanks had reached the start line. One came up on the right of the 46th Battalion's line at about 4:45, the time that the infantry was supposed to jump off, and its first action was to drive along the assembly trench and open machine gun fire on the waiting troops. Obviously the crew had become hopelessly lost and thought that they had already reached the German line. No-one appears to have been hit, and a chorus of shouts soon attracted the attention of the tank commander. He was firmly informed of where he was and where the enemy was. The tank set off again but this time headed too far to the right. It was soon hit by a shell and disabled. At about 5 am, by which time the fifteen-minute field artillery barrage on Bullecourt had just ceased, a second tank appeared. This one crossed the centre of the jumping-off line but then stopped a short distance out, either broken down or hit by a shell. By now the battalions' leaders were becoming concerned at the lack of action. At 5 am the 48th Battalion CO, Lieutenant Colonel Leane, 'thinking perhaps they might be waiting for signals from tanks,' sent a message to his company commanders saying 'You do not wait for signals from tanks. When the first objective is taken, you go on and take the second.'[76] The reference to signals from the tanks suggests that the 48th Battalion leadership was not as fully conversant with the plans as is usually supposed—the actual issue was not one of signals, but rather of timing. If the 48th's battlefield leaders were certain that the infantry was to jump off at 4:45 regardless of the tanks, then they would have done so— the senior company commander and attack leader, Captain John Mott, was a resourceful and determined officer, presumably not prone to indecision. Colonel Leane's after-action report strongly suggests that he himself believed that the infantry had to wait for the tanks: 'The men would have gone forward at once under cover of darkness instead of having to wait in the open from 4 am until 5:16 am by which time it was daylight, for tanks that never arrived.'[77] Probably the 48th officers could see that the 46th in front of them had not moved (although it was not yet dawn, there was enough illumination from shell bursts and flares). If they believed that this was contrary to the orders, an officer could have been sent forward to ask the 46th what they thought they were doing, but nothing like that seems to have happened. It does appear that both battalions were not clear on the exact timing arrangements, not just the 46th; Colonel Denham makes an easy target for criticism because he committed his instructions to writing. The clarity of the briefing given by the 12th Brigade staff comes further into question.

At 5:10 am by the unit War Diary, Captain Henry Davis, commanding the 46th's 'C' Company in the centre of the line, called Colonel Denham on the field telephone—still working for the time being—to ask for instructions: 'Only one tank has passed our jumping off trench—we can't see any of the others—are we to advance?'[78] The CO gave the order to move off at once and the 12th Brigade advance finally got under way, half an hour late and with daylight just appearing. The troops of both battalions went forward at the double and immediately ran into a storm of fire from in front and on both flanks, particularly on their left from the enemy trenches in front of Bullecourt, where the Germans were undisturbed by either artillery or tanks. At 48th Battalion HQ, 'a wretched niche in a four-foot bank,'[79] Colonel Leane sent a message to Brigade (timed at 5:19 am) asking 'have arrangements been made to keep barrage longer on flanks of Bullecourt?'[80] But the barrage had already ceased and the request was refused on the grounds that renewed shelling would interfere with the tanks. No-one seems to have grasped that there were no tanks. The 12th Brigade's supporting artillery ('P' Group, the 4th Division's own guns) would have presumably been in the process of re-laying their weapons on to the 'SOS' line, but probably something could have been done if the issue had been pressed.

As it was, the German fire continued unabated, not just the flanking machine guns and rifles but also the defensive artillery barrage, now falling even more heavily on the open approach. 'A tornado of thunder and flame fell upon us, beyond anything I had known or imagined,' recalled Lance Corporal George Mitchell of the 48th Battalion, doubling forward with his Lewis gun team. 'The air was dense with crackling bullets, and thick with the blood-chilling stink of explosives. The plain was carpeted with bodies ...'[81] As with the 4th Brigade on the right, several battlefield leaders were among the early losses in the advance across No Man's Land. In the 46th Battalion Captain Davis was killed, and the 48th lost two company commanders badly wounded and carried back, Lieutenant William Caldwell and Captain A G 'Johnny' Moyes, the future sports journalist and broadcaster.[82] Losses were particularly heavy on the flanks. One of the tanks allocated to the central depression had managed to reach the wire on the 46th Battalion's extreme right, near the western edge of the depression. A party of infantry tried to follow its path but they were caught by enemy machine guns and almost annihilated. Enfilade fire from Bullecourt on the left cut down more men but the Victorians pushed on and reached the wire belts protecting OG 1. As the 4th Brigade units had found on the right, there were a few gaps in the wire made by shelling but the entanglements were mostly undamaged. Nevertheless, the 46th troops forced their way through somehow and got into the enemy trench. There was some close-quarter combat but many of the garrison did not stay to fight, running back to their support line, OG 2.

Coming up behind the 48th Battalion troops were running the same gauntlet of fire and in their turn forced a way through the wire belts, leaving many dead and wounded hanging from the barbs. The survivors went on to the OG 1 trench where some were briefly involved alongside the 46th in fighting the few enemy troops remaining in the trench, but the 48th's task was to pass through and attack OG 2. Led on by Captains Mott and Allan Leane (a nephew of the 48th CO) the remaining troops climbed out into the open again, kept going through the next line of wire and drove the defenders out of the German support trench—but the battalion's strength was melting away under the unceasing fire from the flanks.[83]

Captain Mott, already hit twice, went back to OG 1 in search of reinforcements but there he was shot in the neck, a serious wound that temporarily paralysed him; Lieutenant Robin Morris was also wounded twice in the fighting for OG 2. Captain Leane in OG 2 was now the 48th's only company commander remaining in action. The 48th now held a substantial length of OG 2 with the 46th behind them occupying a sector of OG 1. It was then about 6 am. Despite their heavy losses, both units had established strong footholds in their objectives. The next task was to consolidate their positions and try to extend them.

On the right of the battlefield, the four battalions of the 4th Brigade faced the same task. Captain Murray of the 13th, making his way along the captured position, organised the placement of men and weapons. Eight of the 4th MG Company's Vickers gun crews, advancing with the final waves of the infantry, had come up by now—the other eight had been put out of action in No Man's Land—and these were positioned along the two trench lines. Their firepower was supplemented by the battalions' Lewis guns, some of which were outposted in shell-holes beyond OG 2. Two of the 4th LTM Battery's Stokes mortars had survived the approach, although the crews had very little ammunition with them—some of the carriers having been killed by 'friendly fire' from a tank at the start line. These were emplaced in a cross-trench towards the left flank. The trenches were very deep, with walls well above head height, and work was started making firesteps in what had been their rear walls. Barricades were built on the right flank in both trenches, where bombing parties had managed to push on for some distance beyond the limit of the original objective. Two early German counter-attacks on that flank of OG 2 were easily repulsed with grenades; Captain George Gardiner, 13th Battalion, was in charge there. On the left, however, the flank was open where the central depression made a 400-metre gap between the two brigades. The plan to bridge this with tanks had obviously failed, and it was now up to the infantrymen to fight their way along the trenches and join hands with the 12th Brigade to complete the front.

The troops from the 4th Brigade's different battalions had become mixed together in the confused fighting, and it was a combined bombing party under Lieutenant William Parsonage (13th Battalion) and CSM Charlie Emerson (15th) that attacked westwards along OG 1. As long as the supply of hand and rifle grenades held out the group made progress against determined resistance, extending the flank by about 100 metres. Their own grenades were soon used up, however, and they were reduced to using German stick-grenades found in the trench—an indication to their opponents that all was not well. Unable to advance further, Parsonage's group barricaded the trench and went on the defensive, still 100 metres short of the Central Road. Attempts to extend the left flank in OG 2 were forestalled by strong German counter-attacks coming down the communication trench Ostrich Avenue from the direction of Riencourt. The left of the 14th and 15th in OG 2 was pushed back for some distance, but an attempt by the Germans to attack OG 1 over open ground was stopped by fire from Vickers and Lewis guns. The situation in the 4th Brigade's objective was at a stalemate for the time being, and the priority now was to defend the ground gained. For this ammunition was needed urgently, particularly grenades, and defensive artillery support was equally important. At 7:15 am Captain Murray wrote out a message for his battalion HQ setting out the situation clearly and sent it off by runner:

> We hold first objective and part of second. Have established block on right of both objectives ... Expect heavy bomb fighting in evening ... Quite impossible to attack village [i.e. Riencourt] ... We will require as many rifle and hand grenades as you can possibly send, also SAA [small arms ammunition] ... Look out for SOS signals ... With artillery support we can keep the position till the cows come home.[84]

At about the same time, Captain Jacka, observing from somewhere near the main line at the railway, was reporting to Colonels Peck and Drake-Brockman that the tanks had failed completely but both objectives had been taken with heavy losses.[85]

The two 12th Brigade battalions on the other side of the battlefield were also fighting to extend their positions in the captured trenches. Captain Leane, leading the 48th in OG 2, now the Australian advanced line, sent bombing parties down the trench to right and left. By about 7 am Lieutenant Samuel Jones' group on the right had succeeded in pushing that flank as far as the Central Road. Here the troops dug in to establish a post in the road-bank. On the 48th's left, Lieutenant Edwin Dennis led another group bombing down the trench. This party made steady progress until it reached an open gap where the sunken Bullecourt-Riencourt road intersected the trench at a sharp angle. Here the Germans, sheltering behind the road bank, prevented the 48th from crossing the gap. At the same time neither side could attack the other across the open ground between the trench and the road. Here again the situation was deadlocked, and Lieutenant Dennis ordered a barricade constructed. Several Lewis guns were positioned along the occupied section of trench and those sniped at targets in the enemy back area towards Riencourt.

Behind the 48th, the 46th Battalion in OG 1was also engaged in heavy fighting up and down the trench, particularly on its left towards Bullecourt. Here Captain Frederick Boddington led his 'B' Company in a grenade duel against determined opposition. It had been intended that the company would be following the tanks into the Bullecourt position, and for that reason it had been reinforced by two platoons of 'A' Company. With no tanks anywhere near, the aim was now to extend the flank as far as possible. By 6:30 am Boddington's men had pushed close to the nearest corner of the village site, but by then their supply of grenades was exhausted and no further progress could be made. After a half-hour pause, a German counter-attack came in, and with no grenades the troops on this flank were forced back for some distance along the trench. The Germans had also set up a trench mortar in Bullecourt, and bombs from that weapon increased the pressure on the left in OG 1. On the 46th's right, where Major Waine was in charge, the almost total loss of the right-hand platoon in the central depression meant that the Battalion was some distance short of its objective on that flank. The major undertook a head count, which showed only 65 officers and men in the trench, 12 of whom were wounded (those figures, stated to C E W Bean in a post-war interview, were taken to mean the numbers for the whole battalion, but Major Waine may well have meant just his own 'D' Company, which would have been his main focus at this point, and which was somewhat separated from the other companies; if so, this would explain an apparent discrepancy in the numbers for the 46th[86]). Feeling that his company was too badly weakened by its casualties to attempt any more than holding the ground already gained, Major Waine ordered the trench barricaded against counter-attacks. He established company HQ in a big German dugout near the barricade and sent a series of messages back to Battalion HQ requesting desperately-needed ammunition and reinforcements.

The first of these, reaching Colonel Denham shortly after the 46th had entered the enemy line, resulted in a carrying party being sent forward with grenades. One of the attached companies of the 47th Battalion, 'A' under Captain Francis North, was ordered up from reserve. They collected 600 grenades from the dump at the railway and set out for the fighting line, Colonel Denham ordering that two platoons were to reinforce the 46th in OG 1 and the other two to pass on to the 48th in OG 2.[87] Shortly afterwards another message from Major Waine arrived reiterating the need for grenades, and the 46th's few remaining carriers were sent up with further supplies, followed shortly afterwards by a further group from the 47th. Many of the carriers were cut down crossing the fire-swept No Man's Land but enough got through to enable the left company to renew their attack. Some of the ground lost was regained but Captain Boddington was killed in the fighting, by some accounts in attempting to lead a bayonet charge before the additional grenades arrived; 'he was the finest officer out there, a soldier both in the trenches and out,' wrote one of his men later.[88] Lieutenant James Stanton took charge of the left flank. By now there was also enemy pressure on the right flank, but an exchange of grenades resulted in no gains for either side and the fighting in that area died down temporarily. With the reinforcements from the 47th, the 46th was able to stabilise its position in OG 1, which was further strengthened by two Vickers guns of the 12th MG Company. Those gun crews had been sent forward at 7:20 and apparently got through unscathed. The guns were emplaced near the left of the 46th's position in OG 1,[89] from where they could sweep the area to the north, past the left flank of the 48th Battalion where the sunken road intersected OG 2.

The 48th had also received reinforcements from the 47th, bringing with them supplies of grenades, and a carrying party from their own unit led by Lieutenant Norm Imlay brought up Lewis gun ammunition and stayed to assist in the fighting. Captain Leane now ordered another attempt to push past the sunken road junction on the left. The Germans below the road bank, aided by the topography, still proved difficult to shift, however, even with the addition of the reinforcements. Although the 48th could make no progress, the Germans were equally frustrated in trying to push them back, and the stalemate on this flank continued. It was a similar situation over all of the 12th Brigade's position. With the right of the 46th held up short of its objective in OG 1 and the left of the 48th stopped in OG 2, each unit had an unsupported flank but overlapped for 250 metres in the centre of the objective, where a cross-trench linked the two lines.[90] There was a pause in the infantry fighting on that side of the battlefield for the time being, although it would soon be apparent that the Germans were preparing powerful counter-attacks. Some of the men took the opportunity to snatch something to eat from their field rations but their meal was soon interrupted by the enemy artillery, which began to shell the trench lines, joined by bombs from the mortar in Bullecourt. From that direction also, machine gun and rifle fire continued to sweep across No Man's Land, making a deadly barrier to the carrying parties trying to bring forward more ammunition.

At 9 am Colonel Leane at 48th Battalion HQ decided to send up four Stokes mortars of the 12th LTM Battery, two to his unit and two to the 46th, in the hope that their fire would counter that from the German mortars. It is one of the minor mysteries of Bullecourt that the order never reached the LTMs. In his report Colonel Leane stated that the message was sent by runner to the position where the battery OC was supposed to be (map reference U 27 d 5.4, a location in the railway cutting directly south of Bullecourt), but 'although my runners searched everywhere, both right and left of this position, they could not be found and I have since been informed that the mortars never went forward. They would have assisted my line materially.'[91] The various reports written after the battle do not explain the missing mortars and there is no record of any repercussions.[92] The deployment of the 47th Battalion's 'B' Company is also uncertain. As one of the two companies attached to the 46th, it has been generally assumed that 'B' Company was sent up to the fighting front shortly after 'A', but this is not mentioned in the war diaries or reports of the brigade and both battalions (the 47th diary did not report on the two companies' activities on 11 April because they were under the orders of the 46th). The remaining two 47th companies were first employed in carrying ammunition from the brigade dump near Noreuil to the battalion dumps in the railway cutting, and in fitting detonators to grenades. At the end of the battle, about midday, all available troops of the 47th's 'C' and 'D' Companies were sent up to the railway to reinforce the main line, where they reported to Colonels Leane (48th) and Denham (46th).[93] 'B' Company may also have been employed on carrying duties, or possibly retained as a last reserve in case of a major enemy counter-attack on the original front line. It is also possible that the commanders, in particular Colonel Denham, simply forgot that they were available. The company may in fact have gone forward to the Hindenburg Line trenches, and their advance gone unrecorded, but details of the 47th's casualties on 11 April suggest otherwise.[94]

The 4th Brigade meanwhile was also battling to maintain its position in the enemy lines. A continuing problem was the German presence in both trenches near the Central Road, where two companies of Württembergers still held a short stretch of OG 2 and a longer segment of OG 1. The latter troops were almost cut off to the rear by the 48th Battalion in OG 2, but the Germans in that sector stubbornly stuck to their guns, and the Australians, short of numbers and grenades, were unable to shift them. An avenue was thus held open between the two brigades through which German counter-attacks could be launched, and at the same time a possible supply route from the main Australian line remained blocked.

Apart from ammunition, artillery support was vital to the 4th Brigade infantry in the trenches and the need had to be communicated to the headquarters in the main line. There were signs of enemy troops gathering to counter-attack and some had occupied buildings in Riencourt, directly to the 4th Brigade's front, from where they kept up a constant fire on the parapet of OG 2. Machine gun fire from the enemy positions in Bullecourt and Balcony Trench/Quéant was sweeping across the re-entrant behind the trenches, making safe movement across No Man's Land almost impossible. At the beginning of the battle, before it was full daylight, runners had brought messages from the fighting line to the railway within fifteen minutes of despatch. When Captain Murray sent his message to 13th Battalion HQ at 7:15 am, although the runners did manage to get through safely, it took ninety minutes for the message to reach its destination at the railway.

The Battalion HQ itself had been badly hit at about 7 am, when a German shell burst close to the dugout and the nearby RAP. Six were killed and five wounded, the dead including the unit RMO, Captain Norman Shierlaw; his AAMC orderly, Sergeant Percival James, took over the running of the RAP for the rest of the battle. Amongst the wounded was the brilliant 22-year-old Major Douglas Marks, the Battalion second-in-command, who was at first not expected to survive. The CO, Colonel Durrant, was the only one unhurt, and for a time was running the headquarters on his own before replacement signallers and runners could be collected. Captain Murray's message was immediately sent on to 4th Brigade HQ by runner; it was apparently the first clear account of the situation, particularly the need for artillery support, to reach the Brigade staff. It was then nearly 9 am and the troops in the Hindenburg Line had sent up the artillery SOS flare signal several times already, the first fired by Murray at 7:20 am, just after despatching his message. The signal was three separate flares, in the sequence green, red, green.[95] Although the SOS was said to have been fired eighteen times altogether during the morning, there is no record of any being observed from the main line. The overcast weather should have helped their visibility in the daylight, but the short delay between colours may have caused the flares to be confused with those of the enemy, who had been observed to fire numerous green flares. Rockets with multi-coloured bursts might have been more distinguishable if they had been supplied; they were mainly intended for night use, but could be used in daylight also.[96]

Regardless of signals, Murray's message ('from an officer everyone could trust,' as C E W Bean put it in a newspaper article[97]) was enough to spur the Brigade staff to call in the artillery. What happened next was described in Brigadier General Brand's after-action report:

> 9.10am: Artillery Liaison Officer at Brigade Headquarters instructed to secure an SOS artillery line 200 yards beyond second objective and 200 yards to right of our right flank which rested on the road in [map square] U 30 a.
>
> Most aggravating telephonic communication took place between the Artillery Liaison Officer and Group Commander [i.e.'Q' Group, Lieutenant Colonel Rabett] as to the wisdom of having the SOS line as indicated in view of the rumour that our men were reported in Riencourt ... Despite very exhaustive enquiries I have failed to gather the slightest clue which would lead anyone to believe that any of our men got beyond the second objective ...[98]

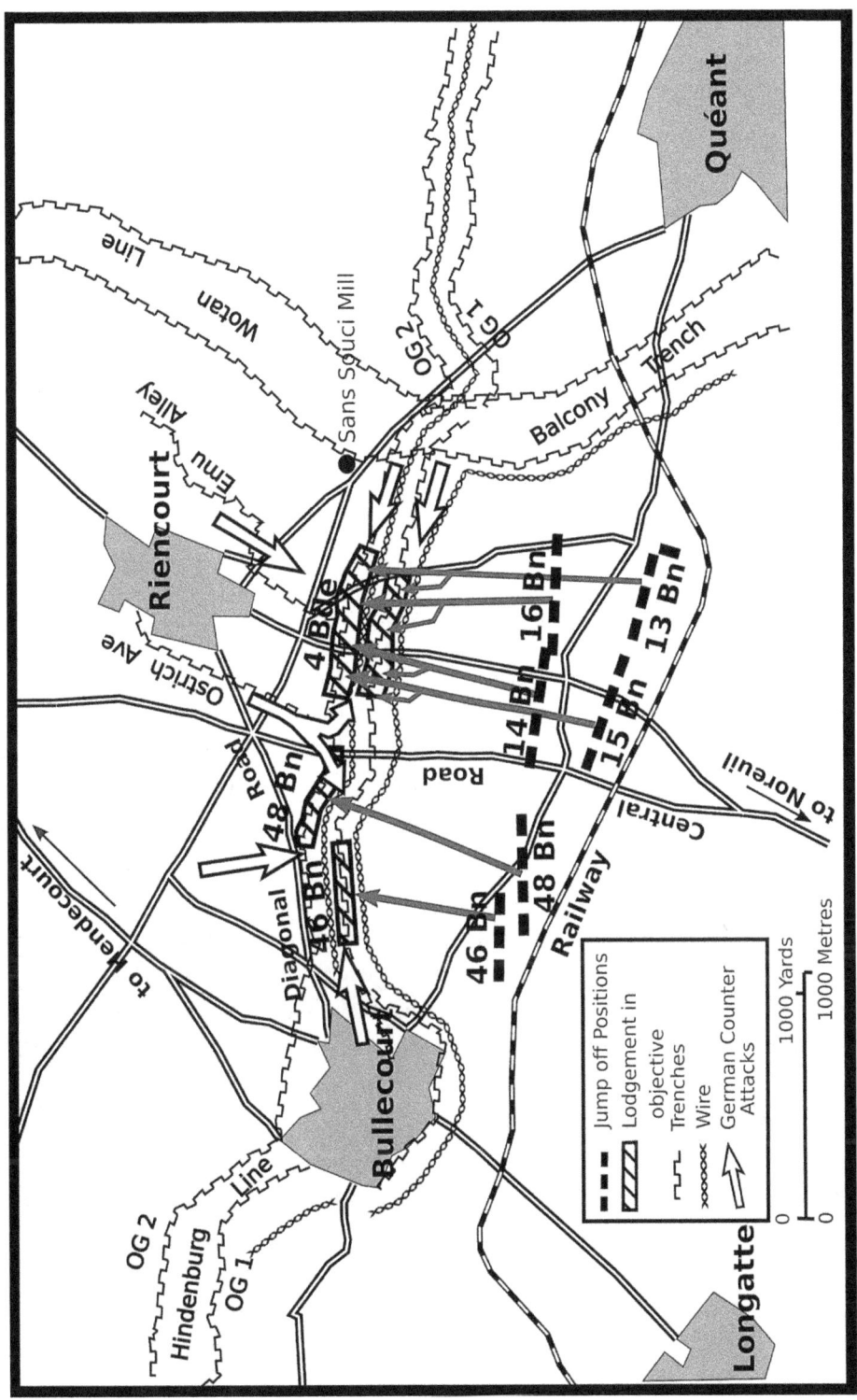

First Battle of Bullecourt, 11 April 1917.

Colonel Rabett declined to order the barrage fired. The artillery liaison officer was not identified,[99] but Brigadier General Rosenthal's final Left Sector artillery order for the operation (Order No 4, 10 April) specified that

> P and Q Groups will find *experienced* officers as Liaison Officers with the 12th and 4th Australian Infantry Brigades respectively. If Battery Commanders can be spared for this, it should be done.

Whether or not the liaison officer was in that category, Lieutenant Colonel Rabett preferred to accept several earlier reports from Forward Observation Officers (FOOs) that Australian troops had been seen advancing beyond the trench lines, and even beyond the further objectives of Riencourt and Hendecourt. Two reports that had come in from RFC aircraft observers were contradictory, one seeing no sign of progress beyond the trenches but the other reporting that the troops were still advancing according to plan; the more optimistic report was the one accepted.[100] The 12th AFA Brigade War Diary commented, apparently referring to the 9:10 am request, that

> the Infantry Brigadier wanted a barrage in a place which upon information at hand was absurd. The CO [Lieutenant Colonel Rabett] had the matter referred ... to the GOC I Anzac [General Birdwood] who decided in favour of CO.[101]

It appears from that statement that Colonel Rabett went direct to the Corps GOC without referring to either 4th Division HQ or Brigadier General Rosenthal, commanding the Left Sector Artillery and so Rabett's direct operational superior (General Rosenthal's report indicates that his HQ received no firm information between 8:30 am and 11:10 am[102]). It is difficult to explain why Colonel Rabett chose to accept brief reports from subaltern FOOs—whose duties were less to do with the overall tactical situation than with directing particular batteries' shooting—over a specific request through a (presumably) experienced liaison officer working directly with the infantry. The field artillery's main task of supporting the infantry appears to have been overlooked; since there had been no preliminary bombardment, the only task for the guns in this battle was protecting the infantry after its advance. It was ironic that Colonel Rabett had played an important part in the original formation of the 4th Division artillery in Egypt but his actions now would contribute to disaster for his old Division. Possibly as CO of an 'Army' brigade, there was an unconscious assertion of independence from his former CRA, now his commander only by virtue of a temporary grouping.

Whatever the reasons, the crucial factor for the 4th Brigade infantry hanging on in the Hindenburg Line was that there would be no protective barrage from 'Q' Group, responsible for most of the 4th Brigade sector. There was some spontaneous assistance, however, from the 101st Howitzer Battery of the 1st Division artillery ('M' Group), positioned near the centre, just behind Noreuil. The battery commander, Major Jeremiah Selmes, had watched the infantry advance into the enemy trenches, then 'Huns were seen with my naked eye to come out of the ground and counter-attack heavily ... it was evident to me that the attack had failed, and I promptly put down my 4.5 barrage just over the second line.' On being instructed by the group commander to revert to his allotted tasks, the forceful Selmes 'refused on the ground that I had a first-hand view of what was actually taking place.'[103] The fire of his six howitzers probably would not have caused great inconvenience to the Germans, and does not seem to have been noticed by the 4th Brigade infantry in the trenches, but the major's commonsense attitude is in striking contrast to the other artillery commanders. If Major Selmes could see the situation with the naked eye from as far back as Noreuil, other observers should also have been able to.

For the 4th Brigade's officers in the Hindenburg Line, the options for communicating with the higher command had almost disappeared. The storm of fire across the re-entrant continued to block runners, or at least seriously slow them down, as well as preventing ammunition carriers from getting through to the fighting zone. Visual signalling was out of the question, as the enemy fire made it fatal for signallers to show themselves above the parapet to get a line of sight to the main line. There were attempts to use 'power buzzer' Morse signals, but none were picked up. The numerous flare signals sent up had been ignored or not seen, and all available flares may have been used up in any case. A few pigeon messages had actually got through, but the time lapse with these made them ineffective. Captain Dunworth (15th Battalion) sent one at 7:10 am, asking for more ammunition, but it was nearly three hours before the details were phoned through to his Battalion;[104] the bird loft seems to have been located at Corps HQ.[105] The 4th Brigade was essentially marooned in the Hindenburg Line, cut off from supplies and communication. During the initial advance and the first fighting before dawn, 'walking wounded' and stretcher bearers carrying incapacitated men had some chance of getting back to the main line, but with daylight the fire sweeping No Man's Land closed off that avenue and the wounded were forced to remain in the fighting line, moved into dugouts for some protection where possible. With ammunition running low, moves were made to economise on what was available. Captain Murray ordered the collection of any grenades that the dead and wounded might still have in their equipment and the trenches and dugouts were searched for German grenades. The troops were ordered to cease long-range shooting and only fire at definite targets. All of these measures could only be temporary but Murray still held out some hope that the brigade could hang on until nightfall, when darkness might enable reinforcements and supplies to get through.

The 12th Brigade troops near Bullecourt faced a similar situation. According to the Brigade report, in mid-morning, probably about 9:30 or 10, the Brigade staff arranged for an artillery barrage to be put down on the enemy trenches on the eastern edge of Bullecourt. This seems to have been prompted by an assessment of the messages sent back from the fighting line rather than by observing an SOS signal—there is no record of either the 46th or 48th Battalion firing SOS flares until almost the end of the battle.[106] It seems from the artillery HQ's report that there was some delay in commencing the barrage because of the continuing problem of contradictory information coming in, but 'finally it was decided to barrage the [South East] face of the village and shell it with heavies.'[107] No timing is given for the start of the barrage, but at 11:10 am artillery HQ received a message from a spotter aircraft stating that troops had been seen in the south-west corner of Bullecourt at 10:30; these were apparently patrols sent out by the 62nd Division (the timing is right[108]). The heavy artillery's shelling was stopped, but 'in view of the precarious position of the left flank of the 12th Infantry Brigade the flank barrage was kept up.' The barrage when it eventually got under way does not seem to have been particularly heavy, although it does appear that messages sent by runner had slightly more chance of getting back to the main line on this side of the battlefield. The Germans were not prevented from building up their strength for a series of major counter-attacks that were now launched against the captured Hindenburg trenches.

The right flank of the 46th Battalion in OG 1 was particularly heavily hit, the enemy in that sector having been reinforced by troops coming down the communication trench Ostrich Avenue into the open gap between the two brigades. At 11:15 am a shower of German grenades drove back the few men in the 46th's right flank post. The enemy advanced quickly along the trench and overran the dugout near the flank, in which Major Waine had his HQ and where many of the wounded had been sheltering. Taken by surprise, the major and several of his officers were captured, although a few others, including the 47th Battalion company commander Captain North, were able to escape through an unguarded entrance. There is an implication in accounts of this incident that there were a few too many officers in the dugout and they spent a little too long in it.[109] In any case, the 46th Battalion had lost a large proportion of its leadership in a few moments. Enemy pressure came in on the left flank also, and without grenades the troops could not hit back effectively. The defence quickly collapsed. Those not killed, wounded or captured were forced out of the trench by the triumphant enemy and attempted to get back to the original line individually. A number did succeed in running the gauntlet back through the wire belts and across No Man's Land, but OG 1 was firmly in German hands again and the 48th Battalion was now isolated ahead in OG 2, with the enemy in their rear. The suddenness of the 46th's defeat and the loss of most of its officers meant that there was no organised attempt to advise the 48th of what had happened, but one man (or boy—he was not yet 19[110]), Private (later Lieutenant) Herbert Dunnett, a member of the reinforcements sent up earlier from the 47th Battalion, took it upon himself to give the warning. Making his way further forward to the 48th in OG 2 instead of retreating, Dunnett sought out Captain Leane and informed him of the situation. Cut off and surrounded by enemies, the 48th was faced with annihilation unless it could fight its way out.

On the Australian right, the 4th Brigade was also under heavy pressure, with counter-attacks coming from in front and both flanks. While their ammunition lasted the Brigade's Lewis and Vickers guns kept the Germans from advancing across open ground, but the enemy exploited the gap between the brigades to send troops down the Ostrich Avenue trench against the left in both OG 1 and OG 2. Attacks in the centre came along Emu Alley against the outpost at that point, and the barricades on the right were assailed by Germans coming from the direction of Quéant. In the duel along the trenches the Württembergers, with the great advantage of an unrestricted supply of grenades, gradually gained the upper hand and began to force back the Australian flanks. Shortly after 10 am, with the situation becoming more serious by the minute, Captain Murray conferred with several other officers to decide the Brigade's next move. The view of Captain Gardiner (13th Battalion) was that the surviving troops should retire a short distance from the Hindenburg trenches and find cover in shell holes, digging in to improve their positions, and call in a barrage to protect their new line. An officer would be sent back to the main line to give a first-hand report of the situation and ensure that the artillery support was given—Lieutenant Aarons (16th Battalion) volunteered for that task and set out on his perilous journey at 10:20. Captain Gardiner was actually the senior officer present in the trenches, but although he had seen combat with the 13th in the Gallipoli campaign, and commanded that unit for a short time, this was his first action in France.[111] Seniority meant that his approach prevailed over that of the far more experienced Captain Murray. The latter 'never seriously entertained the idea of forming a line of shell holes ... because there were practically no shell holes [and] the Germans commanded the position with enfilade, oblique and frontal fire'[112] (some of the German shelling would have been air-burst shrapnel, and it appears that many of their HE shells were fitted with instantaneous fuzes, so the burst did not produce a hole[113]). In the event, the plan was never tested. The Germans closed in strongly behind showers of grenades, the pressure increasing as the Australians, using up their last few grenades, rapidly lost the power to defend themselves. With the position on the verge of collapse the word was passed along the troops in OG 2, in danger of being cut off, to pull back to OG 1. At the same time the Vickers gunners of the 4th MG Company were ordered to wreck their weapons. Covered by a few officers and men under Captain Gardiner, the survivors got back to OG 1, but that position soon became untenable also.

The fight could not be maintained and Captain Murray, still moving ceaselessly along the trench, announced the only remaining options to those of the troops that he could reach: 'Well, men, we are just about out of ammunition and it doesn't look as if anything more can be done. We either stay here and get skittled or taken prisoners, or we can get out while our luck is in.'[114] Of those who tried the second option many were cut down in the attempt to pass through the wire belts in the reverse direction, but a number made it through and dashed for the Australian main line, risking the fire still sweeping across No Man's Land. Groups and individuals who could not get away in time were shot or taken prisoner by the Germans now swarming along the trenches, and the wounded in the dugouts were captured. By 11:45 am the 4th Brigade's position in the Hindenburg Line had been abandoned. Shortly before the final retreat Lieutenant Aarons had reached the combined 14th and 16th Battalion HQ, after a hair-raising journey across the open using every scrap of cover available. Aarons' message, together with another brought back at about the same time by CSM William Boland (14th Battalion) confirmed that the situation was desperate. The troops could now been seen attempting to retire from the line, and finally Brigade HQ was able to convince Colonel Rabett to bring the 'Q' Group artillery into action, too late to do anything except cover the last stage of the retreat. The barrage fell on and beyond the Hindenburg trenches and although it did apparently provide some assistance to the men still trying to get back, the shelling was said to have also killed a number of wounded and captured Australians in the German lines.

Many of the retreating troops were killed or wounded on the way back but a number succeeded in reaching the main line at the railway. Among these was Corporal Patten of the 13th, already twice hit by grenade splinters in the Emu Alley fighting, then badly wounded by a bullet as he covered the retreat of his section.[115] The few officers who got back included Harry Murray, utterly spent physically and emotionally but somehow with only a few scratches after seven hours of desperate close-quarter fighting. He was the only 13th Battalion company commander to return from the attack; Captain Gardiner, covering the right flank to the last, had been cut off and taken prisoner, and Captain Basil Fletcher had been killed as he climbed out of the trench at the start of the retreat. The two surviving 16th Battalion company commanders, Captains Somerville and Hummerston, were both hit and incapacitated in No Man's Land on the way back. The latter was picked up by the Germans and became a prisoner but Captain Somerville was found by stretcher bearers the next morning and brought in. Captain Wadsworth, the only surviving company commander of the 14th, reached the railway safely, but none of the 15th Battalion's officers got back, Captain Dunworth being among the wounded taken prisoner in the Hindenburg dugouts.

Isolated in OG 2 on the left of the battlefield, the 48th Battalion, with its reinforcements from the 47th, was now the only element of the 4th Division infantry still active in the Hindenburg trenches. Captain Leane decided that the best course was to recapture the segment of OG 1 that cut off the Battalion from the rear. The 48th had hoarded enough grenades to maintain a trench-fight and Leane now organised two bombing parties to fight their way down the communication trench back to OG 1, one led by himself and the other by Lieutenant Samuel Jones. In desperate fighting, the bombers forced their way into OG 1 and pushed back the Germans towards both flanks, although both leaders were among the casualties. Lieutenant Jones—in France for only three weeks—was killed and Captain Leane wounded. The 48th now occupied segments of both lines but the situation could not continue indefinitely—the Battalion's numbers had been further reduced in the burst of fighting and the supply of grenades was almost expended. The Germans returned to the attack, making use of the diagonal sunken road intersecting OG 2 to bring up reinforcements. At one stage a Lewis gun crew tried to raise their gun high enough above the trench parapet to shoot down into the road. Private Bill Carr climbed up onto the parapet, got down on hands and knees and used his back to support the gun, fired by Sergeant John Cooper. The gallant attempt failed when the sergeant was fatally hit.[116] To make matters worse the Australian artillery barrage now came down on the trenches, the result of another instance of misinformation. Reports reaching Colonel Leane at 48th Battalion HQ had given the impression that the whole force was withdrawing, and at 11:15 he sent a message to Brigade saying 'Both 4th and 12th Brigades retiring. We hold this line [i.e. the original front line at the railway] but you must assist with artillery barrage.'[117] This was passed on by Brigade and the artillery opened fire as requested, naturally targeting the German trenches instead of the original SOS line beyond them. The error was reverse of that made on the right of the battle area: in the 12th Brigade sector the artillery group responded to a request that was based on wrong information, whereas the group covering the 4th Brigade had refused to respond to one based on correct information.

Just after midday Captain Leane despatched a message to HQ saying 'Our artillery is making the trench untenable.'[118] At about the same time the SOS flare signal was fired, apparently in the hope that it would be interpreted as a request to lift the barrage to the original SOS line beyond OG 2.[119] The signals had no effect, and it was obvious that holding both trenches was out of the question. Those remaining in OG 2 made their way down the communication trench to OG 1, but the enemy was attacking strongly again and Captain Leane soon realised that there was no hope of even holding on to that last position. He gave orders for the troops to evacuate the trench and get back to the main line as best they could. To the anguish of the men, all that could be done for the immobile wounded was to leave them at the dugout entrances in the hope that they would receive medical treatment from their captors. Among these were Captain Mott, lying paralysed by the neck wound that he had received early in the fighting, and Lieutenant Morris, with leg and arm wounds. At 12:25 pm, having held on in the Hindenburg Line for an hour after every other unit had withdrawn, the survivors of the 48th clambered over the parapet, many being hit in the process, and began the long trek back to the railway cutting. More fell dead or wounded to the continuing enemy fire on No Man's Land, but the retreat was unhurried; observers at the main line saw them making their way back 'at walking pace, picking their way through the broken wire.'[120] Lance Corporal Mitchell had decided to carry his Lewis gun out with him instead of disabling it and he walked back in a state of calm fatalism:

> In complete indifference I trudged over the field ... a man reaches a blasé stage after too much excitement ... Five-point-nines burst black on either hand, and futile bullets zipped about. They could do nothing to me.[121]

It appears that the covering artillery barrage did provide some help to the retreating troops, interfering with the aim of the enemy machine guns and rifles in the vicinity; Sergeant Max McDowall, one of the last to leave OG 1, noticed that the shelling was keeping the Germans' heads down, and he and the men with him took advantage of this to make their retreat.[122] Many did not get through, however. Captain Leane himself, already limping from a grenade wound, was badly hit near the wire. Picked up by the enemy, he died of his injuries in a German medical facility three weeks later.[123]

With the arrival of the 48th Battalion's survivors at the railway line the fighting was over, but there was more to be done. The first concern was the possibility that the victorious Germans would launch an immediate follow-up attack on the Australian position, an unlikely event that nevertheless had to be guarded against. The remnants of the two brigades, fatigued and almost disarmed, were in no condition to put up a strong resistance but the 51st and 52nd Battalions of the 13th Brigade were holding the line in strength. As an extra precaution the 12th Brigade brought up 'C' and 'D' Companies of the 47th to reinforce the line on the left, while the artillery continued to shell the German positions. It was soon apparent that there would be no attack—the Germans moving in No Man's Land were soon seen to be medical orderlies tending to wounded men, and at 2 pm the artillery was ordered to cease fire. The principal task now was to help the wounded who had been unable to reach the line and were now lying scattered across No Man's Land. There had already been spontaneous efforts to bring in casualties, groups of volunteers leaving the comparative safety of the cutting to help the regular stretcher bearers in the task. 'Let's go out for some of these wounded,' said Corporal Jack Fennell (48th) to Lance Corporal Mitchell, just returned from the fighting, and 'we laboured at the stretchers till darkness fell.'[124] Forty men of the 47th volunteered to stay at the front line to assist the exhausted bearers after that unit was relieved.[125] Bearers from the 13th Brigade battalions holding the line, the 51st and 52nd, were active also, and the 52nd sent out a party of fifty infantrymen under Lieutenant James Julin. The Red Cross flags carried by that group were observed by the Germans, who ceased their sporadic firing on No Man's Land at about 4 pm. The bearers and volunteers were able to work without interference for the next two hours, before another snowstorm and the coming of darkness put an end to the unofficial truce. 'Nevertheless, throughout the night, which was still and frosty, not a shot was fired.'[126] Several more wounded were recovered or managed to crawl in that night and for several days afterwards.

The Division's medical services were under extreme pressure handling the flood of casualties. The 12th Brigade's RAPs were located in the sunken Noreuil-Longatte road, more than a kilometre behind the front line at the railway. The 4th Brigade had two advanced RAPs in the railway cutting, one of which had been hit by a shell early in the battle, and there were two others further back near Noreuil. This meant that

> The task of the regimental and ambulance bearers respectively differed greatly on the two Brigade fronts. In the 12th Brigade the battalion bearers faced an immense carry but the ambulance one of a few hundred yards only... In the 4th Brigade the situation was reversed...[127]

The closest staging point to the 12th Brigade RAPs was a relay post 750 metres away,[128] so the 12th Field Ambulance stretcher bearers on that side still had some distance to carry, although it was not as far as that faced by the bearers of the 13th Field Ambulance evacuating the 4th Brigade's casualties from its RAPs. Both groups had been reinforced by bearers from the 4th Field Ambulance. The circumstances overrode the ADMS's standing orders, which specified that the infantry's regimental bearers should not go in the rear of the RAPs nor ambulance bearers forward of them. The two groups assisted each other according to need and by the end of the day the bearers were utterly exhausted; 'most of the men were drenched and cold but their suffering was naught as compared to the unfortunate wounded who lay out in the snow.'[129]

Stretcher cases from both sectors were carried to the closest wagon post then by horse-drawn ambulance to the ADS of the 12th Field Ambulance behind Vaulx-Vraucourt. From here they were transferred to the 13th Field Ambulance MDS, which had moved forward from Bapaume to a position behind Beugnatre shortly before the battle. Walking wounded made their way to a second MDS established nearby, administered by the 4th Field Ambulance. Approximately 1,000 patients were treated at the two stations over 24 hours,[130] but the majority of the casualties were still in the Hindenburg Line.

Over a thousand (the generally accepted number is 1,170, 28 officers and 1,142 other ranks[131]) were prisoners, and many of those were wounded. Another 900[132] were dead, their bodies mostly in and near the Hindenburg trenches, hanging from the wire, or lying in No Man's Land. A number of the prisoners did not survive, succumbing to their wounds while in captivity, some like Captain Allan Leane soon after the battle and others later. Others did recover, however, with the benefit of medical attention in German hospitals. The general treatment of the prisoners by their captors varied from reasonable to deliberately malicious. Many of the unwounded prisoners were sent at first to the occupied city of Lille in the north, where they were crammed into cells in the notorious Fort Macdonald and used on working parties within range of Allied artillery. There were several deaths from the shelling before the prisoners were moved on to prison camps in Germany. More deaths occurred in the camps over the long months before the Armistice from disease and general deprivation,[133] and there were also a number of escapes. One took place within six weeks of the battle, when four men of the 16th Battalion cut their way through the wire of a prisoner compound at Marquion, 10 kilometres behind the German front at Bullecourt. Two were recaptured, but Lewis gunners Lance Corporal Hamilton Parsons and Private George Stewart crossed the German trenches after dark on 22 May and reached the Australian front line safely, almost at the point where they had moved out to the attack on 11 April.[134] A famous escape was that of Captain John Mott, the 40-year-old 48th Battalion company commander, seriously wounded and captured in OG 1. His wounds were treated in German hospitals, and his temporary paralysis wore off. By September he was considered well enough to be sent to a camp at Strohen in northern Germany. He succeeded in escaping, apparently by procuring a duplicate key to a gate,[135] and crossed the Dutch border into neutral territory six days later. Captain Mott returned to England on 11 October, exactly six months after the battle. The first Australian officer to escape from Germany, he resumed active duty with the 48th in July 1918.

Most of the dead in the enemy lines were probably buried by the Germans in mass graves and shell holes, although it was said that there were still some desiccated bodies hanging in the wire when the second Bullecourt battle began on 3 May. Perhaps the rough graves will be discovered at some time, as happened at Fromelles in 2008-9, and the dead will receive their proper recognition. Others are buried in the Quéant Road Military Cemetery at Buissy, five kilometres north-east of Quéant. The cemetery has 54 identified graves and special memorials of Australian soldiers killed on 11 April 1917, all members of 4th and 12th Brigade units.

There are 1,441 graves of unidentified Commonwealth soldiers (out of a total of 2,377)[136] at Quéant Road, and these would probably include a number of others who fell in the Bullecourt battles. There is a good chance, for instance, that the remains of Captains 'Lofty' Williamson (14th Battalion), Basil Fletcher (13th), and Frederick Boddington and Henry Davis (46th) are buried there.[137]

The 4th Brigade's casualties, including the MG Company and the LTMs, totalled 2,126 dead, wounded and missing. The 16th Battalion lost 600 officers and ORs, the highest in the Division, out of 717 who were in the attack, a casualty rate of 84%.[138] The 4th MG Company suffered a similar rate of loss, reporting that one officer and 15 ORs (three of them wounded) got back to the line, of five officers and 110 men who went out. The survivors brought back two Vickers guns from 16, and grimly set those up to defend the line until they were relieved at 7 pm that night.[139] The other battalions' losses were: 13th, 503; 14th, 526; 15th, 367. The 4th LTM Battery lost 34 or 35 casualties out of 45 'hop over strength.'[140] Assuming the other battalions sent about the same numbers into the attack as the 16th did (although the 15th was somewhat under strength compared to the others), the Brigade had just over 3,000 troops in action, of whom more than 70% became casualties. The 12th Brigade had total casualties of 909, the majority of which were suffered by its two principal units in the attack, the 46th and 48th Battalions; losses for those units were almost equal, at 373 and 395 respectively. The 47th, with limited numbers in action, had 127 casualties, and the 12th MG Company 14. The Brigade probably had about 2,000 troops engaged, so its overall casualty rate was 45%. The 4th Division's losses in what became known as the First Battle of Bullecourt, the worst day in the Division's history, totalled 3,035.

The survivors of the shattered brigades were withdrawn from the front line during the evening. The 45th Battalion, not used in the battle, came up to the line from support to join the units of the 13th Brigade, which took over the divisional front temporarily. It was snowing again as the battalions slogged along the muddy roads back to the bivouac areas around Vaulx, Favrueil and Beugnatre. Here there was little in the way of accommodation for the weary, hungry troops except for a few canvas shelters on the wet ground. The better-organised units managed to provide their troops with some nourishment—Sergeant Rule (14th Battalion) recalled a feast of sandwiches, hot tea and rum: 'we fairly gorged ourselves ... It was just on twenty-four hours since anyone had had a hot meal.'[141] Some stragglers had fallen out from the units along the way, but most of these had rejoined by the next day when the battalions marched the five kilometres to Bapaume; there the 4th Brigade troops passed by Brigadier General Brand, in tears at the sight of his sadly depleted units. At the Bapaume railhead the brigades entrained for Albert, marching from there in continuing miserable weather to hutments outside the town for several days of rest, the 4th Brigade to Mametz Camp and the 12th to Crucifix Camp. Both brigades had settled in by the morning of 13 April and that night the 13th Brigade, with the attached 45th Battalion, handed over the front line at Bullecourt to the 5th Brigade (2nd Division). The 13th Brigade moved back via Beugnatre and Bapaume to another hutment near Albert, Bécourt Camp, arriving there in the evening on 14 April. The 4th Division infantry brigades were now all away from the battle area and could begin the process of recovering and rebuilding.

The battle plan for First Bullecourt was fatally flawed from the outset in nearly every respect, but it is part of the frustration of hindsight that it need not have been so. The failure was in the beginning due to the personality and command style of General Sir Hubert Gough, the Fifth Army commander. His desire to use his forces to assist the main British attack at Arras is understandable and commendable, and it could be argued that it was his duty. The General's impulsive nature, however, led him to adopt an impractical, badly thought out plan, conceived in extreme haste. There was no influential officer on the Fifth Army staff who was inclined to temper the General's aggression with an injection of caution and common sense—his chief of staff, Brigadier General Neill Malcolm, was of similar impatient personality.[142] Although the Fifth Army leadership staff must bear the major responsibility for the disaster, the staff at the lower levels, I Anzac and the 4th Division's own leaders, missed opportunities to argue for modifications to the plan that might have produced a different outcome. Protests about the plan were certainly made, but more with a view to shelving it altogether rather than coming up with an alternative.

The overall approach of attacking into a re-entrant, highly risky in itself, was made more difficult by the lack of artillery resources for wire-cutting. Presented with the idea of using the tanks to crush the wire instead of waiting another week for the artillery to do that job, General Gough 'adopted, on the spur of the moment, a scheme devised by an inexperienced officer of an experimental arm.'[143] The tanks may well have been capable of the wire-cutting task, but the plan for 10 April gave them the main role in actually taking the German trenches and then signalling the infantry to come forward and mop up before moving on to the more distant objectives. By the next day, after the tanks had failed to arrive on time, their task was changed to the slightly less ambitious one of leading the infantry into an assault the enemy position. The tanks were still to be the means of breaking through the wire and would also be a substitute for a frontal artillery barrage to cover the advance of the infantry. The presence of the tanks was seen as precluding the use of a barrage in any case because of the risk of hitting them; this was the reason given for refusing Colonel Leane's request to continue the flank barrage on Bullecourt soon after the 12th Brigade jumped off.

It does not seem to have occurred to the staff at any level to question why a field artillery barrage could not be used in conjunction with the tanks. The plan assumed that most, if not all, of the machines would get safely through enemy shelling to the Hindenburg Line, implying that they were believed to be in more danger of being hit accidentally by their own artillery than by German guns deliberately aimed at them. The latter would be using HE shells against tanks whereas the Australian barrage would be mostly, if not exclusively, shrapnel. Armour-piercing machine gun bullets could penetrate the hulls of the Mark I and II tanks but they would surely have been proof against the lead balls sprayed out by an air-bursting

18-pounder shrapnel shell. Being hit would be unlikely in any case—the shrapnel is projected forward by the burst, and the original plan called for the barrage to open on the German front line, so a tank would have to have passed over the trench before the barrage had lifted to be hit by shrapnel, which would probably prove harmless anyway. In an advance covered by artillery, infantry were expected to keep as close to the barrage as possible, risking a few casualties for the great advantage of being almost into the enemy trench when the barrage lifted. That was the first point made in the 12th Brigade staff's guidelines for the imminent battle,[144] and it was said of the 4th Brigade that it 'leans up against the barrage, and when it lifts, falls on top of the enemy.'[145] What was an acceptable risk for a foot soldier in a woollen uniform and steel helmet was apparently unacceptable for an armoured fighting vehicle. As stated earlier in this chapter, the operation against the Hindenburg Line was first envisaged as an orthodox infantry attack behind a barrage, and the 4th Brigade's initial concept included a section of four tanks co-operating with the infantry. An approach that retained the barrage and brought in the whole company of eleven or twelve tanks to work with both brigades, with an emphasis on dealing with uncut wire, may well have produced a workable plan.[146] The framework for such a plan already existed, and an attempt could have been made to produce a scheme that would have satisfied General Gough's urgent desire to strike a blow and curbed the dangerous enthusiasm of the tank commanders. Some definite arrangement for relieving the troops after the initial attack would have been desirable as well, beyond the brief mention of a 5th Division brigade being 'available.' Had there been an alternative plan put forward and accepted, the outcome would not necessarily have been the breakthrough sought by General Gough. If the 4th Division had succeeded in taking and holding the enemy lines, the battle would probably have turned into a costly grinding match of attack and counter-attack as the second Bullecourt battle did next month, dragging in fresh divisions to maintain the struggle. Nevertheless, that result might have reduced the total casualty list for the overall period of fighting in the Bullecourt sector.

The operation of 10 April, if it had gone ahead according to plan, would surely have failed. The infantry, waiting in their assembly positions for the 'green disk' signal, would have seen only eleven burning tanks in No Man's Land. Casualties among the unfortunate tank crews would have been high, and the infantry would have suffered losses to the inevitable retaliatory bombardment before they could retreat to protected positions, but such an outcome would have forced a complete re-think of the plans. As it was, the tanks failed to arrive and the only change made for the next day was to specify that the infantry would not wait for signals from the tanks, but rather jump off at 4:45 am, fifteen minutes after the tanks were meant to have moved off from the start line; timing of the flank barrages was fixed on that basis also. Even that change was not clear to the brigades at first—it was late in the night before amendments to the initial orders were issued. Haste made for very brief written orders and many of the details were communicated verbally even at division and brigade levels, fertile ground for misunderstanding. In particular, the intention that the infantry would advance at 4:45, regardless of what progress the tanks had made, assumed that the tanks would have moved off at 4:30 and made no allowance for any alternatives if that was not the case. As noted earlier in this chapter, both battalion COs in the 12th Brigade seem to have had the impression that their men had to wait for the tanks. It is also just possible that the 4th Brigade commanders thought the same—three of their allotted tanks did actually arrive at the start line and advance on time, so there was no need for a decision such as that which faced the 12th Brigade. The operation had been delayed in the first place because the commanders would not send infantry against uncut wire even with the aid of an artillery barrage. If the tanks did fail to arrive as had happened on 10 April, was it really intended by Army, Corps and Division that the infantry, completely unprotected by either a frontal barrage or tanks, should advance against an immensely strong position with the wire still uncut?

In the event, that was what happened, and by an extraordinary achievement of courage, determination and battle discipline the troops did succeed in taking their objectives in the Hindenburg Line, but at such cost in casualties that no more could be done without reinforcements, ammunition resupply and fire support. The difficulties of maintaining battlefield communication, in both senses of exchanging information and conveying supplies, plagued all armies in 1914–18, and Bullecourt was an extreme example of the problem. After the initial assault had reached the objective it proved to be almost impossible to get ammunition up to the fighting line through the enemy fire across the rear of the re-entrant. The artillery support which might have eased this situation, and interfered with enemy counter-attacks, was withheld, particularly in the 4th Brigade's sector. Attempts to communicate the need for guns from the fighting line to the commanders were mostly ineffectual, but even the information that did get through, notably Captain Murray's message, was discounted. There is the possibility that some misunderstanding between infantry and artillery arose over the identification of the objectives. The infantry commanders had consistently designated the German front and support lines as the first and second objectives with Riencourt as the third, but higher command may have interpreted the first objective as comprising both enemy trenches and the second objective as Riencourt. The entry in the 4th Division War Diary for 11 April certainly describes the objectives in the latter way, although the Division's final report on the battle reverts to the infantry's interpretation.[147] It is possible that when the infantry reported capturing the second objective, this was initially interpreted as meaning Riencourt. One would think, however, that if such a misunderstanding had occurred it would have been quickly cleared up.

The failure of the artillery to support the infantry was an issue raised in correspondence between Newton Wanliss, the 14th Battalion's historian, and C E W Bean in 1924[148], in the course of which Wanliss commented that 'the 4th Division artillery appears to have been very poorly handled ... the sum total of its achievement being practically to butcher a lot of our wounded at the end of the battle.' Bean responded that the 'divisional artillery carried out its task as ordered,' and that some losses among the wounded could not be avoided, but Wanliss was unconvinced. Wanliss was concerned mainly with the 4th Infantry Brigade's experiences, but the 4th Division's own artillery, forming 'P' Group, was responsible only for covering the 12th Infantry Brigade on the left. The 4th Brigade was covered by 'Q' Group, comprising the 2nd Division artillery and the independent 12th AFA Brigade and commanded by the 12th's CO, Lieutenant Colonel Rabett. The 4th Infantry Brigade's difficulties were with the '4th Division Artillery' only in the general sense that the 4th Division CRA, Brigadier General Rosenthal, and his staff, were in overall command of the sector artillery, but it appears that Colonel Rabett did not involve the sector HQ in the crucial decisions of 11 April.

The 4th Division artillery as such, the 10th and 11th AFA Brigades forming 'P' Group under Lieutenant Colonel King, could be said to have done all that was asked of them, even if that was not a great deal. The barrage put down at the end of the battle that fell on the trench held by the 48th Battalion was not really the gunners' fault, as the Group was responding to a request from the infantry, made in the belief that the position had been vacated. The Group's flank barrage at the start of the battle, intended to suppress enfilade fire from the German trenches on the eastern side of Bullecourt, was fired according to the orders from 4:45 am to 5 am, the time that the 12th Brigade infantry should have been advancing. In fact the infantry did not jump off until after the barrage had ceased and there was no flexibility in the orders to allow for the infantry to request any changes in the timing as circumstances developed. Liaison between infantry and artillery seems to have taken a backward step after the high level of co-operation achieved in the Stormy Trench fighting in February. When the 13th Battalion attacked on that occasion, the artillery group commander had shared headquarters with the infantry, an arrangement that had worked well. If that could be done for an attack that involved a single infantry battalion, then an attack by six battalions would seem to justify the presence of at least an artillery brigade commander, if not the appropriate group commander, in the infantry brigades' HQs. As it was, General Rosenthal's orders only specified that an experienced officer, a battery commander if possible, be assigned the liaison role. An artillery officer of higher rank at the 4th Infantry Brigade HQ might have made a significant difference when that Brigade's officers in the Hindenburg Line made their desperate calls for a barrage.

In assessments after the battle, the infantry brigades' leaders made some criticisms of the artillery but laid most of the blame for the disaster on the tanks. Captain Albert Jacka, infuriated at the losses of his Battalion and Brigade, produced a report castigating the tank crews for inefficiency and lack of 'pluck,' even implying that some crews had sabotaged their own machines to avoid going into action. His report was fully endorsed by Colonels Peck (14th Battalion) and Drake-Brockman (16th) who sent it up the chain of command over their own signatures.[149] Other reports from battalion and brigade level were only a little less scathing. The Australian attitude was not mollified by exaggerated claims about the tanks' achievements made by their officers, both at

Battalion commanders of the 4th Brigade, May 1917. Left to right: Lieutenant Colonel Edmund Drake-Brockman (16th Battalion); Lt Col James Durrant (13th); Lt Col Terence McSharry (15th); Lt Col John Peck (14th). (AWM E00642)

the time and subsequently. The tank battalion CO's report was criticised by Colonel Denham (46th) as 'absolutely misleading ... one would infer [from it] that the tanks had carried out their allotted task.'[150] The tank company commander, Major Watson, writing in 1920, was still under the impression that two tanks had got all the way to Riencourt and Hendecourt.[151] The Australian view was naturally resented by the tankers and there were some recriminations: another tank officer wrote after the war, also believing that the tanks had broken through the Hindenburg Line,

> the feat ... makes the Australians' complaint, that they were 'let down' by the tanks, seem, to say the least of it, ungenerous. This charge [is one] which Colonial troops are but too ready to fling at everyone except themselves ... [152]

If some of the tank crews showed less determination than might have been expected, others did their best in very difficult circumstances and the company suffered a casualty rate of over 50%. The failure of the tanks was more likely due to ineptitude than to cowardice. The tankers' equipment, resources, training and experience were not up to the task demanded of them, a task for which they had been volunteered by their own senior officers. The real responsibility lay with the commanders and staffs who had come up with the battle plan in the first place, including the 4th Division HQ and to a lesser extent the Brigade leaders, who do not seem to have made any real effort to modify the worst aspects of the plan. The numerous changes from above were simply passed on with little if any comment. As the 1st Division artillery officer Major Selmes put it,

> orders countermanded, orders substituted, orders the like of which I have never before experienced ... One's work at any time in the front line is bad enough with a straight-out order, but with the heterogeneous litter of literature we have had to put up with one needed the wisdom of Solomon.[153]

There were some mitigating circumstances to the staffs' shortcomings also. The pressure from above and the urging of haste in launching the attack worked against careful consideration, and the constant work in the weeks of the advance leading up to the battle would have left many officers on the staff with little opportunity for rest. While it would have seemed laughable to front-line troops that a staff officer could possibly be fatigued, the latter's job was essentially to think, a function that is weakened by lack of sleep.

Regardless of where the responsibility lay, the officers, NCOs and men in the front line gave more than could reasonably be expected of them. Two of the Division's brigades had achieved the apparently impossible, summed up by Brigadier General Brand in reporting on his 4th Brigade's efforts as

> ... one of the most heroic achievements of any body of troops. Unaided by artillery, forsaken by tanks on which so much depended, the Brigade crossed formidable unbroken wire and secured both objectives which they held on to for 7 hours and only then forced to retire owing to overwhelming numbers of the enemy, numerous casualties, shortage of bombs with no immediate hope of getting more up; and hesitating co-operation from the artillery.[154]

By all accounts at the peak of efficiency and morale on 11 April, the 4th Division was 'an incomparable weapon ... woefully mishandled and thrown at an impossible target.'[155] Such was the resilience of people and organisation, however, that the rebuilding Division was back in major battles again by June, and had reached if anything a higher level of effectiveness twelve months later, in the climactic battles of 1918. Many notable deeds would have gone unnoticed in the confusion of the battle, but a number were recognised by decorations. Among the officers, Captains Somerville (16th Battalion) and Murray (13th) received DSOs for their dauntless leadership in the firing line, in the case of the latter a Bar to the award that he had won at Mouquet Farm. Bullecourt was the last time that Harry Murray led troops in close-quarter combat in the trenches; promotions brought different duties and meant that he would have fewer opportunities from now on, although he was rarely far from the front line for the rest of the war. Captain Wadsworth (14th Battalion) was awarded the MC, as was Captain Hummerston (16th) after his release from captivity at the Armistice. The daring reconnaissance patrols of Captain Jacka (14th) on the nights leading up to the battle brought him a Bar to his MC, and the same award was made to the 16th Battalion's intelligence officer, Lieutenant Frank Wadge; the MC seems to have been regarded as the standard reward for particularly outstanding efforts by battalion intelligence officers, who were routinely out roaming No Man's Land most nights when their units were in the line. Among the subaltern officers winning MCs were Lieutenants Rose (13th Battalion), Stanton (46th), Imlay (48th) and Aarons (16th). Captain Allan Leane of the 48th, dying in a German hospital, was recommended for the MC but the decoration was not awarded, a notable injustice. Awards of the DCM went among others to the 48th Battalion Lewis gunners, Lance Corporal Mitchell and Private Carr, and to Corporal Patten (13th). Patten's colleague in the Emu Alley fighting, Private Knight, received one of the numerous MMs awarded, as did the 16th Battalion escapees Lance Corporal Parsons and Private Stewart. Others included Sergeant James of the AAMC and four 16th Battalion stretcher bearers, Privates Ernest England, Patrick Fox (both Bars), Elliott Buswell and Rowland Taylor; the four operated as a group and were recommended jointly. Taylor was badly wounded himself while carrying out the life-saving work and died five days after the battle, while England later returned to combat duties and added a DCM to his decorations in 1918.

The fighting in the Bullecourt sector was by no means over, and would rise to a bloody climax in May as General Gough continued the Fifth Army's efforts to break the Hindenburg Line. While the battered 4th Division infantry was now out of the fight, other elements of the Division were still in the line, in particular the artillery. The gunners would continue in action on this front for another month, including playing a part in dealing with a sudden crisis that confronted the I Anzac troops only a few days after the First Bullecourt battle.

10 Notes

1. *Official History*, Vol IV, p. 345.
2. *Ibid*, pp. 255–6, 261–2,
3. *Ibid*, p.355.
4. Sections set back from the main line, forming a dent in the line seen in plan, the opposite to a salient.
5. 14th Battalion War Diary for April 1917, Appendix 3.
6. *Official History*, Vol IV, pp. 359–60
7. 4th Divisional Train War Diary, 7 April 1917; I Anzac Intelligence Staff War Diary for April 1917, Intelligence Summary 6 to 7 April 1917; AWM Red Cross Wounded and Missing Files 1DRL/0428 (Driver Alfred Knapman). Assuming the Intelligence assessment was correct, German weapons of this size were superseded naval guns, on railway mountings, firing shells weighing 148 kilograms (327 pounds).
8. I Anzac Order No 123, 8 April 1917, Appendix A to I Anzac GS War Diary for April 1917.
9. Lt Arnold's letter of 1 January 1922 in the Bean Papers, AWM38, 3DRL606/247/1.
10. P. Kendall, *Bullecourt 1917*, p. 57.
11. 14th Battalion War Diary for April 1917, Appendix 6.
12. *Official History*, Vol IV, p.266.
13. I Anzac Order No 123, as for Note 8 above.

14　I Anzac Artillery Instructions No 94 of 5 April includes 'On assault day the Corps is attacking ... under a barrage of 18-pdrs of the Left Divisional Artillery. This barrage will lift from front to second line trenches, and ... will subsequently cover the advance on Riencourt'. Instruction No 95 issued two days later orders batteries to practice their barrage fire.

15　4th Brigade Order No 74, Appendix 4 to 4th Brigade War Diary for April 1917.

16　General Rosenthal's diary records a meeting on 6 April with the GOC General Holmes and the infantry brigadiers to discuss the forthcoming operation. The War Diary of the 12th (Army) AFA Brigade notes that the Group Commander (Lt Col Rabett, the Brigade CO) visited the infantry brigade HQ on the morning of 9 April.

17　4th Brigade Order No 74, as for Note 15 above.

18　The 52nd Battalion's War Diary entry for 9 April confirms this; by the next day, the role of the 52nd had changed to holding the line when the 4th Brigade jumped off.

19　12th Brigade War Diary for April 1917, Appendix 2A. The order is dated 8 April, but no time of issue is shown.

20　4th Division GS War Diary for April 1917, Appendix 28.

21　I Anzac Order No 123, as for Note 8 above.

22　W H L Watson, *A Company of Tanks*, pp 44–5.

23　*Official History*, Vol IV, p. 273.

24　4th Division GS War Diary for April 1917, Appendix 39.

25　The narrative in the 4th Division GS War Diary for 9 April says that an instruction was issued at 7 pm and another at 9.30 pm. These are referenced as Appendices XXXIII and XXXIV, but those appendices are missing from the Diary, at least from the scanned copy on the AWM web site. The 14th and 16th Battalion's April War Diaries, however, include in their Appendices two Divisional memoranda dated 9 April, forwarded through 4th Brigade HQ, which I have assumed are copies of the relevant documents. The second of these is endorsed as having been received by Brigade at midnight.

26　*Official History*, Vol IV, p. 275.

27　14th Battalion War Diary for April 1917, Appendix 8.

28　Calculated from the map references given in Capt Jacka's report.

29　This was pointed out by Jonathan Walker, in *The Blood Tub: General Gough and the Battle of Bullecourt 1917* (1998), pp. 84-5. The 16th Battalion War Diary, however, does say in reference to this patrol that the wire was found to be intact in some places.

30　12th Brigade War Diary for April 1917, Appendix 4.

31　C E W Bean heard about this incident in conversation with Colonel Leane a year later, as recorded in his diary entry for 16 April 1918 (AWM38 3DRL606/107/1). The 4th Division's written order for the patrols, issued at 11.30 pm on 8 April, gives the left (western) limit of the patrol area as a map reference directly in front (south west) of the Bullecourt village position, which appears to be within the 62nd Division's area of responsibility. The 12th Brigade's written order the next day, 'confirming verbal instructions given this afternoon', directs the 48th to patrol to a point near the eastern face of the village, 500 yards away from that mentioned in the Division order, and that the line is to be occupied by two platoons (half a company) if not held by the enemy. The origin of the misunderstanding noted by Bean may be that the Division quoted a wrong map reference in its order for the patrols, then corrected it verbally the next day. In Bean's diary entry, his main point was the obstinacy of General Robertson, in contrast to the attitude of General John Gellibrand, then commanding the 12th Brigade. Robertson had, however, shown himself to be reasonably flexible in his handling of the 45th Battalion's attack at Stormy Trench in February (see p. 169).

32. *Official History*, Vol IV, p. 279.
33. Capt David Dunworth (15th Battalion), 'Muddle on Muddle: 4th Bde. At Bullecourt,' *Reveille*, April 1 1933, p. 20–21. Dunworth stated that he was with his CO, Lt Col McSharry, at the briefing.
34. Capt Jacka's report in the 14th battalion War Diary for April 1917, Appendix 8.
35. Mitchell, *Op Cit*, p. 87.
36. *Official History*, Vol IV, p. 281.
37. Apparently at the suggestion of Capt Jacka, who was present at Brigade HQ. See Brig Gen Brand's letter of 6 March 1930 to C E W Bean, in the Bean Papers, AWM 38 3DRL606/247/1.
38. Watson, *Op Cit*, p. 283; *Official History*, Vol IV, p. 282.
39. See Browning, *Leane's Battalion, Op Cit*, pp. 99–100. Lt Tom Arnold, in his letter of 1 January 1922 to CEW Bean referred to in Note 9 above, wrote that Colonel Leane saw the shattered body soon afterwards but did not realise at first that it was his brother.
40. The 62nd Division's War Diary entry is quoted in the *Official History*, Vol IV, p. 283; on p. 282, Bean states that it was 'just 5 o'clock' when General Holmes made his decision, and the 4th Division GS War Diary says 5 am also.
41. See the Bean Papers AWM38 3DRL606/247/1, Bean's February/March 1930 correspondence with Brig Gen Brand, and Colonel Bernard's letter of 23 October 1930 in AWM38 3DRL7953/34 Part 1 (also cited in Walker, *The Blood Tub*, p.90).
42. White, *Op Cit*, p. 93.
43. *Loc Cit*.
44. That is, the written orders for the operation on the next day, 11 April (4th Division Artillery HQ War Diary for April 1917, Left Sector Order No 4). I have assumed that these reflected the informal arrangements made for 10 April.
45. The time endorsed on 4th Division Order No 54. The 12th Brigade's after-action report says that the first word was received at 3.42 pm 'by wire' and the final order at 9 pm, while the brigade's own final order (No 137) was issued at 10.30 pm. The 4th Brigade's written order was timed 6 pm, with a supplementary memo issued at 10.45 correcting the artillery timings.
46. *Official History*, Vol IV, p. 295. Two days earlier, Maj Black had made a similar comment to his friend Capt Harry Murray of the 13th Battalion: 'Well, Harry, we have been in a few stunts together, but this is my last. I'll have that Hun front line first' (Murray, 'Bravest Man in the AIF', *Reveille*, 31 Dec 1929, p.8).
47. Brig Gen Brand's after action report, 4th Brigade War Diary for April 1917, Appendix 4.
48. According to the 4th LTM War Diary. The 4th Brigade warning order (No 74, 9 April) had two mortars per battalion. That order also called for two Vickers guns of the 4th MG Company to be attached to the 15th Battalion and four guns to the other three battalions, but the Company's War Diary says that each battalion had four guns on the day.
49. Brig Gen Robertson's after-action report says that the 48th occupied the assembly trench in map squares C4 a and b, a considerable distance to the south of the railway (a trench had been dug in that location when the brigade first moved in to the front line). This appears to be an error. That position would have put the 48th over 700 metres behind the 46th.
50. As stated in the 12th Brigade's supplementary order (No. 137, 12th Brigade War Diary for April 1917, Appendix 6).

51 4th Division General Staff War Diary for April 1917, Appendix 38.

52 I Anzac Asst Director Signals War Diary for April 1917, Appendix 32. A few of these sets were used by the British at Arras—see the memoir by Sapper B Neyland, RE, on the Internet site www.firstworldwar.com/diaries/awirelessoperator.htm .

53 Although the *Official History* (Vol IV, p. 291) says that Capt Jacka's informant was the subaltern tank commander, the joint after-action report by Colonels Peck and Drake-Brockman (in the appendices of each unit's April 1917 War Diaries) clearly says that he spoke to the tank section commander, as does the 16th Battalion War Diary narrative; the 14th Diary narrative says the 'CO Tanks'; Captain Wyatt was the officer in charge of the four-tank section on the right flank. This seems more reasonable than extracting a tank commander from his vehicle at that stage of the operation.

54 The Battalions' reports say that the request was to postpone the infantry advance by 15 minutes, but the 4th Brigade report (Appendix 4 of the Brigade War Diary for April 1917) says that the request was to 'start the tanks earlier i.e at 4.15 am'.

55 Bean, in the *Official History*, Vol IV, pp 314–316, discusses the actions of each tank and shows the locations where they were knocked out or abandoned; his assessment is generally followed by Kendall, *Op Cit*, and Walker, *Op Cit*. None of these locations is in the sunken track near the 14th Battalion's jumping off position. Major Watson (*Op Cit*, p. 60), whose account is not particularly clear, notes that Lt Morris's tank 'ditched at the bank and was a little late' but did get going at some point. It seems likely that this was the tank that got into the track. It was one of the two tasked with turning right at the enemy line and running past the Balcony Trench/Quéant positions. It was said by Watson to have accomplished this, although Bean points out that neither Germans nor Australians noticed any such action. Having returned to the railway line as ordered, Lt Morris took his tank across to the left sector to assist another ditched tank, Lt Skinner's—Bean (pp. 315–16) says the latter machine was 'towed over the embankment by a tank that had returned from the right.' Although several hours late, Lt Skinner took his tank into Bullecourt, where it was knocked out after a hard fight with the German garrison. Lt Morris's tank was apparently later knocked out by a shell near the central road.

56 6th MG Company War Diary for 11 April 1917. Although the *Official History* (Vol IV, p. 290) states that eight guns were used, the War Diary says that all sixteen of the Company's guns were in action.

57 4th LTM Battery War Diary for 11 April 1917.

58 *Official History*, Vol IV, p. 293.

59 Wanliss, *Op Cit*, p. 198.

60 Rule, *Op Cit*, p. 75.

61 Bean in the *Official History* (Vol IV, p. 299n) estimated that 'at least a quarter, possibly a third, of the whole attacking force was killed or wounded at or near the first entanglement.' The 16th Battalion noted in its war diary that 717 officers and men actually took part in the attack, and the 14th Battalion probably used about the same number, bearing in mind that up to one-third of a unit's total strength would usually be 'left out of battle'.

62 16th Battalion War Diary, 11 April 1917.

63 *Official History*, Vol IV, p. 296.

64 15th Battalion War Diary for April 1917, Appendix 'Narrative of Action.'

65 According to his file in the Red Cross Wounded and Missing records in the AWM Collection.

66 According to the *Official History* (Vol IV, p.299 and p.300n). The battalion history (Chataway, *Op Cit*, p.170) says he was killed attempting to reach Riencourt.

67	Harry Murray's letter of 12 March 1930 to C E W Bean, in the Bean Papers, AWM38 3DRL606/247/1, pp.38–40 in PDF.
68	White, *Op Cit*, p. 95.
69	*Official History*, Vol IV, p. 302.
70	46th Battalion War Diary for April 1917, Appendices.
71	*Ibid*.
72	Bean Papers, AWM38 3DRL606/247/1, p.95 in PDF, interview notes, April 1930.
73	Bean Papers, AWM38 3DRL606/247/1, p. 92 in PDF, Brig Gen Robertson's letter of 9 December 1930, in which he quotes from his personal diary.
74	The initial 4th Brigade order (No. 76) is in the Brigade War Diary as Appendix 4. The Brigade diary does not have a copy of the correcting memo, but one can be found in the Appendices of the 16th Battalion's April 1917 diary.
75	*Official History*, Vol IV, p. 304.
76	48th Battalion War Diary for April 1917, Appendices.
77	12th Brigade War Diary for April 1917, Appendix 11, Colonel Leane's report to Brigade on the operations of the tanks, dated 19 April. There is a similar but not identical document (undated) in the 48th Battalion War Diary for April which does not include that sentence, but does blame the tanks for the failure to start on time. This document may have been the first draft of the final report to Brigade.
78	46th Battalion War Diary for April 1917, Appendices.
79	*Official History*, Vol IV, p. 315n.
80	48th Battalion War Diary for April 1917, Appendices.
81	Mitchell, *Op Cit*, p. 92.
82	Johnny Moyes was at the ABC Radio microphone in Brisbane for the final over of the Australia-West Indies tied test match in 1960.
83	For an excellent detailed account of the 48th Battalion at Bullecourt, see Browning, *Leane's Battalion, Op Cit*, pp. 101-123.
84	Bean Papers, AWM38 3DRL606/149/1, attachment after p.79 of notebook.
85	14th Battalion War Diary for April 1917, Appendix 9. Presumably Jacka had gone some distance out into No Man's Land to make his own observations, and he had probably talked to walking wounded and runners coming back as well.
86	Bean's interview with Waine is in the Bean Papers, AWM38 3DRL606/247/1, and the comment as to numbers reappears on p.311, Vol IV of the *Official History*; p.323 mentions the numbers including attached 47th personnel as over 100 at 9.30 am. The 46th attacked with three and a half companies, with additional troops used as carrying parties. Allowing for a number left out of battle as the nucleus, at a conservative estimate the 46th would have had about 650 troops in the attack (Bean estimated that the battalions averaged 750 in action, which may be a little high). The 46th's total casualties on 11 April, killed, wounded and missing, were 373. The discrepancy is obvious. Also, it seems highly unlikely that the battalion would have lost 90% of its numbers in the advance, unless a very large number of uninjured men had simply turned around and run away, an occurrence which would surely have attracted some comment. On the other hand, it is not unreasonable that 'D' Company, exposed to heavy flanking fire, could have lost two-thirds of its numbers in reaching OG 1.

87   As stated in Col Denham's after-action report in the 46th Battalion War Diary. The 12th Brigade report (Appendix 7 in the Brigade War Diary for April) says that it was Brig Gen Robertson who ordered that both units be reinforced.

88   AWM Red Cross Wounded and Missing Files, p. 10 of Capt Boddington's file. As is often the case with these files, accounts of his death are inconsistent, but three witnesses mention an attempted bayonet charge.

89   The 12th Brigade report (War Diary Appendix 7) says the guns were in the second objective, i.e OG 2, but the map references given are in OG 1.

90   *Official History*, Vol IV, p. 311. The cross trench was probably the sap that George Mitchell, 48th, moved up to get from OG 1 to OG 2 (Mitchell, *Op Cit*, pp. 92–3).

91   48th Battalion War Diary for April 1917, Appendices, Report on Operation 11 April 1917..

92   The battery OC at the time, Capt John Johnstone, was later court martialled over an unrelated issue and eventually discharged. The 12th Brigade command made no attempt to retain him. There is nothing on Capt Johnstone's service record referring to the incident at Bullecourt, however.

93   47th Battalion War Diary, 11 April 1917.

94   The 47th's War Diary notes by name all of the unit's officer casualties, killed, wounded and missing, for 11 April, and all were members of 'A' Company. A check of service records and AWM Red Cross files for the other ranks killed in action on 11 April, as listed in the Roll of Honour in the fine unit history published recently (C Deayton, *Battle Scarred*, 2011) has identified the company to which 29 of the 34 names belonged. Of these, 21 were from 'A' and four each from 'C' and 'D', but none from 'B'. Two witness statements by 'B' Company soldiers in the Red Cross files are of interest: (1) In the file on Pte T E Williams, Corporal P A McDonald of 'B' Company stated that he was 'carrying up bombs and ammunition' when the body of Williams ('A' Company) was pointed out to him; McDonald was told that Williams had been killed by a shell that landed in 'our front line', i.e. the railway cutting position. (2) The file on Pte W E Budgen ('D' Company) includes a statement by Pte J R Jones that he was 'at a place between Lagnicourt and a sunken road where my company was under Captain Miller [i.e. Capt John Millar, OC 'B' Company, later killed in heroic circumstances at Messines]' when he saw Budgen.
None of the foregoing is conclusive, of course. It was not practical to identify and check all of the 47th's wounded for 11 April, and such a check may have produced a different picture. It is curious though, if 'B' Company did advance across No Man's Land through heavy fire to the Hindenburg trenches, fight there for even a short period, then withdraw still under fire, that no fatal casualties can be identified.

95   *Official History*, Vol IV, p. 318n. This appears in C E W Bean's notebook AWM38 3DRL606/149/1, pp. 16-17; his information was obtained soon after the battle from a 14th Battalion source, apparently Capt Wadsworth—but see note 96 below.

96   See Rule, *Op Cit*, p. 112, for example. Although it appears that Capt (later Lt Col) Wadsworth gave Bean the information about the flares (see note 95 above), that officer, in a 1933 article ('14th's Losses: Bullecourt Toll', *Reveille*, 1 April 1933, p. 15) wrote that rockets *were* used for the SOS, 'upwards of twenty', but it was apparently impossible for observers 'to distinguish the colours at so great a distance in the day-time.'

97   *The West Australian*, 22 June 1917.

98   4th Brigade War Diary for April 1917, Appendix 4.

99   According to the 12th AFA Brigade War Diary (Q Group) for April 1917, the OC of the 45th Battery (Maj J R Ellis) was sent to liaise with the 16th Battalion on 9 April, and a Group order of 8 April states that the 5th AFA Brigade was to find a liaison officer to work with the 4th Infantry

Brigade. Both of those references predate the orders for the attacks on the Hindenburg Line, and there is no definite statement that either of these officers was with the 4th Brigade on 11 April.

100 *Official History*, Vol IV, p. 319.

101 12th AFA Brigade War Diary, 11 April 1917. This entry implies that the incident took place between 12.02 pm and 1.45 pm, which presumably is incorrect as the surviving infantry had already withdrawn from the Hindenburg line to the original front line by then. The diary was written up by the unit adjutant, but it would have been read and approved—including the disparaging word 'absurd'—by Colonel Rabett.

102 4th Division Artillery HQ War Diary for April 1917, Appendix 'Report on operations of 11 April'.

103 Quoted in White, *Op Cit*, p. 100.

104 Bean Papers, AWM 38 3DRL606/183/1.

105 Chataway, *Op Cit*, p. 171n.

106 Lt L. Challen's notes, Appendix to 48th Battalion War Diary for April 1917.

107 4th Division Artillery HQ war Diary for April 1917, Appendix 'Report on operations of 11 April'.

108 Kendall, *Op Cit*, p. 104.

109 *Official History*, Vol IV, p. 336.

110 The *Official History* (Vol IV, P. 339n) gives his date of birth as 1 September 1898. When he enlisted, however, Dunnett stated his age as exactly 19 on 1 September 1915, when he would have just turned 17. Obviously he had increased his age to enlist (the official minimum was 18).

111 Injuries from a riding accident in Egypt had kept him away from the front until now.

112 Harry Murray's letter of 12 March 1930 to C E W Bean, in the Bean Papers, AWM38 3DRL606/247/1, pp. 38–40 in PDF.

113 *Official History*, Vol IV, P. 359.

114 D W Blackburn, 'Tank Opens Fire,' *Reveille*, 1 April 1933, p. 60.

115 Rather than getting back to the front line without assistance, Patten may have been picked up by stretcher bearers in No Man's Land after the fighting; his last wound was described as 'severe'. He had also been wounded at Mouquet Farm in 1916. After recovering in hospital, Patten was put on light duties in the Pay Corps. In 1918, this adventurous young man was accepted as a trainee pilot with the Australian Flying Corps, only to be badly injured in a training crash. He spent six months in hospital, and eventually returned to Australia in December 1919.
Wilfred Patten was awarded the DCM for his Bullecourt exploits. In the AWM 'Honours and Awards' database, the medal recommendation shows his name as 'William Francis Paton', but the award notice, correctly, is under 'Wilfred Francis [DeCourcy] Patten'. Patten's service file includes corrected copies of the recommendation.

116 The *Official History* (Vol IV, p. 322) has this incident occurring early in the battle, but Sgt Harry Downes' account in the Bean Papers, AWM38 3DRL606/247/1, pp. 163-4 describes it as in the final stages of the 48th's fight. Mitchell (*Op Cit*, p. 96) agrees with Downes.

117 Bean Papers, AWM38 3DRL606/247/1. This is apparently the message that the 12th Brigade report (War Diary Appendix 7) says was received from the 46th Battalion at 11.40am, although both units' Diaries report contacting Brigade HQ at 11.15 requesting a barrage.

118 48th Battalion War Diary for April 1917, Appendix 'Report on Operation 11 April'.

119 Notes on Bullecourt by Harry Downes (48th Battalion) in the Bean Papers, AWM38 3DRL606/247/1, pp. 163-4 in PDF.

120 *Official History*, Vol IV, p. 340.

121 Mitchell, *Op Cit*, p. 99.

122 Kendall, *Op Cit*, p. 84.

123 AWM Red Cross Wounded and Missing Files.

124 Mitchell, *Op Cit*, p. 99.

125 47th Battalion War Diary, 11 April 1917.

126 *Official History*, Vol IV, p. 341.

127 *Medical History*, Vol II, p. 136.

128 4th Division ADMS War Diary for April 1917, Appendices, map with 'Memorandum on Medical Arrangements.' There are some discrepancies between that document, the War Diaries of the 12th and 13th Field Ambulances, and the account in the *Medical History*.

129 '4th Australian Field Ambulance: History 1916-18', AWM224 MSS 291/1.

130 The *Medical History* (Vol II, p. 137) gives precise figures of 446 stretcher cases handled at the 13th Field Ambulance MDS and 671 walking wounded at the 4th Field Ambulance MDS, a total of 1,117. At the end of the month, the divisional admin staff reported a combined total of 880 wounded for the 4th and 12th Brigade Groups (4th Division Admin War Diary for April 1917, Appendix 7). The numbers treated at the MDS would include those who subsequently died of their wounds, and there would also have been some patients from units outside of the two infantry brigade groups. The 13th Field Ambulance War Diary for April notes a total of 1,930 cases treated at the two MDSs between 1 April and noon on 12 April, which would include the 13th Brigade's casualties in the Noreuil fighting. The 4th Division Admin Staff reported a total of 1,491 wounded for all units in the full month of April. The number of MDS patients reported by the 13th Field Ambulance again would include those who did not survive, and probably also patients who were not 4th Division members.

131 *Official History*, Vol IV, p. 342, citing the German Official History. Bean mentions that other authorities give numbers between 1,125 and 1,168. David Coombes in *Crossing the Wire* (2011), p. 145, gives 27 officers and 1137 ORs, a total of 1164.

132 The AWM's Roll of Honour database shows 846 deaths in 4th Division units on 11 April 1917 and a further 64 over the following two days, some of whom died from wounds received on 11 April. Alternatively, an approximation can be made based on figures compiled by the Admin Staffs of the 4th Division and I Anzac, recorded in their April War Diaries. Working through Division weekly strength reports and Corps casualty figures gives the Division's total losses for the battle as 3,035 in the 4th and 12th Infantry Brigades (allowing for what appears to be an understatement of 68 in the 16th Battalion's losses); this approach gives slightly different figures to those in the *Official History*, Vol IV, p. 343. Using the accepted figure of 1,170 prisoners and the Division staff summary report at the end of the month of 880 wounded for the two brigades (although that figure includes a few wounded prior to 11 April) leaves 985 other losses. Some of these would have died of wounds in the Allied lines, but most would have been killed in action; that figure is, however, somewhat higher than that produced by the Roll of Honour. The Division's summary report shows only 261 killed in the brigades, but that number is only those known definitely as of 30 April 1917; nearly 2,000 were still categorised as Missing at that time. There are several inconsistencies in the figures, for instance that for the 16th Battalion's total casualties appears to omit 68 known to be PoWs, although there is no comparable PoW figure for any of the other battalions. Among the adjustments made after the initial estimates is a reduction of 74 in the 48th Battalion's casualty numbers. It is unlikely that an

exact breakdown of the Division's total losses for 11 April can be arrived at from reports made at the time, hardly surprising in view of the confusion that must have reigned in the immediate aftermath of the battle, when no-one would have been concerned with recording precise statistics of casualties.

133   See Coombes, *Crossing the Wire*, for a detailed study of Australian prisoners in the First World War.

134   Bean Papers, AWM38 3DRL606/247/1, p. 82-88.

135   Letter by Lt H Baker in the Library of NSW collection, available on the internet at: http://acms.sl.nsw.gov.au/_transcript/2011/D12322/a4056.htm.

136   Figures from the Commonwealth War Graves Commission website. Of the 54 identified 11 April deaths, fourteen were members of the 14th Battalion, eleven of the 16th, nine of the 13th, five each of the 15th and 46th, four each of the 47th and 48th, and two of the 4th MG Company.

137   On 24 February 1921, the Army records office wrote to Colonels Peck, Durrant and Denham, COs of the respective battalions at the time of the battle, quoting information received from the Officer in Charge, Australian Graves Service, London, stating that the remains of the four captains were buried in a particular group of numbered grave sites at Quéant Road. It was not certain which body was in which grave, however, and the Army was seeking further information to identify the graves individually. A copy of the letter can be found on each of the colonels' service records. There is no record of any conclusion being reached, and the matter appears to have lapsed. The author represented this to the Commonwealth War Graves Commission in 2011, proposing that the names be recorded as 'possibly buried' at Quéant Road, but the Commission considered the evidence to be insufficient.

138   The I Anzac Admin Staff's final statement of 4th Brigade's casualties for 11 April gives the 16th Battalion's total losses as 532 killed, wounded and missing. Previous estimates in the Admin War Diary, however, also include an additional figure of 68 for definite prisoners of war, as mentioned in Note 132 above. This number also appears in the 4th Division Admin's statements, and there seems to be general agreement in the sources that the 16th's casualties totalled at least 600, supported by a comparison of 'Fighting Strength' numbers for the beginning and end of the month. The Battalion War Diary says that 'about 17 officers and 700 other ranks actually went into the attack and only 3 officers and 87 other ranks got back again.'

139   4th MG Company War Diary, 11 April 1917.

140   4th LTM Battery War Diary, 11 April 1917.

141   Rule, *Op Cit*, p. 81.

142   Walker, *Op Cit*, p. 71. See also Philip Gibbs, *Now It Can Be Told/The Realities of War* (1920), pp. 476–7, for highly critical comments on the Fifth Army staff as a group.

143   *Official History*, Vol IV, p. 351.

144   12th Brigade War Diary for April 1917, Appendix 1, Operation Memo 98.

145   Wanliss, *Op Cit*, p. 191.

146   That was certainly the opinion of the 15th Battalion historian—see Chataway, *Op Cit*, pp. 163–4.

147   4th Division General Staff War Diary for April 1917, Part 2, Appendix 39.

148   Bean Papers, AWM38 3DRL606/247/1, pp. 44–50.

149   Copies of the report are in the brigade and battalion war diaries, and in the Bean Papers.

150   12th Brigade War Diary for April 1917, Appendix 11.

151   Watson, *Op Cit*, p.71.

152 Capt D G Browne, *The Tank In Action* (1920), p. 63. The quote is from an inaccurate account of Bullecourt on pp. 61–4, which is partly sourced from Maj Watson's *A Company of Tanks*.
153 Quoted in White, *Op Cit*, p. 100.
154 4th Brigade War Diary for April 1917, Appendix 4.
155 *Official History*, Vol IV, p. 354.

11: The Gun-Line—Lagnicourt and Second Bullecourt

By 13 April the 4th Division's infantry units had been replaced in the front line by the 2nd Division's 5th Brigade, and the next day command of the left sector of I Anzac's front passed to the GOC 2nd Division. Over the next few days 4th Division HQ moved to Baizieux in the back area west of Albert. The 4th Division medical units had also been relieved by their 2nd Division counterparts by 14 April and the Divisional Train's three linked supply companies followed their infantry brigades to the rear; the 14th (HQ) Company stayed at Bapaume and continued to supply the divisional artillery. The 4th Division pioneers and engineers also remained in the forward zone for the time being, not rejoining the main body until early May. The Pioneers, based at Frémicourt to the east of Bapaume, continued with their never-ending work of extending and maintaining the Decauville light railway. The three engineer field companies were based in the vicinity of Favreuil, working on various construction projects in the sector, mainly road repairs but also sinking wells and strengthening the defences behind the front line. Enemy long-range artillery fire caused some casualties in the units and the pioneers also lost several men to German aerial bombing.

The 4th Division CRA, Brigadier General Rosenthal, continued in command of the left divisional sector field artillery. In the gun-line the three groups of the sector, now covering the 2nd Division infantry in the front line, maintained generally the same positions that they had held for the 11 April battle. The 4th Division's 10th and 11th AFA Brigades—forming 'P' Group, under Lieutenant Colonel King—had one battery each of 18-pounders and howitzers emplaced in the Ecoust-Longatte village site, and the remainder along the high ground running to the south of the village.[1] At the highest level of the terrain, and so the most open to enemy observation, was the 11th Brigade's 43rd Battery, with five 18-pounders emplaced in gun-pits dug into the bank of the Ecoust—Vraucourt sunken road where it crossed the crest of the ridge. The centre of the sector was held by 'Q' Group, the 2nd Division artillery and the 12th 'Army' AFA Brigade, with gun positions in the valley behind Noreuil, through which the Hirondelle stream ran. 'M' Group, the 1st Division artillery, was positioned in the next valley to the right, behind Lagnicourt. That village itself was just within the right-hand divisional sector of I Anzac's front, with the boundary between left and right running along its north-west outskirts. The 1st Division infantry remained holding the right sector, facing the Hindenburg Line east of Quéant and covered by the 5th Division artillery. The 1st Division was responsible for a front 12 kilometres wide, increasing to 13 when the Division advanced closer to the enemy line on the night of 13/14 April.

In order to defend a line of that distance, the 1st Division was deployed according to the method of defence in depth, with successive zones of resistance:

> To the enormous front held by the 1st Australian Division this system could be applied only if the outpost-line was reduced to the thinness of a light screen ... the front would be held, first by a line of sentry posts (4 to 7 men) 166 yards [150 metres] apart, whose duty would be to warn—and if necessary fall back upon—a line of picquets (15 to 20 men and normally a Lewis gun) 330 yards [300 metres] apart. Behind these, from a quarter to half-a-mile [400 to 800 metres] distant, would be the general line of the support platoons—one platoon to 1000 yards [900 metres].[2]

The forward zone was occupied by two brigades, each with two battalions 'up' and providing the screens and picquets, and two in reserve; the third brigade was kept well to the rear as the divisional reserve. Defence in depth meant that higher command was aware of the risk to the isolated posts on the forward edge of the front if the enemy chose to attack: '... it was obvious that so thin a line must be penetrated by any serious thrust, and could only be maintained by employing reserves to retake any part temporarily lost.'[3]

For the moment, however, there were no apparent signs that the enemy had any intention of attacking. The focus of the Fifth Army's planners and the staffs of its subordinate formations was on renewing the attack on the Hindenburg Line as soon as possible. The long-foreshadowed French offensive on the Chemin des Dames front to the south was about to be launched, and it was essential that the British support their allies by keeping up the pressure on the Arras/Bullecourt front. For General Rosenthal's Left Sector artillery, this meant that shelling of targets in the Hindenburg Line continued straight on after the failure of the 11 April operation. The tasks of wire cutting and interfering with enemy repair parties went on, and the guns also laid harassing fire on roads behind the German lines and shelled enemy troop movements detected by observation posts. The heavy artillery concentrated on pounding the Bullecourt village site, steadily reducing it to rubble. The new attack—this time using a conventional barrage—was meant to be launched by the 2nd Division as early as 15 April; preliminary instructions were issued for the operation, but its postponement was notified the night before.[4] In the event it was the Germans who attacked on 15 April.

Following the 11 April battle, the commander of the German forces opposite the 1st Division, General von Moser, had been struck with the idea of retaliating with a sudden offensive against the Australian line, on the principle that attack is the best means of defence. The general decided to use 16,000 men in 23 battalions to strike the blow.

The German objective was not to take and hold ground but rather to break through to the field artillery positions and destroy the guns. Noreuil, Lagnicourt and the five 'outpost' villages to their south-east were to be taken and occupied for 24 hours, military material captured or destroyed and intelligence information gathered, after which the Germans would retire to their own lines. It would be a raid on a massive scale.

Before dawn on 15 April, the German artillery opened a brief barrage along most of the 1st Division's front. This was largely ineffective, serving mainly to alert the defenders in the centre and right of the line. The German infantry, advancing under cover of darkness at about 4 am, was able to isolate and cut off a few of the piquets on the Australian right, but reserve companies were brought up and the German attack on this flank was first stopped and then thrown back after several hours fighting. The situation quickly became critical on the Australian left, however, in the area from Lagnicourt to Noreuil where the 1st and 2nd Division sectors joined. The German battalions attacking at this point achieved surprise by dispensing with a preliminary barrage in their sector, and quickly overran the outposts in front of Lagnicourt. Advancing against the second line of defence, the Germans pushed back the outnumbered piquet platoons comprising the left flank of the 12th Battalion (1st Division) and the right of the 17th (2nd Division). By 5 am the leading elements of the German force had broken through and were thrusting into and beyond Lagnicourt village, while at the same time others were advancing on Noreuil further north. The attack on the 5th Brigade's position at Noreuil was held after desperate fighting over the same ground where the 13th Brigade had fought in the capture of the village two weeks earlier. At Lagnicourt, however, the German force was threatening the field batteries of 'M' Group, the 1st and 2nd AFA Brigades of the 1st Division, emplaced in the valley behind the village.

Apart from a few sentries, the gun teams were snatching some sleep, but they were alerted at about 4:30 am when firing broke out nearby and retreating infantry began passing between the gun positions. The gunners soon came under fire from the advancing German infantry and prepared to bring the guns into action at short range, but they were unable to distinguish friends from enemies in the darkness. At the sector artillery HQ Brigadier General Rosenthal and his staff had also been roused early as reports of enemy activity began to come in. At 4:48 by Rosenthal's after-action report[5] he received the dramatic news from the 'M' Group commander that Lagnicourt was under attack and German infantry was closing in on the guns. The general ordered that the crews prepare to remove the breech blocks and dial sights from their weapons and retire. Twelve minutes later came confirmation that the guns had been lost. The 2nd AFA Brigade's batteries on the southern outskirts of Lagnicourt had been overrun first and the crews fell back on the 1st Brigade positions further to the rear. With the enemy still coming on, those guns were abandoned in turn and the nearby group HQ was forced to withdraw as well. The retreating troops streamed in the direction of Vaulx-Vraucourt:

the withdrawal was accompanied by signs of panic, one party, at least tumbling into the infantry bivouacs and artillery headquarters [of Colonel Rabett's 'Q'Group] near Vaulx-Vraucourt in a manner which might have spread alarm ...[6]

At about 5 am, with the situation far from clear, General Rosenthal ordered 'P' and 'Q' Groups to put down a barrage across the ridge between the Hirondelle valley west of Noreuil and the outskirts of Lagnicourt. The line of the barrage fell just beyond where the 1st Division's outpost line had been, cutting off the leading elements of the German force from their supports. 'Q', with its batteries positioned down in the Noreuil valley, had considerable difficulty moving its guns into locations from where their shells could clear the crest of the ridge. The 4th Division's batteries in 'P' Group did not have that problem, elevated as they were on the plateau behind Longatte, but the guns still needed to be repositioned to obtain the line of fire. The 43rd Battery's crews manhandled their 18-pounders out of the pits in the road bank and into the middle of the road, from where they opened fire on the barrage line. With daylight, the crew of a German observation balloon floating behind the enemy line spotted the battery in the open and called in countering fire from their own medium artillery. A storm of HE shells fell around the 43rd's position as the Germans found the range. The gunners continued firing, but casualties mounted up, guns were damaged and ammunition pits caught fire. One gun was smashed by a direct hit from a '5.9' shell that

> fell right on No. 4 gun while it was still in action, killing Sergeant [Stan] Read [the gun commander or 'number 1'] and the whole gun crew outright; the Battery still kept in action until ordered to cease fire.[7]

Three of the five guns were out of action just after 7 am and shells in the burning dumps were starting to explode. With no more ammunition available, the battery commander, Major Raymond Pybus, a 26 year old Tasmanian, gave the order to take cover, then to withdraw as the enemy shelling went on. Major Pybus and one of his section commanders, Lieutenant E J H 'Jack' Clarke, stayed to ensure that the survivors got clear; both officers were killed by a German shell. Sergeant Donald Macphail took charge of the withdrawal and organised the evacuation of the wounded, assisted by Sergeant John Quick, who had been hit in three places himself. By that time, however, the situation on the battlefield was changing decisively.[8]

The remaining batteries of the 10th and 11th AFA Brigades, less exposed, kept up the barrage across the ridge, and General Rosenthal contacted the Corps heavy artillery and asked them to join in also. The 14th AFA Brigade (5th Division) in the right sector, positioned near Morchies directly south of Lagnicourt, was independently called in by the 1st Division infantry at about 6 am. Those guns also put down a barrage on the ridge, later shifting their fire to roads out of Lagnicourt as the situation developed.[9] The 'Q' group batteries behind Noreuil, still unable to obtain a line of fire for the barrage, instead turned several batteries of 18-pounders and howitzers at short range on to the German troops advancing through Lagnicourt. The infantry fight was building in intensity as the 1st and 2nd Division battalions brought up their reserve companies. The German penetration was held, outflanked, and then driven into hurried retreat by determined counter attacks:

The 43rd Battery, 11th AFA Brigade, under enemy shell-fire during the Battle of Lagnicourt on 15 April 1917.
(Sketch by George Benson, AWM ART03605.035.002)

> ... under the withering fire from numerous Lewis guns from all directions, the very effective barrage, and the threat [to] his line of retreat, the enemy soon began to break. On observing his intention to retire, the barrage was lengthened 200 yards so that the majority still remained between the Lewis gun fire in front and barrage in rear. The enemy then began to surrender freely...[10]

The fighting had already begun to swing in favour of the Australians by 7 am when some concern was caused at artillery HQ by an outdated message that the infantry was withdrawing. As a precaution, General Rosenthal ordered that the batteries' horse teams be brought forward from the wagon lines in case the guns had to be pulled out. The true situation was soon clarified, however, and the batteries kept up their fire, lengthening the range in response to requests from the infantry, who continued to advance to their original defence line. By 8:45 Lagnicourt had been re-occupied and the field and heavy artillery was shelling the German lines of retreat; fire ceased at 10 am. The gunners of 'M' Group, returning to their positions at Lagnicourt, found that only five guns had been wrecked out of 21 that had been temporarily captured by the enemy, although several others had explosive charges attached to them. It turned out that many of the German troops, deprived of any small luxuries by the Allied blockade, had forgotten their duty and spent too long looting the Australian dugouts.

The German attack had been completely defeated despite the defenders being outnumbered four to one. After the initial surprise, the infantry had recovered quickly and outfought their opponents decisively (three VCs were awarded to 1st Division members). The system of defence in depth had succeeded in repelling a major attack and inflicting heavy casualties on the enemy, without needing to call on the reserves behind the front-line infantry brigades. There were some issues that needed attention, however, in particular the ease with which the guns near Lagnicourt had been overrun. It emerged that most of the rifles issued to the battery personnel (ten per battery) had been left at the wagon lines, leaving the gunners defenceless in a situation where the guns could not be used for fear of hitting their own troops. Even with rifles, the artillerymen could not be expected to do the job of infantry, however. The batteries were positioned unusually close to the enemy to increase their effectiveness in the operations against the Hindenburg Line, but it 'had not occurred to the staffs of the corps, divisions or even of the artillery itself to suggest the simple precaution of stationing a company of infantry to protect the Lagnicourt guns.'[11]

Orders went out the same night for the infantry units to allocate several platoons to guard the guns in case of another German sortie, and moves were made to strengthen the field defences that evening also. The 4th Division's 12th Field Company was called up from Favreuil to work on the construction of five strong-points at Lagnicourt.[12] Precautions having been taken, the I Anzac units continued with preparations for resuming the attack on the Hindenburg Line.

For the Australian field artillery, the period in the Bullecourt sector had been one of unusually high casualties. German counter-battery shelling had become increasingly frequent and effective, aided by air superiority which gave their observation aircraft and balloons opportunities to locate the general areas of the artillery groups, then to spot individual battery positions. 'Q' Group in the Noreuil valley noted that on the afternoon of the 11 April battle, two German aircraft had 'hovered against the wind over the valley for 15 minutes' at low altitude while the guns were in action, undisturbed by the RFC or fire from the ground.[13] This incident was assumed to have resulted in the heavy bombardment, including gas shells, of that Group's gun positions that went on all morning on 14 April, the day before the Lagnicourt fight. Shelling on the 4th Division artillery brigades ('P' Group) near Longatte had not been particularly heavy until the morning of the battle, when the 43rd Battery was shattered and lost more than half of its personnel, with fourteen dead and eight wounded. Unused to high casualties in his command, General Rosenthal was clearly shaken. At the funeral of Major Pybus and Lieutenant Clarke the next morning, he 'tried to say a few words to the officers and men present ... I am afraid I made a very poor showing for I certainly spoke from a full heart.'[14] Several surviving members of the battery, including Sergeants Macphail and Quick, were subsequently awarded MMs for their work in getting the wounded away under fire. On 19 April, General Rosenthal arranged for the sector groups to send their batteries in rotation back to the wagon lines for a few days break from the constant pressure.

The day after the Lagnicourt battle the major French offensive in the south got under way. General Nivelle's armies made some gains at first but the Germans, forewarned through extraordinarily lax security, brought up strong reserves that stopped the French advance then forced them back. By the end of the first day it was apparent that the promised breakthrough was out of the question. In the following days Nivelle ordered further attacks that made no significant progress, and the great offensive reverted to another battle of attrition. With the French stalled and some of their units on the verge of mutiny, the British armies on the

Arras front were obliged to maintain their efforts to crack the enemy lines. For I Anzac, this meant that a renewed assault on the Hindenburg Line was imminent. The 4th Division's artillery brigades continued in action as an element of the Left Sector artillery, coming under command of the 2nd Division CRA from 21 April. With his brigades and ammunition column still in the line, General Rosenthal established a temporary office near the main HQ at Favreuil to continue the administrative functions for his units.

Arrangements for the next series of operations progressed through April. In the Arras sector two local attacks produced limited results, and the decision was made that the next effort would be made along the whole front of the Third and Fifth armies from Vimy to Bullecourt. After several postponements, the date for the new attack was settled as 3 May, in the hope—not realised—that the French would be able to resume their own offensive on the following day. By then the weather had improved greatly, with frequent sunny days as the delayed spring arrived at last. With considerably more time available the staffs were able to produce far more thorough plans than those for the 11 April attack, which had provided an example of what not to do. This time I Anzac's attack would be made under a full creeping barrage from the Left Sector field artillery. That force now included the 14th AFA Brigade of the 5th Division, designated as 'R' Group, to support the right flank of the attack against fire from the enemy positions in front of Quéant. The guns in the creeping barrage were to fire a combination of 80% shrapnel and 20% HE at a rate of four rounds per gun per minute. Additional batteries of heavy artillery were brought in, and these set about pounding the German positions and blasting gaps in their wire entanglements; by the time the attack was launched, the damage done made the wire less of an obstacle than had faced the 4th Division in the first battle. Transport of ammunition and supplies to the forward zone steadily improved as engineers, pioneers and infantry working parties continued the constant work of restoring the infrastructure behind the lines. The 2nd Division would use two of its infantry brigades in the attack with the third brigade in reserve. Further infantry reserves would be available from the 1st Division, which was relieved in the right sector of the front line by a British division on 25 April. The infantry attack would go in on either side of the Central Road as in the first battle, but now with no gap between the brigades—and no tanks. The first objective for the infantry was now clearly defined as both trenches, OG 1 and OG 2, of the Hindenburg Line. The second objective was an intermediate position beyond OG 2, roughly along the line of the Moulin Sans Souci road and an adjoining tramline, from where the advance would continue to the final objective, again the village of Riencourt. On the 2nd Division's left Bullecourt village itself would now be attacked head-on as the first objective of the 62nd British Division, which would then go on to take Hendecourt. The postponements to the plan gave the infantry brigades time and opportunity to comprehensively rehearse the attack in the back area. Recognising the 4th Division's problems with ammunition supply on 11 April, the orders now called for each infantryman to carry six grenades in the attack, some of which would be collected into dumps when the enemy positions had been taken. The difficulty of getting additional supplies and reinforcements up to the fighting line does not seem to have received a great deal of attention in the preliminary planning, however. Fortuitously, it became apparent on the morning of the battle that a supply route could be based on the Central Road, partly protected as it was by a bank on its eastern side.

The artillery plans called for the 4th Division's 10th and 11th AFA Brigades to again support the advance of the left-hand infantry brigade, which would be the 2nd Division's 6th Brigade under Brigadier General John Gellibrand. In the confident expectation that the advance would proceed according to plan, three batteries (38th, 42nd and 43rd) from the 4th Division brigades were designated to form a new group ('X') that would move forward as soon as Riencourt was taken, to provide immediate fire support for the successful infantry.[15] In the days leading up to 3 May the artillery of both sides kept up the pounding of their designated targets in the opposing lines. The Australian field artillery groups continued to take accurate counter-battery fire from the German guns, which maintained a measure of superiority in that endeavour throughout the Bullecourt campaign. 'During the month hostile artillery activity has been above anything hitherto experienced by this Brigade,' wrote the 10th AFA Brigade diarist.[16] The field batteries continued with their routine tasks, firing on the enemy wire, transport routes and suspected machine gun positions. There were some special tasks also, as on the night of 28/29 April when the groups' howitzer batteries fired 750 gas shells into Riencourt, followed up by a shrapnel bombardment from the 18-pounder batteries. On 2 May the field batteries carried out registration shooting on their barrage lines for the attack on the next morning and the resting batteries were brought forward from the wagon lines into position. Measures were taken to improve the liaison between infantry and artillery, a crucial failing in the 4th Division's attack on 11 April. 'P' Group appointed Major Thomas Williams, OC 39th Battery, 10th AFA Brigade, as liaison officer with the 6th Infantry Brigade HQ. This time, Forward Observation Officers (FOOs) and their signallers would advance with the infantry and make their reports directly from the Hindenburg Line itself. Another 10th AFA Brigade officer, Lieutenant Peter O'Reilly, was selected for these duties by 'P' Group; he would go with the 24th Battalion on the right of the 6th Brigade's leading waves, advancing alongside the Central Road. In the operation orders, more attention was paid to detailing the flare signals to be used for calling in fire support and reporting progress.

At 3:45 am on 3 May the field artillery groups opened on the first line of the creeping barrage, 400 metres short of OG 1, lifting twice at three-minute intervals to fall on the trench itself where it would stay for a further ten minutes. This gave the infantry, jumping off with the opening of the barrage, sixteen minutes to cross No Man's Land to the enemy line. The German artillery reacted quickly, putting down a violent counter-barrage on the Australian front line and support areas within a few minutes, while more guns shelled No Man's Land. From the preliminary bombardments in the previous weeks the Germans had anticipated that an attack would be launched at some stage, only the exact day and time being in doubt. Consequently, they were ready to retaliate when the covering barrage opened, accompanied as it was by a machine gun barrage that was a sign of an attack in earnest on their lines.[17] For the time being, the German guns shifted target away from their persistent shelling of the field battery positions, but their counter-barrage on the front line had terrible consequences for another element of the 4th Division artillery.

The Division's MTM batteries had been detached in support of the 62nd Division's attack on Bullecourt village, to go in once the village had been secured and assist with defence against counter-attacks. The ill-fortune that had affected the infantry light mortars on 11 April continued for the artillery's mortars on 3 May. The crews, including some from the HTM battery as ammunition carriers, assembled with their weapons and ammunition in the railway cutting south-west of Bullecourt in the British sector of the line. The British infantry went forward at Zero, 3:45 am, and struck trouble almost immediately. Although the village had been reduced to piles of rubble the garrison had mostly survived in dugouts and cellars, resembling the situation at Mouquet Farm on a larger scale, emerging with their weapons when the barrage lifted. Fighting from cover provided by the rubble-heaps, the Germans stopped the British attack at the wire with heavy casualties. The 4th Division mortars contingent, waiting in the cutting to be called forward, came under fire from the enemy artillery and at 4:30 am an HE shell scored a direct hit on the mortar ammunition dump. The rounds—there were said to be 300 of the 19-kilogram shells[18]—blew up in a huge explosion. In that split-second 25 men lost their lives. Many of the mortarmen were literally blown to pieces; 16 were initially reported as 'missing,' in the sense that their remains could not be identified. Another nine men were identified at the time as killed, together with 14 wounded (at least two of whom later died of their injuries) and eight were reported, understandably, as 'shell-shocked,' an overall casualty rate of 50% from about 100 personnel.[19] All nine mortars were wrecked.

In the I Anzac sector, the infantry jumped off on time and followed the barrage towards the enemy line. The 6th Brigade on the left, covered by the 4th Division artillery, advanced with its right-hand companies alongside the Central Road that ran along the shallow depression in the centre of the attack front. It was this depression that had caused so much concern as a potential machine gun trap prior to the 4th Division's attack on 11 April, resulting in the area being left to the tanks. The road now proved to be more of an advantage than otherwise, with its eastern bank providing the 6th Brigade's two battalions on the right with protection from machine gun fire on that side. The right-hand waves of infantry kept up with the barrage, 'dangerously close ... when it lifted they were in the German trench with the last shell, and the enemy garrison, not having had time to leave its dugouts, was easily suppressed.'[20] The barrage fell for six minutes between the two trenches, then lifted onto OG 2 for another eleven minutes. Again the right of the 6th Brigade infantry followed the barrage closely, the rear waves passing over OG 1 and entering OG 2 as the barrage lifted, catching the defenders still in their dugouts. The trench was quickly secured and the troops reorganised for the next part of the advance, while the barrage moved on to the line of the second objective. The two battalions forming the left of the 6th Brigade were not so successful, however.

As they advanced they came under heavy fire from the German positions on the eastern side of Bullecourt, where the barrage had moved on but the 62nd Division infantry had been unable to penetrate. The troops who managed to get through the fire to the Hindenburg trenches were forced to their right, and the western half of the 6th Brigade's objective in OG 1 and 2 remained in the enemy's hands.

On the right of the battlefield, east of the Central Road, the advance had made virtually no progress. There the 5th Brigade was stopped by heavy machine gun fire from positions beyond the front trenches,[21] where the barrage had not yet reached. Heavy flanking fire was also coming from the Quéant/Balcony Trench positions on the right. No heavy artillery had been assigned to that target,[22] although the enemy trenches in that sector were being shelled by the field artillery of 'R' Group (14th AFA Brigade) assisted by 'M' Group's two howitzer batteries and by the 13th AFA Brigade, the 5th Division's other artillery unit.[23] The troops took cover short of the objective and consequently missed their moment when the barrage lifted. The German garrison quickly emerged and manned the parapet, and their fire cut down many of the brigade's leaders, adding to the disorganisation in the ranks. A few men got through to OG 1 near the Central Road, but most of the survivors gave up the attempt and pulled back in some confusion to their starting point at the railway. The Australian lodgement in the Hindenburg Line consisted only of the 6th Brigade's right flank elements to the west of the Central Road.

The field artillery groups, unaware of the true situation for the moment, continued with the barrage timetable. Having lifted away from OG 2, the line of shell-bursts formed a protective barrage beyond the trench for the next hour to give time for the infantry to reorganise before advancing to the second objective, the intermediate position between OG 2 and Riencourt. In the left sector 'P' Group would then creep the barrage up to the objective in another series of lifts. Here the fourth wave of the 6th Brigade's right-hand battalions made the attempt to continue the advance according to the timetable, despite the absence of support on both flanks. At 5:25 the barrage lifted away from the tramline that marked the second objective on the left, and small parties of infantry moved up to occupy positions in that line while the barrage continued on its next protective line, the 'blue barrage.' By this time, however, the commanders were beginning to realise that all was not going according to plan. There followed a frustrating period of order and counter-order for the gunners. Since 5 am Artillery HQ had been getting reports from their liaison officers at both infantry brigades that some of the 5th Brigade infantry had retired back to the start line.[24] By 5:20 it was clear that the right flank had failed. The information was passed on to 2nd Division HQ, which ordered that the barrage was to stay on the second objective for another 30 minutes. By that time, however, the barrage had already lifted and in 'P' Group's sector there were parties of 6th Brigade infantry actually occupying the second objective. The brigadier's protest was just in time to prevent the guns shortening range back onto their own troops, and 'P' Group was instead ordered to continue firing on the 'blue barrage line' for the extra 30 minutes before resuming the barrage timetable. That order was soon countermanded when it became clear that continuing the advance to Riencourt was now out of the question. Early reports that the British had taken Bullecourt were now known to be mistaken also. At 7:43 all field artillery groups were ordered to fire on the blue line protecting the second objective, and shortly afterwards to put half of their guns on to searching a 500-metre strip beyond the protective line. The 6th Brigade troops held on to their lodgement under counter-attacks that began to come in an hour later but the position remained precarious, in particular for the small force in the second objective deep inside enemy territory.

The 4th Division artillery's FOO, Lieutenant O'Reilly, had gone forward with the infantry and established himself with his signallers in OG 2, from where he had been regularly reporting back to the artillery liaison officer at the Brigade HQ. According to General Rosenthal, who was observing the battle from a position in the Noreuil-Longatte road,

> Lt. O'Reilly ... did magnificent work with the infantry in the captured trenches as FOO, his information being the most consistent and reliable of all that came through, which apart from his was very meagre.[25]

At 11:05 am and again at 11:20, O'Reilly reported shells falling short of the protective barrage line and onto the troops in the second objective, apparently from the left-hand batteries of 'Q' Group. These were ordered to lift their range, but by that time the decision had been taken to abandon the untenable position in the second objective and the surviving troops made their way back to the Hindenburg trenches. At midday the barrage was ordered back onto the line of the second objective, protecting the captured positions in OG 2. All groups continued firing for the next forty minutes until ordered from 2nd Division HQ to slow down their rate and then cease; for the time being, further shooting would be in response to requests and SOS signals from the infantry. The gunners, exhausted by the physical labour at their weapons, deafened and shaken by the roar and concussion of nine hours' firing, could now snatch a short rest.[26] Fire tasks soon resumed, however, as the Germans began to counter-attack and calls came in from the infantry to engage particular targets and enemy approach routes. In the Hindenburg Line fierce grenade fighting see-sawed back and forth along the trenches as the heroic survivors of the 6th Brigade infantry, reinforced by a fresh battalion, first repelled the enemy attacks and then extended their own foothold in the objective.

Although the initial advance had captured considerably less ground than had the 4th Division infantry on 11 April, the lessons learnt from that battle gave the infantry at Second Bullecourt some vital advantages in holding their positions in the Hindenburg Line. Artillery support, if sometimes inaccurate, was unrestricted except occasionally by ammunition supply, and the artillery commanders were very conscious of the need to respond quickly to infantry requests. Signal communication between the firing line and forward headquarters was better than before, although still well short of satisfactory. Most importantly a partly protected route, the Central Road, was available for reinforcements and supplies. When it became apparent that there would be no advance beyond the Hindenburg trenches, the 2nd Division's Pioneer Battalion was hurriedly sent in to dig a communication trench along the road at the base of the bank.[27] Completed by 9 pm on that first day of the battle, 'Pioneer Trench' became the infantry's lifeline.

The afternoon and night of 3 May saw the field artillery groups called in to open fire on several occasions, while for its part the German artillery bombarded their lost positions intermittently. Among the casualties from enemy shelling in OG 2 was the 'P' Group FOO, Lieutenant O'Reilly, killed at about 8 pm. The field groups put down a barrage on the designated 'SOS' line between 9 and 10 pm in response to flare signals that seem to have been a false alarm, caused by mistaking similarly-coloured German flares for the SOS signal. During this barrage it appears that the 4th Division guns were responsible for some short shooting that fell on the left of the 6th Brigade's position in OG 2.[28] Such errors were not confined to the 'P' Group guns and were perhaps the inevitable result of the unprecedented expenditure of ammunition on 3 May, with the consequent wear and tear on the guns and the exhaustion of their crews. According to the *Official History*, the field guns fired an average of over 400 shells each, far higher than the accepted normal rate.[29] The 4th Division Ammunition Column reported sending up over 14,000 18-pounder and 1,500 howitzer shells for its brigades in the 24 hours; the DAC took 96 wagonloads of shells direct to the gun-pits instead of dropping them at the batteries' wagon lines, and also brought up grenades and small arms ammunition for the infantry. Colonel Vernon noted that 3 May was the unit's heaviest day since Fromelles in 1916.[30]

During the night the surviving 6th Brigade infantry, after fighting an action that C E W Bean described as one of the finest achievements of the 1st AIF,[31] was relieved by two 1st Brigade battalions from the reserve. The infantry struggle flared up again early in the morning of 4 May. The 7th British Division launched another attack on the ruined Bullecourt village, but could make no progress in savage fighting among the rubble-heaps. In I Anzac's sector the 1st Brigade troops, after beating off an early German counter-attack, extended their foothold in the Hindenburg Line during the afternoon by bombing attacks along both trenches. This was the day on which the French had been expected to resume their offensive in the south, but widespread mutinies and changes in command at the top (General Nivelle was soon to be sacked) left the French with no option but to stand on the defensive. The 'P' Group guns were called on through the day to support the attacks with shelling on enemy troop concentrations and approach routes, and put down several SOS barrages during the night and early morning of the next day. An enemy night attack on the left flank of the 3rd Battalion in the trenches brought barrages from the 'P' Group guns, joined by several batteries of 'Q' and the 7th British Division artillery, as well as the I Anzac 'heavies;'[32] the shooting was effective, but again some shells fell short. The 3rd Battalion CO later reported

> Our 'SOS' barrage was very effective ... [but] ...Heavies, 4.5' howitzers and 18 pounders at different times dropped short in and behind our trench; on one occasion our Field Artillery placed a barrage on my line. Many 18 Pounder shell cases and pieces of our heavy shells [were] picked up in our trench. A number of casualties were traced to our own shells ...[33]

Routine fire tasks continued the following day and night while the infantry struggle went on in the trenches. By now the German artillery had resumed its counter-battery shelling, damaging two howitzers of the 110th Battery (10th AFA Brigade) on 6 May. In the early morning of 7 May, the British made another attempt on Bullecourt. Their 7th Division's objective was now limited to securing the south-east corner of the village on the left of the Australians in the Hindenburg Line trenches, now held by the 9th Battalion (3rd Brigade, 1st Division). The latter was to push west down OG 1 to link up with the British. 'P' Group combined with 'Q' to provide artillery support for both attacks, under the orders of the 7th Division,[34] and by 5:15 am the 9th Battalion and the Gordon Highlanders had gained their objectives and joined up. A foothold in the village site had been taken at last and I Anzac's left flank was secure, but the fighting was far from over. The gunners' tasks continued through the following days and nights in support of both British and Australian infantry at different times. Over the nights of 8 and 9 May, the infantry of the 14th and 15th Brigades (5th Division), their period of back-area rest cut short, came in to relieve the depleted 1st Division units. The British continued to hammer away at the remaining German positions in Bullecourt but made little progress against fierce resistance. Another attempt was organised for 12 May, this time with some success, the British attacking towards the north-east sector of the village and the 5th Division troops pushing along OG 2 to join them. 'P' Group again assisted with the fire support for the British operation, switching to a protective barrage later in the day after most of the infantry's objectives had been secured. The Germans still held out in a few areas of the village site and the battle went on for another week before it was finally secured, but the action of 12 May was the last major operation for the 4th Division artillery in the Bullecourt sector. The 10th and 11th AFA Brigades and the DAC were withdrawn from the line on the night of 13/14 May, handing over responsibilities to the 7th British Division's artillery, and returned to Brigadier General Rosenthal's command. The divisional artillery had been in the line and in action day and night since 5 April, suffering casualties of 53 killed and 133 wounded in the period.[35] They were not being withdrawn to rest, however, but instead to move north for another series of major operations, this time in the Flanders sector of the front, a move that General Rosenthal had been given a warning of as early as 8 May.[36] By the time the Second Battle of Bullecourt, and the wider Battle of Arras, ended on 17 May, it had cost the AIF over 7,000 casualties in the two weeks, to add to the 3,000 lost in First Bullecourt on 11 April, and the British V Corps lost just under 7,000 casualties also. All this bloodshed was for a ruined village and a stretch of trench-line of no real value. The original objective was to break through at least as far as Riencourt, and once that aim became out of the question—on the first day—there was little point in hanging on to an isolated intermediate position, except for reasons of prestige and a perceived need to draw attention away from the disrupted French forces. Before the end of the Arras/Bullecourt fighting the attention of the Commander-in-Chief, Sir Douglas Haig, and his staff at GHQ had shifted to Belgium and the strategic possibilities of the Ypres sector.

The 4th Division infantry, relieved straight after the 11 April battle, had moved back to billets in the vicinity of Albert where the next weeks were spent in re-equipping, rest and training.

The troops welcomed the opportunity to spend their off-duty time in the nearby villages. The area was now well behind the front and beginning to recover from the ravages of war, and the *estaminets* did good business supplying wine and female company, as well as food to vary the monotonous army rations—'*oeufs* and murphs' (fried eggs and potatoes) was a favourite. Reinforcements came in gradually, both recent enlistees coming through from the training battalions and experienced men returning from wounds or illness. The losses among the officers and NCOs at Bullecourt had been disproportionately heavy. Several of the battalions in the attack had lost all of their company commanders killed, taken prisoner or hospitalised, and others had lost three out of four; the 13th Battalion had sent six officers of captain's rank into the battle and only one, Harry Murray, remained on duty by the end of the day. Losses among subaltern platoon commanders had been comparably high. The many officer vacancies were mostly filled by mass commissioning in the field of promising NCOs, although some may not have appeared so promising at first sight—in the 48th Battalion, Lance Corporal George Mitchell, 'the most junior lance-jack' in the Battalion and self-described 'right marker of the bad boys,'[37] was one of nine NCOs selected for commissions by Lieutenant Colonel Leane. Like all good COs, Leane could see the potential in a soldier who could lead others naturally and knew his way around a battlefield. These citizen soldier officers, enlisting in the ranks and in many cases with no previous military training, formed close ties with each other within and outside their battalions: 'Welcome to the brotherhood,' said Captain Jacka to newly-commissioned Second Lieutenant Ted Rule,[38] one of twelve new officers in the 14th Battalion. Those selected for commissions in the 13th Battalion included the unusual case of one Sergeant Ciam MacMilville, posted in from the 9th Battalion. The new Second Lieutenant shortly revealed that his real name was Charles Macnaghten—previously Lieutenant Colonel Macnaghten, CMG, British-born former CO of the 4th Battalion on Gallipoli, where he had been wounded leading his men from the front in the battle for Lone Pine. Invalided back to Australia after Gallipoli, Macnaghten did not accept that he was unfit for active service and re-enlisted, at the age of 38, as a private under the assumed name of MacMilville, working his way up to sergeant before the commission in the 13th came through. Unfortunately, Macnaghten's health soon deteriorated again and a breakdown resulted in his final resignation from the AIF as permanently unfit in October 1917.[39] Another older subaltern of unusual background, although not a new promotion, was 46-year-old Lieutenant Montague Prior of the 47th Battalion. Prior, who had been wounded at both Pozières and Bullecourt, was an English-born veteran of the Boer War, in which conflict he had won the DSO as an officer with a British irregular unit, Bethune's Mounted Infantry.[40] Something of an Imperial drifter, Prior was also noteworthy for a reprehensible private life, shown by the letters from his abandoned South African wife that are in his service file. There were other sources of officer reinforcements also; it appears that something of a combing-out occurred of officers who had previously been detached to other units and were now returned to their original battalions, and there are signs that at least some of these were not particularly welcome. One who certainly was welcome, however, was Captain Bill Lynas, MC and Bar, formerly the 16th Battalion's intelligence officer.

He had been posted to a training unit in England earlier in the year, then selected for a posting to the new 6th Division in the process of forming. Hearing the news of Bullecourt, Lynas made his way to France, quite unofficially, and rejoined his old battalion at the end of April. The irregularity was smoothed over by some means and Lynas resumed his career as one of the 16th Battalion's finest officers. The nascent 6th Division was soon disbanded; the AIF's losses at First and Second Bullecourt meant that the numbers were not available for forming and reinforcing another division.

Most of the 4th Division's infantry battalions had been well under normal fighting strength when they came out of the line. The 4th Brigade units had suffered the heaviest losses on 11 April, and by the end of the month the four battalions were still collectively more than 1,500 short of full strength. The two 12th Brigade battalions, the 46th and 48th, that had been fully engaged at Bullecourt were 500 under strength between them, and the 13th Brigade was still 450 short of making up the losses suffered at Noreuil, mainly by its 50th and 51st Battalions.[41] By 12 May, the situation had improved slightly, with the division's total infantry numbers within 1,900 of full strength, although 580 of the reinforcements in the ranks were categorised as still needing further training.[42] On that day, with all of the Division except the artillery now billeted in the vicinity of Albert, a full parade for inspection by the Corps Commander, Lieutenant General Sir William Birdwood, was held on the 4th Brigade's rifle range, a field between Bresle and Ribemont. The general presented medals and ribbons awarded for the Bullecourt fighting, in a relaxed atmosphere with the men seated casually on the grass and applauding as each name was announced. Sir William then addressed the parade. The key point in his speech was the announcement that the 4th Division was about to be detached from I Anzac and sent north to

4th Division parade at Ribemont: General Sir William Birdwood (in slouch hat) presenting a medal ribbon to Captain Albert Jacka, 14th Battalion; Major General Holmes looks on. (AWM E00438)

Flanders, to join II Anzac in the Ypres sector. The implication was that the Division would be involved in further heavy fighting in the near future, and the troops would have had plenty to contemplate as they marched past the general to conclude the parade.

The HQ administrative staff was already working on the arrangements for moving the Division to its new area. The Division entrained over a three-day period, 15 to 17 May, on a total of 38 trains leaving from three railway stations. The Division's artillery, arriving in the Albert area from the Bullecourt front during 14 May, had only two days away from the forward area before packing up again to board its allocated trains for the north. Travelling separately by motor vehicle, Major General Holmes and his immediate staff arrived at Bailleul in French Flanders, a few kilometres from the border with Belgium, on 16 May and Divisional HQ was established in the townsite that evening. The troop trains pulled in over the next few days. The 4th Division units marched from the stations to billets in areas that the veterans would have recalled from eleven months earlier when the Division had first arrived on the Western Front and also from the period following the Mouquet Farm battles, so this would be its third stint in the region. For the time being the infantry brigade groups, the battalions and their associated arms and services units, were located around the villages of Doulieu and Vieux Berquin in the back area, engaged in refitting, training and various labouring tasks. The artillery, however, arriving in the area during 17 May, was sent into the line almost immediately. After a brief rest for men and horses and a quick overhaul of the guns,[43] seriously worn after the heavy firing during the Bullecourt operations, the 10th and 11th AFA Brigades moved up to their allocated sector of the gun line on 20 May. Here they came under the tactical control of the New Zealand Division artillery, as did the DAC. The trench mortar batteries, partly reconstituted since the disaster of 3 May, were sent forward also and attached to the 3rd Australian Division artillery. Facing the German lines along the Messines-Wytschaete ridge, the artillery was the first element of the 4th Division to go into action in what would be known as the Battle of Messines.

11 Notes

1. 4th Division General Staff War Diary for April 1917, Appendix 48 (disposition report for 14 April).
2. *Official History*, Vol IV, p. 357.
3. *Ibid*, p. 358.
4. 2nd Division General Staff War Diary, 14 April 1917.
5. 4th Division Artillery HQ War Diary for April 1917, Appendices.
6. *Official History*, Vol IV, p. 379.
7. AWM Red Cross Wounded and Missing file on Sergeant E S Read, p. 9, report from Bombardier Henry Forsey. This record incorrectly shows Sgt Read as a member of the 11th [Infantry] Battalion rather than the 11th AFA Brigade.
8. As well as the *Official History* (Vol IV, p. 388), see AWM26 170/12 '43rd Battery, 11th Aust FA Brigade' for an account of this action.

9   14th AFA Brigade War Diary for April 1917, Appendix XVIII.
10 5th Infantry Brigade War Diary for April 1917, Appendix 5.
11 *Official History*, Vol IV, p. 402.
12 4th and 2nd Field Company War Diaries for April 1917. Labour was supplied by 9th Battalion infantry.
13 12th AFA Brigade War Diary for 14 April 1917.
14 Rosenthal Diary, *Op Cit*, 16 April 1917.
15 2nd Division Artillery HQ War Diary for May 1917, Appendices.
16 10th AFA Brigade War Diary, 30 April 1917 (Summary).
17 *Official History*, Vol IV, p. 422n.
18 The quantity of bombs in the dump is mentioned in two accounts by survivors in the AWM Red Cross files.
19 The author originally located 24 names in a search of the Roll of Honour records on the AWM website, but that was corrected by Stephen Brooks's excellent article 'Tragedy in the 4th Division Heavy and Medium Trench Mortar Batteries' in the March 2020 issue of *Digger*, the magazine of the Family and Friends of the First AIF Inc. There is some inconsistency in the records as to the unit name, but most are recorded as members of the '4th Division Heavy and Medium Trench Mortar Battery, Field Artillery.' The Division reported a figure of 25 missing plus killed, and two others died of wounds in the next few days. The 27 names are: H A Beck, F Bermingham, J Bladen (died of wounds), J G Campbell, S D Cockshell, P B Dwyer, G Hunter, J T Jenner, J J Kelly (died of wounds), L G Langdon, A L Lodge, W E McDonald, W C Meldrum, S J Michell, W Mitchell, C L Mitchener, H Moore, R J Mortimer, J Moss, G H Olive, J H Parkes, A E S Parsons, A Pascall, F J Powell, J Reid, M S Reidy and H W B Smith. All of those soldiers except Bladen and Kelly have no known grave, their names being recorded as 'missing' on the Australian memorial at Villers-Bretonneux. The 4th Division members killed on 3 May 1917 make up more than a quarter of the 88 names shown on the Roll of Honour as deaths in all AIF 'Medium Mortar' units for the entire war.
20 *Official History*, Vol IV, p. 437.
21 *Ibid*, p. 434.
22 E M Andrews and B G Jordan, 'Second Bullecourt Revisited,' *Journal of the Australian War Memorial*, 1989; E M Andrews, 'Bean and Bullecourt,' *Review Internationale d'Histoire Militaire*, No 72, 1990.
23 Not being part of the creeping barrage, this task is not shown on the barrage map. The 2nd Division artillery orders, however, state that 'R' Group and the howitzers of 'M' Group were to place a separate barrage on the enemy front and support trenches in map squares U 30, C 6 and D 1, facing the right flank of the 5th Brigade's advance. The tasks are specified in 'Left Sector First Anzac Artillery Instructions No 12' dated 27 April 1917, in the Appendices to 2nd Division Artillery HQ War Diary for April 1917. Those orders are reiterated in the memorandum 'Howitzer Tasks and Tasks for 'R' Group', dated 1 May 1917, in the Appendices to the May 1917 HQ Diary. Appendix 44 to the 14th AFA Brigade's May 1917 War Diary is the brigade's own order detailing the tasks for each battery in the barrage (the 14th also had the 106th Howitzer battery attached from the 6th AFA Brigade); the order includes a clear sketch map of the barrage lines. The diary entry for 3 May states that the barrage was fired from 3.45am to 1 pm. Andrews (Note 22 above) points out that the weight of fire was inadequate to suppress the German machine gunners, a task that needed heavy artillery.
The task for the 13th AFA Brigade, arranged at short notice, was to fire a 30-minute lifting barrage on the next section south in the Quéant trenches, facing the Right Sector of the Allied line, to

simulate an attack at that point. There is no indication as to whether or not this succeeded in deceiving the enemy.

The Artillery HQ Memorandum 'Instructions for the Defence of the Line after Zero plus 3.44 and During Consolidation,' also dated 1 May and in the May War Diary Appendices, has been cited elsewhere as showing that little or no provision was made to barrage the Quéant trenches during the infantry advance. That document, however, describes the artillery arrangements to be implemented after the third objective (i.e. Riencourt) had been taken, an event that did not occur.

24   2nd Division Artillery HQ War Diary, 3 May 1917. The entries include minute-by-minute notes of information coming in and going out of the HQ. Bean, in the *Official History*, Vol IV, p.452n, comments on the difficulties of communication between infantry and artillery on 3 May.

25   Rosenthal Diary, *Op Cit*, 3 May 1917. General Rosenthal had set up his observation post in the road two days earlier, including a telephone connection to 'P' Group HQ.

26   There was some rotation of personnel within the gun crews during the action. See Horner, *Op Cit*, p. 145, quoting Mant (ed), *Soldier Boy*.

27   2nd Division General Staff and 2nd Pioneer Battalion War Diaries, 3 May 1917.

28   *Official History*, Vol IV, p. 481.

29   *Ibid*, pp 467–8 and 468n. The 2nd Division Artillery HQ (Appendix 2 of its May War Diary) reported expenditure of ammunition on 3 May as 37,110 shrapnel and 12,181 HE shells by the 18-pounders, plus 7,910 howitzer shells, amounts far higher than on any other day of May. If these figures included every battery in the four groups under 2nd Division command, and each was fully equipped with six weapons which remained in action through the day, the average would be 333 shells per 18-pounder and 165 per howitzer.

30   4th Division DAC War Diary, 4 May 1917; the alternative name of Fleurbaix was used for Fromelles.

31   *Official History*, Vol IV, p. 488.

32   2nd Division Artillery HQ War Diary, 4-5 May 1917.

33   3rd Battalion War Diary for May 1917, Appendices.

34   A copy of the orders is in the 4th AFA Brigade's War Diary for May 1917.

35   4th Division Artillery HQ War Diary, May 16/17 1917. Similar figures can be found in the 2nd Division Artillery HQ War Diary for May 1917 (Appendix 1), and the I Anzac Admin Staff War Diary for April 1917. The latter document reported casualties under the controlling division, which was the 2nd for the latter part of April, and also the 4th Division figures up to then would include casualties in attached artillery units when the division was in command of the sector.

36   Rosenthal Diary, *Op Cit*, 8 May 1917.

37   Mitchell, *Op Cit*, p. 103.

38   Rule, *Op Cit*, p. 83.

39   See the *Official History*, Vol I, p. 53 for Bean's estimate of Macnaghten. The latter's service record shows that at one stage he was considered to have deserted: he was supposed to have taken up a training appointment in Australia after returning from Gallipoli, but did not report for that duty, having re-enlisted instead.

40   Announced in the *London Gazette*, April 19, 1901, p. 2702.

41   4th Division Admin HQ War Diary for April 1917, Appendix 13, Strength Return for 28 April 1917.

42   *Ibid*, May 1917, Strength Returns in Appendices. The 52nd Battalion had an unusually high sick list that month, contributing to the 13th Brigade's shortage of numbers.

43   11th AFA Brigade War Diary, 18 May 1917.

12: Black and Green Lines at Messines

Since the early months of the war in 1914, the BEF had been holding the Ypres Salient, the great bulge in the British line, 16 kilometres wide and projecting ten kilometres into enemy territory. The German lines were along the ridges east of Ypres city and extended to more high ground to the south. There the opposing lines formed a smaller salient, this one held by the Germans, along the Messines-Wytschaete ridge. Although only averaging 45 metres in height, the ridges gave the Germans the significant military advantage of observation in that flat country. General Sir Herbert Plumer had commanded the British Second Army in the Ypres Salient since May 1915, and for much of that time he and his chief of staff, General C H 'Tim' Harington, had been planning the means of forcing the enemy off the dominating heights. The Messines ridge, overlooking the British positions from the south, was of particular concern. General Plumer, a careful, meticulous planner, was conscious that the situation along the Western Front, at Ypres in particular, had many of the characteristics of siege warfare. Included in his plans was one of the oldest of siege techniques, undermining the enemy's fortifications. Beginning early in 1916, engineers and specialist miners had been driving more than 20 tunnels beneath No Man's Land to locations under the German positions on Messines ridge. Those mines, once completed, were packed with huge charges of high explosive below the German front line, ready to destroy it and open the way for an infantry attack. As well as the mines, the infantry would also be supported by an immense concentration of artillery.

By May 1917, the Second Army's proposed operation had become absorbed in a far more ambitious scheme of strategy in Flanders. With the Arras campaign winding down and the continuing need to support the demoralised French armies, the Commander-in-Chief, Sir Douglas Haig, revived his long-favoured plan of driving the Germans away from the occupied Belgian coast and eventually achieving a decisive breakthrough. Ypres is about 50 kilometres from the Channel coast, and an advance north-east from the Salient would threaten to cut off the German coastal garrisons. With pressure added by a smaller frontal advance along the coast and possibly an amphibious landing, the Germans could be forced into a precipitate retreat. Clearing the coast would also have the advantage of depriving the Germans of their submarine bases at Zeebrugge and Ostend. The U-Boat campaign, although it had brought the United States into the war, was causing enormous losses to British and neutral merchant ships and there was a real chance that the Germans could achieve their aim of starving Britain out. Sinkings in April 1917 reached a record of 860,000 tons of shipping and reinforced the British Admiralty's support for any efforts by the Army to turn the Germans out of the Belgian ports.

Second Army's original planning was for the attack at Messines to be a stand-alone operation. The new strategy saw the capture of the ridge as securing the right flank, a necessary preliminary to capturing all of the high ground east of Ypres. Once that had been achieved the advance would turn north-east through Roulers towards the coast. Haig ordered an extension of the original objectives of what was now to be the preliminary operation at Messines, and it was that change that saw the 4th Australian Division become involved. General Plumer had intended to capture the German first line on the forward slope of the ridge, destroyed by the explosion of the great mines, after which the infantry would follow through to take the second line along the crest, including the villages of Wytschaete and Messines. A strong defensive position would then be established, impregnable to counter attacks, with a further line of outposts beyond the crest to screen the main position. This was not enough for the C-in-C, who directed that the first day's objectives include a further advance of 800 metres to the German third line, which ran south from the village of Oosttaverne near the eastern foot of the ridge. From the colours used to mark up the staff maps, the main position to be occupied beyond the crest was designated as the Black Line, the outposts were the Black Dotted Line (or Red on some maps), and the new final objective was the Green Line; the latter was also referred to as the Oosttaverne Line. The German lines were held on the principle of defence in depth, with reserves towards the rear ready to counter-attack if the forward positions were lost. General Plumer intended to forestall these tactics by catching the advancing reserves with artillery before they could reach the battle area. The German defensive lines were studded with concrete block-houses ('pillboxes') serving as strong-points and shelters for infantry; these could resist all but the heaviest artillery shells. Other strong-points and machine gun posts were scattered between the main lines. Second Army's preparations for the attack went on through May. The artillery arrangements were particularly elaborate, laid down in a series of orders known as the 'Magnum Opus,'[1] and Second Army received massive reinforcements of artillery pieces and ammunition, of all calibres; British factories were now producing guns and shells in the quantities needed for operations on the Western Front. Many of these were gas shells, the most effective way of delivering the deadly vapours on to the enemy, and both sides made heavy use of gas in the Ypres sector. By the time the battle opened Second Army had over 2,000 guns and howitzers available to support the attack.[2] The 4th Division artillery became a small cog in this mighty machine, contributing two of the sixty-four field artillery brigades that would take part in the battle. The German artillery in the sector was outweighed four to one, but they would nevertheless prove capable of striking effective blows.

II Anzac, commanded by Lieutenant General Sir Alexander Godley, was the southernmost of Second Army's three Corps, and in mid-May it comprised the New Zealand Division, Major General John Monash's 3rd Australian Division and the 25th British Division. For the Messines operation a further division was to be attached to each Corps as a reserve, and the extended objectives now meant that the reserve division would be sent in to attack the final 'Green Line.' The 4th Division, its units arriving in the area from 16 May, became II Anzac's reserve and would therefore be put in on the first day of the upcoming battle. It was just over a month since First Bullecourt and the Division was still recovering from the carnage of that battle, but assuming that II Anzac's reserve division had to be Australian—which was not necessarily the case, the Corps having had two British divisions under command at times—then there was no real alternative to the 4th at that time. The 1st and 2nd Division infantry had been heavily engaged at Second Bullecourt less than a fortnight earlier and that of the 5th Division was actually still fighting in the Hindenburg Line trenches; the artillery of those three divisions was also still in action on the Bullecourt front.

On 20 May the 4th Division's artillery brigades had been attached to the New Zealand Division and sent up to the gun-lines, in the area between Wulverghem village and the low rise called Hill 63 (from its height in metres above sea level), near Ploegsteert. In the line, the brigades were re-grouped to conform to Second Army's overall artillery plan. Each of II Anzac's three front-line divisions was allocated three field artillery groups of 18-pounders, each group comprising the guns of two field brigades (that is, six batteries per group) from its own and other divisions, plus several 'Army' brigades. Each division also had one separate group of six 4.5-inch howitzer batteries, detached from the same brigades, in a temporary reversion to the organisation of a year earlier.[3] The six 18-pounder batteries of the 10th and 11th AFA Brigades were combined to form 'E' Group of the NZ Division field artillery, under the command of Lieutenant Colonel Waite, the 11th Brigade CO. The Brigades' two howitzer batteries were allocated to 'H' howitzer group. Colonel Waite found that his group's gun positions had 'been excellently prepared by [the] New Zealanders,'[4] characteristic efficiency from that outstanding division. Ammunition was being dumped at the gun pits, and the batteries moved into position during the night of 21 May. The guns were soon firing for registration on their allotted zones for the offensive. Most of the main body of the 4th Division, the infantry brigades and their associated arms and services, stayed in the Second Army back area for the remainder of the month, except for the 45th Battalion, and later the 48th, which were detached to work on unloading artillery ammunition at the railhead. The other elements of the Division continued with routine training, interspersed with a series of inspections by the high commanders, including Field Marshal Haig, General Plumer and the Corps Commander, General Godley, a sure sign of action in the near future. There may have been some veterans of the old NZ & A Division who had hoped that they had seen the last of General Godley after Gallipoli and their first short stint in Flanders, but on the other hand, General Plumer was known to be a believer in reducing casualties by careful planning. In the conditions on the Western Front in 1917, however, that was no guarantee that events would always go according to plan in the heat of battle.

The 4th Division G-staff conferred with Corps and on 28 May issued a preliminary instruction outlining the Division's part in the forthcoming battle. Following the opening stage, the capture of the German line on the crest of the ridge and establishment of the Black Line defensive position, there would be a long pause during which most of the artillery would continue bombarding the enemy reserve positions while some batteries moved forward into position to fire on the Green Line objective. During the pause the reserve divisions would begin moving up to reach their jumping off positions a little in advance of the Black Line. Covered by a creeping barrage from the repositioned field artillery, the attack on the Green Line was to begin 10 hours after the battle opened. The day before the battle, the timing was reconsidered by Army HQ and it was decided that the time would instead be determined on the day depending on the progress of the early attack, and to allow for possible delays in the reserve units getting into position. The time for the afternoon attack could therefore be more than 10 hours after Zero, and it was now referred to as 'New Zero'. In II Anzac's sector of the front the 4th Division would attack the sector in front of the trenches captured by the 25th and NZ Divisions, flanked on the left by a IX Corps division and on the right by the reserve battalion (the 37th) of the 3rd Division. The 4th Division's attack would be mounted by the 12th Brigade on the right and the 13th on the left, each with two battalions up front and two in reserve; the 4th Brigade, the most damaged in the April fighting, would be in divisional reserve. Having captured the first trench of the Oosttaverne system the battalions would go on to take the German support trench 100 metres further on, the final Green Line. It may not have been apparent at this point that the 4th Division, still recovering from its recent experiences, had been given the most difficult task of the battle.

Orders were issued at the same time for the Division to move up to the 'D' or reserve area behind the front, around Neuve Église (Nieuwkerke). Most units were to move during 30 and 31 May, but several were sent forward a few days earlier, including the three machine gun companies. The 4th and 13th MG Companies were attached to the 3rd Division in the forward zone and the 12th came under command of the NZ Division. The 12th Company had recently received a new commander, Major Ernest Radford, who came in from the 7th MG Company (2nd Division) to replace the unfortunate Captain Edgar Sawer, struck down earlier by cancer (Major Radford himself was taken seriously ill at the end of June, and Captain David Martin then took over as OC). Several other units had also received new COs since Bullecourt. In the 12th Brigade, poor health caused the departure of the 47th Battalion's Lieutenant Colonel Lewis shortly after that battle and the unit second-in-command, Major Alexander Imlay, was promoted into the vacancy. The new CO, a Gallipoli veteran, had served in the 16th and

48th Battalions (his brother Norman was a captain in the 48th) before transferring to the 47th in January 1917. A hard man and a strict disciplinarian, Lieutenant Colonel Imlay quickly made himself unpopular with the men in his new capacity,[5] and C E W Bean was later to raise doubts about his general ability as a battalion commander. Nevertheless, he did provide firm leadership of the 47th at a crucial time. There had also been a change in the 12th Brigade HQ staff, Captain Eric Terry having been posted in from the 47th Battalion as staff captain in place of Major Inglis, on sick leave. The 13th Brigade had appointed a permanent commander for the 49th Battalion at the end of April, Lieutenant Colonel Harold Paul coming in on promotion from the 20th Battalion (2nd Division); his period in command was destined to be a short one, however. In the 4th Brigade, the 14th Battalion suffered a blow when its popular and efficient CO, Lieutenant Colonel Peck, was posted to the 3rd Division staff. It would be some time before Brigadier General Brand, who seems to have had something of a blind spot where the 14th Battalion was concerned, was able to find a satisfactory permanent CO for the unit, and temporary commanders filled the position for several months; Major Eliazar Margolin, a Russian-born Western Australian transferred from the 16th Battalion, was acting CO at the time of the Messines battle.

Outside of the front-line units, a change of senior officer took place in the 4th Division's veterinary services. When the ADVS, Major Bill Kendall, had departed on sick leave several months earlier, Major Robert Macindoe had filled the posting initially. The latter officer had been posted to the 2nd Division in April, and since then Majors C T McKenna and G G Heslop had acted as ADVS for short periods. Kendall returned to the Division on 24 May, with a promotion to lieutenant colonel (divisional senior veterinary officers were re-titled D[eputy]ADVS in July, when postings of ADVS were set up at Corps level). A number of the Division's draught animals would soon be used for special duties once the offensive got under way. On arriving in the sector, Colonel Albert Holdsworth's Divisional Train had fitted into the supply infrastructure behind Second Army's front line; the system had become fairly well established with long occupation of the sector, and included an elaborate system of water pipes. If the offensive went according to plan, however, it would be some time before the troops could be reached by the normal transport network for vital supplies of food, water and ammunition, as well as basic stores (sandbags and wire) for consolidating captured positions. Water was particularly important—in mid-summer, the weather was expected to be hot on the day of battle, and in the event it turned out to be sweltering. To fill the gap, the divisions were ordered to set up pack transport troops of horses and mules to come into operation when the offensive began. The 4th Division Train had some experience of such units from the operations at Mouquet Farm in 1916. Captain Septimus Robertson, OC 27th Company AASC, was nominated as overall commander of the troop with a subaltern and several NCOs from the Train to assist, and 179 animals with their drivers and transport NCOs were allocated from the infantry brigades and engineer units. The Pack Transport Troop would do vital work under fire in the first few days of the battle.

The medical arrangements for the battle saw the 4th Division's medical units pooled with those of the other II Anzac divisions in an overall Corps scheme for evacuating and treating casualties. In effect, each Field Ambulance would be split into its component bearer and tent sub-divisions which would then be allocated as required to the different medical stations in the system. The presence of Hill 63 behind the centre of the Corps front meant that the evacuation routes were split to its north and south, each with a corresponding MDS and CCS. Casualties on the 4th Division's front would be evacuated on the northern route through the MDS near Westhof Farm to the CCS at Bailleul. Most of the Division's medical personnel were allocated to the stations on that route, under command of the NZ Division ADMS, with an ADS at both Kandahar Farm and Underhill Farm.[6] Up to the day of the battle, the 4th Division's engineering elements were also employed in duties with the Corps, working on infrastructure projects—the Pioneers were temporarily attached to the NZ Division for road works, while the engineer field companies worked on a variety of tasks, including construction of gun positions and battery commanders' dugouts for the artillery, and manufacture of carrying racks for the Pack Transport Troop.

While these tasks were going on in the background, the Division's cutting edge, the infantry units, made ready for 'Z-day,' as the opening day of the battle was designated,[7] and their attack on the Green Line. The two attacking brigades selected the battalions that had suffered the least in April to lead the advance, the 45th and 47th Battalions in the 12th Brigade on the right and the 49th and 52nd in the 13th Brigade on the left, the other battalions being held in support for their respective brigades. The battalions would form two waves, each wave comprising two companies, the first wave to take the German front line and the second to leapfrog through and attack the support line. The attacking front covered most of the area between the Douve river on the right (south) and the Wambeek stream on the left (north). Between those features ran the Blauwepoortbeek stream and the main road known as Hun's Walk running east from Messines on the crest of the low spur between the Douve and the Blauwepoortbeek. The 12th Brigade's line of advance crossed Hun's Walk obliquely on the south of the Blauwepoortbeek, while the 13th Brigade would move along the spur south of the Wambeek, with its right on the Blauwepoortbeek alongside the left of the 12th. Artillery cover, including the creeping barrage, would be provided by the groups supporting the divisions that would be holding the Black Line objective—the 25th British for the 13th Brigade on the left and the NZ Division (including the 4th Division's guns) for the 12th Brigade on the right.[8] Those divisions would continue in overall control of the Black Line, which would by then have become the defensive support line, while the 4th Division controlled only its own infantry units in the advance. This arrangement contained the seeds of future difficulties, with the infantry firing line and its artillery support coming under different commands. Each brigade allocated eight Vickers guns of its MG Company to directly support the attacking infantry, the remainder of the machine guns remaining attached to the other II Anzac divisions to take part in the barrage covering the first attack.

The brigades' LTM batteries would provide further fire support, each sending four Stokes mortars forward with the infantry. A dozen British tanks were made available also, assistance that would have seemed of dubious value to 12th Brigade members who had survived First Bullecourt; the tanks' role was envisaged as only secondary, however. The 12th and 13th Field Companies and the Pioneer Battalion would move up once the objective was taken to assist with consolidating the captured trenches and to open up communication routes to the new front line. Much attention was paid to fully briefing the infantry, officers and men, on the details of the operation, including visits to a large-scale relief model of the battlefield that had been constructed in a field behind the lines.

Battalion commanders of the 13th Brigade, May 1917. Left to right: Lieutenant Colonel Harold Paul (49th Battalion); Lt Col Alfred Salisbury (50th); Lt Col John Cecil Ridley (51st); Lt Col Harold Pope (52nd).
(AWM E00641)

The Second Army's artillery bombardment had been building up in intensity through May. The 4th Division's field brigades, as part of the NZ Division's artillery, joined in the preliminary tasks of wire cutting and shelling of communication routes behind the enemy lines, firing by night and day. The batteries also registered their guns on their allocated barrage lines and took part in practice barrages fired in the last few days before the main attack. The 18-pounder batteries of the 4th Division brigades, 'E' Group, were selected to move their guns forward to advanced positions once the morning attack's objectives had been gained, from where they would cover the advance to the Green Line on their front. The forward positions were being prepared up to the night before the attack, and a party of linesmen from the divisional Signal Company under Sergeant Alexander Townsend went out to lay telephone wires to the new gun pits under heavy enemy shelling. The Division's Medium and Heavy Trench Mortar batteries, operating under the 3rd Division on the right of II Anzac's line, were also in action during the lead-up period. The MTMs concentrated on wire cutting while the awkward, slow-firing HTMs, sparingly used in previous campaigns, lobbed their huge shells on to the enemy front line trenches and strong-points. Z-day being set for 7 June, the shelling intensified from 31 May. The heavy artillery paid particular attention to counter-battery fire. British methods of locating enemy batteries by sound ranging and flash spotting had become increasingly accurate by this time in the war, aided by a heavy programme of aerial reconnaissance—the RFC held a clear advantage in the air above the Ypres/Messines sector, thanks to superior numbers and the recent introduction of improved aircraft. Initially the German guns retaliated to some effect, hitting a number of British batteries and ammunition dumps; three members of the 4th DAC, Sergeant Alfred Miles and Drivers Jock Noble and William Comrie, were each awarded the MM for extinguishing a fire in an 18-pounder dump, ignited by enemy shelling on the night of 27 May. The German guns were steadily silenced, however, and by Z-day the weight of their artillery retaliation had declined sharply.

Zero time for the great attack was set for 3:10 am on 7 June and on the previous night 4th Division HQ had moved forward from Bailleul to Westhof Farm, where the NZ Division HQ was also located. For the 4th Division infantry, who would not jump off for the second phase of the advance until 1:10 pm at the earliest, reveille in the reserve bivouacs near Neuve Eglise would be several hours after Zero, but many rose early and found vantage points to watch the show.[9] Precisely on time the first of nineteen huge mines under the German front line was detonated, the others going up in succession over the next twenty seconds:

> we see a movement as of an enormous black tin hat slowly rising out of the hill. Suddenly the great rising mass is shattered into a black cloud of whirling dust as a huge rosette of flame bursts from it and great flames lick, dancing and flickering. High up in the sky above the explosion we see a bank of dark clouds turn red from the reflection of the terrible burst below ... we get the appalling roar ... the ground rumbles, shivers and vibrates under us.[10]

Almost simultaneously the full force of the artillery opened up with over 2,000 guns and howitzers of all calibres, joined by batteries of machine guns sweeping their fire ahead of the shells, and the infantry of Second Army's three corps went forward behind the creeping barrage. In II Anzac's sector the 3rd Division infantry on the right had struck trouble earlier during their approach march through Ploegsteert Wood, having the ill-fortune to be caught in a German gas bombardment that incapacitated at least 500 men, but overall the first stage of the battle was the closest thing to a walkover that had occurred on the Western Front up to that time. The mines had utterly shattered the German front line. The few enemy troops who had survived there were completely demoralised and could only surrender. The attacking infantry then swept on to the German second line on the crest close behind the devastating creeping barrage. The Germans put up some resistance here, fighting in some places from their concrete 'pillbox' emplacements, but the shaken defenders were methodically overcome.

By 5:30 am the New Zealanders had captured Messines village, and the Black Line position had been occupied. The troops then turned to their picks and shovels to dig in and consolidate the new line—'to entrench themselves so strongly that the enemy could not retake the ridge, no matter how vehement his efforts.'[11] The Germans attempted several local counter-attacks but those were quickly shattered by the British artillery. It was now the turn of the 4th Division.

At 7:40 am the attacking battalions of the 12th and 13th Brigades left their camps and began the march to their jumping-off lines. The equipment to be carried by the troops in action, as recently specified by the staff,[12] consisted of: 170 rounds of ammunition; two Mills grenades; an entrenching tool; two sandbags; gas mask (box respirator and helmet); haversack with a spare pair of socks, an 'iron' ration and a preserved ration; waterproof sheet; and water bottle—one was specified, but the troops carried two on this day in the hot weather, a provision that proved to be inadequate. It was laid down that officers would be dressed the same as their men so as not to be too obvious to enemy snipers, but would carry revolvers rather than rifles. The leading elements reached the first assembly point, the old British front line below the ridge, at about 11 am, where they halted to await the next stage of the advance, due to begin in forty minutes. By that time the 4th Division artillery had brought up its horse teams and was on its way forward. At 10 am the guns had limbered up and moved off for their new positions in the vicinity of the presumably aptly named Stinking Farm, just behind the old front line. The batteries went through some scattered enemy shelling. One shell-burst killed the 11th AFA Brigade's veterinary officer, Captain William Ridley, who had volunteered to go forward with the column; he was one of only two AAVC officers to be killed in action on the Western Front.[13] The signaller Sergeant Townsend, 4th Division Signal Company, went up with the batteries to connect up their telephone lines as they came into position. By noon the guns were all in position and firing again.[14] It was probably one of these batteries that Private Ted Lynch (45th Battalion) noticed while his unit was waiting to continue the advance:

> The horses halt in a cloud of dust, the guns are swung round, horses unhitched and galloped back. A few curt orders are given and the guns roar into action doing rapid fire. We watch the gunlayer on the nearest gun ... his body jerks to the kicking recoil. Blood is streaming from his nose and ears but he never lets up—bleeding from concussion.[15]

At around the same time the Germans began to make effective countermeasures—artillery was brought up from reserve, and batteries to the south of the battle area, unaffected by the British counter-battery fire of previous days, began to fire methodically on the ridge. Infantry reinforcements began to reach the Oosttaverne Line. While the main body of the Australian infantry waited, intelligence officers and scouts went forward over the ridge and made their way down to the new outpost line to lay tapes marking the final jumping off position for their units, risking the artillery of both sides and fire from German infantry manning the Oosttaverne Line trenches. Here the 45th Battalion lost Lieutenant Robert Murray, who had distinguished himself in the Stormy Trench operations in February, and his assistant Lance Corporal Eric Kingel,[16] both killed by a shell just as they finished the task.

The final time of 'New Zero', although generally understood to be 1:10 pm, was still subject to final confirmation from Army HQ. The possibility of units being delayed in their approach was of particular concern in the centre of the front, where the IX Corps troops would have to cross the widest part of the original salient, a march of eight kilometres, to reach their jumping-off line. That force was late in starting anyway, and at 10 am General Plumer and his staff had decided to postpone the Green Line attack by two hours, to 3:10 pm. Communications through the various command levels were slow. Word of the postponement reached the 13th Brigade units just in time to delay their advance to the final jumping-off line until 1:40; the troops were held back in their assembly position behind the ridge. The message reached 12th Brigade HQ at 10:35 am but did not get through to its attacking units in time,[17] so the 45th and 47th Battalions, with carrying parties from the 46th, moved off at 11:40.[18] Initially forming files to cross the ridge, the troops first had to pass through the German barrage now dropping just behind the crest. This was accomplished with some losses, and the men formed into lines and continued down the slope towards the Black Line where the New Zealanders were dug in. One of the 47th's company commanders, Captain Francis Davy, was killed by a shell splinter during the approach. The 45th and 47th had passed over the Black Line and were nearing the tapes, coming under heavy machine gun fire from the right flank, when runners reached them with the word that the attack had been delayed by two hours. At first the troops went to ground and tried to find some cover from the increasing enemy fire, which now included shrapnel shelling, but some were pulled back to the New Zealanders' trench to wait out the postponement.[19]

An hour before New Zero was due the Germans mounted a counter-attack on their lost positions in this sector, but the attempt was broken well short of the line by artillery and machine gun barrages and by rifle and Lewis gun fire from the New Zealanders and the waiting 12th Brigade infantry. That task accomplished, with half an hour to go before New Zero, the 45th and 47th troops dashed forward through still-heavy enemy fire to the final jumping-off tapes. In the meantime the 13th Brigade's attacking battalions had moved off from their first assembly position at 1:40 pm for the advance to their jumping-off line. As they crested the ridge the troops came under fire from the flanking German artillery. Among the 52nd Battalion's casualties was the unit CO, Lieutenant Colonel Harold Pope, going forward with his staff to set up an advanced HQ. Colonel Pope was hit by a bullet or a piece of shell that broke his thighbone, a wound severe enough to end his active service career. Command of the 52nd devolved to the senior company commander, Captain Claude Stubbings, for the time being, leaving Captain Arthur Maxwell as the senior officer in the fighting line. On reaching the jumping-off line, the 49th Battalion on the 13th Brigade's right gained touch with the 45th on the left of the 12th Brigade, but the 52nd on the left flank found that their own left was 'in the air.' The troops of the 33rd British Brigade should have been in that position but they had been unable to complete their approach on time, and the 52nd's patrols found that there was a 400- metre gap to the nearest British troops. For the moment, Captain Maxwell sent a platoon across to extend his line, and a section of Vickers guns from the 13th MG Company took up positions to provide covering fire on the flank. Behind the two infantry brigades, the half-dozen tanks assigned to support them were lumbering over the crest of the ridge.

At 3:10 the covering artillery barrage began its creep towards the objective. The waiting infantry, bayonets fixed, advanced behind the curtain of shells, the leading battalions in two waves with two companies per wave, each company in four lines. The 4th Division troops were going into conditions quite different from those that had faced the morning attack. There had been no mines to obliterate the enemy garrisons, and the preliminary bombardment, directed largely at the first and second German lines and known battery positions, had left the trenches of the Green Line and the countryside beyond them relatively undamaged. The area was a patchwork of agricultural fields separated by thick hedgerows that gave cover and concealment to defensive outposts. Scattered across the fields were numerous farmhouses, many occupied by German detachments. The enemy trench line itself was strengthened by many concrete pillboxes. Most of these were shelters against shell-fire, from which the occupants had to emerge to fight, but others were self-contained strong-points with machine guns firing from loopholes. The new infantry platoon structure, with integrated sections of riflemen, Lewis gunners, 'bombers' and rifle grenadiers, would prove to be effective in overcoming isolated pillboxes, but those that were supported by crossfire from neighbouring positions formed highly dangerous obstacles to the attackers.

In the 52nd Battalion on the extreme left of the advance, Captain Maxwell was faced with the crucial dilemma of dealing with the wide gap to his left. To cover the empty area as well as his battalion's objective would thin out the line dangerously towards the right, but at least that flank had the rest of the 4th Division troops in position. Maxwell decided that the gap on the left had to be filled, and 'the huge Tasmanian, six feet five [195 cm] in his socks'[20] led his own company, in the second wave of the advance, angling across to the north-east towards the Wambeek valley. The Battalion's other three companies conformed by inclining to their left also, and inevitably a gap opened up between the right of the 52nd and the left of the 49th. The German trench that was the 52nd's intended objective was designated Odious Trench—the code names given to the trenches were arbitrary words beginning with the letter of the map square in which they were located, 'O' here and the adjoining 'U' to the south[21]—but the Battalion's frontage had now shifted to the northern segment of Odious and part of its continuation further north, Odour Trench. The creeping barrage had passed over the trench by the time the 52nd reached it and had changed to a protective barrage 300 metres beyond, but opposition was comparatively light and the 52nd quickly occupied the first enemy line. The second objective, the enemy support line, was thought to be a complete trench but it turned out to consist of only a few isolated segments. The Oosttaverne-Warneton road ran parallel to the front here, however, and Maxwell formed an advanced line along a stretch of the road, with its right just south of the Wambeek and its left at Joye Farm. From those points flanking posts were bent back to the main (Odious/Odour) trench, with further posts extending to the left and right along that trench. A short line of supports was dug in 100 metres to the rear of the main trench. Thinly spread, the 52nd now held part of the Green Line, but not the part that had been intended originally, and Captain Maxwell now set out to locate the tardy British troops.

The 49th Battalion, next on the south in the advance, became extended as it tried to conform to the 52nd's movement while keeping touch on the right with the 12th Brigade. The 49th ran into very tough opposition, particularly on its right advancing down the Blauwepoortbeek valley. Here two roads ran parallel to the stream, on the north and south slopes of the valley, the southern road forming the boundary between the brigades. Near that road German machine gun groups were posted in concrete shelters and a fortified farm, and others were in pillboxes further south near the German support line, all supported by more machine guns further to the east. These guns had survived the barrage and had an unobstructed field of fire down both sides of the valley, and they now opened intense fire on the leading elements of the 49th's right flank companies. The troops were stopped short of their objective, Odd Trench, with heavy losses to both the machine gun fire and the defensive shelling that was still sweeping over the area. Two parties from the companies on the left flank reached Odious Trench, one under Lieutenant Byrne Hart near the right-hand post of the 52nd, and the other, led by Lieutenant Frank Berriman, 300 metres to the south. Those two subalterns were the only officers of the 49th still in action of the twelve that had jumped off with the attack. All four company commanders—Captains Francis Bridgman, Francis Kay, Herbert Rhead and Hubert Selwyn-Smith, all original members of the Battalion—had been killed[22] and six of their juniors wounded. Lieutenant Berriman probed further south down the trench almost to the Blauwepoortbeek, finding neither friend nor foe in the trench on either side of the stream. He then swung his group back behind the occupied line and formed a flank guard facing south. The 49th, with losses of over 300 dead and wounded, could do nothing more for the moment.

On the southern flank the 12th Brigade battalions' advance made good progress at first. The creeping barrage was described as 'excellent,'[23] and several tanks came up in time to accompany the infantry as they went forward. One tank assisted the 45th Battalion on the Brigade left to capture Oxygen Trench, a section of communication trench that the Germans had manned as an outpost of their main line, with over 100 prisoners. The 47th on the right took the southern end of Oxygen Trench and fought its way along another communication trench, Unbearable. The 45th carried on to assault its objective in the enemy front line, Owl Trench in this sector. Machine gun fire from pillboxes near the trench forced the two wings of the attacking line to split and diverge to the flanks and the two waves of each wing became mixed together. The companies on the right, led by Captain Arthur 'Tubby' Allen—in the next war, Major General Allen, GOC 7th Division on the Kokoda Track—entered Owl Trench and worked along it to outflank a pillbox on that side.[24] The defenders were eliminated with grenades by a party under Second Lieutenant Alexander Muir. The final objective was the incomplete German support trench, Owl Support, 200 metres beyond, and Allen's men on the right resumed the advance to capture that position as well. The left-flank companies, however, ran into the devastating fire from the enemy machine gun nests and pillboxes where the trench crossed the roads running south of the Blauwepoortbeek. So many of the troops were cut down that the attack faltered and the survivors were forced to ground, although it appears that some elements managed to gain a foothold in Owl Trench[25]. Most of the leaders fell: the commander of 'C' Company, Captain William Young, was killed, as were his platoon commanders, and the only two sergeants who survived were both wounded. Private Lynch was in that charge:

> We are without officers to direct us, without NCOs except one lone corporal as far as I can see. We work onwards still. No longer charging, but just a few of us worming our way from shell hole to shell hole with men falling every metre or so … we crouch in shell holes, a mere handful of worn-out men, just a little isolated mob out of touch with the men on either side, facing an impossible task …[26]

(Lynch was in 'D' Company; according to the *Official History*, at the end of the Messines fighting, 'C' company was reduced to two corporals, two lance corporals and 19 privates unhurt).[27]

It was now 4:15 pm[28] and the 45th was holding at least the right segment of its first and second objectives in Owl Trench and Owl Support. On the 12th Brigade's right, the 47th Battalion, advancing behind the barrage into the tangle of enemy trenches straddling Hun's Walk, had taken thirty prisoners in clearing most of the outlying Unbearable Trench. Beyond this was the 47th's first objective in the main German line, the southern sector of Owl Trench and its continuation south of Hun's Walk, Uncanny Trench. The two companies forming the two waves of the 47th's left, north of the road, were forced to combine after heavy losses in the second wave company. Captain Edward Williams led those troops on to take both of their objectives in the enemy front and support lines, where they began to consolidate the captured trenches.[29] On the other side of the road the right flank companies encountered stiff resistance. 'B' Company in the lead came under machine gun fire as the barrage lifted but its commander, Captain John Millar, dashed ahead of his men along the trench, firing his revolver. He was not seen again, yet another company commander killed. The other officers in the company were killed or wounded as well and the survivors lost direction, angling off to their right. The second wave company came through the resulting gap and assaulted the enemy front line. Near the junction of Owl and Uncanny trenches the ground was studded with several pillboxes and the troops took those on in close-quarter fighting that reached a peak of savagery. Few prisoners were taken in that part of the battle—the troops who got up to a pillbox after seeing their friends cut down by the fire of its machine guns were in no mood to accept a last-moment surrender from the gunners. Many of the Germans in the front-line position fled for the rear to escape the bayonets, pursued by fighting-mad groups from the 47th's right-flank companies. The supposed support line trench ('Uncanny Support' in this area) was almost non-existent here and the charge went on for some distance beyond the line of the final objective before losing its impetus.[30] The troops then went to ground in whatever cover they could find among the hedges and shell holes, the few surviving officers organising a rough defensive line near a building that the troops called Hun House. Here they came under machine gun and sniper fire from positions concealed in the hedgerows, trees and ruined buildings of the countryside in the enemy rear. In the distance German infantry could be seen forming up to counter-attack.

By then, about 5 pm, the 4th Division's advance had reached the general line of its objectives along most of the front, but the situation was far from stable. On the left (north), the 52nd Battalion had established a thin line of posts in parts of the first and second objectives but mostly in the sector of the 33rd British Brigade. Scattered groups of British infantry had reached the battle zone after their excessive approach march and Captain Maxwell located some of these and sent them into the line, interspersed with his own troops. Others, assisted by two tanks, ousted the Germans from a strong point in the buildings of Van Hove Farm, just beyond the occupied line. For the time being, however, not enough British troops had come up for Maxwell to safely hand over the sector. The 49th Battalion, much reduced by casualties, held some posts further south but was prevented from extending further by the hornet's nest of German machine guns that dominated the Blauwepoortbeek valley. Lieutenant Berriman still held his flank guard post overlooking the valley, later strengthened by a section of Vickers guns from the 13th MG Company posted in the vicinity.

There was a gap of a kilometre south across the valley to the left of the 12th Brigade, the remnant of the 45th Battalion's two left flank companies stopped short of the second objective. On their right but out of touch on that side, Captain Allen with the other two companies was holding both objectives, in sight of the left flank of the 47th. That unit's two left companies under Captain Williams also held their final objective, but in turn were out of touch with the two companies on the right, which were holding a rough line beyond the objective. From there a further gap existed to the 3rd Division's 37th Battalion, advancing in the next sector to the south. By this time communications between the front line and the various headquarters had all but broken down. The continuing German shelling from beyond the right flank constantly cut field-telephone wires and hit or seriously delayed runners, as did the machine gun fire coming from ahead. Commanders at battalion level and above had little idea of where their men actually were, and in at least one instance the troops themselves made matters worse. Those of the 47th's right that had overrun their objective were spotted by the RFC's contact patrol aircraft, which signalled them with its klaxon horn. The arrangement was that the infantry would respond by lighting green flares so that the aviators could identify them and pinpoint their position, but 'most foolishly'[31] they did not do so, fearing that flares would give away their position to the Germans—who, as Private Denver Gallwey noted in his diary,[32] already knew where the Australians were located and were shooting at them. It was their friends who did not know their position, and it is possible that the aircraft crew mis-identified them as German in the absence of the agreed signal. There were apparently no officers involved in the decision not to use the flares, but another method of signalling to the rear was tried. Private Caleb 'Charlie' Shang, a diminutive 33-year-old of British-Chinese ancestry from Cairns, had taught himself the basics of signalling and he was now ordered by an unidentified officer[33] to signal to the rear giving the company's estimated location and requesting artillery support. This he did, using either semaphore flags or a signalling lamp that he had found and repaired (accounts differ[34]), standing up with only a tree for cover from enemy snipers, one of whom was later found to be hiding in the same tree. The 47th would gain no real advantage from his gallant act, but the fearless and tireless Shang continued to excel over the next few days of action, scouting, running messages under fire back to Battalion HQ, and returning to the firing line with ammunition and water.

It was the 12th Brigade units on the right that first faced enemy counter-attacks. At 5:30

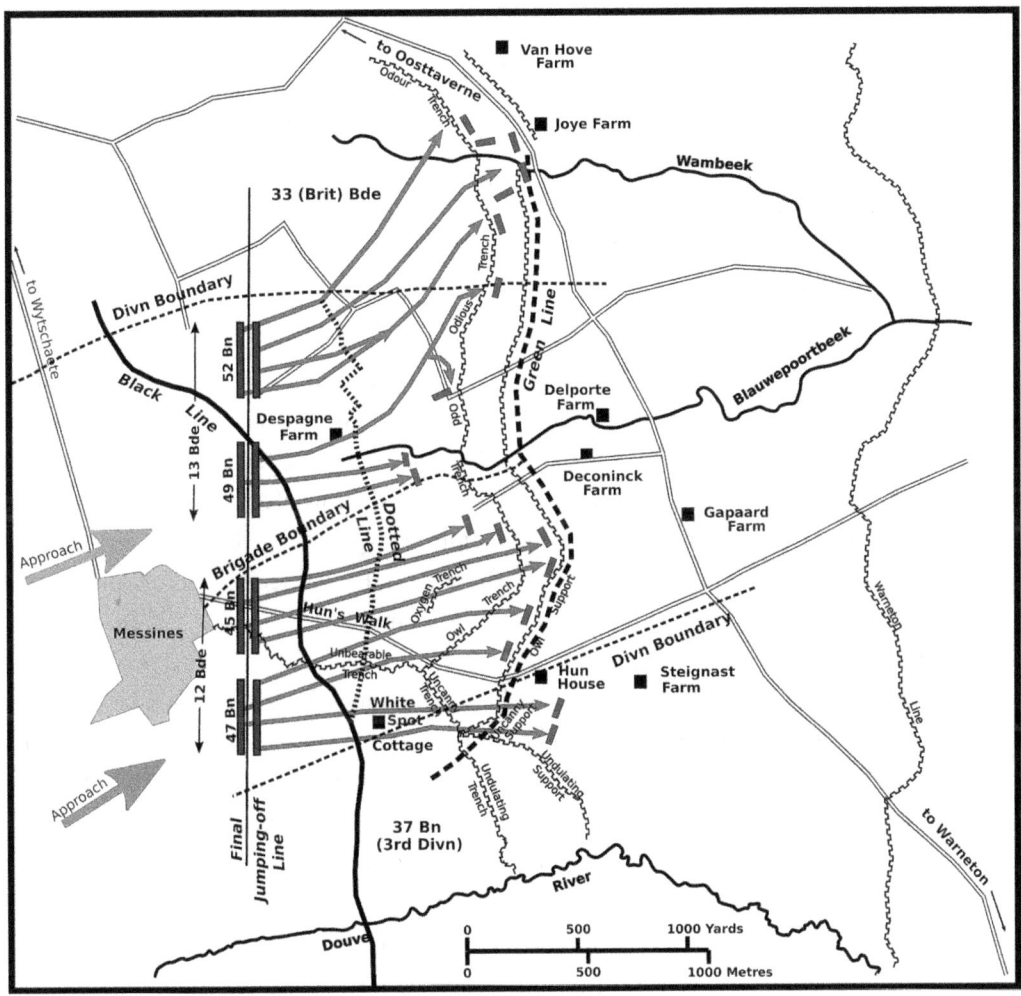

Battle of Messines, 7 June 1917, 4th Division's attack on the Oosttaverne Line; positions reached before retreat in the evening.

pm the enemy shelling died away and several lines of German infantry began to advance against the positions held by the 45th and 47th. The attack in front was broken up by rifle and Lewis gun fire, but on the left a part of the German force began to work around the open flank where the isolated remnants of the 45th's left companies had been hanging on in or near Owl Trench. In danger of being surrounded, the troops on that side pulled back towards the New Zealand line. That withdrawal seems to have been the immediate cause of a disastrous misunderstanding with the supporting artillery. The defensive barrage came down, falling not on the Germans but along a line to the rear of the Australian positions, then quickly lifting to engulf the men in the captured lines. Being shelled by their own artillery can break the morale of any troops, and most of the overstrained men in both battalions abandoned their positions and ran back for the Black Line. Even those in the firmly-held centre of the 12th Brigade's line, the two right companies of the 45th and the two left companies of the 47th, broke for the rear. Captain Williams of the latter unit was unable to stop the retreat, and as he later wrote

> I looked towards the 45th and could see Captain Allen standing up alone. The shelling had by this time passed over us so I went to him and told him the position; he was in great distress and said the same thing had happened to his company; we decided to go back and pick up some of our men; it seemed as if every machine gun in Germany was sweeping the area at this time.[35]

A few of the troops had stayed in position, probably those who had found some cover below ground level and had seen that it was more dangerous to run back in the open than to stay where they were. It seems that the barrage did move beyond the occupied objective line but was brought back to that line some time later.[36] How the mistake happened at all was never fully explained, although the divided command between the firing line and the support line must have been an underlying factor. In the 12th Brigade's report after the battle[37] Brigadier General Robertson stated that a New Zealand battalion CO had called for a barrage in front of the 'Dotted Line', the outposts ahead of the Black Line, having seen the left companies of the 45th Battalion retreating and assumed that the whole line was falling back. 12th Brigade HQ had not been consulted; there was a senior 4th Division artillery officer—Lieutenant Colonel Giffard King, CO of the 10th AFA Brigade—as liaison officer with 12th Brigade, a factor which might have made a difference if Brigade had been promptly informed of the situation. Other versions were that an SOS signal had been made, from 'somewhere in the rear'[38] or perhaps from as far to the left as the 13th Brigade's sector.[39] Private Shang's signal, made at about 5:30 pm, came from near or beyond the Green Line objectives in the 12th Brigade sector, although the position transmitted may have been misread. There were differing reports of the time that the barrage came down, ranging from 5:30 pm to 8 pm and 'just before dark.' 4th Division HQ (co-located with the NZ Division HQ at Westhof Farm) recorded receiving a message from the 47th Battalion 'timed 7:25pm' asking for artillery fire on Steignast Farm, a location beyond the final objective where counter-attack forces were seen to be assembling, but also on map reference U 4 a 8.2, a location in Uncanny Support trench, behind the line that the 47th had apparently reached.[40] None of the infantry accounts speak of artillery FOOs being with the forward troops, in a position to clarify the targets for their batteries. The sector was covered by the guns under control of the NZ Division, including the 4th Division's own 'E' Group artillery, which was firing from its advanced positions by this time. The artillery instructions for SOS barrages after the taking of the Green Line were imprecise,[41] in contrast to the detailed instructions for supporting the morning attack, a consequence of the comparative haste in which the plans for the Green Line attack were made. The batteries were to fire 'on Green' if the call came after 8:40 am, by which time the Black Line should have been consolidated—but did that mean the SOS line selected to defend the captured Green Line, or on the Green Line itself? At 8:40 am there would be no friendly troops forward of the Dotted Line, those of the 12th and 13th Brigades being still in the first stage of their approach march. For the next four to five hours the Oosttaverne (Green) line would not be an unreasonable target for interfering with an enemy counter-attack on the occupied Black Line, although the New Zealand artillery orders only show an SOS line 140 metres in advance of the Black Line in that situation.[42] Those orders also state that after the Green Line was taken the SOS zone would be 180 metres beyond it for all batteries except those of the advanced 'E' Group and the howitzers of 'H' Group, which were to fire on the 'approaches' to the Green Line. Direct communication between infantry and artillery had worked well enough in the morning's set-piece operation but could not cope with the more fluid situation in the afternoon attack. Possibly the barrage did have one positive aspect: it may have finished off the German counter-attacks in the sector, since they failed to re-occupy the trenches that the Australians had been shelled out of, and the enemy force which outflanked the 45th Battalion's left seems to have achieved nothing further.

The 13th Brigade troops north of the Blauwepoortbeek, covered by the 25th Division artillery, also had the unpleasant experience of short shooting, although with less serious consequences than in the 12th Brigade sector. Shells from both field and heavy artillery had been falling on the line held by the 52nd Battalion and even in its rear. Messages sent to the rear had no result, the shelling only increasing in severity after 8 pm, and by 9:15 the 52nd had been forced to withdraw its forward posts back to the support positions in and behind Odour Trench; the British troops holding the outpost in Van Hove Farm were also driven out of their position. Captain Maxwell then went back in person to find his Battalion HQ and get the shelling stopped. The message seems to have got through this time, as the errant guns eventually lengthened their range and the 52nd was able to re-establish its advanced line. Maxwell also came across the HQs of some British units that were now coming up to the forward area, and arranged for reinforcements to be sent up to his thin line. This may have taken some time; the British troops were disorganised after their long march and were described as 'nervy' and 'apprehensive' in several reports. Fortunately the only enemy action in this part of the front was a half-hearted infantry attack at 11:30 pm[43] that was easily dispersed.

The difficulties between infantry and artillery were not confined to the 4th Division sector: to their right, the 3rd Division battalions were also troubled by short shooting by their own Division's guns and were forced to pull back.

The sun had gone down over the battlefield by that time, but the commanders and their staffs from battalion level upwards had figuratively been in the dark for some time already. The disruption of all forms of communication from the fighting line meant that minimal information had come to even the battalions' forward HQs near the Black Line, which themselves had come under enemy shelling; the 47th Battalion HQ in particular had as many as 35 casualties.[44] It appears to have been two to three hours after the event that 12th Brigade HQ became aware that their battalions had been forced back from the captured objectives, and as long or later before 13th Brigade HQ realised that the 49th Battalion had been stopped short of its objective and the 52nd was stretched into the British sector. The information, sketchy as it was, was sent on to Division and Corps and both brigadiers sent up their reserves to retrieve the situation. In the 47th Battalion Lieutenant Colonel Imlay had already sent forward his adjutant, Lieutenant Norman Bremner, to find out what had happened to the companies on the right; early in the battle, the 47th had been getting information from a forward observation post under the intelligence officer, Lieutenant Charles Scott, but Scott had been killed at about 5 pm. Lieutenant Bremner managed to locate and reorganise the scattered elements of 'B' Company, which had lost all of its officers killed or wounded, and by 10 pm had got them into position somewhere near the line of the objective and linked with other groups of the 47th still in the vicinity. Returning to the main line, Bremner picked up Lieutenant Clifford Mendoza, lying severely wounded on Hun's Walk, and began carrying him back. On the way they were attacked by a group of five Germans who had been bypassed during the original advance. They had chosen the wrong opponent—Lieutenant Bremner shot all five with his revolver, killing four and wounding the fifth, who he brought in as a prisoner. The 45th Battalion's adjutant, Lieutenant Arthur Varley, also went up to the firing line from Battalion HQ to help in reorganising the unit.

Nightfall had brought much other activity in support of the infantry in the fighting line. Carrying parties and the Pack Transport Troop brought rations and ammunition forward, while pioneers and engineers began work on improving the positions on the battlefield. At 10:30 pm two companies of the 4th Pioneer Battalion, under Captain John Calder, started a new communication trench from the Black Line in the 13th Brigade's sector past Despagne Farm towards Odd Trench, the objective line north of the Blauwepoortbeek. Digging through for 1,000 metres almost to the trench, the Pioneers expected to find it occupied by the infantry but instead encountered two Germans repairing the wire. These were promptly taken prisoner but the Pioneers then came under enemy machine gun fire. Odd Trench in this area was obviously still in German hands and the Pioneers withdrew to a safer distance. From there work continued on the communication trench although water seepage meant that it had to remain shallow (the Pioneers went out again the next night to lay duckboards and build up the parapets with sandbags). The other two 4th Pioneer companies had been allocated to construct a communication trench to the front line (Owl Trench) in the 12th Brigade's sector. A reconnaissance found that the captured Unbearable Trench was already usable for the purpose, so the pioneers instead dug a trench back from the Black Line across the ridge just south of Messines village, to provide some protection for troops coming forward over the crest.[45] In this sector the 12th Field Company engineers were responsible for organising construction of various fieldworks, and in late afternoon the company OC, Major Consett Riddell, had gone forward himself with a small party of sappers to reconnoitre the area and select positions for new trenches and transport routes. German shelling scattered the group and Major Riddell was stunned by a piece of flying debris. It was 10:50 pm before he regained consciousness and found himself alone on the battlefield. The area was still being shelled, but Riddell was undeterred and continued forward to reach the vicinity of White Spot Cottage, on the way to the objective line that the infantry had been forced out of earlier. The major went on further and reconnoitred along the abandoned Owl Trench before walking back to 12th Brigade HQ to make his report, having discovered a cache of documents in an abandoned German headquarters on the way.[46]

In the meantime, at 9:20 pm Brigadier General Robertson had ordered the 48th Battalion to send two companies forward, one each to reinforce the 45th and 47th. Those reached the respective battalion HQs at about midnight. By that time Division and Corps had become aware of the withdrawal from the Green Line and had ordered its recapture. The problems with artillery barrages had now been reported also and the Corps commander, General Godley, had ordered that the barrage must stay to the east of the Green Line. The 12th Brigade's operation to retake the objective was to begin at 3 am (8 June) and the remaining two companies of the 48th Battalion were also ordered forward to further reinforce the 45th and 47th. The 48th companies themselves were well short of full strength, the Battalion having not yet made up all of its losses from Bullecourt. The 13th Brigade, also operating on sketchy information from the fighting line, brought up its reserves as well. Brigadier General Glasgow had already ordered the 51st Battalion to send two companies forward to reinforce the 52nd at about 9 pm, and an hour later another company was sent to the 49th. The 51st's final company was ordered forward, also to the 49th, at 11:35, by which time it had become known that the 49th had not reached its objective and that a gap existed at the Blauwepoortbeek valley.

Continuing poor communications caused the 12th Brigade's 3 am attack to miscarry, runners with the orders getting to the battalions' forward HQs only a few minutes before Zero. This left not enough time to deploy for an organised advance, particularly as the depleted 47th and 45th would mainly be using the attached reinforcing companies from the 48th, which had only just reached the front and were not familiar with the ground. At 3:50 am the Division GOC, Major General Holmes, went forward in person to the HQs of his brigades to find out why the attack had not started and found that neither of the brigadiers had any information either. The GOC then took Glasgow and Robertson with him further forward to confer with the 45th and 47th Battalion COs, who informed the generals that although the formal attack had not come off an advance was being carried out by the 48th Battalion companies.[47] That unit's two companies with the 47th, under Captains Derwas Cumming and Joseph Mayersbeth, had been instructed by Colonel Imlay to move up to the Black Line and from there to push forward as far as possible, so as to be in a forward position if the attack was re-scheduled. Dawn was approaching when the 48th troops completed lining up and began cautiously advancing in extended formation towards the Green Line. There was very little enemy fire to contend with and after about 150 metres the line came across the traces of an old trench, which gave enough cover to serve as a jumping-off position. The troops paused there and Captain Cumming sent out a small patrol from his company, under Lieutenant Charles Stoerkel, to probe further forward. The patrol found that the outlying Oxygen Trench, captured then abandoned earlier, had not been re-occupied by the enemy, so one platoon (the companies, still below strength after Bullecourt, comprised only two platoons) was sent forward to occupy it. From here Lieutenant Stoerkel's patrol pushed forward again and reached Owl Trench, which was also found to be empty, and the second platoon was sent up to occupy it. Enemy machine gun fire was now coming from the trees beyond the trench but the platoon got through with only four casualties. The rest of the company then moved up from Oxygen Trench, followed by Captain Mayersbeth's company. Captain Williams of the 47th then brought up the 80 men that he had collected from the previous night's retreat and took up position in Oxygen Trench in support. For the third time Lieutenant Stoerkel took his patrol out, now looking for the final Green Line objective, Owl Support, part of which was a complete trench in this sector. This was located and again found to be undefended. Half of the force in Owl Trench was sent forward to occupy the position which they managed with light casualties, even though it was daylight by now and the approaches were still under fire. In Owl Support the troops discovered a Lewis gun team of the 47th, who had decided to hold their ground when most of their battalion had pulled back on the previous evening (presumably, there were other parties of the 47th remaining in either Owl or Owl Support, or both, further to the right, the troops that Lieutenant Bremner had brought into position during the night). Once more Lieutenant Stoerkel took his patrol out into enemy territory but this time his luck ran out and he was seriously wounded by a sniper. The 48th troops then settled in to consolidate, having regained by audacious movement tactics a considerable length of the positions lost the night before.

On the left of the Brigade sector the other two companies of the 48th Battalion reinforcing the 45th, also informed too late of the proposed 3 am attack, had been waiting for further instructions. One of the company commanders, Lieutenant John Stabback, observed the advance of the other 48th companies in the 47th's sector to his right. Word shortly came through that Owl Trench had been entered, and Stabback arranged with Colonels Herring and Imlay to take his and Lieutenant Archibald Allen's company forward also. The troops reached Owl Trench without a casualty, to the left of Cumming and Mayersbeth's men, and began probing further to the left along the trench towards the Blauwepoortbeek. After some distance, just past an empty pillbox captured in the original advance, German troops were encountered and Stabback sent a message to Colonel Herring suggesting a bombing attack up the trench. Herring ordered that this should not take place before nightfall, when he would use the 45th's own troops. A barricade was constructed to guard the flank in the meantime. Three advanced posts were established beyond Owl Trench, north of Hun's Walk—Sergeant Harry Whittle went out into the open to select the positions one at a time and post the men, disdaining to take cover from the enemy fire. Later in the morning Second Lieutenant George Mitchell, now the 48th Battalion Lewis gun officer, came up to the captured position with his sergeant, Herbert Shepherdson, and set about positioning the battalion's Lewis guns to form a bastion guarding the left flank.[48] Shepherdson collected two captured German machine guns, cleaned them and set them up in the new strongpoint also. Enemy snipers were proving dangerous. Private Leigh Kilpatrick, a 42-year old Scottish-born WA goldfields timber worker who had enlisted under the name of Robert Leigh Kirkpatrick, crawled out into the open to stalk and kill two of them.[49] The 48th CO, Lieutenant Colonel Leane, visited the position about midday. He found the troops 'digging hard' and firmly holding a considerable length of the previous day's objectives, particularly in the 47th's original sector.[50]

> Thus, north of Hun's Walk, through an exceptionally fine combination of enterprise and cool judgement on the part of battalion and company leaders, the objectives seized in the original attack had been reoccupied before the Germans had taken advantage of the previous night's withdrawal.[51]

A little later the 3rd Division's 44th Battalion came up on the 48th's right and made contact, but the gap at the Blauwepoortbeek Valley between the 12th and 13th Brigades still remained in German hands. The 13th Brigade had its own issues stabilising its line and completing the capture of its objectives. The brigade's firing line had been reinforced during the night, with the 51st Battalion sending up two companies each to the 52nd and 49th. This left the 51st CO, Lieutenant Colonel Cecil Ridley, with only his headquarters details to command, and Brigadier General Glasgow decided to send him forward to take over the 52nd in place of the wounded Lieutenant Colonel Pope. Ridley reached the 52nd's advanced HQ at 4:10 am and relieved Captain Stubbings, who had been acting CO since the previous afternoon. Ridley then went around the front line with Stubbings to see the situation for himself. It was apparent that the 52nd was still holding a large part of the British sector, and the two officers confirmed that the 49th's objective in the valley was still in enemy hands. Before anything decisive could be done the line would need to be reorganised and troops put into position to attack the Blauwepoortbeek gap. Glasgow decided to withdraw the 52nd and send it around to the south of the 49th's present position, where it would then come back into the line facing the gap and ready to attack (as Colonel Ridley pointed out in his report,[52] a large proportion of the numbers in those units, particularly in the 49th Battalion, were attached troops of the 51st). It was a prerequisite that troops of the 33rd (British) Brigade would be required to take over their correct front and relieve the 52nd. Before this could be organised, Glasgow had to personally take a British battalion commander around the front line to convince the latter that the 33rd Brigade units were not in their allotted sector.[53] That settled, it was arranged that the redeployment would begin at dusk, with the attack to be launched later in the night.

The 13th Brigade units held their positions during the day of 8 June, after a burst of fighting mid-morning. At 9:30 or 10 am, on a section of the front held by part of the 52nd interspersed with Lincolnshire regiment troops, groups of German infantry were noticed creeping forward into shell holes, evidently trying to establish a line from which to launch a counter-attack. The 52nd sent out a bombing party of 20 men under Second Lieutenant Leonard Boase to drive the enemy away. In a short grenade duel Boase's men completely outfought the Germans, who broke and fled, into the fire of Lewis guns and rifles that cut down many of the survivors; 40 prisoners were later brought in. At a cost of three killed and four wounded, the 52nd's small force had virtually annihilated a full German company in a display of ruthless efficiency that was perhaps not previously characteristic of the unit. During the afternoon an SOS artillery barrage was called in to break up another potential enemy counter-attack. The 13th Brigade's redeployment began as planned when British units arrived at dusk to relieve the 52nd Battalion, but the movement was almost immediately disrupted by a deluge of artillery shelling that broke out at 8:45 pm across the battlefield. First the German guns put down a heavy barrage on the support lines behind the 52nd, then the troops in that area, thinking themselves under attack, fired the SOS signal and brought down the British defensive barrage. Once again, at least some of the 'friendly' shelling fell short onto and behind the 13th Brigade's positions, and for the next two hours the 'terrific' firing continued, spreading across most of the II Anzac front.

The 52nd's orders were to pull back at 9 pm in any circumstances, and elements of the battalion vacated their trench and ran back through the barrage, losing casualties and becoming scattered in the process. 'The sight of the troops running gave rise to a score of alarmist reports that the 4th Division was retiring in confusion.'[54] Captain Maxwell decided to hold back the troops under his direct control until the shell-fire slackened, then made sure that the units in the rear, described in more than one report as 'jumpy,' were aware that his withdrawal was a planned movement. The delays and disorganisation caused by the shelling, however, had prevented the 52nd from getting into position in time for the proposed night attack. Meanwhile the 49th Battalion (that is, the two attached companies of the 51st) had extended its right down Odious Trench towards the road on the north slope of the Blauwepoortbeek valley.[55] Those troops now prepared to deploy for the attack into the valley (Captain Charles Duchatel, the 13th MG Company OC, was in the vicinity oversighting his gun teams and took it on himself to lay the tape for the jumping-off line) but the shelling again prevented an orderly assembly. Among the casualties was the 49th CO, Lieutenant Colonel Paul, evacuated with a serious leg wound—the 49th had now lost its CO and all of its company commanders to enemy action. The brigadier turned again to the 51st Battalion HQ for a temporary replacement, sending that unit's second-in-command, Major Albert Rowe, to take command of the 49th until the unit's own second-in-command, Major William Arrell, could come forward and take over (he was with the left-out-of-battle nucleus at the time). With both battalions out of position and in no condition to launch an attack, the operation was postponed.

In the 12th Brigade sector, the companies of the 48th holding the reoccupied lines were joined at about 5:30 pm by the remaining fit men of the 45th who could be collected, probably no more than 50 to 60 men organised as a single company under Captain Allen; he was now the only company commander of the 45th still in action, Major George Knox and Captain John Hand having been wounded during the day. Allen's troops came in on the left of the 48th and began a grenade and bayonet attack that pushed further up the trench towards the Blauwepoortbeek, gaining perhaps 200 metres before being stopped by the pair of heavily-defended pillboxes near the southern road. Nothing more could be done without support, and the extended flank was barricaded. During the evening German infantry were observed assembling for a counter attack on the left, but this was broken up by fire from the troops in the trench and an accurate artillery barrage. At some time during the night, Captain Allen sent Lieutenant Thomas McIntyre to scout across the valley, where he made contact with an outpost of the 51st Battalion. The gap had been reduced but still remained to be taken. During the night Corps HQ had taken steps to resolve the issue of the divided command between the front (Green) line and the support (Black) line. As of the morning of 9 June the one division would control a sector of the battle area from the front line to the rear. This meant that 4th Division HQ continued to control the 12th Brigade's sector of the front and also took over the corresponding sector of the Black Line, presently held by a New Zealand brigade. At the same time 13th Brigade initially came under the 25th British Division's command; it would be relieved by units of that division on the following night (9/10 June) but only after making a further attempt to close the Blauwepoortbeek gap. On that night also, the 4th Brigade came up to relieve the NZ Division units holding the Black Line. Command of the field artillery groups covering the 4th Division's front passed from the NZ Division to the 4th Division CRA, Brigadier General Rosenthal, as of 5 pm on 9 June; the guns of the 25th British Division also came under his control two days later.

The morning of 9 June passed without major fighting, but the German guns continued to play on the ridge, interfering with forward movement of supplies and reinforcements and casualty evacuation. Captain Roy Winn of the 4th Field Ambulance (formerly 14th Battalion RMO) had been working in the forward area under fire throughout the battle, although slightly wounded himself. On this day, leading a group of stretcher bearers to clear the 45th Battalion's RAP, he was badly hit by a shell splinter, losing his right foot.[56] A day earlier, another 4th Field Ambulance member, Sergeant Archibald Wilkins, ignored his own head wound and continued supervising his team of bearers under heavy shelling, at one point staying with a wounded man for three hours out on the slope. Up forward the troops in the firing line worked on consolidating their positions. The 48th Battalion dug to improve its outposts above Hun's Walk, covered by fire from a section of the 12th LTM Battery's Stokes mortars under Lieutenant Harry Coward. In the afternoon, Captain Allen's group of the 45th tried a surprise attack against the nearer of the pillboxes blocking the left flank in Owl Trench, but the German garrison proved to be too alert and responded with machine gun fire and a shower of grenades. The 45th could do no more than advance the flank for a short distance down the trench. A major effort to close the gap would be made that night, mainly in the 13th Brigade's sector. Brigadier General Glasgow brought up his last reserve, the 50th Battalion, to spearhead the attack, with Zero set for 10:30 pm. The attack was to be 'silent', with no artillery support, so as to avoid warning the enemy. The 50th CO, Lieutenant Colonel Alfred Salisbury, had been informed from optimistic reports that the part of the front line still held by the enemy, Odd Trench in this sector, was no more than 410 metres wide, but the 50th soon found that this was at least 180 metres understated.

The attack was launched on time but was immediately detected by the German defenders, who opened fire and called in their artillery. The 50th kept their advance going through a hail of fire, coming particularly from the cluster of fortifications near the road. Near the trench uncut wire was encountered, an obstacle that had not been anticipated, and as Colonel Salisbury ruefully reported, 'our attack came to a standstill, some men dropping into shell-holes in front of the wire, others where they came under the heavier machine gun fire scattering back to the jumping off line.'[57] A small party under Captain James Churchill Smith, who had distinguished himself at Mouquet Farm in 1916, managed to enter Odd Trench and work their way to the right for 50 metres before being stopped by machine gun fire, while another group found some cover just short of the wire. With daylight, the latter party came under fire from the German trench and was forced to withdraw. Earlier the units to the north, the 49th and 52nd Battalions and their reinforcing companies of the 51st, had been relieved by British units and withdrawn to positions behind the Messines ridge. That left the 50th Battalion, mostly back behind its start line, facing the 13th Brigade's original objective line in the valley. South of the gap the 45th Battalion had made another attempt during the night against the pillbox on that side, but were again driven back by the German machine guns. After midnight the 12th Brigade sent up its remaining battalion, the 46th, which up to then had been providing carrying parties to support the other units. The 46th relieved the 48th Battalion in the line, but not the exhausted remnant of the 45th, which continued to hold the left flank on the gap. The 48th withdrew to a support trench to rest and reorganise. On the right of the 12th Brigade sector the 47th Battalion sent forward several fighting patrols to probe the country beyond the captured line, after reports that the Germans appeared to have retreated in that area. Sharp clashes with enemy posts proved that the Germans were still established in strength and the patrols returned with half of their numbers as casualties.[58]

By dawn on 10 June the 4th Division's front was held by the 50th Battalion on the left, with the remaining 13th Brigade troops well to the rear but available to come up in support, and the

45th, 46th and 47th Battalions on the right, supported by the 48th. The night's operations had edged the inner flanks slightly inwards, but the Blauwepoortbeek gap remained as formidable as ever. For the second time in the battle, Major General Holmes went forward to assess the situation in person, accompanied by Brigadier General Robertson and Major Joseph Lee, assistant brigade major (ex-45th Battalion and later the unit historian).[59] Holmes came right up to the flanking barricade in the 12th Brigade's front line in Owl Trench and used a periscope to observe the German pillboxes that were blocking progress. The general decided to have the area bombarded by artillery during the day and to renew the infantry attack that night, with the 13th Brigade attacking the gap from in front and the 12th pushing its flank along the trench. Heavy artillery was brought in to pound the enemy front line and two fortified farms to its rear, Delporte and Deconinck, thought to be the source of long-range machine gun fire. The heavies would cease fire at 9 pm. Direct cover for the infantry attack would be provided by the 4th Division's own 'E' Group 18-pounders. Three batteries would put down a standing barrage just beyond the two farms, and with the attack being on a fairly narrow front two batteries were allocated to fire a creeping barrage on the trench lines. The barrage was to commence five minutes before Zero, then lift at Zero on to the support line for another three minutes before lifting again to the line of the standing barrage.[60] This would have given little time for the 13th Brigade infantry to get up to the objective from a start line 300 metres away, but it appears to have been arranged for the infantry to actually jump off as soon as the barrage fell.[61] The 13th Brigade would use the 50th and 52nd Battalions, the latter unit coming forward from its resting position behind the ridge. The Zero time itself was an issue; it was set for 10:30 pm and Brigade orders were that the jumping-off line was to be marked with tape and the infantry lined out by 10 pm. From the 50th's experience of the previous night, Colonel Salisbury was aware that there would still be some light at 10 pm and the troops were likely to be spotted while moving into position. He felt that the time should have been at least 30 minutes later, but the orders stood.

Coming from well to the rear, the 52nd Battalion began their forward march at 8 pm. The troops were observed as they crested the ridge, and heavily shelled by the German guns. The 52nd took some casualties, and among the wounded was Captain Stubbings, the senior company commander, so Captain Maxwell again took charge. The 50th Battalion also came under enemy artillery fire; the officer detailed to lay the jumping-off tape was wounded, but the 50th managed to assemble without it. Coming up on the 50th's right, the 52nd had been delayed and disorganised by the shelling, and only two companies reached the front, barely on time, in unfamiliar territory and with no tape to indicate the line. Captain Maxwell took it upon himself to crawl forward under fire and mark out part of the frontage with a tape; the 52nd's remaining companies were mistakenly guided into a wrong position, and were further delayed in reaching the start line. The covering barrage came down on schedule and the 50th Battalion went forward behind it. Some gaps had been blown in the wire, and the South Australians were able to get to close quarters, particularly on the left, where

Captain Churchill Smith's small group, still occupying their post in the trench, joined in with covering fire. After a sharp fight with hand- and rifle-grenades and bayonets, the 50th troops entered the trench as the German defenders broke and ran for the rear. On the right the two companies of the 52nd, starting late, were caught by the German defensive barrage and lost heavily as they advanced. Nearing the enemy trench, they were confronted with uncut wire and a shower of grenades, and the attack was stopped. The troops withdrew and reorganised, joining with some from the misdirected companies now coming up, and tried again further to the left. Entering the trench where it was held by the 50th, the 52nd group began bombing down it to the right (south). They were able to push for some distance down the trench, Lieutenant Boase again distinguishing himself in this fighting, before being held up by the still-unconquered machine guns on the southern slope of the valley.

On that flank, the 12th Brigade's efforts to close the gap had once more been blocked by the formidable pillboxes near Owl Trench and the machine guns covering them from the rear. The flank was still held by the remnant of the 45th Battalion, down to their last fifty or so fit men and those utterly spent—it was said that some had fallen asleep in the act of digging during the previous night.[62] They should surely have been relieved before now but instead they were ordered to again tackle the nearer pillbox, still undamaged after the heavy artillery bombardment, which had been unable to get a direct hit on it. A telephone line had been laid through to the trench and the Battalion CO spoke directly to the nominated attack leader, Lieutenant Thomas McIntyre. The account in the *Official History* makes distressing reading:

> ... when Colonel Herring during the afternoon telephoned to Lieutenant McIntyre, who had already led three attempts, and told him that the strong-point must be taken, McIntyre, knowing this was his death-warrant, answered simply: 'All right, Sir, if it is to be taken, it will be taken.' At 10 o'clock he and his men went straight for it, 'over the top.' The surrounding machine guns opened as usual. Five yards from the blockhouse McIntyre and Sergeant [Alfred] Stevenson were killed, and the attack failed.[63]

The survivors of the 45th Battalion were at last relieved after that final effort, the 48th Battalion coming up again from support to take over and completing the relief by 3 am (11 June). It is difficult to understand why the 45th was left in the line for so long after its losses and then again given the task of taking the pillbox. The 46th had just come up to the line and would have been reasonably fresh, while the 48th, although below strength and suffering a number of casualties during its previous short stint in the line, would have been in considerably better shape than the 45th. Possibly 12th Brigade HQ was unaware of the true situation of the 45th, but Colonel Herring must have been aware, considering that he was in voice communication with his front line. It could be concluded that the CO was reluctant to acknowledge that his unit could do no more, allowing considerations of prestige to override both humanity and military common sense.

The 47th Battalion was also relieved overnight, the 46th extending to take over the right

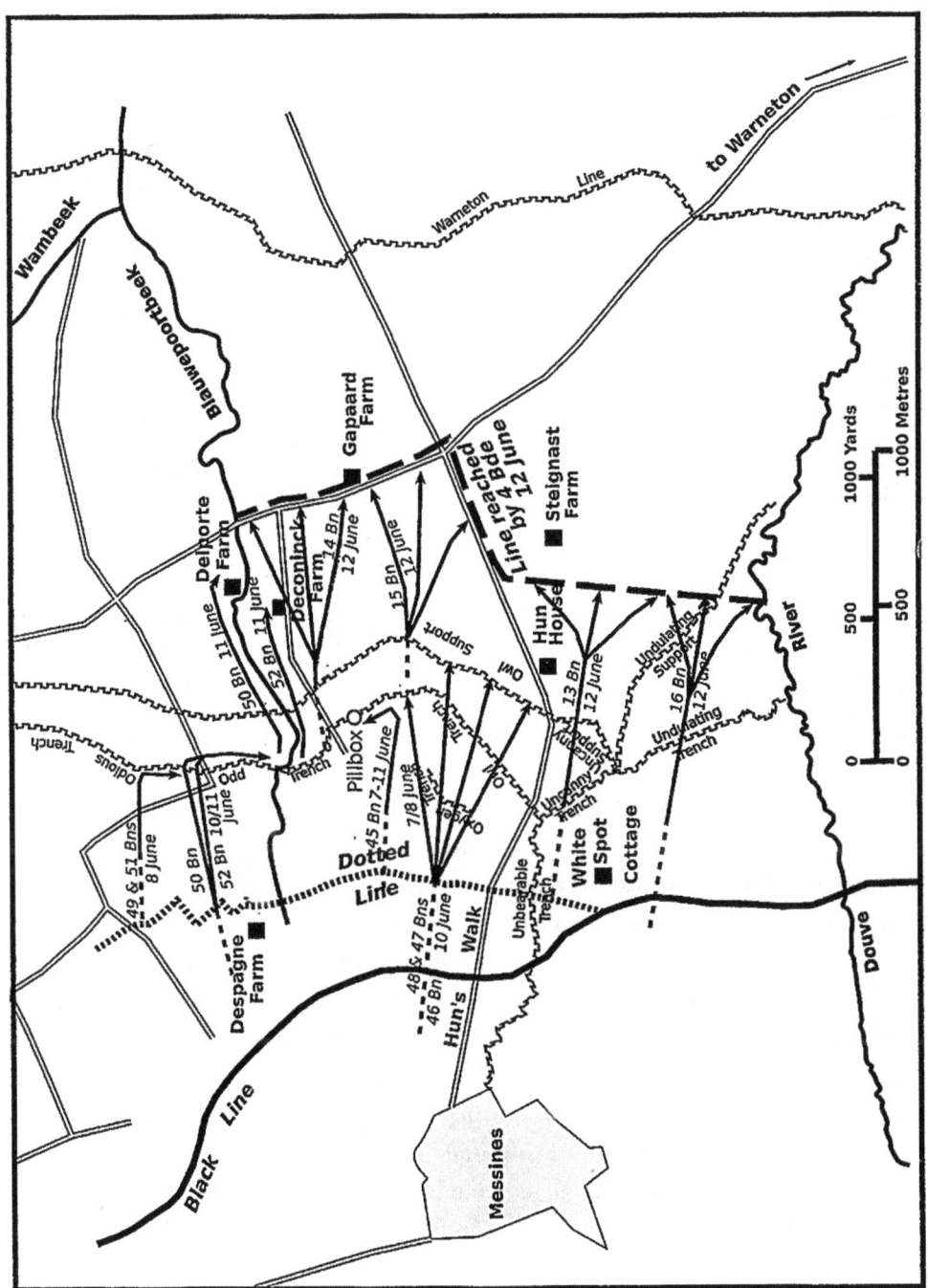

Battle of Messines 8 to 12 June 1917: second phase of 4th Division's operations.

The pillbox in Owl Trench at Messines that resisted several attacks by the 45th Battalion. (AWM E01366)

of the 12th Brigade position. The morning of 11 June found the gap closed somewhat, with the 50th and 52nd Battalions holding the captured line on the north and the 48th and 46th to the south. With daylight, observers in the trench were astonished to see that the Germans were withdrawing from their second line. Patrols from both brigades pushed along the trench and found that the troublesome strong-points had been evacuated by the enemy. The German high command had decided to withdraw to their next line, the Warneton Line, and there was no point in them continuing to occupy the isolated posts in the Blauwepoortbeek valley— the 45th Battalion's final effort had been unnecessary. The German units that had held the fortifications in the valley were not identified, although they were probably part of the 1st Guards Reserve Division; they were certainly troops of high morale, and their determination had cost the Australians dearly. In any case, the two brigades had gained touch on their inner flanks and the gap was at last closed. While the first line was consolidated, patrols probed out towards the enemy second line (Odd Support and Owl Support trenches, the final Green Line), driving away snipers and occupying several strong-points between the lines. The 48th Battalion's daring young scout, Corporal Tom Arnold, led a patrol that occupied two blockhouses containing enemy field guns and later eliminated a machine gun post near Gapaard Farm.[64] At dusk, the Green Line was reported to have been reached and occupied, and both brigades sent further patrols deeper into the fields beyond the line. A party from the 50th Battalion occupied Delporte Farm, and another post was established by the 52nd at nearby Deconinck Farm, 250 metres out from the Green Line. That night both brigades' sectors south of the Blauwepoortbeek were relieved by the 4th Brigade, coming up from support in the Black Line, with British troops taking over north of the stream. The 13th Brigade moved back to the old front line behind the ridge, forming a reserve force for the advanced lines, and the 12th Brigade took the 4th's place in the Black Line.

The 4th Brigade sent its 14th and 15th Battalions in on the left, with the other two units extending to take over part of the 3rd Division front to the south, up to the River Douve. The 15th Battalion patrolled as far forward as Gapaard Farm, a party under one of the unit's best officers, Lieutenant Percy Toft, occupying that point. North of Gapaard the 14th Battalion, relieving the 50th and 52nd, sent the companies of Captains Reg Jones and Albert Jacka to skirmish forward and establish outpost positions. During the relief a curious incident occurred involving Jacka and the 52nd Battalion's Captain Arthur Maxwell. The 52nd's report states that 'the OC of the relieving company of the 14th refused to occupy Deconinck Farm ... on this being reported to Lieutenant Colonel Salisbury [as senior officer in the sector] he refused to consider the relief of the Brigade Sector complete and instructed the Farm be reoccupied by our Battalion.'[65] Jacka believed that the farm was too far ahead of the main line to be tenable but Maxwell intervened, and after some discussion Jacka agreed to take a party of the 14th forward to occupy the post, thereby completing the relief. According to C E W Bean, however, there was rather more to the story. Bean noted at the time that Maxwell went out to the Farm himself with Jacka and some of the latter's men:

> J[acka] took over and at once reported that he had captured Delporte Farm [sic; Deconinck was meant] ... for this he and 14 Bn are at once being given the credit. As a matter of fact Arthur Maxwell and 52 Bn did it.

[Bean then noted his opinion that]

> Jacka is the sort of chap who would probably hang back while Arthur was there, in order to get the credit for himself and 14 Bn by going out later.[66]

Without knowing Albert Jacka's views, it is not easy to judge the full truth of that story; Bean had a family connection with the Maxwells, but although he admired Jacka's accomplishments, he did not particularly like him. Nevertheless, it is interesting as an instance of tension between two strong men, among the 4th Division's most distinguished front-line officers.

In the 24 hours following its relief of the front line, the 4th Brigade advanced II Anzac's perimeter to within 700 metres of the next line of German defences, the Warneton Line. On the night of 12/13 June the brigade was relieved in turn by a brigade of the 25th British Division, and that Division's HQ took over control of the sector from the 4th Division. The 4th Brigade moved back to camps behind Hill 63, temporarily designated as the reserve brigade for the 25th Division. The 12th and 13th Brigades with their supporting arms moved back to billets in the rest and training area south-east of Bailleul, with the medical units, engineers and pioneers coming out of the forward area over the next few days. Division HQ remained at Westhof Farm for the time being and the divisional artillery stayed in the line, but only for a few days this time. The 10th and 11th AFA Brigades, by now with their howitzer batteries rejoined, continued in action with routine fire tasks. These included covering the successful advance towards the Warneton

Line on 14 June, that date marking the official end of the battle. During the action, the 10th AFA Brigade had its main ammunition dump hit by enemy shelling. A fatigue party from the 110th Howitzer Battery was working there at the time and the entire party became casualties in the resulting explosion, with 18 killed and eight wounded.[67] The artillery brigades came out of the line on the night of 17/18 June, moving back to join their wagon lines in the La Crèche area. Division HQ moved back from Westhof Farm to Vieux Berquin next day.

The 4th Division's part in the battle of Messines had finished with the capture of all of its objectives, but only after a desperate struggle and several setbacks. There was some sharp criticism of the Division's performance from high level.[68] The difficulties experienced on the Green Line, which were also encountered by the 3rd Division on the extreme right, made an obvious contrast with the comparative ease of the morning attack on the ridge, which had succeeded with scarcely a hitch. The conditions facing commanders and troops in the afternoon and the following days, however, were so different as to make the Oosttaverne Line attack almost a different battle, particularly in II Anzac's sector on the south. There were no huge mines to destroy the German fortifications, which were mostly intact and strongly garrisoned with fresh troops. While the enemy artillery, swamped by counter-battery fire, had been ineffectual in the first stage of the battle, by the time the Green Line attack began the Germans had brought other batteries into action from the south of the battle area, beyond the Lys River. These guns were able to bombard the ridge and interfere with the assembly, approach and communications of the II Anzac troops, a problem not encountered by the centre and northern corps which were able to reach their Green Line objectives with moderate losses. Having got through the shelling to launch their attack, the 13th Brigade found their left flank in the air and had to thin out their line to cover the gap. The inner flanks of both brigades were then faced with advancing into the shooting gallery of the Blauwepoortbeek valley, which no fire support was able to suppress. The 12th Brigade, having nevertheless occupied a large part of their final objective, was then shelled out of it by their own artillery. The breakdown of communications between infantry and artillery was compounded by the division of command between front and support lines. A Royal Artillery historian has commented

> the divisions which advanced to capture the Oosttaverne Line were controlled separately from those holding the Messines Ridge and, to make matters worse, the FOOs with each were out of contact. ... Towards evening on 7th June, many FOOs on the Ridge, who had no knowledge of the phase two attack and unable to tell friend from foe, engaged many of the forward troops, causing casualties. At the time, neither they nor their superiors knew they were doing it, and there was no way of stopping them ... when one battalion of a forward brigade was withdrawn for relief, they were heavily engaged from Messines Ridge, being mistaken for an enemy counter-attack ... it had been a tragic lapse ...[69]

Mistakes had been made, but by the next morning, all of the objectives had been reoccupied except for the Blauwepoortbeek gap, and it was only that particular tough nut that delayed the final success. Another factor that worked against the attacking brigades was the heavy losses among the officers and senior NCOs. Several battalions lost some or all of their company commanders killed or wounded, and two 13th Brigade battalions had their COs put out of action at crucial times. A number of platoon commanders were lost as well, either as casualties or through having to take charge of their companies. Their platoons were taken over on the spot by NCOs, or sometimes privates, who in the circumstances would probably not have been as conscious as the officers of the need for prompt and accurate reports being sent back to higher command. Those soldiers rose to the occasion and did their best in difficult situations, however. In the 47th Battalion Privates William Brown and George Robertson, and Corporals William Dickson and Oliver Jones were all awarded the DCM for their work in charge of platoons after their seniors had been put out of action; Corporal Jones even found himself in command of his company at one time until a replacement officer came up.[70]

Those were among numerous decorations awarded for the battle, including DSOs to Captain Allen (45th Battalion) and Captain Maxwell (52nd), the latter partly on the recommendation of the British forces that he had worked with so energetically. Lieutenant Bremner of the 47th also received the DSO, after being recommended for the VC. Soldiers awarded the DCM included Private 'Kirkpatrick' (Kilpatrick) and Corporal Arnold of the 48th Battalion, and Private Shang of the 47th. The 52nd Battalion's Lieutenant Boase was awarded the MC, as were Captain Cumming and Lieutenants Stabback and Stoerkel of the 48th, and Lieutenants Muir and Varley of the 45th. Outside of the infantry battalions, decorations included the DSO to the determined engineer officer Major Riddell, 12th Field Company, and MCs to Lieutenant Coward of the 12th LTM Battery, the machine gun officer Captain Duchatel, 13th MG Company, and Captain Calder of the Pioneers. Captain Winn, the 4th Field Ambulance medical officer, was another recipient of the MC, and Sergeant Wilkins of that unit was awarded the DCM. Another DCM went to Sergeant Townsend of the Signal Company. Awards of the DSO to senior officers Lieutenant Colonel Salisbury (50th Battalion), Lieutenant Colonel Denham (46th Battalion), Lieutenant Colonel Waite (11th AFA Brigade) and Major John Fraser (OC 4th Division Signal Company) were also notified during June, from earlier recommendations.

The month of June 1917 had cost the 4th Division a total of 2,688 officers and men as casualties, of whom 787 were recorded as killed or missing.[71] The 45th Battalion was the hardest-hit unit, losing a total of 568 of whom 206 were killed or missing. The unit had gone into the Messines battle as the Division's strongest battalion in numbers and come out the weakest. The 47th Battalion had 157 killed and missing, and 306 wounded, the next highest total casualties in the Division. The 12th Brigade's losses totalled 1,180, slightly higher than the 13th Brigade's total of 1,030. Of the 13th Brigade units, the 49th Battalion had the heaviest losses, with 92 killed and missing from a total of 379 casualties. The 52nd Battalion lost 326 including 98 killed and missing. The 4th Brigade, efficiently mopping up at the end of the battle, reported a total of 268 casualties. Outside of the infantry brigades, the 4th Pioneer

Battalion had the highest casualty total of 102. Coming at a time when the Division was still below strength after its heavy fighting in April, these losses could have justified a lengthy period of rest and rebuilding. The upcoming 'spell' would be all too short, however, and by the end of the month, the Division would be on its way back to the front line.

Officers of the 4th Division engineers in July 1917.
Command group, in second row from front, left to right from second left: Major Horace Reid, OC 13th Field Company; Maj Consett Riddell, OC 12th Field Company; Lieutenant Colonel Gilbert Elliott, CRE; Maj John Fraser, OC Signal Company; Maj Howard Tolley, OC 4th Field Company.
Others mentioned in this book are: (back row, 2nd from left) Captain Robert Park, 13th Field Company; (back row, 4th from left) Capt Robert Smith, Signal Company; (third row, 3rd from left) Capt Coleman Joseph, Signal Company; (second row, far right) Lieutenant Norman Wilkinson, 4th Field Company.
(AWM A00918)

12 Notes

1. This expression is sometimes said to apply only to the battle orders produced by the 3rd Australian Division. Certainly those were voluminous, but the term was used at least as high as Corps level, and appears to relate particularly to the artillery preparations. See Byrne, *New Zealand Artillery in the Field: The History of the New Zealand Artillery 1914-1918*, pp. 162–3.

2. The *Official History*, Vol IV, p. 581n, says the total was 2,338. Farndale, *Op Cit*, p.185 gives a total of 2,266. The difference is in the medium and heavy pieces; both agree that the field artillery amounted to 1,510 18-pounders and 4.5-in howitzers.

3   II Anzac artillery orders, in the Corps GS War Diary for June 1917, Part 3. The 25th Division on II Anzac's left, with more ground to cover in the advance, had an extra group of two field brigades.
4   11th AFA Brigade War Diary, 21 May 1917.
5   See Deayton, *Op Cit*, pp. 105–110 and 246–51. Imlay's birthplace is given there as Bulloo River, NSW, but the state should be Queensland (Comongin South Station on the river, according to the *Australian Dictionary of Biography*).
6   *Medical History*, Vol II, pp. 160–66; *Official History*, Vol IV, pp. 680n–681n; War Diaries of 4th, 12th and 13th Field Ambulances for June 1917.
7   The preceding five days were designated U, V, W, X, and Y for the purposes of orders.
8   II Anzac GS War Diary for June 1917 Part 3, Appendices, 'Artillery Instructions for the Attack, No.4'.
9   Mitchell, *Op Cit*, pp. 131–2; Lynch, *Op Cit*, pp. 138–9.
10 Lynch, *Op Cit*, p. 138.
11 *Official History*, Vol IV, p. 606.
12 4th Division G-staff War Diary for May 1917, Appendix 7.
13 AWM Red Cross files; 4th Division DADVS War Diary, 7 June 1917. The AWM Roll of Honour record incorrectly identifies Captain Ridley as an artillery officer, rather than AAVC. The other veterinary officer killed in action, Major C R Seelenmeyer, was also with the 4th Division (see p. 596).
14 11th AFA Brigade War Diary, 7 June 1917.
15 Lynch, *Op Cit*, pp. 140–41.
16 The 45th Battalion history (Lee, *Op Cit*, p.38) identifies that soldier as 'Corporal Kingsley'. The Red Cross file on Eric Kingel is clear that he was killed laying the tapes on 7 June; witnesses stated that he and Lt Murray were both killed by the same artillery shell burst, but the *Official History* says that Murray was shot through the head.
17 It appears that the first two runners sent by Brigade HQ were killed before reaching the battalions (Bean notebook, AWM38 3DRL606/160/1, p.43).
18 Both the 12th and 13th Brigade's final written orders for the attack (in Appendices to their June 1917 War Diaries), however, are not completely clear as to the 'New Zero' arrangements—the orders still state that the advance to the final jumping-off line is to start at Zero plus 8.30, i.e 11.40am—not to wait for confirmation of New Zero.
19 Lynch, *Op Cit*, p. 143. *Official History*, Vol IV, p. 620.
20 *Official History*, Vol IV, p. 671.
21 Messines was one of those battles fought where two map sheets join, the line between the northern and southern maps running about half-way up square 'O'. Maps issued with orders by the staffs had to be joined into a continuous sheet, or special maps produced.
22 The Red Cross files on Captains Bridgman and Rhead indicate that the officers' remains were buried 'about 1000 yards northeast of Messines', but the location must have been lost, as the four captains' names appear on the Menin Gate memorial as having no known grave.
23 12th Brigade War Diary for June 1917, Appendix 4.
24 Capt Allen was OC 'A' Company of the 45th, which was the lead company on the right flank. The original plan called for 'A' to take the front line trench then the second wave company, 'B', was to leapfrog through and take the support trench. As the companies had become mixed in assaulting the front trench, it appears to have been a composite force, led by Allen, that attacked the support

line. His DSO recommendation indicates that also. 'B' company's OC, Maj George Knox, was the battalion's senior company commander, but since Allen took charge on the right flank, it would seem that Maj Knox was not with his company on 7 June. He was certainly in the fighting on the next day, when he was wounded and evacuated.

25 The *Official History* is not quite clear on this point, but implies (Vol IV, pp. 631–2) that the first objective was not attained on the 45th's left. The 12th Brigade War Diary (June 1917, report in Appendix 4) says the left companies were 'unable to get forward' due to resistance from a strong point at map reference O.34.a.95.15, about where Owl Trench intersected a road south of the Blauwepoortbeek near the 12th Brigade's left boundary. On the other hand, the 45th's Diary (June 1917, Report in Appendix 1) says 'the left Companies gained their first objective only'. The same strong point is identified as the principal source of opposition. The Battalion history (Lee, *Op Cit*, p. 46), apparently follows that report and states that the left captured its objective in Owl Trench. Pte Lynch, as in Note 26 below, describes his company ('D' on the left) taking Owl Trench but being driven back from Owl Support.

26 Lynch, *Op Cit*, pp. 146–7.

27 *Official History*, Vol IV, p. 632n.

28 12th Brigade War Diary for June 1917, Appendix 4.

29 Capt Williams, writing to C E W Bean after the war, said that the 'A' Company commander, Lt Dudley Salmon, was killed earlier in the advance (Bean Papers, AWM38 3DRL606/272/1, p.123), and this is also stated in the *Official History* (Vol IV, p. 628n). Captain Williams wrote that he had been so informed by Lieutenant Charles King, who had come up with a few men from 'A' Company to the second objective. Lt Salmon is, however, officially recorded as having been killed on the next day, 8 June. One of the reports on his Red Cross file does say that he had also been wounded on 7 June but stayed on duty. Bean recorded elsewhere (notebook, AWM38 3DRL606/160/1, p.51) that Salmon positioned a force in Owl Trench (the first objective) to fight off a counter-attack from the left. It may be that Salmon sent Lieutenant King up to assist Capt Williams, while himself maintaining the flank guard, and Williams' memory of the incident was inaccurate.

30 The *Official History* (Vol IV, p. 629) says 250 yards, but Deayton (*Op Cit*, p. 140) puts the distance as a maximum of 130 metres.

31 *Official History*, Vol IV, p.637.

32 Quoted in the Bean Papers, AWM38 3DRL 606/272/1.

33 As stated in the *Official History* (Vol IV, p. 638). The senior officer still on duty in 'D' Company at the time that the incident occurred was Lt John Schulz, acting in command after Capt Davy's death. He, however, in correspondence with C E W Bean, denied any knowledge of it (Bean Papers, AWM38 3DRL 606/272/1, p.116). The officer may have been Lt Joseph Smith, who was also present, though later wounded. When Lt Schulz was seriously wounded shortly after the signalling episode, he handed over command of the company to the CSM, William Parry, which suggests that all of the other officers in the company had also become casualties by then, as stated also in CSM Parry's MC recommendation. The officer concerned may have been from 'B' Company, which was scattered in the same general area as 'D'; at least one, Lt Benjamin Bird, was unwounded and on duty at the time. Official records rarely mention which company that a soldier was in within his battalion, and it is possible that Shang may have actually been a 'B' Company member. Pte Gallwey of 'D'Company, whose diary is the main source for the details of the 47th Battalion's fight at Messines, included happenings that he had not personally witnessed but had heard about from others.

34 C E W Bean in his notes made at the time (AWM38 3DRL 606/160/1, p. 74), and subsequently in the *Official History* (Vol IV, p. 638) states that the method was a signal lamp, and this is also

stated in Shang's DCM recommendation. The Gallwey diary, however, says that he used flags, and this is accepted by Deayton (*Op Cit*, p.140).

35   E O Williams to C E W Bean, 11 July 1931, Bean Papers, AWM38 3DRL 606/272/1.
36   In C E W Bean's notebook (AWM38 3DRL 606/160/1, p. 40) he says that the barrage lengthened to the SOS line 200 yards beyond the Green Line, but later dropped back again on to Owl Trench. Lt John Schulz (47th Battalion), writing to Bean on 13 May 1931 (AWM38 3DRL 606/272/1) says that the barrage initially fell on the 47th's position but then lengthened its range; this was at about the time that Schulz was making his way back after being shot through the jaw.
37   12th Brigade War Diary for June 1917, Appendix 4, report dated 14 June.
38   Williams to Bean, as for Note 35 above.
39   Bean notebook, AWM38 3DRL 606/160/1, pp. 39–40.
40   4th Division GS War Diary, 7 June 1917.
41   11th AFA Brigade War Diary for June 1917, Appendix 11, Magnum Opus Instructions No 12.
42   NZ Divisional Artillery HQ War Diary for June 1917, Appendices, Operation Order 31. A distance of 140 metres (150 yards) out from the Black Line would be inside the Black Dotted Line outposts. Perhaps it was assumed that the troops there would have fallen back in the event of a counter-attack.
43   According to the *Official History*, Vol IV, p. 646. The 52nd Battalion's report has 11.00.
44   Bean notebook, AWM38 3DRL606/160/1, p. 66.
45   4th Pioneer Battalion War Diary, 7/8 June 1917.
46   L Carlyon, *The Great War*, pp. 415–16; Maj Riddell's DSO recommendation, in AWM Honours and Awards files; 12th Field Coy and 4th Division Engineers HQ War Diaries for June 1917.
47   *Official History*, Vol IV, p. 654. This incident is not reported in Division or Brigade War Diaries.
48   Mitchell, *Op Cit*, p. 138; Browning, *Leane's Battalion, Op Cit*, p. 143.
49   According to his DCM recommendation. Mitchell, *Op Cit*, pp. 138–9, says he shot three snipers from the trench. That Kirkpatrick was an assumed name is shown by documents on his service record, which is still under the name Robert Leigh Kirkpatrick. He was fatally wounded in July 1917, and he is entered in the Roll of Honour as Leigh Kilpatrick; that name is also on his headstone in Pont D'Achelles military cemetery, France.
50   Col Leane's report in the Appendices to the 48th Battalion War Diary for June 1917.
51   *Official History*, Vol IV, p. 652.
52   51st BattalionWar Diary fro June 1917, Appendix 3.
53   4th Division General Staff War Diary, 8 June 1917.
54   *Official History*, Vol IV, p.662.
55   13th Brigade War Diary for June 1917, Appendix 3.
56   *Medical History*, Vol II, p. 174.
57   50th Battalion War Diary for June 1917, Appendices, 'Report on Operations'.
58   Colonel Imlay's report (47th battalion War Diary for June 1917, Appendix 4) says that the patrols had 50% casualties but gives no other details.
59   *Official History*, Vol IV, p. 671, stating that Maj Lee was the Brigade Major. Documents in the 12th Brigade War Diary indicate that while Lee was attached to the staff, Maj E L Salier, finally promoted to the rank appropriate to the posting, was still Brigade Major.
60   4th Division Artillery HQ War Diary for June 1917, Appendices, Order No. 73.

61 According to Colonel Salisbury's report in the 50th Battalion War Diary for June 1917.
62 *Official History*, Vol IV, p. 673
63 *Loc Cit*. The report in the 45th Battalion War Diary says the time was 10:30 pm, probably correct as that was the Zero time for the main attack by the 13th Brigade north of the valley; 10 pm was the assembly time.
64 Browning, *Leane's Battalion, Op Cit*, p. 146.
65 52nd Battalion War Diary for June 1917, Appendix 2.
66 Bean Papers, notebook AWM38 3DRL606/161/1, pp. 24–5. Another note here indicates that Bean got his information from Arthur Maxwell's brother Duncan rather than Arthur himself. Biographers of Albert Jacka (I. Grant, *Jacka VC*, pp. 126–7; R Macklin, *Jacka VC*, p. 178) mention that Bean omitted Jacka's part in these operations from the *Official History*, and that a recommendation for a bar to his MC was not approved. The incident as described by Bean in his notes provides a possible explanation, if not a justification, for those points, bearing in mind also that Duncan Maxwell was ADC to General Holmes at the time.
67 10th AFA Brigade War Diary, 14 June 1917.
68 P.A. Pedersen, *The Anzacs*, p. 237, gives examples.
69 Farndale, *Op Cit*, p. 191.(extract reproduced by kind permission of the Royal Artillery Institution).
70 AWM Honours and awards records.
71 4th Division Admin War Diary for June 1917, Appendix 11; the figure would include a few casualties before the Messines battle began on 7 June. The *Official History* (Vol IV, p. 682) has a total of 2, 677 for the actual battle.

13: In And Out Of The Line

The 12th and 13th Brigades spent their first few days out of the line resting and refitting, as well as making the usual welcome visits to the baths. Some light training was begun, and Generals Plumer and Godley visited and inspected both brigades. On 17 June the brigades moved further back to billets near St Omer, the troops travelling by bus for the 30-kilometre distance. The 4th Brigade, which had remained not far behind the front line in support of the 25th Division, also moved back on 17 June, but only as far as tented camps in the Neuve Église ('D') area. Here the 4th Brigade battalions supplied working parties for various projects under the II Anzac Chief Engineer, and some training was undertaken also.

Training in the infantry brigades included refining the new platoon structure and tactics, with several units specifying cross-training of all platoon members in the different weapon sections—Lewis guns, grenades, rifle grenades. Emphasis was also placed on tightening up signalling methods, the commanders having taken note of the breakdown in communications in the Messines battle. The 12th Brigade staff, for instance, passed down the higher command's orders in a four-page memo to all units, 'for guidance and strict compliance,' detailing procedures for all of the methods of signalling—electronic, visual, human (written messages by runners), and avian (pigeons were still a fall-back method). Battalions were instructed to ensure that one-third of their runners and trained signallers were to be held back in reserve when the unit went into an attack.

> The fact that all mechanical means of communication have failed will not excuse a commander remaining in ignorance of the course of events, or neglecting to keep his immediate superior and neighbouring formations constantly informed of what is occurring on his front.[1]

At the end of the month the 12th Brigade set up a specialist signalling school, and communication exercises were included in each brigade's routine training programmes. Those varied slightly between brigades and battalions, but the 50th Battalion's programme for the six days ending 30 June can be taken as representative:

25 June: Battalion route march.

26 June: rifle shooting on the range; bayonet fighting; physical training; gas drill; Lewis gunners shooting on the range in the afternoon; lecture by the brigade signals officer to all officers and NCOs on communications.

27 June: Physical training; bayonet fighting; trench tactics for bombers and rifle grenadiers; close order drill; rifle exercises.

28 June: Route march—during the march, communications by runner and visual signal were practiced. In the afternoon officers and NCOs reviewed the exercise with the brigade signals officer, and all practiced message writing technique.

29 June: Physical training; company attack formation practice.

30 June: Lewis gunners worked on the firing range; remainder of platoons did bayonet fighting and throwing grenades; close order drill.[2]

On most days, the rank and file had the afternoons off duty, or took part in organised sports, although some battalions worked until 3 or 3:30 pm.

Another issue arising from the Messines battle was the use of tanks with infantry. After the 4th Division's unfortunate experience with tanks at Bullecourt (that is, the 4th and 12th Brigades), some units had now found that the machines could be useful in a supporting role. The 52nd Battalion in particular noted that the tanks 'rendered very valuable aid and were untiring in their efforts to help,'[3] mopping up strong-points and generally intimidating the enemy infantry. Other 13th Brigade units had less positive experiences, and there were no tanks available to assist the troops attacking the Blauwepoortbeek Valley strong-points, where they might have made a significant difference. The 12th Brigade had similarly mixed experiences with the tanks. One had materially assisted the 45th and 47th Battalions to capture Oxygen Trench, but had then moved off by the time the infantry assaulted Owl Trench. This was not necessarily through any lack of determination, and could have been due to damage, mechanical problems, fuel or ammunition shortage or simply limited awareness—from their noisy, fume-filled metal boxes, the tank crews could see little and hear less. The pillboxes near Owl Trench that caused so much trouble to the 12th Brigade units at Messines could have been neutralised by a tank or two (if any had been available) attacking them in conjunction with the infantry, a tactic that was used successfully later in the year during the early stages of the Third Battle of Ypres.[4] The point was not lost on Lieutenant Colonel Ray Leane, CO of the 48th Battalion, who noted his

> opinion that the tanks retired too soon from the action. Infantry are at a great disadvantage when confronted with the Cement Strong Points; Artillery even with direct hits make little impression, but the tanks can go forward and engage them at close quarters.
>
> I consider the left of OWL TRENCH and OWL SUPPORT could have been cleaned up much earlier with considerably less loss of life had the policy of the

> tanks been more vigorous ... Of course, I do not know what orders they received but it appears to me that the tank should really be a STRONG point for the infantry ... [with] an efficient Artillery barrage and the good co-operation of the tanks, Infantry should not fail.[5]

Although Leane's unit had suffered heavily from the failures of the tanks at Bullecourt, he could see the potential of the machines if the right tactics were developed.

In the three weeks following the Messines battle the Division received 72 officers and 1,885 ORs as reinforcements, leaving its strength still short of establishment by 38 officers and 2,290 ORs at the end of June. The deficiency was of course mostly in the infantry brigades, although the 4th Brigade, less involved in the recent heavy fighting, was now closer to full strength than the other brigades.[6] Some of the reinforcements would have been experienced men returning from hospital or detachment, but the majority were raw recruits arriving in the fighting zone for the first time. These men would have received basic training in Australia, more advanced work with the training battalions in England, and an unpleasant introduction to France via the BEF's harsh transit depot at Étaples. Now the units took over their training in the requirements of the front line, to which the Division would soon be returning after an all too brief break. The experienced men benefited from regular training also, in the same way as a sporting team knows its game but trains regularly to maintain and improve its performance.

Heavy losses among the officers at Messines meant more commissions of veterans from the ranks, and a number of reinforcement officers, appointed during training, also arrived; the latter would need to quickly pick up experience in action to lead effectively. In the 13th Brigade, Brigadier General Glasgow had to replace two of his battalion COs, Lieutenant Colonels Paul (49th) and Pope (52nd), badly wounded at Messines. The 49th's acting CO, Major Arrell, was left in command for the time being but was not given the permanent posting yet; there was no obvious reason for this—Arrell appears to have been a competent officer, and his service record includes a favourable assessment from a senior officers' training course that he attended later in the year, but he would have to wait until 1918 for promotion. The 52nd Battalion was temporarily led by its second-in-command, Major Herbert McPherson,[7] but a new commander was brought in when Lieutenant Colonel John Whitham was appointed on 1 July. The new CO, a 35 year old Tasmanian, born in British India, was a pre-war professional officer who had already achieved some distinction in the war. He had been through the Gallipoli campaign with the 12th Battalion (the 52nd's 'parent') and had more recently held senior staff appointments in the 2nd Division and at AIF HQ, being made a CMG for his services. Colonel Whitham was nearly 183 cm tall and of a distinguished soldierly appearance, with a calm and courteous manner, an impressive leader for the 52nd Battalion.[8]

The 12th and 13th Brigade groups spent less than a week in the St Omer area before they were once more in motion towards the forward zone. The troops again travelled by bus, arriving at camps in the reserve area, Doulieu and Vieux Berquin, on 21 June; Division HQ had already been established at the latter place. Two days later the 4th Brigade, which had remained closer to the front at Neuve Église, was ordered to relieve elements of the

New Zealand Division holding part of the line on II Anzac's right flank. Moving via Hill 63, the Brigade occupied the front from the River Douve south to the River Warnave on the night of 29/30 June, with its 15th and 16th Battalions in the firing line and the 14th and 13th in close support; the Brigade machine guns and trench mortars relieved their NZ equivalents also. The 4th NZ Brigade continued to hold the extreme right of II Anzac for the time being, coming under command of the 4th Division. The 4th Field Ambulance remained in the back area at Steenwerck administering the divisional rest station, with the 12th Field Ambulance moving up to the ADS at 'Charing Cross' on the western edge of Ploegsteert Wood and taking over responsibility for front-line casualty evacuation. The 12th Brigade units came up to positions at Hill 63 and Underhill Farm as the support brigade to the 4th, with the 13th Brigade moving to reserve at De Seule where its units continued with their training programmes. Division HQ moved forward from Vieux Berquin to Steenwerck on 30 June. That night the divisional artillery, after a fortnight's rest and refitting, also came back into the line to relieve the New Zealand gunners. The engineer field companies conformed with their linked brigades, with the 4th Company oversighting works on the front and support line positions and the other two companies working on projects in the reserve areas. The Pioneer Battalion resumed construction work on tramways and communication trenches on 2 July, but four of the Pioneers' Lewis gun teams were sent forward to reinforce the 4th Brigade units in the front line.

Returning to the fighting zone, the 4th Division troops found the overall situation scarcely changed in the weeks since the Messines battle. The front line was more or less in the same position as it had been when the battle had ended with the elimination of the German salient. The focus had now shifted further north to the main Ypres salient as Sir Douglas Haig continued with his plans for a triumphant advance to the Belgian coast. The next stage of the Flanders offensive was entrusted to the Fifth Army under Sir Hubert Gough, a general whose aggressive attitude was regarded as more likely to achieve a resounding success than the methodical approach of Sir Herbert Plumer. The latter's Second Army, including II Anzac, would continue to hold the southern flank at Messines and make diversionary attacks while Fifth Army assaulted the high ground of Pilckem Ridge and the Gheluvelt Plateau overlooking Ypres. That attack was planned to begin at the end of July, a delay of seven weeks after Messines that the Germans made good use of to strengthen their defences. Successive lines of breastworks and trenches were constructed, interspersed with numerous pillboxes and machine gun posts, and strong infantry and artillery reinforcements were brought up. The German guns were positioned behind the heights and more care was taken over their concealment after the successful British counter-battery fire at Messines. The British batteries were now concentrated in the plain around Ypres, in full view of German observers on the ridges, and it was the Germans who now had an advantage in counter-battery operations.

The 4th Division was now in the sector south of the Douve river, not familiar territory, and was required to occupy a front line that consisted of isolated outposts, often in shell-holes, and a few shallow trenches and breastworks. One thing that had changed since Messines was the weather conditions. The dry hot conditions of early June had given way to periods of rain, with a major downpour on the 4th Brigade's first day in the line. In this low lying area, with its high water table and its drainage systems mostly destroyed by shellfire, it did not take much rain for the terrain to become swampy and waterlogged. 'Trenches are full of water and the mud is as bad as it was on the Somme' noted the 4th Brigade diarist,[9] and the 15th Battalion in the front line found that 'the saps were in many instances knee deep in water, and in other parts nearly waist deep, and through this thick muddy soup the men waded.'[10] In these conditions infantry fighting was infrequent, but patrols and working parties still went into No Man's land at night and there were occasional clashes with enemy troops. The artillery of both sides was active, the Germans frequently shelling the Australian front and support lines. The enemy guns intermittently targeted the rear areas as well, and one dealt a major blow to the 4th Division on the morning of 2 July.

The Premier of New South Wales, Mr W A Holman, was visiting Division HQ and Major General Holmes took him towards the forward area for a view of the Messines battlefield. The general was normally unconcerned about entering dangerous areas, but on this occasion he decided to take what was thought to be a safe route for his civilian guest. The party had left their car near Hill 63 and was proceeding on foot to climb the hill when a chance shell from a German 77mm gun burst near them. General Holmes was hit through the chest by a shell splinter. The rest of the group was unharmed, but the general died while being carried to the dressing station, without regaining consciousness. William Holmes was the second AIF divisional commander to die in action in the war, (Major General Sir William Bridges had been mortally wounded by a sniper at Gallipoli) one of at least eleven BEF officers of his rank to meet that fate on the Western Front.[11] He had made a fine record in six months as the 4th Division's GOC, in command during the battles at Gueudecourt, Bullecourt and Messines. If he could have argued more forcefully for modification to the plans at Bullecourt, the Division under his command had achieved its objectives elsewhere and maintained a reputation as hard fighters. His physical courage was unquestioned, perhaps not always an advantage to his subordinates, and it is ironic that his death came about from a rare instance of caution. C E W Bean called him 'one of the most eminent of Australian citizen-soldiers' and noted that he possessed 'fine moral qualities, transparent sincerity, energy and courage.'[12]

Brigadier General Charles Rosenthal was temporarily appointed to act as GOC, in addition to his responsibilities as CRA. One of his first duties was to attend his predecessor's funeral the next day, with many other high-ranking officers, when General Holmes was buried in the cemetery of the 2nd CCS at Trois Arbres, near Steenwerck, in what is now the Trois Arbres war cemetery. The 12th Brigade's camps in the support positions at Ploegsteert received their share of the frequent enemy shelling, and on 5 July a shell burst near the 48th Battalion's headquarters hut. The unit second-in-command, Major Harold Howden, was hit by a fragment and died within an hour from internal bleeding. Major Howden, one of the 12th Brigade's most promising young officers, was also buried at the Trois Arbres CCS, in the next grave to General Holmes. The next day, in similar circumstances, 4th Brigade's forward headquarters on the northern edge of Ploegsteert Wood was also hit by an enemy shell as the staff were about to dine in their makeshift mess. Lieutenant Gordon Mills, the Brigade intelligence officer, was killed and Brigadier General Brand, Major Johnston (brigade major) and Captain Harry Thomson (acting staff captain) were wounded. The 16th Battalion CO, Lieutenant Colonel Edmund Drake-Brockman, took over as acting brigadier and hastily put together a temporary staff group, with Major Eric Wilton, former OC of the 4th MG Company, coming in as brigade major from Division HQ, where he had recently been attached for staff training. It appears that the German guns had been probing for a battery of 6-inch howitzers 'which were in the vicinity of B[riga]de HQ, in spite of numerous requests for their removal.'[13] Lieutenant Mills's remains are interred near those of General Holmes and Major Howden in the Trois Arbres cemetery.

The routines of holding the line continued for the 4th Brigade infantry. The battalions rotated on the night of 7/8 July, with the 13th and 14th Battalions relieving the 15th and 16th in the front line. Patrols continued at night and occasional skirmishes took place with German troops. The 14th Battalion had an isolated outpost attacked and driven in by a large enemy force, following which the unit set about reorganising its outpost line to improve observation and fields of fire.[14] Enemy snipers presented a frequent danger, and one hit the 14th's great fighter Captain Albert Jacka in the leg on the night of 9 July; Jacka was evacuated to England, but he would be back in time for his unit's next major battle. Work went on improving the trenches and posts in the front and support lines, using infantry working parties under their own officers but often overseen by engineers in a relationship that was not always harmonious. Lieutenant Ted Rule noted in his memoirs that

> ... no matter what we did, we were always in hot water with [the engineers]. It not infrequently happened that an engineer officer would come round, and whoever of us was in charge of the working party would ask him if he thought we had done enough. If he said 'Yes' we would obtain permission to leave. Then another engineer officer would put in a complaint that we had left too soon. There were continual misunderstandings of this sort.
>
> In contrast to this were our dealings with the 4th Pioneers, a battalion which did all the drudgery for our division. They dug trenches, constructed dugouts, and made life a lot easier for the infantrymen ... they very seldom received a rest, as we did, away from the forward areas.[15]

The working conditions were made somewhat easier by a week of fine weather that helped the ground to dry out, followed by another two days of rain before fine weather resumed for the last few days of the 4th Brigade's stint in the line. On the night of 13/14 July the 13th Brigade came up from reserve in relief, sending its 49th and 51st Battalions into the firing line first. The relief was completed by 12:30 am and the 4th Brigade units retired to the 13th Brigade's previous camp in reserve at De Seule, having suffered 226 casualties in the line including

39 killed and missing. The 12th Brigade units remained in the support lines in the Hill 63/Ploegsteert Wood area, while the Pioneer Battalion's Lewis gunners stayed in the front line to support the 13th Brigade infantry. Within half an hour of taking over its sector of the front line, one of the 51st's outposts was attacked by a strong enemy force under cover of a trench mortar barrage. The attack was driven off by Lewis gun fire as was a second attempt shortly afterwards, with no loss to the 51st.

On the morning of 16 July Major General Ewen Sinclair-MacLagan arrived at 4th Division HQ, Steenwerck, to assume command as GOC from Brigadier General Rosenthal. The new commander, a 48 year old Scot, was a regular officer in the British Army but also a member of the AIF. He happened to be serving in Australia when war was declared in August 1914, as a lieutenant colonel and Director of Drill at the Royal Military College, Duntroon. When the 1st Australian Division was raised the GOC, General William Bridges, chose Sinclair-MacLagan to command its 3rd Brigade with the rank of colonel (later brigadier general) and he was appointed to the AIF in that capacity. The 3rd Brigade was first to land at Gallipoli and Sinclair-MacLagan was the senior officer on shore in the vital first hours. It fell to him to make several decisions in the deployment of the landing force, against the original plan,[16] and debate continues to this day as to whether or not his decisions were correct. Both cases have been argued strongly, although rarely with reference to what information Sinclair-MacLagan had to work with at the time.[17] After Gallipoli his brigade was split to form the 4th Division's 13th Brigade and he took the reconstituted 3rd to France, leading it through the Pozières/Mouquet Farm fighting. In December 1916 Sinclair-MacLagan was posted to England as overall commander of the AIF depots there, before the 4th Division command and promotion to major general came. He was a very experienced soldier and administrator, with a somewhat pessimistic temperament—General Monash later wrote that Sinclair-MacLagan 'invariably contrived to do what he had urged could not be done. One could not afford to take him at his own modest estimate of himself.'[18] The new GOC brought Lieutenant Ernest Kemmis in as one of his aides-de-camp, with Captain Duncan Maxwell retaining the other ADC posting.[19] General Sinclair-MacLagan proceeded to familiarise himself with his new command, visiting the brigades accompanied by General Rosenthal. The two generals knew each other well from Gallipoli,[20] and there

Major General Ewen Sinclair-MacLagan CB CMG DSO (1868–1948), GOC 4th Division from July 1917. (AWM 03064)

were probably some officers in the 13th Brigade who had served with Sinclair-MacLagan in his original 3rd Brigade, as well as his former brigade major, Brigadier General Brand, GOC 4th Brigade. The latter was away at the time recuperating from his wound, but would return to duty by the end of the month.

There were several other changes among the 'heads' at Division HQ in July. The GSO2, Major Miles, was posted away to 2nd Division HQ and replaced by Queenslander Major Eric Plant, a 27 year old regular officer of some distinction both in the field and on the staff. A Gallipoli veteran, he had been a subaltern with the 9th Battalion at the Landing, one of the few to reach as far inland as the Third Ridge on that day. Subsequently Plant became brigade major of the 6th Brigade under Brigadier General John Gellibrand, and served in that capacity through all of his Brigade's operations on the Western front, winning the DSO and Bar. There was a new GSO3 on the staff also; the impresario Captain Keighley had been posted to the 1st Division, and he was replaced by Captain James Stanley Rogers, already attached to the HQ staff from the 14th Battalion (post-war, Rogers became a distinguished physicist). Changes took place in the administrative staff as well. The Boer War veteran Lieutenant Colonel Richard Dowse, DAAG, had been selected for transfer to the 1st Division as its AA&QMG, but he had only just 'marched out' when the 4th Division's own long-serving AA&QMG, Lieutenant Colonel Edward Armstrong, received orders to return to the British Army for similar duties, 'much to his disgust.'[21] Colonel Dowse was immediately recalled to the 4th Division to take up the senior administrative position in place of Colonel Armstrong. Captain Walter Fowler-Brownsworth moved from DAQMG to DAAG with a promotion to major, and Major Edmund Milne, senior supply officer in the Divisional Train, came in as DAQMG (Major Milne moved on to I Anzac HQ in September and was succeeded by another Divisional Train officer, Captain Edward Carter). These changes left the GSO1, Lieutenant Colonel Denis Bernard, as the only non-AIF officer on the Division staff.

By the time Brigadier General Rosenthal reverted to his duties as CRA after handing over to the new GOC, his field brigades had once more been detached from the Division. After eight comparatively quiet days in the line the 10th and 11th AFA Brigades were withdrawn on the night of 9/10 July and sent to the left of the Second Army front, the St Eloi sector, together with the artillery ammunition element of the DAC. Here they came under command of the 47th British Division (X Corps) forming part of the artillery cover for Second Army's diversionary attacks in support of the forthcoming assault by Fifth Army to the north (the NZ Division artillery returned to the line, under their own CRA, to cover the 4th Division infantry). Gun pits in the X Corps sector were still being prepared and it took until 20 July for all of the 10th and 11th AFA Brigade batteries to be in position, split between two groups. To their north, the field artillery brigades of the 1st, 2nd and 5th Divisions (I Anzac) were brought up from rest as part of Fifth Army's massive artillery force. All four divisional artilleries were soon shooting in the preliminary bombardments for the next stage of the Flanders offensive, the series of battles collectively known as the Third Battle of Ypres, planned to begin on 31 July.

Rosenthal, with his field brigades under other commands, found himself occupied with administrative issues. Earlier in July, the CRA had noted in his diary that

> I had a powwow with all officers of the 4th Aus Div Artillery and gave them final warning that any officers found unsatisfactory in their work, either due to negligence or incompetence, would be recommended for removal from Artillery and if necessary the AIF.[22]

There is no indication of any particular incidents or people that might have motivated that 'powwow' but General Rosenthal had obviously seen something that had raised his concerns. In a different category was the sudden need that arose later in the month to replace both of the able and long-serving artillery brigade commanders, Lieutenant Colonels Giffard King and William Waite. Both were in poor health and feeling the strain of twelve months' command in the field with minimal rest. Colonel King officially asked to be relieved of his command and a posting was found for him in England as CO of the Australian Artillery Reserve Brigade. Colonel Waite was sent on extended sick leave, diagnosed with 'debility,' indicating exhaustion and stress; in time, he would resume duty with the 4th Division.[23] Both of the 4th Division's artillery brigades therefore went into action at Third Ypres under acting commanders, both fine officers. Major Thomas Williams, OC 39th Battery, took command of the 10th AFA Brigade; he was 37, a citizen soldier from Sydney, a dental surgeon in civilian life. Captain Frederick Forrest, the artillery staff captain, took over the 39th Battery with a promotion to major. His place at Artillery HQ was filled by Lieutenant Arthur Waite, younger brother of Lieutenant Colonel William Waite. Temporary command of the 11th AFA Brigade went to Major Percy Edwards, the 111th Howitzer Battery OC, 40 years old, whose military service went as far back as the Boer War in which he had won the DCM as a sergeant-major with a WA mounted infantry unit.[24]

While these moves and changes were happening at the command level, the 4th Division infantry and supporting arms continued with basic Western Front tasks, holding their front between the Douve and Warnave rivers. The 13th Brigade, having relieved the 4th Brigade on 14 July, had five days in the line before being relieved in its turn. The forward posts of the 49th and 51st Battalions lost casualties to periodic enemy shelling, and infantry patrols from both sides skirmished in No Man's Land at night; a patrol of the 51st, supported by two mortars of the 13th LTM Battery, captured and occupied a German post on the night of 16 July. The enemy troops in the area proved to be dangerous opponents, however, and two nights later they retaliated strongly. A German force surprised one of the 51st's outposts and drove the small garrison back to the main line, capturing two Lewis guns in the process. That setback occurred in the early hours of 19 July, and the West Australians had no opportunity to hit back as the 4th Division was relieved that night, once more by the New Zealand Division. The 13th Brigade reported casualty figures of 33 killed and 74 wounded for its short period in the front line; of those, the 51st Battalion had suffered the highest proportion, with 21 killed and 32 wounded.[25] The 12th Brigade had not been called on to occupy the front line but had still lost 18 killed and 91 wounded since 1 July, mostly to German shelling on the support positions.[26]

The Division moved back to the reserve area, with Division HQ setting up at Vieux-Berquin on 20 July. After three weeks in the front line the units would have about the same time in the rear before moving up again. Training re-commenced on a fairly intensive basis, although most afternoons were reserved for organised sports. It was made clear to the troops that the period was not to be seen as a rest. That applied particularly to the 12th Brigade, which was ordered to be at readiness to move forward again at four hours notice to reinforce the 57th British Division in the Armentières sector if needed (the sector was thinly held, and Second Army was concerned that the Germans could stage an attack there). The Brigade staff prepared contingency plans setting out the transport arrangements and logistics to be employed if the call came, and officers were sent to reconnoitre the sector.[27]

With the troops away from the firing line the commanders, as military hierarchies will, turned their attention to non-combat matters. General Sinclair-MacLagan called his infantry brigadiers, CRA and CRE together on 23 July for a conference on discipline and training.[28] The GOC was particularly concerned that the 4th Division had the worst record in Second Army for cases of absence without leave (AWL) and desertion, and a suggestion was approved that offenders should be sentenced to what the British and Empire armies called 'Field Punishment'. This was a crude penalty of rough treatment that included several hours per day tied to a post in the open, as well as confinement, loss of pay and other inconveniences. The suggestion probably came from Brigadier General Robertson; earlier in the month, the 12th Brigade had already encouraged its unit COs to consider imposing Field Punishment, citing its successful imposition by a battalion commander, apparently Colonel Leane in the 48th, during the Somme fighting.[29] How far this was adopted subsequently by other unit COs is not clear. The 4th Brigade's memorandum to its units, summarising the conference outcomes, does not even mention the matter, and most officers would have been aware of the men's deep resentment of that penalty.

Saluting, a perennial issue with First AIF soldiers, was another disciplinary matter that concerned the conference. Troops usually failed to salute a general's car when it passed and it was agreed that the significance of the distinguishing flag on the car should be explained to the men—of course, most of them already knew perfectly well what the flag meant. The conference also deplored 'the practice of turning away and pretending not to see an officer passing.' There were other more practical matters discussed as well. Correct practices for columns on the march—march discipline—was given some attention. Junior officers were to be reminded of their responsibilities in ensuring that their men's webbing equipment was correctly adjusted to minimise discomfort on the march, and particularly that all had well-fitting boots, something perhaps easier said than done. That item was one of a number directed at instructing platoon commanders in the finer points of their duties—many of those officers had been recently commissioned in the field without the benefit of any formal training courses. Co-operation between infantry and artillery received some attention also. The infantry brigadiers were to arrange for their forward HQs to include accommodation for the artillery group commander, and another item was the use of the SOS signal:

> During the Messines engagement thousands of pounds worth of ammunition was expended through the improper use of the SOS by jumpy subalterns. In future the SOS will only be sent up when the enemy are seen advancing across No Man's Land with fixed bayonets, showing that an attack and not a raid is being made.[30]

– although the situation might not be so easy to assess for a young platoon commander crouched in a muddy shell-hole in the dark, trying to hold a thin line with an unknown number of Germans coming at him.

A housekeeping issue that tended to come up when units were relieved was the sanitary arrangements in the camps, not surprisingly where crude latrines were in use by up to 20,000 men. When divisions changed over the incoming division routinely complained that the area had been left in an unsatisfactory condition by their predecessors, set about cleaning it up, then moved out again and were in their turn criticised by the next division to be stationed in the area. The 4th Division was no exception, finding that the facilities in their reserve area needed much improvement and coming under complaint from the NZ Division for the condition of their previous area. The divisions had lost their specialist Sanitary Sections in March 1917, when the personnel and functions were transferred to Army and Corps control,[31] and Colonel George Barber, the 4th Division ADMS, saw that policy as a prime cause of sanitation problems. Responding to the latest complaints, an exasperated Colonel Barber wrote a strongly-worded memo to the II Anzac DDMS, pointing out firstly that the units denied the accusations, and stating that

> no action has been taken, nor could anything be done owing to the units having left the area.
>
> This is a very good example of the uselessness and ineffectiveness of Sanitary Sections as at present utilised. The Sanitary Section reports the condition of sanitation of Units, as a rule, some days after the Unit has left the particular camp, and then it is impossible to prove who is responsible for the condition complained of. As the essence of good sanitation is prompt remedy I regard the Sections as useless ... the sanitation of Units of this Division has suffered since the detachment of the Sanitary Sections from division to army ... it is a matter of regret that they cannot be returned to Divisions.[32]

The return of the sections was Barber's principal suggestion for improvement. Some changes along these lines were made later in the war, particularly in what was by then the Australian Corps, but the problems would never entirely go away.

Colonel Barber was involved in another back-area medical activity late in July when he accompanied Archdeacon John William Ward[33] on a tour of the units over several days, lecturing the troops on the topic of venereal disease.[34] The ADMS spoke on the medical aspects of VD, while the Archdeacon urged prevention by an attitude of 'continence and purity.'³⁵ One could reasonably assume that this was not particularly effective in the long term (more pragmatic approaches to prevention were adopted later in the war³⁶), and some thought the talks a waste of time: 'Interfered very much with training' noted the 4th Brigade diarist,³⁷ and A G Butler commented that the lectures were 'probably worse than useless.'³⁸ Another event that interrupted training was a formal inspection by the Army commander, Sir Herbert Plumer, on 27 July, at which most of the members of the Division were on parade. By then the Division's return to the front line was imminent, but the short break from combat had produced a 'very noticeable improvement in appearance and smartness of men' as recorded by the 4th Brigade,³⁹ and the training, re-equipping and reinforcement had been of benefit to its effectiveness. For once the numbers aspect came out on the credit side: the Division overall had lost 22 officers and 607 ORs as casualties during July but had taken on 86 officers and 2,541 ORs as reinforcements.⁴⁰ Numbers were not everything of course, as Major Salier, brigade major of the 12th Brigade, reminded the brigade's units:

> ... many of those who were responsible for [the Brigade's] efficiency have become casualties. A greater responsibility rests on those who remain; the responsibility of inculcating in recent arrivals the high standard that has always been maintained in this Brigade by helping them to overcome the difficulties that beset them through want of experience.⁴¹

On 31 July Fifth Army launched its great offensive against the Ypres ridges, supported by the French First Army advancing on the left and by Second Army's diversionary operation on the right. The French made good progress in their sector and Fifth Army's left advanced on to Pilckem Ridge. Further south, however, although some ground was gained the attack stalled against determined resistance with most of the vital high ground of the Gheluvelt Plateau still in German hands. In the afternoon heavy rain began and put a stop to any further fighting. The first day of rain was enough to turn the battlefield, and the supply routes leading to it, into an impassable morass. The downpour would last for seven days before there was any kind of a break. Second Army on the right flank made its demonstration on 31 July also, capturing parts of the German outpost line in its sector. The 4th Division artillery was engaged in this operation as part of the artillery force covering X Corps, firing in the preliminary bombardment and then covering the attacking infantry on the day. A week later the 10th and 11th AFA Brigades were withdrawn and moved back to the south to rejoin their own Division in the Messines sector. By that time the 4th Division infantry had returned from reserve to the forward zone. The 4th and 12th Brigades moved up first, marching in the rain to relieve 3rd Australian Division and British units in the Messines front line.

This time the Division went into the line initially between the Douve and the Blauwepoortbeek. The 4th Brigade, with Brigadier General Brand now recovered from his wound and back in command, relieved the 11th Brigade (3rd Division) over the nights 3/4 and 4/5 August. The 16th Battalion went into the firing line first, with the 13th in support and the 14th and 15th in reserve. Another wearying and dangerous round of routine line-holding began, made worse by the recent wet weather. The front line units worked on the forward defences and patrolled No Man's Land, and the supports and reserves sent fatigue parties to work on the never-ending infrastructure projects, all under constant enemy shelling. The Germans pounded the forward positions particularly heavily at this time, the 16th Battalion losing 26 killed and 87 wounded in five days.[42] On the night of 7/8 August the 12th Brigade came up to relieve the 111th British Brigade from the Blauwepoortbeek north to a point just beyond the line of the Wambeek stream, sending the 48th and 47th Battalions in first. Those units held the front line for a week then were relieved by the 45th and 46th. The 13th Brigade moved to reserve positions at Kemmel on 8 August and Division HQ moved to Dranoutre on the same day. The Division's new front now ran roughly from Steignast Farm on the right (south), across Hun's Walk and the Blauwepoortbeek, then further north across the Wambeek to the crest of the northern slope of that stream's valley.[43] The brigade frontages were divided along the general line of the Blauwepoortbeek. The 4th Brigade held the right sub-sector with one battalion 'up', relieving with its other units in turn, while the 12th Brigade on the left had a two-battalion frontage and would be relieved by another brigade.

The 4th Division artillery arrived back from the St Eloi sector on the nights of 8/9 and 9/10 August and went straight into the line, relieving the batteries of the 37th British Division. The 4th Division's front was now covered by its own artillery and that of the 3rd Division, which had stayed in the line, the combined force coming under Brigadier General Rosenthal's command on 10 August. The CRA himself would soon be the next member of the 4th Division's command group to move on. Rosenthal was seen by Sir William Birdwood, GOC AIF, as a potential divisional commander, but as first needing some experience commanding infantry. A vacancy for an infantry brigadier had recently arisen in the 3rd Division and it was arranged that Rosenthal would be transferred to the posting. He was aware of this move early in August,[44] but it was not until towards the end of the month that the arrangements were complete and a successor appointed as CRA. This was Lieutenant Colonel William Burgess,[45] currently commanding the 3rd (Army) AFA Brigade, an officer with whom Rosenthal had been closely associated earlier in the war. Burgess, now promoted to brigadier general, was a British-born New Zealander, 37 years old, a professional officer of the

Brigadier General William Burgess (later Sir William Sinclair-Burgess) KBE CB CMG DSO (1880–1964), CRA 4th Division from August 1917. (AWM H00045)

New Zealand permanent forces who had been on exchange duty in Australia at the outbreak of war. Appointed to the AIF, he was made a battery commander in the 3rd AFA Brigade (1st Division), under Rosenthal as Brigade CO. He commanded his battery in the Gallipoli campaign during which he and Rosenthal were both wounded by the same Turkish shell. When Rosenthal was promoted to CRA 4th Division in Egypt, Burgess succeeded him as Brigade CO and commanded the unit with the 1st Division in the early fighting in France, and then as an independent 'Army' brigade after the 1917 artillery re-organisation. Now Burgess was again succeeding his former CO in a senior appointment. The changeover occurred on 25 August, three years to the day since Rosenthal had first assumed command of the 3rd AFA Brigade at the beginning of the war.[46] The 4th Division artillery had now replaced its CRA and both unit commanders in little over a month.

Fifth Army's attacks east of the Salient had resumed on 10 August, in conditions of weather and ground that were if anything worse than those that had stopped the first attack. For all of their dogged courage, the British infantry could make almost no progress through the mud against the German artillery and machine guns. Where any ground was gained the Germans counter-attacked in force and drove their opponents back in savage fighting. The optimism of Sir Douglas Haig and Sir Hubert Gough was undiminished, and in the belief that the Germans were about to crack, Fifth Army launched several more attacks over the next two weeks. All failed with heavy losses in the morass. By the end of the month even Sir Douglas Haig had had enough, and he decided that a change of method was needed. Responsibility for continuing the offensive was passed to General Plumer and Second Army.

During that period the 4th Division had been holding the front line at Messines, a quiet sector in the sense that no large-scale fighting took place; 'the Australian infantry was so fortunate as to be spared ... the flooded but quiet trenches east of Messines were sufficiently uncomfortable without the added horrors of the offensive.'[47] The usual patrol clashes and exchanges of harassing fire continued, as did the strenuous and repetitive work of trying to get the infantry's positions into some sort of habitable condition and improve the defences, while the brigades rotated their battalions week-about between front and support lines. In the 4th Brigade sub-sector on the right, the 14th Battalion, relieving the 16th in the front line on the night of 8/9 August, were displeased that the 16th had made little progress on setting up barbed wire. The 14th, perhaps not fully aware of the battering that the 16th had been taking from the German artillery, soon found that they did not have enough men themselves to complete the wiring,[48] before handing over in turn to the 15th Battalion on 14/15 August. Long-range enemy shelling and aerial bombing made life dangerous also for the units behind the front line. On 11 August the 13th Battalion, in the support lines, had both its CO, Lieutenant Colonel James Durrant, and second-in-command, Major Hugh Pulling, wounded and evacuated,[49] leaving Major Harry Murray, senior company commander, as acting CO. Later in the month, the 13th's previous second-in-command, Major Douglas Marks, returned to the unit, having recovered from his near-fatal wound at Bullecourt, and took over as temporary CO. Rotating in and out of the line through the month, the 13th relieved the 15th in the front line positions on 20/21 August, finding conditions that were graphically described by the battalion historian. The route to the front was via the communications trench called Fanny's Avenue,

> but after a few had become bogged in it, the rest kept on top ... we did our best to drain and improve it, but it remained and would always remain an awful trench. The whole area was waterlogged... On our left was the stagnant swamp of [the] Blauwepoortbeek, overflowing towards Gapaard. From Gapaard to Steignast we deepened the trench to nine feet, drove piles to carry a duckboard floor four feet from the bottom, and still the water rose a foot over the duckboards. Out in the Outpost Line where we linked up a series of isolated posts, the men preferred the dangers of the surface to the waist-deep mud of the trenches.[50]

The previous night the 4th Brigade had lost another senior officer when the 15th Battalion veteran Major William Mundell was mortally wounded in the front line. The Battalion CO, Lieutenant Colonel McSharry, was just returning from a long stay in hospital from a serious case of trench fever and Major Mundell was in temporary command of the unit. He was going around the Battalion outposts when he was hit by a German machine gun bullet. He was carried to the RAP but died soon afterwards. Enlisting in 1914 as a private, 'in his quiet way, Major Billy Mundell had firmly established himself in the affections of his men ... he had a premonition of his fate ... for he had openly spoken about it in the mess before entering the line.'[51]

On 23 August the 4th Division changed front to its right, shifting southwards for the Blauwepoortbeek to form its northern boundary again. The 12th Brigade, then manning the front line north of that stream, was relieved by British units and marched back to camps in the Neuve Église area. Division HQ relocated a short distance south to Ravelsburg. The 4th Brigade, now the left brigade of the 4th Division front, stayed in place, while the 13th Brigade was ordered up from reserve near Kemmel to relieve New Zealand units facing the German line at Warneton. That sector now became the right of the 4th Division front. The Division only occupied the new sector for another week and were then relieved by the 30th British Division on the night of 29/30 August, having lost 161 killed and missing and 653 wounded holding the 'quiet' sector for the month.[52] The 4th Brigade was withdrawn that night and the 13th Brigade on the next night. The divisional artillery had already been relieved several nights earlier for a welcome, if brief, rest. The artillery remained in reserve in the Caestre area but the main body of the Division continued further away from the front to billets in a string of villages centring on Bomy, 55 kilometres south-west of Ypres in a region untouched by the war. Division HQ was set up at Bomy on 3 September. The move seemed to confirm what all ranks had been anticipating, a lengthy rest well away from the forward area, as the divisions of I Anzac had been enjoying since late May in 'what was probably the longest, most complete, and most pleasant rest ever given to British infantry in France'[53] (their artillery elements, however, had been sent into action at Ypres in July). Now the I Anzac infantry were on the way up to the forward area, and that of II Anzac was scheduled to rest—but as of 3 September, the same day that its main body arrived in the rest area, the 4th Division was transferred to the control of I Anzac. The break would only be for three weeks before heading for the front line again with I Anzac, and the word spread through the Division with what C E W Bean called a 'sharp shock of disappointment,' probably saying the least. Bean noted that the 4th Division was then 'heavily diluted with new reinforcements ... probably then at its lowest ebb,'[54] with the inexperience of the new troops and the fatigue of the veterans.

The effect of this change in plans was particularly serious in the 4th Brigade's 14th Battalion, at least among its officers, partly because a regrettable situation with that unit's leadership had arisen at about the same time. The story is of interest as an example, if an extreme one, of how issues behind the scenes can result in dissension and affect a unit's morale.[55] Since June, the 14th had been commanded by Major (temporary Lieutenant Colonel) Eliazar Margolin, but that appointment had not been a success. Margolin had been unable to gain the respect of his officers and men. Well aware himself of that situation, he had asked in August to be relieved of the command. This was granted, and Brigadier General Brand asked for Lieutenant Colonel Walter Smith to be transferred from the AIF Depots in England to command the 14th. It is difficult to understand how that choice can have been made. Colonel Smith was a regular officer who had done good work as a brigade major in the 3rd Division, but he had been found wanting when promoted to command the 37th Battalion in that Division. His brigadier had been dissatisfied with Smith's performance at Messines and sent in an adverse report recommending that he be relieved of command. Major General Monash, GOC 3rd Division, concurred and Smith was transferred to England. Less than three months after Smith had been assessed as unsuitable to command a battalion in the field Brand requested his appointment as CO of the 14th, an inexplicable lapse in judgement by the brigadier. General Sinclair-MacLagan, in a memorandum to General Birdwood (as GOC AIF) supporting the request, wrote that 'Brand says that he [Smith] will be just the man to get the battalion going well. He knows him very well and says that he is a second Peck.' How Brand knew Smith and how he came to have such an opinion about his qualities is not clear, but the request was approved and Lieutenant Colonel Smith 'marched in' to take command of the 14th Battalion on 1 September.[56]

At about the same time, the 14th's second in command was replaced as well, also in unusual circumstances. Major Otto Fuhrmann currently held that appointment by virtue of seniority. Although he appears to have been a conscientious officer, by now the higher command had assessed Fuhrmann as not having the right qualities for a battalion second-in-command and Brigadier General Brand wanted him moved elsewhere. This was approved, but General Birdwood pre-empted the choice of a successor by ordering that the vacancy be filled by Major David Thomson,[57] to be transferred from the 53rd Battalion (5th Division). Thomson was also under a cloud in his present unit. A regular soldier who had started the war as a sergeant-major in the 1st Division, he had been commissioned then transferred to the 5th Division, and had initially done well before promotion to major seems to have taken him beyond his capabilities. He was assessed as unsuitable at that level and as being a bad influence on the younger officers—

an incident while on leave in England suggests that drink may have been a factor. In any case, General Birdwood believed that Thomson should be given another chance in view of his earlier record, and ordered that he was to swap postings with Fuhrmann, thereby meeting the wishes of neither the 14th nor 53rd Battalions. The 4th Division GOC, General Sinclair-MacLagan, presumably after consulting Brand, protested to Birdwood: 'replacing Major Fuhrmann by Major Thomson ... would truly be a case of out of the frying pan into the fire.' It was to no avail.

Some accounts suggest that Brand had deliberately brought in both Smith and Thomson, both regulars, with the intention of blocking promotion from within the 14th Battalion, in particular that of the outspoken Captain Albert Jacka. Lieutenant Colonel Smith's posting was Brand's idea, but that of Major Thomson certainly was not, and there is no indication of who Brand might have actually had in mind to replace Fuhrmann. In any case, Jacka was not necessarily next in line within the battalion for promotion. One good officer with seniority over him was Captain Harold Wanliss; although he had less combat experience than Jacka, Wanliss had been commissioned several months before him, and Wanliss's captaincy had also come through earlier, if only by a few days. Another who could have been considered was Captain William Wadsworth, the only survivor of the 14th's four outstanding company commanders who had gone into action at Bullecourt.[58] Wadsworth was currently detached to the 4th Training Battalion, but could well have been brought back in the circumstances, and he had been made captain in March 1916, a year before Jacka. Major Thomson's appearance was thus a potential barrier to promotion for more than one officer in the 14th (the other major's appointment in the 14th was held by Major Arthur Cox, an original officer with the unit and a Gallipoli veteran; it is not clear what part Major Cox played in these events).

Thomson had not even arrived, however, on 4 September, when Brigadier General Brand visited his units to pass on the bad news that the anticipated long rest would not happen. Addressing a parade of the 14th Battalion's officers, he was interrupted by Captain Jacka, recently returned after recovering from his leg wound. Jacka made his feelings known plainly: 'Do you mean to tell me that this battalion is to be flung into the line right away, in spite of all the promises made to the men?'[59] Further harsh words were exchanged in an extraordinary clash between a brigadier and a company commander in one of his battalions, before the fuming Brand departed. The change of orders was hardly the brigadier's fault—the decision to bring the 4th Division back into action had originated with General Birdwood—as Edgar Rule later recognised in his memoirs:

> ... we were unjust to the old Brig. He was not one who offered his brigade for useless stunts, and he was not one who remained out of a fight when his men were in it ... [he] had an unpleasant duty in breaking the news to us, and he could not have done it more straightly and honourably.[60]

The battalions resumed training, concentrating on perfecting platoon and company tactics, but in the 4th Brigade the tension between Brigadier General Brand and the 14th Battalion continued. When the unit first came out of the forward area, a mix-up in orders had resulted in its Lewis guns, a key element of platoon structure, being transported to a wrong location and until they arrived the 14th was restricted to fairly elementary training. The brigadier was unaware of this when he visited the Battalion's training area. Seeing the simple exercises going on, and no doubt still smarting over the recent parade, Brand lost his temper and berated the troops and their officers for inefficiency. Some of the tirade was directed at Captain Wanliss, one of the most admired officers in the Battalion, and such was the resentment that most of the officers agreed between themselves to send in their resignations and request transfers out of the brigade. Brand met the officers the next day and told them that he would not accept their resignations. After another heated clash with Captain Jacka, the brigadier went on to speak to the officers about plans for the upcoming operations, during which he asked Jacka's opinion on tactics. It was an olive branch, but Jacka rejected it with a truculent reply. Overnight the officers wrote out their resignations again; Albert Jacka had tremendous influence in the Battalion, and it is perhaps regrettable that he did not use that influence to smooth over the situation, rather than making it worse by his attitude. His fighting record and unsurpassed value in action, emphasised by the strip of crimson ribbon above his breast pocket, probably saved him from any disciplinary repercussions. By the next morning the brigadier had thought better of things. He visited the Battalion again and apologised for his earlier remarks, acknowledging that he had been unfair and too hasty. 'It is not every superior who can recover from a mistake as the old Brig did, and retain men's respect, and one must hand him high marks for it. It is to the credit of both sides that the incident ended there.'[61] It was not the end of the 14th's internal troubles, however. The doubtful quality of the battalion's leadership remained, exacerbated at about the same time when an unpopular officer returned from a long detachment and shortly afterwards took over the key post of adjutant. With no confidence in Battalion HQ, the 14th's company officers felt that they would be left to their own devices in action. It is greatly to those officers' credit, and particularly to that of Albert Jacka, that the unit put in an outstanding performance in the next battle, but the situation could not go on indefinitely.

The infantry brigades continued with their training through the first half of September, leading up full brigade exercises as the time approached for the Division's return to the front. The 13th Brigade filled its remaining battalion CO vacancy on 15 September when Lieutenant Colonel James Denton arrived to take over command of the 49th Battalion, with Major Arrell reverting once more to the second-in-command role. Colonel Denton came with a solid record as a fighting officer. He was 41 years old, a former militia officer with long service in Western Australia before the war. At Gallipoli, Denton had been awarded the DSO as a major with the 11th Battalion, among the first units to go ashore, in General Sinclair-MacLagan's 3rd Brigade. After Gallipoli, he had gone to France with the 11th and had commanded the unit for a short time, before returning to Australia on leave to be with his dying wife. On his return, he was appointed to command a battalion in the 6th Division before that formation was disbanded and he was transferred to the 49th as CO.[62] By that time, mid-September, enough reinforcements had been absorbed for the 4th Division's numbers to be approaching full establishment. The official war establishment was 762 officers and 18,140 Other Ranks, and the total strength figure was only about 700 short of that. After allowing for the usual absences on leave, courses, detachment and illness, the numbers actually with their units was reported as 612 officers and 15,652 ORs;[63] a few units were slightly over establishment, at least on paper, a situation that was unlikely to recur.

Orders now came out for the Division's movement to the forward area again, while the units finished off their training and brigade sports days were held. The move to the Steenvoorde area, west of Ypres, began on 18 September, with the 4th Brigade Group leading off and the other groups following over the next few days. Division HQ opened at Steenvoorde on 20 September, the same day that the offensive against the heights beyond Ypres was resumed by Second Army, with the 1st and 2nd Divisions of I Anzac going into action. The 4th Division was getting into position to join the battle and the staff were already working on preliminary operation orders. At Steenvoorde a new unit, the 24th Machine Gun Company, joined the Division. Over recent months, each BEF division's firepower had been augmented by an additional MG company, directly controlled from division level; with the existing brigade MG companies, the divisions now had 64 Vickers guns available. The 24th MG Company had been training in England since its formation in June and would shortly be going into action for the first time, only a few weeks after landing in France. The unit was commanded by Captain Fredric Hinton,[64] who had been a machine gunner with the Light Horse at Gallipoli and more recently an officer with the 12th MG Company.

With the number of changes in senior personnel since Messines in June, the 4th Division would be going into its next round of heavy fighting with a somewhat different group of commanders:

4th Australian Division Order of Battle, mid-September 1917

GOC	Major General E G Sinclair-MacLagan
GSO1	Lieutenant Colonel D J C K Bernard
GSO2	Major E C P Plant
GSO3	Captain J S Rogers
AA&QMG	Lieutenant Colonel R Dowse
DAAG	Major W Fowler-Brownsworth
DAQMG	Major E O Milne
ADCs	Captain D S Maxwell, Lieutenant E H G Kemmis
24th MG Company	Captain F B Hinton

Infantry (including brigade machine guns and mortars)

4th Brigade:	Brigadier General C H Brand
Brigade Major:	Major E A Wilton
Staff Captain:	Captain A H Fraser
13th Battalion:	Lieutenant Colonel J M A Durrant (Major D G Marks temporarily)
14th Battalion:	Lieutenant Colonel W J Smith

15th Battalion:	Lieutenant Colonel T P McSharry
16th Battalion	Lieutenant Colonel E A Drake-Brockman
4th MG Company:	Captain A Mitchell
4th LTM Battery:	Captain A W Potts
12th Brigade:	Brigadier General J C Robertson
Brigade Major:	Major E L Salier
Staff Captain:	Captain F G S Cherry
45th Battalion:	Lieutenant Colonel S C E Herring
46th Battalion:	Lieutenant Colonel H K Denham
47th Battalion:	Lieutenant Colonel A P Imlay
48th Battalion:	Lieutenant Colonel R L Leane
12th MG Company:	Captain D S A Martin
12th LTM Battery:	F G S Cherry
13th Brigade:	Brigadier General T W Glasgow
Brigade Major:	Major R Morell
Staff Captain:	Captain A Nicholson
49th Battalion:	Lieutenant Colonel J S Denton
50th Battalion:	Lieutenant Colonel A G Salisbury
51st Battalion:	Lieutenant Colonel J C T E C Ridley
52nd Battalion:	Lieutenant Colonel J L Whitham
13th MG Company:	Captain C F Duchatel
13th LTM Battery:	Captain S C Morris

Artillery

CRA:	Brigadier General W L H Burgess
Brigade Major:	Major C M Bates
Staff Captain:	Lieutenant A C R Waite
10th Field Artillery Brigade: (37th, 38th, 39th, 110th Batteries)	Lieutenant Colonel T I C Williams
11th Field Artillery Brigade: (41st, 42nd, 43rd, 111th Batteries)	Lieutenant Colonel P M Edwards
Divisional Ammunition Column:	Lieutenant Colonel H V Vernon
Divisional Trench Mortar Officer: (X4A, Y4A, Z4A MTM Batteries, V4A HTM Battery)	Captain S J Fox (Captain C A Sherwood temporarily)

Engineers
    CRE: Lieutenant Colonel G C E Elliott
    4th Field Company: Major H G Tolley
    12th Field Company: Major C C Riddell
    13th Field Company: Major H A Reid
    4th Division Signal Company: Major J E Fraser

Pioneers
    4th Pioneer Battalion: Lieutenant Colonel V A H Sturdee

Medical
    ADMS: Colonel G W Barber
    DADMS: Major L W Jeffries
    4th Field Ambulance: Lieutenant Colonel H H B Follit
    12th Field Ambulance: Lieutenant Colonel C E Wassell
    13th Field Ambulance: Lieutenant Colonel J B StV Welch

Veterinary
    DADVS: Lieutenant Colonel W A Kendall
    4th Mobile Veterinary Section: Major E S James

Transport (Divisional Train)
    CO: Lieutenant Colonel A A Holdsworth
    7th Company AASC: Captain C R Walsh
    14th Company AASC: Major S A Robertson
    26th Company AASC: Captain C Reynolds
    27th Company AASC: Captain J Warmington

13 Notes

1. 12th Brigade War Diary for June 1917, Appendix 9.
2. 13th Brigade War Diary for June 1917, Appendix 15.
3. 52nd battalion War Diary for June 1917, Appendix 2.
4. R Prior and T Wilson, *Passchendaele: The Untold Story*, p. 106.
5. 48th Battalion War Diary for June 1917, Appendices, memorandum 'Messines, Operation of tanks at, 7/6/17'.
6. Figures from the 4th Division Admin Staff War Diary for June 1917, various Appendices.
7. This appears to be the correct spelling, although some records have MacPherson. Both spellings appear in documents in his service record, which is registered under McPherson; that spelling is also in the gazettal for his Mention in Despatches. After Lt Col Whitham assumed command of

the 52nd, Maj McPherson returned to his original unit, the 12th Battalion. He survived the war, but tragically took his own life on a ship returning to Australia.

8   'Celebrities of the AIF: Major-General J L Whitham, CMG, DSO', *Reveille*, February 1939, pp. 8–9, 32–33; *Australian Dictionary of Biography*, article on John Lawrence Whitham by Peter Burness.
9   4th Brigade War Diary, 30 June 1917.
10 Chataway, *Op Cit*, p. 181.
11 Holmes, *Op Cit*, pp 212–13.
12 *Official History*, Vol IV, p. 713; Vol II, p. 810.
13 4th Division General Staff War Diary, 6 July 1917.
14 Wanliss, *Op Cit*, p. 227.
15 Rule, *Op Cit*, pp. 89–90.
16 That is, the GHQ plan. Robin Prior maintains, in *Gallipoli: the End of the Myth* (2009), pp. 110–118, 123 and 245, that Sinclair-MacLagan was actually following amended orders issued by General Birdwood, GOC ANZAC.
17 For an exception, see Peter Williams, *The Battle of Anzac Ridge* (2007).
18 Monash, Sir J *The Australian Victories in France in* 1918, p. 244.
19 Lt Kemmis replaced Lt Donald Gillies-Reyburn, who had returned to his British/Indian Army regiment on 13 July, as noted in the Admin Staff War Diary.
20 Rosenthal Diary, 9 July 1917.
21 *Ibid*, 18 July 1917.
22 *Ibid*, 10 July 1917.
23 *Ibid*, various entries in July 1917.
24 A more senior but much less experienced officer, who would need a long period of practical training in the forward zone, was originally considered for the command, but Rosenthal argued successfully that Edwards could take on the duties immediately.
25 13th Brigade War Diary for July 1917, Appendix 12.
26 12th Brigade War Diary, 31 July 1917. The numbers in the divisional Admin War Diary are slightly different.
27 *Ibid*, Appendix 9.
28 Most of the material that follows is sourced from the conference notes in the 4th Division GS War Diary for July 1917, Appendix 38, and from a detailed memorandum produced by the 4th Brigade staff, in their July 1917 War Diary, Appendix 35.
29 4th Division GS War Diary for July 1917, Appendix 38, and 12th Brigade War Diary for July 1917, Appendix 4. See P Stanley, *Bad Characters* (2010), pp. 101–105 etc, for a discussion of this topic.
30 4th Brigade War Diary for July 1917, Appendix 35.
31 See the *Medical History*, Vol II, pp. 595–600. The policy was later modified following protests from senior medical officers, notably those of the AIF.
32 4th Division ADMS War Diary for July 1917, Appendices.
33 At the time, Archdeacon Ward was serving as a chaplain attached to AIF HQ in London. He was requested by General Birdwood (as GOC AIF) to give these lectures to all AIF troops in France, according to documents on his service record.
34 4th Division ADMS War Diary, entries for 27, 28, 30 and 31 July.

35 Stanley, *Op Cit*, p. 117. Sgt Eric Evans, 13th Battalion, mentions the lecture in his diary (*So Far From Home*, p.96).
36 Stanley, *Op Cit*, p. 192–7
37 4th Brigade War Diary, 27 July 1917.
38 *Medical History*, Vol III, p. 155.
39 4th Brigade War Diary, 26 July 1917.
40 4th Division Admin War Diary for July 1917, Appendices 8 and 10.
41 12th Brigade War Diary for July 1917, Appendix 8.
42 4th Brigade War Diary for August 1917, Appendix 15.
43 4th Division GS War Diary for August 1917, Appendix 7. The original order for the 12th Brigade deployment (Appendix 6 in the Diary) quotes the wrong map square, U instead of O.
44 Rosenthal Diary, 6 August 1917.
45 From 1921, he used the surname Sinclair-Burgess, making the change definite in 1926. Burgess was his stepfather's name and Sinclair that of his natural father (*New Zealand Dictionary of Biography*, article on W L H Sinclair-Burgess by W D McIntyre). Burgess was the surname that he was known by throughout the war, and his AIF service record is under Burgess.
46 Rosenthal Diary, 25 August 1917.
47 *Official History*, Vol IV, p. 729 and 729n.
48 Rule, *Op Cit*, p. 104. Rule's chapters 20 and 21 give a graphic account of life for the average infantry platoon in such situations.
49 The circumstances are difficult to determine. The actual incident is not mentioned in the division, brigade or battalion war diaries, except for the two officers' names appearing in casualty summaries. The battalion history (White, *Op Cit*, p. 103) has a bare mention of Lt Col Durrant's wounding, misdating it to July. The officers' service records note both being wounded on 11 August but give no details; Durrant was recorded as receiving a shrapnel wound, but one of the medical reports on Maj Pulling's file says that he was hit by a bomb fragment, which must mean an aerial bomb rather than a grenade. There is a record in the division and brigade war diaries of a German aircraft bombing the 13th Battalion horse lines on the night of 11 August, but no personnel casualties are mentioned.
50 White, *Op Cit*, p. 104.
51 Chataway, *Op Cit*, p. 186. Maj John Corrigan was actually the senior major in the 15th Battalion, but he appears to have been away at this time also. The reason is not clear from his service record, but he had recently recovered from a bout of pneumonia, then gone on a senior officers' course until the end of July, and may have been on leave after that.
52 4th Division Admin Staff War Diary, Appendix 4 to the August diary; that appendix is attached to the September diary in the AWM records, as is the August list of officers joining and leaving the Division.
53 *Official History*, Vol IV, p. 683.
54 *Ibid*, p. 734 and 734n.
55 Most of the following account is sourced from correspondence on the service records of the officers concerned.
56 This assessment is mainly based on reports on Colonel Smith's service record, supported by implications in the Battalion history. There is, however, a very favourable assessment of Smith by an ex-37th Battalion member in the Bean Papers (AWM38 3DRL606/254/1, pp. 145–6). That

57   document states that Smith became unpopular with his superiors because of his tendency to take the side of the ordinary 'digger' against higher authority.

57   Not 'Thompson' as appears in some sources. The account that follows is based on documents in Maj Thomson's service record.

58   See p. xxx [445–6 in draft]

59   Rule, *Op Cit*, p. 109. Rule, who was present at the parade, is the main source for accounts of this famous incident, including that in the battalion history (Wanliss, *Op Cit*, pp. 234–5).

60   *Loc Cit*.

61   *Ibid*, p.110. Some accounts, including Wanliss, point out that the simple training exercises that caused the brigadier's ire were as ordered by Colonel Smith. Certainly the first week of the 14th's training syllabus appears to be undemanding (Appendix 2 of the unit War Diary for September 1917) but Rule makes it clear that the absence of Lewis guns was the main problem. From September 10, the syllabus is at a more advanced level (Appendices 4 and 5). Presumably the guns had arrived by then, and probably General Brand or his staff had given the CO the benefit of their advice also. The 14th Battalion seems to have done well in a full brigade exercise that took place on 14 September.

62   *Australian Dictionary of Biography*, article on James Samuel Denton by R.D. Manley.

63   Figures from the 4th Division Admin Staff War Diary for September 1917, Appendix 3. The *Official History* (Vol IV, p. 734n) gives the 4th Division numbers as 496 officers and 11,543 ORs at the time that it came out of the line at the beginning of September.

64   24th MG Company War Diary for June to September 1917. It is not always easy to determine who was the company OC at different times.

14: Bite and Hold

Sir Herbert Plumer, GOC Second Army, approached the task of advancing the British line on to the Ypres heights with much the same tactics that he had used at Messines. He planned a series of attacks, each with a strictly limited set of objectives, with the infantry advancing under the cover of massed artillery. Having reached a line that was still within range of artillery protection, the infantry would dig in and consolidate the new position, which would be held against counter-attack by their own weapons but particularly by defensive artillery barrages. Once that line was firmly established, the artillery would move their weapons forward and another advance would be launched in the same style, a succession of steps that would keep the front steadily advancing—the 'bite and hold' method. Each step would be limited to no more than 1,400 metres from the jumping-off line, with the attacking divisions rotating for each step.

Second Army's front was extended to the left (north) to face the German positions on the Gheluvelt plateau that had defied numerous attacks by Fifth Army in August. The first step would be capture of a line along the western portion of the plateau, including the various woods—that is, groups of scattered stumps, studded with dug-in machine gun positions—in that area, such as Glencorse Wood, Inverness Copse and the 'indescribable morass'[1] of Nonne Boschen. With Fifth Army advancing on the left, Second Army would attack in the angle formed by the Ypres-Roulers railway and the Menin Road, radiating out from Ypres. I Anzac Corps would be brought up to form the extended left of Second Army, with X Corps on its right, the Menin Road forming the boundary between the two corps, each of which would have two divisions in the line. The first attack was scheduled for 20 September, and I Anzac ordered the 1st and 2nd Divisions, right to left, to go up for this first step. Preparatory work on infrastructure behind the lines went on, helped by a period of fine weather, and Second Army assembled a mighty force of artillery, amounting to 575 'heavies' and 720 field artillery pieces (30 brigades).[2] The 4th Division's 10th and 11th AFA Brigades and the DAC were brought up from their short rest in reserve at Caestre to join this force, to combine with the

2nd Division artillery in covering the left divisional front in I Anzac's sector. The command arrangement was for the CRA of whichever division's infantry was in the line to control both divisional artilleries, so for the first stage of the advance the 2nd division CRA would be in command. The 2nd and 4th Division batteries completed relieving those of the 25th and 47th British Divisions by the night of 10/11 September, with the two DACs taking over from their equivalents also. The 4th Division's field brigades were grouped together and designated as 'C' Group; Lieutenant Colonel Williams, CO of the 10th AFA Brigade, was nominated as group commander, with headquarters in one of the numerous dugouts within the Ypres Ramparts. The 11th AFA Brigade CO, Lieutenant Colonel Edwards, was initially appointed as liaison officer with the 7th Infantry Brigade and also regularly alternated with Colonel Williams as Group Commander over the next few weeks of fighting;[3] where two field artillery brigades were grouped, it was becoming standard practice for the 'spare' brigade commander to work with the appropriate infantry brigade HQ,[4] thereby making an artillery officer of substantial rank responsible for liaison at that level.

On this front the German system of defence in depth had been developed to comprise a thinly held forward zone, an intermediate zone up to two kilometres deep defended by numerous pillboxes and machine gun posts, and then a strongly held line from which powerful counter-attacks could be launched to destroy a weakened and disorganised attacker. The system had been effective against Fifth Army's operations in August but new infantry and artillery tactics had been worked out to overcome those defences. Since enemy resistance was expected to be stronger the deeper the attacking infantry advanced, a light force (typically one battalion on a brigade's front) would be used against the German forward zone, with the strongest wave leapfrogging through to deliver the main punch against the deepest objective line. Artillery fire instead of being directed at a defined enemy line would now deluge a deep zone, the field artillery directly covering the infantry advance and the heavy artillery searching for enemy batteries and strong-points. The 2nd Division CRA, Brigadier General G J Johnston, outlined the method in preliminary instructions to the units under his command:

> ... to deal effectively with the enemy's new system of defence, the old principles of creeping and standing barrages are inadequate. It is necessary to cover the whole ground to be taken to a depth of a thousand yards into successive lines of barrages from different natures of guns. These lines move forward as the Infantry advance. On an objective being gained, a continual searching of the ground beyond the protective barrage is necessary.[5]

Joining in Second Army's week-long preliminary bombardment, the 4th Division's batteries began shooting in their allotted tasks as they came into the line, and also began losing casualties to enemy shelling. On 13 September the Germans hit the positions of the 37th Battery (10th AFA Brigade) and put four of its guns out of action. On the same day at his Ypres headquarters the Brigade's CO and group commander, Colonel Williams, encountered a rare note of natural beauty in the desolation all around when he observed the well-known pair of white swans that still made their home in the old moat of the ruined city. So struck was

Williams by the graceful birds that he made a detailed entry about them in the unit's official War Diary.[6] The field artillery put down harassing fire on identified movement routes in enemy territory, with the howitzers paying particular attention to communication trenches, and on several days all batteries took part in practice barrages. These represented only part of the barrage that would be delivered by the full force of the artillery on the day of the attack but were still intended to inflict damage on the enemy.

> [The practice barrages] would begin sometimes from the enemy's forward area and sweep backwards, sometimes from his back area and sweep forwards. At other times the field-artillery barrages would sweep forwards and those of the heavy artillery backwards until they met, when the combined storm would advance again. The barrage always ended by a jump back to its starting line, or to some area where the enemy's garrison might have emerged from its shelter.[7]

The final attack barrage would consist of five lines of fire—18-pounders, firing shrapnel, starting 140 metres from the infantry forming-up positions, then more 18-pounders combined with 4.5-inch howitzers, firing a mixture of shrapnel and HE, next a barrage of machine gun fire from massed batteries of Vickers guns, and the final two lines from the heavy artillery. Early on 20 September field and heavy howitzers began a four-hour gas bombardment on known enemy battery positions, then at 5:40 am every artillery piece and machine gun battery on Second and Fifth Army's fronts opened fire and the infantry went forward. The combined 4th and 2nd Division artilleries, covering the 2nd Division infantry, were in continuous action for the next eight hours, first firing their creeping barrage up to each stage of the advance, changing to a protective barrage while the infantry re-organised, then creeping on again up to the final objective. It was a complex fire-plan with the rate of creep varying with the stages of the infantry advance. As each stage was reached the guns briefly changed to smoke shell to indicate to the infantry that the barrage had stopped moving, then temporarily increasing their rate of fire to signal when the next creep was about to begin. The infantry attained all of their objectives except on the extreme right where a particularly formidable German stronghold known as Tower Hamlets held out. During the afternoon the field artillery opened fire several times to break up German counter-attacks, and by evening the new line was firmly held; the 10th AFA Brigade reported firing 25,000 18-pounder shells and almost 5,000 howitzer shells in 24 hours.[8] The advance, the Battle of the Menin Road, had gone almost exactly to plan. In Second Army's sector the British front had moved forward more than a kilometre onto the Gheluvelt Plateau and now included the western edge of Polygon Wood. The battle had not been bloodless, however. The German artillery was not as badly affected by counter-battery fire as it had been at Messines and its shelling had inflicted many casualties on the advancing troops. There was considerable resistance also from pillboxes that had survived the bombardment, and many sharp infantry fights took place. The 2nd Division had 2,259 casualties,[9] mostly in the infantry, and casualties over the whole front amounted to about 21,000;[10] stretcher bearers from the 12th and 13th Field Ambulances had been called forward from reserve to assist the 1st Division casualty evacuation.[11]

The first stage of General Plumer's plan had succeeded and preparations started immediately for the next advance, to jump off in six days' time. The 4th Division infantry would now be in the forefront and the main body of the Division was already moving up to relieve the 2nd Division on the left of I Anzac's sector. The 5th Division similarly relieved the 1st on the right. The 4th Division's attack would be carried out by the 13th and 4th Brigades, and the troops moved up from the reserve positions around Steenvoorde to the new front line on the night of 23/24 September. The 12th Brigade was held in reserve, except for its MG company, which would have a task in the attack. Major General Sinclair-MacLagan took over command of the left divisional sector on the morning of 24 September, with forward HQ established at Smyth Camp to the north of Dickebusch. The combined 4th and 2nd Division artillery continued to cover the sector, now coming under the control of the 4th Division CRA, Brigadier General Burgess. Immediately after the Menin Road battle the batteries moved forward and continued with harassing fire and practice barrages on the next objectives. The other arms and services of the Division relieved their 2nd Division equivalents in the usual way.

With the date for the attack set for 26 September the staffs at the various command levels prepared their plans and issued operation orders in the preceding days. The 4th Division would advance a distance of about a kilometre to the final objective line, with its left reaching the southern edge of Zonnebeke village and its right brushing past the northern edge of Polygon Wood, a front of about 1,400 metres. The Wood itself would be attacked by the 5th Division while Zonnebeke was the objective of the 3rd British Division (V Corps, Fifth Army). The advance would be carried out in two stages rather than the three of the Menin Road battle a week earlier, with the first stage to overcome the German outpost line and reach a position designated as the Red Line, about 700 metres from the start. The second stage of 300 metres would take the advance to the final objective, the Blue Line, partly along the low rise called Tokio Spur. Both brigades in the attack, the 13th on the left and the 4th on the right, would use one battalion for the first stage and two for the second, where the strongest resistance was expected. The remaining battalion in each brigade would hold the existing front line and provide carrying parties and general support for the units in the attack. Both brigades detailed the majority of their LTMs to move forward with the infantry to assist in defending the Blue Line when that objective had been gained, and all of the Division's machine gun resources would be used in the attack. Each attacking brigade's MG company had eight of its sixteen Vickers guns allocated to advance in close support of the infantry and then be set up in defence of the Blue Line. The other guns were detailed to form part of the Division's machine gun barrage, overseen by the divisional machine gun officer, a post currently filled by Captain Charles Duchatel, OC 13th MG Company (the ranking machine gun officer, Major Ernest Radford, was seriously ill in hospital at this time). The barrage guns were formed into two groups, one of 24 guns comprising the new 24th MG Company reinforced by eight guns attached from the 6th MG Company (2nd Division), and the other, designated as the SOS group, with 32 guns formed by the full 12th MG Company and the remaining eight guns each from the 4th and 13th Companies. The guns were positioned about 500 metres behind the jumping-off line, firing over the heads of the infantry as they moved forward.[12] Both groups would be in action as part of the creeping and standing barrages covering the infantry advance to the Red and Blue Lines, with the SOS group then ceasing fire and standing by to respond, in conjunction with the artillery, to SOS signals from the infantry.

The artillery arrangements were similar to those for the Menin Road battle. The barrage would open at Zero with its rear edge falling along a line 140 metres in front of the infantry's forming-up line, where it would stay for three minutes before beginning its creep towards the enemy positions. The barrage would take eight minutes to advance over the first 180 metres, a rate of 90 metres in four minutes, then slow down to 90 metres in six minutes up to the first protective line just beyond the first (Red Line) objective, where it would remain until the next stage of the advance. While the infantry was advancing each 18-pounder would be firing two rounds per minute, a rate that could be physically sustained by the gun crews for lengthy periods; the slower-firing howitzers would shoot at one round per minute. Having reached the first protective line each gun would rapidly fire three rounds of smoke shell as a signal to the infantry, then fire on the protective line for 41 minutes at a slow rate of one round per minute. The advance would then resume, the guns signalling the stage to the infantry by briefly increasing their rate to four rounds per minute. For the last 270 metres to the Blue Line the rate of creep would slow down again to 90 metres in eight minutes. The curtain of shell-bursts would then move to the final protective line and continue for three hours at gradually decreasing intensity.

Of the Division's engineer resources, the 12th Field Company and the 4th Pioneer Battalion worked on transportation routes in the forward area while the 4th and 13th Field Companies would directly support their linked infantry brigades in the advance. Once the objectives were taken some of the sappers would select and mark out tracks for runners and carrying parties to use to and from the front line and the various headquarters, while others supervised the location and construction of strong-points to defend the captured positions. Divisional Engineer HQ organised a pack transport troop to bring up engineering stores along the duckboard tracks to dumps in the battle zone, while for carriage of rations and other supplies the Divisional Train again set up its pack troop, under Captain Clement Walsh, 7th Company AASC.

Medical arrangements centred on the 4th Field Ambulance. There were two Advanced Dressing Stations in use in this sector, 'two ruined buildings on the Menin Road about a mile [1,600 metres] east of Ypres [that] had been in use for medical purposes since 1915,'[13] one for stretcher cases and the other for walking wounded. The 4th Field Ambulance took over the latter ADS and became responsible for all evacuations from the 4th Division's front, as well as receiving walking wounded from the 5th Division on the right; that Division's medical units managed stretcher cases at the other ADS.[14] The stretcher-bearers and ambulance wagons of the 12th and 13th Field Ambulances were attached to the 4th to assist with the long carry from the forward RAPs to the vehicle loading post at Birr Crossroads on the Menin Road, from where the wounded would be transported along that crowded thoroughfare to the ADS. The tent section of the 13th Field Ambulance was allocated to the Corps MDS behind Ypres, while that of the 12th Field Ambulance stayed with its linked infantry brigade in the reserve area and managed the divisional rest station.

The 13th Brigade on the 4th Division's left sent its 52nd Battalion in first on the night of 23/24 September to hold the present front line and carry out support duties for the attacking battalions. Those would be the 50th to lead off against the Red Line, followed by the 51st and 49th to leapfrog through and take the Blue Line. During the deployment the 13th Brigade lost its LTM Battery commander, Captain Sydney Morris, severely wounded. The 4th Brigade on the right selected the 16th Battalion to attack the Red Line with the 14th and 15th to go for the Blue Line and the 13th in support, holding the present front line. The 13th was required to dig a communication trench up to the Red Line on the day of the attack, and Major Marks, acting CO, decided to make an early start on the work; the digging party completed the first 150 metres of the trench on the night of 24/25 September.[15] Besides the 13th, several other battalions went into the battle under acting commanders. The 50th Battalion CO, Lieutenant Colonel Salisbury, was detached as liaison officer to the 3rd British Division (Fifth Army), which would be attacking Zonnebeke on the 13th Brigade's left, and Major Noel Loutit, the 50th's second-in-command, was in charge of the unit for the battle.[16] Similarly the 51st Battalion would be led in action by its second-in-command, Major Robert Christie, instead of the CO, Lieutenant Colonel Ridley. Both officers had been away from their unit until recently, Colonel Ridley having been in hospital for a month with a case of mumps, and Major Christie at a senior officers' course in England. It may be that the CO was still feeling the effects of his illness and the opportunity was taken to give Christie experience of commanding the Battalion in action, while Colonel Ridley went with the left-out-of-battle nucleus. It appears that the 16th Battalion may also have been led by its second-in-command, Major Ross Harwood. That unit's CO, Lieutenant Colonel Edmund Drake-Brockman, had spent the past week in hospital with trench fever, but had returned to his battalion on 24 September. Major Harwood had been across all of the preliminary arrangements and it may have been decided that he should continue in command for the actual operation—the 4th Division's summary of its preparations, dated 25 September, shows Harwood as in command of the 16th Battalion.[17]

The formations to be used by the infantry in the attack were laid down in some detail by Division HQ, following guidelines from the higher command. Each Brigade would have its lead-off force of one battalion, attacking the Red Line objective, spread across the brigade frontage ahead of the existing front line, with the heavier Blue Line contingent of two battalions each concentrated on half the frontage behind the front line, the whole force deployed over a depth of 380 metres. The 4th Brigade on the right would occupy a front of

460 metres at the jumping-off line, widening to 620 metres at the final objective, with the 13th Brigade's frontage on the left starting at 570 metres and widening to 690 metres. The first line would be preceded by a thin screen of skirmishers keeping as close as possible to the edge of the barrage.[18] For the early part of the advance the infantry would move in small columns of sections before deploying into line as they neared the objective. Each attacking battalion formed up in three waves per company, with the 4th Brigade units on a four-company frontage and those of the 13th Brigade on two companies.[19]

On 25 September, the day before the operation, Second Army's preparations were disturbed by a sudden German attack on the British X Corps front adjoining I Anzac to the south. Behind a heavy barrage the Germans drove into the British lines on the right of the 5th Division; Brigadier General 'Pompey' Elliott's 15th Brigade became involved in heavy fighting to stop the enemy advance and partly restore the flank. A gap remained in the line, however, and the 5th Division would have to attack the next day while guarding an open right flank. On the night of 25/26 September, after a period of intense activity by unit intelligence officers laying tapes to mark the jumping off positions, the attacking troops moved up and assembled to wait for Zero. At 5:50 am the Battle of Polygon Wood began with the opening of the barrage:

> It seemed to break out ... with a single crash. The ground was dry, and the shell-bursts raised a wall of dust and smoke which appeared to be almost solid. So dense was the cloud that individual bursts, except for the white puffs of shrapnel above its near edge, could not be distinguished. Roaring, deafening, it rolled ahead of the troops 'like a Gippsland bushfire.'[20]

The barrage machine guns joined in seven minutes later, by which time the lines of infantry were well on their way to the objectives. On the right of the Corps front the 5th Division, despite the difficulties on its right flank, succeeded in capturing all of its objectives including Polygon Wood itself with its formidable strong-points, as well as part of X Corps' objective (after the war, Polygon Wood was chosen as the site of the 5th Division memorial). In its sector, the 4th Division went about its tasks methodically. The 50th Battalion, leading off the 13th Brigade's advance on the left, found the going reasonably easy except for the swampy banks of the Steenbeek stream, which ran across the front in this sector. The battalion kept up with the barrage, closely enough to lose a few casualties to their own shells, and occupied the objective line straight after the barrage had passed over it and left most of the surviving enemy infantry in no condition to resist. A group of four concrete bunkers held out at first but mopping-up parties cleared these within ten minutes. By 6:50 am according to Major Loutit's report the 50th had completed the capture of its objective in the Red Line and was beginning to dig in,[21] starting with a series of posts which were later connected into a continuous trench line. Casualties had been minimal and the artillery was now firing on the first protective barrage line as the units in the second stage of the attack, the 49th and 51st Battalions, closed up behind the Red Line. At Zero plus 100 minutes (7:30 am) the batteries fired briefly at the increased rate and the barrage

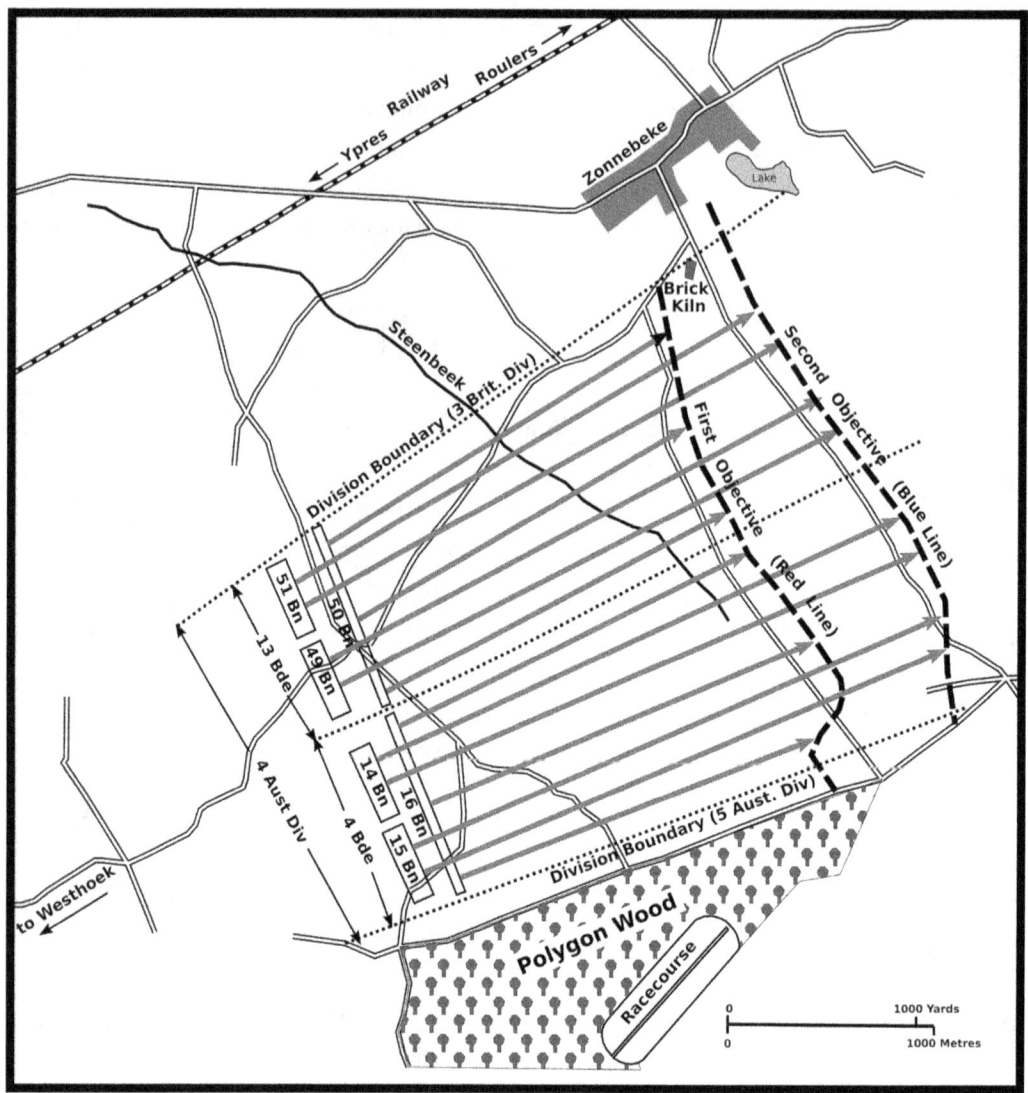

Battle of Polygon Wood, 26 September 1917 (4th Division sector)

began to creep forward again. The 49th and 51st passed through the 50th's line and moved on behind the curtain of shells for the final objective. By 8 am both units were on the Blue Line and digging in, again meeting little opposition from the enemy infantry; 'the effectiveness of the barrage knocked the fight out of the Huns' reported Lieutenant Colonel Denton, the 49th Battalion CO.[22]

Having won their objectives the troops turned their energies to consolidating the captured lines. LTMs and Vickers guns came up and were positioned to defend against counter-attacks, and engineer parties from the 13th Field Company began their tasks. Some groups concentrated on laying out and marking communication routes back to the various headquarters locations, others worked with the infantry on constructing strong-points in advance of the Brigade front, two in the Red Line and three in the Blue Line. These were designed as a curving trench covering a front of 45 metres, shaped in plan view like a flattened letter 'W', with a machine gun post at each end.[23] The enemy was now directing fire on to the position and the engineers lost Captain Robert Park, killed by a machine gun bullet while supervising the construction.[24] The Brigade forward signals party came up to the Blue Line and set about establishing a centre to control telephone and power-buzzer communications with the rear. The signallers were shelled out of two locations by the enemy artillery before the Brigade signals officer, Lieutenant Herbert Carlton, assisted by Lance Corporal Wilfred Paris, reorganised the party and set up in a captured pillbox. From here they established and maintained communication with Brigade HQ in the rear.[25] The battalions' headquarters parties came forward also, taking up positions close behind the captured position; Major Christie, acting CO of the 51st, went ahead to his unit's new front line to personally supervise the work of consolidation. So far there had been little interference from the enemy, and the 13th Brigade had gained touch with the 3rd British Division on its left (Zonnebeke) flank and with the 4th Brigade on the right.

The 4th Brigade's attack had followed a similar pattern to that of the 13th. The 16th Battalion jumped off first at 5:50 am and followed the barrage to their sector of the Red Line, which was occupied with little resistance from the stunned survivors of the German infantry in the area. A working party from the 13th Battalion, following closely behind the 16th, immediately began digging back from the Red Line to the original front line to complete the communication trench that had been started the night before, while at the same time another party of the 13th was digging forward from the old line to join up. Within two hours a usable trench, 1.5 metres deep and 915 metres long, had been completed. The attacking infantry moved off quickly enough to mostly avoid the German counter-barrage that had begun to fall on the old front line and No Man's Land, but earlier a shell had caught the 4th Brigade's forward signalling party during its approach march, scattering the group and causing a number of casualties including the officer in charge, seriously wounded. The Brigade signals officer, Lieutenant Arthur Waring (attached from the 4th Signal Company) came up and took charge, with the 13th Battalion's signal section taking on the work for the Brigade. In the meantime, the Brigade's second-line assault force, the 14th and 15th Battalions, moved off in their turn and closed up to the Red Line behind the 16th to wait for the barrage to move on. According to the 14th Battalion history, Captain Albert Jacka's company of that unit assisted the 16th to silence some troublesome pillboxes on the left flank during the pause.[26] The barrage was timed to begin its creep forward again at 7:30 but a few of the 15th Battalion moved off too soon, apparently through careless synchronisation of watches,[27] and lost some casualties to their own shells. The line was quickly reorganised—Colonel McSharry, the 15th's CO, had come forward to the jumping off line[28]—and the two units went forward for the Blue Line. During the advance some of the 14th Battalion's leading wave also ran into their own barrage through over-eagerness. Part of the line recoiled, but the men were rallied by Captain Jacka and the advance went on.[29] The 14th and 15th had some losses on the way from intermittent enemy shelling and unsubdued machine guns, but the final objective line was reached at about

8 am and occupied against scattered opposition. Some accounts state that the 14th's objective was along the line of a road and Jacka ordered that the battalion advance a further 45 metres to avoid enemy artillery, which could readily range on the road from the map. According to the orders and maps issued before the battle, however, the Blue Line was actually about that distance beyond the road, which ran south-east from a brick-kiln on the outskirts of Zonnebeke.[30] As a company commander, Jacka would have been well aware of this. Probably some of the troops initially stopped at the road, assuming it was the objective line, but Jacka ordered them to keep going and explained that enemy shelling would target the road; the story then later developed that the extra distance was advanced only on Jacka's initiative. The troops were beginning to dig in and consolidate when the 14th's 'A' Company commander, Captain Harold Wanliss, was killed by a burst of machine gun fire from somewhere on the right, beyond the captured position.

The 14th Battalion's task had been complicated by an apparent loss of contact between front line and the CO's forward HQ, but this did not prevent the unit from succeeding in this fight under the inspiring battlefield leadership of Albert Jacka, who assumed overall control of the firing line. The dissensions within the 14th Battalion show up in later accounts of its part in this battle, which imply, sometimes very strongly, that Colonel Smith and his headquarters officers were more interested in seeking safety than in controlling the battle. The new second-in-command, Major Thomson, is often included in that criticism, although he had probably not even been at the forward HQ—it was the usual practice for a battalion second-in-command to stay with the rear party. In the afternoon the forward HQ had relocated from its original position behind the forming-up area to a point about 300 metres out from the original front line, according to the Battalion war diary. The relevant entries in that document, neatly typed, give the impression of being inserted some time after the event and intended to answer criticism that the new HQ location could not be found by runners from the fighting line—considerable detail is given of efforts to inform Brigade and the companies by runner of the new location, and it was stated that a party was also left at the original location to redirect messages. The Diary states that HQ did not move until 12:25, well after the 14th reached the Blue Line; that up to that time messages had been regularly received and sent; and that message traffic through the relocated HQ resumed after 3:30 pm. At least one of Captain Jacka's early messages from the front line, reporting that the objective had been gained, was sent by pigeon, which would have been received further back than Battalion HQ—the 4th Brigade's after-action report and the 4th Division artillery HQ War Diary both record a pigeon message from the 14th between 9 and 10 am, the latter document mentioning Jacka by name. He may also have sent a runner with the same message to Battalion HQ—the unit Diary records such a message at 9:10 am, but without saying by what means it was sent. A report from Major Tolley of the 4th Field Company, timed at 11:30 am, noted that the 14th HQ was 'still in trench', while the 15th and 16th Battalion HQs had by then moved up to a 'very strong concrete blockhouse' not far behind the Red Line. That was an hour before the 14th diary says that their HQ moved up, however, and a later note by Major Tolley indicates that the engineer party marking out communication tracks had no particular difficulty finding the 14th's forward HQ, although he gave a different map reference to that stated in the Battalion diary.[31]

The work of consolidation went on under increasing enemy fire, with the supporting elements of LTMs, engineers, signallers and machine guns coming up to carry out their allotted tasks. In charge of one of the 4th MG Company's mobile machine guns was 27 year old Sergeant John J Dwyer of Bruny Island, Tasmania, who brought his weapon and crew up on the right flank, probably in support of the 15th Battalion, the unit with which he had served on Gallipoli. Spotting a German machine gun firing from that side in the direction of the 5th Division troops to the right, Dwyer took his Vickers further forward, set the weapon up within 30 metres of the German gun and opened fire on it.[32] His shots killed the enemy crew, but Dwyer was not content with that result. Ignoring sniper fire and shelling from both sides, he dashed out to the German post, picked up the gun and brought it back to his own position. The enemy weapon was set up in the 4th Brigade defences, Dwyer sending a message back to the main line for a reserve crew to come forward and operate it.[33] Engineer parties from the 4th Field Company had come up to the Blue Line also with the last infantry waves, an officer and 10 sappers with each of the 14th and 15th Battalions, and these set about marking out communication routes between the infantry company HQs and the forward battalion HQs. One of the engineer officers, Lieutenant Norman Wilkinson, was killed by a sniper while supervising his group's task; Sergeant William Pirie took over to complete the work. The 4th Company OC, Major Howard Tolley, came up himself through the enemy counter-barrage to the Blue Line, reconnoitring likely supply routes on the way. In the new front line he oversaw the consolidation works and located, examined and mapped the dugouts and pillboxes in the captured position.

Across the 4th Division's front both brigades had a respite of about 90 minutes to dig in before the Germans commenced shelling their lost positions and casualties began to build up. Some enemy machine guns and snipers remained active in spite of the protective barrage, and the enemy continued to shell the approaches to the new line. In mid-afternoon enemy infantry forces were observed assembling to counter-attack, but these were broken up by the SOS artillery and machine gun barrages and fire from the machine guns in the new front line. Another attempt was made at about 6 pm but again the Germans could not penetrate the fire of field artillery and machine guns.[34] The new front was reported to be 'quiet' towards nightfall, and after dark the carrying parties and pack animals toiled back and forth with supplies and rations while the troops in the front line continued to improve their defensive positions. The morning of 27 September found the 4th and 13th Brigades in firm possession of their new territory, as were the units all along the line of the Second and Fifth Armies' advance. There were some further alarms during that day, when the German artillery fired heavy bombardments along the front. During the shelling in the 4th Brigade's sector Sergeant Dwyer of the 4th MG Company again distinguished himself. His Vickers gun was wrecked by a shell, and he braved the enemy bombardment to make his way back to the main line, pick up a replacement weapon and return with it to the front line. The last of the bombardments at 6:40 pm was particularly heavy and seemed to presage a counter-attack. The British artillery opened fire on the SOS lines in all sectors and no infantry attack developed—perhaps to the disappointment of the 14th Battalion's Captain Jacka, who had planned a bayonet charge if any Germans appeared on the 4th Brigade's front.

The battle was won and over the next two nights the 4th and 13th Brigade units in the front line were relieved by units of the 12th Brigade. The 12th then held the whole divisional front, deployed in depth with its 45th and 46th Battalions both divided between the Red and Blue Lines, and the 47th and 48th occupying support positions in the previous front line.[35] On the last day of the month the divisions changed over again for the next stage of the advance and the 12th Brigade was itself relieved by 1st Division units, except for six Vickers guns and their crews from the 12th MG Company, detached to the 1st Division for barrage tasks. The front was adjusted at this time with I Anzac's sector shifting north, so that the relieving 1st Division was now occupying the right divisional sector; the 2nd Division came in on the left, relieving British units of V Corps. The two days holding the line under heavy enemy shelling had cost the 12th Brigade infantry about 250 casualties,[36] and the relieved brigades also had losses to shelling while in the support areas. Overall the 4th Division had a total of 1,887 casualties in September, including 390 killed and missing (another 700 had been evacuated with sickness during the same period). The 4th Field Ambulance, managing the ADSs on the Menin Road, reported few major difficulties handling the stream of wounded evacuated from the fighting on 26 September. Many of the wounded passed through the 13th Battalion RAP; the 13th's RMO, Captain Charles Kellaway, was said to have 'established what must be a record by passing 400 cases through his RAP in 24 hours.'[37] Temporary bottlenecks did occur at some staging points on the bearers' routes, however, particularly at the Birr Cross Roads vehicle loading post, and alternative routes had to be used to avoid enemy shelling. The 'walking wounded' ADS treated a large number of patients, the majority from the 5th Division's heavy fighting in Polygon Wood, and was reported as being 'glutted' for some time.[38] The routes from the front line to RAPs and back to the dressing stations were lengthy and congested as well as being shelled, and it was pointed out by Brigadier General Glasgow, 13th Brigade, that 'the evacuation of casualties was very slow and, had the casualties been very heavy, the question would have become acute.'[39] The brigadier might have added that if the fine weather ceased, the question would become more acute.

In action for most of September, the 4th Division artillery had 208 casualties for the month, including 31 killed and missing.[40] The 13th Infantry Brigade had 125 killed and missing from a total of 617 casualties for the month, including the last few days under fire in the support lines. The 50th Battalion, which had attacked the Red Line on 26 September, had the highest losses in the Brigade with a total of 211, including 46 killed and missing. Of the 4th Brigade units, the 14th Battalion suffered the highest casualties, with 32 killed and 141 wounded; the Brigade had a total of 125 killed, the same number as the 13th Brigade, from a total of 612 casualties. Among the Division's other elements, the Pioneer Battalion also suffered heavily in September, losing eight killed and 66 wounded.[41] A particularly heavy blow in the 4th Infantry Brigade was the death of that shining young man Captain Harold Wanliss, 14th Battalion. By all accounts Wanliss had deeply impressed everyone that he met with his intellect and uprightness of character, as well as his military prowess. He was thought by many to be a future Prime Minister.[42] Newton Wanliss, Harold's father, never ceased to grieve for his son and after the war became the 14th Battalion's historian, much as Rudyard Kipling wrote the history of his dead son John's regiment, the Irish Guards. Harold Wanliss had been buried where he fell but although the exact map reference of the grave location was recorded, his remains were not found, or at least not identified, after the war.[43]

Before leaving the forward zone for the rear areas, some units remained in the support line on Westhoek Ridge for a few days, supplying working parties for various construction tasks. Here they were still within long artillery range and the German shelling caused a number of casualties, as did night bombing by German aircraft on the back areas. Division HQ was hit by aerial bombing on 28 September, resulting in six killed and 10 wounded in the HQ details,[44] and the next night the DAC lost 10 casualties to the same cause. On the night of 2 October another aerial bomb hit the 4th Pioneer Battalion's HQ at Kruisstraat, close to Ypres; the second-in-command, Major Norman Macrae, and Captain Thomas Graham were killed. Enemy shelling on the roads caught a 4th Division Train wagon convoy near Westhoek on 29 September, blocking the road with damaged wagons and dead horses. Sergeant Kenneth Dowden and Drivers David Browning and Alexander Robinson worked for hours under the shelling to sort out the confusion and clear a path; all were awarded the MM for their efforts. On 30 September a shell burst in the 51st Battalion's area on Westhoek Ridge just as the Western Australians were preparing to march off for the rear, killing Sergeant George Calder and Private George Storey. The bodies were hastily buried nearby, close to the rough graves of several other 4th Division soldiers, including Queenslander Private John Hunter, 49th Battalion, killed in the fighting on 26 September. In time the details of the location were lost and the remains of those men, as with Harold Wanliss and more than 300,000 others of the BEF, could not be identified for honourable interment after the war. For Calder, Storey and Hunter, however, their story was not over.

Decorations won in the Division for the Polygon Wood fighting were headed by the Victoria Cross awarded to Sergeant John Dwyer of the 4th Machine Gun Company. 'His contempt of all danger and his cheerfulness and courage raised the spirits and admiration of all who were in his sector of the lines,' in the words of the recommendation.[45] Dwyer had enlisted as a private with the 15th Battalion reinforcements in 1915, serving with that unit in the later stages of the Gallipoli campaign. He had transferred to the 4th MG Company when the unit was formed in Egypt and had served with it through most of the fighting in France and Belgium, receiving a serious wound at Messines. His was the only 4th Division VC to be awarded outside of the infantry battalions. 'JJ' Dwyer survived the war and went on to a distinguished career in Tasmanian politics. DSOs went to Major Tolley, OC 4th Field Company, and Major Christie, acting CO of the 51st Battalion, outstanding leaders

Sergeant (later Lieutenant) John J Dwyer VC (1890 –1962), 4th Machine Gun Company. (AWM 03691)

of their units. Other decorations included a Bar to his MC for Lieutenant Herbert Carlton, 13th Brigade Signals Officer, and the DCM to Private John Cooper, 51st Battalion, who had taken charge of his platoon at a crucial stage in the Blue Line. There seem to have been comparatively few decorations recommended overall in the 13th Brigade, however, perhaps because the attack had gone fairly smoothly. In the 4th Brigade Group, Sergeant Pirie of the 4th Field Company engineers was awarded the DCM. 4th Brigade officers to receive the MC included the 13th Battalion RMO Captain Kellaway, Captain Robert Glasgow and Lieutenant Simon Porter of the 15th Battalion, and Captain Charles Ahearn, Lieutenant Henry Bradley and Second Lieutenant Basil Minchin of the 16th.

There were no decorations for officers of the 14th Battalion, the highest award in that unit being a DCM to Sergeant Charles Thompson, his third decoration of the war. Three 14th officers, Captain Jacka and Lieutenants Norman Aldridge and John Johnson, were recommended but none was approved (Aldridge was Mentioned in Despatches), another sour note adding to that unit's recent internal troubles. By all accounts of the battle the 14th had put up a fine effort and much of the credit for its performance was due to Jacka's control in the front line. It has been pointed out that Jacka's recommendation did not specify a particular award, a circumstance that has been taken to suggest a deliberate intention to withhold recognition. That may be so, but actually most of the recommendation forms, at least in 4th Brigade units, were initially prepared without an entry in the 'Honour or Reward' column. The recommendations were prepared by the unit COs, as was the standard practice, and are noted as having passed through Brigade. General Sinclair-MacLagan, the GOC, endorsed the details of the award himself and initialled the entry on the form; it appears that the GOC wished to make those decisions himself, at least at this time.[46] In the case of Jacka, the General had endorsed 'Card' on the form—that is, a congratulatory card (a 'soup ticket' as they were called) from the Division commander or higher. That is probably the origin of the later comment that Jacka was 'complimented publicly' by the GOC;[47] it may not have been realised that those compliments were all that was intended. It has been suggested that Jacka was deprived of a decoration by the intervention of Brigadier General Brand, to avoid drawing attention to the less than glorious part played in the battle by 14th Battalion HQ and Lieutenant Colonel Smith. Sinclair-MacLagan's decision may have been influenced in that way, but it also may not have been. Company commanders leading an attack were frequently decorated without that being seen as an unfavourable reflection on the battalion CO, who would be preparing the recommendation. No such reason should have prevented the award to Jacka of, say, another Bar to his MC, if not the DSO that was rumoured at the time. Colonel Smith's recommendation was generous in its praise, but perhaps falls short of the degree of eloquence that was becoming necessary to catch the attention of higher authority in approving decorations, particularly for officers. General Sinclair-MacLagan did recommend MCs for Lieutenants Johnson and Aldridge in the 14th, but neither of those was approved higher up the chain of command. In Jacka's case it is possible that the GOC felt that his deeds as described in the recommendation were no more than could be expected of a senior company commander in action. Whatever the case, Albert Jacka certainly deserved more than a 'soup ticket' for his efforts at Polygon Wood, and the discontent in the 14th Battalion went on.[48]

By 3 October the 4th Division infantry had moved out of the forward zone, on foot and then by motor transport, to billets in the Steenvoorde area for a few days' break for refitting and routine training, while preparations went on for the next step in the offensive. Division HQ also moved to Steenvoorde. The medical units were also relieved by their 1st Division equivalents, although the bearers of the 12th and 13th Field Ambulances were attached to the Corps MDS in reserve for the next round of fighting, and were called forward to assist on the day.[49] The 4th Division's engineer field companies and pioneer battalion remained in the forward area, however, working with other elements of the Corps' engineering resources on the incessant infrastructure projects that supported the fighting front as it edged eastwards. The 13th Field Company had a change in commander during this period when the Royal Engineer officer Major Horace Reid was transferred to command a British field company; Major Reginald Carr came in from the 8th Field Company (5th Division) as the new OC. The further the front advanced, the worse the ground became for transport. Movement forward was now through the zone that had been flayed by the bombardments covering earlier advances. There were never enough firm routes for all the needs of the army, and the enemy artillery did its best to interfere with the work. Both sides made heavy use of gas shells during the Third Ypres operations and the Germans had recently introduced mustard gas, particularly dangerous as it did not have to be breathed in to affect its victims. Contact with exposed skin caused severe blistering, not always fatal but agonising enough to put a man out of action, often permanently. Mustard gas impregnated clothing and contaminated waterlogged ground with an oily residue. Phosgene, the respiratory poison used by both sides, could be counteracted by gas-masks, markedly reducing the efficiency of the wearer, but its odour was hard to detect and the effects were often not apparent for some time after it had been inhaled.

The 4th Division artillery continued in the line covering the left divisional front of I Anzac in conjunction with the 2nd Division artillery, coming again under command of the 2nd Division CRA as the infantry changed over; Brigadier General Burgess and his staff moved back to Oudezeele, near Steenvoorde, pending the next rotation of the artillery command. In the nights after the Polygon Wood battle, designated batteries began moving into position and bringing up ammunition for the next stage of the advance. General Burgess reported that

> the only source of supply was the Westhoek-Zonnebeke road ... east of Zonnebeke this road was a mere mud track ... The forward batteries had a continual fight to get their guns and ammunition forward. It was, however, done and by October 2nd all were ready for the final attack on the ridge.[50]

'The ridge' was the new objective, Broodseinde Ridge, which would be assaulted on 4 October by twelve divisions of Second and Fifth Armies. This time the infantry advance would cover a distance of up to 1,800 metres, most of the divisions on a front of 900 metres each. II Anzac, coming back to the line after a month's rest, had taken over the sector adjoining I Anzac to the left (north) and for the first and only time in the war four ANZAC divisions—New Zealand, 3rd, 2nd and 1st Australian—would be attacking side by side. Again the advance would be in two steps, first to a preliminary Red Line objective then to the final Blue Line over the crest of Broodseinde Ridge. For the field artillery this meant firing a pattern of creeping and covering barrages similar to the method and timing of the previous operations. On the two days preceding the attack the batteries fired practice barrages before the full artillery force opened at Zero, 6 am on 4 October. Half an hour earlier, however, a German barrage had fallen on the I Anzac infantry assembled for the attack. The troops endured heavy casualties while waiting for Zero, then rose and went forward as their own barrage came down ahead. The German barrage ceased at the same time and the advancing infantry soon discovered that the shelling had been intended to cover an enemy attack launched simultaneously with their own. The two infantry forces met in No Man's Land and after a short fire-fight the Germans broke and ran. The leading battalions kept moving to their first objective, getting involved in some sharp fighting around pillboxes; in an attempt to counter the inexorable British advances, the Germans had reverted to manning their forward zone more heavily. The tactic was to no avail and the Red Line was occupied successfully. The units were reorganised in time for the next step at 8:10 am when the barrage began to creep forward again, and before midday the I Anzac infantry was over the crest of Broodseinde Ridge and digging in to establish the Blue Line. II Anzac to the left had also reached its objective, against stiff resistance, and the troops now had observation over the countryside in front to the next ridge, crowned to the north-east by the ruined village of Passchendaele.

For the 4th Division artillery, 'C' Group of the I Anzac guns, the day had followed the routine pattern set in the first two attacks. The 4th Division batteries covered the right infantry brigade of 2nd Division (6th Brigade, the same that they had covered at Second

Bullecourt) with creeping and protective barrages, and responded to SOS calls during the afternoon and evening. The barrage appears to have been not quite as effective as in the previous attacks. The ground was wet from light overnight rain and the shell bursts did not raise a concealing dust-cloud, and the infantry also felt that the barrage was not as dense as before. The *Official History* is somewhat inconsistent on this point, noting that 'the II Anzac barrage was perceptibly denser than that of I Anzac'[51] but also that in the I Anzac sector 'in front of the 2nd Division the 18-pounder barrage was noticeably denser and more regular than that which covered the 1st.'[52] It was also stated that in the Blue Line protective barrage on the 6th Brigade front, at first the shrapnel was bursting too high to suppress enemy sniping,[53] the gunners perhaps being slow to adjust their fuzes to allow for the ground sloping away on the far side of the ridge. Nevertheless, once more an advance had achieved the planned objectives, although at a cost of 20,000 casualties in Second Army overall, and the Germans seemed to have no real answer to the British methods. The situation changed almost immediately, however. The infantry was scarcely in possession of the Blue Line when the rain began, light at first but steadily increasing to a downpour over the next few days. The loose soil was quickly transformed into a quagmire. The deteriorating conditions unfortunately coincided with an excess of optimism in the higher commanders.

Convinced by three successive victories that the Germans were on the verge of collapse, Sir Douglas Haig saw again the vista of a breakthrough and a triumphant advance to the coast. The overriding factor in the recent successes had been the artillery support of the infantry and it was essential that the guns and their ammunition must be moved up to positions within range of the next objective. This required good weather, but the sudden flooding of the ground made movement almost impossible even for a man on foot, let alone artillery pieces, supply carriers and stretcher bearers. Despite that situation the Commander in Chief ordered that the operations continue as planned, even bringing forward the original date for the next step. Even General Plumer, who may have had his doubts initially, abandoned his normal caution to support his chief's view.[54] The next two stages were planned to occur in quick succession and the first of these, an advance of 900 metres to the near slope of the Passchendaele Ridge, was now ordered for 9 October. The axis of the advance was now angling to the north-east and its front was narrower than before, a situation likely to create a salient. The Germans, after the failure of their tactic of heavily manning the front line, had hastily reverted to the system of defence in depth. II Anzac was allocated the main role in Second Army, but I Anzac was required to support the right flank of the attack. The 2nd Division was kept in the line for this operation with the combined 2nd and 4th Division artillery continuing to cover the infantry in this sector. The artillery was now reinforced by the 1st Division's field brigades, combined with the 4th Division guns to cover the 6th Infantry Brigade.

The difficulties were immense for the artillery personnel and draught animals trying to get the guns and ammunition forward through the bog that the forward zone had become.

> I Anzac ... had been unable to provide a third planked road circuit like those undertaken before September 20th and 26th. Forward of Westhoek it had to place chief reliance upon the single road from Westhoek to Zonnebeke, ['Smith's Road'] in which the crowded shell-holes had been filled in with earth. [When] the first echelon of guns was ordered to advance by it ... even in the slight rain it gave way beneath them. As the rains went on, mules and pack-horses, endlessly ploughing their way along the same tracks ... quickly rendered them almost impassable.[55]

In attempting to move up to new positions the 11th AFA Brigade had several guns hopelessly bogged and others put out of action by enemy shelling.[56] Ammunition wagons bogged also, and often shells could only be carried from wagon lines to the battery positions by pack mule. The unfortunate animals frequently slipped off the roads or stumbled into flooded shell-holes, and the ammunition became coated in mud and had to be cleaned before it could be fired. At the gun positions unstable footings meant that the weapons often had to be re-laid after a few shots, losing the advantage of the 'Quick Firing' capability. HE shells landing in the target area often buried themselves in the mud before bursting, minimising their effect. All of these factors meant that the rate of fire, weight and accuracy of the field artillery barrage proved to be inadequate on the day of battle.

Zero was 5:20 am on 9 October. The barrage, such as it was, opened on time and the infantry moved off through the mud. II Anzac used its two attached British divisions, the 49th and the inexperienced 66th, in the attack. After a nightmarish approach march, many of those troops were still coming up to the start line by Zero and the advance in that sector was well behind schedule. In I Anzac's sector on the right the 2nd Division troops made some progress in spite of their weakened condition, some parties reaching the second objective on the Keiberg ridge. They found themselves unsupported on their left, however, and were soon driven back by machine gun fire and counter-attacks. By that time some elements of the 66th Division had managed to get forward, but now found themselves unsupported in their turn and were also forced to fall back. By the end of the day the attacking units were mostly back in their original lines with heavy losses. Only on the northern part of the front was there any success; Fifth Army and French forces had gained some ground in their advance, centring on the village of Poelcappelle, which gave the battle its name. In common with the rest of the artillery, the 4th Division guns had been unable to give adequate support to the infantry in the circumstances. The 6th Brigade noted that 'the barrage was inaccurate, ragged and thin, and the percentage of shorts ... considerable—at no time was it sufficient to prevent sniping and machine gun fire.'[57]

Despite the failure of the latest stage of the plan, the higher commanders accepted inaccurate reports suggesting that the line had been advanced far enough to proceed with the next stage, which was ordered to go ahead on 12 October. The principles that had brought success earlier were now abandoned. The main task was given to II Anzac, an advance of

2000-2,500 yards [1830 to 2300 metres] for their final objective: Passchendaele village and a considerable section of the ridge to its north. This represented a depth of advance of approximately 1,000 yards [900 metres] more than had been achieved in any of Plumer's first three steps, all of which had been carried out after an extended period of fine weather and a preparation time of between six and twenty-one days. Now the weather was continuing abysmal, so that preparation was confined effectively to just 10 and 11 October.[58]

The left division of I Anzac would again be supporting II Anzac's right flank. The exhausted 2nd Division infantry was withdrawn, and that of the 4th Division came forward again to relieve them. The 12th Brigade, in reserve for Polygon Wood, moved to the front line to take on the 4th Division's principle task in the next attack. The 13th Brigade came up to hold the right of the divisional front, with the 4th Brigade in reserve, and 5th Division units completed I Anzac's line on the right. The 45th Battalion was sent in first on the evening of 9 October and relieved the remnants of the 5th Brigade, finding the 'front line' to be a series of shell-holes.[59] Exploring their new front after dark, patrols from the 45th found a number of wounded men in shell-holes, who had been overlooked earlier, an indication of the low ebb to which the 5th Brigade had been reduced. One company was put on the task of carrying the wounded to the nearest RAP.[60] The 45th was now under a temporary commander, the long-serving CO, Lieutenant Colonel Sydney Herring, having been posted to command the Division's training group in England the previous day. Major Hubert Ford came in from the 46th Battalion to take over command, but was himself wounded by artillery fire on 11 October; Major A S 'Tubby' Allen, the second-in-command, then became acting CO. 12th Brigade HQ also had a change in its staff at about this time. Major Edward Salier, the Australian-born British Army officer who had been brigade major from the early days in Egypt, was posted to the Tank Corps; he was replaced by Major Eric Wilton, transferred from 4th Brigade HQ. Major Charles Johnston, recovered from his wound sustained after Messines, resumed as brigade major with 4th Brigade.[61] Another change in the 4th Brigade saw the 16th Battalion's CO, Lieutenant Colonel Edmund Drake-Brockman, detached on 9 October for a term commanding the Brigade's training battalion in England. Major Harwood took over command again, with a promotion to temporary lieutenant colonel; he was a veteran of the 16th, having started as a subaltern in November 1914.

The 12th Brigade completed its deployment on the evening of 10 October, with the 46th Battalion going into the support line (also a rough line of shell holes) behind the 45th, and the 47th and 48th taking up positions further back on Anzac Ridge and Westhoek Ridge. Those two units had been selected to carry out the actual attack, when they would come forward and advance through the front line. Division HQ was set up in the Ypres Ramparts on 11 October. Of the Division's other elements, the engineers and pioneers continued with their infrastructure works in the morass behind the firing line, and the forward brigades' linked medical units came up again to relieve their 2nd Division equivalents. The 12th Field Ambulance took over the stretcher-case ADS on the Menin Road (5th Division units looked after the walking-wounded station), and the 13th Field Ambulance moved to the Ypres city precincts to administer two auxiliary dressing stations recently established there for walking and stretcher cases, in locations that some felt were too exposed to enemy shelling.[62] With the axis of the advance shifting to the north-east, the Ypres stations were closer to the fighting front than those on the Menin Road. The 13th's bearers were responsible for casualty evacuation from the front line brigades, reinforced by the 12th Field Ambulance bearers and vehicles, with those of the 4th Field Ambulance available in reserve if needed; the 4th's tent personnel managed the divisional rest station.

With the 4th Division infantry back in the front line, Brigadier General Burgess again took command of the combined 4th and 2nd Division artillery, now with the 1st Division guns attached for the 'attack day' tasks. The backbreaking work of getting the guns forward to their next positions went on. The 4th Division brigades, ordered to move five batteries up to the Zonnebeke area, found Smith's Road impassable and were diverted to the Frezenberg-Zonnebeke road, north of the Roulers railway in II Anzac's sector,

> which was already packed with transport for the Division on the left [3rd Australian, coming into the line for the next attack]. Finally the effort to get the 41st and 43rd Batteries up had to be temporarily abandoned and all energies were concentrated on the 38th, 39th and 110th (Howitzer) Batteries. In the end at least four guns from each of these batteries were got up into the neighbourhood of Zonnebeke by the evening of the 11th/12th October.[63]

On the eve of the new attack the CRA recorded that the 4th Division artillery had 27 18-pounders in position from a maximum of 36, and seven out of 12 howitzers; 'the balance are either out of action or stuck in the mud in moving.'[64] The attached 1st Division artillery was in a similar situation, although that of the 2nd Division, not required to make substantial moves, had all but three of its pieces available. The DAC faced similar problems getting ammunition forward from the dumps. Lieutenant Colonel Vernon, the 4th DAC CO, adopted the method of sending ammunition wagons up with unloaded pack mules following; when the wagons reached the end of firm roadway, the loads were transferred to the mules for the rest of the journey to the battery wagon lines or all the way to the battery positions.[65] The artillery's forward moves, like the plans for the infantry, were based on the false assumption at Second Army HQ that the attack of 9 October, the fourth step in the series, had advanced the front line to at least somewhere near its objectives. The fifth attack was planned on that basis and II Anzac was given three objective lines for 12 October, of which the final ('Green') line included Passchendaele Ridge and village. The New Zealand Division and the 3rd Australian Division, now back in the line, would have the main tasks, with no time for methodical preparation and insuperable difficulties getting their field artillery into range.

As the flank guard on the 3rd Division's right, the 12th Brigade infantry would advance with their left on the Ypres-Roulers railway, which formed the boundary between I and II Anzac, starting at the point called Defy Crossing where the Broodseinde-Passchendaele road crossed the railway. Direct fire support for the infantry would be provided by two Stokes mortars of the Brigade LTM battery, and the 12th MG Company was ordered to send four Vickers guns forward with the infantry advance. Another four guns were posted in the support line and the remaining eight were attached to the 13th MG Company, which was to provide barrage fire covering the attack, in conjunction with the artillery. Two objectives were set for the 12th Brigade. The 47th Battalion would advance to the Red Line objective, a line running roughly south from the area where the railway crossed the higher ground of the Keiberg spur and its embankment became a cutting; a clump of ragged tree stumps called Decline Copse[66] was located at the near end of the cutting. The 48th would then pass through to move a further 450 metres up the railway and both units would establish a line of posts facing south and southeast, the most advanced being designated as the Blue Line. These positions were intended to continue the second objective line to be reached by the 3rd Division's 9th Brigade (commanded by Brigadier General Charles Rosenthal, the former 4th Division CRA), advancing to the north of the railway, and cover its right flank. The 48th would also push out an advanced post towards the 9th Brigade's final Green Line objective. The operation orders from Division referred to the need for close coordination between the two forces:

> Certain men of the 12th Brigade will be told off to advance with the right of the 9th Brigade attack and a similar party from them will move with the left of the 12th Brigade ... GOC 12th [Brigade] will arrange close liaison with GOC 9th [Brigade].[67]

Down the line, that liaison task was allocated to 'D' Company of the 48th Battalion, ordered to detail a party to work on the north side of the railway; it was expected that a 9th Brigade party would advance with the 48th in their sector.[68] The 9th Brigade's written orders were less precise about liaison on their right, however,[69] and in the event there is no record of these arrangements actually being carried out on the day of the battle.

With the uncertainty as to exactly where the existing front line was, the 9th Brigade's start line turned out to be 270 metres further back than that of the 12th Brigade. That situation would make close battlefield liaison between flanking units difficult, although 12th Brigade HQ apparently did send a liaison officer (Captain Arthur Varley, attached to the staff from the 45th Battalion) to 9th Brigade HQ. The difference in the start lines does not seem to have caught the attention of the staffs at Corps, Division or Brigade level, and there is no mention of that factor in the written orders. After-action reports, at least in the 4th Division, indicate that officers at unit level were unaware of it until after the battle had started and there was enough light to see what was happening on the flanks. Maps issued with the orders to units, in both 3rd and 4th Division, show only their own start lines and not those of the units on the flanks. Rushed preparation had worked against effective co-ordination across the Corps boundary. The 9th Brigade's artillery plan had to change at the last minute also. The first line of the barrage would now start 180 metres in front of the infantry start line and its first four lifts of 90 metres would be every four minutes instead of eight, doubling the rate at which the infantry would be expected to advance. These changes were conveyed by signal and verbally rather than by written orders.[70]

Zero for the barrage was set as 5:25 am on 12 October. Around midnight the 47th and 48th Battalions began the move to their jumping-off positions, which the Brigade and unit intelligence officers had earlier taped out. Optimistically, it was expected that the troops would be in position 30 minutes (47th) to an hour (48th) before Zero, but darkness and the state of the ground made that impossible. Duckboards had been put down by the engineers for part of the way but those were slippery with mud and broken in places by enemy shelling, which continued during the approach march. The conditions deteriorated further when rain began to fall at 2 am, and the troops took five hours to cover five kilometres, reaching the jumping-off line with only a few minutes to spare and already exhausted. Behind the attacking companies, both battalions established a shared HQ in a captured concrete blockhouse on Broodseinde Ridge, its three chambers accommodating the two units' HQ personnel and the 47th's RAP.[71] The barrage came down on time, starting 140 metres in front of the infantry and then beginning to advance eight minutes later, but all of the gunners' efforts could not achieve fully effective cover for the infantry. The weight and accuracy of the barrage were inadequate and it moved too quickly for the troops to keep up in the heavy going.[72] The 48th Battalion reported that some shells dropped as much as 90 metres short and caused losses while the troops were still on the start line.[73] It is possible, however, that those shells came from one or more of the 3rd Division's guns, through an error in direction rather than elevation—with only four minutes between lifts, the 3rd Division barrage would have reached a line about level with the 12th Brigade's start line before the latter's own barrage began to advance. The German counter-barrage came down within a few minutes of the start, mostly falling behind the moving infantry, but at 5:45 am a salvo of three shells fell around the pillbox housing the two battalions' HQs. The 47th's headquarters details—runners, signallers and scouts—were waiting around the walls and in a nearby trench, and the shells killed 24 and wounded 10 of those men, leaving only two runners and three signallers to maintain communications.[74]

The lines of infantry pressed on through mud and around flooded shell-holes. Keeping formation was almost impossible and the two battalions were soon intermingled. Enemy infantry ahead of the line of the advance put up only weak resistance, but the troops came under heavy fire from the far side of the railway, in the 3rd Division's sector on the left flank. Most dangerous was the close-range fire from 'Vienna Cottage,' a strongpoint on higher ground. It was apparent that the 3rd Division had not come forward and the flank was open on that side. The 48th Battalion's two left companies wheeled to their left and lined out along the railway embankment, opening fire with rifles and Lewis guns on the enemy positions while the remainder of the two battalions continued the advance, sweeping through Decoy Wood and reaching the railway cutting at Decline Copse. There Private Albert Yates, a Lewis gunner with the 48th Battalion, attacked an enemy machine gun post in a dugout, capturing the gun and eight Germans. The battalions advanced further to reach the enemy strongpoint known as 'Assyria House' on the right of the first objective line. The German garrison there, together with snipers in the vicinity, kept up a steady fire and presented serious problems for some time. An infantry attack supported by fire from the two Stokes mortars eventually drove the enemy out of the buildings;[75] CSM Lavington Carter,[76] 47th Battalion, was credited with leading the successful assault.

The 12th Brigade had now reached the area of the Red Line objective, close to the scheduled time of about an hour after the start, although casualties had been heavy. The 47th in particular had lost a high proportion of its officers killed or wounded, and NCOs were in charge of platoons and companies. Attempts were made to dig in but little could be achieved in the waterlogged ground. The troops took any available cover and waited for the next stage of the advance. The original intention was for a pause of two hours to reorganise before the barrage moved on and the 48th followed it to establish the Blue Line posts. Part of that unit, however, was fully occupied defending the railway embankment on the left, still waiting with increasing frustration for the 3rd Division units to come up on that flank. The 12th Brigade could not be aware of the situation that the II Anzac divisions had been struggling against in their sector. The New Zealand Division on the left, attacking Bellevue Spur in the mud without an effective covering barrage, had struck a deep belt of uncut barbed wire. Trying to work their way through in the face of murderous fire from massed machine guns, the New Zealanders were stopped with 3,000 casualties in what was their worst day of the war. This exposed the 3rd Division's left brigade, which had managed to reach its first objective—a small party even penetrated to the outskirts of Passchendaele village—to flanking fire and counter-attacks.

The 9th Brigade on the 3rd Division right, with its start line well behind that of the 12th Brigade, went forward on time but immediately ran into heavy machine gun fire, unsuppressed by the feeble barrage, and the advance fell into 'the utmost confusion.'[77] Although the troops were disorganised they pressed on with determination—two pillboxes were captured in desperate fighting by a party under Captain Clarence Jeffries (34th Battalion), who was killed attacking the second one and posthumously awarded the Victoria Cross. Part of the left and centre of the 9th Brigade did succeed in crossing their first objective and almost reached the second, the Blue Line, but their right on the railway was struggling well behind schedule. It was an hour and a half after Zero before any of those troops had even come up as far as the 12th Brigade's start line, according to the report of the 48th Battalion's companies lining the embankment. After another ninety minutes the 9th Brigade's right flank elements had worked their way to a point near the first objective. Some of the 48th troops guarding the flank could now be released to move up from the embankment to positions in the Red Line, where they joined the remainder of their unit and the 47th. Captain Wilfred Hilary crossed the railway to confer with 9th Brigade officers and was informed that those troops were in no condition to continue the advance after their heavy losses. By now the 48th should have begun the next stage of the advance to the Blue Line. The barrage had already moved on but the 48th's officers on the spot decided that it would be unwise to go any further with no prospect of support on their left. The two 12th Brigade battalions now held a position facing outwards in a rough

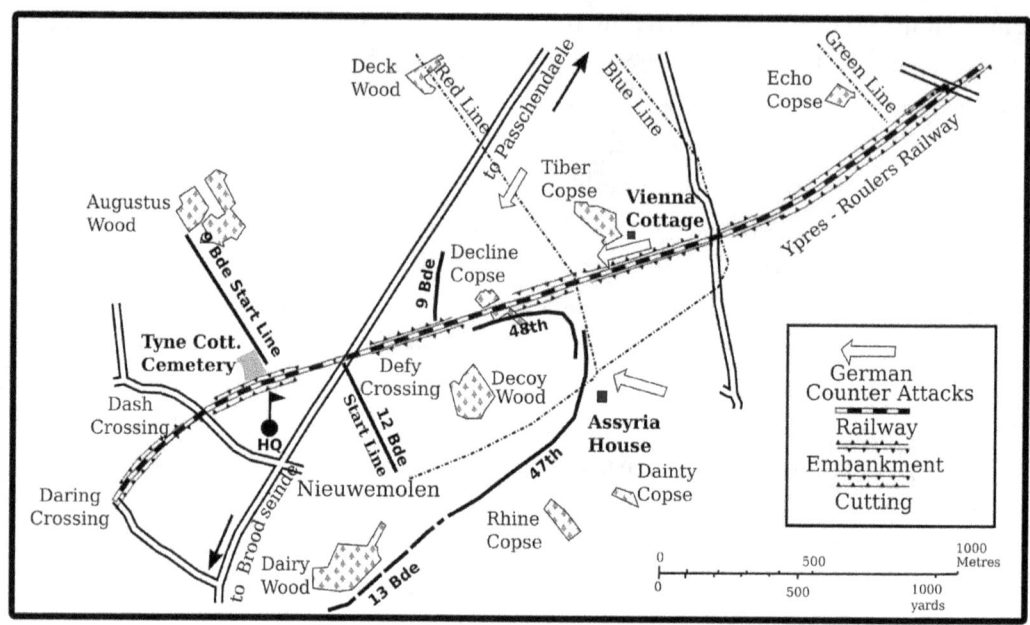

Passchendaele, situation at end of 12th Brigade's advance

'U' shape. The 48th's line ran north-east along the railway from a point 275 metres out from the jumping-off line to Decline Copse, where the railway cutting ran across the higher ground, then south-east to the vicinity of Assyria House. From there, the 47th occupied a line of posts running back to the south-west, more or less on their intended Red Line objective, the southern face of what was a small salient; the 47th reported that they had gained touch with the 13th Brigade, holding the existing line on the right.[78] One of the 48th's companies had also pushed outposts forward in advance of Assyria, towards the Blue Line objective. Two of the 12th MG Company's Vickers guns were positioned in the railway cutting near Decline Copse, right up with the foremost infantry in the north-east corner of the line. The machine gunners had gone through a difficult time getting forward. Four gun teams had started out, but in moving behind the infantry, they came under the enemy counter-barrage and were soon reduced by casualties to an NCO and eight men under two officers (Lieutenant Errol Upton and Second Lieutenant Joseph East, whose commission had been notified only the night before). This was not enough men to handle all four guns and their equipment, so two guns were left behind and the other two brought up to the captured position.[79]

The battalions settled in to defend their line and await developments. An early counter-attack had been attempted by a company of German infantry advancing from the direction of Vienna Cottage, but this had been shattered by fire from the railway cutting. As the day wore on enemy shells, snipers and machine guns continued to cause casualties. The 48th Battalion's Second Lieutenant Wally Pritchard, 'big cheery Englishman,'[80] twice crept out with a rifle to pick off two particularly dangerous snipers, and Corporal Gregory O'Neil led a party that stalked and killed others. The 47th Battalion lost three of its company commanders, Captains Gregory Gibson and Clarence Collins and Lieutenant George Storey, wounded and evacuated. All the other officers in those three companies had also become casualties through the day and the senior NCO on the spot, Sergeant James Heading, found himself commanding elements of all three. Captain Alexander Anderson, in charge of 'D' Company holding the right flank posts, was the only 47th company commander remaining on duty from those who had led off that morning (by coincidence, each Battalion's 'D' Company was commanded by an officer named Anderson; Captain Frederick Anderson was OC 'D' Company in the 48th Battalion[81]). Enemy shelling intensified, and in mid-afternoon a heavy barrage preceded an infantry attack coming from the south-east against the 12th Brigade's right. The Germans, estimated to be in battalion strength, advanced in several 'well-ordered' waves on a front of 360 metres. In the open they made an excellent target for the Australian Lewis guns, rifles and machine guns, and the attack was driven off with heavy losses. An hour later the German infantry tried again from the same direction, this time in greater numbers and with more caution. The enemy pressure gradually pushed back the outposts in front of the south-east corner of the line and re-captured the area of Assyria House, but the main line held firm and the Germans could make no further progress against accurate defensive fire.

Both battalions fired the SOS signal for artillery support but there was no apparent response—it was later reported that the artillery had been wrongly informed that the 3rd Division, with the 12th Brigade on its flank, had reached the Blue Line, and the barrage had been put down to defend that line instead.[82] The 12th MG Company's SOS machine gun battery reported that they had responded promptly to the SOS, but this was not noticed by the infantry.[83] Nevertheless the battalions were holding their line successfully when the situation suddenly deteriorated. At 5 pm the posts of the 48th Battalion holding the left flank on the railway realised that the 9th Brigade troops north of the embankment were withdrawing (they had been ordered to do so) and a massive German force was advancing from that side of the battlefield. 'This attack, which comprised at least a brigade, developed from the direction of Passchendaele, and struck the railway line at about Decline Copse.'[84] The two battalions, now isolated ahead of the main line and under attack from both flanks, were in grave danger of being cut off and annihilated. The only option was immediate withdrawal, and the troops fell back along the railway embankment, which offered some cover on the left. A few Lewis gunners formed rear guards to cover the retreat, among them Lance Corporal William Patterson, 48th Battalion, and Private William Cowen, 47th; Patterson eventually got back to the main line, but Cowen was never seen again.[85] The advanced post of the 12th MG Company in the railway cutting kept up covering fire also. One of the guns was wrecked by a shell but the 'Number One' on the other gun, Lance Corporal Thomas McTye, sent back the survivors of his crew and continued firing, holding off the Germans to his front until the ammunition ran out. Only then did McTye head back himself, after dismantling the gun mechanism. On the way, he was assisting the wounded

Lieutenant East when both men were caught in the explosion of a shell or grenade. East was killed and McTye suffered a broken leg; fortunately a team of stretcher bearers happened to be nearby and McTye was carried out, but his injuries were so serious that he was later discharged from the Army.[86]

The withdrawal was generally conducted in good order, but here was no time to collect all of the wounded and a number were unavoidably left behind. The retreating troops streamed past the pillbox housing the joint battalion HQs. Information from the front line had been scanty and delayed, resulting in what C E W Bean called 'the usual misunderstandings,'[87] and the sight of the troops was almost the first indication to Colonels Leane and Imlay that matters had gone awry up forward. The two COs went outside with the intention of rallying their men, but when the situation became clear they ordered the establishment of a firm defensive position along the original jumping-off line, joining up with the two forward companies of the 45th Battalion already near that line. While they were in the open organising the deployment, a shell burst nearby and both COs were badly wounded by splinters. Both were evacuated by stretcher bearers sent up from the 46th Battalion[88] and temporary command devolved onto the senior officers remaining at the forward HQ, the 47th's signals officer, Captain James Brack, and the 48th's adjutant, Captain David Twining. Those officers continued with the formation of the new defensive line, which was mostly completed during the evening except for the 47th Battalion's 'D' Company, several groups of which were still out in front holding their Red Line posts on the right. That company finished falling back to the main line in the early morning of 13 October and later in the day provided an officer (Lieutenant Joseph Smith) to relieve the hard-working Sergeant Heading in charge of the unit's other three companies.

With the line now stabilised almost in its original position, the battle—officially the First Battle of Passchendaele—was over for the 4th Division. The Armies in the Ypres sector paused to hold their lines while the higher command pondered the next move. As well as Second Army's failure, the Fifth Army advance had made no progress in the northern sector of the front, and overall nothing had been achieved for the loss of 13,000 casualties. The 4th Division regarded its own part in the battle as a successful advance that had been first held up and then forced to withdraw through the failure of the 3rd Division, whose right flank the 12th Brigade was guarding, to push forward. In simple terms, there was no flank to guard. This was a narrow point of view, of course, but understandable given that the officers and men on the ground could only see what was happening in their immediate area on the railway. Further north the 3rd Division's dead strewn through the mud in front of Passchendaele Ridge showed that the failure was not due to any lack of determination. With only 48 hours for preparation there had been no real opportunity for joint planning between the staffs, who were working not only across division and brigade boundaries but between two different corps. If representatives from both staffs had been able to work closely together, an obvious issue like the wide gap between the jumping-off lines of the two brigades could have been identified and resolved before the battle opened.

Recriminations were not confined to the infantry. Because of the lay of the land in the battle area, many 3rd Division regimental stretcher bearers tended to converge with their casualties on the 12th Brigade RAP in the forward headquarters pillbox near the railway. From there it was the 4th Division's field ambulance bearers who were required to carry to their own Division's relay post at the 'Cordial Factory' (also called the 'Soda-water Factory') on the outskirts of Zonnebeke, then further down the line of evacuation to the Ypres ADS. The 4th Division's medical resources were stretched by having to deal with many of the 3rd Division casualties as well as their own, 'an enormous contract' as Lieutenant Colonel John Welch, the 13th Field Ambulance CO, put it,[89] and there was some ill-feeling. Colonel Welch related several tense incidents, including one where 4th Division bearers carried three 3rd Division casualties and one from their own Division to a wagon loading post and began transferring them to a 3rd Division horsed ambulance, the only one available. The driver refused to take the wounded 4th Division man, saying that he had orders to evacuate only casualties from his own Division.[90] According to the *Medical History* the two Divisions had previously agreed to pool their ambulance transport,[91] but this arrangement does not appear to have been understood all the way down the chain of command.

All medical personnel were under great stress working in the terrible conditions, the bearers facing carries of as much as 5,500 metres through a sea of mud. Some sections of the route needed eight bearers per stretcher, and infantry reinforcements had to be brought up from the reserve brigades to assist the bearers. Even when the wounded reached motor ambulances on the Zonnebeke road, traffic was so heavy that the five-kilometre trip to the Ypres ADS took an hour.[92] The dead still lay on the battlefield, as the 47th Battalion RMO, Captain John Jones, recorded:

> Next morning [13 October] the ground around the RAP was littered (with wounded who had died) who had to be piled in heaps to clear the trenches; and along the track from the RAP to Zonnebeke a distance of over a mile, the dead lay every few yards.[93]

The battle cost the 12th Brigade over 1,000 casualties. The greater proportion of these were in the two battalions actually engaged in the attack, the 47th and 48th, but the 45th and 46th Battalions, holding the line and sending carrying parties forward under the incessant shelling, also lost heavily, as did the 12th MG Company. The 47th and 48th recorded unusually high numbers of 'Missing' in their casualty lists, reflecting their necessarily hurried retreat from isolated positions. Initial reports to Division administration showed the 47th losing a total of 351 officers and men, 48 killed, 70 missing and 233 wounded, and the 48th's losses as 47 killed, 134 missing and 192 wounded, a total of 373 casualties.[94] Some of the missing were later found to be wounded at casualty stations or had straggled for one reason or another, but the majority were dead or prisoners. Later histories of the 48th Battalion have adjusted the numbers to 108 killed and 52 taken prisoner on 12 October; several of the prisoners died in captivity.[95] Similarly the 47th Battalion history establishes that 78 of its members were actually killed in action on that day,[96] meaning that up to 40 were prisoners. These were serious losses, particularly for an operation that had produced no positive results.

A number of individuals had distinguished themselves and were later awarded decorations for their efforts in the battle. The machine gunner Lance Corporal McTye, 12th MG Company, was recommended for the Victoria Cross but was awarded the DCM instead. DCMs also went to 47th Battalion NCOs Sergeant Heading and Sergeant Charles Brook, both of whom had shown outstanding leadership under fire when their officers had been put out of action. The 48th Battalion Lewis gunner Private Yates was another recipient of the DCM and a number of soldiers were awarded MMs, including 48th Battalion stretcher bearers Lance Corporal Walter Webb and Private Oskar Tuami (Tuami was a Finn who had worked his sea-passage to Australia in 1915, and was currently under a suspended sentence of two years imprisonment for a disciplinary offence). MM recipients in the 47th Battalion included Sergeant Ernest Maywood and Private Henry Adcock, who both worked with pack mules getting supplies forward through the barrage, and runner Private Edgar Turner. Among the officers, the wounded battalion COs, Colonels Imlay and Leane, were each awarded a Bar to their DSOs. There were comparatively few decorations approved for junior officers, and some unsuccessful recommendations provide further examples of General Sinclair-Maclagan reducing a recommended MC to a congratulatory card. The 48th Battalion's RMO, Captain Archibald Collins, was awarded the MC, however, for leading stretcher parties through heavy shelling and attending the wounded under fire at an improvised RAP. Captain Lionel Carter[97] of the 48th also received the MC for his gallantry in command of the unit's 'B' Company throughout the battle and the following days.

The 12th Brigade continued to hold its re-established front line for the next two days before being relieved by the 4th Brigade during 14 October. The 12th Brigade units moved back to the environs of Ypres, where they were accommodated in dugouts and the cellars under the old Infantry Barracks. These offered some protection from the intermittent long-range shelling by the Germans but it was hardly a period of rest for the Brigade, which would be recalled to the front within a few days. For the relieving 4th Brigade, the 14th Battalion was first into the chain of flooded shell-holes that constituted the front line, with the 15th in support and the 13th and 16th in reserve on Westhoek Ridge.

> In front was a swamp several hundred yards wide tenanted on its other side by the enemy ... the locality was strewn with the bodies of dead Australians ... who had fallen in the disastrous battle of October 12.[98]

The 4th Brigade rotated its battalions through the front and support positions every few days, with the reserve units supplying the usual large working parties for such projects as burying telephone cables and carrying up duckboards. Frequent bursts of shelling by the German artillery disrupted traffic and brought a steady stream of losses, both in the front line and behind it. On 20 October two 4th Field Ambulance stretcher bearers were killed and 17 wounded when shells hit a relay post on the casualty evacuation route, and a team of four bearers and their patient were killed the next day by a single shell.[99] The same night a Divisional Train convoy bringing up engineering stores was involved in an enemy bombardment on Westhoek Ridge that blocked the road with dead horses and broken wagons. The officer in charge of the convoy, Second Lieutenant Francis Cawley of the 14th Company AASC, took charge of clearing the road and got the traffic moving again under continued shelling; he was later awarded the MC for his efforts.

The 4th Brigade put in the next ten days holding the line, a stint that cost 396 casualties including 63 killed and 31 gassed; the latter were all from the 13th Battalion, caught in a heavy gas bombardment of the reserve positions on Westhoek Ridge. Over 100 were evacuated with illness in the same period.[100] In the meantime the 12th Brigade, after its brief rest underground in Ypres, was brought up to the front again on 20 October to relieve the 13th Brigade, holding the right of the divisional front on Broodseinde Ridge. Although not required to take part in the recent attacks, the 13th Brigade units had spent the past ten days under continual enemy shelling that had inflicted 641 casualties, 189 of whom had been killed. Over 250 had been hospitalised with sickness also.[101] 'The period in the line was one of the hardest put in by this Brigade', was the comment in its Diary.[102] Among the dead was the 51st Battalion's admired chaplain, Father Michael Bergin, hit by a shell splinter while attending wounded at the RAP. The 13th Brigade troops trudged wearily back to the Ypres dugouts while those of the 12th Brigade took over the line of shell-holes, sending up the 45th and 46th Battalions to the front positions with the battered 47th and 48th in support and reserve. There was no respite from the shelling but the period was mercifully short, with the Brigade being withdrawn in turn 24 hours later, on the night 20/21 October. Its line was taken over by the 4th Brigade, extending to its right, and by units of the 5th Division extending to their left, the I Anzac divisional fronts adjusting and thinning out; the inter-divisional boundary now followed the line of the Zonnebeke-Broodseinde-Droogenbroodhoek road.

By that time the Canadian Corps had come into the line to relieve II Anzac in the sector north of the railway, and the 4th Division was scheduled to be relieved by the 1st Division on 24 October. At first it was intended that the 4th Division artillery would stay in the line as before, but Brigadier General Burgess made strong representations that his gunners were in no condition to continue. The CRA pointed out that the 10th and 11th AFA Brigades had been in action almost continuously since early April, taking part in eight major attacks. Just over 1,000 casualties had been suffered in that time, almost half of those (486, including 72 killed) in September and October;[103] 'they had been in this period [only] 12 days in reserve, and about a week out of the line at the beginning of September.' In the current series of operations, added to the difficulties of the terrain,

> the enemy was using large numbers of gas shells which seriously affected all ranks; men in consequence could hardly speak above a whisper. Gassed, wet through, under shell-fire night and day and rapidly diminishing in numbers these batteries had carried out their task ... but in doing so their strength had been absorbed and

it was realised that this state of affairs could not continue if the 4th Australian Divisional Artillery Brigades were to remain organised units.[104]

Corps agreed and orders came through to withdraw the artillery with the rest of the Division. It was arranged for selected battery positions to be taken over by the 2nd Division artillery and a number of serviceable 4th Division guns would also be taken over, in exchange for damaged or bogged guns which would then go back with the 4th Division batteries.[105] The relief was to be completed by 25 October but General Burgess's HQ remained in overall command of the sector artillery, now consisting of the 1st and 2nd Division brigades, for the next attack, ordered for 26 October.

The main thrust was an advance by the Canadians on the same front as II Anzac had attempted on 12 October but over a much shorter distance—the Canadian Corps GOC, General Currie, had insisted on a return to the method of limited objectives. As for the previous battle I Anzac was responsible for covering the right flank of the main attack and events in that part of the battlefield followed a very similar pattern to those of 12 October. Troops of the 1st Division advanced along the railway to the Keiberg Spur and Decline Copse, this time with better liaison with the units on their left, but eventually had to fall back when the Canadian right flank was forced to withdraw. The Canadians had, however, taken their objectives further north and were in a position to go ahead with the next stage of their advance. The shooting of the I Anzac artillery covering the 1st Division's attack had again been less than ideal—part of the opening barrage fell short on to the troops on the start line and the leading waves had been forced to cross the railway and advance on its north side, using the embankment as cover from their own artillery.[106] After this operation General Burgess and his staff handed over to the 1st Division artillery HQ on 27 October and rejoined their troops, now withdrawn to the wagon lines at Reninghelst and Ouderdom and working on salvaging damaged and bogged guns. That task occupied several days, during which period (on 1 November) German aircraft bombed the 10th AFA Brigade's wagon lines, killing two men and wounding 19 others; 35 horses were also killed in the raid.[107] The artillerymen then prepared to follow the main body of the 4th Division moving to the back areas. Lieutenant Colonel William Waite returned from sick leave on 27 October and resumed command of the 11th AFA Brigade, Major Edwards returning to his battery. The artillery command changed again a fortnight later when the 10th AFA Brigade CO, Lieutenant Colonel Williams, was temporarily posted away from the Division to command the 12th (Army) AFA Brigade. Major Edwards then moved across from the 11th Brigade to take Colonel Williams' place until the latter returned in the following February. The infantry brigade groups had been relieved by their 1st Division equivalents on 24 October. Over the next few days the troops moved by train and motor transport to the areas of Bomy and Lisbourg, well to the rear. Division HQ was established at Bomy on 27 October. This was the same region that the Division had been sent to at the beginning of September, when hopes of a long rest had been first raised and then dashed. History would soon repeat itself.

This famous photograph by Frank Hurley shows members of the 4th Division artillery (110th Howitzer Battery, 10th AFA Brigade) crossing a duckboard track through Chateau Wood, Ypres sector, on 29 October 1917. There is some doubt about the identification of several soldiers in this picture, but the first two from the left are Gunner James Fulton and Lieutenant Anthony Devine. (AWM E01220)

14 Notes

1. *Official History*, Vol IV, p. 725.
2. *Ibid*, p. 743n.
3. 2nd Division Artillery HQ War Diary for September 1917, Appendix 8. The 10th and 11th FA Brigades' War Diaries for September and October record Colonels Williams and Edwards taking over the group command at various times.
4. Horner, *Op Cit*, p. 157.
5. 2nd Division Artillery HQ War Diary for September 1917, Appendix 5.
6. 10th AFA Brigade War Diary, 13 September 1917.
7. *Official History*, Vol IV, p. 745.
8. 10th AFA Brigade War Diary, 20 September 1917.
9. *Official History*, Vol IV, p. 789n.
10. Prior and Wilson, *Passchendaele, Op Cit*, p. 119; the authors point out that in comparing casualties to area of ground gained, the successful Menin Road battle was more than twice as costly as Fifth Army's attack on 31 July.
11. *Medical History*, Vol II, p. 207.
12. 12th MG Company War Diary for September 1917, Appendix V.
13. *Medical History*, Vol II, p. 201.
14. *Ibid*, p.215.
15. 13th Battalion War Diary for September 1917, Appendix 99A, and diary of Lt Col D G Marks, 26 September 1917. The battalion history (White, *Op Cit*, p. 109) says 200 yards.
16. 50th Battalion War Diary, 23 September 1917.
17. 4th Division GS War Diary for September 1917, Part 2, Appendix 21.
18. 4th Division GS War Diary for September 1917, Part 1, Appendix 16, and Part 2, Appendix 33.
19. 13th Brigade, 49th Battalion and 51st Battalion War Diaries for September 1917, Operation Orders and after-action reports. The orders are sometimes inconsistent in the use of the terms 'wave' and 'line'.
20. *Official History*, Vol IV, p. 813.

21　50th Battalion War Diary for September 1917, Appendices. It appears that the information reached Battalion forward HQ half an hour later, and was then sent on to Brigade HQ by pigeon; that message was timed 7.25 am (13th Brigade War diary, September 1917, Appendix 10).

22　49th Battalion War Diary for September 1917, Appendices, report dated 29 September.

23　4th Division Engineers HQ War Diary for September 1917, Appendix 1 (report from 13th Field Company). It appears that a fourth post was constructed in the Blue Line in the next day or two.

24　From correspondence on Capt Park's service record (page 20). Although that document gives an exact map reference for his burial place, his remains were not found after the war; see note 43 below for a similar instance.

25　13th Brigade War Diary for September 1917, Appendix 10, and award recommendations for Carlton and Paris.

26　Wanliss, *Op Cit*, p. 241. There is no report of such an incident in the relevant Brigade and Battalion reports.

27　Chataway, *Op Cit*, p. 190 –91.

28　*Loc Cit*.

29　Wanliss, *Op Cit*, p. 242. That passage has been interpreted (eg. in Grant, *Jacka VC*, p. 144) as meaning that the 16th Battalion ran into the barrage, but it is clear that Wanliss meant the first wave of the 14th Battalion, in the second stage of the advance (it will be recalled that the 4th Brigade battalions were each advancing in three or four waves).

30　The Blue Line intersected the road on the right of the 4th Brigade front, in the 15th Battalion's sector.

31　The 14th Battalion War Diary gave the reference as J.3.b.3.4, that of the 4th Field Company as J.3.d.4.4. The difference in the final co-ordinates is not significant, but the discrepancy between the two sub-squares 'b' and 'd' makes the positions 500 yards apart. The 14th Battalion version seems more likely to be in error, as that position is well inside the 13th Brigade's sector, whereas J.3.d.3.4 is an early point in the general line of the 4th Brigades advance. The sources for this section in general are mentioned in the text..

32　Dwyer was probably using a Vickers fitted with an auxiliary tripod, a folding light stand under the barrel. It would have been extremely difficult for one man to carry the gun, its heavy standard tripod and at least one box of ammunition over some distance and then set up the weapon single-handed, and there is no indication that he had any assistance. The German machine gun, although it was firing to Dwyer's right (south) when he sighted it, was in a position where it might have been the one that killed Capt Wanliss, 14th Battalion.

33　The 4th MG Company's War Diary for 26 September records messages requesting crews for two captured German guns, one each in the Red and Blue lines, although the messages did not arrive at Company HQ until evening.

34　The 4th Division's report (Appendix 35 in the September GS War Diary) notes up to four attempted counter-attacks. The 12th MG Company, controlling the 4th Division's SOS machine gun barrage, reported in its War Diary that it had responded to three SOS calls on 26 September.

35　12th Bde War Diary for September 1917, Appendix 17.

36　As is often the case, discrepancies in casualty figures arise depending on which sources are used. The 4th Division Admin Staff War Diary for September 1917, Appendix 4, gives a total of 248 casualties (69 killed and missing) for the four 12th Brigade battalions during the month of September; the figure would include some losses from shelling to working parties behind the lines before the brigade moved up. The *Official History* (Vol IV, p. 831n) gives a total of 208 in the Brigade, including

25 for the 12th MG Company, which was in action from the beginning of the battle. The *History* numbers appear to be understated, particularly for the 46th Battalion (32, compared with 94 in the Admin report), perhaps due to late reporting and because the more detailed Weekly Strength Reports include the last day of the month in the first weekly report for October.

37   Wording from Capt Kellaway's MC recommendation, in the AWM Honours and Awards files. His name is spelled 'Kelleway' in the 13th Battalion history.

38   4th Field Ambulance War Diary, 26 September 1917.

39   13th Brigade War Diary for September 1917, Appendix 10.

40   4th Division Admin Staff War Diary for September 1917, Appendix 4. The Artillery HQ's September War Diary reported the total as 235, including 28 in the DAC.

41   Numbers are all taken from the Admin Staff report, as above, for the full month. The figures quoted for the infantry brigades include their MG companies and LTM batteries but not their linked Engineer companies and Field Ambulances (the 24th MG Company, not linked to a brigade, had 24 casualties).

42   *Official History*, Vol IV, p. 828n; 'AIF Celebrities', *Reveille*, May 1932, pp 7, 26–7; Wanliss, *Op Cit*, p.248.

43   In 1926, Newton Wanliss wrote to the Imperial (later Commonwealth) War Graves Commission advising the map reference, which was J.4.b.4.4, definitely a location in the Blue Line of 26 September. He gave the map sheet name as Becelaere, which appears to have been a special series map taken from the regular series sheets entitled Zonnebeke and Gheluvelt (adjoining north/south; Gheluvelt includes Becelaere village). This should not have been difficult for the Commission to interpret. His informant, who happened to be Albert Jacka, further advised that 'if a trench is dug five yards in each direction from the above point ... his remains should be found.' The letter is on Harold's Service Record. Lt Norman Aldridge, second in command of Harold's company, also recorded the map reference, according to his letter on the AWM Red Cross file. Despite these details, the Commission could not locate the body, unless it was actually exhumed but not identified. Mr Wanliss noted that, in the absence of any other indications, Harold's boots would have had non-standard rubber strips across the soles. Another 14th officer, 2nd Lt Lloyd Gill, was also killed in the vicinity two days later, and his remains lie in Aeroplane Cemetery, near Ypres. It is possible that Harold Wanliss is among the unidentified soldiers buried in that cemetery (there are at least three unknown Australians buried in the same row as Lt Gill who were found at locations with similar map references).

44   4th Division General Staff War Diary, 28 September 1917.

45   AWM Honours and Awards files. The recommendation was written by Captain Albert Mitchell, the Company OC. Mitchell, who was in his proper place with the unit HQ near the existing front line, would not have seen Dwyer's exploits in person and would have relied on reports from officers in the firing line. Regrettably, none of those reports is readily available, and Dwyer does not seem to have left a personal account.

46   In most cases, the AWM Honours and Awards files include two copies of 4th Division recommendations for the 26 September fighting, one with the specific award noted and initialled by hand by the GOC, the other with that information typed in.

47   Grant, *Op Cit*, p. 147.

48   The author is aware that a disproportionate amount of space has been taken up with the internal politics of one infantry battalion out of twelve in the Division. This was in the hope of drawing attention to a number of issues relating to the 14th Battalion that do not appear to have been fully resolved. Perhaps the time has come for a new unit history of the 14th.

49   *Medical History*, Vol II, p. 225. Only the 12th Field Ambulance is mentioned, but it is also stated that 'all reliefs' were used.

50 4th Division Artillery War Diary for October 1917, Appendices, CRA's report on operations 9 September to 26 October 1917, dated 30 October.
51 *Official* History, Vol IV, p. 849.
52 *Ibid*, p. 856.
53 *Ibid*, p.861-2. Bean's source for the shrapnel bursts was his interviews at the time with 21st Battalion (6th Brigade) officers (Bean Papers, AWM38 3DRL606/168/1, p.15). The after-action reports by 6th Brigade and the 21st and 24th Battalions only say that the protective barrage was too thin and the rate of fire too slow to fully suppress the snipers. On the other hand, the 6th Brigade also noted after the failed operation of 9 October that 'Had we had the barrage of October 4th there could have been no doubt of our complete success' (6th Brigade War Diary for October 1917, Appendix 14). That comment probably refers to the creeping barrage.
54 Prior and Wilson, *Passchendaele, Op Cit*, pp. 160-61; *Official History*, Vol IV, pp. 884-5.
55 *Official History*, Vol IV, p. 883.
56 11th AFA Brigade War Diary, 7 to 9 October 1917.
57 6th Brigade War Diary for October 1917, Appendix 14.
58 Prior and Wilson, *Passchendaele, Op Cit*, p. 166.
59 Lee, *Op Cit*, p. 53.
60 45th Battalion War Diary for October 1917, Appendices. The New Zealanders, coming into the line in II Anzac's sector, had a similar experience, finding many casualties left behind by the 49th Division (C. Pugsley, 'The New Zealand Division at Passchenedaele,' in P. Liddle (ed), *Passchendaele in Perspective:The Third Battle of Ypres*, p. 283).
61 Maj Johnston had returned to duty in September, as supernumerary on the 4th Brigade staff.
62 13th Field Ambulance War Diary for October 1917, Appendices, memos dated 19 and 22 October.
63 4th Division Artillery HQ War Diary for October 1917, Appendices, report dated 30 October.
64 *Ibid*, 12 October 1917.
65 4th Division DAC War Diary, 13 October 1917.
66 The name of this landmark was incorrectly transcribed as 'Dead Line' Copse in the 48th Battalion's after-action report.
67 4th Division General Staff War Diary for October 1917, Appendix 14.
68 48th Battalion War Diary for October 1917, Appendices, Operation Order 95.
69 9th Brigade War Diary for October 1917, Appendix 118.
70 *Ibid*, Appendices 120 and 121.
71 Browning, *Leane's Battalion, Op Cit*, p. 180.
72 The 47th Battalion's report, however, described the barrage as 'excellent' (Battalion War Diary for October 1917, Appendix 5).
73 48th Battalion War Diary for October 1917, Appendices, report dated 17 October.
74 47th Battalion War Diary for October 1917, Appendix 5. C E W Bean's notebook entry at the time (AWM38 3DRL606/178/1, p. 40) gives 27 killed and 12 wounded. There is no report of casualties to the 48th Battalion HQ personnel, who were sharing the building, and the differences may represent casualties in that unit.
75 12th Brigade War Diary for October 1917, Appendix 6a.

76. Lavington Lewis Carter was later commissioned, and transferred to the 48th Battalion when the 47th was disbanded in 1918. The 48th had another officer named L L Carter, Captain Lionel Lewin Carter.
77. *Official History*, Vol IV, p. 912.
78. 47th Battalion War Diary for October 1917, Appendix 5.
79. 12th MG Company War Diary for October 1917, Appendix 1.
80. Mitchell, *Op Cit*, p. 111.
81. Alexander Anderson transferred to the 48th when the 47th was disbanded in 1918, and won the DSO with his new unit in the fighting at Le Verguier (Hindenburg Outpost Line).
82. 12th Brigade War Diary for October 1917, Appendix 6.
83. 12th MG Company War Diary for October 1917, Appendix 1; Bean Papers, AWM38 3DRL606/178/1, p.64.
84. 4th Division General Staff War Diary for October 1917, Appendix 28.
85. Deayton, *Op Cit*, p. 178.
86. 12th MG Company War Diary for October 1917, Appendix 1; AWM Red Cross file on 2nd Lt J T East, which contains two statements by Lcpl McTye; AWM Honours and Awards files, recommendation for Lcpl T M McTye.
87. *Official History*, Vol IV, p. 926n.
88. Browning, *Leane's Battalion, Op Cit*, p. 180.
89. 13th Field Ambulance War Diary for October 1917, Appendices, memo dated 12 October. The *Medical History* (Vol II, p. 237) mentions this issue, but puts the RAP concerned as located at the Cordial Factory. The account in Colonel Welch's memo, however, clearly refers to the RAP established in the pillbox housing the 47th and 48th Battalion forward HQs. The Cordial Factory was being used as a relay post on 12 October, but when the 12th Brigade withdrew, the pillbox and the co-located RAP were abandoned and the Cordial Factory was then used as an RAP serving the re-established front line.
90. *Ibid*, memo dated 16 October. This incident seems to have occurred after the 12 October fighting, as the complaint came from the 15th Battalion RMO (the 4th Brigade had relieved the 12th on 13/14 October).
91. *Medical History*, Vol II, p.236.
92. 13th Field Ambulance War Diary, 11 October 1917.
93. *Medical History*, Vol II, p. 238.
94. Figures from the weekly Strength Returns, in Appendices to the 4th Division Admin Staff War Diary for October 1917.
95. These figures are extracted from the Roll of Honour lists in Devine, *The Story of a Battalion*, and Browning, *Leane's Battalion*; the number of fatalities is confirmed by the AWM Roll of Honour. Browning also lists all 48th members taken prisoner during the war. Two other 48th members died of wounds the next day.
96. Deayton, *Op Cit*, from Appendix 3, Roll of Honour; the AWM Roll of Honour confirms 78 deaths in the 47th on that date..
97. See Note 76 above.
98. Wanliss, *Op Cit*, pp. 249–50.
99. 13th Field Ambulance and 4th Field Ambulance War Diaries, 21/22 October 1917 (the 4th Field Ambulance bearers were attached to the 13th for duty).

100 Figures from the 4th Brigade War Diary for October 1917 and 16th Battalion War Diary for October 1917, Appendix L.
101 Figures from the 13th Brigade War Diary for October 1917. The Division Admin staff reported a slightly higher casualty total of 663. The Brigade figure may have omitted those wounded in the MG Company and LTM Battery.
102 13th Brigade War Diary, 20/21 October 1917.
103 Figures from reports in the Artillery HQ War Diary for September and October 1917, and January 1918. The 4th Division Admin HQ reports for September and October show slightly lower numbers.
104 4th Division Artillery HQ War Diary for October 1917, Appendices, report dated 30 October.
105 *Ibid*, Order No. 99, 24 October.
106 *Official History*, Vol IV, p. 934 and 934n. The report in the 6th Battalion War Diary for October 1917 says that some of the troops had already been detailed to advance on the north of the railway.
107 10th AFA Brigade War Diary, 1 November 1917. It appears that these casualties were included in the October figures—the November Artillery HQ War Diary says that there were no battle casualties in November.

15: Depot Division

During the later stages of the 4th Division's involvement in Third Ypres, momentous events had been taking place in other theatres of the war. In the East the Russian army, its morale fatally weakened by inept leadership and domestic political turmoil, was rapidly collapsing under German attacks. The Germans were able to spare large numbers of troops for other fronts where they were under greater pressure; several divisions were sent to reinforce the defences on the Ypres front, others to assist their Austrian allies fighting the Italians on the line of the Isonzo River. In that region the two sides had fought to a bloody standstill over two years of failed offensives, but on 24 October a combined German-Austrian army launched a powerful attack centred on Caporetto that broke through the Italians' lines and drove them back in rout and disaster. By the time the front stabilised, the Austro-German forces had advanced 100 kilometres and the British and French were hurriedly transferring divisions from the Western Front to shore up their allies. Early November saw the Bolsheviks seize power in Russia and begin armistice negotiations with Germany. It was apparent that the Germans would soon be able to concentrate the great majority of their forces in the West. The allies could expect to be greatly strengthened by the huge resources of the United States, but the expanding American army was still many months away from being ready for combat. At Passchendaele the Canadian Corps edged towards the final ridge in a series of short advances, capturing the village site and part of the high ground on 6 November. Following further minor gains over the following few days the battle was closed down. The Flanders armies, after the grandiose ambitions at the start of the campaign, had succeeded only in pushing their line out to positions on the Ypres ridges, ending in a small exposed salient that could not be held against a full-scale attack. Certainly Sir Douglas Haig's forces had inflicted heavy losses on the German army, but their own losses were even greater and left the BEF seriously weakened for the fighting to come in 1918.

In the smaller world of the AIF there were high-level administrative decisions being made behind the scenes at this time that seemed likely to have a significant effect on the

4th Division's future role. Maintaining manpower numbers up to strength in the face of enormous casualty lists was a constant issue for all national armies, and it was particularly acute for the AIF, dependent as it was on all-volunteer enlistment. All other nations had sooner or later adopted conscription but Australian voters had rejected the idea via the referendum (strictly speaking, the plebiscite) of October 1916. Another referendum was proposed for December 1917 but there was no reason to suppose that the vote would be 'yes' this time. With voluntary enlistments steadily declining, it was feared that the AIF would soon face a manpower crisis. This situation was connected to another ongoing issue, the desire of the Australian authorities for all of the nation's troops in France to be placed under a unified operational command. Since 1916 the government had been pressing for the formation of an Australian (or Australasian) Army, but it was now apparent that there insufficient resources for such a step. The possibility still existed, however, of forming the five Australian divisions into a single corps, and the government raised that proposal in late 1917, with the strong support of General Birdwood. GHQ and Sir Douglas Haig, however, were firmly of the view that four divisions was the optimum number for a corps, and five would be too difficult for a corps staff to manage. This suggested that the aim could be achieved by disbanding one of the Australian divisions and distributing its personnel to the others, but there were moral factors that had to be considered.

> Such a step would have caused intense heartburning among the troops and also in Australia. The divisions were no longer mere accidental groupings of battalions; from harsh experience of fighting each had emerged as a definite entity, with a distinct character, firm comradeship and fiery pride.[1]

If those considerations were ignored, however, it would probably be the 4th Division that would go. Overall the 4th had spent the longest time in the line, was collectively worn out in morale and physical condition and was well under strength in numbers –although not actually the weakest: the 3rd Division had lost heavily during Third Ypres and its numbers were lower than the 4th's at the end of October.[2]

> But Birdwood never forgot that the Australian Government, which itself had formed that division in Australia ... might be specially interested in its welfare; moreover, though it was now lowest in strength, it seemed fitter for the line than the 4th.[3]

General Birdwood and Major General Brudenell White, I Anzac chief of staff, now suggested that the proposed new corps could comprise four active divisions, with the remaining division, instead of being disbanded, withdrawn into reserve well to the rear and designated as a 'depot division,' providing an additional source of reinforcements for the other four. The depot division would itself be reinforced only by its own returning sick and wounded. If (or more likely when) one of the active divisions suffered heavy battle losses it would be rotated to the rear and become the depot division in its turn, with the original depot division coming forward to relieve. This approach both avoided disbandment and answered the objections to a five-division corps, while also making some allowance for the looming manpower shortfall. Sir Douglas Haig accordingly gave his approval for the change on 1 November. The 3rd Division was transferred from II Anzac to I Anzac a fortnight later, bringing all five Australian divisions under General Birdwood's command in one corps. I Anzac Corps would in future be known as The Australian Corps, although that designation was not used officially until 1 January 1918. At that time the title of II Anzac also ceased to exist, changing to XXII Corps, a formation that then still included the New Zealand Division, 'probably the all round best and strongest division in the British Army.'[4]

It was in fact the 4th Division that would be the initial depot division for the unified Corps, although few of its members outside of the staff would have been particularly conscious of the change in status. Following the Division's relief from the front line, late October and early November was a period of reorganising and relocation. While the main body of the Division settled into billets in the Bomy-Lisbourg area, the Pioneer Battalion and the 4th and 13th Field Company engineers stayed in the forward area for two weeks completing various works around Ypres before following the main body. The divisional artillery completed its task of salving abandoned guns and moved back to Morbeque, near Hazebrouck, on 2 and 3 November. While in that area, on 14 November the artillery held its first full ceremonial parade since arriving in France in 1916. Despite the heavy strain of recent months the gunners put on a fine turnout for the inspection by Sir William Birdwood, to Brigadier General Burgess's great satisfaction.[5] The next day the artillery units moved out for Estrée-Blanche, near Bomy, to join the rest of the 4th Division. The month of October 1917 had cost the Division a total of 2,739 casualties, 738 of them killed or missing.[6] Sick evacuations had totalled about 850 for the month and 1,879 reinforcements had come in, leaving the Division's total strength, in terms of personnel actually on duty, as 612 officers and 13,219 ORs. After allowing for those on leave or detachment the Division was about 4,000 short of full strength on coming out of the line. This period saw another round of changes in senior officer appointments in a number of units. The 12th Brigade had lost three of its four battalion commanders wounded during the 12 October fighting, the 45th, 47th and 48th Battalions completing their battle assignments under acting COs. Major A S Allen, the 45th's second-in-command, was in charge of that unit initially before Major Stanley Perry, promoted to temporary lieutenant colonel, was appointed as CO on 16 October. Colonel Perry, a 27 year old from New South Wales, had first shown his abilities when a platoon commander with the 13th Battalion on Gallipoli,[7] before transferring to the 'daughter' 45th in Egypt. He had recently returned from England after completing a senior officers' course, having been assessed as 'an excellent type of young Australian officer ... determined, cheerful and conscientious.'[8] With 'Tubby' Allen as second in command, the 45th had a strong leadership group.

With their COs wounded in hospital but expected to return in due course, the 47th and 48th Battalions had several temporary commanders in the short term. The 47th's appointed second in command, Major Denis Hannay, was away on a course in October and

Captain Charles Symons, next in seniority, succeeded to the command after the 12 October fighting, taking over from Captain James Brack who had been in charge following Lieutenant Colonel Imlay's wounding. At the end of the month Lieutenant Colonel Arthur Deeble was posted in from England to assume command, but for reasons that are not obvious he only stayed with the 47th Battalion for a week before being transferred to the 48th as CO. Command of the 47th reverted to Captain Symons until Major Hannay returned to the unit in December. On moving over to the 48th Battalion on 4 November, Colonel Deeble took over from the unit's second in command, Major Montague Brearley, who had assumed temporary command following the battle of 12 October. Deeble, a former Light Horse officer, had spent most of his war service in training postings in England before being appointed to a command in the short-lived 6th Division. His only front-line service had been three months on Gallipoli, although that period had included the harrowing experience of taking part in the Charge at the Nek, when he had been one of the few officers to survive that disastrous engagement.[9]

A 13th Brigade unit, the 51st Battalion, also had a change of CO in October. Lieutenant Colonel Cecil Ridley was posted to the senior officers' school at Aldershot as an instructor, and the unit second in command, Major Robert Christie, moved straight into the vacancy on 23 October with promotion to lieutenant colonel. Colonel Christie was the first member of the 4th Division to rise to substantive unit command from the ranks, although not from private—a regular soldier before the war, he had originally been appointed to the AIF Light Horse in 1914 as a quartermaster sergeant.[10] During his service at Gallipoli Christie was granted the traditional honorary commission as unit quartermaster. This was relinquished when he left the posting after Gallipoli to transfer to the 51st Battalion infantry, but he was immediately given a full commission and quickly rose to major. Christie's promise was confirmed by his faultless command of the 51st at Polygon Wood, and the tall, 34 year old Queenslander was to lead the unit for the rest of the war. The Brigade's medical unit, the 13th Field Ambulance, also received a new CO. Lieutenant Colonel Welch returned to Australia for personal reasons and was replaced on 1 November by Lieutenant Colonel Kenneth Fry, promoted from DADMS in the 2nd Division. Colonel Fry had been with the 2nd Division on Gallipoli, and had later been awarded the DSO for his work at Pozières.

In the 4th Brigade Lieutenant Colonel James Durrant, recovered from his wound, returned from hospital on 29 October and resumed command of the 13th Battalion from Major Douglas Marks, who reverted to second in command. As of 4 November, Major Ernest Radford, the divisional machine gun officer, took on the command of the 24th MG Company in addition to his HQ duties. The Pioneer Battalion was another unit to have a change of CO, Lieutenant Colonel Vernon Sturdee leaving on 26 October to take up the post of CRE of the 5th Division, the next step in his distinguished career. The 5th Division provided his replacement, Lieutenant Colonel Harold Morrison, promoted from major in the 5th Pioneers; Colonel Morrison, 34 years old from NSW, was a pre-war militia infantry officer who had developed an interest in field engineering. At this time Major Howard Tolley,

4th Field Company, was acting as 4th Division CRE while Lieutenant Colonel Elliott was on leave, and Captain Edwin Norman was acting OC 12th Field Company in the absence of Major Riddell.[11] It fell to Major Tolley to submit the engineers' comments for a divisional review of the Ypres operations, and he noted that 'it was freely acknowledged that the Field companies worked on the right lines in assisting the Infantry in the assault,'[12] an observation that is supported by comments in the infantry brigades' after action reports. The acting CRE made several suggestions for further improvements in future operations, and also turned to the vexed topic of infantry working parties on engineering projects. Major Tolley's view, probably not unjustified, was that

> the work that is accomplished is sometimes done grudgingly. It is often regarded by Officers and men as a sort of extra fatigue, and ... considered ... as time wasted

The infantry attitude was often

> 'I came out here to fight not to sling mud about.' ...they must be taught that in these days, slinging mud about is a very necessary part of the fighting.[13]

To accomplish this change in attitude he suggested several ways to tighten up the organisation and methods of working parties, and also that as a means of improving the prevailing mental approach,

> The phrases 'RE [Royal Engineers] Fatigue' and 'RE Working Parties' should be abolished ... and disciplinary action taken against anybody using the phrases

and that orders should instead be couched in terms of an infantry task with technical assistance from engineers. To what extent this approach was implemented is not clear, but Major Tolley may have been over-optimistic in believing that such a piece of 'spin' could overcome the boundless cynicism of the average infantryman. Nevertheless, there were positive signs that co-operation between the two arms was improving and the contribution of the engineers in the firing line was being appreciated.

By mid-November the 4th Division units were billeted in the general area Estrée-Blanche—Lisbourg—Fruges—Bomy, continuing with refitting, sports and light training as well as the always-welcome hot baths. The usual off-duty diversions were now augmented by cinema films and by the recently-formed divisional concert party, 'The Smart Set', who gave their first performance on 3 November.[14] The opportunity was taken to grant leave to a number of soldiers and Major General Sinclair-MacLagan himself took a fortnight's break. He was relieved at first by Brigadier General Robertson, then by Brigadier General Glasgow when the latter returned from his own period of leave. General Robertson had earlier applied for and been granted a long furlough in Australia and he relinquished command of the 12th Brigade as of 15 November. Robertson had commanded his brigade competently for a year without perhaps making any great impact as a personality,[15] but his successor was somewhat more colourful. This was Brigadier General John Gellibrand, who had arrived from England earlier in the month to familiarise himself with his new command. The incoming brigadier was 45, born in Tasmania but raised in England. He had become a regular officer in the British Army, served in the Boer War, and passed the Staff College course before lack of career prospects led him to resign his commission and return to his native Tasmania. At the outbreak of the war Gellibrand was making a living as an orchardist. He was soon appointed to the AIF as a staff officer at 1st Division HQ, one of the few AIF officers who held the 'psc' qualification. He served on Gallipoli then commanded the 6th Brigade (2nd Division) in France. As a brigadier Gellibrand's finest moment was the Second Battle of Bullecourt, where his men had taken their objective in the Hindenburg Line and held it unsupported under extreme pressure. Shortly after that battle Gellibrand had a serious falling-out with 2nd Division HQ and asked to be relieved of his command. Pending the availability of another operational command, he was posted to training duties in England, which he tackled with typical energy before the vacancy arose in the 12th Brigade.

Brigadier General Gellibrand's bearing seemed casual—he often wore a private soldiers' tunic and an old slouch hat instead of the usual finery of a general—but he went everywhere and saw everything. The 48th Battalion historian noted that young officers would receive unexpectedly incisive critiques of their performance on the training field, prompting remarks that 'the new Brig. knew too dam' much.'[16] Gellibrand's former brigade major, Eric Plant, was now on the 4th Division HQ staff as GSO2, and on 24 November the brigadier brought in another former colleague, Major Reginald 'Babe' Norman, as brigade major of the 12th Brigade. Norman, whose active duty had begun in August 1914 on the staff of the New Guinea expedition,[17] had been Gellibrand's staff captain in the 6th Brigade. There had been a rapid turnover of brigade majors in the 12th Brigade in recent times. Major Wilton, who had replaced Major Salier early in October, had himself been evacuated sick two weeks later, and then posted to training duties in England when he recovered. Captain Thomas Louch, detached from 13th Brigade HQ, had been acting as brigade major before Major Norman arrived. With that recent instability in the Brigade staff and three of his four battalion commanders new to their duties, it was not surprising that General Gellibrand began by holding a tight rein.

The 4th Division was on the move again in mid-November. In keeping with its status as depot division the 4th was now transferred from the direct control of I Anzac to GHQ Reserve, deep in the rear zone or Lines of Communication area. The Division's new area was close to the channel coast, centring on Gamaches south-west of Abbeville, a journey of about 100 kilometres from the present billets around Bomy. The commanders decided that the move would be made as a march by the whole Division, men, vehicles, weapons and animals. The troops were to proceed along the roads by easy stages, in seven marches with one rest and inspection day, and each days march planned to finish early in the afternoon. Marching would keep the troops fit and provide opportunities for improving march discipline and transport methods. The movement began on 15 November, with the 12th Brigade Group leading off followed on successive days by the other two brigade groups and a final group consisting of the artillery, pioneers, 24th MG Company, veterinary section and HQ details. Between 22 and 25 November all of the 4th Division units arrived at their allotted sub-areas in a 12 kilometre-wide strip of territory from Bourseville south to Gamaches, with Division HQ at the latter place. Although the weather was cold and sometimes squally, the locality was a boost to morale in itself. The 48th Battalion was billeted at Friaucourt,

> a short distance from the coast. The smell of the sea was in the billets of the troops. The breakers could be sighted from their training ground. ... In the country around them, there was nothing ... to suggest the existence of war. The sound of a gun was never heard, and an aeroplane ... was never seen. The district lay far away from the main roads of traffic, civil or military. The people of the district knew almost nothing concerning the war, and were indeed a much more kindly and pleasant people for that fact.[18]

It seemed that the promised long rest would take place at last, and some units set up committees to plan Christmas celebrations. A programme of afternoon sports was soon instituted and the command groups conferred to develop comprehensive training agendas to take advantage of the period in the back area. One of the tasks was to select suitable training grounds and rifle ranges in the surrounding countryside, areas that had to be rented from the owners and then prepared for use. Lieutenant Colonel Bernard, the GSO1, outlined the staff's intentions in a preliminary memorandum to all units:

> The Division will now have a long period in which to carry out thorough and systematic training. Owing to never having had a long period in which to train it has always been necessary to carry out more advanced training without ever having had a thorough grounding.[19]

Such was the aspiration, but dramatic events at the fighting front would once again upset calculations. The Third Battle of Ypres had petered out and winter was approaching rapidly when GHQ decided to launch one more offensive before the weather closed in. The Tank Corps had been building up its strength and now had several hundred vehicles available, of improved type, and had been pressing for the massed use of tanks in suitable terrain—this time in conjunction with artillery. The German positions in the Hindenburg Line in front of Cambrai offered an opportunity and the attack was launched on 20 November (the 4th Division was on the march from Bomy to Gamaches at the time). A hurricane bombardment by 1,000 guns, firing without previous registration, and an assault by over 300 tanks backed up by infantry took the Germans completely by surprise and tore a nine-kilometre wide gap in the Hindenburg Line. Exceeding all expectations, the attack penetrated to a depth of five kilometres by the end of the day. Church bells were rung out in Britain to celebrate the triumph. Reserves for further exploitation were inadequate, however, and progress over the succeeding days was minimal against stiffening enemy resistance. The resilient Germans were able to bring up strong reserves and on 30 November they launched a powerful counter-attack that not only recaptured most of the lost ground but penetrated into original British territory. There were fears that the Germans were on the verge of a major break-through, and GHQ was compelled to bring up its reserves.

Those reserves included the 4th Australian Division at Gamaches, and on 3 December Division HQ received a signal from GHQ ordering that the Division make urgent arrangements to move again. Later that day the staff issued a warning order for all units to be ready to leave 'by rail at short notice ... destination at present unknown,'[20] with 5 December the likely date. This was not long after the memorandum announcing a long period of rest and systematic training, but since leaving Bomy the Division had experienced 'seven days on the road for eight days rest, the whole of which were taken up with preparing for the future training,' as the 13th Battalion historian put it.[21] After the inevitable resentment the troops seem to have accepted the sudden change of plans with resignation, aware that the purpose was to help stave off potential disaster. Entraining at three stations in the area, on seven trains per brigade group and a dozen for the artillery, the Division started its next journey up to the forward zone on 5 December. The destination was now known to be the VII Corps (Third Army) area around Péronne on the Somme, behind the front of the Cambrai battle. There were few other details, however. Major Plant, the GSO2, travelled ahead by car and sought further orders at VII Corps HQ, but 'Corps [was] unable to state any facts regarding any instructions for 4th Australian Division and advised Division to make itself comfortable.'[22] The Division did so as far as possible, the units arriving at various times of the day and night over the next few days. By the evening of 7 December all units had reached their billets at villages near Péronne, the 4th Brigade Group at Moislains, the 12th at Haut Allaines and the 13th at Etricourt initially, then Templeux-la-Fosse closer to the front line. The artillery brigades were based at Doingt, moving to Flamicourt on the outskirts of Péronne later in the month. Division HQ was set up at Haut Allaines. It was confirmed that the Division was now attached to VII Corps and had to be ready to move to the front line at short notice—the 4th Division's role as a depot division in the back area had lasted all of three weeks.[23] In the New Year the Division would rejoin the Australian Corps and the depot idea quietly faded away.

As it happened, the danger had all but passed as the 4th Division arrived. Third Army succeeded in establishing a firm defensive line against the German attacks and the Battle of Cambrai petered out with no real advantage to either side. The opposing armies along the Western Front settled in to hold their winter lines and await developments in the spring. In the short term the 4th Division was to remain near Péronne, an area that had been devastated in the German withdrawal to the Hindenburg Line. In contrast to the previous pleasant accommodation near the coast, the troops were now in 'a bleak and desolate place, whilst Péronne was but a ruin and with its surroundings was destitute of all civilian population,'[24] and the weather was approaching the freezing stage. The danger of further enemy attacks had now receded, however, and the terrain did offer realistic training grounds. The commanders were determined to continue with the interrupted training scheme, and the infantry brigades resumed their programmes whenever the weather permitted. Another change in unit commanders had taken place on the day the 4th Brigade had left Bomy for Péronne when the 13th Battalion's long-serving CO, Lieutenant Colonel James Durrant, had left to take up duty as AA&QMG of the 2nd Division. There was a seamless transition of command with the unit's second-in-command, Major Douglas Marks, moving up to CO with promotion to lieutenant colonel, at the age of only 22 years and eight months; Marks' close friend Major Harry Murray became second-in-command. Marks had first come to notice as a platoon commander with the 13th on Gallipoli and since then he had risen steadily through the unit's hierarchy, showing maturity and military acumen far beyond his years.

Officers of the two NSW infantry battalions in the 4th Division. Left to right: Lieutenant Colonel Douglas Marks, CO 13th Battalion; Major Henry 'Harry' Murray, second in command 13th Battalion; Major Arthur 'Tubby' Allen, second in command 45th Battalion; Captain Ernest Davies, company commander 45th Battalion.
(AWM H15106)

For the next few weeks the 4th Division's activities behind the Péronne front were divided mainly between working parties and training, with voting for the (ultimately unsuccessful) second conscription referendum being held on 11 December. The three infantry brigades conducted open-warfare tactical exercises, starting at company level and working up to full brigade exercises later in the month. This approach was in anticipation of the type of fighting that the troops might be faced with in the New Year. After the endless months of trench warfare, the brigadiers found that their officers, NCOs and men had much to learn, and the exercises were rigorously reviewed then repeated to correct identified errors. The 4th Brigade staff noted that the first exercise on 13 December 'was not a great success ... [but] ... as it was full of mistakes much was learnt;' the next attempt two days later 'was a great improvement ... and showed that everyone had taken a keen interest in it.'[25] With many junior officers and NCOs being recent promotions to replace casualties, much attention was paid to the front-line leaders' responsibilities for fire control and communications. The training was conducted in adverse weather conditions, frequently with snow or sleet, sometimes so bad as to cause exercises to be abandoned. Freezing temperatures made movement hazardous for men trying to march in military boots on cobbled roads coated with ice, and the transport horses were equally affected. On 19/20 December the 13th Brigade moved back from Templeux-la-Fosse, changing over with the 4th Brigade coming up from Moislains. The 13th Brigade had 100 men throwing dirt on to the road and others on drag ropes to help the horses and wagons negotiate the slippery surface, and the 4th Brigade experienced similar problems moving in the opposite direction. The 15th Battalion had the misfortune to be reviewed by General Sinclair-MacLagan along the way. Military protocol overcame common sense:

> The men had been picking their way with considerable care ... [and] ... the sudden call to the men to march at attention was disastrous ... [an officer's] feet shot from under him and, falling heavily upon his buttock, he split that part of his anatomy open and had to receive medical attention. Several other men sustained nasty falls, one man having his collarbone broken ... the water cart horse sprawled heavily upon the roadway when his driver attempted to salute, and a general mix-up ensued ... By the time Templeux-la-Fosse was reached, the men in the unit were seething with rage. When it was learnt that a special parade was called for the afternoon, at which the Brigade Commander, General Brand, would inspect the men, they were almost on the verge of revolt ... [however] ... the good humour of the unit was restored, and the parade, the briefest ever held in the 15th Battalion, passed off without a hitch.[26]

At Templeux the 4th Brigade was employed on major construction tasks, supplying large parties to work on the VII Corps defence lines, a task in which the Pioneer Battalion was also engaged. Other groups were put on to road works, the battalions taking turns to supply the working parties while the others continued with training. The 13th Field Company engineers managed the defence line construction and the field companies also assisted their brigades with improvements to the troops' accommodation and bathing facilities. The latter was one aspect where the Péronne area was actually an improvement over the Division's previous billets in the rear at Gamaches. The ADMS, Colonel George Barber, noted that the British administration at the latter area had little interest in providing baths for the troops; at Péronne, however, transportable bath 'sets' had been obtained and were in regular use, keeping down lice to some extent with consequent improvements in the health of the troops.[27]

As well as grouping all of their divisions together the Australian government had also pressed for commanders and staffs to be Australians as far as possible, or at least members of the AIF, and the policy was being implemented as opportunities arose. In the 4th Division the GOC, Major General Sinclair-MacLagan, was a professional officer of the British Army but also an AIF member, as was the CRE, Lieutenant Colonel Elliott, while the CRA, Brigadier General Burgess, was a member of both the New Zealand regular forces and the AIF. Lieutenant Colonel Denis Bernard, GSO1 since the early days in Egypt, was the only non-AIF officer on the Division HQ staff and on 18 December he relinquished those duties on being posted to GHQ. His replacement was Lieutenant Colonel John Dudley Lavarack, promoted from GSO2 in the 1st Division. Pre-war the new GSO1 had been an artillery officer in the regular Australian Army. As a captain he was attending the

British Army staff college course at Camberley when war was declared in August 1914. The course was cut short, but the students were deemed to have graduated, so Lavarack joined the small group of Australian officers with the 'psc' qualification. Although he had been appointed to the AIF in February 1915, Lavarack was at first attached to the staff of various British formations and it was over a year before he actually served with the AIF, in the 2nd Division artillery. Several staff appointments followed before he was posted to the 4th Division, a specialist staff officer apart from a brief period as a battery commander in the 2nd Division. Colonel Lavarack, a Queenslander, turned 32 the day after he took up his duties with the 4th Division. A man of impressive appearance, 'determined intelligence and unpredictable volatility,'[28] Lavarack was to become an important and controversial figure in the Army before and during World War Two.

Commander and HQ officers of the 12th Brigade, at Haute Allaines, France, on Boxing Day 1917. Left to right: Lieutenant Thomas Deam (4th Division Signal Company, attached to 12th Brigade); Captain Eric Terry (Staff Captain); Brigadier General John Gellibrand; Major Reginald 'Babe' Norman (Brigade Major); Lt John Stabback (Intelligence Officer); Lt George Sharp (Signal Company, attached to 12th Brigade).
(AWM E01551)

All ranks had Christmas Day off duty with a substantial meal, the fare including gifts of food supplied by the Australian Comforts Fund and an issue of wine and beer. The celebrations were muted with the Division still being in close reserve and ready to move at short notice, but there was now little possibility of any serious fighting. Normal working days of training and fatigues resumed on 26 December, before the troops had another holiday for New Year's Day 1918. With enemy action against the reserve lines confined to infrequent aerial bombing at night, the Division had recorded only three battle casualties in December 1917 but over 700 members had been evacuated with sickness. At this time new reinforcements were being sent only to the four active divisions, but those returning from hospital or detachment added 1,300 to the numbers on duty. The Division began 1918 with a total of 15,168 personnel actually with their units and another 1,288 on leave, courses or detachment. The Imperial New Year's Honours list brought a number of awards to senior 4th Division officers, including the Companion of the Bath (CB) to Brigadier General Glasgow, 13th Brigade, and the CMG to Lieutenant Colonel Leane, 48th Battalion. DSOs went to Lieutenant Colonels Dowse (AA&QMG) and Vernon (commanding the DAC), and to Majors Eric Wilton, former brigade major of the 4th Brigade, and Cecil Bates, brigade major of the divisional artillery. Major John Corrigan (15th Battalion) was another awarded the DSO, his first decoration during a long period of courageous and efficient service with his unit. Major Hubert Ford (46th Battalion) also received the DSO in the New Year list, a few days after he became temporary CO of the 46th in place of Lieutenant Colonel Howard Denham, who had been sent on sick leave on 30 December.[29] Major Ford had commanded the divisional training school in early 1917 and since then had served in the 45th, 46th and 47th battalions at different times. He had only recently returned to duty after suffering a serious head wound at Passchendaele, but although he had seemingly recovered, the after-effects of the injury would become apparent several months later.

For the time being all of General Gellibrand's battalions in the 12th Brigade were under recently-appointed or temporary commanders (in February 1918, it was confirmed that Colonel Denham would not be returning and Major Ford was made temporary lieutenant colonel). On 10 January Captain Arthur Varley (ex-45th Battalion) replaced Captain Eric Terry as staff captain on the 12th Brigade staff when the latter went on extended leave (both of those officers served in World War II and both lost their lives at sea as a result of the fall of Singapore[30]). The 4th Brigade also changed its staff captain in January when Captain Alexander Fraser resumed his regimental posting with the 52nd Battalion. His replacement was another 13th Brigade officer, Capt Harry Thomson of the 50th Battalion, Rhodes Scholar in 1910 and a barrister in civilian life; Captain Thomson had acted as staff captain previously, having been among those wounded when 4th Brigade HQ was hit by a shell in July 1917. Also in January the Division GSO3, Captain Stanley Rogers, was posted to the 4th British Division staff; his place was taken by Captain Leslie Craig, who had been on attachment to the staff for some months from the 46th Battalion.

The infantry brigade groups continued their training programs in the first days of January with brigade-strength exercises, but the 4th Division's period at Peronne was coming to an end. A move back to Flanders had been foreshadowed and the divisional artillery had already left for the north at the end of December. The artillery's trains reached Bailleul behind the Messines front, where the gunners came under the orders of IX Corps, in the afternoon of 30 December; there I Anzac (about to be renamed the Australian Corps) was holding the adjoining sector to the right of IX Corps. After a few days in billets at Godewaersvelde, north-west of Bailleul, the field brigades moved into the line over 3 and 4 January to relieve the 37th British Division artillery, covering a sector of the front astride the Ypres-Comines canal. The 37th Division CRA continued in command of the sector artillery pending relief of his Division's infantry, which would be by that of the 4th Division coming north from Péronne. The main body of the 4th Division began its move on 8 January when the 12th Brigade Group entrained at Péronne for Bailleul, arriving the following day and going into temporary billets at Godewaersvelde. Over successive days the 13th Brigade, 4th Brigade and HQ groups followed. On the night of 11/12 January the 12th Brigade infantry and supporting arms moved up to the front line south-east of Ypres, in relief of a 37th Division brigade (by now, movement behind the front lines had been much improved by extension of the light rail network). The 13th and 4th Brigades relieved their British equivalents as reserve and support brigades, and the 4th Division was once more holding a sector of the Flanders front.

The Division's right flank rested on Hollebeke from where the line ran roughly northeast across the canal for about 4,000 metres to the landmark called Bitter Wood, beside the Bassevillebeek stream that ran across the front. All four of the 12th Brigade's battalions went in to the front line system, which consisted of a series of grouped outposts in shell holes and pillboxes, backed up by a support line in segments of trench and a reserve line in a continuous trench. A brigade reserve was formed from elements of all battalions, occupying dugouts at the Spoil Bank location on the canal. Medical facilities for the front line were provided by the 12th Field Ambulance, which took over the management of ADSs at Voormezeele, Spoil Bank and Larch Wood near Zillebeke, and became responsible for evacuations from the forward RAPs. The 13th Field Ambulance took over the sector MDS at Kemmel and the 4th Field Ambulance ran divisional rest stations at Keersebrom and Magilligan Camp near Bailleul. Both of those units provided bearer teams to assist the 12th Field Ambulance in the forward zone. The CO of the 12th, Lieutenant Colonel Wassell, another officer who had been awarded the DSO in the New Year's Honours, had been seriously ill for some time and was evacuated early in January, unfit for further duty. He was replaced next month by Lieutenant Colonel Arthur Gibson, promoted in from the 15th Field Ambulance (5th Division). Another change in the medical leadership occurred in January when the DADMS, Major Jeffries, was posted out to AIF HQ in London. Major Frank Lind, who had been an RMO with the 1st Division on Gallipoli, came in from XXII Corps (formerly II Anzac) as DADMS.

The 4th Division took over command of the sector on the morning of 12 January, with HQ at Scherpenberg near Mount Kemmel, and at the same time the Division came under command of the Australian Corps.

> The arrangement, intended to be temporary, proved permanent. The Australian Army Corps thus at last comprised five active divisions; and, by the irony of chance, when three months later a great emergency arose, it was the 4th Australian Division that was first thrown into serious fighting.[31]

The Australian Corps held its front with three divisions in the line, one in support at Merris and one in distant reserve, 80 kilometres to the rear at Samer near the coast. The 4th Division now held the left sector of the Corps line, with the 1st Division next on its right and the 20th British Division on its left. After the 12th Brigade had held the front line for a week, the Division's front line dispositions were rearranged so that the sector was split into two brigade zones. The right brigade would hold its front with two battalions and the left brigade with one, each brigade rotating its battalions every seven or eight days. Accordingly, the 12th Brigade battalions were relieved over the nights of 19/20 and 20/21 January by the 4th Brigade on the right and the 13th Brigade on the left; the 12th Brigade moved back to bivouacs in the area around La Clytte (De Klijte) and Locre (Loker) as reserve brigade. The 4th Brigade sent up the 13th and 15th Battalions first, with the 16th in support and the 14th in reserve and scheduled to relieve the front line units a week later. The 50th Battalion was first in the firing line on the 13th Brigade's one-battalion front, with the 49th in support and the 51st and 52nd in reserve. The front line system was thinly held, each battalion using two companies in its outposts, another in close support and the fourth further back in established dugouts as a reserve. The support and reserve battalions were accommodated in hutted camps such as Ridgewood (or Ridge Wood) and Tournai camps near Vierstraat and in dugouts or tunnels at Spoil Bank. Two of the MG companies, periodically relieved by the other two, were posted in positions for defence and for indirect fire into the enemy lines.

The infantry in the front line settled in to the Western Front routine of mainly nocturnal activity, dividing their time between strengthening the defences with sandbags and barbed wire, and patrolling No Man's Land, while the artillery and machine guns put down regular harassing fire on roads and approaches behind the enemy front line. The reserve brigade, at this time the 12th, was required to provide large working parties of 100 or more men each to labour on construction of the Corps defences behind the front line. Other groups were put on to salvaging abandoned engineering equipment and stores scattered around the area. Brigadier General Gellibrand later estimated that out of 2,000 men in his Brigade available for work, up to 1,700 daily could be on working parties, with minimal opportunity for rest or training;

> the very great importance of the work [is recognised] and the men generally understood that there was nothing else for it ... [but] it is considered by all ranks that the period spent in Reserve is much more strenuous and fatiguing than the period of actually holding the Line ...[32]

The reserve battalions of the 4th and 13th Brigades also provided parties for salvage and other works as well as working on their own lines in the forward area. Despite the recent good intentions for improving engineer/infantry co-operation the arrangements did not always go smoothly:

> Working party of 10 officers 300 other ranks 47th Battalion entrained at Parrett Farm for work on Corps Line under 4th Field Company. On arrival at work it was found that only 220 were required. This bungling has been reported to Division to prevent any possible reoccurrence.[33]

That construction work on the secondary zone of the Corps defence lines was the main focus of the engineer field companies. In the 4th Division's sector the lines ran north-east from the area around St Eloi at a distance averaging about 2,000 metres behind the outposts of the front line system. They were built up with camouflaged strong-points and machine gun or Lewis gun posts with interlocking fields of fire, protected by barbed wire entanglements. Some effort was made to excavate deep trenches but the high water table worked against this and many old German pillboxes were incorporated into the defences instead.[34] Other works behind the front were fell to the 4th Pioneer Battalion, with most of the unit's personnel employed on maintenance and improvements to communication trenches, a task often frustrated by frequent heavy rain that caved in the trench sides and necessitated long stretches of revetments being installed. The Pioneers also had parties working on the tramways and on drainage of underground billets, particularly the tunnels at Spoil Bank. All ranks worked well under difficult circumstances and the new Pioneer CO, Lieutenant Colonel Morrison, expressed satisfaction with his unit: 'General condition of the men is now good, and moral[e] high. They are fit for anything. Percentage of sickness small; discipline excellent; a fine Battalion.'[35]

The attention paid to defensive preparations reflected changes in strategic thinking in the new year. Sir Douglas Haig's original intention had been to resume the Flanders offensive as soon as the weather permitted, but the situation had now changed. In the first place the BEF was well short of the numbers needed to mount a major offensive. Reinforcements were available in England, even if a high proportion of those were conscripted youths, but were being withheld by the British government. The Prime Minister, David Lloyd George, had been horrified by the carnage of the Third Ypres battles and he feared that the more men supplied to Haig the more would be consumed to no significant purpose. The troops in the field were believed to be sufficient to hold the existing line, even though the British front had recently been extended by taking over a sector from the French and several divisions had been sent to Italy. Essentially the Allied approach was now to remain on the defensive until the Americans arrived in sufficient numbers to make victory certain (several American officers were attached to 4th Division units for training during February[36]). On the other hand, German resources on the Western Front continued to grow with the transfer of further divisions and guns from the east, where Russia was virtually powerless and would shortly have to accept a ruinous peace treaty. The German high command, dominated by General Erich Ludendorff, for the moment held the advantage of numbers and the strategic initiative but that was a situation that could not last. Once the American forces were fully deployed the defeat of Germany would only be a matter of time, and Ludendorff decided to gamble on one great offensive against the Allied armies while the opportunity was there. If the offensive failed Germany would also lose the war in the long run, but success could force the Allies to negotiate for peace from a position of disadvantage.[37]

The Allies had no difficulty in assessing their enemy's intentions, hence the stepping up of work on the defensive positions during the winter. The German method of defence in depth had been adopted, with a lightly held forward zone and progressively stronger positions further to the rear. Once the defences were completed it was confidently expected that enemy attacks would shatter against them and leave the Germans too weakened to resist the Allied counterstroke. For the 4th Division holding its sector of the Australian Corps line, work on the rear defences continued through January and February 1918 while the units in the front line confronted the enemy on the other side of No Man's Land. The weather continued snowy and freezing into January, turning to several days of heavy rain towards the end of the month. The rain and the beginnings of the thaw turned the ground muddy at first before a period of cold but fine weather started to dry it out; morning fogs reduced visibility on most days. The front was quiet for much of the time but savage little fights broke out occasionally as patrols and raiding parties from both sides endeavoured to gain intelligence about their opponents. The Australians generally had the better of these clashes, although the Germans struck some blows of their own at times. The 14th Battalion, which relieved the 15th in the 4th Brigade front line on 29 January, began its stint with a bad few days. The forward outposts were fully manned only at night, usually by six to eight men, the garrison being reduced to two before daylight. The morning of 31 January was foggy, enabling a German patrol to approach a post of the 14th near Potsdam Farm unseen and capture its occupants, Corporal Edward Frost and Lance Corporal John Jeffreys; the loss was not discovered until the night garrison went out to relieve them.[38] The previous night the enemy artillery had commenced a heavy gas bombardment on the 14th's lines, most of the shells falling in the vicinity of Battalion HQ at Fusilier Dugouts and on the support and reserve companies. The shelling went on with few pauses for fourteen hours, continuing into the morning of 31 January, and over 60 personnel were evacuated with gas poisoning on that day. The effects of the gas continued to appear for nearly two weeks, by which time the 14th had been relieved in the front line, and altogether the unit had more than 250 gassing victims hospitalised.[39] Among those casualties were a number of senior officers: the senior company commander Major Charles Cox, adjutant Captain Arthur Blainey, and on 12 February the CO, Lieutenant Colonel Walter Smith. The unit second-in-command, Major Thomson, was also absent on sick leave, leaving Captain William Wadsworth as the senior officer still on duty. Major Charles Johnston, brigade major of the 4th Brigade, was immediately posted to the 14th as temporary CO.

A third of the battalion had been incapacitated, losses that should have been minimised by the established anti-gas procedures. A court of enquiry was quickly convened and came to the conclusion that responsibility lay with Colonel Smith for failing to ensure that all possible precautions were taken in his command. Brigadier General Glasgow, temporarily commanding the Division at this time (Major General Sinclair-Maclagan was away on special leave), wrote to General Birdwood that 'the [14th] Battalion is really in a bad way, and I am convinced that the fault lies with the Battalion Commander.'[40] Colonel Smith did not return to the 14th Battalion and neither did Major Thomson; the temporary command arrangements were retained for the time being, pending the return of Brigadier General Brand from a short detachment to Corps HQ.

In Brand's absence the 4th Brigade was initially commanded by Lieutenant Colonel McSharry, 15th Battalion CO, then from 17 February by Lieutenant Colonel Drake-Brockman, 16th Battalion CO, when the latter returned from his posting to the 4th Training Battalion. While Glasgow was acting as Division GOC from 3 February the 13th Brigade was commanded by the 52nd Battalion CO, Lieutenant Colonel Whitham. Glasgow was concerned that identification of the enemy units opposite the 13th Brigade was lacking and he directed that plans for a trench raid be prepared. The 51st Battalion was currently holding the Brigade's front line and a small party was sent out on the night of 10/11 February to reconnoitre the enemy lines for a likely raid objective. Lieutenant Arthur Castles, the 51st's Intelligence Officer, led the patrol himself, accompanied only by a scout, Private Denis Whitfield, and Lieutenant Irvine Barton, IO of the 52nd Battalion (the 52nd would shortly be relieving the 51st in the front line). The group penetrated the German wire and surprised an eight-man enemy patrol, which they attacked with grenades and pistols. Four of the Germans went down killed or badly wounded and the others fled. The patrol searched the casualties for documents and cut the shoulder straps with regimental numbers from their uniforms, then made their way back to the Australian line. The items taken identified the enemy formation as the 239th Division and the required information had been gained without the need for a potentially costly raid. Private Whitfield was later awarded the MM[41] and the two officers each received the MC.

The 13th Brigade on its one-battalion front was relieving its front line units from within the Brigade, but the two-battalion segment on the right of the Division's front was held by the 4th and 12th Brigades relieving each other in turn. During the 12th Brigade's period in reserve the two battalion commanders wounded at Passchendaele had returned to duty, Lieutenant Colonel Leane resuming with the 48th Battalion on 25 January and Lieutenant Colonel Imlay with the 47th on 4 February. The 12th Brigade moved forward again on the night of 5/6 February to relieve the 4th, sending the 45th and 47th Battalions into the front line first. The 45th took over the left sub-sector of the front from the 14th Battalion and immediately found that the area remained something of a hot spot, with the German unit or units opposite being unusually active and resourceful. At about 10 pm, just after the relief, a post of the 45th at Belgian Wood was rushed by a German party suddenly appearing out of the dark. An NCO and five men, the whole garrison of the post, were taken prisoner. The Brigade staff theorised that the Germans had crept out soon after dark and lain up close to the post. Noticing the movements of the relief, they had waited until it was completed and then attacked before the new troops had settled in.[42] Belgian Wood was the group of posts next north from Potsdam Farm where the 14th Battalion had lost two men captured less than a week earlier. The remainder of the 12th Brigade's period in the line was comparatively uneventful, regular patrols rarely encountering the enemy. The 47th Battalion obtained an identification on 8 February when one of that unit's posts shot and killed an enemy soldier who had apparently lost his way and was trying to run back to his own lines. A patrol went out after dark to search the body, the German unit being identified as the 76th Reserve Infantry Regiment.[43] The low level of activity in No Man's Land was not to Brigadier General Gellibrand's liking and at a conference on 16 February he pressed for a more aggressive approach, ordering each battalion to prepare a scheme for a raid on the enemy positions.[44] The 12th Brigade battalions had changed over on 13 February, with the 46th and 48th Battalions taking their turn in the front line. The Brigade was then relieved by the 4th Brigade on 20 February, a relief for which orders had been issued three days earlier. This would have left insufficient time to plan and mount any formal raids, but the 12th Brigade staff reported that the front-line units carried out 'vigorous patrolling' in their last few nights in the line and 'the enemy did not dispute our right to own No Man's Land during the night as our whole front was continually patrolled without any interference by the Germans.'[45]

It may have been during this period that a certain amount of tension arose between General Gellibrand and Colonel Leane, the 48th Battalion CO. The strong-willed Leane had at times asserted a degree of independence towards the two previous brigadiers, and he was said to have initially taken the same attitude towards Gellibrand, a character as strong as himself. Captain Thomas Louch left an account of a dispute between the two officers that originated with the arrest by military police of a 48th Battalion member. Leane decided to hold his 'orderly room' hearing of the case

> in the front line and insisting that he required the personal attendance of the two policemen to give evidence before him. Gellibrand said that he would speak to Leane about the matter the next day; and as we were on the move he decided to be at the starting point at the time the 48th were due to pass, and talk to Leane then. We ... had a long wait before the 48th showed up. When asked why he was late, Leane said that the time fixed in the Brigade order was too early and did not suit him ... the climax came when Gellibrand said he would inspect the 48th on parade and that he wanted a full attendance of all ranks. When we [i.e the brigadier and staff] got there the parade looked rather thin, and Gellibrand told the staff captain to make an actual count of the number present ... [there was] a big discrepancy. Gellibrand demanded to know where the missing men were, and was not pleased to be told that the band, the orchestra and the Battalion concert party were rehearsing.[46]

There are some difficulties with that account. Louch in his memoirs said that the incident occurred 'immediately' after Gellibrand's arrival in mid-November 1917, when he (Louch) was with the 12th Brigade staff. That cannot be correct, however, since at that time Leane was in hospital recovering from wounds received at Passchendaele and did not resume with the 48th until late January 1918, as noted above. Louch was on the 12th Brigade staff as acting brigade major only until the end of November when he returned to his former posting at 13th Brigade HQ, making it highly unlikely that he observed the events in person; Louch is more likely to have heard the story from an acquaintance at 12th Brigade. That does not mean it is not true, but the accepted timing must be wrong.[47] If the incident did take place in November, the 48th CO at the time would have been Colonel Deeble, not Colonel Leane. A possible occasion for the contentious battalion parade could have been 3 March or one of the preceding few days, by which time the 48th was at Meteren. That date being the second anniversary of the Battalion's formation, its band performed items during the day and the annual officers' dinner was held in the evening. As it happened, the invited guest of honour at the dinner was Brigadier General Gellibrand, accompanied by Major Norman, the brigade major. That may have been a matter of protocol rather than indicating a reconciliation, of course. The Battalion Diary noted that

> A most enjoyable evening was spent but unfortunately we had to cease at 10.30, just as things were going well. Surely officers who are out of the line could be allowed more latitude than this![48]

The implication is that it was the brigadier who brought proceedings to a close (the 48th Battalion diary was now being written up by Major 'Johnny' Moyes, in an entertaining style that foreshadowed his post-war career as a sports writer).

The 4th Brigade had relieved the 12th in the forward zone on 20 February, with the 13th and 15th Battalions taking over the front line positions; the 13th Brigade now had the 52nd Battalion in the front line of its part of the 4th Division front. These were the final dispositions before the whole Division was due to be relieved in the Corps line by the 1st Division and for the most part the pattern of recent weeks in the front line continued. The usual patrols roamed No Man's Land each night and the Germans for their part attempted to repeat their earlier successes against the Australian outposts. On the night of 25 February the enemy again targeted the Potsdam Farm positions to mount a raid but found the 15th Battalion too alert; the raiders were driven off, leaving two of their number behind as prisoners. It was only on the Division's final night in the line, 1/2 March, that the front flared up and the 13th Battalion became involved in the heaviest fighting of the tour. Intelligence reports had warned that the Germans were planning a large-scale attack for 28 February, but although nothing happened the warning remained current as preparations for the relief went ahead for the following night.

At about 9:40 pm on 1 March, the 13th Battalion had just completed handing over to incoming troops of the 10th Battalion when a shower of German mortar bombs fell on and around the pillbox housing the front line company headquarters, followed by an artillery box barrage on the front and support lines. The final platoon of the 13th to be relieved was caught by the shelling while moving to the rear in a communication trench, losing four killed and four wounded. Telephone wires to the rear were immediately cut by shells, but the SOS flare signal was fired and the Australian defensive barrage opened fire on the enemy lines. A German infantry force numbering at least 100 rushed the HQ pillbox and captured the occupants, who included the 10th Battalion company commander, Major Horace Henwood, and Captain Robert Browning of the 13th Battalion, who had stayed behind to complete the hand-over. The enemy force was retiring with their prisoners when they were counter-attacked from neighbouring posts of the 10th Battalion. The Germans lost heavily in the fighting; 25 of their dead were counted near the Australian wire the next morning and another four were taken prisoner, and they may have had more losses regaining their lines through the counter-barrage. During the exchange of fire, however, Major Henwood was killed and Captain Browning badly wounded, casualties that may have been caused by friendly fire. The 10th Battalion had 18 killed or wounded with another seven missing and assumed to be prisoners; casualties in the 13th Battalion totalled 10.

The day after this sharp burst of fighting the main body of the 4th Division completed its move back to the support division zone, occupying an area centring on Bailleul. The 12th Brigade Group was billeted at Meteren, the 13th at Locre and the 4th at Neuve Église; Division HQ was established at Merris. The divisional artillery once again stayed in the forward zone, but the field brigades were withdrawn slightly to form a supporting, or 'superimposed' group backing up the 1st Division artillery, which took over the forward battery positions covering their infantry. The period in the line had cost the 4th Division over 400 casualties, but more than half of those had been the unfortunate gassing victims in the 14th Battalion. Reinforcements coming in, the great majority of whom were returning from wounds or illness, balanced out the losses from casualties and sick evacuations, and on coming out of the line the Division had 14,953 personnel actually with their units.[49] That figure was slightly less than the numbers present at the beginning of the line period but there were 2,700 members on leave or detachment, making the overall total about 1,000 higher, although still well below full establishment. As always it was the infantry battalions that accounted for most of the deficiencies in numbers, but oddly the number of officers on the Division's strength was actually well over establishment when those absent from their units were included. That situation had existed for several months; the reasons are not immediately obvious, but a factor would have been wounded officers returning to their units after others had been commissioned to replace them in the short term (units were permitted to retain some officers as supernumeraries). In January the 4th Brigade, noting that there were 'many officers in excess of those required for regimental duty,' took the opportunity to set up a training course on tactical and administrative skills, presumably for the more recently-commissioned officers.[50] There were also some concerns at command level that some officers were not up to standard. In late January an administrative conference at Division HQ noted that

> ... Brigadiers all expressed the opinion that they were handicapped in not being able to get rid of officers who were virtually being carried ... cases have occurred in which officers on promotion have failed to exhibit the keenness that actuated their COs in recommending their promotion. [Also] during the stress consequent of past fighting direct commissions were granted and some mistakes made ... it is essential for efficiency that officers of this class should be removed.[51]

Among other items, the conference also discussed the likelihood that some battalions would have to be disbanded as recruiting continued to fall, an issue that would come to a head later in the year.

Commander and HQ officers of the 4th Brigade, at Neuve Église, Belgium, 12 March 1918. Left to right, back row: French interpreter; Lieutenant Henry Davis (Intelligence Officer); Lt Stanley Larkins (Signal Officer, attached from 4th Division Signal Company); Lt Leonard Barnes (Gas Officer). Front row: Major Raymond Tovell (Acting Brigade Major); Maj Charles Johnston (substantive Brigade Major, acting CO 14th Battalion); Brigadier General Charles Brand; Captain Harry Thomson (Staff Captain); Lt Leslie Tweedie (Assistant Staff Captain). (AWM E01729)

Among the officers 'removed', or at least not to return from absence, was the 14th Battalion CO, Lieutenant Colonel Smith. Returning to command of the 4th Brigade from detachment at the end of February, Brigadier General Brand sought to correct the unsatisfactory leadership of that unit, a situation that was mostly of the brigadier's own making. The choice for a new CO fell on Major Henry Crowther, a 30-year-old former schoolteacher from Victoria, who had made a fine record with the 6th Brigade (2nd Division).[52] Crowther took command of the 14th on 15 March with promotion to lieutenant colonel. As it happened, Colonel Crowther had little time to settle into his new command before the unit was in action again, but he soon proved himself to be a good choice, affable in the mess, efficient in the office and a good tactician, no stranger to the front line—the CO that the 14th had needed since Colonel Peck had been posted away after Bullecourt. Major Johnston, who had earlier come in from 4th Brigade HQ as temporary CO, stayed on with the 14th as second-in-command and Major Raymond Tovell was appointed brigade major in his stead. Tovell was an officer of the 4th Pioneer Battalion who had been attached to the 4th Brigade staff for several months as Johnston's assistant. In the next war Tovell would command an infantry brigade under General Morshead at Tobruk.

After a long period as OC 4th LTM Battery, Captain Arnold Potts returned to infantry duty with the 16th Battalion early in March; Captain Arthur Loveday took over the Brigade light mortars in his place. The artillery-controlled medium and heavy mortars had undergone a major re-organisation during February. As with all BEF divisions, the divisional heavy mortar batteries were disbanded and the resources transferred to Corps control to form one battery per Corps. The 'flying pigs' had not been particularly effective, at least at division level, being cumbersome to handle and difficult to find suitable targets for; the huge shells could crack a pillbox, but the weapons needed a very solid footing, something difficult to find in Flanders. At the same time the medium batteries were reduced in number from three to two per division, each battery equipped with six of the new Newton 6-inch (152 mm) mortars, which had replaced the old 'plum pudding' weapons. The Newton was essentially a scaled-up version of the infantry Stokes mortar, with the propellant at the base of the shell igniting when the shell was dropped into the barrel; extra propellant could be added to increase the range. The reorganised batteries were also renumbered, those of the 4th Division becoming the 7th and 8th MTM Batteries. The Division had three of the Newtons emplaced forward during the recent period in the line and they had fired nearly 700 of their 24-kilogram shells at selected targets in the enemy trenches—machine gun posts, dugouts, *Minenwerfer* positions, and pillboxes. Captain Fox, the divisional trench mortar officer, believed that the mortars had inflicted considerable damage on their targets but doubted if they would be useful in open warfare situations.[53]

Also in early 1918 another important reorganisation of supporting weapons took place with the BEF's machine gun units. Since mid-1917 machine guns had been increasingly used for barrage work, both for covering fire in attacks and for 'SOS' defensive barrages. Elements of two or more MG companies were often combined for these tasks and each division had been given an additional company (the 24th in the case of the 4th Division), added to the three companies that formed part of the infantry brigade groups. The trend in machine gun organisation was towards centralised control, and the final development was the grouping together of each division's four MG companies as a battalion directly under divisional HQ. On 11 March Corps issued orders to divisions to proceed with establishing their MG Battalions, to be numbered according to division number. The constituent companies, although having now become sub-units, were allowed to retain their traditional numbers rather than being designated by an anonymous lettering system, a recognition of the *esprit de corps* that they had built up as separate units in their own right. Major Harry Murray, currently second-in-command of the 13th Battalion, was selected as CO of the new 4th Machine Gun Battalion, appointed as of 15 March with promotion to temporary lieutenant colonel. The promotion was made permanent two months later, Murray joining a select group of AIF members who rose from private to lieutenant colonel during the war. Now 37, he was the second officer in the 4th Division (after Robert Christie) to rise to that level from the ranks, but the first to have enlisted in the AIF as a private. Having started with the original 16th Battalion MG section in 1914, Murray had learned machine gun work from the ground up, and in the closing stages at Gallipoli had commanded the 13th Battalion's MG section. Since then, as an infantry leader of unexcelled skill and courage, he had not been directly involved in the technical developments in machine gun tactics, but he knew what the infantry needed as support. It was a popular appointment in the Division, although Murray would not have been the only officer considered; Major Ernest Radford, divisional machine gun officer and commander of the 24th MG Company, had nearly a year's seniority over Murray as a major and was one who might have expected the appointment (Radford, who was on leave at this time, was nominated as second-in-command of the new unit). With the four companies already operational, the main administrative task was to establish a headquarters staff for the new battalion, and Murray also continued to administer command of the 13th Battalion in the absence of Colonel Marks on leave.

Before being relieved by the 1st Division the 4th Division general staff had prepared a comprehensive review of the defensive preparations on their sector of the front. The document,[54] which ran to 20 pages plus another 15 of appendices and maps, gives an idea of the complexity of Western Front defences in both physical structure and operational procedures in just a single divisional sector. It provided an overview of all elements the system: infantry positions in forward and second zones, field and heavy artillery locations, machine guns, Lewis guns, mortars and the communications network. The latter showed increasing use of wireless telegraphy links and power buzzers as well as buried telephone cables, although the enemy raid of 1 March showed that in some circumstances troops in the front line had to fall back on flare signals and runners to call for support. The report also covered accommodation for troops, administrative and medical arrangements, supply and ammunition dumps, works policy, liaison arrangements between the various arms and services, and prescribed tactics for the defending troops in case of attack: 'The main principle of Defence is resistance to the utmost in every portion of each successive Infantry Defensive System and in the ground between them.' As of late January when the report was prepared, some sections of barbed wire were incomplete and extra machine gun and artillery positions were under construction, but the defences should be ready to receive the expected German offensive in the spring. In the event, the first blow would fall in the south and the 4th Division would not return to the line in Flanders that it had laboured to construct.

Shortly after taking command in July 1917 General Sinclair-MacLagan had expressed concern at the 4th Division's poor record for absence without leave and desertions. The situation appears to have improved considerably by early 1918, the 13th Brigade reporting that the February figures for those offences were a 15-month low for the Brigade.[55] The results were similar for the following month spent in the support area, although there was a rise in short-period AWLs (as opposed to overstaying official leave); the proximity of Bailleul, a functioning civilian town, was a strong temptation to take an unauthorised night off.[56] Actual desertion was often the result of heavy fighting in impossible conditions, such as at Pozières/Mouquet Farm and the later stages of Third Ypres. The cumulative strain proved too much for some men, who could no longer force themselves back into the fighting, and conversely periods in rest or on an inactive front saw a noticeable reduction in desertions—the 4th Division's latest period in the line had been comparatively quiet with generally low casualties and the troops now had a few weeks in the support role to look forward to.

A proportion of the absentees, of course, were not essentially-decent men broken by stress but rather those of darker character who had never had any intention of doing their duty.

It will be recalled that during the AIF expansion in Egypt the 4th Division had been forced to accept a large number of rejected wrongdoers from the older divisions. A proportion of these eventually 'made good,' at least to the extent of taking out some of their aggression on the Germans although continuing to cause trouble out of the line. Many, however, proved to be incorrigible and spent little if any time at the front, being either regularly incarcerated for military and civil crimes or on the run following desertion. As well as desertion and other military crimes, another major criticism directed at the AIF was the disproportionate tendency of its personnel to contract venereal diseases. Perhaps that was only to be expected for a large group of virile young men on the other side of the world from their normal homes and social connections, and in constant danger of death or disablement. Opportunity was available, if for short infrequent periods, and knowledge of preventative measures was minimal. Statistics are difficult to verify, but Peter Stanley mentions a figure of 144 cases per thousand men (presumably a per annum average) in mid-1917 for the AIF as a whole in all theatres,[57] the highest by a large margin of the national groups in the British armies. The *Medical History* has a figure of 72.6 per 1,000 per annum for Australian troops actually in France with the BEF over all of 1917.[58] The 4th Division medical staff reported a total of 332 personnel evacuated with VD over the five months of November 1917 to March 1918 inclusive;[59] assuming an average strength of 15,000, that works out to 53 cases per 1,000 on strength. Certainly that is not a direct comparison, with the discrepancy in the periods considered, but it would appear that the 4th Division was no worse or better than the rest of the AIF on the Western Front in this respect.

Consideration of such issues, added to the undoubted inclination of AIF troops to unruly behaviour in their periods off-duty, could give the impression of an undisciplined, disease-ridden rabble, with the 4th Division as a particularly notable example. The 4th had its uniquely high proportion of men from the 'outer states,' many from rural occupations that suited tough individualists, and its members in general were probably even less inclined to accept restraints on their behaviour than the other AIF divisions. They would no doubt have been pleased with C E W Bean's characterisation of the 4th Division as the 'most rugged'[60] and 'perhaps the toughest of all Australian divisions.'[61] That toughness may have resulted in a questionable standard of discipline behind the lines, but there was no lack of battlefield discipline. The examples of the 4th and 12th Brigades at Bullecourt, advancing into a storm of fire with no support from artillery or tanks, breaking through uncut barbed wire and capturing an apparently impregnable objective; the remnant of the 45th Battalion at Messines, shelled out of the position they had just taken by their own artillery, returning to the attack again and again until beyond the limits of exhaustion; and the 49th Battalion's capture and holding of the Fabeck Graben at Mouquet Farm are only a few instances of the type of discipline that could keep men risking their lives to achieve a collective aim. An individual who made an extreme example was Private Nathaniel Lunt of the 48th Battalion.

Constantly in trouble out of the line, his misdemeanours included a charge of attempting to shoot another soldier (a sentence of five years penal servitude was never applied), but he was equally prominent in the fighting.

> ... the best known man in the Battalion and the hero of many fights both in the line and out of it, for he gave as much trouble to his friends as he did to the enemy. With Punch Donovan [Private Percy Donovan, MM and Bar] and Cork Daly [Corporal Gordon Daly, MM] and some others he formed a small party that one learned to look on as essential to the identity of the 48th.[62]

(Lunt was killed towards the end of the war). Another factor in the 4th Division's reputation was its seeming destiny to be sent into the line more frequently than the others, and if this caused some resentment against 'the heads' it also contributed to the Division's *esprit de corps*. As Thomas Louch (13th Brigade) recalled:

> The 4th Division had begun to take pride in the fact that other divisions might need long rests, but if there was a job to be done the 4th was sent to do it ... The Smart Set Concert Party put over a wisecrack : 'After the war General Birdwood visited Australia and gave a long address extolling the 1st, 2nd, 3rd and 5th Divisions. When asked about the 4th Division, he replied: "Good Lord, I had forgotten all about them; they must still be in the line".[63]

That tradition would continue, and the Division's level of discipline and training on the battlefield would be severely tested over the coming months.

Once in the support zone, the 4th Division units resumed training, although a shortage of suitable grounds in the area ruled out large-scale tactical manoeuvres, and programmes were mostly limited to individual and specialist training. Weapons and musketry was a priority, making the most of the few available shooting ranges and some new ones constructed by units. Lectures on a variety of military topics were given to officers and NCOs, and officers of the 4th Signal Company presented signalling courses. The restriction on new reinforcements meant that the majority of personnel had at least some experience of the front line, but even the old hands could still benefit from practicing and improving their skills. As Lieutenant George Mitchell (48th Battalion) saw this period:

> Daily the Lewis gunners, with furious bursts of speed, clipped seconds off their assembling times. Cracking of rifles came from many miniature ranges. Bombers slinging their grenades gained inches in distance over their previous best. Rifle grenadiers, with thoughtful expressions, lobbed grenades dead on the mark. Signallers wagged uncomplimentary [flag] messages to each other ... the battalion was being hammered into a higher state of efficiency, reaching a pinnacle of perfection, such as that attained early in 1917, before Bullecourt.[64]

An infantry shooting competition was instituted, to be contested by platoons, with elimination rounds within the brigades and a final between each brigade's champion platoons at the end of the month. Much attention was also paid to inter-unit competitive sports ('recreational training') in the afternoons. In his memo outlining the Division's training requirements, Colonel Lavarack, the GSO1, sternly enjoined units 'to ensure that every man takes part in the Recreational Training and that it is not confined to competitions between selected teams, with the bulk of the units taking the part of onlookers only.'[65] The extent to which this instruction was followed is questionable—brigade and unit records mention numerous representative contests in all football codes, with plenty of onlookers, and great interest was taken in a keenly-contested boxing competition. There were several grim reminders, however, that the war was not far away. As March wore on and the weather improved (some days late in the month were described as 'glorious'[66]), there were signs of increasing enemy activity, particularly long-range shelling of the back areas. Several shells landed in Bailleul and some of the villages in its vicinity, causing casualties among the civilians still living there and to 4th Division troops. On 22 March the 13th Battalion's tug-of-war team was in a field near Neuve Église, training for the unit athletics day, when a high-velocity shell burst nearby. It was a 'daisy-cutter,' instantaneously fuzed, and the hurtling splinters swept the field and killed or wounded the entire group of 15. Among the dead was the team coach, the popular Lieutenant John Browne, who had been with the 13th since its formation in 1914. The shell was assessed as British, fired from a British gun supplied to the Russians and captured by the Germans.

The sports went ahead despite that tragedy, and all units went into the final stages of their programmes in the last few days in support prior to returning to the front line in routine rotation. The expectation was that the 4th Division would relieve the 5th in the central sector of the Corps front at the end of the month. Word began to ripple through the Division, however, that the long-anticipated German offensive had begun on 21 March and that the blow had fallen in the south, on the Somme front to the east of Amiens. Definite information was sparse but it quickly became apparent that so far from meeting with the expected repulse the massive German attack had broken through on the fronts held by Fifth and Third Armies. The situation has suddenly become desperate for the Allies. In the absence of any orders to the contrary the Division went ahead with its current activities—after all of its recent troubles the 14th Battalion produced the 4th Brigade's champion rifle-shooting platoon—but the feeling spread that the Australian Corps would soon be called south to join the decisive fighting. The divisions currently out of the line, the 3rd in reserve at Steenvoorde and the 4th as support division at Merris, were the obvious candidates to be sent into the battle first, and on their past record the 4th Division collectively expected nothing else. That assumption had been verified a few days later when a 4th Division staff officer told a group of war correspondents, anxious for the latest news, 'Our fellows were offering bets all over the place that we would be here [on the way to the Somme front] this week, but found no takers anywhere. Worst of belonging to this Division—can't make any money that way at all.'[67] George Mitchell put it more simply: 'The old Fourth Divvy, the "Stormy Petrels," were for it again.'[68]

The Division went into that crucial period of the war with the following units and senior officers:

4th Australian Division Order of Battle, late March 1918

GOC	Major General E G Sinclair-MacLagan
GSO1	Lieutenant Colonel J D Lavarack
GSO2	Major E C P Plant
GSO3	Captain L C A Craig
AA&QMG	Lieutenant Colonel R Dowse
DAAG	Major W Fowler-Brownsworth
DAQMG	Captain E W Carter
ADCs	Captain D S Maxwell, Lieutenant E H G Kemmis

Infantry

4th Brigade: Brigadier General C H Brand
Brigade Major: Major R W Tovell
Staff Captain: Captain H Thomson
13th Battalion: Lieutenant Colonel D G Marks
14th Battalion: Lieutenant Colonel H A Crowther
15th Battalion: Lieutenant Colonel T P McSharry
16th Battalion: Lieutenant Colonel E A Drake-Brockman
4th LTM Battery: Captain A C Loveday

12th Brigade: Brigadier General J Gellibrand
Brigade Major: Major R H Norman
Staff Captain: Captain A L Varley
45th Battalion: Lieutenant Colonel S L Perry
46th Battalion: Lieutenant Colonel H C Ford
47th Battalion: Lieutenant Colonel A P Imlay
48th Battalion: Lieutenant Colonel R L Leane
12th LTM Battery: Captain F G S Cherry

13th Brigade: Brigadier General T W Glasgow
Brigade Major: Major R Morell
Staff Captain: Captain A Nicholson
49th Battalion: Lieutenant Colonel J S Denton
50th Battalion: Lieutenant Colonel A G Salisbury
51st Battalion: Lieutenant Colonel R Christie
52nd Battalion: Lieutenant Colonel J L Whitham
13th LTM Battery: Captain C O Long

Artillery

CRA:	Brigadier General W L H Burgess
Brigade Major:	Major C M Bates
Staff Captain:	Captain A C R Waite
10th Field Artillery Brigade:	Lieutenant Colonel T I C Williams
(37th, 38th, 39th, 110th Batteries)	
11th Field Artillery Brigade:	Lieutenant Colonel W C N Waite
(41st, 42nd, 43rd, 111th Batteries)	
Divisional Ammunition Column:	Lieutenant Colonel H V Vernon
Divisional Trench Mortar Officer:	Captain S J Fox
(7th and 8th MTM Batteries)	

Machine Guns

4th Machine Gun Battalion:	Lieutenant Colonel H W Murray VC
(4th, 12th, 13th, 24th MG Companies)	

Engineers

CRE:	Lieutenant Colonel G C E Elliott
4th Field Company:	Major H G Tolley
12th Field Company:	Major C C Riddell
13th Field Company:	Major R B Carr
Signal Company:	Major J E Fraser

Pioneers

4th Pioneer Battalion:	Lieutenant Colonel H L Morrison

Medical

ADMS:	Colonel G W Barber
DADMS:	Major E F Lind
4th Field Ambulance:	Lieutenant Colonel H H B Follit
12th Field Ambulance:	Lieutenant Colonel A H Gibson
13th Field Ambulance:	Lieutenant Colonel H K Fry

Veterinary

DADVS:	Lieutenant Colonel W A Kendall
4th Mobile Veterinary Section:	Major E S James

Transport (Divisional Train)

CO:	Lieutenant Colonel A A Holdsworth
7th Company AASC:	Captain C R Walsh
14th Company AASC:	Major J W Blanch
26th Company AASC:	Captain J Warmington
27th Company AASC:	Captain S A Robertson

15 Notes

1. *Official History*, Vol V, p. 4.
2. At least in terms of infantry, the principal arm. The *Official History* (Vol V, pp. 21-2) gives the 4th Division's infantry strength as 9787 and the 3rd's as 8503 at the end of October. The October 1917 Admin Staff War Diaries of the two Divisions confirm those figures, or very nearly in the case of the 4th Division. The 3rd Division diary only gives strength figures for its infantry battalions and not for the other elements.
3. *Official History*, Vol V, p. 4.
4. F M Cutlack, *The Australians: Their Final Campaign 1918*, p. 18.
5. 11th AFA Brigade War Diary for November 1917, Appendices, memo dated 14 November.
6. 4th Division Admin Staff War Diary for October 1917, Appendices. The 'Missing' figure was given as 177, as was known at the time; probably these were about evenly divided between killed and taken prisoner.
7. *Official History*, Vol II, pp 208–9.
8. Document on S L Perry's service record, National Archives.
9. The then-Major Deeble's report in the 3rd Light Horse Brigade's War Diary for August 1915 gives some idea of what the troopers faced in the charge. See also M Emery, *They Rode Into History* (2009), p.35.
10. Col Ridley, then a lieutenant, was the officer who signed Christie's attestation form when he enlisted in the AIF.
11. From the unit War Diary, it appears that Capt Norman was in temporary command of the 12th Field Company from mid-September 1917 until Major Riddell returned to the unit in February 1918. Riddell's service record shows that he was on leave from 28 October, then with the engineer training depot in England, but is not clear why he was apparently away from the unit for about six weeks before going on leave.
12. 4th Division Engineers HQ war Diary for October 1917, Appendix 6.
13. *Ibid*, Appendix 8.
14. 4th Division GS War Diary, 3 November 1917. The Smart Set continued after the war as a professional touring company, with original member Charles Holt (former private in the 13th Field Ambulance) as producer/director—see the Australian Variety Theatre Archive on the internet, ozvta.com/troupes-digger-companies.

15 In the entry for James Campbell Robertson in the *Australian Dictionary of Biography*, K R White notes that 'Strangely, in view of his record, Robertson was largely ignored by Charles Bean in the *Official History*.'
16 Devine, *Op Cit*, p. 104.
17 The nickname 'Babe' probably dates from that time - then not yet 21, Norman was unusually young for a staff officer. The Babe Norman Scholarship, for clinical nursing research, is granted through a foundation established by his daughter Rosemary.
18 Devine, *Op Cit*, p. 102.
19 Division HQ memorandum dated 24 November 1917, copy in 13th Battalion War Diary for November 1917, Appendix 120.
20 4th Division GS War Diary for December 1917, Appendix 1.
21 White, *Op Cit*, p. 115.
22 4th Division GS War Diary, 5 December 1917.
23 Calculating from 15 November when the 3rd Division joined I Anzac Corps to 5 December when the first elements of the 4th Division came under VII Corps.
24 Devine, *Op Cit*, p. 104.
25 4th Brigade War Diary, 13 and 15 December 1917.
26 Chataway, *Op Cit*, pp. 196–7.
27 4th Division ADMS War Diary, 2 and 19 December, 1917.
28 B. Lodge, *Lavarack: Rival General*, p. xiv.
29 According to the 46th Battalion War Diary for January 1918. Colonel Denham's service record shows that he was on leave from 31 December 1917 but not declared unfit until 5 February 1918. He had been suffering recurrent bouts of trench fever for a year, and it appears that General Gellibrand sent him on leave to the UK with instructions to report to AIF HQ for a thorough medical examination.
30 Terry was among those evacuated in the final stages of the fighting, but was killed when his vessel was bombed by Japanese aircraft. Varley was taken prisoner at Singapore, but later in the war he was with a draft of prisoners being transferred on a Japanese freighter and was among those drowned when the ship was sunk by an American submarine.
31 *Official History*, Vol V, p. 19.
32 12th Brigade war Diary for February 1918, Appendix 1.
33 12th Brigade War Diary, 21 January 1918.
34 4th Field Company War Diary for February 1918, Appendices 1 and 2.
35 4th Pioneer Battalion War Diary, 31 January 1918.
36 4th Division Admin War Diary, 9 February 1918; 4th Brigade War Diary, 28 February 1918.
37 See the *Official History*, Vol V, pp. 93–102 for a summary of the issues facing Ludendorff.
38 14th Battalion War Diary, 31 January 1918; see also J A Jeffreys' POW report on his service record. The two men were members of Captain Albert Jacka's 'D' Company, holding the left of the Battalion's sector. The Battalion history (Wanliss, *Op Cit*, p. 260n) states that after his capture, Cpl Frost was told by a German interrogator that 'they were anxious to capture one of our men (i.e. Capt Jacka), who spent his nights patrolling No Man's Land single handed.' One of Jacka's biographers (Grant, *Op Cit*, pp 150–51), citing a poem in *Reveille*, adds that Jacka took revenge for the loss of his men by capturing or killing eight Germans in lone excursions on succeeding nights; another biography (Macklin, *Op Cit*, p.200) states that this took place over a period of

several weeks. It is difficult to know what to make of those stories. According to the unit Diary, the 14th went into the front line at 7.30pm on 29 January and was relieved in turn at 8.30 pm on 5 February. At the time of the outpost incident, the battalion had only been in the line for two nights. Several patrols from 'D' Company had gone out in that period, but the majority were led by NCOs, with only one on each night led by an officer—not identified in the patrol reports, but more likely to be a subaltern than the company commander. None of those patrols reported any contact with the enemy (the reports are in the appendices of the Battalion War Diaries for January and February 1918). It seems unlikely that the Germans would have become aware of any particular opponent in those circumstances.

It is possible that Frost's interrogation occurred some time after his capture, and the interrogator was referring to subsequent events. Patrol reports for the remaining five nights of the 14th's time in the line follow a similar pattern, however, again mostly NCO's patrols and with no enemy contact reported. Captain Jacka compiled 'D' Company's reports himself, and on only one occasion recorded that he led a patrol in person. That was on the night of 1/2 February, a special patrol that unsuccessfully searched for the body of an Australian that had been reported seen somewhere in front of the 14th's line; that patrol was also mentioned in the 4th Brigade Intelligence Summary, Appendix 2 of the Brigade's February 1918 Diary.

The story of Jacka seeking out Germans in No Man's Land implies that he was operating alone and unofficially and so may not have reported his activities. It would be unusual for a company commander in the front line to have so much spare time on his hands, but leaving that aside, he was said to have taken several prisoners on his patrols. It would be very difficult to avoid reporting a prisoner, at a time when it was important to gain intelligence of enemy dispositions, but nothing is mentioned in the battalion, brigade or division records; taking prisoners was a matter of prestige to a unit, rather than something that would be concealed.

On balance, it appears that these accounts are no more than old soldiers' tales, and it is safe to assume that Albert Jacka himself had nothing to do with their circulation.

39   Figures from the 14th Battalion and 4th Division Admin Staff War Diaries for February 1918. It appears that the Battalion was hit by gas several more times during the week, but much less heavily than on 30/31 January.

40   Correspondence on Walter John Smith's service record, which also includes his protest about the findings of the enquiry.

41   The AWM Honours and Awards files have his recommendation recorded under 'Dennis Whitfeld', but the actual award record has the correct spelling.

42   12th Brigade War Diary, 5 February 1918, possibly written up later from the results of a court of inquiry on 7 February. The post-war statement by the NCO in charge, Corporal Alfred Hemming, is consistent with the account in the Diary. Privates Hugo Blomquist, Cyril James and Matthew Sowden are known to have been among the five others taken prisoner. The 45th Battalion War Diary mentions the court of inquiry but not the incident itself, and it does not appear in the battalion history; it is also difficult to find in the *Official History* (Vol V, App 2, p. 687).

43   47th Battalion War Diary, 8 and 9 February 1918.

44   P S Sadler, *The Paladin; A Life of Major-General Sir John Gellibrand* (2000), p. 148, citing AWM 1473/67. The conference is not mentioned in Brigade or Battalion War Diaries, and there does not appear to have been a written order issued for the raid proposals.

45   12th Brigade War Diary, 18 and 19 February 1918.

46   T S Louch, *Personal History of the Great War*, Pt III, p.10.

47 Louch wrote that he was relying on memory, assisted by reviewing letters he had written home and occasional references to the *Official History*, when preparing the memoirs, which are dated 1970.
48 48th Battalion War Diary, 3 March 1918. There is no obvious instance of a discrepancy in march timing between corresponding movement orders issued at Brigade and Battalion level around this time.
49 Figures from 4th Division Admin Staff War Diary for March 1918, Appendix. The Admin documents do not include a casualty report for January 1918.
50 4th Brigade War Diary, 23 January 1918, and Appendix 11 for January.
51 4th Division Admin Staff War Diary, 1 February 1918.
52 Brig Gen Brand's attention may have been drawn to Maj Crowther by Brig Gen Gellibrand, who would have known Crowther from the 6th Brigade and had signed his recommendation for the DSO.
53 4th Division DTMO War Diary, 29 March 1918 and March 'Summary of Operations' appendix.
54 4th Division GS War Diary for February 1918, Part 1, Appendix 13.
55 13th Brigade War Diary for February 1918, Appendix 49.
56 13th Brigade War Diary for March 1918, Appendix 19. The other Brigades do not appear to have reported specifically on disciplinary issues.
57 Stanley, *Op Cit*, p. 118.
58 *Medical History*, Vol III, p. 187; see Chapter III, *passim*, of that volume for Butler's full account of the VD problem.
59 4th Division ADMS War Diaries December 1917 to April 1918, Appendices. For the same period there were 748 cases of trench fever ('PUO').
60 *Official History*, Vol IV, p.579 and Vol V, p.4.
61 Bean, *Anzac to Amiens*, p.349.
62 Devine, *Op Cit*, p.151.
63 Louch, *Op Cit*, p.12.
64 Mitchell, *Op Cit*, p. 174.
65 4th Division GS War Diary for March 1918, Appendix 4.
66 4th Brigade War Diary, 22 and 23 March.
67 Cutlack, *Op Cit*, p. 81.
68 Mitchell, *Op Cit*, p. 178.

16: *Vous Les Tiendrez*–Hébuterne

Although the allies had no doubt that the Germans would be launching a major offensive in the spring, the focus of the attack remained unclear. The German preparations that had been detected seemed to indicate three simultaneous thrusts, in the areas of Armentières in the north, Arras and Péronne further south, and Rheims on the French front. In fact the Germans had managed to conceal, by careful night movements, their main concentration of strength at the centre of that line, where their attack was aimed through St Quentin, Péronne and Bapaume towards Amiens. This was the area of the junction between the British and French forces, held in the British sector by the Fifth and Third Armies on an 80-kilometre front. The Fifth Army on the right was the weakest in numbers and most thinly spread, and its limited resources meant that construction of in-depth defensive lines in the sector was still in progress. Against the 26 infantry divisions of the two British armies the Germans had concentrated 76 divisions and an unprecedented artillery force of over 6,400 guns (a third of medium and heavy calibre) and 3,500 mortars.[1] At 4:40 am on 21 March the German artillery opened a tremendous bombardment on the British lines, firing from the map without previous registration. After five hours the barrage lifted and the German infantry, under cover of morning fog, advanced against the stunned survivors of the shelling. Using infiltration tactics developed on the Eastern front and used in the Cambrai counter-attacks, the German storm troops penetrated the British line, bypassing strong points for mopping-up forces to deal with later. Under that pressure the front collapsed. By the end of the day Fifth Army had lost 38,000 casualties, the survivors were in full retreat and the Germans had taken 250 square kilometres of territory. By way of comparison, the British had captured the same amount of territory in the Battle of the Somme in 1916 but that had taken more than four months, at enormous cost. The Germans were now approaching their original 1916 front line.

The pace slowed somewhat over the next two days as the German logistic systems struggled to keep up with their spearheads, but they continued to press forward and threatened to cut off the right flank of Third Army, exposed by Fifth Army's retreat. It was at this point that the 4th Australian Division, waiting at Merris in Flanders, became involved. On 23 March preliminary orders were issued for the Division to move at some time in the following two days to the area of Busnes and Estaires in First Army's sector, well to the north of the crucial front. The divisional artillery, still in the line behind Messines when the crisis arose, pulled out of its positions and began moving back on Merris towards the main body of the Division. Urgent telegrams were sent recalling a number of senior officers who were on leave at this time, among them Brigadier General Glasgow, whose 13th Brigade was again temporarily commanded by Lieutenant Colonel Whitham, 52nd Battalion; Lieutenant Colonel Elliott, the CRE, currently being relieved by Major Riddell, 12th Field Company; and Brigadier General Burgess, the CRA, relieved by Lieutenant Colonel Waite, 11th AFA Brigade. Before the move even got under way the destination had been changed three times, reflecting the high command's uncertainty as to the battle situation. By the night of 24 March Hermaville, west of Arras and in the Third Army area, had been substituted. By that time the infantry brigades' heavier weapons, the Vickers and Lewis guns, had been sent off by transport to Busnes and had to be urgently brought back—the troops would now carry the guns with them in case they had to go straight into action. The Divisional Train also had to hurriedly retrieve part of the provisions that had been dumped in position to supply the original Busnes location. The artillery and the transport wagons, unit and Train, would travel independently, with the foot-soldiers carried on a fleet of buses and lorries, about 160 vehicles per brigade group.[2]

By the time the long convoys of vehicles began to move off early on 25 March the destination had been changed again, from Hermaville to the area around Basseux and Bavincourt, further south. The 4th Brigade found billets at Bavincourt, La Herlière and Saulty, where the Brigade arrived late in the day. The 13th Brigade group reached its area, Gouy, Monchiet and Barly, at about the same time, but the 12th Brigade group had been delayed on the road by a large convoy of artillery blocking the way. It was about midnight before the 12th's vehicles reached Beaumetz, still five kilometres short of their allocated area (Bailleulmont, Bailleulval, Berles-au-Bois) where the vehicles stopped and the troops had to march the rest of the way, not settling in until 2 am. Major 'Johnny' Moyes, 48th Battalion, did not hesitate to express his feelings in that unit's official War Diary:

> There was a good road to Berles-au-Bois, but the pigheaded and stupid officer in charge of the buses could not see the necessity for going there ... men who might have been called on to fight at any moment had to march the 5 kilo[metre]s and carry Lewis guns and all [ammunition] panniers, which are not light ...[3]

It was during the 4th Division's journey south that the famous incidents took place where French townsfolk, loading up their belongings and preparing to evacuate their homes with the Germans approaching, changed their minds on realising that the Australians had arrived. In particular an encounter between villagers at Barly and 13th Battalion troops passing through in their lorries was recorded in the *Official History* and the Battalion's unit history:

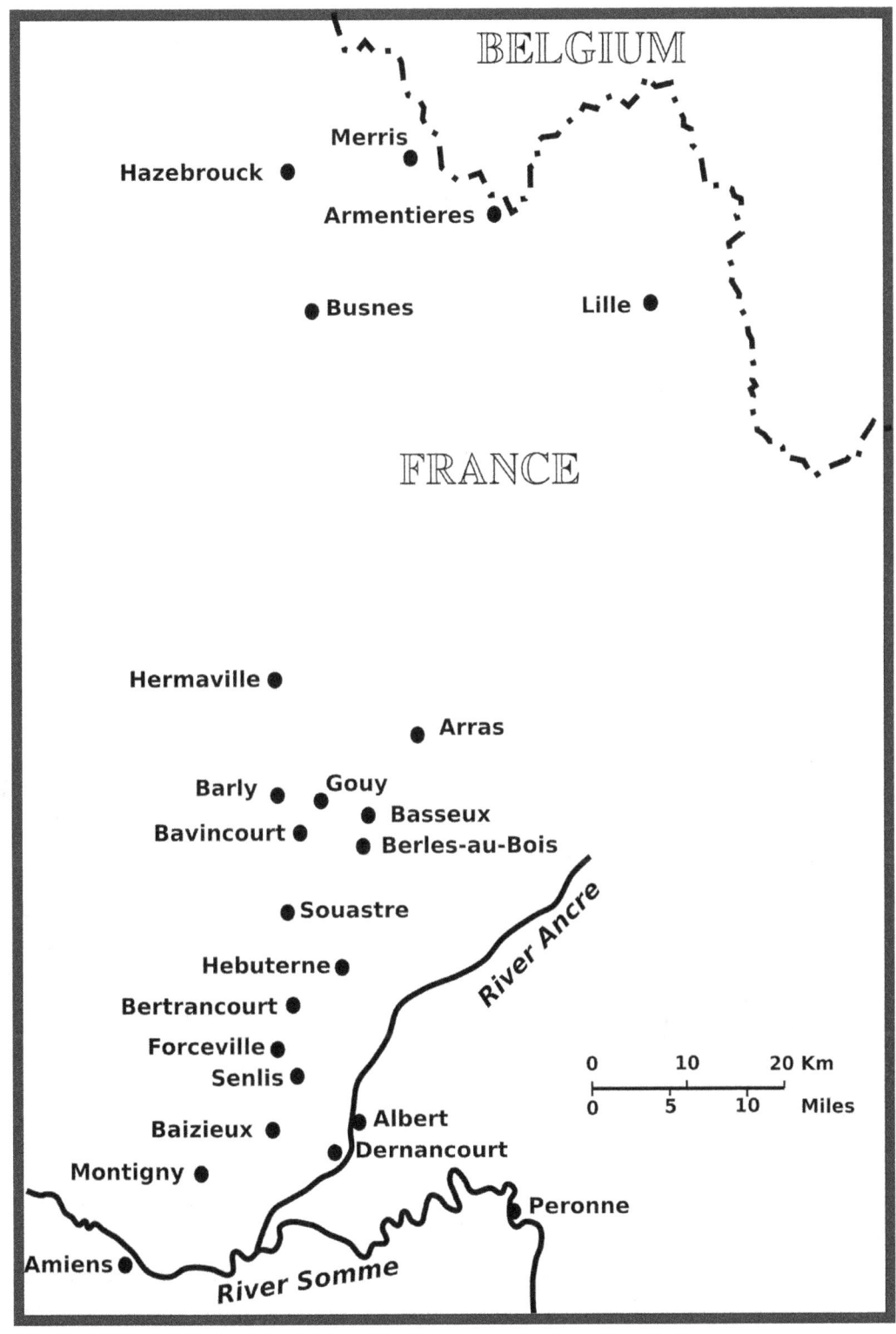

Area of 4th Division's movement from Flanders, March 1918.

> As lorry-load after lorry-load of cheerful men bumped past, each crowd shouting and waving to the old folk, these paused in their loading ... The gazing villagers could be heard calling from one house to the other, 'Les Australiens.' A few minutes later ... they began unloading their carts, and the furniture was carried indoors again. An old man said to one of the 13th Battalion, whose lorries halted there for a while, 'Pas necessaire maintenant—vous les tiendrez ['Not necessary now—you will hold them'].' 'We'll have to see the old bloke isn't disappointed,' said the digger, when the remark was translated to him.[4]

The mood of the Australian troops in that incident, cheerful, confident and determined to succeed, is attested to in many accounts. It seemed to the troops that they were the only ones heading towards the front as their convoys passed crowds of refugees and retreating troops moving in the opposite direction. Far from being depressed by the atmosphere of defeat and confusion, the Australians were collectively elated by the thought that it was up to them to stem the tide at this decisive point in the war, and they felt themselves quite capable of meeting the challenge. 'Here was a situation in which it was obvious that every effort must help directly towards beating the Boche. This, at last, was the job for which they had come oversea.'[5]

4th Division HQ was temporarily set up at Basseux, south-west of Arras, on 25 March. The Division was now in Third Army's sector, attached to X Corps as part of GHQ reserve, and General Sinclair-MacLagan drove to Third Army HQ at Beauquesne seeking definite orders. Information was scarce, however, and it was apparent that the higher command was still trying to decide how best to employ the Division. The situation changed again towards midday on 26 March when a report came through that the Germans, spearheaded by armoured cars or tanks, had captured Hébuterne, 15 kilometres south of Basseux, and were continuing to advance into a gap in the British line. In fact, the report was no more than a rumour; German forces were advancing in that direction, but there were still some remnants of British units in the village and the enemy had no armoured vehicles. It could well have been true, however, and the immediate task of the 4th Division was to defend its area in front of Basseux against the supposed threat. A good defensive position was available, old trenches along the crest of a ridge running south-west to north-east, a short distance forward of the roads between Souastre on the right and Bellacourt on the left. The line faced south-east towards the reported enemy advance, with a view over part of the old Somme battlefield, now overgrown with long grass. Elements of the 12th Brigade's 47th and 48th Battalions went forward to block the roads leading to the Division's area while the Brigade prepared to occupy the left sector of the position on the ridge, between Berles-au-Bois and Bellacourt. The 4th Brigade was ordered forward to the right of the line, from Souastre to Bienvillers, with the 13th Brigade waiting in reserve at Gouy but ready to move at a moment's notice (it was on this day that the British and French high commands, meeting at Doullens 21 kilometres to the east, appointed France's General Ferdinand Foch as supreme commander on the Western Front).

The 4th Brigade moved out from billets for its allotted position with the 13th Battalion leading off. That unit's CO, Lieutenant Colonel Marks, had been urgently recalled from leave, and he caught up with the 13th at La Herlière just as the marching orders arrived;[6] Marks resumed command from Lieutenant Colonel Murray, the MG Battalion CO, who had been doubling as acting CO of the 13th (the sudden emergency had interrupted the orderly transition of the brigade MG companies to the new battalion structure; for the time being they continued to operate with their brigades). On the way into position the Battalion passed groups of fugitives heading in the other direction, who were convinced that the rumoured German armoured cars were right behind them and advancing through Souastre. Colonel Murray took a platoon of the 13th and pushed ahead to investigate. They soon saw that there were in fact some strange vehicles approaching, and Murray dispersed his men into cover on both sides of the road, ready to open fire as the enemy passed. The tension broke, however, when the machines came closer and he realised that they were actually French agricultural ploughs towed by a tractor. The 4th Brigade, infantry units and MG Company, continued the march and reached the Souastre-Bienvillers line about 2 pm. The troops had just begun to dig in when another change of orders came through—Hébuterne was still believed to be in the hands of the enemy, and the 4th Brigade was now ordered to advance and recapture the village. As a preliminary move the Brigade was to concentrate at a windmill between Bienvillers and Fonquevillers on the road that continued south to Hébuterne, with the 12th Brigade moving to Hannescamps in support. Artillery cover was to be provided by the 11th AFA Brigade of the divisional artillery, just arriving in the area after force-marching from Flanders. The movements had barely begun when the orders were changed yet again. The 4th Brigade's operation against Hébuterne was still to proceed, but it was now detached from its own Division and placed under command of the 62nd British Division (IV Corps). The remainder of the 4th Division, including all of the artillery, would immediately move further south towards Albert to fill another breach in the line.

While the other units hurriedly reorganised for this latest move, those of the 4th Brigade marched to their concentration area at the windmill. The Brigade's spirits remained high despite the constant changes of orders. The 4th MG Company's transport wagons had not yet come up, meaning the gun teams had to manhandle their heavy weapons and equipment along the congested roads, but 'the spirit displayed by the whole of the men was excellent as they marched along singing to step ... [while] they discussed the good shooting that all accounts promised at the massed attacks of the Hun.'[7] Patrols were sent out by the 13th and 15th Battalions to reconnoitre Hébuterne, under Lieutenants Herbert Brown and Jack Rae respectively, and Brigadier General Brand decided to make a personal reconnaissance as well. On horseback and accompanied only by his groom, the brigadier rode down to the village himself and made a quick survey. Instead of bristling with German troops it appeared to be deserted, and General Brand spurred back to the windmill to give his orders to the battalion

COs. It appeared that the situation was not as serious as first thought and the brigadier made the bold decision to give the troops a hot meal before continuing the advance. They had not eaten since early morning and there might not be another chance for some time, but the decision entailed a long delay while the cookers were brought up and the food prepared and distributed—C E W Bean thought that General Brand took too great a risk in leaving Hébuterne open to a German advance.[8] As it happened the village was not completely empty, as the advance patrols of the 13th and 15th Battalions found. A few isolated detachments of British troops were there, exhausted but hanging on grimly, and it was said some broke down and wept on seeing the Australians and realising that relief was at hand. Some German advance parties had also reached the village, and an enemy outpost with several machine guns was positioned in the cemetery at its southern corner.

Not all of the 4th Brigade Group's units were to be employed in the Hébuterne operation. The machine guns and LTM battery were retained but the 4th Field Ambulance was ordered to go with the main body of the Division on the march south,[9] leaving medical services to be provided by the 62nd Division. The 4th Field Company engineers were also detached from the Brigade Group, although that decision was made at a very late stage. At first the engineer company was designated as an extra reserve of riflemen for the Brigade's operation; the sappers were issued with rifle ammunition and went through a hasty refresher of musketry drill before marching off to join the infantry advance. They had reached the vicinity of Hébuterne when at 10 pm further orders came through to retrace their steps and join the rest of the Division on the march to Albert.[10] With all sections of the DAC also moving to Albert, small arms ammunition would have to be replenished through the 62nd Division, which also became responsible for artillery fire support; the 7th Company AASC, however, remained with the Brigade for transport of rations.

Daylight was fading when the infantry and supporting arms of the 4th Brigade began their march at 7:30 pm, taking the direct road through Fonquevillers. The area was the northern end of the old Somme battlefield where the opposing trench-lines had been situated, running roughly north-south. Hébuterne was just inside the original British front line of July 1916. Close by to the east of the road, on the other side of the former No Man's Land and less than a kilometre north-east of Hébuterne, was Gommecourt, scene of a costly attack on the first day of the Somme battle. Civilians had only recently been permitted to re-settle Hébuterne[11] and now they had been forced out again by the German advance. The area was criss-crossed by numerous old front and communication trenches, still deep enough to provide temporary cover, and the rusted remnants of barbed wire entanglements. The 13th Battalion led off, with orders to form the centre of a line taking in the southern boundaries of Hébuterne village. The 15th Battalion would take the left flank, with the 16th on the right and the 14th to the rear in reserve. The 13th reached the outskirts of Hébuterne shortly after 9 pm and began to push through the narrow streets, coming under scattered fire as they cleared the village and approached its southern end.

At the cost of a few casualties the 13th Battalion troops had reached and occupied their designated positions by 11:40 pm, taking two prisoners from a German patrol. Two of the 13th's companies now held a line incorporating the south-east and south-west extremities of the village, close up to the enemy position in the cemetery at about the point where the two companies joined. Rising ground there put Captain Robert McKillop's 'C' Company on the right in an awkward position, blocking their view of the cemetery and beyond. The 15th Battalion[12] was coming up to its position on the 13th's left at about that time. The 15th made use of an old trench to extend the line further to the north-east beyond the village limits, but the 16th on the right had been delayed for an unspecified reason. That unit had not started from the windmill until 10:30 pm and it was after midnight before it was in its ordered position, a line extending out from the western edge of the village, angled back from the 13th's position and facing directly south. The 4th MG Company had arrived about 10 pm, met by guides from the infantry units who took the Vickers gun teams to selected positions in the new line.[13] The 4th LTM Battery had reached the village by now also, and began selecting positions for the Stokes mortars; during this time the Battery lost its senior NCO, Sergeant Joseph Ross, shot through the head by a sniper.[14] A forward Brigade HQ was set up a kilometre north of the village with the 14th Battalion, in reserve, standing by in the same area (as was the 4th Field Company until its changed orders came through). There had perhaps been no need to be so concerned about food before the advance, at least for the 13th Battalion stationed within the village precincts—in their haste to evacuate, the inhabitants had left their livestock behind, 'and many ownerless fowls and rabbits went to swell the rations.'[15] Stocks of wine were also discovered; although there would have been some drinks taken when opportunity permitted, by all accounts there was no misbehaviour. The troops were well aware that this was not the time to render themselves incapable, unlike a few German scouts who had been unable to resist the temptation and were picked up in a state of inebriation.[16]

With no other troops nearby both flanks of the 4th Brigade line were in the air, but in the early morning (27 March) the welcome news came through that the New Zealand Division was coming up to the south and would fill the gap on the right flank. There could be no better reinforcement, and at 3:45 am the 16th Battalion was ordered to swing its line south-east and link up. The 16th was in position by dawn, finding that a New Zealand battalion had arrived and was posted in front of the right flank. Only the left company of the 16th was directly facing the enemy and the dispositions would need to be adjusted, but the right of the Hébuterne position was now reasonably secure. On the left, however, where the 62nd British Division was meant to be linking up, there was no sign of any friendly troops and the 15th Battalion's flank remained in the air. Evidently the Germans were not yet aware of that gap; at 11 am aerial reconnaissance reported enemy infantry assembling a kilometre to the south-east, with the obvious intention of launching an attack, but when it came at 1:45 pm, the attack was directed towards the village of Sailly-au-Bois, beyond the New Zealanders on the 4th Brigade's right. The Germans, one or more battalions in twelve waves, advanced in a north-westerly direction and in doing so presented their flank to the 15th and 13th Battalions. A storm of enfilade fire from rifles and Lewis guns cut the enemy force to pieces and the survivors were forced to retreat, without getting close enough to do any damage to the entrenched defenders. There was some shelling of the village, although most of the German artillery was still getting into position, and another danger to the 4th Brigade troops was strafing by enemy aircraft. The 13th Battalion's 'B' Company commander, Captain Edgar Moseley, was severely wounded by that fire;[17] his place was taken by Lieutenant Thomas White, the future unit historian. Despite the repulse of their main attack, the Germans made further efforts later in the afternoon. The 13th Battalion reported observing an assembly at 3 pm that was broken up by artillery fire—some of the 62nd Division guns were in position by now and their CRA had been in touch with Brigade HQ.[18] Forty minutes later a party of 150 German infantry was observed advancing directly towards the village. The column was sent to ground by Vickers guns firing at long range,[19] but a number of the enemy soldiers persisted, finding cover and gradually making their way to the village limits and their outpost in the cemetery. By evening the 13th Battalion estimated that 30 German reinforcements had managed to trickle into the cemetery, and it was apparent that the strong-point would have to be eliminated. Colonel Marks worked out a plan with Brigade HQ to attack the enemy post, with the 16th Battalion advancing its left-flank company at the same time to straighten the line connecting to the New Zealanders.

The 13th got its orders out at 4:30 pm but for some reason the 16th's communications were still not working properly, and it was 1:20 am on 28 March before that unit's company had linked up and the 13th could begin its attack. A section of the 4th LTM Battery's mortars under Lieutenant Leo Waterford provided a short preliminary bombardment before the companies of Captain McKillop and Lieutenant White began bombing down several old trenches leading in to the cemetery. The attackers had entered the position within 10 minutes, most of the enemy not staying to fight, and the troops began mopping up and clearing dugouts. By dawn the position had been secured in a well-conducted small operation that cost one man killed, and the 13th Battalion's line was beyond the village outskirts. It had happened so quickly that eight Germans, coming forward unknowingly in ones and twos to reinforce their comrades, walked straight into the hands of the 13th and were taken prisoner. The 16th Battalion's left company also pushed forward over the crest, with the New Zealanders conforming further to the right, and the 4th Brigade now held a firm line with observation over the territory to their front. A gap of unknown size remained on the left of the 4th Brigade line in front of Gommecourt, and there were signs that the enemy was beginning to probe forward in that area. Earlier in the night General Brand had ordered the 14th Battalion, in reserve, to move forward and extend the line on the left (north) of the 15th Battalion and gain touch with any British troops in the area; the 14th was replaced in reserve by a company of the 16th, freed up by the shortening of that unit's line on the west of the village.[20] The 14th's advance had begun at 7 pm, Colonel Crowther sending one company to link up with the 15th Battalion's left.[21] The other three companies and Battalion HQ moved across open country through the area between Hébuterne and Gommecourt, in loose 'artillery formation' with a screen of scouts in front. The 14th made steady progress in bright moonlight and by 11 pm had reached its first position, a ridge running north between the two villages. The 14th had been able to maintain communications back to Brigade and the Battalion was now ordered to make a further advance, swinging its left across to meet the old German front line ahead of the landmark called Nameless Farm. The 14th reached that position before daylight on 28 March, overrunning a German sentry outpost on the way. Its right flank company was in touch with the 15th Battalion's left on the outskirts of Hébuterne, giving the Brigade a fairly continuous line to the New Zealanders on the right, but the extended left flank was still in the air. The 14th had only encountered a few scattered British troops in that area during its advance. Colonel Crowther now sent out patrols eastwards but no substantial formed bodies of infantry could be located. In fact a German attack on the previous day had pushed back the right of the 62nd Division to a position behind Rossignol Wood, 1,500 metres east of the 14th Battalion's left.

28 March (Good Friday) saw sporadic fighting along much of the local front. The 62nd Division attempted a counter-attack to retake Rossignol Wood, only to see it fail disastrously—three companies of infantry were cut off and forced to surrender to the Germans.[22] A small enemy force then penetrated the gap as far as Nameless Farm, behind the 14th Battalion's left flank. The Germans now had a strong force of artillery available and during the morning a heavy bombardment by guns and trench mortars descended on the 4th Brigade's positions at Hébuterne. The shelling went on for several hours, demolishing much of the village, but casualties were relatively light. Those killed in the 13th Battalion included the 'B' Company CSM, Andrew Tennant; the same shell also killed his colleague, Sergeant Edward Robertson.[23] There was little activity from the German infantry in this part of the front, however, except for two attempts by small groups to probe the 15th Battalion's sector east of the village. These were driven off with heavy losses by fire from rifles and machine guns,[24] actions in which Sergeant Patrick Sammon's platoon was prominent. Further east the 14th Battalion had some encounters with enemy patrols:

> Two or three half-hearted thrusts to find out our strength throughout the day proved most satisfactory targets for our Lewis guns and rifles which took an appreciable toll of him all day. Two prisoners, two light enemy machine guns, one Lewis gun [i.e a captured weapon used by the enemy] were captured and a wounded British soldier rescued. Active patrolling located the enemy in strength in the vicinity of the Crucifix and Rossignol Wood but was unable to gain touch with the troops on the left [the Crucifix landmark was 500 metres west of the Wood].[25]

One of the prisoners was a German sentry snatched from 'under the very nose of the enemy' by Second Lieutenant Victor Hall (called 'Harry Danman' in E J Rule's *Jacka's Mob*) and his batman Private Percy O'Dowd, who stealthily worked their way up an old sap to the enemy post.[26]

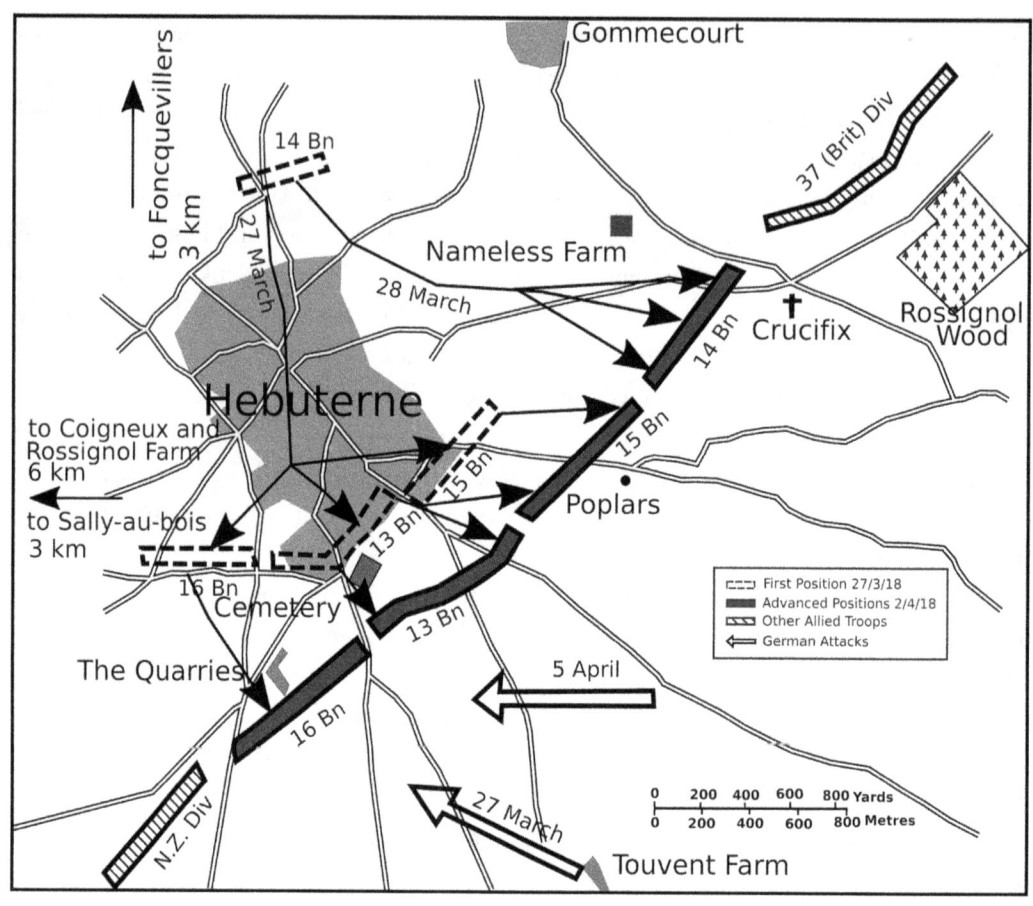

4th Brigade's defence of Hébuterne, March/April 1918.

That night the 62nd Division made another attempt to drive the Germans out of Rossignol Wood. Heavy rain and the pitch-dark night hampered the British attack, as it did a company of the 14th Battalion that had been sent up in support, and hardly any progress was made. Another patrol of the 14th went to Nameless Farm to check the report of Germans in that location but found that the enemy had already withdrawn. The patrol then approached Rossignol Wood, which was found to be still strongly held by the Germans; again there was no sign of British troops in the area. In daylight the next day, 29 March, the 14th sent out another patrol led by the Battalion intelligence officer, Lieutenant John Johnson, together with the Brigade IO, Lieutenant Henry Davis. That patrol finally made contact with elements of the 62nd Division 'in the top of [map square] K.12.a,' outside the north-west fringe of Rossignol Wood. A further attempt to recapture Rossignol Wood was to be made that night and again the 14th Battalion was required to advance in support of the British right. One or two companies of the 16th Battalion were sent from Brigade reserve to reinforce the 14th, with the 15th to send bombing parties against enemy positions in the old saps in their sector.[27] At 3 pm the 14th noticed an enemy force, estimated at 100 strong, advancing down a trench to their front, apparently preparing to attack. Second Lieutenant Hall's platoon was sent to forestall them. The platoon was the same that had won the Brigade shooting competition a week ago in Flanders, and they proved to be equally well-trained in grenade-fighting, driving the enemy back and capturing 150 metres of the trench. Hall himself, leading his men with great dash, was killed by machine gun fire towards the end of the fight. 'We've never had an officer as good,' said a member of the platoon when relating the story to Edgar Rule several weeks later.[28] Hall was recommended for a posthumous VC by Colonel Crowther but the award was not granted.[29]

The British attempt on Rossignol Wood that night was again unsuccessful. Elements of the 14th and 15th Battalions, attacking on the British right with inadequate fire support from mortars and a thin artillery barrage, could make little progress against strong opposition. Brigade reported, perhaps optimistically, that some parties had pushed down the trenches of the old German front line before more heavy rain put a stop to further efforts.[30] During the day the German artillery had continued its bombardment of Hébuterne village and the lines of the 13th and 16th Battalions. Although the strain was heavy on the weary men in the trenches, which were now deep in the inevitable Somme mud from the persistent rain, casualties from the shelling were still fairly light. The bombardment continued during the next day (30 March) as did the rain, which stymied a planned attack for that night by the 15th Battalion on the enemy lines to their front. Four mortars from the 4th LTM Battery had commenced firing a supporting barrage for the attack before it was called off, losing three men killed on one gun when a faulty round went off in the barrel. It had been a bad day for the Battery, three other members having been killed earlier when a shell made a direct hit on their dugout in the village.[31] There was only minor infantry activity in the 4th Brigade sector during that day, but further south the New Zealanders carried out a brilliant operation in the afternoon, an advance by parts of two battalions to secure enemy-held high ground overlooking their positions. The Germans were taken by surprise and heavily defeated, losing an estimated 250 killed, and the 'Enzeds' captured 110 machine guns and at least 230 prisoners.[32]

The following day the 14th Battalion on the Brigade left continued to 'nibble' forward and by evening had occupied the ridge west of Rossignol Wood, the enemy withdrawing before them. On the 14th's right the 15th Battalion advanced in conformity and established their front on the higher ground also. In this sector of the front, except for Rossignol Wood, the trend of movement had been reversed and it was the Germans who were falling back. Easter Monday 1 April saw aggressive action by the 16th and 13th Battalions in front of Hébuterne. At the suggestion of two 16th company commanders, Captains Dan Aarons and Charles Ahearn,[33] the 16th mounted a daylight operation to advance their line 250 metres ahead to higher ground with a commanding field of fire. The objective was held by a strong German post. At 1:30 pm the two 16th companies began a converging attack on the enemy position. Captain Ahearn led from the front as his company forced its way along an old sap on the right with grenade and bayonet, supported by Captain Aarons' men attacking down a sunken road on the left. Covering fire was provided by Lewis guns and rifle grenades, the latter weapons controlled by the unit RSM, James Leunig.[34] At the same time a company of the 13th Battalion advanced from the cemetery on the 16th's left and joined in the fight. The enemy garrison was overwhelmed; 71 prisoners were taken, and 'at a low estimate, over 100 dead Germans were found in the road and saps.'[35] Others were shot down as they tried to flee by a Vickers gun crew of the 4th MG Company posted in 'The Quarries' on the right of the 16th's line, who got off 4,000 rounds firing at the fugitives.[36] So one-sided was the fight that the Brigade recorded its total casualties as only two killed and three wounded.[37]

The troops immediately set about consolidating the captured position against counter-attacks, while the 13th Battalion established Lewis gun posts in continuation of the new line and linking with the 15th's positions on the left. The whole operation had taken 25 minutes.[38] Late in the day the enemy made two counter attacks on their lost position, but these were not in any great strength and were easily beaten off.[39] That evening the 15th Battalion also advanced part of its front by 200 metres without opposition. The day's success, coming so soon after the New Zealand operation two days earlier, was a great boost to morale throughout the sector and the 4th Brigade received a number of congratulatory messages from the higher commanders. At this time the battered 62nd Division had been relieved by the 37th Division. The 4th Brigade now came under the orders of the latter formation, the GOC of which 'seemed full of pleasure at having this Brigade under him'[40] (this was Major General H B Williams, who had commanded a brigade in the fighting at nearby Gommecourt on 1 July 1916). IV Corps had now managed to form a reasonably continuous line in the sector, although Rossignol Wood remained in the hands of the enemy.

There was something of a pause on the front for the next few days, which continued rainy. Apart from some skirmishing both sides confined themselves to artillery shoots and harassing fire from machine guns and snipers while planning their next major operations. The 37th Division decided to make another attempt on Rossignol Wood. On 2 April as part of the preparations for the attack a battalion of that Division's 63rd Brigade relieved three companies of the 14th Battalion in the line to the west of the Wood. Those troops moved back into Brigade support while the remaining 14th company stayed in position, attached to the 15th Battalion next in the line; the latter unit would be required to support the British right flank. The 13th Battalion also had a task in the operation, creating a diversion by raiding enemy posts to its front. The new attack was planned for 5:30 am on 5 April and as it happened the Germans had also chosen that date for a renewed offensive thrust. The British operation at Rossignol Wood got underway on time, two battalions advancing behind tanks and a creeping barrage of artillery and machine guns; some of the 4th MG Company's guns joined in the barrage. At almost the same time German artillery commenced a violent bombardment on the Hébuterne positions, both front line and rear areas, and also on the New Zealander's lines further south. The shelling, which included gas as well as HE and shrapnel, continued for several hours but fortunately it was generally inaccurate and caused few casualties. It was apparent that an infantry attack was on the way in this sector, but fighting had already commenced near Rossignol Wood. The 63rd Brigade troops managed to enter the fringes of the Wood but were stopped and gradually pushed back again by determined German resistance. By the end of the day the British force was back on its start line. The 15th Battalion advance on the British right also stalled. Lieutenant George Fewster's platoon had the task of connecting up with the 63rd Brigade right flank, and the troops had begun moving forward down an old trench before the covering barrage fell. At Zero the platoon advanced with the intention of establishing a post at the landmark called The Poplars, but the troops had to stop when they found that not only was the area strongly defended but it was also dominated by enemy machine guns on higher ground to the left. Fewster decided to hold his present position in the expectation that the British advance would soon overrun the machine gun post. The company commander, Captain Percy Toft, came forward to assess the situation himself, and concurred with Fewster's judgement. German infantry made several attempts to oust the 15th troops from their position during the day but they were held off by Lewis guns, rifle grenades and sniping. Towards evening word came through that the 63rd Brigade was retiring and the 15th's advanced party pulled back in conformity. The Battalion reported losses of two killed and four wounded during the day's fighting near The Poplars and estimated that they had inflicted 40 casualties on their opponents.[41]

The 13th Battalion's diversionary raid also got under way at 5:30. The allotted troops moved forward behind covering fire from Lieutenant Waterford's mortar section, while at the same time the German barrage crashed down on the Hébuterne positions behind them. The Stokes guns dropped 30 rounds accurately onto the enemy machine gun post that was the 13th's first target and the rifle sections had no difficulty overrunning the position. The intention was to send another patrol further forward to reconnoitre, but British 18-pounder shells were now falling in the area and blocking the way. The shooting was coming from the guns covering the New Zealand line further to the right, firing in enfilade across the front to interfere with the expected German infantry attack. At 9:30 am the enemy barrage lifted away from the 4th Brigade's front line and a regiment of infantry appeared, advancing obliquely against the 16th Battalion's sector south of the village, held by the companies of Captains Aarons and Ahearn. As had happened on 27 March the German right flank was open to enfilade fire from the left and centre of the Brigade line. The attack melted away under heavy fire from the 16th Battalion line in front and the 13th and 15th on the left, joined by some of the Stokes mortars and Vickers guns; the 15th Battalion reported that its right-hand company sent Lewis gunners out into No Man's Land to fire on the enemy flank.[42] At 10 am according to Colonel Drake-Brockman's report the German barrage came down again on the 16th Battalion front line, then lifted after 30 minutes to allow another infantry attack. This was beaten off like the first: 'Fritz well and truly towelled up' reported Captain Aarons.[43]

Further south the New Zealand Division had smashed similar attacks on their front, also launched after a very heavy but strangely ineffective barrage. Like Aarons, a New Zealand company commander sent a confident message to his CO: 'we have beaten off two attacks by the Hun and are wanting him to put in a third.'[44] In their sector the 4th Brigade and the NZ Division had established superiority over a disheartened enemy, already worn down by their exertions since the launching of the great offensive and now facing determined, confident and aggressive opponents. Of the prisoners taken earlier, on 1 April, the 16th Battalion noted that although 'a good class of man,' the Germans were tired and hungry, and in this latest engagement, Captain Aarons observed that of an estimated 500 men assembling in front of his position only about half had the determination to form up and take part in the attack.[45] The 4th Brigade men were weary also, of course, having had minimal rest since leaving Flanders eleven days earlier: 'the boys are in the highest spirits but are tired and weary for the want of a relief,' wrote the 4th MG Company diarist; 'It is simply grand to see them, and it gives me extreme pleasure to put this on record.'[46] Despite the heavy shelling and bursts of infantry fighting the Brigade's casualties for 5 April were fairly low, the heaviest being the nine killed and 28 wounded suffered by the 16th Battalion.[47] Evacuation of the wounded from the unit RAPs to the 37th Division ADS at Fonquevillers and the MDS at Souastre was now being conducted by the 4th Field Ambulance's bearer division, which had relieved the British 50th Field Ambulance bearers on the previous night.[48] Having originally remained with the main body of the 4th Division when the 4th Brigade was detached, the bearers had been sent back to the Brigade from the Division's sector near Albert, 17 kilometres to the south—a move that may have been premature, since it was also on 5 April that the 12th and 13th Brigades fought their victorious but costly battle at Dernancourt.

The next few days were quiet, the main difficulty being continuing rain that made the already muddy trenches impassable in places. Congratulatory messages flowed in to the 4th Brigade from the higher commanders, but the troops were more interested in finding out when they might be relieved. There was some discussion at command level about relieving the whole Brigade, but eventually the decision was made by IV Corps that only the 15th Battalion on the left would be relieved by a British unit at this stage; any other reliefs would have to be arranged internally by the Brigade for the time being. The Corps commander, General Sir George Harper, after more than two weeks of retreating from the German advance, found that he now had what seemed to be a brigade of snarling wildcats under his command, firmly holding a key position, and was naturally reluctant to let them go. On 8 April General Harper sent a message for promulgation to the Brigade:

> The Corps Commander desires to thank all ranks of the 4th Australian Brigade for their gallant behaviour in the defence of Hébuterne against all attacks during the past 14 days. Without relief and without complaint they have held their positions and in many cases have advanced and improved their line. Heavy attacks on the Brigade on the 1st and 5th April were repulsed with severe loss to the enemy ... a very fine performance which reflects great credit on all ranks of the Brigade.[49]

Vous Les Tiendrez–Hébuterne

'The Corps Commander is afraid to let the defence of Hébuterne out of our hands,' wrote General Brand to Colonel Marks, the 13th Battalion CO, on the same day, when giving the latter the bad news that his unit would have to stay in the line for the time being.[50] The 13th had to be content with rotating two companies at a time between front line and support, making use of the old catacombs in the village, which had been cleaned out to provide safe underground accommodation for resting troops. On 8 April the 14th Battalion came up from reserve to relieve the 16th on the right of the Brigade line, a daylight relief with no casualties. The 15th on the left was relieved the next evening by a British unit. Both Battalions moved back to a new reserve location at Rossignol Farm near Coigneux, where the Brigade transport was also now based (this was six kilometres west of Hébuterne, and so nowhere near Rossignol Wood). Baths had been arranged there and the troops were able to get a change of underclothes and socks. Here also the reserve units were visited on 11 April by General Sinclair-MacLagan; with the main body of the 4th Division now relieved after its heavy fighting at Dernancourt, the GOC took the opportunity to motor north and visit his detached Brigade.[51] The 13th Battalion, still in the wet trenches in front of the village, was at least able to ensure that the men's feet were attended to when they had a chance of a rest in the catacombs, with dry socks provided whenever possible. Cases of trench foot were kept to a minimum throughout the Brigade by such precautions.

Enemy activity was now mostly confined to intermittent shelling, but on the morning of 11 April a heavier bombardment than usual covered a raid by German infantry on the 13th Battalion's left-hand advanced post. The shelling isolated the post from support and the enemy force was able to outflank and surprise it, taking Lance Corporal James Baillie and his four men prisoner.[52] There was some resentment in the 13th directed at the British unit on its left over this incident. The 13th had understood that a post covering the left of the lost one would be manned at all times by the British, but it had actually been withdrawn at daylight, leaving Baillie's position open to attack from that flank. The 13th resolved to man the flanking post themselves in future.[53] As it happened, the 13th was not to be in the line for much longer—with the front now appearing to be stabilised, the higher command relented and decided that the Battalion could now be relieved by a British unit. The move was part of a general rearrangement to frontages and boundaries in the sector, with the 4th Brigade's front moving to the right (south) and taking over 500 metres of the NZ frontage, and so no longer including Hébuterne village itself. The Brigade back area now extended to the west of the revised front line, with HQ moving to Sailly-au-Bois between Hébuterne and Coigneux on 12 April; a new ADS was established at Sailly also.

On the following night the 13th Battalion handed over the Hébuterne trenches, coincidentally to the 13th Battalion of the Rifle Brigade, and moved west to Coigneux and a well-earned rest,

> so weary that ... many were quite unable to walk. Officers and men helped each other along to the bivouacs at Coigneux, but many dropped along the roadside and slept until transport could be spared to pick them up. It was less than four

> miles [6.4 kilometres] to Coigneux, but dozens took eight hours to cover it. [Brigadier General Brand] himself was at Sailly helping to issue coffee to the weary troops ... men who had been cheerful and active to the very last lost their reserve of strength all at once upon relief, and the strongest found themselves forced to sit on the road bank and then unable to rise.[54]

The 4th Brigade was now disposed with one battalion in the front line south of Hébuterne, one in close support west of the village, and two resting in reserve at Rossignol Farm and Coigneux. The front line and support battalions each had their left-out-of-battle nucleus at the reserve billets also, and some training was initiated for the troops in those locations, with particular emphasis on Lewis gun work. The 16th Battalion relieved the 14th in the front line on 13 April, the latter unit moving back to Rossignol Farm with the 15th coming up to the close support positions. General Williams, the 37th Division GOC, visited the reserve units on 15 April and addressed the troops to express his appreciation for their efforts under his command. Australian transport details had a reputation for replacing losses among their draught animals from neighbouring units by unofficial means, and the General commented that the 4th Brigade transport seemed to always be at full strength—but 'even my transport people believe that it's been worthwhile having you with us.'[55] Those British 'transport people' had previously been to the 4th Brigade lines looking for missing animals but could find none with their brands. It seems that the Brigade had taken precautions against discovery, through its Train company, Captain Clement Walsh's 7th AASC:

> The animals we had 'souvenired' ... had been sent down south ... to the other battalions of the 4th Division while their 'souvenirs' had been sent up to us ... Major [sic] Walsh, MC, of the 7th ASC was always a popular visitor to any battalion in the 4th Division.[56]

Although there were several intelligence warnings of imminent German attacks in the next few days, nothing eventuated and the front continued quiet, so much so that the 15th Battalion was able to detach a 100-man party to work on digging a support trench (the 'Purple Line') behind Hébuterne. The 16th Battalion in the front line sent out night patrols that penetrated deep into No Man's land without encountering the enemy. The 16th was ordered by 37th Division to secure an identification from the German units opposite by whatever means available, and in daylight on 15 April three NCOs crept out due east along an old communication trench seeking enemy outposts. About 500 metres out they came across a German machine gun near a dugout, in which the gun crew were evidently sheltering. Deciding that they were too few to be starting a fight so far from their own lines, the group quietly collected the gun and made their way back for reinforcements. An officer and six ORs then went back through the trench to the enemy post, and in a short skirmish with grenades and rifles killed one German and captured five others, three of them wounded, without loss. The prisoners were brought back along the communication trench to the 16th's lines, a successful result in an early example of the type of operation later known as 'peaceful penetration.' The next day the

37th Division was relieved by the 42nd, with the 4th Brigade now coming under the latter formation's orders ('handed over as trench stores'[57]). As yet the only relief for the Brigade was by rotating units, and on 20 April the 15th Battalion took over the front line from the 16th, which moved back to Rossignol Farm for a rest and a bath. The 14th Battalion came forward again into close support in place of the 15th, with the 13th moving up to forward reserve near Sailly-au-Bois where the troops were kept occupied with Lewis gun training and work on the 'Purple Line.' Finally on 22 April orders came through from 42nd Division that the 4th Brigade would be released in the next few days, to rejoin its own Division in the Amiens area further south. Units of the 1st New Zealand Brigade came in to relieve those of the 4th Brigade over 23 and 24 April, the latter moving back and assembling at Coigneux to embus for the journey south on the latter date. The troops boarded the buses in record time,[58] and by Anzac Day morning all units had arrived at their new billets, at Allonville and Cardonette just north of Amiens, and were settling in (while the 4th Brigade vehicles were on the road overnight, the 13th Brigade had been fighting its great battle at Villers-Bretonneux, within sight of Amiens).

The cost in casualties to the 4th Brigade in the fighting between 26 March and 24 April, though serious, was considerably lower than might have been expected, at 76 killed and 307 wounded, as well as the five 13th Battalion men captured and classified as missing.[59] With reinforcements arriving to balance the losses—the 4th Division was now receiving some new recruits through the training depots again—units were generally close to full strength. Decorations awarded for Hébuterne included those for the 16th Battalion officers Captains Ahearn and Aarons, who had led their companies in the forefront of battle through the whole period in the line. Ahearn was recommended for the VC and Aarons for the DSO, but in the event lesser awards were approved, the DSO to Ahearn and a Bar to his MC for Aarons.[60] Lieutenants Joseph Senior and William Burrows of the 16th were awarded MCs for their efforts in the action of 1 April, in the case of the latter a Bar to the decoration that he had won at Bullecourt. Other 4th Brigade officers awarded the MC, or a Bar to a previous award, included the 14th Battalion IO Lieutenant Johnson, and Lieutenants Norman Aldridge and Henry Schutz also of that unit. 13th Battalion officers Captain Robert McKillop and Lieutenants Richard Swinbourne and Herbert Brown were other MC recipients; Brown's decoration was his third of the war, adding to the DCM and MM that he had won while in the ranks. In the 15th Battalion, MCs went to Lieutenants Jack Rae and Cecil Goss; the latter had been temporarily commanding a company that had played a key part in beating off the German attack on 27 March.

Soldiers awarded DCMs in the Brigade included the 13th Battalion's Lance Corporal Edmund Rawdon, leader of a bombing squad, and 'smiling little Frank Massey,'[61] Corporal F E Massey, a tireless patrol leader. 14th Battalion DCM recipients were Lewis gunner Lance Corporal Patrick Brennan, Sergeant George Bullen (both for the action on 29 March in which Lieutenant Hall was killed), CSM William Coleman and

Corporal Thomas French. There were four DCMs awarded in the 15th Battalion, to Sergeants Robert Day, Percival McCoy and Patrick Sammon, and to signaller Corporal Sergia Lockwood. 16th Battalion soldiers awarded DCMs, principally as a result of their unit's combats on 1 and 5 April, were RSM James Leunig, Sergeant Henry Thompson, Corporal Charles Cowain and Sergeant William Prescott, who received his fifth wound of the war in the fighting.[62] Numerous MMs were awarded in the Brigade; at a parade in May, General Birdwood presented over 70 members of 4th Brigade units with MM ribbons, the great majority of which would have been for the Hébuterne battle,[63] but regrettably many of the recommendations have not been preserved, at least in Australian records.[64] Some details are available of 16th Battalion MMs, however, and those include Corporal Augustus Farmer, who was decorated for leadership of a bombing section in that unit's attack on 1 April and its defensive battle on 5 April. Farmer was the only known indigenous member of the 16th to be decorated for gallantry.[65]

Whether the 4th Brigade's defence of Hébuterne is thought of as a distinct battle or as a series of separate but interrelated engagements, it remained a source of great pride for the Brigade troops, who had established decisive superiority over their opponents at a vital stage of the war. It was later accepted that the German advance in the sector had paused temporarily at the time that Australian troops first occupied the village, but within a day the Brigade had begun to frustrate all attempts by the enemy to renew their momentum;

> an abounding virility, which rendered impenetrable a previously precarious defence, and, mastering the failing spirits of the enemy, quickly developed into aggression, was the contribution of the 4th Brigade at Hébuterne[66]

- or, as the 13th Battalion digger passing through Barly might have put it, the old bloke would not have been disappointed. Other dramatic events had been taking place during the same period that the 4th Brigade had been fighting under British command—the rest of the 4th Division had been thrown into intense combat further south, and this account will now return to 26 March when the Division had first been split up.

16 Notes

1   M Middlebrook, *The Kaiser's Battle*, pp. 50, 52, 71-2. Fifth Army also had three cavalry divisions, each considerably smaller than an infantry division; these had been split up to reinforce the infantry.

2   From the 4th Brigade War Diary for March 1918, Appendix 9.

3   48th Battalion War Diary, 25 March 1918.

4   *Official History*, Vol V, p. 120; also White, *Op Cit*, p. 122. White had access to Bean's notes in preparing *The Fighting Thirteenth*, which was published over a decade earlier than Volume V of the *Official History*.

5   *Official History*, Vol V, p. 116.

6   D G Marks diary, 26 March 1918

7   4th MG Company War Diary, 26 March 1918. The diarist was Lt John Kennare.

8   *Official History*, Vol V, p. 126. Bean cited Lt Col Marks's diary for this incident (see Note 6 above); in the relevant entry, Marks did not express an opinion about the decision, and the phrasing suggests that it may have been made jointly with the battalion COs. The 4th MG Company was one unit pleased that its men had the chance for a meal before going into action, as recorded in its War Diary entry for that day.

9   The *Medical History* (Vol II, p. 616n) says that the order came from either Brig Gen Brand or Maj Gen Sinclair-MacLagan.

10   4th Field Company War Diary, 26 March 1918.

11   Bean Diary, AWM38 3DRL606/104/1, 1 April 1918 (p 38 in PDF).

12   According to the 15th Battalion history (Chataway, *Op Cit*, p. 204n), the CO, Lt Col McSharry, went on leave that night, and the unit was commanded 'for several days' by Maj Corrigan. This is not mentioned in the unit or Brigade War Diaries, nor on Col McSharry's service record, which only shows that he had a week's 'Paris leave' in the previous October. At a time when senior officers were being recalled from leave, it is difficult to understand why Brig Gen Brand would approve leave, or why Mc Sharry, something of a fire-eater, would want to go at such a crucial time. On the other hand, Mc Sharry usually countersigned the unit War Diary; his signature does not appear on either the March or April diaries, but he did sign that for May. If he actually was absent, it is possible that illness was a factor.

13   4th MG Company War Diary, 26 March 1918.

14 4th LTM Battery War Diary, 26 March 1918; Red Cross file on J W Ross.
15 D G Marks diary, 26 March 1918.
16 Chataway, *Op Cit*, p. 204.
17 This occurred on 27 March according to his service record and Colonel Marks' diary, although the 13th Battalion history has 28 March.
18 4th Brigade War Diary, 27 March 1918. The 3 pm incident is in the 13th Battalion diary but is not mentioned by Brigade. The latter says that the German force assembling at 11am was shelled.
19 This incident is mentioned in the 4th Brigade and 13th Battalion War Diaries, but not in that of the 4th MG Company; in view of the constant action during this period, inconsistencies can be expected, with the diaries probably being written up some time after the events. Although, or perhaps because, T A White was heavily involved in the fighting, he misdated some of the 27 March incidents to the next day in the 13th Battalion history (*The Fighting Thirteenth*, *Op Cit*, pp. 126–7).
20 16th Battalion War Diary, 27 March 1918, stating that the Battalion had one company in the front line, one in support, one in Battalion reserve and one in Brigade reserve. The 4th Brigade diary says two companies were in its reserve. From a later entry in the Battalion diary, it appears that Brigade used the reserve company on 29 March, and the Battalion reserve was then transferred to replace that company in Brigade reserve.
21 Capt Albert Jacka's 'D' Company, currently commanded by Capt William Beamond; Jacka's service record shows that he was away on a course at Second Army School of Instruction between 23 March and 14 April.
22 C E W Bean recorded an implied criticism in his diary, that the 'Tommies surrendered without our hearing a shot fired' (AWM38 3DRL606/104/1, entry for 1 April 1918, p. 16 in PDF).
23 Both soldiers were buried in the same rough grave, according to Red Cross reports, but only Robertson was identified for formal burial after the war.
24 The 15th Battalion War Diary noted one attack at 10 am and another at 5 pm, on two different posts. The Brigade diary and the *Official History* only mention the first incident.
25 14th Battalion War Diary for April 1918, Appendix 1A, 'Narrative of Operations'.
26 Rule's account (*Op Cit*, p. 116) of this incident and of the death of 'Danman' the next day leaves no doubt that 2nd Lt Hall was the soldier referred to.
27 4th Brigade War Diary, 29 March 1918. The 16th Battalion War Diary is not clear on how many companies were directly working with the 14th. A message in that document (Appendix 22) says that both 'A' and 'C' Companies were attached to the 14th on 29 March, but the main entry for 29 March states that only 'A', as Brigade reserve, was involved in the fighting. The entry for 31 March notes that 'C' Company had returned to the unit as it was no longer required for Brigade reserve while 'A' Company was still in support to the 14th. The 15th Battalion War Diary (May 1918, Appendix 13), however, mentions that two companies of the 16th were operating with the 14th. See also Note 19 above.
28 Rule, *Op Cit*, p. 116.
29 The recommendation, in the AWM files, does not specify a particular decoration, but since it was for a posthumous award, it can only be for the VC (or possibly a Mention in Despatches, but that seems unlikely in the circumstances).
30 4th Brigade War Diary, 29 March 1918. One of the map references given for the line reached is possibly a typing error (K.11.a.4.7. when K.11.d.4.7. may have been meant), and the position given may include the trench taken by Lt Hall's platoon during the afternoon.

31 4th LTM Battery War Diary, 30 March 1918. The casualties from the shelling were Cpl Arthur Wood, L-Cpl Bertie Aspery and Pte Vyvian Ellem (shown on the Roll of Honour as a member of the 15th Battalion, his original unit before being transferred to the LTMs). Those killed by the premature explosion were L-Cpl Walter Binning, Pte Wallace Broom and Pte Patrick Currie.

32 Bean diary, AWM38 3DRL606/104/1, p.46, written into the *Official History*, Vol V, P. 141, and H. Stewart, *The New Zealand Division 1916–1919*, pp. 362–7, stating that '3 officers and close on 300 other ranks' were taken prisoner in that action.

33 Or Ahrens—he was using the name Ahearn at this time.

34 From RSM Leunig's DCM recommendation in the 16th Battalion War Diary for April 1918, Part 4, Appendix 28.

35 16th Battalion War Diary, 1 April 1918.

36 4th MG Company War Diary, 1 April 1918.

37 4th Brigade War Diary, 1 April 1918. The 13th Battalion diary reports no fatalities, that of the 16th one during the actual operation, but a total of four killed for the day; presumably the others occurred through shelling (as was the case with Pte Everard Cream, according to Red Cross reports) or during German counter-attacks on the captured position.

38 From the detailed reports in Appendix 1 to the 16th Battalion War Diary for April 1918.

39 4th Brigade and 4th MG Company War Diaries, 1 April 1918, stating that the attacks took place at 6 pm and 9.30 pm; they are not mentioned in the diaries of the 16th and 13th Battalions.

40 Bean Diary, AWM38 3DRL606/104/1, 1 April 1918 (p. 41 in PDF).

41 15th Battalion War Diary for May 1918, Appendix 13.

42 *Ibid.*

43 16th Battalion War Diary for April 1918, Appendix 3 (folio 33). Aarons' message was timed 11.18am, suggesting he was referring to the second attack. The diary narrative and Lt Col Drake-Brockman's report to Brigade explicitly state that there were two attacks, at 9.30 and 10.30, but the *Official History* (Vol V, pp. 414–16) only describes the first; Bean had access to German accounts, which only mention one attack, with another ordered for late in the day but abandoned.

44 Stewart, *Op Cit*, p. 370.

45 16th Battalion War Diary for April 1918, Appendix 3 (folio 44), and entry for 1 April.

46 4th MG Company War Diary, 5 April 1918.

47 16th Battalion War Diary, 6 April 1918. I have assumed that the figure given there is for the 24 hours ending 6 am on that day. The AWM Roll of Honour confirms nine deaths on 5 April.

48 4th Field Ambulance War Diary for April 1918, Appendix 1.

49 4th Brigade War Diary for April 1918, Appendix 11. The general or his staff may have confused the action of 1 April with that of 27 March.

50 13th Battalion War Diary for April 1918, Appendix 1.

51 The Brigade War Diary says the GOC visited on 12 April, but the Division diary and those of both units have 11 April.

52 Not 'Bayley' as in the Battalion history (White, *Op Cit*, p. 130). The others were J Burrows, L T Lyndon, J Murray and W K Small.

53 13th Battalion War Diary for April 1918, Appendix 1, entry for 10 April—the Diary describes the incident under that date, as does Colonel Marks' own diary, but the Brigade diary and the corresponding intelligence report has 11 April, as does the Battalion history (White, *Op Cit*, p. 130). L/Cpl Baillie's Red Cross file and service record have 11 April also, and the 13th Battalion

diary entry for 12 April refers to the raid being 'yesterday morning'. The Battalion history states that a British Lewis gunner failed to fire on the German party because he had no orders to do so, but a report on the Red Cross file says that the gunner did not want to risk hitting the prisoners being escorted away.

54   White, *Op Cit*, p. 131.
55   *Ibid*, p. 132.
56   *Ibid*. Walsh was not promoted to Major until November.
57   *Ibid*, p. 131.
58   14th Battalion War Diary, 24 April 1918.
59   Figures extracted from the War Diaries of the 4th Brigade and its constituent units for March and April 1918.
60   Ahearn's recommendation, together with others made at the same time, is preserved in the 16th Battalion War Diary (April 1918 Part4, Appendix 28). That Appendix includes several recommendations that, like Ahearn's, did not find their way into the AWM's Honours and Awards files, probably because they were being made through 37th Division/IV Corps rather than the usual 4th Division/Australian Corps channels. A number of award recommendations by other 4th Brigade units, particularly for MMs, are also missing for the Hébuterne period. Most of the gazettals for those awards seem to have appeared in London Gazettes of late August and early September 1918. The DSO for Captain 'Ahearn' was gazetted in July under his true name, Ahrens.
61   White, *Op Cit*, p. 129.
62   Prescott was a nephew of the late Major Percy Black, the 16th's elder statesman.
63   4th Brigade War Diary for May 1918, Appendix 39.
64   See Note 60 above.
65   Gill, *Op Cit*, p. 154, noting that three of Augustus Farmer's brothers also served in the AIF. Two were killed in action, including Augustus at Amiens, 8 August 1918.
66   *Official History*, Vol V, p. 270.

17: Dernancourt

At 5 pm on 26 March the 12th Brigade had begun to march from billets east of Basseux to Hannescamps in support of the 4th Brigade's advance to Hébuterne. An hour later the 45th and 46th Battalions, leading off, had covered four kilometres to reach Berles au Bois when a message came through from Division to halt the march pending new orders. These were outlined to the Brigade staff by Captain Arthur Maxwell, now attached to Division HQ, at 6:30 pm. Except for the 4th Brigade, the Division was now ordered to immediately move south to the area of Senlis-le-Sec, near Albert, a marching distance of up to 30 kilometres. The 13th Brigade, standing by in its billets in villages around Gouy a little further north of Basseux, had already received a similar warning order (only that morning, the Brigade's GOC and brigade major, Brigadier General Glasgow and Major Morell, had arrived at their HQ, having rushed back from leave in England). The 45th and 46th Battalions, halted along the road to Hannescamps, were now ordered to retrace their steps to their original billets. After some discussion between Division HQ and the two brigade staffs, orders came through for the brigade groups to set off as soon as they could from their respective billeting areas to the point where the different roads met at Souastre. They would then form one column and continue to Senlis, whichever group reached Souastre first taking the lead in the march from there on. The 4th Field Ambulance and the 4th Field Company, detached from their own Brigade Group, would march with the 13th Brigade.

The 12th Brigade column, with the 47th Battalion leading, arrived at Souastre first, obliging the 13th Brigade troops to halt by the roadside until the other column had passed.[1] It was to be a flank march, with unknown enemy forces somewhere on the left (east) but apparently no friendly troops. There was a strong possibility that the Division could be in action before the destination was reached; 'We must protect our own flanks and be prepared for anything,' Colonel Leane of the 48th told his officers.[2] The 12th Brigade battalions put out small patrols to the east to act as flank guards, while the 13th Brigade chose to cover the flank by marching a full battalion (the 50th) for part of the distance on an alternative route further east. On leaving

Souastre the 50th diverged through Bayencourt and Corcelles before rejoining the main column at Bertrancourt for the second-last stage to Forceville. With the long infantry group columns taking up the roads, the 4th Division artillery waited until early next morning (27 March) before moving off, each field brigade providing its own flank guards. The artillery's initial destination was the area around Acheux, a little to the west of Forceville.

The infantry battalions had been ordered to travel light, dumping packs and blankets under guard in the villages;

> The night was perfect for marching, cold and clear with a bright moon ... A few miles to the left the flares of the fighting line could be seen, rising and falling continuously. British aeroplanes hummed constantly over, as one after another flew to unload its bombs on the enemy ... The column moved through almost empty villages ... Dawn found it still marching, 108 paces to the minute, with ten-minute halts in each hour.[3]

Some fell instantly asleep in the halts, particularly the 12th Brigade troops, who had had scarcely any rest in the previous 48 hours. It was said that towards the end of the march some men were actually walking while asleep.[4] It says much for the fitness of the men, as well as for their determination, that very few had to fall out along the way. In the 46th Battalion

> one corporal ... carried 270 rounds SAA, 6 rifle grenades and 4 [Mills] bombs the whole distance of 18 miles [29 kilometres]. On this long, trying march, on a cold night, the Battalion did not lose a man, which shows the excellent form they were in.[5]

There were no details yet of the actual situation that the Division was going into or what its tasks were to be, only that it was to come under command of VII Corps, Third Army. While the troops marched General Sinclair-MacLagan and his GSO1, Colonel Lavarack, drove to Montigny, 15 kilometres west of Albert, where VII Corps HQ had just been established, to receive their orders. Arriving at Montigny chateau after midnight the 4th Division officers found that the 3rd Division GOC, General Monash (Sir John since the New Year) had just arrived with some of his staff on a similar quest. The Corps Commander, General Congreve VC, outlined the situation to the Australian officers. The troops meant to be holding the southern sector of Third Army's line between the Somme and Ancre rivers, covering Albert, had retreated the previous afternoon, not through enemy action but by a misunderstanding of orders. The movement had gone too far to be reversed in time and German forces were advancing rapidly into the gap in the line. The way to the vital transport hub of Amiens was open and the 3rd and 4th Divisions were required to bar the enemy's way. The 3rd Division, operating on the Somme front for the first time, was to take up a position running south from Méricourt-l'Abbé on the Ancre to Sailly-le-Sec on the Somme, making use of an old French defensive line in that area. The 4th Division's two brigades were to deploy in the area on the north bank of the Ancre, where the retreating British divisions, the 9th and 35th, were believed to have halted and taken up a line facing south and east, from Buire through Dernancourt to Albert. Depending on the condition of those divisions the 4th would probably have to relieve them in the front line immediately. Colonel Lavarack left the conference and drove east to Baizieux, where Division HQ was to be set up in the chateau.

> On the road he had passed a brigade of British siege artillery, which had been withdrawing before the German thrust. 'You Australians think you can do anything,' said its commander to Lavarack, 'but you haven't a chance of holding them.'
> 'Will you stay and support us if we do?' asked Lavarack. 'Right you are,' said the brigadier—and he did.[6]

The area was familiar territory to the 4th Division. The villages on the Ancre west of Albert had been a rest and training area for the troops during the Mouquet Farm period in 1916 and later that year, then again after Bullecourt in 1917, when Division HQ had also been at Baizieux.

The head of the 12th Brigade's marching column reached Senlis at about 6:30 am on 27 March, the units all coming in over the next two hours.[7] The weary men dispersed into billets, snatched a quick meal and flopped down for some much-needed sleep. At 6 am the 13th Brigade Group's column, bringing up the rear of the Division, had begun to enter Forceville where the troops rested for two hours and availed themselves of food found in the abandoned village. Both Brigade staffs sought out further orders. British officers in Senlis could give the 12th Brigade no information and telephone lines to 4th Division HQ were not yet through, so Major Norman, the brigade major, rode over to Baizieux. Here he was given brief orders by Colonel Lavarack for the Brigade to move south then east, from Senlis to a forward supporting position behind British troops of the 9th Division facing Albert, which was now in enemy hands. The 13th Brigade's initial orders were to move down to the vicinity of Bresle in support of the 12th. The start time for the 12th Brigade's forward move was 10 am, and Brigadier General Gellibrand arranged to meet with his unit COs prior to moving off. Before the conference could begin a staff officer from the 9th British Division arrived with orders to the effect that the 12th Brigade had been placed under command of that Division and was to march immediately, but only as far as the low ground between Hénencourt and Millencourt, concentrating in that area pending further instructions. The brigadier was to report to 9th Division HQ at Hénencourt 'at once' for briefing. General Gellibrand and his staff officers did so, while the units made ready and moved off for the ordered concentration area. At Hénencourt the brigadier was told that his troops would probably have to relieve those of two 9th Division brigades in the front line that night and he was to arrange the details with the British brigades' HQs in Laviéville, the next village to the south. At Laviéville the 12th Brigade staff found that their counterparts 'did not ... appear to know very much about the situation or dispositions of the line, and very little information could be obtained from them.'[8] While this discussion was going on, new and urgent orders arrived from 9th Division. Dernancourt village was apparently in the hands of the enemy, and it had been reported (wrongly, as it turned out) that British troops were falling further back from defensive positions outside the village. The 12th Brigade was to go forward immediately to block any further enemy advance—the position to be occupied, as it happened, was close to that in the original orders issued by the 4th Division staff earlier in the morning.[9]

Shortly after midday the orders had been confirmed and the 12th Brigade units had arrived in the Hénencourt-Millencourt area, where General Gellibrand went to pass on the orders to the units. The 47th and 48th Battalions, each with a section of the 12th MG Company, were selected to take up the forward blocking positions. The 45th and 46th would remain at Millencourt in reserve, together with the LTM battery and the remainder of the MG company. Brigade HQ was set up in a cellar in Laviéville, probably the same used by the two 9th Division brigade staffs. The brigadier personally gave the orders to Colonel Imlay, the 47th Battalion CO, and the unit moved off immediately, but there was some delay before the 48th started. That Battalion had moved from its original position to avoid enemy shelling, and General Gellibrand sent a British staff officer to find Colonel Leane and pass on the orders verbally. No-one at Brigade HQ thought to give the officer (un-named but probably the 9th Division officer who had delivered the preliminary orders) any written authority, even a scribbled note on a message form. There had been rumours of Germans impersonating British officers to spread false information and Colonel Leane was suspicious of the stranger when he arrived at the 48th's position, particularly when the latter could not remember the name of the brigadier who had sent him. Leane 'fixed him with his murderous stare'[10] and asked in what direction the Battalion should march. By now thoroughly rattled, the young man pointed the wrong way, and Leane then placed him under arrest and went to find the brigadier himself.

It was 1:30 pm before the orders had been confirmed as genuine and the 48th began its advance. In the meantime the 13th Brigade had also been positioning its units in response to a series of changes in orders. Initially the Brigade was to occupy the ground from Bresle south to the Ancre at Ribemont, and the units resumed their march from Forceville at 11 am. The unit COs went ahead to meet with Brigadier General Glasgow at Bresle church at midday to receive the detailed dispositions, but changed orders arrived from Division HQ almost immediately. The Brigade was now to take up a line with two battalions between Hénencourt and Millencourt, facing east astride the road between those places and backing up the advancing 12th Brigade. The 49th and 50th Battalions were allocated to the forward positions with the 51st and 52nd behind them in close support. The two lead battalions had begun their movement by 1:30 pm when yet another change of orders came through. The position to be occupied was now further east and south, in front of Laviéville and with the left of the line on the Hénencourt-Millencourt road and the right on the Amiens-Albert road where it crossed the Laviéville-Buire road. The 49th Battalion took the right of the new line and the 50th the left with the other two units in support north and south of Bresle Wood, to the north-west of Bresle village. This deployment put the two forward 13th Brigade units directly in front of the 12th Brigade's HQ in Laviéville, an unusual situation. The 13th Brigade established its own HQ in a dugout 800 metres west of Bresle Wood, a location about three kilometres west of 12th Brigade HQ. Both brigades were reasonably up to strength and each was able to leave a substantial nucleus in reserve with the transport lines, at Contay and later Bavelincourt.

The terrain was a combination of natural and man-made features, scarcely changed today, that would have a significant influence on the way that the fighting was conducted over the ensuing week. The 4th Division infantry brigades were deploying on the high ground above the valley of the Ancre, a region where that river runs south through and beyond Albert then curves south-west and continues its course to meet the Somme 15 kilometres east of Amiens. The village of Dernancourt is situated near the bend in the river, about three kilometres from Albert. A broad grassy hill slopes up north and west from the valley, with several minor sunken roads running across it at angles. The straight Roman road from Amiens to Albert (now the D929) runs along the crest of the hill before passing through a steep gully outside Albert. North of that road, below the crest, the villages of Hénencourt, Millencourt and Laviéville form a close triangle, with Bresle a little to their south-west. The south-easterly slopes of the

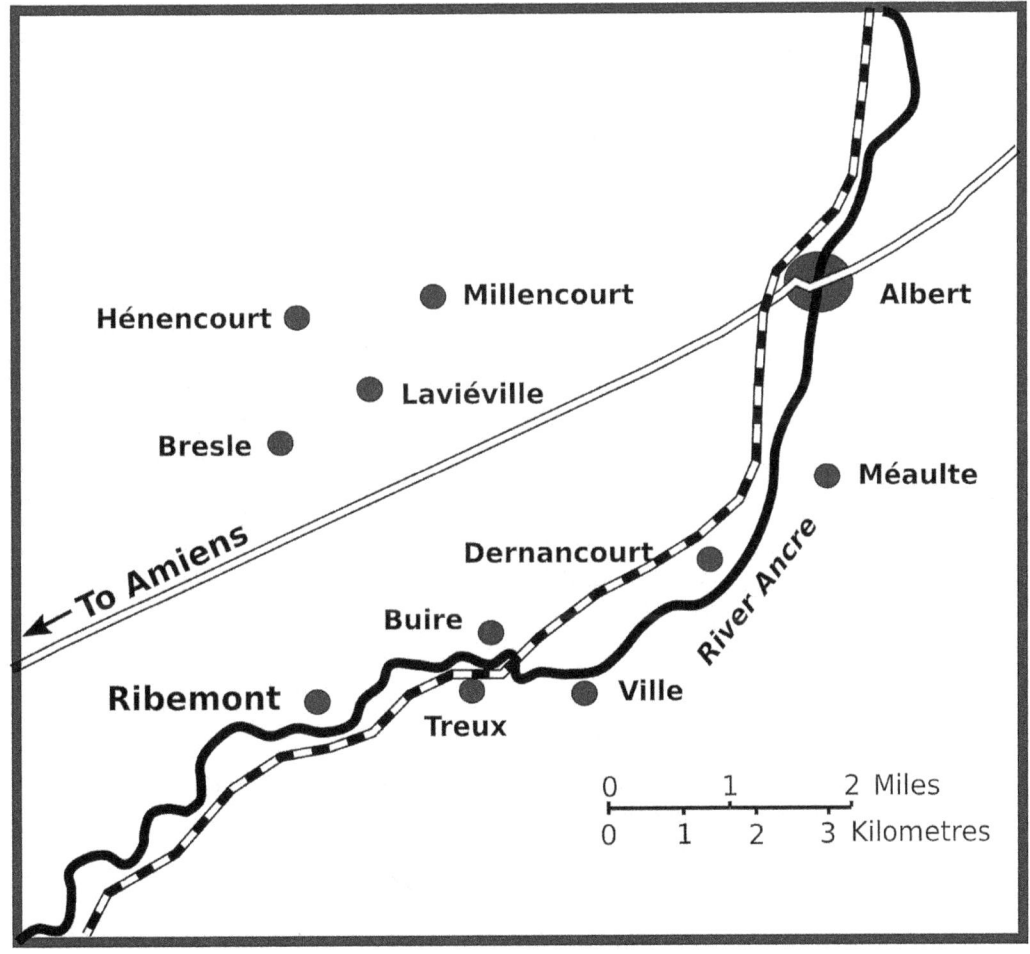

Dernancourt area.

hill are fairly open and featureless, but further west the ground is indented by a wide valley running down towards Buire on the north bank of the river; in 1918, that depression gave useful concealment to troops in that part of the battlefield. There are, or were, several chalk-pit quarries scattered over the hill. On the flats at the foot of the high ground is a railway conforming roughly to the course of the river, running south from Albert and curving south-west past the near edge of Dernancourt, which is between the railway and the river. The railway passes under the Amiens road near Albert and is then built up on an embankment for most of the distance towards Dernancourt, before variations in the ground contours cause it to pass into a cutting about 500 metres long that runs as far as the northern corner of the village; there is a level crossing at each end of the cutting, the northern of which was used for a cart track in 1918.[11] A further embankment then begins and runs along the edge of Dernancourt and beyond, towards Buire to the south-west, with a road underpass at the western corner of the village where the road to Millencourt and Laviéville runs through the embankment.

From the heights the troops had a view over the countryside east and south, with the green fields and woods of early spring. Although shell-bursts were beginning to scar the ground, there had not been the sustained weeks-long bombardment by heavy guns that had reduced other battlefields to desolation; shellfire was damaging but not yet demolishing the local villages. Albert could be seen in the distance, with the damaged statue of the Virgin atop the cathedral still hanging precariously over the streets. The enemy army's activities were visible on the rising ground on the other side of the valley, an unusual sight for men who were used to spending weary weeks below ground level in the trenches, hardly sighting a single German unless a raid was on. From the enemy lines any movement in daylight on the bare hillside above Dernancourt was plainly visible also, and this presented a highly dangerous situation to the Australians. Fire from German artillery and machine guns could be brought down on them as soon as they were sighted, and Colonel Imlay was very aware of this as he led the 47th Battalion forward in loose artillery formation towards the front line—the positions to which they had been ordered were on the forward slope of the hill. By about 1:30 pm the Battalion had reached the Amiens road where they halted while the CO made a personal reconnaissance further along the road, until he came under machine gun fire from somewhere ahead. At 2:30 pm orders arrived from Brigade confirming that the two battalions were to continue advancing to an interim position on the forward slope, prior to relieving the 9th Division troops in the line from Dernancourt around to Albert that evening. After its late start the 48th Battalion was only just arriving at 2:30, and Colonel Leane also called a halt with the 48th on a line north of the Amiens road on the 47th's left. It is not clear whether or not Leane got in touch with Imlay at that time, but the former undertook his own reconnaissance, walking over the slope with Lieutenant Harry Downes, the assistant adjutant. The Germans were shelling the road area by now and Downes was slightly wounded by a splinter during that period.

Leane succeeded in making contact with elements of Scottish regiments from the 9th Division. Although the situation was still obscure, it had been established by now that the railway embankment in front of Dernancourt was still occupied by British troops, even though the village itself could be in German hands. At 3 pm 12th Brigade HQ had received an order from 4th Division HQ confirming that the forward battalions were to take over the railway position, and this was passed on to the battalions an hour later, with the relief to take place 'as soon as possible after dusk.'[12] No change had been made to the timing of the previous orders to occupy positions on the open hillside, however, and Colonel Imlay had already ordered the two leading companies of the 47th Battalion to commence that stage. 'This necessitated movement on the forward slope of [the] hill in full view of the enemy who shelled us causing casualties which were minimised by adopting loose formations and dribbling the men through.'[13] The troops found an old training trench near a sunken road, somewhat short of the specified line but offering some cover from the shelling, and this became the line. The 47th's forward companies were in position by 5 pm, at which time they reported that they were in touch with 48th Battalion troops on their left. By all accounts Colonel Leane had decided on the spot to hold the 48th back out of direct enemy observation until dark, but the report by the 47th indicates that at least some element of the 48th had been pushed forward across the road to link up.[14] Whereas the final front designated for the 47th faced south-east towards Dernancourt, that for the 48th faced directly east, with its left close to Albert. The terrain where the 48th waited for dusk was not as open as that forming the 47th's intermediate position, with a steep depression intersecting the Roman road as it neared Albert. It was apparently that area where the main body of the 48th waited—Lieutenant George Mitchell described a 'steep bank' where his company sheltered.[15] Both units had taken casualties from shell fire in the afternoon, particularly the 47th with around 50 hit, eight of those fatally. The 48th's casualties were considerably lower, probably a total of about ten, with six fatalities.[16] The casualties included several men hit when low-flying British aircraft machine-gunned their positions. There was much anger at the time, but it was later established that the airmen had been told that any troops east of Laviéville would be German (since 21 March, the RFC had put in a supreme effort across the whole front, constantly in action strafing and bombing the advancing German columns).

Both battalions established their HQs in trenches behind the line of the Amiens road. Sunset would have been at about 7:15 pm, and by 8 pm the shelling had died down and guides from the British units at the railway had reported to the HQs to bring in their reliefs. The 48th Battalion sent two companies into the front line to relieve the exhausted but undaunted Scots, holding the other two companies as supports in the depression where they had halted in the afternoon. The 48th's left was meant to follow the railway embankment as far as the Amiens road near Albert, linking with British troops of V Corps, but the section of embankment there was found to be in German hands. Contact was made with the British slightly west of the intended position, and the 48th's extreme left platoons took up a position facing north-east towards Albert, bent back from the railway. From there the 48th's line ran south for 1,300 metres along cuttings and embankments to link with the 47th Battalion. That unit held the elbow of the railway where it curved in front of the northern outskirts of Dernancourt along to the road underpass, a front of about 1,500 metres; the 47th's right linked with British troops of the 35th Division at the underpass. Colonel Imlay sent the two companies on the forward slope down to the railway, replacing them with the two previously held in reserve.

By about 9:30 pm both 12th Brigade battalions had their forward elements moving into position along the railway, sheltering behind the banks in a series of one-man niches or rifle pits previously dug by the Scots. The reserve 46th Battalion sent 90 men to assist with carrying ammunition to the front line.[17] It was 1:30 am before the relief was reported as complete. The designated sections of the 12th MG Company also went into the line after dark. Six Vickers guns under Lieutenant James Pontin were spread in pairs along the railway in the 47th Battalion's sector, with two reserve guns in a chalk pit or quarry on the slope 800 metres above the railway. Pontin's right flank gun was near the underpass, adjacent to the left of the 35th Division's sector, held by the 19th Battalion Northumberland Fusiliers, a pioneer unit operating as infantry. The thinly-spread companies sent out scouting patrols ahead of the line, while sentries in the rifle pits strove desperately to stay awake after 48 hours of minimal sleep. George Mitchell recalled dozing

> in a slit with my head against the clay ... every twenty minutes or so, without apparent reason, I would climb to my feet, patrol the line, and awaken sleeping sentries. Doubt if I was really awake myself as I did it![18]

After midnight Brigadier General Gellibrand sent the 45th Battalion forward to form a further support behind the front line units. The 45th took up positions at the northern end of the Buire valley, above the 35th Division's sector, forming two lines of two companies each. The rear line occupied a sunken road, but the forward line troops had to dig a new trench a short distance ahead of the road, near the lip of the depression. The task was completed by 5 am[19] (Major A S Allen was commanding the 45th during this period—Colonel Perry was on leave and presumably out of contact for recall).

While the infantry had been moving to the front line the 4th Division's other arms and services were deploying through the sector. The divisional artillery, leaving Souastre early on the morning of 27 March, reached Acheux, 10 kilometres north of Baizieux, about midday and halted for further orders. The two field brigades were temporarily placed under command of the 9th Division CRA, forming a group under Colonel Williams, CO of the 10th AFA Brigade, to cover the 12th Brigade infantry. The group also included two British brigades that were already in position but overdue for relief. Battery commanders reconnoitred likely gun positions on a general line between Millencourt and Laviéville, finding that there was little cover available; the guns would have to be positioned in the open until they could be dug in. The batteries began moving down from Acheux to the front during the afternoon, advancing into the gun line after dark. The deployment was completed in the early hours of the morning (28 March) with wagon lines established at Frechencourt and Behencourt, west of the gun line. The DAC was set up nearby at Agnicourt, an outlier of Bavelincourt. The 13th Brigade infantry, with their attached machine guns and mortars, had been positioned at Laviéville and Bresle to give depth to the defence of the sector. The 24th MG Company was initially used to strengthen a further defensive position known as the GHQ Line, with its guns spread along a north-south ridge behind Bresle.

Of the engineer units, the 13th Field Company allocated a section of sappers to each of its Brigade infantry battalions. Its first task was organising construction of a series of platoon strong-points for the Brigade's forward and support lines at Laviéville and Bresle Wood, dug by the 4th Pioneer Battalion overnight. The Pioneers would play a notable supporting role in the events of the coming days. At first the 12th Field Company was not assigned to work directly with the 12th Brigade infantry, instead being put on to accommodation works initially, then to road repairs within a few days as enemy shelling began to damage the approach routes. The 4th Field Company was also available, having been detached from its own Brigade Group at Hébuterne. On arriving at Forceville with the 13th Brigade, the Company was assigned to keep order in that village:

> the town was full of fugitive English troops, whose sole aim appeared to be to loot the houses and estaminets of the inhabitants who had evacuated the town ... armed guards were placed by the 4th Field Company, and NCOs of the Company took an active part in restoring order[20]

(The Company OC, Major Tolley, noted that the sappers had not completed the overnight march in good shape, having done very little route march training). The Company remained at Forceville until the next day (28 March), then moved down to the Division area where it was put on to various tasks, including laying out strong-points in the area just to the north of Ribemont and Buire for construction by the 4th Pioneers that night; those were later joined up into trenches as part of the third line of defences in the sector. The Signal Company had reached Baizieux at 5:30 am on 27 March and was soon at work establishing communications at Division and Brigade level. There were no existing telephone wires in the area, and the signallers had to roll out new cables, using cable-laying wagons for the first time since arriving in France.[21] The lines were connected during the day, linking Division HQ with the infantry brigade and artillery group HQs by telephone and telegraph, as well as interconnecting the brigades; lines from that command level to units were installed by unit signals personnel. The cables were laid on the ground, there being no time to bury them, and hence they were frequently cut by enemy shelling and also damaged at least as often by the Division's own vehicles: 'Transport was continually cutting the wires and stripping insulation,'[22] and the linesmen were under high pressure making repairs. The Signal Company also established wireless sets at Division and Brigade HQs, as well as visual signalling relay stations at various points, with the main station in the steeple of the Baizieux church.

The medical units were soon set up and functioning. On the way down to the sector overnight the ADMS, Colonel Barber, had found much confusion over medical arrangements at the Army and Corps level. Things were more organised closer to the front, however, with the 35th and 17th Division casualty evacuation procedures working reasonably well.[23] The 12th and 13th Field Ambulances took over the existing ADS in the stables of Hénencourt Chateau, and were receiving wounded evacuated from the 12th Brigade infantry units on the evening of 27 March. An initial shortage of stretchers and blankets was alleviated by using equipment salvaged from an old CCS ('Edgehill Siding') near Dernancourt, abandoned on the approach of the Germans. The original intention was to run the Hénencourt facility as an MDS, but enemy shelling in that area caused a change of plans. An MDS was established instead at Warloy, four kilometres further west, managed by the 13th Field Ambulance, with Hénencourt remaining as an ADS under the 12th Field Ambulance, reinforced with elements of the 13th. An intermediate post was set up at Millencourt, from where Major Archibald Collins supervised the overall evacuation arrangements. From Warloy MDS the wounded faced a journey of 25 kilometres by Motor Ambulance Convoy (MAC) to the nearest functioning CCS, at Doullens. The 4th Field Ambulance, detached from its Brigade, was used to administer a Divisional Collecting Station at Toutencourt, six kilometres north-west of Warloy, where casualties were transferred to vehicles for the journey to the CCS. Over subsequent days continued shelling of Hénencourt forced personnel and patients into the cellars, and the 4th Field Ambulance bearers were returned to the 4th Brigade at Hébuterne, but the arrangements remained basically the same during the period on the Dernancourt front. The Divisional Train established its HQ at Vadencourt, three kilometres from Division HQ at Baizieux, with its 26th and 27th AASC Companies nearby at Contay to supply the 12th and 13th Brigades and the 14th Company at Agnicourt (Bavelincourt) servicing the artillery and HQ elements. The railhead was at Belle Église Farm near Acheux initially, changing to Vignacourt a week later. The Division proceeded with the usual Western Front tasks of setting up its systems in a new area of operations while its cutting edge, the infantry garrison at the outpost line on the railway, waited for the enemy.

In the 47th Battalion's sector on the elbow of the railway, the tracks ran atop an embankment in front of Dernancourt village then into a cutting as they curved north, then on a further embankment on the way to Albert. With the garrison as thinly spread as it was, a steep 100-metre section on the right of the northern embankment had been left unoccupied. Troops were posted along the cutting to its south, in niches dug in to the reverse of the foremost bank, on the village side of the rails.[24] A cart track crossed the rails where the ground levelled for a short distance between the northern embankment and the cutting, and a Lewis gun team was posted to guard that point. Behind the end of the embankment just north of the crossing was stationed a sentry group of two privates and an NCO, Sergeant Stanley McDougall, the Battalion scout sergeant, a rugged 27-year old Tasmanian blacksmith. The night passed fairly quietly and a misty dawn approached in the early hours of 28 March. The officers on duty, Lieutenants George Reid and Ernest Robinson, had just walked by McDougall's post on their rounds of the posts when the sergeant heard noises from the far side of the tracks. He recognised the sound as bayonet scabbards flapping on the thighs of marching men, and it seemed to be coming from 50 to 100 metres away. Shouting 'I think they're coming at us!' McDougall began to run north along the top of the embankment to alert the nearest troops beyond the unoccupied section. Through the mist he could now see a mass of German troops advancing towards the 47th's line. Collecting seven men from the flanking platoon, he ran back along the embankment towards the crossing while the two officers set about organising the firing line on the left.

The details of what happened next are not entirely clear, with several different versions recorded at the time and later. C E W Bean's account in the *Official History*, based on an interview that he conducted with Stan McDougall three weeks after the event, says that a German grenade thrown over the embankment wounded the platoon's Lewis gunners, and McDougall, formerly a Lewis gunner himself, picked up the weapon. Continuing to run along the top of the bank, he saw two German light machine gun teams crossing the rails right in front of him. McDougall, not a tall man but strongly built,[25] held the Lewis across his chest, opened fire at point-blank range and mowed down the German gunners. McDougall kept going, now on the German side of the rails, and spotted more enemy troops crouching below the bank. He turned the Lewis on to those, hitting some and sending the others running back for cover. It was probably about that time that McDougall was joined by Sergeant James Lawrence. He would almost certainly have used up his ammunition by now—a Lewis gun drum held 47 rounds, enough for only five or six seconds sustained firing—and it may have been Lawrence who brought up more drums.[26] McDougall continued towards the level crossing, then to his right sighted a party of about fifty Germans who had overrun the isolated post guarding the crossing and penetrated behind the Australian lines. McDougall opened fire on them with the Lewis, which was now so hot that he badly burned his hand on the barrel casing; Sergeant Lawrence then held it steady for him as he fired with the other hand. The garrison in the cutting south of the crossing turned to their rear and opened fire also, and half of the Germans were hit. The remainder broke away northwards in confusion. Sergeant Lawrence and another sergeant were walking across to secure any surviving prisoners when a German officer appeared from concealment and aimed a pistol at them. McDougall shouted a warning, the German's shot missed and he was killed by Lawrence's colleague. The other part of the German group had meanwhile wandered into the area behind the 48th Battalion's line where they were sighted by Lieutenant George Mitchell, who charged straight at them brandishing his revolver.

Sergeant Stanley McDougall VC MM (1889–1968), 47th Battalion. (AWM A05155)

Mitchell 'picked out the officer and jammed my pistol barrel into his Adam's apple,'[27] the Germans dropping their weapons and raising their hands as more of the 48th troops arrived on the scene. As well as taking 30 prisoners there, the 48th also freed two captured 47th Battalion men, perhaps the sentries at the level crossing.[28] All of the enemy troops who had crossed the railway were now either dead or prisoners.

Of Stan McDougall's part in the fighting, five witnesses described what they had seen in statements made to Colonel Imlay over the next few days. With events happening so quickly in mist and half-light it is not surprising that the accounts differ in detail, but all stated that McDougall had originally attacked the German force with rifle and bayonet before using a Lewis gun, and most said that he had picked up a second Lewis at some stage, perhaps a captured British weapon that the Germans had been carrying. When he first ran along the bank to get reinforcements and then led them back towards the crossing, McDougall must have been carrying a weapon of some sort, and presumably would have used that when he first encountered the Germans—but he may have only had a revolver with him.[29] When Bean interviewed McDougall on 15 April, however, there was no mention of any bayonet-work or of using more than one Lewis gun. Bean does not appear to have asked about ammunition for the Lewis, although Sergeant Lawrence, who could have answered such a question, was present for at least part of the interview.[30] Lawrence, in his written statement made on the day of the battle, had said that McDougall used both bayonet and revolver as well as a Lewis gun. Whatever had actually happened, it was clear that Stan McDougall had done something extraordinary in destroying a strong enemy attack almost single-handed, and in due course Colonel Imlay recommended him for the Victoria Cross.

Dramatic as the early morning fight was, it was only the beginning of a series of heavy actions through most of day. It later emerged that the initial German attack had been launched prematurely, without waiting for covering fire, but paradoxically it had achieved surprise and could have resulted in the enemy force gaining a dangerous lodgement behind the Australian line ahead of the main attack. The enemy company had started at 5 am, fifteen minutes before their barrage was due to start, while the full infantry advance was not planned to move off until 6 am.[31] The full attack got under way with the German artillery barrage falling on the Australian support and rear areas first then sweeping towards the front line, several *minenwerfer* trench mortars joining in to drop shells along the railway position. The German infantry came on from assembly positions behind the Ancre, crossing by footbridges, and advanced directly against the railway, all along the line from south of Albert to the underpass at Dernancourt. The 12th Brigade infantry opened up with rifles and Lewis guns on the mass of targets, the troops stationed at the embankments standing up to get a line of fire over the forward edge or lying on top of the double line of rails. The pressure was particularly heavy on the 47th Battalion's front, and several of the 48th's Lewis guns fired across their own front into the enemy attacking their neighbours. The 12th MG Company's Vickers guns joined in, firing at up to a kilometre range on enemy troops moving down the valley slopes on the far side of the river (the gunners fired 20,000 rounds during the day's fighting[32]). The methods of emplacing the guns are not fully described in the records. The six forward weapons were all in the 47th Battalion's lines, probably through issues with fields of fire in the 48th's sector, but the four on the left and centre were positioned in the cutting just north of the village;[33] the banks of the cutting would have enabled gun positions to be dug unobstructed by the rails and they would presumably have allowed fire on to the 48th's front.

The German infantry could get no closer than grenade-throwing range before the survivors fell back, but as they receded the enemy artillery and mortars increased their fire. The troops at the embankments were exposed to shells and mortar rounds bursting behind them, and also to enfilading fire from a machine gun on the Albert railway bridge on the left and another in a building in Dernancourt on the right. The shelling was heavy near the underpass where Lieutenant Pontin's two Vickers guns formed the extreme right of the 12th Brigade, on the left flank of the Northumberland Fusiliers. The troops crouched against the embankment for cover, and at about 9:30 am Pontin realised that the shelling was slackening off. He 'crawled to the top of the embankment to see what was going on, and found a row of enemy bayonets lining the other side of the metals.'[34] The German infantry had evidently advanced from the village right up to the railway under cover of the bombardment; they were now so close that the machine guns behind the bank could not get at them. Pontin and a senior officer of the Fusiliers quickly conferred and decided to immediately charge the enemy force before the latter could organise their own attack—the Germans had advanced in such haste that they had not been issued with grenades and were throwing rocks over the embankment. Two enemy soldiers tried to come through the underpass tunnel but both were immediately shot by the sentry there, Private James Gray. While the crew of the right-hand Vickers began to manhandle their weapon up on to the rails to get a line of fire, Lieutenant Pontin organised most of his men to join in the charge, using their revolvers. Pontin himself with Privates John Sheehan and Stanley Bigg covered the gun's crew as they dragged it forward, shooting a number of Germans who tried to rush it. With that protection Private Thomas Bruce and his 'Number 2, 'Private William Johnston, quickly got their Vickers into action, opening fire at point-blank range on the enemy to their front. 'The Germans fell back in disorder under its demoralising fire'[35] and the impetus of the charge by the British pioneers and the rest of the Australian machine gunners. Private Bruce followed the retreating enemy troops with his fire, shooting into the houses of Dernancourt when the Germans sought cover there, but the gun crew was also under fire. Johnston, who had tried to shield his 'Number 1' with his body,[36] was hit in the shoulder and Private Sheehan went to the gun to do the 'Number 2' duties. Bruce was then killed by a shot to the head and Sheehan, who was said to have already killed seven Germans with his pistol,[37] took over the gun. The garrison resumed their positions behind the embankment and the fighting at that end of the line died down.

Further north the German infantry resumed their efforts to advance against the railway, meeting steady fire from the defenders that stopped every attempt, nine in all over the course of the day. In between infantry assaults the enemy artillery and mortars increased their fire and snipers from both sides emerged to pick off opponents; the 48th Battalion lost one of its company commanders, Captain Thomas Elliot, shot through the head by an enemy sniper that he was trying to locate. During pauses in the attacks a few men at a time would take the opportunity to step down from the banks and clean their fouled rifles, while others refilled empty Lewis gun drums from loose rounds. At one stage the 48th's right company had all four of its Lewis guns damaged by the shells, but Lance Corporal Joe Pitt assembled two working guns from the intact parts. The main German assembly points were in and behind a narrow wood that ran south from Albert on the 48th's front, between the railway and the Ancre, and the area around Vivier Mill on the river and the village of Méaulte on the far side, facing the 47th. Enemy movement in these areas was sighted from observation posts in the support line on the hill, and artillery support was called in. The 4th Division's artillery, only just in position, was in the process of registering on its SOS lines; that of the 10th AFA Brigade ran through the wood, so the registration rounds would have been hitting live targets, adding to the shooting of the two British field brigades already established in the line. The methodical shelling disrupted the enemy infantry's preparations, and one attack was broken up by the explosion of an old British ammunition dump, hit by a chance shell. Casualties continued to mount up in the Australian positions, however, the ranks of the 47th Battalion, still under great pressure, thinning out steadily under the German shelling and grenades from enemy infantry who got close enough to throw. Among the 47th's casualties were two company commanders, Major Denis Hannay and Captain Edward Williams, wounded and evacuated, and a company second-in-command, Captain Gregory Gibson, who was badly hit and died in the CCS the same day.[38] At one point Lieutenant John Schulz led 25 men in a charge over the embankment north of the level crossing, clearing away the German grenadiers in front and pursuing them for some distance before falling back again to the main line. Losses were heaviest on the 47th's right; the remaining troops edged in that direction to cover the gaps, with the right of the 48th extending in turn to maintain a continuous, though thinning, line. Colonel Imlay meanwhile ordered two platoons from the companies in the support trench to make their way down the hill to reinforce his right. Although spread out and advancing in short rushes, the reinforcements lost 25 casualties[39] in running the gauntlet of artillery and machine gun fire that broke out as soon as they emerged from cover. Among those killed were two platoon commanders, Lieutenants Christian Nommensen and Frederick Lane.

Late in the morning, word came through to 12th Brigade HQ that the 35th Division was considering an attack to retake Dernancourt village, a highly unrealistic intention that was confirmed shortly after noon. The Northumberland Fusiliers, after their spirited defence of the railway in the morning, were now tasked with sending strong patrols against the village at 2 pm following an artillery bombardment. The 47th Battalion was ordered to cooperate by extending its line still further to the right to cover the line vacated by the Fusiliers. If

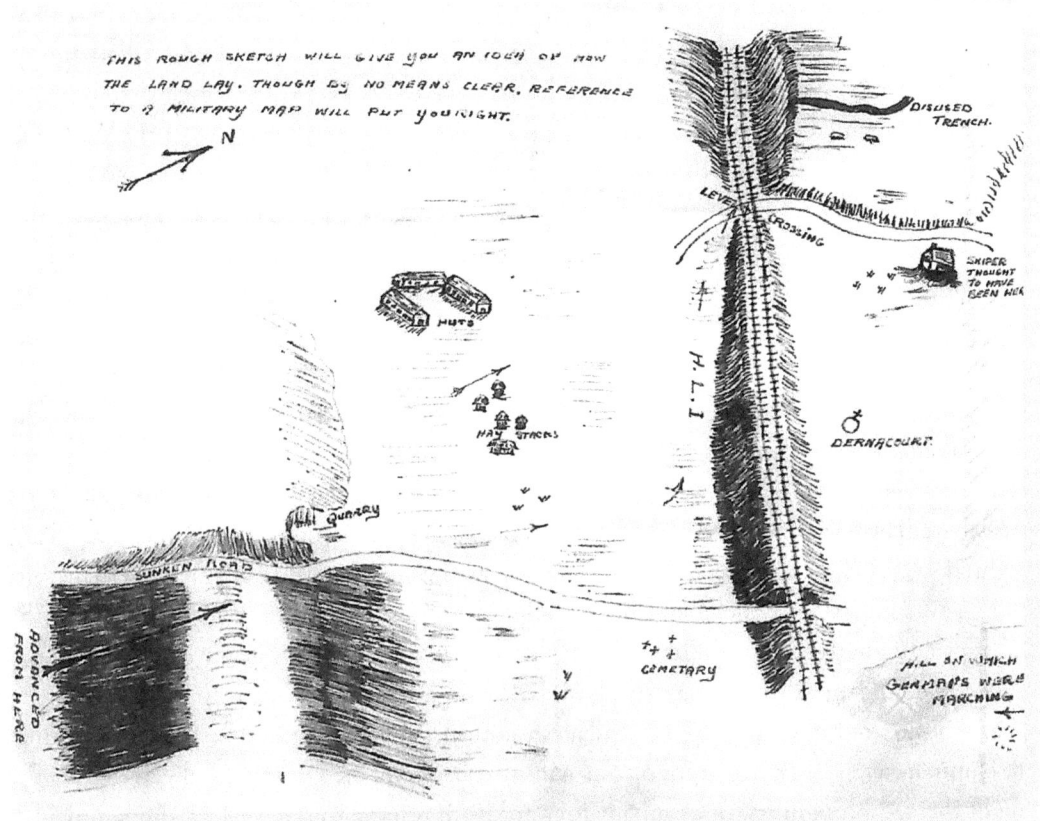

Sketch of the railway embankment and cutting outside Dernancourt village, made by Pte Ian Galloway, 45th Battalion. North is actually in the opposite direction to the arrow. (in AWM 3DRL606/251/1)

the attack succeeded the 47th was to send a company forward to assist in occupying the objective, and Colonel Imlay was allocated a company of the 45th Battalion to restore his numbers. The 45th was currently occupying the support trench that it had dug during the night on the edge of the depression in the hill above Buire, and at about 2 pm Captain Leon Ferguson's 'B' Company left the trench and advanced toward the railway. Inexplicably, the company moved off in normal artillery formation, somewhat spaced out but making no allowance for the fact that they were under direct enemy observation. They immediately came under heavy machine gun fire and shelling that killed or wounded a number of men, particularly a group who bunched up in a sunken road. Others scattered and used any scrap of cover to make their way individually down to the railway embankment. Having taken the shortest distance to the railway rather than diagonally across the hillside towards the 47th's position, the 45th troops found themselves in the British sector, somewhat west of their intended location. The company closed up and moved along the embankment to reach their position, incurring more losses on the way, when several attempted to pass the level crossing near the northern corner of Dernancourt where the village embankment transited to the cutting. A particularly dangerous German sniper was watching the gap and Lieutenant James Terras, Private Joseph Phelan and Private George Henry were all killed by his shots. Those fatalities made the company's total casualties 12 killed and 40 wounded, with one missing, from 125 who had started out[40] (C E W Bean commented that the company commander 'had possibly received no special warning of the difficulty of getting his troops down the hill,'[41] which may have been the case, but one would have thought that a special warning would not have been necessary in the circumstances). By this time, the Northumberland Fusiliers attack on the village had failed under heavy machine gun fire, precluding the backup operation. There was obviously no point in sending the 45th company back over the open, so Colonel Imlay retained them to reinforce his defensive line on the right.

By 4 pm the infantry fighting was dying down in front of Dernancourt, with the Australian line unbroken and the German effort almost spent. In front of the 48th Battalion's left, however, enemy troops were observed at 4:30 concentrating in the southern outskirts of Albert. The 48th called in the artillery to disperse these, and retreating columns were later sighted and shelled also. The notion persisted at the higher command that Dernancourt village was not strongly held, and the 47th Battalion was ordered to send a patrol into the village at 10 pm to test the German strength. The patrol was met by heavy machine gun fire that settled the question. The approach of darkness gave an opportunity for carrying parties to reach the front line with supplies and ammunition, particularly grenades, which were used to eliminate a few isolated groups of Germans that had remained near the railway. During the night the 48th brought its 'B' Company forward from reserve to relieve 'C' Company, which had borne the brunt of the assault on the unit's sector. Two Stokes mortars of the 12th LTM Battery came into the front line also, one to each battalion sector.[42] An unsuccessful enemy raid against a post of the 48th during the night concluded the fighting for 28 March, a day when four companies had stopped nine strong enemy attacks, at a cost of 28 killed[43] and 85 wounded in the 47th Battalion, and 12 killed or died of wounds and 45 wounded in the 48th,[44] as well as the 45th Battalion's losses mentioned earlier; the 46th Battalion also had a dozen casualties from enemy shelling on the reserve lines. The outstanding individual action of the day had been that of the 47th Battalion's Sergeant Stan McDougall in the early morning mist, and it would be confirmed in May that he had been awarded the VC, the first for a 12th Brigade soldier. From Recherche, Tasmania, he had enlisted in August 1915. Originally allocated to the 15th Battalion in Egypt, he had been among those transferred to the 47th when that unit was first formed, rising steadily to sergeant's rank on the Western Front, a natural fighting man. Lieutenant Mitchell of the 48th Battalion, who had captured the enemy troops that had escaped McDougall's Lewis gun and also shown dynamic leadership of his platoon during the attacks on the railway, was awarded the MC. Lieutenant Pontin of the 12th MG Company was also awarded the MC and his gunner Private Johnston the DCM for their actions in support of the Northumberland Fusiliers on the right flank. The fighting of 28 March is not usually given a particular name, overshadowed as it would be by the culminating battle on this front that took place soon afterwards on 5 April. That action became known as the Battle of Dernancourt, but 28 March could well be called the First Battle of Dernancourt.[45]

Rain fell the next day, 29 March, adding to the discomfort of the unsheltered troops in the front line, but the enemy did not renew the attack on the railway. For the next few days the Germans were regrouping and reinforcing, building up infantry and artillery resources for another attempt, their commanders rethinking the crude tactics that had seen their attacks fail with heavy losses. Activity was confined to intermittent shelling by both sides while the infantry sniped with rifles and Lewis guns at enemy movement. 'The men of the 12th Brigade, who had now been moving, marching, digging and fighting for three days and three nights almost without sleep, were in a daze of exhaustion'[46]—particularly the troops of the 47th and 48th Battalions who had beaten off the German assaults on the previous day, and the Brigade arranged to relieve those units by rotating with the reserve battalions. On the night of 29/30 March the 45th Battalion took over the right of the railway position from the 47th, and on the following night the 46th Battalion relieved the 48th in the left (northern) sector of the line near Albert.

With the pause in the fighting, the Division continued with organising the defences of its area. For the forward defence of the railway in the left brigade sector Captain David Martin, OC 12th MG Company, reconsidered the disposition of his 16 Vickers guns. The battle had been fought with six in the front line, two held further back in the quarry on the slope and the remaining eight in reserve, spread out in pairs back towards Laviéville. With the approval of Brigadier General Gellibrand, Captain Martin decided to resite the guns, moving those that were right in the front line and repositioning them further back, presumably because their original fields of fire were too restricted. With some changes also in the reserve locations, there would now be a battery of four guns in the quarry, four in two pairs along an old section of trench on the slope 350 metres to the east of the quarry, another four further up the slope above the 47th Battalion's support line, two more beyond the eastern end of the support line within the 48th Battalion's area, and the remaining two on the reverse slope of the hill near Millencourt, where they could face up the Albert road in case of an enemy breakthrough from that direction.[47] The guns were repositioned during the night 28/29 March and carrying parties distributed a total of 100,000 extra rounds of ammunition to the new positions. From their more elevated locations the guns 'commanded approaches from Albert- Méaulte and Morlancourt [south of Dernancourt]'[48] and were better placed to cover a withdrawal by the infantry if they were forced to abandon the railway position. They were also more open to observation by the enemy, however, particularly those in the quarry and the trench to its east. Those batteries were given

> instructions that neither men nor guns were to be shown in daylight except in emergency. The guns therefore were normally only mounted at night, but if the SOS signal was sent up, or if the infantry was driven back from the railway, it was the duty of the crews to accept all risks of exposure.[49]

The supporting artillery was reorganised also. Brigadier General Burgess, the CRA, had been recalled from leave and caught up with the Division on the evening of 28 March, resuming command from Lieutenant Colonel Waite, who returned to his 11th AFA Brigade. The following morning, General Burgess took over command of all field artillery covering the Division, including several British brigades. Over the next two nights three of the British units were withdrawn to refit after the strains of the retreat. That reduced the Left Group to the Division's own 10th and 11th AFA Brigades covering the 12th Infantry Brigade. The three remaining British field brigades, the 95th, 108th and 150th RFA, with batteries positioned between Laviéville and Bresle, formed the group covering the right sector, where the British troops of the 35th Division were about to be relieved by the 13th Infantry Brigade. Lieutenant Colonel Williams (10th AFA) was designated as the artillery liaison officer with the 12th Brigade and his Group HQ was co-located ('lived with') the infantry Brigade HQ. At about that time, Major Cecil Bates, the British officer who had served as brigade major of the divisional artillery since the early days in France, was posted back to the Royal Artillery. His successor was an Australian officer, Major T A J 'Jack' Playfair, who took up the duties as of 31 March; he had been attached to the staff for the previous two weeks, transferring from the 3rd Division. It was perhaps not a good time to be making a change in a key posting at artillery HQ, but Major Playfair was an experienced officer, twice wounded at Gallipoli as a subaltern with the 1st Division guns, and he proved to be an able replacement.[50]

The 4th Division's policy for the defence of the Dernancourt sector was generally one of defence in depth, and had to allow for the difficulties of the terrain while conforming to the higher command's order that a line on the forward slope of the high ground must be occupied. The railway position was regarded as the outpost line, with the second line (the main line of resistance or firing line) on the slope consisting at this stage of little more than the section of sunken road and the old practice trench occupied by two companies of the 47th Battalion on the first day. The trench, 1,000 metres from the railway, was only a straight ditch without traverses and therefore vulnerable to fire from an enemy that managed to outflank it. Further back and to the right was the shallow trench dug by the 45th Battalion over the night of 27/28 March, now unoccupied. More field works were needed to develop the defences, and the engineers and pioneers set about the task. Half of the Pioneer Battalion (two companies) was allocated to each infantry brigade, the 13th Brigade having received a warning order on 29 March to take over the right brigade sector from the 35th Division on the next night. In the 12th Brigade's sector, work was commenced on a support trench at the top of the slope, running diagonally across the Amiens-Albert road to form a further defence line in case both the outpost and main positions were lost. The new trench was designed and marked out by 12th Field Company engineers[51] and 300 pioneers carried out the major part of the digging in the chalky soil over the next three nights, 29 to 31 March, a task made more difficult by the rain that began on the first night. The engineers put out barbed wire entanglements, limited in coverage by a shortage of wire, and the pioneers finished off the traverses on 1 April. The new position, Pioneer Trench, was

> eight feet [2.4 metres] in depth and well traversed and fire-stepped, had an excellent field of fire at the top of the slope, and was so defensible that officers of the 47th in the support line wondered why it was not held as the main line of resistance and their difficult position a few hundred yards down the slope given up.[52]

There appears to have been little or no work done, however, to improve that 'difficult position,' even though it was still considered to be the main line of resistance.

More field works were needed on the right of the front, from Dernancourt to Buire, where it had been confirmed that the 13th Brigade would relieve the British troops on the night of 30/31 March. The 51st Battalion was sent in to the outpost line on the railway, completing the relief in the rain at 1:35 am at a cost of three killed and six wounded by enemy shelling. The 51st put three companies into the line and held the fourth in support, with Battalion HQ in the valley above Buire, over a kilometre back but out of enemy observation. The unit's left linked with the 12th Brigade's right (now held by the 45th Battalion) at the railway underpass and its right was in touch with the 3rd Division's left at Buire. Australian troops were now holding the line from Albert along the Ancre to Buire and thence south to the Somme. The 52nd Battalion moved up in support of the 51st, taking up positions further west in sheltered ground from a point south of Laviéville, across the main road and down the valley north of Buire. The Brigade's other two battalions, the 49th and 50th, were held back as divisional reserve, the Division being short of one brigade which would normally form the reserve. The 13th MG Company, now commanded by Captain William Cory, also went in that night to relieve their British equivalents. At first eight Vickers guns were posted along the front line and eight in supporting positions 500 metres in the rear, but on the following night four of the forward guns were moved further back to locations in the support battalion area. Having occupied what was still regarded as the outpost line, the 13th Brigade now had to establish a main line of resistance. The decision was made to site that line on the slope at an average of 300 metres to the rear of the railway. This main defence line consisted of 10 platoon strong-points designed by the engineers, with firing bays and traverses.[53] This line was open to observation and so not occupied regularly, the garrison being the reserve company of the front line battalion, initially the 51st. Those troops were held back in the Buire valley, which was also to be the location of the support line, positioned on the northern slope of the indentation, below the main road and roughly in line with Pioneer Trench on the left but not directly joined with it.[54] The support line was formed by 14 platoon posts with bays and traverses, similar to the those in the main line; the support posts do not appear to have been joined into a continuous trench as Pioneer Trench was.[55] Officers of the 13th Field Company laid out the new works. The OC, Major Reginald Carr, personally sited the new support line, the right sections of which offered a field of fire straight down the Buire valley. The far right of the support line was in the existing trenches dug by the Pioneers on 28 March, and Colonel Whitham, the 52nd CO, arranged for those works to be extended.[56] The allocated two companies of pioneers began digging the new positions on the night of the relief and completed them over succeeding nights, with the engineers and an infantry working party erecting wire entanglements in front. On 2 April two smaller parties of pioneers were sent down to the railway to begin work on driving tunnels through the embankment in both brigade sectors, to provide advanced firing posts for machine guns and Lewis guns.

The quiet period continued until the morning of 1 April when the 46th Battalion was involved in a sharp burst of fighting in the 12th Brigade sector. At 8:30 am a small German force emerged from cover and advanced against the unit's extreme left post, while the enemy artillery and mortars put down a light bombardment on the outpost and support lines elsewhere in the forward area.[57] The German infantry, a leading group estimated at between 30 and 45 men and a larger covering party following behind, immediately came under heavy fire from the keen Victorians—the CO, Lieutenant Colonel Hubert Ford, had noted that his men were in high spirits and 'eager for a fight' instead of waiting in the mud under shellfire and never seeing an enemy.[58] The first enemy group was cut to pieces, a few survivors and the covering party hastily falling back to cover except for a remnant of about 10 men who attempted to dig in close to the 46th's position. Those were taken on by Corporal John White, who collected a supply of grenades and went out alone to attack them. White killed some of the enemy group with grenades, both his own and German stick bombs that he picked up, shot two others with his rifle, and brought in a prisoner; the exploit earned him the DCM in due course. The 46th took a total of six prisoners, who were identified as marines of the 3rd Naval Division.

That evening the VII Corps heavy artillery supporting the Division, together with the field brigades' howitzers, conducted a fifteen-minute 'hurricane' bombardment of Dernancourt village, with the intention of destroying the concealment used by enemy machine gunners. Much damage was done to the buildings, but patrols sent in after dark by the 45th and 51st Battalions found that the village remained strongly held, with machine guns still active. Earlier in the day German long-range artillery had shelled 4th Division HQ at Baizieux chateau, forcing the staff into pre-prepared dugouts nearby; the next day, the HQ moved to the Beaucourt chateau, five kilometres to the west. Signal Company personnel had worked through the night to re-route the HQ communications. The 12th Brigade moved its HQ during the night of 1 April, relocating from its cellar in Laviéville to purpose-built dugouts constructed by the 12th Field Company in a quarry a short distance outside the village. The 12th Brigade began to rotate its battalions again on the night of 2 April when the 47th returned to the front line to relieve the 45th. The latter unit moved back to the reserve area near Laviéville, except for one company that took up a position in Pioneer Trench, attached to the 47th as a tactical reserve. The 47th again posted two companies on the railway line and its other two in the old trench on the slope, still referred to by the units as the support line. Arrangements were also made to relieve the 12th MG Company by the 24th Company, brought forward from their defensive line near Bresle. Major Hinton, OC 24th Company, inspected the gun positions on the night of 31 March/1 April and the relief was arranged to take place in two stages, over the nights of 2/3 and 3/4 April; the MG Battalion CO, Colonel Murray, had also visited the positions earlier.[59]

The 46th Battalion was still in the front line on 3 April when it again came under attack. At 8:15 am on 3 April a heavy barrage of artillery and mortar fire descended on the railway then lifted to reveal an enemy infantry force, estimated at 300 men, advancing towards the junction of the 46th and 47th Battalions. Sergeant Patrick Coll of the 47th was out in front of the line with a patrol and was one of the first to sight the enemy. In returning to the line to give the alarm, he was shot in the neck but refused to be evacuated with a battle about to start. A hail of fire from the rifles and Lewis guns of both units broke the attack. A few Germans got close to the embankment but Captain George Milne of the 46th led a charge that drove them back in disorder. He was later awarded the MC, and the 47th's Sergeant Coll, who was credited with killing seven of the enemy after being wounded, received the DCM. At the same time a smaller enemy force made an attempt on the 46th's left (northern) flank but was easily repulsed. The infantry action was over in ten minutes; the German force was identified as again the 3rd Naval Division. Including losses caused by the preliminary bombardment, the fight cost the 46th 19 killed and 32 wounded. In their eagerness, the troops had stood up on the railway tracks to get a clear shot at the enemy and had been fired on from both flanks by the enemy machine guns on the Albert bridge and in Dernancourt. That night the 46th Battalion was relieved by the 48th, coming in for its second stint in the firing line. The same night, 3/4 April, the 24th MG Company completed the relief of the 12th Company in the Brigade machine gun positions, the 12th moving back to the rear defence line near Bresle. On the right of the Division's sector, the 13th Brigade also rotated its front line troops on 3/4 April. After a comparatively quiet few days in the line the 51st Battalion was relieved by the 52nd coming forward from the support line, with the 51st moving back to the 52nd's original positions; the 49th and 50th Battalions remained in divisional reserve.

Up to that point the Division's approach to the defence of its sector had been to treat the line along the railway as a strongly held outpost system, 'to deny the enemy the advantage of the cover it offered, and to cramp ... any forming-up operations.'[60] The curve of the outpost line formed a salient protruding into enemy territory and the defences behind it were very roughly aligned as chords across the salient. The next line back from the railway, consisting of the various positions on the forward slopes of the spurs, was referred to as the Forward System or the Main Line of Defence. Pioneer Trench on the left and the trench segments aligned with it in the right brigade sector formed the third line or Support System. There was also a fourth line, the Laviéville Line or the Reserve System, comprising the trenches and posts running from Millencourt south-west in front of Laviéville towards Ribemont on the river.

The deployment conformed to the defence policy expressed in Divisional Order 105 issued on 29 March,[61] but late on 4 April a change of approach was decided on by General Sinclair-MacLagan. The line along the railway was now to be held as the 'main line of resistance', and if lost, reserves were to be used for its recapture.

> Thus the policy given out to the forward Brigades was the retention, at all costs, of the railway line. As, however, this line was not absolutely vital to the defence of the sector, and there was no reserve infantry brigade available, the Divisional Commander reserved his decision as to whether, in the event of the loss of the whole or part of the railway line, the divisional reserve should or should not be employed in its recapture.[62]

That comment appears in the Division's final after-action report on the Dernancourt operations, written two months later, and the *Official History* adds that if the forward line happened to be outflanked on the left the subordinate commanders were authorised to withdraw to the second line without referring to the GOC.[63] Bean also noted that it was uncertain how far down the chain of command the order penetrated (one can imagine that if it reached the diggers in the ranks, they might have referred to it as a 'two bob each way' approach) and there is no formal numbered Divisional order to that effect, but a memorandum was issued by Colonel Lavarack to the brigades on 4 April outlining the change of policy.[64] Neither of the Brigade war diaries has a record of receiving the memo, but that does not necessarily mean that its contents were not known; the gist was probably conveyed by telephone in advance of written confirmation. Two days earlier Colonel Leane's order for the 48th Battalion to move forward to the railway had included the instruction 'the line will be held at all costs,'[65] so it appears that some commanders at least may have been aware of the changed approach, even prior to 4 April.

That does not seem to have been consistent throughout the Division, however, and Bean doubted that the 13th Brigade units were operating on that basis.[66] Brigadier General Glasgow's report after the fighting noted that the original intention had been to hold the prepared positions parallel to the railway and 300 metres behind it as the Brigade's main line, but 'it was subsequently decided to hold the railway line in order to conform with the 12th [Brigade].'[67] As of 4 April, however, the two Brigades do not seem to have been operating on the same principles, indicating that the liaison between them was not as close as it could have been. The two HQs were a considerable distance apart geographically, and although they were connected by telephone closer personal contact between the staffs would have reduced the chance of inconsistencies. There may even have been an advantage in the HQs being co-located at the 12th Brigade's dugouts—although there may not have been enough space available, since the artillery group HQ was also accommodated with the 12th Brigade.[68] In any case, Colonel Whitham, the 52nd Battalion CO, intended in the event of an attack that his line on the railway should be held as long as possible, but if the garrison was forced out, it would fall back to the second line and 'fight to the last there,'[69] reinforced by the supporting 51st Battalion if necessary.

After completion of overnight unit reliefs, by the morning of 4 April the 4th Division was deployed with three battalions in the forward area and elements of three others further back in brigade reserve and supporting positions. The extreme left of the foremost line was held by one company of the 48th Battalion angled back from the railway with three platoons, facing north-east, along the south side of the gully leading down to Albert, and one platoon posted on the north side. Next on the right were two further companies of the 48th lining the railway embankment, facing east. To their right came two companies of the 47th Battalion. The left of that unit held the remainder of the northern section of embankment to the point where it transited to the cutting on the north-east of Dernancourt village; the centre was posted on the forward bank of the cutting and so was somewhat in advance of the remainder of the line; and the right was along the next embankment, in front of the village itself, as far as the railway underpass bridge. The 13th Brigade sector, which included the bridge itself, began there, with the line along the embankment occupied by three companies of the 52nd Battalion as far as Buire, where the 3rd Division's sector began. In both Brigade sectors the railway positions were studded with Lewis gun posts, and the 13th Brigade had four Vickers guns in the 52nd Battalion's front line in two pairs, near the left flank and in the centre. The remaining guns of the 13th MG Company were positioned in depth on the rising ground above the railway. Apart from two reserve weapons to the rear, the 12th Brigade had all of its machine guns (now the 24th MG Company) in intermediate positions on the heights, up to the general area of the second line of infantry positions.

The second line was not continuous, consisting in the 12th Brigade's sector of the old practice trench and nearby sunken road on the slope above the curve of the railway, manned by the other two companies of the 47th Battalion, and the line of platoon posts closer to the railway in the 13th Brigade sector, including the Edgehill CCS site. The latter posts still did not have a permanent garrison but the remaining company of the 52nd was standing by in sheltered ground further back, available to move into the posts at short notice. Pioneer Trench in the 12th Brigade sector was the strongest segment of the third line, and was manned by one company of the 48th Battalion and one of the 45th, the latter company being under the orders of the 47th. The 13th Brigade's third line consisted of trenches and platoon posts in the valley above Buire, occupied by three companies of the 51st Battalion. The 51st's remaining company was located on the reverse slope of the main height, south of Laviéville, part of a further defence line that also included the other three companies of the 45th Battalion between Laviéville and Millencourt, with three of the 46th bivouacked to the north behind the latter village. The remaining company of the 46th was located further east behind the crest, attached to the 48th as a reserve.

The day of 4 April was quiet on the 4th Division's front with intermittent rain showers. There was heavy fighting elsewhere though, as the Germans resumed their advance against Amiens astride the southern route through Villers-Bretonneux. Here the 3rd Division's detached 9th Brigade under Brigadier General Rosenthal, the former 4th Division CRA, stopped the enemy thrust at the First Battle of Villers-Bretonneux. The Germans had also built up their forces for another attempt to advance on Amiens from the Albert/Dernancourt direction, and three enemy divisions now faced the 4th Division's two brigades. A large artillery force of all calibres, including heavy trench mortars, had been assembled. The Germans now had a better idea of the Australian dispositions through ground and air observation—the previous day, the 12th Brigade had seen as many as 20 enemy aircraft flying low over the lines[70]—and had improved their plans since the attacks a week earlier. Their broad objective was to capture the crest of the high ground then wheel to their left and advance on Amiens astride the main road. It was a not a great surprise when intelligence reports came in from Corps to the Division during the night with very strong indications that the Germans intended to launch a powerful attack along the Ancre the next morning. The warning went out to the Brigades at 11:20 pm and was passed on to the units. In the 52nd Battalion's sector Colonel Whitham's first reaction was to order up his reserve, Captain William Kennedy's 'C' Company, to the forward system, the line of platoon posts 300 metres back from the railway; a company of the 51st moved forward to take their place in reserve, coming under the orders of the 52nd. It appears that the original intention was to establish a line through the Edgehill CCS site and to its east, backing up the left-centre of the railway position. Kennedy, a regular army NCO before the war, later reported that 'it was raining steadily and very dark, and I had some difficulty in locating the positions; but eventually I got settled down at about 4 am in four strong points.'[71] Kennedy's left-flank platoon was in the post just west of the CCS, leaving his line somewhat to the right of its intended location,[72] but Whitham, personally inspecting the 52nd's positions in the early hours and talking with his officers, was satisfied with the situation. The 12th Brigade did not make any immediate changes to dispositions in its sector, but the 45th and 46th Battalions were ordered to be ready to move up from reserve at short notice. By the chances of routine reliefs the 47th and 48th Battalions, which had taken the heavy attacks of 28 March, were back in the 12th Brigade's front line for what would be the next major enemy assault if the intelligence reports proved correct.

Lieutenant Colonel John Whitham CMG DSO (1881–1952), Commanding Officer 52nd Battalion, and later 49th Battalion. (AWM H00108)

As an anticipatory counter-measure, Corps had ordered the artillery of the 4th and 3rd Divisions and the 'heavies' to bombard likely enemy assembly positions starting at

7:30 am (5 April), but this program was overtaken by events. The infantry brigades ordered their firing-line battalions to send out strong dawn patrols to look for signs of activity in the enemy lines. Concentrations of German infantry were detected at several points along the front, and early reports to 12th Brigade HQ at about 5 am caused Brigadier General Gellibrand to call for assistance from his covering artillery. The 10th and 11th AFA Brigades, standing-to since 4 am, opened a slow fire at 5:15 on their standard SOS lines, generally about 500 metres beyond the railway, periodically searching back for a further 500 metres to interfere with likely assembly points. The brigadier also ordered the three companies of the 45th Battalion near Laviéville to move forward to support the 48th; their place in the Laviéville line was taken by the three reserve companies of the 46th. Ahead of the front line some of the infantry patrols now became involved in skirmishes with parties of the enemy. On the 47th Battalion's front Lieutenant Harry Taylor went out into hostile territory with a Lewis gun and emptied two magazines into a group of Germans, killing some and dispersing the remainder. The 48th Battalion's platoon on the extreme left broke up an enemy probe at about 6 am with fire from rifles and Lewis guns. There was some sharp fighting on the 52nd Battalion's front also, concentrated around the railway underpass at the north-west corner of Dernancourt. Lieutenant Leonard Boase, who had made his mark as an aggressive leader at Messines, was in charge of the platoon at this point, and he led out a small patrol that exchanged shots with an enemy force. Boase returned to report that the Germans were concentrating in the village, and his company commander, Captain Alexander Fraser (former staff captain in 4th Brigade), called on the nearby section of two 13th LTM Battery Stokes mortars under Lieutenant James Williams to open fire on the location at 5:20 am. Lieutenant Boase went out again to spot the fall of shot, and for the next hour the mortars steadily bombarded targets in the village buildings.

The Right Group field artillery had begun to fire also and the morning mist had thickened, when at 6:55 am the German artillery opened up with every weapon in their arsenal in an increasingly intense bombardment that some veterans thought was the heaviest that they had experienced since Pozières. At first most of the shelling, HE, shrapnel and gas, fell on the support and reserve lines, catching part of the 45th Battalion in the open as the unit was coming into position in support of the 48th; the 44 casualties included the RMO, Major Wade Garnett, who died of his wounds ten days later. The bombardment disrupted communications almost immediately, a situation that was to continue through the day. Most of the telephone wires from the front line and further back were quickly cut by shell-bursts. Signallers did all they could to make repairs under fire, only to find that the lines were broken again within minutes. Lieutenant Jack O'Brien's Signal Company detachment worked continuously under the bombardment to maintain communications between the brigades and Division HQ. The shell-smoke combined with the thick mist to interfere with visual signalling, and few of the courageous runners could get through the shelling unscathed to deliver written messages. Regimental stretcher bearers began carrying the first wounded to the unit RAPs from where the bearers of the field ambulances took over for the next stage of evacuation, the carry to the Hénencourt ADS. All day the bearers laboured, using the sunken lanes for cover when they could but often in the open under fire that killed or wounded a number of both bearers and patients. Among those prominent in this work were Lance Corporal Charles Smith (48th Battalion), Lance Corporal Robert Bolger (12th Field Ambulance) and Private Augustin Siebert (13th Field Ambulance).

From about 7:30 am the bombardment began to reach back into the artillery gun-line. The Australian artillery officers noted with professional interest that it was an 'area shoot,' not aimed at particular battery positions, but casualties began to mount up among the gunners. The early losses included the commander of the 37th Battery (10th AFA Brigade), 24 year old Major Terence Garling, mortally wounded by a shell splinter; Lieutenant John Harrison of the Signal Company, attached to the 10th AFA, was another killed in the bombardment. The 50th Battalion, waiting in divisional reserve, was also hit by the rear-zone shelling, losing nine dead and 43 wounded. The artillery groups, with no information getting through on particular targets, continued to fire slowly on the SOS lines. Shortly before 9 am the main weight of the enemy bombardment began to concentrate on the front line; that seemed to presage an infantry attack and the defending artillery groups responded by increasing their rate of fire. For the forward posts along the railway, the first appearance of enemy troops had come on the front of Captain Fraser's company holding the left of the 52nd Battalion line, soon after the bombardment began. A German infantry advance was stopped and driven off by Lewis and rifle fire, the defenders including Lieutenant William Reid's party of pioneers working on the tunnels through the embankment, who joined the infantry in the fight. Half an hour later the Germans resumed the attack, with a large body of infantry observed moving up the road at the edge of the village leading to the underpass. Captain Fraser tried to call in artillery support, but with the telephone lines cut he had to use flares and these went unseen in the mist. Fire support was limited to Lieutenant Williams's two Stokes mortars and those kept up a steady rain of bombs on the enemy force. Early in the fight the support legs of one mortar collapsed, but Corporal George Blake held the barrel in position with his hands and knees while the rest of the crew kept the weapon firing, wrapping sandbags around the barrel when it became too hot to hold.[73]

The 13th MG Company's left-hand pair of Vickers guns under Sergeant Walter Waters, positioned 450 metres along the railway from the underpass bridge, joined in, firing into the enemy flank and forcing the survivors to ground. At the bridge Lieutenant Boase's platoon had a concealed Lewis gun positioned on the enemy side of the railway and 'the man at the gun [Lance Corporal Walter Whitmore] quickly cleared the enemy from the road, but numbers of other were advancing out of the houses and back-gardens on either side of it.'[74] For the moment, however, the Germans could make no progress in that sector, and the 52nd's centre and right companies had not yet been attacked. The right company of the 47th Battalion, thinly spread north-eastwards from the underpass, had been assaulted at about the same time as the left of the 52nd. Another pioneer tunnelling party was in this area, 27 men under Lieutenant Reginald Pennefather, and they assisted the 47th in repelling the attack (Pennefather was among those wounded in the fighting). At one stage a group of German infantry penetrated the line between two posts but was soon ejected, and another attempt shortly afterwards was stopped also.[75] At some time between 8:30 and 9 am (accounts vary—few would have been closely checking their watches) the German bombardment shortened on to the railway positions, as the artillery observers had noticed. The enemy artillery was backed up by numerous machine guns firing across the valley on to the Australian positions on the hillside. The Germans had concentrated a number of heavy mortars in Dernancourt village and those weapons targeted the embankment from the overpass along the northern edge of the village;

> here the range to our positions on the railway line averaged 150 to 200 yards [137 to 183 metres]. The bombardment put down here was devastating and the garrison, 'A' Company 47th Battalion and a platoon of the 4th Australian Pioneer Battalion ... ceased to exist, as such, before 9 am.[76]

The enemy barrage lifted away from the front line at about 9:30 and their infantry attacked again at several points along the railway. On the right the 52nd Battalion's centre and right companies saw a German force advancing on them from the village of Ville-sur-Ancre on the far side of the river. The attack was broken up by the 52nd's rifles and Lewis guns, and the two Vickers guns in that part of the line. The 3rd Division's machine guns at Treux futher to the right joined in also. After attempting to continue their advance by short rushes, the survivors of the enemy force diverged towards Dernancourt and eventually withdrew to their starting point. Captain Claude Stubbings, commanding 'A' Company on the right, believed that this attack was only a diversion,[77] but a more determined effort was made by the enemy at the other end of the line, against the 48th Battalion's left flank.

There Captain Derwas Cumming's 'B' Company, holding the posts overlooking the gully running to Albert, was attacked by waves of German infantry. Heavy fire shattered several assaults, the surviving enemy seeking cover in the gully. The isolated platoon on the north side of the gully, posted at a ruined farmhouse, was also heavily attacked. Some of the enemy troops got to grenade-throwing range and the platoon commander, Lieutenant Herbert Shepherdson, was hit in the chest by a grenade splinter that lodged in his right lung. The tough young Yorkshireman refused to be evacuated, continuing to lead his men as they beat off every attack on the post.[78] German infantry also launched unsuccessful attacks on the remainder of the 48th's line and the left of the 47th, running north-south along the embankment and cutting, but the heaviest pressure came in the area of the underpass, on the junction between the right of the 47th and the left of the 52nd. Here the enemy mortar bombardment had shattered the 47th's right half-company at the embankment, and the few survivors of the garrison in that area now came under fierce assault from the 230th Reserve Infantry Regiment of the 50th (Prussian) Reserve Division. The German attack swept over the embankment and drove into the Australian position, killing or capturing most of the outnumbered defenders. A few men got away from the immediate area and reached the adjoining 'B' Company of the 52nd Battalion, where they reported to Captain Fraser that their line beyond the underpass bridge had been broken.

Fraser was unconvinced (Company HQ was about 200 metres away from the bridge, and the thick mist hampered visibility[79]) and he sent the men back to their position with his acting CSM, Sergeant Howard D'Alton. The group soon returned to confirm that the report was true, and the 47th men were posted with the 52nd's line. By then Lieutenant Boase's platoon at the archway had become engaged in desperate fighting as the German attack extended into their sector. The Lewis gun forward of the railway continued to hold up the enemy troops pressing up the road until it was knocked out by a mortar bomb that killed or wounded the crew; the 'Number One,' Lance Corporal Whitmore, later returned to the fight after his wound had been dressed. Another gun, further to the right on top of the embankment, was still firing but the German infantrymen were able to get close enough to begin a grenade duel. While some of his men stood up on the rails to throw, Boase collected a few others and ran down the embankment on the village side, throwing Mills bombs himself into the enemy ranks until a German grenade burst almost at his feet. He fell unconscious and apparently dead.[80] Corporal Edward Morrison, although twice wounded, continued the fight but the supply of grenades was running out. The Germans finally gained the upper hand and began pouring through the underpass and over the embankment, joining those who had broken through the 47th's position. The left of the 52nd's line was outflanked and short of ammunition, and they now came under enfilade fire from a machine gun that the Germans had set up behind the embankment. Captain Fraser sent a runner to the centre company's commander, Captain Henry Williams, advising him to fall back on the next line. The two LTM crews had expended their ammunition by now, 300 rounds or more, and Fraser instructed them to wreck the mortars and withdraw. At this point some of the 'B' Company men lost heart and ran for the rear, behind the bank of a minor road angling uphill past the village cemetery. It seems to have been this group, estimated at about twenty[81] and probably including some of the pioneers from the tunnelling party, that reached as far back as the artillery positions at Millencourt by noon.

> Lieutenant Colonel Waite of the 11th AFA Brigade, whose headquarters were in Millencourt, ran out and ordered some of these men to the front. 'But where are we to go?' they asked, 'and what are we to do?' The question was not easy to answer ... eventually, when someone was found to direct them, [they] went forward again.[82]

Fraser ordered the remainder of the company to pull back to the support line near the CCS, but delayed himself to return to his HQ and destroy his secret papers. In then trying to retreat he was pinned down in a shell hole by a German machine gun and taken prisoner. Captured with him was Sergeant William Murray, who had hung on to the last at the railway bridge in spite of wounds that were to cause his death in prison camp six weeks later. From their positions further along the bank the two Vickers guns under Sergeant Waters kept up their fire into the flank of the enemy troops, giving some cover to the retreat; 'one gun fired

1,250 rounds without stopping.'[83]

At 10:15 Captain Kennedy, commanding the 52nd's 'A' Company in the support positions 300 metres above the railway, realised that something was wrong at the front line when he noticed Australian troops retreating up the hill east of the CCS. At about the same time, a message arrived by runner from Captain Williams of the centre company ('D'), advising that the left company had fallen back and asking Kennedy's views on how to deal with the situation. It was evident that the plan for an orderly withdrawal to the support line was not working, and Kennedy saw that it would be up to him to hold the crumbling

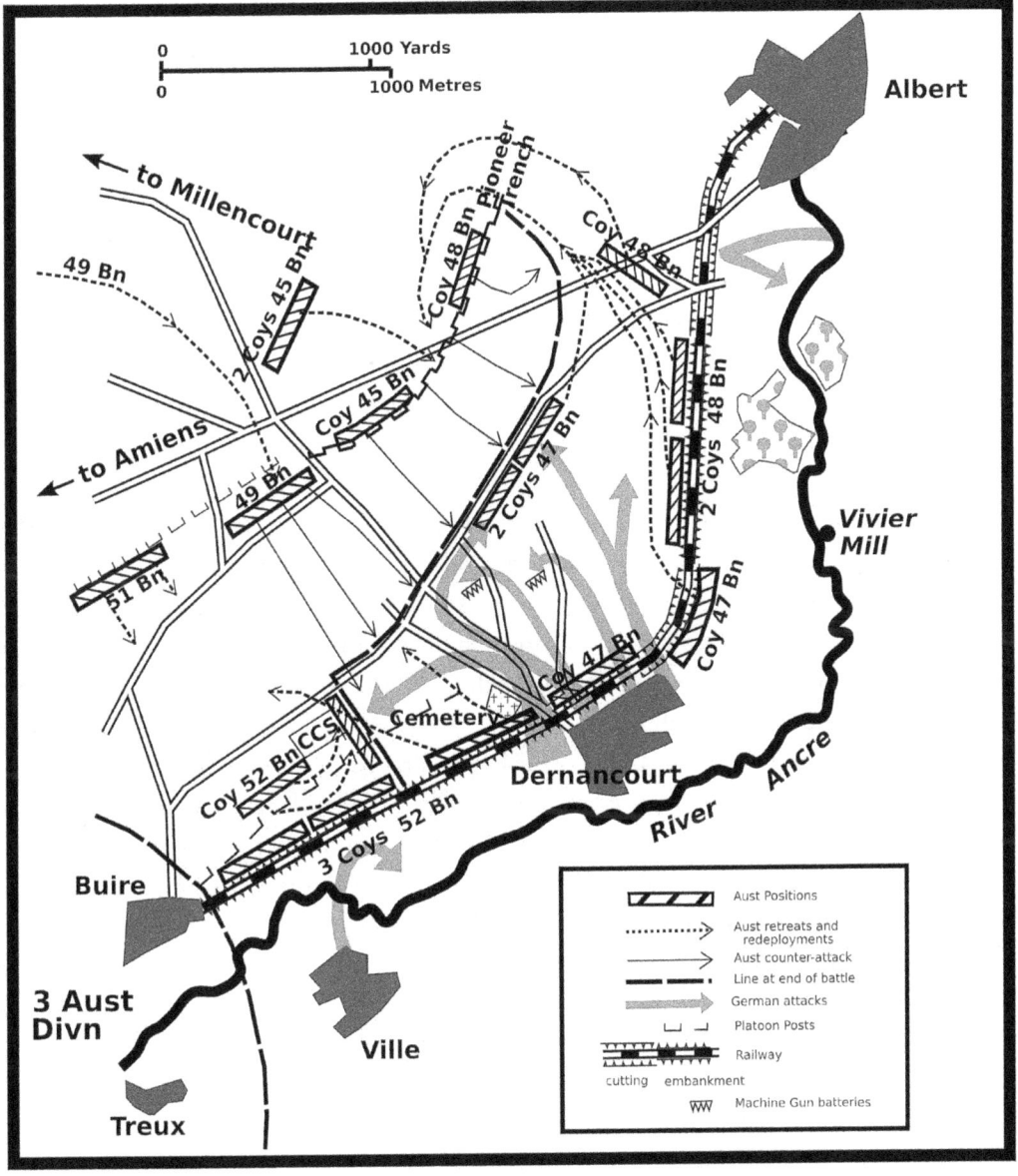

Second Battle of Dernancourt, 5 April 1918.

flank. He wasted no time, sending a reply advising Williams to hang on at the railway and ordering three of his own platoons to change front and form a defensive line up the hillside, the southernmost linking its right to 'D' Company's left at the railway, the centre in one of the prepared strong-points east of the CCS site, and the left at the north-east corner of the CCS. Kennedy kept the fourth platoon as a reserve with his HQ behind the CCS. He then sought out Captain Williams to explain the dispositions in person. Some members of the left platoon became caught up with the retreating troops and headed for the rear with them, but the remainder were rallied by the platoon commander, Lieutenant Frank Rogers, and held their ground. Kennedy himself collected a group of 20 to 30 'rather shaken' stragglers from 'B' Company [84] and deployed them in his line; they included several Lewis gun crews, adding to his available fire-power. The new line was in place by 11:15 am and ready to defend the open flank, Captain Kennedy having decisively conceived and executed his plans on the spot under great pressure.

On the other side of the breakthrough at the underpass, the centre and left of the 47th Battalion were engaged with the enemy to their front, not immediately aware of what had happened on their right, where visibility was still hampered by mist and smoke as well as variations in the ground contours. The information available to the acting commander of 'A' Company, Captain Edmund Hurd, was further restricted because he had chosen to establish his HQ at some distance from the railway—an unspecified location but said to be in a 'concrete dugout.'[85] He later stated that he was not aware of any attack on his line before noon, a claim that was contradicted by some of his men when they returned from prison camp after the war.[86] By contrast the commander of the 47th's 'B' Company on the left, Captain Charles Young, described by C E W Bean as a 'hard wiry wizened little Queensland pastoralist,'[87] was fighting in the front line with his men. On the far side of the valley, the Germans brought up two field guns which opened fire at close range on the 47th's position, and Young took a rifle himself to snipe at the gun-crews. The situation deteriorated rapidly. As soon as the attacking Germans had gained the embankment, they were already in the rear of the platoons posted on the forward bank of the cutting, and now the enemy dragged a field gun through the gap to the near side of the railway and opened fire on the flank and rear of the 47th's line. The pressure was too great, and Captain Young ordered a retreat northwards across the rear of the 48th Battalion's position. He seems to have originally intended to form a flank facing south and then launch a counter-attack in conjunction with the 48th,[88] but the enemy penetration had already made too much progress and Young, with only one unwounded officer (Lieutenant Taylor) to assist him, had his hands full controlling the withdrawal. The two Stokes mortars behind the line, each of which had fired 200 rounds into the advancing enemy, were in danger of being overrun also; the crew of the left-hand gun wrecked their weapon and retreated with the infantry, but the other mortar was knocked out by a German shell that killed or wounded all of the crew.[89]

In the centre of the line a strong force of German infantry, evidently following a preconceived plan, advanced directly from the breakthrough point against the two batteries of machine guns on the slope and the 47th Battalion's support line beyond. The 24th MG Company crews, on their second night manning the four guns each in the quarry and the nearby trench, had dismounted their weapons at dawn in accordance with standing orders for those posts. The early German shelling, followed by a stream of machine gun fire that 'was clipping the grass all around the edges'[90] of the quarry position, kept the gunners' heads down until after 10 am when the fire eased off. Observers then saw German infantry moving on the slope below, but before the guns could be set up shots were fired from the rear and the gunners found themselves covered by the rifles of an enemy squad lining the edge of the quarry. Those Germans had apparently used the sunken road running east of the quarry to approach unseen in the mist and get behind the position, and the gunners could only surrender. The other four-gun battery in the trench had also been taken in identical fashion, and most of the 12th Brigade's machine guns had been lost without firing a shot. Four other Vickers guns west of the support line had no field of fire, blocked by their own retreating infantry, and only Lieutenant Tom Jack's two guns on the left above the 48th Battalion's position remained in action. The German unit had carried out a well-planned subsidiary operation that had worked perfectly, the infantry timing their approach to arrive at the objective as the covering fire eased. In a sense most of the 24th MG Company personnel probably owed their lives to their delay in getting their guns mounted—if they had managed to set up for firing it was unlikely that the surrounding Germans would shown the forbearance to take them prisoner, but would have simply shot them down. Strangely, the Germans seem to have made no attempt to use the guns themselves—their infantry was already in possession of the ground in front of the quarry battery, but one or more of the captured guns in the trench to the east could have been in a position to fire down into the backs of the Australians further around the curve of the railway line. Later in the battle hostile fire was noticed coming from an automatic weapon in the area, but it was identified as either a captured Lewis gun or a German light Maxim. Although there were differences between the mechanisms of the German Maxim and the British Vickers they were from the same family of weapons, but it seems that the German force did not have anyone who could operate the Vickers—certainly the Australians, and the BEF in general, were trained to use Maxims and routinely used captured guns against their former owners. It may have been just as well that the guns were not set up on their tripods, loaded and ready to fire; is hard to imagine that the Germans would not have at least tried to use them in that case.

    The powerful enemy thrust through the centre of the position now closed on the 12th Brigade support line, the two companies of the 47th Battalion in the old practice trench halfway up the slope. That position had been heavily hit by the German bombardment during the morning, both companies suffering numerous casualties—as early as 8:30 am 'C' on the right, under Lieutenant William Goodsall as acting commander, reported only 24 men left unwounded out of 108, with all of its officers hit, including Goodsall himself, wounded in the back but remaining on duty. Captain Symons' 'D' Company on the left had lost 74 of 124.[91] The layout of the trench, no more than a ditch without protective traverses, would have contributed to the high rate of loss. It is puzzling that no attempt seems to have been made to improve it in the preceding week, particularly considering that it was originally intended to be the main line of resistance. The Pioneer Battalion had had a heavy schedule since arriving in the sector, but they could have been assigned to work on the trench ahead of the embankment tunnels, and in any case the infantry was routinely used for digging earthworks. Probably Brigade HQ and the 47th Battalion, which had spent the most time occupying the position, assumed that the machine gun batteries would stop anything in front of the trench, but events had turned out differently.

The reported casualties from shelling caused Colonel Imlay to send a platoon from his attached 45th Battalion company forward from Pioneer Trench, that group also taking losses on the way down. At 11 am the men on the left of the support line opened fire on German infantry who were observed crossing to the near side of the embankment below them; the 47th's garrison on that flank included the hero of 28 March, Sergeant Stan McDougall, again behind a Lewis gun that he made expert use of. The fire caused those enemy troops to seek cover but within minutes the right flank was assailed by more German infantry with machine guns, coming up the slope past the quarry and firing in enfilade into the Australian position, fire made more deadly by the lack of traverses. The recently arrived platoon from the 45th was sent across to form a flank guard with Lieutenant Goodsall's company on the right, but the platoon quickly lost 12 men and was forced back to the dubious cover of the trench. With the pressure increasing on the right and the Germans now closing in on the left as well, the defence rapidly collapsed. There was some confusion and perhaps some panic as casualties mounted up. Goodsall had decided on a withdrawal to the left but he was overruled by his senior Captain Symons, who insisted that the position must be held to the last. Goodsall accordingly tried to hold on with his remnant, but

> no defence was possible; the enemy could only be seen by lying out in the open, which meant certain death, and men were being quite uselessly killed; the dead and wounded of the 47th now lay everywhere underfoot ... [the officers] ... decided to withdraw their men through Captain Symons' position. To their horror they found the Germans holding it, Symons and the survivors of his men having already gone.[92]

It appears that Symons had been badly shaken by a close shell-burst, and if so his judgement may have been impaired.[93] With the Germans now all around them the remnants of 'C' Company had no option but surrender; those taken prisoner included the commander of the 45th Battalion platoon, Lieutenant Joshua Allen, brother of Major 'Tubby' Allen. Some of the survivors of 'D' Company were also captured but others, including Captain Symons, got back to Pioneer Trench, the third defence line. It appears that a few men held on a little longer on the extreme left of the support line before retreating—Sergeant McDougall was in that area, and he was later decorated for his determined Lewis gun work. So too was Private 'Charlie' Shang, who had been operating as an observer and runner through the morning then took over a Lewis and stayed to the last covering the retreat.[94] Beyond the left flank of the position, the two remaining Vickers gun crews found themselves coming under fire from the right and German infantry were getting around them on three sides. Lieutenant Jack nevertheless managed to extricate his men with the guns, tripods and ammunition and re-establish them in Pioneer Trench.

Those developments had occurred between 11:30 and midday, four hours or more after the first shots, but the continuing disruption to communications meant that it was only a short time earlier that any information had begun reaching the higher commanders. Colonel Leane, the 48th Battalion CO, had been receiving reports from 10:30 of a serious situation developing on his right, with either the 13th Brigade or the 47th Battalion or both believed to be falling back. At 47th Battalion HQ Colonel Imlay, having already sent a platoon of his attached 45th Battalion company to the support trench, now had a runner return from that position to inform him that it was occupied by the enemy. Leaving his HQ to see for himself, Imlay noticed troops of the 52nd Battalion retreating to his right and assumed that the breakthrough had come through that unit's front at the railway—unaware that the right of the 47th had been virtually wiped out and the left was withdrawing northwards along the railway. Imlay formed a party from his HQ details and sent it to back up the support line, and also ordered the 45th company to feed its remaining platoons forward. The other three companies of the 45th had earlier moved up to positions behind the crest in support of the 48th. Colonel Leane of the latter unit had already sent two platoons from his own reserve to reinforce his left near Albert. Shortly afterwards, apprehensive that the reported enemy breakthrough would develop into a strong thrust against the centre of the position, he sent orders to Major Allen commanding the 45th to move his unit forward and to the right, re-occupying the shallow trenches that the 45th had dug on the first night in the sector. That position, at the top of the Buire valley and slightly on the reverse of its southern slope, seemed well-placed to block an enemy coming up from the railway. Before Allen could organise the movement, however, he received a verbal order from 12th Brigade HQ to instead move two companies to Pioneer Trench and leave the other where it was as a reserve (the telephone lines between battalion and brigade were still working, through the efforts of signaller teams repairing the lines under fire). Information was beginning to trickle through to Brigade, and General Gellibrand evidently though it advisable to strengthen the garrison in Pioneer Trench, which had been denuded to reinforce the 47th in the support line. Allen thought that Leane's idea was the better one, resulting in an exchange that apparently still rankled 15 years later—in a 1933 letter to Leane, Allen recalled that 'I remonstrated with Babe Norman, Brigade Major, and was curtly told to carry out the orders of the Brigade commander.'[95] It is not clear whether or not Norman went to the brigadier for the final decision, but Allen resignedly obeyed the order and got his two companies into Pioneer Trench with no losses, the men making their way in small groups of six at a time.

Down at the railway the 47th Battalion's surviving forward troops were still being forced back by the swarming Germans. The Battalion intelligence officer, Lieutenant George Reid, and his scout sergeant, William Brown, had made their way from Battalion HQ to the front line and were helping to cover the retreat with Lewis guns. The pressure was continuous and the two 48th Battalion companies on the right and centre were now in danger of being cut off as well. Captain Frederick Anderson, the senior 48th officer in the area, gave the order to withdraw and both units fought rearguard actions as they fell back up the hill, seeking the refuge of Pioneer Trench. The last man out of the 48th's position was Lance Corporal Wilfred Thomas, in charge of his platoon after its officer had been wounded. Thomas organised his surviving men in an orderly withdrawal before going back himself, carrying a wounded man. The retreat reached Lieutenant George Mitchell's platoon of the 48th's reserve company, posted in an intermediate position near what had been the left flank. Mitchell, who had only 12 men with him, had been following the progress of the mist-shrouded battle by sound and had become increasingly alarmed. Now as the retreating men began moving past his position he posted his platoon to give covering fire. To Mitchell's right a small party of the 47th under a young sergeant (Eric Watson[96]) made a stand, lying down and firing steadily at the advancing Germans. All died where they lay. The firing reached a crescendo, the noise so great that, according to Mitchell, his men could not hear their own rifles when they fired and only knew from the recoil that they had got their shot away.[97] A number of Mitchell's men had also been hit by the time he at last received permission to withdraw, his reliable Lewis gunner, Private William Connaughton, firing off his last drum to cover the retreat. The usually unsentimental Mitchell found himself in tears at the thought that an Australian force had given ground, but his mood improved as his 'remnant of a remnant' reached Pioneer Trench: 'to my delighted eyes there stretched a well-sited, new dug trench lined with capable-looking Australians.'[98] By then the German force was losing its impetus, and there does not appear to have been any organised assault on this final defensive position. Colonel Leane sent his second-in-command, Major Montague Brearley, forward to organise the new line, occupied as it was by mixed elements of the 48th and 47th Battalions and the two companies of the 45th that had moved down shortly before.

It was 1:30 pm by then, and for all of that time the 48th's 'B' Company on the extreme left had been fighting almost a private battle against the Germans pressing forward from the direction of Albert. The company held its ground for another two hours before continuing enemy pressure on his now-open right flank compelled Captain Cumming to order a retirement. First he had to get word of the movement to the British troops beyond the Amiens road to his left, but the signallers could not attract their attention. A signaller from the platoon on the north of the gully, Private Frederick Tregoweth, volunteered to take a message in person across 200 metres of open ground swept by enemy machine gun fire. He was hit three times but struggled on, finally crawling to within 50 metres of the British position. Two Tommies ran out and carried him in, and shortly the British signallers flagged acknowledgement. 'B' Company then withdrew in good order and reached the vicinity of Pioneer Trench about 4 pm, the left flank platoon swinging around to the north to get clear before making their way back. Not until then did the badly-wounded platoon commander, Lieutenant Shepherdson, go to the rear for treatment. In the 13th Brigade's sector Captain Kennedy's company of the 52nd Battalion continued to hold its posts facing the axis of the enemy penetration, the 800-metre gap that the Germans had torn in the Australian line. Kennedy's men were coming under heavy fire from machine guns and artillery that caused a number of casualties, but for the moment there was no direct infantry assault. The 13th MG Company's two pairs of Vickers guns above the Edgehill CCS site were heavily in action also. The two easternmost guns were heard firing until 1:30 pm, when they were cut off and captured by enemy infantry with the loss of eight men reported missing.[99] The other two, under Lieutenant Richard Tuckett, were almost surrounded also, but Tuckett managed to extricate one of the guns and set it up in a new position; his crews lost three killed and eight wounded in the retreat.

By noon enough information had come through to the higher commanders for it to be apparent that at least part of the line along the railway had been lost, but for some time the true situation remained obscure. Partly because of inaccurate information from the 47th Battalion, under the impression that its right company was still in place at the railway, 12th Brigade HQ at first believed that the breach in the line was confined to the 13th Brigade sector and reported to Division accordingly. That information, passed on by Division, came as an unpleasant surprise to 13th Brigade HQ, which had received no reports from its own units at that stage. Brigadier General Glasgow and Major General Sinclair-MacLagan conferred by telephone, and the decision was reached that the 13th Brigade would 'restore the situation at once by working along the railway line.'[100] At 12:50 orders were issued to the 52nd Battalion to carry out the operation. The message took an hour to reach Colonel Whitham,[101] who informed his company commanders but was concerned, correctly, that Brigade was unaware that the enemy had penetrated well beyond the railway and the 47th had been driven back. He sought clarification before committing his unit, but was soon informed that the orders were now cancelled. Division HQ had become aware that the situation in the centre was more serious than was first thought, and General Sinclair-MacLagan now decided to launch a large-scale counter attack with fresh troops. The 49th Battalion had earlier been moved up from divisional reserve behind Bresle to a position in trenches between Laviéville and the Amiens road, and that unit, nominally restored to 13th Brigade control, would be used as the principal force in the proposed counter-attack (the 50th Battalion moved forward to take up the 49th's original position near Bresle). The initial orders sent to Lieutenant Colonel James Denton, the 49th CO, were so brief that for some time he remained unaware of the situation at the front line and the intended role of his battalion. The 49th's orders were being passed through 12th Brigade HQ, located nearby on the other side of Laviéville, the two Brigade HQs being still connected by telephone. The proposed operation required considerable co-ordination between brigades and units, with artillery support to be arranged if possible. All of this took time, and before the counter-attack could be launched the Germans had completed their regrouping and resumed the offensive, this time directed south-west against the left flank of the 52nd Battalion.

The artillery groups, anxious to play their part in the battle, had been frustrated all day by the lack of information from the forward area. The gun positions were themselves under continued shelling from the enemy artillery, and when retreating infantry reached the Left Group's gun-line at midday it appeared that the batteries might soon come under attack themselves.

> But the guns-crews were making the battle their own, and they fought as if they were in the front line. When, after the arrival of the withdrawing infantry, the gun-teams came up at the gallop, ready to pull out the guns, the gunners themselves waved them away with a shower of rough jests. It was known that the orders given to the division were that this crest was to be held to the last.[102]

The gunners could only continue firing on their SOS lines in the absence of any definite information, with the howitzers bombarding Dernancourt village from 11:30 am. Artillery liaison officers were stationed with infantry battalion HQs, but were prevented by cut telephone lines and casualties to runners from maintaining a regular flow of information to their batteries, information that may not have been entirely accurate in any case.[103] By around 2 pm it was fairly certain that the line on the railway had been lost and the 12th Brigade troops had fallen back at least as far as the support line. The Left Group guns then put down a barrage along a new SOS line about 500 metres back from the railway, 'after much seeking and enquiry ... and satisfied our infantry.'[104] At 2:30, with improved visibility, some of the guns were switched to shelling observed enemy movement and the approaches to Dernancourt, while others pounded the lost positions in the quarry and the nearby sunken road. The heavy artillery had earlier been called in to shell the village itself and some of the 3rd Division's guns were assisting as well, firing in enfilade along the railway. Word of the proposed counter-attack came through at 3 pm, and although there were still few details the artillery officers worked out a barrage plan to support the attack.

The company of the 45th Battalion attached to the 47th had already sent one of its platoons to reinforce the support line, only for it to be lost when the Germans took the position. Lieutenant Stuart Perry, the acting company commander, following his orders from 47th HQ had sent a second platoon down, but those troops had taken casualties from heavy enemy fire and the survivors were pinned down short of the support trench, as were the other two platoons when Perry tried to bring them forward also. Unsure of what was happening in front of him, Perry was holding back the rear platoon and considering his next move when a more senior officer, Captain William Adams, arrived to take over command of what remained of the company (Adams had been in Pioneer Trench leading one of the other companies, but when its substantive OC arrived on the field from leave and resumed command, Major Allen sent Adams forward to assist his less experienced colleague[105]). Observing with binoculars, Adams saw Australian troops being escorted away as prisoners by German guards and realised that the ground to the front had been lost. More enemy troops were moving up the slope towards his position. Some of these were apparently wearing British helmets, but once Adams had positively identified the men as German he decided to hold his ground and delay the enemy advance as long as possible. There were only 14 men in the 45th group, with no real cover, but they opened a heavy fire on the Germans and sent them to ground. The one Lewis gun with the group was particularly effective. The gunner, Lance Corporal William Bannister, could not get a field of fire with the gun in its usual position on the ground so he stood up to fire the weapon, with his mate, Private Alfred Squires,[106] supporting the barrel on his shoulder. Standing in full view of the enemy, Bannister was hit three times during the fight, and when he could no longer continue Squires took over the gun. After two hours of fighting the Germans had succeeded in bringing up a machine gun to fire in enfilade from Adams' right flank, and he decided that it was time to pull back. Only eight men were now left on their feet, Lieutenant Perry being among the wounded, and these fell back one at a time to Pioneer Trench; Adams and Squires with the Lewis gun stayed until last to cover the retreat. Captain Bill Adams, who was only 21, had already proved to be a tower of strength for the 45th during its period in the sector—C E W Bean wrote that 'he had done the work of a superman'[107]—and his part in the battle was not yet finished.

It was 2 pm by then, and something of a pause settled over the battlefield as both sides regrouped and organised their next move. The German units that had taken the embankment in the 13th Brigade sector had moved on to capture the area around the village cemetery north of the railway (a German regimental commander, leading his men in the front line, was mortally wounded in the fighting). Part of the enemy force now redeployed to form a front facing south-west and extending up the hill, with its left on the railway, in position to advance against the left flank of the 52nd Battalion. The movement began at 4 pm and quickly exerted heavy pressure on Captain Kennedy's 'C' Company guarding the flank. The Germans brought up machine guns and a field gun in close support of their advance, and Kennedy's left and centre forward platoons were gradually forced back from the CCS site on to his headquarters trench. From there the Lewis gunners and riflemen maintained fire on the enemy to their front and succeeded in stopping the advance from that direction, but the company came under heavy fire from up the hill to the north, where part of the German line had reached a position overlapping the company's left. Kennedy switched most of his men's fire to that direction, and although he could not drive the enemy away from their flanking position he managed to keep them pinned down, while one platoon kept up the frontal defence. Kennedy was in desperate need of reinforcements, however. Before noon Colonel Whitham had ordered his attached company of the 51st Battalion forward to join Kennedy, but for reasons that remain unclear those troops had only gone forward a short distance and had stopped on the southern slope of the Buire depression, well back from their intended position.[108] It was only when urgent messages from Kennedy got through to Battalion HQ in the late afternoon that the CO realised that the original reinforcements had not arrived.

Another 51st company had been attached to the 52nd in place of the first and Colonel Witham now ordered those troops forward, but again the attempted reinforcement miscarried. At the railway line, enfilade machine gun fire had forced Kennedy's right flank platoon back along the line for 300 metres, and the centre and right companies came under fire from flank and rear. Those companies pulled back from the railway, initially in disorganised fashion, but were able to re-establish themselves with the right flank remaining anchored on the railway at Buire and still in touch with the 3rd Division troops there. The centre found cover in some of the pre-constructed support posts above the railway and the left extended north-east towards Kennedy's position. A weak German attack across the river from Ville-sur-Ancre was quickly stopped by fire from the 3rd Division and danger on the 13th Brigade's right dissipated. At about 5 pm Captain Stubbings ordered the right and centre companies to advance again and re-occupy their original positions at the railway (Captain Williams, the other company commander, had been seriously wounded) and the men began to move forward a few at a time. At that point the second company of the 51st intended to reinforce Captain Kennedy reached the vicinity and became caught up in the advance—it (particularly the officers) '[seemed] to have forgotten all its instructions and joined in with the one piece of movement which it saw and went with Stubbings to the railway embankment.'[109] Kennedy, still unreinforced, continued to face the main danger, the strong German infantry force pushing south-west beyond the CCS site and outflanking him on the left.

Relief was finally at hand, however. The staffs of the Division and the two brigades, conferring by telephone, had now settled on plans for the counter-attack. The broad intention was for the 49th Battalion to drive through the gap between the brigades, joined by elements of the 12th Brigade troops from Pioneer Trench. Major General Sinclair-MacLagan's orders were that the final objective was to be the re-capture of the original positions on the railway, an objective that his subordinates had their doubts about. Given the current situation as it was understood, it appeared to be unrealistic; C E W Bean felt that the General's decision was made under pressure from above.[110] A section of four British 'Whippet' tanks (a light tank armed with machine guns, somewhat faster than the heavy tanks) had been made available for the attack, and those were another point of contention. The GOC urged that the tanks be used in direct support of the infantry attack but the 12th Brigade senior officers, remembering Bullecourt, strongly opposed any plan that depended heavily on tanks. The most that they would accept was to bring in the tanks to follow up the attack and protect the infantry while they dug in at the objective. General Sinclair-MacLagan gave way on that point but insisted on the recapture of the railway. Between themselves, the senior 12th Brigade officers could not see that the objective could reasonably be achieved in their sector of the battlefield; Brigadier General Gellibrand 'rang up [Lieutenant Colonel] Leane, [who] told him it was impossible to push down to the railway. "Yes, I know it is," said Gelly.'[111] They decided to restrict the objective to the sunken road that ran diagonally across the slope and the support line. The 12th Brigade leaders seem to have had no qualms about circumventing higher authority in that manner; the situation was slightly different in the 13th Brigade sector, where the defenders had fallen back for a considerably shorter distance and still retained a foothold on the railway. 12th Brigade HQ being located closest to the 49th's advanced position, orders were co-ordinated through that point, and at 1:30 pm Colonel Denton received an order to move his unit further forward to a potential jumping-off position. That was a line 500 metres ahead of the Amiens road, along the road on the reverse slope at the head of the Buire depression, with the left on the Millencourt–Dernancourt road adjacent to the western end of Pioneer Trench, which was occupied by the 45th Battalion. Denton's right flank was open, although one of the 51st Battalion's stray companies was in the vicinity. The 50th Battalion again moved up behind the 49th, taking up a reserve line astride the Amiens road facing east.

By 3:15 the 49th's movement had been completed and touch established between the left of that unit and the right of the 45th, and at 4:00 the 49th CO received an operation order from 13th Brigade for the actual counter-attack—'up to this time I had no instructions that my Battalion was to attack,' noted Colonel Denton.[112] The attacking line would be prolonged on the left by 12th Brigade units, the two reasonably intact companies of the 45th Battalion and the remnants of the 47th. The 48th Battalion holding the extreme left, facing east, provided supporting fire but was not required to advance, although Colonel Leane, as the senior officer in the forward area, directed the overall effort of the 12th Brigade; the 48th would maintain links with the advancing line. The timing was left to Colonel Denton, who called in his company commanders for briefing, and at 4:45, satisfied that his unit and the rest of the force was fully deployed and ready for action, he advised that the attack would jump off in 30 minutes. The artillery was notified and the Left Group requested to put down a barrage in support—short notice, but the task that had been anticipated by the artillery officers and some preliminary planning had already been done.[113] Other support was not as prompt. A few minutes before Zero, a message was sent to Colonel Denton through the 48th Battalion that 'four whippet tanks will assist you as soon as you have gained your objective,'[114] but nothing was seen of these (they finally turned up too late to play any part in the battle, thereby confirming the 12th Brigade's negative view of tanks in general). The artillery was operating under difficulties. The 10th and 11th AFA Brigades had lost 89 casualties to German shelling during the day, 22 of them killed or died of wounds, as well as having four guns put out of action.[115] Some pieces had only two men to operate them from the usual crew of six, and the battery officers joined in serving the guns.[116] Several officers and NCOs had continued on duty in spite of wounds, among them Lieutenants Gordon Linsley and John Pidcock, and Sergeants Harry Cole and Basil Henderson; the latter had remained with his gun in spite of a shattered elbow until his battery ceased fire, and he was about to be evacuated when an SOS call came in and he returned to the fray. The rate of fire was inevitably slowed and the effectiveness of the barrage reduced, but the gunners did what they could—even if they had been at full strength, two field brigades were a small enough force for an adequate barrage. For six minutes from Zero the barrage fell on the line of the lost support positions, the howitzer batteries concentrating on the quarry, before lifting 500 metres on to the SOS line established earlier in the day, then again on to the railway[117] (the Group fired 12,300 rounds during the day's fighting). The right segment of the barrage lines extended well into the 13th Brigade's sector and was probably fired by some of the guns in the Right Group, the three RFA brigades supporting the 13th Brigade, which throughout the day had been engaging targets requested by the infantry or identified by artillery observers.[118]

At 5:15 the Australian line went forward down the hill, the 49th Battalion advancing over the crest of the depression and the 45th and 47th climbing out of Pioneer Trench to join them; the force included the few survivors of the 45th's 'C' Company under Captain Adams, who took it upon himself to get information back and forth between the front line and Battalion HQ. As the troops came into view of the Germans ahead, they were taken under heavy fire, 'a machine gun barrage like a blast from a furnace,' as Captain Archibald Gledhill, in command of the 49th's left company, later described it,[119] from numerous enemy machine guns positioned in the captured ground and across the valley. The attackers lost heavily, particularly in the two centre companies of the 49th, the most exposed to the fire; both company commanders, Captains John Willenbrock and James Atkinson, were among those killed, as were five of their platoon commanders. The thinning ranks kept going, quickening the pace to a charge when they were close enough to the enemy positions. The German infantry was driven back in disorder all across the battlefield, but continuing heavy machine gun fire eventually forced the Australian left and centre to ground short of the support line positions, an advance of 500 to 700 metres from their start line. On the right, however, Lieutenant James Graham's company of the 49th swept on to the area of the Edgehill CCS, where Captain Kennedy of the 52nd and his depleted company were still hanging on under extreme pressure. At first Kennedy had feared that the approaching troops were yet more Germans, but he soon realised that reinforcements were arriving at last and the fire on his front was slackening. The German force facing Kennedy suddenly found that they had opposing troops coming down on their right flank, and turned their weapons in that direction. The 49th troops were slowed by the fire but steadily continued their advance, and by 6:30 the Germans were in full retreat to the railway, pursued by fire from the 52nd positions.

That proved to be the final infantry action of the day—the opposing forces had fought each other to a standstill. The powerful German assault had taken a large chunk out of the original Australian line, but in doing so the Germans had spent their collective energy and had nothing left to carry on to their overall objective, the crest of the rise and the road to Amiens. The 4th Division staff, when they had time later to assess the battle, saw the attack as an example on a small scale of the enemy's tactics employed since their great offensive opened on 21 March, beginning with an intense bombardment on a particular point, followed by a strong infantry force breaking through at that point, then rolling up the flanks on either side of the penetration.[120] The Germans had succeeded with the first stage—C E W Bean rightly noted that it had been an outstanding achievement by the 230th Regiment of the 50th Prussian Reserve Division[121]—but were then foiled by the determined resistance of the Australian units on the flanks against heavy odds. The enemy attack was held up just long enough for the counter-attack to be launched, which although it could not restore the original line had stabilised the front with the Germans gaining no real advantage from their efforts. The salient had been flattened out but the chord was held. The 4th Division now occupied an irregular line across the hill from a point in front of Albert down to the railway at Buire. The 48th Battalion held the left, that unit now forming a north-south line across the Amiens road facing Albert, with its right flank having swung forward from Pioneer Trench. The new front continued through the 47th, 45th and the left of the 49th, those elements stopped down the slope a little short of the original support line. Next was the right of the 49th in the CCS area near the 52nd's left, with that part of the line facing north-east across the slope, and the right of the line formed by the centre and right of the 52nd, now back on the railway position. Touch had been maintained with the left of the 3rd Division at Buire. There was a gap between the left and right companies of the 49th, where the centre of that unit had suffered heavily from the German machine guns, and another near the CCS. After dark the two previously-misdirected companies of the 51st Battalion were sent in to fill those gaps. The 13th Brigade retained those dispositions for the time being, but in the 12th Brigade sector the 46th Battalion was sent forward during the night to take over the new front, where the troops had been digging in to make a line of outpost positions. The 46th, close to full strength, relieved the depleted and weary 45th, 47th and 48th, those units moving back to Pioneer Trench to rest and reorganise. The 12th Brigade also brought forward 300 troops from its left-out-of-battle nucleus to fill the gaps in the ranks. The 4th Pioneer Battalion was placed under 12th Brigade orders and brought forward to man the Laviéville-Millencourt reserve line, with two companies moving further up before dawn to take over support positions from the 45th—the first time in their history that the 4th Pioneers had been tasked with holding trenches as infantry. The two tunnelling parties in the original front line had also earned considerable credit for their fighting alongside the infantry in the early stages of the battle, although the Pioneer leaders regretted that there had been few opportunities for infantry training in the past, the unit having usually stayed in the line when the main body of the Division had gone out.[122] With those dispositions the troops settled in to await developments. The remaining wounded were moved to the rear area for treatment; Corporal William Cooper of the 49th Battalion worked tirelessly organising the unit stretcher bearers to bring out the 49th's many casualties. The 13th Field Ambulance reported that the backlog of cases at the Warloy MDS had been cleared by 11 pm, by which time about 1,000 patients had passed through.[123]

It was expected that the Germans would renew their attacks in the morning, but 6 April proved to be uneventful apart from a heavy exchange of artillery fire. That night the 52nd Battalion was relieved by the 50th on the right of the 13th Brigade sector, while despite its losses the 49th Battalion continued to hold the line on the Brigade's left. The Division now had its only two reasonably-fresh infantry units in the front line with the weakened 49th, while the other units, all more or less affected by the strain and losses of twelve hours' desperate fighting, were still in the forward area as supports. The situation supported General Sinclair-MacLagan's natural pessimistic outlook, and he feared that his troops would not be able to withstand an attack by fresh enemy forces;

> 'The fighting has been harder than we realise,' he said to the corps commander on the telephone. 'I don't think, if we are hammered by artillery, we shall be able to hold the line.' General Congreve asked where the Germans were going to get fresh divisions from; the information from the few captured prisoners showed that they had used up the only three that had been available.[124]

Reinforcements were now arriving in the sector, however, in the shape of the 2nd Division coming down from the north, and it was agreed that the 4th Division should be relieved in the front line by the 2nd. Troops of the 6th Brigade took over the line from the 12th Brigade on the night of 6/7 April and the 13th Brigade was relieved by the 7th Brigade on the following night. The brigade groups moved back down the Amiens road to the area of Lahoussoye, Pont-Noyelles, Bussy-les-Daours and Corbie, between the Ancre and Hallue rivers. Divisional headquarters moved to Allonville, just outside of Amiens, on 8 April, by which time all units had been relieved by their 2nd Division equivalents or were in the process, with the usual exception of the artillery. The gunners remained in the line as a group covering the 2nd Division infantry, with the CRA, Brigadier General Burgess, initially in overall command until the 2nd Division artillery came up, then handing over to their CRA on 12 April. The breathing space for the infantry and their linked arms and services proved to be brief, with further dramatic events to come in the remainder of the month.

17 Notes

1. It appears that the marching arrangements may not have been fully understood at 13th Brigade HQ. The Brigade War Diary entry for 26/27 March notes that 'The march started well but at Souastre it was blocked by [the] 12 Bde column moving on [the] same road, several hours late.'
2. Mitchell, *Op Cit*, p. 177.
3. *Official History*, Vol V, p. 151.
4. Mitchell, *Op Cit*, p. 179.
5. 46th Battalion War Diary, 26 March 1918.
6. *Official History*, Vol V, p. 159.
7. The time is from the 12th Brigade's report on operations, Appendix 3 of the April 1918 War Diary. The narrative in the March Diary gives 5.30 am.
8. 12th Brigade War Diary, 27 March 1918.
9. The 4th Division orders were for two forward battalions to take up a line in map squares E7 and E13, the later orders specified squares E2 and E8, a kilometre on average north and east of the first position, according to the Brigade War Diary for 27 March (the report in the April diary gives slightly different references).
10. Devine, *Op Cit*, p. 113.
11. *Official History*, Vol V, p. 193.
12. 12th Brigade War Diary for March 1918, Appendix 7 (order No. 194B).
13. 47th Battalion War Diary, 27 March 1918.

14   See also Leane's letter of 20 October 1933 to C E W Bean, in which he states that 'I decided to occupy the trenches built on the forward slope' (Bean Papers, AWM38 3DRL606/251/1, p. 181 in PDF). He also says that it was 5 pm when he got in touch with Colonel Imlay.

15   Mitchell, *Op Cit*, p. 184. If at least part of the 48th had moved across the Amiens-Albert road, then those troops would have been somewhere near the unit's intermediate position—map squares E2 and E8. The orders from 12th Brigade do not give any more specific map references than 'central', suggesting that the COs on the spot had the latitude to choose their position within those broad boundaries. The written order to occupy posts on the railway line (see Note 12 above) clearly states that the final advance was not to take place until after dusk.

16   Lt Col Leane's official report, written about 10 days later, (48th Battalion War Diary for April 1918, Appendix 4) says there were no casualties at all to shellfire, but this is apparently not correct. There were at least three men killed by shelling on 27 March and another by aircraft strafing, plus two who died of wounds on the following day—see Browning, *Leane's Battalion, Op Cit*, pp. 209-10. The deaths are confirmed by the AWM Roll of Honour. Browning suggests the casualties from shelling may have occurred after the advance to the railway line in the evening, but the AWM Red Cross reports on one of the victims, Pte W. McNee, say the incident was in the afternoon, near the Amiens-Albert road; it appears to be the same as that described in Mitchell, *Op Cit*, p.183 (Mitchell's account gives an impression of heavy losses, but he may have been referring to the 47th also). Casualty figures for the 47th Battalion are in that unit's March War Diary (Appendix 13), with a slightly higher total in the Brigade diary (Appendix 16); the AWM records six killed on 27 March and two died of wounds the next day. With the intense activity of that period, it is not surprising that there are some discrepancies in the statistics.

17   46th Battalion War Diary, 27 March 1918.

18   Mitchell, *Op Cit*, p.186.

19   45th Battalion War Diary, 28 March 1918 and Appendix 11.

20   4th Field Company War Diary, 27 March 1918.

21   4th Division Signal Company War Diary, 27 March 1918. A photograph of a 4th division cable wagon or limber is in the AWM collection, ID E03265.

22   *Ibid.*

23   *Medical History*, Vol II, pp.624–5; 4th Division ADMS War Diary, 26 March 1918.

24   Bean Papers, notebook AWM38 3DRL606/184/1, p.23 (p. 25 in PDF).

25   His army service record says that McDougall was 5 ft 5 1/2 in (166 cm) tall and weighed 12 st 11 lb (81 kg) in 1915.

26   In his statement describing the fight (a copy is on McDougall's service record, together with those of other witnesses), Lawrence said that 'fresh magazines for the gun were brought, when he continued firing,' although Lawrence did not say whether or not he brought them himself. Lawrence also stated that McDougall had fought the Germans with a revolver before the extra Lewis gun ammunition arrived.

27   Mitchell, *Op Cit*, p. 187.

28   C E W Bean at first believed that the German party had already surrendered to the 47th Battalion and had in effect been captured twice (Bean Papers, notebook AWM38 3DRL606/184/1, p.21, p. 24 in PDF), but states in the *Official History* that they had actually surrendered to the 48th. The matter is also mentioned in Leane's letter referred to in Note 14 above.

29   See Note 26 above.

30   Bean Papers, notebook AWM38 3DRL606/184/1, p.15 (p. 18 in PDF). See also 3DRL606/185/1, p. 62 (p. 50 in PDF), in which McDougall seems to be saying that although the 47th did recapture a Lewis gun from the Germans, it was not by him personally. There is a German light Maxim on display at the AWM, identified as one captured by McDougall at Dernancourt.

31   Devine, *Op Cit*, pp. 116–118; *Official History*, Vol V, p. 198. Mitchell (*Op Cit*, p. 186) also mentions that the 48th Battalion's first indication of an attack was the sound of small arms fire from the 47th's sector.

32   12th MG Company War Diary for March 1918, Appendix A.

33   Indicated by the map references on page 4 of Appendix A in the Company's April 1918 War Diary. The MM recommendation for Pte J F Coyle of the 12th MG company suggests that his gun was on the forward bank of the cutting.

34   12th MG Company War Diary for March 1918, Appendix A.

35   *Ibid*.

36   According to his DCM recommendation in the AWM honours and awards files.

37   Also from an award recommendation.

38   Capt Gibson appears to have been in charge of 'D' Company in the front line at the time. Captain W A Symons was the company commander, but commanders and 2ic's often alternated between the line and the nucleus. Capt Symons was in command for the next major action, on 5 April.

39   This figure comes from a Red Cross report on the death of Private W J Summerfield, as noted by Deayton, *Op Cit*, p. 205.

40   Casualty figures from the 12th Brigade War Diary for March 1918, Appendix 16 (the AWM Roll of Honour confirms 12 fatalities). The 45th Battalion initially reported 11 killed, 31 wounded and 6 missing. The figure of 125 for the company strength is mentioned in a report on the Red Cross file for Pte J A Littlewood, one of those killed.

41   *Official History*, Vol V, p. 205.

42   12th Brigade War Diary for March 1918, Appendix 10; Mitchell, *Op Cit*, p. 194..

43   From Deayton, *Op Cit* (Appendix 3) and the AWM Roll of Honour, showing 28 killed and two died from previous wounds on that day. The 12th Brigade report (April 1918 War Diary, Appendix 3) still shows Capt Gibson as wounded when he had actually died of his wounds on 28 March.

44   From Browning, *Leane's Battalion, Op Cit*, pp. 213–215 and the AWM Roll of Honour. The 12th Brigade report shows the 48th as having 13 killed on 28 March, and also 13 on 29 March, which must be an error.

45   The map facing p. 402, Vol V, of the *Official History* is entitled 'Second Dernancourt, 5th April 1918,' however.

46   *Official History*, Vol V, p. 208.

47   12th MG Company War Diary for April 1918, Appendix A, p.9. There is an obvious error in one of the map references where first given, where D 8 b is written instead of E 8 b; later in the report, the correct reference is used.

48   *Ibid*.

49   *Official History*, Vol V, p. 359.

50   Playfair had a distinguished career in NSW business and politics after the war; see the article on him by G P Walsh in the *Australian Dictionary of Biography*.

51 12th Brigade War Diary, 29 March 1918. Oddly, the 12th Field Company diary does not mention this task.
52 *Official History*, Vol V, p. 358.
53 13th Field Company War Diary, 31 March 1918 and 1 April 1918, and Appendix 1 to the March diary. The diaries of the 13th Field Company and the 4th Pioneer Battalion are not consistent as to the dates that the main and support lines were dug.
54 The *Official History*, Vol V p. 358, refers to the line closest to the railway as the 'support line' but the 13th Field Company war diary uses that term for the next line back, near the Amiens road, which is consistent with Division order No 105. The engineers called the line closest above the railway the 'front line,' which Division referred to as the 'main line of resistance', as opposed to the outpost line on the railway embankment itself.
55 The divisional staff's report on the battle of 5 April, however, states that the support system was 'a continuous traversed trench known as Pioneer Trench running from just N[orth] of Buire ... to [a point near Albert]' (4th Division GS War Diary for June 1918, Appendix 33, folio 105). This statement is inconsistent with reports of the infantry brigades, engineers and pioneers.
56 52nd Battalion War Diary for April 1918, Appendix C.
57 Although the *Official History* (Vol V, p. 361) says that the 46th's post was shelled, the unit War Diary for 1 April states that there was no preliminary bombardment. The divisional intelligence report for that day (4th Division GS War Diary for April 1918, Appendix 1) gives the map references for enemy shelling, and these do not include the location of the 46th's left flank.
58 46th Battalion War Diary, 30 March 1918.
59 12th MG Company War Diary for April 1918, Appendix A, Capt Martin's after-action report. By the time the report was written, the battle of 5 April had taken place and the positioning of the machine guns as chosen by Capt Martin had come under question, particularly the eight guns in the quarry and the trench to its east on the slope. Understandably, Martin pointed out in his report that three senior officers, Brig Gen Gellibrand, Lt Col Murray and Maj Hinton, had all been aware of the gun positions, and, by implication, had not raised any objections.
It was not until 14 April that the full organisation of the machine guns into the new battalion structure came into force (4th Division Admin Staff War Diary, 7 April 1918), the MG Battalion having just begun the process of formation when the Division was suddenly thrust into action. The MG Companies continued to be controlled more by their original Brigades; the location statements for the Division's various units, up to and including the statement for 10 April (in the appendices to the April GS War Diary), continued to list the Companies under the Brigade headings, with only the divisional company, the 24th, appearing under the heading of the 4th MG Battalion. It is only in subsequent statements that all four companies are listed as part of the MG Battalion. When the 24th Company relieved the 12th between 2 and 4 April, it came under control of the 12th Brigade.
60 4th Division GS War Diary for June 1918, Appendix 33, p.105 (the Staff's final report on the Dernancourt and Villers-Bretonneux operations).
61 4th Division GS War Diary for March 1918, Appendix 15.
62 4th Division GS War Diary for June 1918, Appendix 33, p. 105.
63 *Official History*, Vol V, p. 364.
64 The memo is in the AWM Operations Files, AWM26 item 407/13.
65 48th Battalion War Diary for April 1918, Appendix 1.
66 *Official History*, Vol V, p. 365.
67 13th Brigade War Diary for April 1918, Appendix 10A. This view is also mentioned in the VC

recommendation for Lt L C Boase (52nd Battalion), an unusual type of document in which to find such comments.

68   A week later, the 4th Division staff issued an operational memo recommending, *inter alia*, that where two brigades were engaged in joint operations, their HQs should be co-located (4th Division GS War Diary for April 1918, Appendix 16).

69   *Official History*, Vol V, p. 365. Bean got his information here directly from Col Whitham; their conversation is detailed in the notebook AWM38 3DRL606/185/1, pp. 6–11.

70   12th Brigade War Diary, 3 April 1918.

71   52nd Battalion War Diary for April 1918, Appendix H (D), folio 42.

72   Kennedy reported, in the above reference, that it was only when daylight came that he was able to see the next two posts to his left in the CCS area.

73   As described in his award recommendation.

74   *Official History*, Vol V, p. 377. A relevant entry in Bean's notebook on Dernacourt has the soldier's name as 'Whitcombe?' (AWM38 3DRL606/185/1, p.15). W L Whitmore's DCM recommendation indicates that he was the gunner under the bridge. See also Browning, *The 52nd Battalion*, p. 210.

75   *Ibid*, p. 379. The author has been unable to identify Bean's source for that statement, either in his papers or in unit/formation diaries.

76   4th Division GS War Diary for June 1918, Appendix 33, folio 109. That document is the staff's final report on Dernancourt, presumably compiled with considerable reference to the outcomes of the Court of Inquiry conducted after the battle. The account in this book generally follows the report.

77   52nd Battalion War Diary for April 1918, Appendix H, folio 45.

78   Shepherdson's wound was reported as a gunshot, but the medical records on his file describe a 'bomb wound' and a 'piece of grenade'. The fragment was still there when he was passed fit in August.

79   The position is shown on the sketch map appended to Lt Col Whitham's report (52nd Battalion War diary for April 1918, Appendix H, folio 27). The report says (folio 40) 'about 7 men of the 47th Battalion came to 'B' Company Headquarters situated West of the Railway Arch ... [Capt Fraser] sent the CSM back with this party of men, and he went a couple of hundred yards along the road and embankment into 47th Battalion sector but saw no one; he then returned with the 7 men and allotted them a post near his own, near 'B' Company's Headquarters.' This statement is sometimes understood (including by C E W Bean) to mean that D'Alton travelled 200 yards beyond the inter-battalion boundary, and doubts have accordingly been cast on it—adding the distance from Company HQ, he would have had to cover about 800 yards altogether to get back and report. It may mean, however, only that he went as far as the boundary i.e. 200 yards from 'B' Company HQ, plus 200 yards back (Edgar, *To Villers-Bretonneux, Op Cit*, p. 201, just says that D'Alton 'ran 200 yards to the left flank [of the 52nd].'). On the other hand, it appears that Capt Fraser had left his HQ for a position closer to the railway bridge just before the incident—see the Bean Papers, AWM38 3DRL606/227 p.325 (130 in the digitised PDF).

The seven (or five, depending on the source) 47th men have not been identified, although three members of that unit, Privates Leonard Ward, Arthur Jolly and Howard Dillon, made statements in May (47th Battalion War Diary for May 1918, Appendix 61) that they had been with the 52nd at the time of the enemy breakthrough, having been sent across to obtain grenades. Their accounts are different to those from 52nd sources, of men from the 47th arriving to report that their unit had been driven back, but it is still possible that they are different recollections of the same events.

80   The *Official History* (Vol V, p.377) has this incident occurring during the first attacks, at about 7 am, as does Capt Anderson's report (Appendix H, folio 51 in the 52nd Battalion's April 1918 Diary). The way that Colonel Whitham wrote up the award recommendation for Boase, however (he was recommended for the VC but awarded the DSO), indicates that it occurred in the 9 to 10am attack, when the Germans succeeded in breaking through; N Browning (*The 52nd Battalion*, p.213) takes that view also. The badly wounded Boase was taken prisoner by the Germans, while if he had been hit during the earlier fighting his men could have brought him back to the Australian line when the Germans fell back. While recognising that award recommendations are not always reliable, I believe that this one represents the most likely scenario.

81   Edgar, *Op Cit*, p. 201. The 52nd Battalion reported (War Diary April 1918, Appendix H(B)) that 'B' Company suffered the highest casualties of the four companies, a total of 67 among the ORs, of whom 15 were killed and nine missing (some or all of the missing had probably been taken prisoner); 43 were wounded. The company had 116 men in the battle, so 49 were unhurt. All companies were understrength, the other three averaging 131 men in the front line (13th Brigade War Diary for April 1918, Appendix X (O) (B)).

82   *Official History*, Vol V, p. 374.

83   13th MG Company War Diary for April 1918, Appendix A.

84   See Note 81 above

85   From a prisoner of war statement by Sgt J M F Ryan (PoW statements, AWM 30 B10.5). Company HQ locations are not specified in either the Battalion or Brigade records, although a map with the 12th Brigade report on the battle (Appendix 3 in the April 1918 War Diary) shows a strong-point about 400 metres back from the railway in the 47th's sector.

86   Capt Hurd's statement is documented in the Division's final report on the battle (GS War Diary for June 1917, Appendix 33, folio 109). The issue is discussed by Deayton, *Op Cit*, on pp. 237–8.

87   Bean Papers, AWM38 3DRL606/185/1, p. 92 (p. 65 in PDF).

88   48th Battalion War Diary, 5 April 1918.

89   12th Brigade War Diary for April 1918, Appendix 3 (folio 45). Although that report states that the whole mortar crew 'were casualties', the included casualty summary only shows one OR wounded in the 12th LTM Battery as does the *Official History* (Vol V, p.412n). The final strength report for the week (Appendix 9), however, records three killed, two wounded and one missing on 5 April, in a table that includes some arithmetical errors. From the Roll of Honour, those killed were Pte W H Davey (shown on the Roll of Honour as a 47th Battalion member), Cpl L M Henderson, and L-Cpl A A Howard. Also, L-Cpl P Maher died on 5 April from wounds received the same day.

90   Bean Papers, Folder AWM38 3DRL606/251/1, p.191.

91   Bean Papers, AWM38 3DRL606/185/1, p.72 (55 in PDF).

92   *Official History*, Vol V, p.390.

93   Bean Papers, AWM38 3DRL606/185/1, p.88 (63 in PDF). This is not mentioned in the *Official History*.

94   Shang's recommendation for a bar to his DCM does not make it clear where he was, but Bean's notes mention that he was with 'D' Company on 5 April (AWM38 3DRL606/185/1, p.90, p. 64 in PDF).

95   Bean papers, AWM38 3DRL606/251/1, p.190.

96   Identified by Deayton, *Op Cit*, p. 223.

97   Mitchell, *Op Cit*, p. 204.

98 *Ibid*, p. 205.
99 Some PoW statements in AWM30 B10.5 suggest, however, that those guns did not actually fire—see the statements from Ptes A V Postle, G C Simmonds, C Pounsett and D J Roberts.
100 13th Brigade War Diary for April 1918, Appendix 10A.
101 According to his report (52nd Battalion War Diary for April 1918, Appendix H) the message, numbered B340, was received at 1.55pm; the copy of that message in the Brigade diary is timed as sent at 12.50.
102 *Official History*, Vol V, p.375.
103 As exemplified by the report of the gunner officer with the 47th Battalion: 'communication during the bombardment [7 to 10.30am] barely existed ... I would say that 50 percent of the information received at Battalion headquarters was very faulty and had to be accepted with reserve [sic]. A lot of this stuff I did not send to [Group HQ] as I thought it would cause confusion, but the news I got from Colonel Imlay and the adjutant appeared to be correct but I might add this to some extent had to be drawn out of them. My opinion is that the infantry should take the liaison officer a little more into their confidence.' (10th AFA Brigade War Diary for April 1918, Appendix 2. The signature on this report is not clear, but the officer was from the 37th Battery).
104 10th AFA Brigade War Diary for April 1918, Appendix 2.
105 Notes of C E W Bean's conversation with Adams, undated but probably from 1935, are in the Bean Papers, AWM38 3DRL606/251/1, pp. 203-4. That document says that Adams was acting in command of 'B' Company and was displaced by Capt L D Ferguson returning from leave, the other commanders being Capts E Davies and J H Holman, as well as Lt Perry, who was in turn succeeded by Adams. There is no mention in Ferguson's service record of him being on leave at that time, however, and the 45th Battalion War Diary entry for 25 March 1918 notes that the company commanders at the time were Capts Holman, Ferguson, O B Dibbs and Adams. Capt Davies' service record shows that he was on leave about that time and returned on 3 April, a date which may well be a clerical error for 5 April. Capt Dibbs had been killed in action on 1 April, and Lt Perry had taken his place commanding 'C' Company, before Adams became available to take over during the battle, and it appears that this was because of the return of Davies rather than Ferguson.
106 Squires' award recommendation has the wrong given name ('Frederick') but the gazettal has the correct one (he was recommended for the DCM but awarded the MM).
107 *Official History*, Vol V, p. 398.
108 'C' Company of the 51st. C E W Bean noted that 'the company commander didn't realise what was expected of him' and had halted on the reverse of the slope in map square D18.d (AWM38 3DRL606/185/1, p. 14 and 28). The company had started in square D18.c, so could not have moved more than about 700 metres. Edgar (*Op Cit*, p. 205) notes that a 13th Brigade order instructing the company to join up with the 12th Brigade may be the cause of the misunderstanding, but that order seems to be rather for the 51st's 'A' Company to take the place of 'C'—to move from 'north of Amiens road to posts in D18' ; 'A' was the only 51st company located north of the road on the morning of the battle (13th Brigade War Diary for April 1918, Appendix 10E, and 51st Battalion War Diary for April 1918, Appendix 11).
109 Bean Papers, AWM38 3DRL606/185/1, p. 34 (p. 33 in PDF).
110 *Official History*, Vol V, p. 402.
111 Bean Papers, AWM38 3DRL606/185/1, p. 41 (p. 39 in PDF).
112 49th Battalion War Diary for April 1918, Appendix 8, folio 33.

113 10th AFA Brigade War Diary for April 1918, Appendix 2.
114 49th Battalion War Diary for April 1918, Appendix 8, folio 25.
115 4th Division Artillery HQ War Diary for April 1918, Appendix 1, and 10th AFA Brigade War Diary for April 1918, Appendix 2; the latter reference has 84 casualties for the Left Group.
116 Bean Papers, AWM38 3DRL606/223/1, p. 69..
117 April 1918 War Diaries for: 12th Brigade, Appendix 3, folio 45; 4th Division Artillery HQ, Appendix 1; 10th AFA Brigade, Appendix 2. The artillery reports give different timings to those in the infantry report.
118 The 4th Division Artillery HQ War Diary for April 1918, Appendix 1, says that the two groups combined expended 23,320 18-pounder and 5,263 howitzer shells for the day.
119 A J Gledhill, 'Dernancourt—A Recollection,' *Reveille*, October 1935.
120 4th Division GS War Diary for June 1918, Appendix 33, folio 115.
121 *Official History*, Vol V, p. 417.
122 4th Pioneer Battalion War Diary for April 1918, Appendix 1.
123 13th Field Ambulance War Diary, 5 April.
124 *Official History*, Vol V, pp. 406–7.

18: Three Weeks in April

The 12th and 13th Brigade groups were in need of rest, hot food, refitting and a clean-up as they marched to the rear after ten days in the line with almost constant fighting, culminating in the fierce battle of 5 April. Tired as they were, the men remained in high spirits, aware that their 'two brigades in impossible defences [had] received and repelled with but little bending the blow of two and a half German divisions.'[1] Colonel Leane, the 48th Battalion CO, noted that his men sang as they marched, despite intermittent rain showers.[2] The 12th Brigade units had reached covered billets by the time the rain set in heavily, but those of the 13th Brigade, marching a day later, were bivouacked in the open when 'a steady downpour of rain set in and the discomfort was complete.'[3] Wet through, the troops moved to billets on the night of 8 April and tried to dry out. The divisional staff arranged for baths and a supply of dry underclothing for both brigades. Motor lorries were sent north to collect the men's packs and blankets, which had been dumped at the villages around Basseux when the march to Dernancourt had started on 26 March.

The margin of success in the Dernancourt battle had been a narrow one, and a court of enquiry was instituted to review contentious aspects of the fighting and to put together the full picture of the battle. The record of the enquiry itself has not survived, but it is reasonable to assume that the 4th Division staff's final report on the battle[4] contains information sourced from the enquiry. One point of contention was the loss of the eight machine guns and their entire crews in the 12th Brigade sector. On the day of the battle first reports said that the guns had been heard firing through the morning before falling silent, and it was assumed that the crews had fought to the death (there were certainly Vickers guns in action, those in the 13th Brigade sector and the two 24th Company guns on the extreme left). The truth, that the guns had not fired a shot, came out in an extraordinary manner. On 13 April, two Australian soldiers, escaped from German captivity, came into the 2nd Division's lines above Dernancourt. They proved to be Corporal Charles Lane and Private Reinhold Ruschpler[5] of the 24th MG Company, members of the gun crews posted 'missing' on 5 April, and they soon gave the real story of the incident. The two men's evidence drew attention to the mistakes made in the positioning and tactics of the guns, resulting in firm instructions from higher authority to avoid any similar instances in future. Among other points, defensive machine guns should be mounted at all times, relying on camouflage to conceal them from the enemy. Scouts and sentries were to be posted forward to give warning of an attack, and the gun positions should be covered by infantry squads to forestall attempts by the enemy to outflank them.[6] On the personal side, there is a strong indication in C E W Bean's correspondence of a falling-out between Colonel Murray, the MG Battalion CO, and Major Hinton, OC 24th Company, which if not actually caused by the events of Dernancourt was probably exacerbated by them.[7]

There were recriminations also over the initial breakthrough by the Germans in the area of the railway overpass on the boundary between the 12th and 13th Brigade sectors—specifically the question of which unit, the 47th or the 52nd Battalion, had given way first. It was an emotional issue, one that still bothered Colonel Whitham, the 52nd CO, six years after the war; in 1924 he arranged for the inclusion in the unit's War Diary of his letter reiterating his belief that the enemy penetration had come through the 47th's line first. The letter stated that the 47th 'got the brunt of the enemy's fire and early bombardment and by sheer weight of numbers were forced back (no blame attaching to them)'[8] and that had in turn caused the 52nd's left flank to fall back. Colonel Imlay of the 47th was equally convinced that his unit had held on until after the 52nd withdrew. The divisional staff's final report in June took the view that the enemy had first broken through on the front of the 47th's right company, not because those troops had given way but rather because they had been virtually wiped out by the German close-range mortar fire. Although this meant that there was no misconduct, there seems to be little doubt that Colonel Imlay's credibility was under some question at the higher command level. C E W Bean, talking with the 12th Brigade staff a few days after the battle, recorded their feeling that Imlay was inclined to exaggerate and that '... the work of the 47th Battalion is slapdash ...'[9] Despite Imlay's confident assertion that the 52nd had been first to retreat, Bean noted also that 'the break was almost certainly [through the] right of 47 Bn.'[10] Imlay's case would not have been helped by the circumstance of the company commander at the crucial point, Captain Hurd, somehow being unaware until well after the event that his troops were even under attack. Also, the divisional staff's report was presumably referring to the 47th in the comment

> One Battalion assumed that some troops to its right rear formed the left flank of the front line troops of the next Battalion [i.e. the 52nd], and so reported, whereas the left flank of [that] Battalion was actually about 800 yards to his right front, still holding on to practically its original position.[11]

According to Colonel Leane of the 48th Battalion, there was a feeling that Colonel Imlay was too ready to blame other units for setbacks encountered by his own. Writing to Bean in 1933 Leane stated that 'Imlay was rather noted for forwarding information of this nature in reference to supporting units'[12] (Leane was referring to the deployment of the two units on 28 March rather than the battle of 5 April particularly). In the same letter Leane also gave his opinion that Imlay's reports of inadequate support from the 45th Battalion at Messines had been the cause of Colonel Sydney Herring's removal from command of that unit. Be that as it may, the 12th Brigade's initial report on the battle tended to follow Colonel Imlay's version of events, albeit somewhat cautiously, and 'there was a certain coolness between the 13th and 12th Brigades.'[13] The 13th Brigade staff took the opposite view in their own report, and no doubt would have felt vindicated by the divisional staff's final assessment.

Colonel Imlay was also thought to have a tendency to overstate his unit's casualty rate,[14] presumably to emphasise how hard they had fought. Australian Corps HQ recorded an initial estimate of 383 casualties in the 47th Battalion for the fight of 5 April[15] but by the time the 12th Brigade wrote up its report the figure had been revised to a total of 269, of which a large number, 176, were recorded as 'missing.' The Brigade reports also noted a numerical increase of 82 in the 47th's strength over five days as a result of 'casualties over-estimated.'[16] Regardless of that, the 47th's losses were still the highest in the Division. It is now known that the unit had 56 members killed in action on 5 April 1918;[17] 28 deaths were reported initially, and assuming that the other 28 were at first included in the 'missing,' up to 148, many of them wounded, may have been taken prisoner by the Germans. The actual number of prisoners would be somewhat lower, as some of those missing would have turned up later wounded in hospital (the initial figure for wounded was 65), and others rejoined after losing contact with their unit; at least six of the prisoners subsequently died while in captivity.[18] The 49th Battalion suffered the next most heavily in the Division, losing 62 killed and 159 wounded in their great counter-attack[19] (among the 49th's wounded was Private Duncan Thompson, a promising young rugby league player, who survived a bullet through the chest to become one of the greats of the game after the war). At the other end of the scale, the 48th Battalion, although heavily involved in defending the railway and in the rearguard action up the slope, reported the comparatively low total of 81 casualties, 42 of whom were killed or missing, although that number may be slightly understated; 23 of the missing had been taken prisoner.[20] Although the casualty figures vary slightly depending on which source is used, a total of 1,271 for the Division overall would be fairly accurate from the records of the time, 1,122 of those losses being in the infantry brigade groups. The latter figure includes 483 killed and missing, of whom about 200 had been taken prisoner, including the 35 members of the hapless 24th MG Company teams; not all of the prisoners survived the war.[21] The divisional artillery recorded 89 casualties, as mentioned in the previous chapter, and the pioneers had five killed and 37 wounded.[22] C E W Bean estimated that the German infantry lost between 1300 and 1600 casualties in the battle.[23]

Mistakes had been made, both at the front line and command levels, a few officers had not performed well under pressure, some men had, to put it bluntly, run away—but the vast majority, though heavily outnumbered, had fought it out and held off what C E W Bean believed was the strongest attack ever met by Australian troops on the Western Front. For a long time the officers and men in the front line had been left to their own devices without intervention by the commanders, who had been deprived of the information they needed by the destruction of communication links and by the mist that shrouded the battlefield for much of the morning. It was a rare thing in military history for the defending army to win a battle when the attackers were concealed by mist—from Lake Trasimene in 217 BC, through Austerlitz and as recently as the German assault on 21 March, morning mist had given an important advantage to the attacking force and would do so again in the AIF's offensive battles later in the year.

Many individual soldiers had distinguished themselves in the battle, and numerous decorations were awarded afterwards. Three were recommended for the VC—Lieutenant Boase, who had led the 52nd Battalion platoon at the railway bridge, the 48th Battalion signaller Private Tregoweth, and Lewis gunner Lance Corporal Bannister of the 45th. None of these was approved, however, and lesser decorations were awarded. Boase, at first thought to have been killed but later known to have been wounded and taken prisoner, was awarded the DSO after the war,[24] and both Tregoweth and Bannister received the DCM. Among the infantry officers the 47th Battalion's Captain Young and Lieutenant Taylor were awarded DSOs, as was Captain Adams of the 45th. MCs went to, among others, Lieutenants James Graham and Robert Argue (a Bar in the case of the latter) and Second Lieutenant Percy Blewett, leaders in the 49th Battalion counter-attack, and Lieutenant Shepherdson of the 48th. Captain Cumming, also 48th, was recommended for the DSO but awarded a Bar to his MC instead. Perhaps surprisingly, Captain Hurd of the 47th also received the MC; the recommendation by Colonel Imlay suggests that the CO was not aware of Hurd's inattention in the early part of the battle, but also that Hurd apparently redeemed himself during the counter-attack. Colonel Whitham was more circumspect in his recommendations for his 52nd Battalion, going no further than the MC for Captain Kennedy, whose dynamic leadership had prevented the collapse of the right flank. In the infantry's direct supporting arms, MCs went to the mortar officer Lieutenant Williams (13th LTM Battery) and the machine gun officers Lieutenants Tuckett (13th Company) and Jack (24th Company). The pioneer officers Lieutenants Pennefather and Reid also received MCs for their parts in the fight along the railway embankment. Divisional artillery personnel decorated included Lieutenants Linsley (10th AFA Brigade) and Pidcock (11th AFA Brigade), who were each awarded the MC (both officers died of their wounds, Pidcock on the day of the battle and Linsley two days later, very unusual posthumous awards of the MC[25]); Sergeants Cole and Henderson (both 11th AFA Brigade) were each awarded the DCM.

Multiple decorations were now occurring more frequently among the infantry 'ORs' who had survived earlier actions and continued to distinguish themselves. In the 47th Battalion Sergeant Brown and Private Shang both received Bars to the DCMs they had won at Messines. Sergeant Stan McDougall received the MM to add to his VC for the action of 28 March. For their efforts in the fighting at the railway bridge, Corporal Morrison of the 52nd Battalion won a Bar to his DCM and Lance Corporal Whitmore of the same unit was awarded the DCM, as was Lance Corporal Thomas of the 48th. Machine gunner Sergeant Waters (13th MG Company) was another DCM recipient. Corporal Blake of the 13th LTM Battery, who had supported the barrel of his damaged mortar with his hands, was recommended for the DCM but awarded the MM instead, one of numerous MMs that went to soldiers in the infantry battalions and their supporting arms, including Lance Corporal William Loo Long (45th Battalion), like 'Charlie' Shang of part-Chinese background.

The AAMC officer Major Archibald Collins (12th Field Ambulance) received the DSO for his energetic management of the casualty evacuations. Stretcher bearers, signallers and runners had roamed the battlefield all day carrying out their specialised duties under fire, and a number were decorated in the infantry and artillery units as well as in the field ambulances and the 4th Signal Company. Lance Corporal Charles Smith, stretcher bearer in the 48th Battalion, was awarded the DCM, as was 'bearer' Corporal William Cooper (49th), who already held the MM and Bar. The 48th Battalion's signals officer, Lieutenant Leslie Challen, received the MC for his work in maintaining the unit's communications during the shelling. Another MC went to Lieutenant Jack O'Brien of the Signal Company, his fourth decoration of the war, added to the DCM and MM and Bar that he had won in the ranks.[26] Another Signal Company member, Sapper Thomas Linney, received his third award in the form of a second Bar to his MM. A DCM went to artillery signaller Corporal James Moylan (110th Howitzer Battery), who had continued with the repair of his Battery's telephone lines despite a severe wound. Lance Corporal Bolger (12th Field Ambulance) and Private Siebert (13th Field Ambulance) were among a number of AAMC members awarded MMs. Another MM was awarded to Driver Noel Fordham, 4th Motor Transport Company, who made 19 trips driving an ambulance car over a heavily shelled road, carrying casualties to the ADS.

The Division now had a brief breathing-space away from the forward area except for the artillerymen at Dernancourt, who had no break at all, and the 4th Brigade, still in the line at Hébuterne. The opportunity was taken to make some necessary changes in the higher command appointments. Colonel George Barber, ADMS since the formation of the Division, had been notified at the end of March that he would shortly be posted to similar duties at the next level up, as Deputy Director of Medical Services (DDMS) Australian Corps. This occurred on 8 April and he was succeeded by Colonel Arthur Moseley. The new ADMS was 37, English-born like his predecessor, and had been with the 2nd Division medical services since the later stages at Gallipoli, most recently as CO of the 6th Field Ambulance. Another founding member of the command group was relieved at about the same time. Lieutenant Colonel Gilbert Elliott, the CRE, had been in London on sick leave when the great German offensive broke. He had been unwell for some time, having never fully recovered from the effects of gasses he had inhaled when caught up in the explosion of a mine on Gallipoli, and Colonel Elliott was now declared unfit for further active service. Major Riddell, OC 12th Field Company, had been acting CRE in Elliott's absence, but a substantive appointment was made on 6 April when Lieutenant Colonel John Dyer arrived to assume the duties. The new CRE, promoted from major commanding the Australian engineer training depot in England, at 24 was over twenty years younger than his predecessor and younger also than his company OCs.[27] Colonel Dyer had first made his mark as a subaltern with the 1st Division engineers on Gallipoli where he had achieved the unusual distinction of not only having a landmark named after him but also having created it himself, by laying and firing an explosive charge that wrecked a Turkish tunnel and left a hole known as Dyer's Crater.[28] Rising quickly to major's rank, he had further distinguished himself in France and been awarded the DSO before his posting to the training depot. Also in April the DADVS, Lieutenant Colonel Kendall, was taken ill and evacuated. Major Edward James moved into the posting from the Mobile Veterinary Section, where he was succeeded in turn by Captain Reginald Heywood.

As of 6 April the Division came under command of the Australian Corps again, when General Birdwood's Corps HQ arrived in the Somme area from Flanders and took over the front from VII Corps. The next day the Australian Corps came under the orders of Fourth Army HQ, which several days earlier had replaced that of Fifth Army in control of the southern sector of the British front, astride the Somme. The 4th Division would generally remain under that higher command structure for the rest of the war, although situations continued to arise where units or brigades were temporarily attached to other formations. One such occurred almost as soon as the Division came out of the line after Dernancourt when the 13th Brigade was informed that it was now attached to the 3rd Division as its reserve brigade (the 3rd's 9th Brigade was still under British command in the Villers-Bretonneux sector). On 8/9 April the Brigade group was required to move again, a short distance south to positions near Corbie behind the 3rd Division front. The higher command was working on the basis that the German effort against Amiens had only paused temporarily and the priority was to shore up the defensive lines east of the city. By now the 5th Australian Division had arrived from the north and was in the process of slotting in to the front on the 3rd Division's right (south), and considerable effort was being put into creating successive lines of defences in depth all along Fourth Army's front—which was now held entirely by Australian troops. The 50th and 51st Battalions went into defensive positions along the bank of the Somme canal between Corbie and the front line near Sailly-le-Sec (the 'Bridgehead Line') with their reserve companies and the 49th and 52nd Battalions billeted in the villages, which had been abandoned by their civilian occupants. There was some confusion over the arrangements at first, as the 13th Brigade diarist noted:

> The role of the Brigade in this area is not clear ... The present position is that the Brigade is quartered in 4th Aust Div area, is under tactical command of 3rd Aust Div, and yet the forward troops on the bridgehead line are in the 5th Aust Div area.[29]

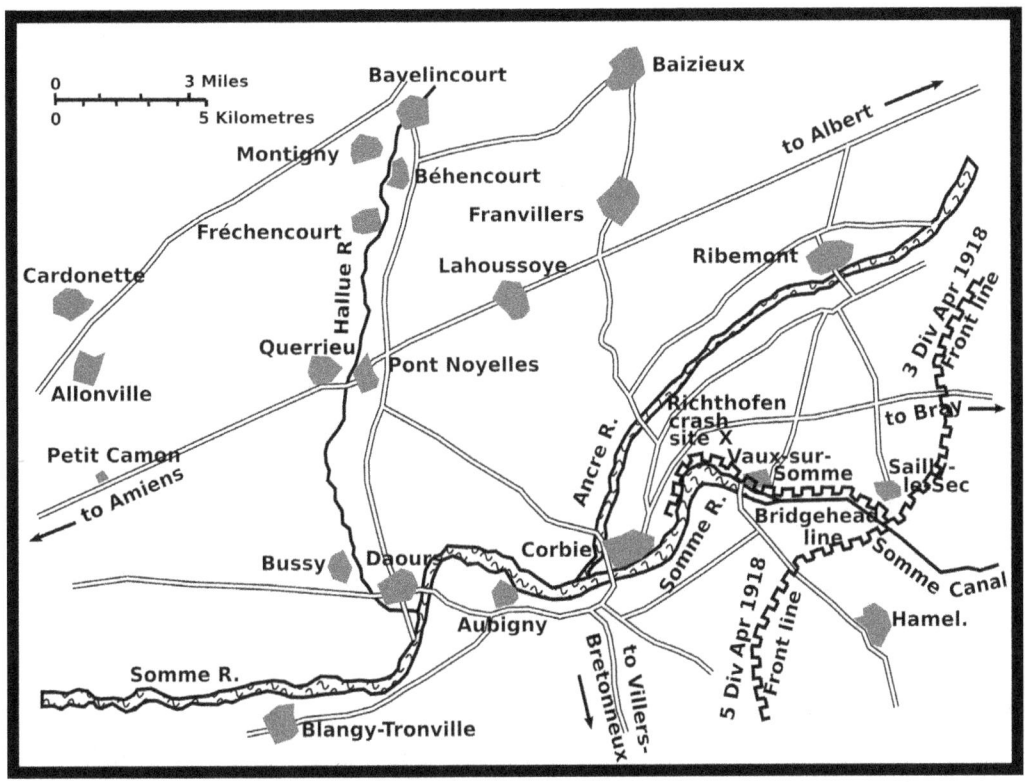

Environs of the Somme, Ancre and Hallue Rivers between Amiens and Albert.

The line faced south and formed a 'switch,' running back at a wide angle to the front line, to protect the 3rd Division's right in case of an enemy breakthrough on that flank. This meant that the 13th Brigade's left battalion (initially the 51st) was close to the front line, with the right further towards the rear and only required to man its posts with a small garrison. The troops in the villages were able to get a bath and a change of clothing despite intermittent enemy shelling, and after two days the battalions changed over to enable the 50th and 51st to clean up and rest; the 13th MG Company was relieved by the 24th at about the same time. It was not long before the inevitable digging began again, as working parties were put on to constructing extra earthworks on the line of the canal.

The 4th Division now had only one of its infantry brigades, the 12th, under its direct command, and even that force was soon diminished. The 12th Brigade units had moved to villages in the area to the north of Amiens on 10 April and over the next few days two of its four battalions were detached to other commands within the Corps. The 45th Battalion moved east to Lahoussoye where it came under the orders of the 3rd Division and manned a defensive position aligning with the village of Franvillers, about three kilometres behind the 3rd Division front line. The 46th was sent back to recently familiar territory at Baizieux and attached to the 2nd Division, now holding the Dernancourt front, where the battalion was given the task of holding a line from Baizieux to Ribemont and the Ancre. While these defensive precautions were being taken in the Amiens area the next German blow actually fell in the north near Armentières on 9 April. The Germans again achieved surprise and struck at a weak part of the front, held by an unenthusiastic Portuguese division supported by weary British troops who had been sent to the area to rest after the recent Somme fighting. The news came through the next day that Armentières had fallen and the Germans were driving hard for Hazebrouck, a vital transport centre, beyond which were the Channel ports. Another German spearhead overran the Messines Ridge and threatened Ypres itself. The 1st Australian Division had just arrived at Amiens from the north to complete the Australian Corps deployment, designated as 'close support' division to occupy the second defensive zone behind the front line. The orders were hurriedly cancelled and on 11 April the 1st Division retrained to return north as a desperately-needed strong reinforcement, and over the following days played the major part in stopping the German thrust in front of Hazebrouck.

The defensive lines on the Somme front still had to be garrisoned, so the 4th Division was sent in again in place of the 1st as the Corps' close support division. The allocated operational area was the defensive zone west of the line from Baizieux to Ribemont on the Ancre, as far as the line of the Hallue river, which ran north/south to join the Somme 10 kilometres east of Amiens. Depending on the situation, the Division could be required to move forward to aid the defence of the second line or to hold along the line of the Hallue. Following the various detachments to other formations the Division's infantry resources for these tasks now comprised only half of the 12th Brigade, the 47th and 48th Battalions. The shortfall was partly made up by forming a scratch group within the Division known as the Composite Force, made up of the Pioneer Battalion and the divisional engineers. The sappers and pioneers were required to proceed with their normal duties with construction of works in the defensive zones, but also to provide small nucleus garrisons for strong-points in the line and be ready to fight as infantry if needed. The field companies issued small-arms ammunition to their troops and initiated musketry and Lewis gun training. The Composite Force was put under command of Lieutenant Colonel Harold Paul, who had been CO of the 49th Battalion for a short period before being seriously wounded at Messines; he had recently been passed fit for duty but had not yet been given a new appointment.[30]

By Division orders of 14 April the Composite Force was allocated the southern (right) half of the Division's line on the Hallue, with the attenuated 12th Brigade group responsible for the northern (left) sector. A machine gun company was allocated to each sector, the 12th Company to the 12th Brigade sector and the 13th Company to that of the Composite Force. With the sector generally quiet except for occasional long-range shelling of the villages, the main task for the troops was the construction of an improved system of strong points in the defensive zone. The divisional staff, inspecting the works on 16 April, noted that progress was 'very satisfactory' and that the 12th Brigade was 'digging splendidly.'[31] During this quiet period, the 12th Brigade had a temporary change in its command group when Brigadier General Gellibrand was sent on a month's sick leave, run-down and unable to sleep with what was described as 'nervous exhaustion.' Lieutenant Colonel Leane of the 48th Battalion was the obvious choice for acting brigadier, and the change in command took place on 19 April. C E W Bean recorded in his diary at about his time that

> Gelly considers [Leane] a magnificent Colonel—and so he is—with a magnificent battalion. Leane thinks the same of Gellibrand ... 'Gelly will let you put your reasons for and against...' said Leane.[32]

Major A S 'Tubby' Allen was transferred from the 45th Battalion to be temporary CO of the 48th. The Brigade's resources began returning to normal on 20 April when the 46th Battalion was released from attachment to the 2nd Division and the next day the 45th returned to the fold from the 3rd Division, both battalions taking up billets along the Hallue line.

For the time being the 13th Brigade remained attached to the 3rd Division, forming a flank guard along the line of the Somme canal, the boundary between the 3rd and 5th Division's sectors. The 52nd Battalion, now holding the left of that line nearest the front, had its HQ and two companies at Vaux-sur-Somme, reporting to the 3rd Division's 11th Brigade and supported by machine guns of the 24th MG Company. Several of the Company's guns were attached directly to 11th Brigade HQ and mounted for anti-aircraft work, a circumstance that led to that element of the 4th Division being involved in one of the most famous incidents of the war—the death of the great German fighter pilot Manfred von Richthofen, the 'Red Baron.' On the morning of 21 April a whirling aerial dogfight developed over the Somme when the Fokker Triplanes of the Baron's 'Flying Circus' attacked two RE8 two-seaters from 3 Squadron Australian Flying Corps (AFC) and were in turn attacked by British fighters. The Royal Air Force (RAF) had been created as recently as 1 April, by amalgamating the RFC and the Royal Naval Air Service (RNAS), and Richthofen's opponents that morning were aircraft of a former naval unit, 209 Squadron RAF. The squadron was equipped with Sopwith Camels, one of the best allied fighters ('scouts') of the war and a good match against the Triplanes. The Baron himself was in fine form. Sometimes unfairly disparaged for attacking inferior reconnaissance aircraft, he had on the previous day in a three-minute dogfight shot down two Camels, one of them piloted by a squadron commander, for his 79th and 80th victories. Now he closed in on another Camel, flown by an inexperienced Canadian pilot, Lieutenant W R May, who dived his aircraft for the ground with Richthofen's red-painted Triplane in pursuit. May's flight commander, Captain A R Brown, also a Canadian, saw what was happening and dived after the other two aircraft to rescue his colleague. May reached low level over the Somme and headed west for the British lines with Richthofen right behind him, endeavouring to get his sights on the Camel. May, though a novice at air-fighting, had the piloting skill to control the tricky Camel at tree-top height and weave enough to prevent the German from getting a clear shot at him. Brown, diving steeply to intercept, got in a burst of fire at the red Triplane before he had to pull up to avoid the ground; he temporarily lost sight of the other two aircraft, but was sure that he had hit the German.

The pursuit of May by Richthofen went on, however, the aircraft roaring over 52nd Battalion HQ in Vaux-sur-Somme and bringing Colonel Whitham and his staff running out to see the show. Richthofen, in his determination to bring down his elusive target, was breaking one of his own rules by flying low behind enemy lines, and he was now being fired at by numerous rifles and machine guns from the ground. Sergeant Cedric Popkin, manning one of the 24th MG Company's Vickers guns attached to the 11th Brigade, got in a short burst at the Triplane as it came almost straight towards him heading west, but without apparent effect. The pursuit reached the artillery gun-line and two anti-aircraft Lewis gunners with a 5th Division battery opened fire on the German as he flew towards them. It may have been this fire that caused Richthofen to break off the chase and turn back for his own lines. Now heading east, he again flew past Popkin's position and the Vickers gunner fired another burst, this time at the right side of the aircraft, from a range of 550 metres. The red Triplane immediately reared upwards, swerved down again, then side-slipped and crashed near the Bray-Corbie road. The wreckage was quickly surrounded by souvenir-hunting Australian troops who had run to the spot from all directions. The pilot was dead, struck by a single bullet that had passed through his chest from right to left, and papers found on the body identified him as Manfred von Richthofen. Ever since the controversy has continued as to who had killed the Red Baron, the principle contenders being Captain Brown in the air and the ground gunners Popkin and the two artillery Lewis gunners (R. Buie and W J Evans, 53rd Battery AFA). On the day, 11th Brigade HQ was referring to Sergeant Popkin in a signal to 13th Brigade HQ: 'One of your A[nti]A[ircraft] machine guns brought down ... pilot Capt. VON RICHTHOFEN. Congratulations,'[33] and a century later there is some consensus that Popkin's claim is the most likely to be correct.[34]

That dramatic incident marked the end of the 13th Brigade's period of attachment to the 3rd Division. That night the Brigade's units were relieved by units of the 8th Brigade (5th Division) and by the next day, 22 April, had moved to positions between Querrieu and Bussy-les-Daours, west of the Hallue. The original intention was for the 13th Brigade to return to 4th Division command and take over the right of the Hallue defence line from the temporary Composite Force of pioneers and engineers, which would then be disbanded. By the time the Brigade had moved, however, that arrangement had been countermanded; instead, the Composite Force remained in place, and the 13th Brigade was designated as Army reserve brigade, under orders of Fourth Army HQ.[35] The reserve was constituted as a brigade group with the usual supporting arms and services, although without a directly-linked engineer company. The opportunity was taken to change over the MG companies, the 13th Company resuming its traditional grouping with the 13th Brigade with the 24th Company coming under Composite Force command. At this time the Pioneer Battalion had a change of CO; Lieutenant Colonel Thomas Rutledge, a 29 year old grazier from New South Wales, came in on promotion from major with the 2nd Pioneers, relieving Lieutenant Colonel Morrison who was posted to command the Pioneer Training Battalion in England.

As Army reserve the 13th Brigade had instructions to be ready to move at short notice in an emergency, and it was becoming increasingly likely that such a situation could arise. For the past 10 days the focus had been on the heavy fighting to the north in Flanders, where the latest German offensive had forced the British to abandon the Passchendaele ridge, captured with such grievous loss in October. The enemy was now threatening the key height of Mount Kemmel and closing in on Ypres. The Germans, however, were also preparing to renew their attack on the Somme front, partly as a diversion from the Flanders fighting but also as a further attempt to capture Amiens, or at least seriously endanger it. For an enemy advance south of the Somme, the key to Amiens, 16 kilometres to its east, was Villers-Bretonneux village, set on a plateau that gave observation over Amiens; capture of the village and the heights would give the Germans an ideal position for directing artillery fire onto the city. Villers-Bretonneux was in the sector held by III Corps, on the immediate right (south) of the Australian Corps. Intelligence reports were giving strong indications that an attack was imminent, and early signs of serious enemy preparations had come on 17 and 18 April with sustained periods of gas shelling on Villers-Bretonneux and its environs. The gas caused 1,000 casualties among the troops holding the area, who included elements of the 2nd and 5th Australian Divisions attached to III Corps. There was no immediate infantry attack, however, and over the next few days Fourth Army began to reorganise the formations holding its front. III Corps retained responsibility for Villers-Bretonneux village and the area to its south, bringing in the 8th British Division to garrison the village and releasing its attached Australian units to their own divisions. The boundary between the Australian and III Corps ran just north of the village, with the 5th Division holding the right of the Australian Corps line including the vital height of Hill 104, the highest point of the Villers-Bretonneux plateau (and subsequently the site of the Australian National Memorial). As of 23 April the 4th Division remained scattered, with the artillery supporting the 2nd Division in the Dernancourt sector, the 4th Brigade still at Hébuterne but due to be released soon, the 12th Brigade north of the Somme garrisoning the Hallue line together with the pioneers and engineers, and the 13th Brigade in the same geographical area but with Army HQ controlling its deployment.

This arrangement was intended to be only short-term, Corps issuing orders for the 4th Division, including the 13th Brigade, to relieve the 3rd Division in the front line sector between the Somme and the Ancre over the period 25 to 27 April. The 13th Brigade was to be replaced in Army reserve by a 3rd Division brigade from 27 April. These orderly arrangements were soon disrupted. On 23 April information extracted from German deserters and prisoners indicated that the attack on Villers-Bretonneux had only been postponed, and it would be launched the next day. If this proved to be true there was a good chance that the 13th Brigade might become involved. The warning came through to Brigade HQ late in the night and was passed on to the units. Captain Tom Louch, assistant brigade major of 13th Brigade, recalled that Brigade HQ, enjoying the luxury of their accommodation in the chateau of Querrieu, also spent time that night pondering what might be done for the troops to celebrate Anzac Day.[36]

Early the next morning (24 April) the roar of a heavy enemy bombardment was heard to the south, seeming to confirm the anticipated attack. At 5:30 am Division HQ telegraphed an order to Brigade HQ for all units to prepare to move but nothing further was heard for over two hours, when word came through that there appeared to have been no infantry action after the bombardment. Another two hours passed uneventfully, but at 9:25 Division telephoned to announce that the Brigade was now attached to the 8th British Division and was to march south to the Somme as soon as possible. News had reached Fourth Army HQ that the Germans had taken Villers-Bretonneux and the GOC, General Rawlinson, had ordered the 13th, as his reserve brigade, to move to the area, where it would probably be required to take part in operations to recapture the town. The brigade staff hurriedly got orders out by telephone and telegraph for the units to form up in fighting order and begin the movement, with the first units, the 52nd Battalion from Pont Noyelles and the 50th from Daours, to lead off at 11:15 am. The first stage of the march was to reach the Somme and cross to the south bank at Blangy-Tronville, where there were two pontoon bridges (a march of about seven kilometres for the units starting from Querrieu and Pont Noyelles). There were no detailed orders yet as to what to do when they got there, although it was apparent that the Brigade would soon be involved in fighting, over ground that they had never seen before and which there was no opportunity to reconnoitre.

A kilometre to the south of Blangy-Tronville another of the straight Roman roads (now the D1029) radiating from Amiens runs west-east, passing along the northern edge of Villers-Bretonneux. The railway from Amiens crosses the road just west of the village and curves to run past its southern edge. To the west of the village and south of the Roman road is a long stretch of woods (*Bois*), divided by cross-roads into three segments: from east to west, the Bois d'Aquenne; the Bois l'Abbé; and the Bois de Blangy. Monument Farm, about 500 metres south of the railway line on the southern side of the village, had a large orchard (Monument Wood) attached to it in 1918. The hamlet of Cachy is located two kilometres south-west of Villers-Bretonneux; in 1918 a British 'switch' trench (at an angle from the front line) called Cachy Switch ran from Cachy past the south-east corner of the Bois d'Aquenne. The HQ of 8th Division was at Glisy, two kilometres west of Blangy-Tronville, where 13th Brigade HQ sent representatives to be briefed on their task. Brigadier General Glasgow went himself by car, with his 'G' staff officers, reaching Glisy around noon. Here he met with Major General Heneker, GOC 8th Division, who confirmed that a powerful German attack by tanks and infantry had overwhelmed the defenders of Villers-Bretonneux several hours earlier and the town was now in enemy hands. Counter attacks had failed and the 13th Brigade was now to take part in another attempt to retake the lost ground. Three of its battalions were to be used in the new counter attack, with the fourth diverted to fill a gap in the reserve line (the 'Aubigny Line') west of the town and north of the railway. The Germans were thought to have penetrated into the woods on the west of Villers-Bretonneux and also advanced beyond the key landmark of Hangard Wood, three kilometres to the south. Their attacks on Hill 104 just north of the town had failed, however, against stout defence by the 5th Division's 14th Brigade and scattered British elements. The 8th Division HQ staff had no clear idea of where any remaining British troops might still be holding out in the southern part of the battle area, so General Glasgow decided to see for himself before continuing the conference. The Brigade intelligence officer, Captain Tennyson Clark, was sent back to give the marching battalions preliminary instructions, while the brigadier, with 'his brigade-major and inseparable companion, Major Roy Morell'[37] and the latter's assistant, Captain Louch, drove east to the nearest British brigade HQ, at the edge of the Bois de Blangy. Here, after some initial difficulty, Glasgow established that the British still held Cachy and the switch trench and also had some troops in the woods west of the village, at least in the Bois l'Abbé. With these assurances the Australian officers set out for Glisy again, narrowly escaping some enemy shelling while walking back to their car.[38] On the way, the group passed the pontoon bridges at Blangy-Tronville, where the battalion columns were in the process of crossing the river.

Glasgow stopped briefly to outline the situation to the unit COs before continuing to 8th Division HQ to resume planning the operation. There had been some minor delays in starting the march, but the closest unit, the 50th Battalion, had reached the bridges by 1:15 pm and commenced to cross, with the 49th following and the others crossing as the way cleared. The 49th, the battalion designated for the Aubigny Line, received its orders there and marched directly east for five kilometres, taking up its positions by 4:30 pm; the unit now came under the orders of the British 24th Brigade. In extended order, the other three battalions continued south-east from the crossings for three kilometres to the Bois de Blangy where the troops took up assembly positions in the fringe of the wood, bivouacking in old trenches and shelters or digging temporary posts. The infantry units had settled into position by 4 pm, while the 13th MG Company dug in a short distance west of the woods. The other supporting units were moving into position also. The 13th Field Ambulance was based at Petit Cambon, a dot on the map between Amiens and Querrieu, and had begun the day with a planned exercise to practice following up a fast-moving infantry attack and maintaining casualty evacuation procedures. The exercise began at 9 am but was cancelled an hour later when an urgent message came through: reality had overtaken theory and the unit would now be required to take part in just such an operation. The Ambulance personnel had to be called in from the field and it was 12:30 pm before the unit was reassembled and moved off for Blangy-Tronville, where it waited while the CO, Lieutenant Colonel Kenneth Fry, sought out the 8th Division ADMS to get details of the situation.[39] In the meantime the allocated small-arms sub-section of the DAC moved from Bavelincourt to Lamotte-Brebière in position to bring ammunition forward for re-supply when needed, while the 27th Company AASC stood by at Querrieu. North of the Somme the 12th Brigade, in the midst of preparations for routine relief of a 3rd Division brigade, was ordered to move into the area vacated by the 13th Brigade and be at readiness to move again to the front line if needed.

It was about 2 pm when General Glasgow arrived back at Glisy and planning resumed with General Heneker and his staff. The 13th Brigade's task was to form the right-hand (southern) pincer of a converging attack, advancing over the open fields past the southern side of Villers-Bretonneux to meet a similar advance on the north beyond the village and cutting it off to be mopped up by other units. The 5th Division's 15th Brigade, under Brigadier General H E 'Pompey' Elliott, had also been attached to the 8th Division and would provide the northern force. Disagreements quickly emerged. According to Captain Louch's recollections, General Heneker was in an ill-temper over an earlier encounter with the volcanic Elliott, who 'was an aggressive and erratic man. He criticised and quarrelled with everyone.' As a result the General 'was at first inclined to treat [Glasgow] as just another Australian brigadier—like Elliott—and consequently we got an undeservedly chilly reception.'[40] General Heneker was somewhat mollified on finding that Glasgow was of considerably less flamboyant temperament than Elliott, although at least as strong-willed. The plans were developed in a better atmosphere, aided by the tact and skill of Heneker's GSO1, Lieutenant Colonel C C Armitage, for whom the Australian officers had nothing but praise.

It appears to have been Colonel Armitage who first proposed the broad plan, 'a common and fairly obvious one for attacks on villages and small towns;'[41] similar tactics had been used in the pursuit to the Hindenburg line and the capture of the villages in front of Bullecourt in 1917, for instance. It remained to work out the details. The original plan was for the 13th Brigade to form up in the vicinity of Cachy and advance from there in a north-easterly direction, more or less parallel to the Cachy Switch trench. General Glasgow pointed out that this would present his right flank to enfilade fire from the German front line established during the day and insisted on making the attack directly to the east, with his left flank on the woods and his right on Cachy. There was disagreement about the time of the attack also, the III Corps GOC, General Butler, having ordered it to commence at 8 pm. That was an hour before full dark and so in clear view of the enemy: 'If it was God Almighty who gave the order, we couldn't do it in daylight,'[42] protested Glasgow. He wanted 10:30 pm for the jump-off time, but after negotiation back and forth up to Corps level he eventually agreed to 10 pm. The brigadier also declined the assistance of a protective artillery barrage, pointing out that the German positions were not known exactly and the British guns had just been pulled back to temporary positions and could not be expected to fire on an accurate barrage line. A barrage would also be an obvious warning to the enemy that an attack was on the way. Instead he asked that the artillery bombard known targets, particularly Villers-Bretonneux village itself, for an hour after the start then lift to what was now the German back area. This was agreed also, and the 2nd Northamptonshire Battalion was placed under 13th Brigade orders to carry out the mopping-up of the village.

It was 4 pm before those matters were settled, and with time growing short the 13th Brigade staff set about allocating tasks to the units and preparing orders. The designated start line ran north-south from the southern side of the Bois d'Aquenne; to reach the start, the units would have to march about 2.5 kilometres from their present positions. The 51st and 52nd Battalions, left to right, would form the first line of the attack with the 50th following close behind in support. The final objective was on the previous British front line about a kilometre east of Monument Farm, an advance of up to four kilometres from the start line. On the objective the left would link up with the 15th Brigade troops advancing past the north of the village; the right would be supported by a battalion of the 54th British Brigade, advancing from a line south of Cachy towards Hangard Wood. All of the 13th MG Company's Vickers guns would go forward, two with each of the first wave battalions and the remainder advancing independently, some to take up covering positions on the left flank and others to go into Cachy Switch trench as a reserve. There was no specific task for the LTM Battery but it was also to go forward to Cachy Switch to be available if needed. A car was sent to collect the battalion commanders and the MG Company OC (Captain William Cory) and bring them in for briefing. By some misunderstanding of earlier signals, the 50th Battalion believed that it had been ordered to join the 24th Brigade in the Aubigny Line—the same task that the 49th Battalion had already been sent on—and Colonel Salisbury, the 50th CO, had gone to 24th Brigade HQ to report.[43] The vehicle picked up Colonels Whitham and Christie, Captain Cory and the Northamptons' CO and brought them to Glisy

Commander and key staff officers of the 13th Brigade at Tronville Chateau on Anzac Day 1918, following the overnight battle at Villers-Bretonneux. Left to right: Brigadier General William Glasgow; Captain Arthur Nicholson (Staff Captain); Capt Thomas Louch (Assistant Brigade Major); Major Roy Morell (Brigade Major). Maj Morell's dog 'Pete' completes the group. (AWM E02135)

to receive their orders and a personal briefing from General Glasgow. The operation orders, necessarily short, were handwritten by Captain Louch and Major Morell on a few message pad pages, one carbon copy per battalion, accompanied by a copy of the area map marked up in coloured pencil to show the battalion boundaries, start lines and objective lines; extra copies of the map were given to the battalions for their company commanders.

The briefing was completed by 7 pm, and with only three hours until Zero the car took the COs back to their units. Colonel Whitham took the 50th Battalion's orders and maps with him, handing them over to Colonel Salisbury when the latter returned from his unnecessary excursion. The battalions, waiting in their uncomfortable temporary bivouacs while the commanders conferred, had lost several casualties to scattered shelling and moreover had eaten little since early morning—the men had moved off before the usual midday meal and the cookers and regular rations had been left behind to speed the march. The 49th Battalion quartermaster had organised a hot breakfast for his unit before the march and the 13th MG Company had brought their cooker down, but most had only their emergency rations or what they could scrounge from British troops in the area. Arriving back at their lines, the battalion COs set about organising their units for the operation. Colonel Whitham, describing the 52nd Battalion's briefing, noted that:

> Battalion HQ was located in an open field ... and consisted of a hastily erected shelter; a few sticks stuck in the ground [and] covered with a piece of canvas.
>
> Company Commanders were sent for immediately on return of CO from Brigade HQ and whilst the Senior Major (Major R F Fitzgerald DSO) and Adjutant (Lieutenant G E C Gill) marked the 4 maps ... with boundaries and limits of attack, CO briefly explained the instructions for the counter-attack.[44]

It was about 8 pm when the briefings finished. The units would have to move off by 8:30 to reach the start line by 10, and by the time the company commanders got back to their own HQs there was barely ten minutes to pass the instructions on to their platoon commanders. While the troops were forming up to begin the advance the battalion intelligence officers went ahead to join the Brigade IO, Lieutenant Clark, for the task of laying tapes to mark the start line.

In the meantime General Glasgow had driven to Tronville Chateau to set up a joint HQ with the 15th Brigade; arriving at 8 pm, he found that his fellow brigadier, 'Pompey' Elliott, had just completed his own briefing of battalion commanders. This was the first chance that day for the two brigadiers to compare plans. The 15th Brigade's lead-up to the imminent battle had been somewhat different to that of Glasgow's men. The 15th had been located not far to the north of Villers-Bretonneux for several weeks and was currently occupying positions between Blangy-Tronville and Aubigny as the 5th Division's reserve brigade. For all his bluster, General Elliott was an outstanding commander. From his reading of the situation in the sector he had become convinced that the Germans would attack Villers-Bretonneux sooner or later, and moreover he doubted that its British garrison, filled out as it was with inexperienced young conscripts, would be able to hold the village. Elliott anticipated that his brigade would then be required to recapture the position, and accordingly he kept one of his battalions in readiness at all times and ordered his senior officers to study the ground. Elliott even had a model of the ground constructed and drew up a contingency plan for a counter-attack (his scheme was very similar to the one adopted on the day, leading to his insistence after the war that he was personally and solely responsible for the Villers-Bretonneux plan, which he compared to that used by Hannibal at Cannae[45]). At the first signs of the German attack that morning, he had ordered patrols sent out to reconnoitre and keep him informed of the situation as it developed. Now that his predictions had been justified, Elliott was in the process of implementing a version of his original counter-attack plan. Keeping one battalion in reserve, two others would sweep north of the village and the remaining unit would swing around the south to link up on the eastern side; the village itself would then be mopped up. When General Glasgow was informed of the 15th Brigade plan he pointed out the battalion advancing on the south side

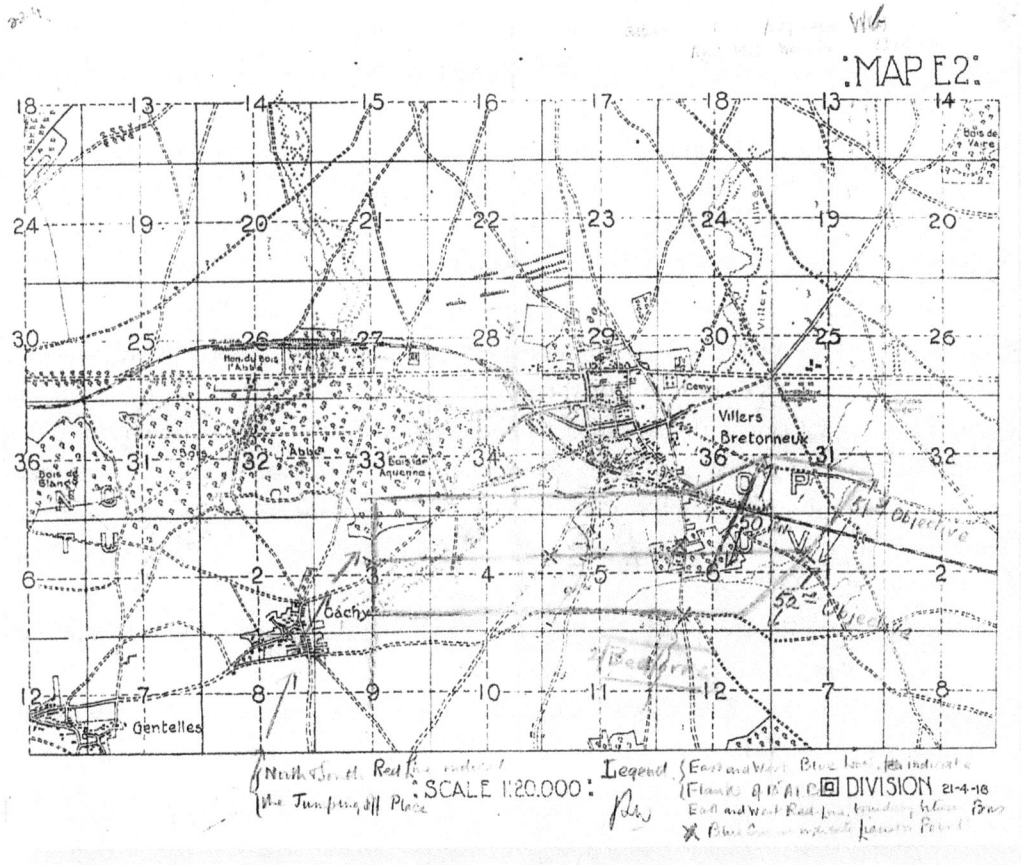

One of the maps used by the 52nd Battalion on 24 April, annotated by Colonel Whitham for the unit's War Diary. The final "start line" was about 300 metres west of that shown and ran from the edge of the woods.
(52nd Battalion War Diary for April 1918)

would almost certainly run into the British units moving directly on the village, as well as the left of the 13th Brigade troops making their advance; there was a good chance of a 'friendly fire' clash in the darkness. Elliott agreed at once and changed his orders to have all of his battalions advance on the northern side; the change necessitated re-briefing of the 15th Brigade COs, contributing to those units falling behind the starting time.

The 13th Brigade intelligence officers with some of their scouts had meanwhile moved forward to the edge of the Bois d'Aquenne where they were to mark the start line with tapes. It was not fully dark when the party came up to the position and they immediately came under fire from a German machine gun in the woods on their left. Lieutenant Norman Phillips, the 51st Battalion IO, called on some nearby British troops to provide covering fire while the tapes were laid and a decision was taken to mark the line 300 metres behind that originally intended and with its left on the edge of the wood.[46] It was apparent that there were German forces in the woods, despite assurances made to General Glasgow that the area would have been cleared by the time the attack went in; in fact it was bristling with enemy machine guns. In briefing the 52nd Battalion company commanders, Colonel Whitham had told them that 'the woods on the west of the town, which are on the left flank of the Brigade attack, are reported to be now practically cleared of the enemy, British troops having been ordered to clear them this afternoon.'[47] This information would have been given to the battalion COs by General Glasgow from his own briefing, and presumably the 51st Battalion was similarly briefed by Colonel Christie. The report appears to have referred to an attack made by a battalion of the Sherwood Foresters regiment on the Bois d'Aquenne some time after 3 pm. The attack had been stopped by intense fire from German positions in the wood and had got no further than the Cachy-Fouilloy road, which divided the Bois l'Abbé from the Bois d'Aquenne. The crucial information that the attack had failed does not seem to have got through to the higher commanders, however. The British battalion CO, up with his troops, had been seriously wounded, a circumstance that would have hindered timely and accurate reporting.[48] The situation at Villers-Bretonneux resulted in battalion commanders going well into the forward zone; the CO of the 2nd Northamptons was killed in action later that night, and Colonels Christie, Whitham and Salisbury and their HQ details went with the advance of their units.

The 52nd Battalion troops, taking the right of the first wave, began moving from their bivouacs at 8:30 pm and the leading files had reached the jumping-off position by 9:45. Ten minutes later the Battalion's deployment was almost complete, with the two lead companies each with two platoons in extended line across the battalion frontage and one[49] in section columns fifty metres behind; the support and reserve companies further to the rear also formed up in columns. The 51st, on the left of the line near the woods, was a little delayed on its approach march and Colonel Christie himself was the first to reach the start line. The leading company came up at 9:53 and Christie began guiding the troops into position on the tapes. The 51st deployed similarly to the 52nd, with two companies in front followed by the support and then reserve companies, except that all of the 51st companies remained in the artillery formation of section columns that they had used in their approach.[50] It was apparent that the 51st would not be fully formed up by 10 pm for the planned jump-off, so Colonels Whitham and Christie agreed to delay the start for ten minutes. Behind the two first-wave battalions, the supporting 50th was on its way forward also. That unit had not started its march until 9:30, having been delayed by the incident of the mistaken orders, and they were moving 15 minutes behind the two leading battalions, the rear elements of which they could just make out ahead in the available light—the moon was up, but heavy cloud cover restricted its effect. As the support battalion, the 50th deployed in a line covering the whole frontage of the Brigade's advance.

At 10 pm the III Corps heavy artillery opened up and began pounding Villers-Bretonneux village, and ten minutes later the 51st and 52nd Battalions began their advance. It was a desperate enterprise. C E W Bean, who had been made aware of the plans at 5th Division HQ, wrote in his diary that night

> One cannot help thinking of our magnificent 13th Brigade going over ... I don't believe they have a chance ... 5,000 yards to go through the enemy, another Brigade to meet in the dark ... I scarcely think it will come off ...[51]

The battalions had already marched at least 10 kilometres to reach their first assembly positions, followed by a further two to three kilometres to reach the start line. With scarcely a pause at that point they then faced a battlefield advance of another four kilometres to achieve the final objective, against a confident, numerous enemy whose positions were not known with any certainty. The attack had to be carried out in the dark across unfamiliar territory with only a superficial briefing, conveyed in mostly hurried verbal outline below the level of company commanders. One thing the troops did know was that they were in for a hard, ruthless fight—'take no prisoners' Captain W R 'Billy' Harburn told his 'C' company of the 51st Battalion, forming the left of the unit's first line near the woods. General Glasgow's rejection of the original plan of advancing north-east from Cachy avoided presenting the right flank of the advance to the enemy front line, but the chosen alternative of advancing directly eastwards had its own drawbacks. The Cachy Switch trench ran diagonally across the line of advance and formed a serious obstacle, particularly its defensive barbed-wire entanglement on the far side (it may be that Glasgow and his staff were not aware of this, but as a 50th Battalion soldier later wrote, it was shown on the printed maps[52]). Also the plan assumed that any German presence in the woods on the left flank would have been neutralised before the attack jumped off, an assumption that would quickly turn out to be false.

Almost as soon as the leading files moved off German flares shot up from the woods and a storm of machine gun fire broke out, enfilading the advancing lines. Lieutenant Clifford Sadlier's platoon on the extreme left of the 51st Battalion's line took the brunt of the fire. Many of the men were hit, the neighbouring platoon suffering heavily as well, and the others were pinned down, unable to move in the light of the flares and the streams of tracer bullets coming from the wood. When the first sheaf of flares died out those men who remained unhurt got to their feet and tried to continue the advance, but more flares rose and the machine guns opened fire again. More men fell dead or wounded and the survivors again went to ground seeking cover. The advance had been effectively stopped on that flank. Lieutenant Sadlier himself was one of the few in his platoon who was unwounded, and he was pondering his next move when Sergeant Charles Stokes from the platoon on the right crawled over to him with a suggestion: 'Collect your bombers and go into the wood and bomb those guns out.'[53] Sadlier realised immediately that Stokes was right, and set about organising the attack. The support company was coming up and Sadlier told one of its officers to fill the gap in the line while he took the surviving men from the two platoons into the wood—as well as Sadlier and Stokes, who carried a bag of grenades, there were only about ten still unhurt. Sadlier set one of these, Lewis gunner Corporal Wilfred Guthrie, to fire on the nearest enemy machine gun post while the rest of the group rushed it. Sadlier tossed a grenade into the post then charged in firing his revolver. The enemy crew was finished off at close quarters, Stokes and the others joining in with rifle and bayonet; in the fight Sadlier was shot through the thigh by a German who had at first held up his hands in surrender and was then either shot by Sadlier or bayoneted by Stokes (accounts differ[54]). The wound did not hamper Sadlier at first and he led on towards the rest of the enemy guns, posted 50 metres apart. A series of small, savage fights went on in the dark around the bushes and trees on the fringe of the wood. Stokes put a machine gun out of action with grenades and Sadlier killed the crew of that or another gun with his revolver. He had been wounded again by now, with a bullet through the right forearm; it was only when he tried to reload his pistol that Sadlier realised that his hand was paralysed. As well, his leg was now stiffening up from the earlier wound and he could do no more, 'so I decided to get out while I could still walk.'[55] Others of the small group had also been hit but Stokes was unhurt and he went on to attack a further gun, accompanied by two remaining men. He had used all of his grenades but he was now joined by Lance Corporal S R 'Bob' West, a signaller, who had two rifle grenades with him. Stokes fired these at the gun position but both missed. West had noticed a dump of German stick grenades, however, and he collected several of these and brought them to Stokes, who threw two of them accurately onto the post and wiped out the crew. Further on, a single German was operating another gun and Stokes killed him with a rifle-shot. The little group had knocked out the four or five machine guns closest to the advancing troops but Sergeant Stokes, who was later described as 'a tall raw-boned Aussie … [with] a Red Indian caste of countenance … a warrior really on the war-path,'[56] was not finished yet and he continued to probe along the fringe of the wood seeking more targets.

While that drama was taking place inside the wood the 51st's right flank and the 52nd beyond it maintained the advance. The ground sloped down from south to north and those troops were to the right of the crest, giving them some protection from the machine guns on the left, but they came under increasingly heavy fire from their right front. Although the fire was coming from long range and was not particularly accurate, casualties mounted up as the men moved forward through the frightening streams of glowing tracer bullets, sometimes standing motionless as a sheaf of flares burst above then resuming the advance as the illumination faded. By this time, the British bombardment had set fire to buildings in the town and the flames helped the advance to maintain direction in the dark, with the moonlight still blocked by clouds. Apart from the platoons on the extreme left the troops had nothing to shoot at yet, and could only passively endure the enemy fire until they got close enough to use their personal weapons. As the front lines came up to the Cachy Switch trench, however, a skirmish with rifles and grenades broke out. This quickly ceased when it was realised that the opponents were British troops manning the trench, who had not been informed of the Australian advance and had opened fire on what they thought was a German attack from the rear. The 51st and 52nd passed across the trench and kept on towards the barbed wire entanglement beyond it. The 50th Battalion, coming on ten to fifteen minutes behind in support, had also encountered machine gun fire from the Bois d'Aquenne on its left flank soon after crossing the start line. The German guns, presumably positioned at longer range than those attacked by Sadlier and Stokes, were firing too high to seriously interfere with the start of the 50th's advance but the volume of fire increased as the troops moved forward. The 50th's left flank company sent two platoons into the trees to deal with the enemy machine guns. A number of posts were knocked out, the Battalion later reporting that seven machine guns were captured in the area.[57]

Ahead, the 51st and 52nd reached the wire and came under fire from machine guns on the far side of the entanglement where the Germans had established their outpost line. Fire was still coming from the right front but the most dangerous was from a single gun on the left, positioned where it could fire in enfilade directly along the line of the wire entanglement. The first troops of the 51st trying to find a way through the wire were cut down, while others tried to outflank the gun; two attempts failed and the advance seemed to be blocked again. At this point Sergeant Stokes, still working his way through the fringe of the wood, located the gun and prepared to attack it with the help of a Lewis gunner, Corporal James Meldrum. The German saw them first and opened fire; Meldrum was wounded and a bullet knocked Stokes's steel helmet off his head. After quickly attending to Meldrum, Stokes went back to try again and found that the gun had been withdrawn.[58] This may have been due to the intervention of the 13th MG Company Vickers gun section tasked with covering the approaches to the village, which had now reached the vicinity. The section commander, Lieutenant Thomas Cowley, detected an enemy machine gun firing from about the same location; he brought two of his own guns into action and reported that their fire had silenced the enemy weapon. It may have been the same gun that Stokes had attacked (or the German crew could have simply run out of ammunition) but that particular menace had been removed. The gun had done great execution among the Australians struggling with the Cachy Switch wire, however, particularly in the 51st Battalion. Still under fire from in front, the troops had lost formation and split into small groups, hesitating as they tried to find a way through the entanglement.

Captain Harburn saw that the advance had to be kept going. He quickly conferred with Captain Clive Cooke, commanding the 51st's right flank company, and the two officers decided to simply blow their whistles, the recognised signal for an all-out assault. The men responded immediately and rushed the wire. Some found gaps to the far side, others forced their way through, but many were hit and hung on the barbs. Captain Cooke was among those killed in the wire and several platoon commanders were wounded and put out of action; Corporal Thomas Sullivan put himself at the head of two platoons and led them on. The survivors of the two companies reached the far side in some disorder, a few drifting to the right where they found themselves mixed in with part of the 52nd Battalion. The men of that unit had also forced their way through the obstacle, under fire that was not quite as intense as that facing the 51st but still caused heavy losses. The commander of the 52nd's 'A' Company on the right of the first line, Captain Claude Stubbings, was wounded at this stage. In the 51st on the left, Captain Harburn collected the remaining men of his battered company together, finding that he had about 40 still on their feet. They were at the enemy outpost line now and a group of Germans appeared with their hands up in an offer of surrender. Harburn could not spare any men to escort prisoners and he could not leave enemies on the loose behind him; 'No prisoners,' he ordered again, and a Lewis gunner mowed them down.

Following that incident there was a short pause while Harburn went back to the 51st's support and reserve companies, now coming up behind, to seek reinforcements. Lieutenant Roy Earl's platoon from the support company hurried forward to fill the gap on Harburn's left while the company commander, Captain Frank Smith, sent a message back to the 50th Battalion requesting that unit to send a company ahead to reinforce the front line. At about that time the 51st's reserve company sent forward an officer, Lieutenant Charles Town, to assist Harburn.[59] At another blast of Harburn's whistle his own depleted company resumed their advance and almost immediately ran into a German infantry force, estimated at 200 men, advancing on them in counter-attack and firing as they came. Harburn had his men lie down in a semicircle and open fire. The enemy force lost heavily but was working around Harburn's left flank when part of the 50th Battalion company called forward earlier came on the scene. Those troops had already lost their company commander, Lieutenant Henry Kay, killed in the Cachy Switch wire but they went straight into the fight against the now-outflanked Germans, most of whom turned and fled for the woods. Others were shot and a party on the right, said to be 60 strong,[60] surrendered and were sent to the rear—a luckier group than those who had first tried to surrender to Harburn's men. All along the line the troops who had run the gauntlet of the flanking machine guns were now coming to grips at close quarters with the previously unseen enemy, targets on whom they could release their pent-up tension. The 52nd Battalion on the right had worked through the wire and closed with the German outpost line. After a fire-fight lasting three minutes the 52nd's right flank company, now led by Lieutenant Neville Hatton, charged and routed their opponents. The battalion continued the advance for 460 metres to reach the next German line; those enemy troops did not stay to fight, and the 52nd pushed on again. After a further 460 metres the leading

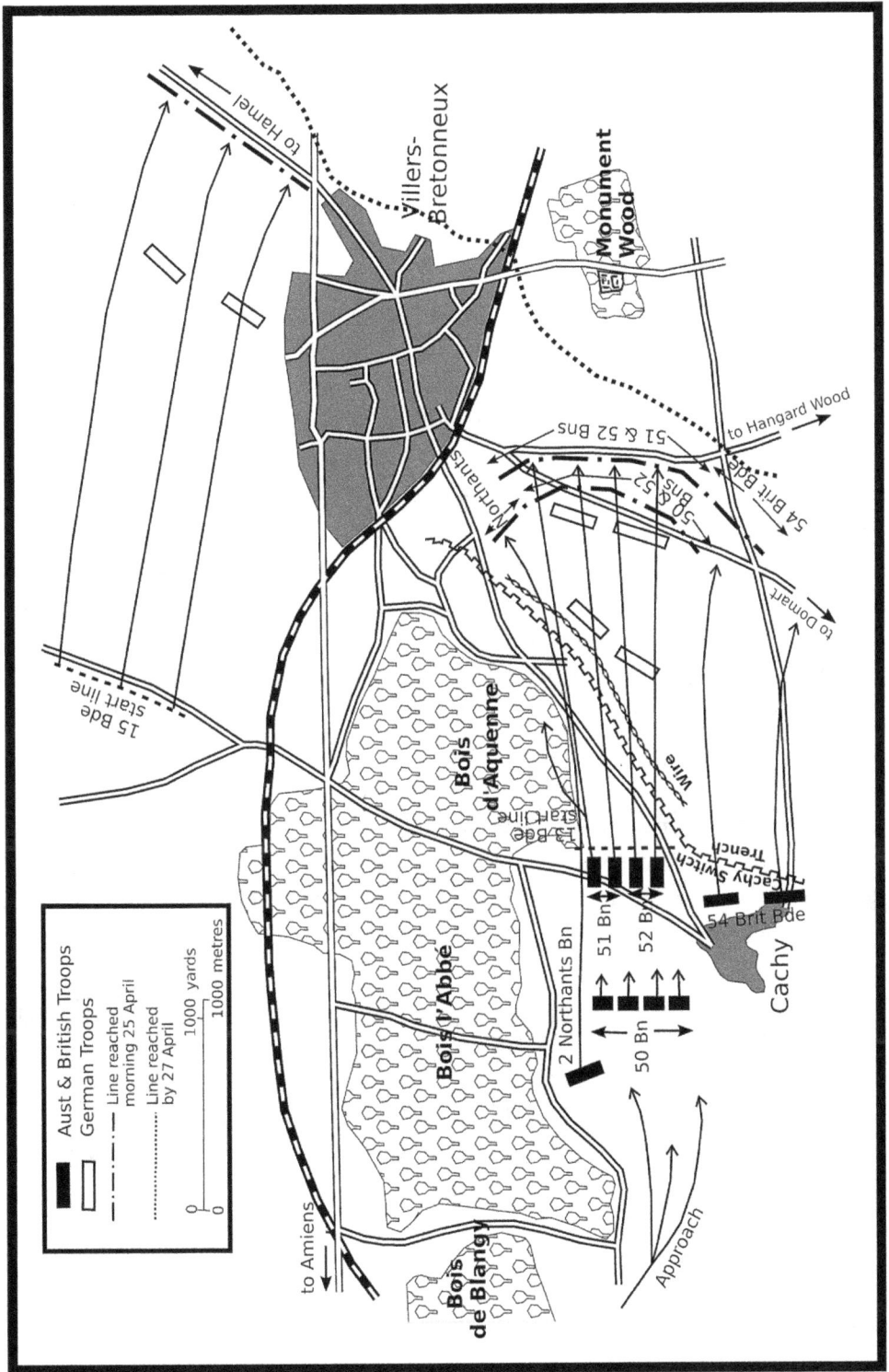

Second Battle of Villers-Bretonneux: counter-attack by the 13th and 15th Brigades, 24/25 April 1918.

companies encountered a stronger line of enemy posts, including eight machine guns; those opened fire on the advancing Australians, who went to ground and returned fire, the Lewis gunners concentrating on the enemy machine gun posts. The Germans were launching flares, illuminating the scene but also giving away their own positions. The fire-fight went on for a few minutes, then 'We let out a wild yell and at them. The Germans ran.'[61] The flares stopped and the 52nd pursued the enemy for several hundred metres, shooting and bayoneting in the dark, to the south-west outskirts of Monument Wood where the impetus slowed.

During that fighting the 52nd had lost two more company commanders, Captains William Kennedy of 'C' (who had led so well at Dernancourt three weeks earlier) and William Wilmott of 'D', both wounded, the latter fatally. All of Kennedy's platoon officers were also hit, and 21-year-old Sergeant Alfred White found himself in command of the company, leading it capably through the remainder of the battle. Other NCOs took charge of the platoons, while Lieutenant William Hall moved across from 'A' Company to take command of 'D'. The 52nd had reached a point fairly close to the final objective, and on the left near Villers-Bretonneux village the much-depleted 51st was making some progress also. Captain Harburn's force moved up level with the town-site, coming under fire from enemy machine guns on the railway embankment running along its southern fringe. To cut off the retreat of the Germans fleeing from their failed counter-attack, Harburn sent Lieutenant Earl's platoon into the valley on that side of the village, where those troops encountered and defeated an enemy force, capturing three machine guns and a number of prisoners. Earl, who had first made his mark at Noreuil a year earlier, then deployed his 20 men and two Lewis guns to form a strong-point covering the left flank. In this area, the Lewis gun team of Lance Corporal Cecil Burt and Private Reg Helyar, scouting ahead, suddenly came across an enemy post of 40 men with four machine guns. Helyar threw a grenade into their midst, then Burt threatened the shaken Germans with the Lewis and bluffed them into surrender—his gun had been damaged and would only fire single rounds.[62] Captain Harburn pushed on into the area between Monument Wood and the village, reaching the road running south into the wood; there he called a halt to regroup.

At some stage in this period of intense fighting, wristwatches had ticked past midnight and it was Anzac Day. Until then the 13th Brigade had been the only jaw of the pincers that had been in action. On the northern side of the village the 15th Brigade's attack had been delayed, firstly by the last-minute changes in the orders and then by a battalion losing direction on the approach to the start line. The advance finally began two hours late but soon made up for lost time. Unopposed at first, the leading elements of the 15th Brigade contacted the enemy line at 12:40 am and smashed it with a ferocious bayonet charge. Few prisoners were taken until the troops grew weary of killing, and the battalions began to consolidate a line along the road to Hamel, beyond the north-eastern outskirts of the village. This was some distance short of the correct final objective, the old British front line, which the 15th Brigade probably could have reached but for confusion in their orders over how far they were meant to go.

The left flank of the 13th Brigade sector comprised Captain Harburn's small force of the 51st Battalion north of Monument Wood. During the halt it appears that he managed to collect a number of the troops scattered during the advance, as he later recalled that his force had built up to 120 men, although he had only one other officer with him, Lieutenant Town.[63] There was no sign of any other troops on his right, so Harburn left Town in charge and set out to find the 52nd Battalion's flank. That unit, after overwhelming the several lines of enemy in front of them, was re-grouping near the southern fringe of Monument Wood. The 52nd also found that their right flank was open, the British unit on that side, the 7th Bedfords, having been held up by machine gun fire to their front. Part of the 52nd's right attacked those positions and drove off the enemy troops, but a firm link could not at first be established with the Bedfords. The movement caused a gap to open between the 52nd's right and left, which was soon filled when the Battalion's reserve company came up. This was 'B' Company under Major William Craies, an officer whose career had started unpromisingly with the 25th Battalion (2nd Division) at Gallipoli. Then he had been sent home and had his appointment terminated as unsuitable, for 'malingering on the beach,' when in fact he was suffering from dysentery, as C E W Bean understood the circumstances.[64] Craies had managed to clear his name and regain his commission in Australia, securing a posting to the 52nd, where Colonel Whitham now regarded him as 'lion hearted ... one of the bravest men we had.'[65] As the senior officer on the spot and the only one of the Battalion's company commanders to have come through the advance unscathed, he now set about re-organising the line, first sending one of his platoons to fill the gap in the 52nd's centre.

The main body of the 50th Battalion was now coming up in support, having earlier sent several rifle sections forward to plug gaps in the other units' front lines. Among its casualties during the advance, the 50th had also lost three of its starting company commanders, Lieutenant Kay and Captain Frank Hancock killed and Captain Patrick Auld taken prisoner; one of the companies was now led by an NCO, Sergeant Hamilton Brakenridge. Major Craies redeployed the troops in the area to set up a connected front and consolidate the ground gained. On the right flank he found that the Bedfords had retired further from their original position, having found that they were unsupported on their own right towards Hangard Wood, where the units in that sector had been stopped by heavy German machine gun fire. Sergeant Henry Wright went across from the 52nd to steady a shaken group of young Tommies who had lost their officers, getting them organised to dig in and set up a defensive line. To maintain touch with the Bedfords, Major Craies pulled the 52nd back to form a position along the Villers-Bretonneux to Hangard Wood road[66] with two companies forward and two 150 metres behind in support, and the 50th Battalion prolonging the support line to the left. He was assisted by an officer identified in some reports as Captain James Churchill Smith of the 50th, but who was more likely to have been Lieutenant William Beresford, that unit's remaining company commander, or Captain Frank Smith of the 51st Battalion.[67] The troops dug in, making use where they could of old segments of trench and the German machine gun posts that they had just captured.

There the officers were found by Captain Harburn of the 51st, who had made his way across from the left flank. Harburn's blood was still up from the drama of the night and he wanted the other units to keep the advance going into Monument Wood, but Major Craies felt that was unwise in view of the uncertain situation on the right. There was some discussion before Harburn agreed to withdraw his own men from their advanced position and conform with the 52nd. He returned to his command and organised the movement, pulling back to take position along the road on the 52nd's left, with Lieutenant Earl's strong-point still guarding the extreme left flank to the south of the village. The 13th MG Company's four Vickers gun teams attached to the battalions came up and were positioned in the front line, having lost their section commander, Lieutenant Francis Burt, killed on the way. The difficulties that the machine gunners faced getting their awkward weapons and equipment through the Cachy Switch wire were not recorded, but they must have been considerable; it was reported that a quantity of ammunition was lost during the advance, a problem that Corporal Raymond Davie, in charge of the guns supporting the 52nd Battalion, solved by making use of two captured German weapons. Although the original final objective had not been reached, the enemy had been pushed back for more than a kilometre from their outpost line near the Cachy Switch wire. It was apparent that the territory in front, and particularly Monument Wood, remained strongly held by the Germans. The situation reinforced the troops' natural inclination to slow down once the enemy to their immediate front had been dispersed. As well, it is likely that the men were worn out after their exertions since mid-morning, culminating in all-out charge and hand-to-hand fighting. A few small groups had penetrated further: a 51st Battalion Lewis gunner, Private Henry Passmore, took charge of his section when its commander was hit and led it well forward to attack an enemy post mounting three machine guns. Passmore, who was 18 years old and had been with the unit for only six weeks, killed seven of the Germans and took two others prisoner. The rest of the enemy crews fled, abandoning their guns. The section then realised that they had got too far ahead of the rest of the company and fell back to the main line, Passmore carrying a severely wounded man. In the 52nd Battalion sector Second Lieutenant Douglas Henderson took a patrol into Monument Wood and captured a few prisoners, but withdrew on realising that there was no support on the flanks.

Behind the infantry rifle companies other elements of the Brigade followed in support. The original intention had been for the COs of the two leading battalions to each move on the inner flank of his unit during the advance and thereby keep in close personal touch. Four liaison points were selected and marked on the map where they were to meet, and a joint forward headquarters was to be established which would also be shared with the support battalion CO. This arrangement had fallen down almost immediately when the 51st Battalion was late to the start line and Colonel Christie was occupied with positioning his men on the tapes. He had no time to rejoin Colonel Whitham of the 52nd before the line jumped off and the advance had reached the vicinity of Cachy Switch before they re-established contact. The joint HQ location had been selected as a depression just ahead of the trench, but when

Colonel Whitham reached the position he found that it was swept by enemy machine gun fire. A better location was found in a shallow trench further back, west of the Switch (apparently part of that system), and Whitham set up his HQ there. Colonel Christie later joined him in the new location and the 50th Battalion CO, Colonel Salisbury, set up his own HQ in another section of trench 200 metres away. An immediate task was to establish communications. The 52nd Battalion's signals officer, Lieutenant Cameron Crocker, with a squad of linesmen from his own unit and the 51st, ran wires forward 1,600 metres to the front line and had a telephone working by 12:40 am, and also set up a connection with 50th Battalion HQ. By 1 am the Brigade signallers under Second Lieutenant Joseph Climpson, attached from the divisional Signal Company, had established a reporting centre on the railway near the Bois de Blangy and run lines connecting Brigade to the forward battalion HQs, having closely followed the advancing infantry. Unit and Brigade linesmen worked through the hours of darkness, under steady shelling, to repair breaks and keep the phones working.

The Brigade's medical services had faced their own challenges. Since arriving in the area south of the Somme during the afternoon, Colonel Fry, the 13th Field Ambulance CO, had been trying with minimal success to extract from the 8th Division medical staff some details of the available facilities and evacuation routes. Referred to the British 24th Field Ambulance at Blangy-Tronville, he found that the CO of that unit was uncertain of his own dispositions. The only definite information was the location of the relevant ADS, at an old prisoner-of-war cage near Blangy-Tronville.[68] There was also no clear direction yet as to what the 13th Brigade's task would be, so Colonel Fry decided to allot three of his stretcher-bearer teams to stay with each infantry battalion, with others in reserve and the tent personnel standing by at Camon just east of Amiens while the situation developed. The bearer teams had been posted with the battalions by 7:30 pm, those allotted to the 50th Battalion having to wait while that unit returned from its fruitless march to the Aubigny Line. The teams were under the direction of Major Leslie Tassie, commanding the Ambulance's bearer division, and Captain Ernest Docker in charge of the teams directly attached to the three attacking battalions. It was not until 9:45—fifteen minutes before the jump off, with the battalions on the move to the start line—that Colonel Fry was informed that the attack was definitely going ahead, and only then because he went to Brigade HQ to confirm an unofficial report.[69] Once the axis of the infantry advance was determined, the Field Ambulance officers followed up to establish the evacuation route and distribute their personnel, setting up a motor ambulance post at a building identified as a 'Red Chateau'[70] and two bearer relay posts between there and the Cachy area.

The battalion RMOs with their orderlies, unit stretcher bearers and allotted Field Ambulance bearer squads went forward at the rear of their units, seeking suitable locations to set up their RAPs once the battalion forward HQs had taken position. The 50th Battalion RMO, Captain Phillip Sewell, halted his party in a segment of trench near Cachy and went ahead to contact the unit HQ. After an hour he had not returned nor had he reached HQ—

three days later he was found dead in a shell-hole, killed by a machine gun bullet. With Captain Sewell missing, two NCOs in the RAP group, Corporal Charles Donnelly in charge of the unit's medical details, and Lance Corporal Arthur Forrester in charge of the three Field Ambulance bearer teams, took the responsibility of organising evacuation of the wounded. Corporal Donnelly formed a temporary RAP in the trench, and the wounded brought there were relayed by the Ambulance bearers to cellars in Cachy village, 450 metres to the west; Corporal Forrester organised that location as a casualty collection post, from where the patients were picked up for the next stage of evacuation to the rear. The only cover that the 52nd Battalion RMO, Captain Robert Forsyth, could find near Battalion HQ was a big pile of harvested beets (mangold-wurzels). Here he set up his post and began bandaging the wounded coming in from the struggle in the wire, unconcerned by the machine gun fire hitting the pile, even though this was the first time that he had been in action; Captain Forsyth was wounded himself during the next day. The location was close to the 50th Battalion post, and the 52nd's wounded were also sent initially to the collection points in the Cachy cellars; with the coming of daylight both RAPs moved from their exposed positions to the cellars. The 51st RMO, Captain Geoffrey Arnold, established his post south of the Bois d'Aquenne and dressed the wounded in the open, placing them in shell-holes to wait for evacuation to the ADS by the Field Ambulance bearers.[71] Captain Arnold also treated some of the 50th's casualties, and later those of the 52nd when Captain Forsyth was hit. A frequent visitor to the RAPs was the senior Anglican chaplain of the 13th Brigade, Rev Donald Blackwood; although he was only expected to perform his duties at the CCS in the rear, Chaplain Blackwood spent much of the night and the next day up in the battle zone, doing what he could to comfort the wounded and assist the medical personnel. He also had the grim task of conducting numerous burial services. The casualty evacuation continued through the day of 25 April and overall worked reasonably well, particularly considering the difficult circumstances faced by the unit medical personnel and the 13th Field Ambulance, as acknowledged in the infantry's after-action reports. The Field Ambulance noted that about 800 wounded men were successfully evacuated over the period of fighting.

Daylight on 25 April gave both sides the opportunity to assess the situation. The 13th Brigade units had consolidated their line along the road facing Monument Wood, although there was no link to the 15th Brigade north of the village and only tenuous touch with the British troops on their right. The plan for clearing of the village itself had gone awry and the German garrison was still ensconced—Captain Harburn's men on the left flank of the 51st found themselves fired on by machine guns from the railway cutting and the woods to their left and left rear. The 2nd Northants, tasked with mopping up the southern part of the village, had struck trouble early in the attack when their CO was killed and adjutant wounded by a shell-burst. After heavy losses getting through the Cachy Switch wire, the Northants turned to advance on the village but were stopped by intense fire from the machine guns along the railway. With nearly 300 casualties, the unit pulled back to dig in on a line facing north; there they gained touch with Harburn's force. The Germans still occupied the Bois d'Aquenne in some strength, but that danger was soon removed when a troop of three British tanks arrived on the scene, their officer keen to make a contribution. Colonel Christie directed them to clear the wood and by 9:30 am the Germans had been driven out by the tanks, with the assistance of some British infantry that had also come up. For the German forces still holding their positions inside Villers-Bretonneux, it was becoming apparent that they were almost surrounded and they began to withdraw eastward before the net could be closed completely. For the 13th Brigade troops south of the town, daylight had brought increasing enemy sniper activity and bursts of machine gun fire from the strong German lines facing them. Lieutenant Town, 51st Battalion, was killed by a sniper early in the morning, and later in the day the same unit also lost company commander Captain Frank Smith to a sniper's shot. At 8 am a large party of troops was observed digging in behind the right flank of the 52nd Battalion. It was difficult to identify them in the prevailing visibility, but they were at first assumed to be British. The arrival at Battalion HQ of three German messengers carrying flags of truce soon corrected that impression. The Germans brought demands from their commanders for the surrender of the Australian and British forces, on the grounds that they were surrounded by superior numbers. The proposal was indignantly rejected and the envoys hustled into captivity, as fire began to come into the Australian positions from the newly-arrived enemy force. At 11 am a machine gun opened fire on Cachy Switch and was quickly answered by the reserve guns of the 13th MG Company positioned in the trench. Any movements from both sides drew fire through the afternoon, and the opposing forces mostly remained under cover. In spite of frequent reports from the front line Brigade HQ and higher command were reluctant to believe that German troops were present so far west, but eventually a troop of three 'whippet' tanks was sent to investigate late in the day. These were directed by Colonel Whitham to the area in question and were soon involved in fighting the definitely hostile force, part of which they drove off in disorder.

Once the dispositions of the two brigades became clear the commanders turned their attention to closing the gap between them and blocking the exits from the town. On the north side the 15th Brigade was holding a line running north-east from the Roman road, with one of its battalions, the 57th, swung around to face south-west towards the edge of the town. The British units assigned to mop-up the northern part of the town had been unable to make progress so the 57th sent in two companies to begin the task, in which they were later joined by the British. An element of the 4th Division played a part in the fighting in that sector of the battlefield. During the night Lieutenant Harold Sheridan's reserve section of the 24th MG Company, billeted at Pont Noyelles, had been ordered to reinforce the 5th Division machine guns. The four Vickers gun teams reached the front line area in the early morning and were assigned to support the 57th Battalion. Sergeant Thomas Liddicoat's gun was set up to cover the right rear of the line towards the village, and he found a position with a field of fire down the Roman road. From there he fired all morning on parties of Germans trying to escape in that direction—Lieutenant Sheridan later estimated that the gun caused at least 100 enemy casualties—ceasing only when the mopping-up troops appeared and rounded up the surviving enemy (for good measure, Sergeant Liddicoat shot down a German aircraft the next day, using a salvaged enemy machine gun). The other guns of the section were in action through the day, shooting at enemy positions across the level ground between the opposing lines.[72]

In the 13th Brigade's sector the railway cutting formed an escape route for the German troops in the southern part of the town, and at 11 am the 50th Battalion received an order from Brigade HQ to fill the gap between the 51st and the railway[73] by advancing across the open ground from its reserve position behind the forward line. The 50th was then to send out patrols to capture Monument Wood,

> but, like other commanders, General Glasgow had little conception of the volume of machine-gun fire, especially from Monument and Hangard Woods, that swept the open fields of the plateau whenever anything moved there by daylight. To reach the railway, the 50th Battalion would have to cross 400-800 yards [365-730 metres] of open plateau ... Colonel Salisbury therefore did not attempt to carry out the order.[74]

Instead Salisbury intended to wait until dark before mounting the operation. Brigade HQ was unaware for some time that the 50th had not moved, and at around midday the attached British battalion, the 2nd Northants, was ordered to also advance to the railway and form a support line. That unit, having been stopped in its attempt to enter the village during the night, was holding a north-facing line linked with the left of the 51st Battalion. From that position it had a considerably shorter distance to cover (140 metres) and its acting commander decided to make the attempt, instructing the troops to sprint straight for the objective. So fast was the movement that the Germans were taken by surprise and most of the Northants had gained cover close to the railway before the Monument Wood machine guns opened up; the British then moved on to occupy the railway station. A few German troops who had not managed to get away along the cutting were picked up in that area.[75]

The evening brought an hour-long bombardment by the German artillery between 7 and 8 pm, but the shelling was not followed by an infantry attack (the Germans had attempted a counter-attack earlier in the day, but their assembly had been broken up by the British artillery). Once the light had faded the rear echelons of the battalions, second in command, quartermaster, transport officer and RSM, organised the task of bringing up food, water and ammunition to the forward troops. Wagons took the supplies to locations near Cachy, where they were picked up by carrying parties from the companies in the front line. The dixies of stew would have been particularly welcome to men existing on emergency rations for more than 24 hours. Another 13th Brigade company commander fell victim to a German sniper during the evening, when the 52nd Battalion's Major Craies, doing the rounds of his posts in the open, was shot through the stomach; he was carried back but died on the way to the dressing station.[76] His death meant that all of the 52nd's company commanders had become casualties—in view of the difficulties of the operation, Colonel Whitham had decided to put all four substantive OCs into battle, rather than following the usual practice of leaving one or two out with the nucleus and having their companies led by the seconds-in-command (he was later admonished by General Birdwood for that decision).[77]

Darkness was also the time for the 50th Battalion to make its delayed advance, and Lieutenant Beresford's company sent out two advanced patrols to probe up to the railway. Two larger parties followed in support and those troops were able to establish posts along the objective line, collecting some more prisoners in the process. The main body of the 50th then moved up and occupied the position in strength, with its left on the railway and the line angled back to the south-west linking with the left of the 51st—'without any difficulty and with no casualties,' as Colonel Salisbury pointed out in his report.[78] A gap remained from the north side of the railway to the 15th Brigade's right flank, but this was filled a little later by the 49th Battalion. That unit had been relieved in the Aubigny Line north of the woods during the day and had marched through the rear of the now-cleared woods to reach a position behind the 13th Brigade's front line in the afternoon. Colonel Denton went forward and established his HQ with that of the 50th Battalion while his men waited in the road through the woods. Well after dark orders came through to move two companies forward into the gap. Those troops passed through the village and progressively established a line of eight posts linking with the 57th on the left and the 50th on the right, the last being in place at 3:40 am; 'thus by the small hours of April 26th the line east of Villers-Bretonneux was complete.'[79]

The enemy still held strong positions forward of the former British front line, however, and the sector from Monument Wood south to Hangard Wood now became the objective of a renewed attack. French forces were brought in for this operation, the elite Moroccan Division of colonial troops, which included a regiment of the Foreign Legion. The French moved up during the night 25/26 April, their left-flank unit (8th Zouaves) passing through the lines of the 51st and 52nd Battalions. Those units were then withdrawn, the 51st moving to a position west of the town, and the 52nd back to its 24 April bivouac area on the edge of the Bois de Blangy; on the way, the 52nd's 'B' Company marched past the spot where Chaplain Blackwood was conducting the burial service of its late commander, Major Craies. The 50th Battalion was ordered to co-operate with the Zouaves by advancing its right flank in conformity and linking up in the vicinity of Monument Farm. The French attack across open country north of Hangard Wood, launched in daylight at 5:15 am behind an inaccurate barrage, failed disastrously in the face of the German machine guns. On the left of the French the 50th attempted to advance on time but was quickly pinned down by heavy fire from Monument Wood, while the Zouaves, arriving late at the start line alongside the 50th after apparently losing most of their command group to hostile shelling,[80] chose to go no further. Another attack on Monument Wood was proposed but soon cancelled, and the fighting in the Second Battle of Villers-Bretonneux closed with a costly small operation by the 15th Brigade to straighten its line north-east of the town. Although the final objective of the attack, the original British front line, had not been reached, the Germans had been thrown back from most of the ground that they had gained in recent days. The town was back in Allied hands and the vital heights had been held. The danger to Amiens, if not entirely removed, had been greatly diminished. The enemy's other purpose, diverting attention from their Flanders operations, had failed also, the defenders only needing to use local reserves to blunt the enemy threat. The principle component of those reserves, the 13th and 15th Australian Brigades, had enhanced the already high fighting reputation of the AIF. Within a few days the German effort in Flanders had petered out also, the British of Second Army holding on outside Ypres almost in the last ditch.

The 50th and 49th Battalions remained holding their positions in the line east of Villers-Bretonneux until the night of 27 April when they were relieved by units of their own Division, the 45th and 46th Battalions of the 12th Brigade—the 4th Division was about to take over responsibility for the sector. Following that relief the 13th Brigade was out of the front line, with the 49th and 50th at Blangy-Tronville, the 51st west of the woods in support trenches, and the 52nd taking over the southern part of the Aubigny reserve line within the woods. It was only three weeks since the 13th Brigade had been in the forefront of the severe fighting at Dernancourt and now it had come through another pitched battle, victorious but at further heavy cost in blood. Many of the dead were still hanging on the barbs of the Cachy Switch wire. The 51st Battalion reported 114 killed and missing with a further 251 wounded; the 50th had 76 killed and missing, 178 wounded. The 52nd Battalion lost 61 killed and missing, and 183 wounded, while the 49th, although not involved in the close fighting, had 145 casualties, 21 of them dead or missing.[81] The 13th MG Company reported seven killed and 23 wounded.[82] At just over 1,000 casualties in total, the 13th Brigade had lost more than twice as heavily as the 15th Brigade in the battle. This reflected the different circumstances that had faced the two brigades:

> ... the 13th Brigade had a much more difficult task—to attack by night over completely unreconnoitred country, trailing its flank past the big wood fringed with machine-guns, through a diagonal wire-entanglement also defended by machine-guns ... The resistance met by the 13th Brigade was much greater, and began at a much earlier stage in the advance, than that confronting the 15th ... The companies of the [German] 4th Guard Division this day mostly fought to the end, without thought of surrender, and to drive them out of position after position, as the 13th Brigade did, was a remarkable achievement.[83]

The casualty rate among the officers had been particularly high. Of the twelve officers commanding companies at the start of the advance, ten had been killed or wounded by the end of the battle (the 50th Battalion had another company OC, Captain Randall Rhodes, wounded by shellfire in the bivouac area), and losses among the platoon commanders were nearly as high; several companies lost all of their officers killed or wounded. Junior officers and NCOs stepped up to take charge of companies and platoons, and it says much for the battlefield discipline within the Brigade that for the most part the units maintained their cohesion under fire and the advance was kept going.

Three Weeks in April

Recognition of individual soldiers in the form of gallantry decorations came in due course after the battle. Considerable attention has been focussed on the awards to Lieutenant Sadlier and Sergeant Stokes (51st Battalion) for their courage and skill in eliminating the German machine guns that menaced their unit's left flank at the start of the advance. It has been generally understood that both soldiers were recommended for the Victoria Cross but only Sadlier's was approved by higher authority, while the recommendation for Stokes was disallowed and he was awarded the DCM instead. It is likely, however, that the circumstances may be slightly different to those usually accepted. Neville Browning has pointed out that Sadlier was actually recommended for the Military Cross (MC) in the first instance;[84] that is how the recommendation document held by the Australian War Memorial reads. The equivalent document for Stokes shows his recommended decoration as the DCM rather than the VC. The 13th Brigade's covering memo to Division lists all recommendations submitted for the battle, including Sadlier for the MC and Stokes for the DCM—and no VC recommendations.[85] If those documents actually do show what went up the chain of command above divisional level, then *neither* soldier was initially recommended for the VC. That would mean that instead of Stokes' decoration being downgraded from a VC to a DCM, he was awarded the same decoration for which he had been recommended. On the other hand, Sadlier was upgraded from the MC to the VC—which represents two steps upward in degree. The DSO, as an officers' decoration, sits between MC and VC in precedence and although it was unusual for subalterns to receive the DSO it was certainly possible. The DCM was a second-level decoration, one 'down' from the VC, and so the Other Ranks equivalent of the DSO; in that sense it can be said that initially Stokes was recommended for a higher decoration than was Sadlier. At some point in the approval process, someone in the higher staffs decided that Sadlier's exploit warranted higher recognition, and it is possible that two successive decisions to upgrade were made as the recommendation passed up the line. No such change was made when it came to Stokes, whose recommendation was not necessarily reviewed by the same individual as that of Sadlier. Whatever the administrative details might have been,

Lieutenant Clifford Sadlier VC (1892–1964), 51st Battalion.
(AWM D00022)

Sadlier had certainly earned his VC but a notable injustice was done to Stokes, who had done virtually the same as Sadlier, had continued the fight after the latter was wounded, and whose suggestion it was to attack the machine gun nests in the first place.

Both men were Victorian-born Western Australians and both had been resident in the Perth suburb of Subiaco when they enlisted. Sadlier, 25 at the time of the battle and a commercial traveller before the war, had served first in 1915 as a private in the AAMC, posted to the 1st Australian General Hospital in Egypt. Returning to Australia early in 1916 he re-mustered as an infantry private, joining the 51st Battalion in France in May 1917. He was commissioned only two months later, an indication that his leadership qualities were obvious. Stokes was 32 in April 1918, a horse driver by occupation and a man of imposing physique. Enlisting in March 1916, a married man with children, he joined the 51st in December that year and had reached lance corporal's rank when he was wounded at Polygon Wood in September 1917. Stokes returned to his unit two months later and his promotion to sergeant had come through only a few days before Villers-Bretonneux. Both men survived the war—Sadlier's wounds took time to heal and he did not return to his Battalion[86]—and slipped quietly back into their civilian occupations on discharge. Regardless of the discrepancy between their decorations, posterity has linked both men's names with the story of that dramatic fight in the dark. The Soldier's Chapel in St George's Cathedral, Perth, has a display commemorating their part in the battle, featuring reproductions of their decorations. The City of Subiaco in WA named two adjacent reserves Clifford Sadlier Memorial Park and the Charles Stokes Reserve. In 1989 the Australian government established the Sadlier-Stokes Memorial Scholarship, awarded annually to outstanding students from the French villages most closely associated with the 1st AIF.

These were of course not the only decorations won for the battle. The COs of the 50th, 51st and 52nd Battalions were each awarded the DSO—a Bar to their previous decorations for Colonels Salisbury and Christie, and the first for Colonel Whitham. A DSO went to Major Tassie of the 13th Field Ambulance also. Infantry officers receiving the MC included Captain Harburn (51st Battalion), Lieutenant Beresford (50th), and Lieutenants Hatton and Crocker (52nd); Lieutenant Earl (51st) was awarded a Bar to his MC. From the supporting arms and services, Captain Docker of the 13th Field Ambulance was decorated with the MC as were the 51st Battalion RMO Captain Arnold, Chaplain Blackwood, and Lieutenants Cowley (13th MG Company) and Climpson (4th Signal Company). DCMs were awarded to Lance Corporal Forrester (13th Field Ambulance), Corporal Sullivan, Lance Corporal Burt, Private Helyar and Private Passmore (51st Battalion), and to Sergeants Wright and White[87] (52nd). Sergeant Brakenridge of the 50th Battalion, who like Sergeant White had led a company during the battle, was recommended for the DCM but received the MM instead. Among many other MM recipients were Corporal Donnelly (50th Battalion RAP), Lance Corporals Guthrie and West (51st), who had both backed up Sadlier and Stokes in the Bois d'Aquenne, and Sergeant Liddicoat (24th MG Company). The 51st battalion's MM recipients included seven regimental stretcher bearers recommended as a group, Privates James Pianto, William Saunders, Edward Gilmour, Ernest Stokes, John Cox, David Shanks and George McKenzie. Similarly, the 52nd had MMs awarded to four battalion pioneers who had volunteered as stretcher bearers, Privates William Bailey, George Armour, Leonard Jarman and William Allan (a Bar in his case). MMs were awarded to soldiers who had braved enemy fire to maintain battlefield communications, including the 50th Battalion's Privates William John, Wilfred Northcott and Thomas Allen (signallers), and Edward Slattery and Frederick Strong (runners).

It was just over a calendar month since the 4th Division had set out south from Flanders to join the fight against the great German offensive. In that time, split into its separate components, it had fought and won pitched battles on three different fronts, the 4th Brigade at Hébuterne, the 12th and 13th Brigades in the two battles of Dernancourt and the 13th Brigade again at Villers-Bretonneux. 'By a strange chance, in the AIF, the heaviest share of the fighting had fallen to the 4th Division, which five months earlier had so barely escaped from being marked for disbandment.'[88] Now the Division was coalescing again, to play its part in what would prove to be the final stages of the Great War on the Western Front.

18 Notes

1. *Official History*, Vol V, p. 417.
2. 48th Battalion War Diary for April 1918, Appendix 4, folio 41.
3. 13th Brigade War Diary, 8 April 1918.
4. 4th Division General Staff War Diary for June 1918, Appendix 33.
5. Australian-born son of an Australian mother and a naturalised father of Polish/Swiss forebears; see the statement made by the father (also named Reinhold) on Pte Ruschpler's service record. No doubt the statement was made to formally declare his loyalty in the light of the German-sounding name. It appears that the younger Ruschpler changed his name to Ronald Clifford Royston after the war.
6. 24th MG Company War Diary for April 1918, Appendix 24. The report also urged the gun crews to fight to the last and give up their lives if necessary.
7. See the Bean Papers, AWM38 3DRL606/270 Part 3/1, folios 110–110a, Maj Hinton's letter to Bean dated 14 October 1929. He was writing about the 'Red Baron' incident of 21 April 1918, a week after the gunners escaped and reported the true story of the Dernancourt machine guns; at that time 'the breach was at its widest' between the two officers, wrote Hinton.
8. 52nd Battalion War Diary for April 1918, inserted between folios 21 and 22.
9. Bean Papers, notebook AWM38 3DRL606/185/1, p.39 (p. 37 in PDF).
10. *Ibid*, p. 78 (p. 58 in PDF).

11   4th Division GS War Diary for June 1918, Appendix 33, folio 116.
12   Bean Papers, AWM38 3DRL606/251/1, p. 179.
13   Louch, *Op Cit*, p. 18.
14   Bean Papers, notebook AWM38 3DRL606/185/1, p. 38 (p. 36 in PDF).
15   Australian Corps Admin Staff War Diary, 9 April 1918.
16   12th Brigade War Diary for April 1918, Appendix 9.
17   From the AWM Roll of Honour and that compiled by Deayton, *Op Cit*, pp. 370–381.
18   Deayton, *Loc Cit.*
19   According to the 13th Brigade's report. The 49th Battalion's own War Diary (April 1918, Appendix 14) gives 60 killed and 131 wounded, in a report compiled up to 9 April. The figures in the Australian Corps Admin Staff War Diary for April 1918 are different again. The AWM Roll of Honour, however, shows 68 deaths in the 49th Battalion on 5 April.
20   The AWM Roll of Honour has 26 48th Battalion deaths on 5 April; the PoW figure is in Browning, *Leane's Battalion, Op Cit*, Appendix F.
21   The *Medical History* (Vol II, p. 630) gives the Division's losses as 358 killed, 837 wounded and 180 prisoners, a total of 1375 casualties; Butler does not show a source for these figures.
22   4th Pioneer Battalion War Diary for April 1918, Appendix 6.
23   *Official History*, Vol V, p. 412.
24   Boase's recommendation in the AWM records is not dated, but it is signed by Brig Gen S C E Herring as GOC 13th Brigade, indicating it was prepared no earlier than late June 1918, well after the battle, Herring having succeeded Brig Gen Glasgow at that time.
25   At this time, only the VC and Mentions in Despatches could be awarded posthumously, in the sense of the soldier's death resulting from the action for which the distinction was awarded; he could be recommended for a decoration for a particular exploit then die in a subsequent action and the decoration still be bestowed. Lts Pidcock and Linsley died in the Canadian hospital at Doullens, where they had been taken from the CCS; it is possible that the administrative channels moved slowly and this was not known to higher authority until after their MCs were approved, a non-regrettable error. The recommendations by the CRA are dated 8 April and do not mention that either had died—Brig Gen Burgess may have been unaware of that fact, or may have chosen to be unaware.
26   Full name John Patrick O'Brien—see the entry in the Australian Dictionary of Biography by R E Cowley. Both his WWI and WWII service files show his given name as 'Jack,' as do some of his items in the AWM Honours and Awards records.
27   Richard John Dyer, who signed official documents as 'R John Dyer.' Of the field and signal company commanders, Maj Tolley was 29, Riddell and Carr 30, and Fraser 40. Lt Col Dyer's service record shows that he corresponded with the Army after the war enquiring whether he or another 4th Division officer, Lt Col N M Loutit, promoted to be CO 45th Battalion in September 1918 at 24, was the youngest AIF officer to reach that rank. Neither seems to have been aware that the 4th Division also included Lt Col D G Marks, CO of the 13th Battalion at the age of 22.
28   See the *Official History*, Vol II, pp. 328–41 for details of the operation.
29   13th Brigade War Diary, 9 April 1918.
30   Colonel Paul's medical clearance seems to have been premature, as two months later he was reclassified as permanently unfit for active service. He died in 1922 at the age of 44.
31   4th Division General Staff War Diary, 16 April 1918.

32 Bean Diary, AWM38 3DRL606/107/1, 16 April 1918.

33 13th Brigade War Diary for April 1918, Appendix XXV.

34 The references for the Richthofen incident are too numerous to list, but C E W Bean's summary of the evidence in the *Official History*, Vol V, Appendix 4 is logical and quite conclusive in favour of Popkin's claim. A more modern work, Franks and Bennett, *The Red Baron's Last Flight* (1997) comes to the same conclusion. Bean's correspondence on the subject, in AWM38 3DRL606/270, is of interest, and shows how different people can view the same events but report them very differently.

35 4th Division General Staff War Diary for April 1918, Appendices 24 and 25.

36 Louch, *Op Cit*, p.20.

37 *Official History*, Vol V, p. 572.

38 Louch, *Op Cit*, p. 21.

39 13th Field Ambulance War Diary, 24 April 1918.

40 Louch, *Op Cit*, p. 20.

41 *Official History*, Vol V, p. 570. See also the Bean Papers, AWM38 3DRL606/273/1, pp. 111–12.

42 *Ibid*, p. 575.

43 This occurrence is not mentioned in the 50th Battalion War Diary, other than a statement in Colonel Salisbury's report to the effect that orders were received at Battalion HQ, implying that the CO did not attend the briefing. Colonel Whitham, the 52nd CO, described it in his later account of the battle (in *Stand-To*, the ACT RSL journal, June-July 1952, p. 4), and further stated that the 50th had actually begun to march to the Aubigny line before being recalled; soldiers' accounts in the 50th Battalion history (Freeman, *Op Cit*, pp. 147 and 151) also state that the Battalion marched most of the distance and then returned to its original position. A message in the 52nd Diary (April 1918, Part 2, Appendix W, folio 158) confirms that the 50th CO understood that his unit had been ordered to the Aubigny line. C E W Bean also made a brief reference to the mistaken orders in his diary (AWM38 3DRL606/108/1, p. 78 in PDF). The original order (signal) for the 49th Battalion (Brigade order B411, Appendix 30 in the 13th Brigade War Diary for April 1918, Part 2) had the other units as information addressees, and it is possible that someone at 50th Battalion HQ misinterpreted the signal as being for action; it was, however, issued much earlier in the day.

44 52nd Battalion War Diary for April 1918, Part 2, Appendix W (folio 133), Colonel Whitham's notes on the briefing. The *Official History* (Vol V, p. 579) says that the briefing took place at the HQ of the 2nd Northamptonshires, but Colonel Whitham specifically refutes this in his article referred to in Note 43 above; it is not clear whether or not the 51st and 52nd Battalions COs conducted a joint briefing for their company commanders, but that is the implication in Whitham's account.

45 Bean Papers, AWM38 3DRL606/273/1, pp. 114–15, and 118–20.

46 Maps in some sources show the left of the start-line within the woods, but Capt T G Clark (Brigade IO at the time, who led the taping party) confirmed in a 1936 letter to C E W Bean that the tape was laid from the edge (Bean Papers, AWM38 3DRL 606/273/1, p.37).

47 52nd Battalion War Diary for April 1918, Appendix W (folio 133).

48 In an account of the Villers-Bretonneux fighting sent to C E W Bean in 1936, the British brigade commander, Brig Gen G W Grogan VC, described this operation (Bean Papers, AWM38 3DRL606/273/1, p.100). Bean mentioned it in the *Official History* (Vol V, p.566) but did not directly link it with the mistaken impression given to the 13th Brigade units that they would probably be free from enemy interference on their left (Vol V, pp.580 and 582).

49 Shortage of numbers meant that some units had organised their companies into three platoons instead of four. The 50th Battalion's 'D' Company went into the battle with only two platoons.

50 Bean Diary, AWM38 3DRL606/108/1, p.66.

51 *Ibid*, pp. 23–4.

52 Freeman, *Op Cit*, pp. 147–8, Cpl Duncan Butler's account.

53 *Official History*, Vol V, p. 583. Bean's source was a 1935 letter from J Mulqueeny, former private in the 51st Battalion, who was on the ground near Lt Sadlier and stated that he had heard the conversation (Bean Papers, AWM38 3DRL606/273/1, p.178).

54 Sources for Bean's account in the *Official History* are in the Bean Papers, referred to in Note 53 above, and include correspondence from Lt Sadlier as well as Pte Mulqueeny, and also a note by journalist and former AIF officer C A Longmore of his interview with Sgt Stokes. There are several discrepancies between those accounts, not surprisingly in view of the nature of the fighting and the lapse in time of 17 years since the events occurred.

55 Bean Papers, AWM38 3DRL606/273/1, p. 196, Sadlier's letter to Bean dated 28 June 1935.

56 *Ibid*, P. 213, C A Longmore's letter to Bean dated 27 July 1935.

57 50th Battalion War Diary for April 1918, Appendix 6. It is possible that some of the seven captured guns may have been from posts already attacked by the 51st Battalion group. The *Official History* (Vol V, p. 584) says that six machine guns were picked up on the edge of the wood, while the 13th Brigade's after action report (April 1918 War Diary, Appendix 31) states that 'a number of light and heavy machine guns' were captured, 'though the exact number cannot be stated as the majority of them were left where they were and were afterwards removed by other troops or set up for action.' In the *Official History* reference above, Bean identified several German units that were operating numerous machine guns in the area, and some of those guns may have been moved into position after Sadlier and Stokes had passed through the area; their 51st Battalion party would have been perhaps ten minutes ahead of the 50th troops. It is also possible that the 50th's fight took place further east on the line of the advance, closer to Cachy Switch.

58 Bean Papers, AWM38 3DRL606/273/1, p. 214.

59 One platoon commander, Lt Sadlier, had been wounded in the fighting with the German machine guns in the Bois d'Aquenne, and had gone to the rear. There are no details of the whereabouts of the other two subalterns commanding platoons in 'C' Company, except that neither had become casualties. Both were inexperienced (one had joined the Battalion only a week earlier) and it possible that they had simply become separated from the Company in the confusion of the night.

60 The 51st Battalion later reported taking a total of 86 prisoners during the whole battle, and the 50th reported definitely 20 and estimated up to a further 30 unconfirmed.

61 Bean Diary, AWM38 3DRL606/108/1, p. 51.

62 Browning, *For King and Cobbers*, *Op Cit*, p. 242.

63 Bean Papers, AWM38 3DRL606/273/1, p. 162.

64 Bean Diary, AWM38 3DRL606/108/1, p. 58.

65 *Loc Cit*. Craies' service record has no details of the events that led to his discharge, effective 15 April 1916, nor to his reinstatement eight months later. He had reached the rank of major when his first appointment was terminated, and he was re-commissioned with the rank of lieutenant and honorary major; he had been promoted to substantive captain, still honorary major, by the time of Villers-Bretonneux.

66 Various sections of the narrative in the *Official History*, Vol V Chapter XVII, as well as several of the marginal maps, indicate that the position reached was along the Domart road i.e. the western fork of the road. The after action reports of the 13th Brigade and of the 51st and 52nd Battalions include sketch-maps showing the forward line established along the eastern fork leading to Hangard Wood, with a support line further back near the Domart road. The large map in the *History* following p.618 of Vol V shows the 51st and 52nd pulling back from the limit of their advance only as far as the eastern fork.

67 The 52nd Battalion War Diary for April 1918, Part 2, Appendix W (but not the 50th Battalion Diary) says that the officer was Capt [James] Churchill Smith, and Bean follows that in the *Official History* (Vol V, p. 596). That officer's personal diary, however, indicates that he was with the 50th's nucleus at their transport lines during the battle (a transcript of Churchill Smith's diary is available on the State Library Service of South Australia website)—no doubt much to his chagrin; Churchill Smith was an outstanding officer, winning the MC and Bar in the Mouquet Farm operations, and according to his instructor on a senior officers' course in early 1918, displaying 'a mastery of the problems faced before him [during the course] which I have seldom seen excelled. His military knowledge is remarkable for one who is not a regular soldier ... a first-rate leader' (the report is in his service record). The 50th Battalion War Diary says that Churchill Smith was not among the four officers commanding companies in the initial advance at least. By the time the front was being re-organised under Major Craies' direction, three of those four were killed or missing; the only surviving company commander was Lt W R Beresford ('B' Company), and Lt P E Nuttall was the only unhurt officer in 'D' Company, to which Capt Churchill Smith belonged. Lt Beresford's MC recommendation for the battle mentions that he 'reorganised and consolidated all [50th Battalion] companies on the position won'. The after-action report from the 52nd Battalion's 'A' Company says that 'Major Craies and Captain Smith 51st were siting the Brigade line of resistance' (52nd Battalion War Diary for April 1918, Appendix W, Folio 124). It appears from C E W Bean's diary (AWM38 3DRL606/108/1, page 73 in PDF) that it was Captain Frank Smith, commanding the 51st's support company, who led forward the 50th Battalion platoon that reinforced the left of the 51st and attacked the German force that had outflanked Captain Harburn's party. Smith may have then stayed with those troops, or a mixed group from both Battalions, and reached the final position with them.

68 The 13th Field Ambulance War Diary for April 1918 says several times that the ADS was north of Blangy-Tronville. These appear to be typographical errors—Blangy-Tronville is on the south bank of the Somme, with its marshes, and the sketch in the Diary shows the ADS as *south* of the village, confirmed by the map reference mentioned in the 4th Division ADMS War Diary for April (Appendix 21); the location is identified as 'Blangy Cabaret.'

69 13th Field Ambulance War Diary, 24 April 1918.

70 This was marked on the 13th Field Ambulance's sketch map as located near the western corner of the Bois de Blangy, about 5 km west of Villers-Bretonneux, south of the railway line, and was apparently a different building to the Delacour Chateau, also called the Red Chateau. The latter building was at the edge of the village and was set on fire by the shelling on 24 April. Its ruins were finally demolished in 2004. See Pedersen, *Battleground Europe: Villers-Bretonneux*, 2004, pp. 146–8

71 4th Division ADMS War Diary for April 1918, Appendix 10.

72 24th MG Company War Diary for April 1918, Appendix G.

73 50th Battalion War Diary for April 1918, Appendix 6 and 13th Brigade War Diary for April 1918, Appendix 31, Attachment C. This would put the 50th Battalion's left at an intermediate point that was meant to have been reached in the advance during the previous night, where the present D23 and the railway intersect, north of Monument Farm.

74   *Official History*, Vol V, p. 628.

75   *Official History*, Vol V, p. 628 and Pedersen, *Villers-Bretonneux*, pp. 132–3 (the latter quoting the 2nd Northants War Diary). In the 51st Battalion War Diary, however, Lt Col Christie's report states that the Northants withdrew from their overnight position at dawn on 25 April (Appendix 11 to the April Diary).

76   The circumstances are described in a letter by Lt Col Whitham, on Maj Craies' service file.

77   52nd Battalion War Diary for April 1918, Appendix W (folio 134); Bean Diary, AWM38 3DRL606/108/1, p. 64.

78   50th Battalion War Diary for April 1918, Appendix 6.

79   *Official History*, Vol V, p. 629.

80   50th Battalion War Diary for April 1918, Appendix 6.

81   These numbers are from the 13th Brigade's report (War Diary for April 1918, Appendix 31L) except for the 52nd Battalion; the Brigade report shows the 52nd as having 46 killed and 60 'unaccounted for,' whereas the Battalion report has 48 killed and 13 missing, which seems more reasonable. The AWM Roll of Honour records 65 deaths of 52nd Battalion members occurring on 24/25 April, with numbers of deaths for the other battalions being: 49th 19; 50th 80; and 51st 107. The casualty totals in the *Official History* (Vol V, p. 637n) are those in the Brigade report.

82   13th MG Company War Diary for April 1918, Appendix C.

83   *Official History*, Vol V, p. 642.

84   Browning, *For King and Cobbers, Op Cit*, p. 419.

85   13th Brigade War Diary for May 1918, Appendix 13.

86   This is probably why, in his earlier personal accounts of the fighting (see the Bean Papers, AWM38 3DRL606/273/1, pp. 191–7, for example), Sadlier hardly mentioned the part played by Stokes. After a few minutes intense close fighting in the dark, wounded twice and evacuated, Sadlier would not have been aware of Stokes' involvement in the next phase of the fight, and it is also possible that, since they were in different platoons, he did not know Stokes personally and may not have been sure who it was that was backing him up. Other correspondence in the Bean Papers (*Ibid*, p.214) says that the story that Stokes suggested the attack was 'current just afterwards' in the Battalion (Capt Harburn being quoted), but of course Sadlier was not there and did not have the opportunity to fill out his own recollections. It was not until C E W Bean had extracted the details and published Volume V of the *Official History* (1937) that the full story became generally known.

87   Sgt White's given names were recorded variously as Alfred Walter and Arthur Willis, but his correct names, according to his service record, were Alfred Willis. By the time his DCM was gazetted, he had transferred to the 50th Battalion.

88   *Official History*, Vol V, p. 657.

19: The Right of the Line

As soon as the Villers-Bretonneux fighting died down the higher command took steps to extend the Australian Corps' area of responsibility southwards to include the town and the lines around it, taking over from III Corps and adjoining the French sector. As far as the 4th Division was concerned, it had been ordered on 26 April to take over command of the sector nominally held by the 8th British Division (that is, by the 13th and 15th Australian Brigades temporarily attached to that formation) the next day. Initially it was intended that the 12th Brigade would relieve the 15th as the left brigade in the line on the night 27/28 April. The following night the 4th Brigade, only just arrived in the area from Hébuterne, would relieve the 13th on the right, with the main (Roman) road forming the inter-brigade boundary. These arrangements were changed almost immediately when the Division staff became aware of how worn down the 13th Brigade actually was. The 12th Brigade was ordered to relieve the 13th on the first night instead, followed by the 4th Brigade taking over from the 15th. The 45th and 46th Battalions were sent into the front line first, moving forward at dusk on 27 April. Both units were in position shortly after midnight, the 46th Battalion relieving the 49th and elements of the 59th (5th Division) north of the railway, and the 45th Battalion relieving the 50th on the south (right) where the line faced south-east towards Monument Wood, in touch with the French 8th Zouaves; 'It may be mentioned,' noted the 45th's diarist, 'that our right flank was the extreme right of the British Army in France.'[1] Behind the front line the 47th Battalion took up posts along a line running south from the Roman road along the eastern edge of the Bois d'Aquenne, in support of the 46th. Similarly the 45th Battalion on the right was supported by the 48th Battalion, relieving elements of various British units in the Cachy Switch trench.

It will be recalled that the 4th Brigade infantry had left the Hébuterne area on 24 April, after the better part of a month in the front line attached to British formations. The Brigade moved overnight by bus to billets at Cardonette and Allonville, north of Amiens, where it came under the umbrella of the 4th Division again. The troops might have expected at least a short break there away from the battle zone but within a day word had come through from Division that the 4th Brigade would be required to go into the front line again, as early as the night of 28/29 April. Major Tovell, the brigade major, described the news as a 'Bomb Shell' in his hurried memo to the battalion COs.[2] On 27 April the Brigade moved to the Querrieu-Pont Noyelles-Daours area recently vacated by the 12th Brigade, then during the next night relieved the 15th Brigade in the left sub-sector of the Villers-Bretonneux front, north of the Roman road. The 13th and 14th Battalions went into the front line with the 15th and 16th in support positions, in continuation of the 12th Brigade's support line west of the town-site. The MG Companies changed over on 28 and 29 April also, the 4th Company going in to the left sub-sector and the 12th to the right. The LTM batteries also relieved their counterparts and both Brigade HQs moved in to the established accommodation in the Tronville chateau. The 13th Brigade now became the divisional reserve, with one of its battalions, the 52nd, providing the garrison for a long section of the Aubigny line.

The 4th Division officially took over command of the sector at 10 am on 28 April, with HQ at Glisy. At the same time command of the field artillery in the sector passed to the 4th Division CRA. Brigadier General Burgess and his staff, also headquartered in Glisy, found themselves in the unusual position of controlling an artillery that initially included no elements belonging to their own Division; the force comprised five British Royal Field Artillery (RFA) brigades in three groups, with another British brigade in reserve. After the Dernancourt battle the 4th Division's 10th and 11th AFA Brigades, together withthe DAC, had remained in that sector under command of the 2nd Division; it would be another week before those units were released to return to their parent division. Among the other arms and services, the engineer field companies moved to billets at Blangy-Tronville; the 4th Company was allocated to administering works in the left sub-sector, resuming its usual link with the 4th Infantry Brigade, while the 13th Company worked with the 12th Brigade on the right. The 12th Field Company was detailed to work in the divisional area generally, beginning with construction of a new switch trench running west from the southern end of the Aubigny Line. The Pioneers, moving down from Lahoussoye on 28 April, were also accommodated at Blangy-Tronville and were first set to work constructing dugouts for Division HQ and a forward battalion HQ, as well as providing labour on the Aubigny switch trench. The 13th Field Ambulance was relieved on 28 April also, moving to Allonville in the rear area. The incoming medical units, the 4th and 12th Field Ambulances, had their bearer sections evacuating from the front line RAPs (which they had some difficulty in locating) and their tent sections administering dressing stations—the 4th taking over the ADS at the crossroads inn (Blangy Cabaret) near Blangy-Tronville and the 12th the MDS further back at St Acheul, a suburb of Amiens. The Divisional Train established itself with HQ at Allonville and the three AASC companies servicing the infantry brigades based at Camon, just east of Amiens (the 14th Company remained in the Dernancourt sector with the divisional artillery for the time being); the supply railhead was established at Ailly-sur-Somme, west of Amiens.

Active operations began as soon as the Division had completed its deployment, with infantry patrols probing ahead of the front line posts. The 45th Battalion on the right reported that its patrols exploring the village itself had brought in 15 wounded Germans who had been hiding in cellars since the battle. On the night of 29/30 April the two centre battalions, the 13th on the left and the 46th on the right, advanced their forward posts on both sides of the Roman road by up to 500 metres. Those two units carried out further operations on the following night but with less success. A derelict aerodrome with several large hangars lay in enemy territory beyond the 13th Battalion's front line, which was now east of the Hamel road, and it was believed that the Germans were using the hangars as observation posts. The 4th Field Company engineers were given the task of destroying the buildings, which were of frame construction covered with fire-resistant canvas. Around midnight a party of sappers under Second Lieutenant Alfred Buckler, escorted by an infantry patrol from the 13th Battalion, went out across No Man's Land with incendiary materials to set fire to the hangars. At about the same time the 46th Battalion sent out two platoons to occupy the buildings of a farm half-way between the main road and the railway, in the German outpost line. The 13th patrol with the engineers worked their way through enemy shelling to reach the hangars but they were detected and came under machine gun fire. The sappers ignited their combustibles in two of the hangars but the machine guns kept them on the downwind side of the structures. Although the coverings began to burn, a strong wind prevented the flames from spreading and the fires died out after an hour. Although accounts differ, it appears that an attempt was also made to fire the third hangar but the fuel refused to ignite—the 13th Battalion history has a story that a petrol-can used here turned out to contain water (the same type of container was used for both petrol and water).[3] While the fires were burning they were bright enough to cause unexpected problems for the 46th Battalion's operation against the farm south of the main road. Silhouetted against the flames, the troops were spotted by the German garrison who threw grenades and opened fire with machine guns. The 46th party fought back but the advantage of surprise had been lost and they eventually withdrew; six had been wounded in the fight, including both platoon commanders. The 46th had made some progress on its right flank, however, where its post in the railway cutting had pushed forward a further 90 metres in conjunction with the left flank of the 45th Battalion.

Those operations, edging the line forward, were the preliminaries to a larger-scale effort initiated from the highest level—the supreme Allied commander, General Foch. Concerned at the continued proximity of the German line to Villers-Bretonneux, Foch proposed an advance in the French sector to drive the enemy back at least to their former position beyond Hangard Wood. As part of that operation the 4th Division would be required to capture the farmhouse and apple-orchard of Monument Wood near the southern outskirts of Villers-Bretonneux, the position that had remained in German hands after the battle of 24/25 April. On 1 May an order for the operation came to the Division from the Australian Corps and on the same day Division in turn issued an order to the 12th Brigade to carry out the attack. The Corps order did not mention the size of the force required but Division specified that the task be carried out using one infantry battalion with supporting arms. Although Corps nominated 3 May as the date of the operation, the Division order left the date open, presumably pending confirmation of the French plans. In the meantime the 12th and 4th Brigades would maintain their efforts to take more ground to their fronts and improve the position for the Monument Wood attack. In the 4th Brigade sector north of the main road the 13th Battalion continued as the principal force for the task. That unit had taken some unlucky losses during 1 May from random enemy shelling: in the morning company commander Captain William Bone was terribly wounded with both feet shattered, the same shell killing his runner, Private James Leonard, and later in the day another company commander, Captain Neville 'Doss' Wallach, was killed and two of his platoon commanders wounded.[4] The next night a patrol skirmish cost the life of the 14th Battalion's admired intelligence officer, Lieutenant John 'Jack' Johnson.

The 12th Brigade decided to relieve the 46th Battalion by the 47th in the front line, the relief being completed by midnight of 1/2 May. The 47th's numbers remained low after its losses at Dernancourt and the unit had to use all four companies to occupy the front line in sufficient strength; two companies of the 46th Battalion therefore stayed in the forward area as close support, under command of the 47th. As soon as the unit had taken over the front line, in the early hours of 2 May, the 47th was required to attempt the capture of a line including the farm buildings that had resisted the 46th's attack on the previous night, with the 13th and 45th Battalions also pushing forward to left and right,. The 13th Battalion's task was to swing its right forward for about 275 metres to conform with the left of the 47th; the movement was accomplished and the 13th dug in on the new line with minimal casualties, despite heavy machine gun fire. The 47th's left flank kept pace with the 13th and began to dig in also, but in the centre the troops found the farm to be strongly held and were driven back by machine guns and grenades. Noticing that group withdrawing, the 47th officer in command on the left decided to withdraw also, thereby uncovering the 13th Battalion's right. Under the direction of their company commander, Captain Bob Henderson, the 13th troops on that side set about forming a flank position facing south. While checking his new posts Henderson was hit by machine gun fire, so seriously that he later succumbed to his wound in hospital, the third experienced and popular officer lost by the 13th within 24 hours.[5] It was nearly daylight when the 47th made another attempt, apparently under instructions from Brigade,[6] to connect up the new line. This time the farm was avoided and a party led by Lieutenant George Storey gained enough ground to establish a satisfactory position and provide some support for the 13th Battalion. On the 47th's right an advance of 140 metres had been made along the railway, but the 45th Battalion's left-flank post, already close to strong enemy positions, had been unable to gain more than 50 metres.[7] This implies a gap in the line, but Colonel Leane, the acting brigadier in General Gellibrand's absence, later reported that since the 12th Brigade had taken over the sector,

> by the morning of 2nd May we had pushed forward 350 yards [320 metres] along Railway Line and 700 yards [640 metres] along Amiens road with connecting Posts in between. We were now in position to carry out operations against Monument Wood with some chance of success.[8]

The line in the vicinity of the railway cutting, from which the attack on the Wood was to be launched, faced the northern side of the Wood then bent south-west to face its western side.

The orders to the 12th Brigade had specified that one battalion was to be used and Colonel Leane chose his own unit, the 48th, currently in the Cachy Switch trench as the right-flank support battalion. As C E W Bean saw it,

> Leane saw that his brigade was faced by a difficult undertaking ... [and] ... adhering to his principle of allotting the worst tasks to himself or members of his family, he gave it to the 48th.[9]

That may be so, but it does not seem to be a sound basis for a brigadier to make a decision of that nature, and although Leane was only acting in the posting he undoubtedly aspired to a permanent appointment in the future. There were other factors that he may have considered also. If it was to be his consistent policy to always employ the 48th for difficult tasks (and few infantry operations in Spring 1918 would have been easy) the unit would soon be used up, even if its morale held up long enough to keep fighting effectively to that point. As it was, the 48th had suffered comparatively low casualties in the Dernancourt battles and was the strongest in numbers of the four 12th Brigade battalions[10] (on the other hand, the 48th had also received the most reinforcements in recent weeks, many of whom were recent recruits with no combat experience[11]). Of the other battalions the 46th had just been relieved by the 47th, the latter unit being badly under-strength, and the 45th, also down in numbers after Dernancourt, was holding the sector of the front line from which the advance would begin—it was not unusual to bring up a unit from support to pass through the forward troops in launching an attack.

The commanders had anticipated that the Monument Wood operation would be 'a rather tough job' as Bean gathered from the 12th Brigade HQ staff,[12] but just how tough was not fully understood. It was known that the original enemy garrison, whose morale might have been expected to be dented following the events of 25 April, had recently been replaced by elements of the Jäger Division, 'first rate troops fresh from Italy.'[13] Only later was it realised, however, that there were actually two full-strength battalions in the Wood, holding trenches protected by wire entanglements and well equipped with machine guns—as many as 152 altogether, according to a prisoner interrogated afterwards.[14] In contrast, immediate fire support for the 48th Battalion consisted of four Vickers guns of the 12th MG Company and two LTMs from the Brigade battery going in with the infantry. Another six machine guns were positioned in two groups to give long-range covering fire at the beginning of the attack. An unconventional scheme of artillery support was adopted. With the intention of achieving surprise for the infantry, the objective would be heavily shelled for only two minutes before the attack jumped off. Similar bombardments were carried out in the few days prior to Zero in the hope that the enemy would be led to believe that the shelling was not the precursor of an infantry attack; a shell partly demolished the farmhouse during this period but its cellars remained intact. Two heavy tanks were allocated to support the infantry but only with consolidation from dawn, with two others and four of the lighter Whippet tanks in reserve.

In the afternoon of 2 May 4th Division HQ confirmed that Zero would be 2 am the next morning.[15] The 12th Brigade staff had already issued an order detailing the tactics to be used by the 48th Battalion and the supporting arms. The plan was for two companies, assembling in line just ahead of the 45th's positions along the railway, to advance from north to south through the Wood on either side of the sunken road running from the town between the farm buildings and the main orchard. A third company, facing south east, would follow up by sweeping across the Wood to its east side after the first two companies had passed through. The fourth company was held in reserve but also provided a force of three officers and 50 men under Lieutenant Charles Stoerkel to follow the main force in as a mopping-up party. The attacking companies would employ a formation of three waves, each wave in one line, with 25 metres between waves. Although the tactics were contained in a Brigade order, on 1 May Major Allen, temporarily commanding the 48th, his company commanders and intelligence officer (Lieutenant Tom Arnold, twice decorated as a daring scout while in the ranks) had gone forward to the 45th Battalion's front line positions and reconnoitred the ground before conferring; 'the scheme was fully discussed, method of attack, disposition[s] and jump off position decided upon.'[16] That evening, Colonel Leane visited the 48th HQ with Major Norman, the brigade major, for further discussions; it appears that the plan proposed by the Battalion officers was then incorporated in the Brigade order issued the next day (although C E W Bean gained the impression that 'it was Norman who really drew the Brigade order for this attack'[17]). Preparations had already commenced, with dumps of ammunition, grenades, sandbags and water established in and near the front line. The steep bank of the railway cutting offered a concealed route to the front line and good observation points, allowing all the officers and NCOs involved in the attack to go forward and study the ground. The 48th also exchanged liaison officers with the French unit on the right, although it had now been established that the French attack on Hangard Wood was not going to be launched simultaneously that night but instead some hours later during the day. Colonel Leane hoped that the French operation, although delayed, might at least interfere with German counter-attacks at Monument Wood.

At 11:30 pm on 2 May the attacking troops began filing out of Cachy Switch and made their way along the cutting to the front line. From there the 48th moved out of the cutting into the assembly area, a phase of the operation that had been recognised as crucial. The troops had been instructed to lie down on the tapes, the orders pointing out that

> It is of the utmost importance owing to the cramped area for forming up and the closeness of enemy Posts to the 'Jumping off' tape that every care is exercised in the forming up with the least possible noise.[18]

Although Major Allen's after-action report stated that the force got into position 'unobserved,' there was a different view in the front line. Lieutenant George Mitchell, commanding a platoon of Captain Norman Imlay's 'C' Company on the left of the main line, later wrote that some of the inexperienced reinforcements were standing up and moving around shortly before Zero, when a flare rising from the enemy lines illuminated them and several machine guns opened up.[19] At 2 am the artillery barrage opened but it proved to be entirely ineffective, at least as far as the troops in the front line could see. Mitchell's impression was that 'a brigade of our guns opened weakly with a shrapnel barrage. Some shells dropped short among us … The shells ceased to fall. We looked around in astonishment. Was that the barrage?'[20] The artillery plan called for a two-minute bombardment of the Wood by the two British RFA Brigades forming the Right Group covering the 4th Division's front—six batteries of 18-pounders and two of 4.5-inch howitzers. The field guns were ordered to fire at the fairly fast rate of five rounds per minute, using half shrapnel ammunition and half HE, with the howitzers firing all HE at four rounds per minute. The 18-pounders were to carry out an area shoot to cover the 'orchard rectangle' while the howitzers targeted the farm buildings.[21] If those orders were followed to the letter, and assuming each battery had all six of its guns available, the two-minute barrage by the 18-pounders would have dropped 360 shells[22] (180 shrapnel and 180 HE) on an area of roughly 250,000 square metres—not a heavy concentration. The guns and howitzers of that group then lifted away from the Wood to fire on selected targets in the enemy rear for the next half-hour, as the remainder of the supporting artillery was already doing. That shooting would have accounted for the bulk of the 7,000-plus rounds that the artillery later reported had been fired during the operation,[23] a number that might have surprised the infantry.

Regardless of the unimpressive barrage on the objective, the die was cast as far as the infantry was concerned and the company commanders led their men forward two minutes after Zero. There was no surprise; the thoroughly-alert Germans sent up sheaves of flares, illuminating the advancing lines, and a storm of machine gun fire broke out. Captain Imlay, commanding 'C' Company, was badly hit almost immediately together with a number of his men, and both companies in the main assault came up against the unbroken enemy wire belt and were pinned down outside it. The confident Germans hoisted several machine guns out of their trench and fired in the open, while many of their riflemen stood up on the trench parapet to fire or fling grenades. The 48th troops took cover in shell holes and returned fire to some effect, but any forward movement was impossible. After half an hour the enemy fire seemed to have eased slightly and the commander of 'B' Company on the right, Captain Derwas Cumming, made a brave attempt to break the stalemate, leading a few men in a charge straight at the enemy position. Within a few yards he was killed, apparently by a mortar shell that also killed signaller Private Alfred Mallyon.[24] In Captain Cumming the 48th had lost one of its best officers, who had been with the unit from its formation and had most recently distinguished himself by his stubborn defence of the left flank at Dernancourt. Part of his company managed to work around the northern edge of the Wood to the western side but could get no further. Most of the assault force went to ground again, but in the centre near the road Lieutenant Max McDowall led a group from both companies that succeeded in breaking through a blind spot in the German defences. The small party of about twenty men worked their way through a wire entanglement and kept going, probing along the line of the road deep into the trees. They actually reached the objective, the southern fringe of the orchard, successfully rushing a German trench there and knocking out a machine gun post. There was no sign of any other Australian troops nearby so McDowall fired the success signal, two green flares, to indicate his position for any reinforcements who might be able to reach him. There was no response, however, and it became clear to McDowall that he and his men were isolated inside the German lines and would have to withdraw. A large enemy force was observed assembling to counter-attack and McDowall prepared to fight his way out.

His was not the only group to have penetrated the German defences. Lieutenant Stoerkel's mopping-up party following the main assault from the north had also found a gap near the road. This group's objective was the farm buildings, particularly the cellars, which as it turned out were occupied by the enemy battalion HQ. Stoerkel's men penetrated the compound and quickly overcame the guards, Sergeant Harry Davies capturing a post of six men despite being wounded in both legs. Second Lieutenant William Carr then rolled grenades down the cellar steps; several of the German HQ staff were killed (one being the battalion commander, it was thought at the time[25]) and others, two officers and 20 men, surrendered and were escorted back through the Wood to the Australian lines—something of a feat in itself considering the fighting that was still in progress. Like McDowall, Stoerkel soon realised that he was unsupported and almost cut off, badly outnumbered by enemy counterattack forces closing in on the farm. He and Lieutenant Carr set about extricating their men from what had become a trap: 'bullets were already flying across the yard and stick bombs were being heaved over the walls'[26] (it was Carr who, as a private, had used his back as the mounting for a Lewis gun at Bullecourt in 1917). The third company in the attack, 'A', had the task of advancing through the Wood from west to east. The company started out as planned but was largely stopped by the wire and machine guns on the outskirts of the Wood and along the central road; the line was steadied there by the example of CSM Thomas Reid, moving along the line under fire and encouraging the men. Part or all of the left-flank platoon, however, seems to have succeeded in working across the battlefield to its objective north-east of the Wood and gaining touch with the 45th Battalion's forward post on the railway; Sergeant James Way distinguished himself there.[27]

Despite the loss of a battalion HQ, which might have been expected to disrupt the German effort, they retained overall control of the battlefield and the 48th Battalion was now in a grim situation. The two companies on the north and the one on the west were pinned down short of the German wire under continuing heavy machine gun fire interspersed with mortar rounds. The two small parties that had managed to penetrate the

The Right of the Line

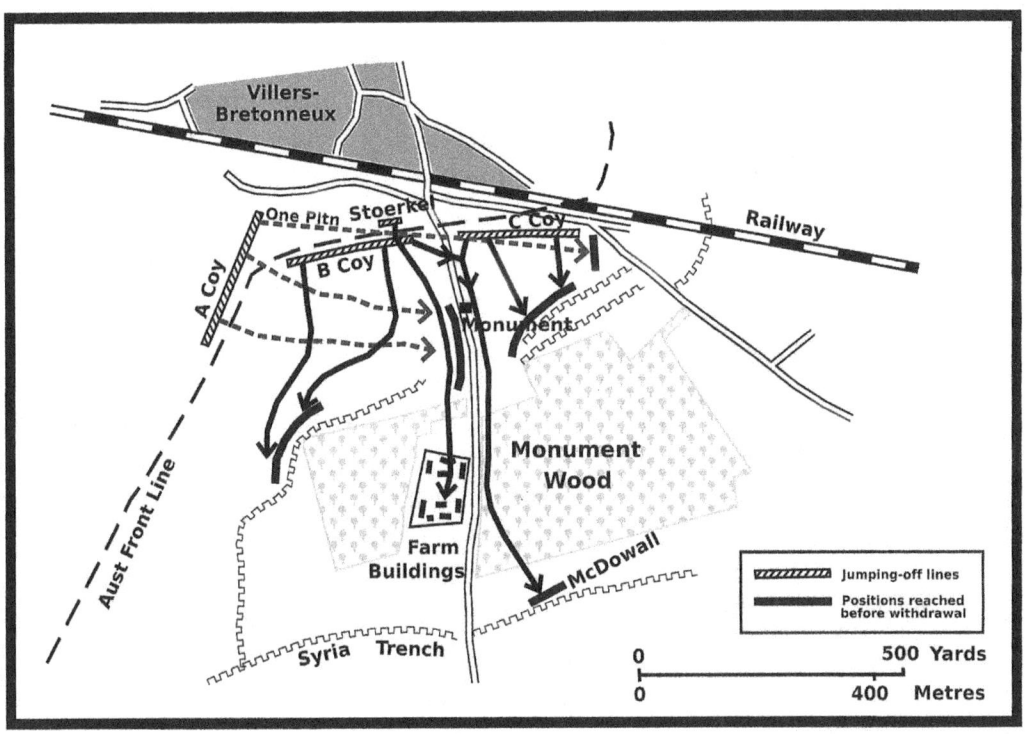

48th Battalion's action at Monument Wood, 3 May 1918.

defences were now withdrawing, fighting rearguard actions against threatening counter-attacks from three sides. It was some time before the situation became clear to Major Allen in his forward HQ near the railway. The success signal from McDowall's group had been seen and the news of the capture of the farm buildings had come in, giving Allen the impression that a line could be held running south from the left on the railway down the road, incorporating the farm, then west beyond the southern edge of the Wood. It was still not clear that most of the force had not been able to advance, even though Lieutenant Mitchell, by then the only unhurt officer in the key area, had sent a message in clear terms: 'Attack hopelessly held up on uncut wire. No chance of success,'[28] and requesting permission to withdraw. Orders were prepared to establish the proposed line but in the meantime the IO, Lieutenant Arnold, had gone out to the battle area, braving the storm of machine gun fire to locate the actual positions of the companies on the ground. His report showed that the enemy still held the western part of the Wood, and Allen had to accept that the operation had failed and the only option was to pull back to the original line. Arnold, who was still a few days short of his 21st birthday, went out again, moving around the firing line 'in his usual untroubled way'[29] to get the word to the troops and organise the movement. In the meantime the two isolated parties managed to fight their way back to the main line, pressed hard by the Germans and losing several men killed along the way, as well as 14 who were cut off and taken prisoner.[30]

Captain George Mitchell MC DCM (1894 – 1961), 48th Battalion

With daylight approaching, the surviving 48th troops under Mitchell had established their line in trenches back at the original front line, facing the enemy trench 90 to 180 metres away across a No Man's Land where the dead and wounded from the night's fighting still lay. This was the planned time for the two heavy tanks to move up and support the infantry consolidating on the objective; a message had been sent informing the tank commanders that the attack had failed but this did not get through and the big machines chugged into the trees and opened fire. One engaged the German troops for twenty minutes, doing 'splendid execution' according to Colonel Leane's report,[31] then withdrew, but the second was disabled by an explosive charge near the south-west corner of the Wood with some of its crew killed and the others captured. The tank fight was followed by a remarkable incident at the front line. In broad daylight a squad of Australian stretcher-bearers carrying a white flag emerged from the railway cutting and walked out into No Man's Land to attend to the casualties. Mitchell, noticing them from his spot in the trench, was sure they would be shot down. Instead a figure arose from the German trench and called out in English, 'Do you want to surrender?' The German had misinterpreted the white flag, an impression that was soon corrected by a chorus of shouts from the Australian line, but he remained in the open and began walking across No Man's Land towards the Australian line. Mitchell, realising that this was the officer in command on the other side, saw that he had to go out himself and meet his opponent half-way—if anyone took a shot at the German the stretcher-bearers would be cut down at once. The two officers came face-to-face and saluted. The German, a tall young fellow with a very strong voice (Mitchell had clearly heard him giving fire orders in the uproar of the fighting) had handled his company with considerable skill in battle and he now proved to be a gentleman as well as a fine soldier (with 'the spirit of a first class sportsman'[32]). The German agreed to a truce of forty minutes, eventually extended to two hours, while the Australians collected their casualties, burying several dead in No Man's Land and carrying others back to the railway. A dozen wounded were carried to the aid posts, while the German stretcher-bearers also worked in the open evacuating their own wounded from the front line. The Germans also returned the body of Captain Cumming, found near their line. While the casualty evacuation went on Mitchell and the enemy officer strolled about chatting, with Mitchell anxious to prevent the German from getting too close to the Australian line and seeing how weak it was. Mitchell's own men also caused him some anxiety:

> The new hands seemed to think this was a regular occurrence, and that the hatchet was buried. So they started to swarm out of the trenches.
> I made some most pointed comments and they got back in again.[33]

Mitchell did, however, take a squad of Jägers near the Australian line to pick up the body of one of their compatriots killed earlier—the Germans cadged cigarettes from him as soon as their officer was out of earshot. Finally the work was done. The two officers saluted again, returned to their trenches and dropped back into cover, ending the brief interlude of peace.[34] This type of fraternisation was strictly forbidden officially and Mitchell had some reason to consider the possibility of a court-martial, but although higher authority was aware of the incident no action was taken.[35]

That night the 48th Battalion was relieved by the 50th, as part of a planned relief of the 12th Brigade by the 13th, and moved back to billets at Blangy-Tronville. The unit had an all too brief few days to reorganise and clean up while the cost of the Monument Wood fight was counted. The Brigade reported the 48th's losses as 18 killed, including four officers, and 24 missing, with 109 wounded and four others slightly wounded and remaining on duty, a total of 155, the figure that appears in the *Official History*.[36] Research by Neville Browning, however, has identified 40 officers and men of the Battalion who were killed in action on 3 May 1918, four who died of wounds soon after the battle, and 14 taken prisoner,[37] so the original casualty total is a little understated. The German casualties were about 150 also,[38] so the 48th Battalion could be said to have given as much as it got, but in the sense that the unit had failed to achieve its objectives and been driven back to the start line, the 48th had for once been outfought. The circumstances were such, however, that their chances of success had been minimal. 'I think it is another case of the uselessness of small attacks,' wrote C E W Bean at the time. '... if the place was worth going for, it was worth attacking on a big scale.'[39] In what was a failure of intelligence, the strength of the enemy defence lines, their numbers and firepower had been seriously underestimated. A garrison of 1,200 good troops with 150 machine guns was unlikely to be overcome by three under-strength companies covered by a two-minute field artillery bombardment, even if they had managed to achieve surprise. Instead it was the Australians who were surprised, to find that the Wood was 'alive with machine guns and wired.'[40] Officers and men had done all that they could and several were recognised with decorations. MCs went to Lieutenants McDowall, Carr, Arnold and Stoerkel (a Bar), with Sergeant Davies and CSM Reid each receiving the DCM. A number of MMs were awarded, including five to runners who had gone back and forth through the storm of machine gun fire to pass messages: Privates Walter Bing, Keith Jarvis (who was badly wounded), Cecil King, William Pengelly and William Pope. Monument Wood remained in German hands until July.

On 4 May, the day after the attack, the 4th Division's 10th and 11th AFA Brigades together with the main body of the DAC and the 14th Company AASC began arriving at the gun- and wagon-lines west of Villers-Bretonneux to rejoin their parent formation. The medium mortar elements had already arrived, the 7th MTM Battery having gone into the line on 2

May in relief of an equivalent British battery; the 7th Battery had fired 100 rounds from their 6-inch Newton mortars into the buildings of Monument Farm as part of the bombardments leading up to the infantry operation.[41] The two field brigades had spent the previous month on the Dernancourt front in support of the 2nd Division until III Corps took over that sector. There they had carried out the routine duties of field artillery on what was now a static front, regularly delivering harassing fire on to selected targets in the enemy lines, taking part in a creeping barrage to cover an attack by British infantry in the next sector, and suffering a trickle of casualties from enemy counter-battery fire. Initially the 10th AFA replaced a British brigade in artillery reserve on 4 May with the 11th AFA taking over from another British unit as the Superimposed Group the next day. The infantry brigades were carrying out reliefs and adjusting their frontages at the same time. On the night of 3/4 May the left brigade sector's front was lengthened by the 4th Brigade extending its right flank (held by the 13th Battalion) southwards for 460 metres. In the adjusted right sector the 13th Brigade returned to the line in relief of the 12th. As well as the 50th Battalion relieving the 48th, the 49th Battalion took over the positions held by the 45th and the right section of the 47th Battalion's line north of the railway; the 47th's left was replaced by a company of the 13th Battalion, thereby establishing the new boundary between the brigade sectors. The 13th Battalion, with its front line posts close to the enemy front, was involved in frequent skirmishing, including two clashes that night, in one of which the unit's veteran Sergeant Arthur Wolff was killed when a German party rushed his Lewis gun post.[42] The heavy activity at the front caused the 13th to call on its support company in relief of the 47th; that company did not reach its position until after 3 am, to the 47th CO's displeasure.[43]

Following further rotations the following night, the 4th Brigade had its 15th and 16th Battalions in the left sector front line while the 13th Brigade was holding the right with the 49th and 50th Battalions. The 12th Brigade was now in divisional reserve but had its 46th Battalion in the forward area attached to the 13th Brigade as part of its reserve. Now that the strength of the Monument Wood position was known no further infantry attacks were attempted for the time being. Instead on 4 May the field artillery brigades shelled the area in a twenty-minute 'pulverising' bombardment, as it was described, targeting trenches and machine gun positions. Two brigades of heavy artillery co-operated, concentrating on the farm buildings with their cellars, and the artillery of the French 37th Division on the right joined in also. Similar bombardments were carried three more times during the month. The Monument area remained a menace to the Allied line covering the approaches to Amiens, an advanced position that would potentially aid a renewed German offensive on that front. There were enough intelligence indications to suggest that such an attack was imminent and the troops around Villers-Bretonneux remained on the alert while work on constructing defences in depth continued.

On 6 May reports (incorrect, as it turned out) that an enemy attack was expected in two days' time resulted in the 45th and 48th Battalions being ordered to move out of their billets in Blangy-Tronville and occupy the incomplete rear defence trench system nearby to the east (the Blangy Line and its offshoot the Tronville Switch). There was no shelter in the trenches and a downpour that night left the men soaked and miserable.[44] The Villers-Bretonneux townsite, previously battered by the British artillery, was being reduced to rubble by steady German shelling, but efforts were made to turn the ruins into a strong defensive position. A company of the 4th Pioneers was assigned to construct a system of dug-in strong points or 'keeps' within the village, with the Pioneers also supplying the garrison for the posts. The MG Battalion provided a section of four Vickers guns positioned to fire along the principal streets, with wire entanglements laid out to channel an attacker into their fields of fire. Road junctions and bridges were mined by the engineers, ready for demolition should the enemy manage to break through. The village formed the foremost bastion in a system of defence works extending well to the rear, designed to provide a strong reception if the Germans did attack again on this front. The German use of tanks on 24 April stimulated the provision of specific anti-tank defences and three 15-pounder field guns were obtained and set up as a battery for that task, manned by crews detached from the MTM personnel.

Behind the scenes the infantry units were going through significant administrative and organisational changes in May. It had been apparent for some time, with voluntary recruitment declining and conscription ruled out by the defeat of two referenda, that the number of reinforcements coming through was too low to maintain all units at reasonable strength into the future. In February a conference of AIF divisional commanders had decided to follow the precedent set by the British Army and reduce certain infantry brigades from four battalions to three; the personnel from the disbanded battalions would be distributed among the remaining units to bring them up to strength.[45] Implementation of the scheme had been delayed by the crisis of the German March offensive. The initial moves could be put off no longer, beginning with the 4th Division (as well as the 3rd) which had been involved in the heaviest fighting and suffered the highest losses in the period. The time had come to select which units would be disbanded, a process that would inevitably have a heavy emotional effect on the personnel involved; the AIF made some concession to this by ruling that the battalion numbers would be transferred to their brigade's training battalion in England. Such was the prestige of the 4th Brigade, a formation that had begun its war at the Landing and was the foundation of the 4th Division, that there could be no question of disbanding any of its units, so the focus was on the 'younger' 12th and 13th Brigades. Both Brigade HQs had been aware for at least a month that they would have to lose a battalion and had given some thought to the problem.

The 13th Brigade opted to get the unpleasantness over with quickly. The 52nd Battalion had been chosen for disbandment when the question was first raised at Brigade HQ, on the basis that the unit's recruitment was from several States and it would therefore be possible to transfer many of the members to another unit associated with their home State.[46] According to C E W Bean, before any announcement was made an exercise in behaviour modification was conducted:

> Brigadier General Glasgow quietly arranged that in his brigade the men of the disbanding battalion—the 52nd—should previously be kept rather shorter than usual ... of new clothes and edible and other comforts, but, on arriving at their new unit, should immediately be given a good dinner and fitted with new clothes and gear.[47]

The Brigade came out of the front line into the reserve area at Blangy-Tronville overnight on 13/14 May. The disbandment decision was announced at a meeting of COs on 15 May and the process began the next day, leaving minimal time for recriminations. That morning the 52nd set up a wooden memorial cross and honour board, carved with the names of battalion members killed in the fighting of 24 to 26 April.[48] The men were split up between the Brigade's other three battalions. Contrary to other views on the difficulties of recruiting in Queensland, the 52nd had received many reinforcements from that State in recent times and it now provided the largest contingent;[49] 174 Queenslanders went to their State's unit, the 49th Battalion, and the remaining 100 were taken on by the 50th (SA) together with 31 from that unit's own State. The 51st (WA) received all 120 Tasmanians as well as small contingents from NSW, Victoria and WA itself.[50] The 52nd's officers were allocated fairly evenly between the three battalions. It was arranged that the CO, Lieutenant Colonel Whitham, instead of going to the training battalion in England would be posted to the 49th as CO, relieving Lieutenant Colonel Denton in command of that unit, while Denton was posted to command the 3rd Training Battalion.

In the 12th Brigade the disbandment decision was announced earlier but implemented later. The Brigade, in reserve, was scheduled to relieve the 4th Brigade in the left sector of the front line on 9/10 May. A few days earlier the 46th and 47th Battalions, which had only gone back as far as the reserve trenches with no opportunity to clean up and refit, were relieved by the 45th and 48th in Cachy Switch and the Aubigny Line; the 46th and 47th moved back to Blangy-Tronville for a bath before returning to the front line. The blow of disbandment fell on the 47th, a decision announced at a meeting of unit COs on 5 May. The choice was perhaps predictable considering that the 47th was the most under-strength battalion in the Brigade at that time. Another factor in the view of the CO, Lieutenant Colonel Imlay, was that the unit's regional origin was mainly Queensland (with a smaller Tasmanian element), a State that had ten battalions wholly or partly associated with it but had a population that was not large enough for the number of recruits needed to maintain numbers.[51] It seems, however, that the decision was made some weeks before the meeting—C E W Bean was informed by the 12th Brigade staff shortly after the Dernancourt battle of 5 April that the 47th was in line for disbandment[52] (Brigade General Gellibrand had since gone on sick leave, but the acting brigadier, Lieutenant Colonel Leane, would have been briefed on the situation). Imlay was to be posted to command the equivalent training battalion in England together with several of his officers and NCOs as headquarters staff and instructors. The remaining officers were allocated by ballot among the other three battalions, with the ORs being asked to nominate their preferences. The news did not go down well with the troops; the announcement at about the same time that their Battalion, in the person of Stan

McDougall, had just been awarded the first VC in the 12th Brigade probably would not have helped. The actual disbandment of the 47th was not to take place until 24 May, however, so there was some time for the men to accept the situation. In the meantime, the 47th was sent back into the forward area on 9/10 May with the rest of the 12th Brigade, in relief of the 4th Brigade.

The 48th and 46th Battalions went into the front line first with the 45th and 47th behind them in support; a few days later, the 47th Battalion rotated into the front line for the last time in its existence. The 4th Brigade moved back into divisional reserve but with its 14th Battalion attached as a reserve to the 13th Brigade. After four days in reserve the 4th Brigade returned to the front line, this time in the right sector in relief of the 13th Brigade, which now had its turn in reserve (during that time the 52nd Battalion was disbanded). The 14th Battalion took over the right-of-the-line position, linking with the French at the point known as International Post, with the 13th on their left and the other two battalions in the support positions. Despite the frequent warnings of a renewed German offensive the enemy remained static and infantry action was confined to patrols and skirmishes in No Man's Land. Exchanges of artillery fire continued also. On 15 May the Germans put down a ten-minute bombardment of mustard gas shells on the 14th Battalion's lines. Among 32 casualties evacuated with gas poisoning was the Battalion's extraordinary warrior Captain Albert Jacka, his condition so serious as to keep him in hospital for several months and away from the front line for the rest of the war. The long-term effects of the gassing, combined with the previous battering that his body had taken from German bullets, would eventually kill him after the war. He was a legend, not only in the 4th Division but in the 1st AIF as a whole.

The 4th Division's tour of duty in the Villers-Bretonneux sector was now coming to its end. As of early May the Australian Corps, with four divisions under its command (the 1st Division was still in Flanders with Second Army) was holding its sector of the front from Villers-Bretonneux north across the Somme to the Ancre near Dernancourt, with three divisions in the line and one in reserve. The 3rd Division, after ten days out of the line in reserve, was ordered to relieve the 4th in the southern (right or 'A') divisional sector over the period 20 to 22 May with the 4th replacing the 3rd as the reserve division. Over the two nights all units of the Division (with the usual exception of the artillery) moved back to the area Allonville–Querrieu–Bussy–Rivery, north-east of Amiens on the north side of the Somme. The 12th Brigade, last to be relieved in the forward zone, moved to Rivery on the night 21/22 May where the 47th Battalion carried out its disbandment two days later. As well as that significant change in structure, the 12th Brigade experienced considerable movement of senior officers during May: earlier in the month Lieutenant Colonel Sydney Herring, original CO of the 45th Battalion, had returned to that unit from his posting in England, taking over command from Lieutenant Colonel Stanley Perry, who reverted to his substantive rank of major. The move of the Division into reserve coincided with Brigadier General Gellibrand's return from sick leave to resume command of the 12th Brigade, Lieutenant Colonel Leane returning to his 48th Battalion to resume command from the acting CO, A S Allen, who rejoined the 45th. At Division HQ Captain Duncan Maxwell, ADC to General Sinclair-MacLagan, had fallen seriously ill with pleurisy and had been hospitalised late in April; his place was filled by Lieutenant Gavin Baillie from the 15th Battalion.

These moves had scarcely taken place when events at the highest levels of the AIF resulted in another round of changes in the 12th Brigade's command structure. The British Fifth Army, as a headquarters entity, had been deactivated during the March crisis but was now to be reconstituted, and General Sir William Birdwood, GOC Australian Corps, was appointed as its new commander (he continued to be administrative commander of the AIF as a whole). Birdwood recommended that Sir John Monash, currently GOC 3rd Division, should succeed him in command of the Corps, a choice firmly supported by the Commander in Chief, Sir Douglas Haig. Despite a clandestine intrigue against Monash's appointment led by the official correspondent, C E W Bean, the general took over the Corps at the end of the month (Bean later published a *mea culpa* in his *Official History*,[53] telling the story with great frankness even though it was much to his own discredit). This created a vacancy in command of the 3rd Division and John Gellibrand was selected as that formation's new GOC, with promotion to major general. Incidentally, another change of divisional commander in the Australian Corps had occurred recently with the appointment of Major General Charles Rosenthal, formerly 4th Division CRA, as GOC 2nd Division. On 28 May, ten days after returning to the 12th Brigade, General Gellibrand departed again to take up his new command. In turn Lieutenant Colonel Raymond Leane was re-appointed to the command of the Brigade, this time on a permanent basis, with his promotion to brigadier general coming through in due course. Leane's place as CO 48th Battalion went to Stanley Perry, recently displaced as CO of the 45th by the return of Lieutenant Colonel Herring; Perry regained his temporary rank of lieutenant colonel. These bursts of changes in command occurred either side of the break-up of the 47th Battalion and the departure of Colonel Imlay.[54] No doubt the brigade and unit administrations would have been hoping for a period of stability, while making the most of the spell out of the line that had commenced on 22 May when Division HQ was established in the reserve area at Allonville.

The spell was expected to be a short one, however. Although it was the closest thing to a rest that the Division had had for some time, as reserve division it still had responsibilities for the rearward defence lines in case of a renewed enemy attack. This included the Pioneer Battalion at Bussy, and each infantry brigade made a battalion available to take up defensive positions if required, bivouacked at Frechencourt (15th Battalion), Lahoussoye (51st) and Glisy (46th), north to south. Less those units, the brigades took up billets further west, the 4th Brigade between Allonville and nearby Cardonette, the 13th around Querrieu and the 12th between Rivery and Camon, just across the Somme from Amiens. All units, including the three forward battalions, rested for a day or two while enjoying a bath and a swim in the river, in weather that was mostly warm now—the 4th Brigade diarist described several days in late May as 'glorious.' Apart from refitting, making up individual equipment shortages and general cleaning up, most of the troops' on-duty time was then devoted to routine weapons training

4th Division Headquarters, Allonville, France, 29 May 1918. Back row, left to right: Lieutenant Gavin Baillie (ADC); Lt Alan Mitchell (Paymaster); Captain Arnold Moulden (Court Martial Officer); Capt Ernest Kemmis (ADC). Second row: Lt Benjamin Stewart (Intelligence Officer); Major John Fraser (Signal Officer); Lt George Donaldson (Adjutant to CRE); Capt Leslie Craig (GSO3); Capt Arthur Rossiter (Gas Officer); Maj Frank Lind (DADMS); Maj Edward Carter (DAQMG); Maj Joseph Tuckett (DADOS); Capt Cyril Bartlett (assistant to DAQMG); Maj Arthur Hyman (Claims Officer); Maj Edward James (DADVS); Capt Clifton Leake (Adjutant, Reinforcement Wing). Front row: Maj Eric Plant (GSO2); Lieutenant Colonel John Dyer (CRE); Lt Col John Lavarack (GSO1); Major General Ewen Sinclair-MacLagan (GOC); Lt Col Richard Dowse (AA&QMG); Colonel Arthur Moseley (ADMS); Maj Walter Fowler-Brownsworth (DAAG). (AWM E02419)

and drill, and recreation in the form of aquatic sports carnivals. General Birdwood took the opportunity of visiting to present decorations earned in recent actions and to say his farewells to all ranks on his departure to command Fifth Army. During this period the 12th Brigade's remaining battalions absorbed the ex-47th troops into their units as reinforcements; numbers were fairly evenly distributed, although the 45th Battalion, lowest in strength, received rather more than the other two. Some outstanding soldiers joined new units, notably Sergeant Stan McDougall VC MM, moving to the 48th Battalion, and Sergeant William Brown and Private Charlie Shang, both DCM and Bar MM, to the 45th.

Towards the end of the 4th Division's rest period the long-anticipated renewal of the German offensive fell on the allied armies. This time, however, Ludendorff's blow was not against the British line but instead hit the French front on the Aisne River; again the Germans achieved surprise and again the defenders gave way. In three days the Germans had advanced 50 kilometres towards Paris before they were slowed and finally stopped, leaving the French badly shaken but not broken;

> many French people and some–though not all–of their generals had believed that the reverses suffered by the British could not have happened to the French. Consequently the shock of May 27th resulted in a marked change in their tone.[55]

The Division was scheduled to return to the forward area on 31 May, with the troops generally refreshed by the short period out of the line. The spell had been 'very fine,' noted the 48th Battalion. '... [the] men now look ever so much fitter than formerly. No doubt the good food, hot weather and excellent facilities for sport are responsible for this.'[56] The back areas had not been free from danger, however. German aircraft were active most nights, dropping bombs on Amiens and the surrounding countryside and villages where the troops were billeted. These caused a few casualties, including two officers of the 15th Battalion mortally wounded when a bomb exploded near their tent. More deadly was the intermittent shelling by German long-range guns, particularly for two companies of the 14th Battalion billeted in two large barns near Allonville. In the early hours of 31 May a high velocity shell, later thought to be from a nine-inch (23-cm) gun, made a direct hit on the roof of one of the barns, smashing the frames and bringing the heavy timbers down on the sleeping men below. The results were horrifying:

> The whole debris had tumbled down on the boys, disembowelling many, cutting off legs and arms ... Under it the dead lay silent; the rest made one long moan of agony. Of those unhurt, all but about half a dozen still stood petrified, unable to move; the others were working like fiends, pulling away the timber to get at the victims ... we saw things that we never want to see again.[57]

The men in the second barn, jerked awake by the sudden uproar, were about to go to help their comrades when another shell hit their building, exploding on the floor and collapsing part of the structure but fortunately causing considerably fewer casualties. The German gun then ceased fire, having in a few moments killed or fatally wounded 29 men and wounded another 57, an event that was remembered in the 14th Battalion as the Allonville Disaster. The first shell caused 69 of the total casualties, thought to be the highest number from a single shell in the history of the 1st AIF.[58] The German gun may have been shooting randomly and scored chance hits, but the Division reported that it had first fired air-burst shrapnel, ranged by an enemy spotter aircraft which had signalled with flares when the shots were on target.[59]

That distressing incident occurred only a few hours before the 14th was due to march off with the rest of the 4th Brigade on the first stage of its return to the forward area. The other units moved off at 6:30 am with the 14th following at 10, after hurried reorganisation to allow for the losses in men and equipment. For this stint in the line the 4th Division was to relieve the 5th in the centre (or 'B') divisional sector of the Australian Corps front, where the front line ran roughly from Sailly-le-Sec on the north side of the Somme River and canal across the river south-west to Hill 104 north of Villers-Bretonneux, curving around the German salient centred on Hamel,

> ... a trench length of 9,900 yards [9,052 metres]. The area is marked by distinct tactical features and has great defensive qualities of commanding observation. The country is undulating and quite open except for a few isolated woods. The river valleys and numerous other valleys and depressions form tactical features which can all be woven into a scheme of defence.[60]

This was mostly new territory for the Division, except that elements of the 13th Brigade had garrisoned the Bridgehead Line, just west of the present front, in late April. The 4th Brigade took over the right of the Division sector facing Hamel, completing the relief by 10 pm on 31 May. On the following night the 13th Brigade moved in on the left where the line straddled the Somme at Sailly-le-Sec. To hold the fairly long front, both brigades put three battalions in the line. The 4th Brigade, having retained its four-battalion structure, had one (the 13th) available to use as support but the 13th Brigade had all three of its battalions 'up.' To back up the front line in the left brigade sector the 4th Pioneer Battalion was designated as the support unit, available as infantry if necessary (but not for regular front-line reliefs) while continuing with their usual construction tasks.

Fire support for the front line was provided by three companies (4th, 24th and 13th) of the MG Battalion, relieving their equivalent 5th Division guns. The 12th Brigade took up positions around Aubigny as reserve brigade, with the 12th MG Company in the same area. The 4th Division assumed command of the 'B' sector on the morning of 2 June when Division HQ opened at Bussy-les-Daours on the Hallue. For the time being artillery support was provided by the 5th Division artillery, which included several attached British units; otherwise the 4th Division arms and services relieved their equivalents in the usual way. The overall stance of the allied armies remained defensive for the moment, and in the first half of June much of the 4th Division's activity was directed at improving the defences in its sector, continuing work started by the 5th Division. The units in the forward zone carried out a 'gigantic' programme of works, designed, organised and managed by the divisional engineers. The infantry and pioneers worked on joining up their front line posts into wired continuous trench lines and digging support and reserve lines with communication trenches connecting them. Other constructions included

> mined dugouts for Brigade and Battalion headquarters, Machine Gun emplacements, Regimental Aid Posts, Advanced Dressing Stations and Relay Posts for stretcher bearers, and living accommodation for personnel of field batteries and heavy artillery as well as forward observation posts.[61]

The 12th Field Company was given responsibility for all prepared demolitions in the area—explosive charges placed at road junctions and on railway and river bridges (the Somme, Ancre and Hallue all ran through the divisional area) to deny their use to the enemy in case of a breakthrough. Many of the charges and fuses set up earlier were found to have deteriorated in the weather, and a programme was initiated to replace them and generally improve the scheme. Behind the front in reserve, the 12th Brigade supplied large working parties, up to 500 men, to bury telephone cables and otherwise strengthen the rearward defensive systems. The effort, physical and mental, put into designing and building these defences was commendable but in hindsight probably not vital—the time was fast approaching when the strategic outlook would change dramatically.

19 Notes

1. 45th Battalion War Diary, 27 April 1916.
2. 4th Brigade War Diary for April 1918, Appendix 42.
3. White, *Op Cit*, p. 134. The 4th Brigade's Intelligence Summary for the period (April 1918 War Diary, Appendix 49) has an account of the operation. See also Lt Buckler's report in the 4th Field Company's April Diary (Appendix 2).
4. The 13th Battalion history (White, *Op Cit*, p. 134) says that Bone and Leonard were hit on 'the night of 29 April' but official records, as well as the unit War Diary and Col Marks' own diary have 1 May.
5. Henderson died on 13 May at Etaples; he was awarded a Bar to his MC for the action of 2 May, the recommendation having gone through before his death was announced. See White, *Op Cit*, pp. 134–5, and the unit War Diary.
6. 12th Brigade War Diary for May 1918, Appendix 4. There are some discrepancies between that report and the narrative in the 47th Battalion's Diary; the latter document also includes a handwritten report (Appendices 2 and 3) which gives a slightly different version. The 13th Battalion's report in its May Diary takes a different point of view again.
7. 45th Battalion War Diary for May 1918, Appendix 9.
8. 12th Brigade War Diary for May 1918, Appendix 6.
9. *Official History*, Vol V, p. 647.
10. 12 Brigade War Diary for April 1918, Appendix 9.
11. See Mitchell, *Op Cit*, pp. 214–216 for a subaltern's view of the material now joining the unit.
12. Bean Diary, 2 May 1918, AWM38 3DRL606/109/1.
13. *Official History*, Vol V, p. 646.
14. Bean Diary, 3 May 1918, AWM38 3DRL606/109/1.
15. 4th Division GS War Diary for May 1918, Appendix 6.
16. 48th Battalion War Diary for May 1918, Appendix 7.
17. Bean Diary, 2 May 1918, AWM38 3DRL606/109/1 (p. 3).
18. 12th Brigade War Diary for May 1918, Appendix 5.
19. Mitchell, *Op Cit*, p. 217 (Mitchell's account has different timings to the official version—he says that the artillery opened at 2.10 am and the infantry attack was timed for 2.20). The *Official History* (Vol

20 V, p. 649) states that the standing troops were seen by the Germans two minutes before 'Zero.'
20 *Official History*, Vol V, p. 649, quoting Mitchell's diary. In his book (*Op Cit*, p. 217), which was based on the diary, Mitchell says that 'Six eighteen-pounders [i.e. one battery] fired for three minutes, then stopped.'
21 4th Division Artillery HQ War Diary for May 1918, Appendix 7 (Order No 133). It appears that two 18-pounder batteries from the RFA brigade forming the 'Superimposed Group' were added to the Right Group's resources; those guns were required to barrage the SOS line, beyond the Wood.
22 Or 396, depending on how the calculation is made—if a gun fired its first round on the stroke of Zero, and then maintained a rate of five rounds per minute, it would have fired eleven rounds by the end of two minutes, rather than ten.
23 4th Division Artillery HQ War Diary for May 1918, Appendix 1. The figures given may include the preliminary bombardments fired in the days leading up to the attack.
24 From the AWM Red Cross report on Pte Mallyon's death. There are documents on Capt Cumming's service record, however, stating that he was killed by machine gun fire (his unusual given name is recorded as 'Derwus' in the National Archives system). Although Capt Cumming's original gravesite was recorded at the time, his remains could not be identified after the war, and his name therefore appears on the Villers-Bretonneux memorial.
25 Cutlack, *Op Cit*, pp. 175–6; Bean Diary, 3 May 1918, AWM38 3DRL606/109/1; narrative in the 48th Battalion Diary for 3 May 1918. In the *Official History*, however (Vol V, p. 651 and pp.653–4), Bean only says that several German officers were killed or mortally wounded, one of whom was the battalion adjutant.
26 Cutlack, *Op Cit*, p.176.
27 The narratives in the Brigade and Battalion Diaries and appended reports are vague as to 'A' Company's part in the battle, but two sketch maps with those documents both show one platoon of the company as having reached a line north of the north-east corner of Monument wood, facing east with its left on the railway. For his part in the operation, Sgt Way was awarded a Bar to his MM, the recommendation for which states that he had 'reached his objective.' He may have been acting in command of the platoon.
28 Mitchell, *Op Cit*, p. 220.
29 *Ibid*, p. 222.
30 Browning, *Leane's Battalion*, *Op Cit*, p. 246–7 and Appendix F.
31 12th Brigade War Diary for May 1918, Appendix 6.
32 12th Brigade War Diary, 3 May 1918.
33 Mitchell, *Op Cit*, p. 224.
34 Regrettably, the name of this gallant foe is not recorded. Under interrogation, one of the prisoners captured at the farmhouse named the 20th Jäger Battalion's company commanders as Lts Korte, Maelitsch, Spintzyck and Müller. He may have been one of those, assuming the prisoner was telling the truth, and the spellings were recorded correctly (4th Division General Staff War Diary for May 1918, Appendix 8).
35 The truce is not mentioned in the official after-action reports on the Monument Wood action, but it does appear in the 12th Brigade Diary for 3 May. The main source for the details is Mitchell himself, in his diary (which Bean used for the account in the *Official History*, Vol V, p.653), book *Backs to the Wall* and a *Reveille* article. An earlier account can be found in Cutlack (*Op Cit*, p. 177) and at least one of the Red Cross reports on Monument Wood casualties (Cpl E C Inglis)

mentions the 'armistice' also.
36. Vol V, p. 654.
37. Browning, *Leane's Battalion, Op Cit*, Appendices C and F; the AWM Roll of Honour confirms the figure of 40 fatalities.
38. *Official History*, Vol V, p. 654.
39. Bean Diary, 3 May 1918, AWM38 3DRL606/109/1 (p. 18).
40. 12th Brigade War Diary. 3 May 1918.
41. 4th Division DTMO War Diary, 2 May 1918.
42. Another soldier whose place of burial was recorded by map reference at the time but whose remains could not be identified after the war.
43. 47th Battalion War Diary, 4 May 1918.
44. 48th Battalion War Diary, 6 May 1918.
45. 4th Division General Staff War Diary, 2 February 1918.
46. 13th Brigade War Diary, 15 May 1918.
47. *Official History*, Vol V, p. 659.
48. The 51st Battalion (WA) set up a similar cross, which has survived and is displayed in St George's Cathedral, Perth.
49. 13th Brigade War Diary, 15 May 1918.
50. *Ibid*, Appendix 24.
51. 47th Battalion War Diary, 5 May 1918. The *Official History* (Vol V, p. 657) takes this view also.
52. Bean Papers, notebook AWM38 3DRL606/185/1, p.40 (p. 38 in PDF). The entry was undated but it was before Brig Gen Gellibrand went on sick leave (19 April).
53. Vol VI, pp. 196–8.
54. The movement of 12th Brigade senior officers in this period invites speculation on what may or may not have been going on behind the scenes. In particular, Lt Col Imlay was still present at Querrieu, finalising the disbandment process for his 47th Battalion, when General Gellibrand was appointed to the 3rd Division and the consequent domino-effect movements were taking place. Was Imlay considered for command of the 48th Battalion in place of Leane, and if not, why not? He was a substantive Lt Col and therefore senior to Maj (temporary Lt Col) Perry, who was given the 48th command. Imlay had also served with the 48th before commanding the 47th. Of course, he may have been prepared to accept the training battalion command without much protest, after two years at the front, twice wounded, and decorated with the DSO and Bar; in any case, an army officer goes where he is ordered, and his new posting was also a Lt Col's command.
55. Bean, *Anzac to Amiens*, p. 448.
56. 48th Battalion War Diary, 31 May 1918.
57. Rule, *Op Cit*, p. 124.
58. Wanliss, *Op Cit*, pp. 290–91, records the names of all of the fatal casualties.
59. 4th Division General Staff War Diary, 31 May 1918, recounted in the *Official History*, Vol VI, p.109n. The Diary entry also says that the German gun continued firing until 8 am, and the Corps Diary for the same date says that 30 shells were fired into Allonville.
60. 4th Division Engineers HQ War Diary, 1 June 1918.
61. *Ibid*, 2 June 1918.

20: Astonishment of a Continent

When the 4th Division's main body had been withdrawn on 22 May, the divisional artillery, with its attached British brigades, remained in the line to cover the relieving 3rd Division infantry. The field brigades' routine work went on under 3rd Division command, while the DAC undertook the task of salvaging the large quantities of abandoned artillery material in the area.[1] Late in May Brigadier General Burgess received the welcome news that the 4th Division artillery would shortly be withdrawn from the line, its first real break from the battlefront for five months. The destination was the Fourth Army artillery training area at Hallencourt, south of Abbeville near the mouth of the Somme; the 3rd Division artillery was completing a stint at Hallencourt, and would be coming up to rejoin its own division in relief of the 4th Division guns.

The batteries and DAC handed over to their reliefs during 2 June and moved back to the wagon lines for the night. The march to Hallencourt got under way next morning, a six-kilometre column of men, horses, guns, limbers and wagons. The column staged through Hangest-sur-Somme, about half-way, for the night and arrived at billets in villages near the training area during the afternoon of 4 June; the artillery's supply unit, the 14th Company AASC, travelled with the guns. General Burgess intended to make the most of what would be a fortnight in the rear, and the artillery staff organised a combination of intensive training and recreation for the troops. The training programme anticipated that the present stalemate at the front would change in the near future:

> Our chief aim will be mobile training and every effort will be made to bring Units to a state of high efficiency and preparation for a possible participation in moving warfare ... the system to be adopted will be progressive, commencing with small commands at most elementary work ... until finally the Battery works as a whole, and later the Brigade ... the same energy will be spent in providing recreation [mainly sports]. Wednesday and Saturday half days and Sunday whole day will be devoted to recreation entirely.[2]

To provide entertainment in the off-duty evenings, in addition to the *estaminets* in nearby villages (Abbeville itself was declared out of bounds) the divisional concert troupe, the Smart Set, came down also, together with the highly-regarded band of the 13th Infantry Battalion for musical backing.[3]

A typical day's activities began with reveille at 5 or 6 am followed by marching drill before breakfast. Specialised training periods for the gunners, horse drivers and signallers were then conducted for the remainder of the day, with a break for lunch; work ceased at 5:30 pm except for the specified half-days and whole Sundays of sports.[4] The schedule also included preparation and practice for a grand ceremonial review of the full artillery by General Birdwood, as part of his farewell to the Australian Corps, to be conducted on 9 June. A detailed format for the parade had been promulgated before the brigades left the forward area,[5] and the various complex movements of men, horses and vehicles were rehearsed two days before the event, on a 17-hectare field near Pont Remy on the Somme. As well as Birdwood, other generals in attendance included his Chief of Staff Major General White, his successor as Corps GOC Lieutenant General Sir John Monash, and Major Generals Sinclair-MacLagan, GOC 4th Division, and Rosenthal, recently appointed GOC 2nd Division, come to see his old command on parade. The review went off without a hitch, an impressive display that produced warm congratulations from General Birdwood; as part of the ceremony, he presented medals or ribbons to recently-decorated personnel, including General Burgess, awarded the CMG for his work in the Third Ypres battles.

Review of the 4th Division artillery at Pont Remy, France, 9 June 1918. General Birdwood takes the salute.
(AWM E02525)

The progressive training programme continued during the second week at Hallencourt, including two days taken up with special recreational events. On occasion BEF formations in rest areas held race meetings, featuring races with officers' chargers and draught horses, and sometimes mules, and including bookmakers, judges, stewards, clerk of the course and the rest of the traditional features of horse racing. Race meetings were popular with the troops, and the 4th Division artillery held one on 12 June at Epagne on the Somme, drawing a crowd of 3,000. To conclude the recreation for the fortnight, an athletic sports meeting, organised by the 10th AFA Brigade, was held on 16 June. Next day, the units began packing up for returning to the forward area;

all units and all ranks have benefited greatly by this period of training and rest. In efficiency, health and general well being, the 4th Australian Divisional Artillery returns to the Line in first class order and condition.[6]

For this tour at the front, the artillery would return to its own Division's command in the central or 'B' sector of the Australian Corps line, relieving the 5th Division artillery, which would then have its turn at Hallencourt.[7] The return march began on 18 June and the relief was completed by 22 June, with artillery HQ established at Bussy-les-Daours. The available field artillery, the two AFA brigades and three attached British RFA brigades, was deployed in three groups covering the divisional front, plus a 'superimposed' group and another brigade in reserve. The 10th and 11th AFA Brigades, each reinforced by a British battery, formed the right and centre groups respectively, with the British brigades making up the left and superimposed groups and the reserve. During the period out of the line Lieutenant Colonel William Waite, CO of the 11th AFA Brigade, had gone to England on leave; he was, however, seriously ill, and a medical board later found him to be unfit to resume service in the field. Major Percy Ross was appointed acting CO shortly after the unit returned to the line.

While the 4th Division infantry, engineers and pioneers worked on defensive systems in early June, the higher command was giving some thought to more aggressive activities. The supreme commander, General Foch, issued a request for the British army to begin conducting minor offensives along its front, both raiding and operations to take and hold ground. At this stage the intention was more to interfere with any German plans for further attacks than to swing over to an offensive policy, and also to obtain intelligence of movements of the enemy's reserves. The Australian Corps already had just such an operation in hand. The 2nd Division, holding the northern (left) sector of the Corps front, had been chipping away at the enemy positions opposite during May, and on 10 June its right-flank brigade (the 7th) mounted an operation to take the high ground running south from Morlancourt. The 4th Division co-operated with that advance, sending its left-flank battalion, the 51st, forward to conform with the 7th Brigade's right. The attack was launched behind a creeping barrage at the unusual time of 9:45 pm, just before dark with daylight saving, and was a complete success. The 7th Brigade gained all of its objectives, destroying a German battalion in the process. The 51st Battalion advanced at the same time, using elements of three companies to overcome several enemy posts, capturing 19 prisoners and a machine gun, then digging in on a line 460 metres forward of its original position. Enemy opposition was weak for the most part, but pockets of resistance and snipers cost the 51st eight killed and 23 wounded. A week later the 13th Brigade was relieved in the front line by the 12th.

General Monash, keen for the Australian Corps to make more contributions on its front, now requested his divisional commanders to submit new proposals. The Morlancourt advance had created a situation that suggested a further such operation: the 2nd Division's right flank had moved far enough forward to be vulnerable to enfilade fire from German artillery positioned in the projecting Hamel salient to the south (in front of the 4th Division), and an attack to push back that part of the enemy line was an obvious move. Intelligence indicated that the enemy troops holding their line were not of particularly good quality, but the features of the Hamel salient meant that an attack on that front would nevertheless not be easy. The Australian line was situated along one of several spurs of higher ground running roughly south-north towards the Somme from the Villers-Bretonneux plateau. The German front line opposite lay an average of 360 metres away along the next spur to the east, on the other side of a flat plain that offered no cover to an attacking force. Towards the southern end of the sector the German trench passed in front of a wooded area split by a road into two segments, Vaire Wood west of the road and Hamel Wood on the east. The enemy front line trench was believed to be in poor condition overall, but it incorporated two formidable strong points or redoubts, named for their shapes on the map—Kidney Trench in front of Vaire Wood, and the larger Pear Trench located about half way between the woods and the village, on a reverse slope and out of direct sight from the Australian line. Hamel village itself, long since abandoned except for German troops, lay to the north-east of the woods, below the spur. Behind Hamel the ground rose again to a knoll known as the Wolfsberg, which was entrenched as a reserve and command position, giving the Germans good observation of the ground over which an attack would come. Intelligence estimated that the enemy had 2,800 men in the forward zone and about the same number in reserve. The Germans had first occupied the area early in April during their advance towards Amiens, stopped at the first battle of Villers-Bretonneux. Shortly afterwards a counter-attack (by the 5th Division) to recover the lost ground was proposed, but had not gone ahead—the possible gains would not justify the likely casualties. Although the situation had changed since then, the risk of unacceptable losses remained, particularly if an attempt was made to retake the entire salient.

A programme of raids on the enemy line opposite the 4th Division was proposed, to be undertaken by the 4th Brigade, holding the right flank sector of the Division front. The plan developed by the Brigade called for its centre battalion, the 16th, to send two raiding parties against Pear Trench, while at the same time the 14th Battalion on the right raided the trench in front of Vaire Wood with three parties;[8] each party was 30 strong under an officer.[9] The raiders would be covered by a creeping barrage on both objectives fired by the field artillery (still the 5th Division artillery at this time), with other fire support provided by a machine gun barrage from the 4th MG Company and by mortar fire from light and medium batteries on selected key points. The Corps heavy artillery would also co-operate, with counter-battery fire and shelling of enemy approach routes. The general outline of the operation was decided at a conference with the Brigade staff and the battalion COs, and the units then went about developing detailed proposals. As usual with trench raids, the attackers planned to get in and out quickly, 10 to 15 minutes at most, with the aim of 'information, identification, destruction and killing.'[10] The 14th Battalion appointed its raiding party commanders by lot and chose the raiders from volunteers; the officers then reconnoitred the terrain and worked out their attack plans, co-ordinated by Battalion HQ. The 16th Battalion took a slightly different approach, designating one company, 'D' under Captain Bill Lynas, to carry out the raid. Lynas conducted the preliminary nocturnal reconnaissance personally—he probably knew as much about that type of work as anyone in the BEF—worked out the best approaches and tactics, then took the raiding parties' officers and NCOs out to the enemy wire to familiarise them with the ground. Lynas set out a plan that included detailed suggestions for the artillery barrage, and instead of relying on the guns for wire cutting, his idea was to use Bangalore torpedoes—tubular explosive charges that produced a long narrow area of blast and splinters, intended to cut a gap in a wire entanglement. Brigade arranged for two of these devices to be designed and manufactured by the 4th Field Company, and the engineers allocated Sappers William Ross and Albert Thompson to go with the raiders and set off the torpedoes. To give them a look at the ground, Captain Lynas took the sappers with him on one of his excursions to the enemy trench (he went out six times in the lead-up to the raid).

Zero was set for 15 June at 11:30 pm, by which time the raiding parties had moved out to their jumping-off positions in No Man's Land. At Vaire Wood the barrage came down promptly, if not perfectly, and the three 14th Battalion groups followed it closely up to the wire. The left party overran several enemy outposts, but on reaching the wire found it mostly uncut and too strong to get through in the limited time allowed for the raid; they were restricted to an exchange of grenades and rifle fire with the German garrison, but sent back two prisoners taken in the outposts. In the centre, the raiders got through the wire and entered the trench, to find that the garrison had made themselves scarce. By contrast, the party on the right encountered opposition, and in a stiff fight killed a dozen of the enemy and took nine prisoners for the loss of nine casualties, two of them fatal. After 15 minutes the recall flare signal was fired and the raiding parties returned to their line with the prisoners and their own wounded. The 14th lost three dead and ten wounded in total, the fatalities including two of the unit's best NCOs, Sergeants Herbert Anderson and Edward 'Darky' Harrison ('A gamer boy never crossed the seas'[11]). Nevertheless the raid was accounted a notable success in view of the German unit identifications obtained, as well as the estimated enemy casualties. Two of the group leaders, Lieutenants Harold Thompson and Alexander Bruford, were each subsequently awarded the MC for their efforts.

The 16th Battalion's raiders at Pear Trench crept across No Man's Land behind the two sappers carrying their awkward eight-foot (2.5-metre) Bangalore torpedoes. Sappers Ross and Thompson slid the explosives under the German wire but were detected by a sentry, who threw a grenade that badly wounded Thompson. He nevertheless started his fuse as did Ross, and the two charges blew a nine-metre gap in the entanglement through which the raiding parties entered both arms of the looping trench. The officer leading one group was wounded at the start as were both of his sergeants, resulting in some disorganisation, but the second party moved along the trench according to plan, tossing grenades into dugouts as they went. A mopping-up party, operating along the sunken road that intersected the position, also got into some sharp combat with the garrison. Some shells from the covering barrage began dropping short and causing casualties, so after nine minutes Captain Lynas (who was controlling the raid from a position 64 metres in front of the trench) fired a flare to signal the recall.

Five German prisoners were brought back, but considerably more had surrendered in the fighting. Raiding was a particularly ruthless business: Lynas reported that many prisoners 'could not be persuaded to leave their trenches and left no alternative but to do them in, about 15 were punished in this way.'[12] He estimated that the enemy had lost 50 men altogether against the raiders' casualties of one dead (Sapper Thompson, who died of his wounds the next day) and 15 wounded; there was also one man missing, Private Hubert Cook, who was subsequently reported killed.[13] The surviving prisoners represented the necessary enemy unit identification, and three captured machine guns were also brought in. Lynas had expected better results, regretting that 'the show went a bit wrong,' but Army, Corps and Division HQ were all satisfied with the night's work and officially congratulated both the 14th and 16th Battalions. Bill Lynas was later awarded a second Bar to his MC and Sapper Ross the DCM; Sapper Thompson was also recommended for the DCM but his death meant that the recommendation could not proceed under the rules of the time.

Even as the raids were being carried out, a way had presented itself that could well make the larger operation a practical proposition. The 5th Tank Brigade's 13th Battalion had just arrived in the sector, equipped with the latest Mark V tanks, machines which offered major improvements in performance over the older models. Both Monash and the Fourth Army commander, Sir Henry Rawlinson, were given a demonstration of the new tanks and briefed on their capabilities. Both generals saw that the tanks offered a solution to the problem of minimising infantry casualties in an attack on Hamel ('Deus ex machina' was Bean's marginal heading in the *Official History*[14]). At a meeting on 18 June, Monash was asked to submit a detailed proposal to Rawlinson; 4th Division HQ was made aware also, since it would be responsible for an operation on its front. Monash consulted with Brigadier General Courage, commanding the tank brigade, and they developed a broad plan, submitted to General Rawlinson on 21 June, for an operation to be mounted in the first week of July. The scheme envisaged that the tanks, initially 48 but later increased to 60, would take the lead in capturing the ground, supported by three brigades of infantry; the latter would play the secondary role, following behind the first line of tanks to mop up and consolidate the captured ground. The artillery's task was directed towards supporting the tank operation, laying down a barrage line 275 metres ahead of the tanks rather than a close creeping barrage to cover the advancing infantry. They would also target the enemy's guns and strong-points. Additional artillery, field and heavy, would be brought in to reinforce the batteries already in place. It was inevitable that the infantry would suffer losses, and with the shortage of reinforcements, Monash decided that the 2nd and 3rd Division would each contribute a brigade to join one from the 4th Division, thereby sharing around the likely casualties. As the only four-battalion brigade remaining in the 4th Division, the 4th Brigade would be the Division's infantry component; the other brigades nominated were the 6th (2nd Division, Brigadier General J Paton) and the 11th (3rd Division, Brigadier General J H Cannan). The 4th Division's other two brigades would hold the original line and then move up to relieve the attacking force in the captured position.

When the outline of the Corps scheme reached the 4th Division command group there was some consternation about the proposed tactics. Bullecourt had not been forgotten, and although General Sinclair-MacLagan had joined the Division after April 1917, his brigadiers and most of their battalion commanders had been there at the time; any plan that relied on tanks to clear the way for the infantry, without a creeping barrage, was unlikely to be received with much enthusiasm. Paton and Cannan attended a conference with Sinclair-MacLagan and his command group at 4th Division HQ on 25 June to discuss the proposed operation. Brigadier General Brand was away on a week's leave and the 4th Brigade was represented by Lieutenant Colonel Edmund Drake-Brockman, CO of the 16th Battalion, as acting brigadier; it was his unit that had suffered the most heavily at Bullecourt. Brigadier General Leane (12th Brigade) had commanded the 48th then, and that unit's heavy losses had included his brother and nephew.[15] The meeting strongly recommended that the plan be changed to have infantry and tanks advancing together behind a conventional creeping barrage, with the infantry having the primary role. That constituted a significant departure from the original concept, but Monash appreciated the importance of his subordinate commanders having confidence in the plan, and the 4th Division's view was also supported by the Corps chief of staff, Brigadier General Thomas Blamey. Monash accepted the changes with good grace and the revised proposal was then approved by General Rawlinson and by GHQ. The detailed planning process now began.

While the higher command was deliberating, the routines of life and death went on for the lower levels of the armies in the line—the drudgery of working parties, and the usual trickle of casualties from patrolling, sniping, aerial bombing and exchanges of artillery fire. On 19 June, German shelling on the 24th MG Company's positions badly wounded the conqueror of Richthofen, Sergeant Cedric Popkin, who had his right leg amputated in hospital (he recovered from the operation and lived until 1968; another 24th Company soldier, Private Thomas Livingstone, was fatally hit in the same shelling). Enemy long-range guns sometimes reached as far back as the headquarters areas, and on 24 June the 4th Division ADMS, Colonel Arthur Moseley, was badly wounded when a shell hit the chateau at Bussy-les-Daours where he was billeted; he too lost a leg. Lieutenant Colonel Roy McGregor, recently appointed CO of the 4th Field Ambulance in relief of Lieutenant Colonel Follit, became acting ADMS.[16] Major Hugh Lewers, also a comparative newcomer to the 4th Field Ambulance, took over as acting CO of the unit. The 13th Field Ambulance had also had a change of CO during the month, Lieutenant Colonel Fry being succeeded by Lieutenant Colonel Frank Wooster, posted in from the 1st Australian General Hospital, Rouen, on 12 June.

The 4th Brigade was given a spell in the rear to prepare for the coming battle, relieved by the 13th Brigade on the night of 26/27 June. The 13th went through some changes in command personnel during June. Lieutenant Colonel John Whitham had assumed command of the 49th Battalion when his 52nd was broken up, but only a month later, on 15 June, Whitham was posted away to be an instructor at the senior officers' school in England. The second-in-command of the 49th, Major William Arrell, took over as CO. A 33 year old Queenslander, a school teacher in civilian life, Major Arrell had been acting CO for short periods several times in the past, but he was now given an extended term in command with promotion to temporary lieutenant colonel.

The 13th Brigade's most notable change took place towards the end of the month, when the final step in the "Australianisation" of the AIF higher command saw the highly-respected 1st Division GOC, the British regular Major General Sir H B 'Hooky' Walker, posted to command a British Army division His chosen replacement was William Glasgow, promoted to major general, who left the 13th Brigade on 28 June and departed for the north to assume his new command, currently with XV Corps in Second Army. Glasgow's promotion meant that all five divisional commanders, as well as the Australian Corps commander, were now members of the AIF, if not all Australian-born.[17] Of the six generals, all except Hobbs (5th Division) had served with the 4th Division at some time, and all except Monash had served with the 1st Division. Glasgow's successor as 13th Brigade commander was Sydney Herring, promoted from lieutenant colonel commanding the 45th Battalion (12th Brigade). In a further inter-brigade posting, Major Charles Johnston transferred from second-in-command of the 14th Battalion (4th Brigade) to the 45th as CO, with promotion to temporary lieutenant colonel. Victorian-born Colonel Johnston, a Gallipoli veteran who had also served on the 4th Brigade staff, was 26 and had been a law student before the war.

Preparations for the Hamel attack gathered pace in the last few days of June. The immediate responsibility for planning and implementation lay with the 4th Division, but the burden was eased by considerable assistance and oversight from the Corps staff. Sir John Monash's gifts as a commander were apparent in the process, as he ensured that all of the threads were brought together into an integrated scheme and every detail was given careful, thorough consideration. Corps issued a brief order formally authorising the operation on 28 June and Generals Rawlinson and Monash called at 4th Division HQ the next day to talk over the operation with General Sinclair-MacLagan and Colonel Lavarack; the Division's formal written order for the attack was issued by the latter that night.[18] Monash chaired a series of conferences at his Corps HQ at Bertangles Chateau, that progressively filled in the details of the plan;

> attendances increased gradually as the development of the plan necessitated the involvement of commanders and staffs from other branches and services. Two hundred and fifty officers were present at the final meeting on 30 June, which lasted four and a half hours. Monash's agenda listed 133 separate items from the arrangements for spare Lewis guns and water supply to the equipment of the assaulting troops and their relief after the battle.[19]

The 4th Brigade held its own final conference that night with the commanders of the infantry battalions, 4th MG Company, 4th Field Company, 4th LTM Battery and the allocated tank companies. The Brigade's operation orders were issued the next day.

Although Monash and his staff developed the broad plan mainly through the conference process with little formal documentation (except for artillery aspects), there was no lack of paperwork below Corps level. The 4th Division's order of 29 June was a five-page document (plus maps), to which was progressively added a series of eight instructions, some with subsequent amendments, laying down details of all aspects of the operation such as signals, engineering, handling of prisoners, and aircraft. As well as the artillery, the infantry brigades and the other arms and services issued their own written orders, as did the tank battalion, and some of these had extra instructions added. At infantry battalion level, most also put out written orders. An exception was the 13th Battalion: the CO, Douglas Marks, later reported that 'there were so many orders written by other people to be read ... that instead of writing my own,' he relied solely on a series of conferences with his company commanders and officers from all the other units involved with the 13th's task, through which a detailed scheme was developed for the day of battle.[20]

The final objective, the 'Blue Line,' was set as a line from a point near the Somme on the left (north) running for 6,800 metres along the high ground that formed the chord of the salient, incorporating Hamel village and the Wolfsberg beyond it. The attacking force of infantry and tanks would break through the German front line and then drive for the Blue Line in the enemy rear, a maximum advance of 2,500 metres on the left and centre of the attack frontage. Monash was not prepared to extend the objective as far as the enemy gun-line, preferring to limit the advance and thereby almost guarantee success. The advance was divided into three sectors: on the left, the 11th Brigade would go for the village and the Wolfsberg; the 4th Brigade in the centre would attack the woods area and the redoubts, then the area beyond those features up to the final objective, while the 6th Brigade's smaller right (south) sector completed the objective line and linked it with the existing Australian front. Most of the battalions employed were below full strength and had to leave a proportion out as the nucleus, giving a strength of 5,500 men in the attack. This was a small force averaging less than one man per metre of the objective line, but the shortage of men was compensated by the weight of supporting arms. Of the 60 tanks available, 48 would go forward with the first infantry wave, leaving the remainder available as a reserve. With the revised plan calling for the tanks and infantry to work together, Monash ruled that the infantry commander on the spot had authority to direct the action of the tanks. Also available were four 'carrier' tanks to bring up ammunition and engineer stores (mostly barbed wire and screw pickets for consolidation work), each capable of taking a load that would have required up to 500 men to carry forward by hand.[21]

As well as the tanks the Division was given heavy reinforcements in artillery and machine guns to boost the supporting firepower. Artillery was an aspect where Corps HQ was more directly involved with planning, as the 'heavies' were under its command. The arrangements were worked out between Corps and Division artillery staffs and the Corps artillery commander, Major General W A Coxen. Coxen issued the overall artillery plan on 29 June, followed over the next two days by the instructions and barrage maps for the field and heavy artillery tasks, as well as supporting tasks for the divisions on both flanks.[22] At divisional level, Brigadier General Burgess and his staff expanded on those instructions with a more detailed order, issued on 1 July, that included designation of command groupings and their specific tasks, and also detailed the requirements for FOOs and liaison officers.[23] The CRA, who held his own conference of group and brigade commanders on 2 July,[24] noted in his after-action report that

> The Barrage Map supplied by Australian Corps RA was excellent. Clear, well drawn and unmistakeable in 'times', all Battery Commanders have expressed their satisfaction with it and the assistance it provided. An ample supply for all was received.[25]

Corps orders were stringent in some aspects but allowed flexibility in others:

> The Field Artillery Commander will conform most carefully to the instructions which will be issued for the barrage, but it will be left to him, if he so wishes, to thicken the barrage in any particular part of the front, covering it more lightly in another part, according as his Divisional Commander considers that the line is more or less strongly held.[26]

In late June the artillery force under Burgess comprised five field brigades, the two of the 4th Division and three British RFA units. This was progressively increased to 16 by adding both brigades of the 5th Division artillery (the 13th and 14th AFA, their break at Hallencourt cut short) and of the 17th and 47th British Divisions, and five other British brigades.[27] Three of the latter constituted the Left Group of the guns covering the right divisional sector ('A' at Villers-Bretonneux), temporarily transferred to 4th Division command for the operation.[28] Each brigade was designated as a sub-group for command and control purposes. Another British brigade, positioned on the high ground north of the Somme, was designated as a reserve to engage targets of opportunity outside the barrage line. Three of the British units had three batteries each instead of four and another had an extra battery attached, making a total of 62 batteries.[29] Of those, 49 were required to move into new camouflaged emplacements, at night to preserve secrecy—not easy at that time of the year when darkness lasted less than six hours. The task was accomplished over four nights, with the guns positioned an average of 2,100 metres from the planned start line for the barrage. Ammunition was supplied at 600 rounds per 18-pounder and 500 per howitzer, requiring a significant logistical effort; 132,000 rounds had to be brought up to the new battery positions, at night, in time for Zero. For the work of moving the ammunition from two dumps in the rear to the wagon lines, the 4th DAC was assisted by elements of the British ammunition columns. The Corps heavy artillery was also reinforced, provided with a total of 200 guns for counter-battery work and 100 to join the creeping barrage. The field artillery of the divisions on both flanks would be given tasks to support the main attack and create diversions.

The 4th MG Battalion under Lieutenant Colonel Harry Murray was also given additional resources. Murray had attended the 25 June conference, where his unit's anticipated tasks had been outlined, with the intention that another complete machine gun battalion of 64 guns would be made available. This was later changed to eight sections (four guns each) detached from the 3rd and 5th MG Battalions, plus a contingent from the 2nd MG Battalion that was progressively increased to 41 weapons.[30] Some of the guns would be detailed to go forward with the attacking infantry while others provided barrage fire to supplement the artillery. The scheme proposed by Murray included positioning some barrage guns near Bouzencourt and Sailly-le-Sec on both sides of the Somme canal in the area where the left of the 4th Division met the right of the 5th Division (which had relieved the 2nd in the northern sector of the front). From there machine guns would take the German line in enfilade from the north, and also provide defensive fire against counter-attack after the objective was taken, without changing position. Suitable emplacements were constructed in the area, where over three nights working parties dug and camouflaged positions to accommodate eight batteries of four guns each. They brought up 8,000 rounds of ammunition, a can of water for the cooling jacket and a tripod baseplate to be stored at each gun's position. More emplacements for barrage guns were built in and around the existing front line, and the construction work was completed by the night of 30 June. In the event, only five of the northern battery positions were used,[31] once the final allocation of additional machine guns was decided. The 3rd and 5th MG Battalions provided 20 barrage guns in the northern positions, while in the centre along the present front line the 4th MG Battalion (12th, 13th and 24th Companies, plus one section of the 4th Company) had 52 guns available. Some of these were kept in reserve for defence and others were positioned to fire on either barrage lines or on identified enemy strong points over the heads of the advancing infantry. Guns of the 2nd MG Battalion (initially 12 but later increased to 35) at the southern end of the attack front covered the 6th Brigade infantry over the flatter ground of the Villers-Bretonneux plateau. The remaining machine guns were allocated to go forward to directly support the advancing infantry and then defend the captured position. The guns were allocated according to the traditional brigade groupings, 12 weapons of the 11th MG Company with the 11th Brigade, four of the 6th Company (plus two of the 7th Company) with the 6th Brigade and 12 of the 4th Company with the 4th Brigade; of the latter, six would be posted in the new front line once the objective was taken, with the others paired in three strong-points that would form the basis of a new support line.

The engineers and pioneers were given various tasks in the build-up period, including establishing forward dumps of entrenching equipment, supply of camouflage material for artillery and machine gun positions, and the maintenance of transport routes. The 4th Field Company and the 4th Pioneers provided parties to patrol the roads behind the line to locate and repair any damage from hostile shelling, while the 12th Field Company was responsible for maintaining the numerous bridges over the Somme in the divisional area. This task included the construction of several floating bridges that were used at night and concealed during daylight hours. The 4th Field Company's duties in the attack and afterwards included supporting the 4th and 6th Infantry Brigades, while the 13th Field Company was allocated to work with the 11th Brigade in establishing the new defensive lines required at the objective and in construction of forward brigade and battalion headquarters. Each brigade allotted three infantry platoons to dig strong points in selected positions 360 metres behind the Blue Line objective, to be joined up later as a support line. The platoons each had an engineer officer and three sappers attached, and undertook several days of training with the engineers in construction and wiring techniques. Once the new front and support lines were established, the pioneers had the job of digging communication trenches to link them. The Signal Company, in conjunction with the artillery, infantry and machine gun unit signallers, had the complex task of providing communication links between formation headquarters and units, with new units coming into the line and temporary battle headquarters being set up in the last few days before Zero. In addition to the network of telephone and telegraph lines, wireless telegraphy facilities were set up at Division HQ and transportable wireless sets were allocated to the three infantry brigade HQs and their designated forward parties. Wireless links were also provided for artillery HQ and the main artillery observation posts on the north and south of the battle area. At this time, wireless was regarded as a backup to land-line communications, and in the event was not used a great deal at Hamel as the German artillery was unable to cause much damage to the phone cables.

An opportunity now arose to reinforce the ranks of the infantry also. In recent weeks, numbers of personnel from the United States Army had spent time attached to AIF units for familiarisation with conditions at the front. These had been mostly small groups of specialist officers in the fields of intelligence, artillery, machine guns and medical services. In mid-June a full US infantry division, the 33rd of Illinois, had arrived in Fourth Army's rear area, for training and availability as an emergency reserve should the Germans renew their offensive. The 65th Brigade of that Division was attached to the Australian Corps. Preliminary discussions on the Hamel operations were under way at the same time, and

> ... it occurred to General Rawlinson—why not give the Americans experience of a model set-piece attack beside the highly-skilled Australians, and at the same time strengthen the Australian battalions by attaching to each of them a company of these fine-looking troops?[32]

Why not indeed, and General Monash readily accepted. He was at first allocated four American companies, then a further six shortly afterwards, with the ten being split five each between the 4th and 11th Brigades, the centre and left of the attacking force.[33] The American companies, at their full strength of 250, had more than double the numbers of most of the Australian companies, undermanned as they were by casualties and illness (an epidemic of influenza had recently broken out). Using an American company as a complete sub-unit would unbalance a battalion as well as increasing the difficulty of giving guidance to the inexperienced troops, so the decision was made to split the American companies into their constituent platoons which were then distributed among the Australian companies. Despite the administrative difficulties, the reinforcement was welcomed, and the troops from the two nations got on famously from the start, with much in common that many observers noticed:

> They bear themselves with the same sturdy self-reliance ... They move with the same easy free-limbed carriage. Their discipline is a thing which force could never impose, but is rather contributed voluntarily to a common good in some violation of temperament and upbringing.[34]

The battalions drew up their attack plans to include the extra men.

A fundamental feature of the plan was co-operation between infantry and tanks, and Monash recognised the importance of overcoming the serious doubts that the infantry held about the effectiveness of the machines. The tanks gave a series of demonstrations at their training area north of Amiens, to show the infantry the capabilities of the new model. The negative feeling was particularly an issue for the 4th Brigade, which was refitting and training in the Aubigny reserve area, and over three days the 4th Brigade sent 500 personnel by motor-lorry to see the tanks in action. The third group on 30 June included 25 Americans from the two companies of the 132nd US Regiment that had arrived the previous night. The 'open house' put on by the tanks had the desired effect:

> The Diggers climbed all over [the tanks], inside and out, rode across trenches and over walls and banks, and even drove them.
>
> 'They'll do us,' was the general opinion. What a change to the feelings about the tanks of Bullecourt ... these Mark 5 tanks were really marvels and a great advance on the clumsy, imperfect and more weighty monsters of 1917 ... Dummy machine-gun posts were quickly seen and dealt with ... 'This is how we squash Jerry and his gun,' proudly remarked a driver as his tank pirouetted on top of one of these positions.
>
> All remarked the tremendous improvement in the morale of the tankmen since Bullecourt, the crews themselves feeling that they had in the minds of the 4th Division, something to wipe out.[35]

The improved relationship was cemented in the last few days before the battle when

> many of the tank officers came up to the bivouacs of the battalions with whom they were serving, and not merely discussed the plans but lived and messed with the Australian officers, establishing friendship and mutual understanding.[36]

Medical arrangements were co-ordinated by the acting ADMS, Lieutenant Colonel McGregor, who discussed the issues with his Field Ambulance COs and the unit RMOs at a conference on 30 June. The basic elements of the rear medical infrastructure were already in place in the divisional sector—the MDS at Les Alençons just outside Amiens, managed by the 4th Field Ambulance, and the ADS west of Daours managed by the 13th Field Ambulance. The latter unit was also responsible for clearance of the wounded from the left and centre of the battlefront (11th and 4th Brigades), using its own bearer teams and vehicles and those of the 4th and 12th Field Ambulance, while the smaller right sector (6th Brigade) would be looked after by the 6th Field Ambulance. Elements of the 11th Field Ambulance were assigned to assist at the MDS and with bearer duties. Several forward ambulance posts and relay posts were established closer to the front line, dug in to provide some protection from shell fire, including a post near the 4th Brigade forward HQ, which was tunnelled into the bank of a quarry off the Hamelet road. RMOs were instructed to move forward with their battalions and select a position for their RAP in consultation with the battalion CO.

Aircraft were another key factor in the integrated plan. The RE8 two-seater crews of 3 Squadron AFC, appropriately the 'corps squadron' for the Australian Corps, undertook a heavy programme of reconnaissance in the lead-up period, producing numerous aerial photographs of the enemy position. The squadron also reconnoitred the Corps' own lines to ensure that the signs of the build-up were not obvious from the air. On the day of battle, 3 Squadron carried out ground-support duties,

> the ordinary contact-patrol work of sketching an advancing line from flares, of marking down hostile batteries in action, and of bombing and machine-gunning in advance of the infantry line to co-operate in the reduction of hostile strong-points.[37]

A novel use proposed for aircraft was the dropping of ammunition by parachute, an idea picked up from a captured German document. Using modified bomb racks designed by Captain Lawrence Wackett of 3 Squadron, an RE8 could carry two 1000-round boxes with parachutes, to be released at dropping points where infantry or machine gunners set out a specified symbol of white cloth on the ground.[38] This task was given to No. 9 Squadron RAF, also equipped with RE8s, since 3 AFC would be fully occupied with contact patrols. Aircraft also had an important role in the deception aspects of the plan. To conceal the sound of the tanks in their approach to the start line, arrangements were made for a particularly noisy type of aircraft, the old FE2Bs of 101 Squadron RAF, to fly over the German positions dropping bombs and flares through the night before Zero, and also during the preceding nights to give the impression of routine operations.

A conference of intelligence officers was held on 1 July at which the Corps staff issued quantities of photographs and maps, 'to assist all ranks in their knowledge of what to do.'[39] The documents included copies of the area map, the artillery barrage maps, annotated vertical and oblique aerial photographs, maps showing the known enemy dispositions with a brief history of the identified regiments, and 'message maps'—a small map of the battlefield with a message form printed on the back. The material was distributed at least to the level of company commanders, with some items going as far down the chain as platoon commanders and NCOs. In some cases area maps still had to be marked up by the units— the MG Battalion recorded that it had draftsmen 'working very hard' completing maps the next day. Each infantry company commander was given a colour-shaded map showing the battalions' objectives.

Much attention was paid to deception and secrecy to ensure that the attack would fall on the enemy with no warning. Corps laid down that all potentially observable activity was to be done by night. This restriction was particularly important to the artillery, as it needed considerable movement of horses and vehicles to bring forward and emplace the large number of reinforcing guns and their ammunition. The usual registration process for newly-positioned guns was restricted to the firing of a few ranging rounds during the usual harassing fire so that there would be no obvious variations that might alert the enemy; the guns would largely be firing from the map when the battle opened. Another deception tactic was to ensure that harassing fire using gas shells also included smoke shells ('flavoured smoke'), so as to induce the Germans to assume that smoke would always mean gas as well; only smoke would be used on the day, but those Germans who put on gas masks would be much inconvenienced in close combat. Regular early-morning harassing shoots were instituted at a set time so that the shelling would not seem unusual on Zero day, when its purpose would change to drowning-out the rumble of the tanks coming up on the last leg to the start line. Officially the troops and junior officers were not informed of the higher command's intentions until the last moments to maintain security, but concealment of all but the final details was impossible. The greatly heightened activity in the rear area, the tank exercises and movements of guns and transport, made it obvious that something big was on. The signs were noticeable further forward also: the 13th Brigade, in the front line on 1 July, noted

> a great deal of movement over the whole area during the day. Americans, Tank Officers, Artillery people, in fact everyone co-operating in the coming attack seemed to be making a reconnaissance.[40]

Remarkably, none of this was detected on the other side of No Man's Land.

Aside from some final details, the plans were settled and most preparations complete one or two days before it before it was officially notified that Zero hour would be 3:10 am on 4 July. The date allowed time for the units involved to complete their arrangements, and also gave recognition to the American presence in the attack force.[41] The infantry, issued with ammunition, grenades and rations, began moving forward in the afternoon of 2 July, making their way into the front line after dark and taking over from the units then holding the line south from the Somme. The 13th Brigade and the right-flank battalion of the 12th Brigade were relieved by the 11th and 4th Brigades (the 4th Brigade sent half of each unit up on the first night, to avoid overcrowding in the front line, with the remainder to follow on Zero night). The relieved units moved back to reserve positions temporarily, prepared to take over the new front line from the attacking units after the objectives were attained. The final plan called for the tanks to begin their approach from dispersal at 10:30 pm on Zero night and halt at their start line, 800 metres behind that of the infantry. At eight minutes before Zero, 3:02 am, they would move off to join the infantry line. Their noise was to be covered by the bombing aircraft and the regular harassing bombardment by a few guns of the field artillery, also beginning at 3:02. Those guns would gradually shorten their range until they were firing on the start line of the creeping barrage, 180 metres ahead of the infantry.

At Zero, 3:10 am, all guns would open fire, the first line fired by the 18-pounders using 75% shrapnel, 15% HE and 10% smoke, with the 4.5 inch howitzers firing 90% HE and 10% smoke 200 yards beyond the 18-pounders, then 100 guns of the heavy artillery (mostly 6-inch howitzers) starting a further 180 metres out. The other 200 heavy weapons would fire into the enemy gun-line on counter-battery tasks. The Left Group of field brigades did not have infantry advancing on its front, but would conform to the main barrage, protecting the left flank of the attack. The artillery of the divisions on either flank would also assist, firing smoke shell on to enemy-held high ground to screen the battle area from observation; the flanking divisions would also lay a barrage on their own fronts and launch limited diversionary attacks by their infantry. The barrage was planned to stay on its start line for four minutes, while the infantry moved forward to get as close as possible to the line of bursting shells and the tanks caught up to join the infantry line. The barrage would then begin its creep, firing at three rounds per minute and lifting 90 metres every three minutes, flaying the enemy territory in depth while the infantry and tanks advanced behind it. After half an hour, the barrage would have passed over and beyond the German front line and would then pause at a 'halt line' about half-way to the final objective, signalling the halt with three rounds of smoke. Ten minutes later the barrage would begin to creep again, now with lifts of 90 metres every four minutes, finally reaching a protective line 360 metres beyond the Blue Line final objective to break up potential counter-attacks. That last lift was timed for Zero + 93 minutes, by which time the infantry, if all had gone to plan, would be on the objective and starting to dig in. The barrage machine guns, starting three minutes after the artillery, would lay down their fire between the lines of the 18-pounders and the 4.5s. At the start line the infantry would deploy with the three forward battalions nominally in two waves (although some battalions decided on different formations to meet their local situation) and the reserve battalion forming a third wave to the rear. In the 4th Brigade the 15th, 16th and 13th Battalions, left to right, made up the forward waves, jumping off from a taped line in No Man's Land, with the 14th in reserve to start from the present front line. The task of the 16th in the centre of the Brigade line was to clear the woods and the trench skirting them. The 15th and 13th on the flanks would move around the woods on either side and advance to the Blue Line with one company of the 15th and three tanks diverting to capture Pear Trench north of the woods. The 14th Battalion was responsible for preparing the support line behind the final objective.

With everything in place, two last-minute hitches arose, one an annoyance but the other with potentially serious consequences. On 2 July, at minimal notice, the Australian Prime Minister, W M 'Billy' Hughes, and the Minister for the Navy, Sir Joseph Cook, arrived to visit Corps HQ and speak to some of the troops. The politicians had been unaware that a major operation was so close and their visit was an unwanted distraction at such a time.

Monash arranged for Hughes and Cook to call on several representative gatherings of troops and the incident passed off without much disruption to the preparations. More seriously, on 3 July orders arrived that six of the ten American companies were not to take part in the attack and must be withdrawn immediately. Approval to use their troops in the battle had been given by the American corps and division commanders, but no-one had thought to inform their Commander-in-Chief, General J J Pershing, when the arrangements were being made. Pershing's firm policy was that his army should operate as a distinct entity rather than scattered through the French and British armies, and that his men should not go into all-out combat before they were fully trained, except in a real emergency. Once Pershing was aware of the Hamel scheme, he refused to allow American participation, but through some misunderstanding at Rawlinson's HQ, it was assumed at first that the directive did not apply to the original contingent of four companies but only to the second six. The 4th and 11th Brigades were ordered to each return three American companies to the reserve area. When word reached those troops, keyed-up as they were and anxious to prove themselves alongside their new friends, there was much indignation among both Americans and Australians; 'I never saw such disgust and disappointment in my life. Our boys were just as disappointed as they were, and amid many good-byes they moved to the rear,' wrote Lieutenant Rule (14th Battalion).[42] The affected battalions had re-organised their dispositions when word came through to Monash late in the day that the remaining four companies had to be withdrawn also. In the beginning, Monash had been prepared to undertake the operation with just the available Australian troops, but the final plans had been drawn up to include the American reinforcements. Commanders down the line were dismayed: the first withdrawal was disruptive enough, while another change at such a late stage was 'very strongly opposed by the [4th] Brigade as it will seriously affect our disposition of troops.'[43] Accordingly Monash confronted Rawlinson and insisted that there was no time to make any more changes and the attack must either go ahead with the remaining Americans included, or be cancelled. The question went up the line to GHQ, and Sir Douglas Haig ruled that the attack must go ahead and the Americans were to be retained if they could not be withdrawn in time.

With that settled, the early moves began after dark. Intelligence officers went forward to lay the tapes marking the start line 300 metres out from the front trench, in places strung on the growing crops in No Man's Land. Other groups opened gaps in the defensive wire to allow passage for the infantry. The relays of RAF bombing missions over the German line drowned out the noise of the tanks as they made their way forward at 10:30 pm. The tanks reached their assembly line towards midnight, and between 1 and 1:30 am on 4 July the troops began climbing out of the front trenches and moving forward to the tapes. By 2:30, still dark and with a heavy mist over the ground, the 4th Brigade riflemen were in their jumping-off positions waiting for Zero. At 3:02, exactly to plan, the regular harassing fire opened, but without gas this time, gradually working back towards the barrage line. The tanks, engines already running, began rolling forward. Eight minutes later the main barrage broke out with a deafening crash and a wide sheet of flame on the horizon behind the line of infantry, followed moments later by the burst of the first rounds of smoke-shells ahead along the barrage line. The field guns switched to shrapnel and HE (with smoke reduced to one round in ten) and continued on their starting line while the infantry, 'lighting their cigarettes and with rifles slung,'[44] closed up to the optimum distance from the barrage, about 65 metres. After three minutes the barrage machine guns opened fire, sweeping between the 18-pounder and howitzer lines. Many of the tanks, groping their way forward in the poor visibility, had not managed to catch up when at 3:14 am the barrage made its first lift and the infantry went ahead into the pall of dust, smoke and mist.

Aerial photograph of Pear Trench in the German front line near Hamel, with the Australian front line on the left. The road intersecting the trench continues south-east to pass between Vaire and Hamel Woods.
(15th Battalion War Diary, July 1918, AWM4 23/32/40)

For the most part, the barrage was accurate, but having to range from the map made it inevitable that some short shooting occurred. This seriously affected the units near the junction of the 11th and 4th Brigades. On the left flank of the 15th Battalion (which used a four-wave formation), Captain Ernest Carter's 'A' Company was hard hit, losing twelve dead and thirty wounded while still on the tapes. The short-firing guns prevented the company from closing up to the main barrage and those guns continued to drop shells 200 metres behind the rest of the barrage line as it lifted. It was 'A' Company that had the task of capturing Pear Trench, the forward edge of which was nearly on the artillery start line, but instead of being almost on top of the enemy position when the barrage first lifted, the company was now forced to advance one or two lifts behind the curtain of shells. By the time they reached the enemy trench the barrage had moved on, and in any case it had actually missed most of the position, leaving wire, trench and garrison almost undamaged (an outcome that seems to have been overlooked when drawing up the barrage plan[45]). A line of German infantry appeared out of the mist throwing grenades, while machine guns opened fire from the trench ahead. In such a situation the infantry was meant to take cover and leave the tanks to do the heavy work, but the three allocated to this area had lost their way in the darkness and mist. The 15th Battalion often seemed to have more than its share of ill-fortune, and now one of its companies was faced with a small-scale Bullecourt, with neither tanks nor artillery to help against uncut wire and a determined enemy. Undeterred, the company launched a bayonet charge on the enemy skirmishers, drove them off, reached the wire, and forced their way through patrol gaps and thinner sections. Firing from the hip, Lewis gunners took on the German machine guns and were in the process of silencing two of the enemy guns when a third opened up from the left at the point where the sunken road through the position intersected the trench. Number two in one of the Lewis gun teams, carrying spare ammunition, was Private Henry Dalziel, a 25 year old railway fireman from Atherton, Queensland. He was nominally a horse-transport driver but had volunteered for Lewis training and been picked for the assault force. Dalziel replaced an empty ammunition drum for his Number One, then, armed only with a revolver, charged the German machine gun alone and captured it. He shot two of the crew and the other three surrendered, but Dalziel had part of his trigger finger shot off in the fight and was ordered to the rear for treatment. He had no intention of leaving the battlefield, however, and rejoined his company when the advance went on.

The forward section of the trench was rushed with grenade and bayonet, and there was more intense fighting as the company, including its attached American platoon, moved on around the curving arms to the sunken road running through the position. Corporal Mainard Goodger distinguished himself in the trench fighting, throwing grenades and leading his section along the trench even after receiving a serious arm wound (the fourth time he had been wounded in the war). He afterwards tried to continue with the advance but 'fell down exhausted and had to be carried away.'[46] Some of the garrison surrendered while others further back continued to throw grenades and more machine guns opened fire. Captain Carter was badly wounded by a burst of fire that broke both of his legs and hit one arm as well. 'This made the men rather wild,'[47] and for a while there was little mercy shown as the riflemen fought their way along the road and into the remaining section of trench. Finally the position was secured, prisoners were sent back, and 'A' Company, now led by Lieutenant Jack Hynes, resumed the next stage of the advance towards the 'Halt Line' (Captain Carter, evacuated in critical condition, lost a leg but eventually recovered). The 15th CO, Lieutenant Colonel McSharry, then arrived with his forward HQ and set up in Pear Trench, where the battalion RAP was also established. Examining the area, McSharry came across a trench-mortar pit in which there were several Germans who he realised were shamming dead. The CO amused himself by throwing dirt at them until they got up and surrendered. The southern (right) part of the 15th Battalion's line had a more accurate barrage to follow up to the enemy front line (Vaire Trench), but with the delay to the left of the line, machine gun fire from the latter position interfered with the adjoining companies before those guns were knocked out. Captain Robert Glasgow's 'C' Company came under this fire and also encountered strong wire in front of Vaire Trench, which for a moment 'rather rattled'[48] the men. Glasgow, who had been slightly wounded by a piece of shell at the start line, came forward and rallied his troops, leading from the front as they picked their way through the wire and assaulted the trench. After a quick close-quarter fight, the surviving Germans surrendered, many being found wearing gas masks, tricked by the smoke shells. The 15th pushed on to reach the Halt Line, where the tanks caught up in the improving light.

The objective of the 16th Battalion was to clear Vaire Wood and the adjoining Hamel Wood. Vaire Trench continued along the western edge of the woods, incorporating the redoubt called Kidney Trench on the left, near the north-west corner of the woods. Several strong-points and machine gun posts were scattered in depth through the trees. The 16th advanced up the sloping ground behind the barrage, which was mainly accurate in this sector, and reached the wire in good order. Captain Bill Lynas's 'D' Company on the left got into Kidney Trench and pushed through to the sunken road that formed its rear segment. There they captured 47 prisoners, found still sheltering in a dugout after the barrage had passed, and a trench mortar battery. Lynas had been hit twice by pieces of shell at the start line, either by short 'friendly' shelling or the enemy response to the early harassing fire, but he brushed aside suggestions that he should leave the field. 'B' Company under Captain Harold Wilkinson, next on the right, advanced through Kidney Trench and along Hun's Walk, the long communication trench that ran back to the German rear area in Accroche Wood, beyond the final objective. The wire was fairly easily penetrated along most of the Vaire Trench position, but part of 'C' Company, which was led by Captain Frederick Woods, struck trouble near Kidney Trench when a machine gun opened fire as the men were working their way through the entanglement. Woods and CSM Harold Blinman, both mortally wounded, were among the casualties as the advance was held up at that point. Lance Corporal Thomas 'Jack' Axford, in the next platoon along, got through the wire and tackled the machine gun himself. Axford tossed his two grenades among the gun crew, then jumped into the enemy trench and took the bayonet to its surviving occupants, altogether killing ten and taking six more as prisoners. He then threw the gun on to the parapet, called out to the others to come on, and went back to his own platoon.[49] The platoon commander was Lieutenant Basil Minchin, 'Minch' or 'Trump' to his friends,[50] a cheerful little larrikin whose time in the ranks had included varied stints as a sniper and a company cook, and who was now 'one of the outstanding leaders of an outstanding battalion.'[51] Minchin led on into the enemy positions and personally wiped out a machine gun post, killing several enemy soldiers and capturing 20, along with their gun and a trench mortar. Further into the wood he led a few men to rush another post, taking two machine guns and killing another six Germans. At this stage, learning of the loss of Captain Woods, Minchin took over command of the company and led it successfully through the rest of the fight (Woods, Blinman, Lynas and Minchin were all original members of the 16th and all had first gone into action at the Landing).

The 16th broke through Vaire Trench and worked its way through the woods in two waves, the troops firing from the hip as they advanced. The leading wave moved rapidly to keep up with the barrage, taking on whatever enemy trenches and dugouts were in their path, while next wave mopped up anything missed by the first. The tanks offered useful support, although restricted to travelling on the existing paths through the trees. Many of the German infantrymen were found to be still wearing gas masks, and their resistance was ineffective. Some tried to run but were caught in the barrage, which was now in their rear, and many surrendered—the 16th took 400 prisoners that day. The aggressive, confident Australian troops performed many individual acts of bravery, with officers and NCOs setting the example and many privates using their initiative in tight situations. The 'D' Company OC, Captain Lynas, was hit again on the way through the woods but he continued to control his company's advance, 'repressing the eagerness of some and ... urging on the more cautious ... he was always to be found [where] the fighting was heaviest.'[52] His CSM, William Rogers, was also prominent in keeping the company together and maintaining the momentum.[53] The leading elements were reaching the far edge of the woods just after 4 am, by which time the barrage had begun to move on after the ten-minute halt and the two flanking battalions were starting the second phase of the advance. Mopping up in the woods was completed shortly afterwards, or so the leaders in the field believed, but a pair of runners, Privates James Northey and Percy Carter, found otherwise when they were sent back to Battalion HQ with a message. At the western edge of Vaire Wood they came near a concealed party of eight Germans overlooked in the advance who made the fatal mistake of opening fire on them. Northey and Carter went for their assailants with rifle and bayonet; in no mood for taking prisoners, they killed all eight enemy soldiers at the cost of a bayonet wound each, then continued on to deliver the message before being evacuated to have their wounds treated.[54]

The 4th Brigade's right-flank battalion, the 13th, had what was probably the most challenging tactical task. Starting from a comparatively narrow front of 360 metres, the battalion had to push past the woods on the south, penetrate the German front line posts in that area, wheel left and open out across the eastern edge of the woods, and finally wheel right and advance to the Blue Line, extending their front to over 900 metres. The CO, Douglas Marks, had given much thought to the problem and worked out a tactical scheme in conference with his company commanders and officers of the supporting arms. One company (less a platoon allocated to construction of a strong-point) led off, deployed across the starting attack frontage, followed by two companies abreast in deeper formation, then the fourth in section columns. The leading company ('D') followed the barrage to be first through the enemy front line, then dug in to form a covering position. 'C' Company in the second line then leapfrogged through 'D' to take up the right of the 13th's final line, linking with the 6th Brigade further on the right. The other second line company ('A') was assigned to make the long advance north behind the woods then wheel into line on the left, linking with the 15th Battalion, while 'B' Company, starting in the rear, moved up to fill the centre of the line between 'A' and 'C'. The 13th Battalion was one of the units that had retained its American reinforcements, the four platoons of 'A' Company, 132nd Regiment. One platoon was attached to each company of the 13th.

The 13th jumped off on schedule and its three allocated tanks had joined up by the time the artillery made its first lift. One tank was soon put out of action, hit by a short-falling 18-pounder shell which also killed battalion scout Private Thomas Parrish who was guiding the tank. Close behind the barrage, 'D' Company overran a few enemy posts and reached its covering position, through which 'C' Company passed before pausing at the Halt Line, also meeting minimal opposition. 'A' Company, commanded by Yorkshire-born Captain George Marper, had to complete its movement across the rear of the woods to the left flank and then reform for the final stage by the time the barrage resumed its creep. The company encountered an early obstacle in the form of a machine gun that opened fire and killed or wounded all of a section. Marper collected a few men and led a rush that took the gun, personally shooting three of the enemy crew. The company moved on and had reached the point for its second wheel when the troops suddenly came under heavy close-range fire from two more machine guns in a well-camouflaged trench that had not been detected on aerial photographs. The company was pinned down, but this was a situation that suited tanks and one was coming up 50 metres behind. Marper left cover and dashed across the open, waving his arms to direct the tank on to the enemy trench. The machine guns caught him and he was shot in the chest and arm, but the tank drove on to one of the gun positions, flattening gun and crew 'much as a man's heel would crush a scorpion,' in General Monash's vivid image.[55] The crew of the other 'scorpion' had seen enough and quickly surrendered. Once he was satisfied that the way was clear for the advance to the Halt Line, Marper handed over to Lieutenant Thomas Dwyer and went to the rear for medical attention. The attached American troops

> behaved magnificently throughout and proved themselves to be of excellent material. However it is only to be expected with new troops they were very inexperienced, were inclined to bunch, and very often their dash took them too close to our barrage.[56]

Following a barrage was an art best learnt through experience, and in stopping some Americans from walking into their own shells the 13th's Corporal Michael Roach was fatally wounded. C E W Bean reflected that putting the Americans into this operation was like teaching a boy to swim by throwing him into the deep end,[57] although once they got to close quarters there was no lack of aggression—in the 11th Brigade's sector, Corporal Thomas Pope of Chicago won the US Army's first Medal of Honour of the war, as well as the British DCM, for taking out an enemy machine gun nest.

At Zero plus 39 minutes, the field guns, which had slowed their rate of fire on the Halt Line, quickened up again to three rounds per minute as a signal to the infantry, then two

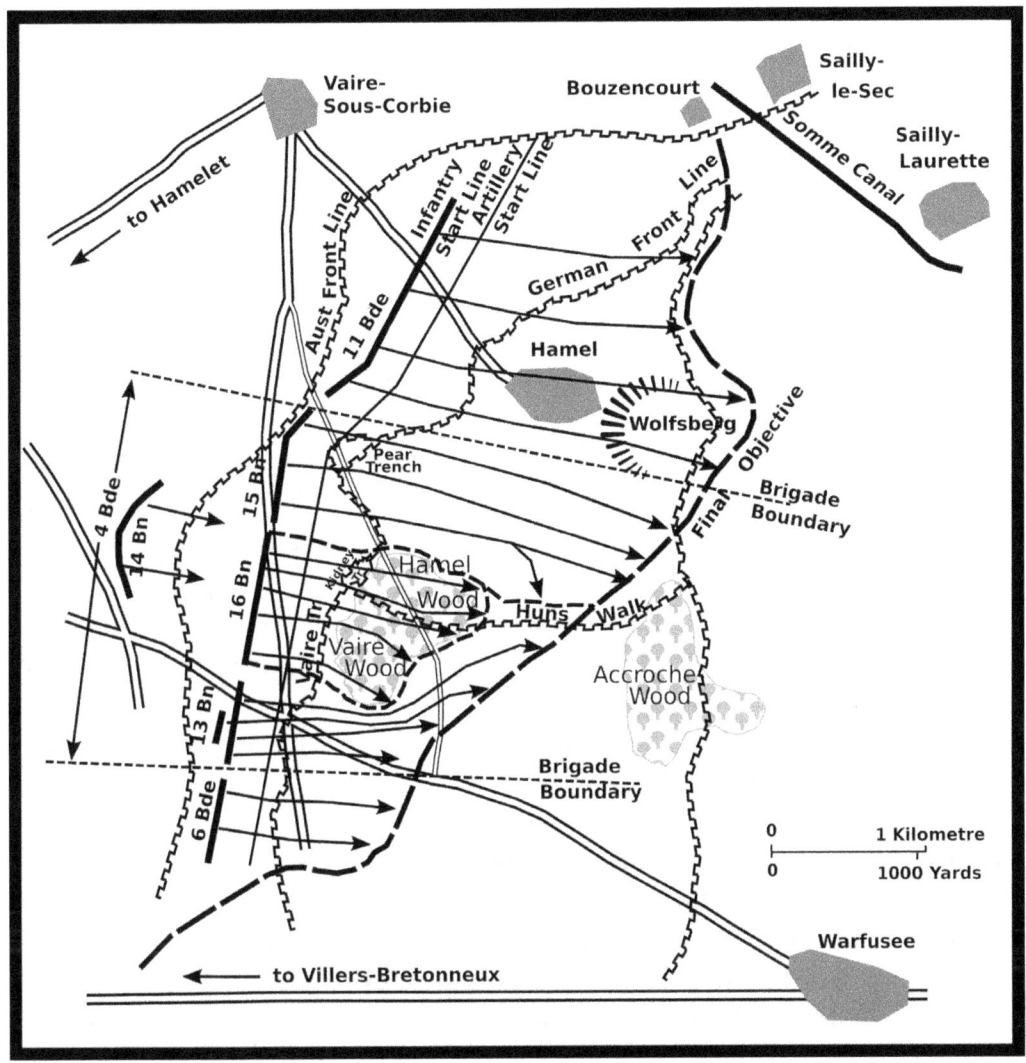

Battle of Hamel, 4 July 1918.

minutes later the barrage resumed its creep. The 6th Brigade on the south, with the smallest area of the attack front but against very tough resistance, had reached its objectives by that time and begun consolidation. Along the rest of the line, infantry and tanks went forward again against haphazard German second-line defensive positions. The 11th Brigade in the northern sector now assaulted Hamel village and then pushed on for the Wolfsberg while the 4th Brigade in the centre resumed the advance to their Blue Line final objective. The 15th Battalion, now with its tanks in attendance, moved on with its right flank brushing past the north-east corner of the woods then inclining further to the right, towards the eastern part of the Hun's Walk trench. Both flanks met some resistance from enemy machine guns near the objective line, but these were eliminated with strong assistance from tanks. Sergeant George Goodwin led his platoon against one post, capturing two machine guns and ten prisoners.

At some point during this stage, Private Dalziel, who was supposed to have gone back to the RAP to have his injured hand dressed after knocking out the machine gun at Pear Trench, joined up again for the advance to the final objective. He carried up a box of ammunition from an aircraft drop and when ordered to the rear again, instead came back to the front line with another box. He was filling empty Lewis gun drums with the loose rounds when he was finally put out of action with a dangerous head wound, the bullet taking a piece out of his skull and exposing the brain. The main body reached the Blue Line, 90 minutes after Zero by Captain Glasgow's account,[58] and began digging in. A screen of patrols and Lewis gun teams, together with a tank, pushed out ahead of the objective line, clearing the scattered German posts in the crops to the immediate front. Of the three tanks with the 15th, Colonel McSharry later reported, one 'was put out of action and another was not very keen, but the third tank made up for the other two and was gallantly handled and saved us a great number of casualties at the final objective.'[59] The arrival of a carrier tank with its load of engineer stores enabled the battalion to string a basic wire entanglement out in front of the new trench.

The 13th Battalion moved off again from the Halt Line behind the resumed barrage and reached its final objective, mostly without serious opposition, but on the right 'C' Company encountered an active machine gun post. Lewis gunner Corporal Jimmy Lihou, standing up and firing from the hip, kept the German post under fire while a bombing section outflanked and destroyed it (probably the strong point that 'C' Company reported as mopped up with the capture of three machine guns and a number of prisoners[60]). 'A' Company, now under Lieutenant Dwyer, kept up with the barrage and reported as early as 4:18 am, 68 minutes after Zero, that it was on the final objective and in touch with the 15th Battalion on the left.[61] 'B' Company, coming up last to fill in the centre of the line, came under fire from a German machine gun post to their front. This resistance was quickly eliminated by the company Lewis gun sergeant, Walter Phillips, who charged the gun at the head of three men and captured it, shooting five of the crew with his revolver.[62] The 13th's line was established on the objective, although with some gaps, and at Zero plus 90 minutes the contact patrol aircraft came over and ground flares were lit to signal the position. The Battalion got on with the hard work of consolidation, with the help of equipment dropped off by a carrier tank, while patrols went out and two tanks rumbled back and forth seeking out enemy posts beyond the objective.

The six forward Vickers gun teams of the 4th MG Company came up and positioned themselves in three pairs along the Brigade frontage. A short 'friendly' shell had hit the centre sub-section during the advance, killing the officer in charge, Lieutenant Reginald Dovey, and Corporal Percy Davis, and putting most of one crew out of action. Sergeant Henry Tyler, in charge of two support line guns coming up behind, ran forward to take command, redistributed the surviving crew members and set up the guns in the front line. On the right, near the 13th Battalion's right flank, the gun position was troubled by sniper fire from the crops ahead. The NCO in charge, Sergeant Patrick Lynch, spotted the location, worked his way close and made a rush on it. The position turned out to be a post occupied by eleven Germans, and Lynch killed two and brought the rest back as prisoners. Soon afterwards an enemy machine gun opened up but was quickly silenced by fire from Lynch's crew. He then led out a party that captured the gun and two wounded survivors of the German crew.[63] Lieutenant Phillip Wright's two guns near the left flank of the 15th Battalion cut up a group of enemy infantry trying to change position near Accroche Wood, inflicting an estimated 50 casualties on them. At Zero plus 93 minutes the barrage made its final lift and settled on the Protective Line, 365 metres out from the new front. The task now was to set up the captured area as a firm front line system and defend it against counter-attacks, under oversight of the engineer personnel who had gone forward with the infantry. The task presented some differences in priorities, particularly with the strong points that would form the basis of the support line. The engineers found some difficulty in getting the infantry started on the labouring work 'due to over-impetuousness and excitement to get into the fight, rather than do the job for which they were detailed. The platoons were finally collected, however, and the strong-points dug.'[64]

By 5 am the 16th Battalion had completed the mopping up of Vaire and Hamel Woods and then withdrew to take up positions in the original front and support lines as brigade reserve. The 14th Battalion moved through on its task to dig the new support line, 360 metres to the rear of the final objective and ahead of the artillery Halt Line for most of its length. Two of the 14th's companies followed the 13th Battalion on the right of the 4th Brigade frontage, one was behind the left of the 16th and the fourth with the right of the 15th. The Brigade orders were for the 14th to stay out of the fighting, at least in the initial stage, but circumstances intervened at several points. One of the platoons moving with the 13th had trained with the engineers for the task of constructing the central of three strong points in the support line. On the way forward the platoon got into a skirmish with a machine gun post missed by the forward troops and eliminated it. Construction of the strong point was begun soon after the barrage moved on from the Halt Line and was completed by 5:15 am. This post provided an alignment point for the support line, which the remainder of the 14th proceeded to dig, although apparently not entirely according to plan in the view of the 4th Field Company officers.[65] Ahead, the 15th and 13th Battalions, both weakened by losses in the advance, were still shaking out along the final objective line. At several points, sections and platoons of the 14th went forward on their own initiative to fill temporary gaps, clashing with scattered enemy troops and picking up a number of prisoners. Lieutenant Ted Rule's platoon, supported by a tank, took on a German trench, the occupants of which first waved a white flag in surrender then opened fire, killing Corporal Stan Cochrane. Showing unusual restraint in the circumstances, the troops took some prisoners in dugouts—a group of terrified teenage conscripts—and drove 40 others into a dead end from which they later surrendered. During the skirmish, a short-falling shell from the barrage fatally wounded Rule's batman, Private Dave Floyd, and shortly afterwards Lieutenant Ramsay Wood, one of the Battalion's 'characters,' was killed by a sniper.

The 13th Battalion's special platoon got on with digging the right-flank support line strong-point, despite the platoon commander and his sergeant both being wounded during the advance. On the left, the 15th Battalion's strong-point digging party had struck a setback early in the advance when the engineer officer, Lieutenant Eric Davidson, was killed in the vicinity of Pear Trench. At some point also, according to Colonel McSharry's report, 'my strong point platoon was knocked out and Lt [Charles] Black wounded, and I cannot spare any men yet to do this.'[66] Sapper Roy Miller, a member of the small engineer element, took it on himself to mark out a location and collect a group of Australians and Americans, with whom he organised to get the bastion dug. Through the morning the troops worked on improving the line with the 6th and 4th Brigades digging mostly new positions and the 11th Brigade working on old British trenches in their area. In front of the line, infantry patrols and tanks skirmished with isolated bodies of enemy troops. The artillery barrage stayed on the protective line for 30 minutes, after which the guns ceased firing but remained on alert in case of counter-attack. There was very little organised activity by the enemy infantry for the rest of the day, however, and good progress was made on the earthworks.

Behind the lines, the evacuation of casualties went on, efficiently for the most part but striking a hitch at the motor ambulance loading post in the quarry near 4th Brigade HQ off the Hamelet road. This was the post for the right (south) sector of the battlefront and Major Laurence Elwell, in overall charge of the evacuation process for that sector, had placed his HQ there. From early in the fighting, wounded men (stretcher cases, including wounded prisoners) were brought back to the 'Quarry Post' from the forward RAPs

> with quite abnormal rapidity ... the stretcher squads being supplemented by German prisoners on their way to the rear as well as by infantry volunteers looking about for something to do; a number of urgent cases were brought in, through previous arrangement, by tanks. Many cases drifted in also from the left flank. By 5.30 am, the incoming stream at the post was so great that the cars allotted to the circuit were quite unequal to the demand, and cases banked up until over 100 were waiting.[67]

Elwell sent urgent messages to the ADMS requesting more vehicles and stretchers to help clear the bottleneck. Over the next few hours, every available vehicle was despatched to the quarry, including spare horse-drawn ambulances and six pontoon wagons from the engineers (the latter were used for transporting German wounded). At 12:30 pm, with the heavy fighting having been over for several hours, Elwell reported that the flow had slowed and no more extra assistance was needed. Clearing the ambulance post had in turn resulted in banking-up at the next evacuation stage, the ADS, so the spare vehicles were switched there for clearance of the more serious cases further back to the MDS. The 13th Field Ambulance CO, Lieutenant Colonel Frank Wooster, reported that the ADS was clear by 5 pm, having treated over 900 wounded, walking and stretcher cases, during the day, a figure that included 180 German prisoners.[68]

The evening was fairly quiet on the 4th Brigade front, but at about 10 pm the Germans launched a counter-attack on the left (north) against the 11th Brigade's line on the Wolfsberg where a strong enemy force got inside the SOS barrage and took 180 metres of the 44th Battalion's trench. The intrusion was stopped and sealed off, then at 2 am the 44th bounced back and ejected the Germans in savage fighting, for good measure following up and capturing their jumping-off trench also. Hostile artillery fire fell on the 4th Brigade area where two companies of the 4th Pioneer Battalion had come up to dig two communication trenches back from the new front line to the support line. The trench on the south was completed by dawn without serious incident, but the northern company was caught by the enemy shelling, losing four killed and 12 wounded. Part of the work was done despite the disruption and both companies returned the following night to complete the trench. The day of 5 July continued quietly apart from exchanges of artillery fire, and that night the 12th and 13th Brigades began the process of relieving the assaulting units, including the return of the 11th Brigade to its own division. The 4th Division front was progressively re-organised with the 48th Battalion, one of the two units north of the Somme, relieved on the night of the battle by 5th Division troops moving southwards. Overnight of 5/6 July, the 45th Battalion relieved the 41st and 42nd, and the 49th relieved the 15th and two companies of the 14th in the new front and support lines.

These and other movements resulted in the 4th Division front on 7 July being held, north to south, by the 12th Brigade, with two battalions in the front line, either side of the Somme, and one in support; the 13th Brigade next, also with two battalions in front and one in support; and the 4th Brigade with one battalion in front, one in support, one in brigade reserve and one in divisional reserve. That day was a notable one in the 4th Division's history. News of the success at Hamel had reached the Versailles meeting of the Supreme War Council of the Allies, the highest military and political leaders. The *Official History* notes that

> Lloyd George and the Prime Ministers of Canada, New Zealand and Newfoundland asked Mr Hughes to telegraph to General Monash their congratulations. [French Prime Minister] Clemenceau was directing a secretary to send his also, when 'No,' he said, 'I'll go and see them and congratulate them myself.'[69]

The 77-year old 'Tiger of France' arrived at 4th Division HQ, Bussy, on the afternoon of 7 July, where he was greeted by Generals Rawlinson, Monash and Sinclair-MacLagan, as well as the brigadiers and a representative group of soldiers from the three infantry brigades concerned. This was the occasion on which Clemenceau delivered the much-quoted speech that still sends a thrill of pride through Australians:.

> ...[Hamel] is not such a very great battle; but I am ready to hold that in a comparatively small battle the man, the fighting man, who goes in to give all he has—his home, his hopes, his life itself—in a small battle his qualities show in all the brighter light, the action of each individual man having more influence in the final result. In a very big action it is not possible to notice so well the qualities of particular men ...

> It is such a wonderful thing that this should happen in history on these old fields of battle which you had read of in books, hearing of wars which you had not seen and the consequences of which you had never expected to see. It is a wonderful thing that you should be fighting beside us on these old battlefields of history... The work of our fathers, which we wanted to leave unharmed to our children, [the Germans] tried to rob us of ... but the free nations of the world said that the Boche should not do this as long as they were there to come and prevent it ... and that is what you did. And that is what made us greet you when you came. We knew that you would fight a real fight.
>
> But we did not know that from the very beginning you would astonish the whole continent.
>
> ... I am going back tomorrow to see my countrymen and tell them: 'I have seen the Australians. I have looked in their eyes. I know that these men who have fought great battles beside us in the cause of freedom will fight alongside us again until the cause of freedom for which we are battling is safe for us and for our children.'[70]

As the French leader had acknowledged, Hamel was a small battle, but it was also one of considerable significance as a key point in the development of the tactics that would eventually bring victory to the British Army in the last months of the war. Tanks, guns and infantry had been used together before, notably at Cambrai in 1917, where the infantry played a subordinate role to the tanks and artillery had fired on deep lines, more to soften up the enemy ahead of the tanks than to protect the infantry. Hamel had shown the effectiveness of co-ordinating the available weapons into an integrated force operating as one, all under cover of secrecy and deception—the whole greater than the sum of its parts. The planning process was a model of careful, thorough attention to detail, aided by the direct involvement of subordinate formations and units, a process that took over two weeks from the first concept and culminated in a battle that lasted an hour and a half. The battle did not necessarily become widely known in the BEF as a whole ('Hamel' would probably have meant Hamel on the Ancre, north of Albert, to the average British soldier). The higher command, however, was eager to promulgate the lessons that had emerged from the battle, and

> a steady stream of commanders and staff officers from other corps and armies in the BEF arrived at [Australian Corps HQ] Bertangles to study the methods [Monash] had employed. GHQ included his orders in two instructional pamphlets it published on the battle.[71]

Another assessment is that Hamel gave Fourth Army 'methods of attack which stood a substantial chance of subduing—at tolerable cost to [the] infantry—*whatever* defences the enemy placed in their path.'[72] The cost of victory was approximately 1,400 casualties, of whom 176 were US troops and 257 were incurred by 2nd and 5th Divisions in the diversionary attacks on both flanks. In the main attack, the 6th Brigade had 131 casualties and the 11th Brigade 312, 154 of those in the 44th Battalion. The 4th Brigade's losses were 89 killed or died of wounds and 410 wounded, the largest proportion of them in the 15th Battalion, which was involved in the heaviest fighting and lost 44 dead and 196 wounded. The experience of the 15th showed that not everything had worked perfectly—when the mechanical aids of tanks and artillery had failed for one reason or another, the infantry still had to take on the foe face to face with bayonet and grenade. The 15th succeeded 'by determined and skilful fighting,'[73] but lost heavily in the process. It was estimated that the Germans had lost 1,000 men killed or wounded in the battle, and another 1,600 were prisoners. The German forward garrison had been virtually wiped out. About half of the prisoners had been taken by the 4th Brigade, which also claimed the capture of a great deal of military equipment, including 60 machine guns and 12 trench mortars.[74]

On the same day as Clemenceau's visit, planning was completed for a further operation that night in the Hamel sector with the aim of further straightening the line on the 12th Brigade's front. Here the advance of 4 July had left a small enemy salient protruding into the Australian line on either side of the Somme canal. The plan called for the 46th and 45th Battalions, north and south of the canal respectively, to each send two companies forward to capture the area. On the 45th's front it was apparent that the Germans had already vacated the objective so the task was simply to occupy the ground and dig in, but it was expected that the 46th would encounter opposition north of the canal. The operation was therefore organised as a formal attack, with a creeping artillery barrage, twelve machine guns from the 12th MG Company firing on rear-area targets, and two of the 12th LTM Battery's mortars in close support. The ground had already been patrolled on earlier nights so the troops had some idea of what to expect ahead of them. The barrage fell at 12:15 am, pounded the German front for three minutes, then moved out in lifts of 45 metres per minute. The two battalions had little trouble in gaining their objectives according to plan with minimal casualties. The 46th on the left encountered several enemy posts but these were easily overcome, and the 45th met no opposition from ground troops. The enemy artillery had responded quickly with a counter-barrage, including gas, and it was that which caused most of the losses to the attacking force—eight killed and missing, 43 wounded (of which 25 were regarded as 'slight') and seven gassed. The 46th picked up 32 prisoners and five machine guns, and estimated that the enemy had lost 25 killed as well. After some further skirmishing the new line was complete and firmly established.

That was the last action for the 4th Division in the Hamel operations, apart from some minor clashes between opposing patrols and outposts. Fortnightly reliefs of divisions had become the regular pattern for the Corps, and the 4th Division was now due to be relieved from the front line. Orders went out on 10 July for all units to prepare for relief by the 3rd Division—with the usual proviso 'less artillery.' The relief was carried out in stages over the next two nights. The 4th Division troops moved to the reserve lines, north-east from the outskirts of Amiens, the 12th Brigade to the area Fréchencourt–Cardonette–Allonville, the 13th to Rivery–Camon–Glisy and the 4th around Querrieu. Reliefs of the brigades' associated arms and services followed the same pattern. Divisional HQ opened at Coisy, west of Cardonette, on 13 July. So far as the divisional artillery was concerned, the extra brigades provided for the 4 July battle had been progressively withdrawn so that by 11 July the force covering the centre ('B') division front was down to six brigades in groups and another in reserve—the four brigades of the 4th and 5th

Divisions and three British units. By this time, 'owing to the system of fortnightly Divisional reliefs (less artillery) it was found that none of the Australian Divisions [was] covered by [its] own artillery at this period.'[75] Corps decided to regularise the situation, ordering a series of moves to take place between 13 and 16 July that would have the effect of restoring the divisional connections as much as possible. The artillery pieces themselves stayed in position while the personnel changed over progressively so that no guns were out of action at any time. By 16 July the 4th and 5th Division's field brigades had completed their transfer from the centre to the left ('C') divisional sector, presently held by the 5th Division infantry. Here the 10th and 11th AFA Brigades came under 5th Division command for the time being, but it was expected that the next fortnightly relief would bring the infantry of the 4th Division into that sector. In the event, things did not work out that way as the situation continued to change rapidly. For the main body of the 4th Division though, the immediate concern was to make the most of the break from front line duty, and the commanders aimed to put the emphasis on recreation this time, recharging batteries for the challenges ahead.

20 Notes

1 4th Division DAC War Diary for May 1918, Appendix 35. The DAC reported salvaging nearly 60,000 rounds of unused artillery ammunition, among other items.
2 4th Division Artillery HQ War Diary for May 1918, Appendix 7 (Order No. 147).
3 4th Division Artillery HQ War Diary for June 1918, Appendix 1.
4 The 10th AFA Brigade's May 1918 War Diary has a syllabus at Appendix 8, as does the 11th AFA diary at Appendix 4.
5 4th Division Artillery HQ War Diary for June 1918, Appendix 9.
6 *Ibid*, 17 June 1918.
7 Curtailed to only one week before being recalled for the Hamel operations.
8 It was also intended that the 15th Battalion on the left would advance its line near the brigade boundary, but that part of the operation was cancelled. The 15th sent out fighting patrols while the raids were taking place.
9 Some documents show the 14th Battalion parties as having 50 men, but this appears to be an error; the Battalion's own orders and reports (Appendix 8 in the June 1918 War Diary) have each party consisting of one officer in command, five NCOs and 25 privates, including the officer's runner.
10 14th Battalion War Diary for June 1918, Appendix 8.
11 Rule, *Op Cit*, p. 129.
12 16th Battalion War Diary for June 1918, Appendix 1 (folio 26).
13 According to the Red Cross file on Pte Cook, he was slightly wounded during the raid and was sent back escorting a German prisoner. They never reached the Australian line, and it seems likely

that Cook was overpowered by the prisoner. A rough grave was found in the area during the Hamel advance next month which may have been Cook's, but his remains were never identified and he was eventually categorised as killed in action, with no known grave.

The 4th Brigade War Diary entry for 15 June in stating the casualties for the raid includes 3 ORs killed, but those are more likely to have died in other circumstances on the same date; at least one, Pte J S Carroll, was killed by shelling behind the front line, according to his Red Cross file. The others were Ptes J J Taylor and W Wilkie (listed in the Roll of Honour compiled by Ian Gill, *Bloody Angle, Bullecourt and Beyond*, pp 516–540).

14 Vol VI, p. 245.

15 There does not appear to be a record of the full attendance at this meeting, but the 12th Brigade War Diary entry for 4 July indicates that Brig Gen Leane attended the meeting. Lt Col Drake-Brockman signed the 4th Brigade's initial summary of the discussions.

16 Lt Col McGregor had previously served with the 4th Field Ambulance, before being posted as DADMS to the 5th Division. Coincidentally, he had also relieved Lt Col Follit in that position, when the latter was promoted to command the 4th Field Ambulance.

17 General Hobbs (5th Division) was born in Britain, as was General Sinclair-MacLagan, who was a member of both the AIF and the British regular army.

18 4th Division GS War Diary, 29 June 1918, and Appendix 47 to June Diary.

19 P A Pedersen, *Monash as Military Commander*, p. 396.

20 13th Battalion War Diary for July 1918, Appendix 1. The other 4th Brigade battalions issued written orders as well as holding conferences. For some reason, the 14th Battalion order does not appear in its Diary, but there is a copy in the 16th Battalion Diary's July 1918 Appendix 2.

21 4th Division Engineers HQ War Diary, 27 June 1918.

22 Australian Corps Artillery HQ War Diary for July 1918, Appendices 2, 3 and 4.

23 4th Division Artillery HQ War Diary for July 1918, Appendix 7 (Order 163).

24 10th AFA Brigade War Diary for July 1918, Appendix 98. Presumably General Burgess would have attended the first Divisional conference on 25 June, as well as the conferences at Bertangles.

25 4th Division Artillery HQ War Diary for July 1918, Appendix 1.

26 Australian Corps Artillery HQ War Diary for July 1918, Appendix 2.

27 The *Official History* (Vol VI, p. 257) is somewhat misleading as to the number of field artillery units and pieces. Bean wrote 'For the whole front of his corps Monash was given twenty-nine brigades of field artillery—326 guns or howitzers—of which eleven brigades came from outside the corps. Sixteen brigades were allotted to the main attack and controlled by the 4th Division'. The last sentence is correct, but 29 brigades, each with four six-gun or six-howitzer batteries would amount to 696 pieces (at maximum establishment), not 326. There were 18 field brigades under Corps command, already in place at the beginning of June rather than 'given' for the Hamel operation—six with each of the three divisions holding the corps front, including a reserve brigade each. The Australian field artillery comprised 13 brigades in total, 10 divisional and 3 unattached 'Army' brigades, but the two 1st Division brigades and one of the Army brigades were in Flanders, and two of the divisional brigades with the Australian Corps were 'resting' in the rear training area at different times.

The 18 field brigades on the Corps front in early June thus comprised eight Australian and ten British brigades. Bean seems to have inferred an increase to 29 brigades from General Monash's briefing to the war correspondents just before the battle (Bean Diary, AWM38 3DRL606/116/1, p.16, 3 July 1918), adding the stated 11 additional brigades to the 18 existing ones—but one of those in the left sector was withdrawn in late June, and three of the 11 came from those already in place in the right sector, temporarily transferred to 4th Division command in the centre. One of the British brigades on the 4th Division front had been briefly withdrawn (leaving five in place), but it was then restored as one of the 11 (nine British and two Australian) brigades added to make the 4th Division force up to 16 brigades. That leaves the Corps field artillery at the beginning of July as five brigades on the left, 16 with the 4th Division in the centre and three on the right, a total of 24 brigades (576 pieces at full establishment) rather than 29. Bean's figure of 326 pieces must apply to the 4th Division's allocated brigades (probably allowing for some batteries not being at full establishment), not the whole Corps field artillery force. The figure of 326 field artillery pieces also appears in 'Notes Compiled by Fourth Army' on Hamel, as 'strength of artillery available for the operations on the Australian Corps front' (copy in the Monash Papers, AWM 3DRL/2316, Book 19, 23 June to 7 July 1918).

28   3rd Division Artillery HQ War Diary for July 1918, Appendix 3. This group was renamed the Southern Group and became one of four designated command groups, the others being, south to north, the Right Group, comprising the 10th AFA Brigade and four British brigades under the 10th Brigade CO, Lieutenant Colonel Thomas Williams; the Centre Group, with the 11th AFA, the 13th and 14th AFA from the 5th Division, and a British brigade, with Lieutenant Colonel H O Caddy, the 13th AFA CO, in command; and the Left Group of three British brigades.

29   General Burgess's after action report (4th Division Artillery HQ War Diary for July 1918, Appendix 1) gives the number of batteries as 61, but the relevant order (Appendix 7, Order No 163) includes a schedule that lists 62 batteries, and the communication diagram with the report also indicates 62. The odd one out is in the Southern Group (ex-Left Group of the 3rd Division artillery in the right sector): the 23rd Brigade RFA had an extra howitzer battery (D of the 86th RFA) attached, presumably because the other two brigades in that group were equipped with all 18-pounders.

30   4th and 2nd MG Battalion War Diaries for July 1918, various appendices.

31   Two four-gun batteries at Sailly-le-Sec (both from the 8th MG Company, 5th MG Battalion) and three south of the canal at Bouzencourt (one 8th Company, two from the 11th Company, 3rd MG Battalion) (ref: 4th MG Battalion War Diary for July 1918, Appendix A).

32   *Official History*, Vol VI, p. 262.

33   *Ibid*, pp. 266 and 264n.

34   Cutlack, *Op Cit*, pp. 222–3.

35   White, *Op Cit*, p. 142.

36   *Official History*, Vol VI, p. 268.

37   *Official History*, Vol VIII (Cutlack, *The Australian Flying Corps*) p.272.

38   4th Division GS War Diary for July 1918, Appendix 5 ('Aircraft' instruction). Five drop points were designated for the infantry and three for the machine gunners, and an additional one of each point was ordered by the 6th Brigade. The latter's instruction (Appendix 3 to the July 1918 Diary) indicates a difference in the type of ammunition supplied for machine guns and rifles. Standard containers for rifle ammunition included boxes containing 1,000 rounds of .303, in 5-round rifle clips (20 bandoliers, 10 clips each), so Lewis and Vickers gunners using these would have had to transfer rounds to drums or belts for their weapons. A full box weighed 75 pounds (34 kg); plus its parachute, two would make quite a load for an RE8. Vickers guns used 250-round belts. The *Official History* (Vol VI, p. 308) says that the aircraft carried two 1,200 round boxes each and dropped 111,600 rounds, meaning 93 boxes of that capacity. The boxes could, of course, have been able to fit an extra four bandoliers crammed in for the operation. The author has been unable to find a reference to a standard 1,200 round box of belted Vickers gun ammunition, only one for 500 rounds (two belts). Possibly four belts could have been transferred to a standard

rifle ammunition box for the drops. It seems that there may have been some difference in the packaging, given also that the sites were specified, and marked accordingly, as being for either infantry or machine guns, and particular aircraft were designated for each type of site.

39 4th Brigade War Diary for July 1918, Appendix 96.

40 13th Brigade War Diary, 1 July 1918.

41 The 4th Brigade Diary notes on 1 July that it was 'certain' the operation would take place on the morning of 4 July, but Corps HQ did not confirm this until the day before. The 11th Brigade also anticipated that 4 July would be the day.

42 Rule, *Op Cit*, p. 132.

43 4th Brigade War Diary 2 July 1918 (apparently wrongly dated).

44 *Official History*, Vol VI, p. 285.

45 The barrage map shows the field artillery start line touching the westernmost curve of Pear Trench, then the line of the first lift running across the open ground enclosed by the loop of the trench, and therefore intersecting the trench itself at only two points, and the second lift falling beyond the rear segment of the trench. The start line for the heavy artillery barrage was 250 metres east of the trench. The 15th CO, Colonel McSharry, reported afterwards that 'our barrage did little or no damage to Pear Trench or its garrison. I examined the ground and saw where our shells fell on either side of it.' (15th Battalion War Diary for July 1918, Appendix 3).

46 From his DCM recommendation (recorded as 'Maynard Goodyer').

47 Bean Papers, AWM38 3DRL606/190/1, p.22.

48 As noted in Capt Glasgow's DSO recommendation.

49 L Cpl Axford's exploit was stated in the *Official History* (Vol VI, pp. 290–91) to have taken place at Kidney Trench itself. Axford was a member of Lt Minchin's platoon in 'C' Company (Capt Woods). According to the 16th Battalion's operation order (in Appendix 2 of the July 1918 War Diary) the companies lined up in the order A, C, B, D, right to left. The order gives the width of each company's front also, putting D and B Companies on the left of the 16th's line facing Kidney Trench, over a combined frontage of 360 yards. Bean's notes (AWM38 3DRL606/190/1 p. 44) confirm that 'D' was on the left, and Capt Lynas's comments on the MC recommendation for Capt H A F Wilkinson confirm that 'B' Company was the next right. Assuming that the companies maintained their alignment in the early stages of the attack, 'C' Company would have advanced on Vaire Trench a little to the south of Kidney Trench. The German machine gun in question would not necessarily be firing straight ahead, but would as likely have been positioned in Vaire Trench firing in enfilade at 'B' Company and holding up one of that company's platoons, or in Kidney Trench firing at 'C' Company; in the latter case though, it would be more likely that 'B' Company would have dealt with the gun. If this was the gun that hit Capt Woods and CSM Blinman, it still seems more likely that it was in Vaire Trench; the Red Cross reports on Woods have several different versions of his death, including that it resulted from shelling near the start. Bean's notebook entries on the 16th at Hamel mentioned above are undated, but his diary (AWM38 3DRL606/116/1) indicates that he interviewed the Battalion officers on 21 July, and that he inspected the battlefield a week later, identifying Kidney Trench and Pear Trench, but apparently not accompanied by anyone who had taken part in the battle.

50 Gill, *Op Cit*, p. 515.

51 *Official History*, Vol VI, p. 292.

52 Quoted from a supporting statement in the original award recommendation attached to 16th Battalion's report (Appendix 2 to the July 1918 War Diary); the final official recommendation was abbreviated to exclude the extra comments.

53 The author has assumed from 16th Battalion Routine Orders that Rogers was the CSM of 'D' Company.
54 Account extracted from award recommendations for both men on the AWM website, and in the 16th Battalion report referred to above.
55 Monash, *Op Cit*, p. 50.
56 4th Brigade War Diary for July 1918, Appendix 100.
57 Bean, *Anzac to Amiens*, p. 462n.
58 15th Battalion War Diary for July 1918, Appendix 4 (folio 26).
59 *Ibid*, Appendix 3.
60 13th Battalion War Diary for July 1918, Appendix 1 Page 4.
61 The 13th Battalion's forward signallers used captured German wire-reels to run out their circuits. These were found to be very efficient devices, enabling quick connection of telephones to the companies.
62 White, *Op Cit*, p. 146. Routine Orders items in the 13th Battalion War Diary confirm that Sgt Phillips was a member of 'B' Company.
63 This account is taken from the 4th MG Company's report on the action, in Appendix 8 of the unit's July 1918 Diary, with a copy in Appendix A of the MG Battalion's July Diary; Sgt Lynch's DCM recommendation does not mention the incident with the sniper post.
64 4th Division Engineers HQ War Diary for July 1918, Appendix 2.
65 See Maj Tolley's 'Report on Recent Operations' in Appendix 1 to the 4th Field Company's July 1918 War Diary. The report implies, incorrectly, that the 14th Battalion supplied all three platoons allocated to build the strong-points in the support line, rather than one each from the 13th, 14th and 15th.
66 4th Brigade War Diary for July 1918, Appendix 109.
67 *Medical History*, Vol II, p. 671.
68 13th Field Ambulance War Diary, 4 July 1918. The figure is close to that given in a full statistical report by the ADMS (4th Division ADMS War Diary for July 1918, Folio 85 in appendices). 2nd Division medical services handled a further 250 cases.
69 *Official History*, Vol VI, p. 334.
70 There are slightly different versions of this speech in the sources. That recorded by Sir John Monash, for instance (Monash, *Op Cit*, pp. 62–3, found also in Cutlack, *Op Cit*, pp. 230–31) differs in detail from that used in abbreviated form here, which is taken from a transcript printed and circulated by the Australian Corps; the text probably comes from C E W Bean who was present and took down most of the speech in shorthand (Bean Diary, AWM38 3DRL606/116/1, 7 July 1918). There is a copy of the printed document at Appendix 2A of the 13th Battalion War Diary for July 1918, and no doubt elsewhere too. Whichever version is preferred, the message is the same, of course.
71 Pedersen, *Battleground Europe: Hamel*, p. 115.
72 Prior and Wilson, *Command on the Western Front: The Military Career of Sir Henry Rawlinson 1914-1918*, p. 298.
73 *Official History*, Vol VI, p. 329.
74 4th Brigade War Diary for July 1918, Appendix 96.
75 4th Division Artillery HQ War Diary, 13 July 1918.

21: The Monash Touch

Decorations awarded for the Hamel battle began to come through over the next few weeks from mid-July. There were many awards for bravery in hand to hand combat—regardless of the weight of support from tanks and artillery, the fight often still got down to the individual footsoldiers and their leaders in the front line. Two men received the Victoria Cross, adding to the 4th Brigade's already impressive list of VC winners—Private Henry Dalziel (15th Battalion) and Lance Corporal Thomas Axford (16th Battalion). Dalziel's VC, the 1,000th awarded since the decoration had been instituted in 1856, was the first and only one for the 15th Battalion.[1]

Private Henry Dalziel VC (1893–1965), 15th Battalion. (AWM A05444)

He had joined the 15th as a reinforcement on Gallipoli, but had spent long periods away with illness and then with a wound received near Ypres in October 1917. When fit, Dalziel seems to have just quietly gone about his duties in the battalion before the battlefield crisis at Pear Trench brought him to the fore; he was to remain in hospital for many months recovering from the dangerous head wound that he had received in the fight. Axford, 24, was born in South Australia but had spent most of his life in Western Australia, where he was working as a labourer at a Goldfields brewery when he enlisted in July 1915. He was among the reinforcements who joined the 16th Battalion in Egypt during the AIF expansion after Gallipoli. Earlier in the year, Axford had been awarded the MM, the recommendation for which has not survived but which was presumably for an exploit during the Hébuterne fighting.

Corporal Thomas Axford VC MM (1894 –1983), 16th Battalion. (AWM J03060A)

Axford's friend and platoon commander, Lieutenant Minchin, was recommended for a Bar to the MC that he had won at Polygon Wood, but in an unusual—and well justified—decision, the reviewing authorities upgraded his eventual award to the DSO. Other DSOs were awarded to 4th Brigade company commanders who had led from the front into the enemy positions—Captains Glasgow (15th Battalion), Marper (13th) and Lynas (16th); that gave the latter officer the rare combination of DSO, MC and two Bars to his name. Lieutenant Colonel McSharry, the 15th Battalion CO, received a Bar to his DSO DCMs went to Sergeant Phillips and Corporal Lihou (both 13th Battalion), Sergeant Goodwin and Corporal Goodger (15th), and CSM Rogers (16th); Rogers had previously been awarded the MM and Bar, and he was commissioned shortly after the battle. Sergeant Lynch (MG Battalion) and Sapper Miller (4th Field Company) were other DCM recipients. Among awards of the MC were those to Lieutenant Wright (MG Battalion), Captain Wilkinson (16th Battalion) and Lieutenant Dwyer (13th Battalion). The 16th Battalion runners Privates Northey and Carter, who had overcome odds of four to one in their skirmish, were among numerous soldiers awarded the MM.

Away from the drama of the Hamel fighting, the early days of July saw further changes in the 4th Division command group. A new ADMS arrived to replace the wounded Colonel Moseley, in the person of Colonel Kenneth Smith, who took up duty as from 6 July (Lieutenant Colonel McGregor returned to his position as CO of the 4th Field Ambulance). Like his two predecessors as ADMS, Colonel Smith was British-born. He was 33, and was posted from a period in command of the 15th Field Ambulance; before that, he had spent most of his service in various hospital appointments. In the 12th Brigade, the 46th Battalion had a change of commander, in unusual circumstances. Brigadier General Leane had developed an unfavourable opinion of Lieutenant Colonel Hubert Ford, the present CO, and in June had formally assessed him as unsuitable for battalion command and recommended that he be relieved. Part of the problem seems to have been a susceptibility to even small amounts of alcohol, which was attributed to the lingering effects of the serious head wound that Ford had sustained at Passchendaele. In any case, the brigadier's recommendation was accepted at higher level and Ford was ordered to proceed to England prior to returning to Australia, reverting to his substantive rank of major. The choice of his successor was between two outstanding officers, each presently second-in-command of his respective battalion—Majors Arthur Allen (45th) and John Corrigan (15th). Leane was in favour of Allen, but General Sinclair-MacLagan chose Corrigan, who had a year's seniority over Allen in major's rank. In an inter-brigade posting, Corrigan took command of the 46th on 10 July, with promotion to temporary lieutenant colonel, one of the few AIF members to rise to that rank from private.[2] Colonel Corrigan was 26 (the three 12th Brigade battalion commanders were now all under 30), born in New Zealand and resident in Tasmania at the beginning of the war. Giving his occupation as 'labourer'[3] he had enlisted as a private with the 15th, reached the rank of sergeant by the time of the Landing, and then was commissioned shortly afterwards. In France, Corrigan had made a fine record in various duties with the 15th, both at Battalion HQ and in the front line (he had survived being shot through the chest at Pozières).

Some changes also took place in the infantry brigade staffs at about this time. Captain Arthur Nicholson, 13th Brigade staff captain, was sent on a formal staff training course, replaced by Lieutenant William Conwell from the 49th Battalion. Later in the month Major Roy Morell, the brigade major, was detached to Corps HQ as machine gun officer; Captain Thomas Louch, having spent a long apprenticeship as assistant brigade major, took on the duties. The 4th Brigade also had a change of staff captain when the Rhodes scholar Captain Harry Thomson was posted to the new AIF Education Service in London, shortly becoming deputy director of that organisation; Lieutenant Royal Lackman, ex-50th Battalion and a staff trainee at 13th Brigade HQ, moved across to take up the posting.

Once the units had settled into the reserve area billets, attention was turned to organising sports and recreation for the men. It was the beginning, in one 4th Brigade battalion's view, of

> one of the most enjoyable fortnights in our history. After bathing, changing [uniforms] and cleaning up generally, all engaged in sport of every kind—swimming, cricket, racing and athletic events—and every evening there was a concert. Company sports, inter-company cricket, battalion sports, brigade sports and a divisional race meeting, kept all sport organisers busy. All seemed to 'let themselves go' this fortnight, from General to Digger, for the interlude was to be followed by big things... In addition to the sports, lorries conveyed [leave] parties to spend a day in Abbeville or Doullens.[4]

The 12th and 13th Brigades mostly left it to the units to arrange sports and recreation, but the 4th Brigade in particular gave much attention to organising activities for the Brigade as a whole. Some light training was conducted in the mornings, and most afternoons were devoted to a keenly-contested cricket competition between units, which was eventually won by the 14th Battalion team, defeating the 4th Field Ambulance by an innings in the final on 26 July. The Ambulance had made the final by earlier defeating the 16th Battalion, much to that unit's chagrin—its War Diary entries show how seriously the matches were taken. The 16th had the consolation, however, of winning the Brigade Australian Rules football grand final, also against the 4th Field Ambulance.

Athletic and aquatic sports featured highly as well. The 4th Brigade held a gala sporting carnival on 20 July in the grounds of Querrieu Chateau on the Hallue river, with a swimming competition in the morning and track and field in the afternoon, in front of an enthusiastic crowd. Among the invited spectators were Generals Birdwood and Monash, and off-field entertainment included a circus with side-shows put on by the 7th Company AASC and musical numbers from the band of the 132nd US Infantry Regiment. Bookmakers and a totalisator were authorised for those inclined to a wager. In the evening, more American guest performers, the concert party of the 108th US Engineers, put on a show in front of the chateau,

> ... the end of a perfect day, and all then dispersed—most lighter in pocket, all lighter in heart. The war was temporarily forgotten, and all day the air had been filled with the sound of jests, laughter, shouts and music.[5]

The day produced a profit of 2,500 francs, which was donated to the Red Cross for prisoner of war assistance. The Brigade Cup for the highest overall points score was won by the 4th MG Company, which was now a sub-unit of the 4th MG Battalion but had participated on the basis of its traditional links with the 4th Brigade (the MG Battalion held its own sports day on 25 July, and the 4th Company won that competition also).

The crowning event of this fortnight was the divisional race meeting, held on 22 July at a disused aerodrome near Allonville. The meeting attracted many spectators from resting Allied formations in the area as well as all ranks of the 4th Division itself. Sixteen pilots of 2 Squadron AFC flew their SE5a scouts down from Flanders for the day, landing on the airfield.[6] There had been something of a panic in the 14th Battalion's ranks a few days earlier, when 'some villain' stole the unit's payroll money, but more cash was obtained just in time for the troops to try their luck with the bookmakers.[7] The first race resulted in a tragedy. A bad fall caused the deaths of two officers, Captain Robert Smith of the Signal Company[8] and Captain Ernest Kemmis, ADC to General Sinclair-MacLagan; as secretary of the meeting committee, Captain Kemmis had played a big part in organising the event. There could hardly have been a worse start to the proceedings, but the festive mood of the crowd picked up again as the programme went on without further trouble, and was declared a great success overall. After the last race, it was rather fortunate that there were no further accidents when the AFC planes took off to return to base. With their natural fighter pilots' daring reinforced by a few drinks, one or more of the aviators put on a spectacular but highly risky display of aerobatics and very low flying—some spectators were said to have 'barely escaped decapitation.'[9]

Two days later another race meeting was held on the same course, this time organised by the 12th Brigade. All went well, and with the expected fortnight out of the line nearing its close, all units began getting back to business, with the emphasis turning towards training. The place of the unfortunate Captain Kemmis as ADC was filled by Captain Cyril Bartlett, an AASC officer on the divisional administrative staff. It had been anticipated that the 4th Division would relieve the 5th in the left sector of the Corps front, and orders to that effect were issued by Corps and Division but were cancelled almost immediately.

There was some uncertainty for a day or two. At first it was thought that the Division would get a further period in the rear, moving to an area near the south-western outskirts of Amiens, but then came the surprising announcement on 28 July that the Division would instead be relieving the French 37th Division in the front line south of Villers-Bretonneux. The Australian Corps front was shifting to the south, with British units of III Corps taking over the sector of the front line north of the Somme from the 5th Division. The movements were to be completed by 2 August.

The changed plans were a result of significant developments elsewhere on the Western Front in the previous two weeks. On 15 July the Germans had launched another powerful offensive, this time against the French on the Marne near Rheims. The attack had been anticipated, however, and the French, defending in depth, at first absorbed the blow then struck back three days later in a devastating counter-attack, an operation that included four American divisions. By the time the Germans managed to stabilise their front two weeks later, they had lost 170,000 men and 600 guns. The defeat also caused General Ludendorff to abandon plans for an intended decisive attack in Flanders. The Allies now clearly held the initiative, and the aggressive supreme commander, General Foch, turned to pressing home the advantage with his own offensive operations. The Germans seemed particularly vulnerable in the sector in front of Amiens, held by Fourth Army (III Corps and the Australian Corps). An attack in that area had been under consideration since May, with the intention of clearing the enemy well away from the positions they had reached, which remained in threatening proximity to the vital transport links centred on Amiens. Now it appeared that more could be achieved.

The Hamel battle had shown that the German defences in the area were in poor condition and the quality of the troops manning them was not high. The Germans appeared to be making no real effort to improve their defensive works, a symptom of low morale among the troops and lack of an organised plan by their commanders. This had been confirmed in the weeks following Hamel by the ease with which small forces from the AIF divisions in the line had been able to infiltrate enemy forward posts, bite off pieces of territory, and move their own line forward, a process termed 'peaceful penetration.' Even the bugbear position of Monument Wood was taken by those methods. General Monash was now pressing his superior, the Fourth Army commander General Sir Henry Rawlinson, for the Australian Corps to take part in a large-scale offensive, and Monash's ideas fitted in with the broad intentions of the higher command—the Corps report on the subsequent events noted that its 'conclusions coincided with those already arrived at by Fourth Army.'[10] On 17 July, with the French counter-offensive on the Marne about to be launched, Rawlinson had met with the British Commander in Chief, Field Marshal Sir Douglas Haig, to revive the earlier proposal for an operation east of Amiens. Haig had agreed to transfer the Canadian Corps to Rawlinson's command to form the striking force alongside the Australian Corps if the operation went ahead. The force would be completed by III Corps, already under Fourth Army, and General Glasgow's 1st Australian Division would finally be released from Flanders to rejoin its own Corps. Rawlinson then conferred with Monash and the Canadian commander, Lieutenant General Sir Arthur Currie, on 21 July to initiate the planning process pending final approval, which was forthcoming from Foch and Haig three days later. The higher command, unable to shake off the vision of a sweeping cavalry breakthrough, also included the Cavalry Corps in the plan, to operate mainly in the Canadian sector.

The need for secrecy and surprise had by now been accepted as a priority by the British high command, a principle that had been applied firmly in the Hamel plan and had contributed greatly to its success. The much bigger operation now proposed offered more chances for detection by the Germans, and consequently secrecy measures were applied even more stringently. To begin with, particular attention was paid to concealing the movements of the Canadian Corps. The Canadians were just coming into the line at Arras after a long rest when the decision was made to include them in the Amiens force. This would entail a move by motor vehicle and railway of 48 kilometres south to take up positions on the right of the Australian Corps, a sector presently held by French troops. Such was the fighting reputation of the Canadians that any indication that they had suddenly been moved to the front line in a different sector would immediately alert the Germans. The decision was taken that the Canadians would first move to the area in the rear of their eventual jumping-off position; at the same time, it was let out that the Canadians were moving north to the Ypres sector, and two of their battalions were actually sent north, together with a wireless station to transmit false messages. On the Amiens front the French would instead be relieved by Australian troops at first. The Germans had good reason to be aware that the Australians were already in the nearby area, and it would be reasonable for them to assume, if they detected the change, that the French forces were being moved to take part in the Marne fighting. Accordingly the 4th Division, as the available reserve formation due to return from rest, was ordered to take over the French line.

Division HQ, unaware at first of the reasons behind the change, decided to use the 4th and 13th Brigades forward, left to right, with the 12th Brigade in reserve. On 31 July, with the units on the march for the front line, General Monash called in all divisional commanders to a conference 'to discuss a confidential matter,'[11] at which the broad plan for the offensive was revealed. That night, the 4th Brigade began moving into the line in relief of the French, with the 14th and 15th Battalions forward, the 13th in support and the 16th further back in reserve; the relief was reported complete in the early hours of 1 August. Differences in language, systems and tactical dispositions complicated the relieving process somewhat but were for the most part overcome, although the divisional staff's comment that the relief was completed 'without incident'[12] was not entirely correct. A platoon of the 14th Battalion was mistaken for Germans by the French troops whom they were relieving and grenades were thrown, killing Corporal Herbert Lewis and wounding another NCO before the error was realised.[13]

The 13th Brigade moved into the right (southern) part of the sector on the following night, sending the 49th and 51st Battalions into the front line with the 50th in support. Each brigade had fire support from a company of the MG Battalion and an attached American MG company, with artillery cover provided by the guns of the 12th British Division. The new front extended from Monument Wood on the 4th Brigade's left to the river Luce at Hourges, south of Hangard, on the 13th Brigade's right. Divisional HQ was established at Cagny, on the Avre river near Amiens. On 1 August General Sinclair-MacLagan had met with his brigadiers and supporting-arms commanders to explain the coming operation, still with heavy emphasis on secrecy. The date for the attack had been set as 8 August—little enough time for preparations, but the high command was anxious to strike the blow before the Germans roused themselves to improve their defences. The time factor was particularly challenging to the Canadians, moving a long distance to an unfamiliar sector and obliged to establish their back-area communication and supply systems.

Fourth Army would advance over a front of 18 kilometres, with III Corps on the left (north of the Somme), the Australian Corps in the centre, and the Canadian Corps on the right; a French corps would co-operate to the right of the Canadians. The front of the Australian Corps would cover seven kilometres at the start, with its left on the south bank of the Somme opposite Sailly-Laurette (which was just inside the German lines) and its right on the railway line running south-east from Villers-Bretonneux. The widening angle of the railway to the river meant that the Australian front would open out to nine kilometres at the final objective. The front was almost bisected by the straight Roman road that ran through Villers-Bretonneux between the river and the railway. The ground was fairly flat for the most part—good tank country—but indented by several gullies running to the river across the direction of the advance. In what would be the 4th Division's area, the gullies close to the riverbank villages of Cérisy-Gailly and Morcourt were the most important. The Somme took several horseshoe bends in that area, the western bend forming a peninsula of higher ground, the Chipilly Spur, on the far bank opposite Morcourt. From there the Germans, if undisturbed, would be able to fire across the river into the left flank of the Australians advancing to the final objective, so it was vital for III Corps, operating north of the river, to capture that ground.

The offensive was intended to go deep, up to 10 kilometres from the start line. The distance would be achieved in three stages, with the successive objective lines designated as the Green, Red and Blue Lines. The depth of the advance required fresh forces to leapfrog through as each stage was reached and take up the fighting for the next objective. As far as the Australian Corps task was concerned, the attack plans as developed by Monash and his staff required the infantry of their four divisions then in the sector (the 1st Division, due to arrive just before the Zero date, would be in reserve) to deploy with two divisions side by side to lead off and take the first objective, followed by the other two continuing the advance to the next objectives. The first objective, the Green Line, was set at 3,200 metres from the start; the original scheme had called for a shorter advance, but this had been extended, at the urging of General Monash, so as to take the German gun line in the Cérisy valley. That phase would follow the pattern set at Hamel, infantry and tanks advancing together behind a creeping barrage. The next objective, the Red Line, was a further 4,500 metres away, well beyond the effective range of the field artillery in its starting positions, and so precluding the use of the standard barrage. Instead, some of the batteries from the barrage force were to come forward and join the second-stage infantry brigades as mobile guns, with tanks now pushing ahead of the infantry in an open-warfare situation. Finally, reserve elements from the second wave would advance a further 1,400 metres to the final objective. The plan developed further to designate the 3rd and 2nd Divisions, left to right, to lead off and capture the Green Line, then the 4th and 5th Divisions passing through to complete the drive to the Red and Blue Lines.

The arrangements for the 'leapfrogs' showed Monash's originality as a planner. Moving one body of troops through another to attack more distant objectives was nothing new in itself, but it was usually done at the level of battalions or brigades, not entire divisions. Furthermore, the standard practice was for the force attacking the first objective to start from the existing front line and that for the second objective to march up from the rear, cross the front line and the first objective (assuming the first wave had succeeded), and continue on to fight for the next objective. The consequence was that the following waves had to cover far more ground than the first, fight their battle and then probably have to defend the captured line against counter-attacks—that is

> the individual man, who was to be required to march and fight his way furthest into enemy country, and therefore was to be the last to enter the fight, would also be called upon to march furthest from his rearmost position of assembly before even reaching the battle zone ... an altogether unreasonable demand upon any infantryman during the stress and nervous excitement of battle. It would have been courting a breakdown from over-fatigue ...[14]

To equalise the strain across the whole infantry force, Monash decided to reverse the usual procedure, by placing the divisions for the second and third phases closest to the start line, and those attacking the first objective to the rear.

Those dispositions meant that the first-stage force (the 2nd and 3rd Divisions) would make its approach march from the rear, leapfrog through the next-stage force (the 4th and 5th Divisions) waiting near the start line, and advance to take the first objective. At the appropriate time, the 4th and 5th Divisions would start their own advance, pass through the 2nd and 3rd, then move on to the more distant objectives; the distance to be covered by the 4th and 5th Divisions on the day of battle would be up to five kilometres less than if the conventional method had been used. Monash characterised the scheme as 'a manoeuvre unique in the history of war, namely a 'double leapfrog,' simultaneously carried out by two separate pairs of divisions, operating side by side.'[15] Another deceptively-simple departure from the usual was his directive that the barrage plan for the first phase should be comprised of straight lines for the successive lifts—instead of the barrage having to conform to an uneven infantry line, the infantry would be required to adjust their frontages to make their start line straight. This simplified the field artillery task and considerably reduced the chances of error. Monash further laid down that once the second-stage divisions passed over the Green Line their commanders would take over tactical control of their sectors or zones from the starting divisions. This was a lesson learnt from Messines, when the 4th Division, advancing to its distant objective, had been hit by 'friendly' artillery controlled by the force holding the first objective.

> Drafted on 22 July, Monash's preliminary notes dealt with every major facet of the attack ... [he] had conceived what was essentially the corps plan of attack less than one day after the Army commander explained the wider scheme.[16]

A huge force of artillery, field and heavy, was progressively assembled, amounting to about 2,000 pieces for Fourth Army overall, 700 heavy and 1,300 field. Two-thirds of the heavy artillery was allocated to the counter-battery role. By the time the battle began most of the German battery positions would have been identified and targeted, through an intensive effort with the improved detection techniques now available to the gunners—aerial reconnaissance, flash spotting and sound ranging. Of the field artillery, 18 brigades (including all 13 AFA brigades) would cover the front of the Australian Corps to fire the creeping barrage covering the advance to the Green Line. Six of those brigades, as soon as their barrage task was completed, would then limber up and advance to provide the mobile artillery covering the second pair of divisions attacking the Red and Blue Lines. A mobile heavy battery of four 60-pounders was also attached to each division. A high proportion of the BEF's available tank force was allocated to Fourth Army for the operation, amounting to about 450 heavy and light vehicles.[17] Of these, the Australian Corps would have 168 tanks, of which 24 were 'carriers' to bring up supplies. Each division was allocated 24 heavy tanks, with the two second-stage divisions each having an additional 18 for the drive to the final objective. The latter vehicles were the longer Mark V* ('Mark Five Star') type, which were intended for a novel tactic—they would be used as personnel and weapon carriers, to bring up troops with machine guns and drop them at the final objective, making an advanced force that would then hold on until the main body came up. The remaining 12 fighting tanks would make up a linking force between the divisional zones. Those tanks of the Green Line force that remained serviceable were to continue on and reinforce those allocated to the further objectives. Air support amounting to 800 aircraft was assembled, covering all types of task—scouts for both ground attack and air superiority work, bombers to attack key points in the enemy rear, reconnaissance machines, artillery spotters, and infantry co-operation (one RAF squadron was particularly tasked to work with the tanks). Number 3 Squadron AFC would perform its usual contact patrol work for the Australian Corps, and the eight scout squadrons of the 22nd Wing RAF would carry out low-level ground attack missions.

The machine gun resources of the four attacking divisions were divided between forward guns moving with the infantry and barrage guns supplementing the artillery creeping barrage, with the barrage force controlled by the 2nd and 3rd Divisions conducting the first stage of the advance. To deal with the numerous infrastructure tasks required before and during the battle, the divisions' engineer and pioneer units were regarded as a pool of resources, with several units allocated to work directly under the Corps Chief Engineer, particularly on road-making, and some detached from their own divisions to work with others according to need. The great distance planned for the advance presented complications for the medical arrangements in evacuation of the wounded and establishment of dressing stations, RAPs and collecting posts. The approach adopted was to combine the medical resources of the two divisions in each half (zone) of the Corps front, with the field ambulances of the second-stage divisions moving up once the Green Line was captured.[18] Distance was also an issue for communications, as was the mobile nature of the operation in its later stages. Telephone communications from forward positions to the various HQs required laying long stretches of ground cable, which would then be liable to frequent damage from tanks criss-crossing the area. Wireless telegraphy sets were supplied to infantry brigades and artillery groups, and detachments of the Corps mounted troops (the 13th Light Horse Regiment) were given to the divisions and would be available to assist with carrying written messages.

The broad plans made known to the division GOCs on 31 July were developed in more detail by the divisional staffs. In the 4th Division, General Sinclair-MacLagan and his staff met with the brigadiers and other senior commanders on 1 August.[19] Unit COs were brought across the scheme later in the day, when the Division was in the process of relieving the French. It was expected that the Division would in turn be relieved by the Canadians several days before the operation, and the plan was worked out to have the 4th and 12th Brigades making the attack on the Red and Blue Lines, with the 13th Brigade in reserve. To carry out mobile tactics for that stage, the infantry force was constituted as brigade groups, expanded to include field artillery, machine guns and light horse. The 13th Light Horse provided a half-troop to each of the two forward brigades, and the British 16th Royal Horse Artillery (RHA) Brigade formed the mobile artillery for the 12th Brigade infantry, with the other arms and services coming from the Division's own resources. The 4th Field Company engineers and a company of the Pioneer Battalion were allocated to the 4th Brigade, with another pioneer company attached to the 12th Brigade. One platoon from each of those pioneer companies was assigned to work with the mobile artillery brigades, to make trench crossings and generally clear routes for the guns. The other two companies of the 4th Pioneers were detached to assist the 5th Division. The 12th Field Company was nominally attached to the reserve infantry brigade, with special responsibility for repairing the bridges across the Somme in the captured territory and constructing new bridges if necessary. The remaining Field Company, the 13th, was among those working directly under the Corps Chief Engineer.

The two forward brigades each had 24 of the MG Battalion's Vickers guns attached, drawn from all four MG Companies. The 16 guns of the 4th Company would go with the 4th Brigade, 10 carried in tanks for the final attack on the Blue Line and the other six to be brought up by horse-limber to operate between the Red and Blue Lines. Close support for the actual attack on the Red Line would be provided by eight guns of the 24th Company.

Similarly the 12th Brigade would have the 12th Company attached, providing 10 guns in tanks for the Blue Line and six on limbers, plus eight guns of the 13th Company for the Red Line. The gun crews designated for the Blue Line were given special training with the tanks in the back area. The remaining 16 guns, eight each from the 13th and 24th Companies, were part of the opening barrage (under command of the 3rd Division), following which they would move to join the reserve brigade. The firepower of the brigade groups was completed by mobile artillery elements, including both brigades of the 4th Division's own artillery. The 10th AFA Brigade would work with the 4th Infantry Brigade and the British gunners of the 16th RHA with the 12th Brigade. The 11th AFA, nominally in reserve, had the task of advancing behind the attack and providing close support as circumstance demanded. As with the allocated machine guns, the artillery would begin the battle as part of the creeping barrage force under the 3rd Division CRA, the three units forming a sub-group commanded by the 16th RHA CO. Once the advance reached the Green Line those units would cease fire and move to their mobile tasks, and command of the left zone artillery would pass to the 4th Division, including three other brigades forming a defensive group.

The 4th Division artillery at the beginning of the planning period had still been in the line under 5th Division command, in what was then the 'C' Division sector north of the Somme. During this period a permanent CO was appointed to the 11th AFA Brigade in place of the ill Lieutenant Colonel Waite. This was Lieutenant Colonel Cyril Spurge, a 40 year old English-born Western Australian promoted from major commanding the 39th Battery (10th AFA); Colonel Spurge was a Gallipoli veteran whose military experience went back to the Boer War, when he had served as a private in the British Army. Another change in July was in the posting of Divisional Trench Mortar Officer (DTMO), when Captain Stanley Fox was transferred to the 110th Howitzer Battery and replaced by Captain Keith Ewan, moving up from MTM battery officer. Activities in the sector had been mostly routine except for an operation on the night of 29 July, when the brigades took part in a barrage fired to cover an advance by the 5th Division's 8th Brigade south of Morlancourt, centred on a landmark called the Brick Beacon. Lieutenant Colonel Williams, CO of the 10th AFA Brigade, commanded a group made up of the 4th Division brigades and several British units. The operation was a complete success, advancing the line 460 metres and depriving the enemy of an area of high ground. The next night units of III Corps began relieving the 5th Division in that sector as the Fourth Army front was adjusted, and over the next few nights the Australian artillery was withdrawn also, initially to its wagon lines. Over the following two days all guns were put through a calibration process at the artillery range near Vaux-en-Amienoix, north of Amiens. This involved each piece firing six rounds through a set of wire mesh screens placed at set distances apart. The passage of the shells through the successive screens was recorded and the true muzzle velocity of an individual piece calculated. The gun-layers could then make corrections to allow for the wear on the barrel of their weapons, thereby reducing errors when firing from the map—as at Hamel, for the purpose of surprise there would be no preliminary registration shooting. Following calibration, the batteries moved to the area near Aubigny in the rear of the 3rd Division zone and prepared to take up positions for the barrage.

The 4th Division's medical services, working in conjunction with those of the 3rd Division, would be distributed from the forward area to the rear, with dressing stations being established and then changing their functions as the advance went forward. Four stretcher bearer squads were assigned to each of the seven infantry battalions in the advance, working with the battalion RMOs, and a senior medical officer was attached to each of the 4th and 12th Brigade HQs, to be in charge of evacuations from the brigade sectors. These officers were Majors David Steele (13th Field Ambulance temporarily attached to the 4th) and Frederick Le Messurier (12th Field Ambulance). When the battle opened, the existing MDS west of Daours would continue to be managed by the 3rd Division, with the tent personnel of the 12th Field Ambulance attached. The 13th Field Ambulance, assisted by 3rd Division personnel, would open a dressing station at Fouilloy, just south of Corbie; this would be set up as an ADS at first. Once the Green Line was taken, with command of all medical services in the zone passing to the 4th Division ADMS, a team from both divisions under command of the 4th Field Ambulance would be moving up to the vicinity of Hamel to establish a forward ADS. When that became operational, the Fouilloy station would be upgraded to become the MDS for the zone. Bearer personnel and vehicles from all units would be distributed along the evacuation routes, with collection points set up as the advance went on.

With less than a week's notice of the operation, infantry brigade staffs worked on their own detailed plans, operational and administrative, as did the commanders of the supporting arms and services. The troops of the 4th and 13th Brigades holding the front line south from the Villers-Bretonneux railway were meant to be relieved by the arriving Canadians two nights before Zero, allowing time to reposition and organise for the attack. The plans for that relief were unwittingly disrupted by the enemy. It had become apparent to the Germans opposite that the French troops had been relieved—an alert observer would have detected the different uniforms and helmets, and possibly some telephone conversations in two languages were intercepted, but in any case the level of activity on that front had suddenly increased. Among other signs, some 49th Battalion troops had found an old dump of rifle grenades and amused themselves by firing them off into the German lines. In the early hours of 4 August, behind an artillery bombardment, the Germans raided several posts of the 51st Battalion at Hourges, seeking identifications. They outflanked one post, and after a brief but intense fight, the German force left ten of their own men dead or dying in front of the post but brought away five prisoners—in the arithmetic of raiding, that constituted a success. The immediate fear at the command level was that the captured men might have heard of the imminent arrival of the Canadians and might reveal their knowledge under interrogation. That was unlikely, however, since the men had gone into the front line before there had been any mention of the Canadians, and in fact they gave nothing away. There was no further reaction from the Germans. They would have identified the battalion and brigade, but they already knew that the Australians were in the area and had not moved very far. Nevertheless, if they then identified Canadians in the same area a day or two later, it would be obvious that something special was building up. The decision was made to retain the 13th Brigade holding the front line until the last moment, spreading the troops out to cover the whole of the future Canadian front and releasing only the 4th and 12th Brigades to prepare for the 4th Division's attack; the 13th Brigade put all three battalions into the front line.[20] This left the 4th Division without a reserve brigade, so the 1st Division's 1st Brigade (Brigadier General I G Mackay), arriving in the area by train on 6 August, was placed under 4th Division orders as the reserve. The Canadians were also arriving, but went only as far as the support areas at this stage.

The 4th and 12th Brigade troops carried out their move over two nights, and by the early hours of 5 August were bivouacked in the area south of the Somme between Hamelet and Hamel, to the rear of the 3rd Division sector and in the general area of the gun-line. The march took some time, 'due to the enormous traffic on the roads, vehicles of all descriptions—tanks down to pack mules—moving forward towards the front'[21] (as at Hamel, such movement was only permitted at night). The bivouac area was mostly open fields, made more uncomfortable by periods of heavy rain. That day 4th Division HQ moved north-east from Cagny on the Avre to Fouilloy Chateau, just outside Corbie on the Somme. At night the artillery batteries moved into position, guns were camouflaged and ammunition was brought up. The selected emplacements had been carefully surveyed by engineers of the Topographical Section, fixing the exact locations to aid in firing from the map. Infantry brigade and battalion leaders continued refining their plans, using the conference technique from corps down to battalion. Officially the lower ranks had not yet been informed that they were about to take part in a major 'stunt,' but the traffic in the rear areas made it fairly obvious. Confidence was high, based on the impressive fighting reputations of the two Dominion corps, both having efficient commanders and staffs and aggressive, experienced troops. The four Canadian divisions were well rested and strong in numbers, and the five Australian divisions, although somewhat more war-weary and below full strength, had a hard core of tough soldiers eager to achieve something decisive. The Army commander, Sir Henry Rawlinson, was no military genius, but he was usually prepared to accept advice from his subordinate commanders and had a good chief of staff in Major General A A 'Archie' Montgomery. The weak link was III Corps. The Corps commander, Sir Richard Butler, ineffectual and in poor health, led a force in which at least two of his four divisions were

> anything but well equipped for their task ... Both divisions had been almost destroyed in the March retreat ... [both] had been rebuilt (cobbled together might be a more accurate description) with the rawest of conscripts brought hastily from Britain in the post-March panic ... The training of these new arrivals ... had at best been sketchy ...[22]

Monash was aware of those difficulties, and of the crucial role that III Corps had been given in guarding the Australian left flank from the other side of the Somme. He had pressed for the Australian Corps to also have responsibility for the north bank of the river, but on that point Rawlinson was unconvinced. The III Corps sector included the area where the 5th Division had recently captured the slice of territory near Morlancourt, just before being relieved by the British. The Germans were determined to recapture the ground and had brought up high-quality troops for the purpose, a force that the Australians, particularly the 4th Division, may have remembered from 1917—the 27th (Württemberg) Division, 'of Bullecourt fame, perhaps the toughest enemy ever met by the Australians.'[23] In the early morning of 6 August the Germans attacked and drove back the III Corps troops, at some points penetrating for more than a kilometre and getting among the British forward ammunition dumps. The Germans took 270 British prisoners and again there were fears that someone would let out the secret of the coming offensive under interrogation. Again, however, the Germans learned nothing. British counter-attacks regained much of the lost ground later in the day but the Germans retained a foothold inside the original front line. Those events confirmed Monash's fears about his left flank and he insisted that III Corps must counter-attack to regain all of the lost territory and restore their start line. A day of see-saw fighting on 7 August saw little progress made, but the offensive would go ahead regardless and III Corps had to modify its plans for the next day. Off-balance and depleted by casualties, the British were not in good shape to begin the battle.

The German attack of 6 August had been covered by a brief but intense artillery bombardment, some shells of which fell into the 4th Brigade's bivouac area south of the Somme. In the 15th Battalion's lines Lieutenant Colonel McSharry and his adjutant, Captain Tom Heffer, dashed into the shelled area to help a wounded man but were caught by another shell-burst. Both officers were badly wounded by splinters; Captain Heffer eventually recovered but Colonel McSharry died an hour later at the dressing station. Another shell killed the battalion intelligence officer, Lieutenant Walter Hines. Terence McSharry had commanded the 15th for most of its service on the Western Front, and his irascible but fair presence would be sorely missed. His funeral at the Corbie cemetery was held the same evening, attended by Major General Sinclair-MacLagan and most of the senior officers of the 4th Brigade, as well as Brigadier General Cannan of the 3rd Division, original CO of the 15th. Mass attendance by the troops was not permitted, to keep noticeable movement to a minimum, 'but in the evening small groups made their way to the cemetery to spend a few moments' contemplation of the grave ... of their much-loved Commanding Officer.'[24] Three key members of the 15th Battalion command group had been lost 48 hours before the unit's biggest battle of the war was to start. Major Burford Sampson, the second in command, took over as acting CO immediately, and two experienced officers were quickly brought in to fill the other places. Major Sampson, a 34 year old Tasmanian, was a sound, hard-working officer who had served with the 15th for most of its history, in Gallipoli and France.[25]

Most of the details of the Australian divisions' plans had been decided and documented, in a plethora of secret orders and instructions, by the evening of 6 August, and final preparations occupied that day and the next. In the 4th Division, the 12th Brigade, attacking on the right in the second phase, put the 45th and 46th Battalions, left to right, forward to attack the Red Line objective. Each battalion had six tanks and four Vickers guns allocated to it. The 48th Battalion, following 460 metres behind, was given the task of making the final jump to the Blue Line, using the predetermined tactics with weapon-carrying tanks. The 48th would rely on nine Mark V* tanks to carry forward 10 Vickers guns and 16 Lewis guns to be dropped at the Blue Line and hold the line while the rest of the Battalion came up. The 48th designated an officer to the overall command of the automatic weapons, one who already had an adventurous past with the battalion: Major 'Jack' Mott, 41 years old, 'a stern-faced Westerner with a vein of humour under a rough exterior.'[26] He had been wounded and captured at Bullecourt, then escaped from prison camp and made his way back to England, the first Australian officer to do so, and had recently returned to active duty with the 48th.

The 4th Brigade, on the left alongside the Somme, had a less straightforward task for its four battalions, with the river bends and villages as features of its objectives. The principle task of the 15th Battalion on the left of the brigade front was the capture of Cérisy village on the river where the first bend began, a short distance beyond the Green Line; the 15th was allocated three tanks. Next on the right, the 14th Battalion, also with three tanks, would go for Morcourt and the northern part of the spur beyond it near the tip of the Chipilly Peninsula, spreading out to its right to occupy the centre of the objective. The 4th Brigade's sector of the Red Line would be completed by the 13th Battalion, advancing the longest distance to cross the Morcourt valley and climb the spur on its far side; six tanks were assigned to the 13th. Each battalion would also have two Vickers guns in close support. The Blue Line would be taken by the 16th Battalion, coming up behind the three other units and like the 48th on the right (the 16th's 'daughter' from the Egypt expansion) also using the tactic of transporting Vickers and Lewis guns in Mark V* tanks. Captain Bill Lynas, an obvious choice for an enterprise of that nature, was put in charge of the tank-borne force.

At battalion and company level 6 August was taken up with issuing battle supplies and equipment—ammunition, grenades, flares, emergency rations. As Kipling pointed out, 'when it comes to slaughter, you will do your work on water,' and each man was issued a second water bottle. Extra water was supplied in cans, and each brigade had a wagon allocated to carry water tanks containing 1,300 litres, in addition to the units' water carts. To bring extra supplies up during the battle, the technique of using carrier tanks, that had proved so successful at Hamel, would be used again on a larger scale. Each of the 4th and 12th Brigades was allocated four supply or carrier tanks, with each tank loaded with coils of barbed wire and screw pickets for consolidation, Stokes mortar ammunition for the LTM batteries, extra grenades and rifle ammunition and more water in cans. During the night the carrier tanks of both the 4th and 5th Divisions moved forward to a concentration point in an orchard just north of Villers-Bretonneux.

7 August, the final day before Zero, was fine and warm after several days of wet weather, and the units worked on the final details of their preparations, while sporadic fighting continued north of the river in the III Corps sector. The 2nd and 3rd Divisions, undertaking the advance to the first objective, were each holding the front line with their reserve brigade, with their attacking brigades waiting towards the rear in the area between Villers-Bretonneux and Corbie. Interposed between there and the front line, the attacking brigades of the 4th and 5th Divisions were bivouacked close to their first assembly points for beginning their advance to the further objectives. In the evening, the machine gun crews allocated for the attack on the final objective met their Mark V* carrier tanks near Fouilloy and packed the weapons and ammunition into the vehicles. Zero hour was set as 4:20 am the next morning, and all was in readiness when the enemy again intervened to upset the arrangements. Late in the day a chance German shell hit one of the supply tanks parked in the orchard at Villers-Bretonneux and set it on fire. The smoke drew the attention of enemy artillery observers and shortly a number of guns were concentrating on the area. Within minutes most of the vehicles had been hit and were burning beyond control, their loads of trench mortar bombs, grenades and rifle ammunition exploding in the heat. By the time the inferno died down, 13 out of 16 vehicles and their contents had been destroyed—with only a few hours to go, the planned means of re-supplying the advancing units was gone. Everything had to be replaced and alternative transport found at the eleventh hour. There was no intention, however, of falling back on the old method of wasting a battalion or more to manhandle supplies forward. In a testing few hours, urgent action was taken under the direction of Colonel Dowse's 'A & Q' staff at Division and the brigade staff captains, firstly to collect and bring up replacement material from depots (fortunately there were few shortages of supply at this stage of the war), then to allocate transport and assemble and load it. Lieutenant Colonel Holdsworth, the Train CO, was summoned to Division HQ at 10 pm, informed of what had happened and requested to supply 20 General Service (GS) wagons and teams (10 per brigade) to carry the replacement engineer stores, to be picked up from dumps in both brigade areas. It was midnight before he got back to the Train camp to rouse his officers and drivers and make the arrangements, the wagons getting under way at 3 am. The DAC small-arms sections similarly organised wagons to follow up the advancing infantry with ammunition and grenades.

During the night the Canadian units moved into their allotted sector and relieved the three 13th Brigade battalions holding the line, the latter moving back to settle into the reserve area near Blangy-Tronville in the early hours. From midnight the 3rd and 2nd Division units attacking the first objective were on the move towards the Australian Corps front line, making their way past those of the 4th and 5th Divisions. Tanks began their movements also, the noise being covered as at Hamel by RAF aircraft flying over the enemy lines, on this occasion a huge Handley Page 0/400 twin-engine bomber. After the first phase troops had passed through, the 4th Division battalions moved from their concentration area to form up in the first assembly area nearby, and were in position between 2:30 and 3:30 am. While the infantry waited the mist rose and thickened just before sunrise. At 4:20 am the barrage opened with a deafening crash and the two leading divisions jumped off from the tapes, the troops groping their way through the mist as they tried to keep up with the advancing curtain of shell-bursts. Apart from the first few rounds of smoke, the 18-pounders were firing HE with standard fuzes, the howitzers, shooting 180 metres ahead, using instantaneous '106' fuzes—shrapnel had mostly been dispensed with for the creeping barrage.[27] The machine gun barrage joined in 10 minutes later, firing at specific areas beyond the field guns. Further ahead the heavy artillery sought out the German batteries and strong points. Two hours was allowed for the first wave of infantry and tanks to reach the Green Line, then a further two hours to secure and consolidate the line while the second wave of the assault moved up and the selected mobile artillery batteries pulled out of the barrage line to join the advance. The remaining guns continued firing a protective barrage ahead of the captured position.

The 4th Division troops waited in their first assembly position, amid the continuing roar from the nearby field artillery gun-line, for about an hour after Zero before moving off for the second position, a kilometre ahead of the old front line. The fog persisted, cutting visibility to 30 metres or less, and leaders navigated by compass to find the way. At around 7 am the 4th and 12th Brigades units were approaching their next assembly area and their allocated tanks were rumbling out of the mist to join up. Intelligence officers and scouts went ahead to tape out the jumping-off line, about 500 metres behind the Green Line, while columns of German prisoners began to hurry through from in front heading for the cages in the rear, an early indication of success in the first phase. Enemy artillery reaction was minimal and it appeared that the heavy artillery had already virtually eliminated the German guns as a factor in the battle, at least on the Australian Corps front. At the second assembly points the force sorted itself out and formed up with tanks in front and an infantry screen just behind them, followed by the main body of the infantry in platoon columns. The force then moved again on to the jumping-off tapes. Pack mules carried heavy gear, such as the machine gunners' weapons and ammunition, and battalion headquarters equipment, as far as the start line. Behind the artillery lines the horse teams and ammunition wagons of the selected mobile brigades began their move forward to pick up their guns from the barrage line. The final lift of the barrage from the first objective to the protective line took place at 'Z + 143'—6:43 am—when the mobile batteries fired three rounds of smoke to signal the lift then hooked up to their horse teams for the advance, while the remaining batteries maintained the protective barrage. At about the same time, the wagons of the Train and the DAC small-arms sections, replacing the destroyed carrier tanks, were loading engineer stores and ammunition to bring forward. Zero hour for the second phase was 8:20 am, four hours after the barrage had first opened. The 4th Division units reached the taped lines with time to spare despite the poor visibility, and were joined there by the supply wagons and shortly afterwards by the allocated artillery batteries. The normal duties of the Divisional Train personnel rarely took them close to the firing line, but on the right, the wagons of the 7th and 26th AASC Companies 'were in advance of our Field Artillery in action, who wanted to know what the hell the ASC was doing there,' as the Train CO was pleased to record in the unit diary.[28]

At 8 am the mist began to rise

> like a curtain, gradually disclosing a scene that will never be forgotten by any who saw it. The Somme valley came into view ... across the summit of the Villers-Bretonneux plateau ... were scattered parties of Australian infantry, some still digging, others looking out from their newly-dug trenches, others strolling or standing between the groups in the easy attitude by which Australians were recognisable on all their battlefields since the first sunrise at Anzac. Behind them was every arm of the Fourth Army's offensive in motion. First, in rear of the spur on which the line was digging, were the infantry of the 5th and 4th Divisions ... Beside them ... like elephants accompanying an Oriental army, were processions of the tanks, sixty machines in all, that were allotted for those divisions ... behind these ... came battery after battery of field and horse artillery, chains jingling, horses' heads and manes tossing ... with these ... rolled the ammunition waggons, water-waggons, and waggons with engineer stores hurriedly packed to replace those lost in the carrier tanks ... Parties of pioneers and engineers who had pushed out along the roads as soon as the advance started were still at work upon them while others were making trench-crossings for the artillery.[29]

A spectacular sight, and a situation which also allowed the supporting RAF aircraft the necessary visibility to join the battle in full force—but the lifting of the mist also disclosed the scene to the enemy, removing the advantage of concealment that the first phase troops had enjoyed.

At 8:20 the barrage ceased and the 4th Division moved off, crossing the Green Line where the 3rd Division troops were digging in, to play its part in what one unit later described as the Australians' 'biggest adventure since arriving in France.'[30] On the right of the Division front the 12th Brigade's two lead-off battalions, the 46th and 45th, both advanced through clearing mist on a two-company front behind their tanks. The 46th's left company met some resistance at Lena Wood, at the head of the Cérisy gully about 460 metres beyond the Green Line, but this was quickly overcome and the 46th captured five field guns there. The battalion had by now caught up to where the heavy artillery bombardment was falling, and had to pause for five minutes waiting for the guns to lengthen their range. Half-way to the Red Line, near Jean Wood, the 46th captured two more field guns, then brought up its support companies to take over the lead and continue the advance. The next landmark reached was Valerie Wood, a kilometre short of the Morcourt valley, where a German regimental headquarters staff surrendered. So far casualties in the assembly and advance had been minimal (among them was the CO, Colonel Corrigan, who had received a slight wound at some point but remained on duty), but as the unit approached the valley enemy resistance stiffened. The 46th came under heavy fire from German positions on the far side of the valley, in terraces on the slope and a brick building, as well as from two patches of woods, Hope on the left and Richmond on the right. The valley wall was too steep here for the 46th's tanks to negotiate, but they gave covering fire onto the German positions while the infantry advanced in section rushes. Company commander Lieutenant John Hall was killed here while directing his men; Lieutenant Arthur Kemp took charge of the company and led it into the enemy position.

The guns of the 16th RHA Brigade had reached the vicinity by now and were also firing at targets across the valley. Led brilliantly by Major Francis North, the 46th infantry pushed forward relentlessly, working their way past the woods and into the open on the far side of the valley as resistance collapsed and the Germans surrendered or ran. The 46th reached the Red Line objective, just beyond the valley, at about 10 am, well into the German back area—the brick building and a group of huts near it turned out to be a field hospital, where the Battalion found 'some very good lager.'[31] By that time, the tanks had found a way across the valley but had come under fire from a pair of enemy field guns near the Roman road. Three tanks were hit and disabled before two Lewis gunners, Lance Corporals William Collyer and Ralph Field, worked into position and opened fire on the gun crews, who abandoned their weapons and made off. On the left another party outflanked a German post holding up the advance of the next unit to the north, the 45th Battalion, and forced its surrender; it was probably in this part of the fighting that Private Richard Nicholls distinguished himself, charging a group of the enemy on his own. The 46th later reported having captured seven field guns and 250 prisoners that day, at a cost of 11 killed and 65 wounded.

The 45th Battalion, jumping off like the 46th with two companies in front and two in support behind the tanks and a screen of scouts, also had little trouble from the enemy in the first part of its advance. Several machine gun posts were encountered in patches of woods in the line of the advance, and these were dealt with by the tanks or by the infantry, the two leading companies skirting either side of the woods while the support companies moved through and mopped up. In this way the 45th passed Reginald Wood and Susan Wood, capturing prisoners and artillery pieces, and advanced steadily to the Morcourt Valley, where the only serious resistance was met. Here, as the 46th Battalion had found, the Germans were manning positions on the far side and appeared ready to put up a fight, and the steep slope halted the tanks. These eventually moved off to the right and joined the tanks with the 46th to find a crossing point. Here also British heavy artillery shells were still falling in the vicinity for the moment. As soon as the shelling lifted Lieutenant James Vincent, the unit intelligence officer, with his scout sergeant William Brown (one of the outstanding soldiers from the disbanded 47th Battalion) led five of their scouts across the valley and up to the enemy position. They found themselves in the German rear area, a complex of field canteens, stables, headquarters dugouts, workshops and stores. The scouts were armed with Lewis guns that were described as 'light' or 'stripped' (presumably with the cooling shroud removed) and with these weapons they shot up the disorganised enemy in the area while the main body of the 45th came up. Many Germans surrendered wholesale, 200 of them—an entire under-strength battalion—being taken prisoner in this area, while others ran for the rear. Vincent and Private Frederick Sellick then used grenades to attack and capture a machine gun post on the right that was firing at the 46th. The 45th was on the Red Line at 10:19 am. The fighting had been so one-sided that the battalion had not found it necessary to extend into line, keeping its formation of section columns throughout the advance. Overall the 45th had taken about 400 prisoners and captured 25 field guns and numerous machine guns and mortars: 'This huge haul of prisoners and guns must surely be a record for any battalion in one attack, especially when the small losses are taken into account,' wrote the unit historian;[32] the 45th reported four killed and 44 wounded in the operation. The 12th Brigade had reached its first objective on schedule and the two forward battalions now began digging in and consolidating on the Red Line, with the eight Vickers guns of the 13th MG Company positioned to strengthen the line. Behind, the 48th Battalion was moving up for the assault on the final objective. The captured position came under fire from two field guns near Proyart, which were taken on by some of the battalion Lewis guns and a Vickers; firing at long range, the machine guns forced the German teams to limber up and withdraw. More enemy shelling was coming in from well away to the left, near the river, and it was apparent that things had not gone quite so smoothly in that part of the battlefield.

The three forward battalions of the 4th Brigade had jumped off on time behind their allotted tanks. The 15th Battalion, on the left beside the river, had the shortest distance to its objective—the village of Cérisy-Gailly, the far side of the valley leading to it and the riverbank, 1,000 metres out from the Green Line. The 15th, coming under fire from machine guns in the village and along a sunken road to its south-east, opened out into line while the tanks went ahead. A machine gun firing from a house at the edge of the village was taken on by a tank, which rammed the building and brought the walls down on the gun and its crew. Other tanks led three companies of the 15th into and through the village, meeting little resistance and taking over 300 prisoners—'in the whole history of the Battalion no easier victory had been won.'[33] The situation was more difficult outside the village precincts, where the 15th's right-flank company faced the high ground to the south, on the far side of the valley. The enemy machine guns on that spur were still active, firing at the 14th Battalion next on the right as well as the 15th, and the terrain at first prevented the tanks from getting at them. Worse, enemy machine guns and artillery now opened close-range fire from positions on the northern riverbank. It was apparent that III Corps had not reached its objectives in that sector.

> This was not by any means the first occasion [on] which the 4th Brigade had suffered through the failure of troops on its left flank. By an extraordinary coincidence, exactly three years before (August 8, 1915), and almost at the same hour, the failure of the Suvla Bay force to support the attack of the 4th Brigade [on Hill 971, Gallipoli] resulted in the loss of the battle and extremely heavy casualties in the Brigade.[34]

The British had started well, easily taking Sailly-Laurette on the river, but had then been held up west of Chipilly, leaving the Germans in that area free to turn their attention to the Australians across the river to the south. At least two field guns in Célestins Wood, a kilometre away from Cérisy near the top of the Chipilly peninsula, others in nearby Malard Wood, and four more at closer range in Chipilly village proved particularly dangerous. The enemy gunners concentrated on the tanks at first, knocking out one that was trying to assist a platoon of the 15th assaulting the German position below the ridge south of Cérisy. A machine gun on

Chipilly then caught the infantry with a burst, killing the platoon commander, Lieutenant Bernard Shaw,

> ... very popular in the Battalion ... This young Tasmanian's service with the unit was dated from the early days of Quinn's Post [at Gallipoli] ... He had been in practically every engagement of importance in which the Battalion had taken part.[35]

For the moment the 15th's right company was pinned down in a sunken road running along the high ground, parallel to the enemy position. Here Lance Corporal Reginald Treloar, 24th MG Company, set up his Vickers gun and took on the German artillery positions at Chipilly, harassing the gun crews with his fire, while the enemy machine guns there were taken under fire by Lewis gunner Private James Pringle.

In the centre of the 4th Brigade's line the 14th Battalion advanced with three companies in front, each following a tank, and the fourth company in support. During the 14th's approach to the Green Line, persistent short shooting by a heavy howitzer caused a dozen casualties, including a wound to the RMO, Captain Hugh Trumble (nephew and namesake of the pre-war Test cricketer). The howitzer was firing 'at least 1,500 yards [1,370 metres] short of its target ... [this] would appear absolutely inexcusable.'[36] The first serious opposition was met when the 14th crossed the Cérisy valley and came under fire from the German machine guns posted on the reverse slope beyond the ridge crest; this was the position that was also holding up the right company of the 15th to the north. Here the Germans put up a determined resistance, and it was in this phase of the fighting that the 14th suffered most of its casualties. Among the 15 killed were company commander Lieutenant Harold Thompson, platoon commander Lieutenant Frederick Appleton, and two outstanding veteran NCOs, Corporals Jack Moriarty and Harry Lamprell; another company commander, Captain Norman Harris, was wounded. The German guns at Chipilly were a menace also, knocking out several more tanks in quick succession. Nevertheless the 14th continued to advance by short rushes, supported by its only remaining tank and one or two others that were thought to have moved across from the 13th Battalion on the right.[37] The tanks succeeded in outflanking the German position on its south, and with the infantry pressing forward enemy resistance collapsed. Some surrendered, running out with their hands up, while others broke for the rear. From the 15th Battalion's line, Captain William Domeney led a party around the northern flank of the position and secured it, with 12 abandoned machine guns and 50 prisoners in dugouts, thereby completing the occupation of the 15th's objectives. Enemy fire was still coming from the other side of the river, so the CO, Major Sampson, sent Lieutenant Eric Simon, the unit intelligence officer, across to find out what was holding up the British. Near Cérisy, Simon found a passable bridge, which a short time earlier had been the scene of a dramatic burst of action involving the divisional engineers.

A section of the 12th Field Company under Lieutenant Ralph Hunt had followed the infantry closely alongside the river, its task to ensure the bridging of the waterway (the canal and two branches of the river itself) in the vicinity of Cérisy. For construction of a new bridge if necessary, five pontoons on wagons were brought up behind them. The existing bridge over the canal north-west of the village appeared to be still usable, so Lieutenant Hunt with several of his men went across to inspect it and reconnoitre on the far side. The area should have been in British hands by then (about 10 am) but the party soon came under fire from an enemy machine gun 270 metres away. With his runner, Sapper George Hook, Hunt pressed on to check the two small bridges over the river branches, but Hook was hit by a machine gun bullet that broke his leg. Hunt carried him back, still under fire, but before they could reach cover Hook was hit again, badly. Hunt got him to assistance, then returned to the north bank and organised his men to repair the shell-damaged roadway leading to the canal bridge. The enemy machine gun nest was still active, its fire deterring the approach of a British unit to the west as well as shooting at the engineer party. Sapper Arthur Dean spotted the German position and decided to take it on. He and Sapper William Campbell charged the guns across an open field several hundred metres wide, with such obvious determination that the Germans were intimidated and raised a white flag. As the two sappers reached the enemy post, a nearby group of German infantry, 30 or 40 strong, took the opportunity to surrender also. 'The two men then beckoned to the English troops who were sitting down on top of the rise and they came down and took charge of the prisoners.'[38] The engineers retained the two machine guns taken with the post, one of which was a captured Lewis gun. It was about this time that Lieutenant Simon, the 15th Battalion IO, arrived on the scene, having noticed on the way 'the kit of an engineer on the bridge and some blood'[39]—Sapper Hook had discarded his webbing equipment and jacket to make it easier for Lieutenant Hunt to carry him. Unfortunately Hook did not survive his wounds.[40] The British troops were collecting the prisoners ('more Tommies there than prisoners'). They had got that far, thanks to the two engineers, but they should have been beyond Chipilly by now. Simon pointed out to the officers present that his men were being killed by the fire from Chipilly, but his urging did not seem to have much effect. After returning to the south bank he 'saw the Tommies slowly going forward. There was no firing. But presently he saw them slowly going back ... The men saw the Germans clear in one direction while the Tommies cleared in the other direction.'[41] For the moment the 4th Division was left to its own devices in dealing with the enemy on the north bank. After this incident, Lieutenant Hunt conducted the pontoon train to the water's edge at Cérisy, working the awkward wagons through narrow village streets under fire from Chipilly, a risk that turned out to be unnecessary, as the German bridge there proved to be intact.[42]

The 14th Battalion had further to go after passing Cérisy. Its final objective lay on the high ground ('Red Line Spur') beyond Morcourt, the next village on the river bend, opposite the tip of the peninsula. The 14th's left companies were slowed down by the fire from the north bank, and also by machine guns positioned on Red Line Spur south-east of Morcourt. Those were taken on by the artillery of the 39th Battery (10th AFA), which was working with the 16th Battalion, advancing as the reserve to tackle the final objective. Seeing that the

14th Battalion ahead was held up, the battery commander, Captain Alan Smith, sent a section of two 18-pounders galloping to the crest of the Morcourt ridge, from where they fired 100 rounds at a range of 1,200 metres and silenced the machine guns. The 14th was still taking fire from the far side of the river, and more of the 16th Battalion's support weapons were diverted to assist, four Vickers guns of the 4th MG Company under Sergeant Henry Tyler coming up on limbers and opening fire on the enemy field guns. Their fire temporarily silenced some of the guns, scattering the crews, before the machine gun teams rejoined to resume their assigned task, less six casualties to German retaliation.. The 14th Battalion CO, Lieutenant Colonel Crowther, who was up with the firing line, realised that his southern flank was not as exposed to the enemy fire and kept it moving forward. 'A' Company on the right was protected by the shoulder of the hill, and its commander, Captain Norman Wilson, took the chance of assaulting Morcourt without waiting for support. The company, which numbered only 65 men at the start,[43] got into position with no casualties and entered the village from the south. 'A' Company was shortly joined by the support company, 'D', which followed through to mop up. The infantrymen were led in by the 14th's one remaining tank, which was handled to great effect by the British NCO in command, Sergeant A J Mitchell.[44] The Germans in the village did not resist for long, demoralised by the tank and the aggressive riflemen, and in time about 300 prisoners were collected. Morcourt was being used as a headquarters for several German units, and the area commander got away in a car; two of his officers trying to escape on horseback were not so fortunate, killed by the deadly marksmanship of Private Joe Marmo.[45] With the village secured Captain Wilson sent back a message by pigeon: 'Am through Morcourt. 100 prisoners. Casualties nil. Bloody dry work.' The message was meant for Battalion HQ, but the bird flew to the Division loft instead, giving an early notice of success to that command level.[46] The right flank companies then worked their way through and beyond Morcourt to dig in on the Red Line, 500 metres east of the village along the spur; Colonel Crowther moved his HQ up to Morcourt a little later.

On the right of the 4th Brigade's sector, the 13th Battalion advanced over a narrower front but a longer distance than the other first-line units. 'D' Company of the Pioneer Battalion (less one platoon working with the mobile artillery) was attached as extra infantry to the 13th, which lined up on a 550-metre front with two companies forming the first line, one across the whole front as the second line, and a third line with the fourth rifle company and the Pioneer company alongside. The infantry companies' strength averaged only 95 men each, organised into three platoons, with the Pioneer company being slightly larger. In the first part of the 13th's advance, enemy resistance was minimal, only a few isolated machine gun posts that were quickly eliminated. One opened fire from a concealed position as the Battalion was crossing a waist-high wheatfield. While his colleagues dropped into cover, Sergeant Gerald Sexton, leading a Lewis gun section, remained standing in full view while searching for the enemy gun. Spotting the muzzle flashes, he emptied a magazine into the location and silenced the gun;

he later knocked out three more. Other exponents of the Lewis gun, Corporal Edward Bourke, Sergeant John Prescott and Lance Corporal Algernon Williams, also successfully tackled enemy machine guns during the advance, as did Lance Corporal Cleave Heydon of the Pioneers; the Lewis gunners were firing from the hip, using shoulder slings. With the 14th Battalion held up at Morcourt for the moment, the 13th got ahead, opening up a gap on the left that was filled by Captain Robert McKillop's company, moving across from its place in the third line of the Battalion's formation. So far the pickings had been slim for the inveterate souvenir hunters in the Battalion, but once into the Morcourt valley the 13th was in the German back area, a complex of camps, transport parks, canteens and messes; the unwarlike enemy troops in this area were not inclined to fight, most emerging with hands raised. These were rounded up and sent into captivity, escorted by the two mounted Light Horse troopers working with the 13th—it was reported that one batch numbered 387.[47] There was plenty of loot to be souvenired, 'and the spirits of the troops rose considerably.'[48]

Of more practical use, a number of German wagons and horse teams were pressed into service to bring up stores, and shortly for carrying wounded back—so far the 13th had suffered scarcely any casualties, but that situation changed abruptly. After a brief ransacking of the enemy camp, the 13th re-formed and resumed serious business. Advancing up to the crest of Red Line Ridge, the far side of the valley, they suddenly ran into heavy small-arms fire from in front and shelling from the German guns near Chipilly. The 13th suffered 60 casualties here in a few minutes, mostly inflicted by the hostile artillery. Of these, 13 were killed including two company commanders, Captains John Geary and Ken Pattrick; the Pioneer company commander, Captain Ronald Bingle, was mortally wounded, among the company's losses of eight killed and 18 wounded.[49] The shelling disconcerted part of the 13th, but they were rallied by CSM William 'Jerry' Oswald, who set the example and led the troops up the slope to the objective line on the crest. A Lewis gun team was put out of action by a German machine gun firing from in front, but Lieutenant Leslie Cleland picked up the Lewis and opened fire, wiping out the enemy gun crew. Lieutenant Leo Waterford of the 4th LTM Battery, in charge of two Stokes mortars working with the 13th, used one to knock out a machine gun that was firing from a well-covered position, and was then wounded while assisting one of his men who had been hit by a sniper. Lance Corporal Murray O'Connor, who had already eliminated two other enemy guns with his mortar, brought Waterford and two other wounded men to cover. The Battery later reported that these two mortars had fired 40 rounds during the advance, destroying three machine guns and causing another three gun crews to surrender.[50]

By about 10 am the Battalion was on the Red Line and had begun digging in to consolidate, while engaging a few enemy posts beyond. Private Charles Finch, Number Two on a Lewis gun and the only unwounded member of his team, carried the gun, its extra ammunition drums and spare parts bag to a position covering the consolidation. When an enemy machine gun opened up on the digging troops Finch replied with the Lewis, forcing the enemy crew to move to another position, where they were protected from his fire.

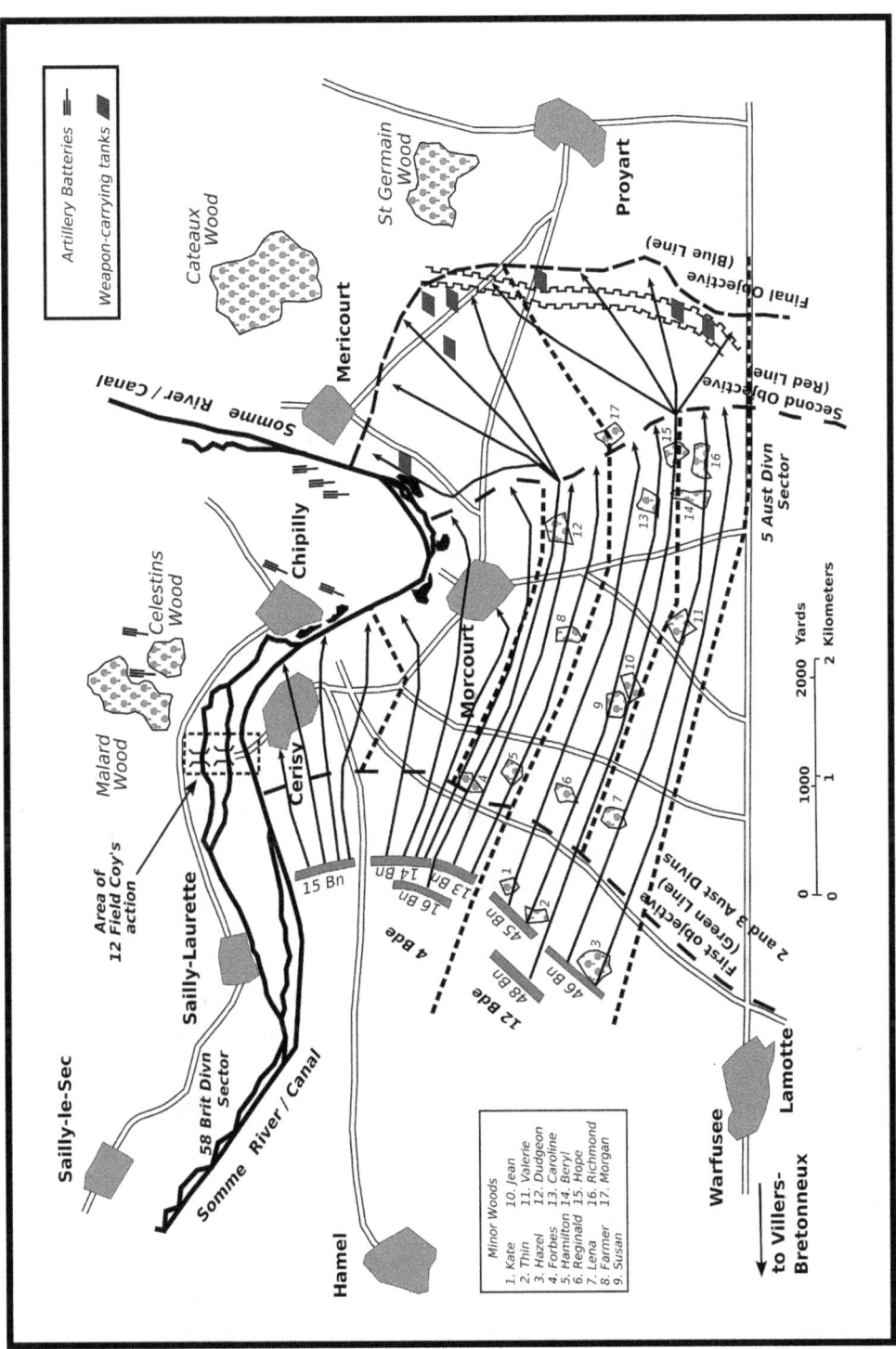

Battle of Amiens, 8 August 1918, 4th Division sector.

Finch instead charged the gun and tossed a grenade that killed two of the enemy crew, then brought in the five survivors as prisoners, carrying their own gun. On the Red Line the 13th was in touch with the 14th on the left and the 45th on the right; the latter unit reported reaching the objective at 10:19 am, and assumed they were the first unit to do so.[51] All of the 4th Division's first-line battalions reported themselves on the Red Line at around the same time, between 10 and 10:30, and at 10:40 the 5th Division's left-flank battalion (the 30th) arrived on the Red Line, in touch with the 46th on the 4th Division's right. On the 4th Division front, barbed wire and pickets for the defences were brought up by the wagon drivers of the Divisional Train, covering a round trip of 30 miles [48 kilometres] from their base and back 'without a scratch, but covered with honor and dust ... [as did] the good horses.'[52] Two groups of wagons from the DAC small-arms section did similar duty, carrying rifle ammunition and grenades for the 4th and 12th Brigade battalions, dumping loads near Cérisy and Morcourt and behind the Red Line in both brigade sectors (the DAC wagons made a second trip that night when the objectives had been secured).[53] The fighting from this stage would now involve the assault on the final objective, the Blue Line, and the continuing struggle with the enemy troops on the Chipilly heights.

The mobile field artillery, moving up close behind the infantry advance, took up successive positions to lay down supporting fire, the horse teams unhooking and galloping away to find cover and wait to be called forward for their battery's next change of position. In the early stages of the 4th Division's advance, the guns were in action covering infantry attacking the enemy positions on the spurs and gullies running across the front. As the morning went on the 10th AFA Brigade and some batteries of the 11th, on the left in the 4th Infantry Brigade's zone, came into range of the German guns north of the Somme. An extraordinary duel began, fought across the river by opposing guns firing at targets under direct observation ('over open sights'). The 4th Division guns were at first restricted by orders that they could only fire on their own side of the river. The situation was exacerbated by British reports coming in to both infantry and artillery HQs stating that the III Corps objectives had been taken. To the officers in the field that was manifestly untrue, and Captain Alan Smith, the 39th Battery OC, requested permission from the CRA to open fire; this was withheld by General Burgess, because of the false reports, but Smith persisted and the CRA finally agreed that he could fire if he could see the enemy gun-flashes. Other artillery officers turned some of their guns on to the Chipilly heights without waiting for permission (in his report, General Burgess endorsed 'their action in departing from these orders' and acknowledged 'their initiative and quick decision at a very critical period, and particularly the bold and decisive action of the battery commanders'[54]).

The gunners of the 10th AFA Brigade batteries found themselves having to divide their attention between their primary task of direct support for the infantry in front, and defending themselves against the German presence on the north bank. Each of the three infantry battalions in the 4th Brigade's first line had a two-gun section working directly with it

—the 13th Battalion with a 37th Battery section, the 14th with the 38th Battery, and the 15th with the 110th Howitzer Battery—with each battery's remaining two sections co-operating more flexibly with the advancing infantry; the full 39th Battery was allocated to operate with the 16th Battalion in attacking the final objective. The 15th Battalion having captured Cérisy village with minimal opposition, its section of the 110th Battery was released and rejoined the rest of the battery on the high ground south of Cérisy. At 9:30 am the battery was shooting at enemy movement east of the Red Line when it came under rapid fire from two of the German howitzers near Célestins Wood. Five of the 110th's pieces were quickly withdrawn to cover, from where they resumed firing infantry support, switching to the ground beyond the Blue Line. The sixth howitzer could not be moved at first. Lieutenant Frederick Chapman took a volunteer crew out to it and engaged the enemy battery, but they could only get off two rounds before the Germans, who already had the range, landed several salvos on the spot. Chapman was mortally wounded and the attempt was abandoned. Overall, the brief action had cost the battery three dead and 13 wounded, as well as 10 horses killed and 12 wounded; three ammunition wagons were also destroyed.[55]

At about the same time the 38th Battery, south of Cérisy in support of the 14th Battalion, spotted another pair of German guns, those that had just knocked out the tanks assisting the 14th and 15th Battalions and were now shelling the infantry. The battery commander, Major Harold de Low, had one of his sections (two guns) up with the 14th infantry, another section below the Cérisy spur and the third on the spur. The latter section, under Lieutenant Arthur Lintott, took the German position under fire only to be hit by the enemy's accurate reply. The crew of one gun were all killed or wounded, including Lintott himself, who died the next day.[56] The enemy fire was too hot to stand, forcing the survivors of the section to seek cover. The section on lower ground had meanwhile retired to a position where its shots could clear the crest of the spur. After a few rounds, however, those guns were also silenced by the German gunners' response. Some time later, Major de Low managed to get two guns recovered and repositioned in trees near the river, from where they again fired on the enemy battery: 'our first shell landing under the muzzle of one of the [German] guns. In this way they were silenced but not before they had done considerable damage.'[57] Further south, Lieutenant Clive Smith's section of the 37th Battery advanced with the 13th Battalion, taking the surrender of two enemy machine gun crews overlooked by the infantry on the way to the Red Line. There the Battalion was shelled by the north bank guns, which were then taken on by the 18-pounders, firing almost directly north at the pair of enemy guns east of Chipilly village. Lieutenant Smith later reported that his section had 'materially assisted in silencing'[58] the German battery. The main body of the 37th Battery engaged likely areas of enemy troop concentrations through the morning ('spraying shells around the countryside'[59]), changing position several times for concealment from the enemy observers on the north bank heights.

The 39th Battery, working with the 16th Battalion for the assault on the Blue Line, had been in action during the earlier stage of the advance, clearing the enemy machine guns off Red Line Spur. Following that action the Battery fired at targets near the 16th Battalion's objective south-east of Méricourt-sur-Somme, the next village around the river bend. Like the other batteries, the 39th was shelled by the enemy guns across the river. Its wagon lines were hit also, and it was there that the 10th AFA Brigade's brave young veterinary officer, Major Cyril Seelenmeyer, lost his life. In previous actions, notably in the Ypres sector, he had ignored shellfire to attend to wounded horses, and had recently been decorated with the MC for his gallantry. Now he was again treating a horse under fire when his luck ran out. With one leg shattered by a shell splinter, he died before reaching the dressing station, the second 4th Division AAVC officer to fall in action: 'our veterinary officer since Egypt days ... his loss is greatly felt by all.'[60] The 39th continued its task of covering the 16th Battalion's advance, as well as turning a section on the German battery in Malard Wood, once Captain Smith had convinced Artillery HQ that the enemy was still in possession of the north bank.

In the meantime the 11th AFA Brigade, coming up in support, had advanced into the battle area. The 41st, 42nd and 43rd Batteries moved from the barrage line to Susan Wood near the Cérisy valley, from where they covered the 12th Brigade infantry, backing up the 16th RHA Brigade in that task. The latter unit contained the famous 'Chestnut Troop' ('A' Battery), the senior battery of the Royal Artillery. The 111th Howitzer Battery's move towards the concentration area was closer to the river, via the Hamel-Cérisy road, where the battery was observed and fired on by the Malard Wood guns, those that had been picking off the tanks at Cérisy. The battery commander, Captain William Cox, got a message to Brigade HQ asking permission to depart from orders and return fire to the far side of the river. This was not granted, but the enemy soon found the range and a shell hit one of the horse teams, killing a driver[61] and several horses. Captain Cox took the responsibility himself and turned a section onto the German battery, later reporting that his howitzers had scored several direct hits and silenced the hostile guns.[62]

So far the problem of the north bank had been responded to by individual initiative. As well as the mobile artillery brigades diverting some of their weapons from direct infantry support to targets on the Chipilly heights, some machine gunners and battalion Lewis gunners also fired on the German batteries, and on machine gun posts closer to the river-bank. The two 12th Field Company engineers had also eliminated the post across the river from Cérisy. There were thought to have been 16 German artillery pieces (77 mm 'Whizzbangs' and '4.2' howitzers) around Chipilly firing into the 4th Division's left flank at different times.[63] A few of these were knocked out through the morning by shells from the 10th and 11th AFA Brigade batteries, and Vickers and Lewis gunners shooting at the gun positions caused casualties among the crews and drove them away from their weapons, even if only temporarily. Shortly after midday the III Corps troops edged forward enough to force the westernmost guns in Malard Wood, and later in Célestins Wood, to pull out. Other batteries along the eastern arm of the river bend would seriously interfere with the 16th Battalion's advance in the next phase of the battle, causing casualties to men and

The Monash Touch

tanks and forcing its left company to take up a position short of the intended objective. Thereafter their effectiveness declined, but on a day when most of the German front collapsed (General Ludendorff famously called it the 'black day of the German Army') their artillerymen in the Chipilly area could hold their heads high, as some of their foes acknowledged. Charles Bean, who was observing the battle from close up, described how the German gunners were

> placing their shells most beautifully around four of our guns... German shells in pairs bracketing them two or three times a minute. [Our] gunners had been driven from their guns ... The shooting was absolutely deadly—and very quick.[64]

The 16th Battalion's Captain Lynas noted in his report the difficulties caused by 'a few good brave [German] 77 artillerymen.'[65] In mid-afternoon some action was initiated from the higher command level, when it was at last accepted that the objectives north of the river were still in German hands; the British heavy artillery opened a bombardment on Chipilly village, turning it into '...a volcano of red dust.'[66] The German garrison was observed running east from the village to cover behind high ground, but there was no apparent move from the British infantry.

With the Red Line taken and in the process of consolidation, the two battalions designated to the Blue Line resumed their approach to their jumping-off lines. In the 12th Brigade sector on the right of the 4th Division zone, the 48th Battalion followed behind the 45th and 46th, pausing several times to maintain spacing and allow their weapon-carrying tanks to join up. On reaching the high ground forming the western side of the Morcourt valley, the 48th came under machine gun fire from the next ridge. Battalion HQ was up with the companies, and the CO, Lieutenant Colonel Perry, was slightly wounded there, hit by a bullet in the left arm. He remained on duty, as did RSM Arthur Baker, who was hit twice.[67] Shepherded by the wounded RSM, the 48th spread out and ran over the crest into the protection of the valley (called 'Richmond Wood Gully' in that area), where the companies reformed for the final stage with the right flank on the Roman road, three companies in front and the fourth with Battalion HQ behind. Here the troops paused for 15 minutes to catch their breath and wait for the carrier tanks, while the 45th Battalion was securing the Red Line ahead. At the initial starting point eight of the 48th's nine allotted Mark V* tanks had joined up and moved off with the infantry on time. The other had broken down and its machine gun crews continued forward on foot, manhandling their weapons. Before long, the gun crews in the other tanks had found the fumes and stifling heat inside to be too much and got out to walk alongside. Heavier than the standard tanks, the carriers were slower and had some trouble finding practicable routes over the terrain. By the time the infantry reached Richmond Wood all but three of the machines had fallen by the wayside for one reason or another.[68] Colonel Perry decided not to wait any longer for the others, and at 10:55 am the 48th jumped off, crossing the Red Line and advancing in skirmishing order over open grain-fields. The objective incorporated the old trenches that had once formed the outer line of the French defences in front of Amiens, at a distance from the start line that varied from 800 metres on the right to 1,600 metres on the left. The frontage at the objective was about twice that of the start line, requiring the battalion to fan out as it advanced (the left and centre companies, with a greater distance to cover, probably jumped off before the right[69]). The three remaining tanks, directed by Major Mott, went forward to cover the advance, two with the right flank company and one with the left. On the right opposition was negligible, probably due to the presence of the tanks, and the company's objective was secured by noon with a loss of only 10 casualties.[70] The tanks dropped their machine gun garrisons then retired, one of them later returning with a gun crew that had been advancing on foot.

The other companies faced more difficult tasks. Lieutenant Roy Potts's 'C' company in the centre, without assistance from tanks or artillery, advanced in short rushes, under long-range machine gun fire from the direction of Proyart to the north-east. Making use of every scrap of cover, the company reached a sunken road half-way to its objective and paused to re-organise. When the advance was resumed, the company encountered a machine nest hidden in a copse near the old trench line, on the final objective. Heavy fire from that position forced the company to take cover again, but Potts directed parties that worked around the flanks and along the trench; led by Sergeants Richard Kealy and George Seal, the troops attacked the post with grenades and Lewis guns. The Germans were quickly induced to surrender, 'C' Company collecting 50 prisoners and four machine guns and establishing themselves on the objective. The left company, 'D' under Captain William Caldwell, had the support of one weapon-carrying tank, which appears to have reached the objective line slightly ahead of the infantry, as was the intention of the original plan. Firing its 6-pounder guns, the tank (named 'Orpheus') penetrated beyond the objective line and came under heavy fire from an enemy concentration. The tank turned back to drop its machine gun teams, two Vickers guns of the 12th MG Company under Lieutenant Claude King, in a less-exposed area, but was hit by a shell and caught fire. The surviving tank crew and machine gunners baled out, saving one machine gun and its ammunition.[71] A squad of German infantry tried to rush the survivors, but Corporals Daniel Pritchard and George Prentice got the Vickers set up in the nick of time and cut down the enemy party at close range. A few minutes later Lieutenant King was killed by a sniper while the troops were pulling back to the objective line.[72]

The gunners were soon joined by the leading platoons of 'D' Company, advancing over ground swept by fire from enemy machine guns. The company had taken losses approaching the German outpost trench, and the advance could have been stopped there had not 'the enemy 'dropped his bundle' as we neared the objective ... Much to our surprise the Germans suddenly stood up with their hands raised ... we were on them in quick time.'[73] The troops were in no mood to show mercy, but Captain Caldwell kept them under control, and the prisoners were packed off for the rear. It was another 180 metres to the main trench at the final objective, an area also covered by enemy machine guns. These could not prevent the leading two platoons from rushing the position on the right; Private Rupert Barrie was first into the trench, tossing grenades into dugouts as he moved along it. He was soon joined by the rest of the two platoons, and the Germans in that part of the line put up no more fight. The machine guns had pinned down the other two platoons and hit a number of men, but several Lewis gunners then crept forward under cover and suppressed much of the enemy fire. With the assistance of a platoon coming forward from 'B' Company in reserve, the held-up troops went ahead again and got into their section of the enemy trench. A stubborn German machine gun in a commanding position still held out, however, and was causing difficulties for the men trying to complete the capture of the trench. The Battalion adjutant, Captain David Twining, having come forward from HQ, collected a few men and worked around behind the enemy post, charging and capturing gun and gunners.[74] By 12:10 pm as Colonel Perry reported, all of the 48th's objective line had been reached, its front extending 270 metres into the 16th Battalion's sector on the left. At about the same time, Captain Allan Taylor, OC 12th MG Company, brought up six supporting Vickers guns at the gallop on horse-drawn limbers, in time to set up and harass the retreating enemy. Infantry patrols went out in front to eliminate a few strong-points still holding out, while the machine guns from the delayed tanks were brought up and positioned to cover the new front. Four Stokes mortars of the 12th LTM Battery arrived also and were emplaced, and by 2:30 pm the position had been consolidated and secured against counter-attack.[75]

On the left of the Division front, the 4th Brigade had assigned its 16th Battalion ('parent' of the 48th) to the final stage of the advance, using eight Mark V* tanks as weapons carriers with a ninth in reserve and carrying the Battalion HQ details. By the time the 16th reached the Green Line four of its tanks had already dropped out with mechanical trouble, but the Battalion pushed on accompanied by the remaining tanks with their machine guns from the 4th MG Company, the supporting field artillery of the 39th Battery, and a further six Vickers guns on limbers. During the advance to the final jumping-off position on the Red Line, those machine guns and two of the 18-pounders had been temporarily diverted to fire on enemy positions that were holding up the 14th Battalion. The machine gunners from the broken-down tanks collected their weapons and equipment, and set out to manhandle them forward to reach the firing line. Shortly after 10 am the 16th infantry reached the Morcourt valley just behind the Red Line ridge, where they came to the attention of the German guns across the river and began to incur casualties; Second Lieutenant William Rogers, decorated and commissioned following Hamel a month earlier, was killed there. In this area the four remaining advance-guard tanks soon joined up, with Captain Lynas, in charge of that element, travelling in one together with Lieutenant Herbert Allan, 4th MG Company, commanding its complement of machine gunners. The weapon teams in the other three tanks were commanded by 16th Battalion officers Lieutenants Basil Minchin and Charles Garratt,[76] and Lieutenant Tom Lydster, 4th MG Company. The vehicles had been forced by the terrain to take a roundabout route through Morcourt village. Up to then the gun teams had been walking alongside, but enemy fire around Morcourt forced them to crowd into the hot, fume-filled interiors of the tanks. With the tanks in position, Captain Lynas gave the order to advance at 10:25, under the impression that the infantry was also ready—that was not the case, and it was another half an hour before the infantry jumped off.

The 16th Battalion's task involved passing through the 14th and 13th on the Red Line then swinging north-east, with its left on the Somme bank, and advancing up the eastern arm of the Chipilly bend. The objective line for the 16th ran past the outskirts of Méricourt and along the old Amiens outer defence line. With the Chipilly peninsula still in German hands, the further the movement went the more exposed the battalion would be to fire from the left flank and from the rear. As well as the guns near Chipilly village, as the Battalion's advance guard swung forward it came within easy range of several guns close to the riverbank on the eastern side of the peninsula. These opened fire on the four tanks as they came over the ridge, but no serious damage was done before they got down to the lower ground and were screened from sight. Here the tanks set about clearing parties of Germans in the valley below the objective—70 surrendered to Lynas's tank, which turned and hustled the prisoners back to the Red Line where they were handed over to 13th Battalion troops. The tanks resumed the advance, sticking to the low ground wherever possible, first turning north towards the river and then following the Morcourt—Méricourt road. They soon ran out of cover, and were faced with moving across open ground and up the slope in front of the objective. The German guns opened up again as the tanks came back into sight. Lieutenant Garratt's tank, still in the road, was hit by a German '77' that its enterprising crew had transported across the river to get a clear shot.[77] The tank caught fire and the occupants baled out, some wounded or burnt, but Garratt's gun crews rescued their weapons and pressed on under cover of woods.

The other three tanks were all hit and damaged while climbing the hill. That carrying Lieutenant Minchin succeeded in dropping its weapon teams on the objective before being hit. Lieutenant Lydster's tank was set on fire short of the line with many of the occupants wounded. Four Lewis gunners got out unhurt with their gun and were led forward by Private John Hagan, who had taken charge when their NCO was killed. Hagan got the gun set up in a shell hole and opened covering fire as the infantry came up, then went back to the burning tank and helped to extricate the wounded. The tank carrying Captain Lynas was hit on the way up the slope by a shell that failed to explode but knocked metal splinters off the inside of the tank, killing two of the occupants and wounding others, including the MG officer, Lieutenant Allan. The shell also broke the exhaust pipe, letting choking fumes directly into the cabin. Lynas directed the tank crew to drive along the line and drop off gun crews at intervals, but another hit forced the tank to retire to cover behind a bank. Here Lynas found that everyone inside was in a fainting state from the heat and fumes, including those who should have got out with their weapons. He was barely conscious himself, but managed to get out of the tank before collapsing. By that time, the leading elements of the infantry had arrived, and some of them helped the other occupants outside into the air. Most of the men were incapable of movement for at least an hour, but it appears that two 16th Battalion Lewis gunners, Privates Clarence Buckenara and Herbert Lyon, recovered fairly quickly and got their gun forward in time to get into the fighting on the objective line.[78] Other automatic weapons arrived at the line later, carried forward from tanks that had broken down or been hit. Corporal Hugh Hamill, 4th MG Company, brought a Vickers gun up from well in the rear, catching lifts for the weapon and equipment from any passing vehicle heading towards the front. Sergeant Charles Disney's Vickers team, walking all the way outside their tank because of the conditions inside, helped the infantry to mop up several overlooked enemy posts on the way. At the firing line, Disney joined Sergeant Raymond Sinclair, who had brought up two guns from one of the tanks knocked out near the riverbank (probably Lieutenant Garratt's[79]), in setting up their guns to cover the 16th's left flank.

For all of their determination, circumstances had prevented the tankers and the gun teams from establishing the planned forward strong points at the Blue Line ahead of the infantry. The main body of the 16th Battalion infantry jumped off from the Red Line at 11 am, the advance beginning with three companies abreast forming the first line and the fourth close behind in support. It was soon apparent that a gap existed on the right, where the 16th should have been in touch with the 48th Battalion, so 'B' Company, in support, moved up onto the right flank. With the 48th extending its left, contact was made during the advance. The troops were met by frontal machine gun fire from Méricourt village, Cateaux Wood to its east, and St Germain Wood further south, as well as the continuing fire from the enemy artillery and machine guns on Chipilly coming from the left and the rear. The 39th Battery guns gave support by firing on Cateaux Wood and the ground south-east of Méricourt, as well as giving some attention to the Chipilly guns, but the infantrymen mainly relied on their own resources for close covering fire as they moved forward. 'D' Company on the left, commanded by Lieutenant Eric Piercy in the absence of Captain Lynas with the tanks, had to advance within close range of the north-bank guns. Piercy organised a few men, presumably with Lewis guns, to form a flank guard in the swampy flats on the south bank and fire on the enemy battery. The rest of the company advanced in short rushes, reaching its objective without much direct opposition from their own side of the river, although Piercy was badly wounded while supervising consolidation. The other three companies, assaulting the trenches of the old defensive line on the right and centre, met determined resistance at first. Under fire from front, flank and rear, the troops advanced in loose skirmishing order, using fire and movement tactics to get close to the enemy positions. The centre-left company, 'C' under Lieutenant Harry Smith, encountered several machine gun posts, Smith personally knocking out one of these. Another was eliminated by Sergeant William Murray, leading a platoon in this operation. Eventually, continuing heavy fire from further ahead and from Chipilly forced the company to ground, Smith establishing a line in some old gun-pits short of the final objective.

'A' Company (Captain Daniel Aarons) and 'B' Company (Captain Charles Ahearn) attacked on the right. Ahearn was badly wounded in the final stages of the advance, but the two companies made a rush at 12:30 pm that took them into the enemy trench. After a sharp burst of heavy fighting in which CSM Douglas Phillips and Sergeants Harry Hutchings, William Sweetnam and William Marshall[80] were prominent, enemy resistance ceased and the 16th troops held the position, capturing 200 prisoners and a dozen machine guns. Towards the centre and left the 16th was thinly spread in a few small posts. These faced an immediate counter-attack by a scratch German force that emerged from Méricourt, 200 strong but not well organised. The attack was easily beaten off, more than 50 of the enemy surrendering once they came to close quarters. Captain Aarons, senior officer in the field, assessed the situation as he worked his way north along the captured trench. Although the 16th was in places somewhat short of the entire objective and had not reached Méricourt, the line achieved was reasonably secure apart from the exposure of the left flank to the continuing fire from across the river. Aarons organised consolidation of the line, pulling back some outposts and adjusting the left to a line running west-east from the river to the Méricourt-Proyart road, with the right positioned along the road to the south-east and linked with the left of the 48th Battalion. The line was further secured by the arrival of two tanks, repaired after breaking down, with more machine gun crews. Several Vickers crews on the river flank kept the enemy artillery positions on the north bank under fire.

The 16th had lost 120 casualties in the advance, a third of its battle strength, and was holding the whole 2,000-metre front of the 4th Brigade, so later in the afternoon the 13th Battalion was moved up from the Red Line to take over the right of the new front line (that deployment had been anticipated before the battle, but not so early[81]). The 16th closed up to its left, while the 14th Battalion extended to cover the 4th Brigade's portion of the Red Line, which now formed the support line. Towards evening the 1st Brigade, temporarily under the 4th Division as its reserve, moved to protect the left flank by establishing an outpost line along the river from Morcourt to Bouzencourt, west of Sailly-Laurette. The 2nd Battalion took over part of the Morcourt frontage from the 14th, allowing that unit to adjust its deployment on the Red Line. The 1st Battalion relieved the 15th in the Cérisy area across the river from Chipilly village, with the 15th moving behind the Red Line as 4th Brigade reserve. The 3rd Battalion occupied the canal bank west to Bouzencourt to form the left of the flank guard. Twelve machine guns from the 13th and 24th MG Companies, attached to the 1st Brigade in reserve after taking part in the opening barrage, were also moved up with the infantry and took position along the bank between Cérisy and Morcourt.

That night the 12th Brigade redeployed similarly in its sector, with the 45th Battalion moving up to take over the right half of the Blue Line from the 48th, which closed up to its left. The 46th remained on the Red Line in support. The 4th Division's line now ran south-north from the main road on the right, then curving around north-west to the left flank on the Somme south of Méricourt, somewhat short of the original final objective in that sector. The line was completed by the 1st Brigade with three battalions strung out facing north along the canal bank from Morcourt through Cérisy to Bouzencourt, and one battalion in reserve behind that line. Behind the front line, the brigade HQs moved forward to locations in the captured territory, the 4th Brigade setting up in Morcourt and the 12th Brigade in Jean Wood, about half-way between the Green and Red Lines. Brigadier General Leane had earlier gone further forward to Beryl Wood in search of a suitable location, but he and Captain Arthur Varley, the staff captain, had been pinned down there in a shell-hole for two hours by enemy shelling.[82] Varley and Major 'Babe' Norman, the brigade major, had spent much time in the field during the operation, to oversight movement of supplies and ensure contact with the forward elements.

All day, the medical units had been transporting and treating the wounded behind the firing line, the 4th Division units taking over in the northern zone from those of the 3rd Division when the Green Line was reached. Initially the 13th Field Ambulance established an ADS for stretcher cases at the 'Hospice,' Fouilloy; the facility would also attend to walking wounded. At 7:30 am the 4th Field Ambulance and attached personnel went forward to set up a new ADS for the zone, just east of Hamel. The tents had hardly been erected there when a direct hit by a German shell destroyed one. It was obviously not the place to be treating wounded men, so the station was packed up again and relocated to a spot about a kilometre north-west of Hamel. That took time, but fortunately casualties from the firing line were still light. A little before midday the new ADS had been opened, and the 13th Field Ambulance converted their Fouilloy location to MDS status, with additional personnel from the 3rd Division providing assistance. There urgent surgery, including limb amputations, would be performed. The numbers of wounded now increased rapidly, carried back from the RAPs by a combination of motor and horse-drawn ambulance vehicles. The motor ambulances, with the great advantage of speed over the horsed vehicles, were now assuming more importance in the evacuation process. The vehicles, particularly in the northern sector, were also subjected to the enemy shelling from the Chipilly peninsula, which forced them to cease using the Hamel-Cérisy road (it is highly unlikely that the Germans were deliberately firing on medical vehicles—the road was an obvious target for interfering with transport in general). Alternative routes were used instead and the flow of casualties through the ADS to the MDS went on fairly smoothly. At the MDS there was some congestion with stretcher patients moving on to the CCS, which was 30 kilometres away at Vignacourt—turnaround time for motor vehicles making the long round trip was up to five hours, including delays in unloading at the destination. Some of those patients were diverted to the light railway terminus at Vequemont, also used to evacuate walking wounded. The process was managed by 12th Field Ambulance personnel, that unit being in charge of a divisional collecting post further west. The forward area was reported clear of casualties about nightfall. The 13th Field Ambulance noted that 832 casualties had passed through their MDS by 9 pm, many of whom were wounded German prisoners[83]— perhaps up to one-third, the total wounded reported by 4th Division units being about 560, not all of whom necessarily passed through the Fouilloy MDS.[84]

The fighting died down in the afternoon apart from some scattered shelling, with the German force that had occupied the front that morning now reduced to a few demoralised remnants. The Australians settled down to the task of consolidation, fortifying the second and third objective lines against counter-attack—highly unlikely to occur now, but tactical doctrine demanded that the line reached be so strengthened. After all, most of the ground gained at Cambrai last year had been lost again to counter-attacks. During consolidation Captain Godfrey Manning, now in command of the Pioneers' 'D' Company working with the 13th Battalion, was killed by a shell while marking out a strong-point for the new front line; the work was completed by his colleague, Sergeant Ernest Sumner. There were signs of a counter attack on the 12th Brigade front during the afternoon when a German force estimated at 400 men was seen advancing from Proyart. The 48th Battalion stood to arms and the 16th Brigade RHA was called on. The artillery fire broke up the enemy advance, some of them retreating and others digging in 700 metres out from the Australian trench, where they remained passive. The field artillery, including batteries moved forward from the original barrage line, was now positioned to defend the front and support lines. Wiring and digging parties worked steadily on improving their positions, finding that the old trenches reached on the third objective made a good basis for the front line. Through the afternoon and into the night unit quartermasters organised hot meals to be brought up to the troops in the successive lines. 'Most of the Australian front-line posts dug, slept or discussed the marvels of the day.'[85]

Marvels indeed, certainly on Fourth Army's front south of the river: except for the 4th Division's extreme left and a small area on the 5th Division's right, all of the Australian Corps objectives had been taken, and the Canadian Corps had been equally successful on its front. Further south, the French First Army, although not reaching all of its objectives, had also gained considerable ground. Fourth Army had torn a huge gap in the enemy positions, 10 kilometres deep and 18 kilometres wide, eliminating the German forward garrison and reserves. The Germans lost 13,000 prisoners and perhaps another 17,000 in dead and wounded. The Australian Corps had taken nearly 8,000 of the prisoners, as well as 200 guns. The 4th Division's share was about 1,900 prisoners and 47 guns. It was an overwhelming victory, and the Australian troops were aware that much credit was due to their Corps commander. C E W Bean later wrote that

> the actual working out of the assembly of the Australian corps for the Battle of August 8 was Monash's masterpiece. Never in his career ... was his genius for minute organisation more perfectly employed. The placing of his brigades, the timing of their advance when they moved off to take up their successive tasks, the co-ordination of the services of supply behind them, has provided the classic example of such operations.[86]

The Battle of Amiens was not quite over yet, however. Several more days of action in the battle zone would follow for the soldiers of the 4th Division until they could have a brief break out of the line. This was the beginning of the period later called the Hundred Days, the great offensive that would bring the War to its end.

At this time, the 4th Division's units and senior officers were as follows:

4th Australian Division Order of Battle, early August 1918

GOC	Major General E G Sinclair-MacLagan
GSO1	Lieutenant Colonel J D Lavarack
GSO2	Major E C P Plant
GSO3	Captain L C A Craig
AA&QMG	Lieutenant Colonel R Dowse
DAAG	Major W Fowler-Brownsworth
DAQMG	Captain E W Carter
ADCs	Captain C Bartlett, Lieutenant G R Baillie

Infantry

4th Brigade:	Brigadier General C H Brand
Brigade Major:	Major R W Tovell
Staff Captain:	Captain R H Lackman
13th Battalion:	Lieutenant Colonel D G Marks
14th Battalion:	Lieutenant Colonel H A Crowther
15th Battalion:	Major B Sampson
16th Battalion:	Lieutenant Colonel E A Drake-Brockman
4th LTM Battery:	Captain A Martin
12th Brigade:	Brigadier General R L Leane
Brigade Major:	Major R H Norman
Staff Captain:	Captain A L Varley
45th Battalion:	Lieutenant Colonel C M Johnston
46th Battalion:	Lieutenant Colonel J J Corrigan
48th Battalion:	Lieutenant Colonel S L Perry
12th LTM Battery:	Captain F G S Cherry
13th Brigade:	Brigadier General S C E Herring
Brigade Major:	Captain T S Louch
Staff Captain:	Lieutenant W H Conwell
49th Battalion:	Lieutenant Colonel W L Arrell
50th Battalion:	Lieutenant Colonel A G Salisbury
51st Battalion:	Lieutenant Colonel R Christie
13th LTM Battery:	Captain C O Long

Artillery

CRA:	Brigadier General W L H Burgess
Brigade Major:	Major T A J Playfair
Staff Captain:	Captain A C R Waite
10th Field Artillery Brigade:	Lieutenant Colonel T I C Williams
(37th, 38th, 39th, 110th Batteries)	
11th Field Artillery Brigade:	Lieutenant Colonel C H Spurge
(41st, 42nd, 43rd, 111th Batteries)	
Divisional Ammunition Column:	Lieutenant Colonel H V Vernon
Divisional Trench Mortar Officer:	Captain K Ewan
(7th and 8th MTM Batteries)	

Machine Guns

4th Machine Gun Battalion:	Lieutenant Colonel H W Murray, VC
(4th, 12th, 13th, 24th MG Companies)	

Engineers

CRE:	Lieutenant Colonel R J Dyer
4th Field Company:	Major H G Tolley
12th Field Company	Major C C Riddell
13th Field Company:	Major R B Carr
Signal Company:	Major J E Fraser

Pioneers

4th Pioneer Battalion:	Lieutenant Colonel T L F Rutledge

Medical

ADMS:	Colonel K Smith
DADMS:	Major E F Lind
4th Field Ambulance:	Lieutenant Colonel R S McGregor
12th Field Ambulance:	Lieutenant Colonel A H Gibson
13th Field Ambulance:	Lieutenant Colonel F C Wooster

Veterinary

DADVS:	Major E S James
4th Mobile Veterinary Section:	Captain R H Heywood

Transport (Divisional Train)

CO:	Lieutenant Colonel A A Holdsworth
7th Company AASC:	Captain C R Walsh
14th Company AASC:	Major J W Blanch
26th Company AASC:	Captain T B Lloyd
27th Company AASC:	Captain S A Robertson

21 Notes

1 If the identification of the 1000th award depends on its publication in the *London Gazette*, then Cpl Axford's VC was the 999th—the notice for his award comes (alphabetically) immediately before Pte Dalziel's, on page 9660 of the 17 August 1918 edition.
The *Official History* (Vol VI, p. 289n) says that Dalziel had 'discovered the Dalziel gold-mine.' It was actually a tin mine, later called the Great Boulder mine, at Emuford, Qld.

2 This account is taken from correspondence on Maj H C Ford's service record. In the event, Maj Ford was not sent home as originally intended. No details seem to be available, but it appears that Ford was not prepared to quietly accept his relegation from active duty. AIF HQ in London decided, within a few weeks of his arrival there, to return him to France and he was found a posting with the 26th Battalion (2nd Division). He acted in command of that unit for two periods during September and October.

3 Presumably at the Renison Bell tin mine in Tasmania, which locality he gave as his home address. The *Official History* gives his occupation as 'miner' in a biographical footnote.

4 White, *Op Cit*, p. 148.

5 Wanliss, *Op Cit*, p. 312.

6 2 Squadron AFC War Diary for July 1918 (misdated to 23 July). The *Official* History (Vol VI, p. 509n) says that some pilots from 4 AFC (Sopwith Camels) also flew in; a photograph in the AWM collection shows a Camel on the field together with SE5As, but the visit is not mentioned in No 4's Diary.

7 Rule, *Op Cit*, p. 136.

8 Capt Smith was 41, a telecommunications lines inspector with the Postmaster General's Dept in civilian life. He had been awarded the MC and Bar for gallantry at Mouquet Farm and Polygon Wood respectively (the original recommendation in the latter case was for the DSO).

9 *Official History*, Vol VI, p. 509n.

10 Aust Corps General Staff War Diary for October 1918 Part 2, Appendix 22.

11 4th Division GS War Diary, 31 July 1918.

12 *Ibid*.

13 Wanliss, *Op Cit*, p. 314. Several of the statements on Cpl Lewis's Red Cross file confirm this.

14 Monash, *Op Cit*, p. 93.

15 *Ibid*, p. 95.

16   Pedersen, *Monash as Military Commander*, pp. 371–2.
17   The *Official History* (Vol VI, p. 496) gives '432 fighting tanks' while the Fourth Army Chief of Staff, General Sir Archibald Montgomery, in *The Story of the Fourth Army in the Battles of the Hundred Days*, says 456 including 96 light Whippet tanks (p.23n). B Cooper (*Tank Battles of World War 1*, p. 68) gives a grand total of 604, including 162 in reserve or used as supply vehicles.
18   *Medical History*, Vol II, pp. 685–8.
19   Divisional HQ was still at Coisy on 1 August, moving to Cagny the next day. The Division's after action report (Appendix 65 to the August GS Diary) says that the CRA was present at the meeting but the Diary entry for 1 August says the Artillery representative was the brigade major. According to the Artillery diary, Brig Gen Burgess was on leave until 2 August, when he returned on recall, and Lt Col T I C Williams was acting CRA until then.
20   It had been intended that the 13th Brigade would take over the whole front in any case, releasing the 4th Brigade to prepare for the operation, but only for one night until the Canadians arrived.
21   12th Brigade War Diary, 5 August 1918.
22   Prior and Wilson, *Command on the Western Front, Op Cit*, p.325.
23   *Official History*, Vol VI, p. 522.
24   Chataway, *Op Cit*, p. 219.
25   Burford Sampson served several terms as a Senator in the federal parliament after the war; see his biography by Kevin Newman in the *Australian Dictionary of Biography*.
26   A G Moyes, '48th Battalion: Gates of Memory,' *Reveille*, 31 January 1931. By 'Westerner' Moyes meant Western Australian—Maj Mott was born in Victoria but was living in Norseman, WA, when he enlisted.
27   The use of standard short-delay fuzes for the 18-pounders was mandated in Corps artillery HQ orders (War Diary for August 1918, Appendices 4 and 5) and repeated in orders by the 2nd and 3rd Division artillery (controlling the barrage in their zones)—yet the *Official History* (Vol VI, p. 499) says 'The Australian infantry preferred to follow a barrage of high-explosive shell with instantaneous fuses.' If the 18-pounders really were firing daisy-cutters, it would have been an uncomfortable proposition for the front rank of the infantry, given that the usual practice was to move as close as possible to a creeping barrage.
28   4th Division Train War Diary for August 1918, Appendix 27, Col Holdsworth's memo to unit personnel. The right flank was the 12th Brigade sector, where the British 16th RHA Brigade provided the mobile artillery; the artillerymen may have been from the 11th AFA Brigade, however, as that unit was following in support across the 4th Division front.
29   *Official History*, Vol VI, pp. 545–7.
30   46th Battalion War Diary, 8 August 1918.
31   Bean Papers, AWM38 3DRL606/227/1, p.182 (folio 377).
32   Lee, *Op Cit*, p. 71. The figure of 25 captured guns is given in the 12th Brigade's after-action report (Appendix 6 in the August 1918 War Diary). The 45th's original report claimed 29, and Lt Col Johnston gave a total of 27 when later interviewed by Bean (AWM38 3DRL606/227/1, folio 279).
33   Chataway, *Op Cit*, p. 222.
34   Wanliss, *Op Cit*, p. 324n.
35   Chataway, *Op Cit*, p. 223.
36   14th Battalion War Diary for August 1918, Appendix 25.

37 The *Official History* (Vol VI. p. 567) says the tanks were those with 'the right of the 14th Battalion and the left of the 13th'. The 13th Battalion's report, (August 1918 War Diary, Appendix 2) says, however, that there was only one tank with the battalion at that stage, and this went all the way to the final objective, but 'three tanks detailed for liaison duty ... may have done good work with the 14th Battalion.'

38 4th Division Engineers War Diary for August 1918, Part 9, Appendix 6, Maj Riddell's report to the CRE, Col Dyer. That document is the main source for the account given above; some details are from the 12th Field Company's August diary, and from Spr Hook's service record and Red Cross file.

39 Bean Papers, AWM 38 3DRL606/227/1, folio 274–5 (Lt Simon's interview with Bean; Simon mistakenly identified the engineer unit as the 4th Field Company).

40 Spr George Hook has no known grave owing to a combination of circumstances. It appears that he was passed through the medical evacuation system in the normal way, but his wounds were too serious for recovery and he died the same day, at the 20th CCS, Vignacourt, as was determined later. Unfortunately, he could not be identified at the successive medical facilities at the time because he had neglected to wear his identity discs when going into action— they were found later at camp among his personal effects. In such circumstances a deceased soldier could be identified by any documents carried in his coat pockets, such as letters or his pay-book, but Hook had discarded his coat (which also carried the shoulder patches that would have identified his unit, and that he was Australian) after being hit. He had given the documents he was carrying to Lieutenant Hunt for safekeeping; Hunt, who was obliged to return to his combat duties immediately, was then unable to trace what had happened to Hook afterwards—because his identity was unknown in the medical system. For some time later, Hook was recorded as missing, and it was months before a post-mortem photograph of an unknown soldier who had died at the CCS was identified as being Hook. It was then confirmed that he had died of wounds received in action on 8 August 1918, well after the CCS had relocated and too late to identify his grave—a situation which must have added to the distress of his family. The Red Cross file on George Hook gives the story, and his service record includes further details in a letter from Lt Hunt to the family.
Soldiers who died at casualty clearing stations were buried nearby, and there can be little doubt that Hook's was among those burials. The CCS cemeteries so formed were later developed into official CWGC cemeteries. The Vignacourt cemetery contains 586 burials, only one of which (Plot IV, Row C, Grave 18) is that of an unidentified soldier. The headstone inscription does not show a date, but the graves in that row are of soldiers, mostly Australian, who died there between 7 and 10 August 1918; burials for August 1918 begin in Plot IV and continue in V and VI. It is very likely that George Hook is buried in Plot IV Row C Grave 18 at Vignacourt British Cemetery. The author has referred this matter to the CWGC.

41 Bean Papers as for Note 39 above, folio 275.

42 See the 4th Division Engineer HQ War Diary for August 1918, Appendix 6, which gives a summary of the 12th Field Company personnel's actions.

43 Wanliss, *Op Cit*, p. 323n.

44 Identified from information on the website google.com/sites/landships, and from the citation for Sgt Mitchell's DCM award in the London Gazette supplement of 16 January 1919, issue 31128, p. 839. Possibly Mitchell also went on to assist the 16th Battalion's advance—see the Bean Papers, AWM38 3DRL606/228/1, p. 470; the 16th Battalion's report on the battle (August 1918 Diary, Appendix 2A) mentions being joined by a Mark V tank near the Red Line, but that appears to have been knocked out shortly afterwards.

45 Wanliss, *Op Cit*, p. 322. Pte Marmo was awarded the MM for his part in the battle; the recommendation indicates that he was with the screen of scouts.
46 Bean Papers, AWM38 3DRL606/228/1, folio 470.
47 13th Battalion War Diary for August 1918, Appendix 2.
48 Bean Papers, AWM38 3DRL606/228/1, folio 310.
49 The *Official History* (Vol VI, p. 564) says that the Pioneer company was commanded by Lt H J Storey in the battle, but does mention the presence and deaths of Capt Bingle and of Capt Godfrey Manning (Vol VI, p. 595n), stating that they were both killed by the same shell; the Red Cross file on Manning suggests, however, that the statement is incorrect. From that report and information in the Pioneers' August 1918 War Diary, it seems that Capt Bingle was the substantive company commander and led it in the advance. When he was wounded, the second-in-command, Capt Manning took over, but was himself killed by shell-fire after the Red and Blue Lines had been gained. Probably Lt Herbert Storey was the next senior officer in the field and so took command at that point. The Pioneer Diary notes that both the OC and 2ic of 'D' Company were killed, and Captains Bingle and Manning are named in a list of casualties at Appendix 11 of the Diary. That list names 12 men wounded on 8 August. Storey was promoted to captain after the battle, now appointed as the company commander, and in a report dated 7 September (Appendix 6 in the August diary) he gives the figure of eight killed and 18 wounded, used here.
It was the policy that infantry companies did not send both the company commander and his second-in-command into battle at the same time. The 4th Pioneer Battalion, rarely operating as infantry, may not have been familiar with that rule.
50 4th LTM Battery War Diary, 8 August 1918. Shortage of ammunition, resulting from the destruction of the supply tanks, reduced the effectiveness of the mortars; two guns with the 15th Battalion had run out of bombs by the time they could have been used against the Germans north of the river. Lt Waterford's crews with the 13th Battalion seem to have used their limited ammunition supply to the best effect.
51 Bean Papers, AWM38 3DRL606/227/1, folio 278.
52 4th Division Train War Diary for August 1918, Appendix 27.
53 4th Division DAC War Diary for August 1918, Appendix 3.
54 4th Division Artillery HQ War Diary for August 1918, Appendix 1.
55 10th AFA Brigade War Diary for August 1918, Appendix 1, (p. 21, report by the battery commander, Maj E K Smart).
56 Some details of this incident can be found in the Red Cross files on Lt Lintott, Sgt E T Cornish and Gnr N L Critten.
57 10th AFA Brigade War Diary for August 1918, Appendix 1, page 15, Maj de Low's report; he stated that 'a section was then got into action' after two sections had been silenced. This could have been the section (under Capt C Webber) in direct support of the 14th Battalion, reverting to command of the Battery, but the 14th Battalion report suggests those guns were in action against the enemy position on Cérisy ridge that was holding up the left of that unit. It was the 39th Battery, supporting the 16th Battalion coming up behind, that shelled the machine guns on the more distant 'Red Line Ridge' to cover the 14th's right flank.
58 *Ibid*, Appendix 1, p. 13. Lt Smith stated in his report that the section was positioned near Farmer Wood, which was about a kilometre west of the 13th Battalion's objective on the Red Line, when it opened fire on the Chipilly guns. The 13th's report says that the 18-pounders opened at 10.15 am, i.e. 15 minutes after the infantry reached the Red Line. This suggests

that the section was not right up with the infantry, turning its attention to Chipilly instead, or perhaps Lt Smith had mistaken his position; there were many small patches of woods in the area—Dudgeon, for example, on the slope below the Red Line.

59 *Ibid*, Appendix 1, p. 12.
60 10th AFA Brigade War Diary, 8 August 1918. Statements on Maj Seelenmeyer's Red Cross file say that he was 'with the 39th Battery horse lines', and 'going up with the ammunition waggon' when he was hit.
61 Dvr John Lobegeiger, whose grave could not be located after the war.
62 11th AFA Brigade War Diary, 8 August 1918.
63 This figure appears in the 13th Battalion's report (August War Diary, Appendix 2), and is supported by the *Official History* (Vol VI, p. 595n).
64 Bean Diary, AWM38 3DRL606/116/1, 8 August 1918 (p. 59).
65 16th Battalion War Diary for August 1918, Appendix 2A.
66 Bean Papers, AWM38 3DRL606/227/1, folio 275.
67 RSM Baker's DCM recommendation says that his wounds were serious, but the lack of a corresponding entry in his service record indicates that he did not need to be evacuated. He had reached the rank of RSM at the age of 26.
68 The 12th MG Company's report states that four of their five tanks reached the Red Line and took part in the 48th Battalion's advance to the final objective (12th MG Coy War Diary for August 1918, Appendix 2). The 12th Brigade's report says both four and three in places (August 1918 Diary, Appendix 6). Other infantry reports only mention three—possibly one reached the jump off position a little late, or was disabled at that point.
69 This is not stated anywhere, but is implied by the timings and distances involved. The 48th Battalion reported that the advance jumped off at 10.55am. 'A' Company on the right had to advance 800 metres, met little opposition, and was reported to have reached its objective at midday. The other two companies had to cover up to twice that distance to their objectives, met considerably stiffer opposition, and were on their objectives only 10 minutes later. This suggests that the respective companies jumped off at staggered times. The tank on the left, if it had started near the point on the main road that the other two did, would have had to travel more diagonally and therefore cover a still longer distance than the elements on the right flank. It may, however, have approached the final jumping off area more directly and gone straight to the left of the start line.
70 As in Col Perry's report (48th Battalion War Diary for August 1918, Appendix 8). The *Official History* (Vol VI, p. 586) says there were only two casualties here.
71 'Orpheus' would have been carrying one or two Lewis gun teams as well—a statement made to C E W Bean by a 48th officer says that two Lewis gunners were killed while getting out the tank after it was hit (Bean Papers, AWM38 3DRL606/227/1, p.292). The *Official History* (Vol VI, p. 586) says 'three Lewis gunners of the 48th were shot at close range.' One of these may have been Pte Charles Tidmarsh, whose Red Cross file includes statements that he was a member of 'D' Company and was killed while getting a Lewis gun out of a tank. Pte Tidmarsh was buried at a map reference about 600 metres short of the Blue Line objective. His body was not identified after the war, but a statement on his Red Cross file says that the initial burial was 'beside Cpl [H A] Talbot.' Talbot's body was recovered and re-interred at CWGC Heath Cemetery, Harbonnières. According to the cemetery records, two places away from Talbot's grave is that of an unidentified 48th Battalion soldier whose body had been found at the same location as Talbot's. It seems very likely that Charles Tidmarsh rests in Plot III Row H Grave 13 in Heath Cemetery.

72   Lt King's place of death was identified by map reference (noted in a report on his Red Cross file) but his remains could not be found after the war.
73   R E Barrie, 'Enemy on Run: August Fighting,' in *Reveille*, 1 August 1934 (Pte Barrie won the DCM for his part in the battle).
74   It was Twining who, as a sergeant, had held the isolated post near the windmill at Pozières in 1916, the scene that is depicted in an AWM diorama.
75   The mortars had first been placed in the supply tanks, and so were destroyed when the tanks were hit by artillery on 7 August; replacement weapons were issued and taken forward by horse-limber. The MG Company reported that all 16 of their Vickers guns were positioned in the line. At least one had been lost earlier, in the tank 'Orpheus', indicating that a replacement gun was brought up.
76   As an NCO, Lt Garratt was the only 16th Battalion member to be awarded the DCM and Bar, for deeds at Bullecourt and Polygon Wood. He died of influenza two days before the Armistice (Gill, *Op Cit*, pp. 164–5).
77   *Official History*, Vol VI, p. 591.
78   Inferred from the MM recommendations for both soldiers. The distribution of the automatic weapons and personnel across the 16th Battalion's tanks is not clear from readily available documents. There is an incomplete schedule in the 4th MG Battalion's War Diary for August 1918 (Part 1, p. 38 in PDF) that shows the 4th MG Company officers and a number of the other ranks allocated to each of eight tanks, indicating that the 10 Vickers guns and 16 Lewis guns were spread across all eight. One way this could have been arranged was to have two Vickers in each of two tanks and one in each of the other six, plus two Lewis guns per tank. The MC recommendation for Lt H A Devenish (16th Battalion) mentions that his tank carried two Vickers and two Lewis guns and their crews.
79   Or possibly Lt Lydster's tank; Sgt Sinclair's DCM recommendation says that his section commander was wounded, probably referring to Lydster, but the document mentioned in Note 78 above shows Sinclair as being in another tank, which would be one with a 16th Battalion officer in charge. The tanks with Lydster and Garratt were hit at about the same time but a short distance apart. A report by Capt Lynas (16th Battalion War Diary for August 1918, Appendix 2A) indicates that the only unhurt men from Lydster's tank were the four Lewis gunners including Pte Hagan. That report also says that the other tank, that directed by Lt Minchin, got to a position almost on the Blue Line before it was hit.
80   It is not always easy to determine which company a soldier belonged to within a battalion, particularly with ORs. From 16th Battalion Routine Orders, included in the units War Diary, it appears that CSM Phillips and Sgt Hutchings were with 'A' Company, Sgt Sweetnam in 'B', and Sgt Murray in 'C'. Lt Rogers, killed near the start line, was probably with 'A'.
81   General Brand's notes for the 4th Brigade's pre-action conference state that the Blue Line would be held by the 16th (left) and 13th (right) Battalions on 'Z' night (copy in, among others, the 4th MG Company's August 1918 War Diary, Appendix 4).
82   Bean Papers, AWM38 3DRL606/227/1, p.304.
83   13th Field Ambulance War Diary, 8 August 1918.
84   The ADMS noted that some of the 12th Brigade's wounded were sent to the 5th Division MDS near Villers-Bretonneux (4th Division ADMS War Diary for August 1918, Appendix 20).
85   *Official History*, Vol VI, p. 603.
86   'General Sir John Monash,' *Reveille*, 1 May 1937.

22: Etinehem and Madame Wood

The morning of 9 August began quietly for the 4th Division units, dug in on their objectives of the previous day. Overnight, patrols sent out by the 16th and 13th Battalions, on the left of the new front line, had found the area near Méricourt to be still strongly held by the enemy, and daylight confirmed the continuing enemy presence on the Chipilly peninsula across the river. Fire from there forced the 16th Battalion troops to keep their heads down for much of the day, and further nuisance was caused by German aircraft making frequent strafing attacks on Morcourt and the nearby trenches.[1] It was apparent at the higher command level that the Chipilly situation had to be corrected by III Corps as soon as possible. The US 131st Regiment, then based well to the rear, was allocated to III Corps as reinforcements. At the same time the offensive would be continued on the southern flank, between the main road and the railway line. Here elements of the Canadian Corps, with the 1st Australian Division coming through from reserve on their left, would aim at a line just beyond the village of Lihons near the railway. The 2nd Division would move through a little later to support the 1st. The 4th Division would hold its ground to begin with until its left flank was cleared, then move up to complete the occupation of yesterday's Blue Line objective.

After the well-organised ruthlessly efficient operation of 8 August, the standard of Fourth Army's staff work faltered overnight. As the Chief of Staff, General Montgomery, ruefully acknowledged years later, 'everyone was so busy congratulating everyone else on their share in the victory that valuable time was lost in preparing for an advance next day.'[2] The attacks were poorly co-ordinated, and although some ground was taken in piecemeal fighting the objectives were not reached on the day. It would be another two days before the Lihons line was occupied. The 1st Division had begun the operation with only two infantry brigades, its 1st Brigade still being attached to the 4th Division and lined out along the south bank of the Somme, guarding the left flank. On the north bank the III Corps operation to clear the enemy from Chipilly was slow to get under way, to the extent that by late afternoon the British were still nearly a kilometre short of Chipilly village, as could be seen by troops of the 1st Battalion at Cérisy-Gailly. Early that morning, two of that unit's NCOs, Company Quartermaster Sergeant (CQMS) Jack Hayes and Sergeant Harold Andrews of the reserve company, had crossed a bridge into Chipilly—unarmed—to look for souvenirs. They went into the western side of the village, where they found no enemy troops but collected two German rifles and a machine gun abandoned in a chalk pit. They then returned and reported to their company commander, who requested permission to send a strong patrol across and occupy the village. This was declined by Brigade HQ on advice that the British attack would finally go in at 5:30 pm. That time came and went with no apparent action, and the brigadier then ordered that the two NCOs cross to Chipilly again with a small patrol and ascertain what, if anything, was happening.

CQMS Hayes and Sergeant Andrews took four riflemen with them on the expedition, crossing the bridge at the north end of Cérisy then working through the riverside marsh to the road north-west of Chipilly. Here they joined up with the stalled British company sighted earlier and Hayes undertook to move his patrol forward to reconnoitre the village. The six Australians extended into a loose line and charged for the western edge of the village, which they reached safely, despite coming under fire from a machine gun to the north. Two platoons from the British company then followed to the location. The 1st Battalion patrol split up to scout the area, two men working their way through the village while Andrews and another man moved up the road running north-east to the far side of the high ground. Hayes and the remaining man directed one of the British platoons into position at a chalk pit north of the village. The patrol re-assembled there just as a barrage of smoke shells came down close by. The British platoon pulled back, but the Australians went the other way. Leaving two men to guard the village, Hayes, Andrews and Private Albert Fuller took advantage of the smoke to return along the north-east road, where they knocked out a small German machine gun post. After dropping two prisoners back at the chalk pit the three were joined by Private William Kane and went up the road again, this time sighting a larger enemy post further along. The patrol split into two pairs, got in position and then charged the Germans from two directions, firing from the hip. A grenade dropped into a dugout flushed out the enemy garrison of an officer and 31 men. The prisoners were collected by the British company, which had come up by now, and seven machine guns were found in the post. Kane and Fuller kept going and found another enemy post which they rushed and captured with another nine prisoners and two machine guns. Sergeant Andrews meanwhile had noticed enemy troops retiring across the river further north and he opened fire on them with one of the captured machine guns. The British resumed their advance until the combined group came under fire from somewhere to their left. This turned out to be coming from the 131st US Regiment, which was in the process of clearing the Germans out of Gressaire Wood at the northern end of the peninsula—they had not expected to see Allied troops so far forward. The effort of the American regiment had been notable, the inexperienced troops succeeding after a long, tiring approach march, made more difficult by shamefully poor staff work that had left the fighting men short of rations and water. The friendly fire soon ceased and the Australian patrol then joined in mopping up the Chipilly Spur, collecting 28 more prisoners in the process. The patrol reported back at dusk, with a note from the British company commander confirming its remarkable performance in leading the whole successful advance.[3]

The peninsula was now in Allied hands, and with the riverside flank now covered the 4th Brigade's front line battalions, 16th and 13th, moved forward during the night to occupy the full Blue Line objective, close to the outskirts of Méricourt on the left. The 4th Division's right, the 12th Brigade, also advanced its front line, conforming to the movement on its right by the 2nd Division (which had just relieved the 5th) as part of the Lihons operation in the southern zone of the battlefield. That night also, the 1st Brigade was released to rejoin its own division, relieved by the 13th Brigade resuming under 4th Division command. The 13th Brigade took over the line along the river, from Morcourt on the right (east) through Cérisy to Bouzencourt on the left.

The 4th and 12th Brigades spent the day of 10 August adjusting and improving their positions, preparatory to being relieved that night by 3rd Division units. On relief the seven battalions moved to locations north of the river between Sailly-le-Sec and Sailly-Laurette in the newly captured territory. This marked the end of the Battle of Amiens for the Division as a whole, although the 13th Brigade was about to get involved in the next stage of the fighting. Overwhelming success, particularly on the first day, had come at a human cost that was unusually low, at least by Western Front standards up to then. The 4th Division suffered about 780 casualties, 119 of them fatal, in the northern zone fighting (in that area the 2nd, 3rd and 5th Divisions had comparable casualty lists, but in the different circumstances of the Lihons fighting the 1st and 2nd Divisions lost at least 2,500 men). The 4th Division artillery had 17 killed of a total casualty list of 96, all except 18 of whom were 10th AFA Brigade members;[4] that unit also had 40 of its horses and mules killed. The 10th had of course been the most exposed to the German guns on the Chipilly peninsula, and similarly it was the 16th Battalion that incurred the heaviest casualties among the infantry units, with 27 killed and at least 77 wounded on 8 August. Including those losses, the 4th Brigade had 70 killed and approximately 230 wounded, and also the Pioneer company attached to the 13th Battalion lost seven killed and 15 wounded. Losses in the 12th Brigade's three battalions amounted to 33 killed and approximately 150 wounded.[5] The MG Battalion reported 16 killed and missing, and 74 wounded.

For their parts in the skirmish at the bridge near Cérisy the three 12th Field Company engineers involved, Lieutenant Hunt and Sappers Dean and Campbell, were all recommended for the VC by the CRE, Colonel Dyer.[6] The recommendations were not approved by higher authority, however; Hunt was awarded the DSO instead, and the two sappers each received the DCM. Major Norman, brigade major of the 12th Brigade, was another DSO recipient, as were Colonel Perry, the 48th Battalion CO, and Major Sampson, commanding the 15th. Soldiers awarded the DCM included RSM Baker, Sergeant Kealy and Private Barrie of the 48th Battalion, CSM Oswald, Sergeant Sexton and Private Finch (all 13th), CSM Phillips and Sergeant Murray (16th), Private Sellick (45th), Private Nicholls (46th), Sergeant Sinclair and Corporal Pritchard (MG Battalion), Sergeant Sumner (Pioneer Battalion) and Lance Corporal O'Connor (4th LTM Battery). Among recipients of the MC, or Bars to previous awards, were Captain Varley (12th Brigade staff), Major Mott and Captain Twining (48th Battalion, Captain Domeney (15th), Lieutenants Piercy and Smith (16th), Captain Wilson (14th), Lieutenant Cleland (13th), Major North and Lieutenant Kemp (46th) and Lieutenant Vincent (45th). Outside of the infantry battalions, MCs were awarded to Captains Cox (11th AFA Brigade) and Taylor (MG Battalion), and Lieutenants Waterford (4th LTM Battery) and Clive Smith (10th AFA Brigade). Numerous MMs or Bars were awarded, including those to Lewis gunners Privates Hagan, Buckenara and Lyon (16th Battalion), Corporal Bourke and Lance Corporal Williams (13th), Private Pringle (15th), Lance Corporals Collyer and Field (46th), and machine gunners Sergeant Disney, Corporal Prentice and Lance Corporal Treloar (MG Battalion). Lewis gunner Lance Corporal Heydon of the Pioneer Battalion also received the MM, as did Private Charles Watson, a medical orderly with the Pioneers, for treating wounded men under fire on Red Line Ridge —his recommendation stated that he 'in two cases saved the lives of men who would have otherwise bled to death.'[7] The awards came through over the following weeks, while the fighting continued with scarcely a pause.

On 9 August General Rawlinson had finally agreed to transfer responsibility for the north bank of the Somme to General Monash and the Australian Corps. That night the 13th Brigade's 50th Battalion was ordered to cross the river from Cérisy to Chipilly, initially to back up the 131st US Regiment holding positions forward of the latter village. The move was completed in the early hours of 10 August, with the 49th shifting to its right (east) along the south bank to fill the vacated area. In the meantime Monash and his staff had produced a plan for an advance on both sides of the Somme, aligning with the Lihons advance further south. Astride the waterway, the principle features were the series of horseshoe river bends and the fingers of land running alternately north and south between them. The southward-pointing finger of the Chipilly peninsula was now in Allied hands, although the exact dispositions of the forces there were not yet clear. The enemy held the territory east from there; next on the east was the bend enclosing the spur of land on the southern bank where Méricourt was situated. At the base of the next peninsula, on the northern bank, was the village of Etinehem. Next came a further northward-pointing finger, with the village of La Neuville at its tip and the larger town of Bray-sur-Somme across the river on the northern bank. The new northern boundary of the Corps ran roughly along the road from Bray west to Corbie. On the south side of the river the operation required the 10th Brigade (four battalions) of the 3rd Division, now holding the front line in that area (that is, the Blue Line of 8 August), to advance east in column, along the Roman road, across the base of the Méricourt peninsula and then swing to the left and march north to reach the Somme. That advance would cut off the peninsula and a considerable area to its south, including the town of Proyart. On the north bank the 13th Brigade (three battalions) would carry out a similar manoeuvre, advancing along the

Bray-Corbie road past Etinehem village then turning south down the eastern side of that peninsula, thereby getting behind the enemy's line to cut off their forces in the area. Both attacks were to be spearheaded by tanks—there were, however, few of these available now, following their heavy losses on 8 August and in the continuing Lihons operations.

The attack was to be carried out on the night of 10 August, leaving minimal time for preparations. At noon that day Monash held a conference at 4th Division HQ, Corbie, where the 3rd and 4th Division senior officers received their orders. It appears that Monash dealt directly with the two brigadiers concerned, but with both divisional GOCs also present.[8] The 13th Brigade commander, Brigadier General Herring returned to his own HQ 'with some pencil notes on the back of an envelope'[9] and called in his battalion commanders for a 2:30 pm meeting, to brief them and work out a detailed plan. The original Corps plan had one battalion passing through the American front and marching east along the Corbie road to a point before Bray and forming a line facing generally north. A second battalion would move east along an intermediate road further south, then swing south to make a line down the eastern side of the peninsula above the steep banks on that side. In those positions both battalions would have enemy forces behind them, so they would have to be watchful to both their front and rear. The third battalion would cut off and encircle Etinehem village, to be mopped up in the morning together with the area around it. Zero was set for 9:30 pm. The brigadier had been told that four tanks would be brought up to lead the attack, but when the tank commander joined the meeting he was not confident that these could be available on time—the heavy work of the last few days had left the machines in poor condition and petrol was short. In any case, working in the dark they would have to keep to the roads and could not assist the battalion moving in the open country down the east side of the spur. The battalion COs and the brigade staff quickly worked out a scheme for the attack that did not rely on the effect of the tanks. Aside from that, their main modification from the Corps plan was that the route taken by the northern force, for which the 49th Battalion was allotted, would run a short distance south of the Corbie road, which would be used by whatever tanks that could reach the start. The 50th Battalion would make up the southern force, with the 51st providing one company to cut off Etinehem. The latter unit's other three companies would form the Brigade reserve. The situation did not suit a conventional artillery barrage, but the Vickers guns of the 13th MG Company, then located at Jean Wood a kilometre south of Morcourt, would be attached to the Brigade to provide some fire support. The company OC, Captain William Cory, was called in to 13th Brigade HQ at 3 pm to receive his orders, sending word back to his gunners to pack up and be ready to move. Four mortars of the 13th LTM Battery were allotted to the 51st Battalion to assist with blockading Etinehem.

In order to jump off at 9:30 pm the troops would need to be in position half an hour earlier. Assembly was to be at the edge of Gressaire Wood, near the line then held by the 131st US Regiment—there was some uncertainty about their exact positions, so the Brigade intelligence officer, Lieutenant James Loudon, made a personal reconnaissance of the area during the afternoon.¹⁰ The Americans were confirmed to be holding the whole area in strength, thereby protecting the Brigade's planned assembly area. The 49th Battalion with the furthest to march was ordered to move off from its present position at 6:30, while the 50th, with three of its companies already north of the river at Chipilly, would march an hour later. The 51st would follow the 50th, aiming to get into its planned position covering Etinehem village. With the short time available the instructions were mostly verbal, and as soon as the details were settled the COs hurried back to their units to brief their officers. Extra ammunition was issued along with picks and shovels and the troops were given a hot meal, in time to begin the approach marches in fighting order on schedule. The 49th Battalion led off across the river and reached its jumping-off position at the north-eastern edge of the wood, a little south of the Bray-Corbie road, in good time. Two tanks were waiting in the road, short of petrol but with their crews anxious to help as much as they could. The tank officers conferred briefly with the 49th Battalion CO, Lieutenant Colonel Arrell, and it was arranged that the tanks would simply proceed straight ahead down the road, 180 metres apart, shooting into enemy territory as they went. The leading tank would fire to its front and both fire to their left, and after half an hour they would turn about and come back along the road, both now firing to their right. The tanks started on time and were soon out of sight, getting well ahead of the infantry. Having probed ahead as instructed, they then chugged back to Battalion HQ 'and asked Arrell what he wanted them to do [now]. He told them they had done it already and they were very surprised and pleased—and went off home.'¹¹ The infantry had followed on with a few scouts in front then Captain Richard Tambling's company leading off the main body. Ahead, flares rose and enemy machine guns loosed off a few bursts, but the fire went harmlessly high and the Germans did not stay to fight, perhaps panicked by the tanks as well as the advancing infantry. Further along the road the 49th encountered more machine gun posts. One of these was taken on alone by a scout, Private Alfred Hockey, who tossed a grenade into the post and then charged it with the bayonet; two of the enemy crew were killed and the other five surrendered.¹² The leading platoon, turning south to link up with the left of the 50th Battalion, came under fire from another machine gun, but the enemy post was quickly knocked out by the scouts. With its left in touch with the Americans holding the original line, the remainder of the 49th deployed according to plan, three companies lining out along the road and forming a flank facing north and the fourth facing east towards Bray. Eight of the 13th MG Company's machine guns were studded along the 49th's line.

In the meantime the 50th Battalion had also been advancing, up the next road to south; the Battalion was short on numbers, so each of its companies had only two platoons. It had been hoped that the 50th would have two tanks to assist, but none turned up. Nevertheless the Battalion pressed forward in the darkness, each company moving with one platoon on either side of the road. Past the first cross-road, German flares went up and a dozen machine guns opened fire from five positions in a line near the next cross-road. The leading companies took cover momentarily, then on hearing the firing from the 49th's area to the north they rose up and charged the enemy line. Again the shaky morale of the Germans was apparent—the machine gunners ran without putting up any serious resistance. With that obstacle out of the way the leading company sought to find the point for the wheel to the south and then pick its way down the east side of the peninsula to the final position. For Lieutenant Ernest Hodge, the company commander, this was no easy task in the dark in unfamiliar territory; as another officer later said

> the ground became a number of divergent trails used by transport ... the direction had seemed simple on the map. It made the direction very difficult to decide as the track was the only guide ... the tracks on the map were wrong—there should have been a road crossing but the track really curved gently in to the road leading to the crucifix [probably meaning one of the two north-east of Etinehem]. Lieutenant Hodge presently realised that he was on the wrong road—too far to the left.[13]

Hodge prudently called a halt and several of the battalion officers made their way to the head of the column, where maps were consulted by the light of electric torches and the area was scouted. Contact was made with a post of the 49th, helping to fix the correct location, and after half an hour the 50th moved off again onto its objective line, where the troops began digging in. Those on the right flank heard a challenge called in English from somewhere ahead. Thinking it was a misplaced 'Tommy' some of the men shouted a response, only to have a German machine gun open fire on them from close range. Lieutenant Arthur Bills and five others were killed and several more were wounded. A grenade was thrown at the gun position, but the cunning German abandoned his gun and got away in the darkness. That incident was the last piece of fighting for the night and the men got on with making a trench line on the heights above the riverbank.

Lieutenant Rupert Finlason's company of the 51st Battalion, with the task of sealing off Etinehem village, followed the 50th column along the road, breaking off to the right take up a position across the two roads leading to the village from the north and north-east. The company's line was strengthened by four Vickers guns and four trench mortars. The 13th Brigade was in position on the peninsula by midnight or shortly afterwards, with the remaining three companies of the 51st in reserve forward of Gressaire Wood and advanced Brigade HQ moving up to a location just south of the Wood. The 50th Battalion was meant to have gained touch with the advanced elements of the 10th Brigade on the other side of the river, but that part of the operation had failed, in what was something of a minor disaster. The 10th Brigade's senior officers had had their doubts about the plan from the first, but the attacking column had started without difficulty, the infantry following three tanks along the Roman road. The column had made steady progress without opposition when a German aircraft flew low along the road and dropped several bombs, scoring a direct hit on one of the tanks. The commotion attracted the attention of numerous enemy machine guns ahead and on the flank, and they raked the road with a storm of fire. The tanks were damaged by armour-piercing bullets and the leading infantry battalion lost over 100 casualties, including its CO killed. There was now no chance of success and the Brigade was forced to withdraw to its original line.

BRAVE DAYS

At dawn on 11 August, Lieutenant Finlason took his 51st Battalion company into Etinehem expecting a fight, but the village proved to be empty except for a single unlucky German who was shot as he ran off—the garrison had evidently withdrawn across the river on a small footbridge.[14] The company moved through the village and took up a position along its south-west edge, with observation over the river crossings. It was now realised that the southern attack had failed and the Méricourt spur was still in enemy hands. As the morning mist dissipated, it became apparent that the 50th Battalion's right flank was not as far south as had been supposed. Following the curve of the high ground, it had bent back somewhat towards the west. The southern part of the Etinehem spur was still open, and some parties of German troops remained in that area. The 13th Brigade's position on the heights was detected by a low-flying German aircraft, and by the mid-morning the line was being heavily and accurately shelled by guns firing mostly from the enemy-held territory on the south bank of the river. The 50th's right flank company, enfiladed by a gun near Proyart, lost eight men killed, and at least another four were killed elsewhere in the unit's line. The 49th had seven killed and 23 wounded during the day, mostly in Captain Tambling's company holding the left of the east-facing line.[15] In unusual circumstances, the 49th also had an officer and four men taken prisoner, recorded as 'missing.' Lieutenant Frank Fearnside was

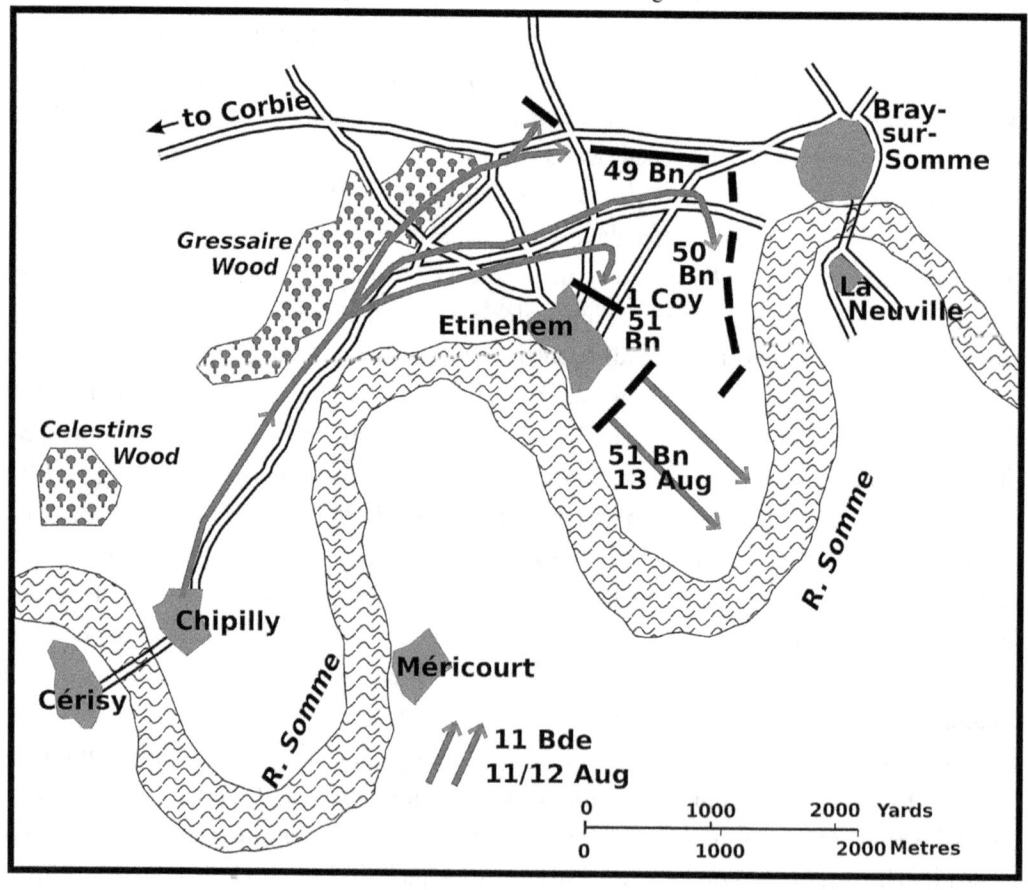

Etinehem Peninsula, Somme River: 13th Brigade's operations 10 to 13 August 1918.

wounded by a shell splinter, and with four other 'walking wounded' was making his way back to the RAP when the party lost direction. They wandered into enemy territory north of the Corbie road where they were picked up by a German outpost. The shelling seemed to presage a counter-attack, particularly as large bodies of Germans were seen moving up to and beyond Bray on the north bank. No attack eventuated, however, and it was later realised that the Germans had evacuated Bray during the night and were now coming back to re-establish their position. More troops were seen moving and digging in the southern corner of the peninsula, but for some time observers could not tell whether they were Germans or Australians. Until they could be certain, the commanders were reluctant to call in their artillery.

The 4th Division artillery had also crossed the river during the previous evening to provide cover for the 13th Brigade, emplacing their weapons in the area to the north of Chipilly. Here three British field brigades came under Brigadier General Burgess's command, becoming the Left Group of batteries. The 10th and 11th AFA Brigades formed the Right Group, under Lieutenant Colonel Thomas Williams, CO of the 10th AFA. To ensure close liaison with the infantry, Williams established himself with 13th Brigade HQ. An infantry officer commented that this arrangement worked well, as 'one good senior officer in liaison is better than a lot of juniors.'[16] The artillery officers were keen to turn their guns on to the troops seen in the south of the peninsula, but Brigadier General Herring would not allow this until he had confirmation that the troops were definitely Germans. A lengthy debate took place at Brigade HQ, and 'as the news spread scores of eyewitnesses looked curiously down from Gressaire heights.'[17] Eventually the 51st company outside Etinhem sent a patrol to investigate and the unit CO, Lieutenant Colonel Christie, also went forward to see for himself. The figures were definitely Germans, they reported, and in late afternoon the gunners were authorised to open fire. The area was bombarded with shrapnel and HE. C E W Bean, observing from near Brigade HQ, thought the shells were mostly falling 100 metres too short of the line where the enemy troops had been spotted. Most of the guns ceased fire after 15 minutes, but one battery had found the right range by then and continued firing for some time afterwards until all movement in the area had ceased.[18] That particular body of the enemy had been neutralised, but it was known that others were still in occupation of the tip of the peninsula.

That evening an operation on the south bank by the 3rd Division captured Méricourt and Cateaux Wood, bringing their front closer to Proyart and now partly covering the 13th Brigade's right flank. Through the next day, 12 August, the 3rd Division continued its advance against stubborn resistance, taking Proyart and establishing a line on the south bank of the Somme across from the tip of the Etinehem spur. The immediate task for the 13th Brigade on the north bank remained to clear the whole spur, an operation that would be spearheaded by two companies of the 51st Battalion. A fairly straightforward plan was worked out by the Brigade staff with the battalion COs and Lieutenant Colonel Williams, the artillery group commander. The 51st troops would line up in front of Etinehem viilage then sweep south-east behind a creeping barrage fired by the 10th and 11th AFA Brigades. At the same time the 50th Battalion would push forward on its right to establish posts beyond its present line on the heights, and also establish a forward position on its left overlooking Bray. The start time was set for 1 am on 13 August. In the meantime, the 13th Brigade was informed that it had been placed under a different command structure. To manage operations on the north bank, Corps had created a new formation, a quasi-division called the Liaison Force, under Brigadier General E A Wisdom who was detached from the 7th Brigade (2nd Division). The infantry element consisted of the 13th Brigade and the 131st US Regiment and the artillery would be the British field brigades currently under the 4th Division CRA's command. Once the operation of 13 August was completed, the 10th and 11th AFA Brigade would be redeployed. The 13th MG Company would remain with the 13th Brigade under Liaison Force command, and other elements of the brigade group—the 13th Field Ambulance, 13th Field Company and 27th Company AASC—now came under Liaison Force also. That day, King George V visited Australian Corps HQ at Bertangles and formally invested Sir John Monash with the knighthood (KCB) previously announced in the New Year's Honours.

At Etinehem the barrage opened promptly at 1 am on 13 August and the 51st Battalion infantry jumped off in moonlight, with 'C' Company on the right commanded by Captain 'Billy' Harburn, and Captain Edward McBurnie's 'D' on the left. Spread across a front of 2,300 metres, the troops followed the accurate barrage closely, meeting weak opposition apart from a few machine gun posts that resisted briefly before the crews surrendered or fled. In an hour, the line had advanced 1,600 metres and reached its objectives along the river, collecting over 170 prisoners in the process, at a cost of five men wounded.[19] Sixty of the prisoners were taken by Sergeant William Lehane, 13th MG Company, who had brought his section of two Vickers guns forward with the infantry. While his men were setting up the guns in the captured position, Lehane scouted the nearby area and spotted a group of men carrying rifles. He could not identify them in the poor light, so he called out a challenge. The response was a few rifle shots, so Lehane charged at them firing his revolver. The group fled into a dugout with Lehane in pursuit. At the dugout entrance he fired a shot into it and called on the occupants to surrender. Two Australian infantrymen came up to assist him as sixty Germans filed out of the dugout and surrendered. Sergeant Lehane was awarded the DCM for this exploit, and both of the infantry company commanders received the MC, in Captain Harburn's case a Bar to the decoration that he had won for his dynamic leadership at Villers-Bretonneux in April.

The 50th Battalion had a somewhat more difficult time. The unit's task was to occupy two gullies leading from the heights to the river, and then establish several platoon posts along the narrow flat stretch at the water's edge. The intention was for two fighting patrols, each of 15 men, to work their way down the gullies as advance guards to cover a following platoon. The small force was all that seemed to be necessary, but unfortunately a number of German troops, estimated at 150 to 200, had accumulated unseen near the heads of the gullies and were prepared to fight. A nest of four machine guns opened up on the supporting platoon, firing upwards at the men silhouetted on the skyline; the platoon was forced to pull back, with the loss of two killed and several wounded, including the platoon commander.[20] Meanwhile Lieutenant George Livesey's patrol in the southernmost gully had attacked and eliminated an enemy post, capturing 14 prisoners and two machine guns. The patrol was then counter-attacked from two sides by a force of German infantry. Almost surrounded by superior numbers, the patrol fought its way out and got back to its original position, bringing in the prisoners and guns. His leadership in this fight earned Livesey the MC in due course.[21] The patrol in the northern gully, commanded by Corporal Irwin Mengersen, a 19 year old South Australian farm boy, reached its intended position but was then taken under fire by several enemy machine guns. Mengersen organised his men to fight back with grenades; the patrol may have knocked out some of the guns, but the 'bombers' were throwing uphill and other guns could not be reached. The patrol was now the only part of the original attack force still in enemy territory, but Mengersen was undaunted and hung on with his men for several hours, until he received a direct order from his company commander to withdraw. The young man was later awarded the DCM.[22]

The Etinehem peninsula, except for that small pocket of German troops, was now in Australian hands. The 13th Brigade held its positions through the day on 13 August, and that night the 50th Battalion set out to finish the job when Lieutenant Livesey took a party down the gully again to the river's edge. Preceded by a mortar bombardment, the troops rushed the enemy position, tossing grenades into the dugouts, only to find that the remaining Germans had already departed across the river to the next peninsula. Together with the capture of Lihons and of Proyart, 'on the Australian front, the objective set on August 9th had everywhere been attained.'[23] It was originally intended by the Allied supreme commander, Marshal Foch, that Fourth Army would keep the offensive rolling on its front, which for the Australian Corps meant that its divisions that had been fighting in the last few days would need relief. To that end the 4th Division, having spent three days resting in the areas of Sailly-Laurette and Sailly-le-Sec, was ordered to return to the south of the river, initially to the area around Harbonnières south of the Roman road, and subsequently to relieve the 1st Division on the Lihons front and take part in the next attack. The 4th Division now had the 132nd US Regiment attached as its reserve infantry, in place of the 13th Brigade under Liaison Force command. The move of the 4th and 12th Brigades to Harbonnières was carried out late on 13 August. While on the march past Bayonvillers, the often-unlucky 15th Battalion was caught by harassing fire from enemy artillery—a heavy shell hit in the midst of No 3 Platoon, killing an outstanding young NCO, Corporal William 'George' Williams, and eight others in an instant.[24] The battalions camped for the night, the 4th Brigade noting that the bivouac area was 'an open plain ... Brigade headquarters is in a drain under the railway line.'[25] Fortunately, the weather was again 'glorious.' The 4th Division artillery, having completed its task at Etinehem, was on the move that day also, to establish a gun line in the vicinity of Rosières, west of Lihons, in position to cover the proposed attack in the next few days.

The overall scheme was for the Canadians and French to advance in the area south of the railway on a front between Chaulnes and Roye, with the Australian Corps on the left of that force making a shorter advance in support. The 4th Division would form the centre of the Corps operation, between the 2nd and 5th Divisions. Division HQ issued an order on 13 August for the infantry brigades, 12th on the right, 4th on the left and 132nd US in reserve, to move further forward and relieve the 1st Division in front of Lihons on the night of 14 August, with the intention of launching the attack the next morning. The divisional artillery would have the 1st Division's guns and two British field brigades added to its command to provide the covering barrage. Almost immediately, the relief and the attack were postponed for 24 hours. Within another day it was announced that the attack was now postponed indefinitely (in effect, cancelled) but the relief of the 1st Division in the front line was to proceed as arranged, while the 5th Division would move to the sector immediately south of the Somme. The high command had reconsidered the strategy for its next move. The direction of Fourth Army's planned offensive would have taken it through the area of the 1916 Somme battlefield, a wilderness of collapsed, overgrown trenches, shell-craters and rusted barbed-wire entanglements. The difficult country, the stiffening German resistance demonstrated in the Lihons fighting, and the effect on the Fourth Army troops of the preceding week's exertions meant that a success would come at a heavy cost, if it could be gained at all. These points were made forcefully by the Canadian Corps commander, Sir Arthur Currie, to his superiors. As the commander of what was in effect a national army, General Currie's views could not be disregarded. Those views also happened to fit in with Sir Douglas Haig's preference for shifting the focus further north to Third Army's front between Albert and Arras. Haig was able to persuade Marshal Foch to agree to the change in plans, and Fourth Army's full-scale offensive was called off. That did not mean that fighting ceased—an aggressive attitude was to be maintained by the forward troops, both infantry and artillery, with frequent patrolling and harassing fire on the enemy lines.

The relief of the 1st Division infantry by that of the 4th Division went ahead as scheduled overnight of 15/16 August. The 12th Brigade, on the right of the new front alongside the Canadians, put its 45th and 46th Battalions into the front line, supported by four trench mortars (12th LTM Battery) and eight Vickers guns (12th MG Company). The 48th Battalion took up the reserve position. The forward area, part of the old French system from 1916, was

> a maze of trenches in a dilapidated state overgrown with weeds, revetments broken down and the present front line has a communication trench into the enemy front line every 100 yards [90 metres] or so ... the enemy is close on the right [45th] Battalion front about 50 yards [45 metres] away, but on the left is some distance out, anything up to 600 yards [550 metres] ... It is anticipated that on the right battalion front bombing encounters will take place at frequent intervals, and the troops opposed to the Brigade are a fair material and appear to be very alert.[26]

The French system continued on the left, where the 4th Brigade found that their trenches were in a better state of repair, with much of the defensive wire entanglement still in place and more communication trenches extending towards enemy territory. The Brigade used its 15th, 13th and 14th Battalions in the front line with the 16th in reserve and the 4th LTM Battery and 4th MG Coy providing supporting weaponry as in the 12th Brigade sector. Both Brigades established headquarters in a former German dugout system two kilometres south-west of Harbonnières. The other elements of the 4th Division moved up in the rear of the infantry in the usual way in place of their 1st Division equivalents. Forward Divisional HQ took over accommodation at the 'Red Chateau' in Villers-Bretonneux.

Enemy shelling was frequent, sometimes extending to the back areas—the HQ of the 16th Battalion, located in a building in Guillacourt, was hit by a long-range shell that penetrated to the cellar before it exploded, killing three men, with another two pulled out of the wreckage alive. In the front line the 4th Brigade's forward troops followed the policy of an aggressive attitude, adopting the technique of 'peaceful penetration' to chip away at German territory. Patrols found that the old communication trenches were not permanently occupied by the enemy. On 17 August, in daylight, the forward battalions used those trenches to advance their front line by 460 metres, occupying another old system of fire-trenches, and including Madame Wood near the northern boundary of the Division's sector. Another advance the next day by the 15th Battalion secured the landmark of Lihu Farm. The 12th Brigade had a tougher time in its sector. The 45th Battalion on the right where the enemy lines were closest found that the German unit opposite them was active and aggressive. On the second day in the line, several duels with grenades broke out, patrols from both sides creeping down the old communication trenches and trying to surprise each other's posts.

On the left of the Brigade's front, the 46th Battalion was not as close to the enemy lines and was subjected to frequent heavy shelling by the German guns day and night, reporting nine killed and 44 wounded over 18 and 19 August.[27] Nevertheless, that night the Battalion was able to move its left company forward to occupy the next trench line in the complex. A brigade relief was planned for that night and the next two, when the 132nd US Regiment, strong in numbers, would come up to the front line from divisional reserve to relieve the 12th Brigade and the right battalion (the 15th) of the 4th Brigade. This move was quickly cancelled amid a more extensive rearrangement of the Australian Corps front, with the inclusion of British troops temporarily under Corps command. On 19 August the 3rd Division commenced taking over from the Liaison Force north of the river. That move released the 13th Brigade and supporting units to return to 4th Division command. Next morning the 13th Brigade relieved the 132nd US as the 4th Division's reserve infantry. Liaison Force was disbanded that day, and the Americans left the area to rejoin their own forces. Over the next few days, the Canadian Corps would be progressively withdrawn to rejoin First Army at Arras, replaced by French troops, leaving Fourth Army consisting of only III Corps and the Australian Corps.

As the 12th Brigade's relief had been cancelled, a battalion rotation took place instead, with the 48th Battalion replacing the 45th in the front line on the night of 19 August. During that day the 4th Brigade had become involved in a burst of fighting on its immediate left. In that sector the 2nd Division had been advancing its line also, and in costly fighting had captured a trench where its front adjoined that held by the 14th Battalion. Overnight (18/19 August) the 32nd British Division had relieved the 2nd Australian, and in the morning the Germans made a determined effort to retake the trench, now manned by the 2nd Manchesters. At 10:25 am the enemy put down a heavy artillery barrage on to their lost position, some shells hitting the 14th Battalion line, then followed up with an infantry attack that got into the trench and drove back the Manchesters. Sergeant William Boyes, in charge of the 14th's left flank post, saw what was happening and raced across to the scene with a few men. There he rallied some of the Manchesters and led a counter-attack—'he himself shot the leading Hun and began to attack with rifle grenades.'[28] Boyes led his party along the trench and succeeded in ejecting the Germans and restoring the position, but he was severely wounded towards the end of the fight. By then, the company commander, Lieutenant George Trewheela, had arrived to join the fight, and went on to reorganise the defence of the post; Boyes later received the DCM and Trewheela the MC.[29] That day also, the 4th Brigade commander Brigadier General Brand left on a month's leave and Lieutenant Colonel Drake-Brockman, CO of the 16th Battalion, took over temporary command of the Brigade; Major Ross Harwood in turn assumed command of the 16th. On the following night, the 16th relieved the 14th in the front line.

By then plans were well advanced for the resumption of the offensive on Third Army's front north of Albert. The operation was due to commence on 21 August, and the next day Fourth Army would advance in support of Third Army's left flank, with III Corps on the left and the Australian Corps on the right. At this point the latter's front line was held, left to right, by the 3rd Division at Etinehem facing Bray north of the Somme, the 5th Division at Proyart on the other side of the river, then the attached 32nd British Division at Framerville, and on the right the 4th Division ahead of Lihons. The 1st and 2nd Divisions were currently in reserve. On 22 August, in conjunction with the advance of III Corps, the 3rd Division would advance to cut off Bray and later capture it. That night the 1st Division would come forward from reserve and pass through the 5th to attack Chuignes and the Froissy Plateau at dawn the next day, while the 32nd Division alongside went for Herleville. The 4th Division had a minor role, advancing 460 metres to protect the right flank of the 32nd, in the network of old trenches that had formed the French front line in 1916. Only the 4th Brigade on the Division's left would be engaged.

On 21 August Third Army jumped off and by the end of the day had reached most of its objectives. Next day III Corps began its advance, succeeding in capturing Albert on its left, and also reached its objectives on the right. The 3rd Division also advanced to capture the ground above Bray according to plan, but in the afternoon the right of III Corps was counter-attacked by the Germans and driven back almost to its start line. Suddenly the 3rd Division found that its left flank was dangerously exposed, but they faced left and held on, maintaining what was 'theoretically an impossible position.'[30] Although the situation was unsatisfactory north of the river, it would not interfere with the operation on the south. At dawn on 23 August the 1st Division attacked, overcoming stubborn resistance to win a brilliant victory. On the 1st Division's right the 32nd Division's left brigade generally kept pace and achieved its objectives, but its right, adjoining the 4th Division's 16th Battalion, was held up short of Courtine Trench running north near Madame Wood. The 16th was required to advance in conformity with the British right battalion, the 16th Lancashire Fusiliers, and at 4:45 am had jumped off behind the barrage and reached its own objective against slight resistance. Lieutenant Charles Garratt and Sergeant Frederick Robbins took a bombing-squad of about ten men from 'D' Company along the communication trench Courtine Alley with the intention of linking up with the Fusiliers in Courtine Trench.[31]

Near the trench junction they came up to a barricade, above head height, at a point where Courtine Trench split around an island of earth then joined up again. The two branches were blocked by timber and wire. A German stick grenade thrown over the barricade made it apparent that the British troops were not there. A quick look over the obstacle showed several groups of Germans, with a machine gun within 40 metres pointing down the trench. A grenade fight broke out. At one stage a Lewis gun was set up to fire over the barricade but this was soon knocked out by a German grenade. After more than an hour's fighting the Australians had almost run out of grenades, so Lieutenant Garratt went back to organise more supplies,

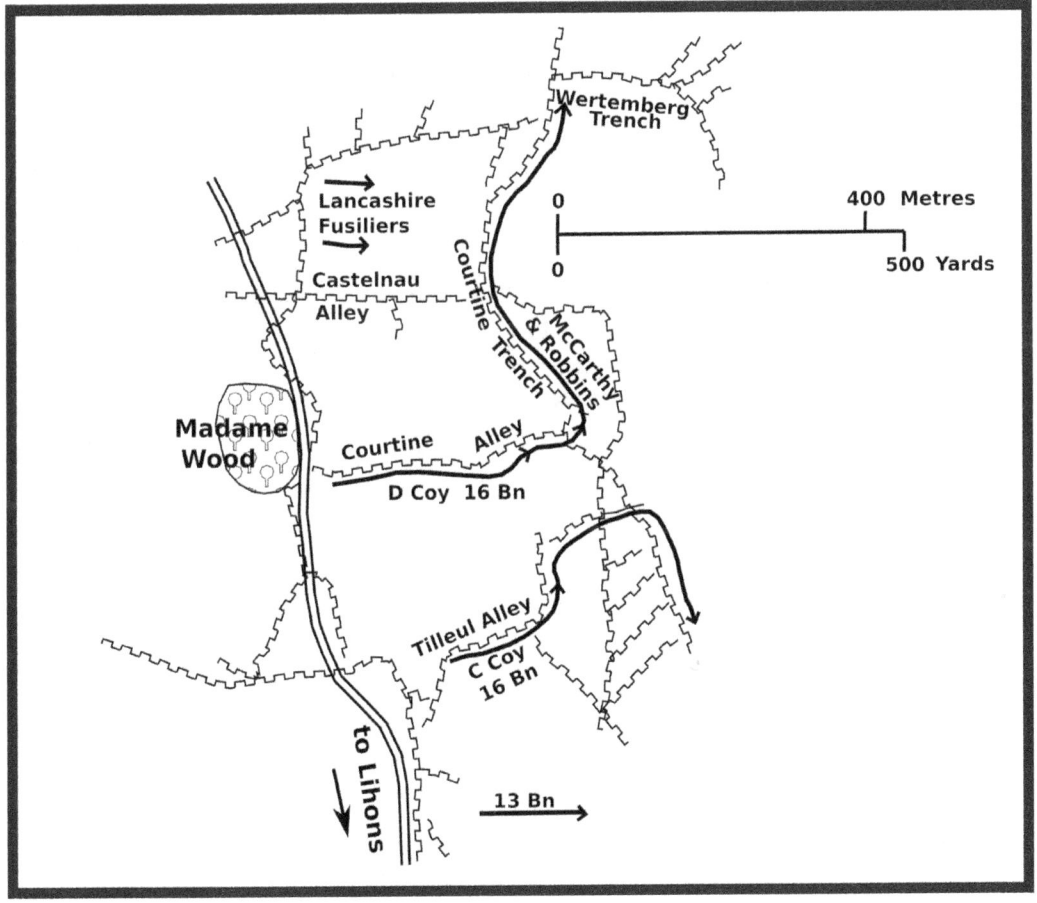

Lieutenant Lawrence McCarthy's exploit near Madame Wood, 23 August 1918.

Lieutenant Lawrence McCarthy VC (1892–1975), 16th Battalion. (AWM H13822)

leaving Robbins in charge. Shortly afterwards, Lieutenant Lawrence McCarthy, acting in command of 'D' Company in place of Captain Lynas, came up to see what was causing the delay. McCarthy decided that the only way to end the stalemate was to charge straight at the enemy. A British sergeant and one or two privates had joined the Australians, and McCarthy set them to digging through the block of earth dividing the trench, while he and Robbins jumped over the top and dropped into the enemy's section of the trench. Robbins had found eight grenades and McCarthy was armed with his revolver. Ten metres down the trench, McCarthy shot a German sentry, then came around a corner and surprised the nearest machine gun with its crew of three. He shot two of them and Robbins killed the other with a grenade. McCarthy kept going, on his own for the moment, having outdistanced Robbins. He next came across a German officer waving his arms and shouting orders to his disorganised men. McCarthy shot the officer and chased the other Germans into a narrow trench leading off the main one. Robbins had now come up, and he joined McCarthy in throwing grenades into the second trench, using German stick grenades when their Mills bombs ran out. Soon the surviving Germans waved a white flag, in the form of a bloodstained handkerchief, and trooped back into the main trench as prisoners—40 or more surrendered, and at least 15 and up to 20 had been killed. McCarthy took charge of the captives, and in another extraordinary scene, attested to in the unit War Diary, the Germans crowded around him and patted him on the back! At this point, the British soldiers who had dug through the block arrived (the sergeant 'was a first class man,' Robbins later said) as did some of the Australian platoon, and McCarthy sent Robbins further up Courtine Trench with two Lewis gun teams to establish defensive posts. Lieutenant Garratt, who had hurried back to the firing line, now noticed parties of the Lancashire Fusiliers cautiously coming forward through an old communication trench. He went out over the top and guided them forward to join the Australians in the main trench. At about the same time, Corporal George Payne led a small squad against another machine gun post. Using rifle grenades for covering fire, he rushed the post, capturing the gun and 12 survivors of the garrison. Eventually the British troops occupied the objective and the Australians were able to withdraw, although some 16th Battalion NCOs stayed for a while to assist the inexperienced Tommies.

Sergeant Robbins was later decorated with the DCM for his part in this fight, and Corporal Payne received the MM, but the outstanding figure was obviously Lieutenant McCarthy. In describing the fight, the 16th's diarist wrote of his 'amazing audacity' and of how

> in 20 minutes [he] had killed 20 Germans, taken 50 prisoners, and captured a fair proportion of the trench which was to have been wrested from the enemy by the Lancashire Fusiliers [at least 500 yards of trench]. But for his act it is more than likely that the Brigade's position would have been seriously menaced.[32]

It was no surprise that he was awarded the VC, announced in December 1918. Lawrence McCarthy was 26 at the time of the fight, and had been with the 16th Battalion since the early days at Blackboy Hill training camp in WA, where he had been a contemporary of such men as Percy Black, Harry Murray and Bill Lynas. While working at a sawmill before the war he had lost several fingers on his left hand in an accident. This resulted in him being at first rejected by the AIF, but he was able to show that he had won prizes for shooting, thereby proving that he would not be hampered by the missing fingers.[33] He served with the 16th at Gallipoli, reaching the rank of sergeant, and on the Western Front, where he was wounded and hospitalised on 2 April 1917. He had previously been selected for an officer's commission, which came through while he was in hospital. Returning to his unit three months later, he served until early in 1918 when he was posted for a stint with the training battalions in England. He had only been back with the 16th for about two weeks when the VC exploit took place, having returned on the day of the Amiens battle, 8 August. McCarthy was a bulky man, of average height but weighing 182 pounds (82.5 kg) on enlistment, resulting in the nickname 'Fat'—he must have made an imposing sight to the Germans as he charged along the trench firing his revolver.[34]

On the same night of 23 August an adjustment of the Corps front's southern boundary began. As the first stage of a progressive relief of the 4th Division, the British 32nd Division extended its right in the newly captured line to take over from the 16th and 13th Battalions. On the following night, the remaining front line units, the 15th Battalion and the 48th and 46th of the 12th Brigade, would be relieved by two French regiments; French units would also relieve the 13th Brigade in the reserve positions. The Division's destination was the rest area north of Amiens, which was now well behind the front line. The 4th Brigade's movements took place mostly according to plan, with the 16th Battalion in particular making sure that they got out quickly— the troops expected that the relieving British, inexperienced as they were, would fire off flares despite advice not to do so, and thereby bring down a German barrage on their positions, and so it proved.[35] The relief of the 12th Brigade by the French on the next night was more difficult, partly due to the language barrier but also to what was seen as a lack of organisation on the part of the French. Eventually some sort of contact was made between units—'How they did this I do not know,' wrote the Brigade diarist[36]—and the relief was completed very late. By the time the movement was in progress the Germans had started a heavy bombardment with gas shells, which lasted for over three hours, using mainly mustard gas ('Yellow Cross'). The 46th Battalion in particular was caught in this, which was described as the most severe gas bombardment that the unit had ever experienced. The effects were not immediately apparent, but the gas had been absorbed into the men's clothing and began to take effect as they were arriving at their new billets later in the morning. Before long 150 men were suffering from blistering and eye irritation, many of them severely enough to be evacuated.

Transported by motor vehicles for the latter part of the journey, the various units were settling into their billets by the morning of 25 August, in areas familiar from the recent past. The 4th Brigade units were accommodated at Coisy, Poulainville, Cardonette and Allonville. The 12th Brigade was located further west at Longpré, St Vast and Vaux-en-Amienois, while the 13th Brigade was at Rivery, just outside Amiens. Other elements of the Division were located in the same general area, and also to the east of the city, with the engineers and pioneers at Longeau and the MG Battalion at Lamotte-Brebière. The divisional artillery was also relieved by the French division's guns on 25 August, and marched via Corbie to Camon, another outlier of Amiens, arriving there the next day—it was rare for the artillery to receive an extended period of rest, particularly one at the same time as the Division's main body. Division HQ was set up at Bussy on the Hallue river. The divisional staff specified that the first three days in the back area would be taken up with re-organisation and refitting, with training not to begin until the fourth day. The men were to rest as much as possible, taking the opportunity to bathe and change clothes and underwear. Canteens were open and well stocked, and a payday ensured that the men were 'able to buy beer, cigarettes and groceries.'[37] The weather was mostly fine, and a thunderstorm one night proved to be an advantage as the rain laid the dust created by a long spell of hot weather, and also grounded enemy night bombers.

The infantry battalions returned to business from 28 August, training in the mornings but playing sports most afternoons. As well as brushing up on individual skills, the troops practiced sub-unit tactics, with platoons and sections working on open-warfare exercises in anticipation of the fighting still to come. The artillery carried out a program of training at battery level, and also took the opportunity to have all of the 18-pounders recalibrated at the Vaux range. At the end of the month the infantry brigades reported their numbers, in terms of personnel actually available for duty, as: 4th Brigade (four battalions) 2,227, an average battalion strength of 556; 12th Brigade (three battalions) 2,024, average battalion strength 674; 13th Brigade (three battalions) 2,222, average battalion strength 740, giving a total of 6,473 infantry officers and men available. The Division as a whole totalled 12,546 officers and men.[38] The 1st Division had also been withdrawn to rest at about the same time, while the 2nd and 5th Divisions joined the 3rd in the front line. The advance of the Australian Corps continued in the meantime, and in a fortnight the resting divisions could expect to take their next turn in action.

22 Notes

1. 16th Battalion War Diary, 9 August 1918.

2. Gen Sir A A Montgomery-Massingberd, 'August 8, 1918,' *Reveille*, 1 Sept 1932 (reprinted from *The Royal Artillery Journal*).

3. *Official History*, Vol VI, pp. 650–2; 1st Battalion War Diary 9 August 1918 and Appendix 8 to August Diary; 'Chipilly Stunt: Brave Diggers,' *Reveille*, 1 Sept 1933; award recommendations in AWM records—CQMS Hayes and Sgt Andrews were each awarded the DCM (Hayes having shown that the reputed skills of army quartermaster-sergeants can include knocking out machine gun nests), and MMs went to Ptes Kane and Fuller.

4. The total of 118 in the divisional artillery War Diary (Appendix 1 to the August 1918 Diary) and the *Official History* (Vol VI, p. 684n) includes casualties in other units under the orders of the 4th Division CRA at the time.

5. The figures for infantry fatalities are based on the AWM Roll of Honour for deaths on 8 August in the various battalions. Those numbers are somewhat higher than the original reports (except for the 45th Battalion), probably because some individuals were originally reported as wounded and the records later corrected. The figures for soldiers wounded were estimated by subtracting the corrected figures for deaths from the total casuaties reported by brigades and battalions at the time—the author acknowledges that such a method is less than rigorous.

6. See the 4th Division Engineers War Diary for August 1918, Pt 9, for correspondence from Maj Riddell (OC 12th Field Company) to the CRE concerning the recommendations. After the war, Ralph Hunt joined the Victorian State Electricity Commission, under general manager Sir John Monash; in 1948 Hunt himself became general manager of that organisation (Australian Dictionary of Biography, article on R A Hunt by D Langmore).

7. From the recommendation in the AWM files.

8. The 4th Division General Staff War Diary entry for 10 August 1918 says that the meeting was attended by the Corps commander (Monash), GOCs 3rd and 4th Divisions, and the brigadier of the 10th Brigade (3rd Division) but oddly does not mention Brig Gen Herring, GOC 13th Brigade; the Division's report on the Amiens fighting (Appendix 65 to the August Diary), however, has it the other way around, saying that the GOC 13th Brigade was in attendance, but not mentioning the 10th Brigade. These may simply be mistakes, but a 1937 account by Herring ('Monash's Genius,' *Reveille*, November 1937) implies that Monash spoke to him separately but by arrangement with the 4th Division GOC. The later memoirs of the brigade major at the time,

Capt T S Louch, state that 'Herring was summoned to a conference where he received verbal instructions direct from General Monash (thus by-passing the Divisional commander General MacLagan)' (Louch, *Op Cit*, p. 34). It is also possible that Herring, whose HQ was south of Cérisy, was unable to reach Corbie in time for the main meeting.

9   Louch, *Op Cit*, p. 34.

10 The 13th Brigade's report on the operation (August 1918 War Diary, Appendix 30) states that 'During the afternoon the Brigade Intelligence Officer made a reconnaissance of the forward area and it was found definitely that American troops were holding the whole of Gressaire Wood.' The *Official History*, however (Vol VI, p. 693n) says that the 13th Brigade's reconnaissance was carried out by 'Captain T S Louch, Intelligence Officer.' At this time, Capt Louch was certainly the brigade major, not the IO, and Lieutenant Loudon's service record shows that he had been Brigade IO since June. In his memoirs (Louch, *Op Cit*, p. 34) on the other hand, Louch stated that he had reconnoitred Gressaire Wood himself in the morning, before the brigadier was summoned to the meeting with Monash at which the operation was ordered. If the reconnaissance did take place in the afternoon rather than the morning, it seems unlikely in view of the urgency of the Brigade's preparations that the brigade major would have had the time available to make his own reconnaissance over such a distance—doing another officer's job. The Brigade report, although signed by Brig Gen Herring, would probably have been drafted by Capt Louch.

There are other difficulties with T S Louch's memoirs, which were written many years after the events. He recalls that the 13th Brigade changed the Corps plan considerably, with the staff and battalion COs persuading a reluctant Brig Gen Herring to agree; the brigadier then feared that he would be removed from his command if the attack failed. The documented orders from Division and Brigade, however, show little difference apart from the changed emphasis on the tanks, a not unreasonable change in the circumstances that is explained in the Brigade report. Louch also says that Herring 'received the immediate award of the CMG' for the Brigade's success in the operation; AWM records show, however, that Herring was recommended for the CMG in January 1919 (the recommendation does not mention the Etinehem operation) and that the award was gazetted on 3 June 1919. There are also recommendations for a Mention In Despatches and a brevet promotion which broadly fit with the Etinehem dates, however.

11 Bean Papers, AWM38 3DRL606/227/1, folio 224.

12 Hockey was awarded the MM. According to Capt Tambling's account ('Etinehem and Corbie-Bray Road,' *Reveille*, 1 Aug 1937), only one German was actually killed in the fight—the second was shot by Hockey while escorting the prisoners to the rear, in his anger when the German tried to misdirect him.

13 Bean Papers, AWM38 3DRL606/227/1, folio 220. In the *Official History* (Vol VI, p. 697), Bean interprets the 'crucifix' reference as meaning the one just west of Bray, on the Corbie road. That was well into the 49th Battalion's area, but the map shows two crucifixes on roads running south-west to Etinehem from the direction of Bray, more in the general direction that the 50th had to move.

14 *Official History*, Vol VI, p. 698.

15 The figure for the 49th Battalion's casualties on 11 August is taken from the AWM Roll of Honour. The unit's August 1918 War Diary, Appendix 26, has six fatalities, but one soldier reported missing was subsequently found to have been killed. The *Official History* (Vol VI, p. 699) says 'Mainly at this stage Tambling's company had 49 out of 110 men hit.' That figure seems to be an aggregate from several days of fighting.

16 Bean Papers, AWM 38 3DRL606/228/1, p. 460.

17 *Official History*, Vol VI, p. 699n. C E W Bean was himself among those observers, and wrote a detailed account in his diary for 11 August.

18 Bean Diary, AWM38 3DRL606/116/1, 11 August 1918, p. 77 (p. 84 in PDF).

19 As in the battalion's report (Appendix 13A to the 51st's August 1918 War Diary). Browning (*For King and Cobbers, Op Cit*, p. 299) notes that Pte Thomas Moir died from a head wound received in this fighting; Moir's record, however, says that he was wounded on 12 August and died on the same date, not 13 August.

20 Bean Papers, AWM38 3DRL606/227/1, folio 222.

21 The footnote on Lt Livesey in the *Official History* (Vol VI, p. 712n) does not mention that decoration, a most unusual omission. The AWM records on decorations show both the recommendation and the gazettal (London, 2 December 1918), so there would seem to be little doubt that the award was made.

22 The recommendation says that his patrol silenced several of the machine guns, but the account in the Bean Papers referred to in Note 20 above only says that they tried several times but could not reach the guns with grenades; Bean followed that account in the *Official History* (Vol VI, p. 712). Irwin Mengersen had joined up before his 18th birthday, and so had to gain his parents' permission first. He had two older brothers in the AIF, one of whom, Lt Herman Mengersen, was killed at the Menin Road in 1917.

23 *Official History*, Vol VI, p. 712.

24 Williams was 21, having enlisted at 18; he had served with the 15th throughout its Western Front campaigns, winning the DCM in 1916 for several days of heroic efforts as a runner and guide in the Pozières-Mouquet Farm fighting. His correct name was William Cecil Williams, but he had enlisted as George Williams, for what are described on his service record as 'family reasons.' His DCM was gazetted as George Williams, but he is buried as William Cecil Williams, in the CWCG's Heath Cemetery on the D1029 (the old Roman road) near Harbonnières. Seven of the other victims of the shell are also buried there: Ptes H P Bailes, J C Beacom, P J Frostrop, J S Hagevole, H H Harp, C Regan and W J T Rowe. The remaining victim was probably Pte Harold H Lawrence, whose record shows that he was wounded on 13 August and died the next day at the CCS; he is buried in Daours Communal Cemetery Extension.

25 4th Brigade War Diary, 13 August 1918.

26 12th Brigade War Diary, 16 August 1918.

27 46th Battalion War Diary for August 1918, Appendix 9.

28 DCM recommendation for Sgt Boyes in AWM records.

29 The AWM records list the gazettal of the MC award under the name of 'Trewhella' but the actual notice (11 January 1919) has the correct spelling of Trewheela.

30 *Official History*, Vol VI, p.731.

31 This account comes from C E W Bean's notes of an interview with Sgt Robbins (Bean Papers, AWM38 3DRL606/228/1, folio 479–81), re-told in the Official History, Vol VI, pp. 742–3. The exact location of the action is not entirely clear. Maps in the battalions' War Diaries identify Courtine Alley and Courtine Trench but there is another un-named segment of trench nearby, to the east of Courtine, which does not appear to have figured in the fighting – it may have been overgrown or collapsed by August 1918, of course. The 16th Battalion's Diary entry for 23 August refers to "Foch Alley – a communication trench leading into Courtine" where a "particularly violent encounter took place" but without saying where Foch Alley was or stating a map reference. The Diary gives what appears to be an incorrect map reference of S.7.a.7.3 for the location of one incident during the fight – "square" S.7 was one of the strip of half-squares

at the western edge of the relevant map, as happened occasionally, and only had sub-squares 'b' and 'd' (the adjoining half-square in the next map was X.12 with two sub-squares 'a' and 'c'). S.7.a is probably a typo for S.7.d, but that location is somewhat further north than where McCarthy appears to have reached. Reference S.13.b.7.3 in the next section to the south is a location in Courtine Trench, however, and the latter reference may have been the one intended..

32 16th Battalion War Diary, 23 August 1918. An intelligence report in the Diary states that McCarthy reached as far as Wertemberg Trench, which is about 500 yards in a straight line from the junction of Courtine Alley and Courtine Trench.

33 Gill, *Op Cit*, p. 248; R K O'Connor, *Super VC and Two Croix de Guerre—The Life of Lt Lawrence Dominic McCarthy VC*, transcript of lecture given in 2012. McCarthy's service record makes no mention of missing fingers under the heading of 'Distinctive Marks' although several comparatively minor scars are noted, suggesting that the medical examiner turned a blind eye rather than giving official acceptance.

34 The recommendation for McCarthy's VC is different in some respects from the account in the *Official History*; in particular, the recommendation states that he personally tunnelled a hole through the earthen block in the trench and then crawled through it. Bean preferred to go by the account of Sgt Robbins, who was an eyewitness and participant. A man of McCarthy's bulk might have found some difficulty forcing his way through a narrow tunnel in the earth.

35 Bean Papers, AWM38 3DRL606/228/1, folio 472.

36 12 Brigade War Diary, 24 August 1918.

37 48th Battalion War Diary, 26 August 1918.

38 Figures from the strength returns in the 4th Division Admin Staff War Diary for August 1918, Appendix 3. The Brigade numbers do not include battalion COs. The average battalion strength in the 13th Brigade is somewhat skewed by the 49th Battalion, which was near full strength. The figures shown in the 4th and 12th Brigade August Diaries are higher than those shown here, and probably include personnel on strength but temporarily absent from their units.

Rivery, near Amiens, August 1918: 50th Battalion's HQ and RAP were located in this substantial building during the 4th Division's period in rest. The Battalion flag is attached to a tree in front, with a Red Cross flag on the left indicating the RAP. The main body of the Battalion was billeted further along the road.
(Sketch by 3362 Cpl William Brewster in 50th Battalion War Diary, September 1918, AWM4 23/67/27. Several more examples of William Brewster's artistic skills are included in the 50th Battalion's 1918 Diaries.)

23: Outpost Line

For the 4th Division, the routines of life in reserve went on for the next two weeks, with regular training and sports, and the occasional ceremonial parade. On 3 September the divisional artillery was inspected by General Sinclair-MacLagan and conducted a full march-past. The General also visited each infantry brigade and most of the other units to observe training and watch the usual sports days. Changes among senior officers during this period included the appointment of new COs for the 15th and 45th Battalions. Higher authority chose not to retain Major Burford Sampson permanently in command of the 15th, and instead transferred Lieutenant Colonel Charles Johnston in from his present posting as CO of the 45th. Colonel Johnston did not take up the duties straight away, since he had just gone on a fortnight's leave, but his replacement at the 45th took over that command as of 2 September. This was the youthful Gallipoli veteran Noel Loutit, promoted to temporary lieutenant colonel from major in the 50th Battalion. An engineering student in South Australia before the war, as a platoon commander with the 10th Battalion at the Landing he had reached further inland than any other officer. He was transferred to the 50th when the 4th Division was formed and had risen to the rank of major with that unit, winning the DSO and Bar in Western Front operations. His service also included a period commanding the 13th Training Battalion in England. Colonel Loutit was still only 24, among the youngest of AIF battalion commanders.

Another change took place in the medical services, when the long-serving DADMS, Major Frank Lind, received command of the 2nd Field Ambulance (1st Division) with promotion to lieutenant colonel; Lind was subsequently awarded the DSO for his service with the 4th Division. His replacement as DADMS was Major Thomas Evans from the 13th Field Ambulance, also a holder of the DSO, for his work at the Passchendaele battles. A little earlier, the officer commanding the divisional Signal Company, Major John Fraser, had been posted to command the Signal Training Depot in England, having been in command of the Company since its formation in Egypt in 1916. In that time its establishment strength had increased from about 200 officers and men to 372 as signals had increased in importance and new methods, notably wireless telegraphy, had been developed. Major Fraser was succeeded by Major Coleman Joseph, promoted from captain within the Signal Company. In the divisional artillery the DTMO, Captain Ewan, was evacuated sick and replaced by Captain William Pinder from the 7th MTM Battery.

On 6 September preliminary orders were issued for the Division's next forward move, to begin later the same day. Most of the journey would be carried out by vehicle, in the interests of speed and the distance to be covered to catch up with the fighting front. While the 4th and 1st Divisions had been resting Fourth Army, and the Australian Corps, had pushed on eastwards, following the German retreat along the line of the Somme towards Péronne. The Corps now had the 2nd and 5th Divisions in the line south of the river, each advancing on a one-brigade front, with the 32nd British on their right. The 3rd Division, no longer fresh, still pressed forward on the north bank. Just west of Péronne, the Somme, flowing north to that point, takes a right-angled bend and continues west to the sea, the south-north stretch forming an obstacle across the line of the advance. By the end of August the Australian Corps had driven the Germans off the western bank of the river but on the east the enemy still held the formidable strongholds of Péronne city and the nearby height of Mont St Quentin. Monash was pushing his weary troops hard at this stage, keeping the Germans off balance, and was prepared to exceed his instructions in order to maintain the pressure. On 31 August and the following two days, in brilliant manoeuvres devised on the spot by Monash, the 2nd and 5th Divisions crossed the river and captured both Mont St Quentin and Péronne, to the amazement of both the Germans and the Army commander, General Rawlinson.

The Germans now had no alternative but to withdraw to the Hindenburg Line further east. Fourth Army followed them up, with the Australian divisions in the line almost at the limit of their endurance after three weeks of fighting every day against the enemy rearguards. Leaving the Somme behind, they reached a line running north-south through the village of Hesbécourt, between the Cologne and Omignon rivers. This was the area where the British front line had been before the great German offensive of March 1918, and it was unfamiliar territory to the Australians. Travelling in brigade groups with the 13th Brigade leading, the 4th Division began arriving and debussing in the area on 8 September to relieve the 5th Division. The next day the 13th Brigade moved into the support area around Bouvincourt, then on 10 September and during that night moved to the front line. The 50th and 51st Battalions, left to right, went into the line first, with the 49th in close support. The 13th MG Company and 13th LTM Battery took up positions covering the front line and the 13th Field Company made their base closer to Bouvincourt. The other two brigade groups were disposed in support and reserve positions, also near Bouvincourt. The divisional artillery meanwhile had moved in stages to the area north and south of Hancourt, with artillery HQ to the west at Catelet,[1] a tiny spot south-west of the larger village of Cartigny. Two British field brigades initially came under the CRA's command here, replaced within a few days by the 6th and 12th 'Army' Brigades, AFA.

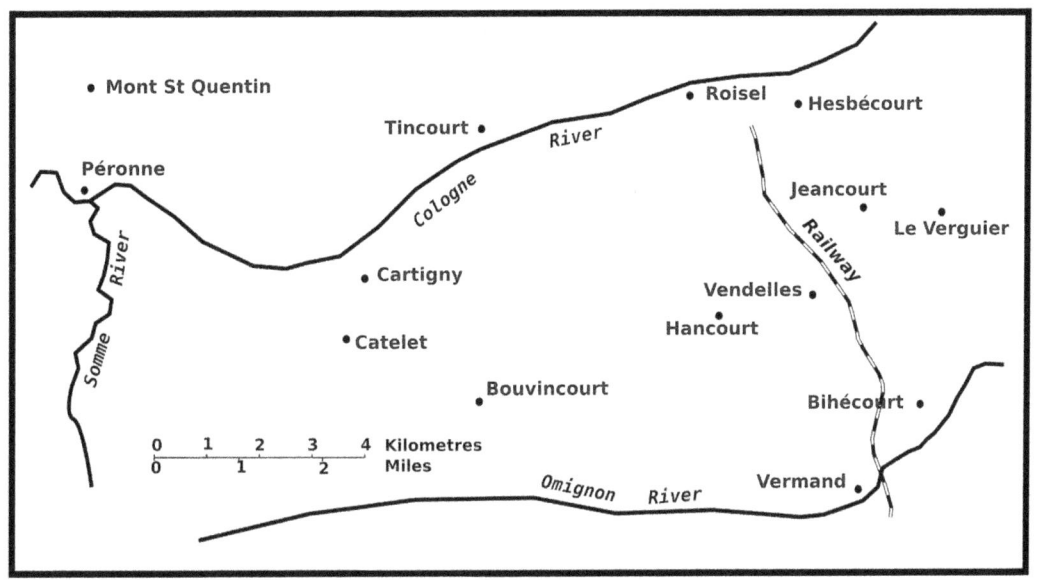

Péronne to the Hindenburg Line, September 1918

4th Division HQ also moved to the vicinity of Catelet, opening there on 11 September. The supply railhead was close to Péronne, initially at La Chapelette then at Flamicourt. On the 4th Division's left (north), the 1st Division had relieved the 3rd at the same time, while on the right the 32nd British Division was also relieved, ceasing attachment to the Australian Corps. The newly-established IX Corps, soon built up to four divisions, came into the line to reinforce Fourth Army.

The immediate task was to advance the line to within striking distance of the Hindenburg system. The 13th Brigade was in action without delay, both the 50th and 51st Battalions despatching nocturnal reconnaissance patrols into No Man's Land as soon as they took over the sector from their weary predecessors. During the afternoon of the next day (11 September) the 50th and 51st conducted a speculative advance along their fronts, the 50th sending out two platoon-strength fighting patrols, each with another platoon in support, and the 51st on the right using two companies. Minimal resistance was met from isolated German observation posts, and by evening the front had been advanced up to two kilometres. The troops reached the line of the disused Péronne—St Quentin railway, which here ran north-south through a series of cuttings between the villages of Vendelles and Vermand. The following day the 50th Battalion advanced a further 360 metres north-east beyond the railway by aggressive patrolling, and Colonel Salisbury moved his HQ forward to the railway cutting just east of Vendelles. On the right the advancing 51st encountered the first serious opposition, in the form of heavy machine gun fire directed at its two forward companies. This slowed down the advance but did not stop it, and by the end of the day the 51st occupied a line facing generally north-east, with its right on the Omignon river at Bihécourt and its left in touch with the 50th near Vendelles. That night the 50th sent out a strong patrol of 27 men under

Lieutenant Arden Hawker, a 37-year old ex-militia officer who had been on active duty with the battalion for only about six weeks,[2] to probe further ahead. The patrol moved out beyond a cross-road near the front line and encountered a German force in a trench. Hawker was about to attack with part of the patrol when another enemy party appeared, apparently the relief for the first. The outnumbered South Australians opened fire on both groups, inflicting an estimated 10 casualties, then started to fall back. A third group of Germans then appeared, but also lost several men to the patrol's fire. Hawker extricated his men with only two slightly wounded. The other part of the patrol had pushed further down the road and encountered a strong enemy force, estimated at a company, wiring a trench intersecting the road. Both groups withdrew to the Australian line and reported their information. It was apparent that the advance had reached a point where stiff resistance could be expected, and the battalion quickly organised an attack for the morning. Hawker, who was said to have personally shot six Germans in the fight, was later awarded the MC.[3]

The next morning (13 September) at 4 am, three platoons from the 50th, spread across a front of 1,600 metres, attacked the detected enemy positions. The Germans were pushed back for 500 metres and the 50th troops captured 40 prisoners and eight machine guns. Unfortunately, the centre platoon lost touch with those on its flanks, advanced too far and was cut off by the enemy. The platoon fought its way back to the line but lost four men wounded and taken prisoner in the process. Nevertheless the new front was firmly established and resisted two counter-attacks by the Germans during the day. The first, at 9:30 am, was a feeble effort easily beaten off but the second, in the evening, was more serious. A heavy enemy artillery bombardment came down on the new front line at 7:15 pm, followed at 8 by infantry attacks at two points. The Germans managed to drive in one outpost but the main line held firm and repulsed the attacks with fire from Lewis guns and rifles, inflicting an estimated 100 casualties. The 51st Battalion on the right was involved in some sharp fighting that day also. Their advance during the previous evening had penetrated between the German positions to their front and in the morning it was discovered that a sizeable enemy force was isolated in a trench between two posts in the new Australian line. Lieutenant John Salter's platoon was sent up from the support company to deal with the Germans, which was done with great efficiency. Concealed by a sunken road, the platoon approached the enemy position while the nearby posts kept the Germans' heads down with Lewis gun fire. When close enough, Salter and his men threw a shower of grenades then rushed the trench. The German force soon surrendered, the platoon gathering 46 prisoners, including two officers, and six machine guns.[4] For this exploit Lieutenant Salter was awarded the MC.

The next day saw a pause in combat activity, during which the 50th Battalion on the left was relieved in the evening by the 49th coming forward from reserve. At the same time the frontage was rearranged, the 49th taking over a section of the 1st Division line to the north. The 51st meanwhile shifted its frontage to conform, with its right flank company on the Omignon being replaced by troops of the 1st British Division, part of the recently-arrived IX Corps.

The effect of these moves was to shift the overall 13th Brigade front (and therefore the front of the 4th Division) to the north, bringing the 49th's left flank up to the village of Jeancourt, with Le Verguier directly east in the German front line. The advance was resumed on 15 September when the 51st Battalion made another 460 metres of ground, conforming with the British unit to the right and again meeting only slight resistance. In turn the 49th Battalion sent forward its right flank platoon, under Lieutenant Michael McCabe, to extend the new line taken by the 51st. McCabe, with a section of four men, rushed and eliminated a German position, capturing 22 prisoners and several machine guns; he received the MC in due course. That evening two companies of the 49th advanced to occupy the new line in force, pushing the Germans off the hill south-west of Le Verguier and capturing nine machine guns and eight prisoners in the process (a German gas bombardment at the time obliged the 49th troops to attack while wearing their gas masks). Some outposts of the 49th's line had reached to within 500 metres of the outskirts of Le Verguier. The 13th Brigade had completed its task of seizing a jumping-off line in the 4th Division's sector for the imminent formal attack on the Hindenburg system, and now prepared to hand over to the 4th and 12th Brigades for that operation.

Those forces had been moving up as the front line advanced and were at first concentrated in the vicinity of Bouvincourt, about nine kilometres behind the new front line. Here the 4th Brigade received a visit from the Australian Prime Minister, W M 'Billy' Hughes, on 15 September. Hughes had just seen one of his ideas come to fruition, the granting of home leave to Australia for some of the longest-serving AIF members. Faced with assurances that the war would continue well into 1919 (or even 1920), Hughes was insistent that the Australian Corps be withdrawn as soon as the current series of operations was finished. The troops would be given a long rest well to the rear before returning refreshed for the anticipated campaigns of the next year. He had also demanded that the surviving veterans who had signed up in 1914 be granted two months furlough in Australia. This had been postponed due to lack of shipping, but some ship space suddenly became available. The window of opportunity was short and the divisions were told to release the first batch of '1914 men' immediately. They departed on 13 and 14 September, the 4th Division's quota being 192.[5] The higher command was not pleased at losing experienced troops almost on the eve of a major operation, but the men themselves were delighted.[6] The 48th Battalion's diarist, Major 'Johnny' Moyes, recorded in his usual humorous style that a 'terrific cloud of dust' was caused by 'various old timers en route for Australia—by the rate they were going they should almost do the trip by nightfall.'[7]

In the 4th Brigade, both the 15th and 16th Battalions had changed their COs just before going into the front line. Lieutenant Colonel Johnston, appointed CO of the 15th in place of Major Sampson, returned from leave and took over the command during 16 September, while Sampson went to Division HQ for liaison duties (the tone of the battalion history suggests some disappointment within the unit that Sampson was displaced at such a moment[8]). In the 16th Major Harwood had been acting CO in place of Lieutenant Colonel Drake-Brockman, who was still commanding the 4th Brigade, but on 14 September he had taken advantage of the home furlough for 1914 men and departed for Australia. The senior officer with the Battalion was now Captain Bill Lynas, who was appointed temporary CO and would command the unit in the coming battle. Lynas was of course a 1914 original himself, but married men were given preference, and unlike Harwood he was single.

Fourth Army's coming assault on the Hindenburg Line system would begin with the capture of its outer defences. In this sector the enemy main line was located behind the St Quentin Canal, which formed a formidable obstacle in its own right, but the position had the great disadvantage of being overlooked by higher ground, Hélène Ridge, to the west, 1,600 metres distant on average. An enemy occupying that ridge would have direct observation over most of the main line, so the Germans had established and progressively strengthened an outer line along the feature. Originally an outpost line, it was now a heavily wired and strongly garrisoned forward defensive line, although it was still usually referred to as the Hindenburg Outpost Line by the British. Further west and also occupied in some strength were the former British outpost and front lines, captured by the Germans at the outset of their March offensive. Beyond these was the old British reserve line, now largely in the possession of Fourth Army following the advances of the previous week, which would mark the start line for the coming attack.

The decision to proceed with a set-piece operation against the outer lines had been made on 13 September, and that afternoon the GOCs of the 1st and 4th Divisions attended a preliminary conference at Australian Corps HQ. The broad plan, after the experience gained at Hamel and Amiens, did not need detailed exposition at Corps level—General Monash later made a well-known comment that the

> methods of the Corps were becoming stereotyped, and by this time we all began to understand each other so well that most of what I had to say could almost be taken for granted. Each Commander was ready to anticipate the action that would be required of him, almost as soon as I had unfolded the general plan.[9]

The Australian Corps was to form the centre of the attack, between III Corps to the north and IX Corps to the south. The first two objectives, the old British positions, were designated as the Green Line and the Red Line. If all went well success would then be exploited by an advance to take the 'Outpost' line on Hélène Ridge, designated as the Blue Line. Recognising that this final stage would be the most difficult, Monash did not insist that the attack be pressed there if it seemed likely to be too costly. The 4th Division would be on the Australian right with the 1st Australian Division on its left and the 1st British Division (IX Corps) on its right. General Sinclair-MacLagan and his staff briefed the infantry brigadiers and supporting arms commanders next morning (14 September). The 4th and 12th Brigades would carry out the advance after relieving the 13th Brigade in the front line just before 'Z-day,' which was anticipated to be 18 September. The brigadiers met with their staffs and battalion commanders in the afternoon to pass on the information and get the detailed planning under way.

Moving forward from reserve, the 4th and 12th Brigades duly relieved the 13th Brigade in the front line overnight of 16/17 September, with the 13th becoming divisional reserve. The deployment of both incoming brigades anticipated their roles in the coming battle. The 4th Division plan required the 4th Brigade to attack on the left, where the fortified village of Le Verguier stood directly to the front in the first objective, and the 12th Brigade on the right where the German lines ran across open country. Accordingly on the right of the 4th Division sector the 12th Brigade came into the line on a one-battalion frontage of 1,400 metres, with the 48th forward, the 45th close behind in support and the 46th next behind them. On the left the 4th Brigade put the 13th, 16th and 15th, right to left, into the front line, each on a front of one company with their other companies behind in succession, covering an overall width of about 1600 metres. The 14th Battalion was further to the rear as brigade reserve. On the day of battle, the 13th and 15th would pass on either side of Le Verguier village to capture the first line of trenches, while the 16th in the centre assaulted the village itself. Beyond Le Verguier, the 13th and 15th would link up and after a short halt move on to capture the next objective, the Red Line, on Ascension Ridge (or Spur). That line was the original British outpost position, in the 4th Division sector consisting of a string of short trenches and posts rather than a continuous trench line. The 14th would then pass through the other units and make an attempt on the Blue Line, a further 1,600 metres away across open country. The 12th Brigade planned a leapfrogging arrangement on a one-battalion front, with its three units deployed one behind the other. The 48th Battalion would lead off to capture the first German line, followed by the 45th passing through and going for the next objective, the Red Line, and finally the 46th with the Blue Line as its objective.

Artillery support followed the now-familiar pattern. The heavy weapons concentrated on counter-battery work and hitting identified strong-points, while the field artillery directly supported the attack with a creeping barrage—only on the first two objective lines, however. The Blue Line would be bombarded by a proportion of the heavy artillery, and several field batteries were allocated to advance with the infantry attacking that objective. As before, no preliminary registration shooting would be allowed unless concealed by normal harassing fire. In the 4th Division sector the field artillery would comprise the brigades of the 4th and 5th Divisions, two AFA 'Army' brigades and a British RFA Brigade, seven brigades altogether under the command of Brigadier General Burgess. The artillery barrage would be supplemented by a machine gun barrage, for which the 3rd and 5th MG Battalions were brought forward and attached to the 1st and 4th MG Battalions respectively, thereby doubling each attacking Division's machine gun resources.

The boosting of the machine guns was partly intended to offset a serious shortage of available tanks, a key aspect in which the battle plan differed from those of Hamel and Amiens. Combat losses, low serviceability and the need to retain as many machines as possible to attack the main Hindenburg Line meant that only 20 tanks were available to the whole of Fourth Army. The share of the Australian Corps was eight, four to each attacking division. Of the 4th Division's share, three were allocated to the 4th Brigade and the fourth to the 12th Brigade. They would advance behind the infantry, and on the 4th Division's front were not to go beyond the first objective. In an attempt to make the Germans think the numbers were greater, a scheme was devised to construct dummy tanks and position them where they could be seen by the enemy. In the 4th Division the 4th Field Company was given the task at short notice of designing and building 10 of these, using wooden framework with painted hessian covering. All hands worked through the day and night of 17 September to complete the task in time for the jump-off. Five dummies were allocated to each infantry brigade, to be moved by squads from the Pioneer Battalion. The remainder of the Pioneers would be employed mainly on road maintenance and marking of forward roads and tracks behind the advance. The 13th Field Company would work closely with the infantry, a half-company to each brigade, on forward engineering work, including searching for booby traps and for water sources. The 12th Field Company was given bridge-building tasks to improve transport routes after the advance. The Signal Company's work included establishing wireless telegraphy equipment at key locations, as well as providing the standard telephone lines linking Division with the infantry brigades and the artillery. Wireless sets would be provided at each infantry brigade's forward HQ and at artillery HQ and the field brigades, communicating with the set at Division. The two battalions attacking the Blue Line would each carry a wireless set with them also. Unit and brigade signallers would have their usual tasks of running telephone lines forward to the battalions and batteries.

The 4th Division's medical arrangements included establishing an MDS at Hancourt by expanding the present ADS at that location. The work was carried out by parties from the 13th Field Ambulance, which would be in reserve on the day of battle apart from the bearers and an element operating a gas treatment centre. The MDS would then be administered by the 4th Field Ambulance, while the 12th Field Ambulance would be responsible for the evacuation of casualties from the forward RAPs. For that task the 12th would have control of the bearers and ambulance vehicles of all three Field Ambulances. A location for an ADS, between Hancourt and the front line, would be chosen once the advance was under way (in the event, Vendelles was selected). Transport of supplies to the forward troops, in the absence of carrier tanks, was organised in a similar manner to 8 August when the allotted carrier tanks had been destroyed. Once the second objective had been taken, horse-drawn wagons of the DAC small-arms sections would carry ammunition and grenades forward and establish brigade dumps just in rear of that line. The Divisional Train provided three wagons per infantry brigade to bring up engineer material, barbed wire and pickets for consolidation, also to be dumped near the Red Line.[10]

Monash held the final conference of higher commanders on the morning of 16 September, 'in a YMCA marquee erected near MacLagan's headquarters,'[11] finishing in only 75 minutes. It was confirmed that Zero day would be 18 September. The brigades and battalions continued with finalising plans and preparing orders, while the troops were issued with battle stores and made preparations for their overnight move to the front line. 17 September was fairly quiet apart from occasional enemy shelling, and junior officers and the troops were officially informed of the following morning's operation and the part their unit and sub-unit was to play —although 'of course they knew all about it even though they did not know details'[12] from the unmistakeable signs of the previous few days. Late in the day, a security scare occurred when the CO of the 5th MG Battalion, Lieutenant Colonel T R Marsden, misinformed as to the location of the front line, was taken prisoner when he walked into a German post while making a personal reconnaissance. Although he was carrying a map showing the objectives, the Germans fortunately failed to take advantage of their capture.

The battle would be opened at 5:20 am on 18 September by the artillery barrage, delivered on the 4th Division front by the seven field artillery brigades under the command of Brigadier General Burgess. The guns were organised in three groups: the Right Group, covering the 12th Infantry Brigade's advance, comprised the 4th Division's 10th and 11th AFA Brigades; the Left Group, the 6th and 12th AFA Brigades covering the 4th Infantry Brigade; and the 'Superimposed' Group shooting across the whole of the 4th Division front, made up of the two 5th Division brigades (13th and 14th AFA) and the British 232nd Brigade.[13] At Zero the creeping barrage would open, falling 180 metres ahead of the infantry start line for the first three minutes. It would then lift at the rate of 90 metres every three minutes in the early stages then changing to every four minutes as the curtain of shells neared the first objective. Having taken the first objective, the infantry would move about 180 metres further forward to a halt line[14] where the advance would pause for nearly two hours (on the 4th Division's front) while the artillery fired on a protective barrage line beyond. At Z + 190 minutes the barrage would resume its creep to cover the advance to the Red Line second objective. Another protective barrage would be placed beyond that line for 15 minutes, then the guns would cease fire to allow the force attacking the Blue Line to pass through. There would be no barrage on the final objective, but each of the two attacking battalions would be directly supported by a battery of 18-pounders—the 37th Battery (10th AFA) working with the 46th Battalion and the 41st Battery (11th AFA) with the 14th Battalion, moving forward as soon as the Red Line was reached. The rest of the artillery force would move up after the protective barrage ceased, to positions north and south of Le Verguier from where they could cover the Blue Line defensively.

Further fire support was provided by the machine guns, both in covering barrages and in direct support to the infantry. With the guns of two full MG battalions available, the 4th Division plan called for all 64 Vickers guns of the attached 5th MG Battalion to fire the opening barrage, sweeping ahead of the artillery barrage to the Green Line, while the companies of Colonel Murray's 4th MG Battalion were assigned to work with the infantry force more directly. The 13th and 24th MG Companies, right to left, with 32 guns in total, would move behind the first waves of the infantry to the first objective. There they would set up in batteries and lay down barrage fire ahead of the infantry advance to the Red Line, in conjunction with the resumed creeping barrage by the artillery. The 4th and 12th MG Companies were attached to the 4th and 12th Infantry Brigades respectively, with their sections distributed among the battalions to provide direct support.[15] The 1st Division on the left used a similar deployment, giving a total of 128 Vickers guns in the opening barrage on the Australian Corps front.[16]

There had been several heavy rain showers in the past few days and the early morning of 18 September was no exception. The downpour started as the troops left the front-line trenches and moved to the jumping-off line. All were soaked by the time they reached the tapes and flopped down in the mud to wait for Zero, an hour away. 'I can't get any wetter,' said a 13th Battalion digger resignedly.[17] The rain gradually died away to a light drizzle and the usual early-morning mist arose. The 4th Division battalions had occupied the front line in the correct relative positions and had shaken out into their battle formations as they moved to the tapes for the attack. The 4th Brigade on the left formed up with the 13th and 15th Battalions, right and left of the first line, each with two companies in front and two in support, and the 16th in the centre with three companies forward and one in support. The 14th Battalion, in reserve to make the attempt on the Blue Line, was not yet in battle formation. The 13th, 14th and 15th Battalions each had a section of Vickers guns from the 4th MG Company with them, the fourth section being held in reserve, and the 13th, 15th and 16th Battalions were each accompanied by a crew of sappers from the 13th Field Company carrying Bangalore torpedoes in case they were needed for wire cutting. The 12th Brigade formed up with the 48th Battalion leading off and the 45th next, each on a three-company front with one in reserve, then the 46th for the Blue Line task with two companies in front and two in support.[18] The 12th MG Company had Vickers gun sections working with each battalion (two sections with the 45th). The direction of the advance would be generally north-east. Half an hour before Zero the men out in front on outpost duty withdrew to the start line, then promptly at 5:20 the barrage crashed out and the troops moved off, closing up to the line of shell-bursts in anticipation of the first lift. The machine gun barrage opened also, filling the air over the German trenches with lead—prisoners later said it was impossible to raise one's head above the parapet without being shot.[19] Visibility for the attacking troops was poor, the drizzle and mist made worse by smoke-shells, the amount of which many regimental officers thought excessive. Nevertheless, direction was maintained for the most part.

The 16th Battalion in the centre of the 4th Brigade's line made for Le Verguier, following the barrage closely. In a quarter of an hour the leading elements had crossed the 800 metres from the jump-off line and were on the outskirts of the village. Working their way through several belts of wire, the 16th entered the village. The buildings had been mostly demolished by shell-fire and the German defences were based on three strong-points in the ruins, designated as Fort Bell, Fort Lees and Fort Bull.[20] Strongly manned and mounting numerous machine guns, these should have put up strong resistance but apart from a few isolated bursts of fire most of the garrisons stayed in their dugouts—'the enemy having had the fight knocked out of him by the artillery barrage,' as company commander Captain Harry Wilson later reported.[21]

'D' Company, led by Lieutenant Lawrence McCarthy (hero of the recent Madame Wood action) attacked and surrounded Fort Bell at the northern corner of the village. A brief resistance was quickly overcome and 70 prisoners emerged from the dugouts, including a regimental commander and his staff. McCarthy pushed on to the far side of the village where the company captured and occupied the northern part of Orchard Trench near the Green Line objective, taking more prisoners there. Meanwhile Lieutenant John Kerr's company captured Fort Bull on the eastern outskirts with another bag of prisoners, and Fort Lees on the south-west edge was taken by Lieutenant Henry Bradley's company. There Private Alfred Lawrence led a section to rush two enemy posts, capturing over 40 prisoners and six machine guns. Captain Wilson's company followed the others through the village to mop up, and an hour after Zero the battalion was holding Orchard Trench east of the village and awaiting the next stage. The 16th's diminutive intelligence officer, Lieutenant Vic Ketterer, was making one of his frequent trips bringing information between the firing line and Battalion HQ when he spotted an enemy machine gun that had been missed in the mopping-up. With his runner he attacked the gun and captured it, killing two of the crew and taking the other three prisoner. So high was the battalion's skill level and so low the German morale that the 16th had captured 450 prisoners, 60 machine guns and several artillery pieces, while recording the extraordinarily low loss of five killed and approximately 17 wounded on the day.[22]

In the meantime the 15th Battalion troops were skirting the north of the Le Verguier, following the barrage and working their way through several wire entanglements in the area of the old British lines. In the mist and smoke it was difficult to keep direction, and Colonel Johnston was obliged to use his compass to assist his officers—the conditions proved to be too much for the two tanks allocated to support the 4th Brigade's left, which did not show up at the start line on time and made no contribution.[23] The major obstacle was a sunken road across the line of the advance, with a barbed wire fence on each side, concertina wire in the roadway and German troops manning a trench beyond it. This line was quickly outflanked on the north by the left company, however, and the Germans soon surrendered. At the other end of the road, Sergeant Joseph Holt and Private Evan Williams, the only unwounded members of their section, took on a German post which surrendered to them. While they were rounding up the prisoners, a German NCO drew a pistol and killed Holt. Williams immediately shot the German and held the others until a few men arrived to assist him. It appears that they shot a few more of the prisoners before sending back the rest, who were fortunate to survive in the circumstances.[24] The Battalion passed over the Green Line, extending its right to link with the 13th Battalion, then reached the halt line beyond. There the troops sought cover in shell holes and re-organised for the next stage, while exchanging fire with Germans near Dawes Copse a further 200 metres on.[25]

To the south of Le Verguier the 13th Battalion experienced some problems with short firing from a few guns in the opening barrage. One shell from the first salvo killed company commander Lieutenant Norman McGuire, a Gallipoli veteran. Nevertheless the Battalion jumped off on time and moved towards its first objective, despite some disorganisation caused by the thick smoke and mist. As with the 15th Battalion on the left, tank support did not eventuate. The CO, Colonel Marks, had had an unsatisfactory experience during the lead-up period in attempting to liaise with the tank officer, and on the day he

> did not see *any* tanks in the attack. I know that the tank attached to the 13th Battalion did not reach the tapes. The Battalion Scout detailed to ride in the tank was not impressed. He said the tank got lost and then stuck in a sunken road.[26]

The poor visibility did, however, enable the 13th to overrun the enemy outposts and get within grenade range of the main line. Some elements of the German troops in this area put up a fight, resulting in several dramatic clashes. On the left a troublesome machine gun post was eliminated by Sergeant Gerald Sexton, standing up and firing his Lewis gun from the hip, the same tactics that he had used at Amiens on 8 August. Taking the lead in the advance, Sexton then used his Lewis again as he charged two more enemy positions in succession, killing or capturing the garrisons. The 13th's left company moved past the southern edge of Le Verguier, preparing to swing north to meet the 15th and complete the line east of the village. Here the company was held up by a German field gun and several mortars firing from a line of trees (Mill Spinney) further east. Sergeant Sexton took these on also. Calling to his section to follow him, he charged at the gun and a party of German infantry nearby, firing short bursts from the Lewis as he went. His shots killed the gun crew and a dozen others further on, and he then ran back to the field gun position, now under fire himself from machine guns. He began shooting into dugout entrances, and shortly 30 of the enemy came up and surrendered. The prisoners included a battalion commander.[27] With the hazard out of the way, the company continued its wheel to the left and made contact with the 15th Battalion's right flank moving down from the north along the Green Line.

The 13th's right flank company, groping forward in the gloom, could not locate the left of the 48th Battalion, so the support company on that flank came up to fill the gap. The troops on that side were split into small groups by the poor visibility and one party under Sergeant 'Jimmy' Lihou encountered a machine gun post that opened fire on them at close range. Lihou tossed a grenade into the post then charged in, taking the survivors of the crew prisoner. Pressing on, the group reached the objective line at the northern end of Dean Trench where another machine gun opened fire. Lihou also knocked that one out with grenades then began to work his way along the trench towards the 48th, throwing grenades ahead as he went. Sighting another machine gun some distance away holding up the 48th, he jumped out of the trench and charged the gun across the open. The Germans spotted him and fired, and he fell with a bullet in the chest; 'Jimmy is hit,' someone called. It seems that the wound was not immediately fatal and Lihou was able to get up and start for the rear, but somewhere along the way he collapsed and died. His body was never recovered.[28] The machine gun post was shortly knocked out by a party of the support company under Captain Harry Turner. Those troops linked up with the 48th on the right and then worked their way back up the trench to complete the capture of the first objective. At some point during the early fighting Private Thomas Denny, a company runner, was returning to the firing line after delivering a message to Battalion HQ. On the way he encountered a group of six diggers who had become lost in the fog, so Denny took charge and led them towards the objective (his duties as runner suggest a good sense of direction). The party reached the trench, but at a section that had been missed by the advancing companies and was still occupied by the enemy. Denny at once led the little group to the attack, moving up and down the trench throwing grenades and finally joining up with troops on both flanks. Denny and his men took 100 prisoners with seven machine guns in a remarkable display of courage and initiative.[29]

To the south the 48th Battalion, leading the 12th Brigade's advance, jumped off behind the barrage on a three-company front, with the single tank allotted to the 12th Brigade following close behind. The tank moved ahead and led the infantry to the Green Line, firing as it went, then crossed the objective line, turned right and moved into the British sector, having played its part in distracting the Germans. The 48th's Green Line objective ran about 180 metres beyond (east of) the enemy positions at the top of a spur, Dean Trench and its southern extension Cooker Trench. The Germans also had outposts in Dean Copse and along the sunken road west of the trench. On the left (north) flank, there was little resistance from the Germans who had survived the barrage, many emerging from dugouts with their hands up as the 48th troops approached. Things were a little more difficult in the centre, where enemy machine guns in Dean Copse took the advancing troops under fire. Two posts were outflanked and eliminated by sections making clever use of cover, and Corporal Hugo Rathke used rifle grenades to knock out a third.[30] On the right flank Captain Alexander Anderson led his 'C' Company against the enemy outposts in front of Cooker Trench, in the continuation of the sunken road and a further trench lying between the road and Cooker. The intermediate trench in particular formed a strong line and fire from that position caused many of the 48th's casualties for the day, including three men killed. The company pressed forward and Lewis gun teams, notably that of Private Arthur Lines, got into position to enfilade the trench and provide covering fire while the riflemen and 'bombers' jumped in and soon overcame the garrison.

The companies quickly reorganised and moved on against the main enemy line in Dean and Cooker Trenches in an irresistible drive. The support company came up to join in and Anderson's men on the right swung through part of the British sector to outflank the position. The trench system was taken in a burst of close

Sergeant James Lihou DCM and Bar MM (1895–1918), 13th Battalion.
(AWM A05757)

fighting, which cost the 48th several more killed. Lance Corporal Harold Jones distinguished himself by capturing an awkward strong-point and Lieutenants Robert Cameron and Arthur Gelston showed outstanding leadership in the fight. Those of the enemy garrison that were not killed or captured fled to the rear, taking refuge in another sunken road 460 metres further east—unfortunately for them, about where the protective barrage would descend.[31] The 48th kept its line moving forward on the far side of the trench to reach the Green Line, which on the right ran past the edge of Parker Copse, the location of the German unit's HQ dugout. Corporal Thomas Price led a party to attack the dugout with grenades, capturing the battalion commander and 60 others. The Germans tried to form up for a counter-attack from the sunken road but Captain Anderson had positioned some of his Lewis gunners on the spur near the captured trench. From there they opened a heavy fire on the German force. Many were cut down and the rest promptly surrendered.[32] Private John Rochford in particular got into a good firing position and was credited with killing 34 of the enemy, 'and all day long our ambulances were carrying back their wounded.'[33] At 7:35 am the 48th reported that their whole objective had been secured and that although there was some doubt about the British on their right they were in touch with the 13th Battalion on their left. The 48th lost 13 killed and up to 55 wounded in the day's fighting.[34]

The 4th Brigade troops had reached the objective a little earlier, between 6:30 and 7, and the 4th Division front was complete on the Green Line. While the infantry moved further forward to the halt line, the artillery barrage continued on its protective line until Z + 190, about two hours after it had reached that stage. Some thought the halt was too long, giving the enemy a chance to reorganise,[35] but a shorter time 'could not be arranged ... owing to the needs of their neighbours,'[36] which presumably meant the two British corps (the 1st Division, with a longer distance to cover before reaching their first objective, halted for an hour and a quarter). As well, while the barrage was stationary several field artillery brigades (the Superimposed Group on the 4th Division front) had to change position and be ready in time to resume the creep to the second objective. The dummy tanks had not proved successful. Two details of 35 men each from the Pioneer Battalion had been allotted to the two groups of five dummies, but the number of men turned out to be inadequate to handle all of the awkward constructions simultaneously. The dummies weighed a quarter of a ton (250 kilograms) each and were meant to roll on two big wooden wheels while being pushed by men inside them. The idea was to move them on to the skyline in front of the jumping-off line, there to be seen by the enemy, but the muddy, uneven ground was a serious handicap. There were not enough men in each group of pioneers to move all of their five dummies at once so they started with three. On the 4th Brigade front, the first three sustained broken wheels and could not be moved into position and the other two took too long to be of any use. Somehow the pioneers on the 12th Brigade front got four of their dummies into position only to find that the mist and smoke hid them from the enemy, thereby defeating the purpose. A legend arose, nevertheless, that the dummy tanks had deceived the Germans and instilled panic in their ranks, a view not supported by the facts.[37]

During the halt the Vickers gun crews of the 13th and 24th MG Companies (right and left brigade sectors respectively) worked at setting up their batteries in the Green Line, 32 guns altogether, to provide a machine gun barrage covering the advance on the Red Line. The gunners, manhandling all of their equipment, had started 10 minutes after the infantry and reached their pre-selected positions in good time, in some cases while the infantry fight for the first objective was still going on. Second Lieutenant Colin Colquhoun, in charge of the 13th Company's right four-gun section, found himself facing a trench still occupied by the enemy. Several men were hit by machine gun fire from the trench but Colquhoun drew his revolver and charged the gun at the head of a small party. He shot the German gunner and took the surrender of 20 to 30 others.[38] The Vickers guns were in place and sighted on to the barrage line by 8:15 am. At 8:30 the artillery barrage began its creep again towards the second objective while the machine guns in the main barrage ceased fire and those in the Green Line opened up, again firing ahead of the line of bursting shells. As the barrage lifted, the infantry went forward again, the 15th and 13th Battalions going on from the halt line on the left and the 45th passing through the 48th on the right. As the 15th and 13th moved off, the 16th came up to the halt line and spread out across the 4th Brigade frontage to hold the position and act as a reserve. For this stage of the fight, the 15th changed its deployment during the halt so that the two companies originally in support now took over the lead. The German outpost at Dawes Copse was quickly overrun and the Battalion moved on steadily behind the barrage, finding the going easier with a clear light now and less barbed wire.

Opposition was heaviest about half-way to the Red Line in the area between Dawes Quarry and Priel Crater ahead of the left company, 'A' under Lieutenant Jack Hynes. Hynes led a few men to outflank a trench near the Crater, forcing the surrender of a battalion commander and his headquarters staff, then led the company on to their final objective. Also on the left, fire from a pair of German 77mm field guns held up the advance until they were taken on by Lewis gunners Corporal Alfred Edwards and Corporal Percy Sutherland. Their bursts put the gun crews out of action and the weapons were captured. The 15th swept on to the German line along Ascension Spur, the former British outpost line, cutting off many 'little isolated MG nests and positions with which this country is covered. Our men who were fighting like veterans simply walked around these places—it was their last fight and their best' said Colonel Johnston later.[39] At the main position, the Germans did not put up a fight, only emerging from their dugouts to surrender. The Battalion arrived right behind the barrage as it lifted—one young 15th platoon commander, Lieutenant Francis Livingston, told C E W Bean on the battlefield that his main difficulty had been keeping his men from walking into the barrage; Livingston was proud that he had not lost a man killed in his platoon.[40] By 9:30 am the 15th was digging in on the Red Line a little east of the captured trenches, having taken a reported 400 prisoners in the operation (probably an over-estimation[41]), as well as 28 machine guns and the two field guns. The price on the day had been 10 deaths and 40 wounded; several of the latter did not survive their injuries.[42]

On the right of the 4th Brigade's advance, the 13th Battalion had also started this phase with two companies leading and two in support, but soon extended with all four in one line. The German positions at the objective, as on the 15th's front on the left, consisted mostly of a series of short lengths of trench protected by barbed wire, with some longer stretches like the one running from the point called Coronet Post. Lieutenant Henry Baker, scouting ahead on the right, encountered an enemy outpost in Collins Copse and immediately attacked it with grenades, resulting in the surrender of 20 Germans. After handing over the prisoners he resumed advancing and led a small party in a charge on another post, capturing that also. Baker had been hit in the leg by then, but he continued on towards the objective line, on the way charging a further machine gun position. He killed some of the crew with revolver fire and captured the rest. Some opposition was encountered in approaching the area from Coronet Post to Ascension Farm but this was met by the extraordinary Sergeant Sexton, continuing his one-man war. Three machine guns held up the company's advance, but Sexton, again firing his Lewis gun from the hip and disdaining to take cover, knocked the guns out one after the other with accurate bursts. Still not satisfied, he then captured a trench and several other small posts, killing some of the occupants and capturing others. Elsewhere along the line, the 13th troops continued the assault. By 9:30 am they had secured their whole objective and were digging in on the forward slope of the spur, linking with the 15th on their left. About 200 prisoners were taken in this phase, and in the overall operation the unit reporting taking a total of 560 prisoners (an estimate that again, as with the 15th Battalion, was probably too high[43]), with two field guns, eight mortars and 30 machine guns. This was achieved with a 'hop-off' strength of 415 officers and men, at a cost of 12 killed and 93 wounded.[44]

The 12th Brigade used a leapfrog approach between battalions, with the 45th Battalion, tasked with the attack on the Red Line, beginning its advance a kilometre behind the 48th at Zero. Ten minutes after the start the German counter-barrage came down, missing the 48th in the lead but falling on the 45th behind and continuing there as the German guns shortened their range. The shelling hit Battalion HQ particularly hard. The signals officer, Lieutenant Samuel Hill, was killed and the intelligence officer, Lieutenant Leslie Hughes, mortally wounded. Captain William Adams, the adjutant, was wounded in both hands and had to withdraw. The CO, Lieutenant Colonel Loutit, was hit in the chest by a piece of shell but was able to continue (the 48th Battalion was warned that it might have to take the 45th under command in view of its losses in key officers). One of the company commanders, Lieutenant William Horne, was also fatally hit, and most of the 45th's casualties for the day occurred in that phase. The 45th reached a position behind the Green Line and waited in a sunken road while the 48th finished securing that objective and the covering barrage remained stationary on the protective line. The 45th paused there for over an hour, in that period losing another officer, Lieutenant Hubert Hines, killed by a sniper. Moving on again, in battle formation with three companies in front and one in support, the 45th passed through the 48th and caught up to the barrage as it began its next creep forward. As the 45th troops crossed the ridge crest they encountered the German force attempting to counter-attack the 48th's line. Caught by the barrage, the Lewis guns of the 48th, and the advancing 45th, the surviving enemy surrendered *en masse*, passing through the 45th with their hands up on the way to the rear.[45] The Battalion pressed on for the Red Line together with two sections of the 12th MG Company (eight guns and their crews) providing close support. It was apparent that the British on the right had not kept up, and Captain Jack Holman, commanding 'A' Company on that side, altered his dispositions to cover the open flank while maintaining the pace of the advance. The German line, another series of small posts on the crest of Ascension Spur, was reached at 9:20 am against opposition that was limited to a few sharp skirmishes.[46] For the most part the demoralised enemy either surrendered at the first opportunity on ran to the rear. The 45th overran a number of field guns also, first a two-gun section of '77's at Red Wood, and then Captain Holman led one of his platoons to attack a battery of 5.9-inch (15 cm) howitzers spotted near the objective line south of Somerville Wood. The German crews were in the process of hitching the horses to the howitzers to pull them out but the platoon's Lewis gunners, in a cruel necessity of war, opened fire and shot the horses, thereby immobilising the weapons and enabling their capture.[47] The 45th had now reached the Red Line on the far slope of Ascension Spur. While some dug in others sniped at retreating Germans running across the open country of Ascension Valley towards the next ridge, on which the actual 'Outpost' line stood. Riflemen, Lewis gunners and machine gunners joined in the sport. Sergeant Clifford Pugh, 12th MG Company, in charge of a pair of Vickers guns in the centre of the advance, got his guns up to the objective even before the infantry arrived, opening a particularly destructive fire on the fugitives.

The Hindenburg Outpost Line. Part of the 45th Battalion on the Red Line objective (Ascension Spur). The Lewis gunner is firing at retreating German troops. (AWM E03249)

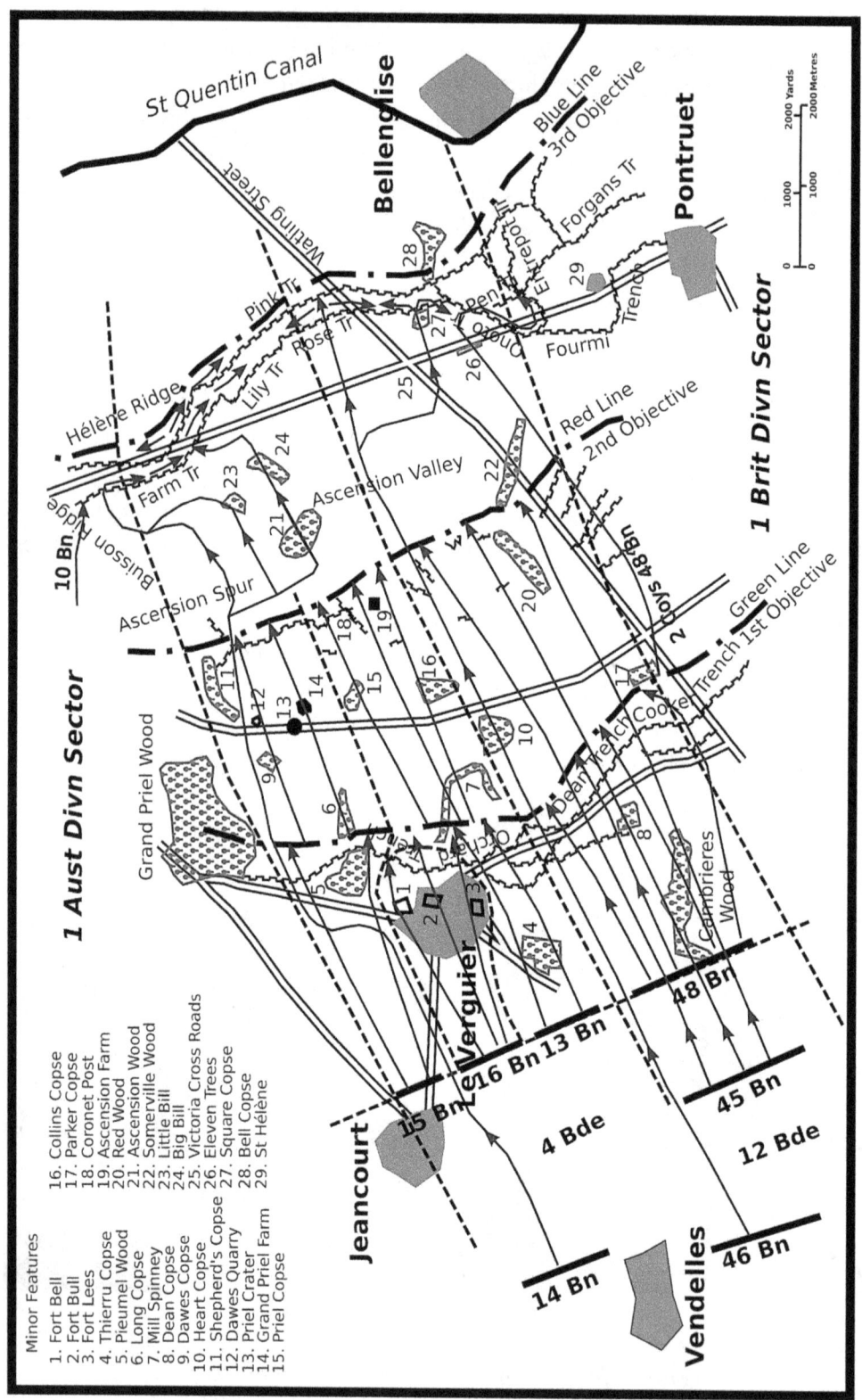

Battle of the Hindenburg Outpost Line, 18 September 1918, 4th Division sector.

While consolidating the captured ground the 45th came under close-range fire from a German field gun battery in Pontruet village to the south-east. The shelling was scattered and did not last long before the British barrage reached the village and silenced the battery, but one of its shots killed Second Lieutenant Joseph Dietze while he was directing his men in consolidation. Dietze had received his commission only a fortnight earlier. As a '1914 man' he had been offered the opportunity of staying out of the battle and then going on furlough, but since it would be his first fight as an officer he had asked to be included.[48] The 45th had lost an unusually high proportion of its officers as casualties in the operation, with four killed and four others wounded, in addition to nine other ranks killed and 60 wounded. The 45th claimed 474 prisoners taken, almost exactly the number of its own troops engaged in the battle, although the correct prisoner figure was probably closer to 400.[49] A group from the 4th Pioneer Battalion, a dozen men under Second Lieutenant William Calder, had been following along behind the advancing battalions, laying direction tapes from 12th Brigade HQ to the battalion HQs, to guide runners and carrying parties. The Pioneer party steadily lost casualties to enemy shelling until Calder had only two men, his runner Private Duncan McDonald and Private Arthur Robb, left unwounded. The remnant persisted and completed the task, later going out beyond the Red Line to link with the 46th Battalion in the final stage.

With the second objective now in Australian hands and being consolidated, the designated units for the exploitation objective, the Blue Line on the next ridge, moved up into position for their task. Corps orders had specified that an attempt be made on that line, but not if the cost was likely to be excessive and not by throwing more and more troops at it—if the line could not be taken easily, it was to be left for another day.[50] If the commanders had decided not to press home the attack,

> Monash's order would have completely exonerated them.
>
> But the troops knew the plans. Not only battalion commanders, but company and platoon leaders, sergeants, and men, knew as well as their brigadiers that what was desired was to obtain a position looking down on the Canal, so that the main Hindenburg Line behind it could be attacked in the next battle. All realised that the attack would really have failed if the Hindenburg Outpost Line on the watershed screening the Canal remained in German hands; and this knowledge decided the day's results.[51]

At 9:59 am, after 15 minutes firing on the protective line ahead of the second objective, the artillery ceased fire to let the final attacking units through. In broad daylight, without an artillery barrage or tanks, two under-strength battalions would be attacking a continuous defensive system, mounting numerous machine guns and protected by uncut wire entanglementss – at the end of a 'nice walk' of over five miles [eight kilometres] as the 46th Battalion diarist put it.[52] On the left the 14th Battalion had waited near Vendelles behind the first jump-off line for the first two hours after Zero, taking the opportunity to give the troops a hot breakfast in spite of the rain. At 7:15, the battalion moved off on a one-company front in artillery formation, accompanied by a section of four Vickers gun crews from the 4th MG Company. The planned approach route to the forming-up position lay through the space between Le Verguier village and Pieumel Wood to its north, but as the leading company neared that area they could see that the enemy artillery was shelling it heavily. Major William Wadsworth, the company commander, immediately took the whole battalion wheeling to its left, passing north of the wood and around Long Copse beyond it and so avoiding the shelling; Captain Lynas, watching from the 16th Battalion HQ in Le Verguier, recalled the 14th's manoeuvre under fire as 'a most marvellous sight'[53] (Wadsworth later commented that such on the spot decision-making 'is the way things are done nowadays as compared with the old way,' simply advising Lieutenant Colonel Crowther at the tail of the column of the reason for the departure from orders[54]). At 9 am the Battalion reached its first forming up position, the north-south road about half-way between the Green and Red lines, extending with two companies in front and two close behind in support, on a frontage of 1,500 metres. The battalion's strength going into battle was only 350,[55] so the two leading companies would have been about half that.

At 9:49 the protective barrage ceased and the battalion advanced to the attack through the 13th and 15th Battalions digging in on the Red Line. Men of those units 'made no effort to hide their misgiving about our part of the show.'[56] Within minutes of starting down the near slope, the 14th came under heavy machine gun fire from the German line on the opposite crest. Fire was also coming from outposts in woods ahead of the enemy line, Ascension Wood and two smaller patches called Big Bill and Little Bill. The advance continued in short rushes, but the leading companies had lost a number of casualties by the time they reached the bottom of the valley. There the Germans were quickly driven out of Ascension Wood, but the centre platoons were then pinned down by heavy fire from further ahead: 'as soon as we showed ourselves, we received such a hail of bullets that we had to go back,' wrote Lieutenant Ted Rule.[57] The company commanders, Major Wadsworth and Captain Joe Mackay, conferred and decided to strengthen the line by bringing up the support companies. The Battalion's Lewis gunners then drove the German garrisons out of Big Bill and Little Bill with concentrated fire; Corporal Vivian Lalor was particularly effective with his Lewis in the fighting at Big Bill. Fighting in platoons and sections, the Battalion pressed forward gradually and by 11 am the companies on the right had worked their way into the sunken road below the objective line. There they were stopped by thick wire to their front. On the left the other companies were held up on the high ground of Buisson Ridge by machine gun fire, along with the 1st Division's right flank battalion, the 10th.

Further north, however, the German line was closer to the second objective. Other 1st Division units succeeded in penetrating it and began to work south down the German trench. This opened the way for the 10th Battalion, which then attacked to their front and also got into the trench. In turn, Captain Mackay's 'B' company of the 14th passed behind the ridge crest and entered the trench through the 10th Battalion sector. They then began to 'bomb' their way to their right down the German front line, called Farm, Lily and Rose Trenches in this area. The second left-flank company, 'D' under Lieutenant Eugene Chubb, then joined in and took over from 'B' while the latter made an attempt on the German second line. Lieutenant Rule's platoon of 'C' Company was withdrawn from the road and sent into the fight on the left also. At some point the 41st Battery (11th AFA Brigade) of 18-pounders had come up in support, and although no details of their contribution were reported, the 14th Battalion noted that they assisted in this part of the operation. There was disappointment, however, at a lack of covering machine gun fire from the Red Line.[58] The push down the front trench was held up by a 45-metre straight stretch with no cover, down which a German machine gun was firing. Captain Allan Martin's 4th LTM Battery was right up with the infantry, and Rule organised for a mortar to fire two bombs into the machine gun position. This distracted the Germans long enough for most of Rule's men to get through the straight section safely, but they could get no further against effective opposition. After an exchange of grenades the platoon had to withdraw back along the trench, with many men wounded.[59] The rest of the force on that flank was stopped also but 270 metres of trench had been gained and a foothold established in the final objective. It was then about 3 pm, and the decision was made to hold on until dark and then make another attempt.

On the 12th Brigade front, the 46th Battalion had the Blue Line task, beginning its advance at 6:50 am a kilometre in rear of the 45th. Four Vickers guns from the 12th MG Company and four Stokes mortars from the 12th LTM Battery advanced with the infantry. Pack horses and mules carried the machine gun gear and mortar ammunition as far as the Red Line where the men took over. After a short halt on the Green Line, the battalion moved on and caught up with the 45th below Ascension Spur as that unit was assaulting the Red Line objective over the crest. The 46th shook out into its attacking formation, two companies forward and two in support, and waited half an hour for the protective barrage to cease. The men were glad of the short rest after the tiring approach march, and their morale received a boost when the sun came out.[60] The 46th then jumped off in the final phase of the advance, passing right through many surrendering Germans heading the other way for the Australian line. At the start its left forward company ('D,' Lieutenant Alexander Wallace) was in touch with the 14th Battalion next on the left, but the situation on the right was not so straightforward. Here the British unit concerned did not propose to advance for another two hours, and then only by patrolling, a decision that had been made before the battle.[61] Major Frank Couchman, commanding 'C' company on that flank, was obliged to use two of his platoons, echeloned back from the main line, to maintain touch with the British force. The latter, difficult as it is to believe at this period of the War, 'instead of leapfrogging fresh troops at each stage, was using … one battalion, the 2nd Royal Sussex, to make the three successive efforts. The strain on the troops was thus very great.'[62]

Like the 14th to the north, the 46th faced heavy machine gun fire from the German line on the high ground opposite, Hélène Ridge. The sunken road parallel to the crest continued from the north, leading through the tiny village of St Hélène to Pontruet at the southern end of the ridge. The road running north-east from Vermand ('Watling Street,' a continuation of the Roman road) crossed it at a point called Victoria Cross Roads, roughly in the centre of the 46th's frontage. Sending his men forward in small groups, Lieutenant Wallace slowly worked his company forward to a position near the St Hélène road. He found that there was no actual road-bank at that point, despite what was shown on the map. The troops found what cover they could but could get no further under the enemy machine gun fire. Here Lieutenant Leslie Byrne, bringing up a reinforcing platoon from the support company, was killed. Another 1914 enlistee and Gallipoli veteran due for home furlough, 'Curly' Byrne was the only 46th officer killed that day.

South of the crossroads, Major Couchman called his two detached platoons forward, leaving a small patrol to maintain tenuous contact with the British. The company then made for the stretch of road known as the Eleven Trees, passing two unmanned enemy artillery batteries on the way. By that time the six 18-pounders of the 38th Battery AFA had reached a forward position and the battery commander, Major Harold de Low, went further up to make contact with 46th Battalion HQ. At Lieutenant Colonel Corrigan's request the battery put down covering fire for the advance, shooting at enemy machine gun positions in the vicinity then lengthening range to bombard the trench beyond. At Eleven Trees there was a road bank but it was only 18 inches (45 cm) high. Couchman's company reached the road by 2 pm without being seen by the enemy, but a storm of machine gun fire suddenly broke out, forcing the company to ground behind the minimal cover of the bank. 'You could not move,' said Couchman later, but the company was not entirely passive. Just above the road was a thick overgrown belt of wire that looked impassable, but a Lewis gunner, Private Harold Greenwood, 'burrowed' under the wire with his team and set up his gun in position to sweep the German parapet up the slope. Whenever an enemy machine gun opened up, he fired back, and succeeded in keeping down the German fire to some extent. This enabled Couchman to hold his position until 5 pm, when the British heavy artillery began to bombard the German position, landing many shells very close to the company. Several casualties were caused by that fire and the company quickly pulled back 450 metres to a minor road along the valley floor that they had passed over earlier in the advance. The 38th Battery's 18-pounders were shelling the wire entanglement at the time and some of their fire may have fallen short also. Close artillery support to the 46th was meant to have been provided by the 37th Battery, but that plan had miscarried somewhat when the Battery commander, Major George Hall, was unable to locate the Battalion HQ, which was on the move. The Battery had reached a position near Heart Copse, south-east of Le Verguier, but was then withdrawn a kilometre to a position just east of Dean Trench. Major Hall finally made contact with the 46th, only to have the telephone lines to the guns cut by shell-fire. 'My battery's part in the show was very unsatisfactory,' he reported ruefully.[63] The guns did manage to get off some shots at various targets before rejoining the rest of the 10th AFA to take part in the operation that night.

Along the line both the 14th and 46th Battalions had been stopped short of the final objective and were depleted by casualties. There was no intention of giving up, however, and battalion and brigade commanders were already planning the next move. Colonel Corrigan, the 46th CO, had earlier sent back asking for artillery support to cover a renewed attack. Brigadier General Leane came up to Battalion HQ in a trench on the Red Line, to ask that the 46th attack again as soon as the artillery could be arranged. Corrigan wanted to wait until well after dark, giving the men a chance to rest and eat, and the brigadier concurred. The 4th Brigade also intended a night attack, and arrangements were agreed with the 12th Brigade (both brigade HQs were located in the railway cutting outside Vendelles), with the attack to be launched at 11 pm. The field artillery was now within range, having moved up to positions near the Green Line, and a brief 20-minute barrage on the enemy front line was organised. Two field brigades, 6th and 10th, would hit the German front line south from the point already occupied by the 14th Battalion. The barrage would start on the wire for three minutes, lift onto the trench for five minutes, then hit the support trench for another five minutes and finally lift to a protective line for the final seven minutes. A machine gun barrage was also set up. To deliver it, the 13th and 24th MG Companies moved all of their barrage guns up from the Green Line to the Red Line, while the two sections of the 12th Company that had gone with the infantry to the Red Line were given barrage tasks as well, reinforced by another section coming up from the rear. The remaining section was to stay with the 46th Battalion in its advance. The 4th Company had two sections forward working with the 14th Battalion, one having moved up from reserve during the afternoon, and the other two in defensive positions. The guns would fire for ten minutes on the enemy support trench, then lift onto a protective line for a further five minutes, except on the left where, since the 14th Battalion already held the northern part of the objective, the 24th Company would fire only on the protective line for the 15 minutes.

In view of the uncertainty on the right flank Brigadier General Leane ordered the 48th Battalion, now in reserve on the first halt line, to support the 46th with an attack by two companies in the area towards St Hélène village. This was in the British sector, however, and the British commander insisted that his own troops would do the job. The 48th attack was cancelled accordingly but Leane took the precaution of ordering the 48th to instead form a protective flank inside the Australian zone. Leane later expressed his frustration in his after-action report:

> ... the 2nd [British] Brigade Headquarters seemed to be absolutely in the dark regarding the position of their troops ... The advance from the Red Line had to be carried out with our flank right up in the air, and the 46th suffered considerably from machine gun fire from the direction of St Helene and Pontrue[t]. The English gave this brigade no assistance whatever during the advance to the Blue Line and the information as to the position of their troops was absolutely inaccurate and misleading.[64]

Meanwhile, during the long pause the 14th and 46th Battalions redeployed for the new operation. The 14th lined up in the captured segment of trench with two companies in front and two behind, waiting against the front and back walls of the trench. As soon as the barrage lifted, the right rear company, 'A' under Lieutenant Norman Aldridge, would work to their right down the front line trench with grenades and bayonets, followed by the left rear company,

'D', as a reserve and mopping-up force. The front two companies would attack straight ahead and get into the German support line (Pink Trench) then work in opposite directions, 'C' moving to the right parallel with 'A', and 'B' to the left aiming to join up with the 10th Battalion. Lieutenant Colonel Crowther put Major Wadsworth in overall charge of the operation and Lieutenant Rule took over 'C' Company temporarily. The 46th meanwhile had changed over its starting forward and support companies and formed up with 'B' Company, commanded by Lieutenant Eric Leith, on the left and 'A', Lieutenant Arthur Muriel, on the right. The other two companies were now in support but would each provide a platoon for mopping up and also 'carry' for the attacking troops. It was to be a frontal attack, the two forward companies entering the front line trench then passing straight on to the enemy support line while the mopping-up platoons finished off the first line. Under cover of darkness the whole force moved up to the upper road close to the German line to wait for Zero. Both battalions' rear echelons worked to organise a meal and resupply of ammunition and grenades for the firing line. For the most part these were brought up in good time, although one company of the 46th missed out on their meal which arrived while they were forming up for the attack; those men had to be content with iron rations. 'It has since been a wonder to me how we ever managed to be ready in time,' wrote Lieutenant Rule later.[65]

At Zero, just as the artillery and machine guns opened up in the barrage, the heavens also opened and a downpour soaked the troops to the skin (the 12th Brigade diarist, in a burst of pessimism, made an entry 'Barrage down. Weather rotten. Everything points to failure.'[66]). Nevertheless, the two Victorian battalions, parent and daughter units from the early days in Egypt, went forward into what would be the last major action of the 4th Division infantry in the War. To the immediate front, a few minutes firing by the artillery had been insufficient to seriously damage the wire, but the troops forced their way through. The wire was not strong facing Lieutenant Rule's company of the 14th, attacking the German support line but enemy machine guns there immediately opened fire. The Germans were using tracer ammunition and the company hesitated at the frightening sight of the glowing balls passing just overhead. After a few moments Rule got his men going over the top. Fortunately the machine guns had ceased just then, perhaps from the effects of the barrage passing over the enemy trench. Rule's company made 90 metres before the guns opened fire again, sending them to ground, but several Lewis gunners took the initiative and began to sweep the enemy parapet with their bursts. The disconcerted enemy gunners began to fire high and Rule led his company in a rush over the final distance to the trench, all 'yelling like lunatics.'[67] The Germans in front gave way and ran for the rear while the company entered the trench and started bombing down it to the south, Sergeant Loftus 'Lofty' Bauchop leading the way. His picked group overcame all resistance, tossing grenades into dugouts as they passed if the occupants hesitated to surrender. In the enemy front line Aldridge's men, pressing down the trench as soon as the barrage moved to the support line, worked their along in the same way with the aggressive Lieutenant Tom Griffith setting the example. Those of their opponents who fled to the support trench were caught by 'C' Company and the two companies had taken possession of both German lines half an hour after the start, 800 metres of double trench system. On the left, 'B' Company was equally successful, getting into the enemy support line with effective aid from the machine gun barrage, as Captain Mackay reported.[68] Working along the trench to the left the company gained touch with the 10th Battalion, and the 14th's objective had been fully attained. On the right (south) however, it was several hours before contact was made with the 46th.

That unit had also jumped off in the rain at 11 pm behind the barrage, which here fell across the full frontage of the attack. The troops moved forward from their positions in the road while the barrage was on the wire entanglement, then worked their way through the almost-intact obstacle as the line of shell-bursts shifted to the enemy front trench. Dashing for the trench after the barrage lifted again on to the support line, the two forward companies found that they had taken the enemy by surprise. The German unit there, said to have come into the line only that night to mount a counter-attack in the morning, was not expecting to be attacked themselves and was sheltering in dugouts from the rain and the shelling.[69] They put up little resistance at first, although Lieutenant Leith, commanding 'B' Company on the left, was shot in the right shoulder by a sentry (his fifth wound of the war). Leith continued on nevertheless, losing no time in the first trench and leading his company on to the second, while the mopping-up platoon from 'D' Company took over in the first trench. In the second line the enemy put up more of a fight but resistance was soon overcome there also, over 100 prisoners and six machine guns being captured. It was probably in that part of the fighting that Sergeant Albert Bainbrigge made a single-handed attack with grenades along the trench, personally taking many of the prisoners. After satisfying himself that his sector of the enemy trench had been secured, Leith handed over to Lieutenant Alfred Willison and made his way to the rear for medical attention.

Lieutenant Muriel's 'A' Company on the right encountered stronger opposition. Inclining somewhat too far to its left, the company struck the trench directly beyond Square Copse instead of keeping that landmark on the left. In a hard fight, the forward troops, led by platoon commanders Lieutenants Thomas Carter and Ralph Brittain, overcame the enemy in that part of the first trench. Lieutenant Muriel took a few men and pushed on to the second line at Bell Copse through a knot of communication trenches, picking up 20 prisoners and two machine guns. The section of the front trench (Onoto Trench) south of Square Copse had not been attacked, however, and the troops of Lieutenant George Storey's mopping-up platoon found themselves fighting to capture the position. They went at the task with great resolve and fighting skill, despite being seriously outnumbered by the defenders. Storey's men forced their way down Onoto Trench past its offshoot Pen Trench, near the southern limit of the objective. Here they could find no friendly troops, only signs of increasing German activity, so barricades were established in both trenches to defend the ground gained. That was at about 1 am (19 September) and the 46th now set about re-organising and dealing with the hundreds of prisoners on their hands. These were channelled via Major Couchman's HQ.

where it was beginning to dawn on one large group of prisoners how few in numbers their captors actually were. The Germans began get restless, but the escort under an unidentified lance corporal avoided trouble by quickly hustling them to the rear. The 12th Brigade had sent a staff officer, Lieutenant Harry Downes (ex-48th Battalion), up to the forward area to arrange the orderly collection of prisoner groups and send them on to Brigade HQ, where military police took custody. He had a challenging task, the 12th Brigade having taken over 1,400 prisoners since the morning. Of these the 46th Battalion had captured an estimated 550, a remarkable achievement by a unit that had made the final attack with its two forward companies having a total strength of only 160 men, plus the two mopping-up platoons. The odds against them were said to have been as much as six to one at times.[70] Even if that was an exaggeration, the total of prisoners plus whatever other casualties the Germans would have suffered shows how badly the 46th was outnumbered. The Battalion's overall losses for the fighting over the day and night amounted to 13 killed and 100 or more wounded.[71]

There was still much to do. As well as the usual task of consolidation after a successful attack, both of the 46th's flanks were in the air, not in contact with the 14th Battalion on the left or the British on the right. The promised British attack had jumped off, but the weary and disheartened troops, who had been in action all day without relief, had been unable to make any headway and had returned to their start line. The gap was filled by the two companies of the 48th Battalion ordered forward by General Leane earlier. One company was strung out in a series of posts from the right of the 46th to the withdrawn British left. The second company came under the orders of the 46th and Major Couchman sent two platoons into the trenches on the right. Here Onoto Trench made a fork with Pen Trench, with a cross-trench (Entrepot) further south connecting the two, making a roughly triangular shape on the map. The two platoons probed down Pen and Onoto Trenches, eliminating a few small enemy posts as they went. The platoon in Onoto, having passed the point where the St Hélène road intersected the trench, set up a block as did the platoon in Pen Trench to the east. The British division on the right had been reporting that they had taken their objectives in the next segment of trench, Fourmi, but there was no sign of friend or foe there. A small patrol was sent to investigate further, comprising Lieutenant Robert Reid and two volunteer privates, James Woods and another, not definitely identified but probably either Ernest Reed or Walter Reid.[72] The patrol probed down Onoto for some distance, finding it deserted, then moved along Entrepot towards Pen. At the junction of Entrepot and Pen, near the highest point on the southern end of the ridge, they encountered a German post held by 25 to 30 men with six machine guns, first spotting them by the light of a German flare. Private Woods, a small man of 160 cm in height, charged straight at the enemy, firing his rifle. He shot one German and captured another, while the others, thinking themselves attacked in force, abandoned the machine guns and took to their heels. Private Reed had been wounded by then, so Lieutenant Reid sent him to the rear with a report for the company commander. Reid soon realised the importance of the position, on high ground with all-round observation and two further trenches joining close by, Entrepot continuing north-east and Forgans running to the

The Hindenburg Outpost Line. Lieutenant Colonel John Corrigan (standing, left), CO 46th Battalion, in the final objective trench captured by his unit. Others in the picture are: standing, right: Lt Nevinson Faulkner. Front, left to right: Lt Alfred Willison; "Signaller Harvey" (probably 3162 Private James H Harvey); Lance Corporal Robert Hogg. (AWM E03366)

south-east. He decided to go back himself and bring up reinforcements to hold it. Woods was willing to man the post alone in the meantime. It was not long before the German garrison regained composure and tried to retake their position, attacking from several directions over the top. Undaunted, Woods climbed up and lay on the parapet, the better to see the attacks coming, and fought back with grenades and rifle fire. He kept the enemy at bay for two hours (at least it must have seemed that long to him) before Lieutenant Reid found his way back with a few more men. Some opened fire on the Germans while Woods stayed in his place on the parapet, flinging grenades that the others handed up to him. Eventually the surviving enemy gave up and withdrew. Woods could now climb down from his perch, having somehow escaped being hit, although he had inhaled some gas at one point during the night. Woods had certainly earned a break from the firing line and Lieutenant Reid sent him back to company HQ to report the situation. Having done that, Woods then guided a reinforcing platoon back to the position.

To the north the 46th and 14th Battalions were still trying to make contact with each other and join up their inner flanks. A gap of 550 metres existed to begin with, and it was getting on for dawn when Lieutenant Rule of the 14th and a 46th officer made contact, each looking for the other unit. The 14th's 'A' Company came down to fill the gap, and both units formed a thinly-held line in the former German support trench, now the 4th Division front line. The morning of 19 September saw fighting continue on the right, where Lieutenant Reid's

Troops of the 46th Battalion in the captured Hindenburg Outpost Line, overlooking the village of Bellenglise in the main Hindenburg Line. (AWM E03390)

platoon of the 48th Battalion was still holding the post at the junction of Pen and Entrepot trenches. For five hours Reid and his men fought off determined efforts by the Germans to retake the position. Grenade fighting swayed backwards and forwards along the trenches radiating from the strong-point, which changed hands several times during the day. Corporal Sydney Lawson's section was pushed back at first, but he led a counter-attack that ejected the Germans in turn, and then repelled a further strong attack on his position. The situation had stabilised by 2 pm, but then artillery supporting a renewed British attack further south landed several misdirected shells on the 48th's position and forced a withdrawal. One shell killed Lieutenant Leslie Ward. The errant shelling cleared the way for the Germans to move into the trench junction again. The 48th barricaded Pen Trench and held off German attempts to go further, then after dark mounted another counter-attack that once more drove the enemy out. Barricades were put up in the trenches leading to the strong-point, and the troops held off renewed enemy attacks. Lieutenant Hurtle Burnett led the defence on the far right, with Private Robert Wells, in charge at one of the blocks, twice fighting off strong assaults. Eventually the fighting died down with the 48th firmly in control. A British force was finally established in the southern part of Fourmi Trench also.

During that night the remaining two companies of the 48th came forward and took over the right half of the 46th's front, relieving two of that unit's companies. Both of the former German trench lines were now occupied in that sector. The 46th's sector of the new front line was defended by two sections (eight Vickers guns) from the 12th MG Company spread along the front, backed up by nine of the Battalion's Lewis guns and five captured German machine guns.[73] Further north, the 14th Battalion, reinforced by a company from the 15th, had spent the day of 19 September setting up their new line for defence, mostly undisturbed by the enemy. Here also eight Vickers guns were mounted by the 4th MG Company, together with infantry Lewis guns and 15 captured German machine guns—the 14th had collected so many of those, at least 50, that the rest were dropped along the bottom of the muddy trench to act as duckboards.[74] The number of machine guns indicated that the 14th had overcome a numerous garrison. Although the Battalion's total of 75 prisoners taken was not high by comparison with other units, numbers of the enemy had been seen escaping into the night and the troops had not hesitated to use grenades on those who were slow to surrender. The 14th had also captured 11 German artillery pieces during the operation, and—perhaps just as important to the troops—the enemy dugouts had yielded a rich harvest of souvenirs.

From vantage points in the captured position, observers looked down on long stretches of the main Hindenburg line itself, running along the far bank of the St Quentin Canal no more than 1,500 metres away in places, with the village of Bellenglise on a bend in the canal to the east of Pen Trench. That night the 14th troops moved out 250 metres in front to dig a line of outposts and to cover a company from the 4th Pioneers erecting a wire entanglement. Daylight on 20 September brought a short but intense bombardment on the position by enemy artillery that killed two outstanding NCOs, Sergeant Bauchop, who had played a big part in the success of the 14th's night attack, and Sergeant Archibald Johnstone. Overall, the battle had cost the unit 20 dead and over 70 wounded.[75] The 12th Brigade battalions also lost some casualties to the shelling. Those killed included the 48th's unconventional character Private Nathaniel Lunt, 'hero of many fights both in the line and out of it,'[76] who had survived all of those fights except the last. Throughout the fighting the medical arrangements had worked smoothly, the wounded being evacuated in good time with no serious bottlenecks. Stretcher cases were now mostly being carried back at speed in motor ambulances for treatment, although horse-drawn vehicles still came in handy when roads were non-existent or impassable to motor vehicles.[77] Captain John Mackay, 12th Field Ambulance, particularly distinguished himself in the management of the bearers working with the 12th Brigade.

Under interrogation some German prisoners from a pioneer unit had mentioned the existence of anti-tank minefields protecting their first line, the Green Line objective. During 19 September some sappers of the 13th Field Company investigated the report, taking the Germans with them, and found that the minefields consisted of several lines of buried mortar (*minenwerfer*) bombs. The bombs were to be set off by the simple method of pressure on a wooden plank just below the ground surface and covered with earth, the plank contacting the bomb's detonator if a tank ran over it. Part of the detonator mechanism was a wire pin that would resist the weight of a man but snap under the weight of a tank. The minefields had still been under construction, and the next day a party of sappers under Lieutenant Robert McKay dug up 54 mines, of which 36 had been fitted with detonators.[78]

Having spent two weeks in the line culminating in a pitched battle, the 4th Division was due for relief (as was the 1st Division). Over several nights the 4th Division units handed over to British and American replacements, with the final infantry battalion, the 15th, coming out on the night of 23/24 September. As their reliefs occurred, the infantry brigades marched away from the forward area, at first moving to Tincourt, on the Cologne River east of Péronne. Six hours marching the next day took the battalions via Cartigny and Biaches to the area between Herbecourt and Belloy, in the angle of the Somme bend. From there on 24 September they travelled by motor vehicle, to billeting areas west of Amiens, now far behind the lines. The 4th Brigade was accommodated near Picquigny and other villages on the Somme, the 13th Brigade at and around Bovelles to the south, and the 12th Brigade further south in the vicinity of a village with the odd name (to English speakers) of Pissy. The 15th Battalion arrived at the 4th Brigade billets on 26 September, having travelled by train most of the way from Tincourt to catch up.

The supporting arms and services, with some exceptions, had been relieved in the normal way and had also moved to the rear area. The Field Ambulances were located at villages near their linked brigades, and the engineers in the centre of the divisional area at Saisseval. Division HQ was set up at Cavillon, with the MG Battalion nearby at Le Mesge. For the time being, the Divisional Train remained in the area between Catelet and Cartigny, while the Pioneer Battalion moved back only as far as Roisel, about half-way between the front line and Péronne. A large element of the 12th Field Company stayed in the forward area for a few more days, constructing a road bridge near Vendelles, where just east of the village the important road to Le Verguier crossed the 9-metre deep railway cutting. The original masonry bridge at the crossing had been demolished and the engineers set about building a timber trestle bridge to replace it, using mainly captured German materials. The new bridge, spanning a total of 27 metres, was opened to transport vehicle traffic on 28 September, saving long detours. The engineer party joined the rest of their company at Saisseval two days later. The 4th Division artillery, as usual, remained in the forward area, but was briefly relieved by that of the 46th British Division and withdrawn into reserve positions for a few days' break and refitting, prior to taking part in the next major operation—the assault on the main Hindenburg Line.

The Australian Corps had won a remarkable victory, in which two under-strength divisions had advanced over a distance of five kilometres and captured three successive defence lines, strongly held by garrisons that outnumbered the attackers and defended by barbed wire and numerous machine guns. The attacking force had been supported by an effective barrage from artillery and machine guns for the first two stages, but did not have the advantage of the sizeable tank force that had been present in previous battles. Essentially, the battle had been won by superior tactics, down to section and even individual level, and superior morale, with the crafty, battle-wise veterans guiding the newcomers. The victory had laid bare the enemy's main position to a future assault. On the day of the battle, C E W Bean recorded of the 4th Division his surprise at finding

> that the men were in such good heart. One could expect to find them depressed owing to the morning's rain and to the excessively hard work ... there is about these Australians an extraordinary buoyancy which surprises even those who know them best ... [General Monash] was clearly right in his estimate—that the Germans in front of us were so broken that it did not matter what trenches his Infantry was in—that Infantry would not stand and face our men.[79]

Brigadier General Leane wrote of the qualities of the troops:

> The operations of 8th August and 18th September have proved the value of spending a lot of time on Sports and Competitions when out of the line against using all the time on hard training. The best results are obtained from Australians by keeping them fit both in body and mind.
>
> Australians have ever proved ideal Storm Troops. They have the Offensive spirit, are keen and alert, and have great dash. It would be well if this were fully realised ...
>
> A German Battalion Commander captured by this Brigade on the 18th September made the following reply when I asked him how it was possible for us to capture so many prisoners and positions ideal for defence:
>
> 'Your men are so brave and have so much dash it is impossible to stop them.'[80]

The battle of 18 September, great achievement though it was, has not had the commensurate high profile in public knowledge of some other AIF battles, perhaps partly because there is some inconsistency with its naming. Officially, the fighting across the whole front was called by the BEF the Battle of Épehy, a village in the III Corps sector to the north. That name has limited relevance to the part played by the Australian Corps, however.[81] The 1st Division tended to use Hargicourt, a key point in its first objective, and similarly the 4th Division referred to Le Verguier or sometimes Jeancourt. The *Official History* calls the battle the Hindenburg Outpost Line, however, and this seems to be a good compromise for Australian purposes.

The 12th Brigade claimed 1,411 prisoners taken in total, the 4th Brigade 1,137, making 2,548. The tally was later reported by the Division administration as 2,442 unwounded taken in the field and 166 wounded and passing through the medical system.[82] There was no official report of enemy killed and wounded, but the 4th Brigade noted a quick count of 230 dead in the objective positions, before the dugouts had been checked. The several days in action had cost the 4th Brigade units 270 casualties, including 53 deaths, while 12th Brigade had 300 casualties including 56 deaths. The MG Battalion had four killed and 45 wounded over the period, the Pioneers five killed and 11 wounded.[83] The 4th Division's casualty list, though tragic enough in itself, was not excessive in actual numbers, which in the infantry brigades were similar to those for the Amiens battle. The loss was, however, somewhat greater as a proportion of the numbers of men engaged, given the depleted strength of the battalions.[84] 'The fewer men the greater share of honour,' and unit commanding officers put in much time writing numerous recommendations for awards, and in some cases collecting eyewitness statements. Lieutenant

Colonel Marks, the 13th Battalion CO, had found it difficult to credit the early reports of Sergeant Sexton's extraordinary bravery in the advance until his enquiries confirmed the story.[85] A recommendation for the Victoria Cross was duly put forward, and the award of the VC to Gerald Sexton was gazetted in December (there could hardly have been any doubt that it would be approved). Early next year, while still awaiting repatriation after the Armistice, he made the surprising admission to his superiors that 'Gerald Sexton' was an assumed name and his real name was Maurice Vincent Buckley. It further emerged that Buckley, as he was now known to be, had first joined the AIF at the age of 23 in December 1914, in Victoria, and had been posted to the Light Horse. He travelled to Egypt with his unit, where he was somewhat incautious in his choice of off-duty female company, and as a result was sent back to Australia for medical treatment while his unit went on to Gallipoli. Confined to the Langwarrin camp with numerous others in what was then regarded as disgrace, he had absented himself early in 1916 and was struck off as a deserter. He went to NSW, changed his name and enlisted again, a move that was said to have been suggested by his mother on the grounds that the Army would not be looking for him in its own ranks.[86] His *nom de guerre* was made up of his deceased brother's given name and his mother's maiden name. In his second enlistment, 'Sexton' was assigned to a reinforcement contingent for the 13th Battalion, joining his unit in France in January 1917.

Whatever his initial motivation may have been for re-enlisting, it does seem that Buckley felt that he had something to prove, hence the exploits that won him the DCM and the VC in the 13th's final two battles of the war. In the circumstances, the authorities chose to take no further action in the matter of his earlier desertion. His VC was the eighth awarded to a 4th Brigade soldier.

Another Victoria Cross was awarded to a soldier who may also have had something to prove, although for quite different reasons. Private James Woods of the 48th Battalion, like Buckley 27 years old in 1918, was originally from South Australia. He had tried to join the AIF early in the war, only to be rejected because he was below the minimum height. He moved to Western Australia, found work at a vineyard and made further unsuccessful attempts to enlist. His determination to serve was finally rewarded when he was accepted late in 1916 as a 48th Battalion reinforcement, the Army's requirements no longer being so stringent in view of the growing casualty lists. Woods was next frustrated by ill-health, and he suffered several bouts of illness before and after arriving in France in September 1917. In the next year he spent about as much time in hospital as on active duty. Woods was with the Battalion at the time of Passchendaele, when he probably first saw action, but was absent in hospital for the fighting of April and May 1918, and again for Amiens in August. It is quite possible that his courageous fight on 18 September was no more than the second time that he had been in close combat. Woods's VC was the only one awarded to a 48th Battalion member in the war, and it came in the unit's last battle. Appropriately, Woods personified the 48th's origins as both South Australian and Western Australian.

Many other decorations were recommended and approved, as was the case for the BEF as a whole in these times of triumph. Among those awards were DSOs or Bars to Colonel

"Gerald Sexton" – Sergeant Maurice Buckley VC DCM (1891–1921), 13th Battalion. (AWM A05136)

Private James Woods VC (1891–1963), 48th Battalion. (AWM A02640)

Corrigan (CO 46th Battalion), Major Couchman and Lieutenant Leith (both 46th), Major Wadsworth (14th), Lieutenant Baker (13th), Captain Anderson (48th) and Lieutenant Hynes (15th). Although the 14th Battalion's Lieutenant Rule downplayed his own deeds in his memoirs,[87] his superiors thought otherwise and recommended him for the DSO, but he was awarded the MC instead. Among numerous other officers receiving MCs or Bars were Lieutenants Burnett, Reid, Gelston and Cameron (48th Battalion), Griffith and Aldridge (14th), Ketterer (16th), Carter, Brittain, Storey and Wallace (46th; Wallace was another recommended for the DSO), and Holman (45th). Outside of the infantry units, MCs went to Lieutenants Colquhoun (MG Battalion) and Calder (Pioneer Battalion), and to Captains Martin (4th LTM Battery) and Mackay (12th Field Ambulance), among others.

The 13th Battalion's Sergeant Lihou was awarded a Bar to his DCM even though he had lost his life in the battle. DCMs were not awarded posthumously but at the time of the recommendation he was thought to have only been wounded and was not declared killed in action until 30 October. By that time the recommendation was well on its way through the system. Other DCMs were awarded to Corporal Lalor (14th, his third gallantry decoration), Corporals Lawson and Price, Lance Corporal Jones and Private Wells (all 48th), Private Denny (13th), Sergeant Bainbrigge (46th),[88] Private Lawrence (16th), and Corporals Edwards and Sutherland (15th). Numerous MMs were awarded, the recipients including, to name only a few, Private Greenwood (46th Battalion), Privates Lines and Rochford (48th), Private Williams (15th), Sergeant Pugh (MG

Battalion), and Privates McDonald and Robb (Pioneer Battalion). Corporal William Boswell, a courageous stretcher bearer in the 45th Battalion, was awarded a second Bar to his MM.

The troops could be fairly confident of a long break in the rest area this time, and it must have been apparent that a victorious end to the war was now only a matter of time. Even so, the fighting was still expected to go on into the next year, and a further stint in the line might still have to be endured. Another danger was the insidious menace of the deadly influenza virus that was beginning to spread in Europe and across the world. As it transpired, the war would be over in seven weeks and the infantry of the 4th Division would not be required to fight again, although the divisional artillery remained at the front and would be in action again until the last few days of the war.

23 Notes

1. Not to be confused with the larger Le Catelet to the north-east, at the time within the German lines.
2. He was an older brother of the late Major Lanoe Hawker VC, a pioneering RFC aviator who had lost his life in combat with the Red Baron, Manfred von Richthofen, in 1916. The brothers were sons of Henry ('Harry') Colley Hawker, a naval officer born in South Australia who later settled in England, where Lanoe was born. Their grandfather, George C Hawker, had been a prominent pastoralist and politician in pre-Federation South Australia. Arden Hawker was lord mayor of Adelaide in the early 1940s.
3. Lt Hawker did not mention his personal fighting in his report (50th Battalion War Diary for September 1918, Appendix 14) but it appears in the recommendation for his MC.
4. Browning, *For King and Cobbers, Op Cit*, pp. 313–14; 51st Battalion War Diary for September 1918, Appendix 15.
5. *Official History*, Vol VI, p. 896.
6. Pedersen, *Monash as Military Commander, Op Cit*, p. 278.
7. 48th Battalion War Diary, 13 September 1918.
8. Chataway, *Op Cit*, p. 231.
9. Monash, *Op Cit*, p. 222.
10. Noted in the after-action reports of both the 4th and 12th Brigades; the September 1918 War Diaries of the DAC and the Train do not give any details.
11. Monash, *Op Cit*, p. 222.
12. 48th Battalion War Diary, 14 September 1918.
13. This grouping was changed when the field artillery moved forward to cover the Blue Line (4th Division Artillery War Diary, 18 September 1918).
14. Marked in brown on the maps—the terms Green Line and Brown Line were used interchangeably depending on which unit's account is used, but most maps, including the artillery barrage map, show an infantry halt line (Brown) forward of the first objective (Green).
15. 4th MG Battalion War Diary for September 1918, Appendix A1.
16. The 1st Division mixed its own MG companies and those of the 3rd MG Battalion across the various tasks.

17 White, *Op Cit*, p. 156.
18 As in the battalion orders and after-action reports. A map attached to the 12th Brigade War Diary for September1918 shows the 45th with four companies abreast and the 46th with three in front and one in support, however.
19 4th Division General Staff War Diary for October 1918, Appendix 12.
20 Called Fort Dyce on earlier British maps, it was Fort Bull on the maps used by the Australian Corps at this time.
21 16th Battalion War Diary for September 1918, Appendix 5a.
22 The number of fatalities comes from the AWM Roll of Honour. The 4th Brigade War Diary (September 1918, Appendix 40) reported 3 killed and 17 wounded but one of the latter was later found to have been killed and another died of wounds the same day. The number of wounded varies depending on which source is used. The *Official History* (Vol VI, p. 931n) gives a total of 22 casualties for the 16th Battalion.
23 4th Division General Staff War Diary for October 1918, Appendix 12.
24 Bean Papers, AWM38 3DRL606/228/1, folio 483; MM recommendation for Pte Williams.
25 This seems to be the same landmark rendered as 'Danger Copse' in the Bean papers referred to in Note 24 above.
26 13th Battalion War Diary for September 1918, Appendix 14.
27 White, *Op Cit*, p. 157.
28 Details from the relevant Red Cross file. One of the reports there says he was hit at Collins Copse, near the second objective, but an account in the Bean Papers (AWM38 3DRL606/227/1, folio 313) is definite that it happened at Dean Trench.
29 White, *Op Cit*, p. 159; DCM recommendation for Pte Denny. It is not clear where this incident occurred, but it would have been at one end or the other of the 13th's line, since the recommendation says that there was a different unit on one flank of the section of trench.
30 See Browning, *Leane's Battalion, Op Cit*, pp. 306–10 for a detailed account.
31 Devine, *Op Cit*, pp. 148–9.
32 Bean Papers, AWM38 3DRL606/227/1, folios 307 (account by Brig Gen Leane) and 295.
33 *Ibid*, folio 296.
34 The 48th initially reported seven killed and 55 wounded (12th Brigade War Diary for September 1918, Appendix 19). The AWM Roll of Honour shows 13 fatalities on 18 September, included several soldiers who died of wounds the same day and others who were at first incorrectly reported as wounded. The *Official History* (Vol VI, p.931n) has a total of 65 casualties for the 48th.
35 The 4th Brigade report (War Diary for September 1918, Appendix 24) makes this comment, as does White, *Op Cit*, p. 158.
36 *Official History*, Vol VI, p. 894.
37 4th Pioneer Battalion War Diary for September 1918, Appendix 15; 16th Battalion War Diary for September 1918, Appendix 5A; 4th Division GS War Diary for September 1918, Appendix 12. A full account of the episode is given in C Goddard, 'It's A Tank Dummy,' *Wartime*, Issue 38, Summer 2015.
38 4th MG Battalion War Diary for September 1918, Appendix A1.
39 Bean Papers, AWM38 3DRL606/228/1, folio 483.
40 Bean Diary, AWM38 3DRL606/116/1, 18 September 1918 (folio 133).

41 The 4th Brigade's final report (Appendix 24 to the September 1918 War Diary) gives a total of 1137 prisoners taken, a figure also used in the reports of Division and Corps. The total included 165 handed over to 1st Division authorities because of enemy shelling on the route back to 4th Brigade HQ. The latter were stated as having been taken 'on the left of our advance' suggesting they were captured by the 15th Battalion. The Brigade report accepts the 16th Battalion's figure of 450 prisoners, but only says that the other units captured 'a large haul' in the advance to and capture of the Red Line. The 14th Battalion, as noted later in this chapter, reported taking 75 prisoners at the final objective, a number which would appear to be fairly accurate. Accepting the numbers for the 16th and 14th Battalion (525 total) leaves 612 between the 15th and 13th Battalions combined. At a guess, perhaps 200 to 250 should be credited to the 15th and 350 to 400 to the 13th. Custody of the prisoners was taken by Military Police from the escorts, but there appears to be no readily available report by the 4th Division Assistant Provost Marshal on the subject. In a situation where over a thousand prisoners were streaming back through the Australian front with whatever minimal escorts could be spared from the firing line, it is not surprising that there was a lack of precision in the initial count.

42 The AWM Roll of Honour records the deaths of 13 members of the 15th Battalion on 18 September. Of these, however, one died in Australia, one died of wounds received on the previous day, and one was attached to the 4th LTM Battery (but not recorded for that unit in reports). Of the remaining 10, seven were recorded as killed in action and three as died of wounds on the same day. Another three 15th members died on 19 September from wounds received on 18 September. Lt Col Johnston's report (15th Battalion War Diary for September 1918, Appendix 19) stated the losses for the 15th as seven killed, eight died of wounds and 40 wounded over the period in the front line.

43 See note 41 above.

44 Deaths include those who died of wounds on the same day, as recorded on the AWM Roll of Honour. The figures for captures and for casualties as estimated at the time are in the 13th Battalion War Diary for September 1918, Appendix 14. The casualty numbers include one soldier (presumably Sgt Lihou) first reported missing then deemed to have been killed in action.

45 Bean Papers, AWM38 3DRL606/227/1, folio 281.

46 Lynch, *Op Cit*, pp 294–8.

47 Bean Papers, AWM38 3DRL606/227/1, folio 282. In this interview, Maj Loutit stated that two batteries (12 pieces) of 5.9s were captured altogether. This appears to be an error. Also, the 12th Brigade report, signed by Brig Gen Leane on 28 September credits the 45th with capturing three 77 mm guns and two 15 cm howitzers, out of the total of six of the latter captured by the Brigade overall (12th Brigade War Diary for September 1918, Appendix 19).

48 Joseph Dietze was born Joseph Sandoe, in England. Dietze was the name of his step-father, from his mother's second marriage, and he used that name from childhood, nominating his step-father as next-of-kin on his army enlistment form. On his death, his original name Sandoe had become known to the authorities, apparently through a statutory declaration (in the form of a letter countersigned by a JP) made by his step-father and enclosing his baptism certificate. The reason for making the declaration is not immediately clear, but may have been to clarify the next-of-kin status. His headstone in Bellicourt British Cemetery was originally engraved as Sandoe, against the instructions of his family. On becoming aware of this, his mother and sister (a Mrs E McKenzie) raised strong objections and insisted that the headstone be re-engraved to show Dietze instead, on the basis that he had chosen to use that name, and had been known to all as Joseph Dietze; there was also a privacy issue as the family did not wish it publicly known that Mrs Dietze had been married twice (the correspondence is on the service record file for 2nd Lt Dietze, which is cross-referenced to Sandoe). In the 1930s, Commonwealth War Graves eventually

agreed, and the headstone inscription was changed to Dietze with no mention of Sandoe, as listed in the CWGC database records for Bellicourt British Cemetery in France (the present author has seen the headstone). There is no entry for Sandoe in the database.

Australian records, however, still show Sandoe as the primary name—that is, the Roll of Honour database has a listing of the name J H Dietze, but when selected the full entry is found to be for J H Sandoe. The Roll of Honour engravings at the Australian War Memorial show J H Sandoe, not J H Dietze. In other words, the soldier's actual war grave and the AWM Roll of Honour show different names for the same individual.

49 Casualty figures from the Brigade report as in Note 47 above, with fatalities corrected from the AWM Roll of Honour. One officer (Lt L R Hughes) died of wounds on 1 October, another was wounded on the day before the battle, and a number of other casualties occurred over the following few days in the line. The number of 474 prisoners is given in Maj Loutit's account, also Note 47, but the 12th Brigade report only gives a total of 1411 taken by the Brigade as a whole. Brig Gen Leane gives approximate numbers of prisoners for each battalion in the Bean Papers, AWM38 3DRL606/227/1, folio 310 (45th 400 prisoners, 46th 550, 48th 500).

50 Australian Corps GS War Diary for September 1918, Appendix 30.
51 *Official History*, Vol VI, p. 914.
52 46th Battalion War Diary, 18 September 1918.
53 Bean Papers, AWM38 3DRL606/228/1, folio 479.
54 *Ibid*, folio 467.
55 14th Battalion War Diary for September 1918, Appendix, Narrative of Operations. The Diary entry for 17 September says 361.
56 Rule, *Op Cit*, p. 141.
57 *Ibid*.
58 14th Battalion Narrative, as in Note 55 above.
59 Rule, *Op Cit*, p. 142.
60 Bean Papers, AWM38 3DRL606/227/1, folio 379, account by Maj F M Couchman. That interview with C E W Bean is a main source for the account that follows.
61 12th Brigade War Diary for September 1918, Appendix 19 ('Instructions No 4' of 17 September 1918).
62 *Official History*, Vol VI, p. 921.
63 10th AFA Brigade War Diary for September 1918 Part 2, Appendix 148. Some of the map references in that report appear to be wrong—he gives the intermediate position of the battery as G5c, a square well to the north, on the 1st Division front. In Maj Couchman's account of the 46th Battalion's fighting (Bean Papers, AWM38 3DRL606/227/1, folio 380-81), he states that the battery got to Heart Copse, which was in square L35c, before withdrawing to Dean Trench. Couchman said that the gunners were told erroneously that the figures they could see on the Red Line ridge were Germans, so they withdrew presumably to get a better line of fire.
64 12th Brigade War Diary for September 1918, Appendix 19. Those comments were toned down somewhat in the Division's report.
65 Rule, *Op Cit*, p. 143.
66 12th Brigade War Diary, 18 September 1918.
67 Rule, *Op Cit*, p. 143
68 14th Battalion War Diary for September 1918, Appendix 9.

69 Bean Papers, as for Notes 60 and 63 above (folio 382).
70 46th Battalion War Diary for September 1918, Appendix 15.
71 Fatalities from the AWM Roll of Honour database. The number of the 46th's wounded differs between the 12th Brigade's Report and the 46th's own Diary. The Battalion suffered several more deaths over the next two days in the line.
72 The account of the fight that follows is based on Browning, *Leane's Battalion, Op Cit*, pp. 314–319. Browning is of the view that the other private was W J Reid—in his diary entry covering the action, Lt R B Reid used that spelling for the surname, the same as his own, without a given name or initials. Most accounts mention that the other private in the patrol was wounded during the fighting. W J Reid's service file does not show a wound, although he could have been slightly wounded and stayed on duty without any record being made. Pte E W G Reed's record, however, does show that he was wounded on 18 September, with a gunshot to the upper left arm (the fight took place in the early hours of 19 September, however). The present author has opted to go with E W G Reed as the other member of the patrol.
73 Information from the sketch maps appended to the 46th Battalion War Diary for September 1918. There are no details of the 48th Battalion's automatic weapons.
74 14th Battalion War Diary for September 1918, Appendix, Narrative of Operations.
75 The 14th Battalion War Diary recorded 19 killed or died of wounds and 75 wounded over the three days (entry for 30 Sept 1918 and appended Narrative of Operations). The AWM roll of Honour database shows 20 fatalities for that period. The 4th Brigade War Diary for September 1918, Appendix 40, gives lower numbers for the 14th Battalion's losses.
76 Devine, *Op Cit*, p. 151.
77 12th Field Ambulance War Diary for September 1918, Appendix 4.
78 13th Field Company War Diary for September 1918, Appendices G1 and G2.
79 Bean Diary, AWM38 3DRL606/116/1, 18 September 1918, folio 133 (page 142 in PDF).
80 12th Brigade War Diary for September 1918, Appendix 19 (folio 75).
81 A modern British book on the fighting in the Épehy area over the course of the war scarcely mentions the Australian Corps in the battle of 18 September
82 Figures from each Brigade's after-action reports appended to the September 1918 War Diaries, and that of the 4th Division, Appendix 12 to the October War Diary; the Division figure may include captures credited to non-infantry units, such as the machine gunners.
83 Again, numbers of fatalities are from the AWM Roll of Honour database. Total casualties are from the Brigade War Diaries as for Note 81 above, and September 1918 War Diaries of the 4th MG Battalion and 4th Pioneer Battalion.
84 The Corps report gave the total 'hopover strength', including battalion and company headquarters personnel, as 1635 for the 4th Brigade (four battalions) and 1413 for the 12th Brigade (three battalions); the latter formation was credited with taking 1406 prisoners, rather than 1411, still virtually one for every man in the attack (Australian Corps GS War Diary for October 1918, Appendix 22).
85 White, *Op Cit*, p. 158.
86 *Sydney Morning Herald*, 30 May 2009.
87 Rule, *Op Cit*, pp. 141–5.
88 The recommendation is listed in the AWM system under 'Bainbridge' although the actual document has the right spelling. The gazettal record is spelled correctly.

24: Armistice

The main body of the 4th Division settled again into the slower tempo of life in the back area, beginning with the always-welcome baths and reissue of clothing and equipment. After a few days' break, varying between units, the standard pattern of rest-period activities began, with training in the mornings, usually from 9 am to 12:30 pm, then organised sports after a meal break. Evenings were off-duty, when the troops could make use of wet and dry canteens or spend time in the little villages where they were billeted. As far as anyone knew, the Division would be going into the line again at some point, and plans were made to ramp up the training programme for October to include advanced exercises. Early in October the Pioneer Battalion was withdrawn to rejoin the Division in the rest area as was the Divisional Train, except for the 14th Company AASC which remained forward to supply the artillery.

More of the 1914 officers and men were released for furlough to Australia during the rest period, as well as those taking normal leave to London or Paris. This contributed to another round of changes in senior officer postings around this time, in addition to changes for operational reasons. The 45th Battalion CO, Lieutenant Colonel Loutit, wounded in the chest on 18 September, had stayed with his unit to see its Red Line objective taken but the next day he had to seek treatment and was evacuated to the CCS. He was replaced by Lieutenant Colonel Cecil Ridley, the former 51st Battalion CO, who had recently returned to the 4th Division from a posting at AIF HQ in London. Colonel Ridley assumed command the same afternoon. In the 16th Battalion Captain Lynas went on leave (to England rather than Australia) when the unit was relieved in the line, having handed over command to Major Edward Parks, just returned from a senior officers' course. The latter was soon given promotion to temporary lieutenant colonel.[1] Lieutenant Colonel John Whitham had returned to the 49th Battalion from his England posting, resuming command as of 18 September from Lieutenant Colonel William Arrell who reverted to his substantive rank of major. The 12th Field Ambulance also had a change of CO in late September, when Lieutenant Colonel Arthur Gibson was posted to No 1 Australian CCS. He was succeeded by Lieutenant Colonel Frederick Le Messurier, promoted from major within the unit. Earlier in September the long-serving Divisional Train CO, Lieutenant Colonel Albert Holdsworth, had left on Australia furlough. The next senior Train officer, Major Leslie Sando, assumed command and next month was promoted to temporary lieutenant colonel. Numerous other regimental and staff officers were temporarily absent on local leave or courses in this period, their places being filled by acting appointees.

Eighty kilometres to the east, the 4th Division artillery was preparing to play its part in the assault on the main Hindenburg Line. So far the BEF had been fighting its way back to the positions held before the great German spring offensive. Now the next step would be to penetrate into territory occupied by the enemy since the first weeks of the War. The reliefs immediately after the Outpost Line battle had resulted in the Australian Corps front shifting north to take over most of the former III Corps sector. The new Australian front was now held by the 27th and 30th US Divisions, relieving the 1st Australian Division and placed under Australian command by agreement with their Corps commander. Those divisions, recently moved south from a brief taste of the front line in the Ypres sector, comprised II American Corps, the only US formation still working with the BEF rather than with the French forces. They were equipped with British weapons and their field artillery was made up of BEF units.[2] Both American divisions had three times the infantry numbers of the depleted Australian divisions. Within a week, the 3rd and 5th Australian Divisions moved forward from rest near Péronne and took up positions in support to the Americans, followed by the 2nd Division going into Corps reserve further back. The US divisions would make the initial attack on the Hindenburg Line followed closely in the next phase by the 3rd and 5th Australian Divisions. Concerned at the relative inexperience of the Americans, both tactically and in staff work, Monash decided to send a team of selected officers and NCOs to each American division to give the benefit of their experience. The teams would be provided by the Australian divisions just relieved, the 1st and 4th, and Major General Sinclair-MacLagan was appointed Chief of Mission, attached to II US Corps. Also with the II Corps HQ was Lieutenant Colonel Harry Murray, 4th MG Battalion CO, to advise on the employment of machine guns. The remainder of the 4th Division contingent was sent to the 27th US Division. Brigadier General Brand, just returned from leave, went to 27th HQ with a small staff, headed by Major 'Babe' Norman, brigade major of the 12th Brigade. Two battalion COs, Lieutenant Colonels Salisbury (50th) and Crowther (14th), were assigned to the next level of command down, called brigades in the US system but considerably larger than a British brigade, the equivalent to which was the US regiment. Officers assigned to the four regiments included the 48th Battalion adjutant Captain David Twining, Major William Wadsworth (14th Battalion), Captain Norman Owen (51st), Captain Basil Atkinson (15th) and Lieutenant Harry Downes (12th Brigade staff). Major Howard Tolley, OC 4th Field Company, was added to the party when a field engineer officer was requested. Quartermaster officers and sergeants were assigned to the regiments together with specialist weapons NCOs. Members of the mission were detached from their units on 24

September. In Major General Sinclair-MacLagan's absence, Brigadier General Leane of the 12th Brigade took temporary command of the 4th Division.

A key feature of the Hindenburg defences in the Australian/American sector was the Bellicourt Tunnel, where the St Quentin Canal ran underground for 5,500 metres north from Bellicourt village. Elsewhere the Canal itself, with its steep banks and defensive works on both sides, was a considerable obstacle, but the ground over the tunnel was in effect a wide bridge across the Canal. Hence the Germans had constructed even stronger defences in that area. Monash's original plan, formulated while the Outpost Line battle was still in progress, envisaged an assault on the tunnel region after several days of an old-style preliminary bombardment that would cut lanes in the extensive wire entanglements and suppress the defending garrison. A creeping barrage would cover the troops in the first phase (the two American divisions, 27th on the left and 30th on the right) as they passed over the tunnel and the enemy front line. They would then go on to capture the support position, the Le Catelet Line, an overall advance of four kilometres. Following on, the two Australian divisions (3rd and 5th, left and right) would leapfrog through and advance another four kilometres to take the German reserve position, the Beaurevoir Line, using open warfare tactics without a creeping barrage. Troops from the two flanking British corps would follow and extend north and south behind the initial penetration. Sufficient tanks were now available to support the infantry. The operation would form part of a coordinated offensive by the Allied armies to both north and south along the front. Fourth Army's operation was planned to take place on 29 September, by which time it was assumed that the start line, that is the Outpost Line facing the tunnel sector, would have been captured. That was the case in the southern part of the sector, taken by the 1st Australian Division, but in the northern part 'so comprehensively had III Corps failed on 18 September that it must have been open to doubt whether further attacks by these worn-down forces would ever succeed.'[3]

So it proved, and by 24 September when the 27th US Division took over the northern portion of the Tunnel front from III Corps the line there was still a kilometre short of the Outpost Line objectives, with several key strong-points remaining in German hands. The plan for the assault on the Hindenburg Line consequently had to be modified at short notice. To get onto its start line for the operation the 27th Division first had to capture it from the enemy, and it was ordered that a regiment of that Division would make the attempt on 27 September, two days before the main operation. Another change was made by order of General Rawlinson, who baulked at confining the main attack only to the comparatively narrow front formed by the ground above the tunnel. There would be too great a risk of the enemy containing the penetration and then concentrating reserves against it. Overruling Monash, Rawlinson approved an attempt by the 46th Division (IX Corps) to cross the Canal south of the tunnel by frontal assault, heavily supported by artillery. That action would widen the attack frontage to 10 kilometres.

The 27th Division's attempt to seize its start line would be covered by the field artillery allocated to the Australian Corps left divisional sector. This force was under command of Brigadier General Burgess, the 4th Division CRA, whose HQ moved from Vendelles to Buire Wood, north of Tincourt, on 25 September. Burgess had nine brigades in three groups: Left, the Division's 10th and 11th AFA Brigades with one British brigade, under Lieutenant Colonel Williams, 10th AFA, and the Centre and Right Groups, each of three British brigades under their respective senior unit COs. On the night of 26 September the left sector guns opened their part in the preliminaries with a bombardment of mustard gas shells and HE on detected enemy artillery positions and strong-points. This was the first time British-manufactured mustard gas had been used by the BEF.[4] The gas shelling went on intermittently for eight hours, timed to cease 48 hours before the main attack, allowing a minimum time for the gas to disperse and lessen the risk of the attacking troops running into it. The preparatory bombardment would then continue with HE shells, concentrating on counter-battery work and wire cutting. At 5:30 am on 27 September, the left sector guns switched to firing the creeping barrage covering the 27th Division's operation to capture their start line for the main attack. The 18-pounders began 180 metres ahead of the infantry, each gun shooting at three rounds per minute (the howitzer barrage started a further 180 metres out at two rounds per minute), the lines of shell-bursts lifting at the rate of 90 metres yards every three minutes until the protective barrage line was reached after 45 minutes. The artillery barrage was supplemented by a machine gun barrage from two 27th Division MG battalions with a total of 96 British Vickers guns.[5] The protective barrage ceased after another 30 minutes and the commanders waited for reports to come in from the front line. First indications were of success, but as the day went on the situation became less certain as contradictory reports followed. It transpired that the Americans had captured part of the northernmost strong-point in the Outpost Line, a feature called The Knoll, but had later been pushed off by a counter-attack. Other strong-points apparently remained in German hands, but little definite information came through. The inexperienced troops, unable to keep direction in the mist and smoke, had inadvertently bypassed many German posts, which then opened fire on them when the mist lifted. The American brigade was also handicapped by a shortage of officers, and most of that small number had been hit, leaving the troops without leaders. The enemy units in this area appeared to be of somewhat different mettle to those that had put up minimal resistance on 18 September, and their morale had been boosted by the successful defence against the attacks of III Corps.

As far as the commanders could ascertain the objectives had not been taken and most of the attack force was back on its start line, but an uncertain number of American troops remained isolated out in what was still mainly enemy territory. This created a dilemma for the barrage to cover the left wing of the main attack scheduled for 29 September—whether to begin the barrage close to the original American start line, meaning it would fall on the troops who were still hanging on or lying wounded in front, or to begin beyond the Outpost

Line as originally planned, leaving the infantry to fight their way over the intervening distance without artillery support. In the end the higher commanders decided that the first option was unacceptable and the original barrage plan would proceed. Additional tanks were allocated to the 27th Division, which would start its advance an hour earlier than the rest of the attacking force and try to reach the barrage line by Zero.[6] Monash asked for a postponement of one day, but this could not be granted because of the need to co-ordinate Fourth Army's operation with the armies in other sectors of the line.

Over the two nights leading up to the main attack the field brigades moved forward into new positions to fire the creeping barrage. As part of the Left Group, the 10th and 11th AFA's batteries moved to locations north-east of Ronssoy. Artillery HQ moved also, to a location in a sunken road south-west of Épehy. The batteries experienced some retaliatory shelling from the enemy artillery, an indication that the Germans had improved their measures for avoiding counter-battery fire. The forward gun positions also began to come under long-range machine gun fire, an unusual situation confirming that the 27th Division had not succeeded in advancing the front line to any great extent. Shortly before Zero on 29 September a German shell hit the gun-line of the 43rd Battery (11th AFA), killing Lieutenant Ernest Battye and three gunners, and wounding most of the crews of two guns. Lieutenant James Diamond, with Sergeants William Richards and John Croll, got both guns into action in time for the barrage, operating them until reinforcements could be brought up from the wagon lines. Diamond was later awarded the MC and the two sergeants received DCMs.

The creeping barrage opened at 5:50 am and followed the standard pattern of lifts and rates of fire, lifting 50 times to reach the final protective line 200 minutes after Zero. The 27th Division advance again failed to reach the forward start line, however, and the barrage line moved on and left the infantry behind, still involved in heavy combat. The three main German strong-points, The Knoll, Gillemont Farm and Quennemont Farm, held out against the Americans, most of whose supporting tanks were knocked out by anti-tank guns. Troops of the 3rd Australian Division, coming up later in the morning to leapfrog through and advance on their distant objective of the enemy reserve line, instead found themselves immediately involved in desperate fighting. Late in the day, they captured Gillemont and Quennemont Farms, but the advance in that sector had gone no further than the planned start line.

The Australian officers and NCOs attached to the Americans had done what they could to instil the benefits of their Western Front experience, but it was a challenging assignment to pass on two and a half years of hard-won knowledge in a few days, and for the Americans to absorb it. The 4th Division members working with the 27th US Division had been instructed that their function was advisory only, but several had found it necessary to become more directly involved. The 12th Brigade assistant staff captain, Lieutenant Harry Downes, was attached to the 107th Regiment, which attacked on the left of the 27th Division front. Downes took personal responsibility for the carriage of ammunition and rations to the firing line, guiding pack animal columns forward while under heavy enemy fire; he was awarded the MC in due course, partly for that work.⁷ Major Howard Tolley, OC 4th Field Company, working with the 102nd Engineer Regiment, went forward with several American engineers to set up a forward report centre. In the confused fighting the party found that the selected position was still in German hands. All except Tolley, who had gone out unarmed, were hit by enemy fire. He pressed on alone, picking up a German stick grenade on the way, and captured a squad of seven enemy soldiers by threatening them with the grenade. Later that day he set up one or more machine guns for anti-aircraft work ('for which no provision had been made'), which shot down a German plane that had been strafing the troops. For these exploits Major Tolley was recommended for the US Distinguished Service Medal (DSM); the decoration was not awarded, however.⁸

On the right of the Australian Corps front the 30th US Division, with the benefit of a suitable start line, was able to gain some advantage from the barrage in the early stages of the attack. The left of the 30th was held up by enemy fire from the north, where the 27th had not been able to advance, but the right had some success. On that flank elements of the 30th crossed the Hindenburg main line over the tunnel near Bellicourt, captured the southern mouth of the tunnel and entered Bellicourt village. The Americans here also lost cohesion in the poor visibility, and they were unable to continue the advance to their final objective, the Le Catelet support line. They had also inadvertently bypassed a number of German posts. These opened fire on the 5th Australian Division, coming forward to pass through and advance on the next objective. The 5th pressed on, joining up with scattered parties of Americans to capture Nauroy on the right. Other elements swung south and linked up with the 46th British Division, which had just carried out an extraordinary feat of arms, against most expectations. A brigade of the 46th, jumping off from the line secured by the 4th Australian Division on 18 September, had attacked the line of the Canal. With the way prepared by a concentrated artillery bombardment, the British infantry crossed the steep-banked water barrier using anything that would float and rushed the German trenches on the far side. The other brigades then leapfrogged through and pressed on to break through the main line on their front and penetrate to their final objective.

The day ended with success in the south, partial success in the centre, and failure in the north. The difficulties of the American troops were more the result of inexperience rather than any lack of courage. Colonel Harry Murray, who reconnoitred the battlefield the next day, wrote to General O'Ryan (27th Division) that the American dead all lay facing the enemy.⁹ Lieutenant Leonard Coulson, a 46th Battalion officer in the Australian advisory group, commented that whereas AIF infantrymen had long since learned to work around machine gun posts and take them in the rear, the Americans were inclined to charge straight ahead into the enemy fire.¹⁰ Captain Hubert Wilkins, polar explorer and the Australian Official Photographer, went out to take pictures and encountered a leaderless group of Americans sheltering in a trench. Wilkins, who had spent his share of time under fire, could see German infantry tossing stick grenades into the trench further down, but the 'Americans were unaware of the danger, imaging that the bombs they heard were shells.'[11] Once the error had been pointed out, the Americans were more than willing to get into the fight. Wilkins directed their efforts until the situation had stabilised then returned to his camera work.

The 4th Division artillery completed the creeping barrage task at 9:10 am, unaware through lack of reliable information from the front that the infantry had not reached the objective. At different times over the rest of the day the batteries engaged various targets on the northern flank of the Corps sector. The gun teams had lost 39 casualties for the day, the majority in the 11th AFA Brigade which had seven killed and 26 wounded; four of its guns were also put out of action. That night, orders went out for the Americans to be withdrawn to reserve as soon as possible. The 3rd Australian Division assumed command of the left sector, with that formation's CRA taking over six of the British field brigades in the sector artillery. The 10th and 11th AFA Brigades, with one British brigade, remained under command of Brigadier General Burgess, responsible for defending the left flank towards Vendhuille while the 3rd Division disentangled itself from stray American troops and renewed the attack on the main Hindenburg Line. Over the next two days the 3rd Division pushed ahead and succeeded in crossing the tunnel in a battle of platoons and sections. By the night of 1 October the line on the left stood beyond Bony in the main Hindenburg Line but short of Le Catelet in the enemy support line. On the right the 5th Division had advanced well beyond the support line. The front now faced north-east, with only the reserve Beaurevoir Line still fully held by the enemy. That night the 5th Division was relieved in the line by the 2nd coming up from reserve, and on the following night the 3rd Division was relieved by a British division of XIII Corps, which had replaced the ineffective III Corps in Fourth Army's left sector.

The Australian Corps experienced no serious fighting on 2 October[12] and on that day the 10th and 11th AFA Brigades moved to the vicinity of Bellicourt. There both units came under command of the 2nd Division CRA for operations in the near future. The 4th Division brigades were not required for the action of 3 October, when the thinly-spread infantry of the 2nd Division took a 5,500-metre segment of the Beaurevoir Line, the final breach in the Hindenburg defences. Two days later, however, both units were included with eight field brigades firing the barrage covering the attack on Montbrehain, a village on high ground just to the east, by the 2nd Division's 6th Infantry Brigade. The guns were brought up into position during the previous night, designated as part of the Right Group for the operation, which got under way at 0605 on 5 October (the BEF had adopted the 24-hour clock system at the beginning of the month). Montbrehain fell that day at a heavy cost in casualties in what proved to be the last action of Australian infantry in the war. The 2nd Division (except its artillery) withdrew that night to join the other divisions in rest, the final division of the Australian Corps to come out of the line. The sector was handed over to II US Corps, coming forward again from reserve. The 30th US Division went into the line first, now with a brief experience of Western Front combat, but still struggling with administrative issues: 'some of the infantry [arrived] without water, rations, Lewis guns, ammunition or telephones.'[13]

The field artillery brigades that had been covering the 2nd Division infantry, including the 4th Division units, remained in the line to cover the incoming 30th US Division. The force was increased to 10 brigades, all Australian, by the addition of the 3rd Division artillery. The next operation would require two regiments of the 30th Division to move the line forward by advancing between Beaurevoir and Montbrehain under a creeping barrage, with British divisions to the right and left. The artillery command arrangements were unusual, with Brigadier General Burgess designated as one of two group commanders under the overall command of the 2nd Division CRA, Brigadier General O F Phillips. The latter officer was in effect divisional artillery commander for the 30th US Division. Later, when the 30th Division was relieved in the line by the 27th, General Burgess assumed those duties for the incoming division. For the forthcoming operation his Right Group consisted of the two 4th Division brigades, the two 5th Division brigades and the 6th 'Army' Brigade. At this time, the 10th and 11th Brigades, numbers depleted by casualties and release of men on furlough, were reinforced by most of the personnel of the divisional MTM batteries, then languishing in the rear at Villers-Faucon without tasks in the recent operations.

The American infantry carried out a minor operation on 7 October to occupy a straighter start line. That day the 4th Division batteries moved forward to positions near Ramicourt to the south-west of Montbrehain, while artillery HQ moved to a location near Nauroy. The creeping barrage opened at 0510 on 8 October and the infantry attack proceeded to timetable against weak opposition. All along the Fourth Army front the first objectives were taken and the infantry went on to capture the second, the 'line of exploitation.' The 30th Division reached its final objective line by 1415, capturing the village of Brancourt-le-Grand on the way and taking 1,500 prisoners out of a Fourth Army total of 4,000.[14] The Army line had advanced by up to six kilometres. This attack began a period of frequent advances in pursuit of the retreating enemy, with constant changes in position for the Australian field artillery and sometimes bewildering changes in groupings and command structure. Signallers followed close behind the batteries to complete the vital communication links, with the DAC keeping pace and the 14th company AASC following up to maintain the supply of rations. The DAC's SAA section had taken on the infantry ammunition supply function for the American division in the line (the DAC was now commanded by Major Alfred Ford, Colonel Vernon having departed for home on furlough).

The attack was followed up next day (9 October) when Fourth Army continued to advance, aiming to reach a line between Bohain on the south and Honnechy on the north. In the centre the 30th Division leapfrogged its two big infantry brigades to reach its second objectives, the villages of Becquigny and Busigny and the ground in between, in the course of the afternoon. The artillery arrangements were made at such short notice that no barrage map was issued. The batteries instead began firing at 0520 on designated lines and simply lifted 90 metres every four minutes until they had reached their extreme range.[15] A two-gun section of the 43rd Battery (11th AFA) moved off with the American infantry at Zero, engaging a pair of German '77's and various parties of enemy troops during the advance. The batteries moved forward again during the afternoon to re-position for the next stage. The Germans fell back to the line of the River Selle with the intention of making a stand behind the water obstacle. Fourth Army continued to press forward in pursuit and attacked again the next day, with the Americans assigned to the villages west of the river crossings, Vaux-Andigny, La Haie Menneresse and St Souplet. Again the field artillery covered the 30th Division by a creeping barrage up to maximum range, starting at 0530. This time it was the 41st Battery that provided a section to advance with the infantry. In the villages the German infantry resisted strongly, supported by heavy machine gun fire from the high ground on the far side of the river. The 30th Division gained footholds in the western outskirts of the villages, but could make no further progress that day. The two flanking Corps were also held up west of the river. The field batteries moved up again, to positions outside Busigny. Another attempt was made on 11 October, again starting at 0530, behind a creeping barrage which this time stayed on its start line for 20 minutes before beginning the creep. The 30th Division completed the capture of Vaux-Andigny, La Haie Menneresse and the major part of St Souplet on the west bank of the river, and some minor progress was made on left and right. In four days of fighting, Fourth Army had advanced 17 kilometres, in the process liberating numerous occupied villages, with a total civilian population estimated at 12,000.[16] It was now apparent, however, that enemy resistance had stiffened considerably and a planned formal attack would be needed to push the Germans off the line of the Selle.

On the night of 11/12 October the 27th US Division came into the line to relieve the 30th. The field artillery in the sector was transferred to the incoming division, with command passing to Brigadier General Burgess as the nominated artillery chief for the 27th Division. Brigadier General Phillips took his turn as a group commander (of the Left Group) under Burgess. The latter moved his HQ up to Busigny on 15 October, close to the Division HQ. Major operations were suspended for several days to enable reorganisation and preparations for the resumption of the offensive. The spearheads of Fourth Army had temporarily outrun the supply chain:

> the date of the attack was postponed subsequently until October 17th, on account of the enormous difficulties experienced with regard to bringing up ammunition and supplies ... the only main line of railway for supply ran through St Quentin, Bohain and Busigny. This line, which had to serve both the Fourth Army and the northern corps of the First French Army, had been considerably damaged by the enemy ... [delayed action mines] causing considerable anxiety to those responsible for supplying the army with food and ammunition.[17]

– which included the ammunition columns and supply companies supporting the Australian artillery. The 4th Division elements, the DAC and the 14th Company AASC, had moved up to the vicinity of Busigny, near the artillery HQ, by late October.[18]

Despite those difficulties the necessary preparations were made and the artillery force was built up to over 1,300 guns of all calibres.[19] The preliminary bombardment of the German positions steadily increased in intensity while plans were being finalised. For the operation of 17 October the sector assigned to II US Corps presented a formidable task for one division, so the 30th was brought back into the line on the night of 15/16 October to take over the right of the American front. The 27th closed up its frontage to form the sub-sector on the left. This produced another change in the field artillery groupings. The existing Left and Right Groups, now reinforced by the artillery brigades of the 3rd and 5th Australian Divisions (back in the line after a brief rest), became the artillery for the left and right divisional sectors, that is for the 27th and 30th US Divisions respectively. Consequently Brigadier General Burgess, as artillery commander for the 27th Division, now had five brigades under his command that did not include the 10th and 11th AFA. Four were drawn from the 2nd, 3rd and 5th Australian Divisions, plus one Army brigade. The two 4th Division brigades, having been part of the previous Right Group, now covered the 30th US Division on the right together with a brigade each from the 3rd and 5th Australian Divisions and an Army brigade. Brigadier General A J Bessell-Browne, the 5th Division CRA, became artillery commander for the 30th US Division. Within that force the 10th and 11th AFA Brigades formed a group under Lieutenant Colonel Williams, the 10th Brigade CO.

The operation of 17 October on the II US Corps front called for an attack by both divisions crossing the river, which was shallow enough to wade and not very wide, and then advancing for 2,700 metres to a halt line. Here there would be a pause of 30 minutes to reorganise. The advance would then go on for a further 1,800 metres to the first objective, a line running roughly from Jonc de Mer Farm on the left to Ribeauville village on the right. A fairly standard creeping barrage would cover the infantry up to the first objective, starting at 180 metres ahead of the infantry start line and lifting at a rate of 90 metres every three minutes. The final lift would be to a protective barrage line beyond the first objective, fire then ceasing at Zero plus 222 minutes. After a three-hour halt by the infantry, fresh troops would leapfrog through and attempt to gain the second objective by open warfare methods without a barrage, a further advance of up to three kilometres to a line close to the Sambre-Oise Canal—clearly an ambitious programme. As soon as the creeping barrage finished the 10th and 11th AFA Brigades would cease their assignment with the 30th Division and revert to the command of General Burgess, the 11th becoming the 'Advanced Guard' artillery supporting the 27th Division. Both brigades would then move up to the Selle near St Souplet and cross the river, using bridging equipment to be erected by American engineers, the 11th AFA in advance followed by the 10th in support. Both brigades would move close behind the infantry as the advance continued to the second objective.

The Battle of the Selle began on 17 October. Continuing the pattern of previous operations, the barrage opened at 0520, the field guns lengthening their range more than 50 times in three hours to reach the protective barrage line beyond the first objective. The American infantry started well: the 30th Division captured the villages of Molain and St Martin Rivière on the river and gained the far bank, while the 27th took the eastern part of St Souplet in the process of making their crossing.[20] Next they faced strong enemy resistance along a steep railway embankment with high ground beyond. The railway position was taken after severe fighting, which held up the infantry advance and resulted in them losing the barrage.[21] Once past the railway both divisions pressed on, now well behind time, and succeeded in reaching the intermediate halt line. This was partly along the main road running south from Le Cateau, through Arbre Guernon at the centre of the II Corps front, to Ribeauville on the right. The 27th advanced to the road and captured Arbre Guernon but was later forced back by a strong enemy counter attack that also fell on the British division to their left. The Americans then rallied and retook most of the lost ground, but could go no further in the face of heavy machine gun fire from strong-points ahead. The Germans still held the line of the main road north from Advantage Farm, a point just north of Arbre Guernon. By evening the II Corps divisions were dug in along the road south of there, holding firm but still well short of the day's first objective. The British corps on both flanks were similarly held up, but not before XIII Corps on the left had taken Le Cateau, scene of a famous rearguard action by the BEF in the dark days of August 1914.

In the meantime, once the creeping barrage had ceased the 11th AFA Brigade limbered up and set off north-east to the river at St Souplet. Here there was no definite information on the infantry's progress, but the 11th sent a section each from the 42nd and 43rd Batteries across the river to make ready for the continuation of the advance. The uncertainty of the situation and reports that the left flank had fallen back resulted in the guns being withdrawn to the west bank again, where battery positions were established. The 10th AFA meanwhile moved up to the vicinity of Escaufort, three kilometres west of St Souplet. The 10th had been hit hard by enemy counter-battery fire during the morning, losing 29 casualties, including Lieutenant Norman Taylor killed. One of the 110th Battery's howitzers had all of its crew hit except for Corporal Hugh Macleod, who continued firing the weapon on his own, an effort that earned him the DCM. Both brigades settled into position and awaited further developments. The operation resumed the next day along the whole Fourth Army front, with the infantry advancing from the line reached so far and attempting to reach yesterday's second objective. The artillery would fire a creeping barrage using the recent method of making regular lifts until maximum range was reached. The two 4th Division field brigades were again assigned to cross the river and give close support to the advancing infantry of the 27th Division. A difference of opinion arose over the artillery start line, planned as 200 yards east of the main road along the whole front. In the 27th Division sector, on that part where the Germans still held the road, the barrage would therefore miss the enemy front line. Brigadier General Burgess proposed that the start line in that area be changed so that the barrage would open directly on the road. This was not accepted by the British officer in overall command of the II Corps artillery, who wanted a consistent start line across the whole front. The question was escalated to the Fourth Army artillery commander, who ruled in favour of the 27th Division's view. There was little time to get the changed orders out, but 'due to the great zeal and energy of General Burgess, all batteries of the divisional artillery were notified in time.'[22]

The infantry attack got under way on time, easily sweeping over the Germans on the line of the main road with the aid of the barrage. Thereafter steady progress was made against heavy machine gun fire—the Germans always seemed to have an abundance of machine guns—over a terrain of farming fields enclosed by thick hedges. The hedges provided good concealment for machine gun positions, which were gradually overcome by the barrage and the infantry. There was heavy fighting at Jonc de Mer Farm before that strong-point was taken, and by evening Ribeauville village on the American right had also been captured and patrols had probed Mazinghien, beyond yesterday's first objective. The two 4th Division artillery brigades completed their barrage tasks then moved across the river, taking up positions two kilometres north-east of St Souplet near Bandival Farm. The American infantry advanced their line another kilometre during the night, and early next day (19 October) completed the capture of Mazinghien. By the end of the day Fourth Army's line had reached positions overlooking the Sambre-Oise Canal, the next major obstacle.[23] During the day the 11th AFA batteries, as the advanced guard artillery of the 27th Division, moved again, closer to the new front line. Here the batteries came under hostile shelling and also indirect machine gun fire. That night the 11th's batteries fired on various targets ahead of the infantry line, but next morning Colonel Spurge decided to move the 42nd and 43rd Batteries back to an intermediate position (Le Quennelet Grange) to avoid the enemy shelling.[24] The 27th Division made another advance early on the morning of 20 October, pushing its line another two kilometres north-east to the Bazuel-Catillon road against light opposition—the Germans were in the process of withdrawing most of their troops to the far side of the Sambre Canal.

The American divisions were exhausted by now and much depleted by heavy casualties after a fortnight of almost continuous fighting. No reinforcements had been sent forward to replace the losses, another example of the American rear echelons letting down their fighting men at the front. Over two nights, 19/20 and 20/21 October, both divisions of II American Corps were successively withdrawn and relieved in the line by two British divisions of IX Corps, extending its front to the left. The 6th Division relieved the American 27th with the British CRA taking over command of the field artillery on that part of the front. Brigadier General Burgess reverted to group commander, his Right Group comprising four brigades—the 4th Division brigades, the 7th AFA (3rd Division) and a British RFA brigade. The artillery units—both men and horses—were feeling the strain of continuous action: 'the health of personnel is low as a result of constant strenuous time in the line and a spell is ardently looked for. The condition of the animals is also low as a result of constant hard work.'[25] The 110th Howitzer Battery (10th AFA) also suffered from an outbreak of influenza, with high fever and body pains; there were 77 cases altogether. The unit medical officer put the outbreak down to the battery personnel occupying enclosed billets previously used by the Germans, since the other batteries used tents in the open and mostly escaped the infection.[26] At this time the 10th AFA batteries moved forward from Bandival Farm to positions near those of the 11th, in readiness for the next operation. This would be an advance to the Sambre Canal line,

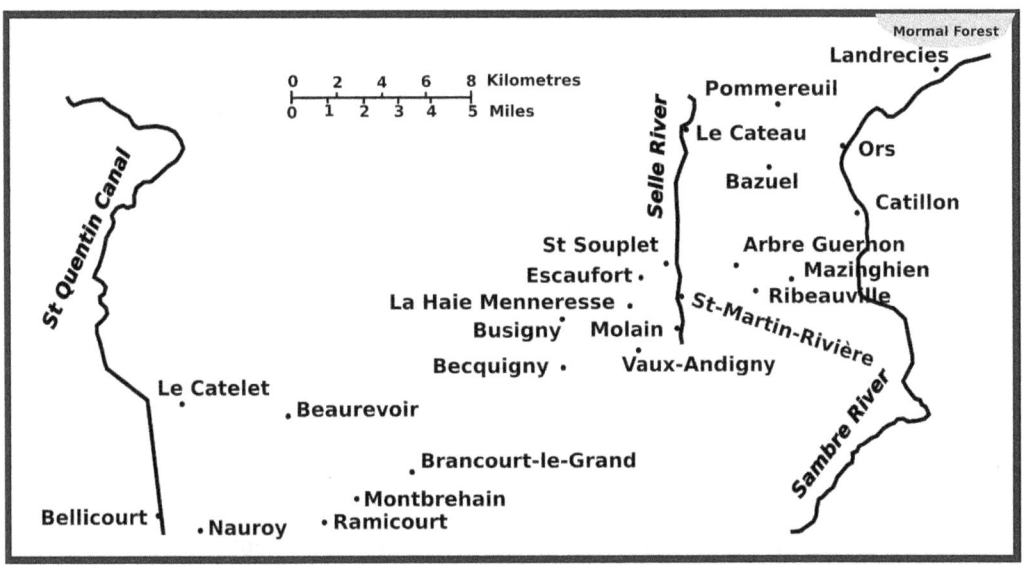

Area of Fourth Army's advance east of the Hindenburg Line, October/November 1918

planned for 23 October, to guard the right flank of Third Army advancing beyond the Selle further north. Zero was set as 0120, a time chosen to take advantage of the full moon and achieve a degree of surprise; Third Army would jump off 40 minutes later.

The task for the 4th Division artillery, as part of the Right Group, was to fire the creeping barrage covering the 18th Infantry Brigade on the right of the 6th Division's advance. The 111th Howitzer Battery had a special task, firing smoke shell into the village of Ors on the canal-bank to screen that enemy strongpoint, followed by a gas bombardment. The barrage was somewhat more complex than usual, with the infantry spreading out during the advance to form a line following the curve of the Canal at its final objective. The protective barrage for the objective had to conform to the curving line. Lifts were timed at 90 metres every four minutes, and after reaching the protective barrage line the guns carried out a programme of searching fire further east, ceasing after 15 minutes. At three hours after Zero a further 'creeper' began, moving to the east at 90 metres every six minutes up to maximum range. The advance of the 18th Brigade made good progress, reaching the objective west of the Canal without much difficulty, but elsewhere the Germans resisted strongly. 'No ground was gained without fighting, and on one occasion, a party of our troops was surrounded and only hacked its way out after hand-to-hand fighting.'[27] Disrupted by an enemy counter-barrage at the start and by the tangled undergrowth of L'Evêque Wood, the 6th Division's 71st Brigade on the left, with a considerably greater distance to cover, was held up short of its final objective.

That evening the Right Group's attached British field brigade was withdrawn to reserve. The attack on the left flank continued the next morning and made some progress in an operation that did not directly involve the Right Group artillery. The 11th AFA batteries moved forward again, to positions south of Bazuel during the day and night, keeping up with the infantry advance. In the evening the 7th AFA was withdrawn, leaving the Group with just the two 4th Division brigades in the line, then on the following day (25 October) the 10th AFA was also withdrawn to its wagon lines. This left the 11th AFA as the sole field artillery brigade in the 6th Division's Right Group for the time being—the unit diarist commented that the Brigade was now the only unit of the Australian Corps in the line.[28] For the next few days the 11th's batteries carried out routine harassing fire at targets on the far side of the canal while Fourth Army consolidated its positions and prepared for an offensive that would force the canal line. This period saw an influx of encouraging news from the outside as the collapse of the Central Powers gained pace. General Ludendorff was forced to resign as German chief of staff on 26 October, in despair as his plans unravelled, while famine and civil unrest spread through the German population. Bulgaria had already signed an armistice and Turkey followed on 31 October. Holding the line of the Sambre-Oise Canal might give the Germans some leverage in the now-inevitable armistice negotiations, and the British general staff was determined to break it and drive home the advantage.

The 32nd British Division relieved the 6th on 31 October and the CRA of the 32nd took over command of the sector field artillery next day. The assault on the canal line was planned for 4 November, Fourth Army to attack in conjunction with the French on the right and Third Army on the left. XIII Corps would form the left of Fourth Army, IX Corps the right, the latter with the 1st Division as its right and the 32nd its left. The terrain presented serious difficulties for the attacking infantry. First there was the canal itself, 21 metres wide from bank to bank and up to 12 metres wide at the water level. The water was up to 2.4 metres deep, and a wide stretch of ground on either side, flooded by the Germans, was waterlogged and swampy—by comparison the Selle had been a trivial obstacle. Fourth Army engineers constructed a variety of portable bridges and rafts for use by the infantry on the day. A section of the 1st Tunnelling Company, Australian Engineers (now trained in above-ground work) was attached to the 1st British Division engineers and tasked with laying a tank-carrying bridge at the canal lock south of Catillon.[29] On the left XIII Corps would have to fight its way through the southern part of the vast Mormal Forest, a region ideal for defence by the enemy. The country around the forest was a continuation of the thickly-hedged enclosed fields east of the Selle.

General Burgess had command of the 32nd Division's Left Group field artillery, covering the 96th Infantry Brigade. His force would comprise the 10th and 11th AFA Brigades and four British brigades. Another British brigade was held in reserve for exploitation of the attack if required (the 3rd Australian Division artillery was included in the force covering the 1st British Division on the right). The 4th Division artillery HQ moved from Busigny to Le Cateau on 2 November, and during that night the five additional brigades moved forward to join the 11th AFA, still in the line. Battery positions were taken up in L'Evêque Wood, east of Pommereuil. The barrage plan for the Left Group again departed from routine, to allow for the presence of the canal. Whereas the direction of Fourth Army's advance in the past month had been to the north-east, the canal ran generally north-east to south-west, so to cross it the advance of the 32nd Division would divert to the south-east. The line of the creeping barrage, moving parallel to the line of the canal, would begin on the eastern bank and remain on that line for five minutes. The first lift would be of 270 metres. The barrage would then stay on the second line for 30 minutes while the infantry crossed the water and established a bridgehead. The creep would then resume, but at the slow rate of 90 metres every six minutes until the protective line ahead of the first objective (the Yellow Line on the map) was reached. The barrage would stay on that line for 15 minutes before resuming, still at 90 metres per six minutes up to the protective line for the second objective (the Dotted Blue Line). The second protective barrage would also last for 15 minutes. If the infantry was then able to go on to the final (exploitation) objective, a further 1,500 metres to the Red Line along the main Landrecies road, a signal would instruct the batteries to resume the barrage, starting from the Dotted Blue Protective line and lifting at the same rate as before.[30]

The batteries spent 3 November organising their positions and completing ammunition stocks. The brigade commanders conferred with the Group staff on the arrangements for tomorrow and afterwards briefed their battery commanders. The guns did not fire during the day or night to avoid detection of their advanced positions by the Germans. Nevertheless scattered shelling from enemy guns found the 11th AFA Brigade area, and two 43rd Battery gunners were killed.[31] The barrage opened next morning at 0545 on the 32nd Division front and continued according to the plan to reach the second protective barrage line. The guns fired on that line for 15 minutes as ordered, then ceased fire and waited for reports to come in from the infantry. At 0720 German retaliatory shelling hit the 43rd Battery again, killing 21 year old Gunner Carl Gerler of Moreton Bay, Queensland—the last member of the 4th Division to be killed in action. The 1st Australian Tunnelling Company had four fatalities that day also.[32] Word arrived that the canal had been bridged and crossed against weak opposition on the right brigade front, but the 96th Brigade on the left had been held up by fierce German resistance. Among those killed there was the poet Lieutenant Wilfred Owen. Under heavy machine gun and artillery fire the engineers had managed to get one bridge over but it had quickly been destroyed by a shell. For all the courage shown—four VCs were won in this area—the infantry was pinned down on the near bank. A German machine gun nest situated where the canal made an s-curve, towards the left flank, was particularly troublesome.

At 0900 the Left Group artillery brigades received orders to shorten their range to a line 730 metres east of the canal and open fire at a slow rate. At about midday the barrage had lifted again to the protective line for the first objective until fire ceased at 1340. Captain William Sanderson, 11th AFA, was later awarded the MC for his work under fire in this period as liaison officer with the infantry and forward observer. By then a battalion of the 96th Brigade had moved to the right and crossed the water by the bridges in the neighbouring sector. The Tommies steadily worked their way up the eastern bank, overcoming the enemy positions in the area as they went, although the machine gun post on the canal bend kept firing all day.[33] Eventually the whole brigade was across and advancing on the first objective. By evening the right of 32nd Division had gone on to almost reach the Landrecies road, its final objective. The pocket on the left at the canal bend was evacuated by the Germans during the night. Fourth Army as a whole had broken through and the Germans were in full retreat to the east:

> a bridgehead on a front of at least fifteen miles [24 km] and to an average depth of three miles [4.8 km] had been established, while Mormal Forest had been penetrated to a depth of some 6,000 yards [5,500 metres]. Over 4,000 prisoners and nearly 80 guns had been captured.[34]

The 4th Division batteries got in some shooting at enemy lines of retreat during the night, and on the morning of 5 November they received the welcome orders to stand down and withdraw to the wagon lines at Le Cateau—the last elements of the 4th Division to see combat in the war (the 3rd Division guns were withdrawn that day also). In other parts of the front the attacks by Third Army, and First Army further north, had also succeeded, as had those by the French and Americans to the south. In the far north Second Army and the Belgians were driving east from the Ypres salient. The German army was melting away, Austria had signed an armistice on 4 November and peace was imminent.

The main body of the 4th Division, billeted in the vicinity of Amiens, had continued its extended period of rest and training through October. As well as the normal back-area routine of training exercises and organised sports, a start was made on a programme of educational courses, with guidance from the AIF Education Office—now that the end of the War in the near future was foreseeable the intention was to prepare the men for a return to civilian life. Knowledgeable instructors in such subjects as mathematics, English, French, carpentry and bookkeeping were found from within the units, and there was no shortage of volunteer pupils. In keeping with the intellectual trend, the 49th Battalion started up a literary and debating society under the patronage of Colonel Whitham, which attracted large attendances to sessions. The idea was soon taken up by other units, and inter-battalion debates were held at times. Regular evening entertainment was provided by the Smart Set divisional concert party and the brigade troupes. The programme of releasing 1914 enlistees on furlough to Australia continued, although some preferred local leave to Paris or London. Some senior officers went to Australia, including Brigadier General Brand, 4th Brigade commander, and the 13th Battalion CO, Lieutenant Colonel Marks, both leaving for home in October, as did Major Riddell, OC 12th Field Company, Lieutenant Colonel Rutledge, the Pioneer CO, and Lieutenant Colonel Le Messurier, CO 12th Field Ambulance. Lieutenant Colonel Edmund Drake-Brockman had been acting in command of the 4th Brigade and he resumed that posting when he returned from his own short leave break, with promotion to temporary brigadier general. At Division HQ

Major Eric Plant, GSO2, was detached to the staff at Fourth Army HQ. Major Reginald Norman, brigade major of 12th Brigade, departed to attend a staff course in England. His replacement was Captain Arthur Nicholson, formerly staff captain at 13th Brigade HQ, who had just returned from a similar course.

The comparatively long break was approaching its end on 1 November when General Sinclair-MacLagan and the brigadiers attended a conference at Australian Corps HQ, Belloy, for preliminary discussions on the Division's return to the front line. A definite date was not set but it was understood that the 1st and 4th Divisions would begin to move in about a week. Before that, however, an unusual operation took place in the Corps billeting areas. By orders classified as 'Secret,' the resting divisions undertook a sweep of the nearby villages to round up any Australian deserters who might be in hiding there—'sandbaggers,' whose activities included assaulting and robbing soldiers and civilians. At 0900 on 2 November the 4th Division held a muster parade with every member required to attend and be accounted for except those on essential duty and covered by a special pass. The men were not dismissed until 1300. Meanwhile checkpoints with selected squads were set up on roads leading to and from camps and villages, and all local leave was stopped. Other patrols were detailed to search the villages in their unit's billeting area: 'special attention is to be given to Estaminets and Brothels which it is thought absentees may frequent.'[35] The Pioneer Battalion patrol that searched Ailly-sur-Somme, thought to be a favourite haunt, arrested nine miscreants. Another who refused to surrender was shot and killed.[36] Units of the 13th Brigade collected seven absentees, three of whom turned out to be British, but no other results were reported in the 4th Division area.

On 4 November came the news that Austria had signed an armistice, leaving Germany the only one of the Central Powers still in the field. Orders came out on 7 November for the Division to move up to the forward area and rejoin Fourth Army on the Sambre front. The Division would travel most of the distance by train and motor vehicle, in brigade groups, beginning in two days' time. A 24 hour postponement meant that the move would now start on 10 November with the first contingent, the 13th Brigade Group, boarding six trains at three stations. That day the abdication of the Kaiser was announced and a German republic was proclaimed. Some of the 13th Brigade trains got away reasonably on time, others were subject to long and frustrating delays, including the one carrying Brigade HQ. More hours of delay occurred at St Quentin, lasting well into the next morning—that is, 11 November, the day of the Armistice. The 13th Brigade troops spent all day on the trains, hearing only rumours at the stations that the War was actually over. It was not until the next day that Lieutenant Colonel Christie of the 51st Battalion, after his unit had arrived at Roisel, could get anything definite, via

> a passing Despatch Rider who had a copy of the *Daily News* which contained all the news and terms. It is interesting to note that no official notification was received by the Battalion.[37]

In the absence of confirmation the brigade major, Captain Tom Louch, noted that

> the cold and discomfort of the railway trucks and the uncertainty as to the next meal were matters of greater moment. Not even a cheer was heard. It may have dawned on some that if the news was true the only chance they now had of being killed was in an accident but a far more important point was that [heating] braziers would not have to be extinguished at sundown on account of enemy aeroplanes.[38]

The 13th Brigade Group detrained at Épehy, Tincourt and Roisel, camped overnight, then went on partly by light rail and partly on foot to reach their billets at Fresnoy-le-Grand, 12 kilometres east of the Hindenburg Line, on 13 November.

Back at the villages near Amiens where the remaining units of the Division were still in camp following a further delay in their trains, the news came through early on 11 November that the Armistice had been signed and would take effect at 1100 that morning. In the 4th Brigade area the bands of the 13th and 16th Battalions assembled in the Picquigny village square and played the national anthems of the allies, the villagers having swiftly decorated their houses and streets with flags and bunting. 'The village bells rang out the good tidings amid great rejoicing among both civilians and soldiers,'[39] The 15th Battalion band similarly performed in the square at Crouy, and the troops were then dismissed for the rest of the day. That seems to be as far as celebrations went on the day, and the reaction in the 12th Brigade area was similarly restrained. The move east was still going ahead as trains became available. The 12th Brigade units began entraining in the morning of 12 November, although again some of the trains did not get going until hours after boarding. The route happened to be along the rails outside Dernancourt, passing the embankment defended by the 12th and 13th Brigades in April. The 12th Brigade Group reached the billets at Fresnoy-le-Grand on 14 November and the 4th Brigade Group arrived the next day. At Fresnoy the troops spent the next week cleaning up at the generous bathing facilities and keeping occupied with the training and sports programmes.

The 46th Battalion diarist commented that this was the first time that all of the 4th Division brigade groups had been billeted in the one town. The town was damaged but not heavily and although there were few civilians, the former inhabitants were beginning to drift back to their homes. The weather was mostly clear and frosty, and something of a carnival atmosphere prevailed,

> an air of gaiety and bustle about the place. There is an abundance of music, the various battalion bands playing their battalions to and from their parade grounds, then playing in the afternoon, either at a football match or in the town, and also playing at Guard Mounting.[40]

The training periods, now that it was peacetime, began to lean towards parade ground drill and saluting practice, never popular with the troops, and time was even spent polishing brass. The commanders were soon given an outline of the Division's next duties, which was passed to the men after Sunday church parades. As part of the army of occupation Fourth

Army, including the Australian Corps, would be advancing to the Rhine and then probably into Germany. The Corps was restricted to four divisions for administrative reasons, so the 3rd Division was detached and left in camp near Abbeville. For the 4th Division the first stage of the march began on 21 November, the 13th Brigade Group leading off as before, followed by the other two Groups on successive days. The march was generally north-east, through the territory covered in Fourth Army's victorious advance during October. On the morning of the first day the 13th Brigade Group marched 16 kilometres to the area of St Souplet on the Selle, scene of 27th US Division's battle on 17 October. Resuming the march next morning, the troops covered 23 kilometres in the day, passing through Ors to cross the Sambre-Oise Canal and reaching Favril late in the afternoon. Next day the units marched a further eight kilometres to Grand Fayt. The 12th and 4th Brigade Groups followed on successive days.

Several changes in command took place over this period. The 13th Battalion CO, Lieutenant Colonel Douglas Marks, had left for Australia a few weeks earlier, and Major Theodore Wells had been in command temporarily. Now Major Arthur 'Tubby' Allen was appointed to the command, with a well-earned promotion to lieutenant colonel coming through in due course. Allen was still only 24, and he was now rejoining his original Gallipoli unit as its CO. At about the same time Lieutenant Colonel Henry Crowther relinquished command of the 14th Battalion and set off for home on furlough; he had taken over the 14th when the unit had been at a low ebb and had led it with great success, yet he received no decoration for his efforts. The new CO was Major William Arrell from the 49th Battalion, promoted to temporary lieutenant colonel for the second time. The 45th Battalion CO, Lieutenant Colonel Cecil Ridley, left for a staff appointment in England, and shortly afterwards Lieutenant Colonel Noel Loutit returned to command the unit again, having recovered from wounds received in the Outpost Line battle. The Pioneer Battalion received a new CO in the person of Lieutenant Colonel Frederick McClean, promoted from major in the 5th Pioneers.

The divisional artillery had moved from the line to reserve positions around Le Cateau less than a week before the news of the Armistice came through; 'the good news was received very placidly by the troops but all wore a very self-satisfied expression.'[41] Brigadier General Burgess took the opportunity for a month's leave in England and Lieutenant Colonel Williams took over as acting CRA. On 14 November Major General Sinclair-MacLagan re-established close contact with a visit to artillery HQ, returning a few days later to carry out a formal inspection of the brigades. Arrangements were then put in hand for the artillery to link up with the main body of the Division, marching up from the west. On 21 November the artillery brigades moved from Le Cateau to the area of La Groise and Le Sart, just east of the canal, with artillery HQ moving to Catillon two days later. As of 24 November, all elements of the Division were across or on the canal and ready for the next stage of the march, destination being the area from Avesnes-sur-Helpe south-

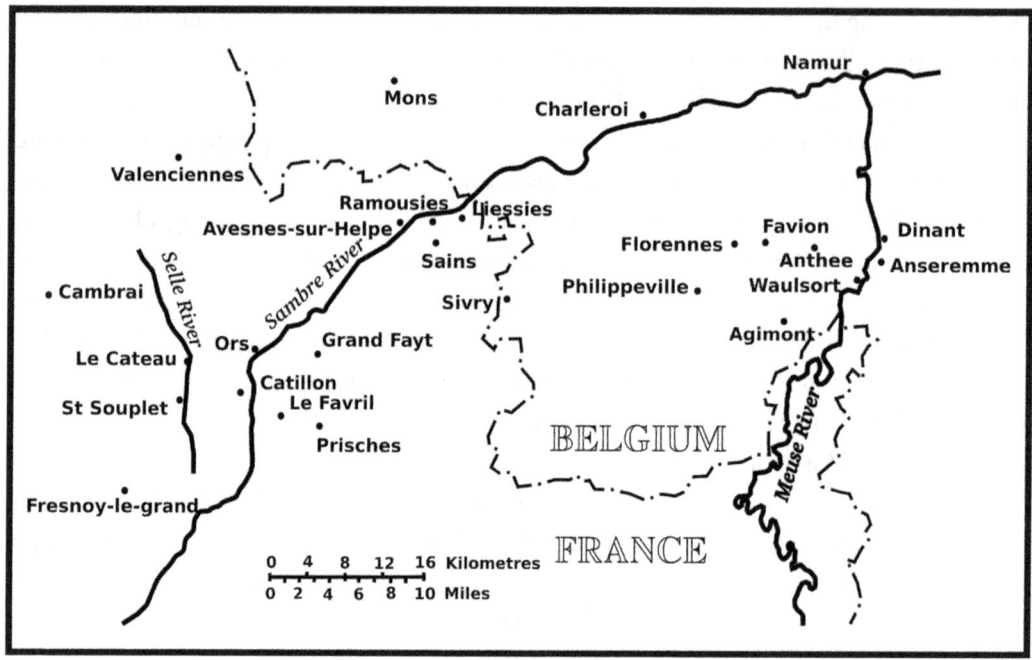

Area of advance into Belgium after the Armistice

east to Sains. All brigade groups had reached that location by 26 November and on that date the 13th Brigade Group led off on the next stage, which would take the Division out of France and into Belgium. A tiring day's march on muddy roads brought the 13th to the town of Sivry, just over the border, where it was expected to remain for up to 10 days. For the time being, the other groups stayed in the Avesnes/Sains area, and Division HQ also moved to Sains; Captain (temporary Major) Herbert Watson was posted in from the 1st Division as GSO2, replacing Major Plant, at about that time. The artillery meanwhile had moved to Liessies and Ramousies, north-east of Sains. At Liessies food shortages had left the civilian population in a bad way, so the artillery brigades shared their rations with the civilians. The brigade medical officers made their skills available to the people also.[42] On 1 December King George V came to the Australian Corps area at Avesnes in the course of touring the liberated areas and visiting his victorious armies. Troops from the 12th Brigade, based closest to the town, provided the 4th Division element that joined those from the 1st Division lining the road into Avesnes to greet the King, who met the commanders then walked for a mile along the column.

December brought cold weather and a swelling of discontent among the troops. The remarkably efficient British supply system was beginning to deteriorate in peacetime and delivery of rations became less reliable as the distance from the coastal bases increased. Shortages combined with frequent marching on poor roads and dull routines when in camp produced negative reactions in some units. The 15th Battalion historian noted that

> the ration situation was most unsatisfactory and the men were getting worse and less food than at any period during the years of fighting.
>
> Matters were not improved with irritating parades, during which most of the time was spent in learning to salute … things went from bad to worse, so bad indeed that on December 4, after the Battalion had gone on strike, Brigadier Drake-Brockman came down to the billets at Sains and ordered everybody out on parade.
>
> … the men refused to leave their billets. When ordered to fall in, they hung out of the windows and told the Brigadier if he had anything to say he had better say it to them from where he stood in the lane.[43]

Wisely, Drake-Brockman chose not to continue the confrontation, instead ordering a special delivery of rations so that the men got a decent meal, and the trouble soon blew over.

The 13th Brigade also went through a difficult time for similar reasons. Two companies of the 51st Battalion refused to parade one morning, but Lieutenant Colonel Christie, by listening to the men's grievances and responding tactfully, persuaded them to start work. A similar incident occurred in the 49th Battalion on 3 December, this proving a little more difficult to resolve, due to the absence of the CO, Lieutenant Colonel Whitham, who had moved over to the 12th Brigade as temporary commander. Major James Churchill Smith from the 50th Battalion had come in as acting CO less than two weeks earlier, and was largely unknown to most of the 49th personnel. Churchill Smith, an excellent officer, handled the situation much as Christie had with the 51st, listening to the complaints and agreeing to investigate them. An address to the Battalion the next day settled the matter peacefully.[44] As it happened Whitham did not return to the 51st, except to say his farewells, having been posted later in the month to the new Repatriation and Demobilisation Branch at AIF HQ in London. This body was charged with the task of extracting all Australian soldiers from Europe and transporting them home to the other side of the world; it had been established just after the Armistice, although the process had been under consideration for some time by then.[45] Sir John Monash was placed in overall charge of the project, arriving in London on 1 December, after handing over command of the Australian Corps to Major General Hobbs of the 5th Division. Monash gathered together a staff to assist in managing the immense undertaking, including a number of current or former 4th Division officers. As well as Colonel Whitham, the Division's ADMS, Colonel Kenneth Smith, went to the new branch early in December. Colonel Roy McGregor, CO 4th Field Ambulance, moved up to ADMS, and Major John James crossed from the 12th Field Ambulance to assume command of the 4th, with temporary promotion to lieutenant colonel; command of the 12th was taken over by Lieutenant Colonel Ernest Culpin coming in from the 2nd Division. Major Fowler-Brownsworth, the DAAG, also joined the demobilisation staff, replaced at Division HQ by Captain Arnold Moulden. Lieutenant Colonel Ridley, Major Plant and Major Norman, who had all left the Division recently on other duties, were others who went to the new branch. The 4th Division Order of Battle about this time, before the repatriation exodus gathered pace, was:

4th Australian Division Order of Battle, November/December 1918

GOC	Major General E G Sinclair-MacLagan
GSO1	Lieutenant Colonel J D Lavarack
GSO2	Major H F Watson
GSO3	Captain L C A Craig
AA&QMG	Lieutenant Colonel R Dowse
DAAG	Captain A M Moulden
DAQMG	Captain E W Carter
ADCs	Captain C Bartlett, Lieutenant G R Baillie

Infantry

4th Brigade: Brigadier General E A Drake-Brockman
Brigade Major: Major R W Tovell
Staff Captain: Captain R H Lackman
13th Battalion: Lieutenant Colonel A S Allen
14th Battalion: Lieutenant Colonel W L Arrell
15th Battalion: Lieutenant Colonel C M Johnston
16th Battalion: Lieutenant Colonel E J Parks
4th LTM Battery: Captain A Martin

12th Brigade: Brigadier General R L Leane
Brigade Major: Captain A Nicholson
Staff Captain: Captain A L Varley
45th Battalion: Lieutenant Colonel N M Loutit
46th Battalion: Lieutenant Colonel J J Corrigan
48th Battalion: Lieutenant Colonel S L Perry
12th LTM Battery: Captain F G S Cherry

13th Brigade: Brigadier General S C E Herring
Brigade Major: Captain T S Louch
Staff Captain: Lieutenant W H Conwell
49th Battalion: Major J C Smith
50th Battalion: Lieutenant Colonel A G Salisbury
51st Battalion: Lieutenant Colonel R Christie
13th LTM Battery: Captain C O Long

Artillery

CRA: Brigadier General W L H Burgess
Brigade Major: Major T A J Playfair
Staff Captain: Captain K Ewan
10th Field Artillery Brigade: Lieutenant Colonel T I C Williams
(37th, 38th, 39th, 110th Batteries)

11th Field Artillery Brigade: (41st, 42nd, 43rd, 111th Batteries)	Lieutenant Colonel C H Spurge
Divisional Ammunition Column:	Major A S Ford
Divisional Trench Mortar Officer: (7th and 8th MTM Batteries)	Lieutenant W H Felstead

Machine Guns

4th Machine Gun Battalion: (4th, 12th, 13th, 24th MG Companies)	Lieutenant Colonel H W Murray, VC

Engineers

CRE:	Lieutenant Colonel R J Dyer
4th Field Company:	Major H G Tolley
12th Field Company:	Major S B Cox
13th Field Company:	Major R B Carr
Signal Company:	Major C H Joseph

Pioneers

4th Pioneer Battalion:	Lieutenant Colonel F S McClean

Medical

ADMS:	Colonel R S McGregor
DADMS:	Major T C C Evans
4th Field Ambulance:	Lieutenant Colonel J A James
12th Field Ambulance:	Lieutenant Colonel E Culpin
13th Field Ambulance:	Lieutenant Colonel F C Wooster

Veterinary

DADVS:	Major E S James
4th Mobile Veterinary Section:	Captain R H Heywood

Transport (Divisional Train)

CO:	Lieutenant Colonel L C Sando
7th Company AASC:	Captain C R Walsh
14th Company AASC:	Major J W Blanch
26th Company AASC:	Captain W I Rogers
27th Company AASC:	Captain C Reynolds

December saw another series of marches that took the Division into winter quarters in the region of the Meuse River in Belgium. The pattern of previous moves continued, with the 13th Brigade Group, already in Belgium at Sivry, leading off and the remainder of the Division following in succession. The movement began on 13 December and was completed in four days. By 17 December the Division was settling into billets in villages from Philippeville east to Dinant on the Meuse. Division HQ and the 13th Brigade Group were at Dinant, a small town in a spectacular setting alongside the river, at the foot of high cliffs crowned by a citadel. Historically a strategic point, Dinant had been taken by the Germans in August 1914 in a battle that was followed by atrocities committed against the civilian population. The 12th Brigade Group area centred on Waulsort, south along the river from Dinant, with the MG Battalion at Anseremme, on the river between Waulsort and Dinant. The artillery brigades were somewhat spread out from Flavion south to Agimont with HQ at Anthée, and the 4th Brigade Group was further to the west of the river, at Florennes and Philippeville. The 4th Division was on the right (south) of the Australian Corps area, with the 1st Division coming into position on the left and the 2nd and 5th Divisions to the west. By that time the high command was having second thoughts about the advance into Germany, mainly because of supply difficulties, and it had now been decided that only Second Army would be the occupation force. Fourth Army halted at the frontier. The Australian Corps would remain about where it was while the process of repatriation was organised and the men were progressively sent home. It was estimated that it would take the best part of a year before the last man left for Australia.

There was some disappointment that after marching so far there would be no triumphant entry into Germany, a feeling that did not necessarily have the noblest of motives—according to the 15th Battalion history, so as 'to treat the Germans in a manner in keeping with their own treatment of the inhabitants of the French and Belgian villages during the years of the German occupation.'[46] The liberated French territory had provided many examples of poverty and mistreatment, but oddly enough once over the border into Belgium, in at least some localities, it was noticed that 'compared with the evacuated areas of France, poultry and stock are seen at every farm and everything appears very prosperous. Shops at Philipeville and Florennes [are] well stocked.'[47] The repatriation scheme worked out by Monash and his staff was based on forming the troops into drafts or quotas of 1,000 (all ranks) grouped by priority, those with the longest service being given preference. Provided ships were available, each division would release a quota every week, meaning that up to 5,000 AIF personnel a week would be starting the journey home. While waiting for their turn the men remaining in camp would have to be kept gainfully occupied. This meant increased attention to the education programme, a certain amount of training and drill to maintain military discipline, and extended recreation time. As before, the latter was mainly in organised sports, and the educational programme was extended to 'Non-Military Employment,' a scheme which placed soldiers in technical training and practical experience in a wide range of industries at various institutions in Britain and Europe.

Social activities now extended to dances held in the villages, usually with ladies admitted free of charge, with music by battalion bands. On New Year's Day 1919 the divisional artillery put on a Fête Day for the village children at Anthée and Agimont. The Smart Set and the brigade concert parties were kept busy with performances in the evenings. Snow falls and freezing temperatures in January produced something of a craze for skating, tobogganing and snowball fights. That month the first drafts left for return to Australia, with their initial destination the demobilisation camp at Le Havre then crossing to England and embarking for home as ships became available. The third and fourth drafts of January were the full complement of 1,000 men each, and from then the drafts continued fairly regularly. At first, release of men from the artillery was restricted because of the need to look after the large number of draught horses and mules with that arm. Through February most of the animals, many of which would have originally been brought from Australia, were sold off locally or sent to British remount depots on the coast, economics driving that poor reward for years of hauling guns and ammunition wagons through the mud under fire. Nevertheless the sales did mean that artillery personnel could be released for repatriation in greater numbers, and during February also the guns and vehicles were handed over to ordnance authorities for storage. A number of senior officers received awards during 1919, recognising leadership in the last months of the war. Brigadier Generals Burgess (CRA), Leane (12th Brigade) and Drake-Brockman (4th Brigade) were made Companions of the Bath (CB), and CMGs went to Brigadier General Herring (13th Brigade) and Lieutenant Colonels Lavarack (Divisional Staff), Salisbury (50th Battalion) and Murray (4th MG Battalion)—thus Harry Murray had received a total of five Imperial awards, headed by the VC, plus the French Croix de Guerre, unrivalled among Australian servicemen. Major General Sinclair-MacLagan was also made a CMG later in the year.[48]

Repatriation was gathering pace now, and the units were steadily being depleted of numbers and losing their identities, a circumstance that caused deep regrets to mix with the elation of heading home. Lieutenant George Mitchell, 48th Battalion, expressed this in an often-quoted passage:

> Wonderful times we had, but underlying all was an indefinable sadness. The battalion, our father and mother of unforgettable years, was drifting to pieces. The links that connected us with the unforgotten dead seemed to be snapping one by one. As each draft left, mateships were sundered, too often never to be renewed in the stress and fierce demands of civilian life.[49]

Such feelings may be difficult to understand if one has not been in that situation, but they are not unique to the 1st AIF. At the end of the devastating American Civil War half a century earlier, for instance, two Union soldiers expressed similar thoughts:

> None of us were fond of war, but there had grown up between the boys an attachment for each other they never had nor ever will have for any other body of men.

and

> I do feel so idle and lost to all business that I wonder what will become of me. Can I ever be contented again?[50]

Perhaps the feeling is confined to soldiers of victorious armies.

As the exodus continued, sub-units and then full units were amalgamated for administrative convenience. At first companies amalgamated within battalions, then the battalions themselves amalgamated, followed by brigades and equivalent units. By April 1919 the 4th and 12th Infantry Brigades had formed a composite Brigade comprising two composite battalions. The 13th Brigade, now one composite battalion, was linked with the divisional artillery for administrative purposes. The MG Battalion was similarly linked with the divisional engineers. As officers in key postings left for demobilisation or to take up duties at AIF HQ they were temporarily replaced by others who then took their turn for home. The final stage was amalgamation of the 4th Division with the 1st, both formations thereby losing their individual identities. The new formation was known as 'A' Divisional Group. Shortly the 2nd and 5th Divisions merged as the 'B' Group (the 3rd Division had not moved to Belgium and was closer to the embarkation ports). The attenuated elements of the 4th Division relocated in stages to villages closer to the railway at Charleroi. One of the final conferences of the 4th Division senior commanders discussed the location for a future memorial. The decision was the high ground overlooking Bellenglise where the Division as a whole had fought its last battle (near where Private Woods had won his VC), the easternmost of the AIF divisional memorials. As of 19 April 1919 the 4th Australian Division effectively ceased to exist, when the divisional staff stood down and all the remaining units, grouped under the command of Brigadier General Drake-Brockman, came under direct command of the Australian Corps, as did the remnant of the 1st Division. Over the succeeding months the remaining personnel took their turn to depart for home via England, the final contingents leaving by the end of the year, those last groups including Monash himself. The final administrative tasks kept the First AIF officially in existence until 1 April 1921.

According to the official statistics compiled up to 30 June 1919,[51] the 4th Division incurred a total of 35,659 casualties on the Western Front, including 9,848 deaths (438 officers and 9,410 other ranks); the 4th Brigade as part of the NZ and A Division had incurred a further 3,451 casualties on Gallipoli, 1,778 of which were fatalities. Of the Western Front deaths, 41 were the result of gas poisoning—perhaps a surprisingly low figure, but the effects of gas were long-lasting; 655 deaths were caused by disease or 'other causes,' which would include accidents. The 4th Division also had 2,076 members taken prisoner by the Germans, by far the highest number of the five divisions, and mostly attributable to the First Bullecourt and Dernancourt battles. Although there is no readily-available figure for how many of those died in captivity, the overall proportion for the AIF on the Western Front was about nine percent, giving an estimate of 186 4th Division prisoners who did not survive the prison camps. The statistics show 21,902 wounded in action (841 officers and 21,061 other ranks) and 1,833 gassed. Not all of these were precluded from further active service though—if a wounded man was not incapacitated in the long term, he would usually be patched up and sent back to duty, sometimes more than once. Lieutenant Ted Rule, 14th Battalion, wrote of his batman, Private Dave Floyd, after the Hamel battle:

> ... he died as he was going out [on a stretcher], and I lost the best lad I'd ever had. He was an old original man [i.e. an original member of the battalion; he was 23], and had been wounded five times [but] the sixth finished him ... doing favours for others was never a trouble to Dave ... though as a batman he was exempt from all parades, he was always ready to take the place of one of the boys in a fatigue party,

if some lad was not well. He was always bright, and a godsend to the platoon. For days afterwards I fancied I could hear his cheery laugh among the boys, and each time it hurt as I 'came back to earth' again.[52]

This highlights a point that is sometimes overlooked, that the total casualty figures do not represent the number of *individuals* who suffered wounds or death in battle. Obviously the number of deaths would be accurate, or very nearly so depending on what time scale is used, but what the 'wounded' figure shows is the number of instances of wounding—that is, if an individual soldier was wounded more than once, he would have been counted more than once. A G Butler, in the *Official History of the Australian Army Medical Services*, touched on this point although did not pursue it,[53] and C E W Bean used the heading 'Number of wounds received by soldiers' rather than 'Wounded' in his concluding statistical summary.[54] It should be added that the same man could be wounded one or more times, return to duty and then be killed, so being counted in two categories. Statistics gave separate figures for officers and other ranks, so a soldier could be wounded as an 'OR,' return to duty and receive a commission, then be wounded or killed, or both, as an officer. To mention just one instance, Lieutenant Eric Leith, 46th Battalion, was

The author at the 4th Division Memorial, near Bellenglise, France.

wounded twice before he was commissioned, then three more times afterwards, the fifth time being in the Outpost Line battle. Separate statistics were recorded for the different theatres of war, so a man wounded at Gallipoli and again in France would be counted in two theatres. A very imprecise calculation suggests that the figure of 21,902 'woundings' for the 4th Division represents 18,664 individuals wounded.[55] This does not allow for any of the 1,833 soldiers recorded as 'gassed' who may also have been wounded at some point (Albert Jacka VC, for one instance, was wounded twice before being gassed), nor for any of the 9,848 who died and might have been wounded on a previous occasion or occasions. This is not to suggest that the impact of the war has been overstated, but rather to emphasise that some men suffered even more heavily than others. It is difficult to imagine the effect on a man having suffered the trauma of one or more gunshot or shrapnel wounds going back to face the bullets and shells again. Escaping wounds was no guarantee of an undisturbed life: Lieutenant Basil Minchin (16th Battalion) went through the war from Gallipoli to Amiens, usually in the front line, without being wounded or even reporting sick, but the accumulated strain of combat was too much in the end and he suffered a breakdown after the battle of 8 August 1918.[56]

The 1919 figures for total casualties were slightly revised in 1921, although there does not appear to be any revised information recorded for each AIF division. It is no simple task to find statistics that can be guaranteed as accurate, not perhaps surprising when the data was extracted from the complex paper-based recording system that was in use at the time, open to interpretation (and error) by clerical staff in medical units and headquarters organisations—Butler's account of the clerical procedures involved shows how comprehensive but also how prone to error they were.[57] At the same time, the 1914–18 War was the first in which the compilation of such statistics on anything like that scale had been attempted. For another illustration, Bean's correspondence with officials of the Defence Department on the subject of AIF casualties in the Third Battle of Ypres shows how difficult it was to confirm statistics even for one period of the War.[58] It has been suggested that perhaps Bean should have taken several years away from his other activities—writing six lengthy volumes of highly detailed narrative history, editing another six, and overseeing the establishment of the Australian War Memorial among other things—to do a detailed study, without the use of computers, to determine the exact number of casualties in the AIF, with source documents being paper files that would have been in use every day by the responsible authorities for normal administrative purposes, such as extracting information for pension assessments. Possibly that may be asking too much, however. In 1936, according to Butler, a complete count of all AIF service files held at the Base Records Office was undertaken to determine the correct number who had embarked for overseas, mainly for estimating future pension liabilities (the original figure included a number who had returned to Australia then re-embarked subsequently). As he remarked, it is regrettable that the opportunity was not taken to do a complete analysis of the files, which might have firmly established the casualty figures.[59] Today, with all the service files having been digitised by the National Archives, such a study could be done remotely in conjunction with the 1st AIF Nominal Roll, which is also available digitally via the Australian War Memorial.⁶⁰

The cut-off date for a soldier's death to be included the Australian First World War Roll of Honour is 31 March 1921, but of course many died subsequently from the effects of their war service. Perhaps the most famous of those is Albert Jacka, who died in 1932 at the age of 39. Officially he died of acute nephritis, but few doubted that his constitution had been fatally weakened by the lingering effects of bullet wounds and gas. He was only one of many thousands who died before their time, not always from physical issues. Martin O'Meara, first soldier to win the VC as a member of the 4th Division, suffered a mental breakdown shortly after returning to Australia, and spent the rest of his life institutionalised until his death in 1935. Sometimes the mental and emotional damage was not so obvious. David Twining, outstanding soldier with the 48th Battalion, returned to civilian life briefly then was commissioned into the regular army on graduation from Duntroon. He was a captain and battalion adjutant when he took his own life in August1931. His friend Harry Downes wrote in *Reveille*:

> To some people the war finished in 1918, but to those of us who understand, the Grim Reaper is still taking his toll, just as surely as he did at Messines or Passchendaele … 'Don Ack Toc' [signallers' phonetic alphabet for Twining's initials DAT] has gone to join his comrades of Gallipoli and Flanders, 'killed in action' just as surely as if he had 'stopped it' in the strenuous days of 1914–18.⁶¹

Downes had also maintained contact with military life, rising to lieutenant colonel in the citizen forces. Less than three months after Twining's death, on Armistice Day 1931, Downes himself committed suicide. Some died in accidents: Douglas Marks, CO of the 13th Battalion at 22, was drowned in 1920 attempting to rescue a swimmer in difficulties at Palm Beach, NSW. Maurice Buckley VC died as a result of a fall from a horse in the following year.

A number of ex-4th Division regular officers served again in the Second AIF during World War Two, the most distinguished of whom was General Sir Vernon Sturdee, former CO of the 4th Pioneer Battalion, who became Chief of the General Staff (CGS) when the incumbent, General Sir Brudenell White, was killed in the Canberra air disaster (1940). General Sir John Lavarack, 4th Division GSO1 in 1917/18, served a period as CGS between the wars then commanded the 7th Division in the Western Desert and I Corps in the Pacific. Eric Plant commanded a brigade in the Desert and later reached the rank of major general with a home command in Australia. William Burgess returned to New Zealand, took the surname Sinclair-Burgess, and rose to command the New Zealand army between the wars. Of non-regulars, Raymond Tovell, long-serving brigade major of the 4th Brigade, was a militia officer between the wars then commanded an infantry brigade in the defence of Tobruk. Duncan Maxwell, ex-52nd Battalion, became a doctor but returned to the infantry in World War Two, rising to command a brigade in the 8th Division. He was taken prisoner by the Japanese at the fall of Singapore and spent the rest of the war in captivity. Two key figures in the New Guinea campaign were Major General Arthur 'Tubby' Allen (ex-13th and 45th Battalions) and Brigadier Arnold Potts (ex-16th Battalion). As division commander and brigade commander respectively, their forces defended the Kokoda

Track under extreme difficulties to eventual success, but both ran afoul of General Blamey (something not difficult to do) and were relieved of their commands. Harry Murray, who had become a grazier in Queensland, commanded a militia battalion during the second war but to his great disappointment was considered too old for a field command overseas. He died in 1966 at the age of 85 as a result of a car accident. Edmund Drake-Brockman took a different course; while continuing as a senior militia officer, he went into industrial relations law and eventually became chief justice of the Arbitration Court, respected across the industrial relations spectrum.

The Second AIF numbered its divisions starting from the 6th, to continue on with the numbering of the First AIF. Formations using the designations 1st to 5th Divisions had been established between the wars as militia forces, but there was limited direct connection with the original First AIF formations. While some elements of the militia troops served overseas, the 4th Division as a formation remained on home defence and it was deactivated in 1944. An echo of the original 4th Division occurred in 2006 when the remains of five Australian soldiers were found during excavations in the vicinity of Zonnebeke, Belgium. Three were identified by DNA testing. George Mitchell had described a soldier's unit as 'our father and mother of unforgettable years,' and now three of the 4th Division's lost children had been found. The remains of Sergeant George Calder, Private George Storey (both 51st Battalion) and Private John Hunter (49th Battalion) were reinterred with honour in Buttes New British Cemetery, Polygon Wood. It is possible that the bodies of the Bullecourt missing may be located in time also.

The old 4th Division of the First AIF had a reputation as tough and effective fighters in battle but particularly unruly and resistant to discipline when out of the line. This may have had something to do with the majority of its recruitment being from the 'outer states' of Queensland, Western Australia, South Australia and Tasmania and the minority from the much more heavily populated New South Wales and Victoria—the opposite of the situation in the other Australian Corps divisions—and hence probably with a larger proportion of independently-minded rural people in the ranks. The idea that a 'country' background produces better soldiers has some currency, and that suggests in turn that the 4th Division may have been more effective on the battlefield than the others. That is not the contention of this history, however. All five divisions had their triumphs and failures, and their differences were more in the intangible factor of collective personality, so to speak. C E W Bean, after four years of war and two decades preparing the *Official History*, wrote that

> the percentage of Australian soldiers who had acquired their powers of determination, endurance and improvisation from country occupations was probably not much more than a quarter.
>
> ... units recruited from the great cities were, at one time or another, probably unequalled in the force. Nevertheless, taking the record over the whole war, Australian leaders would probably give first place to certain units from Western Australia and Queensland, States that were colonies of colonies ...
>
> But the city element in the AIF was so large, and the perceptible distinction between it and the country element was so small, that it seems certain

that, in the case of this force, country training was not the main reason for effectiveness.⁶²

The notion persists, nevertheless, that the knockabout blokes from the bush had a natural talent for fighting that was enough in itself to defeat such opponents as the Prussian Guards. It is true that the more democratic outlook in Australia, by comparison with the far more hierarchical social classes found in Britain, was a very important factor;

> ... the efficacy of the AIF was not in spite of the Australian Jack's being as good as his master, but because of it—or, more accurately, because in the AIF Jack and his master were the same. Social equality in civil life had produced men with the habit of thinking for themselves and acting on their decision ... yet their herd instinct was as strong and irrational as in any people. The Digger's unspoken, unbreakable creed was the miner's and the bushman's, 'Stand by your mate.'⁶³

Commendable, but not enough to succeed at industrialised warfare without battlefield discipline and effective training. Whatever their off-duty attitude might have been, the vast majority of AIF members had a determination to excel at the task they had chosen, which meant mastering the skills of weapons and tactics through training and experience. Parade-ground soldiering was considerably less important, although the men were quite capable of drilling like Guardsmen when the occasion demanded. Front line experience quickly produced acceptance of the need for decisive orders and quick response in battle. That did not preclude individual initiative, and the NCOs and junior officers giving the orders had almost all been chosen on merit from the ranks. Those leaders had worked hard and fought hard to earn their advancement and the respect of their subordinates. The men ranged from decorated heroes to the anonymous diggers who did the best job that they could and slogged their way through the war. Behind the firing line, Australian staff work, from corps through division to brigade level had steadily improved through the war to reach high efficiency in the 1918 offensives.⁶⁴

The conference method of developing comprehensive battle plans, if not invented by the Australian Corps, was perfected by it and formed a model for the BEF, as did the Corps methods of conducting integrated combined arms operations. Good staff work backed up the firing-line combination of intelligent battlefield discipline and individual skill and initiative. Those factors more than compensated for declining numbers, and in the final battles of 1918 enabled Australian troops in attack to overcome defenders who often outnumbered them by a significant margin. In that period the Australian Corps, an elite small force created from an almost entirely amateur base, formed the most effective spearhead of Fourth Army (as did the Canadians and New Zealanders in other BEF Armies) in an unbroken series of victories. The AIF's example in the field made significant contributions to the eventual victory, even though it formed only a small element of the Allied armies (by number of enlistments, Australia accounted for under 1.4% of the Allied men mobilised in Western theatres of war).⁶⁵

While the nation became bitterly divided by the conscription issue, there was little disagreement over the excellence of the serving soldiers—the Anzac Legend as it has developed over subsequent years. All nations have their legends, their origins mostly lost in the mists of time. As a new nation, Australia unusually adopted the Legend of its early years in a time when precise written records were being produced, as well as photographs and motion pictures. Many of the participants survived long after the war and were present as living representatives of the Legend until recently. In those circumstances, it is not surprising that some aspects of the Legend can be shown as exaggerated or simply incorrect, but by the same token it is remarkable how much of the Legend is actually true. If more recent generations can question the less admirable aspects of earlier times and make efforts for advancements in society, then admiration for the great things that our forebears achieved is equally valid. A British reviewer of Bean's first volume of the *Official History* called it 'Australia's *Iliad* and *Odyssey*.'[66] As well as ancient Greece, in Macaulay's vision of the Roman legend of *Horatius*, the hero who held the bridge over the Tiber against overwhelming odds, we can hear echoes of the early Australia at war:

> *Then none was for a party –*
> *Then all were for the state;*
> *Then the great man helped the poor,*
> *And the poor man loved the great;*
> *Then lands were fairly portioned!*
> *Then spoils were fairly sold:*
> *The Romans were like brothers*
> *In the brave days of old.*

Modern times in Australia seem to have moved away from that ideal, even if it never fully existed, and there is a vague discontent with the way our society has developed. Rome in its later centuries had also moved away from the heroic age:

> *Now Roman is to Roman*
> *More hateful than a foe,*
> *And the tribunes beard the high,*
> *And the fathers grind the low.*
> *As we wax hot in faction,*
> *In battle we wax cold;*
> *Wherefore men fight not as they fought*
> *In the brave days of old.*

The memory of the gallant Digger who personified that simpler patriotic time in his fight against militaristic aggression is still present with countless Australian families. Some have always known the story of their AIF forebears, others have only discovered the connection more recently and have found the story to be a revelation. All look back with pride, and often sorrow for those shattered by the war:

> *With weeping and with laughter*
> *Still is the story told,*
> *How well Horatius kept the bridge*
> *In the brave days of old.*

24 Notes

1. Lt Col Parks's service record is not easy to follow for this period of his career. He stated himself that he took over the acting command from Capt Lynas on 19 September, the day after the battle. (16th Battalion War Diary for September 1918, Appendix 18). The Battalion was still in the line at that stage, in close reserve.
2. See M A Yockelson, *Borrowed Soldiers: Americans Under British Command 1918* (Oklahoma USA, 2008) for the history of II Corps.
3. Prior and Wilson, *Command on the Western Front, Op Cit*, p.359.
4. Captured German mustard gas shells had been used against their former owners at the Battle of Cambrai in 1917.
5. Maj Gen J F O'Ryan, *The Story of the 27th Division* (New York, 1921), p.278.
6. Montgomery, *Op Cit*, p.157.
7. The MC recommendation for Downes states that the action took place on 26 September, which would not be correct. It may have been on 27 September, in the preliminary attack to gain the start line, but that operation was carried out by the 105th Regiment, and the recommendation specifies that Downes was attached to the 107th. The latter formation did not go in action until the main attack on 29 September.
8. Account based on the US DSM recommendation in the AWM Honours and Awards files. Another unsuccessful DSM recommendation was made for Lt Col Harry Murray, CO 4th MG Battalion, for his work with the American machine gun units. Howard Tolley was a member of prominent family of engineers, working in the field of irrigation and drainage in South Australia.
9. *The Pictorial Record of the 27th Division* (New York, 1919), p. 7.
10. Rule, *Op Cit*, p. 146.
11. *Official History*, Vol VI, p. 962.
12. Although a member of the 4th Infantry Brigade's training contingent (the IO Lt Henry B Davis) was subsequently declared to have been killed in action that day; the circumstances are unclear.
13. *Official History*, Vol VI, p. 1044.
14. Montgomery, *Op Cit*, p. 195–6.
15. The 4th Division Artillery HQ report on this operation (Appendix 1 to the October War Diary) says that the rate was 100 yards every three minutes, but the telegraphed order from the 2nd Division CRA, issued at 2300 on 8 October, gives the period as every four minutes (Appendix

A13 to the 2nd Division Artillery October War Diary); the 11th AFA War Diary entry for 9 October also says four minutes.

16   Montgomery, *Op Cit*, p. 202n.
17   *Ibid*, p. 203.
18   The movements of the 14th AASC are difficult to determine, as they were detached from the rest of the Train units, but DAC orders for October mention the 14th Company's location as Prémont on 18 October, then as Busigny on 22 October.
19   Prior and Wilson, *Command on the Western Front, Op Cit*, p. 383.
20   St Martin Rivière was on the far left of the 30th Division sector, close to the boundary with the 27th. The commander of the 27th, General O'Ryan, stated that it was one of his battalions, straying into the neighbouring sector, that actually captured the village (O'Ryan, *Op Cit*, p. 371).
21   Montgomery, *Op Cit*, p. 217.
22   O'Ryan, *Op Cit*, p. 376.
23   The Fourth Army Chief of Staff, General A A Montgomery, regarded this as the end of the Battle of the Selle (Montgomery, *Op Cit*, p. 229) but it is generally regarded as finishing on 25 October.
24   There appears to have been some disagreement between General O'Ryan, the 27th Division commander, and General Burgess about the deployment of the advanced guard artillery. General O'Ryan's terminology in his account (*Op Cit*, p. 381) is not entirely clear, but it seems that General Burgess was reluctant to send the field artillery so far forward but General O'Ryan insisted.
25   11th AFA Brigade War Diary, 25 October 1918. The diarist made a similar comment on 18 October.
26   10th AFA Brigade War Diary for October 1918, Appendix 2. Presumably some personnel were temporarily moved from other batteries to cover for the absentees.
27   Montgomery, *Op Cit*, p. 233.
28   11th AFA Brigade War Diary, 25 October 1918.
29   The section commander was Capt O H Woodward, the central character in the film and book *Beneath Hill 60* (W Davies, Sydney 2010).
30   This is only an outline of a complex artillery plan, described in a series of orders and instructions which can be found in the appendices to the 4th Division Artillery HQ War Diary for November 1918, together with the barrage map. The objectives mentioned were as applied by IX Corps and the 32nd Division, and used different terminology to Fourth Army's overall plan.
31   Gunner John Ellis, who had been awarded the MM for his work as a runner at Dernancourt, and Corporal John F Browne (no. 34416). Browne is recorded on the Roll of Honour as a member of the 4th Light Trench Mortar Battery, but he actually belonged to the 8th Medium Trench Mortar Battery (his service record in places says 4th Division MTMs), and was one of the MTM personnel attached as reinforcements to the 11th AFA Brigade in October. His death appears to have at first been overlooked by the 11th, which noted only one killed in action on 3 November (presumably Gnr Ellis) and one on 4 November (Gnr Carl Gerler). The 4th Division DTMO War Diary notes on 8 November that the 11th AFA has advised that one of the attached MTM personnel had been killed in action on 3 November.
32   Cpl A Davey and Sprs C Barrett, A R D Johnson and F N Knight; the latter died of wounds the same day.
33   4th Division Artillery HQ war Diary for November 1918, Appendix 1.
34   Montgomery, *Op Cit*, pp. 255–6.

35 4th Division Admin Staff War Diary for November 1918, Appendices, Administrative Instruction 94.
36 4th Pioneer Battalion War Diary, 2 November 1918.
37 51st Battalion War Diary, 12 November 1918.
38 13th Brigade War Diary, 10 to 12 November 1918.
39 13th Battalion War Diary, 11 November 1918.
40 46th Battalion War Diary, 16 November 1918.
41 11th AFA Brigade War Diary, 11 November 1918.
42 4th Division Artillery HQ War Diary for December 1918, Appendix 1
43 Chataway, *Op Cit*, p. 236. This incident is not mentioned in either the 15th Battalion or 4th Brigade Diary, except that the former says that a route march planned for 3 December was abandoned 'through circumstances.'
44 This account comes from the 13th Brigade War Diary entry for 1 to 12 December 1918, in which Capt Louch attributed most of the trouble to a few 'agitators' but acknowledged that the ration supply difficulties were genuine and that the incidents had released a lot of 'bad blood.' The vacancy at 12th Brigade occurred because Brig Gen Leane was temporarily GOC Division while Maj Gen Sinclair-MacLagan was on leave.
45 See the *Official History*, Vol VI, pp. 1053–73 for details.
46 Chataway, *Op Cit*, p. 235.
47 4th Brigade War Diary, 5 December 1918. The 12th Brigade diarist also noted signs of prosperity (16 December), while the 13th Brigade diary notes that prices for foodstuffs were high in the Dinant area and the quality of the liquor was poor (concluding comments for December 1918).
48 It appears that the general declined a knighthood in favour of promotion to substantive major general in the British Army (article by A J Hill in the *Australian Dictionary of Biography*).
49 Mitchell, *Op Cit*, pp. 280–81.
50 Quoted in Bruce Catton, *This Hallowed Ground*, London 1957, p. 399.
51 *Australian Imperial Force; Statistics of Casualties, Etc; Compiled to 30th June, 1919*, Issued by Records Section, AIF Headquarters, London (copy in AWM collection).
52 Rule, *Op Cit*, p. 134. Pte Floyd's service record shows that he had previously been wounded on one occasion but had been hit in several places, which was probably what Rule meant, but in any case it does not alter the point.
53 *Medical History*, Vol III, p. 894, and also p. 922n, and p. 442. Butler, in Table 51 on p. 923 gives a figure of 53,277 AIF wounded who subsequently rejoined their units, but again a number of individuals may have done so more than once.
54 *Official History*, Vol VI, p. 1099. The AWM website page 'Enlistment Statistics, First World War' mentions the point also.
55 The *Medical History* (Vol II, p. 442n) gives figures for the number of AIF members wounded more than twice; Butler does not name a source, merely saying the number 'is stated to have been;' it presumably applies to the AIF across all theatres of war, but may be only for the European theatre. The figures show: wounded 7 times: 1; 6 times: 10; 5 times: 105; 4 times: 807; 3 times: 5,582. There is no number for twice wounded, but 6,000 would be a conservative estimate.
That gives 32,566 instances of wounding for 12,505 individuals. Subtracting 32,566 woundings

from the total AIF figure of 135,684 (not including gassings) gives 103,118 who were wounded once, and adding back the 12,505 multiple wounded gives 115,623 individuals wounded. Applying a proportional calculation to the 4th Division wounded figure gives 18,664 individuals. The author acknowledges that this cannot be claimed as definitive.

56   Gill, *Op Cit*, pp. 263–5.

57   *Medical History*, Vol III, pp. 846–863.

58   Bean Papers, AWM38 3DRL606/254/1, pp. 188–229 in PDF.

59   *Medical History*, Vol III, p. 957.

60   It is likely that there are enough military enthusiasts in Australia to conduct such a study on a voluntary basis, each taking a set of pages from the nominal roll, checking the relevant service files, and entering information in a suitable electronic database. The present author hereby volunteers for his 20 pages.

61   'Capt Twining: Hero of Pozieres,' *Reveille*, 30 September 1931, p. 4.

62   *Official History*, Vol VI, pp. 1079–80.

63   *Ibid*, p. 1084.

64   Shortly before the Armistice, the highly-respected British General Sir Ivor Maxse, then Inspector General of Training, gave an address to a conference of Australian Corps senior officers. He 'ascribed the great success of our men in recent fighting' to the initiative of the individual Australian soldier. The officers present took exception to this, reminding the General that the 'higher ranks' had great influence on the results also. One hopes that they included junior officers and NCOs in that category (4th Division General Staff War Diary, 5 November 1918).

65   That is, not including the Russian (Eastern) front, the Balkans and the 'Far East.' Excluding Russia and Japan, the Allies mobilised 30,189,000 men including 417,000 Australians (of whom 334,000 served overseas). The inclusion of Russia adds another 12,000,000 men to the Allied total. Australia contributed about 5% of British and Empire enlistments.

66   Quoted in P. Rees, *Bearing Witness*, Sydney, 2015 (a Life of C E W Bean).

Appendix
13th Battalion's attack at Mouquet Farm 14/15 August 1916

Orders

The first written order for operations on the night of 14/15 August was issued to the 4th Division by I Anzac on 14 August (I Anzac Order No. 24); the order was noted as being issued at 7 am that day. The objective was given as the line

R.28.c.95 – 66 – 36 – 03 – R.27.d.94 – 73 – 42 – 12 – R.33.b.29 – 27 – R.33.a.77 – 54

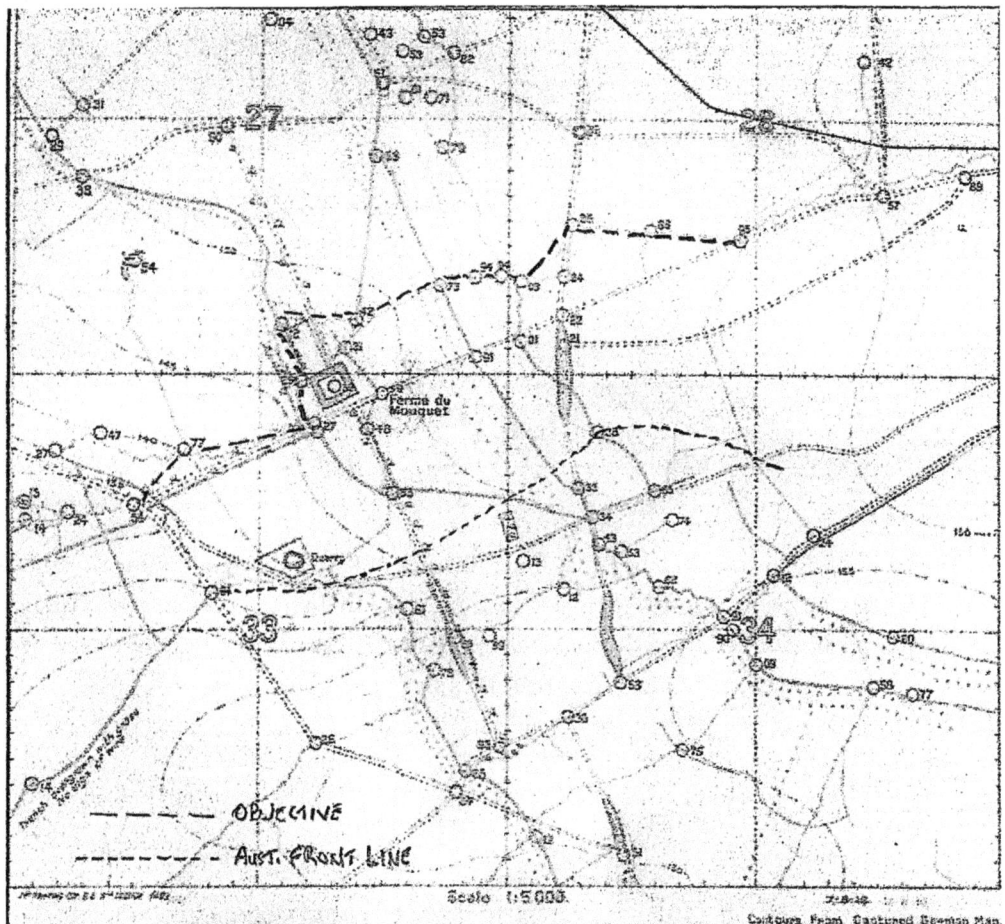

Later in the day, when it became apparent that the situation had changed with the loss of Skyline Trench overnight, I Anzac issued Order No. 25, changing the objective to:

R.28.c.95—66—36—03—R.27.d.94—73—R.33.b.59—48—R.33.a.81 'with left flank refused' (the Farm itself was no longer included).

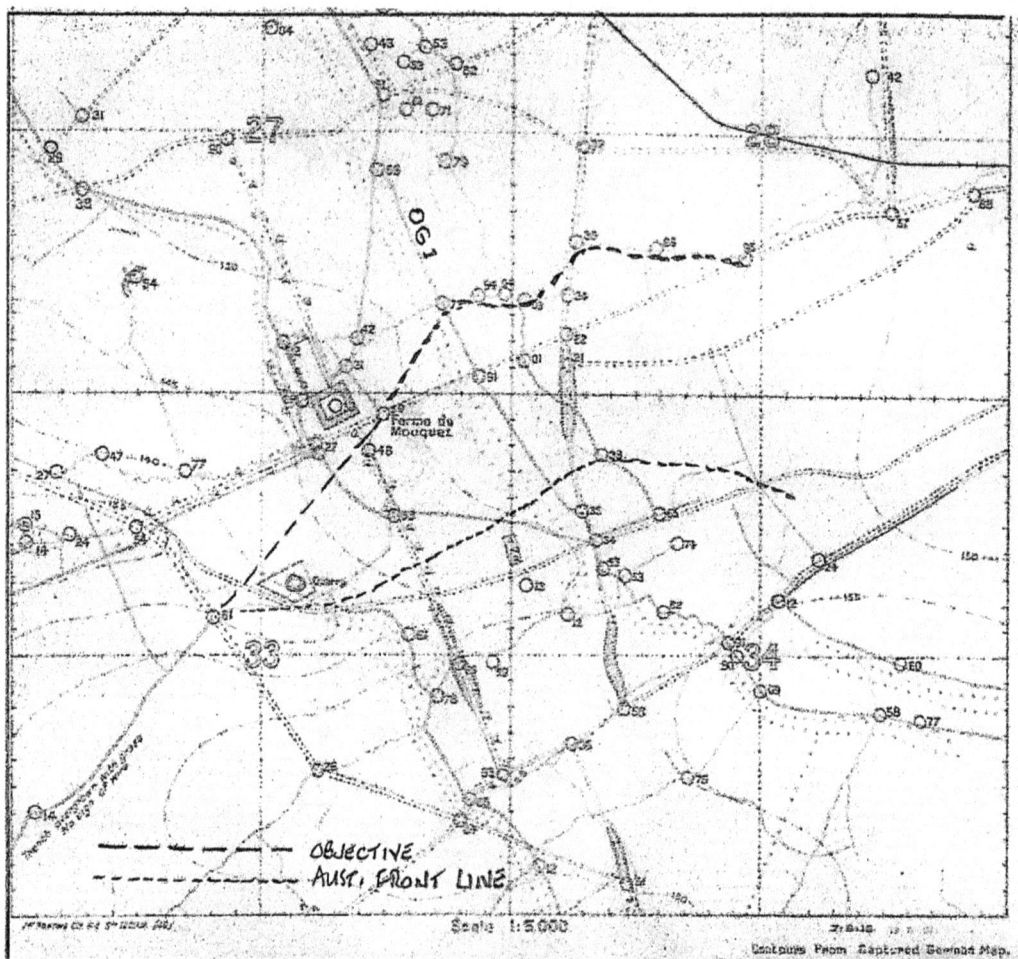

That order, which also specified that 'zero' would be 10 pm, showed its time of issue as 2:45 pm. The 4th Division accordingly issued its Order No. 16 directed particularly at the 13th Brigade for action, and specifying the objective generally as in the amendment to the I Anzac orders, but with a variation about the centre of the line:

R.28.c.95—66—36—24—03—04—R.27.d.94—73—91—R.33.b.48—R.33.a.81

Appendix

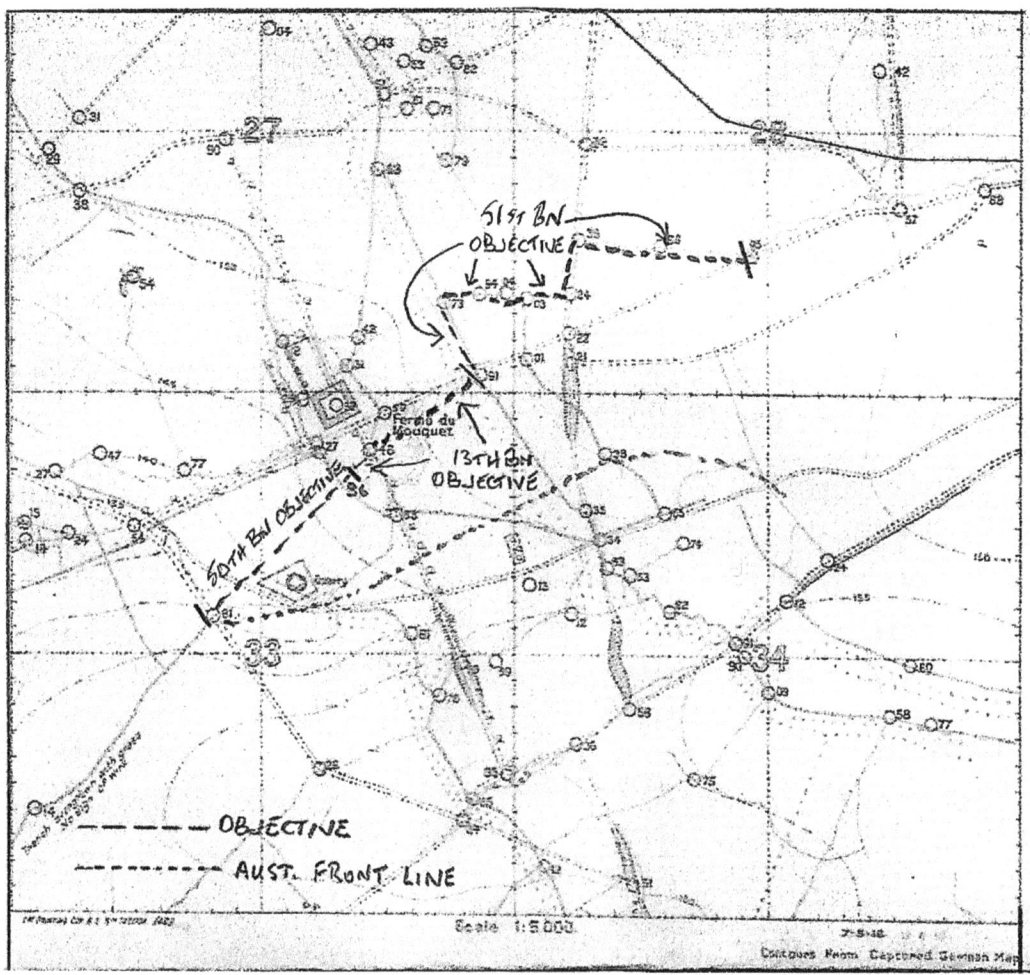

The divisional order showed its time of issue as 2:30 pm, i.e. 15 minutes before that of the Corps order. If this is not a typographical error (say for 3:30) then the amended objective must have been communicated from I Anzac to the division prior to the written order arriving, by telephone or perhaps by handwritten note via despatch rider.

The 13th Brigade War Diary notes that the divisional order was received at 3:45 pm. The Brigade then issued its own written order, Operation Order No. 8, at 5 pm. These objectives were allocated to battalions, from right to left:

> 51st Battalion: R.28.c.95—66—36—24—03—04—R.27.d.94—73 'and back to 91 inclusive' (the last segment was part of OG 1)
>
> 13th Battalion: R.27.d.91 'exclusive'—R.33.b.48—36 'inclusive'
>
> 50th Battalion: 'R.33.b.36 exclusive in front of QUARRY to 33 a 81 inclusive'

as well as instructions for the 49th Battalion to form a defensive flank on the right. A marked-up map was appended showing the Brigade's present positions and its objective.

715

None of the battalions had the time, nor perhaps the facilities, to issue written orders, so briefing at battalion level would have been verbal—the 51st's CO, Colonel Ross, noted specifically in his after-action report[1] that 'all orders were given verbally to Company and Detail Commander[s] at Battalion Headquarters.' The attack leaders would have had to come in to their unit's HQ from the front or support line for briefing then return to their troops to make preparations, running the gauntlet of the German shelling.

The I Anzac artillery staff issued its own order for the supporting barrages; this specified the amended objective as in corps HQ's orders, although the artillery order does not show a time of issue. In turn, the orders issued by the Lahore Artillery (attached to the 4th Division as its divisional artillery at this time) reflected the objective as described in the divisional order, that is, with the further alteration in the centre of the line. The artillery barrage plan and timetable prepared at corps HQ were reproduced in the Lahore orders. On the map, these instructions look more appropriate to support an attack on the *original* objective. The first line of the barrage (of three minutes duration) would fall beyond the new objectives for both the 50th and 13th Battalions, and so would be of little assistance to them.

The *Official History*

C E W Bean's account of the original planning for the operations of 14/15 August is on pages 759 and 760 in Volume III of the *Official History*; a marginal sketch shows the initial objective, and the ground is described in the text. The changes resulting from the loss of Skyline Trench are then mentioned briefly on page 761: 'The acuteness of the salient from whose point the Australian thrust must be now be made is shown in the marginal sketch. The objective was accordingly modified as therein indicated'[2]—there is no description of the new objective in the text, and the sketch is to a smaller scale than that on page 759. The History then goes on to describe the events of the attack itself, on pages 764 to 769. So far as the 13th Battalion's part is concerned, Bean's account says

> ... that battalion had made a most notable advance. It was advancing with two companies and part of a third in two waves, the first about 100 strong, the second 80 ... the 13th, led by Murray, advanced beside OG 1 until near the Fabeck Graben and, when thirty yards from that trench, charged ... after sharp bomb-fights both in the trench and on the parapet the Fabeck Graben was cleared for 200 yards to the right beyond its junction with OG 2 ... posts were stationed at either end as well as 40 yards up OG 1 ...

There is no comment on any reasons why the 13th would have gone so far beyond its specified objective (by about 200 metres on average). Bean's account also implies that the Fabeck Graben was the first and only enemy position encountered by the 13th during its advance.

The Battalion History

Captain T A White's lively unit history, *The Fighting Thirteenth*, describes the operation on pages 67 to 70. Here the 13th's objectives are given as both the line from Point 36 to Point 91 (which White called 'Fox Trench' in the book) *and* the Fabeck Graben (called 'Murray System')[3]. White also wrote that 'the 50th Battalion was to overrun Mouquet and join the 13th near [Point] 63'—the latter point was about 200 metres north-east of Mouquet Farm. These objectives are obviously at variance with the orders from corps, division and brigade; they are compatible with the *original* objective in the I Anzac order, but this did not reach the point of allocating tasks to the battalions before the amended objective was issued and specified in division and brigade orders.

The Fighting Thirteenth then describes the fighting; 'within a few seconds [of jumping off] the attackers encountered an unexpected trench ... 75 yards out.' This was captured, and 'a further 80 yards ahead Fox Trench [i.e. the line between Points 36 and 91, the objective specified in the orders] was found to be full of Germans.' This line was also taken, by 11:15 pm. White states that the 13th then continued to advance and attacked the Fabeck Graben, a long segment of which was also captured after a hard fight. 'All touch with the 50th and 51st Battalions had now been lost, neither battalion having been able to reach its objectives.' There follows an account of the German counter-attacks and Captain Murray's fighting retreat. The 13th Battalion therefore is said to have taken three successive enemy positions: the 'unexpected trench,' 'Fox Trench' and the Fabeck Graben.

War Diaries and Reports

The 13th Battalion War Diary notes the objective for the night of 14/15 August as in the brigade order, R.27.d.91 to R.33.b.48 to 36. The diary records a message received at 10:30 pm stating that 'a trench had been encountered 75 yards from hopping-out trench' and that this had been captured. The next report 'timed 11:15 pm stated that we had captured a further trench 150 yards from hopping-out trench. Trench was full of Germans.' The next message was timed midnight and reported that touch could not be gained with the flanking battalions. Then at 12:45 am (15 August) the Diary notes 'heavily counter-attacked front and flanks and compelled to retire onto original position.' Two enemy trenches are reported as captured, and there is no suggestion of any further advance to a third trench system. The War Diary was presumably compiled by the battalion adjutant, Captain Douglas Marks, who made similar entries in his personal diary, including the map references.

The reports from higher-level formations make similar statements, all speaking of two lines being captured, of course relying on input from the 13th Battalion. Comments by the I Anzac intelligence staff are particularly interesting. As well as confirming that the 13th Battalion 'entered two lines of enemy's trenches' and captured 11 German prisoners from the 69th (Rhineland) Regiment, the intelligence reports include results from interrogation of the prisoners. These stated that several companies of their regiment occupied trenches 'south of Mouquet Farm' which included Points 27, 48, 59 and 91—in other words the 13th Battalion's objective. The prisoners also stated that 'one platoon of the 6th [Company] was deployed as a covering body in shell holes and it is fairly certain from the prisoners' statements that a rough line of occupied shell holes ran right and left of the trench at R.33.b.48.'[4] This is clearly the first German position encountered and captured by the 13th Battalion before going on to its main objective.

Personal Accounts

Major Theodore Wells, who took part in the battle as a lieutenant, contributed an article[5] to the August 1932 issue of the New South Wales RSL magazine *Reveille* in which he stated that the 13th Battalion's objective that night was the Fabeck Graben. It is apparent, though, that he had used the *Official History* to refresh his memory on this point. Interestingly, Wells noted that a 13th Battalion sergeant had taken the opportunity of reconnoitring an enemy front-line trench on 13 August, and stated that this trench would be the 13th's objective for the following night. This incident had happened during an unofficial truce after the failed German attack on the lines of the 50th and 13th Battalions that morning, while German stretcher bearers were picking up their wounded in No Man's Land. Considering where this fight had occurred, it is extremely unlikely that the enemy trench could have been the Fabeck Graben; to reach that position, the sergeant would have had to cross over the enemy's front line and then make his way another 300 metres or more into the German lines before returning the same way. On the other hand, he would have had much less difficulty approaching what would be the 13th's *correct* objective.

Harry Murray (by then Lieutenant Colonel Murray, VC CMG DSO DCM) wrote his own account of the battle for *Reveille* of December 1935. In this article, Murray made no claim of going as far as the Fabeck Graben, merely stating that 'we were attacking in front of Pozières, and 'A' Company of the 13th Bn had better luck than the troops on either flank, having attained its objectives.'[6] Murray's main theme in this piece was his experiences in the subsequent withdrawal, summed up in the secondary title of the article—'When Discipline Mastered Fear.'

Assessment

In summary, the available records of this operation, the orders before it and reports after it, show that the 13th Battalion attacked and captured an outpost line and then its main objective roughly from Point 91 through 48 to 36, a little to the south of the Courcelette road in front of Mouquet Farm—not the Fabeck Graben. The Official History and the Battalion history, on the other hand, state that the 13th captured part of the Fabeck Graben (as does Major Wells's article). Bean is somewhat vague about the lead-up to the attack, making no real comment about the changes to the objective, and also omits any description of the 13th capturing two enemy lines south of the Farm. Those enemy positions are not shown in any of the marginal sketch maps accompanying the text (pages 761 to 766 of Volume III). The next chapter (Ch. XXII) of the Official History deals with the operations of the 3rd Brigade (1st Division) over the same ground, and here the German positions in question are shown in marginal maps—in particular on pages 793 to 795 and 799, relating to the 12th Battalion's part in the fighting.

The Fighting Thirteenth was published in 1924, several years before Volume III of the *Official History*. C E W Bean noted in his preface that he had used it as a reference, but Captain White, the author, had access to Bean's source notes. White was a serving officer in the 13th Battalion, but he did not join the unit until December 1916, so was not present at the Mouquet Farm battles, and thus his account would have been the result of enquiry rather than personal experience. White was definitely in error as to the official objectives of the 13th on the night of 14/15 August (and also the 50th Battalion's objective). It appears that this may have led to inaccuracy in his dramatic account of the fighting—knowing that the battalion took its objective and believing that the objective was the Fabeck Graben, White's conclusion would be that a further advance and further fighting took place after the capture of the trench 'full of Germans.' It is also possible that his sources in the battalion confused the 'stunt' of 14/15 August with that of 29/30 August, the events of which were very similar. On the latter occasion, Captain Murray again led a force of the 13th to capture its objective—which actually *was* the Fabeck Graben.

Bean seems to have based his account on talks with 13th Battalion officers (including Murray) at some later date, recorded in one of his notebooks.[7] Here he writes of a last-minute change of objective but with the original objective still involving part of the Fabeck Graben. Such a change in plans would seem to justify at least a brief mention in the *Official History*. None of the official documents, the orders, diaries and reports of Division, Brigade and the 13th and 51st Battalions, mentions anything supporting those notes, and it is possible that there may have been some misunderstanding as to which of the two attacks was being discussed. Bean's own diary entries at the time of the battle reflect the events as in the official documents.[8] In his account of the battle in the *Official History*, it does appear that Bean relied less on a close study of documentary sources than he usually did, and more on his own notes. My own speculation is that when Bean came to write up the *History*, having reviewed the sources, he began to have some doubts, pushed ahead tentatively, and produced an uncharacteristically vague account.

To consider the practical aspects of the fighting on 14/15 August, it is hard to see what reason Harry Murray might have had for leading his troops so far beyond their correct objective. The orders had been fulfilled and casualties suffered in the heavy fighting that had already taken place; why continue advancing for another 200 to 250 metres? Doing so would virtually guarantee losing touch with the other battalions even if they had managed to reach their objectives. The 13th's left flank would have been well beyond where the 50th would be expecting to link up, and therefore particularly open, with nothing to stop an enemy counter attack penetrating behind it. On the right, the 51st Battalion would be looking for the 13th back at Point 91 to the south, not directly to the west. There would also have been a considerable risk of running into the supporting artillery barrage.

Harry Murray was a bold infantry leader who took many risks to achieve victory, but he was certainly not headstrong or foolhardy. By all accounts he was always able to remain cool and in control of a combat situation even with fighting raging all around him. It is highly unlikely that he would have so far exceeded his instructions as to advance another 200 metres into the unknown. Most accounts note that the 13th Battalion tried to link up with the 50th on the left;

if the 13th had advanced so far, they could hardly have expected the 50th to be alongside them. When the German counter-attacks began to come in from in front, the 13th is said to have needed to challenge before firing, in case the troops they saw were a party of the 51st Battalion trying to make contact. 'Crowds of them could now be seen dimly in the thin moonlight, but our [Lewis] gunners could not fire without challenging even at 20 yards in case they might be our own men.'[9] If the 13th actually was in the Fabeck Graben, any troops approaching from in front, the north, would almost certainly be German. On the other hand, if the 13th was in its *correct* objective, then that direction was exactly where they would expect to see troops of the 51st, probing down OG 1 from Point 73 to Point 91 according to plan, and hence a challenge would be necessary before firing.

Finally, there remains the possibility that the 13th Battalion attack commanders may have been incorrectly briefed and were under the impression that their objective actually was the Fabeck Graben. This is highly unlikely; there were no written orders below corps level which mentioned this, and the objectives for individual battalions were not specified before the 13th Brigade order was issued, giving the correct objectives as modified from the original corps order. The 13th Battalion War Diary records the unit's objective correctly, and the circumstance that the 13th and 51st Battalion HQs were sharing a dugout would also help to ensure that there was no misunderstanding. On the balance of probabilities, it seems very likely that the *Official History* is in error about the events of 14/15 August, and that the 13th Battalion captured its correct objective as ordered before being obliged to withdraw.

Notes

1. 51st Battalion War Diary for August 1916, Appendix 2.
2. *Official History*, Vol III, p. 761.
3. The actual trench line probably ran slightly to the south of that specified, from Point 91 to about 46. A trench in that location was added to the special map 'Ferme du Mouquet' in an edition corrected to 22 August; an example of that map is in the 4th Division General Staff War Diary for September 1916 (Part 1, pp. 46 and 47).
4. I Anzac Intelligence Staff War Diary, August 1916 (AWM4 1/30/7 Part 2). This report says the prisoners were captured 'on the evening of the 15th'. This is probably a mistake for 14 August, but even if the date is correct it does not alter the point.
5. T Wells, 'First Stunt: Vivid Impressions,' *Reveille*, August 1932, p. 34.
6. H W Murray, 'His Hardest Battle,' *Reveille*, December 1935, p. 33.
7. Bean Papers, 3DRL606/140/1, pp 59–78.
8. Bean Papers, 3DRL606/54/1, 14/15 August 1916. He appears to have been present at Division or Brigade HQ that night.
9. T A White, *The Fighting Thirteenth*, p. 69. See also the *Official History*, Vol III, p. 767.

Brave Days

Bibliography

Official Sources:

Australian War Memorial Collection:
    AWM4, AIF formation and unit war diaries 1914–19.
    AWM27 4/11 Australian Imperial Force: Statistics of Casualties etc. Compiled to 30th June 1919.
    AWM30, Prisoner of War Statements.
    AWM38, Papers of C E W Bean (diaries, notebooks, folders, correspondence).
    AWM224, Unit Manuscript Histories
    1DRL/0428, Red Cross Wounded and Missing Files
National Archives of Australia:
    Series B2455, World War I personnel service records.

Other Internet sites:

Australian Defence Force Academy, www.unsw.adfa.edu.au
Landships–British Tank Actions of the First World War, sites.google.com/site/landships
Tunnellers research website, www.tunnellers.net

Books and Journals:

Austin, R. *Gallipoli: An Australian Encyclopedia of the 1915 Dardanelles Campaign.* Rosebud, Vic, 2005.
Australian National University (various authors). *Australian Dictionary of Biography.* Internet edition.
Bean, C E W
    –*The Official History of Australia in the War of 1914–18*, Volumes I to VI. Sydney, 1921–42 and Brisbane, 1981–83,
    –*Anzac to Amiens.* Canberra, 1961.
Belford, W C. *Legs Eleven. The Story of the 11th Battalion in the Great War.* Perth, 1940.

Braga, S. *Kokoda Commander: A Life of Major-General 'Tubby' Allen.* Melbourne, 2004.
Browne, D G. *The Tank in Action.* London, 1920.
Browning, N.
 –*For King and Cobbers: 51st Battalion AIF 1916–1919.* Perth, 2007.
 –*Leane's Battalion: 48th Battalion AIF 1916 – 1919.* Perth, 2009.
 –*The 52nd Battalion.* Perth, 2005.
Bull, S. *An Officer's Guide to the Western Front 1914 – 1918.* London, 2008.
Butler, A G. *Official History of the Australian Army Medical Services in the War of 1914–18*, Volumes I to III. Melbourne, 1930–43.
Byrne, J R. *New Zealand Artillery in the Field, 1914–18.* Auckland, 1922.
Carlyon, L.
 –*Gallipoli.* Sydney, 2001.
 –*The Great War.* Sydney, 2006.
Chataway, T P. *History of the Fifteenth Battalion.* Brisbane, 1948.
Churchill, Sir W S. *The World Crisis 1911–1918.* New York, 2005.
Clayton, D. *Decisive Victory: The Battle of the Sambre, 4 November 1918.* Warwick, UK, 2018.
Conan Doyle, Sir A. *The Great War: The British Campaign in France and Flanders* (Vol VI). London, 1920.
Coombes, D. *Crossing the Wire: the Untold Stories of Australian POWs in Battle and Captivity During World War I.* Newport, NSW, 2011.
Coulthart, R. *Charles Bean.* Sydney, 2014.
Cranston, F. *Always Faithful: A History of the 49th Australian Infantry Battalion 1916–1982.* Brisbane, 1983.
Cutlack, F M
 –*The Australians: Their Final Campaign, 1918.* London, 1919.
 –(ed.), *War Letters of General Monash.* Sydney, 1935.
 –*Official History of Australia in the War of 1914–1918: Vol VIII–The Australian Flying Corps.* Sydney, 1941.
Deayton, C. *Battle Scarred: the 47th Battalion in the First World War.* Newport, NSW, 2012.
Dennis, P et al. *The Oxford Companion to Australian Military History.* Melbourne, 1995.
Devine, W. *The Story of a Battalion: Being a Record of the 48th Battalion AIF.* Melbourne 1919 (reprint by The Naval and Military Press Ltd).
Downing, W H. *To the Last Ridge.* Sydney, 1998.
Edgar, B. *Warrior of Kokoda: a biography of Brigadier Arnold Potts.* Sydney, 1999.
Edgar, P. *To Villers-Bretonneux.* Sydney, 2006.
Ellis, A D. *The Story of the Fifth Australian Division.* London, 1920.
Ellis, J. *Eye-deep In Hell: The Western Front 1914–18.* London, 2002.
Evans, E (ed P Wilson). *So Far From Home.* Sydney, 2002.
Farndale, Sir M. *History of the Royal Regiment of Artillery: Western Front 1914–18.* London, 1986.

Franki, G and Slatyer, C. *Mad Harry: Australia's Most Decorated Soldier.* Sydney, 2003.
Franks, N and Bennett, A. *The Red Baron's Last Flight.* London, 1997.
Freeman, R R. *Hurcombe's Hungry Half Hundred: A Memorial History of the 50th Battalion AIF.* Norwood, SA, 1991.
General Staff, War Office.
- *Field Artillery Training.* HMSO, 1914.
- *Field Service Pocket Book.* HMSO, 1916 (Naval and Military Press Reprint, 2003).
- *Infantry Machine Gun Company Training.* HMSO, 1917 (Naval and Military Press Reprint, 2009).

Gibbs, P. *The Realities of War.* London, 1920.
Gill, I. *Bloody Angle, Bullecourt and Beyond: 16th Battalion AIF 1914–19.* Perth, 2008.
Grant, I. *Jacka VC: Australia's Finest Fighting Soldier.* Melbourne, 1989.
Hatwell, J. *No Ordinary Determination: Percy Black and Harry Murray of the First AIF.* Fremantle, 2005 and 2014.
Holmes, R. *Tommy: The British Soldier on the Western Front 1914–1918.* London, 2004.
Holt, T and V. *Major and Mrs Holt's Battlefield Guide to the Ypres Salient and Passchendaele.* Barnsley, UK, 2011.
Horner, D. *The Gunners: A History of Australian Artillery.* Sydney, 1995.
Kendall, P. *Bullecourt 1917: Breaching the Hindenburg Line.* Stroud, UK, 2010.
Keech, G. *Australians on the Somme 1916: Pozières.* Barnsley, UK, 2016.
Lee, J E. *The Chronicle of the 45th Battalion AIF.* Sydney, 1927.
Lee, R 'The Australian Staff: The Forgotten Men of the First AIF,' in P Dennis and J Grey (eds) *1918 Defining Victory: Proceedings of the Chief of Army's History Conference 1998.* Canberra, 1999.
Liddle, P (ed). *Passchendaele in Perspective: The Third Battle of Ypres.* London, 1997.
Lodge, B. *Lavarack: Rival General.* Sydney, 1998.
Longmore, C. *The Old Sixteenth.* Perth, 1929.
Louch, T S. *Personal History of the Great War.* Perth, 1970 (self-published pamphlets).
Lynch, E P F (ed W. Davies). *Somme Mud.* Sydney, 2006.
Macklin, R. *Jacka VC: Australian Hero.* Crow's Nest, NSW, 2006.
Marks, D G. personal diary, Mitchell Library.
Masters, J. *The Road Past Mandalay.* London, 1961.
McNicoll, R. *The Royal Australian Engineers 1902 – 1919* (Vol II). Melbourne, 1979.
Middlebrook, M.
- *The First Day on the Somme.* London, 1975.
- *The Kaiser's Battle.* London, 1978.

Mitchell, G D. *Backs to the Wall.* Sydney, 1937.
Mitchinson, K W *Pioneer Battalions in the Great War.* London, 1997.
Monash, Sir J. *The Australian Victories in France in 1918.* London, 1920.

Montgomery (later Montgomery-Massingberd), Sir A A. *The Story of the Fourth Army in the Battles of the Hundred Days, August 8th to November 11th, 1918.* London, 1919.

Noonan, D. *Those We Forget: Recounting Australian Casualties of the First World War.* Melbourne, 2014.

O'Ryan, J F. *The Story of the 27th Division.* New York, 1921.

Pedersen, P A.
  –*The Anzacs.* Melbourne, 2007.
  –(with C Roberts) *Anzacs on the Western Front: The Australian War Memorial Battlefield Guide.* Milton, Qld, 2012.
  –*Monash as Military Commander.* Sydney, 2018.
  –*Battleground Europe: Villers-Bretonneux.* Barnsley, UK, 2004.
  –*Battleground Europe: Hamel.* Barnsley, UK, 2003.

Polanski, I L. *We Were the 46th: The History of the 46th Battalion in the Great War of 1914–18.* Townsville, Qld, 1999.

Powell, G. *Plumer: The Soldier's General.* Barnsley, UK, 2004.

Prior, R and Wilson, T.
  –*Passchendaele: The Untold Story.* Melbourne, 2003.
  –*Command on the Western Front: The Military Career of Sir Henry Rawlinson 1914–1918.* Barnsley, UK, 2004.

Prior, R. *Gallipoli: The End of the Myth.* Sydney, 2009.

Rees, P. *Bearing Witness.* Sydney, 2015.

Reveille (journal of the NSW RSL), various issues.

Rosenthal, Sir C. *Diary 1 January 1916 to 31 December 1918.* Mitchell Library, MLMSS 2739 (online transcript).

Rule, E J. *Jacka's Mob: a narrative of the Great War.* Melbourne, 1999 (ed C. Johnson and A. Barnes; originally published 1933).

Sadler, P S. *The Paladin: A Life of Major General Sir John Gellibrand.* Melbourne, 2000.

Snelling, S. *VCs of the First World War: Gallipoli.* Gloucestershire UK, 1995.

Stanley, P.
  –*Bad Characters: Sex, Crime, Mutiny, Murder and the Australian Imperial Force.* Miller's Point, NSW, 2010
  –'Paul the Pimp Reconsidered: Australian "G" Staffs on the Western Front,' unpublished paper presented to the Australian War Memorial History Conference, 1987 (copy made available to the author by Dr Stanley).

Steel, N and Hart, P. *Passchendaele: The Sacrificial Ground.* London, 2000.

Stewart, H. *The New Zealand Division 1916 – 1919.* Auckland, 1921.

Tyquin, M. *Forgotten Men: The Australian Army Veterinary Corps 1909–1946.* Newport, NSW, 2011.

Walker, J. *The Blood Tub: General Gough and the Battle of Bullecourt 1917.* Staplehurst, UK,

1998.

Wanliss, N. *The History of the Fourteenth Battalion AIF.* Melbourne, 1929.

Wartime (Official Magazine of the Australian War Memorial), various issues.

Watson, W H L. *A Company of Tanks.* Edinburgh, 1920.

White, T A. *The Fighting Thirteenth.* Sydney, 1924.

Williams, P. *The Battle of Anzac Ridge.* Loftus, NSW, 2006.

Yockelson, M A. *Borrowed Soldiers: Americans Under British Command 1918.* Oklahoma, USA, 2008.

Index

A

Aarons, Capt Daniel 215, 231, 242, 411, 413–14, 417, 602
Abbeville 47–8, 182, 374, 535, 695
Accroche Wood 554, 559
Acheux 71–2, 424, 430, 432
Adams, Capt Spencer 74
Adams, Capt William 458–9, 462, 476, 652
Adcock, Pte Henry 358
Advantage Farm 687
AFC (Australian Flying Corps)
    2 Squadron 572
    3 Squadron 481, 548, 577
Agimont 700
Agnicourt 430, 432
Ahearn, Capt Charles 108, 165, 344, 411, 413, 417, 602
Ahrens, Capt Charles. *See* Ahearn, Capt Charles
AIF. *See* Australian Imperial Force
Ailly (-le-Haut-Clocher) 133
Ailly (-sur-Somme) 514, 693
aircraft and aerial warfare 60, 74–5, 101, 145, 153, 202, 228, 230, 253, 258, 278, 284, 320, 343, 360, 379, 407, 429, 446, 481–2, 530, 541, 548, 558, 577, 584, 586, 613, 619–20. *See also* RAF; RFC; AFC
Aisne River 154, 529
Albert 69–70, 105, 135, 179, 182, 236, 265, 267, 406, 408, 423–5, 427–9, 435–6, 438–9, 441, 443, 446, 455, 463, 624, 626
Aldridge, Lt Norman 344–5, 417, 659–60, 669
Alexandria 33, 42–3
Allan, Lt Herbert 599–600
Allan, Pte William 507
Allen, Lt Archibald 290
Allen, Maj Gen Arthur ('Tubby') 282, 284, 286, 293–4, 301, 349, 371, 377, 430, 454–5, 458, 481, 518–19, 521, 528, 571, 695, 698, 705–6
Allen, Lt Joshua 454
Allen, Pte Thomas 507
Allonville 417, 464, 513–14, 527–8, 530, 563, 572, 630
ambulance vehicles 138, 235, 357, 432, 560, 603, 665
Amiens 65–7, 133, 394, 401, 417, 424, 427, 446, 461, 463, 478, 480, 483–5, 504, 514, 524, 527–8, 530, 538, 573–5, 629–30, 666, 692, 694
    Battle of 141, 575–604, 613, 615, 642–3, 648, 668
ammunition supply
    artillery 22, 58–9, 61, 70–1, 124–5, 131, 133, 158, 160, 167, 200, 256, 264, 272–3, 333, 346, 348, 350, 544, 581, 585, 691 (*See also* 4th Divn Ammunition Column *under* Australian Imperial Force: Artillery units)

small arms 22, 54, 70–1, 112, 133, 158, 164, 218, 223–5, 229–31, 239, 259, 288, 408, 438, 485, 502, 543, 548, 558, 583–5, 594, 644, 660, 681, 684–5
Ancre River 424–7, 436, 441, 464, 479–80, 483, 527, 531
Anderson, Capt Alexander 355, 649–50, 669
Anderson, Capt Frederick 355, 456
Anderson, Sgt Herbert 539
Andrewartha, Maj Ernest 20, 100
Andrews, Sgt Harold 614
Anseremme 700
Anthée 700
Anzac Day 4, 40, 417, 483, 487, 496
Anzac Legend 707–8
Anzac Ridge 349
Appleton, Lt Frederick 141, 589
Arbre Guernon 687
Argue, Lt Robert 476
Armentières 50–1, 59, 65, 126, 152, 316, 401, 480
Armistice, The (1918) 690, 692–5
Armitage, Lt Col Clement 486
Armitage, Capt Harold 188, 191
Armour, Pte George 507
Armstrong, Lt Col Edward 31, 42, 71, 174, 314
Arnold, Capt Geoffrey 500, 506
Arnold, Lt Thomas (Tom) 203, 298, 301, 518, 521, 523
Arras 154, 173, 179, 184, 202, 254, 271, 401, 574, 624–5
  Battle of 199–200, 205, 208, 211, 259, 265
Arrell, Lt Col William 175, 293, 309, 324, 542, 605, 618, 677, 695, 698
artillery, Australian and British 13–15, 54–5, 58, 65, 67, 77–8, 81–3, 87, 91–2, 102, 106–7, 124–6, 132, 158, 160, 185–6, 194–5, 237–8, 264, 271–4, 277–80, 289, 299–300, 314, 331–3, 342, 347, 380, 408, 425, 436, 440, 462, 486, 502, 514, 519, 537, 543–4, 549, 575–7, 581, 604, 621–2, 664, 680, 690, 716. *See also* Artillery, divisional *and* Artillery units *under* Australian Imperial Force

barrage, creeping 81, 87, 101, 112, 154, 181, 186, 204, 259–62, 274, 276, 278, 281–2, 295, 332–3, 335, 337–9, 346, 348, 351–2, 412, 537–8, 541, 544, 550–2, 554–8, 563, 576–7, 579, 584–5, 621–2, 643, 645–6, 652–3, 679–81, 683–7, 689–91
barrage, protective and SOS 78, 117–18, 145, 158, 160, 163–4, 170, 186, 204, 212, 226, 229, 232, 262–5, 281, 286–7, 292, 317, 333, 335, 337, 341–2, 347, 355, 387, 390, 458, 461–2, 550, 559–61, 585, 645, 650, 652, 656, 659, 680, 686, 689, 691
calibration of weapons 579, 630
co-operation with infantry 68, 81, 91, 102, 116, 131, 159–60, 162, 167, 194, 204, 212, 226, 228, 231–2, 239–40, 242, 258, 260, 262–3, 265, 286–8, 300, 316–17, 347, 440, 458, 519, 562, 576–7, 621
command and control 58, 126, 201, 273, 332, 544, 579, 684, 686
counter-battery fire 60–1, 88, 116, 145, 201, 256, 258, 260, 265, 278–9, 300, 310, 332–3, 524, 538, 544, 550, 577, 585, 643, 680–1, 687
heavy artillery 13, 59–60, 81, 84, 87, 92, 106–7, 112, 116, 124, 156–7, 161, 199–200, 202–3, 211, 215, 229–30, 254, 256, 259, 262, 264, 278, 287, 295, 332–3, 442, 491, 524, 538, 544, 550, 577, 585–7, 597, 643, 658
mobile artillery 576–9, 585, 595–7, 643, 645, 658, 685, 687
organisation 13–14, 43, 143, 155, 389
weapons, field artillery 13
artillery, German 71, 73–5, 77–8, 83, 85–8, 91–3, 100, 105–7, 115, 117–18, 129–30, 135–6, 138, 142, 145, 153, 158, 162–4, 169, 202, 210, 215, 217, 221, 226, 255–6, 258, 260, 264, 273, 278–80, 292–6, 300, 310–12, 315, 319–20, 339, 341–3, 345, 352, 358–9, 384, 394, 401, 409, 411–14, 434, 442, 446–8, 452, 461, 502, 530, 541, 561, 563, 576, 582, 584–5, 588–9, 592, 594–7, 599–601, 603, 615, 620, 623, 626, 652–3, 656, 665, 681

Ascension Farm 652
Ascension Ridge/Spur 643, 653, 657
Ascension Valley 653
Ascension Wood 656
Aspery, Cpl Bertie 421
Assyria House 352, 354–5
Atkinson, Capt Basil 678
Atkinson, Capt James 462
Aubigny 488, 531, 547, 580
Aubigny Line 484–5, 487, 499, 503–4, 514, 526
Auld, Capt Patrick 497
Australian Flying Corps. *See* AFC
Australian Imperial Force (AIF), First
  Anzac Mounted Division 33, 42
  Artillery, divisional
    1st Divn 13, 91, 140, 156, 201, 228, 253, 314, 347, 350, 360, 388, 624
    2nd Divn 13, 56–7, 77, 81, 105, 112, 140, 183, 201, 240, 253, 259, 314, 332–4, 346–7, 350, 360, 464, 514, 684, 686
    3rd Divn 268, 319, 352, 458, 535, 579, 684, 686, 690, 692
    4th Divn 10, 15–17, 33, 37, 39, 42–3, 47, 52–3, 57–9, 61, 124–32, 140, 142–3, 145, 162, 174, 179, 181, 183, 195–6, 242, 253, 259, 268, 310, 314–15, 318–21, 371, 380, 388, 402, 424, 464, 477, 483, 514, 523–4, 527, 535–7, 563–4, 579, 621–4, 630, 637–8, 643, 645, 668, 670, 678, 684–5, 689–90, 695–6, 699–700, 702
      at Amiens 590–1, 594–7, 601, 604, 615
      at Dernancourt 430, 436, 440, 442, 446–8, 458, 461–2, 475
      at First Bullecourt 201, 204–7, 211–12, 215, 219–21, 223, 226, 228–30, 232–3, 239–40
      formation of 14–16, 228
      at Fromelles 59–61
      at Hamel 544, 549–50, 552, 556–7
      at Hindenburg Line 680–1, 683
      at Lagnicourt 256–8
      at Messines 272–3, 277, 279, 286–7, 293, 295, 299–300
      at Outpost Line 646, 651, 658–61
      personnel and training 15–17, 39, 42, 61, 124
      reorganisations 43, 143, 155
      at Sambre 691–2
      at Second Bullecourt 260–5
      at Selle 686–8
      in Third Ypres battles 331–5, 337–8, 340, 342, 346–8, 350, 352, 355, 359–61
    5th Divn 17, 59, 156–7, 254, 314, 531, 537–8, 544, 563–4, 643, 684, 686
  Artillery units
    1st AFA Brigade 201, 255
    2nd AFA Brigade 201, 255
    3rd AFA Brigade 14–15, 319–20
    4th AFA Brigade 185, 201–2
    4th Divn Ammunition Column (DAC) 23, 42–3, 61, 70–1, 125, 140, 264–5, 268, 278, 314, 331–2, 343, 350, 406, 430, 485, 514, 523, 535, 544, 584–5, 594, 644, 684–5
    5th AFA Brigade 185, 201
    6th AFA Brigade 160, 638, 645, 659, 684
    7th AFA Brigade 688, 690
    10th AFA Brigade 15–16, 42–3, 61, 125, 155–7, 160, 174, 181, 201, 240, 253, 256, 260, 265, 268, 273, 299–300, 314–15, 318, 331–3, 360–1, 436, 440, 447–8, 461, 514, 523–4, 536–7, 564, 579, 594–6, 615, 621–2, 645, 659, 680–1, 683–4, 686–8, 690
    11th AFA Brigade 15–16, 42–3, 61, 125, 145, 155–8, 160, 174, 181, 201, 240, 253, 256, 260, 265, 268, 273, 279, 299, 314–15, 318, 331–2, 348, 360, 405, 440, 447, 450, 461, 514, 523–4, 537, 564, 579, 594, 596, 621–2, 645, 680–1, 683–4, 686–91
    12th AFA Brigade 15–16, 42–3, 53, 125–6, 143, 155, 183, 185, 201, 228, 240, 253, 638, 645
    13th AFA Brigade 262, 645
    14th AFA Brigade 256, 259, 262, 645

24th AFA Brigade 15–16, 32, 42–3, 125, 145, 155
37th Battery 332, 448, 595, 645, 658
38th Battery 14, 260, 350, 595, 658
39th Battery 260, 315, 350, 579, 590–1, 594–6, 599, 601
41st Battery 350, 596, 645, 657, 685
42nd Battery 260, 596, 687–8
43rd Battery 253, 256–8, 260, 350, 596, 681, 684, 687–8, 691
48th Battery 61
53rd Battery 482
101st Battery 228
110th Battery 265, 300, 350, 361, 579, 595, 687–8
111th Battery 14, 315, 596, 689

Corps
    Australian Corps, The 371, 376, 380–1, 384, 394, 475, 477–8, 483, 513, 516, 527–8, 530, 537, 541–2, 544, 546, 548–50, 562–4, 571–8, 582, 584–5, 604, 616, 623, 625–6, 629–30, 638–9, 641–3, 646, 666–7, 678, 680, 682–3, 690, 693, 695–7, 700, 702, 707
    I Anzac 32–3, 51, 59, 65, 68, 77, 81, 87, 89–90, 106, 109, 120, 124, 126, 131, 133–4, 136, 138, 140, 154–5, 172–4, 180, 200, 202–3, 206, 208, 211, 228, 237, 253, 259, 265, 267, 314, 321–2, 325, 331–2, 342, 346–9, 359–60, 370–1, 380, 713, 717
        Light Railways Company 146
    II Anzac 32–3, 51, 53, 126, 268, 273–4, 276, 278, 293, 300, 310, 317, 321, 347–50, 353, 359–60, 371

Divisions
    1st 1–3, 5–6, 15, 32–3, 48, 50, 53, 56, 59, 67–8, 70, 90, 94, 99, 103, 109, 118, 124, 126, 131, 133–4, 142, 144, 154, 180, 182, 195, 200, 254–5, 257, 259, 273, 313, 325, 331, 334, 342, 346, 359–60, 381, 480, 527, 542, 574–5, 613, 624–6, 630, 639–40, 642, 646, 650, 666, 678–9, 693, 696, 700, 702

2nd 2–3, 15, 19, 32–3, 48, 50, 56, 59, 67–8, 70, 74–5, 104, 109, 124, 126, 131, 133–4, 136, 152, 154, 181–2, 253, 259, 262, 273, 325, 331, 333–4, 342, 346–9, 464, 479, 483, 524, 528, 537, 540, 545, 562, 576–7, 584, 613, 615–16, 624, 626, 630, 638, 678, 683–4, 700, 702

3rd 3, 67, 123, 273, 278, 288, 299–300, 318–19, 346, 350, 353, 355–7, 370–1, 394, 424, 441, 445, 449, 460, 463, 478–9, 481, 483, 527–8, 540, 563, 576–7, 579, 584–6, 603, 615–17, 621, 625–6, 630, 638–9, 678–9, 681, 683, 695, 702

4th 32, 99–100, 173, 179–81
    advance to Hindenburg Line (1917) 182–96
    advance to Hindenburg Line (1918) 638–42
    amalgamation of units 701–2
    American mission 678, 681–2
    Amiens operations 583–604
    in Armentières sector 50–3, 56–8, 146
    Bullecourt operations 200–43
    canteens 24, 83, 630, 677
    casualties 55, 58, 61, 74–5, 77, 80, 83, 85, 87, 92, 99–100, 105, 107, 109, 119, 132, 136, 142, 158, 179, 194, 217, 234–6, 238, 258, 261, 265, 276, 282, 300–2, 312, 315, 318–19, 321, 333, 342–3, 347, 356–9, 371, 388, 401, 414, 417, 436, 438, 475, 504, 523, 530, 562, 602–3, 615, 620, 665, 667, 683, 687, 702–5
    colour patches 9–10
    Composite Force 480, 482
    as 'Depot' division 370–1, 373–6
    Dernancourt operations 428–64
    disbandment 701–2
    educational courses 692, 700
    Egypt, operations in 33–7, 39–42

in Flers/Gueudecourt sector 135–42, 146, 152–72
formation of 5–10, 14–25, 27–8, 31–2, 146
furlough (home leave) to Australia 641–2, 658, 677–8, 684, 692, 695
in Hamel sector 530–1, 537–63
in Lihons sector 624–9
march to Belgium 695–7, 699
memorial, Bellenglise 702
Messines operations 272–302
in Messines sector 310–15, 318–21
morale 29, 83, 92, 101, 105, 119, 183, 211, 242, 286, 322, 370, 375, 391, 404–5, 414, 418, 517, 573, 581, 657, 666–7, 696–7
movement to France 41–3, 47–8
movement to Sambre sector 693–4
movement to Somme front (1918) 402–6, 408, 423–5, 473, 507
Order of Battle 174–6, 325–7, 395–6, 605–6, 698
Outpost Line operations 642–69
in Péronne sector 376–80
reputation 392–3, 706–7
rest periods 321–2, 371, 374–6, 388, 528, 530, 564, 571–2, 629–30, 637–8, 670, 677–9, 692–3
in Somme sector 59, 65–94, 103–20, 133–4, 477–84, 507, 573–83, 613–24
staff, HQ 25, 28–31, 41–2, 50, 71, 81, 102, 110–11, 124, 133, 143–4, 147, 173–4, 182, 206–7, 210, 212–13, 237, 241–2, 268, 274, 314, 336, 343, 374–5, 378–80, 391, 424, 426, 442, 444, 460, 462, 473–4, 480, 529, 542, 578, 584, 630, 695, 697
strength of, numerical 24–5, 103, 124, 134, 267, 302, 309, 318, 324–5, 370–1, 379–80, 388, 630
in Villers-Bretonneux sector 513–27

Ypres operations 334–59, 373
in Ypres sector 123–4, 126–32, 325, 359–60, 381–94
5th 3, 27–8, 32–3, 36, 42, 48, 53, 59–61, 126, 133, 136, 154–5, 168, 173–4, 182, 184, 195, 204, 265, 273, 334–5, 337, 342, 349, 359, 372, 478, 481, 483, 485, 488, 542, 545, 561–2, 564, 572–3, 576, 578, 582, 584, 586, 594, 604, 615, 624, 626, 630, 638, 678–9, 682–3, 700
6th 267, 324
Education Service 571, 692
Engineer units
    1st Field Company 20
    1st Tunnelling Company 690–1
    4th Field Company 19, 41, 52, 91, 137, 146, 172, 183, 310, 335, 340–1, 371, 382, 406–7, 423, 431, 514–15, 539, 543, 545–6, 559, 578, 644
    8th Field Company 173
    12th Field Company 19, 100, 137, 146, 172, 182–3, 258, 277, 289, 310, 335, 373, 431, 440, 442, 514, 531, 545, 578, 589–90, 596, 644, 666
    13th Field Company 19, 73–4, 91–2, 99, 137, 146, 172, 183, 277, 310, 335, 338–9, 345, 371, 378, 431, 441, 514, 546, 578, 622, 638, 644, 646, 665
    Topographical Section 581
Flying Corps, Australian (*See* AFC)
Infantry Battalions
    1st 2, 9, 602, 614
    2nd 2, 602
    3rd 2, 264, 602
    4th 2
    5th 2
    6th 2
    7th 2
    8th 2
    9th 2, 5–7, 100, 117, 140, 265, 314
    10th 2, 5, 7, 387–8, 656, 661
    11th 2, 5, 7, 36, 324

12th 2, 5–6, 8, 255, 309, 718
13th 2–4, 6, 9–10, 39, 47, 50, 52, 99, 126, 128–30, 141, 266, 310, 312, 318, 320–1, 336, 339, 342, 358–9, 376, 382, 387–8, 390–1, 394, 402, 404–5, 418, 514–16, 524, 527, 531, 535, 574, 613, 615, 624, 629, 643, 694–5
   at Amiens 583, 591–2, 594–5, 600, 602, 604
   at Bullecourt 204, 208, 211, 213, 215, 217–18, 222, 226, 231–2, 236
   at Hamel 543, 550, 555–6, 558–60
   at Hébuterne 405–9, 411–13, 415–18
   at Mouquet Farm 83–94, 104–9, 713–20
   at Outpost Line 646–52, 656
   at Stormy Trench 159–67, 240
14th 2–4, 6, 35, 52, 54, 56–9, 67, 74, 83, 86, 89, 110, 126, 130–1, 138, 141, 144, 162, 164–5, 167, 266, 275, 299, 310, 312, 318, 320, 322–4, 343, 345, 358, 382, 384–5, 388–9, 394, 514, 516, 527, 538–40, 571–2, 574, 624–6, 643, 645, 695
   'Allonville Disaster' 530
   at Amiens 583, 588–92, 594–5, 600, 602
   at Bullecourt 201, 203–4, 207–8, 213–16, 218, 222, 231–2, 236, 239
   at Hamel 550, 559
   at Hébuterne 406–12, 415–17
   at Mouquet Farm 104–5
   at Outpost Line 646, 655–61, 663, 665
   at Polygon Wood 336, 339–45
   at Pozières 77–9
15th 2–5, 41, 66, 74, 86, 89, 110, 123, 126, 128, 130, 141–2, 299, 310–11, 318, 320–1, 358, 378, 382, 387, 514, 524, 528, 530, 571, 574, 582, 623–5, 629, 637, 641, 643, 666, 694, 696, 700
   at Amiens 583, 588–9, 595, 602
   at Bullecourt 204, 208, 213, 215, 217–18, 222, 232, 236
   at Hamel 550, 552–4, 556–60, 562–3
   at Hébuterne 405–17
   at Mouquet Farm 81, 83, 86–7, 104–5
   at Outpost Line 646–8, 651–2, 656
   at Polygon Wood 336, 339–41
   at Pozières 77–9
   at Stormy Trench 156–60, 167
16th 2–7, 33, 36–7, 89, 126, 128, 130, 141, 165, 167, 266–7, 310, 318–20, 349, 358, 382, 389–90, 514, 524, 538–41, 571, 574, 613, 615, 624–6, 629, 641, 643, 677, 694
   at Amiens 583, 590–1, 595–7, 599–602
   at Bullecourt 201, 204, 207–8, 212–16, 218, 231–2, 236, 541
   at Hamel 550, 554–5, 559
   at Hébuterne 406–8, 410–18
   at Madame Wood (Courtine Trench) 627–9
   at Mouquet Farm 81–3, 85–7, 104–9
   at Outpost Line 646–7, 651, 656
   at Polygon Wood 336, 339–40
17th 255
19th 54
21st 104
24th 260
26th 152
30th 9, 144, 594
34th 353
37th 274, 284, 322
44th 291, 561–2
45th 6, 9, 40–1, 53, 74, 105, 109, 126, 131, 135–6, 139, 153, 236, 273, 308, 319, 342, 349, 356–7, 359, 371, 385, 479, 481, 504, 513, 515–17, 520, 524–8, 542, 561, 563, 624–5, 637, 643, 677, 695
   at Amiens 583, 586–8, 594, 597, 602
   at Dernancourt 426, 430, 437–42, 445–7, 454–6, 458–9, 461–3
   at Messines 276, 279–80, 282–4, 286–91, 293–6, 298, 301, 392, 475
   at Outpost Line 646, 651–3, 655, 657
   at Pozières 77–8, 80
   at Stormy Trench 169–72

46th 6, 41, 53–4, 74, 80, 89, 105, 109, 126, 129, 135, 144, 169, 267, 280, 319, 342, 349, 356–7, 359, 386, 424, 479, 481, 504, 513, 515–17, 524, 526–8, 563, 570, 624–5, 629–30, 643, 645, 694
   at Amiens 583, 586–7, 594, 597, 602
   at Bullecourt 201, 205, 208, 212–13, 219–25, 229–30, 236
   at Dernancourt 426, 430, 438–9, 442–3, 445–7, 463
   at Messines 294–6, 298
   at Outpost Line 646, 655, 657–64
   at Stormy Trench 167–9
47th 6, 41, 53, 80, 105, 109–10, 126, 129, 135, 167, 169, 182, 208, 266, 274–5, 308, 319, 342, 359, 372, 382, 385–6, 404, 480, 513, 516–17, 524, 526
   at Bullecourt 205, 213, 219, 224–5, 229–30, 232, 234, 236
   at Dernancourt 426, 428–30, 432–40, 442–3, 445–50, 452–8, 461–3, 474–5
   disbanded 526–8, 587
   at Messines 276, 280, 282–90, 295–6, 301
   at Passchendaele 349, 351–7, 371
48th 7, 28, 38, 41, 53, 74, 100, 105, 109–10, 119, 126, 129, 136, 138–9, 169, 171, 174, 266–7, 273, 311, 319, 342, 359, 372, 374–5, 385–7, 392–3, 402, 404, 480–1, 513, 524–30, 541, 561, 624–5, 629, 641, 643, 668
   at Amiens 583, 588, 597–9, 601–2, 604
   at Bullecourt 201–2, 205, 208–10, 213, 220–5, 230, 232–3, 236, 240, 541
   at Dernancourt 426, 428–30, 433–6, 438–9, 443, 445–7, 449, 452, 455–7, 461, 463, 475
   at Messines 289–91, 293–6, 298
   at Monument Wood 517–23
   at Outpost Line 646, 648–52, 659, 664–5
   at Passchendaele 349, 351–7, 371
   at Pozières 75, 77–8, 80

49th 7, 103, 130–1, 275, 309, 312, 315, 324, 343, 382, 426, 441, 443, 478, 485, 487–8, 503–4, 524, 526, 542, 561, 575, 580, 616, 638, 640–1, 677, 692, 697
   at Dernancourt 457, 460–3, 475
   at Etinehem 617–20
   at Messines 276, 280–2, 284, 288–9, 291–4, 301
   at Mouquet Farm 89, 91, 111–14, 116–19, 392
   at Noreuil 193–4
   at Polygon Wood 336–8
50th 7, 28, 100, 103, 130, 136, 146, 267, 307–8, 382, 426, 441, 443, 448, 457, 461, 463, 478–9, 484–5, 523–4, 526, 575, 616, 637–40
   at Etinehem 617–23
   at Messines 294–6, 298–9
   at Mouquet Farm 87–94, 111, 116–17, 715–20
   at Noreuil 185–95
   at Polygon Wood 336–7, 342
   at Villers-Bretonneux 487–8, 491, 493–5, 497, 499–500, 502–4
51st 7–8, 40, 101, 130, 143, 174, 213, 234, 267, 312–13, 315, 343, 359, 372, 382, 385, 426, 478–9, 526, 528, 537, 575, 580, 638–41, 693, 697
   at Dernancourt 441–3, 445–6, 459–61, 463
   at Etinehem 617–22
   at Messines 289, 291–4
   at Mouquet Farm 89–94, 107, 111, 113–16, 119, 715, 717, 719–20
   at Noreuil 185–8, 193–5
   at Polygon Wood 336–9, 372
   at Villers-Bretonneux 487, 490–503
52nd 7–8, 89, 91, 103, 130–1, 181, 184, 204, 207, 213, 234, 308–9, 336, 382, 385, 387, 426, 478, 481–2, 484, 514
   at Dernancourt 441, 443, 445–52, 455, 457–60, 462–3, 474

disbanded 525–7, 542
at Messines 276, 280–2, 284, 287–9, 291–2, 294–6, 298–9, 301
at Mouquet Farm 111–19
at Noreuil 185, 190, 193–4
at Villers-Bretonneux 487–8, 490–503
53rd 322–3
57th 169, 501
58th 171
Infantry Brigades
1st 2–3, 9, 264, 581, 602–3, 613–15
2nd 2–3, 6
3rd 2–3, 5–7, 10, 53, 69, 313–14, 324
4th 2–6, 8, 10, 17, 22, 27, 32–5, 42, 47–8, 52, 56, 59, 65, 67–9, 99, 101, 119, 124, 126, 129–31, 134, 136, 141–2, 144, 152, 173, 179, 182–3, 236, 267, 274, 307–12, 315, 318–21, 325, 342–3, 349, 358–9, 376–8, 380–2, 385–9, 392, 394, 402, 404–5, 432, 513–14, 516, 524–5, 527–8, 530–1, 538, 569, 571–2, 574–5, 578–81, 615, 623–6, 629–30, 641–3, 645–6, 666, 694–5, 700–2
at Amiens 583, 585, 588–92, 594–7, 599–603
at Bullecourt 201, 203–5, 208–19, 222–3, 225–6, 228–32, 234–6, 238–40
at Hamel 541–3, 545–7, 549–63
at Hébuterne 405–18, 477, 483, 507
at Messines 293, 299, 301
at Mouquet Farm 81–9, 103–4, 106–9
at Outpost Line 646–52, 655–7, 659–61, 665–7
at Polygon Wood 334, 336–7, 339–43
at Pozières 75, 77–8, 80
at Stormy Trench 155–67
5th 146, 151–2, 236, 253, 255, 262, 349
6th 73, 182, 184, 260–4, 314, 346–8, 374, 464, 541, 543, 545–6, 548, 555, 557, 560, 562, 683
7th 182, 184, 332, 464, 537, 622
8th 3, 33, 482, 579

9th 351, 353, 355, 445, 478
10th 616, 619
11th 481–2, 541, 543, 545–7, 549, 551–2, 556–7, 561–2
12th 5–6, 8–9, 32, 35–6, 39–42, 53, 59, 65, 68–9, 86, 89, 99–100, 102–3, 105, 110, 126, 129, 131, 135–6, 141–2, 152, 173, 179, 182–3, 199, 236, 267, 275, 307–10, 313, 316, 318–19, 321, 334, 342, 358–9, 373–4, 376, 379–82, 385–8, 392, 402, 404–5, 414, 423–5, 479–81, 483, 485, 504, 513, 516–18, 523–9, 531, 537, 549, 561, 563, 570, 572, 574, 578–81, 615, 623–5, 629–30, 641–3, 645–6, 666–7, 694–6, 700–1
at Amiens 583, 585–8, 594, 596–9, 602–4
at Bullecourt 201, 203–5, 207–10, 212–14, 216, 219–25, 229–30, 232–40
at Dernancourt 426–30, 432–49, 452–64, 473–5, 507
at Messines 274, 276, 279–80, 282–91, 293–6, 298–301
at Outpost Line 646, 649–53, 655, 657–67
at Passchendaele 349–57, 371
at Pozières 75, 77–8, 80
at Stormy Trench 167–72
13th 5, 7–10, 33, 36, 41–2, 53, 55, 65, 68–9, 99, 103, 105, 119, 126, 130–1, 136, 142–3, 152, 173–4, 179, 181–4, 213, 236, 267, 307–10, 312–15, 319, 321, 324, 342, 349, 354, 359, 374, 376, 378, 381–2, 385–8, 391, 402, 404, 414, 417, 423–6, 430–1, 440, 478–9, 481–3, 513–14, 523–8, 530–1, 537, 542, 549, 561, 563, 571, 574–5, 578, 580–1, 584, 615–16, 625, 629–30, 638–43, 666, 693–5, 697, 699, 702, 720
at Dernancourt 441–52, 455, 457, 459–64, 473–5, 507

    at Etinehem 617–23
    at Messines 274, 276, 279–82, 284, 287–9, 291–6, 298–301
    at Mouquet Farm 87, 89–94, 109–19, 714–15
    at Noreuil 184–95, 201
    at Polygon Wood 334, 336–9, 341–2
    at Villers-Bretonneux 484–504, 507
  14th 36, 61, 181, 265, 485
  15th 167, 265, 337, 486–90, 496, 500–1, 503–4, 513
Liaison Force 622–3, 625
Light Horse 7, 9, 17, 24, 123, 578, 592
Machine Gun units
  1st MG Battalion 643
  2nd MG Battalion 545
  3rd MG Battalion 545, 643
  4th MG Battalion 390–1, 405, 443, 525, 531, 545, 548, 572, 575, 578, 615, 630, 643, 645, 659, 666–7, 700, 702
  4th MG Company 10, 17–18, 52, 78, 80–1, 106, 126, 157, 167, 185, 205, 213, 222, 231, 236, 274, 310, 334–5, 341, 343, 405–8, 412–14, 514, 531, 538, 543, 545, 558–9, 572, 578, 591, 599, 601, 625, 646, 655, 659, 665
  5th MG Battalion 545, 643, 645
  6th MG Company 204–5, 215, 334, 545
  7th MG Company 204–5, 213, 545
  11th MG Company 545
  12th MG Company 17–18, 78, 80, 129, 168, 170–1, 182, 205, 213, 224, 236, 274, 276, 334–5, 342, 350–1, 354–5, 357, 426, 430, 434–5, 438–9, 443, 480, 514, 517, 531, 545, 563, 579, 598, 624, 646, 653, 657, 659, 664
  13th MG Company 18, 41, 89, 91, 111, 130–1, 137, 183, 185, 187, 191–3, 204–5, 274, 276, 281, 284, 292, 334–5, 351, 441, 445, 448–50, 457, 479–80, 482, 485, 487–8, 493, 498, 501, 504, 531, 545, 579, 588, 602, 617–19, 622, 638, 645, 651, 659
  24th MG Company 325, 334, 372, 390–1, 431, 443, 445, 453, 473–5, 479, 481–2, 501–2, 531, 541, 545, 578–9, 589, 602, 645, 651, 659
Medical (AAMC) units
  2nd Australian General Hospital 132
  4th Division Sanitary Section 22, 33, 42, 317
  4th Field Ambulance 22, 33–5, 52, 73, 132, 137–9, 146, 183, 234–5, 293, 310, 335, 342, 350, 358–9, 381, 406, 414, 423, 432, 514, 541, 547–8, 570–1, 580, 603, 644
  6th Field Ambulance 548
  11th Field Ambulance 548
  12th Field Ambulance 22, 34, 73, 132, 137–8, 146, 234–5, 310, 333, 336, 345, 349–50, 381, 432, 448, 514, 548, 580, 603, 644, 665, 677
  13th Field Ambulance 22, 34, 105, 119, 137–8, 146, 183, 234–5, 333, 336, 345, 349–50, 357, 372, 381, 432, 448, 463, 485, 499–500, 514, 541, 547, 560, 580, 603, 622, 637, 644
  15th Field Ambulance 138
Mining Battalion 52
Mortar units
  4th LTM Battery 81–3, 104, 106–7, 126, 159, 205, 213, 215, 222, 236, 310, 334, 389, 406–8, 411, 413, 543, 592, 624, 657
  7th MTM Battery 390, 523–4, 638
  8th MTM Battery 390
  12th LTM Battery 129, 170–1, 205, 225, 277, 294, 350, 353, 426, 438, 452, 517, 563, 599, 624, 657
  13th LTM Battery 89, 111–12, 185, 188–9, 277, 315, 336, 447–8, 450, 487, 617, 619, 638
  V4A HTM Battery 19, 50, 65
  X4A MTM Battery 19, 50, 65, 156, 161, 261
  X5A MTM Battery 156–7

Y4A MTM Battery 19, 50, 65, 261
Z4A MTM Battery 19, 50, 65, 261
Ordnance Corps 23, 30
Pay Corps 24
Pioneer units
   2nd Pioneer Battalion 264
   4th Pioneer Battalion 10, 20–1, 33, 41–2, 52, 65, 74, 91, 99, 110, 119, 127, 137, 146, 172, 183, 253, 276–7, 288, 301–2, 310, 312–13, 335, 343, 345, 371–2, 383, 389, 431, 440–2, 448–50, 454, 463, 480, 482, 514, 525, 528, 531, 545–6, 561, 578, 591–2, 604, 615, 644, 650, 655, 666–7, 677, 693, 695, 705
Provost Corps 24, 33, 386, 662
reorganisation (1917–18) 370–1, 378
reorganisation (infantry) 525–7
Repatriation and Demobilisation Branch 697
Service Corps (AASC) units
   4th Division Train 22–3, 42, 47–8, 70–1, 105, 134, 183, 253, 275, 314, 343, 359, 402, 416, 432, 514, 584–5, 594, 644, 666, 677–8
   7th Company 23, 134, 202, 335, 406, 416, 572, 585
   14th Company 23, 253, 359, 432, 514, 523, 535, 677, 684–5
   26th Company 23, 432, 585
   27th Company 23, 275, 432, 485, 622
   Pack Transport Troop 134, 275–6, 288, 335
Signals units
   4th Division Signal Company 10, 19–20, 33, 105, 110, 277, 279, 339, 393, 431, 442, 447–8, 477, 499, 546, 572, 637–8, 644
Training units
   I Anzac School 144
   3rd Training Battalion 526
   4th Training Battalion 323, 349, 385
   12th Training Battalion 41, 100, 526
   13th Training Battalion 181, 637
   artillery school, 4th Division 143
   infantry school, 4th Division 143
   signals school, 4th Division 143
   signals school, 12th Brigade 307
Veterinary (AAVC) units
   4th Mobile Veterinary Section 24, 140, 478
Australian Imperial Force (AIF), Second 705–6
Australian National Memorial 483
Australian Naval and Military Expeditionary Force (New Guinea) 151, 374
Austria 369, 692–3
Avesnes (-sur-Helpe) 695–6
Avre River 575
Axford, Cpl Thomas ('Jack') 554, 570
   awarded VC 569

B

Bailes, Pte Harold 634
Bailey, Pte William 507
Bailleul 48, 65, 268, 276, 278, 380–1, 388, 391, 394
Bailleulmont 402
Bailleulval 402
Baillie, Lt Gavin 528–9, 605, 698
Baillie, Lcpl James 415
Bainbrigge, Sgt Albert 661, 669
Baizieux 174, 179, 182, 253, 425, 430–2, 442, 479–80
Baker, RSM Arthur 597, 615
Baker, Lt Henry 652, 669
Baker, Maj P K 8
Balcony Trench 200, 207, 212, 215, 218, 226, 262
Bandival Farm 688
Bangalore torpedoes 539, 646
Bannister, Lcpl William 459, 476
Bapaume 70, 133, 173, 181–3, 195, 202, 235–6, 253, 401
Barber, Col George 21–2, 73, 139, 144, 146, 152, 176, 317, 327, 378, 396, 431, 477
Barly 402, 404, 418

Barnes, Lt Leonard 389
barrages, artillery. *See under* artillery
barrages, machine gun. *See under* machine guns
Barrett, Spr Charles 710
Barrie, Pte Rupert 599, 615
Bartlett, Capt Cyril 529, 572, 605, 698
Barton, Lt Irvine 385
Barton, Capt Francis 84
Basseux 402, 404, 423, 473
Bassevillebeek (stream) 381
Bates, Maj Cecil 53, 175, 326, 380, 396, 440
baths 99, 142, 179, 307, 378, 415, 473, 479, 526, 528, 571, 630, 677, 694
Battye, Lt Ernest 681
Bauchop, Sgt Loftus 660, 665
Bavelincourt 174, 179, 181, 427, 430, 485
Bavincourt 402
Baxter, Cpl Thomas 107
Bayonvillers 623
Bazentin 140–2
Bazuel 688
Beacom, Pte John 634
Bean, Charles (C E W) 4–7, 60, 70, 81, 88, 113, 132, 152, 169, 173, 203, 219, 223, 226, 239, 264, 275, 299, 311, 322, 356, 392, 406, 433–4, 438, 444, 452, 459–60, 462, 474–5, 481, 491, 497, 517–18, 523, 525–6, 528, 540, 556, 597, 604, 621, 651, 666–7, 703–4, 706–8, 716, 718–19
Beaucourt 442
Beaumetz 402
Beaumont Hamel 134
Beauquesne 404
Beaurevoir Line 679, 683–4
Beck, Cpl Horace 269
Bécordel 138–9, 146
Bécourt 73, 167, 237
Becquigny 684
Beevor, Lt Col Miles 5, 8, 112
Behencourt 430
Belgian Wood 385
Belgium 48, 123, 265, 695, 699–700
Bell Copse 661

Bellacourt 404
Bellenglise 664–5, 702
Bellevue Spur 353
Bellicourt Tunnel 679, 682–3
Belloy 666, 693
Bennetts, Cpl Frank 193, 195
Beresford, Lt William 497, 503, 506
Bergin, Father Michael 359
Berles-au-Bois 402, 404, 423
Bermingham, Gnr Francis 269
Bernafay Wood 135–7, 139, 142
Bernard, Lt Col Denis 31, 41, 81, 124, 174, 314, 325, 375, 378
Berriman, Lt Frank 282, 284
Bertangles Chateau 542, 562, 622
Bertaucourt (-les-Dames) 65
Bertrancourt 424
Beryl Wood 603
Bessell-Browne, Brig Gen A J 686
Beugnatre 235–6
Biaches 666
Bidstrup, Lt Wilfred 188
Bienvillers 404–5
Big Bill (wood) 656
Bigg, Pte Stanley 435
Bihécourt 639
Bills, Lt Arthur 619
Bing, Pte Walter 523
Bingle, Capt Ronald 592
Binning, Lcpl Walter 421
Birdwood, Gen Sir William 2–3, 9–10, 27, 33, 39, 51, 100, 103, 152, 173, 182, 206, 208, 212, 228, 267, 319, 322–3, 370–1, 384, 393, 478, 503, 528–9, 536, 572
Birr Crossroads 336, 342
Biscuit Trench 135
Bitter Wood 381
Black, Sgt Allan 118–19
Black, Lt Charles 560
Black, Maj Percy 5, 134, 165, 629
  at Bullecourt 212, 214–18
  at Mouquet Farm 83, 85–6, 108–9

Blackboy Hill 629
Blackwood, Rev Donald 500, 503, 506
Bladen, Gnr James 269
Blainey, Capt Arthur 384
Blake, Cpl George 448, 477
Blamey, Brig Gen (Field Marshal Sir) Thomas 541, 706
Blanch, Maj John 176, 396, 606, 699
Blangy-Tronville 484–5, 488, 499, 504, 514, 523, 525–6, 584
Blauwepoortbeek (stream) 276, 282–4, 287–9, 291–3, 295, 298, 300, 308, 318–19, 321
Blenkinsop, Cpl Joseph 195
Blewett, Lt Percy 476
Blinman, CSM Harold 554–5
Blunden, Pte Thomas 172
Boase, Lt Leonard 292, 296, 301, 447–8, 450, 476
Boddington, Capt Frederick 223–4, 236
Boer War 7, 16, 23, 151, 182, 266, 315, 374, 579
Bohain 684
Bois d'Aquenne 484, 486, 490–3, 500–1, 506, 513
Bois de Blangy 484–5, 499, 503
Bois-Grenier 52
Bois l'Abbé 484–5, 490
Bois Quarante 131
Boland, CSM William 231
Bolger, Lcpl Robert 448, 477
bombing, aerial. *See* aircraft and aerial warfare
Bomy 321, 360, 371, 373–4, 376
Bone, Capt William 161–3, 166, 516
Bony 683
Boswell, Cpl William 670
Bourke, Cpl Edward 592, 616
Bourlon Wood 202
Bourseville 375
Boursies 195
Bouvincourt 638, 641
Bouzencourt 545, 603
Bovelles 666
Boyes, Sgt William 626

Brack, Capt James 356, 372
Bradley, Lt Henry 109, 208, 344, 647
Brakenridge, Sgt Hamilton 497, 506
Brand, Brig Gen Charles 67, 81, 83, 86, 100, 104, 141, 152, 156, 159, 174, 204, 209–10, 212, 226, 242, 275, 312, 314, 318, 322–5, 344, 378, 385, 389, 395, 405, 408, 415–16, 541, 605, 626, 678, 692
Bray (-sur-Somme) 482, 616–18, 621, 626
Bray-Corbie road 618
Brearley, Maj Montague 372, 456
Bremner, Capt Norman 288, 290, 301
Brennan, Lcpl Patrick 417
Bresle 173, 179, 267, 425–7, 431, 440, 443, 457
Bresle Wood 426, 431
Brettingham-Moore, Capt Hubert 82
Brewster, Cpl William 635
Brick Beacon 579
Brickfields billeting area 69, 71, 86, 99, 103, 105, 109, 118–19, 123
Bridgehead Line 478–9, 530
Bridges, Maj Gen Sir William 6, 311, 313
bridging 545, 578, 590, 644, 666, 690–1
Bridgman, Capt Francis 282
Brind's Road 77, 81
British Army
   British Expeditionary Force (BEF) 48, 51, 383
   GHQ 51, 58, 131, 163, 180, 200, 265, 374–6, 378, 541, 551
   units and formations
      1 Special Company Royal Engineers 204, 209
      1st Battalion, Sherwood Foresters 490
      1st Division 642, 690
      First Army 59, 199–200, 205, 402, 625, 692
      2nd Battalion, Gordon Highlanders 187, 265
      2nd Battalion, Manchester Regiment 626
      2nd Battalion, Northamptonshire Regiment 486, 490, 500, 502
      2nd Battalion, Royal Sussex Regiment 657, 662

Index

2nd Brigade 659
2nd Division 174
II Corps 87
Second Army 51, 61, 124, 130, 271–3, 275, 280, 310, 314, 316, 318, 320, 325, 331, 333, 337, 341, 346–7, 350, 356, 504, 542, 692, 700
3rd Division 334, 336, 339
III Corps 68, 483, 486, 491, 513, 573–5, 579, 581–2, 584, 588–90, 594, 596, 613–14, 625–6, 642, 667, 678–9, 683
Third Army 184, 199–200, 205, 211, 259, 376, 394, 401–2, 404, 424, 624, 626, 689–90, 692
4th Cavalry Division 203
4th Division 125
Fourth Army 65, 68, 111, 113, 132–4, 142, 155, 173, 478, 482–4, 535, 546, 562, 573–5, 577, 579, 581, 586, 604, 613, 623–4, 626, 638–9, 642–3, 679, 681, 683–5, 687–94, 700, 707
IV Corps 405, 412, 414
5th Brigade Tank Corps 540, 547 (*See also* tanks)
5th RFA Brigade 65, 83
Fifth Army 134, 173, 184, 199–200, 205, 208, 211, 237, 243, 254, 259, 310, 314, 318, 320, 331–3, 341, 346, 348, 356, 394, 401–2, 478, 528–9
V Corps 184, 200, 265, 342, 429
6th Battalion, Lincolnshire Regiment 292
6th Division 688–90
7th Battalion, Bedfordshire Regiment 497
7th Battalion, Suffolk Regiment 82
7th Division 184, 187, 264–5
VII Corps 376, 424, 442, 478
8th Battalion, Yorkshire Regiment 77
8th Division 483–6, 499, 513
9th Division 424–5, 428, 430
IX Corps 274, 280, 380, 639, 642, 688, 690
X Corps 314, 318, 331, 337, 404
11th Company Tank Corps 203–7, 209–10, 212–15, 218, 240–1 (*See also* tanks)
11th RFA Brigade 65
XI Corps 59
12th Division 81, 87–8, 575
13th Battalion, Rifle Brigade 415
XIII Corps 182, 683, 687, 690
15th (Scottish) Division 89
XV Corps 134, 542
16th Battalion, Lancashire Fusiliers 627–8
16th RHA Brigade 578–9, 587, 596, 604
17th Division 432
18th Brigade 689
18th RFA Brigade 65
19th Battalion, Northumberland Fusliers 430, 435–6, 438
20th Division 382
XXII Corps 371
24th Brigade 485, 487
24th Field Ambulance 499
25th Division 273–4, 276, 287, 293, 299
30th Division 321
32nd Division 626, 629, 638–9, 690–2
33rd Brigade 280, 284, 292
35th Division 424, 430, 432, 436, 440
37th Division 319, 380–1, 412, 414, 416–17
41st Division 132
42nd Division 417
46th Division 666, 679, 682
47th Division 314
48th Division 90
49th Division 348
54th Brigade 487
57th Division 316
61st Division 59, 61
62nd Division 200, 203, 207, 210–12, 230, 259, 261–2, 405–12
63rd Brigade 412–13
66th Division 348
71st Brigade 689

95th RFA Brigade 440
  96th Brigade 690–1
  108th RFA Brigade 440
  111th Brigade 319
  150th RFA Brigade 440
  232nd RFA Brigade 645
  Cavalry Corps 574
  Lahore Division artillery 65, 68, 77, 81, 87–8, 91, 105–7, 112, 116, 126, 716
  Reserve Army 68, 74, 80–1, 87, 90, 111, 120, 147
Brittain, Lt Ralph 661, 669
Broodseinde, Battle of 346–7. See also Ypres, Third Battle of
Broodseinde Ridge 352, 359
Brook, Sgt Charles 358
Broom, Pte Wallace 421
Brown, Lt Herbert 405, 417
Brown, Capt Roy (A R) 481–2
Brown, Sgt William 301, 456, 476, 529, 587
Browne, Lt John (N J; 13th Bn) 394
Browne, Cpl John F (8th MTM Bty) 710
Browning, Dvr David 343
Browning, Capt Robert 109, 387–8
Browning, Neville 505, 523
Browse, Lcpl Samuel 168
Bruce, Pte Thomas 435
Bruford, Lt Alexander 539
Buckenara, Pte Clarence 601, 616
Buckler, Lt Alfred 515
Buckley, Sgt Maurice. See Sexton, Sgt Gerald
Buie, Gnr R 482
Buire 142, 146, 179, 181, 424, 426, 428, 430–1, 437, 441, 445, 455, 459–60, 463
Buire Wood 680
Buisson Ridge 656
Buissy 235
Bulgaria 690
Bullecourt 185, 190, 192–3, 202–3, 205, 207–13, 215–16, 218, 220–1, 223, 225–6, 229, 235–6, 240, 254, 258–9, 261–2, 264–5, 486, 582
  First Battle of 200–43, 260, 263, 265–7, 273, 277, 289, 308–9, 323, 392, 425, 460, 520, 541, 547, 583, 702, 706
  Second Battle of 235, 238, 259–65, 267, 273, 347, 374
Bullen, Sgt George 417
Burgess, Brig Gen William 319–20, 326, 334, 346, 350, 359–60, 371, 378, 396, 402, 440, 464, 514, 535–6, 544, 594, 606, 621, 643, 645, 680, 683, 685–8, 690, 695, 698, 701, 705
Burnett, Lt Hurtle 664, 669
Burrows, Lt William 417
Burt, Lcpl Cecil 496, 506
Burt, Lt Francis 498
Busigny 684–5, 690
Busnes 402
Bussell, Grace 37
Bussy (-les-Daours) 464, 482, 527–8, 531, 537, 541, 561, 630
Buswell, Pte Elliott 243
Butler, Col Graham (A G) 318, 703–4
Butler, Gen Sir Richard 486, 581
Buttes New British Cemetery (CWGC) 706
Byrne, Lt Leslie 658

C

Cachy 484–7, 490–1, 499–500, 502
Cachy Switch (trench) 484, 486–7, 491, 493–4, 498, 500–1, 504, 513, 517–18, 526
Caestre 47, 321, 331
Cagny 575
Calder, Sgt George 343, 706
Calder, Capt John 288, 301
Calder, Lt William 655, 669
Caldwell, Capt William 221, 598
Cambrai, Battle of 375–6, 401, 562, 604
Cameron, Lt Robert 650, 669
Camon 499, 514, 528, 563, 630
Campbell, Gnr James 269
Campbell, Spr William 590, 615
Canadian Corps 65, 109, 111, 116–20, 125–6, 200, 359–60, 369, 573–5, 578, 580–1, 584, 613, 623–5, 707

Canaples 65, 99
Cannan, Brig Gen James 5, 8, 81–2, 123, 541, 582
Caporetto, Battle of 369
Cardonette 142, 417, 513, 528, 563, 630
Carlton, Lt Herbert 339, 344
Carlton Camp 138
Carr, Maj Reginald 345, 396, 441, 606, 699
Carr, Lt William 232, 243, 520, 523
Carroll, Pte John S 565
Carter, Maj Edward 314, 395, 529, 605, 698
Carter, Capt Ernest 552–3
Carter, Lt Lavington 353
Carter, Capt Lionel 358
Carter, Pte Percy 555, 570
Carter, Lt Thomas 661, 669
Cartigny 638, 666
Cassel 48
Castles, Lt Arthur 385
casualty evacuation and clearance system 72–3, 137–8, 276, 293, 310, 335–6, 342, 349–50, 356, 414, 431–2, 447–8, 463, 499–500, 547, 560, 578, 580, 603, 644, 665. *See also* Medical units *under* Australian Imperial Force; stretcher bearers
Cateaux Wood 601, 621
Catelet 638–9, 666
Catillon 688, 690, 695
Cawley, Lt Francis 359
Célestins Wood 588, 595–6
cemeteries, military 72, 235–6, 311–12, 582, 706
Central Road (Bullecourt) 207, 213, 218, 222–3, 225, 259–63
Centre Way (Pozières) 77, 87
Cérisy (-Gailly) 575–6, 583, 586, 588–90, 594–6, 602–3, 614–16
Chalk Pit (Pozières) 70, 72, 87
Challen, Lt Leslie 477
Chantilly 153
chaplains 24, 28, 359, 500, 503
Chapman, Maj Duncan 77

Chapman, Lt Frederick 595
Charleroi 702
Charlton, Maj James 23, 176
Chateau Wood 361
Chaulnes 623
Cheese Road 135, 137
Chemin des Dames 254
Cherry, Capt Frederick 326, 395, 605, 698
Chipilly 575, 588, 590, 592, 595, 602, 614, 616, 618, 621
  Peninsula 583, 588–9, 600–1, 603, 613–16
  Spur 575, 594, 596
Christie, Lt Col Robert 7, 144, 174, 336, 339, 343, 372, 390, 395, 487, 490–1, 498–9, 501, 506, 605, 621, 693, 697–8
Chubb, Lt Eugene 656
Chuignes 626
Churchill Smith, Maj James. *See* Smith, Maj James Churchill
Circular Trench 82–3
Clark, Capt Tennyson 119, 485, 488
Clarke, Lt Jack (E J H) 256, 258
Cleeve, Capt Marwood 23
Cleland, Lt Leslie 592, 616
Clemenceau, Georges 561–3
Climpson, Lt Joseph 110, 499, 506
Cloudy Trench 155, 167, 172
Cochrane, Cpl Stanley (H S) 559
Cockshell, Gnr Sydney 269
Coigneux 415–17
Coisy 563, 630
Cole, Sgt Harry 461, 476
Coleman, CSM William 417
Coll, Sgt Patrick 443
Collins, Maj Archibald 358, 432, 477
Collins, Capt Clarence 355
Collins Copse 652
Collyer, Lcpl William 587, 616
Cologne River 638, 666
Colquhoun, Lt Colin 651, 669
Colyer, Capt Moreton 20, 74
Comforts Fund, Australian 24, 379

743

communication trenches. *See under* trenches and defence systems
communications. *See* signalling
Comrie, Dvr William 278
conferences. *See under* planning of operations
Congreve, Gen Sir Walter 424, 464
Connaughton, Pte William 456
conscription referenda 131–2, 370, 377, 525, 707
consolidation, of captured positions 82, 93, 157, 163, 167–8, 170, 172, 191, 272, 275, 277, 279, 283, 294, 331, 338–41, 412, 558–60, 588, 599, 601–2, 604, 644
Contay 427, 432
Conwell, Lt William 571, 605, 698
Cook, Pte Hubert 540
Cook, Sir Joseph 550–1
Cooke, Capt Clive 494
Cooker Trench 649
Coombs, Pte Stanley 188, 195
Cooper, Pte John (51st Bn) 344
Cooper, Sgt John C (48th Bn) 232
Cooper, Cpl William 463, 477
Copse Avenue 72, 74
Corbie 464, 478, 482, 580, 582, 584, 616–17, 620, 630
Corby, Pte Victor 166
Corlette, Lt Col James 20–1
Cornish, Lt Edmund 170, 172
Coronet Post 652
Corrigan, Lt Col John 82, 134, 380, 571, 586, 605, 658–9, 663, 669, 698
Corser, Capt Cyril 82
Cory, Capt William 441, 487, 617
Cosson, Lt Jack 80
Couchman, Maj Frank 657–8, 661, 669
Coulson, Lt Leonard 682
counter-battery fire. *See under* artillery
Courage, Brig Gen Anthony 540
Courcelette 91, 93, 104, 107, 112, 117, 174, 718
Courtine Alley 627
Courtine Trench 627–8

courts of enquiry 141, 384, 473
Cowain, Cpl Charles 418
Coward, Lt Harry 294, 301
Cowen, Pte William 355
Cowley, Lt Thomas 493, 506
Cox, Maj Arthur 56, 323
Cox, Lt Cecil 31
Cox, Maj Charles 384
Cox, Gen Sir Herbert 25, 27–8, 31, 36, 40, 50–1, 53, 56, 59, 69, 81, 83, 89, 101, 106, 110, 119, 134–5, 142, 145–7
Cox, Pte John 507
Cox, Maj Samuel 699
Cox, Capt William 596, 616
Coxen, Maj Gen Walter 544
Craies, Maj William 497–8, 502–3
Craig, Capt Leslie 380, 395, 529, 605, 698
Cream, Pte Everard 421
Crocker, Lt Cameron 499, 506
Croisilles 195
Croix du Bac 61
Croll, Sgt John 681
Crooks, CSM Thomas 172
Cross, Sgt Victor 193, 195
Crouch, Capt Harry 18, 182
Crouy 694
Crowther, Lt Col Henry 389, 395, 408–9, 411, 591, 605, 656, 660, 678, 695
Crucifix (Hébuterne) 409
Crucifix Camp 236
Cullimore, Lt Edward 18
Culpin, Lt Col Ernest 697, 699
Cumming, Capt Derwas 75, 290, 301, 449, 456, 476, 519, 522
Currie, Pte Patrick 421
Currie, Gen Sir Arthur 119, 360, 574, 624
Cutler, Maj Roy 20, 173
Cutts, Sgt Harry 114

D

D'Alton, Sgt Howard 450
Daly, Cpl Gordon 393

Dalziel, Pte Henry 553, 558
  awarded VC 569
Danman, Harry. *See* Hall, Lt Victor
Daours 484, 514, 547, 580
Dare, Lt Col Charles 4, 8, 77, 141, 144
Davey, Cpl Albert 710
Davey, Pte William 470
Davidson, Lt Eric 560
Davie, Cpl Raymond 498
Davies, Capt Ernest 377
Davies, Sgt Harry 520, 523
Davis, Lt Henry B (4th Bde staff) 389, 410, 712
Davis, Capt Henry S (46th Bn) 220–1, 236
Davis, Cpl Percy 558
Davy, Capt Francis 280
Dawes Copse 647, 651
Dawes Quarry 651
Day, Sgt Robert 418
de Low, Maj Harold 595, 658
De Seule 310, 312
Deam, Lt Thomas 379
Dean, Lt Archibald 105
Dean, Spr Arthur 590, 615
Dean Copse 649
Dean Trench 648–9, 658
Decauville tramways. *See* railways, light
deception. *See* secrecy, deception and surprise
Decline Copse 351–2, 354–5, 360
Deconinck Farm 295, 298–9
decorations 103, 109, 118–19, 152, 165–6, 169, 172, 195, 242–3, 267, 301, 343–5, 358, 380, 417–18, 476–7, 505–7, 523, 536, 569, 615–16, 668–70, 701. *See also* Victoria Cross
Decoy Wood 352
Deeble, Lt Col Arthur 372, 387
defence in depth 254, 257, 272, 332, 347, 384, 391, 401, 431, 440, 443–5, 478, 573
Defy Crossing 350
Delporte Farm 295, 298–9
Demicourt 195
demolition works 525, 531
Denham, Lt Col Howard 144, 175, 219–20, 224–5, 241, 301, 326, 380
Dennis, Lt Edwin 223
Denny, Pte Thomas 648–9, 669
Denton, Lt Col James 324, 326, 395, 457, 461, 503, 526
Dernancourt 135, 142, 414, 424–5, 427, 429–30, 440–3, 445, 449, 458, 461, 477, 479, 483, 514, 516–17, 519, 524, 527, 694
  battlefield features 427–8, 440, 443–5
  First Battle of 432–9, 507
  machine guns at 430, 434–5, 439, 441, 445, 450, 453–4, 457, 473
  railway line 428–30, 432–5, 437, 439–45, 449–50, 452, 455–63
  Second Battle of 414, 447–64, 473–7, 496, 504, 507, 526, 702
desertion 391–2, 693
Despagne Farm 288
Devine, Lt Anthony 361
Devine, William 28
Diamond, Lt James 681
Dickebusch (Dikkebus) 334
Dickinson, Maj George 41, 111, 133
Dickson, Cpl William 301
Diependaal Beek (stream) 126
Dietze, 2nd Lt Joseph 655, 674
Dinant 699–700
disbandments, of infantry battalions 388, 525–7
disciplinary issues 39, 47, 316, 391–3, 696–7, 700, 706–7
disease. *See* sickness and disease
Disney, Sgt Charles 601, 616
Docker, Capt Ernest 499, 506
Doignies 184, 195
Doignt 376
Domart (-en-Ponthieu) 65–7
Domeney, Capt William 589, 616
Donaldson, Lt George 529
Donnelly, Cpl Charles 500, 506
Donovan, Pte Percy 393
Doulieu 268, 309
Doullens 65, 123, 404, 432

Douve River 276, 299, 310, 315, 318
Dovey, Lt Reginald 558
Dow, Sgt George 108
Dowden, Sgt Kenneth 343
Downes, Lt Harry 38, 428, 662, 678, 681, 705
Dowse, Lt Col Richard 182, 314, 325, 380, 395, 529, 584, 605, 698
Drake-Brockman, Brig Gen Edmund 5, 36–7, 82, 85, 175, 212, 214, 223, 240–1, 312, 326, 336, 349, 385, 395, 413, 541, 605, 626, 641, 692, 697–8, 701–2, 706
Dranoutre 319
drill, parade ground 38, 308, 694, 696, 700, 707
Drocourt-Quéant Switch (trench) 200, 203
Droogenbroodhoek 359
Duchatel, Capt Charles 130–1, 175, 292, 301, 326, 334
Duncan, Lt Colonel John 31, 33
Dunnett, Lt Herbert 230
Dunworth, Capt David 156–7, 218, 229, 232
Durrant, Lt Col James 31, 100, 152, 159–63, 165, 167, 175, 226, 241, 320, 325, 372, 376
Dwyer, Lt John J 341, 344
   awarded VC 343–4
Dwyer, Gnr Patrick 269
Dwyer, Lt Thomas 556, 558, 570
Dyer, Lt Col John (R J) 478, 529, 606, 615, 699

E

Earl, Lt Roy 187, 195, 494, 496, 498, 506
East, 2nd Lt Joseph 354, 356
Ecoust-Longatte 184–7, 201, 213, 234, 253, 256, 258
Ecoust-St-Mein. *See* Ecoust-Longatte
Edgehill Siding CCS 432, 445–6, 450–2, 457, 462–3
Edward VIII, King 40
Edwards, Cpl Alfred 651, 669
Edwards, Lt Col Percy 315, 326, 332, 360
Egypt 2–44
Elbow, The (Pozières) 78
Eleven Trees 658

Ellem, Pte Vyvian 421
Elliot, Capt Thomas 436
Elliott, Lt Col Gilbert 19–20, 31, 110, 137, 152, 176, 302, 327, 373, 378, 396, 402, 477–8
Elliott, Brig Gen Harold ('Pompey') 337, 486, 488–90
Ellis, Pte Charles 216–17
Ellis, Gnr John 710
Elwell, Maj Laurence 560
Emerson, CSM Charles 222
Emu Alley 218, 230, 232, 243
engineers 19, 119, 142, 146, 152, 172, 174, 253, 276, 302, 341, 345, 349, 373, 382–3, 477–8, 480, 531, 559–60, 578, 586, 589, 630, 666, 702. *See also* Engineer units *under* Australian Imperial Force
   co-operation with infantry 41, 73, 102, 312, 373, 382, 559–60
   engineer stores 71–2, 134, 359, 558, 585, 644
England, Pte Ernest 243
entertainment. *See* sports and recreation
Entrepot Trench 662, 664
Epagne 536
Épehy, Battle of 667. *See also* Hindenburg Outpost Line
equipment, infantry 279
Erquinghem (-Lys) 52
escapes, by prisoners 235, 243, 473, 583
Escaufort 687
Estaires 402
Estrée-Blanche 371, 373
Étaples 309
Etinehem 616–23, 626
Evans, Maj Thomas 637, 699
Evans, Gnr W J 482
Ewan, Capt Keith 579, 606, 638, 698

F

Fabeck Graben (trench) 81, 89–91, 93–4, 106–8, 110–17, 120, 193, 392, 716–20
Falklands, Battle of the 172
Fanny's Avenue (trench) 321

Farm Trench 656
Farmer, Cpl Augustus 418
Faulkner, Lt Nevinson 663
Favreuil 183, 201, 208, 211, 236, 253, 258–9
Favril 695
Fearnside, Lt Frank 620–1
Felstead, Lt William 699
Fennell, Sgt John (Jack) 234
Fennell, Cpl Edwin 110
Ferguson, Lt Keith 174, 183
Ferguson, Capt Leon 171–2, 437–8
Ferry Post 32
Fewster, Lt George 413
Fewtrell, Lt Col Albert 52, 137, 146, 152
Field, Lcpl Ralph 587, 616
Finch, Pte Charles 592, 594, 616
Finlason, Lt Rupert 619–20
First Avenue (Pozières) 87
Fitzgerald, Maj Richard 488
Fitzpatrick, Lt Frank 128–9
Flamicourt 376, 639
Flanders region 47, 50, 123, 265, 268, 271, 274, 310, 314, 369, 380–1, 383, 402, 483, 573
flares. See under signalling
Flavion 700
Flers 133, 137, 140, 152, 154
Flesselles 135, 142
Fletcher, Capt Basil 232, 236
Fleurbaix 53
Flintoff, Lt Col Thomas 110, 136
Florennes 700
Floyd, Pte David 559, 702
Flying Corps, Australian. See AFC
Foch, Marshal Ferdinand 404, 515, 537, 573–4, 623–4
Follit, Lt Col Harold 132, 176, 327, 396, 541
Fonquevillers 405–6, 414
Forceville 424–6, 431
Ford, Maj Alfred 684, 699
Ford, Lt Col Hubert 50, 133, 143, 349, 380, 395, 442, 570–1
Fordham, Dvr Noel 477

Forgans Trench 662
Forrest, Capt Frederick 32, 175, 315
Forrester, Lcpl Arthur 500, 506
Forsyth, Capt Robert 500
Fortescue, Maj Charles 117–18, 193
Forward Observation Officers 60, 102, 131, 202, 228, 260, 263, 287, 300, 544
Fouilloy 490, 580–1, 584, 603
Fourmi Trench 662, 664
Fourteenth Alley 167, 169
Fowler-Brownsworth, Maj Walter 31, 174, 314, 325, 395, 529, 605, 697
Fox, Capt Stanley 175, 326, 390, 396, 579
Fox, Pte Patrick 243
Framerville 626
Franvillers 479
Fraser, Capt Alexander 144, 174, 325, 380, 447–50
Fraser, Maj John 20, 176, 301–2, 327, 396, 529, 606, 637–8
Fréchencourt 430, 528, 563
Frémicourt 253
French, Cpl Thomas 418
French Army 48, 173, 184, 254, 258–9, 264, 271, 318, 348, 383, 401, 503, 513, 518, 524, 529, 573–4, 623, 625, 629, 685, 690, 692
Fresnoy (-le-Grand) 694
Frezenberg 350
Friaucourt 375
Fricourt 135, 140, 182–3
Fritz's Folly (road) 141–2, 169
Froissy Plateau 626
Fromelles, Battle of 59–61, 124, 126, 181, 235, 264
Frost, Cpl Edward 384
Frostrop, Pte Patrick 634
Fruges 373
Fry, Lt Col Kenneth 372, 396, 485, 499, 541
Fugitive Alley 167
Fuhrmann, Maj Otto 322–3
Fuller, Pte Albert 614
Fulton, Gnr James 361
Fusilier Dugouts 384

G

Gallipoli campaign 1–2, 4–7, 10, 15–17, 19–21, 27–8, 36–8, 40, 55, 67, 70, 74, 77, 80, 100, 103, 117, 123, 140–1, 151, 162, 165, 172, 181, 266, 274, 309, 313–14, 320, 324, 343, 372, 374, 390, 440, 477–8, 497, 588–9, 637, 702

Galloway, Pte Ian 437

Gallwey, Pte Denver 284

Gamaches 374–6, 378

Gapaard Farm 299, 321

Gardiner, Capt George 222, 231–2

Garling, Maj Terence 448

Garnett, Maj Wade 447

Garratt, Lt Charles 599–600, 627–8

gas and gas masks 50, 124, 145, 204, 209, 258, 260, 272, 278, 333, 345, 359, 384, 388, 412, 483, 527, 549, 554–5, 563, 629–30, 641, 663, 680, 689, 702, 704

Geary, Capt John 592

Gellibrand, Maj Gen Sir John 182, 260, 262, 314, 373–4, 379–80, 382, 386–7, 395, 425–6, 430, 439, 447, 455, 460, 480–1, 516, 526–8

Gelston, Lt Arthur 650, 669

George V, King 622, 696

Gerler, Gnr Carl 691, 710

German Army
  Aisne Offensive 529
  August 1914 Offensive 48, 687, 700
  final defeat of 692–3
  Flanders Offensive 1918 480, 483, 504
  March 1918 Offensive 383, 394, 401–2, 404–11, 414, 423–5, 462, 476, 507, 525, 638, 642, 678
  Marne Offensive 573
  retirement (1917) 174, 179, 181–2
  retreat to Hindenburg Line (1918) 638
  units and formations
    1st Guard Reserve Division 298
    3rd Naval Division 442–3
    4th Guard Division 108, 158, 504
    6th Bavarian Reserve Division 60
    27th Württemburg Division 215, 225, 230–1, 582
    50th Prussian Reserve Division 54, 449, 462
    63rd Infantry Regiment 78
    69th Rhineland Regiment 717
    76th Reserve Infantry Regiment 386
    119th Reserve Infantry Regiment 191
    230th Reserve Infantry Regiment 449, 462
    239th Division 385
    362nd Regiment 163
    IX Reserve Corps 74
    Jäger Division 517, 522–3

Gheluvelt Plateau 310, 318, 331, 333

Gibson, Lt Col Arthur 381, 396, 606, 677

Gibson, Capt Gregory 355, 436

Gill, Capt George 488

Gillemont Farm 681

Gillies-Reyburn, Lt D 31, 174

Gilmour, Pte Edward 507

Ginchy 111

Glasfurd, Brig Gen Duncan 6, 8–9, 36, 53, 75, 102, 131
  death of 135, 137

Glasgow, Capt Robert 344, 554, 558, 570

Glasgow, Maj Gen Sir William (T W) 7–8, 18, 36, 53, 69, 90, 111, 143–4, 174–5, 182, 185, 193–5, 289–92, 294, 309, 326, 342, 373, 380, 384–5, 395, 402, 423, 426, 444, 457, 484–91, 502, 526, 542, 574

Gledhill, Capt Archibald 462

Glencorse Wood 331

Glisy 484–7, 514, 528, 563

Gocher, Sgt William 170, 172

Godewaersvelde 380–1

Godley, Gen Sir Alexander 2–3, 33, 40–1, 53, 273–4, 289, 307

Goldsmith, Sgt Stanley 168–9

Gommecourt 406, 408, 412

Goodger, Cpl Mainard 553, 570

Goodsall, Lt William 453–4

Goodwin, Sgt George 557, 570
Goodwin's Post 135, 141, 171
Gordon Dump 71–2
Gore, Capt Maxwell 103, 190, 194
Goss, Lt Cecil 417
Gough, Gen Sir Hubert 68, 74, 80, 147, 173, 184, 199, 203, 205–6, 208, 211–12, 237–8, 243, 310, 320
Gouy 402, 404, 423
Gove, Sgt Andrew 166
Graham, Lt James 462, 476
Graham, Capt Thomas 343
Grand Fayt 695
Gray, Pte James 435
Grease Trench 135, 155, 157, 160, 167, 171
Greenwood, Pte Harold 658, 669
Gregson, Lt William 18
grenades, hand 37–8, 56–7, 68, 93, 105, 107–8, 124, 128, 158–60, 162–4, 167–9, 180, 188–9, 191, 218, 222–4, 229, 231–2, 259, 263–4, 282, 292–4, 296, 393, 411, 438, 442, 450, 492, 520, 539, 553, 623, 627–8, 648, 660, 663
grenades, rifle 38, 143, 160, 163–4, 167–71, 180, 222, 296, 393, 412, 492, 580, 626, 628, 649
Gressaire Wood 614, 617, 619, 621
Grieveson, Lt Peter 18
Griffith, Lt Tom 660, 669
Gueudecourt 133, 135, 137, 154–5, 171. *See also* Stormy Trench
Guillacourt 625
Guillemont 67, 111, 113
Guthrie, Cpl Wilfred 492, 506

H

Hagan, Pte John 600, 616
Hagevole, Pte John 634
Haig, Field Marshal Sir Douglas 51, 180, 212, 265, 271–3, 310, 320, 347, 369–71, 383, 528, 551, 573–4, 624
Haking, Gen Sir Richard 59–61
Hall, Maj George 658
Hall, Lt John 586
Hall, 2nd Lt Victor 35, 409, 411, 417
Hall, Lt William 496
Hallencourt 535–7, 544
Halloy (-les-Pernois) 65, 69
Hallue River 464, 480–3, 531, 572, 630
Hamel 496, 530–1, 537–8, 543, 580–1, 603
  Battle of 540–63, 569, 573–4, 576, 642–3, 702
Hamel Wood 538, 554, 559
Hamelet 581
Hamill, Cpl Hugh 601
Hammond, Sgt Frederick 202
Hancock, Capt Frank 497
Hancourt 638, 644
Hand, Capt John 293
Hangard Wood 484, 487, 497, 502–3, 515, 518, 575
Hangest-sur-Somme 535
Hannah, RSM Robert 117–18
Hannay, Maj Denis 371–2, 436
Hannescamps 405, 423
Hansen, Capt Stewart 162, 164
harassing fire, artillery and machine guns 54–5, 71, 86, 91, 112, 126–7, 138, 145, 153, 202, 254, 320, 333–4, 382, 412, 524, 549, 551, 623–4, 690
Harbonnières 623, 625
Harburn, Capt William (Billy) 491, 494, 496–8, 500, 506, 622
Hargicourt 667
Harington, Gen Sir C H ('Tim') 271
Harp, Pte Herman 634
Harper, Gen Sir George 414
Harris, Capt Norman 589
Harrison, Sgt Edward ('Darky') 539
Harrison, Lt John 448
Hart, Lt Byrne 282
Harvey, Pte James 663
Harwood, Maj Ross 108–9, 336, 349, 626, 641–2
Hatton, Lt Neville 494, 506

Haut Allaines 376
Hawker, Lt Arden 640
Hayes, CQMS Jack 614
Hazebrouck 123, 371, 480
Heading, Sgt James 355–6, 358
Heart Copse 658
Hébuterne 404–18, 423, 431–2, 477, 507, 513, 569
Heffer, Capt Thomas 582
Heilly 135
Hélène Ridge 642, 657
Helyar, Pte Reginald 496, 506
Hendecourt (-les-Cagnicourt) 200, 212, 228, 241, 259
Henderson, Sgt Basil 461, 476
Henderson, Lt Douglas 498
Henderson, Cpl Leonard 470
Henderson, Capt Robert (Bob) 107, 516
Heneker, Maj Gen Sir William 484–6
Hénencourt 173, 425–7, 432, 448
Henley, Lt Col Frank 176
Hennessy, Capt Victor 23, 176
Henry, Pte George 438
Henwood, Maj Horace 387–8
Herbecourt 666
Hérissart 69
Herleville 626
Hermaville 402
Hermies 195
Herring, Brig Gen Sydney 6, 8, 135, 152, 169, 175, 290, 296, 326, 349, 475, 527–8, 542, 605, 617, 621, 698, 701
Hesbécourt 638
Heslop, Maj George 275
Heydon, Lcpl Cleve 592, 616
Heywood, Capt Reginald 478, 606, 699
Hilary, Capt Wilfred 353
Hill, Lt Samuel 652
Hill 63 (Ypres) 273, 276, 299, 310–11, 313
Hill 104 (Villers-Bretonneux) 483–4, 530
Hilt Trench 141
Hindenburg, Field Marshal Paul von 179
Hindenburg Line 179–80, 182, 184, 191, 193, 196, 199–204, 206, 208–9, 211–12, 214–15, 225, 228–9, 231, 235, 237–8, 240, 254, 258–60, 262–4, 375–6, 486, 638–9, 641–2, 655, 665–6, 678–9, 694
  Battle of the 680–3
Hindenburg Outpost Line 642–5, 680
  Battle of the 646–69, 678–9, 695, 704
Hines, Lt Hubert 652
Hines, Lt Walter 582
Hinton, Maj Frederick 325, 443, 474
Hirondelle River 253, 256
Hoare-Nairne, Brig Gen Edward 65
Hobbs, Lt Gen Sir J J Talbot 542, 697
Hockey, Pte Alfred 618
Hodge, Lt Ernest 619
Hogg, Lcpl Robert 663
Hoggarth, Lt William 88, 188
Holdsworth, Lt Col Albert 23, 176, 275, 327, 396, 584–5, 606, 678
Hollebeke 381
Holloway, Lt Bernard 192
Holman, Capt Jack 653, 669
Holman, W A 311
Holmes, Maj Gen William 146–7, 151–2, 159, 174, 183, 210, 212, 214, 267–8, 289–90, 295, 312
  death of 311
Holt, Sgt Joseph 647
Honnechy 684
Hook, Spr George 590, 609
Hope Wood 586
Horne, Lt William 652
horses and mules 18–20, 23–5, 42–3, 47, 133–4, 138, 140, 181, 202, 275, 341, 343, 347–8, 350, 359–60, 378, 416, 585, 595–6, 615, 653, 657, 681, 688, 701. *See also* Veterinary units *under* Australian Imperial Force
  race meetings 536, 572
Hourges 575, 580
Howard, Lcpl Albert 470
Howden, Maj Harold 169, 171–2, 311–12

Hughes, Lt Col Francis 16, 145, 152, 155
Hughes, Lt Leslie 652
Hughes, W M ('Billy') 550–1, 561, 641
Hume, Pte Percy 166
Hummerston, Capt Horace 215, 232, 242
Hun House (Messines) 284
Hundred Days, The 604
Hun's Walk (Hamel) 554, 557
Hun's Walk (Messines) 276, 283, 288, 291, 294, 319
Hunt, Lt Ralph 589–90, 615
Hunter, Gnr Gordon 269
Hunter, Pte John 343, 706
Hurcombe, Lt Col Frederick 5, 7–8, 92, 100
Hurd, Capt Edmund 452, 474, 476
Hutchings, Sgt Harry 602
Hyman, Maj Arthur 529
Hynes, Capt John (Jack) 553, 651, 669

I

Imlay, Lt Col Alexander 274–5, 288, 290, 326, 356, 358, 372, 385, 395, 426, 428–30, 434, 436–8, 454–5, 474–6, 524, 526, 528
Imlay, Capt Norman 224, 242, 275, 519
influenza 546, 670, 688. *See also* sickness and disease
Inglis, Maj William 32, 175, 275
International Post 527
Inverness Copse 331
Isonzo River, Battles of 369
Italy 51, 153, 369, 383, 517

J

Jack, Lt Tom 453, 455, 476
Jacka, Capt Albert 4, 6, 78, 86, 134, 144, 166, 266–7, 299, 312, 323–4, 527, 704–5
  awarded VC 4
  at Bullecourt 201, 203, 207–9, 213–16, 223, 240, 242
  at Polygon Wood 339–42, 344–5
  at Pozières 78–80
Jacob, Maj Ross 92
James, Maj Edward 24, 140, 176, 327, 396, 478, 529, 606, 699

James, Lt Col John 697, 699
James, Sgt Percival 226, 243
Jarman, Pte Leonard 507
Jarvis, Pte Keith 523
Jean Wood 586, 603, 617
Jeancourt 641, 667
Jeffreys, Lcpl John 384
Jeffries, Capt Clarence 353
Jeffries, Maj Lewis 93, 146, 176, 327, 381
Jenner, Gnr James 269
Jensen, Sgt Joergen 188–9, 196
  awarded VC 195
Joffre, Gen Joseph 154
Johanson, Sgt Andrew 189
John, Pte William 507
Johnson, Spr Arthur 710
Johnson, Lt John ('Jack') 344–5, 410, 417, 516
Johnston, Lt Col Charles 81, 144, 159, 161, 174, 312, 349, 384, 389, 542, 605, 637, 641, 647, 651, 698
Johnston, Brig Gen G J 332
Johnston, Pte William 435, 438
Johnstone, Sgt Archibald 665
Johnstone, Capt John 175
Jonc de Mer Farm 686, 688
Jones, Lcpl Harold 650, 669
Jones, Capt John 357
Jones, Cpl Oliver 301
Jones, Capt Reginald 299
Jones, Lt Samuel 223, 232
Joseph, Maj Coleman 302, 638, 699
Joye Farm 281
Julin, Lt James 234

K

K Trench 70, 73, 77, 87
Kandahar Farm 276
Kane, Pte William 614
Kay, Lt Henry 494, 497
Kay, Capt Francis 282
Kealy, Sgt Richard 598, 615
Keersebrom 381

Keiberg, The (ridge) 348, 351, 360
Keid, Lt Leonard 112
Keighley, Capt Arthur 133, 144, 174, 314
Kell, Lt Ralph 161
Kellaway, Capt Charles 342, 344
Kelly, Cpl John 269
Kemmel 319, 321, 381, 483
Kemmis, Capt Ernest 313, 325, 395, 529, 572
Kemp, Lt Arthur 586, 616
Kendall, Lt Col William 24, 176, 275, 327, 396, 478
Kennedy, Maj Basil 132, 176
Kennedy, Capt William 446, 451–2, 457, 459–60, 462, 476, 496
Kerr, Lt John 647
Ketterer, Lt Victor 647, 669
Kidney Trench 538, 554
Kilpatrick, Pte Leigh 291, 301
King, Pte Cecil 523
King, Lt Claude 18, 598
King, Lt Col Giffard 16, 155, 175, 201, 240, 253, 286, 315
King, Sgt Walter 193, 195
Kingel, Lcpl Eric 279
Kingsford Smith, Capt Charles 20
Kipling, Rudyard 343, 583
Kirkpatrick, Pte Robert. *See* Kilpatrick, Pte Leigh
Knight, Pte Charles 218, 243
Knight, Spr Frederick 710
Knoll, The 680–1
Knox, Maj George 293
Kokoda Track 105, 705
Kollmann Trench 106–7, 111, 113, 117
Kruisstraat 343

L

La Boiselle 72, 105, 109
La Chaussée 143, 146
La Clytte (De Klijte) 382
La Crèche 48, 300
La Groise 695
La Haie Menneresse 685
La Herlière 402, 405
La Neuville 616
labour, by troops. *See* working parties
Lackman, Capt Royal 571, 605, 698
Lagnicourt 184–6, 190, 192–4, 201, 254–7
  Battle of 255–8
Lahoussoye 464, 479, 514, 528
Lalor, Cpl Vivian 656, 669
Lamotte-Brebière 485, 630
Lamprell, Cpl Harry 589
Landrecies 691–2
Lane, Cpl Charles 473
Lane, Lt Col Denis 112, 116, 175, 181
Lane, Lt Frederick 436
Langdon, Gnr Lewis 269
Larch Wood 381
Lard Trench 141
Larkins, Lt Stanley 389
Lavarack, Lt Gen Sir John D 378–9, 393, 395, 424–5, 444, 529, 542, 605, 698, 701, 705
Laviéville 425–31, 439–40, 442–3, 445, 447, 457, 463
Lawrence, Pte Alfred 647, 669
Lawrence, Pte Harold 634
Lawrence, Gen Sir Herbert 27
Lawrence, Sgt James 433–4
Lawson, Cpl Sydney 664, 669
Le Cateau 687, 690, 692, 695
Le Catelet Line 679, 682–3
Le Hamel. *See* Hamel
Le Havre 47, 700
Le Mesge 666
Le Messurier, Lt Col Frederick 580, 678, 692
Le Quennelet Grange 688
Le Sars 181
Le Sart 695
Le Verguier 641, 643, 645–8, 656, 658, 666–7
Leake, Capt Clifton 529
Leane, Capt Allan 221–4, 230, 232–3, 235, 242–3, 541
Leane, Maj Benjamin 210, 541

Leane, Brig Gen Raymond 5, 7–8, 75, 77, 171, 175, 208, 210, 220–1, 225, 232, 237, 266, 291, 308–9, 316, 326, 356, 358, 380, 385–7, 395, 423, 426, 428–9, 444, 455–6, 460–1, 473–5, 480–1, 516–18, 522, 526–8, 541, 570–1, 603, 605, 659, 662, 667, 679, 698, 701
leapfrogging, by units 101, 276, 332, 336, 555, 643, 652, 657, 679, 681–2, 684, 686
 at Battle of Amiens 575–6
Lee, Lt Col Geoffrey 6, 8, 41, 144
Lee, Maj Joseph 295
Lehane, Sgt William 622
Leith, Lt Eric 660–1, 669, 703–4
Lena Wood 586
Leonard, Pte James 516
Les Alençons 547
Leslie, Capt Francis 217
Leunig, RSM James 412, 418
L'Evêque Wood 689–90
Lewers, Maj Hugh 541
Lewis, Lt Col Eric 136, 175, 274
Lewis, Cpl Herbert 574
Lewis guns 37–8, 85, 88, 94, 102, 117–18, 124, 131, 138, 141, 157–9, 161–3, 180, 187, 222–3, 232, 257, 291, 313, 355, 402, 412–13, 433–4, 436, 445, 447–8, 450, 452, 454–6, 459, 494, 496, 553, 558, 583, 587, 591–2, 601, 648–53, 656, 658, 660
Liaison Force 622–3, 625
Liddicoat, Sgt Thomas 501–2, 507
Liessies 696
Lihons 602, 613, 615–17, 623–4, 626
Lihou, Sgt James 558, 570, 648–9, 669
Lihu Farm 625
Lille 235
Lily Trench 656
Lind, Maj Frank 381, 396, 529, 606, 637
Lines, Pte Arthur 649, 669
Linney, Spr Thomas 477
Linsley, Lt Gordon 461, 476
Lintott, Lt Arthur 595
Lisbourg 360, 371, 373

Little Bill (wood) 656
Littler, Capt Charles 114
Livesey, Lt George 623
Livingston, Lt Francis 651
Livingstone, Pte Thomas 541
Lloyd, Capt Thomas 606
Lloyd, Lt Col Hardress 205
Lloyd George, David 383, 561
Lobegeiger, Dvr John 611
Locke, Capt William 31, 144
Lockwood, Cpl Sergia 418
Locre (Loker) 382, 388
Lodge, Gnr Arthur 269
Long, Capt Charles 395, 605, 698
Long Copse 656
Longatte. *See* Ecoust-Longatte
Longpré 630
Longueval 137, 146
Loo Long, Lcpl William 477
Lorenzo, Lt Col Francis 5, 7–8, 103, 112, 117–18
Louch, Capt Thomas (Tom) 114, 143, 374, 386–7, 393, 483, 485–8, 571, 605, 694, 698
Loudon, Lt James 617
Loupart Wood 181
Loutit, Lt Col Noel 192, 195, 336–7, 637, 652, 677, 695, 698
Louverval 184, 195
Loveday, Capt Arthur 389, 395
Lovett, Capt J H 116, 118
Luce River 575
Ludendorff, Gen Erich 179, 383, 573, 597, 690
Lumbres 61
Lunt, Pte Nathaniel 392–3, 665
Lydster, Lt Tom 599–600
Lynas, Capt William (Bill) 82, 86, 107, 109–10, 266–7, 539–40, 554–5, 570, 583, 597, 599–601, 628–9, 642, 656, 677
Lynch, Pte Edward 139, 170, 279, 283
Lynch, Sgt Patrick 558–9, 570
Lyon, Pte Herbert 601, 616
Lys River 300

M

McBurnie, Capt Edward 622
McCabe, Lt Michael 641
McCarthy, Lt Lawrence 628–9, 647
  awarded VC 629
McCay, Maj Gen Sir James 28, 36, 61
McClean, Lt Col Frederick 695, 699
McCoy, Sgt Percival 418
McDonald, Pte Duncan 655, 670
MacDonald, Capt Norman 161–2
McDonald, Gnr Wilfred 269
McDougall, Sgt Stanley 432–4, 438, 454–5, 476, 526–7, 529
  awarded VC 438, 527
McDowall, Lt Max 233, 520–1, 523
McDowell, Lt George 160, 162–3, 166
McGregor, Col Roy 132, 541, 547, 570, 606, 697, 699
McGuire, Lt Norman 647
machine guns 13, 17, 37, 54, 138, 211, 341, 439, 453, 545, 577, 645. *See also* Machine Gun units *under* Australian Imperial Force
  barrages 205, 213, 215, 261, 276, 278, 280, 333–5, 337, 342, 351, 355, 390, 412, 538, 545, 550, 552, 577, 579, 585, 602, 643, 645–6, 651, 660–1, 680
  organisation 10, 17, 325, 390
Macindoe, Maj R H F 176, 275
McIntosh, Capt Robert 217
McIntyre, Lt Thomas 293, 296
Mackay, Brig Gen Iven 581
Mackay, Capt John 665, 669
Mackay, Capt Joseph 656, 661
McKay, Lt Robert 665
McKenna, Maj Cyril 275
McKenzie, Pte George 507
McKillop, Capt Robert 407–8, 417, 592
McKinley, Lt Harry 215
McLeod, Capt Albert 108–9
Macleod, Cpl Hugh 687
Macnaghten, Lt Col Charles 266
Macphail, Sgt Donald 256, 258
McPherson, Maj Herbert 309
McPherson, Lt Werner 156, 161
McQueen, Pte Frederick 164, 166
McRae, Maj Henry 41–2, 143, 174, 182
Macrae, Maj Norman 146, 343
McSharry, Lt Col Terence 5, 123, 156, 159, 175, 241, 321, 326, 339, 385, 395, 553, 558, 560, 570
  death of 582
McTye, Cpl Thomas 355–6, 358
Madame Wood 625, 627, 647
Magee, Lcpl John 187, 195
Magilligan Camp 381
Maher, Lcpl Peter 470
Mahsama 33, 35
Maiden, Lt Herbert 170
Malard Wood 588, 596
Malcolm, Brig Gen Neill 237
Mallyon, Pte Alfred 519
Mametz 135, 140–1, 146, 152, 167, 173, 181–2, 236
Manning, Capt Godfrey 604
Margolin, Maj Eliazar 275, 322
Marks, Col Alexander 21–2, 146, 152
Marks, Lt Col Douglas 226, 320, 325, 336, 372, 377, 391, 395, 405, 408, 415, 543, 555, 605, 648, 668, 692, 695, 705, 717
Marmo, Pte Joe 591
Marne, First Battle of the 48
Marne, Second Battle of the 573–4
Marper, Capt George 556, 570
Marquion 235
Marsden, Lt Col Thomas 645
Marseille 42–3, 47
Marshall, Sgt William 602
Martin, Capt Allan 605, 657, 669, 698
Martin, Capt David 18, 274, 326, 439
Martyn, Lt Col A M 152
Mash Valley 70
Massey, Cpl Frank 417
Maxwell, Capt Arthur 7, 113, 116, 119, 280–2, 284, 287, 292, 295, 299, 301, 423

Maxwell, Capt Duncan 7, 113–14, 116–19, 183, 313, 325, 395, 528, 705
May, Lt Wilfred 481–2
Mayersbeth, Capt Joseph 290
Maywood, Sgt Ernest 358
Mazinghien 688
Méaulte 436, 439
medical services 21–2, 72–3, 253, 276, 293, 335–6, 349–50, 357, 381, 431–2, 463, 547, 560, 578, 580, 603, 637, 644, 665. *See also* Medical (AAMC) units *under* Australian Imperial Force
Meikle, Lt Col Alexander 22, 132
Meldrum, Gnr William 269
Meldrum, Cpl James 493
Mendoza, Lt Clifford 288
Mengersen, Cpl Irwin 623
Menin Road 331, 335–6, 342, 349–50
  Battle of the 331–5 (*See also* Ypres, Third Battle of)
Méricourt (-l'Abbé) 72, 424
Méricourt (-sur-Somme) 596, 600–2, 613, 615–16, 620–1
Merris 47–8, 53, 65, 381, 388, 394, 402
Messines (Mesen) 51, 268, 271–2, 276, 289, 310, 380, 402, 480
  Battle of 268, 278–302, 307–8, 322, 331, 343, 447, 480, 577
Meteren 387–8
Meuse River 699–700
Michell, Gnr Sidney 269
Miles, Sgt Alfred 278
Miles, Maj Charles 182, 314
Mill Spinney 648
Millar, Capt John 283
Millencourt 425–8, 430, 432, 439, 443, 445, 450, 461, 463
Miller, Spr Roy 560, 570
Mills, Capt Clarence 173, 176
Mills, Lt Gordon 107, 312
Milne, Maj Edmund 314, 325
Milne, Capt George 443

Minchin, Lt Basil (J B) 344, 554–5, 570, 599–600, 704
minefields 665
mining 131, 271–2, 278
Mirams, Maj James 74, 92
Miraumont 174
mist and fog 84, 171, 384, 401, 432, 434, 438, 447–8, 450, 452–3, 456, 476, 551–3, 584–6, 646, 648–50, 680
Mitchell, Sgt A J 591
Mitchell, Lt Alan 529
Mitchell, Capt Albert 80, 175, 326
Mitchell, Capt George 127, 153, 169, 209, 221, 233–4, 243, 266, 291, 393–4, 429–30, 433–4, 438, 456, 519, 521–3, 701, 706
Mitchell, Gnr William 269
Mitchener, Gnr Charles 269
Moascar 2, 5, 33, 35
Moislains 376, 378
Molain 686
Monash, Gen Sir John 3–4, 8, 27–8, 35, 37, 52, 56–7, 67, 123, 172, 273, 313, 322, 424, 528, 536–7, 540–3, 546–7, 551, 556, 561–2, 572–7, 582, 604, 616–17, 622, 638, 642, 644, 655, 667, 678–9, 681, 697, 700, 702
Monchiet 402
Mont St Quentin 638
Montauban 135, 140, 146
Montbrehain 683–4
Montgomery, Gen Sir A A ('Archie') 581, 613
Montigny 424
Monument Farm 484, 487, 503, 518–21, 524
Monument Wood 484, 496–8, 500, 502–3, 513, 515–24, 573, 575
Moore, Gnr Harold 269
Morbeque 371
Morchies 256
Morcourt 575, 583, 586–7, 590–2, 594, 597, 599–600, 602–3, 613, 615, 617
Morell, Maj Roy 18, 130, 174–5, 326, 395, 423, 485, 487–8, 571
Moriarty, Cpl Jack 589

Morlancourt 439, 537, 579, 582
Mormal Forest 690, 692
Morris, Lt Robin 222, 233
Morris, Capt Sydney 175, 326, 336
Morrison, Cpl Edward 450, 477
Morrison, Lt Col Harold 372, 383, 396, 482
Morshead, Lt Gen Sir Leslie 389
mortars 18–19, 43, 50, 55–6, 65, 127, 129, 132, 138, 261, 268, 278, 341, 389–90, 523–4, 538, 579, 638, 684. See also Mortar units *under* Australian Imperial Force
Mortimer, Gnr Ralph 269
Moseley, Col Arthur 477, 529, 541, 570
Moseley, Capt Edgar 408
Moser, Gen von 254
Moss, Bdr Joel 269
Motor Ambulance Convoy 432
motor transport 23, 71–2, 135, 307, 309, 345, 360, 402, 404, 417, 473, 477, 513, 574, 630, 638, 666, 693
Mott, Maj John 220–2, 233, 235, 583, 598, 616
Moulden, Capt Arnold 529, 697–8
Moulin Sans Souci 203, 259
Mount Sorrel, Battle of 65
Mouquet Farm, battles at 70, 81–94, 99, 101–20, 124, 134–5, 140, 143, 146–7, 152, 165, 173, 188, 194, 242, 261, 268, 275, 391, 425, 713–20. See also Pozières, battles at
   battlefield features 84, 90–1, 114
Moyes, Maj A G ('Johnny') 221, 387, 402, 641
Moylan, Cpl James 477
mud 105, 127, 133–5, 137–41, 152–3, 169–71, 311, 318, 321, 346–8, 350–3, 356–7, 384, 411. See also weather conditions
Muir, Lt Alexander 171, 282, 301
Muir, Cpl Percy 165–6
Mundell, Maj William 156–9, 321
Munster Alley 77, 89
Muriel, Lt Arthur 660–1
Murray, Gen Sir Archibald 32, 41–2
Murray, Lt Harold F 47

Murray, Lt Col Harry (Henry W) 4–5, 134, 266, 320, 377, 390–1, 396, 405, 443, 474, 545, 606, 629, 645, 678, 682, 699, 701, 706
   awarded VC 165–6
   at Bullecourt 217–19, 222–3, 226, 229, 231–2, 239, 242
   at Mouquet Farm 93–4, 107–9, 165, 716–19
   at Stormy Trench 160–5
Murray, Lt Robert 170, 172, 279
Murray, Sgt William (16th Bn) 601, 616
Murray, Sgt William (52nd Battalion) 450

N

Nameless Farm 409–10
Naours 67, 143, 146
Nauroy 682, 684
Neuve Église (Nieuwkerke) 274, 278, 307, 309, 321, 388, 394
New Zealand and Australian Division. See NZ & A Division
New Zealand Division 3, 32–3, 53, 56, 273–4, 276, 279–80, 286–8, 293, 310, 315, 317, 346, 350, 353, 371, 407–9, 411–15, 417, 707
   artillery 61, 268, 273, 276–7, 287, 314
Newell, Lt Col John 132
Nicholls, Pte Richard 587, 616
Nicholson, Capt Arthur 174–5, 326, 395, 487, 571, 693, 698
Nielsen, Pte Hans 172
Nivelle, Gen Robert 154, 173, 184, 258, 264
Noble, Dvr Jock 278
Nommensen, Lt Christian 436
Nonne Boschen 331
Noreuil 182–95, 201, 209–10, 213–14, 225, 228–9, 234, 253, 255–6, 258, 267, 496
Norman, Capt Edwin 373
Norman, Maj Reginald ('Babe') 374, 379, 387, 395, 425, 455, 518, 603, 605, 615, 678, 693, 697
North, Maj Francis 224, 230, 587, 616
Northcott, Pte Wilfred 507
Northey, Pte James 555, 570
NZ & A Division 2–3, 5, 22, 273, 702

O

O'Brien, Lt Jack 447, 477
observation, tactical 60, 85, 133, 167, 271, 346, 408, 428, 437, 439, 483, 530, 538, 642, 662
O'Connor, Lcpl Murray 592, 616
O'Connor, Pte William 188
Odd Support Trench 298
Odd Trench 282, 288, 294
Odious Trench 281-2, 292
Odour Trench 281, 287
O'Dowd, Pte Percy 409
off-duty activities. *See* sports and recreation
officers, selection of 9, 124, 209, 266, 309, 315-16, 377, 388, 707
OG Lines (Bullecourt) 199, 216-18, 221-6, 230-3, 259-65
OG Lines (Pozières/Mouquet Farm) 70, 75, 77-8, 89-91, 93-4, 106, 199
Olive, Bdr George 269
O'Meara, Sgt Martin 83, 85-6, 705
  awarded VC 86
Omignon River 638-40
O'Neil, Cpl Gregory 354
Oneux 133
Onoto Trench 661-2
Oosttaverne 272, 274, 279, 281, 287, 300
Orchard Trench 647
O'Reilly, Lt Bernard 18
O'Reilly, Lt Peter 260, 263-4
Orr, Capt Robert 215-16
Ors 689, 695
O'Ryan, Gen John 682
Ostend 272
Ostrich Avenue 218, 222, 230
Oswald, CSM William ('Jerry') 592, 616
Ouderdom 360
Oudezeele 346
Owen, Capt Norman 195, 678
Owen, Lt Wilfred 691
Owl Support Trench 282, 290, 298
Owl Trench 282-3, 286, 289-91, 294-6, 298, 308
Oxygen Trench 282, 290, 308

P

parades, ceremonial 101, 267, 318, 371, 536, 637, 695
Paris, Lcpl Wilfred 339
Park, Capt Robert 302, 339
Park Lane (trench) 81-2, 111
Parker Copse 650
Parkes, Gnr Joseph 269
Parks, Lt Col Edward 677, 698
Parrish, Pte Thomas 556
Parsonage, Lt William 222
Parsons, Gnr Albert 269
Parsons, Lcpl Hamilton 235, 243
Pascall, Gnr Albert 269
Passchendaele (Passendale) 346, 483
  Battles of 347, 349-57, 360, 369, 380, 385-6, 570, 637, 668 (*See also* Ypres, Third Battle of)
Passmore, Pte Henry 498, 506
Paton, Brig Gen J 541
patrolling 54, 84, 126, 129, 138, 153, 174, 201, 203, 206-9, 298-9, 311-12, 315, 319-20, 382, 384, 386-7, 416, 447, 515, 541, 614, 622, 624-5, 639-40, 662
Patten, Cpl Wilfred 218, 232, 243
Patterson, Lcpl William 355
Pattrick, Capt Kenneth 592
Paul, Lt Col Harold 275, 277, 292, 309, 480
Payne, Cpl George 628-9
peaceful penetration 416, 573, 625
Pear Trench 538-9, 550, 552-3, 558, 560, 569
Pearce, Senator George 27
Peck, Lt Col John 6, 32, 41, 100, 127, 144, 175, 223, 240-1, 275, 322, 389
Pen Trench 661-2, 664-5
Pengelly, Pte William 523
Pennefather, Lt Reginald 448, 476
Péronne 376, 381, 401, 638-9, 666, 678
Perry, Lt Col Stanley 371, 395, 430, 527-8, 597, 599, 605, 615, 698
Perry, Lt Stuart 458-9
Pershing, Gen John 551

Petillon 53
Petit Cambon 485
Petrol Lane (trench) 135
Phelan, Pte Joseph 438
Philippeville 699–700
Phillips, CSM Douglas 602
Phillips, Brig Gen O F 684
Phillips, Sgt Walter 558, 570
Phillips, Lt Norman 490
Pianto, Pte James 507
Piccadilly Farm 128
Picquigny 666, 694
Pidcock, Lt John 461, 476
Piercy, Lt Eric 601, 616
Pieumel Wood 656
pigeons, carrier. *See under* signalling
Pilckem Ridge 310, 318
pillboxes 272, 278, 281–3, 293–6, 298, 308, 310, 332–3, 339–40, 346, 352–3, 381, 383, 387, 390
Pinder, Capt William 638
Pink Trench 660
Pioneer Trench (2nd Bullecourt) 264
Pioneer Trench (Dernancourt) 441–3, 445, 455–6, 458–63
Pirie, Sgt William 341, 344
Pissy 666
Pitt, Lcpl Joseph 436
planning of operations 29, 81, 89, 110, 129, 146–7, 156, 160, 167, 169, 184–6, 194–5, 203–7, 211, 237–9, 241–2, 259–60, 271–2, 274, 276–7, 287, 331–2, 334–7, 347, 351, 356, 460, 485–90, 538, 540–51, 562, 574–81, 583, 616–17, 642–5, 659, 679, 707
  conference method 542–4, 547–8, 562, 574, 581, 617, 644, 707
Plant, Maj Eric 314, 325, 374, 376, 395, 529, 605, 693, 696–7, 705
Playfair, Maj Jack (T A J) 440, 606, 698
Ploegsteert 273, 311
Ploegsteert Wood 278, 310, 312–13
Plumer, Gen Sir Herbert 51, 124, 271–4, 280, 307, 310, 318, 320, 331, 334, 347–8

Poelcappelle, Battle of 348
Polygon Wood 333, 706
  Battle of 334–42, 346, 349, 372, 506, 570 (*See also* Ypres, Third Battle of)
Pommereuil 690
Pommiers Redoubt 135, 140, 152
Pont-Noyelles 464, 484, 501, 514
Pont-Remy 133, 536
Pontin, Lt James 430, 435, 438
Pontruet 655, 659
Pope, Cpl Thomas 556
Pope, Pte William 523
Pope, Lt Col Harold 5, 7–8, 36, 61, 181–2, 190, 277, 280, 291, 309
Poperinghe (Poperinge) 123
Popkin, Sgt Cedric 482, 541
Pork Trench 171–2, 174
Porter, Lt Simon 344
Potsdam Farm 384–5, 387
Potts, Brig Arnold 104, 175, 326, 389, 705–6
Potts, Lt Roy 598
Poulainville 630
Powell, Gnr Frederick 269
power buzzer. *See under* signalling
Pozières, battles at 67–8, 70, 73–80, 100, 120, 134–5, 140, 146, 152, 266, 313, 391, 447, 571. *See also* Mouquet Farm, battles at
  battlefield features 69–70, 80–1
Prentice, Cpl George 598, 616
Prescott, Sgt John 592
Prescott, Sgt William 418
Price, Cpl Thomas 650, 669
Prideaux-Brune, Capt F K 24
Priel Crater 651
Pringle, Pte James 589, 616
Prior, Lt Montague 266
prisoners
  taken by Australians and Allies 30, 54–5, 93, 114, 116, 128, 163, 170–1, 189, 217, 282–3, 292, 388, 408–9, 411–12, 414, 416, 433–4, 442, 494, 496, 498, 503, 537, 539–40, 554–5, 557, 559–60, 563, 585, 587–92, 594,

598–600, 602–4, 614–15, 622, 628, 640–1, 647–9, 651–3, 655, 661–2, 665, 667, 684, 692, 717
    taken by Germans 57, 78, 84, 94, 115, 158, 191, 194, 231–2, 235, 357, 384–5, 387–8, 409, 415, 450, 453–4, 475, 521, 523, 580, 582, 621, 645, 702
Pritchard, Cpl Daniel 598, 616
Pritchard, Lt Wallace 354
Proyart 588, 598, 602, 604, 616, 621, 623, 626
Pugh, Sgt Clifford 653, 669
Pulling, Maj Hugh 84, 320
Pybus, Maj Raymond 256, 258

Q

Quarry, The (Mouquet Farm) 83, 85, 87–8, 90, 93, 104, 112
Quarry Siding 138, 142, 146
Quéant 188, 191, 200–3, 205, 207, 211–12, 215, 226, 230, 254, 259, 262
Quéant Road Cemetery (CWGC) 235–6
Quennemont Farm 681
Querrieu 482–5, 514, 527–8, 563, 572
Quick, Sgt John 256, 258

R

Rabett, Lt Col Reginald 16, 143, 155, 201, 226, 228, 231, 240, 256
Radford, Maj Ernest 274, 334, 372, 391
Rae, Lt John (Jack) 405, 417
RAF (Royal Air Force) 481–2, 548, 551, 577, 584, 586. *See also* RFC, AFC
raids 51, 55–7, 126–31, 153, 168, 384–8, 413, 415, 537–40, 580
Railhead camp (Egypt) 39–40, 42
railway transport 33, 35, 42, 47–8, 65, 71, 123, 132, 138, 142, 236, 268, 360, 376, 381, 685, 693–4
railways, light 32, 39–40, 71, 127, 137–8, 146, 172, 183, 253, 310, 381, 383, 603
Ramicourt 684
Ramousies 696
Ramsay, Maj J G 31, 50

Rankin, Lcpl John 164, 166
Rathke, Cpl Hugo 649
Ration Trench 83
rations 71, 83, 105, 133, 139–40, 288, 335, 341, 406–7, 488, 502, 583, 604, 618, 660, 681, 696–7
Ravelsburg 321
Rawdon, Lcpl Edmund 417
Rawlinson, Gen Sir Henry 133, 484, 540–1, 546, 551, 561, 573–4, 581–2, 616, 638, 679
Read, Sgt Stanley (E S) 256
reconnaissance, aerial. *See* aircraft and aerial warfare
Red Line Spur/Ridge 590–2, 596, 599, 616
Red Wood 653
Reed, Pte Ernest 662
Regan, Pte Charles 634
Reginald Wood 587
Reid, Lt George 432–3, 456
Reid, Maj Horace 92, 176, 302, 327, 345
Reid, Gnr John 269
Reid, Lt Robert 662–4, 669
Reid, CSM Thomas 520, 523
Reid, Pte Walter 662
Reid, Lt William 448, 476
Reidy, Gnr Michael 269
reliefs. *See* rotation of units
Reninghelst (Reningelst) 123–5, 130, 360
repatriation scheme 697, 700–2
Reynolds, Capt Chester 327, 699
RFC (Royal Flying Corps) 20, 60, 74, 101, 202, 228, 258, 278, 284, 429, 481. *See also* RAF, AFC
Rhead, Capt Herbert 282
Rheims 401
Rhodes, Capt Randall 504
Ribeauville 686–8
Ribemont (-sur-Ancre) 136–7, 142, 173, 179, 267, 426, 431, 443, 479–80
Richards, Maj E W 32, 53
Richards, Sgt William 681
Richmond Wood 586, 597

Richthofen, Capt Manfred von 202, 481–2, 541
Riddell, Maj Consett C 100, 176, 183, 289, 301–2, 327, 373, 396, 402, 478, 606, 692
Ridgewood Camp 382
Ridley, Capt William 279
Ridley, Lt Col Cecil (J C T E C) 7, 32, 90, 174–5, 185, 277, 291, 326, 336, 372, 677, 695, 697
Riencourt (-les-Cagnicourt) 200, 203–5, 207, 211–12, 214–15, 217–18, 222–3, 226, 228, 239–41, 259–60, 262, 265
Ritter, Cpl Harold 168–9
Rivery 527–8, 563, 630, 635
Roach, Cpl Michael 556
road conditions 137, 200, 253, 259, 276, 335, 346–9, 431, 545, 578, 590, 619, 644
Robb, Pte Arthur 655, 670
Robbins, Sgt Frederick 627–9
Robertson, Sgt Edward 409
Robertson, Pte George 301
Robertson, Brig Gen James 140, 169, 175, 204, 208, 213, 219, 286, 289–90, 295, 316, 326, 373
Robertson, Cpl Malcolm 163–5
Robertson, Maj Septimus 23, 176, 275, 327, 396, 606
Robin, Lt James 107, 159
Robinson, Lt Ernest 432–3
Robinson, Dvr Alexander 343
Rochford, Pte John 650, 669
Rogers, Lt Frank 452
Rogers, Capt Stanley (J S) 314, 325, 380
Rogers, Capt William I (AASC) 699
Rogers, 2nd Lt William R (16th Bn) 555, 570, 599
Roisel 666, 693–4
Roman road (Amiens/V-Bretonneux) 484, 575, 587, 616, 623
Ronssoy 681
Rose, Lt Bernard 218, 242
Rose Trench 656
Rosenthal, Maj Gen Sir Charles 15–17, 32, 43, 50, 140, 145, 159, 175, 195, 201, 212, 228, 240, 253, 255, 258–9, 263, 265, 293, 311, 313–15, 319–20, 351, 445, 528, 536

Rosières 623
Ross, Lt Col Arthur 8, 92, 101–2, 119, 143–4, 716
Ross, Sgt Joseph 407
Ross, Maj Percy 537
Ross, Lt Col Thomas 22, 132, 152
Ross, Spr William 539–40
Rossignol Farm 415–17
Rossignol Wood 409–13, 415
Rossiter, Capt Arthur 529
rotation of units 53–5, 101, 105, 134, 136–7, 142, 153–4, 312, 320–1, 358, 382, 394, 415–17, 439, 442–3, 527, 563–4, 625, 629
Roulers 272, 331
Rowe, Maj Albert 293
Rowe, Pte William 634
Royal Air Force. *See* RAF
Royal Flying Corps. *See* RFC
Royal Naval Air Service (RNAS) 481
Roye 623
Rubempré 69, 99, 119, 123
Rule, Capt Edgar 67–8, 79, 86, 104, 141, 144, 216, 236, 266, 312, 323, 411, 551, 559, 656–7, 660, 663, 669, 702–3
Rule, Lt Esson 192
runners 141, 214, 216, 223, 225–6, 229–30, 284–5, 307, 335, 340, 352, 391, 447, 450–1, 458, 477, 507, 523, 555, 570, 590, 648–9, 655
Ruschpler, Pte Reinhold 473
Russia 51, 153, 369, 383
Rutledge, Lt Col Thomas 482, 606, 692

S

Sadlier, Lt Clifford 491–3, 505–6
  awarded VC 505–6
Sadlier-Stokes Memorial Scholarship 506
Sailly-au-Bois 407, 415, 417
Sailly-Laurette 575, 588, 602, 615, 623
Sailly-le-Sec 424, 478, 530–1, 545, 615, 623
Sailly-sur la-Lys 53
Sains 696
St Acheul 514

St Eloi 125, 319, 383
St Germain Wood 601
St Hélène 657, 659, 662
St Martin Rivière 686
St Omer 59, 61, 124, 130–1, 307, 309
St Ouen 65
St Quentin 401, 639, 693
St Quentin Canal 642, 665, 679, 682
St Souplet 685–8, 695
St Vast 630
Saisseval 666
Salier, Maj Edward 41, 102, 175, 318, 326, 349, 374
Salisbury, Lt Col Alfred 6, 100, 175, 185, 192, 277, 294–5, 299, 301, 326, 336, 395, 487–8, 490, 499, 502–3, 506, 605, 639, 678, 698, 701
Salter, Lt John 640
Sambre, Battle of the 691–2
Sambre-Oise Canal 686, 688–91, 695
Samer 381
Sammon, Sgt Patrick 409, 418
Sampson, Maj Burford 582, 589, 605, 615, 637, 643
Sanderson, Capt William 691
Sando, Lt Col Leslie 678, 699
Sandoe, Joseph. *See* Dietze, Joseph
sanitation 22, 317
Saulty 402
Saunders, Pte William 507
Sausage Valley 70–1, 73, 83
Sawer, Capt Edgar 18, 175, 182, 274
Scabbard Trench 173
Scherpenberg 381
Schulz, Lt John 436
Schutz, Lt Henry 417
Scott, Lt Charles 288
Scott, Sgt Reynold 171–2
scouts, infantry 50, 54, 82, 128, 185, 193, 202–3, 207, 213, 279, 385, 409, 539, 587
Seager, Maj Harold (Harry) 7, 28, 31, 192–3, 195
Seal, Sgt George 598
Second World War. *See* World War Two

secrecy, deception and surprise 78, 154, 186, 255, 401, 434, 480, 529, 548–9, 562, 574–5, 580, 582, 645, 689
Seelenmeyer, Maj Cyril 596
Selle River 685–6, 689–90
    Battle of the 686–8, 695
Sellick, Pte Frederick 587, 616
Selmes, Maj Jeremiah 228–9, 241–2
Selwyn-Smith, Capt Hubert 282
Senior, Lt Joseph 417
Senlis (-le-Sec) 423, 425
Serapeum 16, 21, 32, 37, 39–40
    march to 33–6, 42
Sewell, Capt Phillip 499–500
Sexton, Sgt Gerald (Maurice Buckley) 591–2, 616, 648, 652, 668–9, 705
    awarded VC 668
Shang, Pte Caleb ('Charlie') 285–6, 301, 455, 476, 529
Shanks, Pte David 507
Sharp, Lt George 379
Shaw, Lt Bernard 589
Sheehan, Pte John 435
shell shock 80, 92, 100, 261
Shepherdson, Lt Herbert 291, 449, 457, 476
Sheridan, Lt Harold 501
Sherwood, Capt C A 326
Shierlaw, Capt Norman 166, 226
Shine Trench 155, 160, 164, 166
Shout, Capt Alfred 166
sickness and disease 55, 139, 142, 179, 315, 342, 359, 371, 379, 546, 670, 688, 702. *See also* trench fever; trench foot
    venereal disease 317–18, 392, 668
Siebert, Pte Augustin 448, 477
Siegfried Line. *See* Hindenburg Line
signallers 38, 110, 125, 143, 260, 307, 341, 352, 393, 455–7, 477, 499, 523, 546, 555, 590, 644, 649, 684
signalling 19–20, 30, 107, 143, 159, 181, 213, 220, 238–9, 263, 284–5, 287–9, 300, 307–8, 339, 352, 391, 431, 442, 455, 476, 546, 684. *See also* Signals units *under* Australian Imperial Force

flares and rockets 78, 101, 158, 162–4, 214, 226, 229, 233, 260, 264, 284, 292, 355, 387, 391, 448, 520, 539–40, 558
pigeons 85, 214, 229, 307, 340, 591
power buzzer 181, 214, 229, 339, 391
telephones 19, 57, 105, 110, 125, 128–9, 160, 181, 204, 213–14, 220, 277, 279, 284, 296, 339, 387, 391, 431, 447, 455, 457, 477, 499, 531, 546, 578, 644, 658
visual 19, 209, 214, 229, 285, 307, 393, 431, 447
wireless telegraphy 19, 214, 391, 431, 546, 578, 638, 644
Simon, Lt Eric 589–90
Sinclair, Sgt Raymond 601, 616
Sinclair-Burgess, William. *See* Burgess, William
Sinclair-MacLagan, Maj Gen Ewen 5, 7, 313–14, 316, 322–5, 334, 344–5, 358, 373, 378, 391, 395, 404, 415, 424, 444, 457, 460, 463–4, 528–9, 536, 542, 561, 571–2, 575, 578, 582, 605, 637, 642, 644, 678–9, 693, 695, 698, 701
Sivry 696, 699
Skyline Trench 81, 87, 89–90, 714, 716
Slattery, Pte Edward 507
Smart Set concert party 24, 373, 393, 535, 692, 700
Smith, Capt Alan 591, 594, 596
Smith, Lcpl Charles 448, 477
Smith, Lt Clive 595, 616
Smith, Capt Frank 494, 497, 501
Smith, Lt Harry 601, 616
Smith, Gnr Howard 269
Smith, Maj James Churchill 90, 188, 191, 294, 296, 497, 697–8
Smith, Lt Joseph 356
Smith, Col Kenneth 570, 606, 697
Smith, Capt Robert 302, 572
Smith, Lt Col Walter 322–3, 325, 340, 345, 384, 389
Smith's Road 350
Smyth Camp 334
snipers 50, 54, 127, 138, 162, 172, 183, 191, 284–5, 290–1, 312, 341, 348, 352, 354, 407, 413, 436–8, 501–2, 537, 541, 558–9, 592, 598, 652
Snowden, Lt Col Robert 6, 8, 110

Soissons 179
Somerville, Capt Robert 215, 232, 242
Somerville Wood 653
Somme, Battle of the 56, 58, 61, 133–4, 401, 404, 406, 412, 624
Somme River 48, 51, 131–3, 153–4, 376, 394, 424, 427, 441, 478, 480–1, 483–5, 527–8, 530–1, 535–6, 538, 545, 561, 573, 575, 578, 582–3, 588–91, 594–7, 600, 602, 613, 616, 620, 623–4, 626, 638, 666
Souastre 404–5, 414, 423–4, 430
souvenirs 482, 592, 614, 665
Spence, Capt P A F 31, 41
Spoil Bank 381, 383
sports and recreation 55, 101, 142, 144–5, 152, 266, 308, 316, 325, 373, 375, 379, 392–4, 529–30, 535–6, 564, 571–2, 630, 637, 667, 677, 692, 700
Spurge, Lt Col Cyril 579, 606, 688, 699
Square Copse 661
Squires, Pte Alfred 459
Stabback, Lt John 290, 301, 379
Stanley, Dr Peter 392
Stanton, Capt Frederick 216
Stanton, Lt James 224, 242
Steele, Maj David 580
Steele, Lt Thomas 119
Steele, Capt Alan 7, 32, 130
Steenbeek (stream) 337
Steenvoorde 124, 126, 325, 334, 346, 394
Steenwerck 310–11, 313
Steignast Farm 286, 319, 321
Stevenson, Sgt Alfred 296
Stevenson, Lt Col G I 201
Stewart, Lt Benjamin 529
Stewart, Pte George 235, 243
Stinking Farm 279
Stoerkel, Lt Charles 290, 301, 518, 520, 523
Stokes, Sgt Charles 492–3, 505–6
Stokes, Pte Ernest 507
Storey, Lt George P (47th and 46th Bns) 355, 516, 661, 669

Storey, Pte George R (51st Bn) 343, 706
Stormy Trench 155–72, 174, 179, 209, 240, 279
strategic issues 32, 48, 51, 133, 153–4, 173–4, 179–80, 265, 271–2, 310, 369, 383–4, 401, 424, 537, 573, 624, 638, 690
stress, mental 55, 80, 143–4, 315, 392, 576, 688, 704–5
stretcher bearers 21, 72–4, 80, 93, 109, 119, 138, 146, 166, 183, 229, 232, 234, 243, 293, 333, 335, 342, 345, 349, 356–8, 381, 414, 447–8, 463, 477, 499–500, 507, 514, 522, 547–8, 560, 580, 644, 665. *See also* casualty evacuation and clearance system; Medical units *under* Australian Imperial Force
Strong, Pte Frederick 507
Stubbings, Capt Claude 280, 291, 295, 449, 460, 494
Sturdee, Col Alfred 172
Sturdee, Admiral Sir Doveton 172
Sturdee, Gen Sir Vernon 172–3, 176, 327, 372, 705
Suez Canal 2, 16, 21, 32–3, 39
Sullivan, Cpl Thomas 494, 506
Sumner, Sgt Ernest 604, 616
Sunray Trench 168
Supreme War Council 561
surprise. *See* secrecy, deception and surprise
Susan Wood 587, 596
Sutherland, Cpl Percy 651, 669
Swain, Capt Harry 117–18
Sweetnam, Sgt William 602
Swinbourne, Lt Richard 417
Switch Trench 89, 136
Syme, Lt William 168–9
Symons, Capt Charles 372, 454

T

tactical exercises. *See* training
tactics 80–1, 91, 102, 110, 112–14, 154, 173, 185–6, 194–5, 272, 276, 331–2, 336–7, 391, 401, 462, 486, 518, 541, 555, 562, 666, 707
   open warfare 180–1, 377, 535, 576, 578, 630, 679, 686
   platoon 180–1, 281, 307, 323, 630

Talmas 103
Tambling, Capt Richard 618, 620
tanks 203–7, 209–11, 214–15, 218–19, 221–3, 237–42, 277, 281–2, 284, 309, 375, 412, 460–1, 501, 518, 522, 540–1, 543, 549–53, 555–6, 559–60, 577–8, 583–9, 591, 595–6, 601, 617–19, 643–4, 647–9, 679, 681
   carriers, supply 543, 558, 577, 583–4
   carriers, weapons 577–9, 583–4, 597–602
   co-operation with infantry 204, 209, 212–14, 220, 237–8, 308, 543, 547, 556–8, 562, 576
   dummy 644, 650
tapes, guide 107, 114, 185, 187, 209, 213, 279–80, 292, 295, 337, 352, 488, 490, 518, 551, 585, 655
Tara Hill 70, 81, 99, 105, 119
Tassie, Maj Leslie 499, 506
Taylor, Capt Allan 18, 599, 616
Taylor, Lt Harry 447, 452, 476
Taylor, Pte John 565
Taylor, Lt Norman 687
Taylor, Pte Rowland 243
Tel-el-Kebir 2, 5, 7–8, 16, 19–21, 28, 33, 36
telephones, field. *See under* signalling
Templeux-la-Fosse 376, 378
Tennant, CSM Andrew 409
Terras, Lt James 438
Terry, Capt Eric 275, 326, 379–80
Thiepval 67, 70, 80, 89, 111, 120, 133
Thomas, Lcpl Wilfred 456, 477
Thompson, Spr Albert 539–40
Thompson, Sgt Charles 344
Thompson, Pte Duncan 475
Thompson, Capt Gordon 61
Thompson, Lt Harold 539, 589
Thompson, Sgt Henry 418
Thompson, Lt Stanley 216
Thomson, Maj David 322–3, 340, 384–5
Thomson, Capt Harry 312, 380, 389, 395, 571
Three Trees (Mouquet Farm) 88
Tidmarsh, Pte Charles 611
Tilney, Lt Col Leslie 4, 8, 100

Tincourt 666, 680, 694
Todd, Capt David 188, 190
Toft, Capt Percy 299, 413
Tokio Spur 334
Tolley, Maj Howard 183, 302, 327, 340–1, 343, 372–3, 396, 431, 606, 678, 682, 699
Tom's Cut (trench) 92, 99
Tournai Camp 382
Toutencourt 432
Tovell, Maj Raymond 389, 395, 514, 605, 698, 705
Tower Hamlets 333
Town, Lt Charles 494, 497, 501
Townsend, Sgt Alexander 277, 279, 301
training 8, 15–16, 21, 31, 37–41, 50, 59, 68, 101, 124, 134, 142–5, 179–81, 209, 268, 273, 307–10, 316, 323–5, 345, 373, 375–80, 393, 528, 535–6, 571–2, 630, 637, 677, 692, 694, 700
Tramway Trench 73, 75
transport and supply system 22–3, 54, 70–1, 92, 105, 134, 183, 259–60, 275, 288, 335, 341, 402, 408, 416, 432, 502, 514, 583–4, 603, 644, 684–5, 696, 700. *See also* Service Corps units *under* Australian Imperial Force
Tregoweth, Pte Frederick 456–7, 476
Treloar, Lcpl Reginald 589, 616
trench fever 55, 321, 336
trench foot 55, 127, 139, 415
trench raiding. *See* raids
trenches and defence systems 41, 48–51, 110, 127, 139, 141, 153, 172, 199–200, 272, 310, 338–9, 378, 382–4, 391, 401, 406, 431, 439–43, 445, 454, 478–80, 525, 531, 537, 546, 559–60, 573, 624, 652, 660–2, 664. *See also* pillboxes
  communication trenches 49, 51–2, 54, 70–1, 73, 87–8, 91–2, 102, 105, 110–11, 113–14, 117, 137, 165, 167, 172, 264, 288–9, 310, 336, 339, 383, 531, 546, 561, 624–5
  methods and routines 53–5, 134, 180
Treux 449
Trewheela, Lt George 626
Trois Arbres Cemetery (CWGC) 311–12
Trones Wood 146

Tronville Chateau 488, 514
Trumble, Capt Hugh 589
Tuami, Pte Oskar 358
Tucker, Capt Virgil 215
Tuckett, Maj Joseph 529
Tuckett, Lt Richard 457, 476
Turkey 32, 39, 41, 690
Turner, Pte Edgar 358
Turner, Pte Gilbert 172
Turner, Capt Harry 648
Tweedie, Lt Leslie 389
Twining, Capt David 77–8, 356, 599, 616, 678, 705
Tyler, Sgt Henry 558, 591

U

U-boat campaign 179–80, 272
Unbearable Trench 282–3, 289
Uncanny Support Trench 283, 287
Uncanny Trench 283
Underhill Farm 276, 310
United States 272, 369, 383
United States Army 546, 573, 575, 616, 692
  units and formations
    II Corps 678, 686–8
    27th Division 678–82, 684–8, 695
    30th Division 678–9, 682–6, 688
    33rd Division 546
    65th Brigade 546
    102nd Engineer Regiment 682
    107th Infantry Regiment 681
    108th Engineer Regiment 572
    131st Infantry Regiment 613–14, 616–18, 622
    132nd Infantry Regiment 547, 551, 556, 562, 572, 623–5
units, AIF. *See under* Australian Imperial Force
Upton, Lt Errol 18, 354

V

Vadencourt 103, 123, 432
Vaire Trench 554–5
Vaire Wood 538–9, 554–5, 559
Valerie Wood 586

Van Hove Farm 284, 287
Varley, Capt Arthur 288, 301, 351, 380, 395, 603, 605, 616, 698
Vaulx-Vraucourt 182, 185, 235–6, 253, 255–6
Vaux-Andigny 685
Vaux-en-Amienoix 579, 630
Vaux-sur-Somme 481–2
VC. *See* Victoria Cross
Vendelles 639, 644, 655, 659, 666, 680
Vendhuille 683
Vequemont 603
Verdun, Battle of 32, 51, 154
Vermand 639, 657
vermin, in trenches 55, 153, 378
Vernon, Lt Col Hugh 43, 125, 175, 264, 326, 350, 380, 396, 606, 684
Verrier, Cpl Arthur 195
veterinary services. *See* Veterinary units *under* Australian Imperial Force
Vickers guns. *See* machine guns; Machine Gun units *under* Australian Imperial Force
Victoria Cross 4, 80, 86, 165, 195, 257, 301, 343, 353, 358, 411, 417, 434, 438, 476, 505–6, 527, 569, 615, 668, 691, 701
Victoria Crossroads 658
Vienna Cottage 352, 354
Vierstraat 126, 382
Vieux Berquin 268, 300, 309–10, 316
Vignacourt 134, 142, 146–7, 432, 603
Ville-sur-Ancre 449, 460
Villers-Bretonneux 478, 483, 486, 488, 513, 524–5, 530, 538, 545, 573, 575, 583–4, 625
   First Battle of 446, 538
   Second Battle of 195, 417, 484–504, 507, 526, 622
   battlefield features 484
Villers-Faucon 684
Vimy Ridge 200, 259
Vincent, Lt James 587, 616
Vivier Mill 436
Voormezeele 381

W

Wackett, Capt Lawrence 548
Wadge, Lt Frank 207, 242
Wadsworth, Maj William 216, 232, 242, 323, 384, 656, 660, 669, 678
Waine, Maj Victor 214, 219, 223, 230
Waite, Capt Arthur 315, 326, 396, 606
Waite, Lt Col William 16, 32, 155, 158, 160, 167, 175, 273, 301, 315, 360, 396, 402, 440, 450, 537, 579
Walker, Maj Gen Sir Harold 542
Wallace, Lt Alexander 657–8, 669
Wallach, Capt Neville 516
Walsh, Capt Clement 134, 327, 335, 396, 416, 606, 699
Wambeek (stream) 276, 281, 319
Wanliss, Capt Harold 56–7, 323–4, 340, 343
Wanliss, Newton 132, 239–40, 343
Ward, Lt Leslie 664
Ward, Archdeacon John W 317
Waring, Lt Arthur 339
Warloy (-Baillon) 68, 73, 99, 119, 123, 432, 463
Warmington, Capt James 327, 396
Warnave River 310, 315
Warneton 281, 298–9, 321
Wassell, Lt Col Charles 183, 327, 381
water supply 35–6, 71, 140, 183, 253, 275, 279, 583, 644
Waterford, Lt Leo 408, 413, 592, 616
Waters, Sgt Walter 448, 450, 477
Watson, Pte Charles 616
Watson, Sgt Eric 456
Watson, Maj Herbert 696, 698
Watson, Capt John 217
Watson, Maj William 204–7, 210, 241
Waulsort 700
Way, Sgt James 520
weather conditions 40, 105–6, 133–5, 138–40, 142, 152–3, 155, 169, 181, 183, 187, 193, 200, 202, 208, 210, 213, 236, 259, 275, 279, 311–12, 318–21, 331, 342, 347–8, 352, 375–8, 383–4, 394, 410–11, 414, 439, 473, 525, 528, 530, 581, 584, 623, 630, 646, 660–1, 694, 696, 700

Webb, Lcpl Walter 358
Welch, Lt Col John 22, 152, 176, 327, 357, 372
Wells, Capt Donald 160
Wells, Pte Robert 664, 669
Wells, Maj Theodore 109, 217, 695, 718
West, Lcpl Robert (S R) 492, 506
Westhoek Ridge 343, 346–7, 349, 358–9
Westhof Farm 276, 278, 286, 300
White, Sgt Alfred 496, 506
White, Gen Sir Brudenell (C B B) 3–4, 89–90, 147, 206, 208, 370, 536, 705
White, Cpl John 442
White, Capt Thomas 408, 716–19
White Spot Cottage 289
Whitfield, Pte Denis 385
Whitham, Lt Col John 6, 309, 326, 385, 395, 402, 442, 444, 446, 457, 459–60, 474, 476, 482, 487–91, 497–9, 501–2, 506, 526, 542, 677, 692, 697
Whitmore, Lcpl Walter 448, 450, 477
Whittle, Sgt Harry 291
Wilkie, Pte William 565
Wilkins, Sgt Archibald 293, 301
Wilkins, Capt Sir Hubert 682–3
Wilkinson, Capt Harold 554, 570
Wilkinson, Lt Norman 302, 341
Willenbrock, Capt John 462
Williams, Lcpl Algernon 592, 616
Williams, Capt Edward 283–4, 286, 290, 436
Williams, Lt Col Ernest 21, 31, 41, 52
Williams, Pte Evan 647, 669
Williams, Capt Henry 450–2, 460
Williams, Maj Gen Sir Hugh B 412, 416
Williams, Lt James 447–8, 476
Williams, Lt Col Thomas 260, 315, 326, 332–3, 360, 396, 430, 440, 579, 606, 621, 680, 686, 695, 698
Williams, Cpl William 623
Williamson, Capt Alfred ('Lofty') 165, 216, 236
Willison, Lt Alfred 661, 663
Wilmott, Capt William 496
Wilson, Capt Harry 646–7

Wilson, Sgt James 188, 191, 195
Wilson, Capt Norman 591, 616
Wilton, Lt Vernon 108
Wilton, Maj Eric 18, 80, 312, 325, 349, 374, 380
Windmill, The (Pozières) 77–8, 104–5, 109
Winn, Capt Roy 293, 301
wire-cutting 56, 60, 127–8, 156–7, 161–2, 202–3, 206–9, 216, 237–9, 254, 259, 277–8, 296, 539, 646, 660, 679–80
Wire Trench 87, 89, 110
wireless telegraphy. *See under* signalling
Wisdom, Brig Gen Evan 622
Withers, Capt Roy 163–5
Wolff, Sgt Arthur 524
Wolfsberg 538, 543, 557, 561
Wood, Lt Ramsay 559
Wood, Cpl Arthur 421
Woods, Capt Frederick 554–5
Woods, Pte James 662–3, 668–9, 702
  awarded VC 668
Wooster, Lt Col Frank 541, 560, 606, 699
working parties 41, 55, 73, 83, 102, 105, 110, 127, 137, 141–2, 152–3, 259, 268, 307, 312, 319, 343, 358, 373, 377–8, 382, 479, 531, 541, 545, 559–60
World War Two 104, 133, 173, 282, 379–80, 389, 705–6
Worner, Pte Walter 172
Wotan Line. *See* Drocourt-Quéant Switch
Wright, Sgt Henry 497, 506
Wright, Lt Phillip 559, 570
Wulverghem 273
Wyatt, Capt Wilfred 214
Wynter, Lt Gen Henry 133, 174, 182
Wytschaete (Wijtschate) 125–6, 268, 271–2

Y

Yates, Pte Albert 352, 358
YMCA 24
Young, Capt Charles 452, 476
Young, Capt William 283

Ypres (Ieper) and Ypres Salient 48, 65, 123, 132, 265, 268, 271–2, 310, 321, 325, 332, 335, 349–50, 357–9, 369, 371, 381, 480, 483, 504, 574, 678, 692
    Third Battle of 308, 314–15, 318, 320, 325, 331, 369–70, 375, 383, 391, 536, 704 (*See also* Broodseinde, Battle of; Menin Road, Battle of the; Passchendaele, Battles of; Polygon Wood, Battle of)
Ypres-Comines Canal 125–6, 380–1
Ypres-Roulers railway 331, 350–1, 353–5

Z

Zeebrugge 272
Zillebeeke 381
Zonnebeke 334, 336, 340, 346–7, 350, 357, 359, 706

www.ingramcontent.com/pod-product-compliance
Lightning Source LLC
Chambersburg PA
CBHW081113160426
42814CB00035B/303